D0716654

POCKET VIS...

dictionary

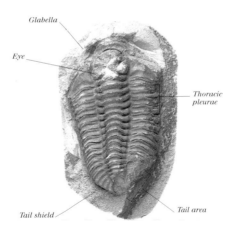

Glabella

Eye

Thoracic pleurae

Tail shield

Tail area

PREHISTORIC TRILOBITE

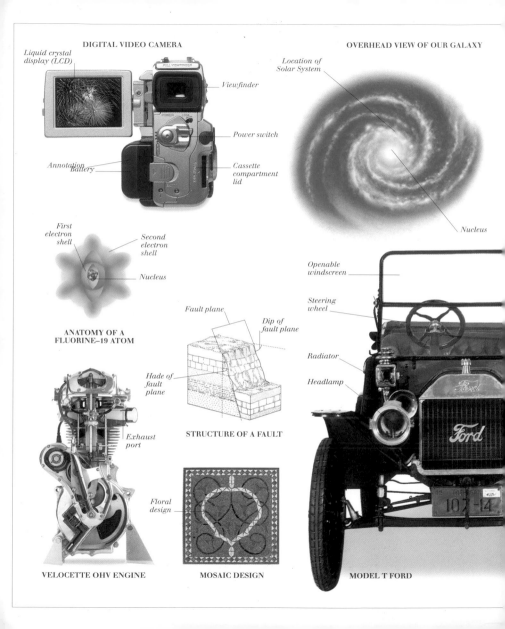

DIGITAL VIDEO CAMERA

Liquid crystal display (LCD)

Viewfinder

Power switch

Annotation

Battery

Cassette compartment lid

OVERHEAD VIEW OF OUR GALAXY

Location of Solar System

Nucleus

First electron shell

Second electron shell

Nucleus

ANATOMY OF A FLUORINE–19 ATOM

Fault plane

Dip of fault plane

Hade of fault plane

STRUCTURE OF A FAULT

Openable windscreen

Steering wheel

Radiator

Headlamp

Exhaust port

VELOCETTE OHV ENGINE

Floral design

MOSAIC DESIGN

MODEL T FORD

POCKET VISUAL dictionary

Pedicel (flower stalk)

Sepal

Achene (one-seeded dry fruit

Remains of stigma and style

STRAWBERRY

A DORLING KINDERSLEY BOOK

LONDON, NEW YORK, MUNICH, MELBOURNE, AND DELHI

Original Edition (*Ultimate Visual Dictionary*)
Project Art Editors Heather McCarry, Johnny Pau, Chris Walker, Kevin Williams
Designer Simon Murrell

Project Editors Luisa Caruso, Peter Jones, Jane Mason, Geoffrey Stalker
Editor Jo Evans

DTP Designer Zirrinia Austin
Picture Researcher Charlotte Bush

Managing Art Editor Toni Kay
Senior Editor Roger Tritton
Managing Editor Sean Moore

Production Manager Hilary Stephens

Anatomical And Botanical Models Supplied By Somso Modelle, Coburg, Germany

Revised Edition
Art Editor Hugh Schermuly
Designers Phil Gamble, Simon Oon, Pamela Shiels
Jacket Designer John Dinsdale
Project Editor Cathy Meeus
Editor Paul Docherty
Jacket Editor Beth Apple
Editorial Consultant Sarah Angliss
Senior Art Editor Ina Stradins

ISBN 1405302364

REPRODUCED BY COLOURSCAN, SINGAPORE
L. REX PRINTING CO., HONG KONG

See our complete catalogue at www.dk.com

Prosoma
(cephalothorax)

Spinneret

Leg

**EXTERNAL FEATURES
OF A SPIDER**

Canopy

Fin

G-BNHB

Main landing
gear

SIDE VIEW OF ARV SUPER 2 AEROPLANE

Heat shield

PAM-D
upper
stage
booster

Launch
vehicle

MARS PATHFINDER

Barrel

Permanent
black ink

FOUNTAIN PEN AND INK

CONTENTS

INTRODUCTION 6

THE UNIVERSE 8

PREHISTORIC EARTH 54

PLANTS 110

ANIMALS 164

THE HUMAN BODY 208

GEOLOGY, GEOGRAPHY,
AND METEOROLOGY 262

PHYSICS AND CHEMISTRY 304

RAIL AND ROAD 322

SEA AND AIR 370

THE VISUAL ARTS 428

ARCHITECTURE 456

MUSIC 500

SPORTS 522

THE MODERN WORLD 564

APPENDIX 616

INDEX 624

Retractable
head light

Pause
button

**SONY AIBO
ROBOT DOG**

Parallel
bands

ONYX

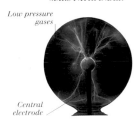

Low pressure
gases

Central
electrode

**BALL CONTAINING HIGH
TEMPERATURE GAS (PLASMA)**

Non-breakable
plastic

Shock
absorber

**AMERICAN FOOTBALL
HELMET**

Introduction

THE VISUAL DICTIONARY is a completely new kind of reference book. It provides a link between pictures and words in a way that no ordinary dictionary ever has. Most dictionaries simply tell you what a word means, but the *Visual Dictionary* shows you – through a combination of detailed annotations, explicit photographs, and illustrations. In the *Visual Dictionary*, pictures define the annotations around them. You do not read definitions of the annotated words, you see them. The highly accessible format of the *Visual Dictionary*, the thoroughness of its annotations, and the range of its subject matter make it a unique and helpful reference tool.

How to use the Visual Dictionary

You will find the *Visual Dictionary* simple to use. Instead of being organized alphabetically, it is divided by subject into 14 sections – The Universe, Prehistoric Earth, Plants, Animals, The Human Body, etc. Each section begins with a table of contents listing the major entries within that section. For example, The Visual Arts section has entries on *Drawing, Tempera, Fresco, Oils, Watercolour, Pastels, Acrylics, Calligraphy, Printmaking, Mosaic,* and *Sculpture.* Every entry has a short introduction explaining the purpose of the photographs and illustrations, and the significance of the annotations.

If you know what something looks like, but don't know its name, find the term you need by turning to the annotations surrounding the pictures; if you know a word, but don't know what it refers to, use the comprehensive index to direct you to the appropriate page.

Suppose that you want to know what the bone at the end of your little finger is called. With a standard dictionary, you wouldn't know where to begin. But with the *Visual Dictionary* you simply turn to the entry called *Hands* – within The Human Body section – where you will find four fully annotated, colour photographs showing the skin, muscles, and bones of the human hand. In this entry you will quickly find that the bone you are searching for is called the distal phalanx, and for good measure you will discover that it is attached to the middle phalanx by the distal interphalangeal joint.

Perhaps you want to know what a catalytic converter looks like. If you look up "catalytic converter" in an ordinary dictionary, you will be told what it is and possibly what it does – but you will not be able to tell what shape it is or what it is made of. However, if you look up "catalytic converter" in the index of the *Visual Dictionary*, you will be directed to the *Modern engines* entry on page 344 – where the introduction gives you basic information about what a catalytic converter is – and to page 350 – where there is a spectacular exploded-view photograph of the mechanics of a Renault Clio. From these pages you will find out not only what a catalytic converter looks like, but also that it is attached at one end to an exhaust downpipe and at the other to a silencer.

Whatever it is that you want to find a name for, or whatever name you want to find a picture for, you will find it quickly and easily in the *Visual Dictionary*. Perhaps you need to know where the vamp on a shoe is; or how to tell obovate and lanceolate leaves apart; or what a spiral galaxy looks like; or whether birds have nostrils. With the *Visual Dictionary* at hand, the answers to each of these questions, and thousands more, are readily available.

The *Visual Dictionary* does not just tell you what the names of the different parts of an object are. The photographs, illustrations, and annotations are all specially arranged to help you understand which parts relate to one another and how objects function.

With the *Visual Dictionary* you can find in seconds the words or pictures that you are looking for; or you can simply browse through the pages of the book for your own pleasure. The *Visual Dictionary* is not intended to replace a standard dictionary or conventional encyclopedia, but is instead a stimulating and valuable companion to ordinary reference volumes. Giving you instant access to the language that is used by astronomers and architects, musicians and mechanics, scientists and sportspeople, it is the ideal reference book for specialists and generalists of all ages.

Sections of the VISUAL DICTIONARY

The 14 sections of the *VISUAL DICTIONARY* contain a total of more than 30,000 terms, encompassing a wide range of topics:

• In the first section, THE UNIVERSE, spectacular photographs and illustrations are used to show the names of the stars and planets and to explain the structure of solar systems, galaxies, nebulae, comets, and black holes.

• PREHISTORIC EARTH tells the story in annotations of how our own planet has evolved since its formation. It includes examples of prehistoric flora and fauna, and fascinating dinosaur models – some with parts of the body stripped away to show anatomical sections.

• PLANTS covers a huge range of species – from the familiar to the exotic. In addition to the colour photographs of plants included in this section, there is a series of micrographic photographs illustrating plant details – such as pollen grains, spores, and cross-sections of stems and roots – in close-up.

• In the ANIMALS section, skeletons, anatomical diagrams, and different parts of animals' bodies have been meticulously annotated. This section provides a comprehensive guide to the vocabulary of zoological classification and animal physiology.

• The structure of the human body, its parts, and its systems are presented in THE HUMAN BODY. The section includes lifelike, three-dimensional models and the latest false-colour images. Clear and authoritative annotations indicate the correct anatomical terms.

• GEOLOGY, GEOGRAPHY, AND METEOROLOGY describes the structure of the Earth – from the inner core to the exosphere – and the physical phenomena – such as volcanoes, rivers, glaciers, and climate – that shape its surface.

• PHYSICS AND CHEMISTRY is a visual journey through the fundamental principles underlying the physical universe, and provides the essential vocabulary of these sciences.

• In RAIL AND ROAD, a wide range of trains, trams and buses, cars, bicycles, and motorcycles are described. Exploded-view photographs show mechanical details with striking clarity.

• SEA AND AIR gives the names for hundreds of parts of ships and aeroplanes. The section includes civil and fighting craft, both historical and modern.

• THE VISUAL ARTS shows the equipment and materials used by painters, sculptors, printers, and other artists. Well-known compositions have been chosen to illustrate specific artistic techniques and effects.

• ARCHITECTURE includes photographs of exemplary architectural models and illustrates dozens of additional features such as columns, domes, and arches.

• MUSIC provides a visual introduction to the special language of music and musical instruments. It includes clearly annotated photographs of each of the major groups of traditional instruments – brass, woodwind, strings, and percussion – together with modern electronic instruments.

• The SPORTS section is a guide to the playing areas, formations, equipment, and techniques needed for many of today's most popular sports.

• In THE MODERN WORLD, items that are a familiar part of our daily lives are taken apart to reveal their inner workings and give access to the language used by their manufacturers. It also includes systems and concepts, such as the Internet, that increasingly influence our 21st century world.

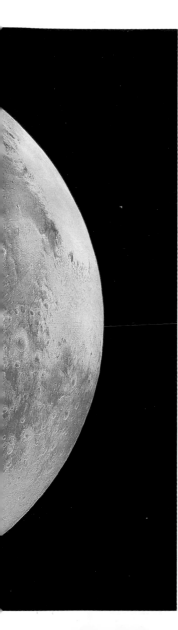

THE UNIVERSE

ANATOMY OF THE UNIVERSE · · · · · · · · · · 10
GALAXIES · 12
THE MILKY WAY · 14
NEBULAE AND STAR CLUSTERS · · · · · · · · 16
STARS OF NORTHERN SKIES · · · · · · · · · · 18
STARS OF SOUTHERN SKIES · · · · · · · · · · 20
STARS · 22
SMALL STARS · 24
MASSIVE STARS · 26
NEUTRON STARS AND BLACK HOLES · · · · 28
THE SOLAR SYSTEM · · · · · · · · · · · · · · · · · 30
THE SUN · 32
MERCURY · 34
VENUS · 36
THE EARTH · 38
THE MOON · 40
MARS · 42
JUPITER · 44
SATURN · 46
URANUS · 48
NEPTUNE AND PLUTO · · · · · · · · · · · · · · · · 50
ASTEROIDS, COMETS, AND METEOROIDS · · 52

Anatomy of the Universe

Fireball of rapidly expanding, extremely hot gas lasting about one million years

THE UNIVERSE CONTAINS EVERYTHING that exists, from the tiniest subatomic particles to galactic superclusters (the largest structures known). Nobody knows how big the Universe is, but astronomers estimate that it contains about 100 billion galaxies, each comprising an average of 100 billion stars. The most widely accepted theory about the origin of the Universe is the Big Bang theory, which states that the Universe came into being in a huge explosion – the Big Bang – that took place between 10 and 20 billion years ago. The Universe initially consisted of a very hot, dense fireball of expanding, cooling gas. After about one million years, the gas probably began to condense into localized clumps called protogalaxies. During the next five billion years, the protogalaxies continued condensing, forming galaxies in which stars were being born. Today, billions of years later, the Universe as a whole is still expanding, although there are localized areas in which objects are held together by gravity; for example, many galaxies are found in clusters. The Big Bang theory is supported by the discovery of faint, cool background radiation coming evenly from all directions. This radiation is believed to be the remnant of the radiation produced by the Big Bang. Small "ripples" in the temperature of the cosmic background radiation are thought to be evidence of slight fluctuations in the density of the early Universe, which resulted in the formation of galaxies. Astronomers do not yet know if the Universe is "closed", which means it will eventually stop expanding and begin to contract, or if it is "open", which means it will continue expanding forever.

FALSE-COLOUR MICROWAVE MAP OF COSMIC BACKGROUND RADIATION

Pink indicates "warm ripples" in background radiation

Pale blue indicates "cool ripples" in background radiation

Deep blue indicates background radiation corresponding to -270.3°C (remnant of the Big Bang)

Red and pink band indicates radiation from our galaxy

Low-energy microwave radiation corresponding to about -270°C

High-energy gamma radiation corresponding to about 3,000°C

ORIGIN AND EXPANSION OF THE UNIVERSE

Quasar (probably the centre of a galaxy containing a massive black hole)

Universe one to five billion years after Big Bang

Protogalaxy (condensing gas cloud)

Galaxy spinning and flattening to become spiral shaped

Dark cloud (dust and gas condensing to form a protogalaxy)

Elliptical galaxy in which stars form rapidly

Universe today (10–20 billion years after Big Bang)

Cluster of galaxies held together by gravity

Elliptical galaxy containing old stars and little gas and dust

Irregular galaxy

Spiral galaxy containing gas, dust, and young stars

OBJECTS IN THE UNIVERSE

CLUSTER OF GALAXIES IN VIRGO

FALSE-COLOUR IMAGE OF 3C275 (QUASAR)

NGC 4406 (ELLIPTICAL GALAXY)

NGC 5236 (SPIRAL GALAXY)

NGC 6822 (IRREGULAR GALAXY)

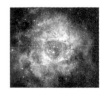

THE ROSETTE NEBULA (EMISSION NEBULA)

THE JEWEL BOX (STAR CLUSTER)

THE SUN (MAIN SEQUENCE STAR)

EARTH

THE MOON

Galaxies

SOMBRERO,
A SPIRAL GALAXY

A GALAXY IS A HUGE MASS OF STARS, nebulae, and interstellar material. The smallest galaxies contain about 100,000 stars, while the largest contain up to 3,000 billion stars. There are three main types of galaxy, classified according to their shape: elliptical, which are oval shaped; spiral, which have arms spiralling outwards from a central bulge; and irregular, which have no obvious shape. Sometimes, the shape of a galaxy is distorted by a collision with another galaxy. Quasars (quasi-stellar objects) are thought to be galactic nuclei but are so far away that their exact nature is still uncertain. They are compact, highly luminous objects in the outer reaches of the known Universe: while the furthest known "ordinary" galaxies are about 10 billion light years away, the furthest known quasar is about 15 billion light years away. Active galaxies, such as Seyfert galaxies and radio galaxies, emit intense radiation. In a Seyfert galaxy, this radiation comes from the galactic nucleus; in a radio galaxy, it also comes from huge lobes on either side of the galaxy. The radiation from active galaxies and quasars is thought to be caused by black holes (see pp. 28-29).

OPTICAL IMAGE OF NGC 4486 (ELLIPTICAL GALAXY)

Globular cluster containing very old red giants

Central region containing old red giants

Less densely populated region

Neighbouring galaxy

OPTICAL IMAGE OF LARGE MAGELLANIC CLOUD (IRREGULAR GALAXY)

Tarantula Nebula

Dust cloud obscuring light from stars

Emission nebula

Light from stars

OPTICAL IMAGE OF NGC 2997 (SPIRAL GALAXY)

Glowing nebula in spiral arm

Spiral arm containing young stars

Galactic nucleus containing old stars

Dust in spiral arm reflecting blue light from hot young stars

Hot, ionized hydrogen gas emitting red light

Dust lane

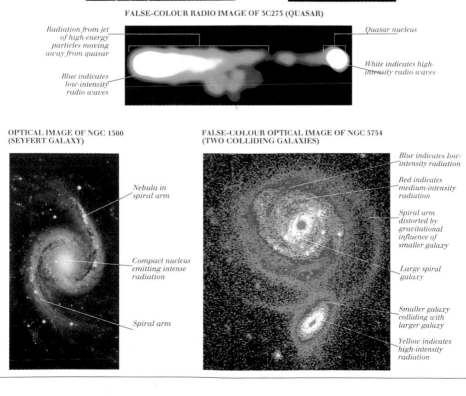

OPTICAL IMAGE OF CENTAURUS A (RADIO GALAXY)

Dust lane crossing elliptical galaxy

Galactic nucleus containing powerful source of radiation

Light from old stars

FALSE-COLOUR RADIO IMAGE OF CENTAURUS A

Red indicates high-intensity radio waves

Blue indicates low-intensity radio waves

Radiation from galactic nucleus

Outline of optical image of Centaurus A

Yellow indicates medium-intensity radio waves

Radio lobe

Radio lobe

FALSE-COLOUR RADIO IMAGE OF 3C273 (QUASAR)

Radiation from jet of high-energy particles moving away from quasar

Quasar nucleus

White indicates high-intensity radio waves

Blue indicates low-intensity radio waves

OPTICAL IMAGE OF NGC 1566 (SEYFERT GALAXY)

Nebula in spiral arm

Compact nucleus emitting intense radiation

Spiral arm

FALSE-COLOUR OPTICAL IMAGE OF NGC 5754 (TWO COLLIDING GALAXIES)

Blue indicates low-intensity radiation

Red indicates medium-intensity radiation

Spiral arm distorted by gravitational influence of smaller galaxy

Large spiral galaxy

Smaller galaxy colliding with larger galaxy

Yellow indicates high-intensity radiation

The Milky Way

**VIEW TOWARDS
GALACTIC CENTRE**

THE MILKY WAY IS THE NAME GIVEN TO THE FAINT BAND OF LIGHT that stretches across the night sky. This light comes from stars and nebulae in our galaxy, known as the Milky Way Galaxy or simply as "the Galaxy". The Galaxy is shaped like a spiral, with a dense central bulge that is encircled by four arms spiralling outwards and surrounded by a less dense halo. We cannot see the spiral shape because the Solar System is in one of the spiral arms, the Orion Arm (also called the Local Arm). From our position, the centre of the Galaxy is completely obscured by dust clouds; as a result, optical maps give only a limited view of the Galaxy. However, a more complete picture can be obtained by studying radio, infra-red, and other radiation. The central bulge of the Galaxy is a relatively small, dense sphere that contains mainly older red and yellow stars. The halo is a less dense region in which the oldest stars are situated; some of these stars may be as old as the Galaxy itself (possibly 15 billion years). The spiral arms contain mainly hot, young, blue stars, as well as nebulae (clouds of dust and gas inside which stars are born). The Galaxy is vast, about 100,000 light years across (a light year is about 9,460 billion kilometres); in comparison, the Solar System seems small, at about 12 light hours across (about 13 billion kilometres). The entire Galaxy is rotating in space, although the inner stars travel faster than those further out. The Sun, which is about two-thirds out from the centre, completes one lap of the Galaxy about every 220 million years.

SIDE VIEW OF OUR GALAXY

Disc of spiral arms containing mainly young stars

Central bulge containing mainly older stars

Halo containing oldest stars

Nucleus

100,000 light years

OVERHEAD VIEW OF OUR GALAXY

Central bulge

Nucleus

Perseus Arm

Crux-Centaurus Arm

Emission nebula

Sagittarius Arm

Dust in spiral arm reflecting blue light from hot young stars

Location of Solar System

Patch of dust clouds

Orion Arm (Local Arm)

PANORAMIC OPTICAL MAP OF OUR GALAXY AND NEARBY GALAXIES

Polaris (the Pole Star), a blue-green variable binary star

Light from stars and nebulae in the Perseus Arm

Galactic plane

Milky Way (the band of light that stretches across the night sky)

Pleiades (the Seven Sisters), an open star cluster

Andromeda Galaxy, a spiral galaxy 2.2 million light years away; the most distant object visible to the naked eye

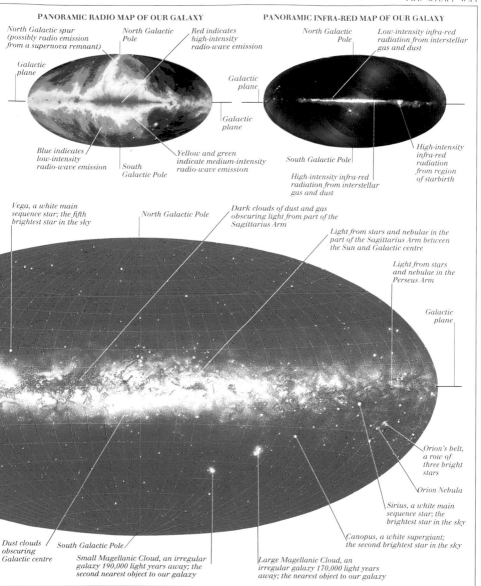

PANORAMIC RADIO MAP OF OUR GALAXY

North Galactic spur (possibly radio emission from a supernova remnant)

North Galactic Pole

Red indicates high-intensity radio-wave emission

Galactic plane

Blue indicates low-intensity radio-wave emission

South Galactic Pole

Yellow and green indicate medium-intensity radio-wave emission

PANORAMIC INFRA-RED MAP OF OUR GALAXY

North Galactic Pole

Low-intensity infra-red radiation from interstellar gas and dust

Galactic plane

Galactic plane

South Galactic Pole

High-intensity infra-red radiation from interstellar gas and dust

High-intensity infra-red radiation from region of starbirth

Vega, a white main sequence star; the fifth brightest star in the sky

North Galactic Pole

Dark clouds of dust and gas obscuring light from part of the Sagittarius Arm

Light from stars and nebulae in the part of the Sagittarius Arm between the Sun and Galactic centre

Light from stars and nebulae in the Perseus Arm

Galactic plane

Orion's belt, a row of three bright stars

Orion Nebula

Sirius, a white main sequence star; the brightest star in the sky

Canopus, a white supergiant; the second brightest star in the sky

Dust clouds obscuring Galactic centre

South Galactic Pole

Small Magellanic Cloud, an irregular galaxy 190,000 light years away; the second nearest object to our galaxy

Large Magellanic Cloud, an irregular galaxy 170,000 light years away; the nearest object to our galaxy

Nebulae and star clusters

HODGE 11, A GLOBULAR CLUSTER

A NEBULA IS A CLOUD OF DUST AND GAS inside a galaxy. Nebulae become visible if the gas glows, or if the cloud reflects starlight or obscures light from more distant objects. Emission nebulae shine because their gas emits light when it is stimulated by radiation from hot young stars. Reflection nebulae shine because their dust reflects light from stars in or around the nebula. Dark nebulae appear as silhouettes because they block out light from shining nebulae or stars behind them. Two types of nebula are associated with dying stars: planetary nebulae and supernova remnants. Both consist of expanding shells of gas that were once the outer layers of a star. A planetary nebula is a gas shell drifting away from a dying stellar core. A supernova remnant is a gas shell moving away from a stellar core at great speed following a violent explosion called a supernova (see pp. 26-27). Stars are often found in groups known as clusters. Open clusters are loose groups of a few thousand young stars that were born in the same cloud and are drifting apart. Globular clusters are densely packed, roughly spherical groups of hundreds of thousands of older stars.

TRIFID NEBULA (EMISSION NEBULA)

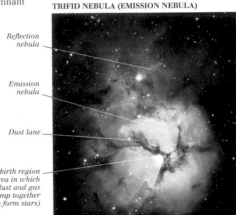

Reflection nebula

Emission nebula

Dust lane

Starbirth region (area in which dust and gas clump together to form stars)

PLEIADES (OPEN STAR CLUSTER) WITH A REFLECTION NEBULA

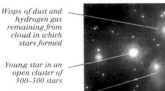

Wisps of dust and hydrogen gas remaining from cloud in which stars formed

Young star in an open cluster of 300–500 stars

Reflection nebula

HORSEHEAD NEBULA (DARK NEBULA)

Glowing filament of hot, ionized hydrogen gas

Alnitak (star in Orion's belt)

Dust lane

Emission nebula

Star near southern end of Orion's belt

Emission nebula

Horsehead Nebula

Reflection nebula

Dark nebula obscuring light from distant stars

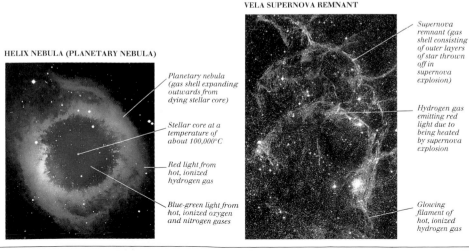

ORION NEBULA (DIFFUSE EMISSION NEBULA)

Glowing cloud of dust and hydrogen gas forming part of Orion Nebula

Dust cloud

Trapezium (group of four young stars)

Red light from hot, ionized hydrogen gas

Gas cloud emitting light due to ultraviolet radiation from the four young Trapezium stars

Green light from hot, ionized oxygen gas

Glowing filament of hot, ionized hydrogen gas

VELA SUPERNOVA REMNANT

Supernova remnant (gas shell consisting of outer layers of star thrown off in supernova explosion)

Hydrogen gas emitting red light due to being heated by supernova explosion

Glowing filament of hot, ionized hydrogen gas

HELIX NEBULA (PLANETARY NEBULA)

Planetary nebula (gas shell expanding outwards from dying stellar core)

Stellar core at a temperature of about 100,000°C

Red light from hot, ionized hydrogen gas

Blue-green light from hot, ionized oxygen and nitrogen gases

17

Stars of northern skies

WHEN YOU LOOK AT THE NORTHERN SKY, you look away from the densely populated Galactic centre, so the northern sky generally appears less bright than the southern sky (see pp. 20-21). Among the best-known sights in the northern sky are the constellations Ursa Major (the Great Bear) and Orion. Some ancient civilizations believed that the stars were fixed to a celestial sphere surrounding the Earth, and modern maps of the sky are based on a similar idea. The North and South Poles of this imaginary celestial sphere are directly above the North and South Poles of the Earth, at the points where the Earth's axis of rotation intersects the sphere. The celestial North Pole is at the centre of the map shown here, and Polaris (the Pole Star) lies very close to it. The celestial equator marks a projection of the Earth's equator on the sphere. The ecliptic marks the path of the Sun across the sky as the Earth orbits the Sun. The Moon and planets move against the background of the stars because the stars are much more distant; the nearest star outside the Solar System (Proxima Centauri) is more than 50,000 times further away than the planet Jupiter.

ORION

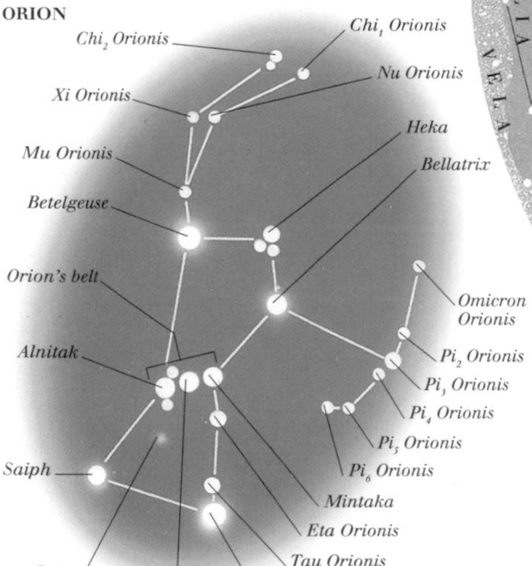

Chi$_2$ Orionis
Chi$_1$ Orionis
Nu Orionis
Xi Orionis
Heka
Mu Orionis
Bellatrix
Betelgeuse
Orion's belt
Omicron Orionis
Alnitak
Pi$_2$ Orionis
Pi$_3$ Orionis
Pi$_4$ Orionis
Pi$_5$ Orionis
Pi$_6$ Orionis
Saiph
Mintaka
Eta Orionis
Tau Orionis
Orion Nebula
Rigel
Alnilam

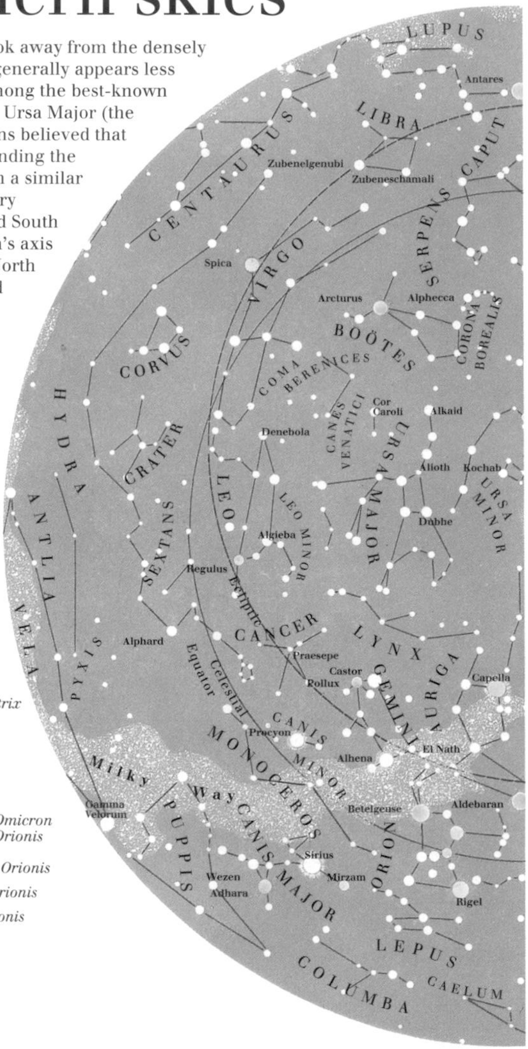

VISIBLE STARS IN THE NORTHERN SKY

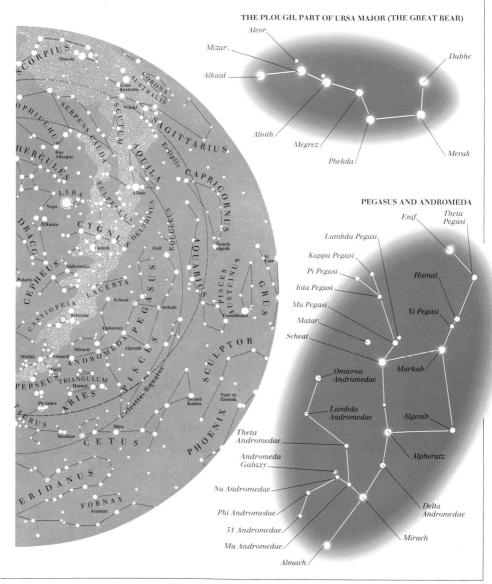

THE PLOUGH, PART OF URSA MAJOR (THE GREAT BEAR)

Alcor
Mizar
Dubhe
Alkaid
Alioth
Megrez
Merak
Phekda

PEGASUS AND ANDROMEDA

Enif
Theta Pegasi
Lambda Pegasi
Kappa Pegasi
Pi Pegasi
Hamal
Iota Pegasi
Mu Pegasi
Xi Pegasi
Matar
Scheat
Omicron Andromedae
Markab
Lambda Andromedae
Algenib
Theta Andromedae
Alpheratz
Andromeda Galaxy
Nu Andromedae
Delta Andromedae
Phi Andromedae
51 Andromedae
Mu Andromedae
Mirach
Almach

SCORPIUS
Shaula
CORONA AUSTRALIS
Kaus Australis
OPHIUCHUS
SERPENS CAUDA
Nunki
SAGITTARIUS
SCUTUM
Ecliptic
CAPRICORNUS
HERCULES
Ras Alhague
AQUILA
VULPECULA
LYRA
Altair
Vega
Eltanin
CYGNUS
DELPHINUS
Deneb Algedi
DRACO
Deneb
Alderamin
Enif
EQUULEUS
AQUARIUS
Al Nair
CEPHEUS
Polaris
LACERTA
PEGASUS
PISCIS AUSTRINUS
GRUS
CASSIOPEIA
Scheat
Markab
Fomalhaut
Schedar
Alpheratz
ANDROMEDA
Algenib
PEGASUS
Mirfak
Mirach
Almach
PISCES
SCULPTOR
Algol
TRIANGULUM
PERSEUS
Hamal
ARIES
Celestial Equator
Deneb Kaitos
Natr Al Zaurak
PHOENIX
Pleiades
TAURUS
Mira
Menkar
CETUS
ERIDANUS
FORNAX
Acamar

19

Stars of southern skies

WHEN YOU LOOK AT THE SOUTHERN SKY, you look towards the Galactic centre, which has a huge population of stars. As a result, the Milky Way appears brighter in the southern sky than in the northern sky (see pp. 18-19). The southern sky is rich in nebulae and star clusters. It contains the Large and Small Magellanic Clouds, which are the two nearest galaxies to our own. Stars make fixed patterns in the sky called constellations. However, the constellations are only apparent groupings of stars, since the distances to the stars in a constellation may vary enormously. The shapes of constellations may change over many thousands of years due to the relative motions of stars. The movement of the constellations across the sky is due to the Earth's motion in space. The daily rotation of the Earth causes the constellations to move across the sky from east to west, and the orbit of the Earth around the Sun causes different areas of sky to be visible in different seasons. The visibility of areas of sky also depends on the location of the observer. For instance, stars near the celestial equator may be seen from either hemisphere at some time during the year, whereas stars close to the celestial poles (the celestial South Pole is at the centre of the map shown here) can never be seen from the opposite hemisphere.

HYDRUS (THE WATER SNAKE) AND MENSA (THE TABLE)

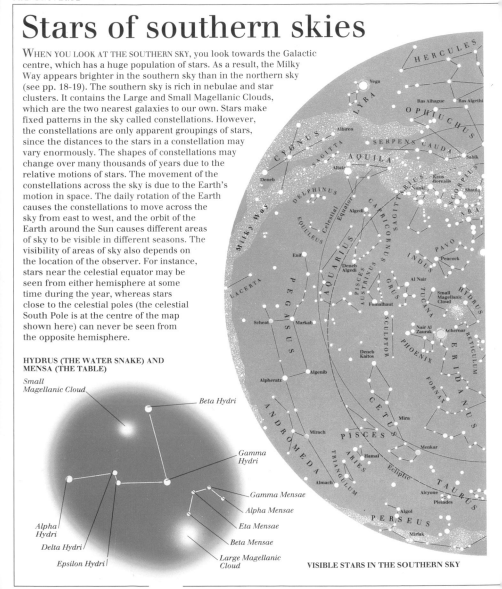

VISIBLE STARS IN THE SOUTHERN SKY

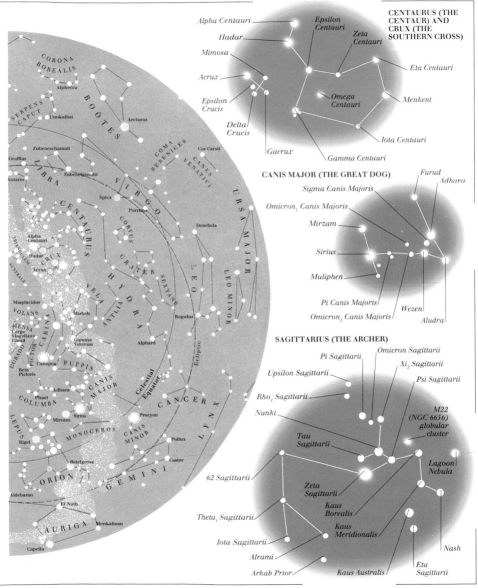

CENTAURUS (THE CENTAUR) AND CRUX (THE SOUTHERN CROSS)

Alpha Centauri
Epsilon Centauri
Hadar
Zeta Centauri
Mimosa
Acrux
Eta Centauri
Epsilon Crucis
Omega Centauri
Menkent
Delta Crucis
Iota Centauri
Gacrux
Gamma Centauri

CANIS MAJOR (THE GREAT DOG)

Furud
Adhara
Sigma Canis Majoris
Omicron₁ Canis Majoris
Mirzam
Sirius
Muliphen
Pi Canis Majoris
Wezen
Omicron₂ Canis Majoris
Aludra

SAGITTARIUS (THE ARCHER)

Pi Sagittarii
Omicron Sagittarii
Xi₂ Sagittarii
Upsilon Sagittarii
Psi Sagittarii
Rho₁ Sagittarii
M22 (NGC 6656) globular cluster
Nunki
Tau Sagittarii
Lagoon Nebula
62 Sagittarii
Zeta Sagittarii
Kaus Borealis
Theta₁ Sagittarii
Kaus Meridionalis
Iota Sagittarii
Alrami
Eta Sagittarii
Arkab Prior
Kaus Australis
Nash

CORONA BOREALIS
Alphecca
SERPENS CAPUT
Unukalhai
BOÖTES
Arcturus
COMA BERENICES
Cor Caroli
CANES VENATICI
URSA MAJOR
Zubeneschamali
VIRGO
Graffias
Antares
LIBRA
Zubenelgenubi
CENTAURUS
Spica
Porrima
CRATER
SEXTANS
Denebola
LEO
LEO MINOR
Alpha Centauri
Hadar
CRUX
Acrux
HYDRA
CORVUS
Regulus
Ecliptic
Miaplacidus
VELA
ANTLIA
Alphard
VOLANS
Markeb
MENSA
Large Magellanic Cloud
DORADO
PICTOR
CARINA
Gamma Velorum
PUPPIS
Regulus
CANCER
LYNX
Canopus
Beta Pictoris
COLUMBA
Adhara
Phact
CANIS MAJOR
Procyon
Pollux
Mirzam
Sirius
CANIS MINOR
Castor
LEPUS
Rigel
MONOCEROS
Betelgeuse
ORION
GEMINI
Aldebaran
El Nath
Menkalinan
AURIGA
Capella
TRIANGULUM AUSTRALE
Celestial Equator
21

Stars

OPEN STAR CLUSTER AND DUST CLOUD

STARS ARE BODIES of hot, glowing gas that are born in nebulae (see pp. 24-27). They vary enormously in size, mass, and temperature: diameters range from about 450 times smaller to over 1,000 times bigger than that of the Sun; masses range from about a twentieth to over 50 solar masses; and surface temperatures range from about 3,000°C to over 50,000°C. The colour of a star is determined by its temperature: the hottest stars are blue and the coolest are red. The Sun, with a surface temperature of 5,500°C, is between these extremes and appears yellow. The energy emitted by a shining star is produced by nuclear fusion in the star's core. The brightness of a star is measured in magnitudes – the brighter the star, the lower its magnitude. There are two types of magnitude: apparent magnitude, which is the brightness seen from Earth, and absolute magnitude, which is the brightness that would be seen from a standard distance of 10 parsecs (32.6 light years). The light emitted by a star may be split to form a spectrum containing a series of dark lines (absorption lines). The patterns of lines indicate the presence of particular chemical elements, enabling astronomers to deduce the composition of the star's atmosphere. The magnitude and spectral type (colour) of stars may be plotted on a graph called a Hertzsprung-Russell diagram, which shows that stars tend to fall into several well-defined groups. The principal groups are main sequence stars (those which are fusing hydrogen to form helium), giants, supergiants, and white dwarfs.

STAR SIZES

Red giant (diameters between about 15 million and 150 million km)

The Sun (main sequence star with diameter about 1.4 million km)

White dwarf (diameters between about 3,000 and 50,000 km)

ENERGY EMISSION FROM THE SUN

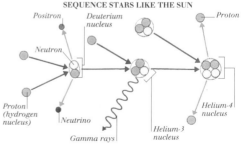

Nuclear fusion in core produces gamma rays and neutrinos

Neutrinos travel to Earth directly from Sun's core in about 8 minutes

Lower-energy radiation travels to Earth in about 8 minutes

Earth

Lower-energy radiation (mainly ultraviolet, infra-red, and light rays) leaves surface

Sun

High-energy radiation (gamma rays) loses energy while travelling to surface over 2 million years

STAR MAGNITUDES

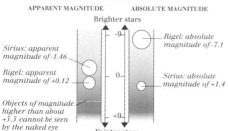

APPARENT MAGNITUDE   ABSOLUTE MAGNITUDE

Brighter stars

Sirius: apparent magnitude of -1.46

Rigel: apparent magnitude of +0.12

Rigel: absolute magnitude of -7.1

Sirius: absolute magnitude of +1.4

Objects of magnitude higher than about +5.5 cannot be seen by the naked eye

Fainter stars

NUCLEAR FUSION IN MAIN SEQUENCE STARS LIKE THE SUN

Positron *Deuterium nucleus* *Proton*

Neutron

Proton (hydrogen nucleus)

Neutrino

Gamma rays

Helium-3 nucleus

Helium-4 nucleus

HERTZSPRUNG-RUSSELL DIAGRAM

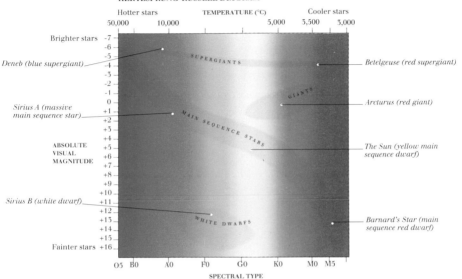

Hotter stars   TEMPERATURE (°C)   Cooler stars

50,000   10,000   5,000   3,500   3,000

Brighter stars −7

Deneb (blue supergiant)   −6 −5 −4   SUPERGIANTS   Betelgeuse (red supergiant)

−3 −2 −1

GIANTS

0   Arcturus (red giant)

Sirius A (massive main sequence star)   +1   MAIN SEQUENCE STARS +2 +3 +4

ABSOLUTE VISUAL MAGNITUDE +5 +6   The Sun (yellow main sequence dwarf) +7 +8 +9 +10

Sirius B (white dwarf) +11 +12   WHITE DWARFS +13   Barnard's Star (main sequence red dwarf) +14 +15

Fainter stars +16

O5   B0   A0   F0   G0   K0   M0   M5

SPECTRAL TYPE

STELLAR SPECTRAL ABSORPTION LINES

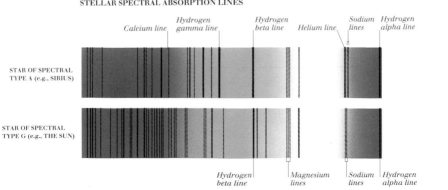

Calcium line   *Hydrogen gamma line*   *Hydrogen beta line*   *Helium line*   *Sodium lines*   *Hydrogen alpha line*

STAR OF SPECTRAL TYPE A (e.g., SIRIUS)

STAR OF SPECTRAL TYPE G (e.g., THE SUN)

Hydrogen beta line   *Magnesium lines*   *Sodium lines*   *Hydrogen alpha line*

Small stars

REGION OF STAR FORMATION IN ORION

SMALL STARS HAVE A MASS of up to about one and a half times that of the Sun. They begin to form when a region of higher density in a nebula condenses into a huge globule of gas and dust that contracts under its own gravity. Within a globule, regions of condensing matter heat up and begin to glow, forming protostars. If a protostar contains enough matter, the central temperature reaches about 15 million °C. At this temperature, nuclear reactions in which hydrogen fuses to form helium can start. This process releases energy, which prevents the star from contracting further and also causes it to shine; it is now a main sequence star. A star of about one solar mass remains in the main sequence for about 10 billion years, until the hydrogen in the star's core has been converted into helium. The helium core then contracts again, and nuclear reactions continue in a shell around the core. The core becomes hot enough for helium to fuse to form carbon, while the outer layers of the star expand, cool, and shine less brightly. The expanding star is known as a red giant. When the helium in the core runs out, the outer layers of the star may drift off as an expanding gas shell called a planetary nebula. The remaining core (about 80 per cent of the original star) is now in its final stages. It becomes a white dwarf star that gradually cools and dims. When it finally stops shining altogether, the dead star will become a black dwarf.

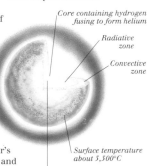

Core containing hydrogen fusing to form helium

Radiative zone

Convective zone

Surface temperature about 5,500°C

Core temperature about 15 million °C

STRUCTURE OF A NEBULA

Young main sequence star

Dense region of dust and gas (mainly hydrogen) condensing under gravity to form globules

Hot, ionized hydrogen gas emitting red light due to being stimulated by radiation from hot young stars

Dark globule of dust and gas (mainly hydrogen) contracting to form protostars

LIFE OF A SMALL STAR OF ABOUT ONE SOLAR MASS

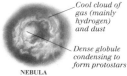

Cool cloud of gas (mainly hydrogen) and dust

Dense globule condensing to form protostars

NEBULA

Glowing ball of gas (mainly hydrogen)

Natal cocoon (shell of dust blown away by radiation from protostar)

PROTOSTAR
Duration: 50 million years

About 1.4 million km

Star producing energy by nuclear fusion in core

MAIN SEQUENCE STAR
Duration: 10 billion years

STRUCTURE OF A RED GIANT

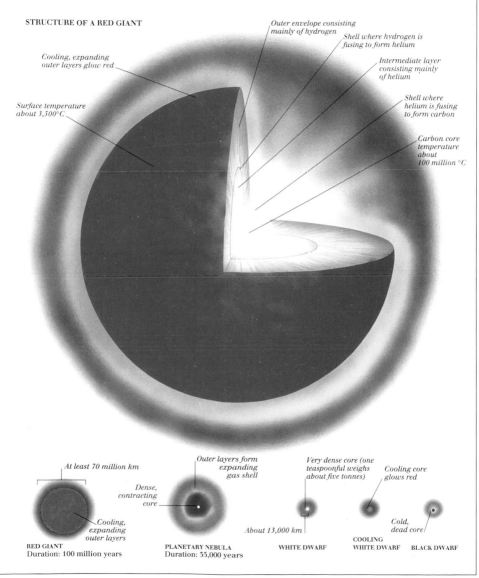

Outer envelope consisting
mainly of hydrogen

Shell where hydrogen is
fusing to form helium

Intermediate layer
consisting mainly
of helium

Shell where
helium is fusing
to form carbon

Carbon core
temperature
about
100 million °C

Cooling, expanding
outer layers glow red

Surface temperature
about 3,500°C

At least 70 million km

Cooling,
expanding
outer layers

RED GIANT
Duration: 100 million years

Outer layers form
expanding gas shell

Dense,
contracting
core

PLANETARY NEBULA
Duration: 35,000 years

Very dense core (one
teaspoonful weighs
about five tonnes)

About 13,000 km

WHITE DWARF

Cooling core
glows red

Cold,
dead core

COOLING
WHITE DWARF

BLACK DWARF

Massive stars

MASSIVE STARS HAVE A MASS AT LEAST THREE TIMES that of the Sun, and some stars are as massive as about 50 Suns. A massive star evolves in a similar way to a small star until it reaches the main sequence stage (see pp. 24-25). During the main sequence, a star shines steadily until the hydrogen in its core has fused to form helium. This process takes billions of years in a small star, but only millions of years in a massive star. A massive star then becomes a red supergiant, which initially consists of a helium core surrounded by outer layers of cooling, expanding gas. Over the next few million years, a series of nuclear reactions form different elements in shells around an iron core. The core eventually collapses in less than a second, causing a massive explosion called a supernova, in which a shock wave blows away the outer layers of the star. Supernovae shine brighter than an entire galaxy for a short time. Sometimes, the core survives the supernova explosion. If the surviving core is between about one and a half and three solar masses, it contracts to become a tiny, dense neutron star. If the core is considerably greater than three solar masses, it contracts to become a black hole (see pp. 28-29).

SUPERNOVA

TARANTULA NEBULA BEFORE SUPERNOVA

STRUCTURE OF A RED SUPERGIANT

Outer envelope consisting mainly of hydrogen

Layer consisting mainly of helium

Layer consisting mainly of carbon

Layer consisting mainly of oxygen

Layer consisting mainly of silicon

Shell of hydrogen fusing to form helium

Shell of helium fusing to form carbon

Shell of carbon fusing to form oxygen

Shell of oxygen fusing to form silicon

Shell of silicon fusing to form iron core

Surface temperature about 3,000°C

Cooling, expanding outer layers glow red

Core of mainly iron at a temperature of 3–5 billion °C

LIFE OF A MASSIVE STAR OF ABOUT 10 SOLAR MASSES

Dense globule condensing to form protostars

Cool cloud of gas (mainly hydrogen) and dust

NEBULA

Glowing ball of gas (mainly hydrogen)

About 3 million km

Natal cocoon (shell of dust blown away by radiation from protostar)

PROTOSTAR
Duration: a few hundred thousand years

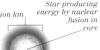

Star producing energy by nuclear fusion in core

MAIN SEQUENCE STAR
Duration: 10 million years

FEATURES OF A SUPERNOVA

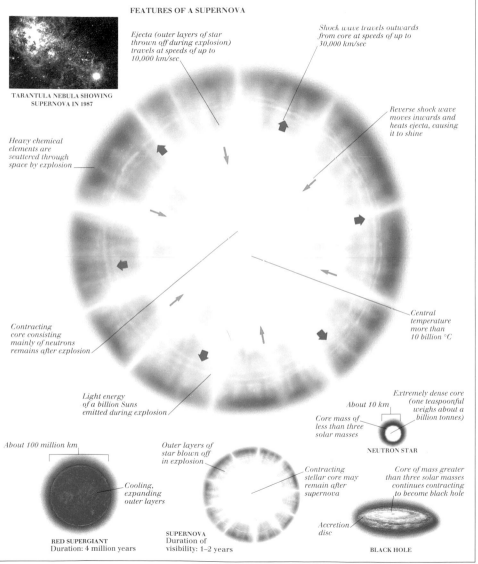

TARANTULA NEBULA SHOWING
SUPERNOVA IN 1987

Ejecta (outer layers of star thrown off during explosion) travels at speeds of up to 10,000 km/sec

Shock wave travels outwards from core at speeds of up to 30,000 km/sec

Reverse shock wave moves inwards and heats ejecta, causing it to shine

Heavy chemical elements are scattered through space by explosion

Contracting core consisting mainly of neutrons remains after explosion

Central temperature more than 10 billion °C

Light energy of a billion Suns emitted during explosion

Outer layers of star blown off in explosion

About 10 km

Extremely dense core (one teaspoonful weighs about a billion tonnes)

Core mass of less than three solar masses

NEUTRON STAR

About 100 million km

Cooling, expanding outer layers

Contracting stellar core may remain after supernova

Core of mass greater than three solar masses continues contracting to become black hole

Accretion disc

RED SUPERGIANT
Duration: 4 million years

SUPERNOVA
Duration of visibility: 1–2 years

BLACK HOLE

Neutron stars and black holes

NEUTRON STARS AND BLACK HOLES form from the stellar cores that remain after stars have exploded as supernovae (see pp. 26-27). If the remaining core is between about one and a half and three solar masses, it contracts to form a neutron star. If the remaining core is greater than about three solar masses, it contracts to form a black hole. Neutron stars are typically only about 10 kilometres in diameter and consist almost entirely of subatomic particles called neutrons. Such stars are so dense that a teaspoonful would weigh about a billion tonnes. Neutron stars are observed as pulsars, so-called because they rotate rapidly and emit two beams of radio waves, which sweep across the sky and are detected as short pulses. Black holes are characterized by their extremely strong gravity, which is so powerful that not even light can escape; as a result, black holes are invisible. However, they may be detected if they have a close companion star. The gravity of the black hole pulls gas from the other star, forming an accretion disc that spirals around the black hole at high speed, heating up and emitting radiation. Eventually, the matter spirals in to cross the event horizon (the boundary of the black hole), thereby disappearing from the visible Universe.

X-ray emission from pulsar (neutron star rotating 30 times each second)

X-ray emission from centre of nebula

X-RAY IMAGE OF THE CRAB NEBULA (SUPERNOVA REMNANT)

PULSAR (ROTATING NEUTRON STAR)

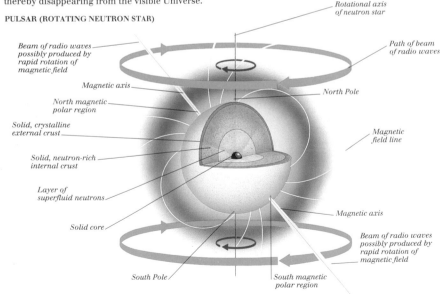

Rotational axis of neutron star

Beam of radio waves possibly produced by rapid rotation of magnetic field

Path of beam of radio waves

Magnetic axis

North magnetic polar region

North Pole

Solid, crystalline external crust

Magnetic field line

Solid, neutron-rich internal crust

Layer of superfluid neutrons

Magnetic axis

Solid core

Beam of radio waves possibly produced by rapid rotation of magnetic field

South Pole

South magnetic polar region

STELLAR BLACK HOLE

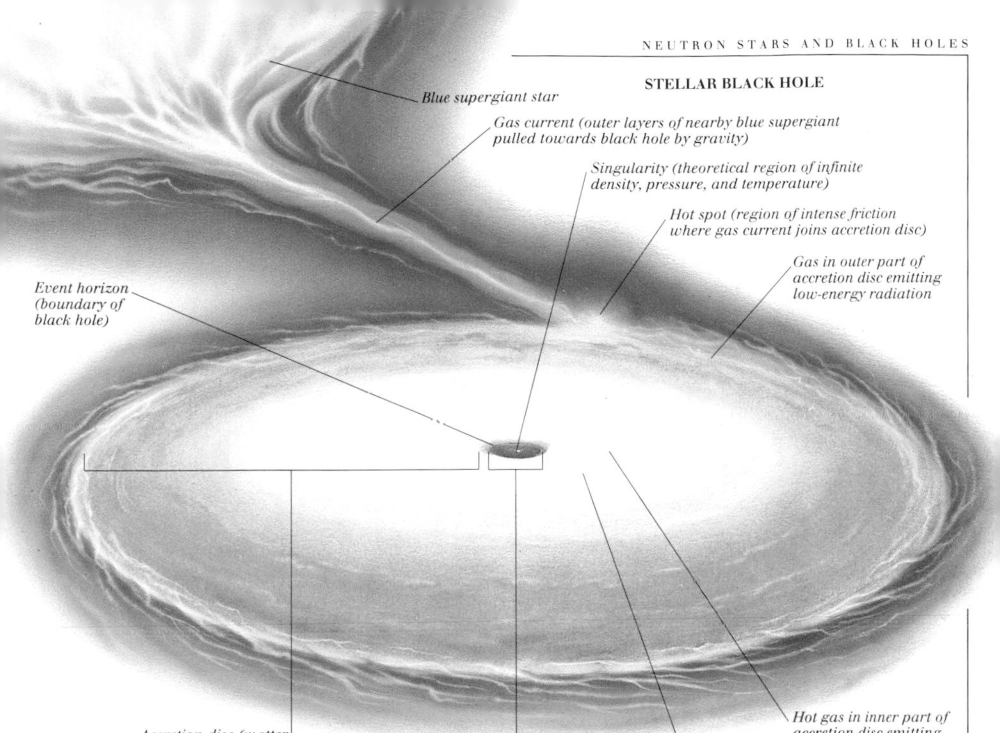

Blue supergiant star

Gas current (outer layers of nearby blue supergiant pulled towards black hole by gravity)

Singularity (theoretical region of infinite density, pressure, and temperature)

Hot spot (region of intense friction where gas current joins accretion disc)

Gas in outer part of accretion disc emitting low-energy radiation

Event horizon (boundary of black hole)

Hot gas in inner part of accretion disc emitting high-energy X-rays

Accretion disc (matter spiralling around black hole)

Black hole

Gas at temperatures of millions °C spiralling at close to the speed of light

FORMATION OF A BLACK HOLE

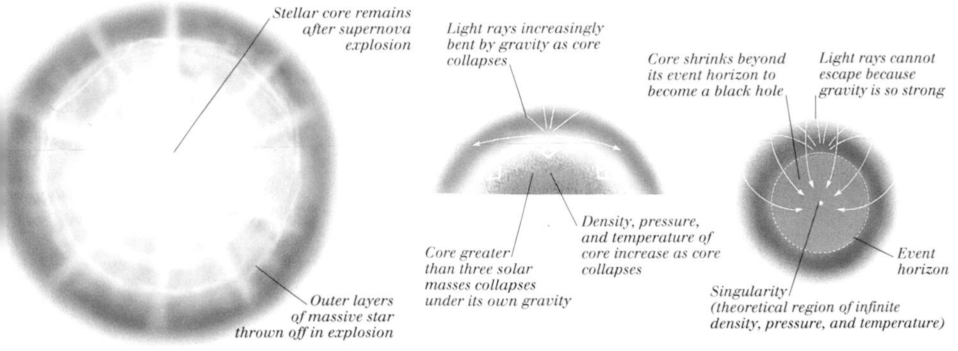

Stellar core remains after supernova explosion

Light rays increasingly bent by gravity as core collapses

Core shrinks beyond its event horizon to become a black hole

Light rays cannot escape because gravity is so strong

Outer layers of massive star thrown off in explosion

Core greater than three solar masses collapses under its own gravity

Density, pressure, and temperature of core increase as core collapses

Event horizon

Singularity (theoretical region of infinite density, pressure, and temperature)

SUPERNOVA

COLLAPSING STELLAR CORE

BLACK HOLE

The Solar System

THE SUN

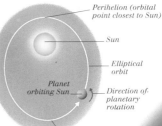

THE SOLAR SYSTEM consists of a central star (the Sun) and the bodies that orbit it. These bodies include nine planets and their 61 known moons; asteroids; comets; and meteoroids. The Solar System also contains interplanetary gas and dust. Most of the planets fall into two groups: four small rocky planets near the Sun (Mercury, Venus, Earth, and Mars); and four planets further out, the gas giants (Jupiter, Saturn, Uranus, and Neptune). Pluto belongs to neither group but is very small, solid, and icy. Pluto is the outermost planet, except when it passes briefly inside Neptune's orbit. Between the rocky planets and gas giants is the asteroid belt, which contains thousands of chunks of rock orbiting the Sun. Most of the bodies in the Solar System move around the Sun in elliptical orbits located in a thin disc around the Sun's equator. All the planets orbit the Sun in the same direction (anticlockwise when viewed from above) and all but Venus, Uranus, and Pluto also spin about their axes in this direction. Moons also spin as they, in turn, orbit their planets. The entire Solar System orbits the centre of our galaxy, the Milky Way (see pp. 14-15).

Perihelion (orbital point closest to Sun)

Sun

Elliptical orbit

Planet orbiting Sun

Direction of planetary rotation

Aphelion (orbital point furthest from Sun)

Aphelion of Neptune: 4,537 million km

ORBITS OF INNER PLANETS

Mercury

Perihelion of Mercury: 45.9 million km
Perihelion of Venus: 107.4 million km
Perihelion of Earth: 147 million km

Average orbital speed of Venus: 35.03 km/sec
Average orbital speed of Mercury: 47.89 km/sec
Average orbital speed of Earth: 29.79 km/sec
Average orbital speed of Mars: 24.13 km/sec

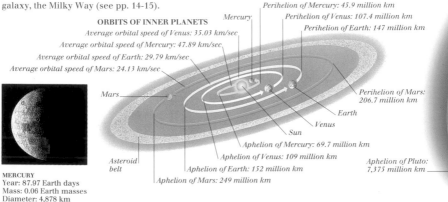

Mars

Perihelion of Mars: 206.7 million km

Earth

Venus

Sun

Aphelion of Mercury: 69.7 million km

Asteroid belt

Aphelion of Venus: 109 million km

Aphelion of Earth: 152 million km

Aphelion of Mars: 249 million km

Aphelion of Pluto: 7,375 million km

MERCURY
Year: 87.97 Earth days
Mass: 0.06 Earth masses
Diameter: 4,878 km

VENUS
Year: 224.7 Earth days
Mass: 0.81 Earth masses
Diameter: 12,103 km

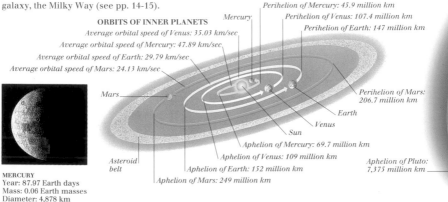

EARTH
Year: 365.26 days
Mass: 1 Earth mass
Diameter: 12,756 km

MARS
Year: 1.88 Earth years
Mass: 0.11 Earth masses
Diameter: 6,786 km

JUPITER
Year: 11.86 Earth years
Mass: 317.94 Earth masses
Diameter: 142,984 km

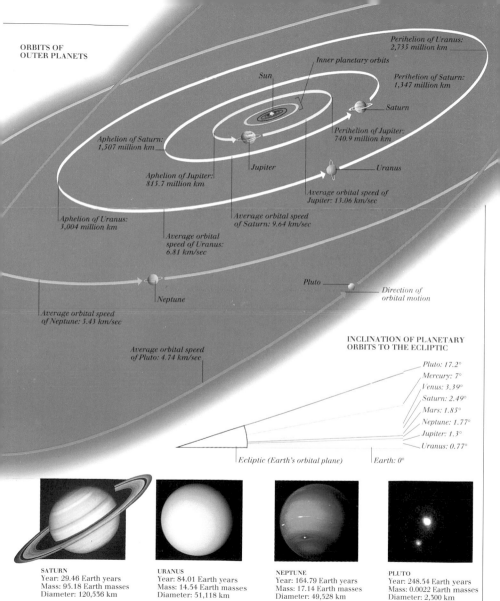

ORBITS OF OUTER PLANETS

Perihelion of Uranus: 2,735 million km

Inner planetary orbits

Sun

Perihelion of Saturn: 1,347 million km

Saturn

Aphelion of Saturn: 1,507 million km

Perihelion of Jupiter: 740.9 million km

Jupiter

Uranus

Aphelion of Jupiter: 815.7 million km

Average orbital speed of Jupiter: 13.06 km/sec

Aphelion of Uranus: 3,004 million km

Average orbital speed of Saturn: 9.64 km/sec

Average orbital speed of Uranus: 6.81 km/sec

Pluto

Direction of orbital motion

Neptune

Average orbital speed of Neptune: 5.43 km/sec

Average orbital speed of Pluto: 4.74 km/sec

INCLINATION OF PLANETARY ORBITS TO THE ECLIPTIC

Pluto: 17.2°
Mercury: 7°
Venus: 3.39°
Saturn: 2.49°
Mars: 1.85°
Neptune: 1.77°
Jupiter: 1.3°
Uranus: 0.77°

Ecliptic (Earth's orbital plane) *Earth: 0°*

SATURN
Year: 29.46 Earth years
Mass: 95.18 Earth masses
Diameter: 120,536 km

URANUS
Year: 84.01 Earth years
Mass: 14.54 Earth masses
Diameter: 51,118 km

NEPTUNE
Year: 164.79 Earth years
Mass: 17.14 Earth masses
Diameter: 49,528 km

PLUTO
Year: 248.54 Earth years
Mass: 0.0022 Earth masses
Diameter: 2,300 km

The Sun

SOLAR PHOTOSPHERE

THE SUN IS THE STAR AT THE CENTRE of the Solar System. It is about five billion years old and will continue to shine as it does now for about another five billion years. The Sun is a yellow main sequence star (see pp. 22-23) about 1.4 million kilometres in diameter. It consists almost entirely of hydrogen and helium. In the Sun's core, hydrogen is converted to helium by nuclear fusion, releasing energy in the process. The energy travels from the core, through the radiative and convective zones, to the photosphere (visible surface), where it leaves the Sun in the form of heat and light. On the photosphere there are often dark, relatively cool areas called sunspots, which usually appear in pairs or groups and are thought to be caused by magnetic fields. Other types of solar activity are flares, which are usually associated with sunspots, and prominences. Flares are sudden discharges of high-energy radiation and atomic particles. Prominences are huge loops or filaments of gas extending into the solar atmosphere; some last for hours, others for months. Beyond the photosphere is the chromosphere (inner atmosphere) and the extremely rarified corona (outer atmosphere), which extends millions of kilometres into space. Tiny particles that escape from the corona give rise to the solar wind, which streams through space at hundreds of kilometres per second. The chromosphere and corona can be seen from Earth when the Sun is totally eclipsed by the Moon.

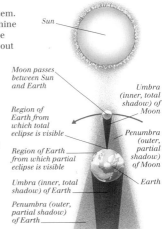

Sun

Moon passes between Sun and Earth

Umbra (inner, total shadow) of Moon

Region of Earth from which total eclipse is visible

Penumbra (outer, partial shadow) of Moon

Region of Earth from which partial eclipse is visible

Earth

Umbra (inner, total shadow) of Earth

Penumbra (outer, partial shadow) of Earth

SURFACE FEATURES

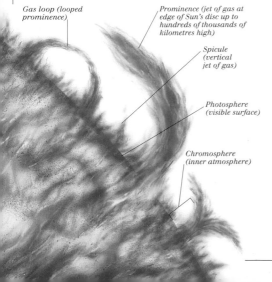

Gas loop (looped prominence)

Prominence (jet of gas at edge of Sun's disc up to hundreds of thousands of kilometres high)

Spicule (vertical jet of gas)

Photosphere (visible surface)

Chromosphere (inner atmosphere)

TOTAL SOLAR ECLIPSE

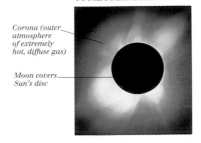

Corona (outer atmosphere of extremely hot, diffuse gas)

Moon covers Sun's disc

SUNSPOTS

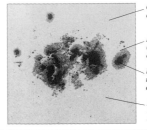

Granulated surface of Sun

Penumbra (lighter, outer region) containing radial fibril

Umbra (darker, inner region) temperature about 4,000°C

Photosphere temperature about 5,500°C

EXTERNAL FEATURES AND
INTERNAL STRUCTURE OF THE SUN

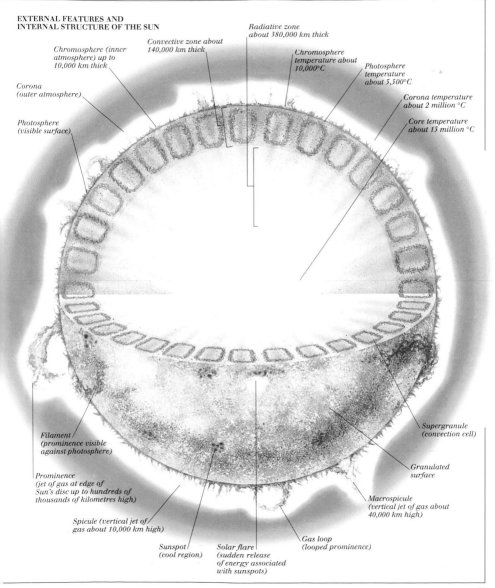

Chromosphere (inner atmosphere) up to 10,000 km thick

Convective zone about 140,000 km thick

Radiative zone about 380,000 km thick

Chromosphere temperature about 10,000°C

Photosphere temperature about 5,500°C

Corona (outer atmosphere)

Corona temperature about 2 million °C

Core temperature about 15 million °C

Photosphere (visible surface)

Filament (prominence visible against photosphere)

Prominence (jet of gas at edge of Sun's disc up to hundreds of thousands of kilometres high)

Spicule (vertical jet of gas about 10,000 km high)

Sunspot (cool region)

Solar flare (sudden release of energy associated with sunspots)

Gas loop (looped prominence)

Macrospicule (vertical jet of gas about 40,000 km high)

Granulated surface

Supergranule (convection cell)

Mercury

MERCURY

MERCURY IS THE NEAREST PLANET to the Sun, orbiting at an average distance of about 58 million kilometres. Because Mercury is the closest planet to the Sun, it moves faster than any other planet, travelling at an average speed of nearly 48 kilometres per second and completing an orbit in just under 88 days. Mercury is very small (only Pluto is smaller) and rocky. Most of the surface has been heavily cratered by the impact of meteorites, although there are also smooth, sparsely cratered plains. The Caloris Basin is the largest crater, measuring about 1,300 kilometres across. It is thought to have been formed when a rock the size of an asteroid hit the planet, and is surrounded by concentric rings of mountains thrown up by the impact. The surface also has many ridges (called rupes) that are thought to have been formed when the hot core of the young planet cooled and shrank about four billion years ago, buckling the planet's surface in the process. The planet rotates about its axis very slowly, taking nearly 59 Earth days to complete one rotation. As a result, a solar day (sunrise to sunrise) on Mercury is about 176 Earth days – twice as long as the 88-day Mercurian year. Mercury has extreme surface temperatures, ranging from a maximum of 430°C on the sunlit side to -170°C on the dark side. At nightfall, the temperature drops very quickly because the planet's atmosphere is almost non-existent. It consists only of minute amounts of helium and hydrogen captured from the solar wind, plus traces of other gases.

TILT AND ROTATION OF MERCURY

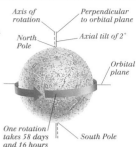

Axis of rotation

Perpendicular to orbital plane

North Pole

Axial tilt of 2°

Orbital plane

One rotation takes 58 days and 16 hours

South Pole

DEGAS AND BRONTË (RAY CRATERS)

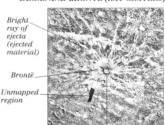

Bright ray of ejecta (ejected material)

Brontë

Unmapped region

Degas with central peak

FORMATION OF A RAY CRATER

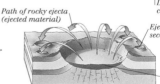

Debris thrown out by impact

Path of meteorite colliding with planet

Wall of rock thrown up around crater

Impact forms saucer-shaped crater

Fractured rock

METEORITE IMPACT

Path of rocky ejecta (ejected material)

Ejecta forms secondary craters

Loose debris on crater floor

SECONDARY CRATERING

Wall of rock forms ring of mountains

Ray of ejecta (ejected material)

Small secondary crater

Loose ejected rock

Central mountain rings form if floor of large crater recoils from meteorite impact

Falling debris forms ridges on side of wall

RAY CRATER

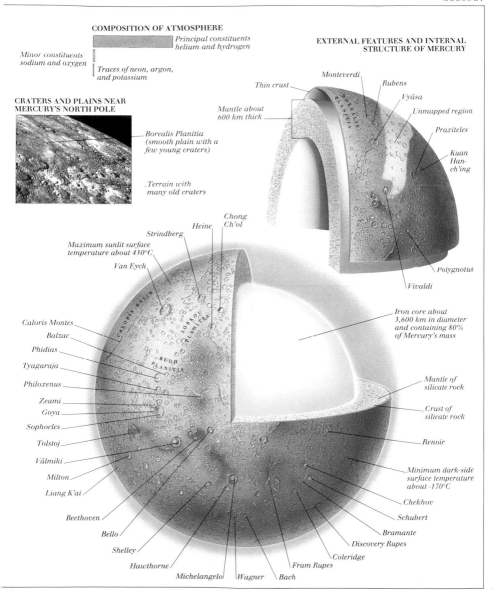

COMPOSITION OF ATMOSPHERE

Principal constituents
helium and hydrogen

Minor constituents
sodium and oxygen

Traces of neon, argon,
and potassium

EXTERNAL FEATURES AND INTERNAL
STRUCTURE OF MERCURY

Monteverdi
Rubens
Vyāsa
Unmapped region
Praxiteles
Kuan
Han-
ch'ing

Thin crust

Mantle
about
600 km thick

Polygnotus

Vivaldi

CRATERS AND PLAINS NEAR
MERCURY'S NORTH POLE

Borealis Planitia
(smooth plain with a
few young craters)

Terrain with
many old craters

Chong
Ch'ol

Heine

Strindberg

Maximum sunlit surface
temperature about 430°C

Van Eyck

Caloris Montes
Balzac
Phidias
Tyagaraja
Philoxenus
Zeami
Goya
Sophocles
Tolstoj
Vālmiki
Milton
Liang K'ai
Beethoven
Bello
Shelley
Hawthorne
Michelangelo
Wagner
Bach
Fram Rupes
Coleridge
Discovery Rupes
Bramante
Schubert
Chekhov

Minimum dark-side
surface temperature
about -170°C

Renoir

Crust of
silicate rock

Mantle of
silicate rock

Iron core about
3,600 km in diameter
and containing 80%
of Mercury's mass

Venus

RADAR IMAGE OF VENUS

VENUS IS A ROCKY PLANET and the second planet from the Sun. Venus spins slowly backwards as it orbits the Sun, causing its rotational period to be the longest in the Solar System, at about 243 Earth days. It is slightly smaller than Earth and probably has a similar internal structure, consisting of a semi-solid metal core, surrounded by a rocky mantle and crust. Venus is the brightest object in the sky after the Sun and Moon because its atmosphere reflects sunlight strongly. The main component of the atmosphere is carbon dioxide, which traps heat in a greenhouse effect far stronger than that on Earth. As a result, Venus is the hottest planet, with a maximum surface temperature of about 480°C. The thick cloud layers contain droplets of sulphuric acid and are driven around the planet by winds at speeds of up to 360 kilometres per hour. Although the planet takes 243 Earth days to rotate once, the high-speed winds cause the clouds to circle the planet in only four Earth days. The high temperature, acidic clouds, and enormous atmospheric pressure (about 90 times greater at the surface than that on Earth) make the environment extremely hostile. However, space probes have managed to land on Venus and photograph its dry, dusty surface. The Venusian surface has also been mapped by probes with radar equipment that can "see" through the cloud layers. Such radar maps reveal a terrain with craters, mountains, volcanoes, and areas where craters have been covered by plains of solidified volcanic lava. There are two large highland regions called Aphrodite Terra and Ishtar Terra.

TILT AND ROTATION OF VENUS

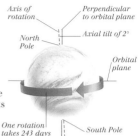

Axis of rotation
Perpendicular to orbital plane
North Pole
Axial tilt of 2°
Orbital plane
One rotation takes 243 days and 14 minutes
South Pole

CLOUD FEATURES

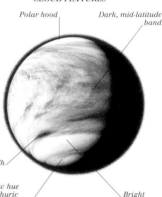

Polar hood
Dark, mid-latitude band
Cloud features swept around planet by winds of up to 360 km/h
Dirty yellow hue due to sulphuric acid in atmosphere
Bright polar band

VENUSIAN CRATERS

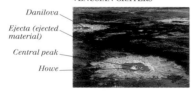

Danilova
Ejecta (ejected material)
Central peak
Howe

FALSE-COLOUR RADAR MAP OF THE SURFACE OF VENUS

Metis Regio
Maxwell Montes
Bell Regio
Tethus Regio
Atalanta Planitia
Sedna Planitia
Leda Planitia
Eisila Regio
Tellus Regio
Guinevere Planitia
Niobe Planitia
Phoebe Regio
Alpha Regio
Ovda Regio
Themis Regio
Thetis Regio
Lavinia Planitia
Aino Planitia
Helen Planitia
Lada Terra

ISHTAR TERRA
APHRODITE TERRA

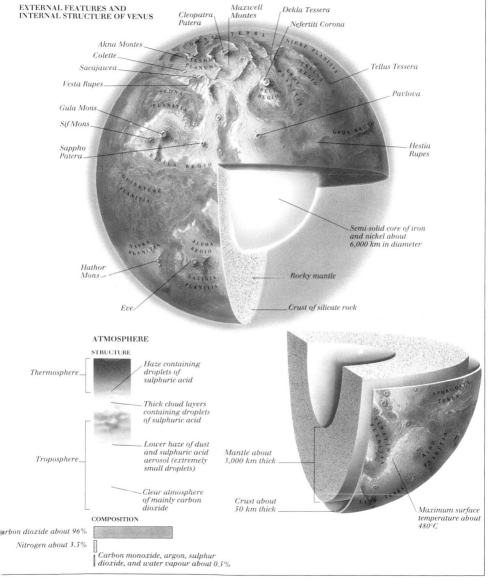

**EXTERNAL FEATURES AND
INTERNAL STRUCTURE OF VENUS**

Cleopatra Patera

Maxwell Montes

Dekla Tessera

Nefertiti Corona

Akna Montes

Colette

Sacajawea

Vesta Rupes

Gula Mons

Sif Mons

Sappho Patera

Tellus Tessera

Pavlova

Hestia Rupes

Semi-solid core of iron and nickel about 6,000 km in diameter

Hathor Mons

Eve

Rocky mantle

Crust of silicate rock

ATMOSPHERE

STRUCTURE

Thermosphere

Haze containing droplets of sulphuric acid

Thick cloud layers containing droplets of sulphuric acid

Lower haze of dust and sulphuric acid aerosol (extremely small droplets)

Troposphere

Clear atmosphere of mainly carbon dioxide

Mantle about 3,000 km thick

Crust about 50 km thick

Maximum surface temperature about 480°C

COMPOSITION

Carbon dioxide about 96%

Nitrogen about 3.5%

Carbon monoxide, argon, sulphur dioxide, and water vapour about 0.5%

The Earth

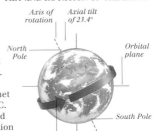

Axis of rotation

Axial tilt of 23.4°

North Pole

Orbital plane

South Pole

One rotation takes 23 hours and 56 minutes

Perpendicular to orbital plane

THE EARTH

THE EARTH IS THE THIRD of the nine planets that orbit the Sun. It is the largest and densest rocky planet, and the only one known to support life. About 70 per cent of the Earth's surface is covered by water, which is not found in liquid form on the surface of any other planet. There are four main layers: the inner core, the outer core, the mantle, and the crust. At the heart of the planet the solid inner core has a temperature of about 4,000°C. The heat from this inner core causes material in the molten outer core and mantle to circulate in convection currents. It is thought that these convection currents generate the Earth's magnetic field, which extends into space as the magnetosphere. The Earth's atmosphere helps screen out some of the harmful radiation from the Sun, stops meteorites from reaching the planet's surface, and traps enough heat to prevent extremes of cold. The Earth has one natural satellite, the Moon, which is large enough for both bodies to be considered a double-planet system.

THE FORMATION OF THE EARTH

The heat of the collisions caused the planet to glow red

Micro-organisms began to photosynthesize, creating a build up of oxygen

The cloud broke up into particles of ice and rock, which stuck together to form planets

4,600 MILLION YEARS AGO, THE SOLAR SYSTEM FORMED FROM A CLOUD OF GAS AND DUST

THE EARTH WAS FORMED FROM COLLIDING ROCKS

4,500 MILLION YEARS AGO THE SURFACE COOLED TO FORM THE CRUST

THE CONTINENTS BROKE UP AND REFORMED, GRADUALLY TAKING THEIR PRESENT POSITIONS

Solar wind enters atmosphere and produces aurora

Magnetosphere (magnetic field)

Solar wind (stream of electrically charged particles)

THE EARTH'S MAGNETOSPHERE

Axis of geographic poles

Axis of magnetic poles

Van Allen radiation belt

Earth

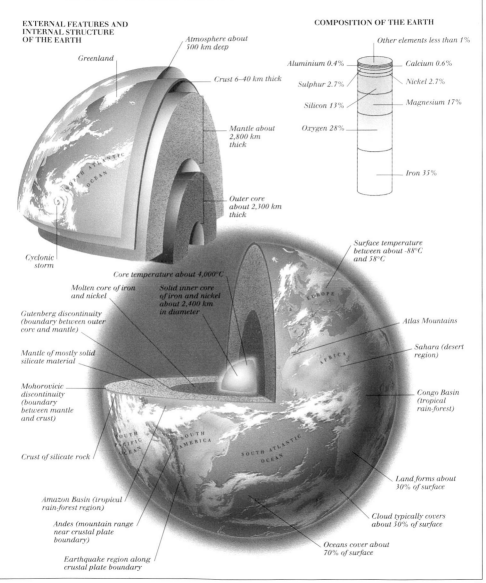

**EXTERNAL FEATURES AND
INTERNAL STRUCTURE
OF THE EARTH**

Greenland

*Atmosphere about
500 km deep*

Crust 6–40 km thick

*Mantle about
2,800 km
thick*

NORTH ATLANTIC OCEAN

*Outer core
about 2,300 km
thick*

*Cyclonic
storm*

COMPOSITION OF THE EARTH

Other elements less than 1%

Aluminium 0.4%

Sulphur 2.7%

Silicon 13%

Oxygen 28%

Calcium 0.6%

Nickel 2.7%

Magnesium 17%

Iron 35%

Core temperature about 4,000°C

*Molten core of iron
and nickel*

*Solid inner core
of iron and nickel
about 2,400 km
in diameter*

*Surface temperature
between about -88°C
and 58°C*

*Gutenberg discontinuity
(boundary between outer
core and mantle)*

*Mantle of mostly solid
silicate material*

*Mohorovicic
discontinuity
(boundary
between mantle
and crust)*

Crust of silicate rock

*Amazon Basin (tropical
rain-forest region)*

*Andes (mountain range
near crustal plate
boundary)*

*Earthquake region along
crustal plate boundary*

EUROPE

AFRICA

Atlas Mountains

*Sahara (desert
region)*

*Congo Basin
(tropical
rain-forest)*

*SOUTH
PACIFIC
OCEAN*

*SOUTH
AMERICA*

*SOUTH ATLANTIC
OCEAN*

*Land forms about
30% of surface*

*Cloud typically covers
about 50% of surface*

*Oceans cover about
70% of surface*

The Moon

THE MOON FROM EARTH

THE MOON IS THE EARTH'S only natural satellite. It is relatively large for a moon, with a diameter of about 3,470 kilometres – just over a quarter that of the Earth. The Moon takes the same time to rotate on its axis as it takes to orbit the Earth (27.3 days), and so the same side (the near side) always faces us. However, the amount of the surface we can see – the phase of the Moon – depends on how much of the near side is in sunlight. The Moon is dry and barren, with no atmosphere or water. It consists mainly of solid rock, although its core may contain molten rock or iron. The surface is dusty, with highlands covered in craters caused by meteorite impacts, and lowlands in which large craters have been filled by solidified lava to form dark areas called maria or "seas". Maria occur mainly on the near side, which has a thinner crust than the far side. Many of the craters are rimmed by mountain ranges that form the crater walls and can be thousands of metres high.

TILT AND ROTATION OF THE MOON

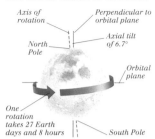

Axis of rotation
Perpendicular to orbital plane
Axial tilt of 6.7°
North Pole
Orbital plane
One rotation takes 27 Earth days and 8 hours
South Pole

CRATERS ON OCEANUS PROCELLARUM

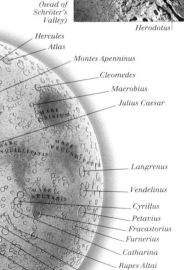

Aristarchus
Cobra Head (head of Schröter's Valley)
Herodotus

NEAR SIDE OF THE MOON

Aristoteles
De la Rue
Aristillus
Plato
Hercules
Atlas
Archimedes
Montes Apenninus
Montes Jura
Cleomedes
Sinus Iridum
Macrobius
Bright rays of ejected material
Julius Caesar
Copernicus
Aristarchus
MARE FRIGORIS
MARE IMBRIUM
MARE SERENITATIS
MARE CRISIUM
MARE VAPORUM
MARE TRANQUILLITATIS
MARE FECUNDITATIS
OCEANUS PROCELLARUM
Langrenus
Kepler
Vendelinus
Encke
MARE NECTARIS
Cyrillus
Flamsteed
Petavius
Fra Mauro
MARE NUBIUM
Fracastorius
Grimaldi
Furnerius
Letronne
Catharina
Gassendi
Rupes Altai
Mersenius
MARE HUMORUM
Albategnius
Ptolemaeus
Arzachel
Pitatus
Walter
Schickard
Stöfler
Alphonsus
Bailly
Tycho
Clavius
Maginus
Deslandres

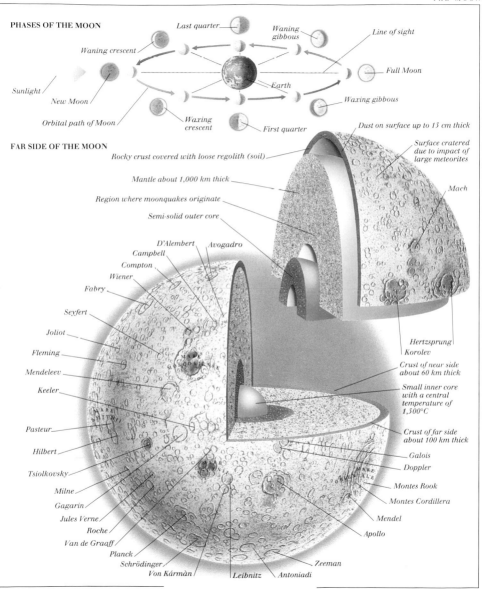

PHASES OF THE MOON

Last quarter

Waning gibbous

Waning crescent

Line of sight

Sunlight

Full Moon

New Moon

Earth

Waxing gibbous

Orbital path of Moon

Waxing crescent

First quarter

FAR SIDE OF THE MOON

Dust on surface up to 15 cm thick

Surface cratered due to impact of large meteorites

Rocky crust covered with loose regolith (soil)

Mach

Mantle about 1,000 km thick

Region where moonquakes originate

Semi-solid outer core

D'Alembert   Avogadro

Campbell

Compton

Wiener

Fabry

Seyfert

Joliot

Fleming

Mendeleev

Keeler

Pasteur

Hilbert

Tsiolkovsky

Milne

Gagarin

Jules Verne

Roche

Van de Graaff

Planck

Schrödinger

Von Kármàn

Leibnitz   Antoniadi

Zeeman

Apollo

Mendel

Montes Cordillera

Montes Rook

Doppler

Galois

Crust of far side about 100 km thick

Small inner core with a central temperature of 1,500°C

Crust of near side about 60 km thick

Korolev

Hertzsprung

Mars

MARS

MARS, KNOWN AS THE RED PLANET, is the fourth planet from the Sun and the outermost rocky planet. In the 19th century, astronomers first observed what were thought to be signs of life on Mars. These signs included apparent canal-like markings on the surface, and dark patches that were thought to be vegetation. It is now known that the "canals" are an optical illusion, and the dark patches are areas where the red dust that covers most of the planet has been blown away. The fine dust particles are often whipped up by winds into dust storms that occasionally obscure almost all the surface. Residual dust in the atmosphere gives the Martian sky a pinkish hue. The northern hemisphere of Mars has many large plains formed of solidified volcanic lava, whereas the southern hemisphere has many craters and large impact basins. There are also several huge, extinct volcanoes, including Olympus Mons, which, at 600 kilometres across and 25 kilometres high, is the largest known volcano in the Solar System. The surface also has many canyons and branching channels. The canyons were formed by movements of the surface crust, but the channels are thought to have been formed by flowing water that has now dried up. The Martian atmosphere is much thinner than Earth's, with only a few clouds and morning mists. Mars has two tiny, irregularly shaped moons called Phobos and Deimos. Their small size indicates that they may be asteroids that have been captured by the gravity of Mars.

TILT AND ROTATION OF MARS

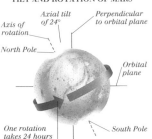

Axial tilt of 24°

Perpendicular to orbital plane

Axis of rotation

North Pole

Orbital plane

One rotation takes 24 hours and 37 minutes

South Pole

SURFACE FEATURES OF MARS

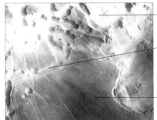

Bright water-ice fog

Fog in canyon about 20 km wide at end of Valles Marineris

Syria Planum

NOCTIS LABYRINTHUS (CANYON SYSTEM)

Summit caldera consisting of overlapping collapsed volcanic craters

Crater

Gentle slope produced by lava flow

Cloud formation

OLYMPUS MONS (EXTINCT SHIELD VOLCANO)

THE SURFACE OF MARS

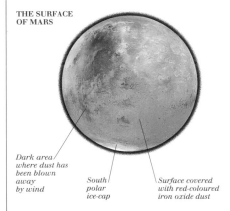

Dark area where dust has been blown away by wind

South polar ice-cap

Surface covered with red-coloured iron oxide dust

MOONS OF MARS

PHOBOS
Average diameter: 22 km
Average distance from planet: 9,400 km

DEIMOS
Average diameter: 13 km
Average distance from planet: 23,500 km

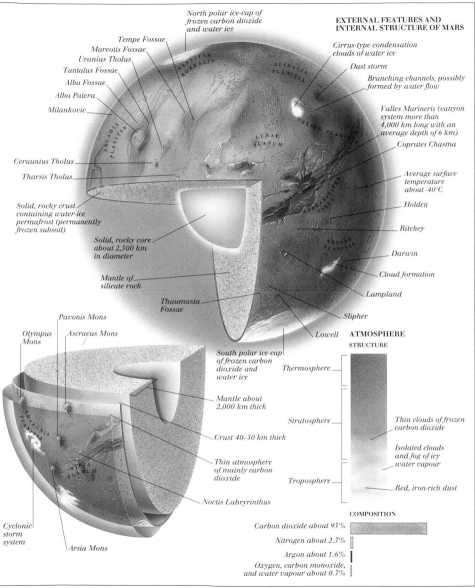

EXTERNAL FEATURES AND
INTERNAL STRUCTURE OF MARS

North polar ice-cap of
frozen carbon dioxide
and water ice

Tempe Fossae

Mareotis Fossae

Uranius Tholus

Tantalus Fossae

Alba Fossae

Alba Patera

Milankovic

Ceraunius Tholus

Tharsis Tholus

Solid, rocky crust
containing water-ice
permafrost (permanently
frozen subsoil)

Solid, rocky core
about 2,500 km
in diameter

Mantle of
silicate rock

Thaumasia
Fossae

Cirrus-type condensation
clouds of water ice

Dust storm

Branching channels, possibly
formed by water flow

Valles Marineris (canyon
system more than
4,000 km long with an
average depth of 6 km)

Coprates Chasma

Average surface
temperature
about -40°C

Holden

Ritchey

Darwin

Cloud formation

Lampland

Slipher

Lowell

South polar ice-cap
of frozen carbon
dioxide and
water ice

Olympus
Mons

Pavonis Mons

Ascraeus Mons

Mantle about
2,000 km thick

Crust 40–50 km thick

Thin atmosphere
of mainly carbon
dioxide

Noctis Labryrinthus

Cyclonic
storm
system

Arsia Mons

ATMOSPHERE
STRUCTURE

Thermosphere

Stratosphere

Troposphere

Thin clouds of frozen
carbon dioxide

Isolated clouds
and fog of icy
water vapour

Red, iron-rich dust

COMPOSITION

Carbon dioxide about 95%

Nitrogen about 2.7%

Argon about 1.6%

Oxygen, carbon monoxide,
and water vapour about 0.7%

Jupiter

JUPITER

JUPITER IS THE FIFTH PLANET from the Sun and the first of the four gas giants. It is the largest and the most massive planet, with a diameter about 11 times that of the Earth and a mass about 2.5 times the combined mass of the eight other planets. Jupiter is thought to have a small rocky core surrounded by an inner mantle of metallic hydrogen (liquid hydrogen that acts like a metal). Outside the inner mantle is an outer mantle of liquid hydrogen and helium that merges into the gaseous atmosphere. Jupiter's rapid rate of rotation causes the clouds in its atmosphere to form belts and zones that encircle the planet parallel to the equator. Belts are dark, low-lying, relatively warm cloud layers, and zones are bright, high-altitude, cooler cloud layers. Within the belts and zones, turbulence causes the formation of cloud features such as white ovals and red spots, both of which are huge storm systems. The most prominent cloud feature is a storm called the Great Red Spot, which consists of a spiralling column of clouds three times wider than the Earth that rises about eight kilometres above the upper cloud layer. Jupiter has one thin, faint, main ring, inside which is a tenuous halo ring of tiny particles extending towards the planet. There are 16 known Jovian moons. The four largest moons (called the Galileans) are Ganymede, Callisto, Io, and Europa. Ganymede and Callisto are cratered and probably icy. Europa is smooth and icy and may contain water. Io is covered in bright red, orange, and yellow splotches. This colouring is caused by sulphurous material from active volcanoes that shoot plumes of lava hundreds of kilometres above the surface.

TILT AND ROTATION OF JUPITER

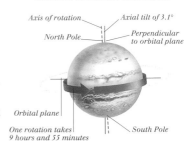

Axis of rotation

Axial tilt of 3.1°

North Pole

Perpendicular to orbital plane

Orbital plane

One rotation takes 9 hours and 55 minutes

South Pole

GREAT RED SPOT AND WHITE OVAL

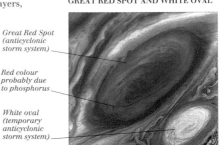

Great Red Spot (anticyclonic storm system)

Red colour probably due to phosphorus

White oval (temporary anticyclonic storm system)

GALILEAN MOONS OF JUPITER

EUROPA
Diameter: 3,138 km
Average distance from planet: 670,900 km

CALLISTO
Diameter: 4,800 km
Average distance from planet: 1,880,000 km

GANYMEDE
Diameter: 5,262 km
Average distance from planet: 1,070,000 km

IO
Diameter: 3,642 km
Average distance from planet: 421,800 km

RINGS OF JUPITER

Main ring

Halo ring

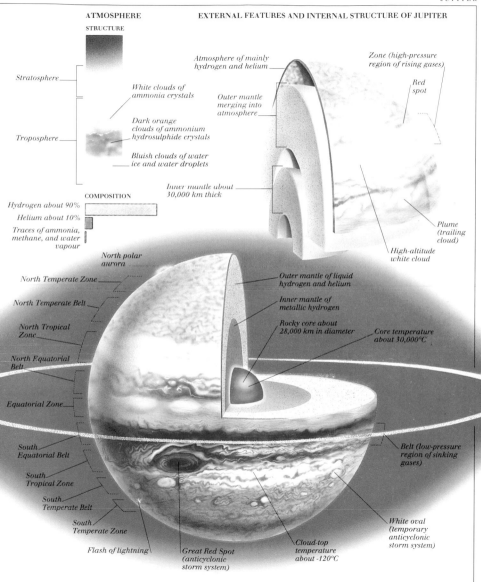

ATMOSPHERE

STRUCTURE

EXTERNAL FEATURES AND INTERNAL STRUCTURE OF JUPITER

Stratosphere

Troposphere

White clouds of ammonia crystals

Dark orange clouds of ammonium hydrosulphide crystals

Bluish clouds of water ice and water droplets

Atmosphere of mainly hydrogen and helium

Outer mantle merging into atmosphere

Inner mantle about 30,000 km thick

Zone (high-pressure region of rising gases)

Red spot

Plume (trailing cloud)

High-altitude white cloud

COMPOSITION

Hydrogen about 90%

Helium about 10%

Traces of ammonia, methane, and water vapour

North polar aurora

North Temperate Zone

North Temperate Belt

North Tropical Zone

North Equatorial Belt

Equatorial Zone

South Equatorial Belt

South Tropical Zone

South Temperate Belt

South Temperate Zone

Flash of lightning

Great Red Spot (anticyclonic storm system)

Cloud-top temperature about -120°C

Outer mantle of liquid hydrogen and helium

Inner mantle of metallic hydrogen

Rocky core about 28,000 km in diameter

Core temperature about 30,000°C

Belt (low-pressure region of sinking gases)

White oval (temporary anticyclonic storm system)

Saturn

FALSE-COLOUR
IMAGE OF SATURN

SATURN IS THE SIXTH PLANET from the Sun. It is a gas giant almost as big as Jupiter, with an equatorial diameter of about 120,500 kilometres. Saturn is thought to consist of a small core of rock and ice surrounded by an inner mantle of metallic hydrogen (liquid hydrogen that acts like a metal). Outside the inner mantle is an outer mantle of liquid hydrogen that merges into a gaseous atmosphere. Saturn's clouds form belts and zones similar to those on Jupiter, but obscured by overlying haze. Storms and eddies, seen as red or white ovals, occur in the clouds. Saturn has an extremely thin but wide system of rings that is less than one kilometre thick but extends outwards to about 420,000 kilometres from the planet's surface. The main rings comprise thousands of narrow ringlets, each made of icy lumps that range in size from tiny particles to chunks several metres across. The D, E, and G rings are very faint, the F ring is brighter, and the A, B, and C rings are bright enough to be seen from Earth with binoculars. Saturn has 18 known moons, some of which orbit inside the rings and are thought to exert a gravitational influence on the shapes of the rings. Unusually, seven of the moons are co-orbital – they share an orbit with another moon. Astronomers believe that such co-orbital moons may have originated from a single satellite that broke up.

TILT AND ROTATION OF SATURN

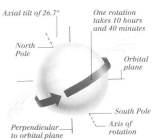

Axial tilt of 26.7°

One rotation takes 10 hours and 40 minutes

North Pole

Orbital plane

South Pole

Perpendicular to orbital plane

Axis of rotation

FALSE-COLOUR IMAGE OF SATURN'S CLOUD FEATURES

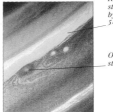

Ribbon-shaped striation caused by winds of up to 540 km/h

Oval (rotating storm system)

INNER RINGS OF SATURN

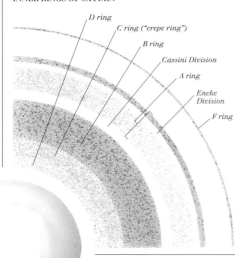

D ring

C ring ("crepe ring")

B ring

Cassini Division

A ring

Encke Division

F ring

MOONS OF SATURN

ENCELADUS
Diameter: 498 km
Average distance from planet: 238,000 km

TETHYS
Diameter: 1,050 km
Average distance from planet: 295,000 km

DIONE
Diameter: 1,118 km
Average distance from planet: 377,000 km

MIMAS
Diameter: 397 km
Average distance from planet: 186,000 km

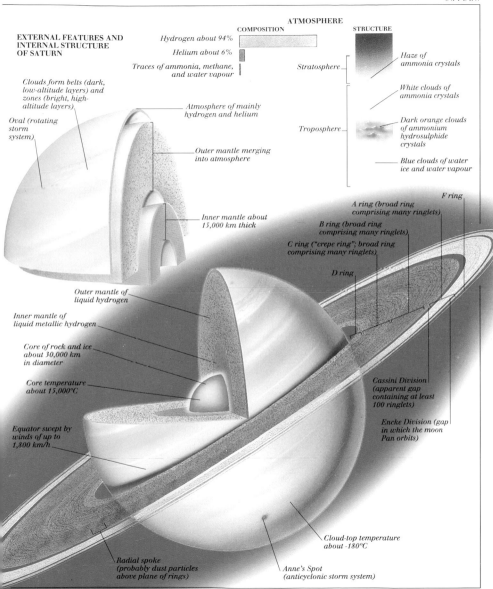

ATMOSPHERE

EXTERNAL FEATURES AND
INTERNAL STRUCTURE
OF SATURN

COMPOSITION

Hydrogen about 94%

Helium about 6%

Traces of ammonia, methane,
and water vapour

STRUCTURE

Stratosphere

Haze of
ammonia crystals

White clouds of
ammonia crystals

Troposphere

Dark orange clouds
of ammonium
hydrosulphide
crystals

Blue clouds of water
ice and water vapour

Clouds form belts (dark,
low-altitude layers) and
zones (bright, high-
altitude layers)

Oval (rotating
storm
system)

Atmosphere of mainly
hydrogen and helium

Outer mantle merging
into atmosphere

Inner mantle about
15,000 km thick

F ring

A ring (broad ring
comprising many ringlets)

B ring (broad ring
comprising many ringlets)

C ring ("crepe ring"; broad ring
comprising many ringlets)

D ring

Outer mantle of
liquid hydrogen

Inner mantle of
liquid metallic hydrogen

Core of rock and ice
about 30,000 km
in diameter

Core temperature
about 15,000°C

Cassini Division
(apparent gap
containing at least
100 ringlets)

Encke Division (gap
in which the moon
Pan orbits)

Equator swept by
winds of up to
1,800 km/h

Radial spoke
(probably dust particles
above plane of rings)

Cloud-top temperature
about -180°C

Anne's Spot
(anticyclonic storm system)

47

Uranus

FALSE-COLOUR
IMAGE OF URANUS

URANUS IS THE SEVENTH PLANET from the Sun and the third largest, with a diameter of about 51,000 kilometres. It is thought to consist of a dense mixture of different types of ice and gas around a solid core. Its atmosphere contains traces of methane, giving the planet a blue-green hue, and the temperature at the cloud tops is about -210°C. Uranus is the most featureless planet to have been closely observed: only a few icy clouds of methane have been seen so far. Uranus is unique among the planets in that its axis of rotation lies close to its orbital plane. As a result of its strongly tilted rotational axis, Uranus rolls on its side along its orbital path around the Sun, whereas other planets spin more or less upright. Uranus is encircled by 11 rings that consist of rocks interspersed with dust lanes. The rings contain some of the darkest matter in the Solar System and are extremely narrow, making them difficult to detect: nine of them are less than 10 kilometres wide, whereas most of Saturn's rings are thousands of kilometres in width. There are 15 known Uranian moons, all of which are icy and most of which are further out than the rings. The 10 inner moons are small and dark, with diameters of less than 160 kilometres, and the five outer moons are between about 470 and 1,600 kilometres in diameter. The outer moons have a wide variety of surface features. Miranda has the most varied surface, with cratered areas broken up by huge ridges and cliffs 20 kilometres high.

TILT AND ROTATION OF URANUS

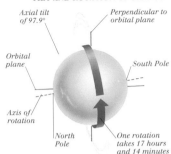

Axial tilt of 97.9°

Perpendicular to orbital plane

Orbital plane

South Pole

Axis of rotation

North Pole

One rotation takes 17 hours and 14 minutes

OUTER MOONS

MIRANDA
Diameter: 472 km
Average distance from planet: 129,800 km

RINGS OF URANUS

Epsilon ring

Ring 1986 U1R

Delta ring

Gamma ring

Eta ring

Beta ring

Alpha ring

Rings 4 and 5

Ring 6

Ring 1986 U2R

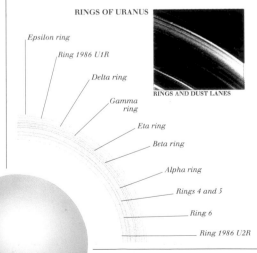

RINGS AND DUST LANES

ARIEL
Diameter: 1,158 km
Average distance from planet: 191,200 km

UMBRIEL
Diameter: 1,169 km
Average distance from planet: 266,000 km

TITANIA
Diameter: 1,578 km
Average distance from planet: 435,900 km

OBERON
Diameter: 1,523 km
Average distance from planet: 582,600 km

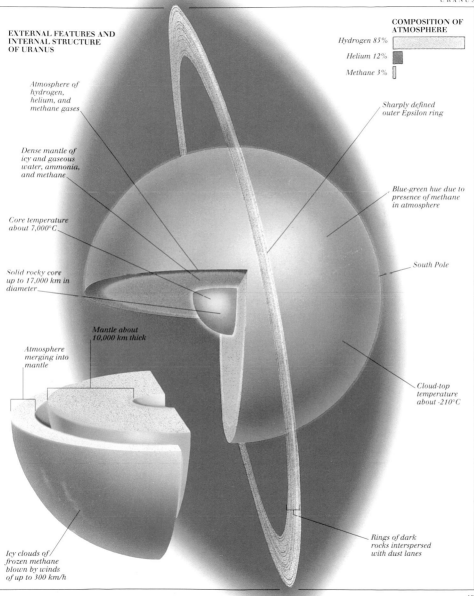

**EXTERNAL FEATURES AND
INTERNAL STRUCTURE
OF URANUS**

COMPOSITION OF
ATMOSPHERE

Hydrogen 85%

Helium 12%

Methane 3%

*Atmosphere of
hydrogen,
helium, and
methane gases*

*Dense mantle of
icy and gaseous
water, ammonia,
and methane*

*Core temperature
about 7,000°C*

*Solid rocky core
up to 17,000 km in
diameter*

*Mantle about
10,000 km thick*

*Atmosphere
merging into
mantle*

*Icy clouds of
frozen methane
blown by winds
of up to 300 km/h*

*Sharply defined
outer Epsilon ring*

*Blue-green hue due to
presence of methane
in atmosphere*

South Pole

*Cloud-top
temperature
about -210°C*

*Rings of dark
rocks interspersed
with dust lanes*

Neptune and Pluto

FALSE-COLOUR
IMAGE OF NEPTUNE

NEPTUNE AND PLUTO are the two furthest planets from the Sun, at an average distance of about 4,500 million kilometres and 5,900 million kilometres respectively. Neptune is a gas giant and is thought to consist of a small rocky core surrounded by a mixture of liquids and gases. The atmosphere contains several prominent cloud features. The largest of these are the Great Dark Spot, which is as wide as the Earth, the Small Dark Spot, and the Scooter. The Great and Small Dark Spots are huge storms that are swept around the planet by winds of about 2,000 kilometres per hour. The Scooter is a large area of cirrus cloud. Neptune has four tenuous rings and eight known moons. Triton is the largest Neptunian moon and the coldest object in the Solar System, with a temperature of -235°C. Unlike most moons in the Solar System, Triton orbits its mother planet in the opposite direction to the planet's rotation. Pluto is usually the outermost planet but its elliptical orbit causes it to pass inside the orbit of Neptune for 20 years of its 248-year orbit. Pluto is so small and far away that little is known about it. It is a rocky planet, probably covered with ice and frozen methane. Pluto's only known moon, Charon, is large for a moon, at half the size of its parent planet. Because of the small difference in their sizes, Pluto and Charon are sometimes considered to be a double-planet system.

TILT AND ROTATION OF NEPTUNE

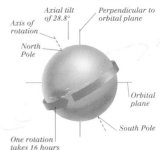

Axis of rotation

North Pole

Axial tilt of 28.8°

Perpendicular to orbital plane

Orbital plane

South Pole

One rotation takes 16 hours and 7 minutes

CLOUD FEATURES OF NEPTUNE

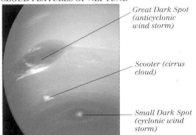

Great Dark Spot (anticyclonic wind storm)

Scooter (cirrus cloud)

Small Dark Spot (cyclonic wind storm)

RINGS OF NEPTUNE

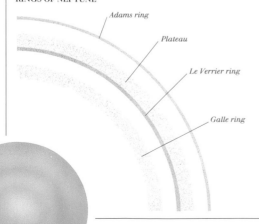

Adams ring

Plateau

Le Verrier ring

Galle ring

HIGH-ALTITUDE CLOUDS

Methane cirrus clouds 40 km above main cloud deck

Cloud shadow

Main cloud deck blown by winds at speeds of about 2,000 km/h

MOONS OF NEPTUNE

TRITON
Diameter: 2,705 km
Average distance from planet: 354,800 km

PROTEUS
Diameter: 416 km
Average distance from planet: 117,600 km

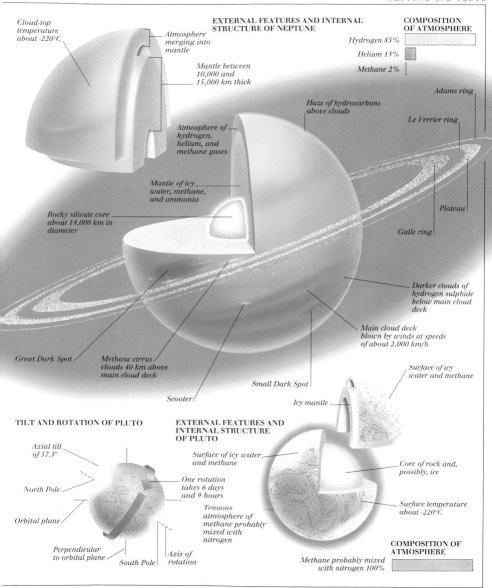

EXTERNAL FEATURES AND INTERNAL STRUCTURE OF NEPTUNE

Cloud-top temperature about -220°C

Atmosphere merging into mantle

Mantle between 10,000 and 15,000 km thick

COMPOSITION OF ATMOSPHERE

Hydrogen 85%

Helium 13%

Methane 2%

Haze of hydrocarbons above clouds

Adams ring

Le Verrier ring

Atmosphere of hydrogen, helium, and methane gases

Mantle of icy water, methane, and ammonia

Rocky silicate core about 14,000 km in diameter

Plateau

Galle ring

Darker clouds of hydrogen sulphide below main cloud deck

Main cloud deck blown by winds at speeds of about 2,000 km/h

Great Dark Spot

Methane cirrus clouds 40 km above main cloud deck

Small Dark Spot

Scooter

Surface of icy water and methane

Icy mantle

TILT AND ROTATION OF PLUTO

Axial tilt of 57.5°

North Pole

Orbital plane

Perpendicular to orbital plane

South Pole

Axis of rotation

EXTERNAL FEATURES AND INTERNAL STRUCTURE OF PLUTO

Surface of icy water and methane

One rotation takes 6 days and 9 hours

Tenuous atmosphere of methane probably mixed with nitrogen

Core of rock and, possibly, ice

Surface temperature about -220°C

COMPOSITION OF ATMOSPHERE

Methane probably mixed with nitrogen 100%

Asteroids, comets, and meteoroids

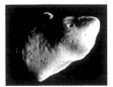

ASTEROID 951 GASPRA

ASTEROIDS, COMETS, AND METEOROIDS are all debris remaining from the nebula in which the Solar System formed 4.6 billion years ago. Asteroids are rocky bodies up to about 1,000 kilometres in diameter, although most are much smaller. Most of them orbit the Sun in the asteroid belt, which lies between the orbits of Mars and Jupiter. Comets may originate in a huge cloud (called the Oort Cloud) that is thought to surround the Solar System. They are made of frozen gases and dust, and are a few kilometres in diameter. Occasionally, a comet is deflected from the Oort Cloud to orbit the Sun in a long, elliptical path. As the comet approaches the Sun, the comet's surface starts to vaporize in the heat, producing a brightly shining coma (a huge sphere of gas and dust around the nucleus), a gas tail, and a dust tail. Meteoroids are small chunks of stone or stone and iron, some of which are fragments of asteroids or comets. Meteoroids range in size from tiny dust particles to objects tens of metres across. If a meteoroid enters the Earth's atmosphere, it is heated by friction and appears as a glowing streak of light called a meteor (also known as a shooting star). Meteor showers occur when the Earth passes through the trail of dust particles left by a comet. Most meteors burn up in the atmosphere. The few that are large enough to reach the Earth's surface are termed meteorites.

OPTICAL IMAGE OF HALLEY'S COMET

FALSE-COLOUR IMAGE OF HALLEY'S COMET

High-intensity light emission

Nucleus

Medium-intensity light emission

Low-intensity light emission

FALSE-COLOUR IMAGE OF A LEONID METEOR SHOWER

METEORITES

DEVELOPMENT OF COMET TAILS

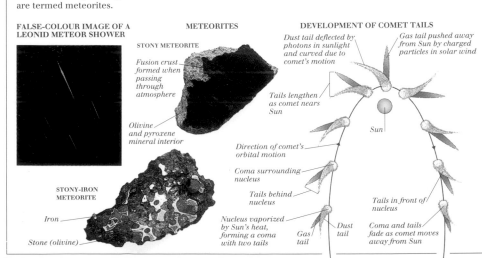

STONY METEORITE

Fusion crust formed when passing through atmosphere

Olivine and pyroxene mineral interior

STONY-IRON METEORITE

Iron

Stone (olivine)

Dust tail deflected by photons in sunlight and curved due to comet's motion

Gas tail pushed away from Sun by charged particles in solar wind

Tails lengthen as comet nears Sun

Direction of comet's orbital motion

Coma surrounding nucleus

Tails behind nucleus

Sun

Nucleus vaporized by Sun's heat, forming a coma with two tails

Gas tail

Dust tail

Tails in front of nucleus

Coma and tails fade as comet moves away from Sun

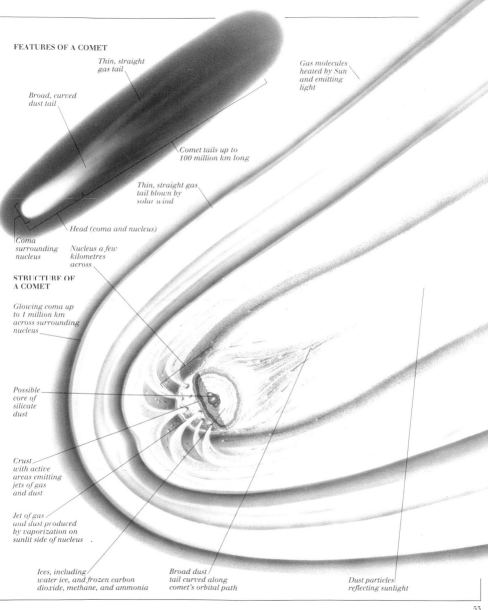

FEATURES OF A COMET

Thin, straight
gas tail

Broad, curved
dust tail

Gas molecules
heated by Sun
and emitting
light

Comet tails up to
100 million km long

Thin, straight gas
tail blown by
solar wind

Head (coma and nucleus)

Coma
surrounding
nucleus

Nucleus a few
kilometres
across

**STRUCTURE OF
A COMET**

Glowing coma up
to 1 million km
across surrounding
nucleus

Possible
core of
silicate
dust

Crust
with active
areas emitting
jets of gas
and dust

Jet of gas
and dust produced
by vaporization on
sunlit side of nucleus

Ices, including
water ice, and frozen carbon
dioxide, methane, and ammonia

Broad dust
tail curved along
comet's orbital path

Dust particles
reflecting sunlight

PREHISTORIC EARTH

THE CHANGING EARTH 56
THE EARTH'S CRUST 58
FAULTS AND FOLDS 60
MOUNTAIN BUILDING 62
PRECAMBRIAN TO DEVONIAN PERIOD 64
CARBONIFEROUS TO PERMIAN PERIOD 66
TRIASSIC PERIOD 68
JURASSIC PERIOD 70
CRETACEOUS PERIOD 72
TERTIARY PERIOD 74
QUATERNARY PERIOD 76
EARLY SIGNS OF LIFE 78
AMPHIBIANS AND REPTILES 80
THE DINOSAURS 82
THEROPODS 1 84
THEROPODS 2 86
SAUROPODOMORPHS 1 88
SAUROPODOMORPHS 2 90
THYREOPHORANS 1 92
THYREOPHORANS 2 94
ORNITHOPODS 1 96
ORNITHOPODS 2 98
MARGINOCEPHALIANS 1 100
MARGINOCEPHALIANS 2 102
MAMMALS 1 104
MAMMALS 2 106
THE FIRST HOMINIDS 108

The changing Earth

THE EARTH FORMED FROM A CLOUD OF DUST and gas drifting through space about 4,600 million years ago. Dense minerals sank to the centre while lighter ones formed a thin rocky crust. However, the first known life-forms – bacteria and blue-green algae – did not appear until about 3,400 million years ago, and it was only about 700 million years ago that more complex plants and animals began to develop. Since then, thousands of animal and plant species have evolved; some, such as the dinosaurs, survived for many millions of years, while others died out quickly. The Earth itself is continually changing. Although continents neared their present locations about 50 million years ago, they are still drifting slowly over the planet's surface, and mountain ranges such as the Himalayas – which began to form 40 million years ago – are continually being built up and worn away. Climate is also subject to change: the Earth has undergone a series of ice ages interspersed with warmer periods (the most recent glacial period was at its height about 20,000 years ago).

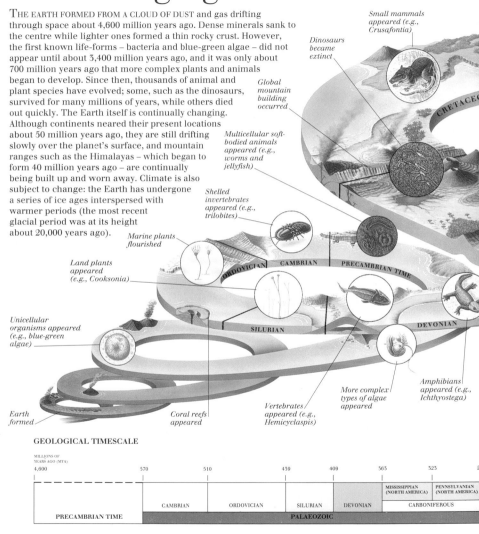

Small mammals appeared (e.g., Crusafontia)

Dinosaurs became extinct

CRETACEO

Global mountain building occurred

Multicellular soft-bodied animals appeared (e.g., worms and jellyfish)

Shelled invertebrates appeared (e.g., trilobites)

Marine plants flourished

Land plants appeared (e.g., Cooksonia)

ORDOVICIAN   CAMBRIAN   PRECAMBRIAN TIME

SILURIAN   DEVONIAN

Unicellular organisms appeared (e.g., blue-green algae)

Earth formed

Coral reefs appeared

Vertebrates appeared (e.g., Hemicyclaspis)

More complex types of algae appeared

Amphibians appeared (e.g., Ichthyostega)

GEOLOGICAL TIMESCALE

MILLIONS OF
YEARS AGO (MYA)

4,600	570	510	439	409	363	323	29

					MISSISSIPPIAN (NORTH AMERICA)	PENNSYLVANIAN (NORTH AMERICA)	
	CAMBRIAN	ORDOVICIAN	SILURIAN	DEVONIAN	CARBONIFEROUS		
PRECAMBRIAN TIME		PALAEOZOIC					

EVOLUTION OF THE EARTH

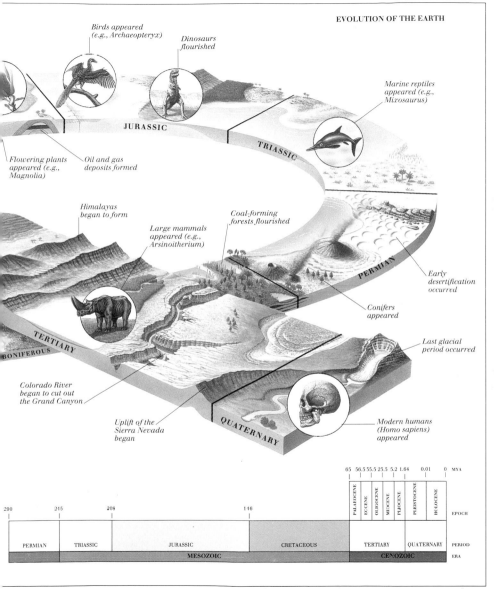

Birds appeared (e.g., Archaeopteryx)

Dinosaurs flourished

Marine reptiles appeared (e.g., Mixosaurus)

JURASSIC

TRIASSIC

Flowering plants appeared (e.g., Magnolia)

Oil and gas deposits formed

Himalayas began to form

Large mammals appeared (e.g., Arsinoitherium)

Coal-forming forests flourished

PERMIAN

Early desertification occurred

Conifers appeared

TERTIARY

CARBONIFEROUS

Last glacial period occurred

Colorado River began to cut out the Grand Canyon

Uplift of the Sierra Nevada began

QUATERNARY

Modern humans (Homo sapiens) appeared

						65	56.5	35.5	25.5	5.2	1.64		0.01	0	MYA
						PALAEOCENE	EOCENE	OLIGOCENE	MIOCENE	PLIOCENE		PLEISTOCENE	HOLOCENE		EPOCH
290		245	208			146									
PERMIAN		TRIASSIC	JURASSIC			CRETACEOUS			TERTIARY			QUATERNARY			PERIOD
			MESOZOIC						CENOZOIC						ERA

The Earth's crust

THE EARTH'S CRUST IS THE SOLID outer shell of the Earth. It includes continental crust (about 40 kilometres thick) and oceanic crust (about six kilometres thick). The crust and the topmost layer of the mantle form the lithosphere. The lithosphere consists of semi-rigid plates that move relative to each other on the underlying asthenosphere (a partly molten layer of the mantle). This process is known as plate tectonics and helps explain continental drift. Where two plates move apart, there are rifts in the crust. In mid-ocean, this movement results in sea-floor spreading and the formation of ocean ridges; on continents, crustal spreading can form rift valleys. When plates move towards each other, one may be subducted beneath (forced under) the other. In mid-ocean, this causes ocean trenches, seismic activity, and arcs of volcanic islands. Where oceanic crust is subducted beneath continental crust or where continents collide, land may be uplifted and mountains formed (see pp. 62–63). Plates may also slide past each other – along the San Andreas fault, for example. Crustal movement on continents may result in earthquakes, while movement under the seabed can lead to tidal waves.

ELEMENTS IN THE EARTH'S CRUST

Other elements 2%

Potassium 2.6%

Calcium 3.6%

Aluminium 8%

Magnesium 2%

Sodium 2.8%

Iron 5%

Silicon 28%

Oxygen 46%

FEATURES OF PLATE MOVEMENTS

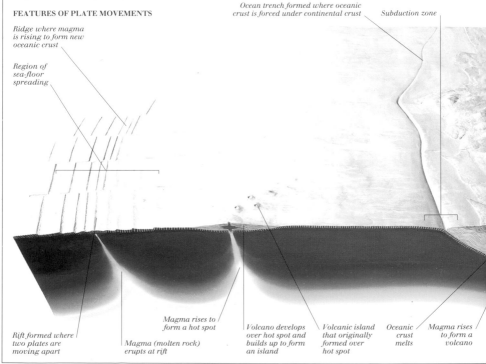

Ridge where magma is rising to form new oceanic crust

Region of sea-floor spreading

Ocean trench formed where oceanic crust is forced under continental crust

Subduction zone

Rift formed where two plates are moving apart

Magma (molten rock) erupts at rift

Magma rises to form a hot spot

Volcano develops over hot spot and builds up to form an island

Volcanic island that originally formed over hot spot

Oceanic crust melts

Magma rises to form a volcano

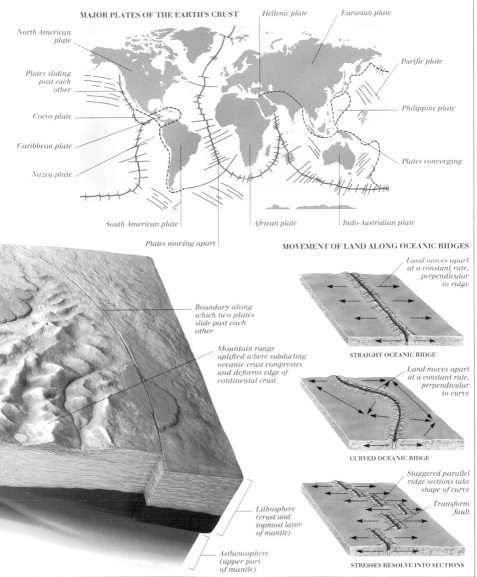

MAJOR PLATES OF THE EARTH'S CRUST

North American plate

Plates sliding past each other

Cocos plate

Caribbean plate

Nazca plate

Hellenic plate

Eurasian plate

Pacific plate

Philippine plate

Plates converging

South American plate

African plate

Indo-Australian plate

Plates moving apart

Boundary along which two plates slide past each other

Mountain range uplifted where subducting oceanic crust compresses and deforms edge of continental crust

Lithosphere (crust and topmost layer of mantle)

Asthenosphere (upper part of mantle)

MOVEMENT OF LAND ALONG OCEANIC RIDGES

Land moves apart at a constant rate, perpendicular to ridge

STRAIGHT OCEANIC RIDGE

Land moves apart at a constant rate, perpendicular to curve

CURVED OCEANIC RIDGE

Staggered parallel ridge sections take shape of curve

Transform fault

STRESSES RESOLVE INTO SECTIONS

Faults and folds

THE CONTINUOUS MOVEMENT of the Earth's crustal plates (see pp. 58–59) can squeeze, stretch, or break rock strata, deforming them and producing faults and folds. A fault is a fracture in a rock along which there is movement of one side relative to the other. The movement can be vertical, horizontal, or oblique (vertical and horizontal). Faults develop when rocks are subjected to compression or tension. They tend to occur in hard, rigid rocks, which are more likely to break than bend. The smallest faults occur in single mineral crystals and are microscopically small, whereas the largest – the Great Rift Valley in Africa, which formed between 5 million and 100,000 years ago – is more than 9,000 kilometres long. A fold is a bend in a rock layer caused by compression. Folds occur in elastic rocks, which tend to bend rather than break. The two main types of fold are anticlines (upfolds) and synclines (downfolds). Folds vary in size from a few millimetres long to folded mountain ranges hundreds of kilometres long, such as the Himalayas (see pp. 62–63) and the Alps, which are repeatedly folding. In addition to faults and folds, other features associated with rock deformations include boudins, mullions, and *en échelon* fractures.

STRUCTURE OF A FOLD

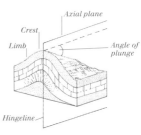

Axial plane

Crest

Limb

Angle of plunge

Hingeline

STRUCTURE OF A FAULT

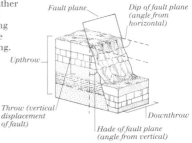

Fault plane

Dip of fault plane (angle from horizontal)

Upthrow

Throw (vertical displacement of fault)

Downthrow

Hade of fault plane (angle from vertical)

STRUCTURE OF A SLOPE

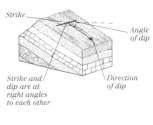

Strike

Angle of dip

Strike and dip are at right angles to each other

Direction of dip

FOLDED ROCK

Steeply dipping limbs

Crest of anticline

Plunge

SECTION THROUGH FOLDED ROCK STRATA THAT HAVE BEEN ERODED

Dipping bed

Anticlinal fold

Monoclinal fold

Mineral-filled fault

Upper Carboniferous Millstone Grit

Lower Carboniferous Limestone

EXAMPLES OF FOLDS

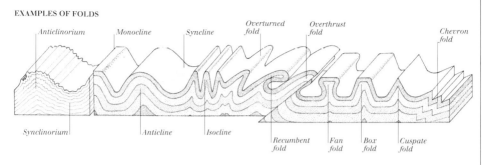

Anticlinorium

Monocline

Syncline

Overturned fold

Overthrust fold

Chevron fold

Synclinorium

Anticline

Isocline

Recumbent fold

Fan fold

Box fold

Cuspate fold

EXAMPLES OF FAULTS

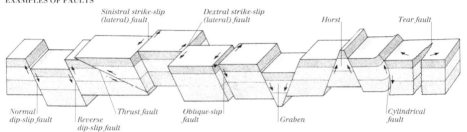

Sinistral strike-slip (lateral) fault

Dextral strike-slip (lateral) fault

Horst

Tear fault

Normal dip-slip fault

Reverse dip-slip fault

Thrust fault

Oblique-slip fault

Graben

Cylindrical fault

SMALL-SCALE ROCK DEFORMATIONS

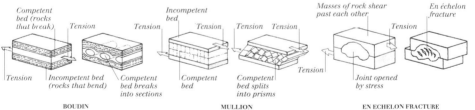

Competent bed (rocks that break)

Tension

Tension

Incompetent bed

Tension

Tension

Tension

Masses of rock shear past each other

En échelon fracture

Tension

Tension

Incompetent bed (rocks that bend)

Competent bed breaks into sections

Competent bed

Competent bed splits into prisms

Tension

Joint opened by stress

BOUDIN

MULLION

EN ECHELON FRACTURE

Horizontal bed

Mineral-filled fault

Dipping bed

Gently folded bed

Mineral-filled fault

Dipping bed

Upper Carboniferous Millstone Grit

Upper Carboniferous Coal Measures

61

Mountain building

THE PROCESSES INVOLVED in mountain building – termed orogenesis – occur
as a result of the movement of the Earth's crustal plates (see pp. 58–59).
There are three main types of mountains: volcanic mountains, fold
mountains, and block mountains. Most volcanic mountains have been
formed along plate boundaries where plates have come together or
moved apart and lava and other debris have been ejected onto the
Earth's surface. The lava and debris may have built up to form a
dome around the vent of a volcano. Fold mountains are formed
where plates push together and
cause the rock to buckle upwards.
Where oceanic crust meets less dense
continental crust, the oceanic crust
is forced under the continental crust. The
continental crust is buckled by the impact.
This is how folded mountain ranges, such as the
Appalachian Mountains in North America, were
formed. Fold mountains are also formed where
two areas of continental crust meet. The
Himalayas, for example, began to form when
India collided with Asia, buckling the sediments
and parts of the oceanic crust between them. Block mountains are formed when a block
of land is uplifted between two faults as a result of compression or tension in the Earth's
crust (see pp. 60–61). Often, the movement along faults has taken place gradually over
millions of years. However, two plates may cause an earthquake by suddenly sliding past
each other along a faultline.

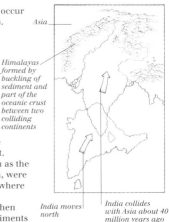

Asia

*Himalayas
formed by
buckling of
sediment and
part of the
oceanic crust
between two
colliding
continents*

*India moves
north*

*India collides
with Asia about 40
million years ago*

BHAGIRATHI PARBAT,
HIMALAYAS

EXAMPLES OF MOUNTAINS

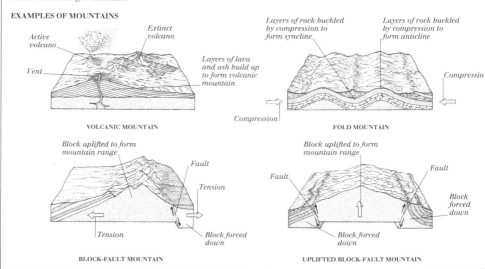

*Active
volcano*

*Extinct
volcano*

Vent

*Layers of lava
and ash build up
to form volcanic
mountain*

VOLCANIC MOUNTAIN

*Layers of rock buckled
by compression to
form syncline*

*Layers of rock buckled
by compression to
form anticline*

Compression

Compression

FOLD MOUNTAIN

*Block uplifted to form
mountain range*

Fault

Tension

Tension

*Block forced
down*

BLOCK-FAULT MOUNTAIN

*Block uplifted to form
mountain range*

Fault

Fault

*Block
forced
down*

*Block forced
down*

UPLIFTED BLOCK-FAULT MOUNTAIN

STAGES IN THE FORMATION OF THE HIMALAYAS

Sediment

India moves towards Asia

Ocean area becomes smaller as plates converge

Sediment

Asia

Volcano

Continental crust

Continental crust

Oceanic crust forced under continental crust

Magma rises to form volcanoes

60 MILLION YEARS AGO

Sediment and part of oceanic crust folded by continental collision

India

Asia

Continental crust

Oceanic crust forced further under continental crust

Continental crust

40 MILLION YEARS AGO

Ganges plain

Sediment and part of oceanic crust folded and uplifted

India

Asia

Continental crust

Continental crust

20 MILLION YEARS AGO

Sediment and part of oceanic crust further folded and uplifted to form Himalayas

Ripple effect of collision forms mountains and plateau of Tibet

Ganges plain

India

Asia

Continental crust

Continental crust

TODAY

SAN ANDREAS FAULT

Faultline along which two plates may slide past each other, causing an earthquake

EARTHQUAKES

Epicentre (point on Earth's surface directly above focus)

Isoseismal lines join places with equal intensity of shock

Shock waves radiate outwards from focus

Focus (point at which earthquake originates)

ANATOMY OF AN EARTHQUAKE

Core (blocks S waves and deflects P waves)

Focus

Crust

S and P shock waves

L wave

Mantle

P wave shadow zone

P wave shadow zone

P wave

PATH OF SHOCK WAVES THROUGH THE EARTH

Precambrian to Devonian periods

North America
Greenland
China
Australia
South America
South Africa
Africa
India
Scandinavia
North East Africa
Europe
Siberia
Central Asia

WHEN THE EARTH FORMED about 4,600 million years ago, its atmosphere consisted of volcanic gases with little oxygen, making it hostile to most forms of life. One large supercontinent, Gondwanaland, was situated over the southern polar region, while other smaller continents were spread over the rest of the world. Constant movement of the earth's crustal plates carried continents across the earth's surface. The first primitive life-forms emerged around 3,400 million years ago in shallow, warm seas. The build up of oxygen began to form a shield of ozone around the earth, protecting living organisms from the sun's harmful rays and helping to establish an atmosphere in which life could sustain itself. The first vertebrates appeared about 470 million years ago, during the Ordovician period (510–439 million years ago), the first land plants appeared around 400 million years ago during the Devonian period (409–363 million years ago), and the first land animals about 30 million years later.

EXAMPLES OF PRECAMBRIAN TO DEVONIAN PLANT GROUPS

A PRESENT-DAY CLUBMOSS
(*Lycopodium sp.*)

A PRESENT-DAY
LAND PLANT
(*Asparagus setaceous*)

FOSSIL OF AN EXTINCT LAND PLANT
(*Cooksonia hemisphaerica*)

FOSSIL OF AN EXTINCT SWAMP PLANT
(*Zosterophyllum llanoveranum*)

EXAMPLES OF PRECAMBRIAN TO DEVONIAN TRILOBITES

ACADAGNOSTUS
Family: Agnostidae
Length: 8 mm (⅓ in)

PHACOPS
Family: Phacopidae
Length: 4.5 cm (1¾ in)

OLENELLUS
Family: Olenellidae
Length: 6 cm (2½ in)

ELRATHIA
Family: Ptychopariidae
Length: 2 cm (¾ in)

THE EARTH DURING THE MIDDLE ORDOVICIAN PERIOD

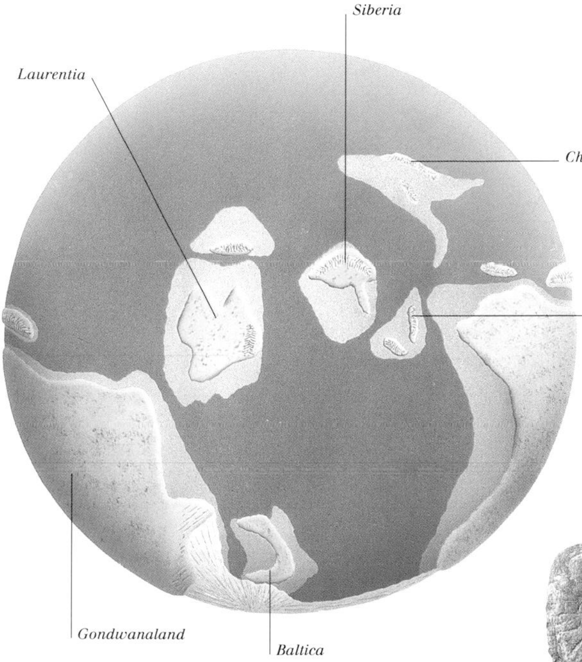

Siberia

Laurentia

China

Kazakstania

Gondwanaland

Baltica

EXAMPLES OF EARLY MARINE INVERTEBRATES

FOSSIL NAUTILOID
(*Estonioceras perforatum*)

FOSSIL BRACHIOPOD
(*Dicoelosia bilobata*)

TRACE FOSSIL
(*Mawsonites spriggi*)

FOSSIL GRAPTOLITE
(*Monograptus convolutus*)

EXAMPLES OF DEVONIAN FISH

RHAMPHODOPSIS
Family: Ptyctodontidae
Length: 15 cm (6 in)

PTERASPIS
Family: Pteraspidae
Length: 25 cm (10 in)

COCCOSTEUS
Family: Coccosteidae
Length: 35 cm (14 in)

BOTHRIOLEPIS
Family: Bothriolepidae
Length: 40 cm (16 in)

CHEIRACANTHUS
Family: Acanthodidae
Length: 30 cm (12 in)

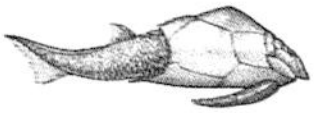

PTERICHTHYODES
Family: Asterolepidae
Length: 15 cm (6 in)

CHEIROLEPIS
Family: Cheirolepidae
Length: 17 cm (6¾ in)

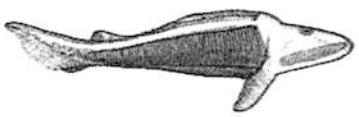

CEPHALASPIS
Family: Cephalaspidae
Length: 22 cm (8¾ in)

Carboniferous to Permian periods

THE CARBONIFEROUS PERIOD (363–290 million years ago) takes its name from the thick, carbon-rich layers – now coal – that were produced during this period as swampy tropical forests were repeatedly drowned by shallow seas. The humid climate across northern and equatorial continents throughout Carboniferous times produced the first dense plant cover on Earth. During the early part of this period, the first reptiles appeared. Their development of a waterproof egg with a protective internal structure ended animal life's dependence on an aquatic environment. Towards the end of Carboniferous times, the earth's continents Laurasia and Gondwanaland collided, resulting in the huge land-mass of Pangaea. Glaciers smothered much of the southern hemisphere during the Permian period (290–245 million years ago), covering Antarctica, parts of Australia, and much of South America, Africa, and India. Ice locked up much of the world's water and large areas of the northern hemisphere experienced a drop in sea-level. Away from the poles, deserts and a hot dry climate predominated. As a result of these conditions, the Permian period ended with the greatest mass extinction of life on earth ever.

EXAMPLES OF CARBONIFEROUS AND PERMIAN PLANT GROUPS

A PRESENT-DAY FIR
(Abies concolor)

FOSSIL OF AN EXTINCT FERN
(Zeilleria frenzlii)

FOSSIL OF AN EXTINCT HORSETAIL
(Equisetites sp.)

FOSSIL OF AN EXTINCT CLUBMOSS
(Lepidodendron sp.)

EXAMPLES OF CARBONIFEROUS AND PERMIAN TREES

PECOPTERIS
Family: Marattiaceae
Height: 4 m (13 ft)

PARIPTERIS
Family: Medullosaceae
Height: 5 m (16 ft 6 in)

MARIOPTERIS
Family: Unclassified
Height: 5 m (16 ft 6 in)

MEDULLOSA
Family: Medullosaceae
Height: 5 m (16 ft 6 in)

THE EARTH DURING THE LATE CARBONIFEROUS PERIOD

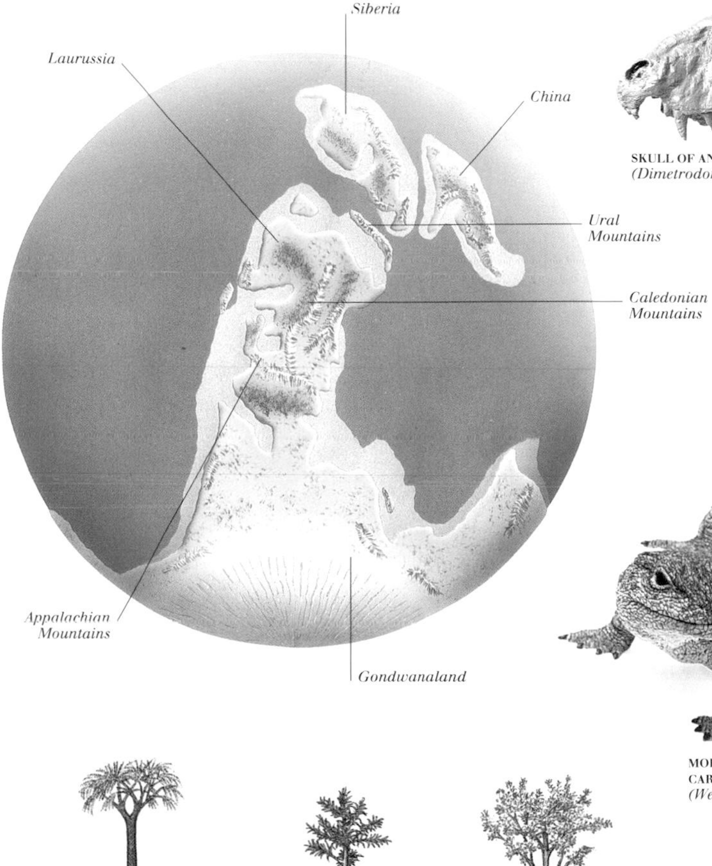

EXAMPLES OF CARBONIFEROUS
AND PERMIAN ANIMALS

Siberia

Laurussia

China

Ural
Mountains

Caledonian
Mountains

Appalachian
Mountains

Gondwanaland

SKULL OF AN EXTINCT SYNAPSID REPTILE
(Dimetrodon loomisi)

FOSSIL TEETH OF
AN EXTINCT SHARK
(Helicoprion bessonowi)

MODEL OF AN EXTINCT
CARBONIFEROUS REPTILE
(Westlothiana lizziae)

LEPIDODENDRON
Family: Lepidodendraceae
Height: 30 m (100 ft)

CORDAITES
Family: Cordaitacea
Height: 10 m (33 ft)

GLOSSOPTERIS
Family: Glossopteridaceae
Height: 8 m (26 ft)

ALETHOPTERIS
Family: Medullosaceae
Height: 5 m (16 ft 6 in)

Triassic period

THE TRIASSIC PERIOD (245–208 million years ago) marked the beginning of what is known as the Age of the Dinosaurs (the Mesozoic era). During this period, the present-day continents were massed together, forming one huge continent known as Pangaea. This land-mass experienced extremes of climate, with lush green areas around the coast or by lakes and rivers, and arid deserts in the interior. The only forms of plant life were non-flowering plants, such as conifers, ferns, cycads, and ginkgos; flowering plants had not yet evolved. The principal forms of animal life included primitive amphibians, rhynchosaurs ("beaked lizards"), and primitive crocodilians. Dinosaurs first appeared about 230 million years ago, at the beginning of the Late Triassic period. The earliest known dinosaurs were the carnivorous (flesh-eating) herrerasaurids and staurikosaurids, such as *Herrerasaurus* and *Staurikosaurus*. Early herbivorous (plant-eating) dinosaurs first appeared in Late Triassic times and included *Plateosaurus* and *Technosaurus*. By the end of the Triassic period, dinosaurs dominated Pangaea, possibly contributing to the extinction of many other reptiles.

EXAMPLES OF TRIASSIC
PLANT GROUPS

A PRESENT-DAY
CYCAD
(Cycas revoluta)

A PRESENT-DAY GINKGO
(Ginkgo biloba)

A PRESENT-DAY CONIFER
(Araucaria araucana)

FOSSIL OF AN
EXTINCT FERN
(Pachypteris sp.)

FOSSIL LEAF OF AN
EXTINCT CYCAD
(Cycas sp.)

EXAMPLES OF TRIASSIC DINOSAURS

MELANOROSAURUS
A melanorosaurid
Length: 12.2 m (40 ft)

MUSSAURUS
A plateosaurid
Length: 2–3 m (6 ft 6 in–10 ft)

HERRERASAURUS
A herrerasaurid
Length: 3 m (10 ft)

PISANOSAURUS
A primitive ornithischian
Length: 90 cm (3 ft)

THE EARTH DURING THE TRIASSIC PERIOD

EXAMPLES OF TRIASSIC ANIMALS

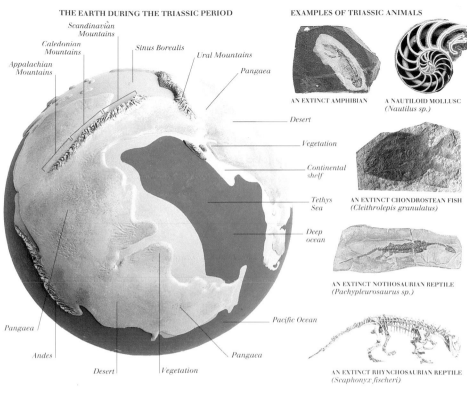

Scandinavian Mountains

Caledonian Mountains

Sinus Borealis

Appalachian Mountains

Ural Mountains

Pangaea

Desert

Vegetation

Continental shelf

Tethys Sea

Deep ocean

Pacific Ocean

Pangaea

Andes

Desert

Vegetation

Pangaea

AN EXTINCT AMPHIBIAN

A NAUTILOID MOLLUSC
(*Nautilus sp.*)

AN EXTINCT CHONDROSTEAN FISH
(*Cleithrolepis granulatus*)

AN EXTINCT NOTHOSAURIAN REPTILE
(*Pachypleurosaurus sp.*)

AN EXTINCT RHYNCHOSAURIAN REPTILE
(*Scaphonyx fischeri*)

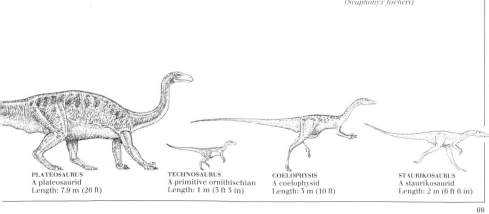

PLATEOSAURUS
A plateosaurid
Length: 7.9 m (26 ft)

TECHNOSAURUS
A primitive ornithischian
Length: 1 m (3 ft 3 in)

COELOPHYSIS
A coelophysid
Length: 3 m (10 ft)

STAURIKOSAURUS
A staurikosaurid
Length: 2 m (6 ft 6 in)

Jurassic period

THE JURASSIC PERIOD, the middle part of the Mesozoic era, lasted from 208 to 146 million years ago. During Jurassic times, the land-mass of Pangaea broke up into the continents of Gondwanaland and Laurasia, and sea-levels rose, flooding areas of lower land. The Jurassic climate was warm and moist. Plants such as ginkgos, horsetails, and conifers thrived, and giant redwood trees appeared, as did the first flowering plants. The abundance of plant food coincided with the proliferation of herbivorous (plant-eating) dinosaurs, such as the large sauropods (e.g., *Diplodocus*) and stegosaurs (e.g., *Stegosaurus*). Carnivorous (flesh-eating) dinosaurs, such as *Compsognathus* and *Allosaurus*, also flourished by hunting the many animals that existed – among them other dinosaurs. Further Jurassic animals included shrew-like mammals, and pterosaurs (flying reptiles), as well as plesiosaurs and ichthyosaurs (both marine reptiles).

JURASSIC POSITIONS OF PRESENT-DAY LAND-MASSES

North America

Europe

Arabia

Asia

Australia

South America

Africa

India

Antarctica

EXAMPLES OF JURASSIC PLANT GROUPS

A PRESENT-DAY FERN
(Dicksonia antarctica)

A PRESENT-DAY HORSETAIL
(Equisetum arvense)

A PRESENT-DAY CONIFER
(Taxus baccata)

FOSSIL LEAF OF AN EXTINCT CONIFER
(Taxus sp.)

FOSSIL LEAF OF AN EXTINCT REDWOOD
(Sequoiadendron affinis)

EXAMPLES OF JURASSIC DINOSAURS

DIPLODOCUS
A diplodocid
Length: 26.8 m (88 ft)

CAMPTOSAURUS
A camptosaurid
Length: 4.9–7 m (16–23 ft)

DRYOSAURUS
A dryosaurid
Length: 3–4 m (10–13 ft)

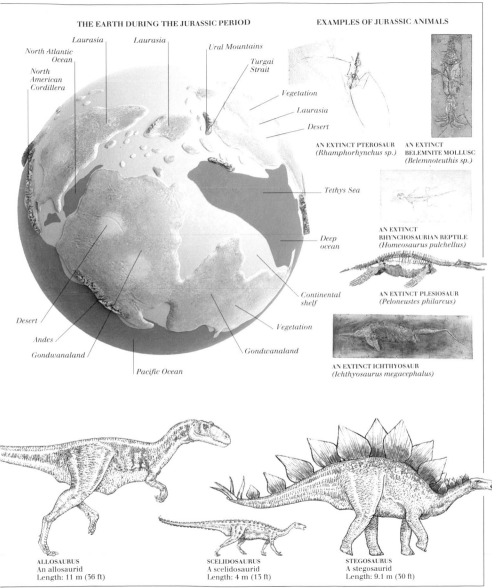

THE EARTH DURING THE JURASSIC PERIOD

North Atlantic Ocean

Laurasia

Laurasia

Ural Mountains

North American Cordillera

Turgai Strait

Vegetation

Laurasia

Desert

Tethys Sea

Deep ocean

Continental shelf

Vegetation

Desert

Andes

Gondwanaland

Gondwanaland

Pacific Ocean

EXAMPLES OF JURASSIC ANIMALS

AN EXTINCT PTEROSAUR
(*Rhamphorhynchus sp.*)

AN EXTINCT BELEMNITE MOLLUSC
(*Belemnoteuthis sp.*)

AN EXTINCT RHYNCHOSAURIAN REPTILE
(*Homeosaurus pulchellus*)

AN EXTINCT PLESIOSAUR
(*Peloneustes philarcus*)

AN EXTINCT ICHTHYOSAUR
(*Ichthyosaurus megacephalus*)

ALLOSAURUS
An allosaurid
Length: 11 m (36 ft)

SCELIDOSAURUS
A scelidosaurid
Length: 4 m (13 ft)

STEGOSAURUS
A stegosaurid
Length: 9.1 m (30 ft)

Cretaceous period

THE MESOZOIC ERA ENDED WITH the Cretaceous period, which lasted from 146 to 65 million years ago. During this period, Gondwanaland and Laurasia were breaking up into smaller land-masses that more closely resembled those of the modern continents. The climate remained mild and moist but the seasons became more marked. Flowering plants, including deciduous trees, replaced many cycads, seed ferns, and conifers. Animal species became more varied, with the evolution of new mammals, insects, fish, crustaceans, and turtles. Dinosaurs evolved into a wide variety of species during Cretaceous times; more than half of all known dinosaurs – including *Iguanodon, Deinonychus, Tyrannosaurus,* and *Hypsilophodon* – lived during this period. At the end of the Cretaceous period, however, dinosaurs became extinct. The reason for this mass extinction is unknown but it is thought to have been caused by climatic changes due to either a catastrophic meteor impact with the Earth or extensive volcanic eruptions.

EXAMPLES OF CRETACEOUS PLANT GROUPS

A PRESENT-DAY CONIFER
(Pinus muricata)

**A PRESENT-DAY
DECIDUOUS TREE**
(Magnolia sp.)

**FOSSIL OF AN
EXTINCT FERN**
(Sphenopteris latiloba)

**FOSSIL OF AN
EXTINCT GINKGO**
(Ginkgo pluripartita)

**FOSSIL LEAVES
OF AN EXTINCT
DECIDUOUS TREE**
(Cercidyphyllum sp.)

EXAMPLES OF
CRETACEOUS DINOSAURS

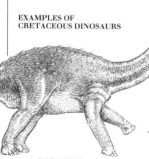

SALTASAURUS
A titanosaurid
Length: 12.2 m (40 ft)

TOROSAURUS
A ceratopsid
Length: 7.6 m (25 ft)

HYPSILOPHODON
A hypsilophodontid
Length: 1.4–2.3 m (4 ft 6 in–7 ft 6 in)

THE EARTH DURING THE CRETACEOUS PERIOD

EXAMPLES OF CRETACEOUS ANIMALS

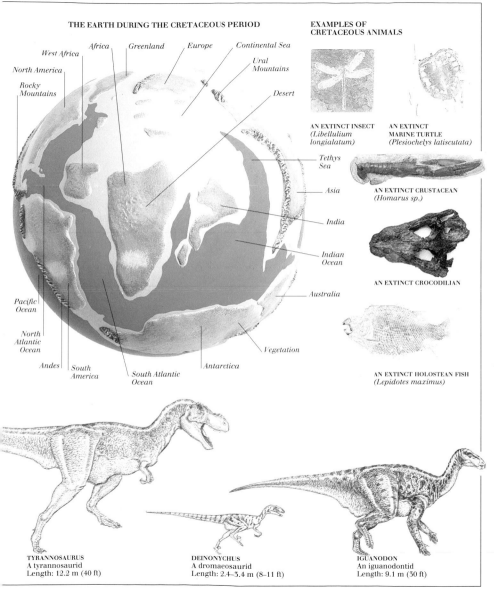

West Africa
Africa
Greenland
Europe
Continental Sea
North America
Ural Mountains
Rocky Mountains
Desert
Tethys Sea
Asia
India
Indian Ocean
Pacific Ocean
Australia
North Atlantic Ocean
Vegetation
Andes
South America
South Atlantic Ocean
Antarctica

AN EXTINCT INSECT
(*Libellulium longialatum*)

AN EXTINCT MARINE TURTLE
(*Plesiochelys latiscutata*)

AN EXTINCT CRUSTACEAN
(*Homarus sp.*)

AN EXTINCT CROCODILIAN

AN EXTINCT HOLOSTEAN FISH
(*Lepidotes maximus*)

TYRANNOSAURUS
A tyrannosaurid
Length: 12.2 m (40 ft)

DEINONYCHUS
A dromaeosaurid
Length: 2.4–3.4 m (8–11 ft)

IGUANODON
An iguanodontid
Length: 9.1 m (30 ft)

Tertiary period

FOLLOWING THE DEMISE OF THE DINOSAURS at the end of the Cretaceous period, the Tertiary period (65–1.6 million years ago), which formed the first part of the Cenozoic era (65 million years ago–present), was characterized by a huge expansion of mammal life. Placental mammals nourish and maintain the young in the mother's uterus; only three orders of placental mammals existed during Cretaceous times, compared with 25 orders during the Tertiary period. One of these 25 included the first hominid (see pp.108–109), *Australopithecus*, which appeared in Africa. By the beginning of the Tertiary period, the continents had almost reached their present position. The Tethys Sea, which had separated the northern continents from Africa and India, began to close up, forming the Mediterranean Sea and allowing the migration of terrestrial animals between Africa and western Europe. India's collision with Asia led to the formation of the Himalayas. During the middle part of the Tertiary period, the forest-dwelling and browsing mammals were replaced by mammals such as the horse, better suited to grazing the open savannahs that began to dominate. Repeated cool periods throughout the Tertiary period established the Antarctic as an icy island continent.

TERTIARY POSITIONS OF PRESENT-DAY LAND-MASSES

North America
Europe
Asia
South America
Africa
Australia
Antarctica

EXAMPLES OF TERTIARY PLANT GROUPS

A PRESENT-DAY OAK
(*Quercus palustris*)

A PRESENT-DAY BIRCH
(*Betula grossa*)

FOSSIL LEAF OF AN EXTINCT BIRCH
(*Betulites sp.*)

FOSSILIZED STEM OF AN EXTINCT PALM
(*Palmoxylon sp.*)

EXAMPLES OF TERTIARY ANIMAL GROUPS

HYAENODON
An hyaenodontid
Length: 2 m (6 ft 6 in)

TITANOHYRAX
A pliohyracid
Length: 2 m (6 ft 6 in)

PHORUSRHACUS
A phorusrhacid
Length: 1.5 m (5 ft)

SAMOTHERIUM
A giraffid
Length: 3 m (10 ft)

THE EARTH DURING THE TERTIARY PERIOD

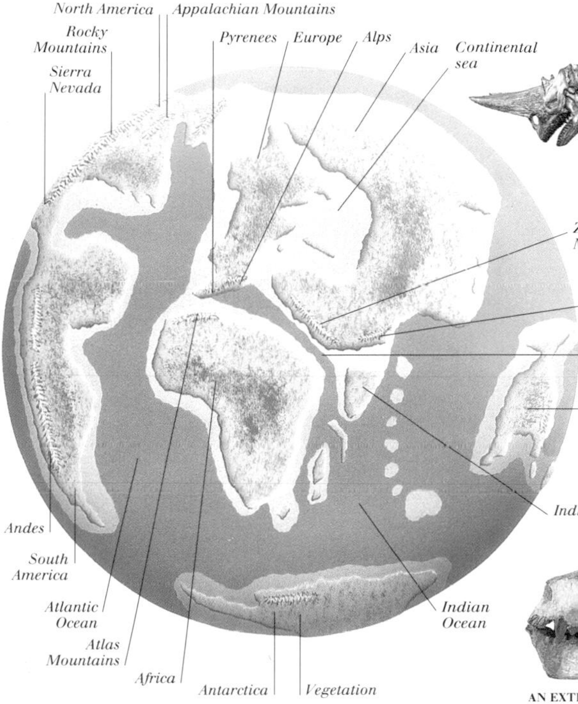

EXAMPLES OF TERTIARY ANIMALS

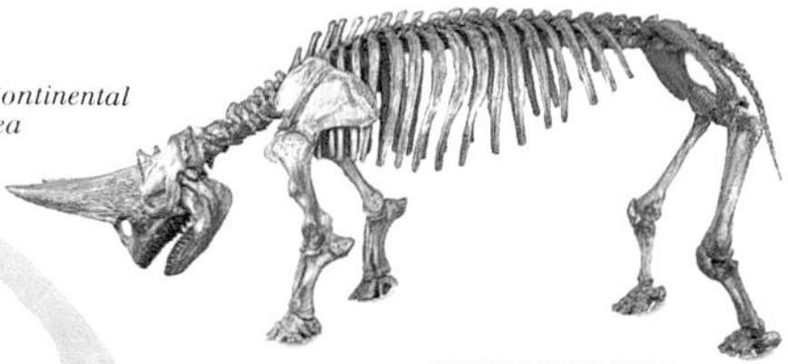

North America
Rocky Mountains
Sierra Nevada
Appalachian Mountains
Pyrenees
Europe
Alps
Asia
Continental sea
Zagros Mountains
Himalayas
Tethys Sea
Australia
India
Andes
South America
Atlantic Ocean
Atlas Mountains
Africa
Antarctica
Vegetation
Indian Ocean

AN EXTINCT MAMMAL
(Arsinoitherium)

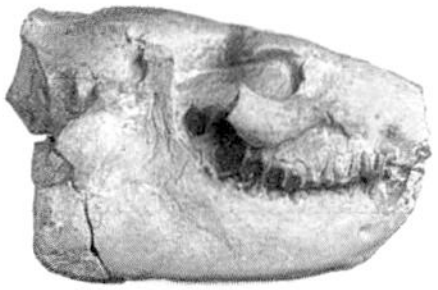

AN EXTINCT MAMMAL
(Merycoidodon culbertsonii)

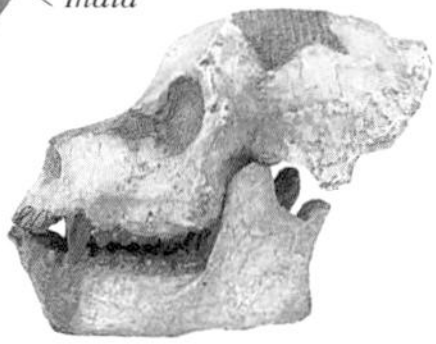

AN EXTINCT HOMINID
(Aegyptopithecus sp.)

**AN EXTINCT
GASTROPOD MOLLUSC**
(Ecphora quadricostata)

MAMMUT
A mammutid
Length: 2.5 m (8 ft)

TETRALOPHODON
A gomphotheriid
Length: 2.5 m (8 ft)

Quaternary period

THE QUATERNARY PERIOD (1.6 million years ago–present) forms the second part of the Cenozoic era (65 million years ago–present): it has been characterized by alternating cold (glacial) and warm (interglacial) periods. During cold periods, ice sheets and glaciers have formed repeatedly on northern and southern continents. The cold environments in North America and Eurasia, and to a lesser extent in southern South America and parts of Australia, have caused the migration of many life forms towards the Equator. Only the specialized ice age mammals such as *Mammuthus* and *Coelodonta*, with their thick wool and fat insulation, were suited to life in very cold climates. Humans developed throughout the Pleistocene period (1.6 million–10,000 years ago) in Africa and migrated northward into Europe and Asia. Modern humans, *Homo sapiens*, lived on the cold European continent 30,000 years ago and hunted mammals. The end of the last ice age and the climatic changes that occurred about 10,000 years ago brought extinction to many Pleistocene mammals, but enabled humans to flourish.

QUATERNARY POSITIONS OF
PRESENT-DAY LAND-MASSES

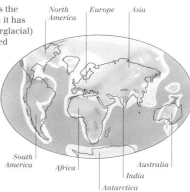

North
America

Europe

Asia

South
America

Africa

Australia

India

Antarctica

EXAMPLES OF QUATERNARY PLANT GROUPS

A PRESENT-DAY BIRCH
(Betula lenta)

A PRESENT-DAY SWEEETGUM
(Liquidambar styraciflua)

FOSSIL LEAF OF A SWEETGUM
(Liquidambar europeanum)

FOSSIL LEAF OF A BIRCH
(Betula sp.)

EXAMPLES OF QUATERNARY ANIMAL GROUPS

PROCOPTODON
A macropodid
Length: 3 m (10 ft)

DIPROTODON
A diprotodontid
Length: 3 m (10 ft)

TOXODON
A toxodontid
Length: 3 m (10 ft)

MAMMUTHUS
An elephantid
Length: 3 m (10 ft)

THE EARTH DURING THE QUATERNARY PERIOD

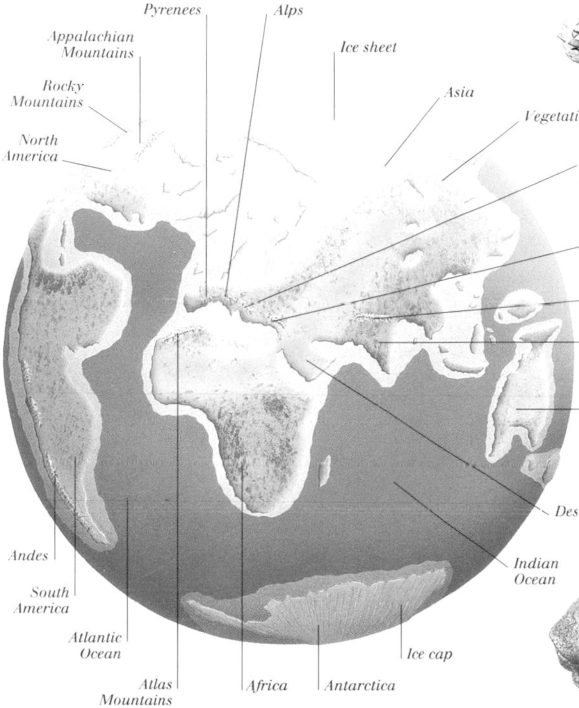

EXAMPLES OF QUATERNARY ANIMALS

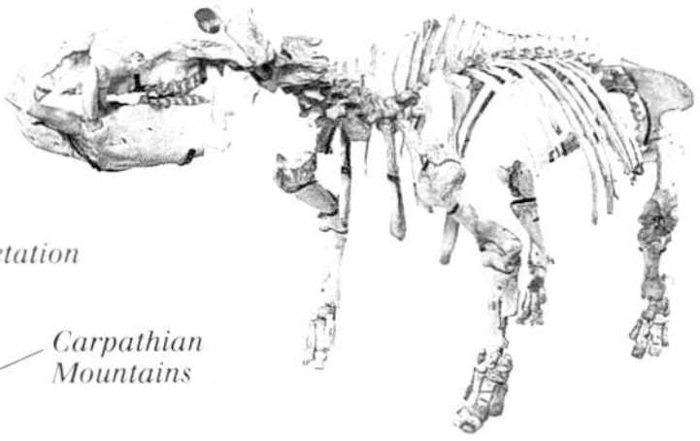

Pyrenees
Alps
Appalachian Mountains
Ice sheet
Rocky Mountains
Asia
North America
Vegetation
Carpathian Mountains
Taurus Mountains
Himalayas
India
Australia
Andes
South America
Desert
Indian Ocean
Atlantic Ocean
Ice cap
Atlas Mountains
Africa
Antarctica

A MAMMAL SKELETON
(*Hippopotamus amphibius*)

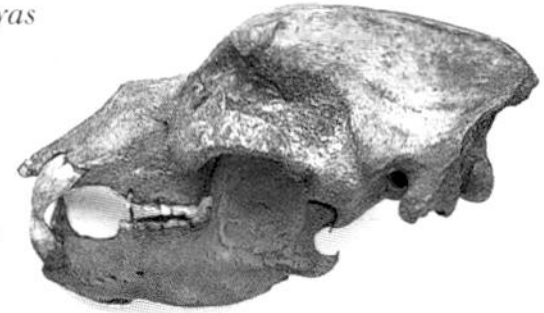

SKULL OF AN EXTINCT CAVE BEAR
(*Ursus spelaeus*)

SKULL OF AN EXTINCT TORTOISE
(*Meiolania platyceps*)

A MAMMOTH TOOTH
(*Mammuthus primigenius*)

DEINOTHERIUM
A deinotheriid
Length: 4 m (13 ft)

COELODONTA
A rhinocerotid
Length: 4 m (13 ft)

AUSTRALOPITHECUS
A hominid
Length: 1.2 m (4 ft)

Early signs of life

FOR ALMOST A THOUSAND MILLION YEARS after its formation, there was no known life on Earth. The first simple, sea-dwelling organic structures appeared about 3,500 million years ago; they may have formed when certain chemical molecules joined together. Prokaryotes, single-celled micro-organisms such as blue-green algae, were able to photosynthesize (see pp. 138–139), and thus produce oxygen. A thousand million years later, sufficient oxygen had built up in the earth's atmosphere to allow multicellular organisms to proliferate in the Precambrian seas (before 570 million years ago). Soft-bodied jellyfish, corals, and seaworms flourished about 700 million years ago. Trilobites, the first animals with hard body frames, developed during the Cambrian period (570–510 million years ago). However, it was not until the beginning of the Devonian period (409–363 million years ago) that early land plants, such as *Asteroxylon*, formed a water-retaining cuticle, which ended their dependence on an aquatic environment. About 360 million years ago, the first amphibians (see pp. 80–81) crawled onto the land, although they still returned to the water to lay their soft eggs. Not until the emergence of the first reptiles would animals with backbones appear that were independent of water in this way.

STROMATOLITIC LIMESTONE

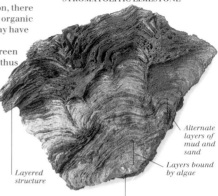

Alternate layers of mud and sand

Layers bound by algae

Layered structure

Limestone

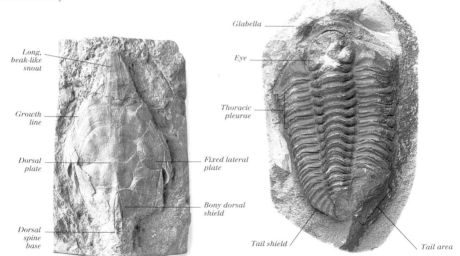

Long, beak-like snout

Growth line

Dorsal plate

Dorsal spine base

Glabella

Eye

Thoracic pleurae

Fixed lateral plate

Bony dorsal shield

Tail shield

Tail area

FOSSILIZED JAWLESS FISH

FOSSILIZED TRILOBITE

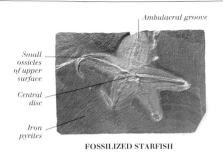

Ambulacral groove

Small ossicles of upper surface

Central disc

Iron pyrites

FOSSILIZED STARFISH

Row of ossicles

Broad disc

Row of ossicles

Short arm

UPPER SURFACE OF FOSSILIZED STARFISH

LOWER SURFACE OF FOSSILIZED STARFISH

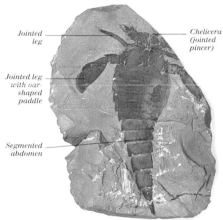

Jointed leg

Chelicera (jointed pincer)

Jointed leg with oar-shaped paddle

Segmented abdomen

UNDERSIDE OF FOSSILIZED EURYPTERID

Telson (tail spine)

Abdominal segments

Shell contains eight somites (thoracic segments)

Hingeless, bivalved shell

FOSSIL OF AN EXTINCT SHRIMP

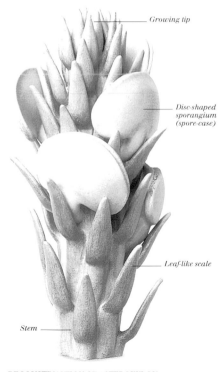

Growing tip

Disc-shaped sporangium (spore-case)

Leaf-like scale

Stem

RECONSTRUCTION OF ASTEROXYLON

Amphibians and reptiles

THE EARLIEST KNOWN AMPHIBIANS, such as *Acanthostega* and *Ichthyostega*, lived about 363 million years ago at the end of the Devonian period (409–363 million years ago). Their limbs may have evolved from the muscular fins of lungfish-like creatures. These fish can use their fins to push themselves along the bottom of lakes and some can breathe at the water's surface. While amphibians (see pp. 182–183) can exist on land, they are dependent on a wet environment because their skin does not retain moisture and they must return to the water to lay their eggs. Evolving from amphibians, reptiles (see pp. 184–187) first appeared during the Carboniferous period (363–290 million years ago): *Westlothiana*, a possible early reptile, lived on land 338 million years ago. The development of the amniotic egg, with an embryo enclosed in its own wet environment (the amnion) and protected by a waterproof shell, freed reptiles from the amphibian's dependence on a wet habitat. A scaly skin protected the reptile from desiccation on land and enabled it to exploit ways of life closed to its amphibian ancestors. Reptiles include the dinosaurs, which came to dominate life on land during the Mesozoic era (245–65 million years ago).

Sculpted or pitted bone surface

Orbit

Pocket enclosing nostril

Spiracle to draw in water

Mandible

Small tooth

FOSSIL SKULL OF ACANTHOSTEGA

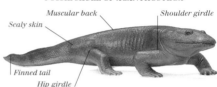

Muscular back

Scaly skin

Shoulder girdle

Finned tail

Hip girdle

MODEL OF ICHTHYOSTEGA

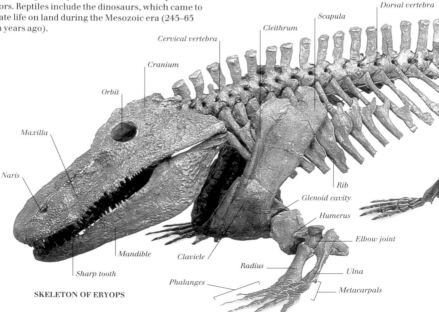

Dorsal vertebra

Scapula

Cleithrum

Cervical vertebra

Cranium

Orbit

Maxilla

Naris

Rib

Glenoid cavity

Humerus

Elbow joint

Mandible

Clavicle

Radius

Ulna

Sharp tooth

Phalanges

Metacarpals

SKELETON OF ERYOPS

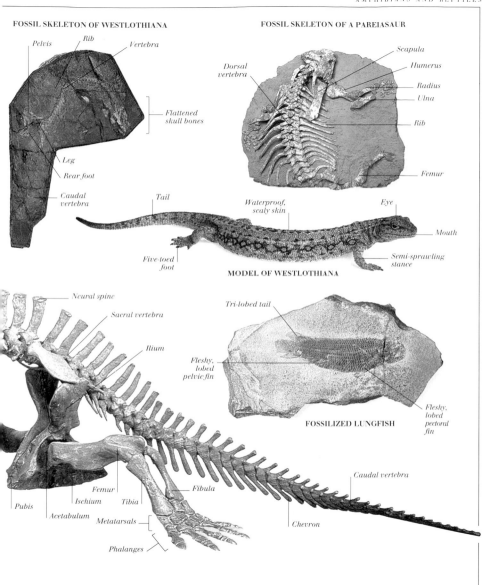

FOSSIL SKELETON OF WESTLOTHIANA

Pelvis
Rib
Vertebra
Flattened skull bones
Leg
Rear foot
Caudal vertebra

FOSSIL SKELETON OF A PAREIASAUR

Scapula
Humerus
Radius
Ulna
Dorsal vertebra
Rib
Femur

Tail
Waterproof, scaly skin
Eye
Mouth
Five-toed foot
Semi-sprawling stance

MODEL OF WESTLOTHIANA

Neural spine
Sacral vertebra
Ilium

Tri-lobed tail
Fleshy, lobed pelvic fin
Fleshy, lobed pectoral fin

FOSSILIZED LUNGFISH

Pubis
Acetabulum
Femur
Ischium
Tibia
Metatarsals
Phalanges
Fibula
Caudal vertebra
Chevron

The dinosaurs

THE DINOSAURS WERE A LARGE GROUP of reptiles that were the dominant land vertebrates (animals with backbones) for most of the Mesozoic era (245–65 million years ago). They appeared some 230 million years ago and were distinguished from other scaly, egg-laying reptiles by an important feature: dinosaurs had an erect limb stance. This enabled them to keep their bodies well above the ground, unlike the sprawling and semi-sprawling stance of other reptiles. The head of the dinosaur's femur (thigh-bone) fitted into a socket in its pelvis (hip-bone), producing efficient and mobile locomotion. Dinosaurs are categorized into two groups according to the structure of their pelvis: saurischian (lizard-hipped) and ornithischian (bird-hipped) dinosaurs. In the case of most saurischians, the pubis (part of the pelvis) jutted forward, while in ornithischians it slanted back, parallel to the ischium (another part of the pelvis). Dinosaurs ranged in size from smaller than a domestic cat to the biggest land animals ever known. The Dinosauria were the most successful land vertebrates ever, and survived for 165 million years, until their extinction 65 million years ago.

STRUCTURE OF SAURISCHIAN PELVIS

Ilium

Postacetabular process

Hook of preacetabular process

Ilio-pubic joint

Acetabulum

Ilio-ischial joint

Pubis

Pubic foot

Ischium

GALLIMIMUS
A saurischian dinosaur

POSITION OF PELVIS IN A SAURISCHIAN DINOSAUR

STRUCTURE OF ORNITHISCHIAN PELVIS

Ilium

Preacetabular process

Postacetabular process

Ilio-pubic joint

Ilio-ischial joint

Prepubis

Acetabulum

Pubis

Ischium

HYPSILOPHODON
An ornithischian dinosaur

POSITION OF PELVIS IN AN ORNITHISCHIAN DINOSAUR

BAROSAURUS
A saurischian dinosaur

COMPARISON OF ANIMAL STANCES

SPRAWLING STANCE
The thighs and upper arms project straight out from the body so that the knees and elbows are bent at right angles.

COMMON IGUANA
(Iguana iguana)
A present-day reptile

ERECT STANCE
The thighs and upper arms project straight down from the body so that the knees and elbows are straight.

SEMI-SPRAWLING STANCE
The thighs and upper arms project downwards and outwards so that the knees and elbows are slightly bent.

DWARF CROCODILE
(Osteolaemus tetraspis)
A present-day reptile

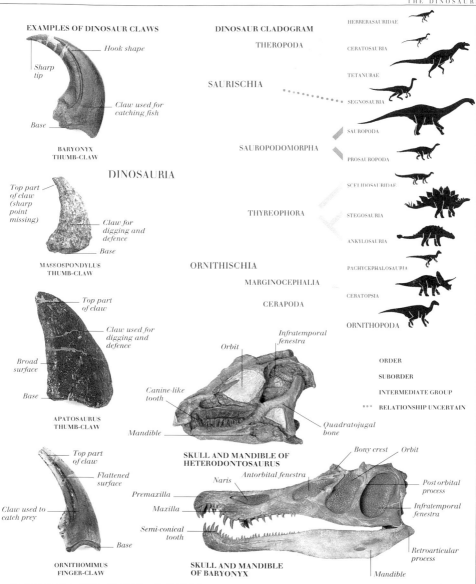

EXAMPLES OF DINOSAUR CLAWS

Hook shape

Sharp tip

Claw used for catching fish

Base

BARYONYX THUMB-CLAW

DINOSAURIA

Top part of claw (sharp point missing)

Claw for digging and defence

Base

MASSOSPONDYLUS THUMB-CLAW

Top part of claw

Claw used for digging and defence

Broad surface

Base

APATOSAURUS THUMB-CLAW

Top part of claw

Flattened surface

Claw used to catch prey

Base

ORNITHOMIMUS FINGER-CLAW

DINOSAUR CLADOGRAM

THEROPODA

SAURISCHIA

SAUROPODOMORPHA

THYREOPHORA

ORNITHISCHIA

MARGINOCEPHALIA

CERAPODA

ORNITHOPODA

HERRERASAURIDAE

CERATOSAURIA

TETANURAE

SEGNOSAURIA

SAUROPODA

PROSAUROPODA

SCELIDOSAURIDAE

STEGOSAURIA

ANKYLOSAURIA

PACHYCEPHALOSAURIA

CERATOPSIA

ORDER

SUBORDER

INTERMEDIATE GROUP

* * * RELATIONSHIP UNCERTAIN

Infratemporal fenestra

Orbit

Canine-like tooth

Mandible

Quadratojugal bone

SKULL AND MANDIBLE OF HETERODONTOSAURUS

Bony crest

Orbit

Antorbital fenestra

Naris

Premaxilla

Maxilla

Semi-conical tooth

Post orbital process

Infratemporal fenestra

Retroarticular process

Mandible

SKULL AND MANDIBLE OF BARYONYX

Theropods 1

AN ENORMOUSLY SUCCESSFUL SUBORDER of the Saurischia,
the bipedal (two-footed) theropods ("beast feet") emerged
250 million years ago in Late Triassic times; the oldest known
example comes from South America. Theropods spanned the
whole of the Age of the Dinosaurs (230–65 million years ago)
and included most of the known predatory dinosaurs. The
typical theropod had small arms with sharp, clawed fingers;
powerful jaws lined with sharp teeth; an S-shaped neck; long,
muscular hind limbs; and clawed, usually four-toed feet. Many
theropods may have been warm-blooded; most were exclusively
carnivorous. Theropods ranged from animals no larger than a
chicken to huge creatures, such as Tyrannosaurus and
Baryonyx. The group also included ostrich-like omnivores and
herbivores with toothless beaks, such as Struthiomimus and
Gallimimus. Many scientists believe that birds are the closest
living relatives to the dinosaurs, and share a common ancestor
with the theropods. Archaeopteryx, small and feathered, was
the first known bird and lived alongside its dinosaur relatives.

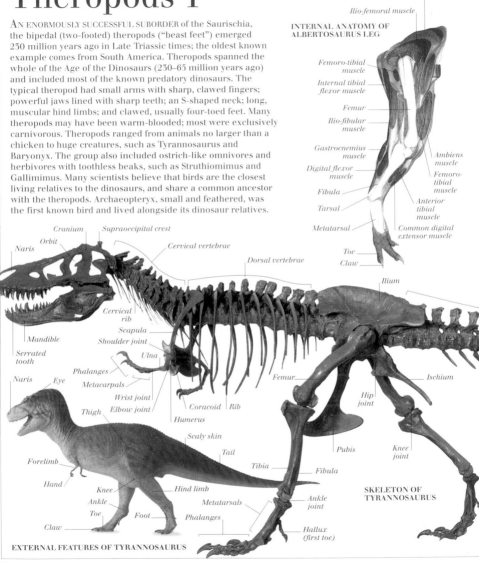

INTERNAL ANATOMY OF ALBERTOSAURUS LEG

Ilio-tibial muscle
Ilio-femoral muscle
Femoro-tibial muscle
Internal tibial flexor muscle
Femur
Ilio-fibular muscle
Gastrocnemius muscle
Digital flexor muscle
Fibula
Tarsal
Metatarsal
Ambiens muscle
Femoro-tibial muscle
Anterior tibial muscle
Common digital extensor muscle
Toe
Claw

SKELETON OF TYRANNOSAURUS

Cranium
Supraoccipital crest
Orbit
Naris
Cervical vertebrae
Dorsal vertebrae
Ilium
Cervical rib
Scapula
Shoulder joint
Mandible
Ulna
Serrated tooth
Phalanges
Metacarpals
Coracoid
Rib
Femur
Ischium
Wrist joint
Elbow joint
Humerus
Hip joint
Pubis
Knee joint
Tibia
Fibula
Ankle joint
Hallux (first toe)
Metatarsals
Phalanges

EXTERNAL FEATURES OF TYRANNOSAURUS

Naris
Eye
Thigh
Forelimb
Hand
Knee
Ankle
Toe
Claw
Foot
Scaly skin
Tail
Hind limb

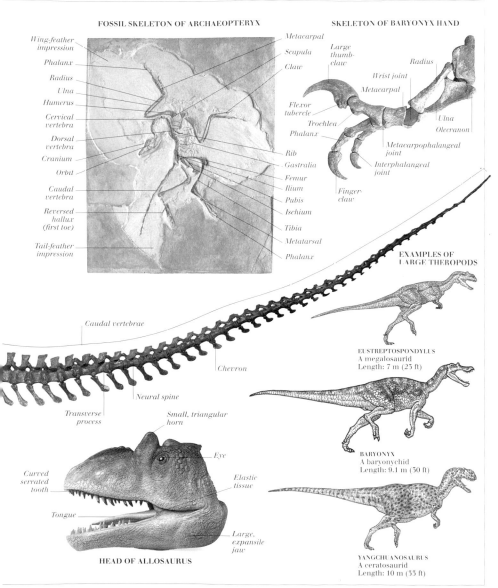

FOSSIL SKELETON OF ARCHAEOPTERYX

Wing-feather impression
Phalanx
Radius
Ulna
Humerus
Cervical vertebra
Dorsal vertebra
Cranium
Orbit
Caudal vertebra
Reversed hallux (first toe)
Tail-feather impression

Rib
Gastralia
Femur
Ilium
Pubis
Ischium
Tibia
Metatarsal
Phalanx

SKELETON OF BARYONYX HAND

Metacarpal
Scapula
Claw
Large thumb-claw
Radius
Wrist joint
Metacarpal
Flexor tubercle
Trochlea
Phalanx
Ulna
Olecranon
Metacarpophalangeal joint
Interphalangeal joint
Finger-claw

EXAMPLES OF LARGE THEROPODS

Caudal vertebrae
Chevron
Neural spine
Transverse process

EUSTREPTOSPONDYLUS
A megalosaurid
Length: 7 m (23 ft)

BARYONYX
A baryonychid
Length: 9.1 m (30 ft)

Small, triangular horn
Eye
Curved serrated tooth
Elastic tissue
Tongue
Large, expansile jaw

HEAD OF ALLOSAURUS

YANGCHUANOSAURUS
A ceratosaurid
Length: 10 m (33 ft)

Theropods 2

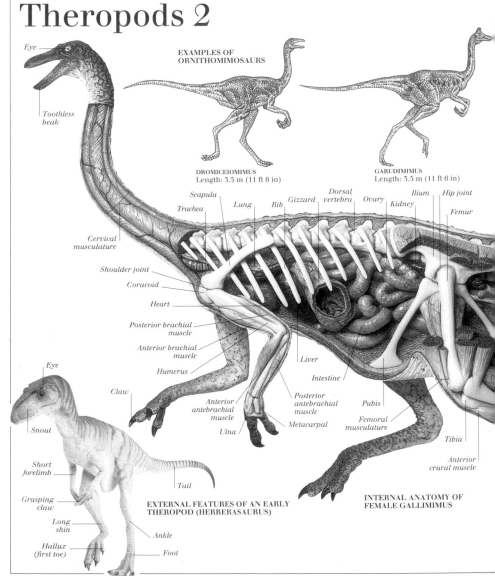

Eye

Toothless beak

EXAMPLES OF ORNITHOMIMOSAURS

DROMICEIOMIMUS
Length: 3.5 m (11 ft 6 in)

GARUDIMIMUS
Length: 3.5 m (11 ft 6 in)

Cervical musculature

Scapula

Trachea

Lung

Rib

Gizzard

Dorsal vertebra

Ovary

Kidney

Ilium

Hip joint

Femur

Shoulder joint

Coracoid

Heart

Posterior brachial muscle

Anterior brachial muscle

Humerus

Liver

Intestine

Eye

Claw

Anterior antebrachial muscle

Posterior antebrachial muscle

Metacarpal

Pubis

Femoral musculature

Tibia

Snout

Ulna

Anterior crural muscle

Short forelimb

Tail

Grasping claw

Long shin

Ankle

Hallux (first toe)

Foot

EXTERNAL FEATURES OF AN EARLY THEROPOD (HERRERASAURUS)

INTERNAL ANATOMY OF FEMALE GALLIMIMUS

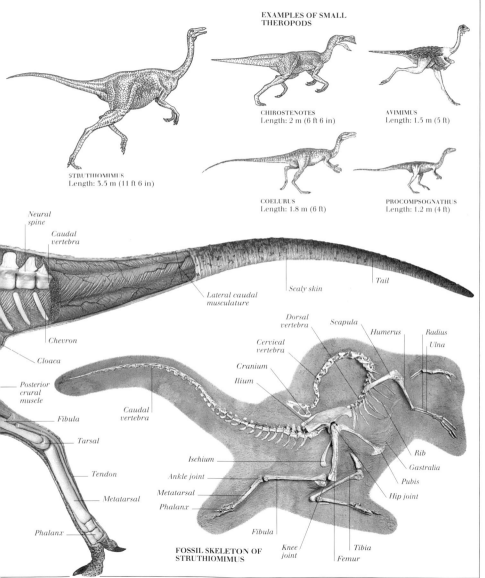

EXAMPLES OF SMALL THEROPODS

CHIROSTENOTES
Length: 2 m (6 ft 6 in)

AVIMIMUS
Length: 1.5 m (5 ft)

STRUTHIOMIMUS
Length: 3.5 m (11 ft 6 in)

COELURUS
Length: 1.8 m (6 ft)

PROCOMPSOGNATHUS
Length: 1.2 m (4 ft)

Neural spine

Caudal vertebra

Lateral caudal musculature

Scaly skin

Tail

Chevron

Cloaca

Posterior crural muscle

Fibula

Tarsal

Tendon

Metatarsal

Phalanx

Caudal vertebra

Dorsal vertebra

Scapula

Humerus

Radius

Ulna

Cervical vertebra

Cranium

Ilium

Rib

Gastralia

Ischium

Pubis

Ankle joint

Hip joint

Metatarsal

Phalanx

Fibula

Knee joint

Femur

Tibia

FOSSIL SKELETON OF STRUTHIOMIMUS

Sauropodomorphs 1

SKULL AND MANDIBLE OF PLATEOSAURUS

THE SAUROPODOMORPHA ("lizard-feet forms") were herbivorous, usually quadrupedal (four-footed) dinosaurs. A suborder of the Saurischia, they were characterized by small heads, bulky bodies, and long necks and tails. There were two infraorders: prosauropods and sauropods.

THECODONTOSAURUS

Prosauropods lived from Late Triassic to Early Jurassic times (225–180 million years ago) and included beasts such as the small *Anchisaurus* and one of the first very large dinosaurs, *Plateosaurus*. By Middle Jurassic times (about 165 million years ago), sauropods had replaced prosauropods and spread worldwide. They included the heaviest and longest land animals ever, such as *Diplodocus* and *Brachiosaurus*. Sauropods persisted to the end of the Cretaceous period (65 million years ago). Many of these dinosaurs moved in herds, protected from predatory theropods by their huge bulk and powerful tails, which they could use to lash out at attackers. Sauropodomorphs were the most common large herbivores until Late Jurassic times (about 145 million years ago), and appear to have survived in southern continents long after they had disappeared from the north.

SKELETON OF PLATEOSAURUS

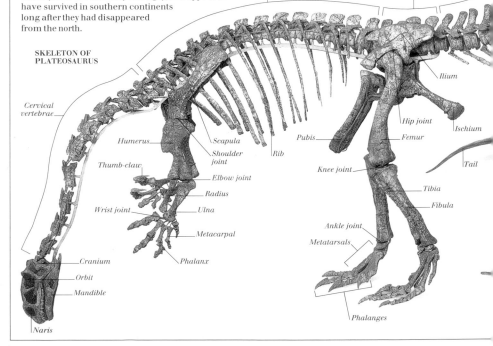

Labels for skull and mandible: Naris, Antorbital fenestra, Orbit, Mandible, Infratemporal fenestra, Paroccipital process, Serrated, leaf-shaped tooth, Mandibular fenestra

Labels for skeleton: Dorsal vertebrae, Sacral vertebrae, Cervical vertebrae, Ilium, Hip joint, Femur, Ischium, Humerus, Scapula, Shoulder joint, Rib, Pubis, Tail, Thumb-claw, Elbow joint, Knee joint, Tibia, Radius, Fibula, Wrist joint, Ulna, Metacarpal, Ankle joint, Metatarsals, Cranium, Orbit, Phalanx, Mandible, Phalanges, Naris

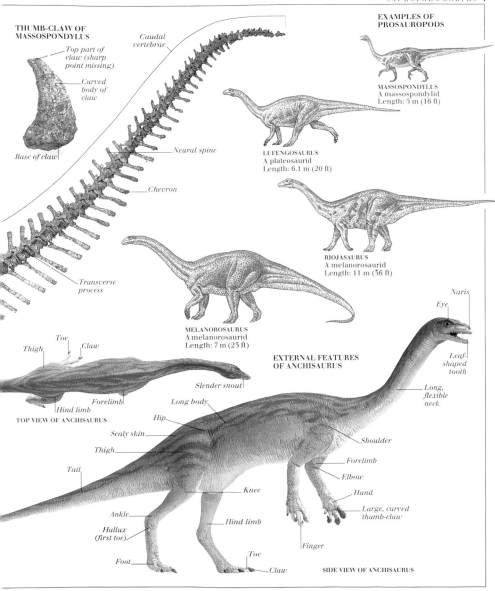

THUMB-CLAW OF MASSOSPONDYLUS

Top part of claw (sharp point missing)

Curved body of claw

Base of claw

Caudal vertebrae

Neural spine

Chevron

Transverse process

EXAMPLES OF PROSAUROPODS

MASSOSPONDYLUS
A massospondylid
Length: 5 m (16 ft)

LUFENGOSAURUS
A plateosaurid
Length: 6.1 m (20 ft)

RIOJASAURUS
A melanorosaurid
Length: 11 m (36 ft)

MELANOROSAURUS
A melanorosaurid
Length: 7 m (23 ft)

EXTERNAL FEATURES OF ANCHISAURUS

Toe
Claw
Thigh

Slender snout

Forelimb
Hind limb

TOP VIEW OF ANCHISAURUS

Naris
Eye

Leaf-shaped tooth

Long, flexible neck

Long body

Hip

Scaly skin

Thigh

Tail

Shoulder

Forelimb

Elbow

Hand

Large, curved thumb-claw

Knee

Ankle

Hallux (first toe)

Hind limb

Foot

Toe

Finger

Claw

SIDE VIEW OF ANCHISAURUS

89

Sauropodomorphs 2

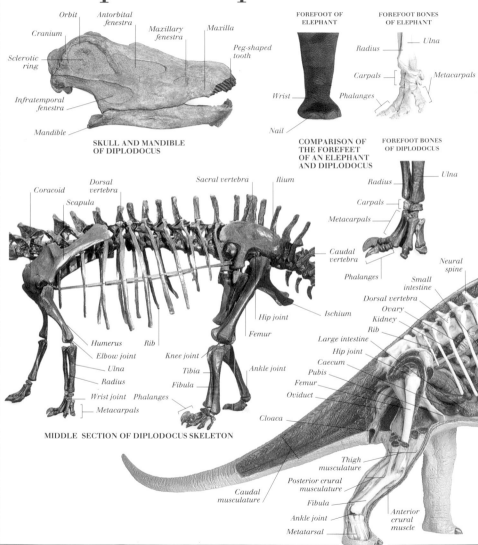

SKULL AND MANDIBLE OF DIPLODOCUS

Orbit
Antorbital fenestra
Cranium
Maxillary fenestra
Maxilla
Sclerotic ring
Peg-shaped tooth
Infratemporal fenestra
Mandible

FOREFOOT OF ELEPHANT

Wrist
Nail

FOREFOOT BONES OF ELEPHANT

Radius
Ulna
Carpals
Metacarpals
Phalanges

COMPARISON OF THE FOREFEET OF AN ELEPHANT AND DIPLODOCUS

FOREFOOT BONES OF DIPLODOCUS

Radius
Ulna
Carpals
Metacarpals
Phalanges

MIDDLE SECTION OF DIPLODOCUS SKELETON

Coracoid
Scapula
Dorsal vertebra
Sacral vertebra
Ilium
Caudal vertebra
Hip joint
Ischium
Femur
Humerus
Rib
Elbow joint
Knee joint
Ulna
Tibia
Ankle joint
Radius
Fibula
Wrist joint
Phalanges
Metacarpals

Neural spine
Small intestine
Dorsal vertebra
Ovary
Kidney
Rib
Large intestine
Hip joint
Caecum
Pubis
Femur
Oviduct
Cloaca
Thigh musculature
Posterior crural musculature
Fibula
Anterior crural muscle
Ankle joint
Metatarsal
Caudal musculature

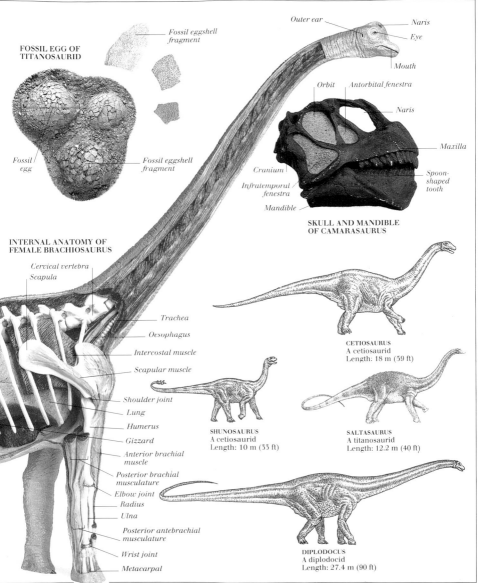

FOSSIL EGG OF TITANOSAURID

Fossil eggshell fragment

Fossil egg

Fossil eggshell fragment

Outer ear

Naris

Eye

Mouth

Orbit

Antorbital fenestra

Naris

Maxilla

Cranium

Infratemporal fenestra

Mandible

Spoon-shaped tooth

SKULL AND MANDIBLE OF CAMARASAURUS

INTERNAL ANATOMY OF FEMALE BRACHIOSAURUS

Cervical vertebra
Scapula

Trachea

Oesophagus

Intercostal muscle

Scapular muscle

Shoulder joint

Lung

Humerus

Gizzard

Anterior brachial muscle

Posterior brachial musculature

Elbow joint

Radius

Ulna

Posterior antebrachial musculature

Wrist joint

Metacarpal

CETIOSAURUS
A cetiosaurid
Length: 18 m (59 ft)

SHUNOSAURUS
A cetiosaurid
Length: 10 m (33 ft)

SALTASAURUS
A titanosaurid
Length: 12.2 m (40 ft)

DIPLODOCUS
A diplodocid
Length: 27.4 m (90 ft)

Thyreophorans 1

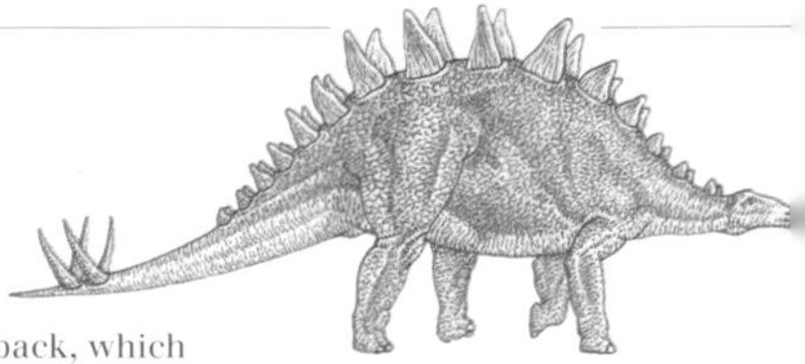

THYREOPHORANS ("SHIELD BEARERS") were a group of quadrupedal armoured dinosaurs. A sub-order of the Ornithischia (bird-hipped dinosaurs), they were characterized by rows of bony studs, plates, or spikes along the back, which protected some from predators and may have helped others regulate body temperature. Up to 9m (30ft) long, with a small head and small cheek teeth, Thyreophorans had shorter forelimbs than hind limbs and probably browsed on low-level vegetation. The earliest thyreophorans were small and lived in Early Jurassic times (about 200 million years ago) in Europe, North America, and China. Stegosaurs, such as Stegosaurus and Kentrosaurus, replaced these older forms. The earliest stegosaur remains come mainly from China. Several genera of stegosaurs survived into the Early Cretaceous period (146–100 million years ago), but only in India did they persist into Late Cretaceous times (97–65 million years ago). Ankylosaurs, with their toothless beaks and cheek teeth adapted for cropping vegetation, appeared later than stegosaurs. They originated in the Late Jurassic period (155 million years ago) and in North America survived until 65 million years ago.

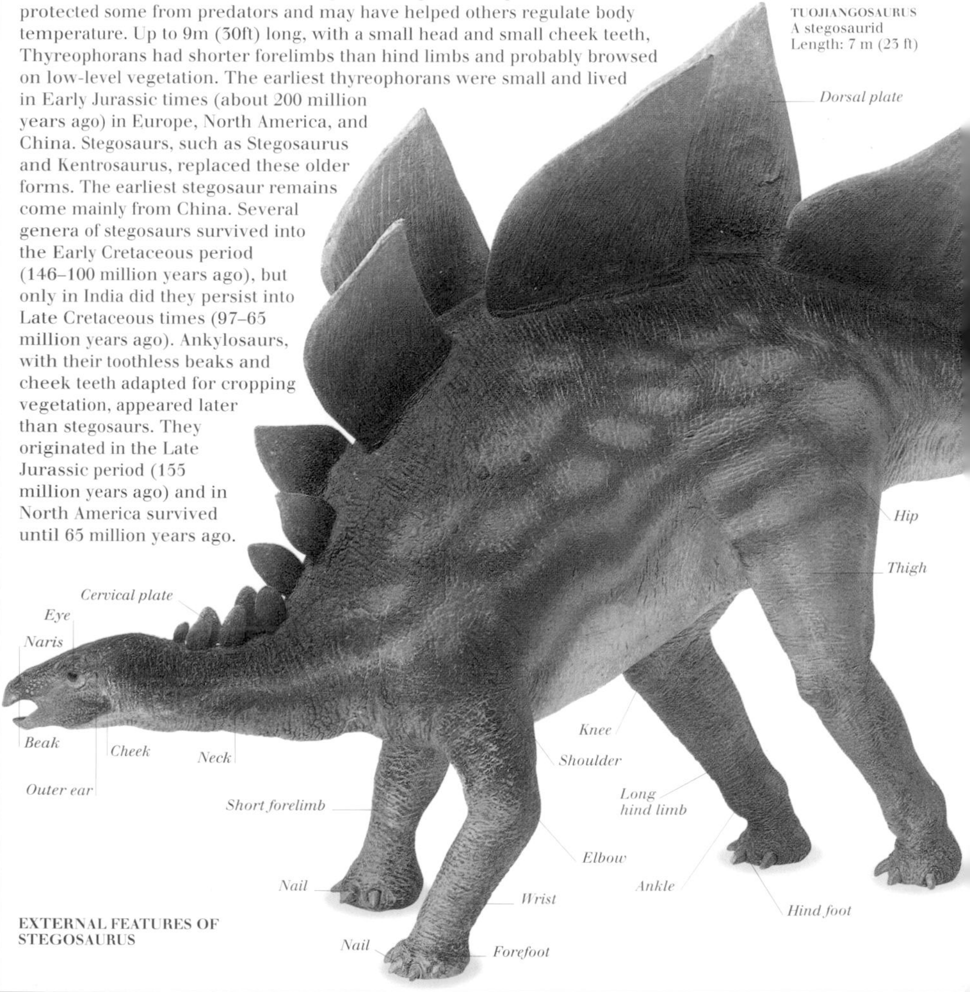

TUOJIANGOSAURUS
A stegosaurid
Length: 7 m (23 ft)

Dorsal plate

Hip

Thigh

Cervical plate

Eye

Naris

Knee

Shoulder

Beak

Cheek

Neck

Long
hind limb

Outer ear

Short forelimb

Elbow

Nail

Wrist

Ankle

Hind foot

**EXTERNAL FEATURES OF
STEGOSAURUS**

Nail

Forefoot

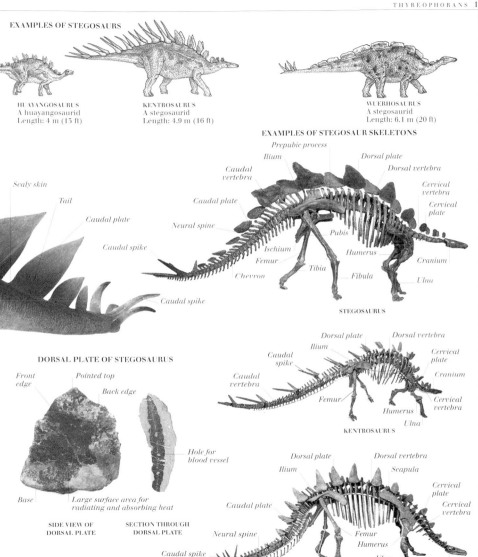

EXAMPLES OF STEGOSAURS

HUAYANGOSAURUS
A huayangosaurid
Length: 4 m (13 ft)

KENTROSAURUS
A stegosaurid
Length: 4.9 m (16 ft)

WUERHOSAURUS
A stegosaurid
Length: 6.1 m (20 ft)

EXAMPLES OF STEGOSAUR SKELETONS

Scaly skin

Tail

Caudal plate

Caudal spike

Caudal spike

Prepubic process

Ilium

Caudal vertebra

Caudal plate

Neural spine

Ischium

Femur

Chevron

Tibia

Pubis

Dorsal plate

Dorsal plate

Dorsal vertebra

Cervical vertebra

Cervical plate

Humerus

Cranium

Fibula

Ulna

STEGOSAURUS

DORSAL PLATE OF STEGOSAURUS

Front edge

Pointed top

Back edge

Hole for blood vessel

Base

Large surface area for radiating and absorbing heat

SIDE VIEW OF DORSAL PLATE

SECTION THROUGH DORSAL PLATE

Dorsal plate

Ilium

Caudal spike

Caudal vertebra

Dorsal vertebra

Cervical plate

Cranium

Cervical vertebra

Femur

Humerus

Ulna

KENTROSAURUS

Dorsal plate

Ilium

Caudal plate

Neural spine

Caudal spike

Chevron

Caudal vertebra

Dorsal vertebra

Scapula

Cervical plate

Cervical vertebra

Femur

Humerus

Ulna

Cranium

TUOJIANGOSAURUS

Thyreophorans 2

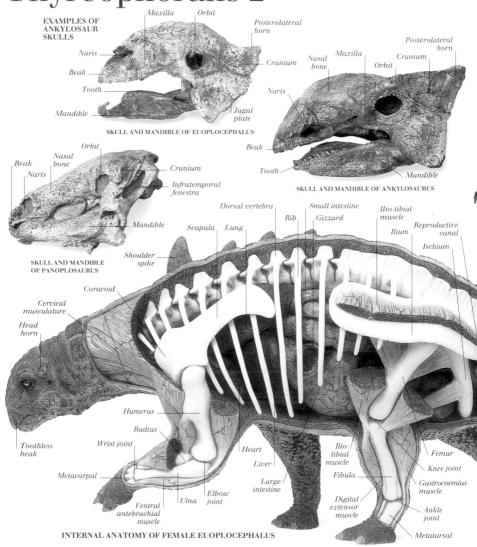

EXAMPLES OF ANKYLOSAUR SKULLS

Maxilla

Orbit

Posterolateral horn

Naris

Cranium

Beak

Tooth

Mandible

Jugal plate

SKULL AND MANDIBLE OF EUOPLOCEPHALUS

Posterolateral horn

Nasal bone

Maxilla

Cranium

Orbit

Naris

Beak

Tooth

Mandible

SKULL AND MANDIBLE OF ANKYLOSAURUS

Orbit

Nasal bone

Beak

Naris

Cranium

Infratemporal fenestra

Mandible

SKULL AND MANDIBLE OF PANOPLOSAURUS

Dorsal vertebra

Small intestine

Ilio-tibial muscle

Rib

Gizzard

Ilium

Reproductive canal

Scapula

Lung

Ischium

Shoulder spike

Coracoid

Cervical musculature

Head horn

Toothless beak

Humerus

Radius

Wrist joint

Heart

Iliotibial muscle

Femur

Liver

Knee joint

Metacarpal

Fibula

Gastrocnemius muscle

Large intestine

Ventral antebrachial muscle

Ulna

Elbow joint

Digital extensor muscle

Ankle joint

Metatarsal

INTERNAL ANATOMY OF FEMALE EUOPLOCEPHALUS

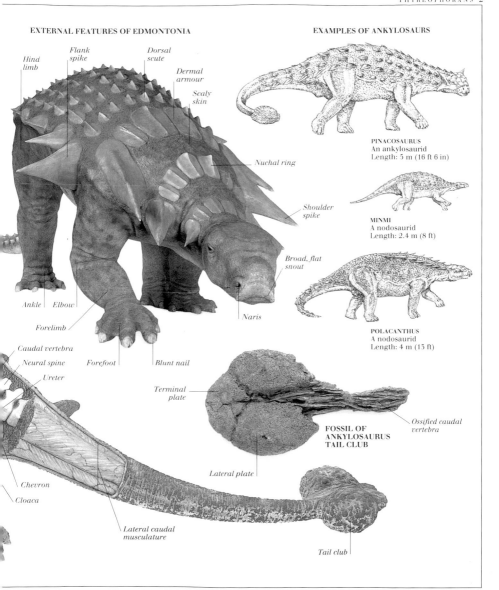

EXTERNAL FEATURES OF EDMONTONIA

Hind limb

Flank spike

Dorsal scute

Dermal armour

Scaly skin

Nuchal ring

Shoulder spike

Broad, flat snout

Naris

Ankle

Elbow

Forelimb

Forefoot

Blunt nail

Caudal vertebra

Neural spine

Ureter

Chevron

Cloaca

Terminal plate

Lateral plate

Lateral caudal musculature

EXAMPLES OF ANKYLOSAURS

PINACOSAURUS
An ankylosaurid
Length: 5 m (16 ft 6 in)

MINMI
A nodosaurid
Length: 2.4 m (8 ft)

POLACANTHUS
A nodosaurid
Length: 4 m (13 ft)

Ossified caudal vertebra

FOSSIL OF ANKYLOSAURUS TAIL CLUB

Tail club

Ornithopods 1

IGUANODON TOOTH

ORNITHOPODS ("BIRD FEET") were a group of ornithischian ("bird-hipped") dinosaurs. These bipedal and quadrupedal herbivores had a horny beak, plant-cutting or grinding cheek teeth, and a pelvic and tail region stiffened by bony tendons. They evolved teeth and jaws adapted to pulping vegetation and flourished from the Middle Jurassic to the Late Cretaceous period (165–65 million years ago) in North America, Europe, Africa, China, Australia, and Antarctica. Some ornithopods were no larger than a dog, while others were immense creatures up to 15 m (49 ft) long. Iguanodonts, an ornithopod group, had a broad, toothless beak at the end of a long snout, large jaws with long rows of ridged, closely packed teeth for grinding vegetation, a bulky body, and a heavy tail. *Iguanodon* and some other iguanodonts had large thumb-spikes that were strong enough to stab attackers. Another group, the hadrosaurs, such as *Gryposaurus* and *Hadrosaurus*, lived in Late Cretaceous times (97–65 million years ago) and with their broad beaks are sometimes known as "duckbills". They were characterized by their deep skulls and closely packed rows of teeth, while some, such as *Corythosaurus* and *Lambeosaurus*, had tall, hollow, bony head crests.

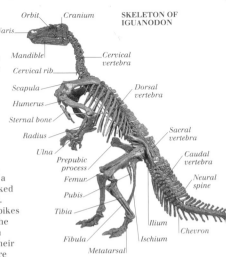

SKELETON OF IGUANODON

Orbit · Cranium · Naris · Mandible · Cervical vertebra · Cervical rib · Scapula · Dorsal vertebra · Humerus · Sternal bone · Radius · Sacral vertebra · Ulna · Caudal vertebra · Prepubic process · Neural spine · Femur · Pubis · Tibia · Ilium · Chevron · Fibula · Ischium · Metatarsal

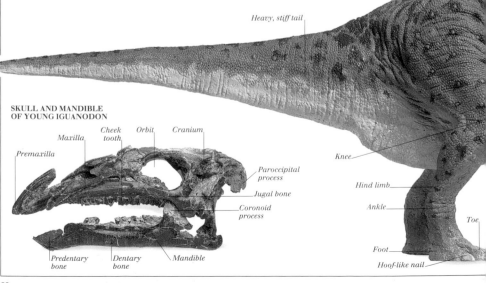

SKULL AND MANDIBLE OF YOUNG IGUANODON

Premaxilla · Maxilla · Cheek tooth · Orbit · Cranium · Paroccipital process · Jugal bone · Coronoid process · Predentary bone · Dentary bone · Mandible

Thigh · Heavy, stiff tail · Knee · Hind limb · Ankle · Toe · Foot · Hoof-like nail

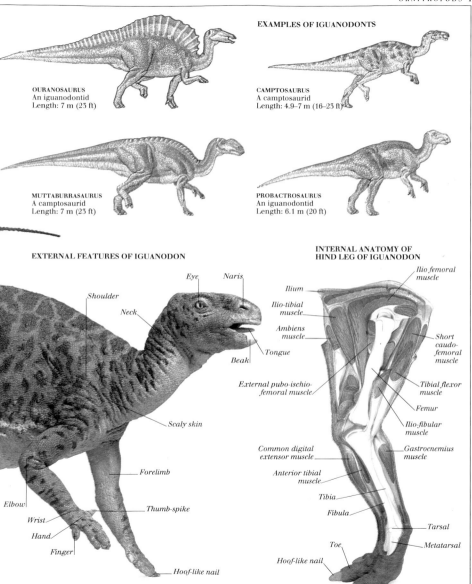

EXAMPLES OF IGUANODONTS

OURANOSAURUS
An iguanodontid
Length: 7 m (23 ft)

CAMPTOSAURUS
A camptosaurid
Length: 4.9–7 m (16–23 ft)

MUTTABURRASAURUS
A camptosaurid
Length: 7 m (23 ft)

PROBACTROSAURUS
An iguanodontid
Length: 6.1 m (20 ft)

EXTERNAL FEATURES OF IGUANODON

Eye
Naris
Shoulder
Neck
Tongue
Beak
Scaly skin
Forelimb
Thumb-spike
Elbow
Wrist
Hand
Finger
Hoof-like nail

**INTERNAL ANATOMY OF
HIND LEG OF IGUANODON**

Ilio femoral muscle
Ilium
Ilio-tibial muscle
Ambiens muscle
Short caudo-femoral muscle
External pubo-ischio-femoral muscle
Tibial flexor muscle
Femur
Ilio-fibular muscle
Common digital extensor muscle
Gastrocnemius muscle
Anterior tibial muscle
Tibia
Fibula
Tarsal
Toe
Metatarsal
Hoof-like nail

Ornithopods 2

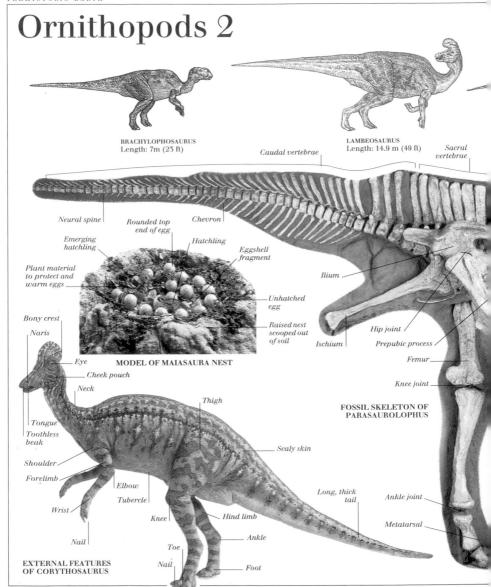

BRACHYLOPHOSAURUS
Length: 7m (23 ft)

LAMBEOSAURUS
Length: 14.9 m (49 ft)

Caudal vertebrae

Sacral vertebrae

Neural spine

Rounded top end of egg

Chevron

Emerging hatchling

Hatchling

Eggshell fragment

Plant material to protect and warm eggs

Ilium

Unhatched egg

Raised nest scooped out of soil

MODEL OF MAIASAURA NEST

Bony crest

Naris

Hip joint

Ischium

Prepubic process

Eye

Cheek pouch

Femur

Neck

Thigh

Knee joint

Tongue

Toothless beak

FOSSIL SKELETON OF PARASAUROLOPHUS

Shoulder

Scaly skin

Forelimb

Elbow

Tubercle

Wrist

Knee

Hind limb

Long, thick tail

Ankle joint

Metatarsal

Nail

Ankle

Toe

Nail

Foot

EXTERNAL FEATURES OF CORYTHOSAURUS

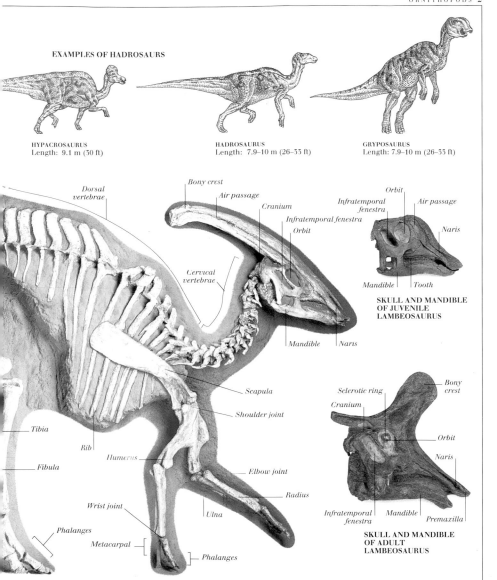

EXAMPLES OF HADROSAURS

HYPACROSAURUS
Length: 9.1 m (30 ft)

HADROSAURUS
Length: 7.9–10 m (26–33 ft)

GRYPOSAURUS
Length: 7.9–10 m (26–33 ft)

Dorsal
vertebrae

Bony crest

Air passage

Cranium

Infratemporal fenestra

Orbit

Cervical
vertebrae

Mandible

Naris

Orbit

Infratemporal
fenestra

Air passage

Naris

Mandible

Tooth

**SKULL AND MANDIBLE
OF JUVENILE
LAMBEOSAURUS**

Scapula

Shoulder joint

Tibia

Rib

Fibula

Humerus

Elbow joint

Radius

Wrist joint

Ulna

Phalanges

Metacarpal

Phalanges

Sclerotic ring

Cranium

Bony
crest

Orbit

Naris

Infratemporal
fenestra

Mandible

Premaxilla

**SKULL AND MANDIBLE
OF ADULT
LAMBEOSAURUS**

Marginocephalians 1

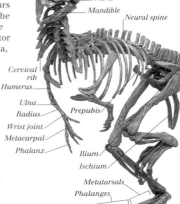

MARGINOCEPHALIA ("margined heads") were a group of bipedal and quadrupedal ornithischian dinosaurs with a narrow shelf or deep, bony frill at the back of the skull. Marginocephalians were probably descended from the same ancestor

HEAD-BUTTING PRENOCEPHALES

as the ornithopods and lived in what are now North America, Africa, Asia, and Europe during the Cretaceous period (146–65 million years ago). They were divided into two infraorders: Pachycephalosauria ("thick-headed lizards"), such as *Pachycephalosaurus* and *Stegoceras*, and Ceratopsia ("horned faces"), such as *Triceratops* and *Psittacosaurus*. The thick skulls of Pachycephalosauria protected their brains during head-butting contests fought to win territory and mates; their hips and spines were also strengthened to withstand the shock. The bony frill of Ceratopsia would have added to their frightening appearance when charging; the neck was strengthened for impact and to support the huge head, with its snipping beak and powerful slicing toothed jaws. A charging ceratops would have been a formidable opponent for even the largest predators. Ceratopsia were among the most abundant herbivorous dinosaurs of the Late Cretaceous period (97–65 million years ago).

Labels on skeleton (img_2): Thick, high-domed cranium; Supraorbital ridge; Orbit; Naris; Mandible; Neural spine; Cervical rib; Humerus; Ulna; Radius; Prepubis; Wrist joint; Metacarpal; Phalanx; Ilium; Ischium; Metatarsals; Phalanges

EXAMPLES OF SKULLS OF PACHYCEPHALOSAURS

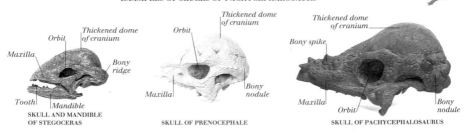

Labels: Orbit; Thickened dome of cranium; Maxilla; Bony ridge; Tooth; Mandible
SKULL AND MANDIBLE OF STEGOCERAS

Orbit; Thickened dome of cranium; Maxilla; Bony nodule
SKULL OF PRENOCEPHALE

Thickened dome of cranium; Bony spike; Maxilla; Orbit; Bony nodule
SKULL OF PACHYCEPHALOSAURUS

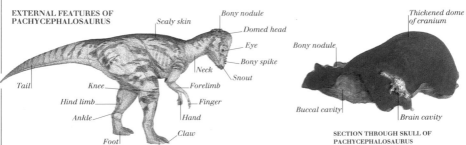

EXTERNAL FEATURES OF PACHYCEPHALOSAURUS

Labels: Scaly skin; Bony nodule; Domed head; Eye; Bony spike; Neck; Snout; Tail; Knee; Forelimb; Finger; Hind limb; Hand; Ankle; Claw; Foot; Toe

Labels: Thickened dome of cranium; Bony nodule; Buccal cavity; Brain cavity
SECTION THROUGH SKULL OF PACHYCEPHALOSAURUS

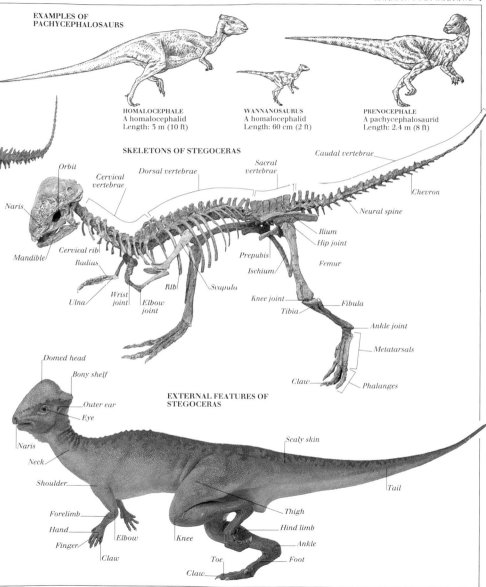

**EXAMPLES OF
PACHYCEPHALOSAURS**

HOMALOCEPHALE
A homalocephalid
Length: 3 m (10 ft)

WANNANOSAURUS
A homalocephalid
Length: 60 cm (2 ft)

PRENOCEPHALE
A pachycephalosaurid
Length: 2.4 m (8 ft)

SKELETONS OF STEGOCERAS

Orbit

Caudal vertebrae

*Cervical
vertebrae*

Dorsal vertebrae

*Sacral
vertebrae*

Chevron

Naris

Neural spine

Mandible

Ilium

Hip joint

Cervical rib

Prepubis

Femur

Radius

Ischium

Ulna

*Wrist
joint*

Rib

Scapula

*Elbow
joint*

Knee joint

Fibula

Tibia

Ankle joint

Metatarsals

Domed head

Claw

Phalanges

Bony shelf

**EXTERNAL FEATURES OF
STEGOCERAS**

Outer ear

Eye

Scaly skin

Naris

Neck

Tail

Shoulder

Forelimb

Thigh

Hand

Hind limb

Finger

Elbow

Knee

Ankle

Claw

Toe

Foot

Claw

101

Marginocephalians 2

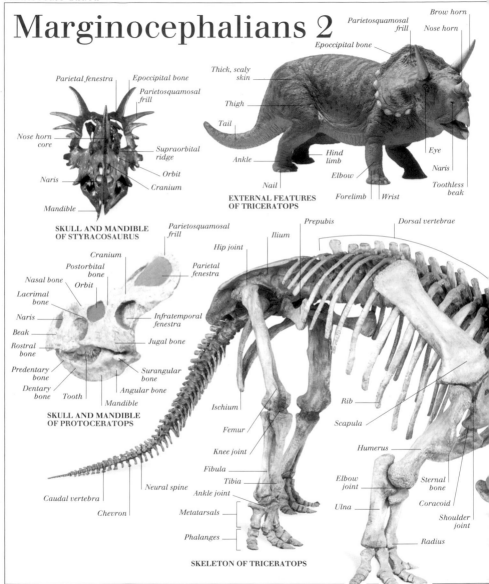

Parietosquamosal frill

Brow horn

Nose horn

Epoccipital bone

Thick, scaly skin

Thigh

Tail

Ankle

Hind limb

Nail

Elbow

Forelimb

Wrist

Eye

Naris

Toothless beak

EXTERNAL FEATURES OF TRICERATOPS

Parietal fenestra

Epoccipital bone

Parietosquamosal frill

Nose horn core

Supraorbital ridge

Naris

Orbit

Cranium

Mandible

SKULL AND MANDIBLE OF STYRACOSAURUS

Parietosquamosal frill

Cranium

Postorbital bone

Nasal bone

Orbit

Lacrimal bone

Naris

Beak

Rostral bone

Predentary bone

Dentary bone

Tooth

Mandible

Surangular bone

Angular bone

Jugal bone

Infratemporal fenestra

Parietal fenestra

Hip joint

Ilium

Prepubis

Dorsal vertebrae

SKULL AND MANDIBLE OF PROTOCERATOPS

Caudal vertebra

Chevron

Neural spine

Ischium

Femur

Knee joint

Fibula

Tibia

Ankle joint

Metatarsals

Phalanges

Rib

Scapula

Humerus

Elbow joint

Ulna

Sternal bone

Coracoid

Shoulder joint

Radius

SKELETON OF TRICERATOPS

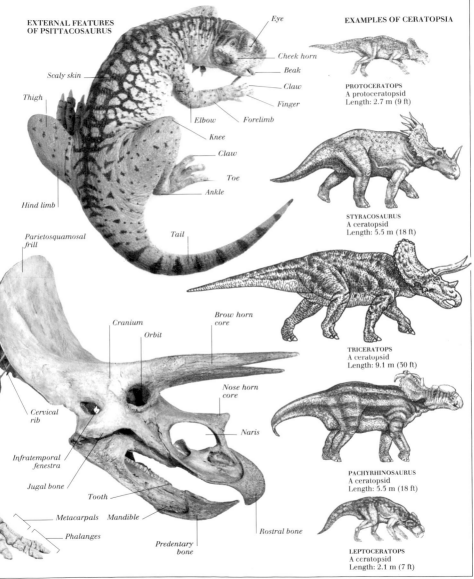

EXTERNAL FEATURES OF PSITTACOSAURUS

- Eye
- Cheek horn
- Beak
- Claw
- Finger
- Forelimb
- Elbow
- Knee
- Claw
- Toe
- Ankle
- Scaly skin
- Thigh
- Hind limb
- Parietosquamosal frill
- Tail

Cranium
Orbit
Brow horn core
Nose horn core
Naris
Cervical rib
Infratemporal fenestra
Jugal bone
Tooth
Metacarpals
Phalanges
Mandible
Predentary bone
Rostral bone

EXAMPLES OF CERATOPSIA

PROTOCERATOPS
A protoceratopsid
Length: 2.7 m (9 ft)

STYRACOSAURUS
A ceratopsid
Length: 5.5 m (18 ft)

TRICERATOPS
A ceratopsid
Length: 9.1 m (30 ft)

PACHYRHINOSAURUS
A ceratopsid
Length: 5.5 m (18 ft)

LEPTOCERATOPS
A ceratopsid
Length: 2.1 m (7 ft)

Mammals 1

TETRALOPHODON CHEEK TEETH

Long tail aids balance

Insulating hair

SINCE THE EXTINCTION of the dinosaurs 65 million years ago, mammals have been the dominant vertebrates on land. This class includes terrestrial, aerial, and aquatic forms. Having developed from the reptilian Therapsids, the first true mammals – small, nocturnal, shrew-like creatures, such as *Megazostrodon* – appeared over 200 million years ago during the Triassic period (245–208 million years ago). Mammals had several features that improved on those of their reptilian ancestors: an efficient four-chambered heart allowed these warm-blooded animals to sustain high levels of activity; a covering of hair helped them maintain a constant body temperature; an improved limb structure gave them more efficient locomotion; and the birth of live young and the immediate supply of food from the mother's milk aided their rapid growth. Since the end of the Mesozoic era (65 million years ago), the number of different mammal orders and the abundance of species in each order have varied dramatically. For example, the Perissodactyla (the order that includes *Coelodonta* and modern horses) was a common group during the Early Tertiary period (about 54 million years ago). Today, the mammalian orders with the most species include the Rodentia (rats and mice), the Chiroptera (bats), the Primates (monkeys and apes), the Carnivora (bears, cats, and dogs), and the Artiodactyla (cattle, deer, and pigs), while the Proboscidea order, which formerly included many genera, such as *Phiomia*, *Moeritherium*, *Tetralophodon*, and *Mammuthus*, now has only three species of elephant. In Australia and South America, millions of years of continental isolation led to increased diversity of the marsupials, a group of mammals distinct from the placentals (see p. 74) that existed elsewhere.

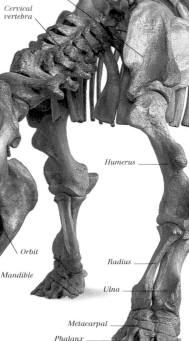

Neural spine

Scapula

Cervical vertebra

Humerus

Nasal horn

Naris

Orbit

Mandible

Predentary bone

Radius

Ulna

Chisel-edged molar

Metacarpal

Phalanx

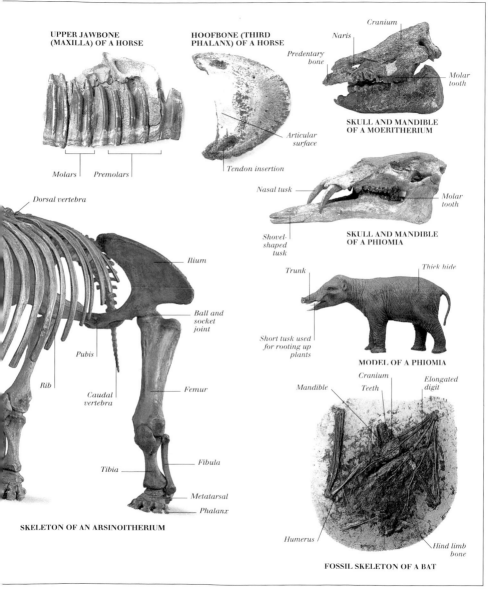

UPPER JAWBONE (MAXILLA) OF A HORSE

Molars

Premolars

HOOFBONE (THIRD PHALANX) OF A HORSE

Articular surface

Tendon insertion

Cranium

Naris

Predentary bone

Molar tooth

SKULL AND MANDIBLE OF A MOERITHERIUM

Nasal tusk

Molar tooth

Shovel-shaped tusk

SKULL AND MANDIBLE OF A PHIOMIA

Trunk

Thick hide

Short tusk used for rooting up plants

MODEL OF A PHIOMIA

Dorsal vertebra

Ilium

Ball and socket joint

Pubis

Rib

Caudal vertebra

Femur

Tibia

Fibula

Metatarsal

Phalanx

SKELETON OF AN ARSINOITHERIUM

Cranium

Mandible

Teeth

Elongated digit

Humerus

Hind limb bone

FOSSIL SKELETON OF A BAT

Mammals 2

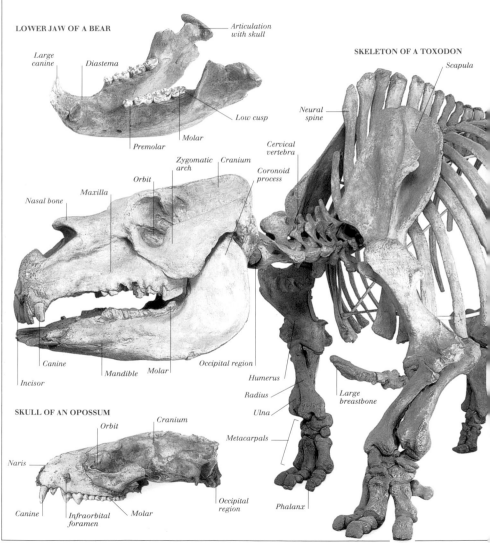

LOWER JAW OF A BEAR

Large canine

Diastema

Articulation with skull

Low cusp

Premolar

Molar

SKELETON OF A TOXODON

Scapula

Neural spine

Cervical vertebra

Zygomatic arch

Orbit

Cranium

Coronoid process

Maxilla

Nasal bone

Canine

Incisor

Mandible

Molar

Occipital region

Humerus

Radius

Ulna

Large breastbone

Metacarpals

Phalanx

SKULL OF AN OPOSSUM

Orbit

Cranium

Naris

Canine

Infraorbital foramen

Molar

Occipital region

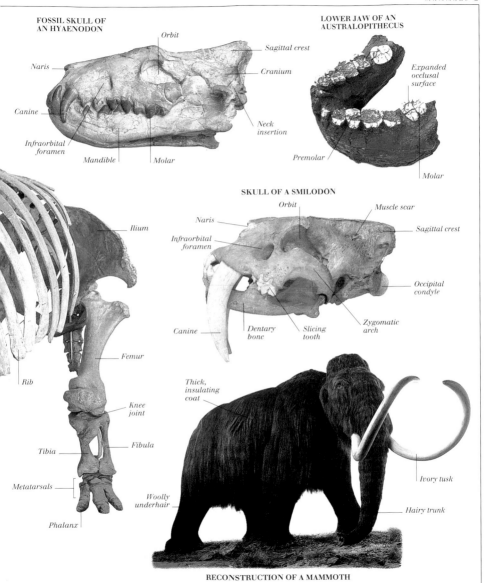

FOSSIL SKULL OF AN HYAENODON

Orbit

Naris

Sagittal crest

Cranium

Canine

Neck insertion

Infraorbital foramen

Mandible

Molar

LOWER JAW OF AN AUSTRALOPITHECUS

Expanded occlusal surface

Premolar

Molar

Ilium

SKULL OF A SMILODON

Orbit

Muscle scar

Naris

Sagittal crest

Infraorbital foramen

Occipital condyle

Canine

Dentary bone

Slicing tooth

Zygomatic arch

Femur

Rib

Knee joint

Tibia

Fibula

Metatarsals

Phalanx

Thick, insulating coat

Ivory tusk

Woolly underhair

Hairy trunk

RECONSTRUCTION OF A MAMMOTH

The first hominids

JAWBONE OF AUSTRALOPITHECUS (SOUTHERN APE)

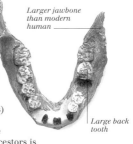

Larger jawbone than modern human

Large back tooth

MODERN HUMANS BELONG TO THE MAMMALIAN order of primates (see pp. 202–203), which originated about 55 million years ago; they comprise the only extant hominid species. The earliest hominid was *Australopithecus* ("southern ape"), a small-brained intermediate between apes and humans that was capable of standing and walking upright. *Homo habilis*, the first known human appeared at least 2 million years ago. This larger-brained "handy man" began making tools for hunting. *Homo erectus* first appeared in Africa about 1.8 million years ago and spread into Asia about 800,000 years later. Smaller-toothed than *Homo habilis*, it developed fire as a tool, which enabled it to cook food. Neanderthals, a near relative of modern humans, originated about 200,000 years ago, and *Homo sapiens* (modern humans) appeared in Africa about 100,000 years later. The two co-existed for thousands of years, but by 30,000 years ago, *Homo sapiens* had become dominant and the Neanderthals had died out. Classification of *Homo sapiens* in relation to its ancestors is enormously problematic: modern humans must be classified not only by bone structure, but also by specific behaviour – the ability to plan future action; to follow traditions; and to use symbolic communication, including complex language and the ability to use and recognize symbols.

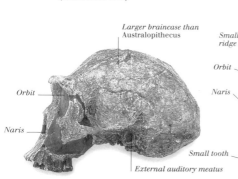

Jutting brow ridge

Cranium

Orbit

Naris

Jutting jawbone

SKULL OF AUSTRALOPITHECUS (SOUTHERN APE)

Orbit

Naris

SKULL OF HOMO HABILIS (FIRST KNOWN HUMAN)

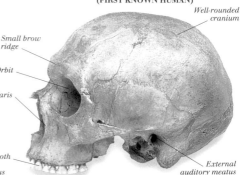

Larger braincase than Australopithecus

Well-rounded cranium

Small brow ridge

Orbit

Orbit

Naris

Naris

Small tooth

External auditory meatus

External auditory meatus

SKULL OF HOMO ERECTUS (UPRIGHT MAN)

SKULL OF HOMO SAPIENS (MODERN HUMAN)

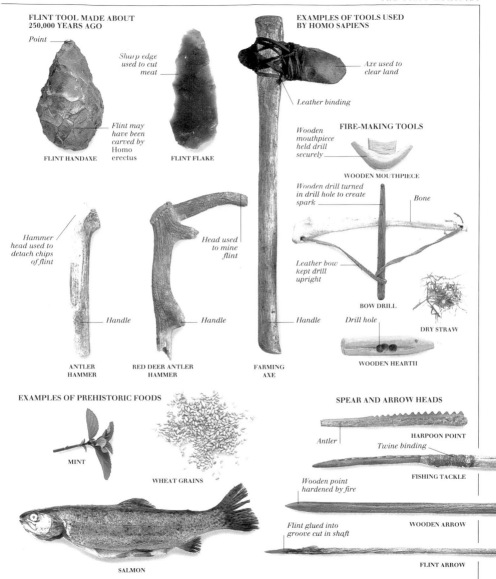

FLINT TOOL MADE ABOUT 250,000 YEARS AGO

Point

Sharp edge used to cut meat

Flint may have been carved by Homo erectus

FLINT HANDAXE

FLINT FLAKE

EXAMPLES OF TOOLS USED BY HOMO SAPIENS

Axe used to clear land

Leather binding

FIRE-MAKING TOOLS

Wooden mouthpiece held drill securely

WOODEN MOUTHPIECE

Wooden drill turned in drill hole to create spark

Bone

Leather bow kept drill upright

Hammer head used to detach chips of flint

Head used to mine flint

Handle

Handle

Handle

Drill hole

BOW DRILL

DRY STRAW

WOODEN HEARTH

ANTLER HAMMER

RED DEER ANTLER HAMMER

FARMING AXE

EXAMPLES OF PREHISTORIC FOODS

MINT

WHEAT GRAINS

SALMON

SPEAR AND ARROW HEADS

Antler

HARPOON POINT

Twine binding

FISHING TACKLE

Wooden point hardened by fire

Flint glued into groove cut in shaft

WOODEN ARROW

FLINT ARROW

PLANTS

PLANT VARIETY 112
FUNGI AND LICHENS 114
ALGAE AND SEAWEEDS 116
LIVERWORTS AND MOSSES 118
HORSETAILS, CLUBMOSSES, AND FERNS 120
GYMNOSPERMS 1 122
GYMNOSPERMS 2 124
MONOCOTYLEDONS AND DICOTYLEDONS 126
HERBACEOUS FLOWERING PLANTS 128
WOODY FLOWERING PLANTS 130
ROOTS 132
STEMS 134
LEAVES 136
PHOTOSYNTHESIS 138
FLOWERS 1 140
FLOWERS 2 142
POLLINATION 144
FERTILIZATION 146
SUCCULENT FRUITS 148
DRY FRUITS 150
GERMINATION 152
VEGETATIVE REPRODUCTION 154
DRYLAND PLANTS 156
WETLAND PLANTS 158
CARNIVOROUS PLANTS 160
EPIPHYTIC AND PARASITIC PLANTS 162

Plant variety

Leaf

THERE ARE MORE THAN 300,000 SPECIES of plants. They show a wide diversity of forms and life-styles, ranging, for example, from delicate liverworts, adapted for life in a damp habitat, to cacti, capable of surviving in the desert, and from herbaceous plants, such as corn, which completes its life-cycle in one year, to the giant redwood tree, which can live for thousands of years. This diversity reflects the adaptations of plants to survive in a wide range of habitats. This is seen most clearly in the flowering plants (phylum Angiospermophyta), which are the most numerous, with over 250,000 species, and the most widespread, being found from the tropics to the poles. Despite their diversity, plants share certain characteristics: typically, plants are green, and make their food by photosynthesis; and most plants live in or on a substrate, such as soil, and do not actively move. Algae (kingdom Protista) and fungi (kingdom Fungi) have some plant-like characteristics and are often studied alongside plants, although they are not true plants.

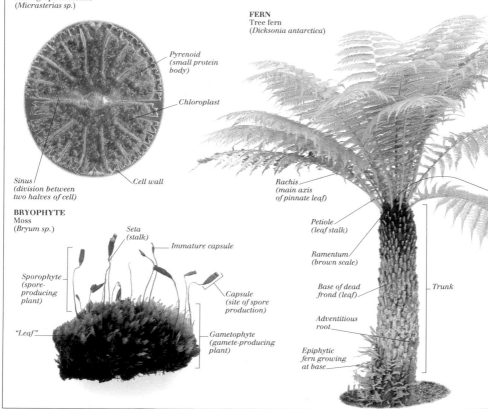

GREEN ALGA
Micrograph of desmid
(*Micrasterias sp.*)

*Pyrenoid
(small protein
body)*

Chloroplast

*Sinus
(division between
two halves of cell)*

Cell wall

FERN
Tree fern
(*Dicksonia antarctica*)

*Rachis
(main axis
of pinnate leaf)*

*Petiole
(leaf stalk)*

*Ramentum
(brown scale)*

*Base of dead
frond (leaf)*

Trunk

*Adventitious
root*

*Epiphytic
fern growing
at base*

BRYOPHYTE
Moss
(*Bryum sp.*)

*Seta
(stalk)*

Immature capsule

*Sporophyte
(spore-
producing
plant)*

*Capsule
(site of spore
production)*

"Leaf"

*Gametophyte
(gamete-producing
plant)*

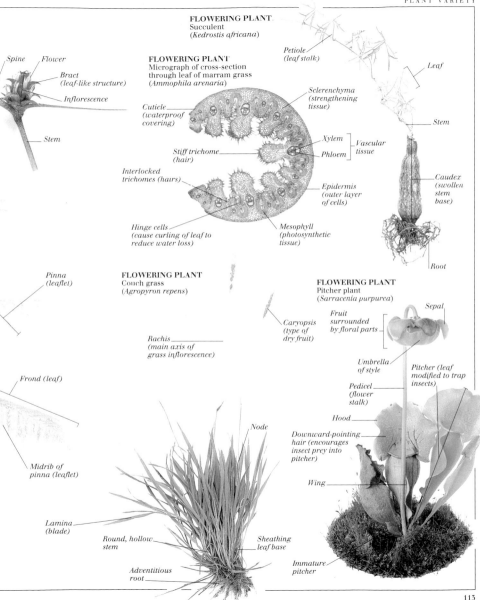

FLOWERING PLANT
Succulent
(*Kedrostis africana*)

Petiole
(leaf stalk)

Leaf

Spine   *Flower*

Bract
(leaf-like structure)

Inflorescence

Stem

FLOWERING PLANT
Micrograph of cross-section
through leaf of marram grass
(*Ammophila arenaria*)

Sclerenchyma
(strengthening
tissue)

Cuticle
(waterproof
covering)

Stem

Xylem   *Vascular*
tissue
Phloem

Stiff trichome
(hair)

Interlocked
trichomes (hairs)

Caudex
(swollen
stem
base)

Epidermis
(outer layer
of cells)

Hinge cells
(cause curling of leaf to
reduce water loss)

Mesophyll
(photosynthetic
tissue)

Root

Pinna
(leaflet)

FLOWERING PLANT
Couch grass
(*Agropyron repens*)

Caryopsis
(type of
dry fruit)

FLOWERING PLANT
Pitcher plant
(*Sarracenia purpurea*)

Fruit
surrounded
by floral parts

Sepal

Rachis
(main axis of
grass inflorescence)

Umbrella
of style

Pitcher (leaf
modified to trap
insects)

Frond (leaf)

Pedicel
(flower
stalk)

Hood

Node

Downward-pointing
hair (encourages
insect prey into
pitcher)

Midrib of
pinna (leaflet)

Wing

Lamina
(blade)

Round, hollow
stem

Sheathing
leaf base

Adventitious
root

Immature
pitcher

Fungi and lichens

FUNGI WERE ONCE THOUGHT OF AS PLANTS but are now classified as a separate kingdom. This kingdom includes not only the familiar mushrooms, puffballs, stinkhorns, and moulds, but also yeasts, smuts, rusts, and lichens. Most fungi are multicellular, consisting of a mass of thread-like hyphae that together form a mycelium. However, the simpler fungi (e.g., yeasts) are microscopic, single-celled organisms. Typically, fungi reproduce by means of spores. Most fungi feed on dead or decaying matter, or on living organisms. A few fungi obtain their food from plants or algae, with which they have a symbiotic (mutually advantageous) relationship. Lichens are a symbiotic partnership between algae and fungi. Of the six types of lichens the three most common are crustose (flat and crusty), foliose (leafy), and fruticose (shrub-like). Some lichens (e.g., *Cladonia floerkeana*) are a combination of types. Lichens reproduce by means of spores or soredia (powdery vegetative fragments).

EXAMPLES OF LICHENS

Emerging sporophore (spore-bearing structure)

Pileus (cap) continuous with stipe (stalk)

Bark of dead beech tree

Secondary fruticose thallus

Branched, hollow stem

Apothecium (spore-producing body)

FRUTICOSE
Cladonia portentosa

Inrolled margin of pileus (cap)

Gill (site of spore production)

Sporophore (spore-bearing structure)

Stipe (stalk)

Hyphae (fungal filaments)

OYSTER FUNGUS
(*Pleurotus pulmonarius*)

Soredia (powdery vegetative fragments) produced at end of lobe

Tree bark

Foliose thallus

Gleba (spore-producing tissue found in this type of fungus)

Sporophore (spore-bearing structure)

Porous stipe (stalk)

Volva (remains of universal veil)

Sporophore (spore-bearing structure)

Toothed branchlet

Branch

Stipe (stalk)

RAMARIA FORMOSA

FOLIOSE
Hypogymnia physodes

STINKHORN
(*Phallus impudicus*)

Soredia (powdery vegetative fragments) released onto surface of squamulose thallus

Apothecium (spore-producing body)

Basal scale of primary squamulose thallus

Podetium (granular stalk) of secondary fruticose thallus

Moss

SQUAMULOSE (SCALY) AND FRUTICOSE THALLUS
Cladonia floerkeana

SECTION THROUGH FOLIOSE LICHEN SHOWING REPRODUCTION BY SOREDIA

Algal cell

Fungal hypha

Upper cortex

Algal layer

Medulla of fungal hyphae (mycelium)

Lower cortex

Rhizine (bundle of absorptive hyphae)

Soredium (powdery vegetative fragment involved in propagation) released from lichen

Soralium (pore in upper surface of thallus)

Upper surface of thallus

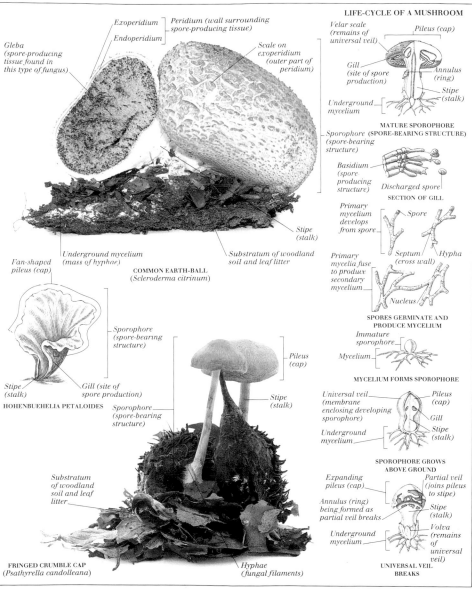

LIFE-CYCLE OF A MUSHROOM

Exoperidium

Endoperidium

Peridium (wall surrounding spore-producing tissue)

Gleba (spore-producing tissue found in this type of fungus)

Scale on exoperidium (outer part of peridium)

Velar scale (remains of universal veil)

Pileus (cap)

Gill (site of spore production)

Annulus (ring)

Stipe (stalk)

Underground mycelium

MATURE SPOROPHORE

Sporophore (SPORE-BEARING STRUCTURE) (spore-bearing structure)

Basidium (spore producing structure)

Discharged spore

SECTION OF GILL

Stipe (stalk)

Underground mycelium (mass of hyphae)

Substratum of woodland soil and leaf litter

COMMON EARTH-BALL *(Scleroderma citrinum)*

Primary mycelium develops from spore

Spore

Septum (cross wall)

Hypha

Primary mycelia fuse to produce secondary mycelium

Nucleus

SPORES GERMINATE AND PRODUCE MYCELIUM

Fan-shaped pileus (cap)

Sporophore (spore-bearing structure)

Immature sporophore

Mycelium

MYCELIUM FORMS SPOROPHORE

Stipe (stalk)

Gill (site of spore production)

HOHENBUEHELIA PETALOIDES

Sporophore (spore-bearing structure)

Pileus (cap)

Stipe (stalk)

Universal veil (membrane enclosing developing sporophore)

Pileus (cap)

Gill

Underground mycelium

SPOROPHORE GROWS ABOVE GROUND

Substratum of woodland soil and leaf litter

Expanding pileus (cap)

Annulus (ring) being formed as partial veil breaks

Partial veil (joins pileus to stipe)

Stipe (stalk)

Underground mycelium

Volva (remains of universal veil)

FRINGED CRUMBLE CAP *(Psathyrella candolleana)*

Hyphae (fungal filaments)

UNIVERSAL VEIL BREAKS

Algae and seaweeds

ALGAE ARE NOT TRUE PLANTS. They form a diverse group
of plant-like organisms that belong to the kingdom Protista.
Like plants, algae possess the green pigment chlorophyll
and make their own food by photosynthesis (see pp. 138-139).
Many algae also possess other pigments by which they can be
classified; for example, the brown pigment fucoxanthin is
found in the brown algae. Some of the ten phyla of algae are
exclusively unicellular (single-celled); others also contain
aggregates of cells in filaments or colonies. Three phyla –
the Chlorophyta (green algae), Rhodophyta (red algae),
and Phaeophyta (brown algae) – contain larger, multicellular,
thalloid (flat), marine organisms commonly known as seaweeds.

Most algae can reproduce sexually. For
example, in the brown seaweed
Fucus vesiculosus, gametes
(sex cells) are produced in
conceptacles (chambers) in
the receptacles (fertile tips
of fronds); after their release
into the sea, antherozoids
(male gametes) and oospheres
(female gametes) fuse; the
resulting zygote settles on a rock
and develops into a new seaweed.

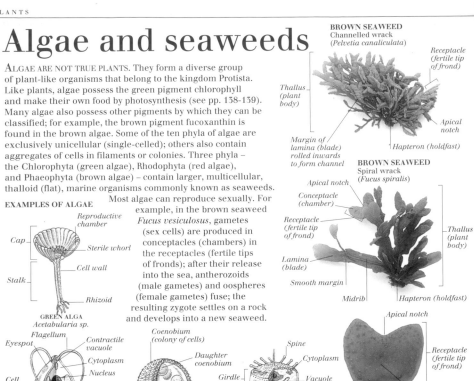

EXAMPLES OF ALGAE

Reproductive chamber

Cap

Sterile whorl

Cell wall

Stalk

Rhizoid

GREEN ALGA
Acetabularia sp.

Flagellum
Eyespot
Contractile vacuole
Cytoplasm
Nucleus
Chloroplast
Cell wall
Pyrenoid (small protein body)
Starch grain

GREEN ALGA
Chlamydomonas sp.

Coenobium (colony of cells)
Daughter coenobium
Girdle
Gelatinous sheath
Nucleus
Biflagellate cell

GREEN ALGA
Volvox sp.

Spine
Cytoplasm
Vacuole
Plastid (photosynthetic organelle)

DIATOM
Thalassiosira sp.

BROWN SEAWEED
Channelled wrack
(*Pelvetia canaliculata*)

Receptacle (fertile tip of frond)

Thallus (plant body)

Apical notch

Margin of lamina (blade) rolled inwards to form channel

Hapteron (holdfast)

BROWN SEAWEED
Spiral wrack
(*Fucus spiralis*)

Apical notch
Conceptacle (chamber)
Receptacle (fertile tip of frond)
Lamina (blade)
Smooth margin

Thallus (plant body)

Midrib
Hapteron (holdfast)

Apical notch

Receptacle (fertile tip of frond)

Conceptacle (chamber) containing reproductive structures

Lamina (blade)
Midrib

RECEPTACLE
Spiral wrack
(*Fucus spiralis*)

BROWN SEAWEED
Oarweed
(*Laminaria digitata*)

Thallus (plant body)

Lamina (blade) palmately divided

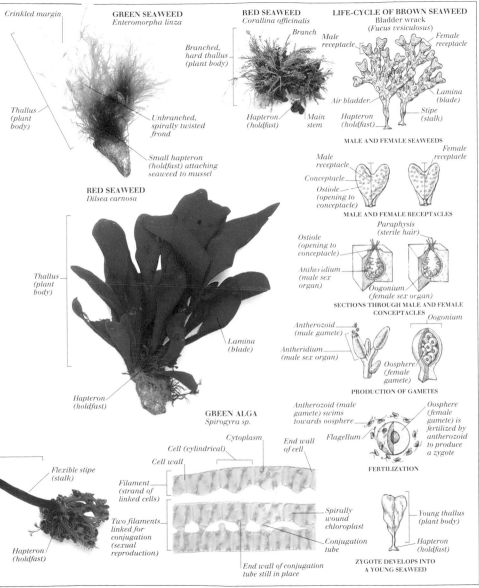

GREEN SEAWEED
Enteromorpha linza

Crinkled margin

Thallus (plant body)

Unbranched, spirally twisted frond

Small hapteron (holdfast) attaching seaweed to mussel

RED SEAWEED
Corallina officinalis

Branch

Branched, hard thallus (plant body)

Hapteron (holdfast)

Main stem

RED SEAWEED
Dilsea carnosa

Thallus (plant body)

Lamina (blade)

Hapteron (holdfast)

LIFE-CYCLE OF BROWN SEAWEED
Bladder wrack (*Fucus vesiculosus*)

Male receptacle

Female receptacle

Air bladder

Lamina (blade)

Hapteron (holdfast)

Stipe (stalk)

MALE AND FEMALE SEAWEEDS

Male receptacle

Female receptacle

Conceptacle

Ostiole (opening to conceptacle)

MALE AND FEMALE RECEPTACLES

Ostiole (opening to conceptacle)

Paraphysis (sterile hair)

Antheridium (male sex organ)

Oogonium (female sex organ)

SECTIONS THROUGH MALE AND FEMALE CONCEPTACLES

Antherozoid (male gamete)

Antheridium (male sex organ)

Oogonium

Oosphere (female gamete)

PRODUCTION OF GAMETES

Antherozoid (male gamete) swims towards oosphere

Flagellum

Oosphere (female gamete) is fertilized by antherozoid to produce a zygote

FERTILIZATION

GREEN ALGA
Spirogyra sp.

Cytoplasm

Cell (cylindrical)

Cell wall

End wall of cell

Filament (strand of linked cells)

Two filaments linked for conjugation (sexual reproduction)

Spirally wound chloroplast

Conjugation tube

End wall of conjugation tube still in place

Flexible stipe (stalk)

Hapteron (holdfast)

Young thallus (plant body)

Hapteron (holdfast)

ZYGOTE DEVELOPS INTO A YOUNG SEAWEED

117

Liverworts and mosses

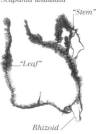

"Stem"

"Leaf"

Rhizoid

LIVERWORTS AND MOSSES ARE SMALL, LOW-GROWING PLANTS that belong to the phylum Bryophyta. Bryophytes do not have true stems, leaves, or roots (they are anchored to the ground by rhizoids), nor do they have the vascular tissues (xylem and phloem) that transport water and nutrients in higher plants. With no outer, waterproof cuticle, bryophytes are susceptible to drying out, and most grow in moist habitats. The bryophyte life-cycle has two stages. In stage one, the green plant (gametophyte) produces male and female gametes (sex cells), which fuse to form a zygote. In stage two, the zygote develops into a sporophyte that remains attached to the gametophyte. The sporophyte produces spores, which are released and germinate into new green plants. Liverworts (class Hepaticae) grow horizontally and may be thalloid (flat and ribbon-like) or "leafy". Mosses (class Musci) typically have an upright "stem" with spirally arranged "leaves".

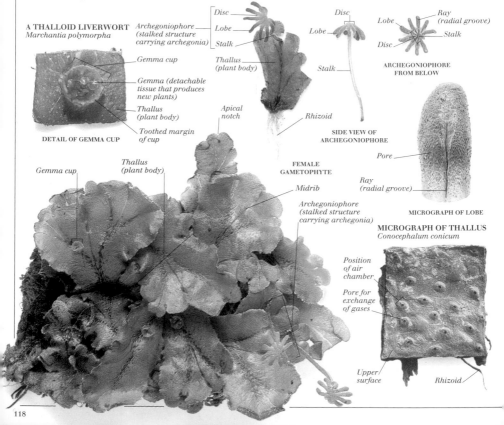

A THALLOID LIVERWORT
Marchantia polymorpha

Gemma cup

Gemma (detachable tissue that produces new plants)

Thallus (plant body)

Toothed margin of cup

DETAIL OF GEMMA CUP

Archegoniophore (stalked structure carrying archegonia)

Lobe

Stalk

Thallus (plant body)

Apical notch

Rhizoid

FEMALE GAMETOPHYTE

Disc

Lobe

Stalk

Disc

Lobe

Disc

Ray (radial groove)

Stalk

ARCHEGONIOPHORE FROM BELOW

SIDE VIEW OF ARCHEGONIOPHORE

Pore

Ray (radial groove)

MICROGRAPH OF LOBE

Gemma cup

Thallus (plant body)

Midrib

Archegoniophore (stalked structure carrying archegonia)

MICROGRAPH OF THALLUS
Conocephalum conicum

Position of air chamber

Pore for exchange of gases

Upper surface

Rhizoid

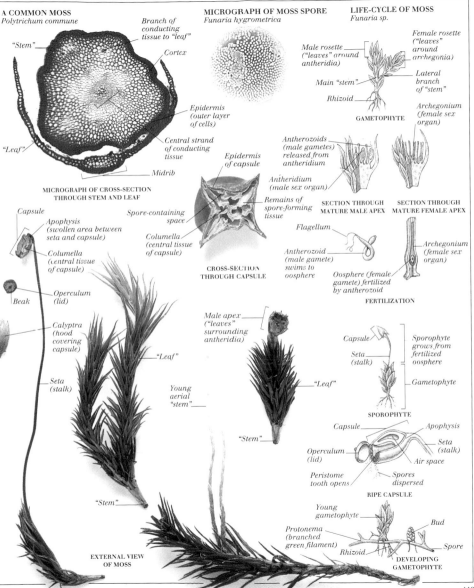

A COMMON MOSS
Polytrichum commune

Branch of conducting tissue to "leaf"

Cortex

Epidermis (outer layer of cells)

"Stem"

Central strand of conducting tissue

"Leaf"

Midrib

MICROGRAPH OF CROSS-SECTION THROUGH STEM AND LEAF

MICROGRAPH OF MOSS SPORE
Funaria hygrometrica

LIFE-CYCLE OF MOSS
Funaria sp.

Male rosette ("leaves" around antheridia)

Main "stem"

Rhizoid

Female rosette ("leaves" around archegonia)

Lateral branch of "stem"

GAMETOPHYTE

Archegonium (female sex organ)

Antherozoids (male gametes) released from antheridium

Antheridium (male sex organ)

SECTION THROUGH MATURE MALE APEX

SECTION THROUGH MATURE FEMALE APEX

Archegonium (female sex organ)

Flagellum

Antherozoid (male gamete) swims to oosphere

Oosphere (female gamete) fertilized by antherozoid

FERTILIZATION

Capsule

Apophysis (swollen area between seta and capsule)

Columella (central tissue of capsule)

Beak

Operculum (lid)

Calyptra (hood covering capsule)

Seta (stalk)

Epidermis of capsule

Spore-containing space

Columella (central tissue of capsule)

Remains of spore-forming tissue

CROSS-SECTION THROUGH CAPSULE

"Leaf"

Young aerial "stem"

Male apex ("leaves" surrounding antheridia)

"Leaf"

"Stem"

Capsule

Seta (stalk)

Sporophyte grows from fertilized oosphere

Gametophyte

SPOROPHYTE

Capsule

Operculum (lid)

Peristome tooth opens

Apophysis

Seta (stalk)

Air space

Spores dispersed

RIPE CAPSULE

Young gametophyte

Protonema (branched green filament)

Rhizoid

Bud

Spore

DEVELOPING GAMETOPHYTE

"Stem"

EXTERNAL VIEW OF MOSS

Horsetails, clubmosses, and ferns

CLUBMOSS
Lycopodium sp.

HORSETAILS, CLUBMOSSES, AND FERNS are primitive land plants, which, like higher plants, have stems, roots, and leaves, and vascular systems that transport water, minerals, and food. However, unlike higher plants, they do not produce seeds when reproducing. Their life-cycles involve two stages. In stage one, the sporophyte (green plant) produces spores in sporangia. In stage two, the spores germinate, developing into small, short-lived gametophyte plants that produce male and female gametes (sex cells); the gametes fuse to form a zygote from which a new sporophyte plant develops. Horsetails (phylum Sphenophyta) have erect, green stems with branches arranged in whorls; some stems are fertile and have a single spore-producing strobilus (group of sporangia) at the tip. Clubmosses (phylum Lycopodophyta) typically have small leaves arranged spirally around the stem, with spore-producing strobili at the tip of some stems. Ferns (phylum Filicinophyta) typically have large, pinnate fronds (leaves); sporangia, grouped together in sori, develop on the underside of fertile fronds.

FROND
Male fern
(*Dryopteris filix-mas*)

Stem with spirally arranged leaves

Branch

Strobilus (group of sporangia)

CLUBMOSS
Selaginella sp.

Epidermis (outer layer of cells)

Cortex (layer between epidermis and vascular tissue)

Shoot apex

Branch

Vascular tissue
Phloem
Xylem

Rhizophore (leafless branch)

Lacuna (air space)

Root

Creeping stem with spirally arranged leaves

MICROGRAPH OF CROSS-SECTION THROUGH CLUBMOSS STEM

HORSETAIL
Common horsetail
(*Equisetum arvense*)

Apex of sterile shoot

Sporangiophore (structure carrying sporangia)

Strobilus (group of sporangia)

Non-photosynthetic fertile stem

Collar of small brown leaves

Young shoot

Lateral branch

Photosynthetic sterile stem

Node
Internode

Node
Tuber

Rhizome

Adventitious root

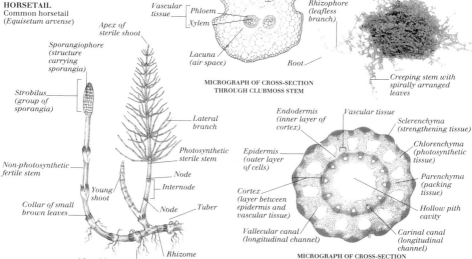

Endodermis (inner layer of cortex)

Vascular tissue

Sclerenchyma (strengthening tissue)

Epidermis (outer layer of cells)

Chlorenchyma (photosynthetic tissue)

Cortex (layer between epidermis and vascular tissue)

Parenchyma (packing tissue)

Hollow pith cavity

Vallecular canal (longitudinal channel)

Carinal canal (longitudinal channel)

MICROGRAPH OF CROSS-SECTION THROUGH HORSETAIL STEM

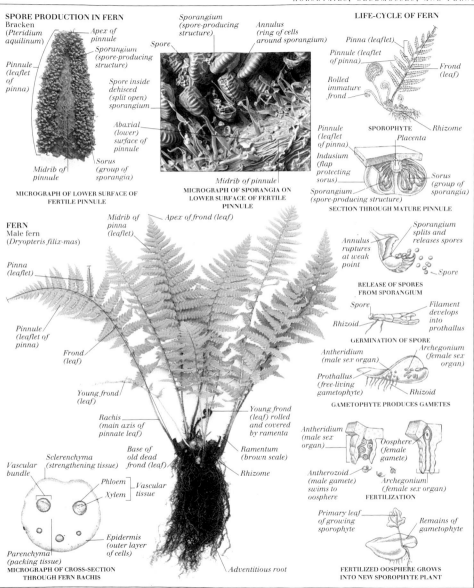

SPORE PRODUCTION IN FERN
Bracken
(*Pteridium
aquilinum*)

Apex of
pinnule

Pinnule
(leaflet
of pinna)

Sporangium
(spore-producing
structure)

Spore inside
dehisced
(split open)
sporangium

Abaxial
(lower)
surface of
pinnule

Midrib of
pinnule

Sorus
(group of
sporangia)

**MICROGRAPH OF LOWER SURFACE OF
FERTILE PINNULE**

Sporangium
(spore-producing
structure)

Spore

Annulus
(ring of cells
around sporangium)

Midrib of pinnule

**MICROGRAPH OF SPORANGIA ON
LOWER SURFACE OF FERTILE
PINNULE**

LIFE-CYCLE OF FERN

Pinna (leaflet)

Pinnule (leaflet
of pinna)

Frond
(leaf)

Rolled
immature
frond

Rhizome

SPOROPHYTE

Pinnule
(leaflet of
pinna)

Indusium
(flap
protecting
sorus)

Placenta

Sorus
(group of
sporangia)

Sporangium
(spore-producing structure)

SECTION THROUGH MATURE PINNULE

FERN
Male fern
(*Dryopteris filix-mas*)

Midrib of
pinna
(leaflet)

Apex of frond (leaf)

Pinna
(leaflet)

Pinnule
(leaflet of
pinna)

Frond
(leaf)

Young frond
(leaf)

Rachis
(main axis of
pinnate leaf)

Base of
old dead
frond (leaf)

Young frond
(leaf) rolled
and covered
by ramenta

Ramentum
(brown scale)

Rhizome

Vascular
bundle

Sclerenchyma
(strengthening tissue)

Phloem ⎫
Xylem ⎬ Vascular
       ⎭ tissue

Epidermis
(outer layer
of cells)

Parenchyma
(packing tissue)

**MICROGRAPH OF CROSS-SECTION
THROUGH FERN RACHIS**

Adventitious root

Sporangium
splits and
releases spores

Annulus
ruptures
at weak
point

Spore

**RELEASE OF SPORES
FROM SPORANGIUM**

Spore

Filament
develops
into
prothallus

Rhizoid

GERMINATION OF SPORE

Antheridium
(male sex
organ)

Archegonium
(female sex
organ)

Prothallus
(free-living
gametophyte)

Rhizoid

GAMETOPHYTE PRODUCES GAMETES

Antheridium
(male sex
organ)

Oosphere
(female
gamete)

Antherozoid
(male gamete)
swims to
oosphere

Archegonium
(female sex organ)

FERTILIZATION

Primary leaf
of growing
sporophyte

Remains of
gametophyte

**FERTILIZED OOSPHERE GROWS
INTO NEW SPOROPHYTE PLANT**

Gymnosperms 1

THE GYMNOSPERMS ARE FOUR RELATED PHYLA of seed-producing plants; their seeds, however, lack the protective, outer covering which surrounds the seeds of flowering plants. Typically, gymnosperms are woody, perennial shrubs or trees, with stems, leaves, and roots, and a well-developed vascular (transport) system. The reproductive structures in most gymnosperms are cones: male cones produce microspores in which male gametes (sex cells) develop; female cones produce megaspores in which female gametes develop. Microspores are blown by the wind to female cones, male and female gametes fuse during fertilization, and a seed develops. The four gymnosperm phyla are the conifers (phylum Coniferophyta), mostly tall trees; cycads (phylum Cycadophyta), small palm-like trees; the ginkgo or maidenhair tree (phylum Ginkgophyta), a tall tree with bilobed leaves; and gnetophytes (phylum Gnetophyta), a diverse group of plants, mainly shrubs, but also including the horizontally growing welwitschia.

LIFE-CYCLE OF SCOTS PINE
(*Pinus sylvestris*)

Needle (foliage leaf)

Cone

Ovuliferous scale (ovule- then seed-bearing structure)

MALE CONES　　**YOUNG FEMALE CONE**

Pollen grain in micropyle (entrance to ovule)

Ovuliferous scale

Pollen grain

Ovule (contains female gamete)

Nucleus

Air sac

POLLINATION

Integument (outer part of ovule)

Pollen tube (carries male gamete from pollen grain to ovum)

Archegonium (containing female gamete)

FERTILIZATION

Seed

Seed

Wing

MATURE FEMALE CONE AND WINGED SEED

SCALE AND SEEDS
Pine (*Pinus sp.*)

Ovuliferous scale (ovule- then seed-bearing structure)

Wing scar

Wing of seed derived from ovuliferous scale

Seed

Seed

Point of attachment to axis of cone

Seed scar

Ovuliferous scale (ovule- then seed-bearing structure)

OVULIFEROUS SCALE FROM THIRD-YEAR FEMALE CONE

Microsporangium (structure in which pollen grains are formed)

Microsporophyll (modified leaf carrying microsporangia)

Ovule (contains female gametes)

Bract scale

Scale leaf

Ovuliferous scale (ovule- then seed-bearing structure)

Axis of cone

Axis of cone

Plumule (embryonic shoot)

Cotyledon (seed leaf)

Root

GERMINATION OF PINE SEEDLING

MICROGRAPH OF LONGITUDINAL SECTION THROUGH YOUNG MALE CONE

MICROGRAPH OF LONGITUDINAL SECTION THROUGH SECOND-YEAR FEMALE CONE

WELWITSCHIA
(*Welwitschia mirabilis*)

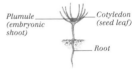

Frayed end of leaf

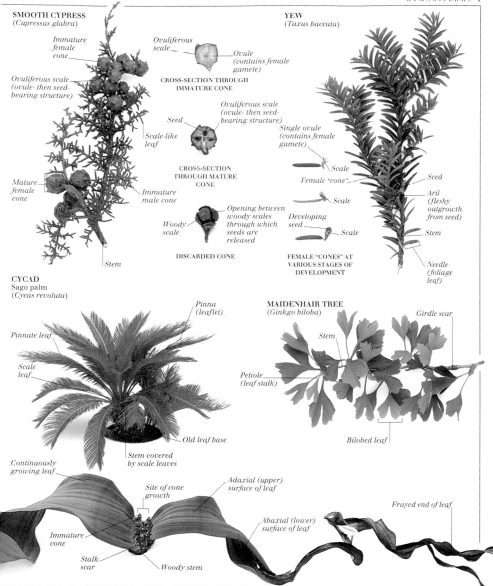

SMOOTH CYPRESS
(*Cupressus glabra*)

Immature female cone

Ovuliferous scale (ovule- then seed-bearing structure)

Ovuliferous scale

Ovule (contains female gamete)

CROSS-SECTION THROUGH IMMATURE CONE

Seed

Ovuliferous scale (ovule- then seed-bearing structure)

Scale-like leaf

CROSS-SECTION THROUGH MATURE CONE

Mature female cone

Immature male cone

Woody scale

Opening between woody scales through which seeds are released

DISCARDED CONE

Stem

YEW
(*Taxus baccata*)

Single ovule (contains female gamete)

Scale

Female "cone"

Scale

Developing seed

Scale

FEMALE "CONES" AT VARIOUS STAGES OF DEVELOPMENT

Seed

Aril (fleshy outgrowth from seed)

Stem

Needle (foliage leaf)

CYCAD
Sago palm
(*Cycas revoluta*)

Pinna (leaflet)

Pinnate leaf

Scale leaf

Old leaf base

Stem covered by scale leaves

MAIDENHAIR TREE
(*Ginkgo biloba*)

Girdle scar

Stem

Petiole (leaf stalk)

Bilobed leaf

Continuously growing leaf

Site of cone growth

Adaxial (upper) surface of leaf

Frayed end of leaf

Abaxial (lower) surface of leaf

Immature cone

Stalk scar

Woody stem

Gymnosperms 2

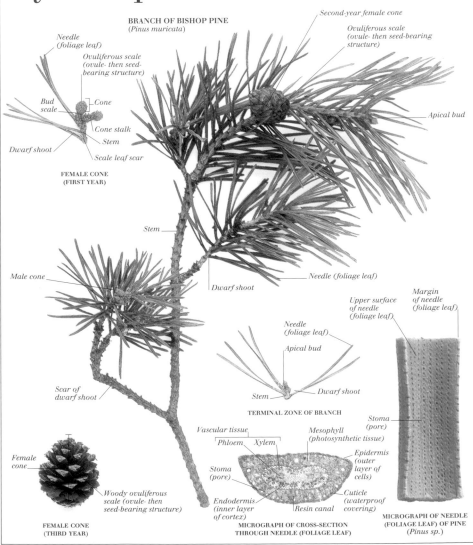

BRANCH OF BISHOP PINE
(*Pinus muricata*)

*Needle
(foliage leaf)*

*Ovuliferous scale
(ovule- then seed-
bearing structure)*

*Bud
scale*

Cone

Cone stalk

Stem

Dwarf shoot

Scale leaf scar

**FEMALE CONE
(FIRST YEAR)**

Second-year female cone

*Ovuliferous scale
(ovule- then seed-bearing
structure)*

Apical bud

Stem

Male cone

Needle (foliage leaf)

Dwarf shoot

*Scar of
dwarf shoot*

*Female
cone*

*Woody ovuliferous
scale (ovule- then
seed-bearing structure)*

**FEMALE CONE
(THIRD YEAR)**

*Upper surface
of needle
(foliage leaf)*

*Margin
of needle
(foliage leaf)*

*Needle
(foliage leaf)*

Apical bud

Stem

Dwarf shoot

TERMINAL ZONE OF BRANCH

*Stoma
(pore)*

**MICROGRAPH OF NEEDLE
(FOLIAGE LEAF) OF PINE**
(*Pinus sp.*)

Vascular tissue

Phloem

Xylem

*Mesophyll
(photosynthetic tissue)*

*Epidermis
(outer
layer of
cells)*

*Stoma
(pore)*

*Endodermis
(inner layer
of cortex)*

Resin canal

*Cuticle
(waterproof
covering)*

**MICROGRAPH OF CROSS-SECTION
THROUGH NEEDLE (FOLIAGE LEAF)**

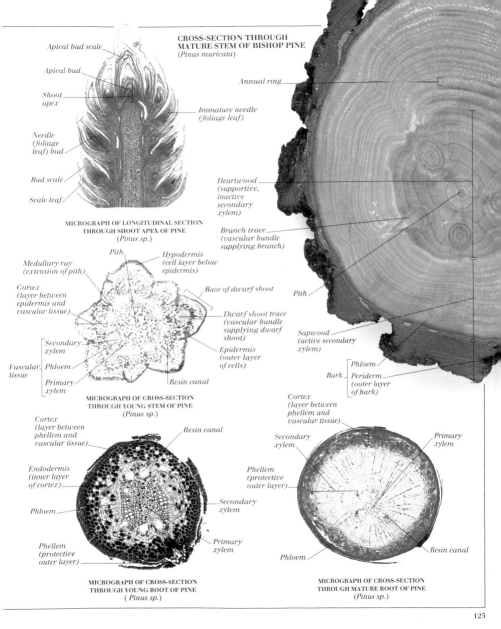

Apical bud scale

Apical bud

Shoot apex

Needle (foliage leaf) bud

Bud scale

Scale leaf

CROSS-SECTION THROUGH MATURE STEM OF BISHOP PINE
(Pinus muricata)

Immature needle (foliage leaf)

MICROGRAPH OF LONGITUDINAL SECTION THROUGH SHOOT APEX OF PINE
(Pinus sp.)

Annual ring

Heartwood (supportive, inactive secondary xylem)

Branch trace (vascular bundle supplying branch)

Pith

Sapwood (active secondary xylem)

Phloem

Bark — Periderm (outer layer of bark)

Medullary ray (extension of pith)

Pith

Hypodermis (cell layer below epidermis)

Cortex (layer between epidermis and vascular tissue)

Base of dwarf shoot

Dwarf shoot trace (vascular bundle supplying dwarf shoot)

Secondary xylem

Epidermis (outer layer of cells)

Vascular tissue

Phloem

Primary xylem

Resin canal

MICROGRAPH OF CROSS-SECTION THROUGH YOUNG STEM OF PINE
(Pinus sp.)

Cortex (layer between phellem and vascular tissue)

Resin canal

Cortex (layer between phellem and vascular tissue)

Secondary xylem

Primary xylem

Endodermis (inner layer of cortex)

Phellem (protective outer layer)

Phloem

Secondary xylem

Phloem

Primary xylem

Resin canal

Phellem (protective outer layer)

Phloem

MICROGRAPH OF CROSS-SECTION THROUGH YOUNG ROOT OF PINE
(Pinus sp.)

MICROGRAPH OF CROSS-SECTION THROUGH MATURE ROOT OF PINE
(Pinus sp.)

Monocotyledons and dicotyledons

FLOWERING PLANTS (PHYLUM ANGIOSPERMOPHYTA) are divided into two classes: monocotyledons (class Monocotyledoneae) and dicotyledons (class Dicotyledoneae). Typically, monocotyledons have seeds with one cotyledon (seed leaf); their foliage leaves are narrow with parallel veins; the flower components occur in multiples of three; sepals and petals are indistinguishable and are known as tepals; vascular (transport) tissues are scattered in random bundles throughout the stem; and, since they lack stem cambium (actively dividing cells that produce wood), most monocotyledons are herbaceous (see pp. 128-129). Dicotyledons have seeds with two cotyledons; leaves are broad with a central midrib and branched veins; flower parts occur in multiples of four or five; sepals are generally small and green; petals are large and colourful; vascular bundles are arranged in a ring around the edge of the stem; and, because many dicotyledons possess wood-producing stem cambium, there are woody forms (see pp. 130-131) as well as herbaceous ones.

CROSS-SECTION
THROUGH
MONOCOTYLEDONOUS
LEAF BASES

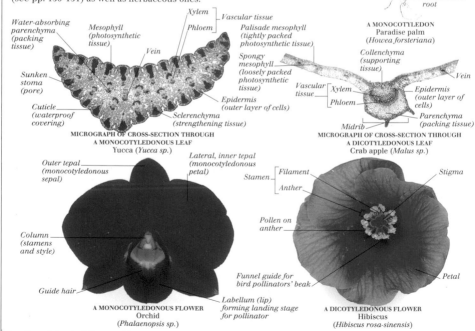

Vein
(parallel
venation)

Leaflet

Petiole
(leaf stalk)

Emerging
leaf

Leaf base

Adventitious
root

A MONOCOTYLEDON
Paradise palm
(*Howea forsteriana*)

Water-absorbing
parenchyma
(packing
tissue)

Mesophyll
(photosynthetic
tissue)

Xylem

Phloem

Vascular tissue

Palisade mesophyll
(tightly packed
photosynthetic tissue)

Vein

Spongy
mesophyll
(loosely packed
photosynthetic
tissue)

Sunken
stoma
(pore)

Vascular
tissue

Xylem

Phloem

Collenchyma
(supporting
tissue)

Vein

Epidermis
(outer layer of
cells)

Parenchyma
(packing tissue)

Cuticle
(waterproof
covering)

Epidermis
(outer layer of cells)

Sclerenchyma
(strengthening tissue)

Midrib

MICROGRAPH OF CROSS-SECTION THROUGH
A MONOCOTYLEDONOUS LEAF
Yucca (*Yucca sp.*)

MICROGRAPH OF CROSS-SECTION THROUGH
A DICOTYLEDONOUS LEAF
Crab apple (*Malus sp.*)

Outer tepal
(monocotyledonous
sepal)

Lateral, inner tepal
(monocotyledonous
petal)

Stamen

Filament

Anther

Stigma

Pollen on
anther

Column
(stamens
and style)

Funnel guide for
bird pollinators' beak

Petal

Guide hair

A MONOCOTYLEDONOUS FLOWER
Orchid
(*Phalaenopsis sp.*)

Labellum (lip)
forming landing stage
for pollinator

A DICOTYLEDONOUS FLOWER
Hibiscus
(*Hibiscus rosa-sinensis*)

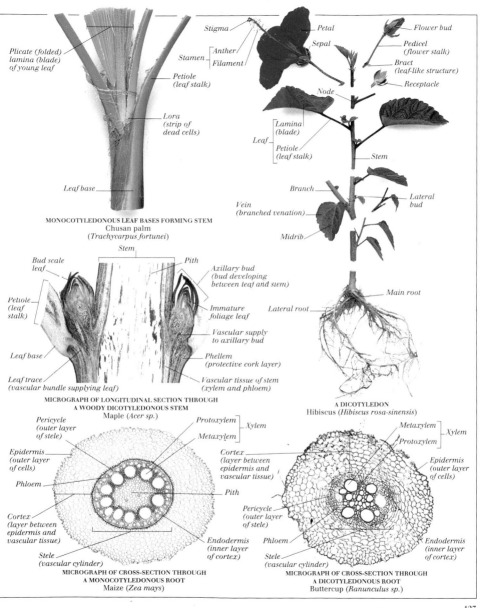

Plicate (folded)
lamina (blade)
of young leaf

Petiole
(leaf stalk)

Lora
(strip of
dead cells)

Leaf base

MONOCOTYLEDONOUS LEAF BASES FORMING STEM
Chusan palm
(Trachycarpus fortunei)

Stigma
Petal
Sepal
Anther
Stamen
Filament

Flower bud
Pedicel
(flower stalk)
Bract
(leaf-like structure)
Receptacle

Node

Lamina
(blade)
Leaf
Petiole
(leaf stalk)
Stem

Vein
(branched venation)

Branch

Midrib

Lateral
bud

Main root

Lateral root

A DICOTYLEDON
Hibiscus (Hibiscus rosa-sinensis)

Bud scale
leaf

Stem

Pith

Petiole
(leaf
stalk)

Leaf base

Leaf trace
(vascular bundle supplying leaf)

Axillary bud
(bud developing
between leaf and stem)

Immature
foliage leaf

Vascular supply
to axillary bud

Phellem
(protective cork layer)

Vascular tissue of stem
(xylem and phloem)

**MICROGRAPH OF LONGITUDINAL SECTION THROUGH
A WOODY DICOTYLEDONOUS STEM**
Maple (Acer sp.)

Pericycle
(outer layer
of stele)

Epidermis
(outer layer
of cells)

Phloem

Cortex
(layer between
epidermis and
vascular tissue)

Protoxylem
Metaxylem
} Xylem

Pith

Endodermis
(inner layer
of cortex)

Stele
(vascular cylinder)

**MICROGRAPH OF CROSS-SECTION THROUGH
A MONOCOTYLEDONOUS ROOT**
Maize (Zea mays)

Cortex
(layer between
epidermis and
vascular tissue)

Pericycle
(outer layer
of stele)

Phloem

Stele
(vascular cylinder)

Metaxylem
Protoxylem
} Xylem

Epidermis
(outer layer
of cells)

Endodermis
(inner layer
of cortex)

**MICROGRAPH OF CROSS-SECTION THROUGH
A DICOTYLEDONOUS ROOT**
Buttercup (Ranunculus sp.)

127

Herbaceous flowering plants

HERBACEOUS FLOWERING PLANTS TYPICALLY HAVE GREEN, NON-WOODY STEMS, and tend to be relatively short-lived. Many herbaceous plants live for only one or two years. Annuals (e.g., sweet peas) grow from seed, produce flowers and then seeds, and die within a single year. Biennials (e.g., carrots) have a two-year life cycle. In the first year, seeds grow into plants, which produce leaves and store food in underground storage organs; the stems and foliage then die back in winter. In the second year, new stems grow from the storage organs, produce leaves, flowers, and seeds, and then die. Some herbaceous plants (e.g., potatoes) are perennial. They grow back year after year, producing shoots and flowers in spring, storing food in underground tubers or rhizomes during summer, dying back in autumn, and surviving underground during winter.

Young plant forming

Petiole (stalk) of young leaf

Lateral root

Stipule (structure at base of leaf)

Node

Trifoliate leaf

Simple ovate leaflet

Root nodule

Main root

STRAWBERRY
(*Fragaria* x *ananassa*)

SWEET PEA
(*Lathyrus odoratus*)

Runner (creeping stem)

Remains of leaves

Lateral root scar

Stem

Leaf scar

Rib

Lateral root

Tap root

CARROT
(*Daucus carota*)

Leaf scar

Leaf base

Slender rhizome

Petiole (leaf stalk)

Spine (modified leaf)

Stem tuber

Adventitious root

Stem

Narrow, succulent leaf

Simple deltoid leaf

ROCK STONECROP
(*Sedum rupestre*)

POTATO
(*Solanum tuberosum*)

Adventitious root

PARTS OF HERBACEOUS FLOWERING PLANTS

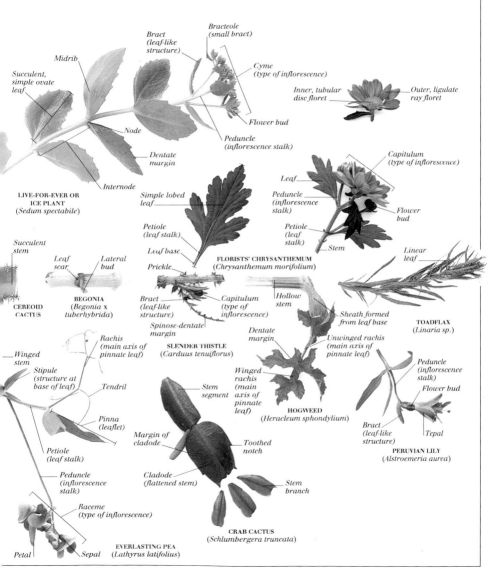

Midrib

Bract
(leaf-like
structure)

Bracteole
(small bract)

Cyme
(type of inflorescence)

Succulent,
simple ovate
leaf

Inner, tubular
disc floret

Outer, ligulate
ray floret

Flower bud

Node

Peduncle
(inflorescence stalk)

Dentate
margin

Internode

**LIVE-FOR-EVER OR
ICE PLANT**
(*Sedum spectabile*)

Simple lobed
leaf

Capitulum
(type of inflorescence)

Leaf

Peduncle
(inflorescence
stalk)

Flower
bud

Petiole
(leaf stalk)

Petiole
(leaf
stalk)

Leaf base

Stem

Linear
leaf

Succulent
stem

Leaf
scar

Lateral
bud

Prickle

FLORISTS' CHRYSANTHEMUM
(*Chrysanthemum morifolium*)

**CEREOID
CACTUS**

BEGONIA
(*Begonia* x
tuberhybrida)

Bract
(leaf-like
structure)

Capitulum
(type of
inflorescence)

Hollow
stem

Sheath formed
from leaf base

TOADFLAX
(*Linaria sp.*)

Spinose-dentate
margin

Dentate
margin

Unwinged rachis
(main axis of
pinnate leaf)

Rachis
(main axis of
pinnate leaf)

SLENDER THISTLE
(*Carduus tenuiflorus*)

Winged
stem

Stipule
(structure at
base of leaf)

Tendril

Winged
rachis
(main
axis of
pinnate
leaf)

Peduncle
(inflorescence
stalk)

Flower bud

Pinna
(leaflet)

Stem
segment

HOGWEED
(*Heracleum sphondylium*)

Bract
(leaf-like
structure)

Tepal

Petiole
(leaf stalk)

Margin of
cladode

Toothed
notch

PERUVIAN LILY
(*Alstroemeria aurea*)

Peduncle
(inflorescence
stalk)

Cladode
(flattened stem)

Stem
branch

Raceme
(type of inflorescence)

CRAB CACTUS
(*Schlumbergera truncata*)

Petal

Sepal

EVERLASTING PEA
(*Lathyrus latifolius*)

Woody flowering plants

Woody flowering plants are perennial, that is, they continue to grow and reproduce for many years. They have one or more permanent stems above ground, and numerous smaller branches. The stems and branches have a strong woody core that supports the plant and contains vascular tissue for transporting water and nutrients. Outside the woody core is a layer of tough, protective bark, which has lenticels (tiny pores) in it to enable gases to pass through. Woody flowering plants may be shrubs, which have several stems arising from the soil; bushes, which are shrubs with dense branching and foliage; or trees, which typically have a single upright stem (the trunk) that bears branches. Deciduous woody plants (e.g., roses) shed all their leaves once a year and remain leafless during winter. Evergreen woody plants (e.g., ivy) shed their leaves gradually, so retaining full leaf cover throughout the year.

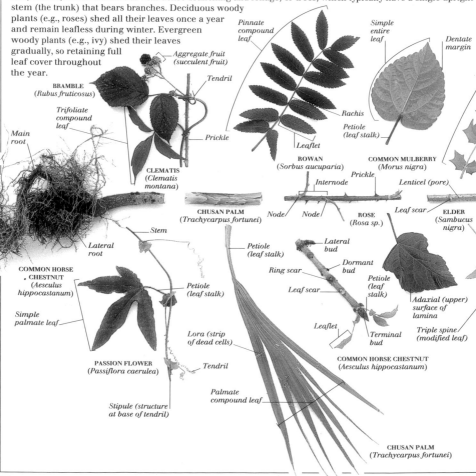

Aggregate fruit (succulent fruit)

Tendril

BRAMBLE
(Rubus fruticosus)

Trifoliate compound leaf

Main root

CLEMATIS
(Clematis montana)

Prickle

Pinnate compound leaf

Rachis

Petiole (leaf stalk)

Leaflet

ROWAN
(Sorbus aucuparia)

Simple entire leaf

Dentate margin

COMMON MULBERRY
(Morus nigra)

Internode

Prickle

Node Node

CHUSAN PALM
(Trachycarpus fortunei)

ROSE
(Rosa sp.)

Lenticel (pore)

Leaf scar

ELDER
(Sambucus nigra)

Lateral root

Stem

Petiole (leaf stalk)

Lateral bud

Dormant bud

Ring scar

Leaf scar

Petiole (leaf stalk)

Adaxial (upper) surface of lamina

COMMON HORSE CHESTNUT
(Aesculus hippocastanum)

Simple palmate leaf

Petiole (leaf stalk)

Lora (strip of dead cells)

Leaflet

Terminal bud

Triple spine (modified leaf)

PASSION FLOWER
(Passiflora caerulea)

Tendril

COMMON HORSE CHESTNUT
(Aesculus hippocastanum)

Stipule (structure at base of tendril)

Palmate compound leaf

CHUSAN PALM
(Trachycarpus fortunei)

PARTS OF WOODY FLOWERING PLANTS

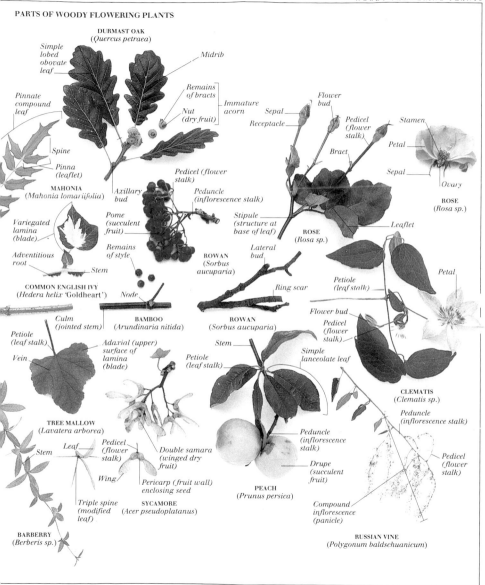

DURMAST OAK
(*Quercus petraea*)

Simple lobed obovate leaf

Midrib

Remains of bracts

Immature acorn

Nut (dry fruit)

Pinnate compound leaf

Spine

Pinna (leaflet)

MAHONIA
(*Mahonia lomariifolia*)

Axillary bud

Pedicel (flower stalk)

Peduncle (inflorescence stalk)

Pome (succulent fruit)

Variegated lamina (blade)

Adventitious root

Stem

Remains of style

COMMON ENGLISH IVY
(*Hedera helix* 'Goldheart')

Node

ROWAN
(*Sorbus aucuparia*)

Culm (jointed stem)

BAMBOO
(*Arundinaria nitida*)

ROWAN
(*Sorbus aucuparia*)

Ring scar

Lateral bud

Flower bud

Sepal

Receptacle

Pedicel (flower stalk)

Stamen

Petal

Bract

Sepal

Ovary

ROSE
(*Rosa sp.*)

Stipule (structure at base of leaf)

Leaflet

ROSE
(*Rosa sp.*)

Petiole (leaf stalk)

Petal

Flower bud

Pedicel (flower stalk)

CLEMATIS
(*Clematis sp.*)

Petiole (leaf stalk)

Vein

Adaxial (upper) surface of lamina (blade)

TREE MALLOW
(*Lavatera arborea*)

Stem

Petiole (leaf stalk)

Simple lanceolate leaf

Peduncle (inflorescence stalk)

Pedicel (flower stalk)

Wing

Double samara (winged dry fruit)

Pericarp (fruit wall) enclosing seed

Leaf

Stem

Triple spine (modified leaf)

SYCAMORE
(*Acer pseudoplatanus*)

Peduncle (inflorescence stalk)

Drupe (succulent fruit)

PEACH
(*Prunus persica*)

Compound inflorescence (panicle)

Pedicel (flower stalk)

BARBERRY
(*Berberis sp.*)

RUSSIAN VINE
(*Polygonum baldschuanicum*)

Roots

Roots are the underground parts of plants. They have three main functions. First, they anchor the plant in the soil. Second, they absorb water and minerals from the spaces between soil particles; the roots' absorptive properties are increased by root hairs, which grow behind the root tip, allowing maximum uptake of vital substances. Third, the root is part of the plant's transport system: xylem carries water and minerals from the roots to the stem and leaves, and phloem carries nutrients from the leaves to all parts of the root system. In addition, some roots (e.g., carrots) are food stores. Roots have an outer epidermis covering a cortex of parenchyma (packing tissue), and a central cylinder of vascular tissue. This arrangement helps the roots resist the forces of compression as they grow through the soil.

CARROT
(Daucus carota)

MICROGRAPH OF PRIMARY ROOT DEVELOPMENT
Cabbage *(Brassica sp.)*

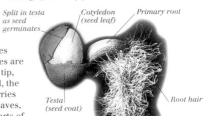

Split in testa as seed germinates

Cotyledon (seed leaf)

Primary root

Testa (seed coat)

Root hair

Root tip (region of cell division)

FEATURES OF A TYPICAL ROOT
Buttercup
(Ranunculus sp.)

Pericycle (outer layer of stele)

Root hair

Air space (allowing gas diffusion in the root)

Stele (vascular cylinder)

Phloem sieve tube (through which nutrients are transported)

Companion cell (cell associated with phloem sieve tube)

Cortex (layer between epidermis and vascular tissue)

Root hair

Epidermis (outer layer of cells)

Xylem vessel (through which water and minerals are transported)

Endodermis (inner layer of cortex)

Cell wall

Nucleus

Cytoplasm

Parenchyma (packing) cell

PRIMARY ROOT AND MICROGRAPHS OF SECTIONS THROUGH ROOTS

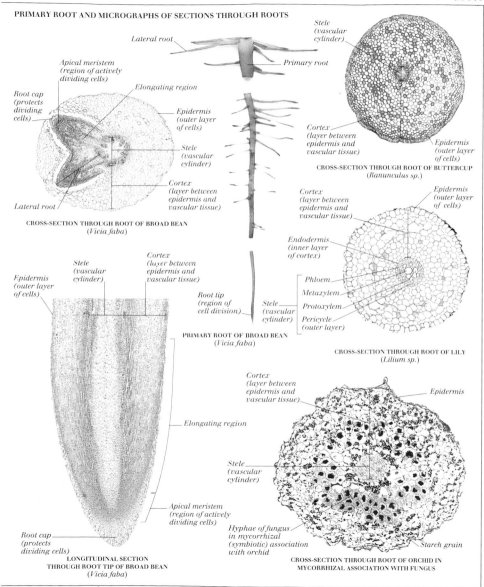

Lateral root

Primary root

Apical meristem (region of actively dividing cells)

Elongating region

Root cap (protects dividing cells)

Epidermis (outer layer of cells)

Stele (vascular cylinder)

Cortex (layer between epidermis and vascular tissue)

Lateral root

CROSS-SECTION THROUGH ROOT OF BROAD BEAN
(Vicia faba)

Stele (vascular cylinder)

Cortex (layer between epidermis and vascular tissue)

Epidermis (outer layer of cells)

CROSS-SECTION THROUGH ROOT OF BUTTERCUP
(Ranunculus sp.)

Cortex (layer between epidermis and vascular tissue)

Epidermis (outer layer of cells)

Endodermis (inner layer of cortex)

Phloem

Metaxylem

Protoxylem

Pericycle (outer layer)

Stele (vascular cylinder)

CROSS-SECTION THROUGH ROOT OF LILY
(Lilium sp.)

Epidermis (outer layer of cells)

Stele (vascular cylinder)

Cortex (layer between epidermis and vascular tissue)

Root tip (region of cell division)

Stele (vascular cylinder)

PRIMARY ROOT OF BROAD BEAN
(Vicia faba)

Elongating region

Apical meristem (region of actively dividing cells)

Root cap (protects dividing cells)

LONGITUDINAL SECTION THROUGH ROOT TIP OF BROAD BEAN
(Vicia faba)

Cortex (layer between epidermis and vascular tissue)

Epidermis

Stele (vascular cylinder)

Hyphae of fungus in mycorrhizal (symbiotic) association with orchid

Starch grain

CROSS-SECTION THROUGH ROOT OF ORCHID IN MYCORRHIZAL ASSOCIATION WITH FUNGUS

Stems

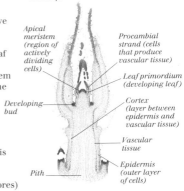

THE STEM IS THE MAIN SUPPORTIVE PART OF A PLANT that grows above
ground. Stems bear leaves (organs of photosynthesis), which grow
at nodes; buds (shoots covered by protective scales), which grow at
the stem tip (apical or terminal buds) and in the angle between a leaf
and the stem (axillary or lateral buds); and flowers (reproductive
structures). The stem forms part of the plant's transport system: xylem
tissue in the stem transports water and minerals from the roots to the
aerial parts of the plant, and phloem tissue transports nutrients
manufactured in the leaves to other parts of the plant. Stem tissues
are also used for storing water and food. Herbaceous (non-woody)
stems have an outer protective epidermis covering a cortex that
consists mainly of parenchyma (packing tissue) but also has some
collenchyma (supporting tissue). The vascular tissue of such stems is
arranged in bundles, each of which consists of xylem, phloem, and
sclerenchyma (strengthening tissue). Woody stems have an outer
protective layer of tough bark, which is perforated with lenticels (pores)
to allow gas exchange. Inside the bark is a ring of secondary phloem,
which surrounds an inner core of secondary xylem.

*Apical
meristem
(region of
actively
dividing
cells)*

*Developing
bud*

*Procambial
strand (cells
that produce
vascular tissue)*

*Leaf primordium
(developing leaf)*

*Cortex
(layer between
epidermis and
vascular tissue)*

*Vascular
tissue*

*Epidermis
(outer layer
of cells)*

Pith

YOUNG WOODY STEM
Lime
(*Tilia sp.*)

*Young
leaves
emerging*

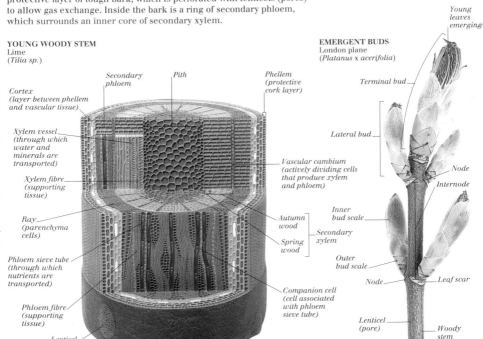

*Cortex
(layer between phellem
and vascular tissue)*

*Secondary
phloem*

Pith

*Phellem
(protective
cork layer)*

*Xylem vessel
(through which
water and
minerals are
transported)*

*Xylem fibre
(supporting
tissue)*

*Ray
(parenchyma
cells)*

*Phloem sieve tube
(through which
nutrients are
transported)*

*Phloem fibre
(supporting
tissue)*

*Lenticel
(pore)*

*Vascular cambium
(actively dividing cells
that produce xylem
and phloem)*

*Autumn
wood*

*Spring
wood*

*Companion cell
(cell associated
with phloem
sieve tube)*

EMERGENT BUDS
London plane
(*Platanus x acerifolia*)

Terminal bud

Lateral bud

Node

Internode

*Inner
bud scale*

*Secondary
xylem*

*Outer
bud scale*

Node

Leaf scar

*Lenticel
(pore)*

*Woody
stem*

MICROGRAPHS OF CROSS-SECTIONS THROUGH VARIOUS STEMS

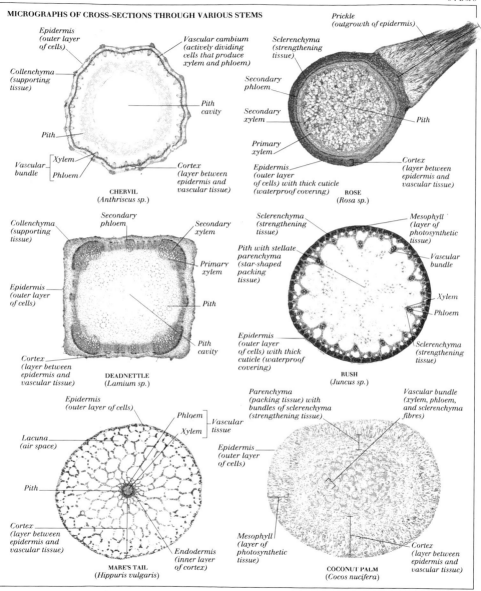

CHERVIL
(*Anthriscus sp.*)

Epidermis (outer layer of cells)

Collenchyma (supporting tissue)

Pith

Vascular bundle

Xylem

Phloem

Vascular cambium (actively dividing cells that produce xylem and phloem)

Pith cavity

Cortex (layer between epidermis and vascular tissue)

ROSE
(*Rosa sp.*)

Prickle (outgrowth of epidermis)

Sclerenchyma (strengthening tissue)

Secondary phloem

Secondary xylem

Primary xylem

Epidermis (outer layer of cells) with thick cuticle (waterproof covering)

Pith

Cortex (layer between epidermis and vascular tissue)

DEADNETTLE
(*Lamium sp.*)

Collenchyma (supporting tissue)

Epidermis (outer layer of cells)

Cortex (layer between epidermis and vascular tissue)

Secondary phloem

Secondary xylem

Primary xylem

Pith

Pith cavity

RUSH
(*Juncus sp.*)

Sclerenchyma (strengthening tissue)

Pith with stellate parenchyma (star-shaped packing tissue)

Epidermis (outer layer of cells) with thick cuticle (waterproof covering)

Mesophyll (layer of photosynthetic tissue)

Vascular bundle

Xylem

Phloem

Sclerenchyma (strengthening tissue)

MARE'S TAIL
(*Hippuris vulgaris*)

Epidermis (outer layer of cells)

Lacuna (air space)

Pith

Cortex (layer between epidermis and vascular tissue)

Phloem

Xylem

Vascular tissue

Endodermis (inner layer of cortex)

COCONUT PALM
(*Cocos nucifera*)

Parenchyma (packing tissue) with bundles of sclerenchyma (strengthening tissue)

Epidermis (outer layer of cells)

Mesophyll (layer of photosynthetic tissue)

Vascular bundle (xylem, phloem, and sclerenchyma fibres)

Cortex (layer between epidermis and vascular tissue)

Leaves

LEAVES ARE THE MAIN SITES OF PHOTOSYNTHESIS (see pp. 138-139) and transpiration (water loss by evaporation) in plants. A typical leaf consists of a thin, flat lamina (blade) supported by a network of veins; a petiole (leaf stalk); and a leaf base, where the petiole joins the stem. Leaves can be classified as simple, in which the lamina is a single unit, or compound, in which the lamina is divided into separate leaflets. Compound leaves may be pinnate, with pinnae (leaflets) on both sides of a rachis (main axis), or palmate, with leaflets arising from a single point at the tip of the petiole. Leaves can be classified further by the overall shape of the lamina, and by the shape of the lamina's apex, margin, and base.

CHECKERBLOOM
(*Sidalcea malviflora*)

SIMPLE LEAF SHAPES

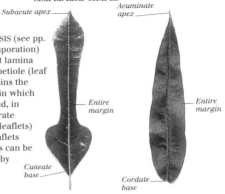

Subacute apex

Acuminate apex

Entire margin

Entire margin

Cuneate base

Cordate base

PANDURIFORM
Croton
(*Codiaeum variegatum*)

LANCEOLATE
Sea buckthorn
(*Hippophae rhamnoides*)

GENERAL LEAF FEATURES

Apex

Midrib

Lamina (blade)

Margin

Lateral vein

Lamina base

Petiole (leaf stalk)

Leaf base

Sweet chestnut
(*Castanea sativa*)

COMPOUND LEAF SHAPES

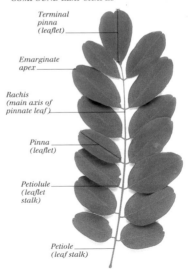

Terminal pinna (leaflet)

Emarginate apex

Rachis (main axis of pinnate leaf)

Pinna (leaflet)

Petiolule (leaflet stalk)

Petiole (leaf stalk)

ODD PINNATE
False acacia
(*Robinia pseudoacacia*)

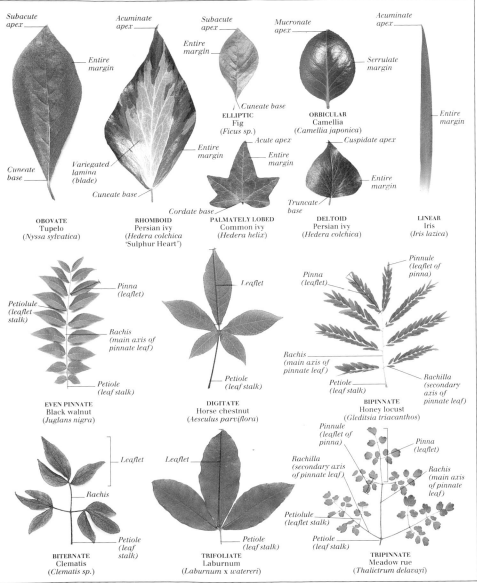

OBOVATE
Tupelo
(*Nyssa sylvatica*)

- Subacute apex
- Entire margin
- Cuneate base

RHOMBOID
Persian ivy
(*Hedera colchica*
'Sulphur Heart')

- Acuminate apex
- Variegated lamina (blade)
- Entire margin
- Cuneate base

ELLIPTIC
Fig
(*Ficus sp.*)

- Subacute apex
- Entire margin
- Cuneate base

PALMATELY LOBED
Common ivy
(*Hedera helix*)

- Acute apex
- Entire margin
- Cordate base

ORBICULAR
Camellia
(*Camellia japonica*)

- Mucronate apex
- Serrulate margin

DELTOID
Persian ivy
(*Hedera colchica*)

- Cuspidate apex
- Entire margin
- Truncate base

LINEAR
Iris
(*Iris lazica*)

- Acuminate apex
- Entire margin

EVEN PINNATE
Black walnut
(*Juglans nigra*)

- Pinna (leaflet)
- Petiolule (leaflet stalk)
- Rachis (main axis of pinnate leaf)
- Petiole (leaf stalk)

DIGITATE
Horse chestnut
(*Aesculus parviflora*)

- Leaflet
- Petiole (leaf stalk)

BIPINNATE
Honey locust
(*Gleditsia triacanthos*)

- Pinnule (leaflet of pinna)
- Pinna (leaflet)
- Rachis (main axis of pinnate leaf)
- Petiole (leaf stalk)
- Rachilla (secondary axis of pinnate leaf)

BITERNATE
Clematis
(*Clematis sp.*)

- Leaflet
- Rachis
- Petiole (leaf stalk)

TRIFOLIATE
Laburnum
(*Laburnum* x *watereri*)

- Leaflet
- Petiole (leaf stalk)

TRIPINNATE
Meadow rue
(*Thalictrum delavayi*)

- Pinnule (leaflet of pinna)
- Pinna (leaflet)
- Rachilla (secondary axis of pinnate leaf)
- Rachis (main axis of pinnate leaf)
- Petiolule (leaflet stalk)
- Petiole (leaf stalk)

Photosynthesis

PHOTOSYNTHESIS IS THE PROCESS by which plants make their food using sunlight, water, and carbon dioxide. It takes place inside special structures in leaf cells called chloroplasts. The chloroplasts contain chlorophyll, a green pigment that absorbs energy from sunlight. During photosynthesis, the absorbed energy is used to join together carbon dioxide and water to form the sugar glucose, which is the energy source for the whole plant; oxygen, a waste product, is released into the air. Leaves are the main sites of photosynthesis, and have various adaptations for that purpose: flat laminae (blades) provide a large surface for absorbing sunlight; stomata (pores) in the lower surface of the laminae allow gases (carbon dioxide and oxygen) to pass into and out of the leaves; and an extensive network of veins brings water into the leaves and transports the glucose produced by photosynthesis to the rest of the plant.

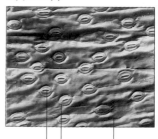

Stoma (pore)

Guard cell (controls opening and closing of stoma)

Lower surface of lamina (blade)

THE PROCESS OF PHOTOSYNTHESIS

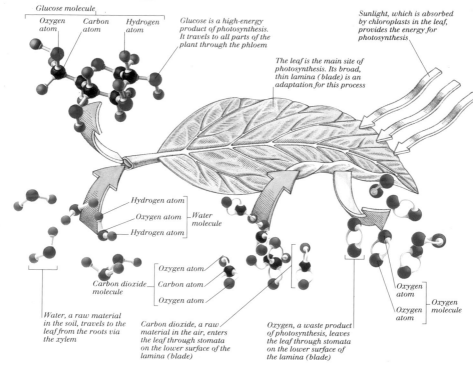

Glucose molecule

Oxygen atom

Carbon atom

Hydrogen atom

Glucose is a high-energy product of photosynthesis. It travels to all parts of the plant through the phloem

Sunlight, which is absorbed by chloroplasts in the leaf, provides the energy for photosynthesis

The leaf is the main site of photosynthesis. Its broad, thin lamina (blade) is an adaptation for this process

Hydrogen atom

Oxygen atom

Hydrogen atom

Water molecule

Carbon dioxide molecule

Oxygen atom

Carbon atom

Oxygen atom

Oxygen atom

Oxygen atom

Oxygen molecule

Water, a raw material in the soil, travels to the leaf from the roots via the xylem

Carbon dioxide, a raw material in the air, enters the leaf through stomata on the lower surface of the lamina (blade)

Oxygen, a waste product of photosynthesis, leaves the leaf through stomata on the lower surface of the lamina (blade)

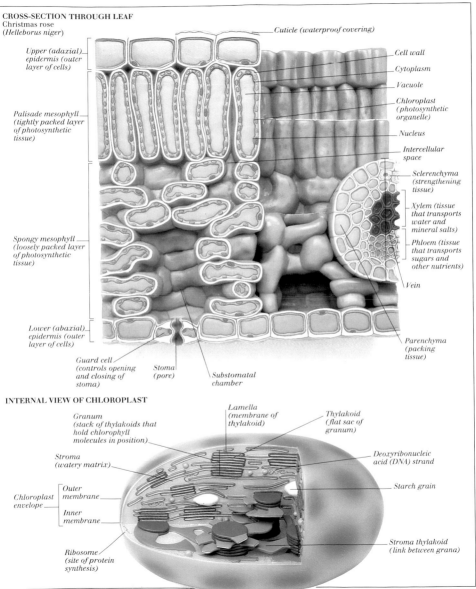

CROSS-SECTION THROUGH LEAF
Christmas rose
(*Helleborus niger*)

Cuticle (waterproof covering)

Upper (adaxial) epidermis (outer layer of cells)

Cell wall

Cytoplasm

Vacuole

Chloroplast (photosynthetic organelle)

Nucleus

Palisade mesophyll (tightly packed layer of photosynthetic tissue)

Intercellular space

Sclerenchyma (strengthening tissue)

Xylem (tissue that transports water and mineral salts)

Phloem (tissue that transports sugars and other nutrients)

Spongy mesophyll (loosely packed layer of photosynthetic tissue)

Vein

Lower (abaxial) epidermis (outer layer of cells)

Guard cell (controls opening and closing of stoma)

Stoma (pore)

Substomatal chamber

Parenchyma (packing tissue)

INTERNAL VIEW OF CHLOROPLAST

Lamella (membrane of thylakoid)

Thylakoid (flat sac of granum)

Granum (stack of thylakoids that hold chlorophyll molecules in position)

Stroma (watery matrix)

Deoxyribonucleic acid (DNA) strand

Chloroplast envelope

Outer membrane

Inner membrane

Starch grain

Ribosome (site of protein synthesis)

Stroma thylakoid (link between grana)

139

Flowers 1

FLOWERS ARE THE SITES OF SEXUAL REPRODUCTION in flowering plants. Their component parts are arranged in whorls around the receptacle (tip of the flower stalk). The sepals (collectively called the calyx) are outermost; typically small and green, they protect the developing flower. The petals (collectively called the corolla) are typically large and brightly coloured; they are found inside the sepals. In monocotyledonous flowers (see pp. 126-127), sepals and petals are indistinguishable; individually they are called tepals (collectively called the perianth). The androecium and gynoecium). The androecium consists of stamens (male organs); each stamen is made up of a filament (stalk) and anther. The gynoecium has one or more carpels (female organs); each carpel consists of an ovary, style, and stigma. Some flowers (e.g., lily) occur singly on a pedicel (flower stalk); others (e.g., elder, sunflower) are arranged in a group (inflorescence) on a peduncle (inflorescence stalk).

EXTERNAL VIEW

Inner tepal (monocotyledonous petal)

Honey guide

Groove secreting nectar

Filament

Style

Outer tepal (monocotyledonous sepal)

Stigma

Anther

A MONOCOTYLEDONOUS FLOWER
Lily
(*Lilium sp.*)

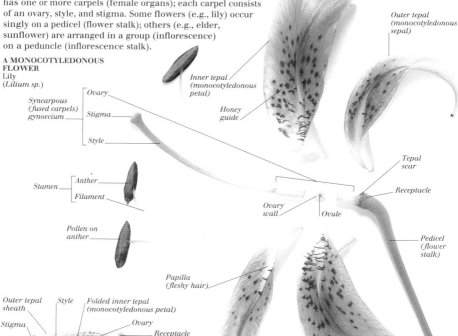

Ovary

Syncarpous (fused carpels) gynoecium

Stigma

Style

Inner tepal (monocotyledonous petal)

Honey guide

Outer tepal (monocotyledonous sepal)

Stamen

Anther

Filament

Pollen on anther

Tepal scar

Receptacle

Ovary wall

Ovule

Pedicel (flower stalk)

Papilla (fleshy hair)

Outer tepal sheath

Style

Folded inner tepal (monocotyledonous petal)

Stigma

Ovary

Receptacle

Anther

Pedicel (flower stalk)

Filament

LONGITUDINAL SECTION THROUGH FLOWER BUD

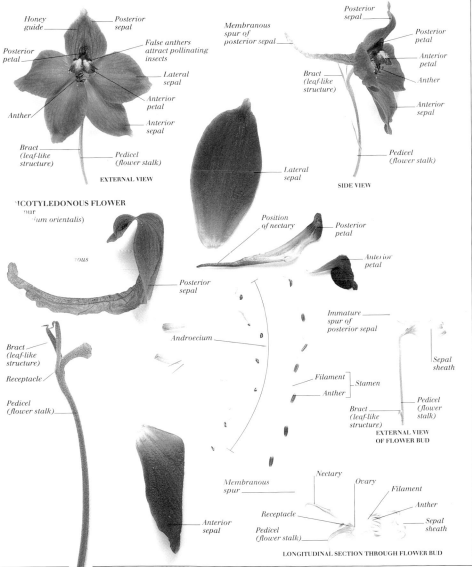

Honey guide

Posterior sepal

Posterior petal

False anthers attract insects pollinating insects

Lateral sepal

Anterior petal

Anther

Anterior sepal

Bract (leaf-like structure)

Pedicel (flower stalk)

EXTERNAL VIEW

Membranous spur of posterior sepal

Posterior sepal

Posterior petal

Anterior petal

Anther

Bract (leaf-like structure)

Anterior sepal

Pedicel (flower stalk)

SIDE VIEW

DICOTYLEDONOUS FLOWER

(Delphinium orientalis)

Lateral sepal

Membranous spur

Posterior sepal

Position of nectary

Posterior petal

Anterior petal

Bract (leaf-like structure)

Receptacle

Pedicel (flower stalk)

Androecium

Immature spur of posterior sepal

Sepal sheath

Filament

Anther

Stamen

Bract (leaf-like structure)

Pedicel (flower stalk)

EXTERNAL VIEW OF FLOWER BUD

Membranous spur

Nectary

Ovary

Filament

Anther

Receptacle

Pedicel (flower stalk)

Sepal sheath

Anterior sepal

LONGITUDINAL SECTION THROUGH FLOWER BUD

Flowers 2

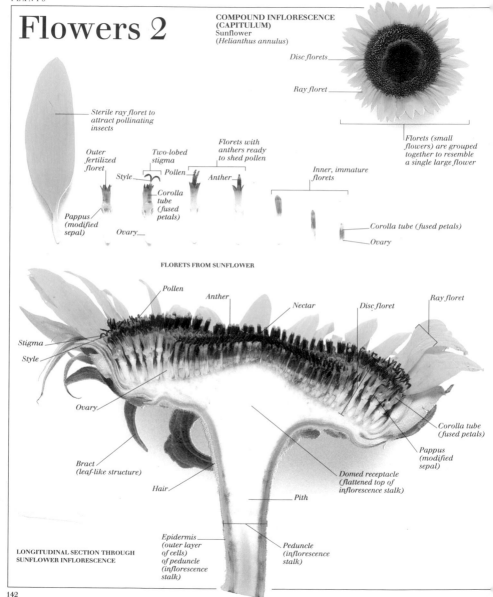

COMPOUND INFLORESCENCE (CAPITULUM)
Sunflower
(*Helianthus annulus*)

Disc florets

Ray floret

Florets (small flowers) are grouped together to resemble a single large flower

Sterile ray floret to attract pollinating insects

Outer fertilized floret

Two-lobed stigma

Style

Pollen

Florets with anthers ready to shed pollen

Anther

Inner, immature florets

Corolla tube (fused petals)

Pappus (modified sepal)

Ovary

Corolla tube (fused petals)

Ovary

FLORETS FROM SUNFLOWER

Pollen

Anther

Nectar

Disc floret

Ray floret

Stigma

Style

Ovary

Corolla tube (fused petals)

Pappus (modified sepal)

Bract (leaf-like structure)

Hair

Domed receptacle (flattened top of inflorescence stalk)

Pith

Epidermis (outer layer of cells) of peduncle (inflorescence stalk)

Peduncle (inflorescence stalk)

LONGITUDINAL SECTION THROUGH SUNFLOWER INFLORESCENCE

ARRANGEMENT OF FLOWERS ON STEM

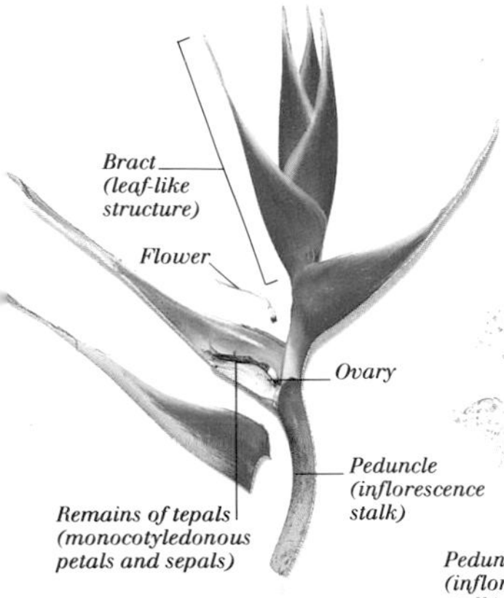

Bract
(leaf-like
structure)

Flower

Ovary

Peduncle
(inflorescence
stalk)

Remains of tepals
(monocotyledonous
petals and sepals)

INFLORESCENCE (SPIKE)
Heliconia peruviana

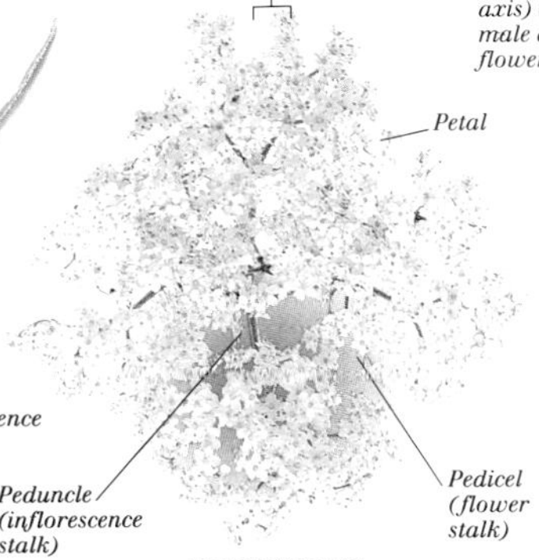

Flower

Petal

Peduncle
(inflorescence
stalk)

Pedicel
(flower
stalk)

**INFLORESCENCE
(COMPOUND UMBEL)**
Common elder
(*Sambucus nigra*)

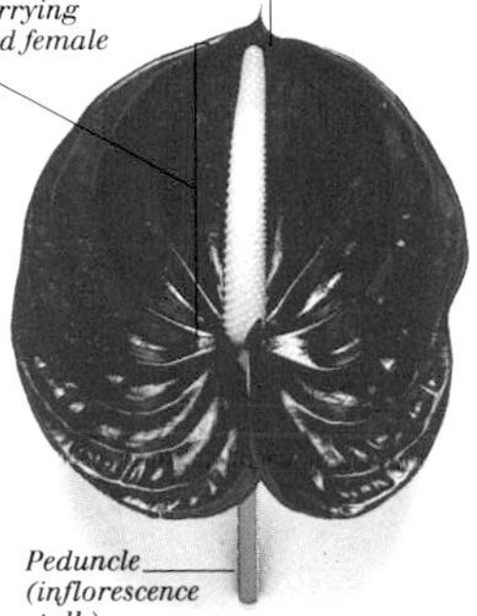

Spathe
(large bract) to
attract pollinating
insects

Spadix (fleshy
axis) carrying
male and female
flowers

Peduncle
(inflorescence
stalk)

INFLORESCENCE (SPADIX)
Painter's palette
(*Anthurium andreanum*)

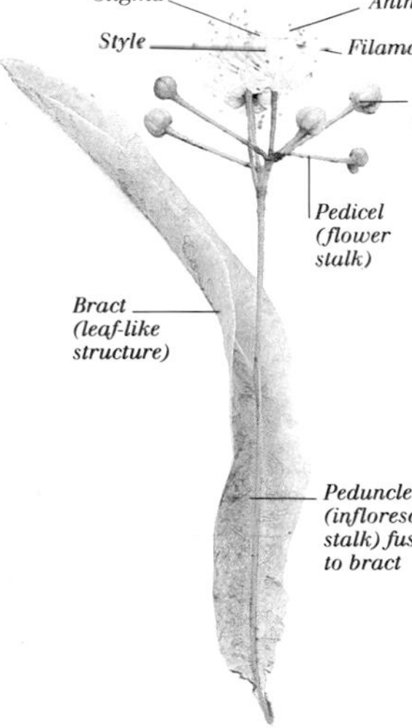

Stigma

Anther

Style

Filament

Stamen

Flower
bud

Pedicel
(flower
stalk)

Bract
(leaf-like
structure)

Peduncle
(inflorescence
stalk) fused
to bract

**INFLORESCENCE
(DICHASIAL CYME)**
Common lime
(*Tilia x europaea*)

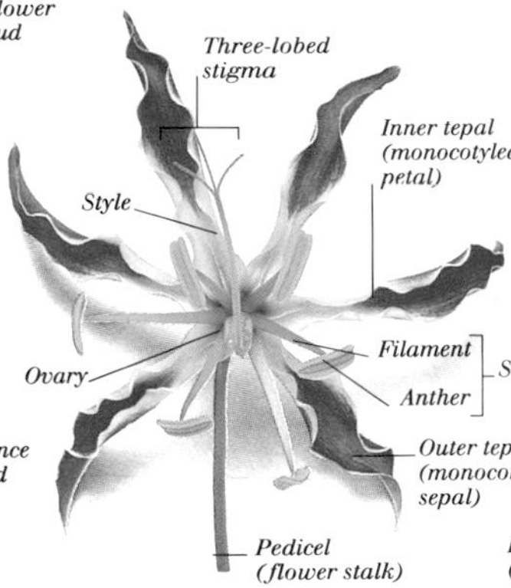

Three-lobed
stigma

Inner tepal
(monocotyledonous
petal)

Style

Ovary

Filament

Stamen

Anther

Outer tepal
(monocotyledonous
sepal)

Pedicel
(flower stalk)

SINGLE FLOWER
Glory lily
(*Gloriosa superba*)

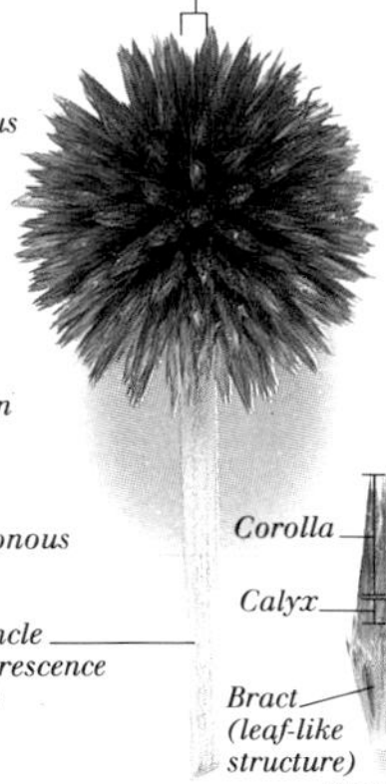

Flower

Peduncle
(inflorescence
stalk)

Corolla

Calyx

Bract
(leaf-like
structure)

**SINGLE
FLOWER**

**INFLORESCENCE
(SPHERICAL UMBEL)**
Allium sp.

Pollination

POLLINATION IS THE TRANSFER OF POLLEN (which contains the male sex cells) from an anther (part of the male reproductive organ) to a stigma (part of the female reproductive organ). This process precedes fertilization (see pp. 146-147). Pollination may occur within the same flower (self-pollination), or between flowers on separate plants of the same species (cross-pollination). In most plants, pollination is carried out either by insects (entomophilous pollination) or by the wind (anemophilous pollination). Less commonly, birds, bats, or water are the agents of pollination. Insect-pollinated flowers are typically brightly coloured, scented, and produce nectar, on which insects feed. Such flowers also tend to have patterns that are visible only in ultraviolet light, which many insects can see but which humans cannot. These features attract insects, which become covered with the sticky or hooked pollen grains when they visit one flower, and then transfer the pollen to the next flower they visit. Wind-pollinated flowers are generally small, relatively inconspicuous, and unscented. They produce large quantities of light pollen grains that are easily blown by the wind to other flowers.

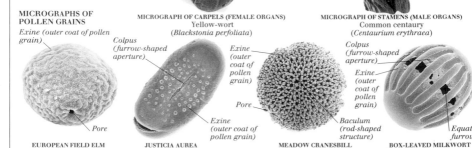

REPRODUCTIVE STRUCTURES IN WIND-POLLINATED PLANT
Sweet chestnut
(*Castanea sativa*)

Flower bud

Prominent stigma protrudes from flower

Female flower

Petiole (leaf stalk)

Bract (leaf-like structure)

Peduncle (inflorescence stalk)

Part of male catkin (inflorescence adapted for wind pollination)

Male flower

Peduncle (inflorescence stalk)

Filament

Anther

FEMALE   **MALE**

REPRODUCTIVE STRUCTURES IN INSECT-POLLINATED PLANTS

Stigma

Style

Dehisced (split open) pollen sac

Boundary between two fused carpels (each carpel consists of a stigma, style, and ovary)

Ovary

Endothecium (pollen sac wall)

Pollen grain

Anther

Filament

Stamen

Calyx (whorl of sepals)

MICROGRAPHS OF POLLEN GRAINS

Exine (outer coat of pollen grain)

Colpus (furrow-shaped aperture)

Pore

EUROPEAN FIELD ELM
(*Ulmus minor*)

MICROGRAPH OF CARPELS (FEMALE ORGANS)
Yellow-wort
(*Blackstonia perfoliata*)

Exine (outer coat of pollen grain)

Exine (outer coat of pollen grain)

JUSTICIA AUREA

Pore

MICROGRAPH OF STAMENS (MALE ORGANS)
Common centaury
(*Centaurium erythraea*)

Colpus (furrow-shaped aperture)

Exine (outer coat of pollen grain)

Baculum (rod-shaped structure)

MEADOW CRANESBILL
(*Geranium pratense*)

Equatorial furrow

BOX-LEAVED MILKWORT
(*Polygala chamaebuxus*)

INSECT POLLINATION OF MEADOW SAGE

Immature, unreceptive stigma

Sepal

Anther pushed on to bee's hairy abdomen

Labellum (lip) forming landing stage for bee

Pollen grains from anther stick to bee's abdomen

1. BEE VISITS FLOWER WITH MATURE ANTHERS BUT IMMATURE STIGMA

Pollen grains attached to hairy abdomen

Long style curves downwards when bee enters flower

Sepal

Mature, receptive stigma touches bee's abdomen, picking up pollen

Labellum (lip) forming landing stage for bee

2. BEE FLIES TO OTHER FLOWERS

3. BEE VISITS FLOWER WHERE THE ANTHERS HAVE WITHERED AND THE STIGMA IS MATURE

SUNFLOWER UNDER NORMAL AND ULTRAVIOLET LIGHT

Central area of disc florets

Ray floret

NORMAL LIGHT

Petal

Ovary

Stamen — *Filament*, *Anther*

Stigma

NORMAL LIGHT

ST JOHN'S WORT UNDER NORMAL AND ULTRAVIOLET LIGHT

Honey guide directs insects to dark, central part of flower

Paler, outer part of ray floret

Darker, inner part of ray floret

Insects attracted to darkest, central part of flower, which contains nectaries, anthers, and stigmas

Dark central area containing nectaries, anthers, and stigmas

ULTRAVIOLET LIGHT

ULTRAVIOLET LIGHT

Pore

Exine (outer coat of pollen grain)

Exine (outer coat of pollen grain)

MIMULOPSIS SOLMSII

Trilete mark (development scar)

Exine (outer coat of pollen grain)

THESIUM ALPINIUM

Columella (small column-shaped structure)

Exine (outer coat of pollen grain)

RUELLIA GRANDIFLORA

Colpus (furrow-shaped aperture)

Exine (outer coat of pollen grain)

Tricolpate (three colpae) pollen grain

CROSSANDRA NILOTICA

Fertilization

FERTILIZATION IS THE FUSION of male and female gametes (sex cells) to produce a zygote (embryo). Following pollination (see pp. 144-145), the pollen grains that contain the male gametes are on the stigma, some distance from the female gamete (ovum) inside the ovule. To enable the gametes to meet, the pollen grain germinates and produces a pollen tube, which grows down and enters the embryo sac (the inner part of the ovule that contains the ovum). Two male gametes, travelling at the tip of the pollen tube, enter the embryo sac. One gamete fuses with the ovum to produce a zygote that will develop into an embryo plant. The other male gamete fuses with two polar nuclei to produce the endosperm, which acts as a food store for the developing embryo. Fertilization also initiates other changes: the integument (outer part of ovule) forms a testa (seed coat) around the embryo and endosperm; the petals fall off; the stigma and style wither; and the ovary wall forms a layer (called the pericarp) around the seed. Together, the pericarp and seed form the fruit, which may be succulent (see pp. 148-149) or dry (see pp. 150-151). In some species (e.g., blackberry), apomixis can occur: the seed develops without fertilization of the ovum by a male gamete but endosperm formation and fruit development take place as in other species.

BANANA
(*Musa 'lacatan'*)

DEVELOPMENT OF A SUCCULENT FRUIT
Blackberry
(*Rubus fruticosus*)

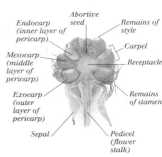

Petal
Stamen — Filament
Anther
Carpel — Ovary
Stigma
Style

**1. FLOWER IN FULL BLOOM
ATTRACTS POLLINATORS**

Endocarp (inner layer of pericarp)
Mesocarp (middle layer of pericarp)
Exocarp (outer layer of pericarp)
Sepal
Abortive seed
Remains of style
Carpel
Receptacle
Remains of stamen
Pedicel (flower stalk)

**4. PERICARP FORMS
FLESH, SKIN, AND A HARD INNER
LAYER (SHOWN IN CROSS-SECTION)**

Exocarp (outer layer of pericarp)
Carpel
Remains of style
Remains of stamen
Remains of sepal
Pedicel (flower stalk)

**7. MESOCARP (FLESHY PART OF PERICARP)
OF EACH CARPEL STARTS TO
CHANGE COLOUR**

Exocarp (outer layer of pericarp)
Drupelet
Remains of style
Remains of stamen
Remains of sepal
Pedicel (flower stalk)

**8. CARPELS MATURE INTO DRUPELETS
(SMALL FLESHY FRUITS WITH SINGLE SEEDS
SURROUNDED BY HARD ENDOCARP)**

Exocarp (outer layer of pericarp)
Drupelet
Remains of style
Remains of stamen
Remains of sepal
Pedicel (flower stalk)

**9. MESOCARP OF DRUPELET BECOMES
DARKER AND SWEETER**

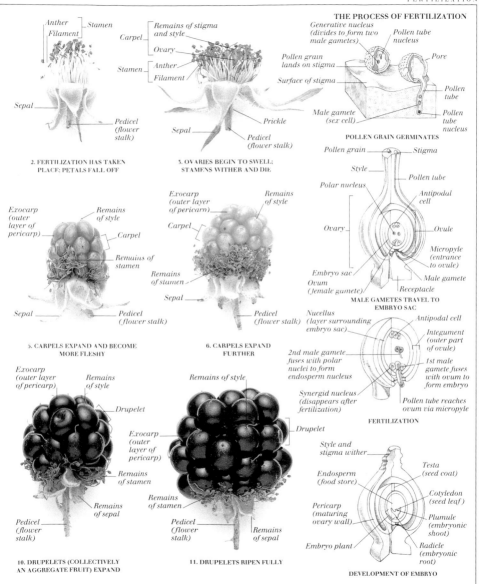

THE PROCESS OF FERTILIZATION

Anther ⌉
Filament ⌉ Stamen
Sepal
Pedicel (flower stalk)

2. FERTILIZATION HAS TAKEN PLACE; PETALS FALL OFF

Remains of stigma and style
Carpel
Ovary
Stamen
Anther
Filament
Prickle
Sepal
Pedicel (flower stalk)

5. OVARIES BEGIN TO SWELL; STAMENS WITHER AND DIE

Generative nucleus (divides to form two male gametes)
Pollen tube nucleus
Pollen grain lands on stigma
Pore
Surface of stigma
Male gamete (sex cell)
Pollen tube
Pollen tube nucleus

POLLEN GRAIN GERMINATES

Exocarp (outer layer of pericarp)
Remains of style
Carpel
Remains of stamen
Sepal
Pedicel (flower stalk)

5. CARPELS EXPAND AND BECOME MORE FLESHY

Exocarp (outer layer of pericarp)
Remains of style
Carpel
Remains of stamen
Sepal
Pedicel (flower stalk)

6. CARPELS EXPAND FURTHER

Pollen grain
Stigma
Style
Pollen tube
Polar nucleus
Antipodal cell
Ovary
Ovule
Micropyle (entrance to ovule)
Embryo sac
Male gamete
Ovum (female gamete)
Receptacle

MALE GAMETES TRAVEL TO EMBRYO SAC

Exocarp (outer layer of pericarp)
Remains of style
Drupelet
Remains of stamen
Remains of sepal
Pedicel (flower stalk)

10. DRUPELETS (COLLECTIVELY AN AGGREGATE FRUIT) EXPAND

Remains of style
Exocarp (outer layer of pericarp)
Drupelet
Remains of stamen
Pedicel (flower stalk)
Remains of sepal

11. DRUPELETS RIPEN FULLY

Nucellus (layer surrounding embryo sac)
Antipodal cell
Integument (outer part of ovule)
2nd male gamete fuses with polar nuclei to form endosperm nucleus
1st male gamete fuses with ovum to form embryo
Synergid nucleus (disappears after fertilization)
Pollen tube reaches ovum via micropyle

FERTILIZATION

Style and stigma wither
Testa (seed coat)
Endosperm (food store)
Cotyledon (seed leaf)
Pericarp (maturing ovary wall)
Plumule (embryonic shoot)
Embryo plant
Radicle (embryonic root)

DEVELOPMENT OF EMBRYO

Succulent fruits

A FRUIT IS A FULLY DEVELOPED and ripened ovary (seed-producing part of a plant's female reproductive organs). Fruits may be succulent or dry (see pp. 150-151). Succulent fruits are fleshy and brightly coloured, making them attractive to animals, which eat them and so disperse the seeds away from the parent plant. The wall (pericarp) of a succulent fruit has three layers: an outer exocarp, a middle mesocarp, and an inner endocarp. These three layers vary in thickness and texture in different types of fruits and may blend into each other. Succulent fruits can be classed as simple (derived from one ovary) or compound (derived from several ovaries). Simple succulent fruits include berries, which typically have many seeds, and drupes, which typically have a single stone or pip (e.g., cherry and peach). Compound succulent fruits include aggregate fruits, which are formed from many ovaries in one flower, and multiple fruits, which develop from the ovaries of many flowers. Some fruits, known as false fruits or pseudocarps, develop from parts of the flower in addition to the ovaries. For example, the flesh of the apple is formed from the receptacle (the upper end of the flower stalk).

BERRY
Cocoa
(*Theobroma cacao*)

HESPERIDIUM (A TYPE OF BERRY)
Lemon
(*Citrus limon*)

Pedicel (flower stalk)

Endocarp

Pedicel (flower stalk)

Exocarp

Mesocarp

Leathery exocarp

Oil gland

Remains of style

Seed

Vesicle (juice sac)

Remains of style

Placenta

EXTERNAL VIEW OF FRUIT

LONGITUDINAL SECTION THROUGH FRUIT

Hilum (point of attachment to ovary)

Embryo

Seed

Carpel wall

Carpel

Testa (seed coat)

Cotyledon (seed leaf)

Placenta

EXTERNAL VIEW AND SECTION THROUGH SEED

CROSS-SECTION THROUGH FRUIT

SYCONIUM (A TYPE OF FALSE FRUIT)
Fig
(*Ficus carica*)

Remains of female flowers

Fleshy infolded receptacle

Peduncle (inflorescence stalk)

Pip (seed surrounded by endocarp)

Remains of male flowers

Skin

Pore closed by scales

EXTERNAL VIEW OF FRUIT

LONGITUDINAL SECTION THROUGH FRUIT

FRUIT WITH FLESHY ARIL
Lychee
(*Litchi chinensis*)

Pedicel (flower stalk)

Pedicel (flower stalk)

Seed

Aril (fleshy outgrowth from seed stalk)

Pericarp (fruit wall)

Pericarp (fruit wall)

Remains of style

Endocarp

EXTERNAL VIEW AND SECTION THROUGH PIP

Drupelet

Pip

Pedicel (flower stalk)

Endocarp

Cotyledon (seed leaf)

Embryo

Testa (seed coat)

EXTERNAL VIEW OF FRUIT

LONGITUDINAL SECTION THROUGH FRUIT

REMAINS OF A SINGLE FEMALE FLOWER

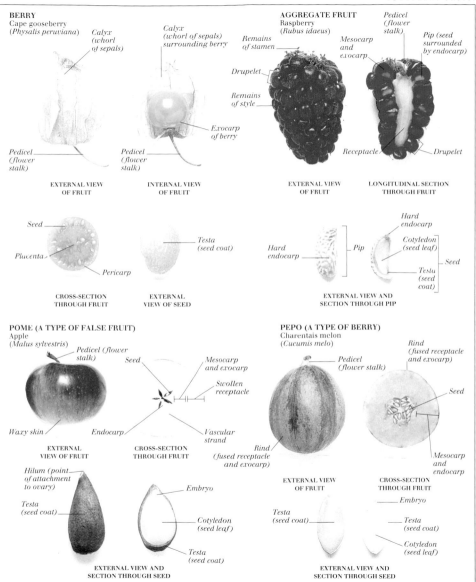

BERRY
Cape gooseberry
(*Physalis peruviana*)

Calyx (whorl of sepals)

Calyx (whorl of sepals) surrounding berry

Pedicel (flower stalk)

Exocarp of berry

Pedicel (flower stalk)

EXTERNAL VIEW OF FRUIT

INTERNAL VIEW OF FRUIT

Seed

Placenta

Pericarp

Testa (seed coat)

CROSS-SECTION THROUGH FRUIT

EXTERNAL VIEW OF SEED

AGGREGATE FRUIT
Raspberry
(*Rubus idaeus*)

Remains of stamen

Drupelet

Remains of style

Pedicel (flower stalk)

Mesocarp and exocarp

Pip (seed surrounded by endocarp)

Receptacle

Drupelet

EXTERNAL VIEW OF FRUIT

LONGITUDINAL SECTION THROUGH FRUIT

Hard endocarp

Pip

Hard endocarp

Cotyledon (seed leaf)

Seed

Testa (seed coat)

EXTERNAL VIEW AND SECTION THROUGH PIP

POME (A TYPE OF FALSE FRUIT)
Apple
(*Malus sylvestris*)

Pedicel (flower stalk)

Seed

Mesocarp and exocarp

Swollen receptacle

Waxy skin

Endocarp

Vascular strand

EXTERNAL VIEW OF FRUIT

CROSS-SECTION THROUGH FRUIT

Hilum (point of attachment to ovary)

Testa (seed coat)

Embryo

Cotyledon (seed leaf)

Testa (seed coat)

EXTERNAL VIEW AND SECTION THROUGH SEED

PEPO (A TYPE OF BERRY)
Charentais melon
(*Cucumis melo*)

Pedicel (flower stalk)

Rind (fused receptacle and exocarp)

Seed

Rind (fused receptacle and exocarp)

Mesocarp and endocarp

EXTERNAL VIEW OF FRUIT

CROSS-SECTION THROUGH FRUIT

Testa (seed coat)

Embryo

Testa (seed coat)

Cotyledon (seed leaf)

EXTERNAL VIEW AND SECTION THROUGH SEED

Dry fruits

DRY FRUITS HAVE A HARD, DRY PERICARP (fruit wall) around their seeds unlike succulent fruits, which have fleshy pericarps (see pp. 148-149). Dry fruits are divided into three types: dehiscent, in which the pericarp splits open to release the seeds; indehiscent, which do not split open; and schizocarpic, in which the fruit splits but the seeds are not exposed. Dehiscent dry fruits include capsules (e.g., love-in-a-mist), follicles (e.g., delphinium), legumes (e.g., pea), and siliquas (e.g., honesty). Typically, the seeds of dehiscent fruits are dispersed by the wind. Indehiscent dry fruits include nuts (e.g., sweet chestnut), nutlets (e.g., goosegrass), achenes (e.g., strawberry), caryopses (e.g., wheat), samaras (e.g., elm), and cypselas (e.g., dandelion). Some indehiscent dry fruits are dispersed by the wind, assisted by "wings" (e.g., elm) or "parachutes" (e.g., dandelion); others (e.g., goosegrass) have hooked pericarps to aid dispersal on animals' fur. Schizocarpic dry fruits include cremocarps (e.g., hogweed), and double samaras (e.g., sycamore); these are dispersed by the wind.

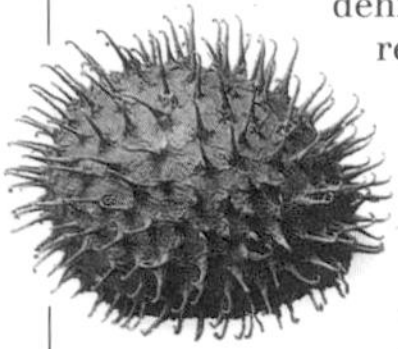

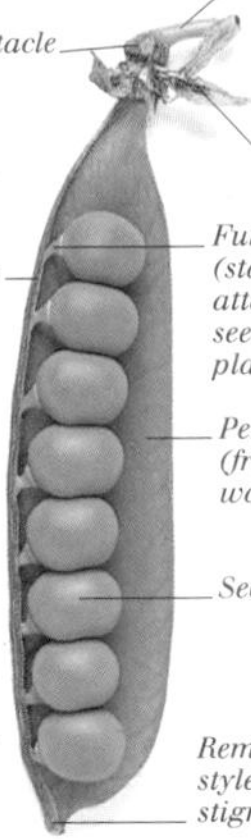

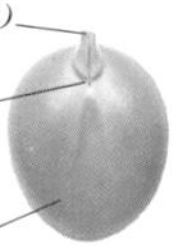

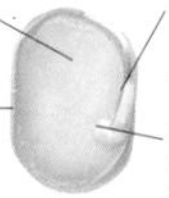

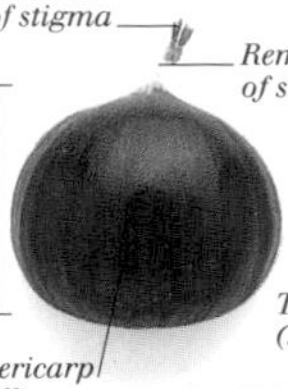

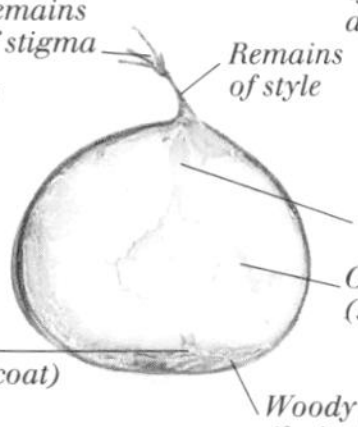

NUTLET
Goosegrass
(*Galium aparine*)

LEGUME
Pea
(*Pisum sativum*)

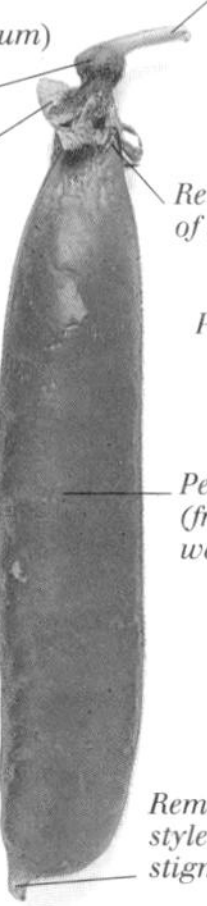

NUT
Sweet chestnut
(*Castanea sativa*)

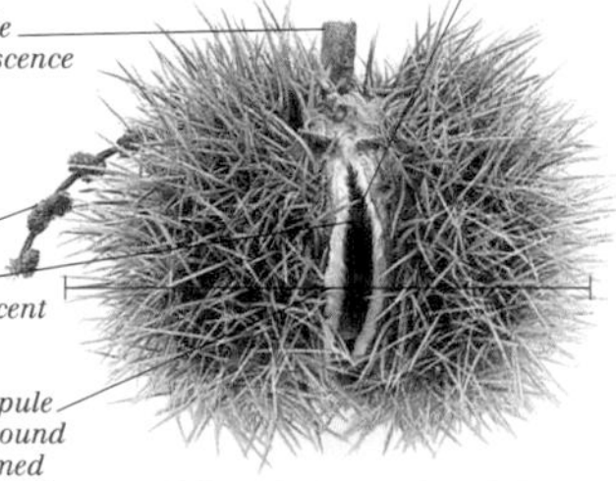

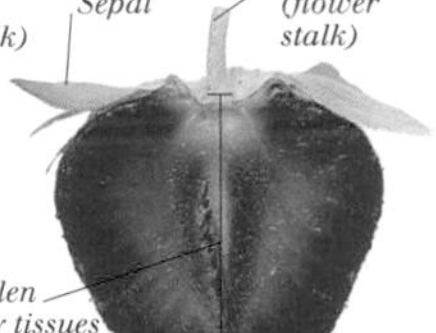

ACHENE
Strawberry
(*Fragaria x ananassa*)

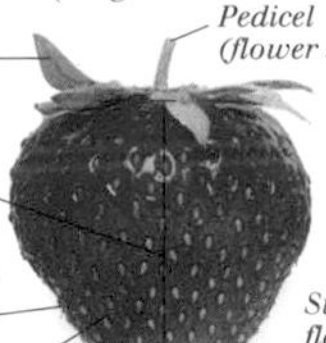

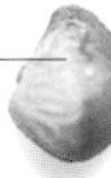

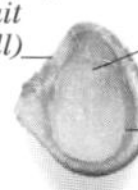

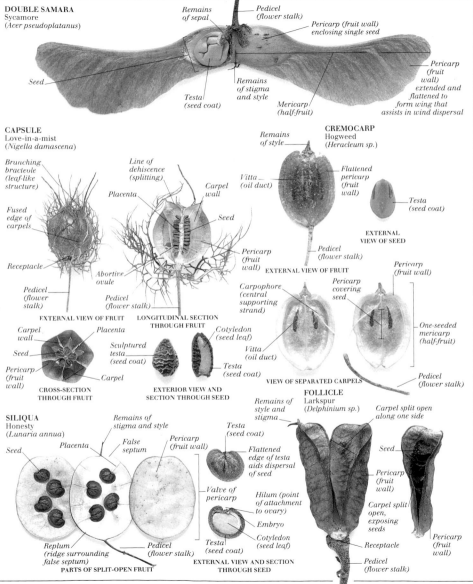

DOUBLE SAMARA
Sycamore
(*Acer pseudoplatanus*)

Remains of sepal

Pedicel (flower stalk)

Pericarp (fruit wall) enclosing single seed

Seed

Testa (seed coat)

Remains of stigma and style

Mericarp (half-fruit)

Pericarp (fruit wall) extended and flattened to form wing that assists in wind dispersal

CAPSULE
Love-in-a-mist
(*Nigella damascena*)

Branching bracteole (leaf-like structure)

Fused edge of carpels

Receptacle

Pedicel (flower stalk)

Line of dehiscence (splitting)

Placenta

Carpel wall

Seed

Pericarp (fruit wall)

Abortive ovule

Pedicel (flower stalk)

EXTERNAL VIEW OF FRUIT

LONGITUDINAL SECTION THROUGH FRUIT

Carpel wall

Placenta

Seed

Pericarp (fruit wall)

Carpel

CROSS-SECTION THROUGH FRUIT

Sculptured testa (seed coat)

Cotyledon (seed leaf)

Testa (seed coat)

EXTERIOR VIEW AND SECTION THROUGH SEED

CREMOCARP
Hogweed
(*Heracleum sp.*)

Remains of style

Vitta (oil duct)

Flattened pericarp (fruit wall)

Testa (seed coat)

EXTERNAL VIEW OF SEED

Pedicel (flower stalk)

EXTERNAL VIEW OF FRUIT

Carpophore (central supporting strand)

Vitta (oil duct)

Pericarp (fruit wall)

Pericarp covering seed

One-seeded mericarp (half-fruit)

Pedicel (flower stalk)

VIEW OF SEPARATED CARPELS

SILIQUA
Honesty
(*Lunaria annua*)

Seed

Remains of stigma and style

False septum

Placenta

Pericarp (fruit wall)

Replum (ridge surrounding false septum)

Pedicel (flower stalk)

PARTS OF SPLIT-OPEN FRUIT

Testa (seed coat)

Flattened edge of testa aids dispersal of seed

Valve of pericarp

Hilum (point of attachment to ovary)

Embryo

Testa (seed coat)

Cotyledon (seed leaf)

EXTERNAL VIEW AND SECTION THROUGH SEED

FOLLICLE
Larkspur
(*Delphinium sp.*)

Remains of style and stigma

Carpel split open along one side

Seed

Pericarp (fruit wall)

Carpel split open, exposing seeds

Receptacle

Pericarp (fruit wall)

Pedicel (flower stalk)

Germination

GERMINATION IS THE GROWTH OF SEEDS INTO SEEDLINGS. It starts when seeds become active below ground, and ends when the first foliage leaves appear above ground. A seed consists of an embryo and its food store, surrounded by a testa (seed coat). The embryo is made up of one or two cotyledons (seed leaves) attached to a central axis. The upper part of the axis consists of an epicotyl, which has a plumule (embryonic shoot) at its tip. The lower part of the axis consists of a hypocotyl and a radicle (embryonic root). After dispersal from the parent plant, the seeds dehydrate and enter a period of dormancy. Following this dormant period, germination begins, provided that the seeds have enough water, oxygen, warmth, and, in some cases, light. In the first stages of germination, the seed takes in water; the embryo starts to use its food store; and the radicle swells, breaks through the testa, and grows downwards. Germination then proceeds in one of two ways, depending on the type of seed. In epigeal germination, the hypocotyl lengthens, pulling the plumule and its protective cotyledons out of the soil. In hypogeal germination, the cotyledons remain below ground and the epicotyl lengthens, pushing the plumule upwards.

HYPOGEAL GERMINATION
Broad bean
(*Vicia faba*)

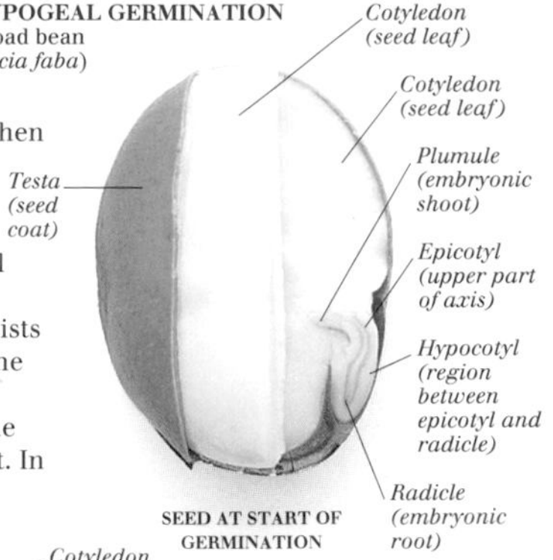

Cotyledon (seed leaf)

Cotyledon (seed leaf)

Plumule (embryonic shoot)

Testa (seed coat)

Epicotyl (upper part of axis)

Hypocotyl (region between epicotyl and radicle)

Radicle (embryonic root)

SEED AT START OF GERMINATION

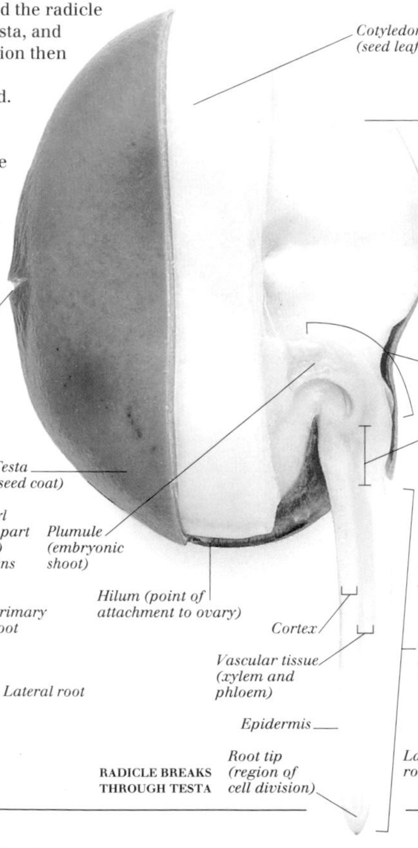

Cotyledon (seed leaf)

Foliage leaf

Cotyledon (seed leaf)

Stipule (structure at base of leaf)

Epicotyl increases in length and turns green

Cataphyll (scale leaf of plumule)

Epicotyl (upper part of axis)

Hypocotyl (region between epicotyl and radicle)

FOLIAGE LEAVES APPEAR

Cotyledons (seed leaves) remain food source for the seedling

Primary root

Radicle (embryonic root)

Lateral root system

Split in testa (seed coat) due to expanding cotyledons

Young shoot

Cataphyll (scale leaf of plumule)

Testa (seed coat)

Epicotyl (upper part of axis) lengthens

Plumule (embryonic shoot)

Hilum (point of attachment to ovary)

Cortex

Vascular tissue (xylem and phloem)

Epidermis

Root tip (region of cell division)

Cotyledons (seed leaves) remain within testa (seed coat) below soil's surface

Primary root

Lateral root

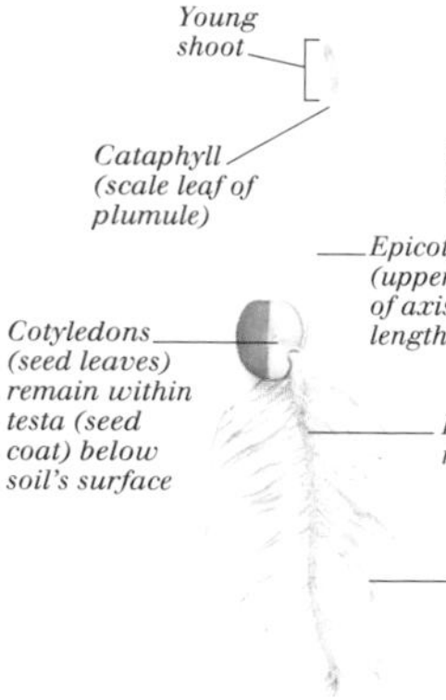

SHOOT APPEARS ABOVE SOIL

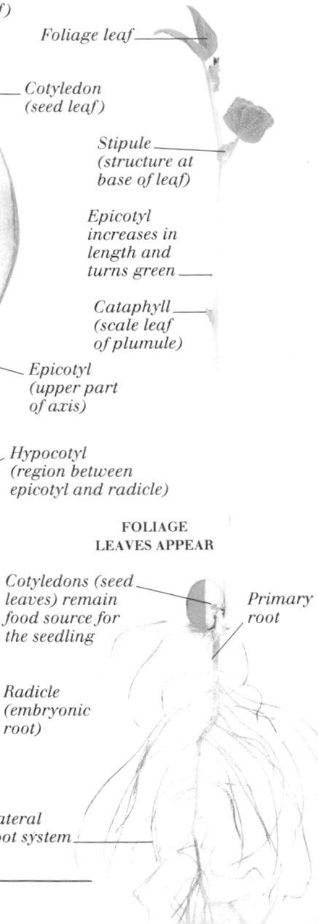

RADICLE BREAKS THROUGH TESTA

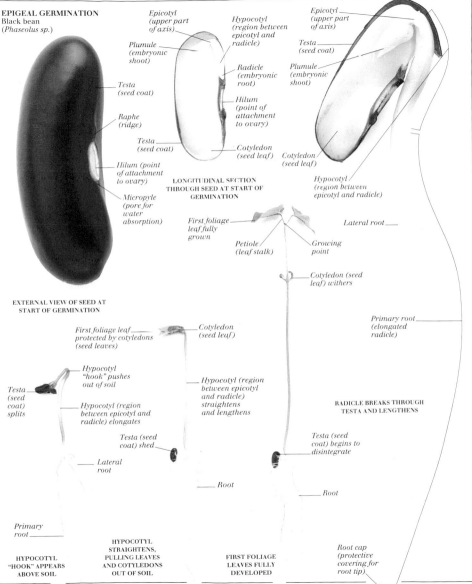

EPIGEAL GERMINATION
Black bean
(*Phaseolus sp.*)

Epicotyl (upper part of axis)

Plumule (embryonic shoot)

Hypocotyl (region between epicotyl and radicle)

Testa (seed coat)

Radicle (embryonic root)

Hilum (point of attachment to ovary)

Testa (seed coat)

Cotyledon (seed leaf)

LONGITUDINAL SECTION THROUGH SEED AT START OF GERMINATION

Epicotyl (upper part of axis)

Testa (seed coat)

Plumule (embryonic shoot)

Cotyledon (seed leaf)

Hypocotyl (region between epicotyl and radicle)

Lateral root

Testa (seed coat)

Raphe (ridge)

Hilum (point of attachment to ovary)

Micropyle (pore for water absorption)

EXTERNAL VIEW OF SEED AT START OF GERMINATION

First foliage leaf fully grown

Petiole (leaf stalk)

Growing point

Cotyledon (seed leaf) withers

Primary root (elongated radicle)

First foliage leaf protected by cotyledons (seed leaves)

Cotyledon (seed leaf)

Hypocotyl "hook" pushes out of soil

Testa (seed coat) splits

Hypocotyl (region between epicotyl and radicle) elongates

Hypocotyl (region between epicotyl and radicle) straightens and lengthens

RADICLE BREAKS THROUGH TESTA AND LENGTHENS

Testa (seed coat) shed

Testa (seed coat) begins to disintegrate

Lateral root

Root

Root

Primary root

HYPOCOTYL "HOOK" APPEARS ABOVE SOIL

HYPOCOTYL STRAIGHTENS, PULLING LEAVES AND COTYLEDONS OUT OF SOIL

FIRST FOLIAGE LEAVES FULLY DEVELOPED

Root cap (protective covering for root tip)

Vegetative reproduction

ADVENTITIOUS BUD
Mexican hat plant
(*Kalanchoe
daigremontiana*)

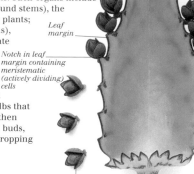

Apex of
leaf

MANY PLANTS CAN PROPAGATE THEMSELVES by vegetative reproduction. In this process, part of a plant separates off, takes root, and grows into a new plant. Vegetative reproduction is a type of asexual reproduction; that is, it involves only one parent, and there is no fusion of gametes (sex cells). Plants use various structures to reproduce vegetatively. Some plants use underground storage organs. Such organs include rhizomes (horizontal, underground stems), the branches of which produce new plants; bulbs (swollen leaf bases) and corms (swollen stems), which produce daughter bulbs or corms that separate off from the parent; and stem tubers (thickened underground stems) and root tubers (swollen adventitious roots), which also separate off from the parent. Other propagative structures include runners and stolons, creeping horizontal stems that take root and produce new plants; bulbils, small bulbs that develop on the stem or in the place of flowers, and then drop off and grow into new plants; and adventitious buds, miniature plants that form on leaf margins before dropping to the ground and growing into mature plants.

CORM
Gladiolus
(*Gladiolus sp.*)

Lamina
(blade) of
leaf

Leaf
margin

Notch in leaf
margin containing
meristematic
(actively dividing)
cells

Adventitious bud
(detachable bud
with adventitious
roots) drops
from leaf

Petiole
(leaf stalk)

BULBIL IN PLACE OF FLOWER
Orange lily
(*Lilium bulbiferum*)

Scar left
by flower

Leaf

Pedicel
(flower stalk)

Terminal
bud

Internode

Node

Node

STOLON
Ground ivy
(*Glechoma hederacea*)

Parent
plant

Stolon
(creeping stem)

Detachable
bulbil formed
in place of
flower

Peduncle
(inflorescence
stalk)

Adventitious root
of daughter plant

Daughter plant
developed from
lateral bud

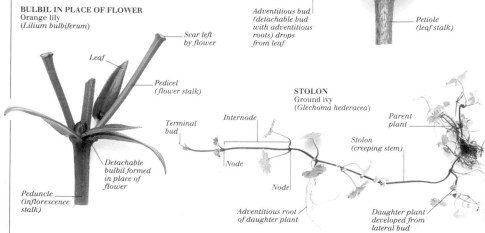

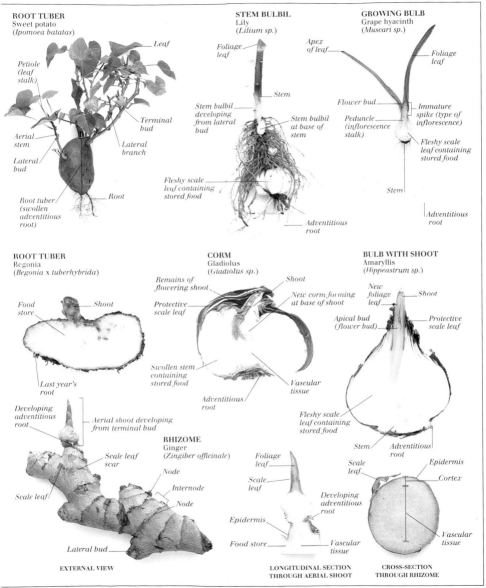

ROOT TUBER
Sweet potato
(*Ipomoea batatas*)

Leaf

Petiole
(leaf
stalk)

Terminal
bud

Aerial
stem

Lateral
branch

Lateral
bud

Root tuber
(swollen
adventitious
root)

Root

STEM BULBIL
Lily
(*Lilium sp.*)

Foliage
leaf

Stem

Stem bulbil
developing
from lateral
bud

Stem bulbil
at base of
stem

Fleshy scale
leaf containing
stored food

Adventitious
root

GROWING BULB
Grape hyacinth
(*Muscari sp.*)

Apex
of leaf

Foliage
leaf

Flower bud

Immature
spike (type of
inflorescence)

Peduncle
(inflorescence
stalk)

Fleshy scale
leaf containing
stored food

Stem

Adventitious
root

ROOT TUBER
Begonia
(*Begonia x tuberhybrida*)

Food
store

Shoot

Last year's
root

Developing
adventitious
root

Aerial shoot developing
from terminal bud

Scale leaf
scar

Node

Internode

Node

Scale leaf

Lateral bud

EXTERNAL VIEW

CORM
Gladiolus
(*Gladiolus sp.*)

Remains of
flowering shoot

Protective
scale leaf

Shoot

New corm forming
at base of shoot

Swollen stem
containing
stored food

Vascular
tissue

Adventitious
root

RHIZOME
Ginger
(*Zingiber officinale*)

Foliage
leaf

Scale
leaf

Developing
adventitious
root

Epidermis

Food store

Vascular
tissue

**LONGITUDINAL SECTION
THROUGH AERIAL SHOOT**

BULB WITH SHOOT
Amaryllis
(*Hippeastrum sp.*)

New
foliage
leaf

Shoot

Apical bud
(flower bud)

Protective
scale leaf

Fleshy scale
leaf containing
stored food

Stem

Adventitious
root

Scale
leaf

Epidermis

Cortex

Vascular
tissue

**CROSS-SECTION
THROUGH RHIZOME**

Dryland plants

DRYLAND PLANTS (XEROPHYTES) are able to survive in unfavourable habitats. All are found in places where little water is available; some live in high temperatures that cause excessive loss of water from the leaves. Xerophytes show a number of adaptations to dry conditions; these include reduced leaf area, rolled leaves, sunken stomata, hairs, spines, and thick cuticles. One group, succulent plants, stores water in specially enlarged spongy tissues found in leaves, roots, or stems. Leaf succulents have enlarged, fleshy, water-storing leaves. Root succulents have a large, underground water-storage organ with short-lived stems and leaves above ground. Stem succulents are represented by the cacti (family Cactaceae). Cacti stems are fleshy, green, and photosynthetic; they are typically ribbed or covered by tubercles in rows, with leaves being reduced to spines or entirely absent.

LEAF SUCCULENT
Lithops sp.

STEM SUCCULENT
Golden barrel cactus
(*Echinocactus grusonii*)

Areole
(modified
lateral shoot)

Trichome
(hair)

Spine
(modified
leaf)

Waxy cuticle
(waterproof
covering)

Water-storing
parenchyma
(packing tissue)

Tubercle
(projection
from stem
surface)

Vascular
cylinder
(transport
tissue)

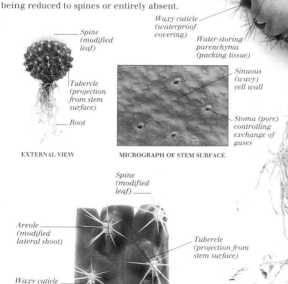

Spine
(modified
leaf)

Tubercle
(projection
from stem
surface)

Root

Sinuous
(wavy)
cell wall

Stoma (pore)
controlling
exchange of
gases

Root

EXTERNAL VIEW

MICROGRAPH OF STEM SURFACE

Spine
(modified
leaf)

Areole
(modified
lateral shoot)

Tubercle
(projection from
stem surface)

Waxy cuticle
(waterproof
covering)

DETAIL OF STEM SURFACE

**LONGITUDINAL SECTION
THROUGH STEM**

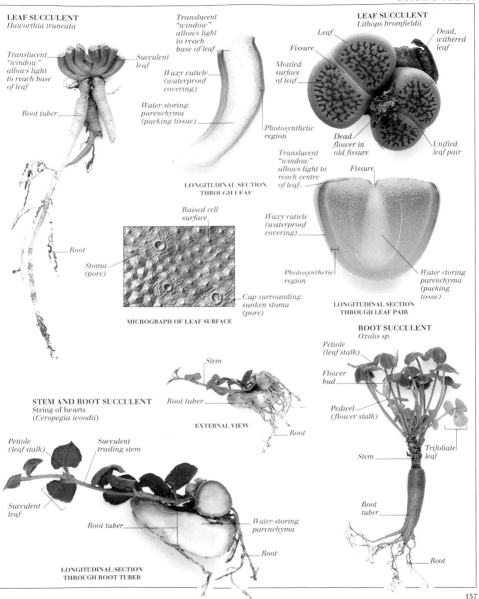

LEAF SUCCULENT
Haworthia truncata

Translucent "window" allows light to reach base of leaf

Succulent leaf

Root tuber

Root

Translucent "window" allows light to reach base of leaf

Waxy cuticle (waterproof covering)

Water-storing parenchyma (packing tissue)

Photosynthetic region

LONGITUDINAL SECTION THROUGH LEAF

Raised cell surface

Stoma (pore)

Cup surrounding sunken stoma (pore)

MICROGRAPH OF LEAF SURFACE

LEAF SUCCULENT
Lithops bromfieldii

Leaf

Fissure

Mottled surface of leaf

Dead, withered leaf

Dead flower in old fissure

Unified leaf pair

Translucent "window" allows light to reach centre of leaf

Fissure

Waxy cuticle (waterproof covering)

Photosynthetic region

Water storing parenchyma (packing tissue)

LONGITUDINAL SECTION THROUGH LEAF PAIR

ROOT SUCCULENT
Oxalis sp.

Petiole (leaf stalk)

Flower bud

Pedicel (flower stalk)

Trifoliate leaf

Stem

Root tuber

Root

STEM AND ROOT SUCCULENT
String of hearts
(*Ceropegia woodii*)

Stem

Root tuber

Root

EXTERNAL VIEW

Petiole (leaf stalk)

Succulent trailing stem

Succulent leaf

Root tuber

Water-storing parenchyma

Root

LONGITUDINAL SECTION THROUGH ROOT TUBER

157

Wetland plants

WETLAND PLANTS GROW SUBMERGED IN WATER, either partially (e.g., water hyacinth) or completely (e.g., pond weeds), and show various adaptations to this habitat. Typically, there are numerous air spaces inside the stems, leaves, and roots; these aid gas exchange and buoyancy. Submerged parts generally have no cuticle (waterproof covering), enabling the plants to absorb minerals and gases directly from the water; in addition, being supported by the water, they need little of the supportive tissue found in land plants. Stomata, the gas exchange pores, are absent from plants that are completely submerged; in partially submerged plants with floating leaves (e.g., water lilies), stomata are found on the upper leaf surfaces, where they cannot be flooded.

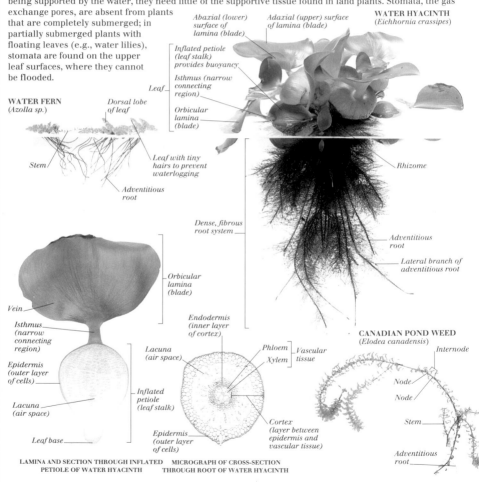

WATER HYACINTH
(*Eichhornia crassipes*)

Abaxial (lower) surface of lamina (blade)

Adaxial (upper) surface of lamina (blade)

Inflated petiole (leaf stalk) provides buoyancy

Isthmus (narrow connecting region)

Leaf

Orbicular lamina (blade)

WATER FERN
(*Azolla sp.*)

Dorsal lobe of leaf

Stem

Leaf with tiny hairs to prevent waterlogging

Adventitious root

Rhizome

Dense, fibrous root system

Adventitious root

Lateral branch of adventitious root

Orbicular lamina (blade)

Vein

Isthmus (narrow connecting region)

Epidermis (outer layer of cells)

Lacuna (air space)

Leaf base

Endodermis (inner layer of cortex)

Lacuna (air space)

Inflated petiole (leaf stalk)

Epidermis (outer layer of cells)

Phloem — Vascular
Xylem — tissue

Cortex (layer between epidermis and vascular tissue)

CANADIAN POND WEED
(*Elodea canadensis*)

Internode

Node

Node

Stem

Adventitious root

LAMINA AND SECTION THROUGH INFLATED PETIOLE OF WATER HYACINTH

MICROGRAPH OF CROSS-SECTION THROUGH ROOT OF WATER HYACINTH

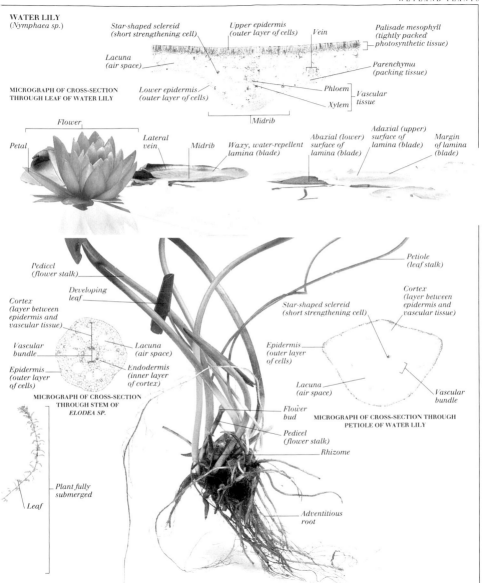

WATER LILY
(*Nymphaea sp.*)

Star-shaped sclereid
(short strengthening cell)

Upper epidermis
(outer layer of cells)

Vein

Palisade mesophyll
(tightly packed
photosynthetic tissue)

Lacuna
(air space)

Parenchyma
(packing tissue)

MICROGRAPH OF CROSS-SECTION
THROUGH LEAF OF WATER LILY

Lower epidermis
(outer layer of cells)

Phloem
Xylem

Vascular
tissue

Midrib

Flower

Petal

Lateral
vein

Midrib

Waxy, water-repellent
lamina (blade)

Abaxial (lower)
surface of
lamina (blade)

Adaxial (upper)
surface of
lamina (blade)

Margin
of lamina
(blade)

Pedicel
(flower stalk)

Petiole
(leaf stalk)

Developing
leaf

Cortex
(layer between
epidermis and
vascular tissue)

Star-shaped sclereid
(short strengthening cell)

Cortex
(layer between
epidermis and
vascular tissue)

Vascular
bundle

Lacuna
(air space)

Epidermis
(outer layer
of cells)

Epidermis
(outer layer
of cells)

Endodermis
(inner layer
of cortex)

Lacuna
(air space)

Vascular
bundle

MICROGRAPH OF CROSS-SECTION
THROUGH STEM OF
ELODEA SP.

Flower
bud

MICROGRAPH OF CROSS-SECTION THROUGH
PETIOLE OF WATER LILY

Pedicel
(flower stalk)

Rhizome

Plant fully
submerged

Leaf

Adventitious
root

Carnivorous plants

Areola ("window" of transparent tissue)

Fishtail nectary

Wing

Hood

Pitcher

Tubular petiole (leaf stalk)

Areola ("window" of transparent tissue)

CARNIVOROUS (INSECTIVOROUS) PLANTS FEED ON INSECTS and other small animals, in addition to producing food in their leaves by photosynthesis. The nutrients absorbed from trapped insects enable carnivorous plants to thrive in acid, boggy soils that lack essential minerals, especially nitrates, where most other plants could not survive. All carnivorous plants have some leaves modified as traps; many use bright colours and scented nectar to attract prey; and most use enzymes to digest the prey. There are three types of traps. Pitcher plants, such as the monkey cup and cobra lily, have leaves modified as pitcher-shaped pitfall traps, half-filled with water; once lured inside the mouth of the trap, insects lose their footing on the slippery surface, fall into the liquid, and either decompose or are digested. Venus fly traps use a spring-trap mechanism; when an insect touches trigger hairs on the inner surfaces of the leaves, the two lobes of the trap snap shut. Butterworts and sundews entangle prey by sticky droplets on the leaf surface, while the edges of the leaves slowly curl over to envelop and digest the prey.

Smooth surface

Nectar roll

Dome-shaped hood develops

Fishtail nectary appears

Immature pitcher

Mouth

Wing

Downward pointing hair

DEVELOPMENT OF MODIFIED LEAF IN COBRA LILY

Immature trap

Interlocked teeth

Closed trap

VENUS FLY TRAP
(*Dionaea muscipula*)

Red colour of trap attracts insects

Phyllode (flattened petiole)

Summer petiole (leaf stalk)

Sensory hinge

Trigger hair

Nectary zone (glands secrete nectar)

Inner surface of trap

Digestive zone (glands secrete digestive enzymes)

Lobe of trap

Midrib (hinge of trap)

Trap (twin-lobed leaf blade)

Tooth

Trigger hair

Spring petiole (leaf stalk)

Digestive gland

MICROGRAPH OF LOBE OF VENUS FLY TRAP

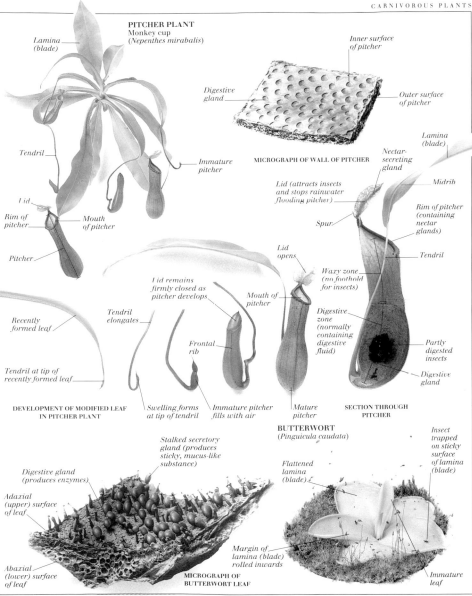

PITCHER PLANT
Monkey cup
(*Nepenthes mirabalis*)

Lamina
(blade)

Tendril

Lid

Rim of
pitcher

Mouth
of pitcher

Pitcher

Immature
pitcher

Digestive
gland

Inner surface
of pitcher

Outer surface
of pitcher

MICROGRAPH OF WALL OF PITCHER

Lamina
(blade)

Nectar-
secreting
gland

Midrib

Lid (attracts insects
and stops rainwater
flooding pitcher)

Spur

Rim of pitcher
(containing
nectar
glands)

Tendril

Waxy zone
(no foothold
for insects)

Digestive
zone
(normally
containing
digestive
fluid)

Partly
digested
insects

Digestive
gland

**SECTION THROUGH
PITCHER**

Recently
formed leaf

Tendril at tip of
recently formed leaf

Lid remains
firmly closed as
pitcher develops

Tendril
elongates

Frontal
rib

Lid
opens

Mouth of
pitcher

Swelling forms
at tip of tendril

Immature pitcher
fills with air

Mature
pitcher

**DEVELOPMENT OF MODIFIED LEAF
IN PITCHER PLANT**

BUTTERWORT
(*Pinguicula caudata*)

Stalked secretory
gland (produces
sticky, mucus-like
substance)

Digestive gland
(produces enzymes)

Adaxial
(upper) surface
of leaf

Abaxial
(lower) surface
of leaf

**MICROGRAPH OF
BUTTERWORT LEAF**

Margin of
lamina (blade)
rolled inwards

Flattened
lamina
(blade)

Insect
trapped
on sticky
surface
of lamina
(blade)

Immature
leaf

Epiphytic and parasitic plants

EPIPHYTIC AND PARASITIC PLANTS GROW ON OTHER LIVING PLANTS. Typically, epiphytic plants are not rooted in the soil; instead, they live above ground level on the stems and branches of other plants. Epiphytes obtain water from trapped rainwater and from moisture in the air, and minerals from organic matter that has accumulated on the surface of the plant on which they are growing. Like other green plants, epiphytes produce their food by photosynthesis. Epiphytes include tropical orchids and bromeliads (air plants), and some mosses that live in temperate regions. Parasitic plants obtain all their nutrient requirements from the host plants on which they grow. The parasites produce haustoria, root-like organs that penetrate the stem or roots of the host and grow inwards to merge with the host's vascular tissue, from which the parasite extracts water, minerals, and manufactured nutrients. As they have no need to produce their own food, parasitic plants lack chlorophyll, the green photosynthetic pigment, and they have no foliage leaves. Partial parasitic plants (e.g., mistletoe) obtain water and minerals from the host plant but have green leaves and stems and are therefore able to produce their own food by photosynthesis.

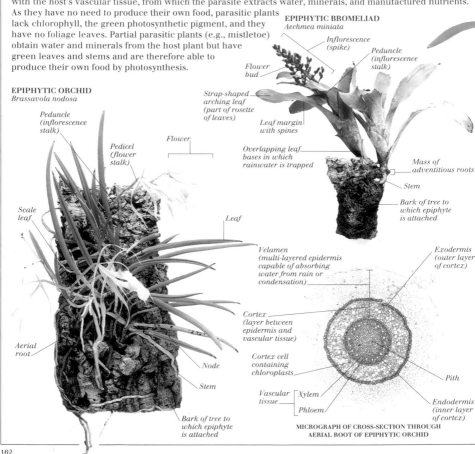

EPIPHYTIC BROMELIAD
Aechmea miniata

Inflorescence (spike)

Peduncle (inflorescence stalk)

Flower bud

Strap-shaped arching leaf (part of rosette of leaves)

Leaf margin with spines

Overlapping leaf bases in which rainwater is trapped

Mass of adventitious roots

Stem

Bark of tree to which epiphyte is attached

EPIPHYTIC ORCHID
Brassavola nodosa

Peduncle (inflorescence stalk)

Pedicel (flower stalk)

Flower

Scale leaf

Leaf

Velamen (multi-layered epidermis capable of absorbing water from rain or condensation)

Exodermis (outer layer of cortex)

Cortex (layer between epidermis and vascular tissue)

Cortex cell containing chloroplasts

Aerial root

Node

Stem

Vascular tissue ⎰ Xylem
⎱ Phloem

Pith

Endodermis (inner layer of cortex)

Bark of tree to which epiphyte is attached

MICROGRAPH OF CROSS-SECTION THROUGH AERIAL ROOT OF EPIPHYTIC ORCHID

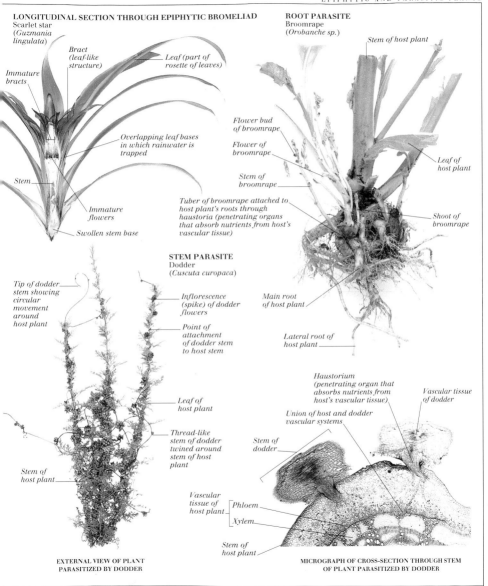

LONGITUDINAL SECTION THROUGH EPIPHYTIC BROMELIAD
Scarlet star
(*Guzmania lingulata*)

Bract (leaf-like structure)

Leaf (part of rosette of leaves)

Immature bracts

Overlapping leaf bases in which rainwater is trapped

Stem

Immature flowers

Swollen stem base

ROOT PARASITE
Broomrape
(*Orobanche sp.*)

Stem of host plant

Flower bud of broomrape

Flower of broomrape

Stem of broomrape

Leaf of host plant

Tuber of broomrape attached to host plant's roots through haustoria (penetrating organs that absorb nutrients from host's vascular tissue)

Shoot of broomrape

Main root of host plant

Lateral root of host plant

STEM PARASITE
Dodder
(*Cuscuta europaca*)

Tip of dodder stem showing circular movement around host plant

Inflorescence (spike) of dodder flowers

Point of attachment of dodder stem to host stem

Leaf of host plant

Thread-like stem of dodder twined around stem of host plant

Stem of host plant

EXTERNAL VIEW OF PLANT PARASITIZED BY DODDER

Haustorium (penetrating organ that absorbs nutrients from host's vascular tissue)

Vascular tissue of dodder

Union of host and dodder vascular systems

Stem of dodder

Vascular tissue of host plant

Phloem

Xylem

Stem of host plant

MICROGRAPH OF CROSS-SECTION THROUGH STEM OF PLANT PARASITIZED BY DODDER

ANIMALS

SPONGES, JELLYFISH, AND SEA ANEMONES	166
INSECTS	168
ARACHNIDS	170
CRUSTACEANS	172
STARFISH AND SEA URCHINS	174
MOLLUSCS	176
SHARKS AND JAWLESS FISH	178
BONY FISH	180
AMPHIBIANS	182
LIZARDS AND SNAKES	184
CROCODILIANS AND TURTLES	186
BIRDS 1	188
BIRDS 2	190
EGGS	192
CARNIVORES	194
RABBITS AND RODENTS	196
UNGULATES	198
ELEPHANTS	200
PRIMATES	202
DOPHINS, WHALES, AND SEALS	204
MARSUPIALS AND MONOTREMES	206

Sponges, jellyfish, and sea anemones

SPONGES ARE MAINLY MARINE animals that make up the simplest of all animals, having no tissues or organs. Their bodies consist of two layers of cells separated by a jelly-like layer (mesohyal) that is strengthened by mineral spicules or protein fibres. The body is perforated by a system of pores and water channels called the aquiferous system. Special cells (choanocytes) with whip-like structures (flagella) draw water through the aquiferous system, thereby bringing tiny food particles to the sponge's cells. Jellyfish (class Scyphozoa), sea anemones (class Anthozoa), and corals (also class Anthozoa) belong to the phylum Cnidaria, also known as Coelenterata. More complex than sponges, coelenterates have simple tissues, such as nervous tissue; a radially symmetrical body; and a mouth surrounded by tentacles with unique stinging cells (cnidocytes).

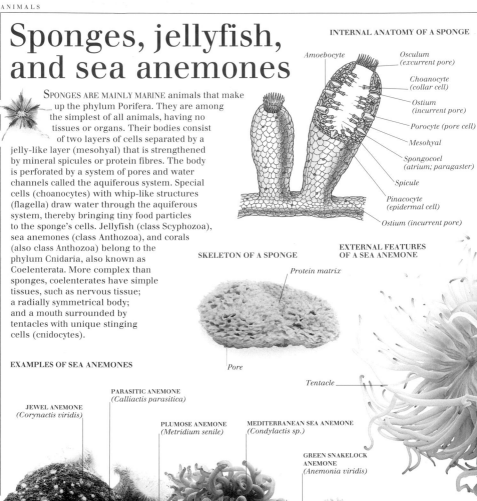

INTERNAL ANATOMY OF A SPONGE

Amoebocyte
Osculum (excurrent pore)
Choanocyte (collar cell)
Ostium (incurrent pore)
Porocyte (pore cell)
Mesohyal
Spongocoel (atrium; paragaster)
Spicule
Pinacocyte (epidermal cell)
Ostium (incurrent pore)

SKELETON OF A SPONGE

Protein matrix

Pore

EXTERNAL FEATURES OF A SEA ANEMONE

Tentacle

EXAMPLES OF SEA ANEMONES

JEWEL ANEMONE
(*Corynactis viridis*)

PARASITIC ANEMONE
(*Calliactis parasitica*)

PLUMOSE ANEMONE
(*Metridium senile*)

MEDITERRANEAN SEA ANEMONE
(*Condylactis sp.*)

GREEN SNAKELOCK ANEMONE
(*Anemonia viridis*)

BEADLET ANEMONE
(*Actinia equina*)

GHOST ANEMONE
(*Actinothoe sphyrodeta*)

Sagartia elegans

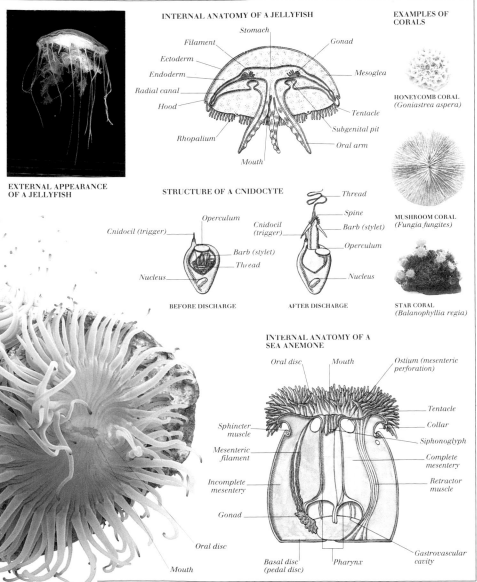

INTERNAL ANATOMY OF A JELLYFISH

Stomach
Filament
Gonad
Ectoderm
Endoderm
Mesoglea
Radial canal
Hood
Tentacle
Subgenital pit
Rhopalium
Oral arm
Mouth

EXAMPLES OF CORALS

HONEYCOMB CORAL
(Goniastrea aspera)

MUSHROOM CORAL
(Fungia fungites)

STAR CORAL
(Balanophyllia regia)

EXTERNAL APPEARANCE OF A JELLYFISH

STRUCTURE OF A CNIDOCYTE

Operculum
Cnidocil (trigger)
Barb (stylet)
Nucleus
Thread

BEFORE DISCHARGE

Thread
Spine
Cnidocil (trigger)
Barb (stylet)
Operculum
Nucleus

AFTER DISCHARGE

INTERNAL ANATOMY OF A SEA ANEMONE

Oral disc
Mouth
Ostium (mesenteric perforation)
Sphincter muscle
Tentacle
Collar
Mesenteric filament
Siphonoglyph
Complete mesentery
Incomplete mesentery
Retractor muscle
Gonad
Oral disc
Mouth
Basal disc (pedal disc)
Pharynx
Gastrovascular cavity

Insects

PUPA (CHRYSALIS)

THE WORD INSECT REFERS to small invertebrate creatures, especially those with bodies divided into sections. Insects, including beetles, ants, bees, butterflies, and moths, belong to various orders in the class Insecta, which is a division of the phylum Arthropoda. Features common to all insects are an exoskeleton (external skeleton); three pairs of jointed legs; three body sections (head, thorax, and abdomen); and one pair of sensory antennae. Beetles (order Coleoptera) are the biggest group of insects, with about 300,000 species (about 30 per cent of all known insects). They have a pair of hard elytra (wing cases), which are modified front wings. The principal function of the elytra is to protect the hind wings, which are used for flying. Ants, together with bees and wasps, form the order Hymenoptera, which contains about 200,000 species. This group is characterized by a marked narrowing between the thorax and abdomen. Butterflies and moths form the order Lepidoptera, which has about 150,000 species. They have wings covered with tiny scales, hence the name of their order (Lepidoptera means "scale wings"). The separation of lepidopterans into butterflies and moths is largely artificial as there are no features that categorically distinguish one group from the other. In general, however, most butterflies fly by day, whereas most moths are night-flyers. Some insects, including butterflies and moths, undergo complete metamorphosis (transformation) during their life-cycle. A butterfly metamorphoses from an egg to a larva (caterpillar), then to a pupa (chrysalis), and finally to an imago (adult).

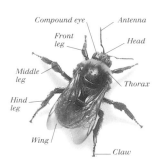

BUMBLEBEE

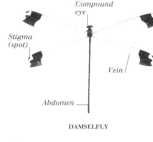

DAMSELFLY

EXTERNAL FEATURES OF A BEETLE

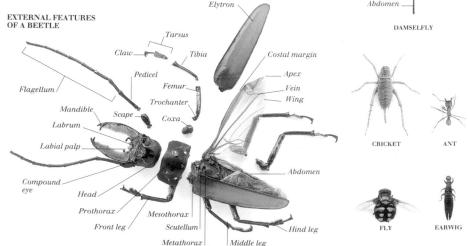

CRICKET

ANT

FLY

EARWIG

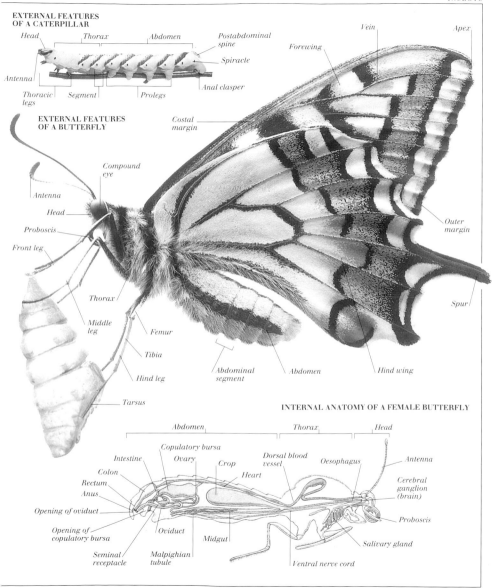

EXTERNAL FEATURES OF A CATERPILLAR

Head
Thorax
Abdomen
Postabdominal spine
Spiracle
Antenna
Thoracic legs
Segment
Prolegs
Anal clasper

EXTERNAL FEATURES OF A BUTTERFLY

Vein
Apex
Forewing
Costal margin
Compound eye
Antenna
Head
Proboscis
Front leg
Outer margin
Thorax
Middle leg
Femur
Tibia
Hind leg
Tarsus
Abdominal segment
Abdomen
Hind wing
Spur

INTERNAL ANATOMY OF A FEMALE BUTTERFLY

Abdomen
Thorax
Head
Copulatory bursa
Intestine
Ovary
Crop
Dorsal blood vessel
Oesophagus
Antenna
Colon
Heart
Cerebral ganglion (brain)
Rectum
Anus
Opening of oviduct
Proboscis
Opening of copulatory bursa
Oviduct
Midgut
Salivary gland
Seminal receptacle
Malpighian tubule
Ventral nerve cord

Arachnids

THE CLASS ARACHNIDA INCLUDES SPIDERS (order Araneae) and scorpions (order Scorpiones). The class is part of the phylum Arthropoda, which also includes insects and crustaceans.

Spiders and scorpions are characterized by having four pairs of walking legs; a pair of pincer-like mouthparts called chelicerae; another pair of frontal appendages called pedipalps, which are sensory in spiders but used for grasping in scorpions; and a body divided into two sections (a combined head and thorax called a cephalothorax or prosoma, and an abdomen or opisthosoma). Unlike other arthropods, spiders and scorpions lack antennae. Spiders and scorpions are carnivorous. Spiders poison prey by biting with the fanged chelicerae, scorpions by stinging with the end of the metasoma (tail).

MEXICAN TRUE RED-
LEGGED TARANTULA
(*Euathlus emilia*)

INTERNAL ANATOMY OF A FEMALE SPIDER

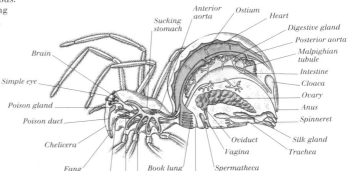

Anterior aorta
Ostium
Heart
Sucking stomach
Digestive gland
Posterior aorta
Malpighian tubule
Brain
Intestine
Simple eye
Cloaca
Ovary
Poison gland
Anus
Poison duct
Spinneret
Chelicera
Oviduct
Silk gland
Vagina
Trachea
Fang
Book lung
Spermatheca (seminal receptacle)
Mouth
Gut caecum
Oesophagus
Spiracle

EXTERNAL FEATURES OF A SCORPION

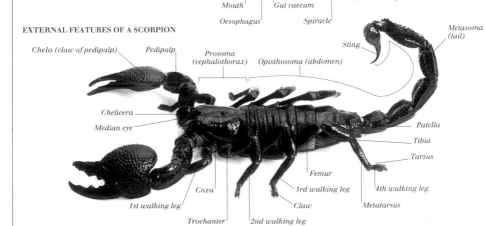

Chela (claw of pedipalp)
Pedipalp
Prosoma (cephalothorax)
Opisthosoma (abdomen)
Sting
Metasoma (tail)
Chelicera
Median eye
Patella
Tibia
Tarsus
Femur
4th walking leg
Coxa
3rd walking leg
Metatarsus
1st walking leg
Claw
Trochanter
2nd walking leg

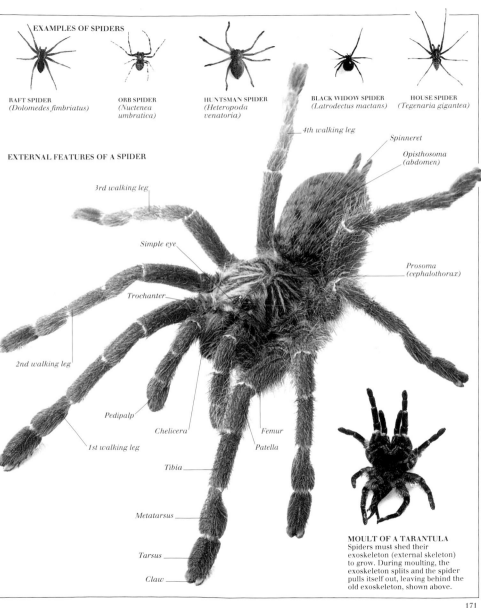

EXAMPLES OF SPIDERS

RAFT SPIDER
(Dolomedes fimbriatus)

ORB SPIDER
(Nuctenea umbratica)

HUNTSMAN SPIDER
(Heteropoda venatoria)

BLACK WIDOW SPIDER
(Latrodectus mactans)

HOUSE SPIDER
(Tegenaria gigantea)

EXTERNAL FEATURES OF A SPIDER

4th walking leg

Spinneret

Opisthosoma (abdomen)

3rd walking leg

Simple eye

Prosoma (cephalothorax)

Trochanter

2nd walking leg

Pedipalp

Chelicera

Femur

Patella

1st walking leg

Tibia

Metatarsus

Tarsus

Claw

MOULT OF A TARANTULA
Spiders must shed their exoskeleton (external skeleton) to grow. During moulting, the exoskeleton splits and the spider pulls itself out, leaving behind the old exoskeleton, shown above.

171

Crustaceans

THE SUBPHYLUM CRUSTACEA is one of the largest groups
in the phylum Arthropoda. The subphylum is divided
into several classes, the most important of which
are Malacostraca and Cirripedia. The class
Malacostraca includes crayfish, crabs,
lobsters, and shrimps. Typical features of
malacostracans include a body divided
into two sections (a combined head
and thorax called a cephalothorax,
and an abdomen); an exoskeleton
(external skeleton) with a large
plate (carapace) covering the
cephalothorax; stalked,
compound eyes; and two
pairs of antennae. The class
Cirripedia includes barnacles,
which, unlike other
crustaceans, spend their
adult lives attached to a
surface, such as a rock. Other
characteristics of cirripedes
include an exoskeleton of
overlapping calcareous plates;
a body consisting almost entirely
of thorax (the abdomen and head
are minute); and six pairs of thoracic
appendages (cirri) used for filter feeding.

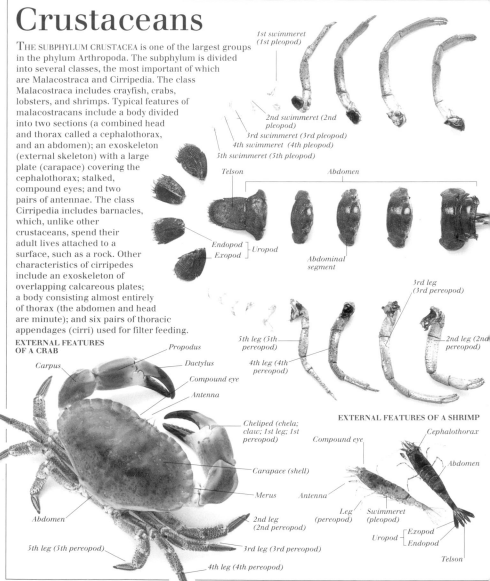

1st swimmeret (1st pleopod)

2nd swimmeret (2nd pleopod)

3rd swimmeret (3rd pleopod)

4th swimmeret (4th pleopod)

5th swimmeret (5th pleopod)

Telson

Abdomen

Endopod
Exopod — Uropod

Abdominal segment

3rd leg (3rd pereopod)

2nd leg (2nd pereopod)

5th leg (5th pereopod)

4th leg (4th pereopod)

EXTERNAL FEATURES OF A CRAB

Carpus

Propodus

Dactylus

Compound eye

Antenna

Cheliped (chela; claw; 1st leg; 1st pereopod)

Carapace (shell)

Merus

Abdomen

5th leg (5th pereopod)

2nd leg (2nd pereopod)

3rd leg (3rd pereopod)

4th leg (4th pereopod)

EXTERNAL FEATURES OF A SHRIMP

Cephalothorax

Abdomen

Compound eye

Antenna

Leg (pereopod)

Swimmeret (pleopod)

Uropod — Exopod
Endopod

Telson

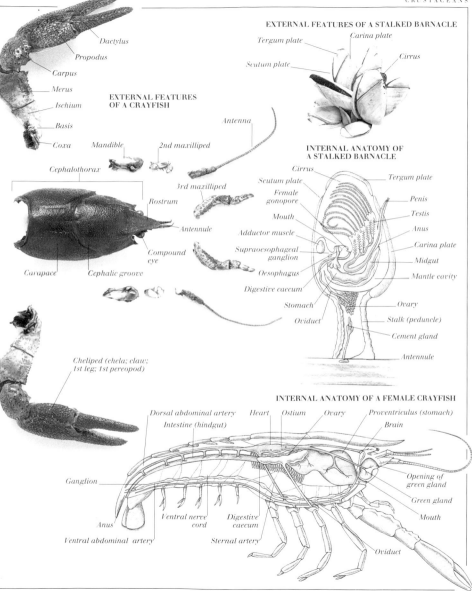

EXTERNAL FEATURES OF A STALKED BARNACLE

Tergum plate

Carina plate

Scutum plate

Cirrus

Dactylus

Propodus

Carpus

Merus

Ischium

Basis

Coxa

Mandible

2nd maxilliped

EXTERNAL FEATURES OF A CRAYFISH

Antenna

3rd maxilliped

INTERNAL ANATOMY OF A STALKED BARNACLE

Cephalothorax

Rostrum

Antennule

Compound eye

Carapace

Cephalic groove

Cirrus

Scutum plate

Female gonopore

Mouth

Adductor muscle

Supraoesophageal ganglion

Oesophagus

Digestive caecum

Stomach

Oviduct

Tergum plate

Penis

Testis

Anus

Carina plate

Midgut

Mantle cavity

Ovary

Stalk (peduncle)

Cement gland

Antennule

Cheliped (chela; claw; 1st leg; 1st pereopod)

INTERNAL ANATOMY OF A FEMALE CRAYFISH

Dorsal abdominal artery

Intestine (hindgut)

Heart

Ostium

Ovary

Proventriculus (stomach)

Brain

Ganglion

Opening of green gland

Green gland

Mouth

Anus

Ventral nerve cord

Digestive caecum

Ventral abdominal artery

Sternal artery

Oviduct

Starfish and sea urchins

STARFISH, SEA URCHINS, AND THEIR relatives (including feather stars, brittle stars, basket stars, sea daisies, sea lilies, and sea cucumbers) make up the phylum Echinodermata. A unique feature of echinoderms is the water vascular system, which consists of a series of water-filled canals from which protrude thousands of tiny tube feet. The tube feet may be used for movement, feeding, or respiration. Other features include pentaradiate symmetry (that is, the body can be divided into five parts radiating from the centre); no head; a diffuse, decentralized nervous system that lacks a brain; and no excretory organs. Typically, echinoderms also have an endoskeleton (internal skeleton) consisting of hard calcite ossicles embedded in the body wall and often bearing protruding spines or tubercles. The ossicles may fit together to form a test (as in sea urchins) or remain separate (as in sea cucumbers).

EXTERNAL FEATURES OF A STARFISH (UPPER, OR ABORAL, SURFACE)

Disc

Madreporite

Spine

Arm

INTERNAL ANATOMY OF A STARFISH

Rectum

Pyloric stomach

Madreporite

Stone canal

Ring canal

Lateral canal

Radial canal

Ampulla

Anus

Rectal caecum

Tube foot

Cardiac stomach

Pyloric duct

Pyloric caecum

Mouth

Oesophagus

Gonad

Gonopore

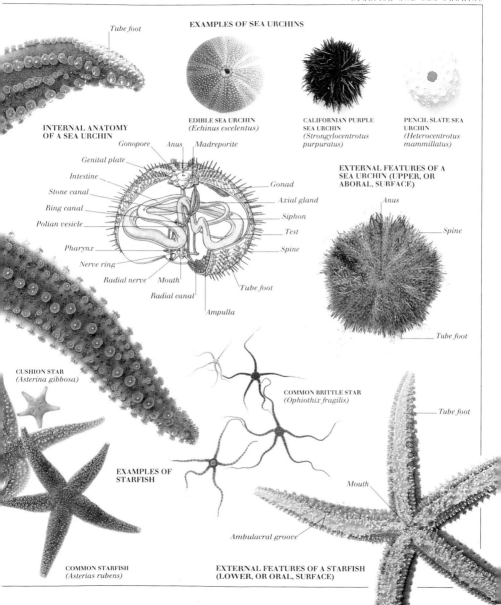

Tube foot

EXAMPLES OF SEA URCHINS

EDIBLE SEA URCHIN
(*Echinus escelentus*)

CALIFORNIAN PURPLE
SEA URCHIN
(*Strongylocentrotus
purpuratus*)

PENCIL SLATE SEA
URCHIN
(*Heterocentrotus
mammillatus*)

**INTERNAL ANATOMY
OF A SEA URCHIN**

Gonopore   Anus   Madreporite

Genital plate

Intestine

Stone canal

Ring canal

Polian vesicle

Pharynx

Nerve ring

Radial nerve   Mouth

Radial canal

Ampulla

Gonad

Axial gland

Siphon

Test

Spine

Tube foot

**EXTERNAL FEATURES OF A
SEA URCHIN (UPPER, OR
ABORAL, SURFACE)**

Anus

Spine

Tube foot

CUSHION STAR
(*Asterina gibbosa*)

COMMON BRITTLE STAR
(*Ophiothrix fragilis*)

Tube foot

**EXAMPLES OF
STARFISH**

Mouth

Ambulacral groove

COMMON STARFISH
(*Asterias rubens*)

**EXTERNAL FEATURES OF A STARFISH
(LOWER, OR ORAL, SURFACE)**

Molluscs

THE PHYLUM MOLLUSCA (MOLLUSCS) is a large group of animals that includes octopuses, snails, and scallops. Octopuses and their relatives —including squid and cuttlefish—form the class Cephalopoda. Cephalopods typically have a head with a radula (a file-like feeding organ) and beak; a well-developed nervous system; sucker-bearing tentacles; a muscular mantle (part of the body wall) that can expel water through the siphon, enabling movement by jet propulsion; and a small shell or no shell. Snails and their relatives—including slugs, limpets, and abalones—make up the class Gastropoda. Gastropods typically have a coiled external shell, although some, such as slugs, have a small internal shell or no shell; a flat foot; and a head with tentacles and a radula. Scallops and their relatives—including clams, mussels, and oysters—make up the class Bivalvia (also called Pelecypoda). Features of bivalves include a shell with two halves (valves); large gills that are used for breathing and filter feeding; and no radula.

EXTERNAL FEATURES OF A SCALLOP

Upper valve (shell)   Mantle   Ocellus (eye)

Lower valve (shell)   Shell rib   Sensory tentacle

Sensory tentacle   Ventral margin of shell   Shell rib

Anterior wing of shell

Umbo   Posterior wing of shell

Dorsal margin of shell

INTERNAL ANATOMY OF AN OCTOPUS

Cephalic vein

Poison gland

Skull

Crop

Digestive caecum

Brain

Dorsal mantle cavity

Siphon (funnel)

Mantle muscles

Buccal mass

Shell rudiment

Beak

Stomach

Caecum

Gonad

Systemic heart

Kidney

Branchial heart

Anus

Ctenidium

Muscular septum

Ink sac

Tentacle

Sucker

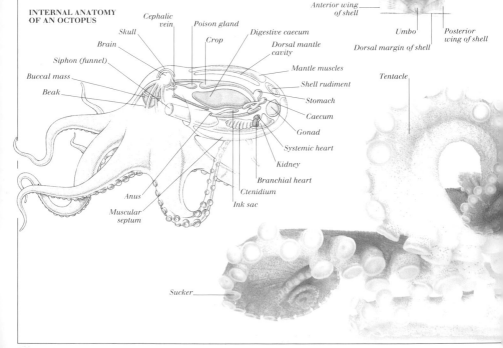

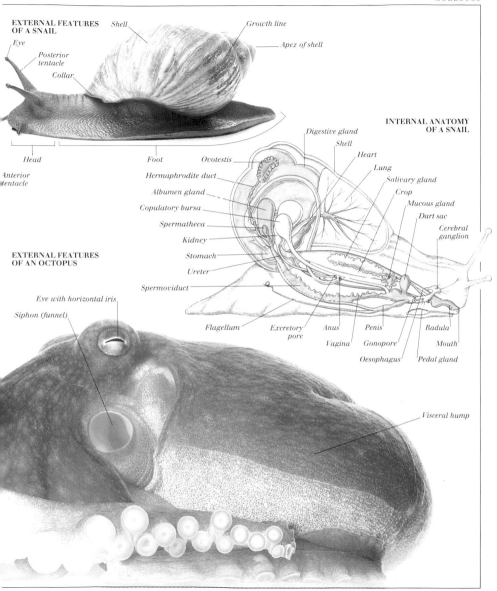

EXTERNAL FEATURES OF A SNAIL

Eye

Posterior tentacle

Collar

Shell

Growth line

Apex of shell

Head

Anterior tentacle

Foot

INTERNAL ANATOMY OF A SNAIL

Ovotestis

Hermaphrodite duct

Albumen gland

Copulatory bursa

Spermatheca

Kidney

Stomach

Ureter

Spermoviduct

Flagellum

Excretory pore

Vagina

Anus

Penis

Gonopore

Oesophagus

Digestive gland

Shell

Heart

Lung

Salivary gland

Crop

Mucous gland

Dart sac

Cerebral ganglion

Radula

Mouth

Pedal gland

EXTERNAL FEATURES OF AN OCTOPUS

Eye with horizontal iris

Siphon (funnel)

Visceral hump

Sharks and jawless fish

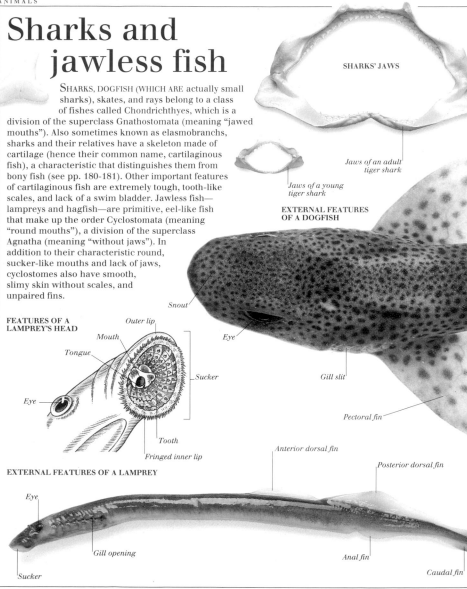

SHARKS' JAWS

SHARKS, DOGFISH (WHICH ARE actually small sharks), skates, and rays belong to a class of fishes called Chondrichthyes, which is a division of the superclass Gnathostomata (meaning "jawed mouths"). Also sometimes known as elasmobranchs, sharks and their relatives have a skeleton made of cartilage (hence their common name, cartilaginous fish), a characteristic that distinguishes them from bony fish (see pp. 180-181). Other important features of cartilaginous fish are extremely tough, tooth-like scales, and lack of a swim bladder. Jawless fish—lampreys and hagfish—are primitive, eel-like fish that make up the order Cyclostomata (meaning "round mouths"), a division of the superclass Agnatha (meaning "without jaws"). In addition to their characteristic round, sucker-like mouths and lack of jaws, cyclostomes also have smooth, slimy skin without scales, and unpaired fins.

Jaws of an adult tiger shark

Jaws of a young tiger shark

EXTERNAL FEATURES OF A DOGFISH

Snout

Eye

Gill slit

Pectoral fin

FEATURES OF A LAMPREY'S HEAD

Outer lip

Mouth

Tongue

Sucker

Eye

Tooth

Fringed inner lip

EXTERNAL FEATURES OF A LAMPREY

Eye

Anterior dorsal fin

Posterior dorsal fin

Gill opening

Anal fin

Sucker

Caudal fin

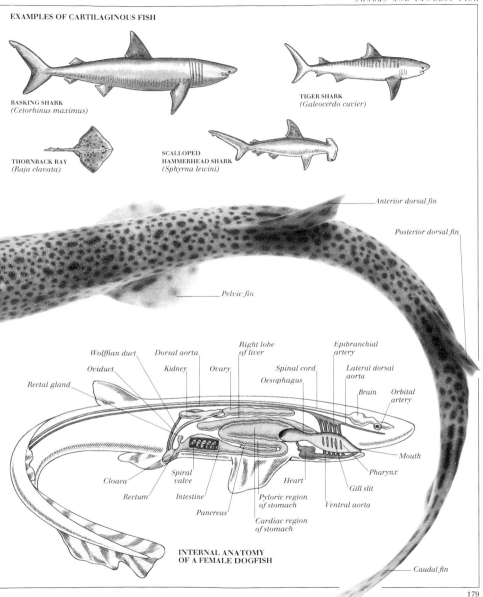

EXAMPLES OF CARTILAGINOUS FISH

BASKING SHARK
(*Cetorhinus maximus*)

TIGER SHARK
(*Galeocerdo cuvier*)

THORNBACK RAY
(*Raja clavata*)

SCALLOPED
HAMMERHEAD SHARK
(*Sphyrna lewini*)

Anterior dorsal fin

Posterior dorsal fin

Pelvic fin

Wolffian duct

Dorsal aorta

Right lobe
of liver

Epibranchial
artery

Oviduct

Kidney

Ovary

Spinal cord

Lateral dorsal
aorta

Rectal gland

Oesophagus

Brain

Orbital
artery

Mouth

Cloaca

Spiral
valve

Pharynx

Rectum

Intestine

Heart

Gill slit

Pancreas

Pyloric region
of stomach

Ventral aorta

Cardiac region
of stomach

**INTERNAL ANATOMY
OF A FEMALE DOGFISH**

Caudal fin

Bony fish

BONY FISH, SUCH AS CARP, TROUT, SALMON, perch, and cod, are by far the best known and largest group of fish, with more than 20,000 species (over 95 per cent of all known fish). As their name suggests, bony fish have skeletons made of bone, in contrast to the cartilaginous skeletons of sharks, jawless fish, and their relatives (see pp. 178-179). Other typical features of bony fish include a swim bladder, which functions as a variable-buoyancy organ, enabling a fish to remain effortlessly at whatever depth it is swimming; relatively thin, bone-like scales; a flap (called an operculum) covering the gills; and paired pelvic and pectoral fins. Scientifically, bony fish belong to the class Osteichthyes, which is a division of the superclass Gnathostomata (meaning "jawed mouths").

HOW FISH BREATHE

Fish "breathe" by extracting oxygen from water through their gills. Water is sucked in through the mouth; simultaneously, the opercula close to prevent the water from escaping. The mouth is then closed, and muscles in the walls of the mouth, pharynx, and opercular cavity contract to pump the water inside over the gills and out through the opercula. Some fish rely on swimming with their mouths open to keep water flowing over the gills.

Pharynx
Gill raker
Water out
Gill slit
Mouth
Water in
Operculum
Gill filament

EXAMPLES OF BONY FISH

MANDARINFISH
(Synchiropus splendidus)

ANGLERFISH
(Caulophryne jordani)

LIONFISH
(Pterois volitans)

STURGEON
(Acipenser sturio)

OCEANIC SEAHORSE
(Hippocampus kuda)

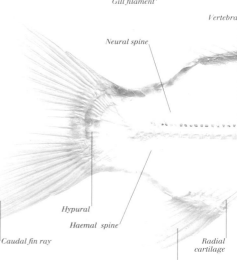

Vertebra
Neural spine
Hypural
Haemal spine
Caudal fin ray
Anal fin ray
Radial cartilage

SNOWFLAKE MORAY EEL
(Echidna nebulosa)

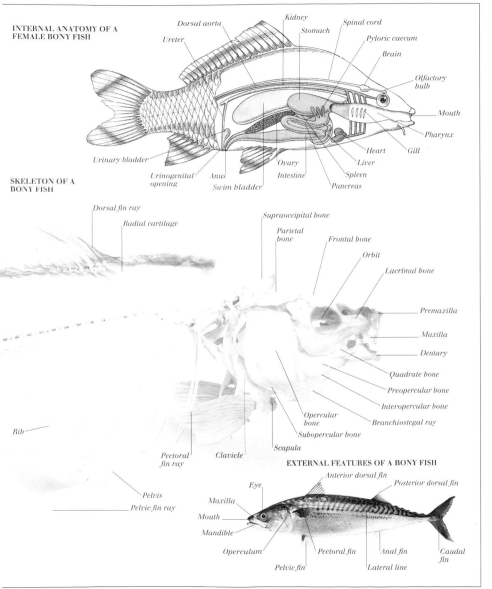

INTERNAL ANATOMY OF A FEMALE BONY FISH

Dorsal aorta
Ureter
Kidney
Stomach
Spinal cord
Pyloric caecum
Brain
Olfactory bulb
Mouth
Pharynx
Gill
Heart
Liver
Spleen
Pancreas
Intestine
Ovary
Swim bladder
Anus
Urinogenital opening
Urinary bladder

SKELETON OF A BONY FISH

Dorsal fin ray
Radial cartilage
Supraoccipital bone
Parietal bone
Frontal bone
Orbit
Lacrimal bone
Premaxilla
Maxilla
Dentary
Quadrate bone
Preopercular bone
Interopercular bone
Branchiostegal ray
Opercular bone
Subopercular bone
Scapula
Clavicle
Pectoral fin ray
Rib
Pelvis
Pelvic fin ray

EXTERNAL FEATURES OF A BONY FISH

Anterior dorsal fin
Posterior dorsal fin
Eye
Maxilla
Mouth
Mandible
Operculum
Pelvic fin
Pectoral fin
Lateral line
Anal fin
Caudal fin

Amphibians

THE CLASS AMPHIBIA INCLUDES FROGS and toads (which make up the order Anura), and newts and salamanders (which make up the order Urodela). Amphibians typically have moist, scaleless, hairless skin; lungs; and are cold-blooded. They also undergo complete metamorphosis, from eggs laid in water through various water-living larval stages (such as tadpoles) to land-living adults. Typical features of adult frogs and toads include a squat body with no tail; long, powerful hind legs; and large, often bulging, eyes. Adult newts and salamanders typically have a long body with a well-developed tail; and relatively short, equal-sized legs. However, newts and salamanders show considerable variation; for example, in some species the adults have minute legs, external gills rather than lungs, and spend their entire lives in water.

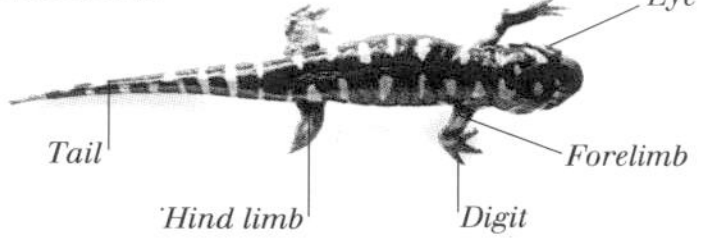

INTERNAL ANATOMY OF A FEMALE FROG

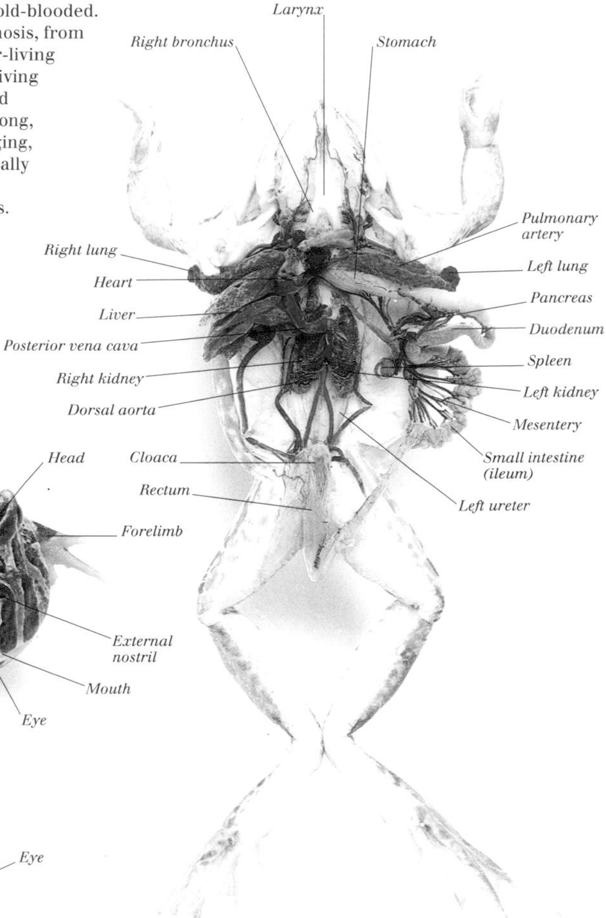

Larynx
Right bronchus
Stomach
Pulmonary artery
Right lung
Left lung
Heart
Pancreas
Liver
Duodenum
Posterior vena cava
Spleen
Right kidney
Left kidney
Dorsal aorta
Mesentery
Cloaca
Small intestine (ileum)
Rectum
Left ureter

EXTERNAL FEATURES OF A FROG

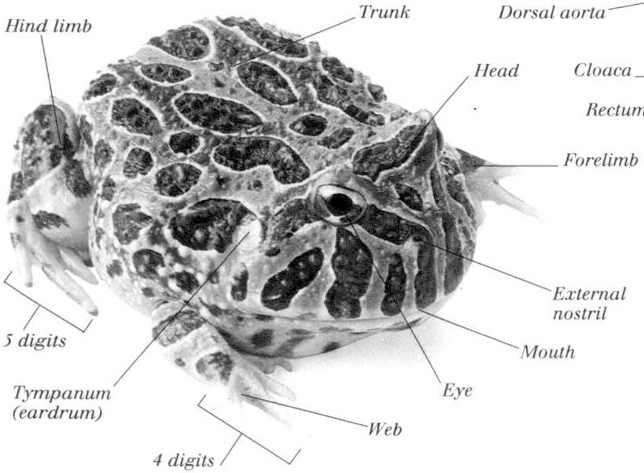

Hind limb
Trunk
Head
Forelimb
5 digits
External nostril
Mouth
Tympanum (eardrum)
Eye
Web
4 digits

EXTERNAL FEATURES OF A SALAMANDER

Eye
Tail
Forelimb
Hind limb
Digit

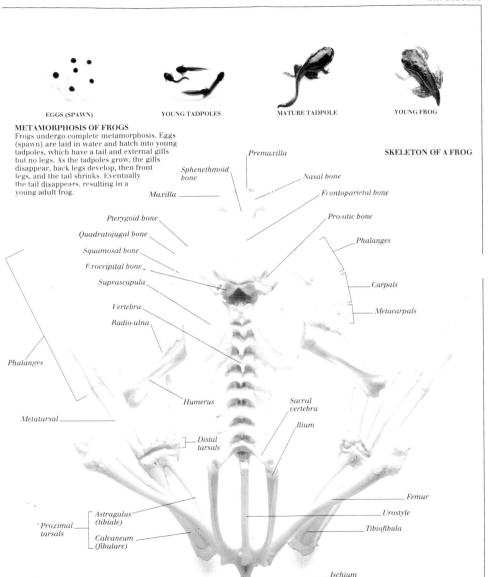

EGGS (SPAWN)   YOUNG TADPOLES   MATURE TADPOLE   YOUNG FROG

METAMORPHOSIS OF FROGS
Frogs undergo complete metamorphosis. Eggs
(spawn) are laid in water and hatch into young
tadpoles, which have a tail and external gills
but no legs. As the tadpoles grow, the gills
disappear, back legs develop, then front
legs, and the tail shrinks. Eventually
the tail disappears, resulting in a
young adult frog.

SKELETON OF A FROG

Premaxilla

Sphenethmoid
bone

Nasal bone

Frontoparietal bone

Maxilla

Pterygoid bone

Pro-otic bone

Quadratojugal bone

Squamosal bone

Phalanges

Exoccipital bone

Suprascapula

Carpals

Vertebra

Metacarpals

Radio-ulna

Phalanges

Humerus

Sacral
vertebra

Ilium

Metatarsal

Distal
tarsals

Femur

Astragalus
(tibiale)

Urostyle

Proximal
tarsals

Tibiofibula

Calcaneum
(fibulare)

Ischium

183

Lizards and snakes

LIZARDS AND SNAKES BELONG to the order Squamata, a division of the class Reptilia. Characteristic reptilian features include scaly skin, lungs, and cold-bloodedness. Most reptiles lay leathery-shelled eggs, although some hatch the eggs inside their bodies and give birth to live young. Lizards belong to the suborder Lacertilia. Typically, they have long tails, and shed their skin in several pieces. Many lizards can regenerate a tail if it is lost; some can change colour; and some are limbless. Snakes make up the suborder Ophidia (also called Serpentes). All snakes have long, limbless bodies; can dislocate their lower jaw to swallow large prey; and have eyelids that are joined together to form a single transparent covering over the front of the eye. Most snakes shed their skin in a single piece. Constrictor snakes kill their prey by squeezing; venomous snakes poison their prey.

EXAMPLES OF SNAKES

MEXICAN MOUNTAIN KING SNAKE
(Lampropeltis triangulum annulata)

BANDED MILK SNAKE
(Lampropeltis ruthveni)

EXTERNAL FEATURES OF A LIZARD

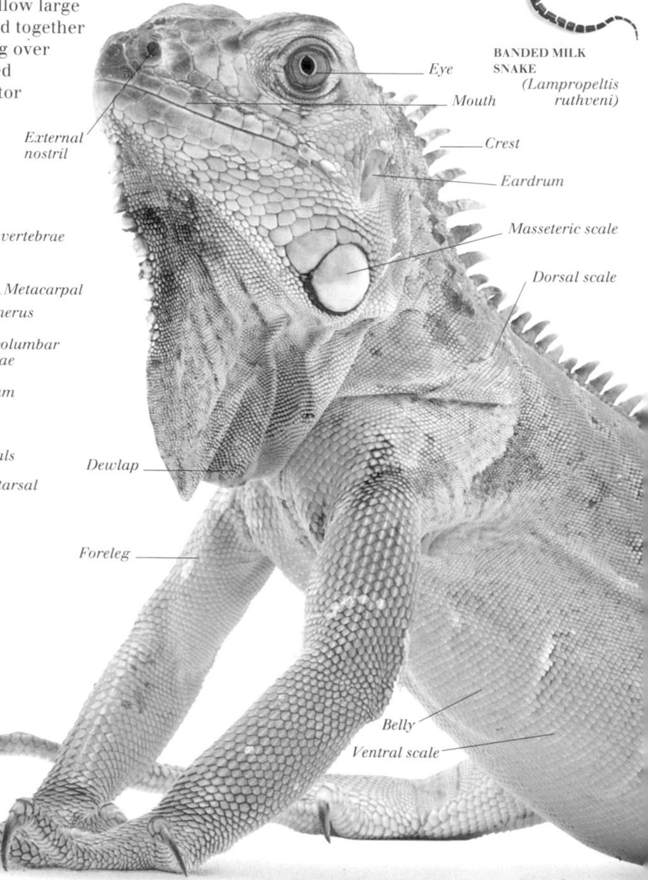

Eye
Mouth
External nostril
Crest
Eardrum
Masseteric scale
Dorsal scale
Dewlap
Foreleg
Belly
Ventral scale

SKELETON OF A LIZARD

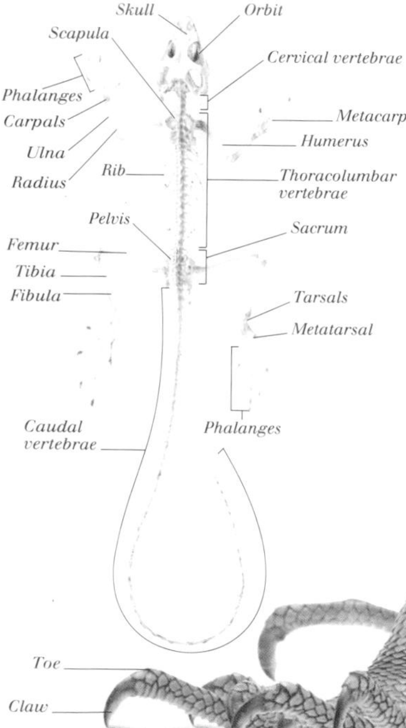

Skull
Orbit
Scapula
Cervical vertebrae
Phalanges
Carpals
Metacarpal
Humerus
Ulna
Radius
Rib
Thoracolumbar vertebrae
Pelvis
Sacrum
Femur
Tibia
Fibula
Tarsals
Metatarsal
Caudal vertebrae
Phalanges
Toe
Claw

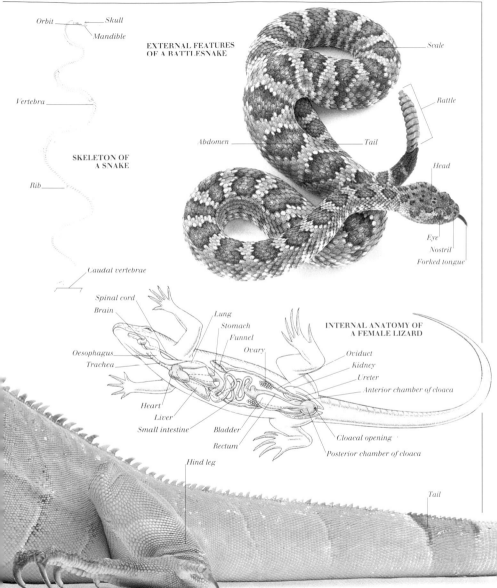

Orbit

Skull

Mandible

**EXTERNAL FEATURES
OF A RATTLESNAKE**

Scale

Vertebra

Rattle

Abdomen

Tail

**SKELETON OF
A SNAKE**

Head

Rib

Eye

Nostril

Forked tongue

Caudal vertebrae

Spinal cord

Brain

Lung

Stomach

Funnel

**INTERNAL ANATOMY OF
A FEMALE LIZARD**

Ovary

Oesophagus

Trachea

Oviduct

Kidney

Ureter

Anterior chamber of cloaca

Heart

Liver

Small intestine

Bladder

Rectum

Cloacal opening

Posterior chamber of cloaca

Hind leg

Tail

185

Crocodilians and turtles

CROCODILIANS AND TURTLES BELONG to different orders in the class Reptilia. The order Crocodilia includes crocodiles, alligators, caimans, and gharials. Typically, crocodilians are carnivores (flesh-eaters), and have a long snout, sharp teeth for gripping prey, and hard, square scales. All crocodilians are adapted to living on land and in water: they have four strong legs for moving on land; a powerful tail for swimming; and their eyes and nostrils are high on the head so that they stay above water while the rest of the body is submerged. The order Chelonia includes marine turtles, terrapins (freshwater turtles), and tortoises (land turtles). Characteristically, chelonians have a short, broad body encased in a bony shell with an outer horny covering, into which the head and limbs can be withdrawn; and a horny beak instead of teeth.

GHARIAL
(Gavialis gangeticus)

NILE CROCODILE
(Crocodylus niloticus)

AMERICAN ALLIGATOR
(Alligator mississippiensis)

SKELETON OF A CROCODILE

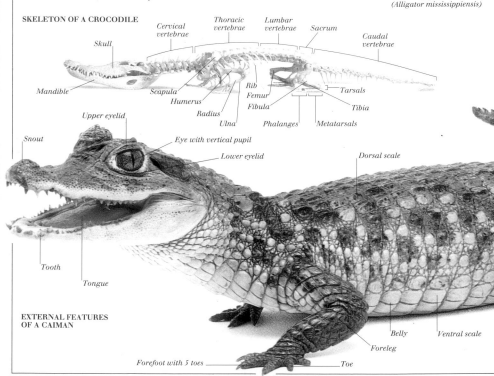

Cervical vertebrae

Thoracic vertebrae

Lumbar vertebrae

Sacrum

Caudal vertebrae

Skull

Mandible

Scapula

Humerus

Radius

Ulna

Rib

Femur

Fibula

Phalanges

Metatarsals

Tarsals

Tibia

Upper eyelid

Snout

Eye with vertical pupil

Lower eyelid

Dorsal scale

Tooth

Tongue

EXTERNAL FEATURES OF A CAIMAN

Belly

Ventral scale

Foreleg

Forefoot with 5 toes

Toe

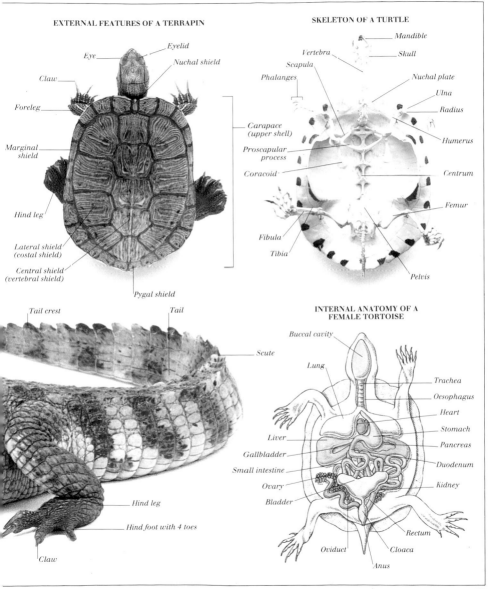

EXTERNAL FEATURES OF A TERRAPIN

Eye
Eyelid
Nuchal shield
Claw
Foreleg
Marginal shield
Hind leg
Lateral shield (costal shield)
Central shield (vertebral shield)
Pygal shield
Carapace (upper shell)

SKELETON OF A TURTLE

Mandible
Vertebra
Skull
Scapula
Proscapular process
Nuchal plate
Ulna
Radius
Humerus
Coracoid
Centrum
Femur
Fibula
Tibia
Pelvis

Tail crest
Tail
Scute
Hind leg
Hind foot with 4 toes
Claw

INTERNAL ANATOMY OF A FEMALE TORTOISE

Buccal cavity
Lung
Trachea
Oesophagus
Heart
Stomach
Liver
Pancreas
Gallbladder
Duodenum
Small intestine
Kidney
Ovary
Bladder
Rectum
Oviduct
Cloaca
Anus

Birds 1

BIRDS MAKE UP THE CLASS AVES. There are more than 9,000 species, almost all of which can fly (the only flightless birds are penguins, ostriches, rheas, cassowaries, and kiwis). The ability to fly is reflected in the typical bird features: forelimbs modified as wings; a streamlined body; and hollow bones to reduce weight. All birds lay hard-shelled eggs, which the parents incubate. Birds' beaks and feet vary according to diet and way of life. Beaks range from general-purpose types suitable for a mixed diet (those of thrushes, for example), to types specialized for particular foods (such as the large, curved, sieving beaks of flamingos). Feet range from the webbed "paddles" of ducks, to the talons of birds of prey. Plumage also varies widely, and in many species the male is brightly coloured for courtship display whereas the female is drab.

EXTERNAL FEATURES OF A BIRD

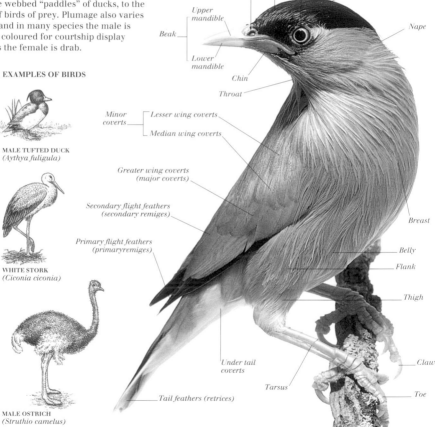

Forehead
Eye
Crown
Nostril
Nape
Upper mandible
Beak
Lower mandible
Chin
Throat

EXAMPLES OF BIRDS

Minor coverts
Lesser wing coverts
Median wing coverts

Greater wing coverts (major coverts)

Secondary flight feathers (secondary remiges)

Primary flight feathers (primaryremiges)

MALE TUFTED DUCK
(*Aythya fuligula*)

WHITE STORK
(*Ciconia ciconia*)

Breast
Belly
Flank
Thigh

Under tail coverts

Tail feathers (retrices)

Tarsus
Claw
Toe

MALE OSTRICH
(*Struthio camelus*)

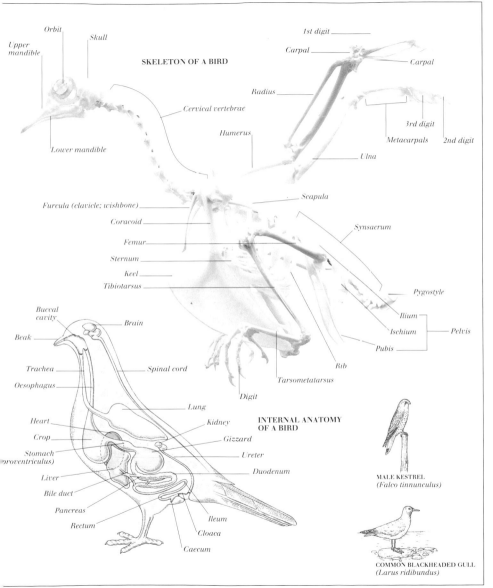

SKELETON OF A BIRD

Upper mandible

Orbit

Skull

1st digit

Carpal

Carpal

Radius

Cervical vertebrae

3rd digit

Humerus

Metacarpals

2nd digit

Lower mandible

Ulna

Furcula (clavicle; wishbone)

Scapula

Coracoid

Synsacrum

Femur

Sternum

Keel

Tibiotarsus

Pygostyle

Ilium

Ischium

Pelvis

Pubis

Buccal cavity

Brain

Beak

Trachea

Spinal cord

Rib

Oesophagus

Tarsometatarsus

Lung

Digit

INTERNAL ANATOMY OF A BIRD

Heart

Kidney

Crop

Gizzard

Stomach (proventriculus)

Ureter

Liver

Duodenum

Bile duct

Pancreas

Rectum

Ileum

Cloaca

Caecum

MALE KESTREL
(Falco tinnunculus)

COMMON BLACKHEADED GULL
(Larus ridibundus)

Birds 2

EXAMPLES OF BIRDS' FEET

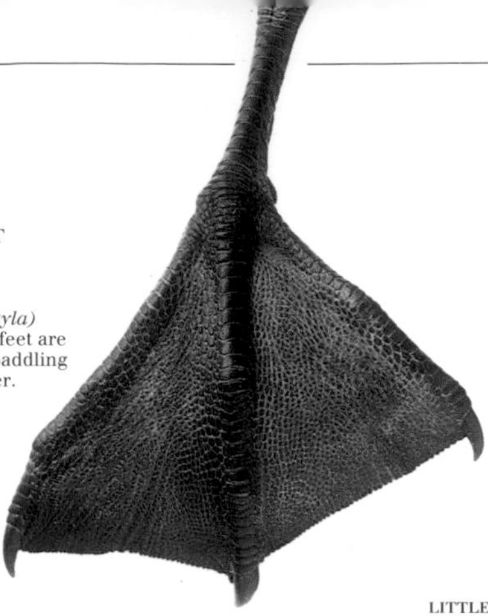

KITTIWAKE
(Rissa tridactyla)
The webbed feet are
adapted for paddling
through water.

LITTLE GREBE
(Tachybaptus ruficollis)
The lobed, flattened feet
are adapted for swimming
underwater.

TAWNY OWL
(Strix aluco)
The clawed feet are adapted
for gripping prey.

EXAMPLES OF BIRDS' BEAKS

KING VULTURE
(Sarcorhamphus papa)
The hooked beak is adapted
for pulling apart flesh.

GREATER FLAMINGO
(Phoenicopterus ruber)
In the living bird, the large,
curved beak contains a
cartilaginous "sieve" for
filtering food particles
from water.

MISTLE THRUSH
(Turdus viscivorus)
The general-purpose beak is
suitable for a wide range of animal
and plant foods.

BLUE-AND-YELLOW MACAW
(Ara ararauna)
The broad, powerful, hooked beak
is adapted for crushing seeds and
eating fruit.

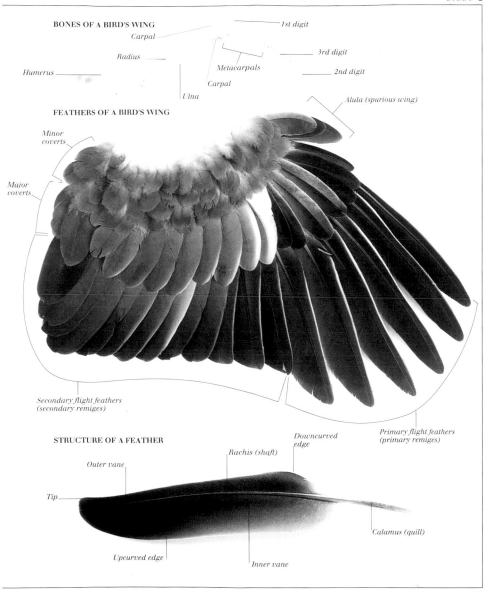

BONES OF A BIRD'S WING

1st digit
Carpal
Radius
3rd digit
Metacarpals
Humerus
Carpal
2nd digit
Ulna
Alula (spurious wing)

FEATHERS OF A BIRD'S WING

Minor coverts
Major coverts
Secondary flight feathers (secondary remiges)
Downcurved edge
Primary flight feathers (primary remiges)

STRUCTURE OF A FEATHER

Outer vane
Rachis (shaft)
Tip
Calamus (quill)
Upcurved edge
Inner vane

Eggs

AN EGG IS A SINGLE CELL, produced by the female, with the capacity to develop into a new individual. Development may take place inside the mother's body (as in most mammals) or outside, in which case the egg has a protective covering such as a shell. Egg yolk nourishes the growing young. Eggs developing inside the mother generally have little yolk, because the young are nourished from her body. Eggs developing outside may also have little yolk if they are produced by animals whose young go through a larval stage (such as a caterpillar) that feeds itself while developing into the adult form. The shelled eggs of birds and reptiles contain enough yolk to sustain the young until it hatches into a juvenile version of the adult.

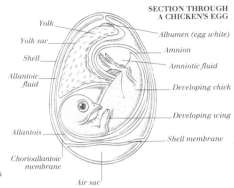

SECTION THROUGH A CHICKEN'S EGG

Yolk
Yolk sac
Shell
Allantoic fluid
Allantois
Chorioallantoic membrane
Air sac
Albumen (egg white)
Amnion
Amniotic fluid
Developing chick
Developing wing
Shell membrane

VARIETY OF EGGS

LEAF INSECT EGGS

Egg capsule
Operculum

GIANT STICK INSECT EGGS

Egg capsule
Operculum

Operculum
Egg capsule

INDIAN STICK INSECT EGGS

Jelly
Developing tadpole

FROG EGGS (FROG SPAWN)

DOGFISH EGGS (MERMAID'S PURSES)

Developing dogfish
Egg case
Tendril

HATCHING OF A QUAIL'S EGG

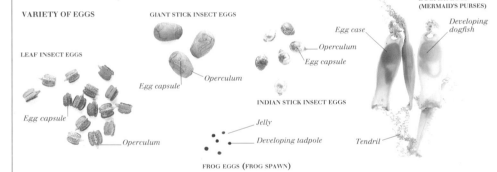

EGG AT THE POINT OF HATCHING

Rounded end of egg
Shell
Pointed end of egg
Shell membrane
Camouflage coloration
Crack caused by chick pecking through the shell

CUTTING THROUGH THE EGG

Chick
Shell
Shell membrane
Crack extended by further pecking by the chick

BREAKING OUT OF THE EGG

Chick pushes off the top of the shell
Shell membrane
Shell
Eye
Beak
Egg-tooth
Crack runs completely around the shell

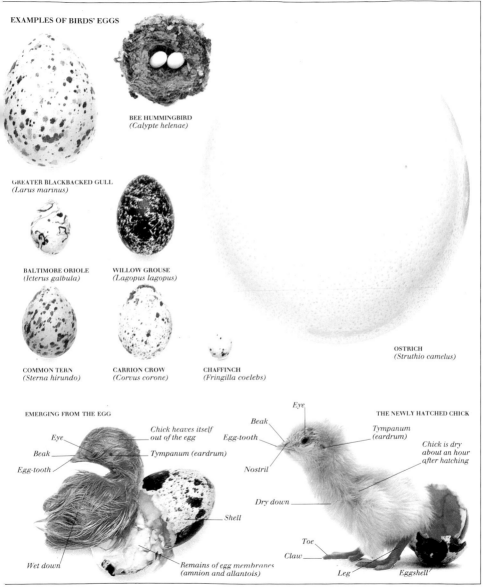

EXAMPLES OF BIRDS' EGGS

BEE HUMMINGBIRD
(Calypte helenae)

GREATER BLACKBACKED GULL
(Larus marinus)

BALTIMORE ORIOLE
(Icterus galbula)

WILLOW GROUSE
(Lagopus lagopus)

COMMON TERN
(Sterna hirundo)

CARRION CROW
(Corvus corone)

CHAFFINCH
(Fringilla coelebs)

OSTRICH
(Struthio camelus)

EMERGING FROM THE EGG

Eye

Beak

Egg-tooth

Chick heaves itself
out of the egg

Tympanum (eardrum)

Wet down

Shell

Remains of egg membranes
(amnion and allantois)

THE NEWLY HATCHED CHICK

Eye

Beak

Egg-tooth

Nostril

Tympanum
(eardrum)

Chick is dry
about an hour
after hatching

Dry down

Toe

Claw

Leg

Eggshell

Carnivores

THE MAMMALIAN ORDER CARNIVORA includes cats, dogs, bears, raccoons, pandas, weasels, badgers, skunks, otters, civets, mongooses, and hyenas. The order's name is derived from the fact that most of its members are carnivores (flesh-eaters). Typical carnivore features therefore reflect a hunting life-style: speed and agility; sharp claws and well-developed canine teeth for holding and killing prey; carnassial teeth (cheek teeth) for cutting flesh; and forward-facing eyes for good distance judgment. However, some members of the order—bears, badgers, and foxes, for example—have a more mixed diet, and a few are entirely herbivorous (plant-eating), notably pandas. Such animals have no carnassial teeth and tend to be slower-moving than pure flesh-eaters.

EXTERNAL FEATURES OF A MALE LION

Nose

Eye

Mane

Nostril

Vibrissa (whisker)

Tongue

Canine tooth

Incisor tooth

Chest

Elbow

Lower arm

Toe

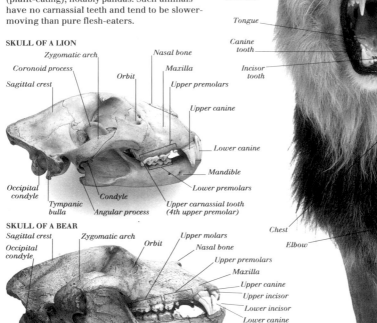

SKULL OF A LION

Zygomatic arch

Coronoid process

Orbit

Nasal bone

Maxilla

Upper premolars

Sagittal crest

Upper canine

Lower canine

Mandible

Lower premolars

Occipital condyle

Tympanic bulla

Condyle

Angular process

Upper carnassial tooth (4th upper premolar)

SKULL OF A BEAR

Sagittal crest

Occipital condyle

Zygomatic arch

Orbit

Upper molars

Nasal bone

Upper premolars

Maxilla

Upper canine

Upper incisor

Lower incisor

Lower canine

Mandible

Lower premolars

Tympanic bulla

Angular process

Condyle

Lower molars

EXAMPLES OF CARNIVORES

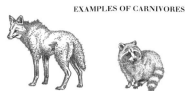

ALSATIAN DOG
(Canis familiaris)

MANED WOLF
(Chrysocyon brachyurus)

RACCOON
(Procyon lotor)

AMERICAN BLACK BEAR
(Ursus americanus)

SKELETON OF A DOMESTIC CAT

INTERNAL ANATOMY OF A MALE DOMESTIC CAT

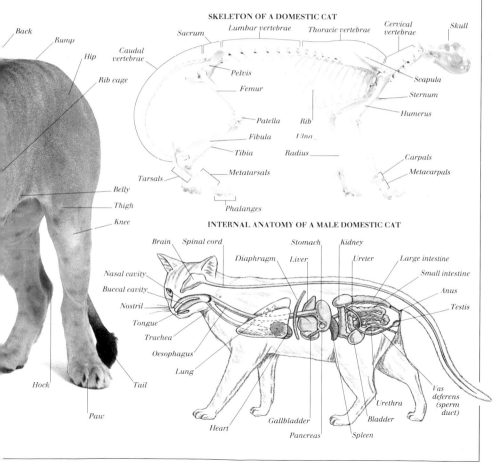

Back

Rump

Hip

Rib cage

Sacrum

Lumbar vertebrae

Thoracic vertebrae

Cervical vertebrae

Skull

Caudal vertebrae

Pelvis

Femur

Scapula

Sternum

Humerus

Patella

Rib

Fibula

Ulna

Tibia

Radius

Carpals

Metacarpals

Tarsals

Metatarsals

Belly

Thigh

Knee

Phalanges

Brain

Spinal cord

Stomach

Kidney

Diaphragm

Liver

Ureter

Large intestine

Small intestine

Nasal cavity

Anus

Buccal cavity

Nostril

Testis

Tongue

Trachea

Oesophagus

Lung

Hock

Tail

Paw

Heart

Gallbladder

Pancreas

Spleen

Bladder

Urethra

Vas deferens (sperm duct)

Rabbits and rodents

EXTERNAL FEATURES OF A RAT

Snout
Eye
Ear
Nose
Pinna (ear flap)
Nostril
Vibrissa (whisker)
Neck
Mouth
Tail
Forelimb
5 digits
Hind limb
5 digits

ALTHOUGH RABBITS AND RODENTS belong to different orders of mammals, they have some features in common. These features include chisel-shaped incisor teeth that grow continually, and eating their faeces to extract more nutrients from their plant diet. Rabbits and hares belong to the order Lagomorpha. Characteristically, they have four incisors in the upper jaw and two in the lower jaw; powerful hind legs for jumping; forelimbs adapted for burrowing; long ears; and a small tail. Rodents make up the order Rodentia. This is the largest order of mammals, with more than 1,700 species, including squirrels, beavers, chipmunks, gophers, rats, mice, lemmings, gerbils, porcupines, cavies, and the capybara. Typical rodent features include two incisors in each jaw; short forelimbs for manipulating food; and cheek pouches for storing food.

EXTERNAL FEATURES OF A RABBIT

Pinna (ear flap)
Ear
Shoulder
Eye
Nose
Nostril
Vibrissa (whisker)
Forelimb
5 digits

INTERNAL ANATOMY OF A MALE RABBIT

Gallbladder
Brain
Liver
Stomach
Kidney
Nasal cavity
Spinal cord
Colon
Ileum
Ureter
Rectum
Bladder
Mouth
Anus
Buccal cavity
Urethra
Tongue
Testis
Vas deferens
Oesophagus
Lung
Pancreas
Appendix
Trachea
Diaphragm
Duodenum
Caecum
Heart

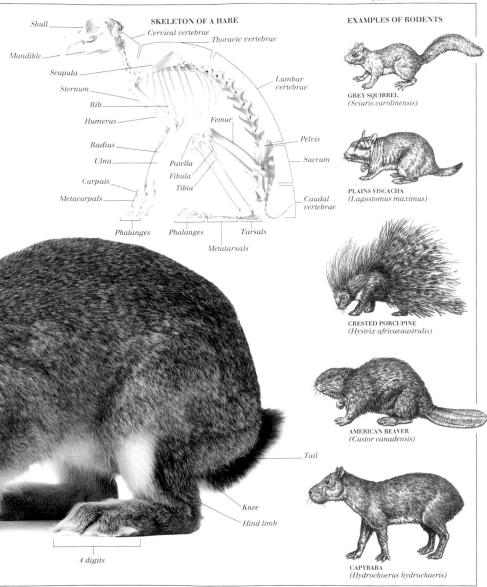

SKELETON OF A HARE

Skull

Mandible

Cervical vertebrae

Thoracic vertebrae

Scapula

Lumbar
vertebrae

Sternum

Rib

Humerus

Femur

Radius

Pelvis

Ulna

Sacrum

Patella

Carpals

Fibula

Metacarpals

Tibia

Caudal
vertebrae

Phalanges

Phalanges

Tarsals

Metatarsals

Tail

Knee

Hind limb

4 digits

EXAMPLES OF RODENTS

GREY SQUIRREL
(Sciuris carolinensis)

PLAINS VISCACHA
(Lagostomus maximus)

CRESTED PORCUPINE
(Hystrix africaeaustralis)

AMERICAN BEAVER
(Castor canadensis)

CAPYBARA
(Hydrochoerus hydrochaeris)

Ungulates

UNGULATES IS A GENERAL TERM FOR a large, varied group of mammals that includes horses, cattle, and their relatives. The ungulates are divided into two orders on the basis of the number of toes. Members of the order Perissodactyla (odd-toed ungulates) have one or three toes. Perissodactyls include horses, asses, and zebras (all of which are one-toed), and rhinoceroses and tapirs (which are three-toed). Members of the order Artiodactyla (even-toed ungulates) have two or four toes. Most artiodactyls have two toes, which are typically encased in hooves to give the so-called cloven hoof. Two-toed, cloven-hoofed artiodactyls include cows and other cattle, sheep, goats, antelopes, deer, and giraffes. The other main two-toed artiodactyls are camels and llamas. Most two-toed artiodactyls are ruminants; that is, they have a four-chambered stomach and chew the cud. The principal four-toed artiodactyls are pigs, peccaries, and hippopotamuses.

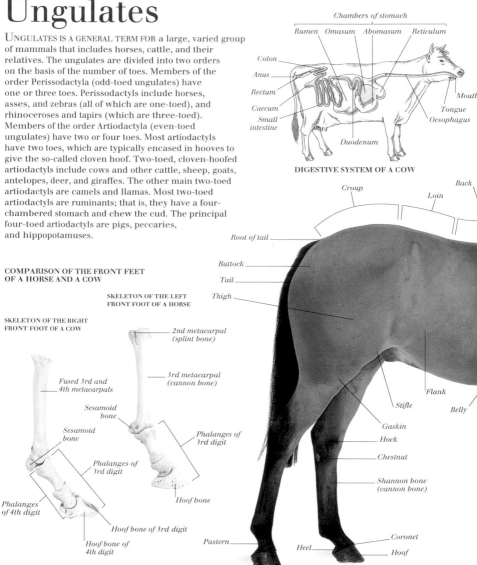

DIGESTIVE SYSTEM OF A COW

Chambers of stomach

Rumen   Omasum   Abomasum   Reticulum

Colon

Anus

Rectum

Caecum

Small intestine

Duodenum

Mouth

Tongue

Oesophagus

Croup

Back

Loin

Root of tail

Buttock

Tail

Thigh

Flank

Stifle

Belly

Gaskin

Hock

Chestnut

Shannon bone (cannon bone)

Coronet

Pastern

Heel

Hoof

COMPARISON OF THE FRONT FEET OF A HORSE AND A COW

SKELETON OF THE LEFT FRONT FOOT OF A HORSE

SKELETON OF THE RIGHT FRONT FOOT OF A COW

2nd metacarpal (splint bone)

Fused 3rd and 4th metacarpals

3rd metacarpal (cannon bone)

Sesamoid bone

Sesamoid bone

Phalanges of 3rd digit

Phalanges of 3rd digit

Phalanges of 4th digit

Hoof bone

Hoof bone of 3rd digit

Hoof bone of 4th digit

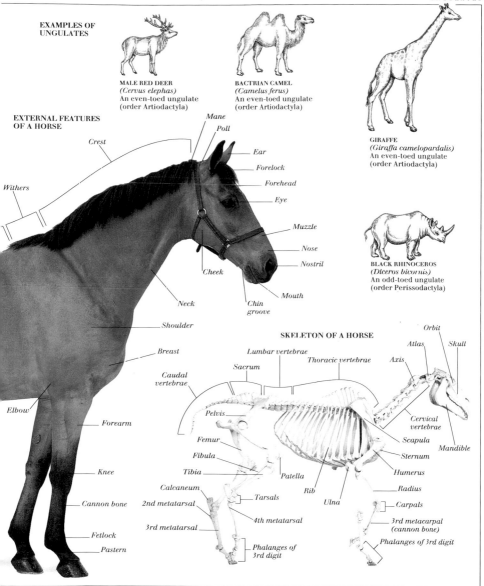

**EXAMPLES OF
UNGULATES**

MALE RED DEER
(Cervus elephas)
An even-toed ungulate
(order Artiodactyla)

BACTRIAN CAMEL
(Camelus ferus)
An even-toed ungulate
(order Artiodactyla)

GIRAFFE
(Giraffa camelopardalis)
An even-toed ungulate
(order Artiodactyla)

BLACK RHINOCEROS
(Diceros bicornis)
An odd-toed ungulate
(order Perissodactyla)

**EXTERNAL FEATURES
OF A HORSE**

Mane
Poll
Crest
Ear
Forelock
Withers
Forehead
Eye
Muzzle
Nose
Nostril
Cheek
Mouth
Neck
Chin
groove
Shoulder
Breast
Elbow
Forearm
Knee
Cannon bone
Fetlock
Pastern

SKELETON OF A HORSE

Orbit
Lumbar vertebrae
Thoracic vertebrae
Atlas
Skull
Sacrum
Axis
Caudal
vertebrae
Pelvis
Cervical
vertebrae
Femur
Scapula
Mandible
Fibula
Sternum
Tibia
Humerus
Patella
Calcaneum
Rib
Radius
2nd metatarsal
Tarsals
Ulna
Carpals
4th metatarsal
3rd metatarsal
3rd metacarpal
(cannon bone)
Phalanges of
3rd digit
Phalanges of 3rd digit

199

Elephants

THE TWO SPECIES of elephants—African and Asian—are the only members of the mammalian order Proboscidea. The bigger African elephant is the largest land animal: a fully grown male may be up to 4 m (13 ft) tall and weigh as much as 7 tonnes (6.9 tons). A fully grown male Asian elephant may be 3.3 m (11 ft) tall and weigh 5.4 tonnes (5.3 tons). The trunk—an extension of the nose and upper lip—is the elephant's other most obvious feature. It is used for manipulating and lifting, feeding, drinking and spraying water, smelling, touching, and producing trumpeting sounds. Other characteristic features include a pair of tusks, used for defence and for crushing vegetation; thick, pillar-like legs and broad feet to support the massive body; and large ear flaps that act as radiators to keep the elephant cool.

DIFFERENCES BETWEEN AFRICAN AND ASIAN ELEPHANTS

Flat forehead
Concave back
Very large ears
2 "lips" at the end of the trunk
4 toenails
3 toenails

AFRICAN ELEPHANT
(*Loxodonta africana*)

Twin-domed forehead
Arched back
Smaller ears
1 "lip" at the end of the trunk
5 toenails
4 toenails

ASIAN ELEPHANT
(*Elephas maximus*)

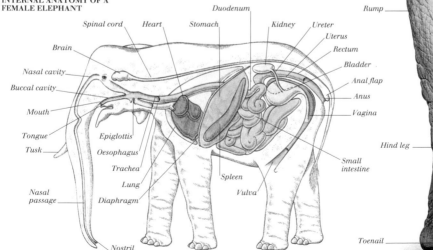

INTERNAL ANATOMY OF A FEMALE ELEPHANT

Spinal cord
Heart
Stomach
Duodenum
Kidney
Ureter
Uterus
Rectum
Bladder
Anal flap
Anus
Vagina
Rump
Brain
Nasal cavity
Buccal cavity
Mouth
Tongue
Tusk
Epiglottis
Oesophagus
Trachea
Lung
Diaphragm
Nasal passage
Spleen
Vulva
Small intestine
Hind leg
Nostril
Toenail

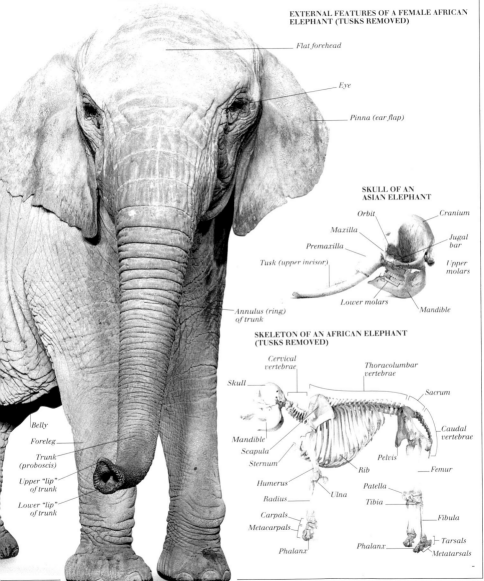

EXTERNAL FEATURES OF A FEMALE AFRICAN ELEPHANT (TUSKS REMOVED)

Flat forehead

Eye

Pinna (ear flap)

SKULL OF AN ASIAN ELEPHANT

Orbit

Cranium

Maxilla

Jugal bar

Premaxilla

Upper molars

Tusk (upper incisor)

Lower molars

Mandible

Annulus (ring) of trunk

SKELETON OF AN AFRICAN ELEPHANT (TUSKS REMOVED)

Cervical vertebrae

Thoracolumbar vertebrae

Skull

Sacrum

Belly

Foreleg

Mandible

Caudal vertebrae

Trunk (proboscis)

Scapula

Sternum

Pelvis

Upper "lip" of trunk

Rib

Femur

Lower "lip" of trunk

Humerus

Patella

Radius

Tibia

Ulna

Carpals

Fibula

Metacarpals

Tarsals

Phalanx

Phalanx

Metatarsals

Primates

THE MAMMALIAN ORDER PRIMATES consists of monkeys, apes, and their relatives (including humans). There are two suborders of primates: Prosimii, the primitive primates, which include lemurs, tarsiers, and lorises; and Anthropoidea, the advanced primates, which include monkeys, apes, and humans. The anthropoids are divided into New World monkeys, Old World monkeys, and hominids. New World monkeys typically have wide-apart nostrils that open to the side; and long tails, which are prehensile (grasping) in some species. This group of monkeys lives in South America, and includes marmosets, tamarins, and howler monkeys. Old World monkeys typically have close-set nostrils that open forwards or downwards; and non-prehensile tails. This group of monkeys lives in Africa and Asia, and includes langurs, mandrills, macaques, and baboons. Hominids typically have large brains, and no tail. This group includes the apes—chimpanzees, gibbons, gorillas, and orangutans—and humans.

**INTERNAL ANATOMY OF
A FEMALE CHIMPANZEE**

Buccal cavity
Brain
Nasal cavity
Tongue
Spinal cord
Trachea
Oesophagus
Lung
Heart
Diaphragm
Liver
Stomach
Pancreas
Spleen
Small intestine
Large intestine
Caecum
Rectum
Appendix
Bladder
Ovary
Urethra
Uterus
Vagina

**SKELETON OF A
RHESUS MONKEY**

Skull
Orbit
Cervical vertebrae
Thoracic vertebrae
Mandible
Clavicle
Scapula
Rib
Humerus
Lumbar vertebrae
Sacrum
Radius
Ulna
Femur
Patella
Tibia
Carpals
Fibula
Metacarpals
Pelvis
Phalanges
Caudal vertebrae
Tarsals
Metatarsals
Phalanges

SKULL OF A CHIMPANZEE

Temporal bone
Suture
Frontal bone
Parietal bone
Supraorbital ridge
Orbit
Occipital bone
Maxilla
Premaxilla
Auditory meatus
Zygomatic arch
Incisor tooth
Mandible
Molar tooth
Premolar tooth
Canine tooth

EXAMPLES OF PRIMATES

RING-TAILED LEMUR
(Lemur catta)
A prosimian

MALE RED HOWLER MONKEY
(Alouatta seniculus)
A New World monkey

MALE MANDRILL
(Mandrillus sphinx)
An Old World monkey

CHIMPANZEE
(Pan troglodytes)
An ape

EXTERNAL FEATURES OF
A YOUNG GORILLA

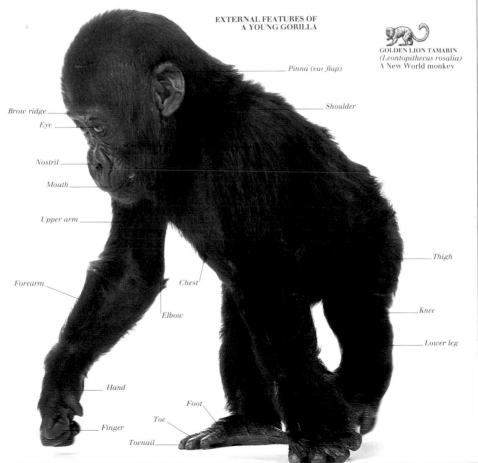

GOLDEN LION TAMARIN
(Leontopithecus rosalia)
A New World monkey

Pinna (ear flap)

Brow ridge

Eye

Shoulder

Nostril

Mouth

Upper arm

Thigh

Forearm

Chest

Elbow

Knee

Lower leg

Hand

Foot

Finger

Toe

Toenail

Dolphins, whales, and seals

DOLPHINS, WHALES, AND SEALS belong to two orders of mammals adapted to living in water. Dolphins and whales make up the order Cetacea. Typical cetacean features include a streamlined, fish-like shape; forelimbs in the form of flippers; no visible hind limbs; a horizontally flattened tail; and thick blubber under the skin. There are two groups of cetaceans: toothed whales, including sperm whales, white whales, beaked whales, dolphins, and porpoises; and the larger whalebone (baleen) whales, including rorquals, grey whales, and right whales. The blue whale—a rorqual—is the largest living animal: an adult may be up to 30 m (100 ft) long and weigh 130 tonnes (128 tons). Seals and their relatives—sea lions and walruses—make up the order Pinnipedia. Characteristically, they have a streamlined, torpedo-shaped body; forelimbs and hind limbs modified as flippers; thick blubber; and no external ears.

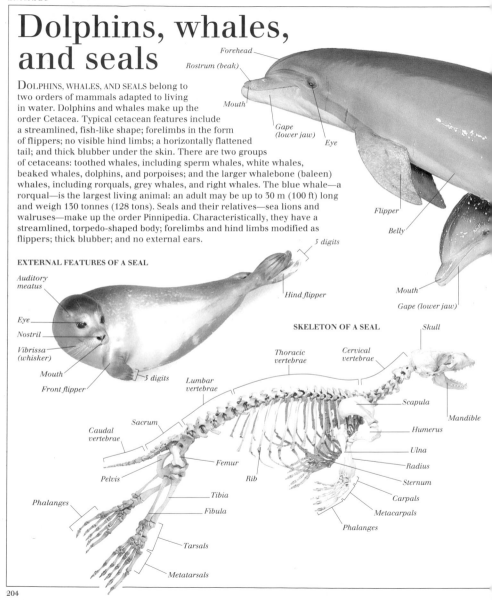

Forehead
Rostrum (beak)
Mouth
Gape (lower jaw)
Eye
Flipper
Belly
Mouth
Gape (lower jaw)

EXTERNAL FEATURES OF A SEAL

Auditory meatus
Eye
Nostril
Vibrissa (whisker)
Mouth
Front flipper
5 digits
5 digits
Hind flipper

SKELETON OF A SEAL

Skull
Thoracic vertebrae
Cervical vertebrae
Lumbar vertebrae
Scapula
Mandible
Caudal vertebrae
Sacrum
Humerus
Ulna
Radius
Sternum
Femur
Rib
Carpals
Pelvis
Metacarpals
Phalanges
Tibia
Fibula
Phalanges
Tarsals
Metatarsals

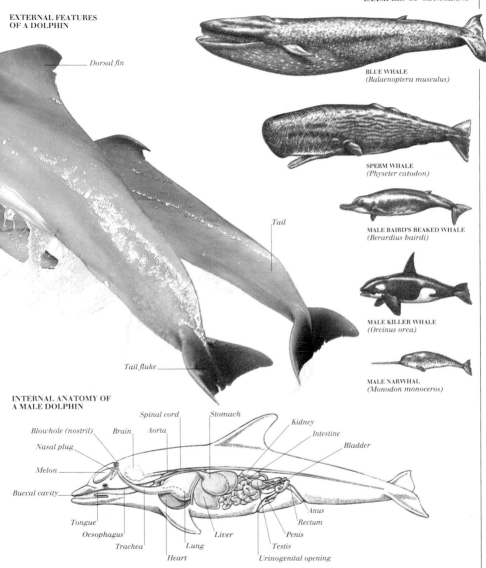

EXAMPLES OF CETACEANS

**EXTERNAL FEATURES
OF A DOLPHIN**

Dorsal fin

Tail

Tail fluke

BLUE WHALE
(Balaenoptera musculus)

SPERM WHALE
(Physeter catodon)

MALE BAIRD'S BEAKED WHALE
(Berardius bairdi)

MALE KILLER WHALE
(Orcinus orca)

MALE NARWHAL
(Monodon monoceros)

**INTERNAL ANATOMY OF
A MALE DOLPHIN**

Spinal cord *Stomach*

Blowhole (nostril) *Brain* *Aorta* *Kidney*

Nasal plug *Intestine*

Melon *Bladder*

Buccal cavity

Anus

Rectum

Tongue *Penis*

Oesophagus *Liver* *Testis*

Trachea *Lung* *Urinogenital opening*

Heart

205

Marsupials and Monotremes

MARSUPIALS AND MONOTREMES are two orders of mammals that differ from other mammalian groups in the ways that their young develop. The order Marsupalia, the pouched mammals, is made up of kangaroos and their relatives. Typically, marsupials give birth to their young at a very early stage of development. The young then crawls to the mother's pouch (which is on the outside of her abdomen), where it attaches itself to a nipple and remains until fully developed. Most marsupials live in Australia, although the opossums—which are classified as marsupials despite not having a pouch—live in the Americas. The order Monotremata is made up of the platypus and its relatives (the echidnas, or spiny anteaters). The monotremes are primitive mammals that lay eggs, which the mother incubates. The monotremes are found only in Australia and New Guinea.

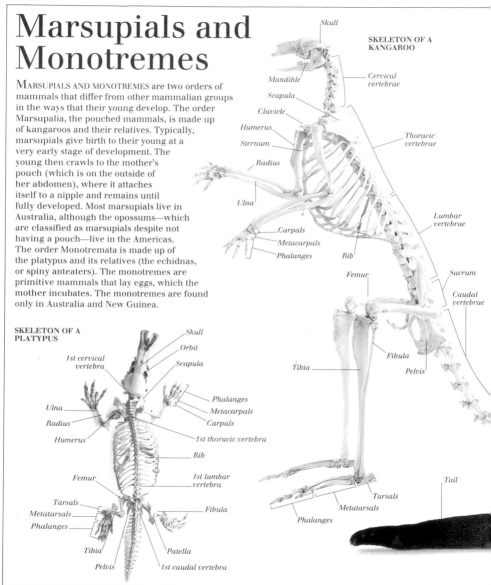

SKELETON OF A KANGAROO

Skull

Mandible

Scapula

Clavicle

Humerus

Sternum

Radius

Ulna

Cervical vertebrae

Thoracic vertebrae

Lumbar vertebrae

Carpals

Metacarpals

Phalanges

Rib

Femur

Sacrum

Caudal vertebrae

Tibia

Fibula

Pelvis

Tail

SKELETON OF A PLATYPUS

Skull

Orbit

Scapula

1st cervical vertebra

Ulna

Radius

Humerus

Phalanges

Metacarpals

Carpals

1st thoracic vertebra

Rib

Femur

1st lumbar vertebra

Tarsals

Metatarsals

Phalanges

Fibula

Tibia

Pelvis

Patella

1st caudal vertebra

Tarsals

Metatarsals

Phalanges

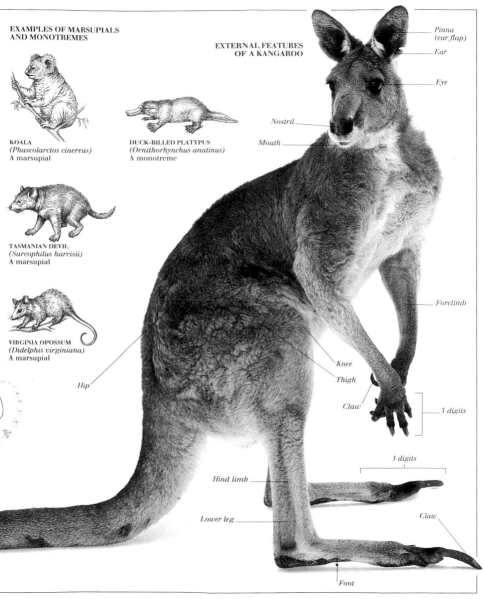

EXAMPLES OF MARSUPIALS AND MONOTREMES

EXTERNAL FEATURES OF A KANGAROO

KOALA
(*Phascolarctos cinereus*)
A marsupial

DUCK-BILLED PLATYPUS
(*Ornithorhynchus anatinus*)
A monotreme

TASMANIAN DEVIL
(*Sarcophilus harrisii*)
A marsupial

VIRGINIA OPOSSUM
(*Didelphis virginiana*)
A marsupial

Pinna
(ear flap)

Ear

Eye

Nostril

Mouth

Forelimb

Hip

Knee

Thigh

Claw

5 digits

3 digits

Hind limb

Lower leg

Claw

Foot

207

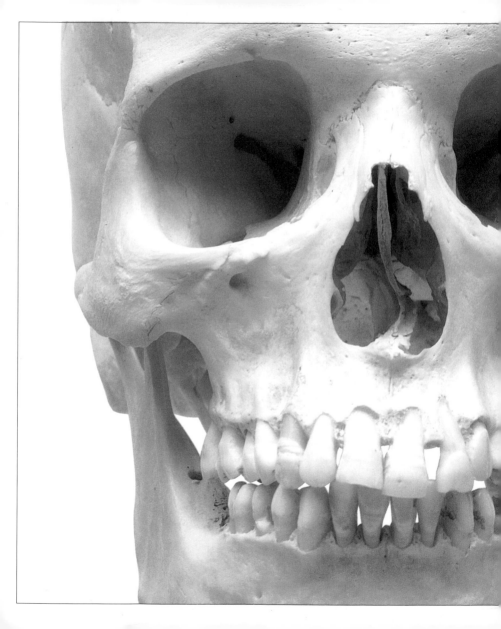

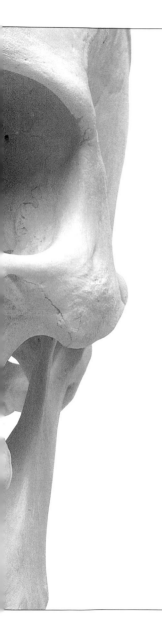

THE
HUMAN BODY

BODY FEATURES	210
HEAD	212
BODY ORGANS	214
BODY CELLS	216
SKELETON	218
SKULL	220
SPINE	222
BONES AND JOINTS	224
MUSCLES 1	226
MUSCLES 2	228
HANDS	230
FEET	232
SKIN AND HAIR	234
BRAIN	236
NERVOUS SYSTEM	238
EYE	240
EAR	242
NOSE, MOUTH, AND THROAT	244
TEETH	246
DIGESTIVE SYSTEM	248
HEART	250
CIRCULATORY SYSTEM	252
RESPIRATORY SYSTEM	254
URINARY SYSTEM	256
REPRODUCTIVE SYSTEM	258
DEVELOPMENT OF A BABY	260

Body features

ALTHOUGH THERE IS enormous variation between the external appearances of humans, all bodies contain the same basic features. The outward form of the human body depends on the size of the skeleton, the shape of the muscles, the thickness of the fat layer beneath the skin, the elasticity or sagginess of the skin, and the person's age and sex. Males tend to be taller than females, with broader shoulders, more body hair, and a different pattern of fat deposits under the skin; the female body tends to be less muscular and has a shallower and wider pelvis to allow for childbirth.

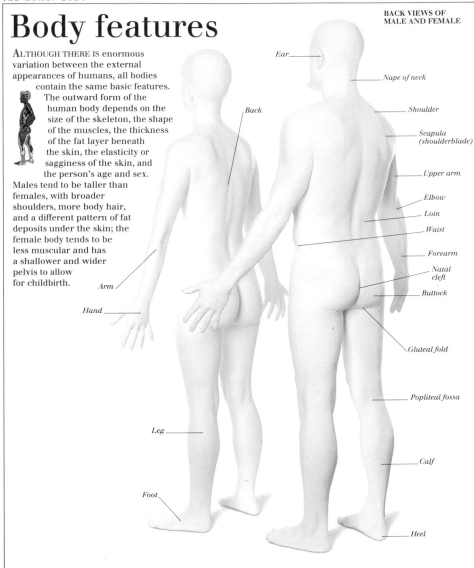

Ear

Nape of neck

Back

Shoulder

Scapula (shoulderblade)

Upper arm

Elbow

Loin

Waist

Forearm

Natal cleft

Buttock

Arm

Hand

Gluteal fold

Popliteal fossa

Leg

Calf

Foot

Heel

**FRONT VIEWS OF
MALE AND FEMALE**

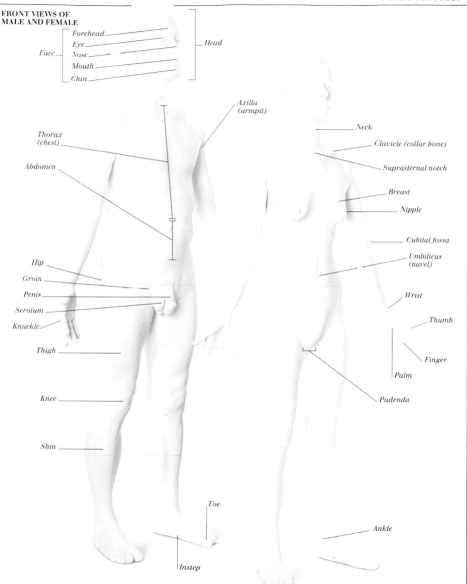

Forehead

Eye

Face — Nose

Mouth

Chin

Head

Axilla
(armpit)

Thorax
(chest)

Abdomen

Neck

Clavicle (collar bone)

Suprasternal notch

Breast

Nipple

Cubital fossa

Umbilicus
(navel)

Hip

Groin

Penis

Scrotum

Knuckle

Wrist

Thumb

Finger

Palm

Thigh

Knee

Pudenda

Shin

Toe

Ankle

Instep

Head

IN A NEWBORN BABY, the head accounts for one-quarter of the total body length; by adulthood, the proportion has reduced to one-eighth. Contained in the head are the body's main sense organs: eyes, ears, olfactory nerves that detect smells, and the taste buds of the tongue. Signals from these organs pass to the body's great coordination centre: the brain, housed in the protective, bony dome of the skull. Hair on the head insulates against heat loss, and adult males also grow thick facial hair. The face has three important openings: two nostrils through which air passes, and the mouth, which takes in nourishment and helps form speech. Although all heads are basically similar, differences in the size, shape, and colour of features produce an infinite variety of appearances.

SIDE VIEW OF EXTERNAL FEATURES OF HEAD

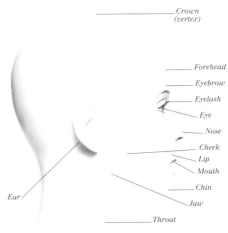

Crown (vertex)

Forehead

Eyebrow

Eyelash

Eye

Nose

Cheek

Lip

Mouth

Chin

Ear

Jaw

Throat

SECTION THROUGH HEAD

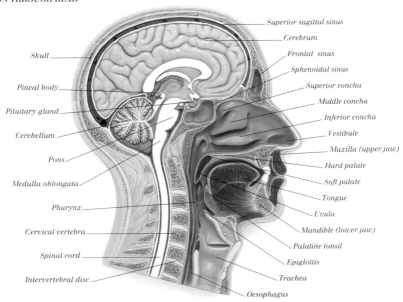

Superior sagittal sinus

Cerebrum

Skull

Frontal sinus

Sphenoidal sinus

Pineal body

Superior concha

Middle concha

Pituitary gland

Inferior concha

Vestibule

Cerebellum

Maxilla (upper jaw)

Pons

Hard palate

Soft palate

Medulla oblongata

Tongue

Pharynx

Uvula

Mandible (lower jaw)

Cervical vertebra

Palatine tonsil

Spinal cord

Epiglottis

Intervertebral disc

Trachea

Oesophagus

**FRONT VIEW OF EXTERNAL
FEATURES OF HEAD**

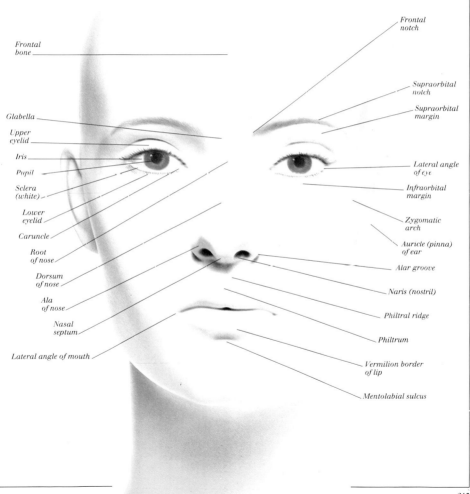

Frontal notch

Frontal bone

Supraorbital notch

Supraorbital margin

Glabella

Upper eyelid

Iris

Lateral angle of eye

Pupil

Infraorbital margin

Sclera (white)

Lower eyelid

Zygomatic arch

Caruncle

Auricle (pinna) of ear

Root of nose

Alar groove

Dorsum of nose

Naris (nostril)

Ala of nose

Philtral ridge

Nasal septum

Philtrum

Lateral angle of mouth

Vermilion border of lip

Mentolabial sulcus

Body organs

ALL THE VITAL BODY ORGANS except for the brain are enclosed within the trunk or torso (the body apart from the head and limbs). The trunk contains two large cavities separated by a muscular sheet called the diaphragm. The upper cavity, known as the thorax or chest cavity, contains the heart and lungs. The lower cavity, called the abdominal cavity, contains the stomach, intestines, liver, and pancreas, which all play a role in digesting food. Also within the trunk are the kidneys and bladder, which are part of the urinary system, and the reproductive organs, which hold the seeds of new human life. Modern imaging techniques, such as contrast X-rays and different types of scans, make it possible to see and study body organs without the need to cut through their protective coverings of skin, fat, muscle, and bone.

MAJOR INTERNAL STRUCTURES

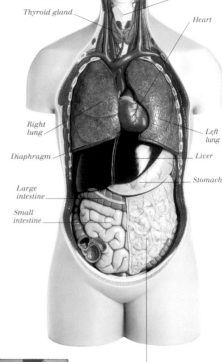

Thyroid gland
Larynx
Heart
Right lung
Left lung
Diaphragm
Liver
Stomach
Large intestine
Small intestine
Greater omentum

IMAGING THE BODY

SCINTIGRAM OF HEART CHAMBERS

ANGIOGRAM OF RIGHT LUNG

CONTRAST X-RAY OF GALLBLADDER

SCINTIGRAM OF NERVOUS SYSTEM

DOUBLE CONTRAST X-RAY OF COLON

ULTRASOUND SCAN OF TWINS IN UTERUS

ANGIOGRAM OF KIDNEYS

ANGIOGRAM OF ARTERIES OF HEAD

CT SCAN THROUGH FEMALE CHEST

THERMOGRAM OF CHEST REGION

ANGIOGRAM OF ARTERIES OF HEART

MRI SCAN THROUGH HEAD AT EYE LEVEL

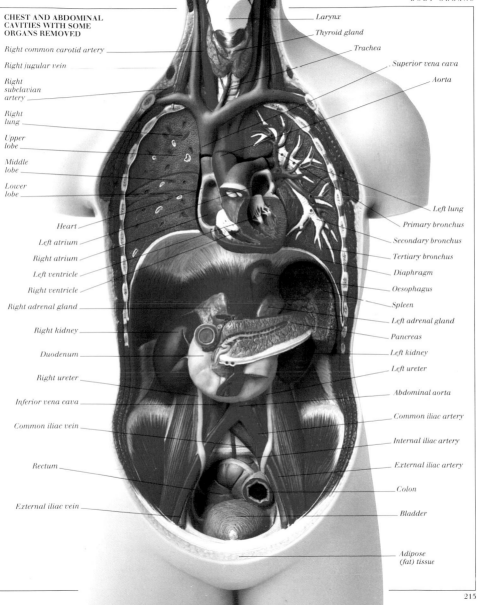

CHEST AND ABDOMINAL CAVITIES WITH SOME ORGANS REMOVED

Right common carotid artery

Right jugular vein

Right subclavian artery

Right lung

Upper lobe

Middle lobe

Lower lobe

Heart

Left atrium

Right atrium

Left ventricle

Right ventricle

Right adrenal gland

Right kidney

Duodenum

Right ureter

Inferior vena cava

Common iliac vein

Rectum

External iliac vein

Larynx

Thyroid gland

Trachea

Superior vena cava

Aorta

Left lung

Primary bronchus

Secondary bronchus

Tertiary bronchus

Diaphragm

Oesophagus

Spleen

Left adrenal gland

Pancreas

Left kidney

Left ureter

Abdominal aorta

Common iliac artery

Internal iliac artery

External iliac artery

Colon

Bladder

Adipose (fat) tissue

Body cells

EVERYONE IS MADE UP OF BILLIONS OF CELLS, which are the basic structural units of the body. Bones, muscles, nerves, skin, blood, and all other body tissues are formed from different types of cells. Each cell has a specific function but works with other types of cells to perform the enormous number of tasks needed to sustain life. Most body cells have a similar basic structure. Each cell has an outer layer (called the cell membrane) and contains a fluid material (cytoplasm). Within the cytoplasm are many specialized structures (organelles). The most important organelle is the nucleus, which contains vital genetic material and acts as the cell's control centre.

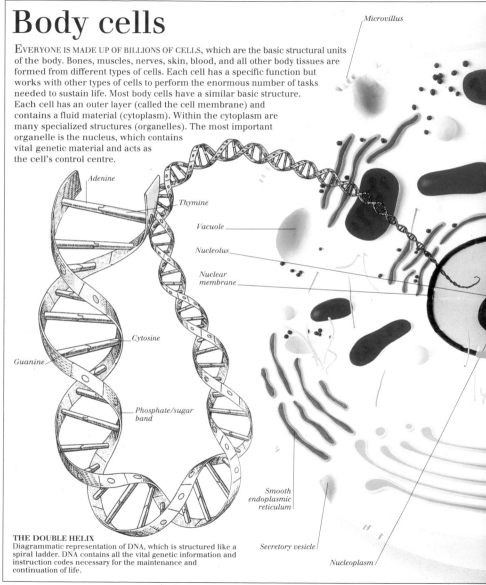

Microvillus

Adenine

Thymine

Vacuole

Nucleolus

Nuclear membrane

Cytosine

Guanine

Phosphate/sugar band

Smooth endoplasmic reticulum

Secretory vesicle

Nucleoplasm

THE DOUBLE HELIX
Diagrammatic representation of DNA, which is structured like a spiral ladder. DNA contains all the vital genetic information and instruction codes necessary for the maintenance and continuation of life.

GENERALIZED HUMAN CELL

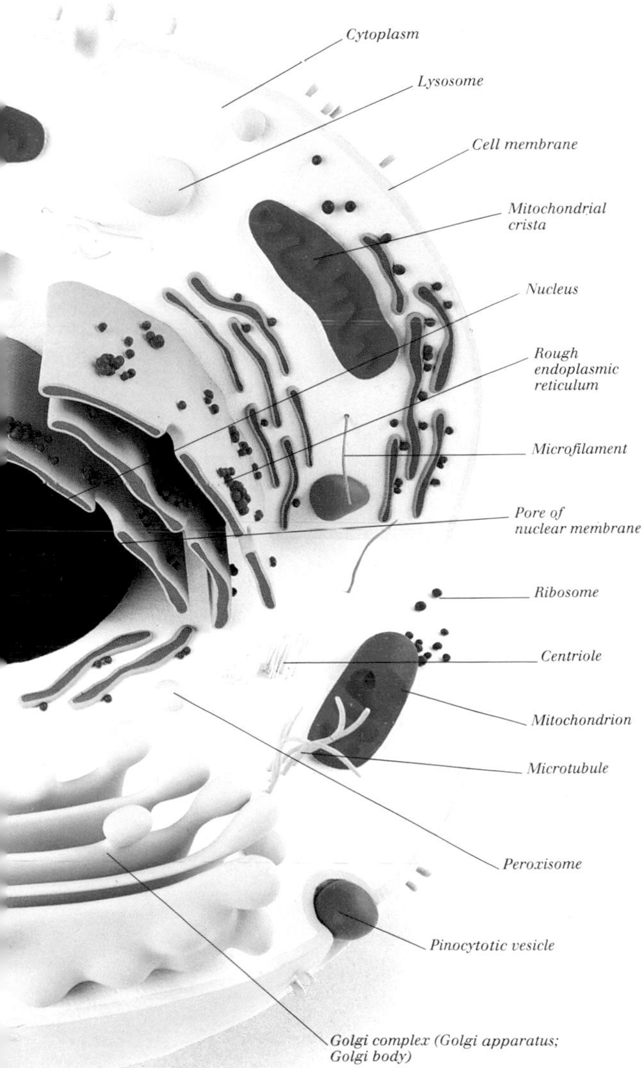

Cytoplasm

Lysosome

Cell membrane

Mitochondrial crista

Nucleus

Rough endoplasmic reticulum

Microfilament

Pore of nuclear membrane

Ribosome

Centriole

Mitochondrion

Microtubule

Peroxisome

Pinocytotic vesicle

Golgi complex (Golgi apparatus; Golgi body)

TYPES OF CELLS

BONE-FORMING CELL

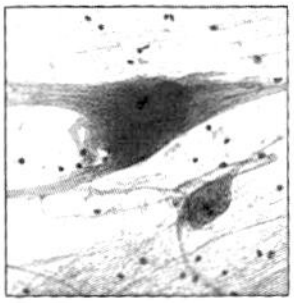

NERVE CELLS IN SPINAL CORD

SPERM CELLS IN SEMEN

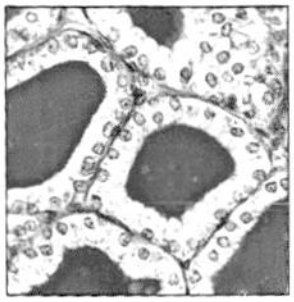

SECRETORY THYROID GLAND CELLS

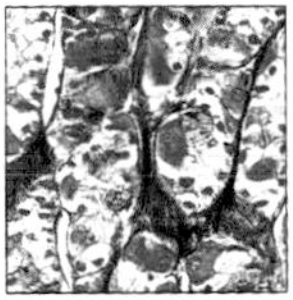

ACID-SECRETING STOMACH CELLS

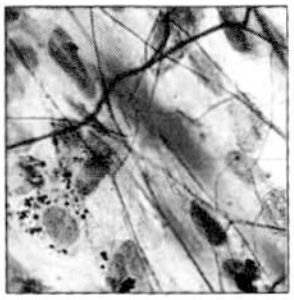

CONNECTIVE TISSUE CELLS

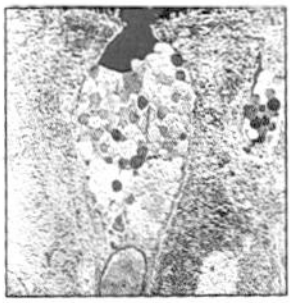

MUCUS-SECRETING DUODENAL CELLS

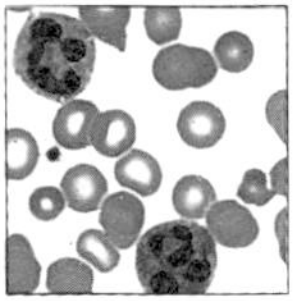

RED AND TWO WHITE BLOOD CELLS

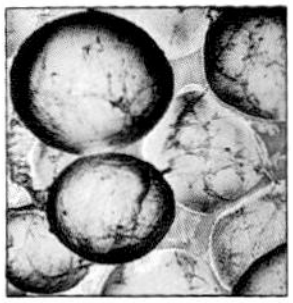

FAT CELLS IN ADIPOSE TISSUE

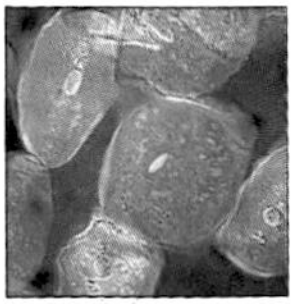

EPITHELIAL CELLS IN CHEEK

Skeleton

THE SKELETON IS A MOBILE FRAMEWORK made up of 206 bones, approximately half of which are in the hands and feet. Although individual bones are rigid, the skeleton as a whole is remarkably flexible and allows the human body a huge range of movement. The skeleton serves as an anchorage for the skeletal muscles, and as a protective cage for the body's internal organs. Female bones are usually smaller and lighter than male bones, and the female pelvis is shallower and has a wider cavity.

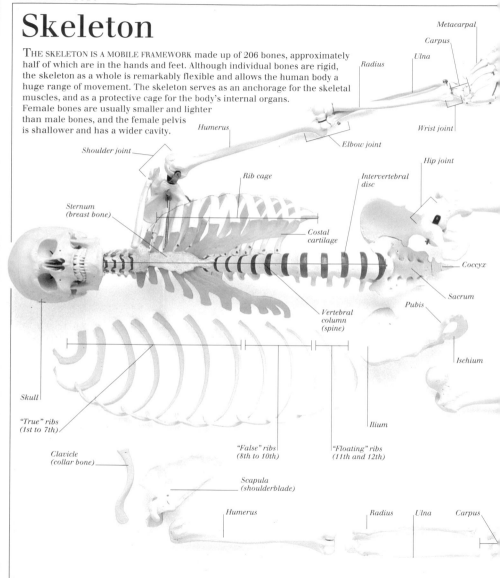

Metacarpal

Carpus

Ulna

Radius

Humerus

Elbow joint

Wrist joint

Shoulder joint

Hip joint

Rib cage

Intervertebral disc

Sternum (breast bone)

Costal cartilage

Coccyx

Vertebral column (spine)

Sacrum

Pubis

Ischium

Skull

Ilium

"True" ribs (1st to 7th)

"False" ribs (8th to 10th)

"Floating" ribs (11th and 12th)

Clavicle (collar bone)

Scapula (shoulderblade)

Humerus

Radius

Ulna

Carpus

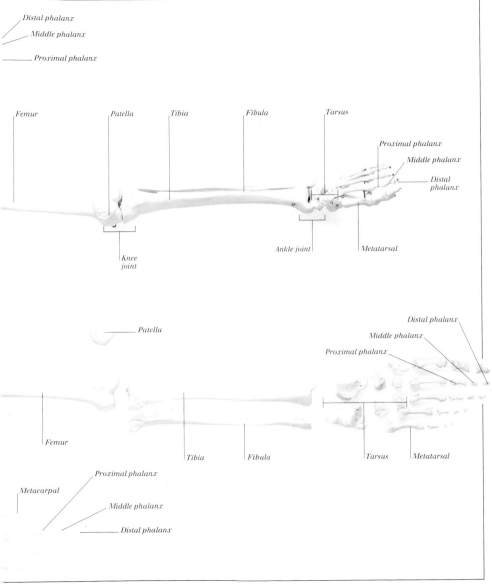

Distal phalanx

Middle phalanx

Proximal phalanx

Femur

Patella

Tibia

Fibula

Tarsus

Proximal phalanx

Middle phalanx

Distal phalanx

Knee joint

Ankle joint

Metatarsal

Patella

Distal phalanx

Middle phalanx

Proximal phalanx

Femur

Tibia

Fibula

Tarsus

Metatarsal

Metacarpal

Proximal phalanx

Middle phalanx

Distal phalanx

Skull

THE SKULL is the most complicated bony structure of the body but every feature serves a purpose. Internally, the main hollow chamber of the skull has three levels that support the brain, with every bump and hollow corresponding to the shape of the brain. Underneath and towards the back of the skull is a large round hole, the foramen magnum, through which the spinal cord passes. To the front of this are many smaller openings through which nerves, arteries, and veins pass to and from the brain. The roof of the skull is formed from four thin, curved bones that are firmly fixed together from the age of about two years. At the front of the skull are the two orbits, which contain the eyeballs, and a central hole for the airway of the nose. The jaw bone hinges on either side at ear level.

RIGHT SIDE VIEW OF A FETAL SKULL

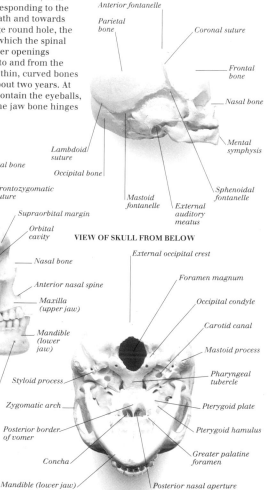

Anterior fontanelle

Parietal bone

Coronal suture

Frontal bone

Nasal bone

Mental symphysis

Sphenoidal fontanelle

Mastoid fontanelle

External auditory meatus

Lambdoid suture

Occipital bone

RIGHT SIDE VIEW OF SKULL

Coronal suture

Frontal bone

Greater wing of sphenoid bone

Frontozygomatic suture

Parietal bone

Supraorbital margin

Squamous suture

Orbital cavity

Nasal bone

Anterior nasal spine

Maxilla (upper jaw)

Mandible (lower jaw)

Lambdoid suture

Occipital bone

Temporal bone

External auditory meatus

Styloid process

Condyle

Coronoid process

Zygomatic bone

Mastoid process

Mental foramen

VIEW OF SKULL FROM BELOW

External occipital crest

Foramen magnum

Occipital condyle

Carotid canal

Mastoid process

Pharyngeal tubercle

Pterygoid plate

Pterygoid hamulus

Greater palatine foramen

Zygomatic arch

Posterior border of vomer

Concha

Mandible (lower jaw)

Posterior nasal aperture

FRONT VIEW OF SKULL

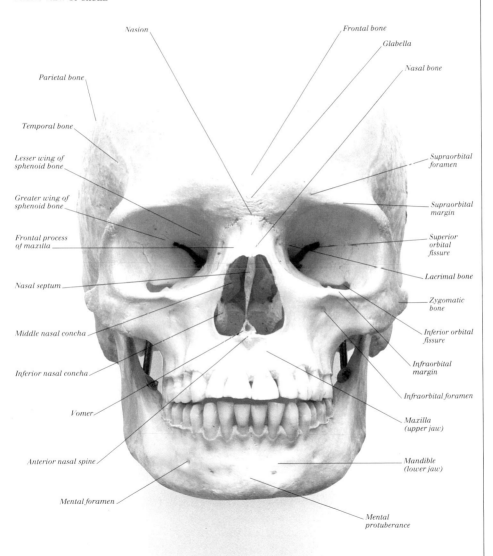

Nasion

Frontal bone

Glabella

Nasal bone

Parietal bone

Temporal bone

Lesser wing of
sphenoid bone

Greater wing of
sphenoid bone

Frontal process
of maxilla

Nasal septum

Middle nasal concha

Inferior nasal concha

Vomer

Anterior nasal spine

Mental foramen

Supraorbital
foramen

Supraorbital
margin

Superior
orbital
fissure

Lacrimal bone

Zygomatic
bone

Inferior orbital
fissure

Infraorbital
margin

Infraorbital foramen

Maxilla
(upper jaw)

Mandible
(lower jaw)

Mental
protuberance

Spine

THE SPINE (OR VERTEBRAL COLUMN) has two main functions: it serves as a protective surrounding for the delicate spinal cord and forms the supporting back bone of the skeleton. The spine consists of 24 separate differently shaped bones (vertebrae) with a curved, triangular bone (the sacrum) at the bottom. The sacrum is made up of fused vertebrae; at its lower end is a small tail-like structure made up of tiny bones collectively called the coccyx. Between each pair of vertebrae is a disc of cartilage that cushions the bones during movement. The top two vertebrae differ in appearance from the others and work as a pair: the first, called the atlas, rotates around a stout vertical peg on the second, the axis. This arrangement allows the skull to move freely up and down, and from side to side.

SPINE DIVIDED INTO VERTEBRAL SECTIONS

FRONT

Cervical vertebrae

Thoracic vertebrae

Lumbar vertebrae

Sacral vertebrae

Coccygeal vertebrae

TYPES OF VERTEBRAE (VIEWED FROM ABOVE)

ATLAS

Anterior arch
Anterior tubercle
Vertebral foramen
Transverse process

Lateral mass with superior articular facet
Posterior arch
Posterior tubercle
Transverse foramen

AXIS

Facet
Dens

Vertebral foramen
Spinous process
Lamina
Transverse process and foramen

CERVICAL VERTEBRA

Body
Anterior tubercle
Posterior tubercle

Superior articular process
Spinous process
Vertebral foramen
Transverse foramen

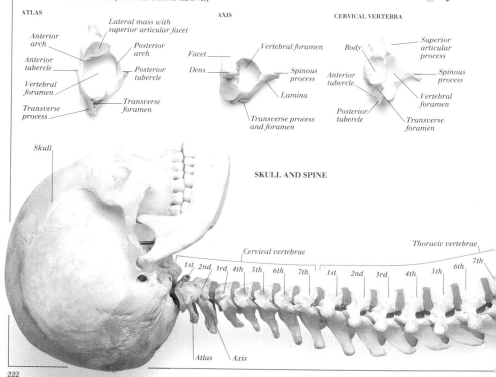

SKULL AND SPINE

Skull

Cervical vertebrae

1st 2nd 3rd 4th 5th 6th 7th

1st 2nd 3rd 4th 5th 6th 7th

Thoracic vertebrae

Atlas   Axis

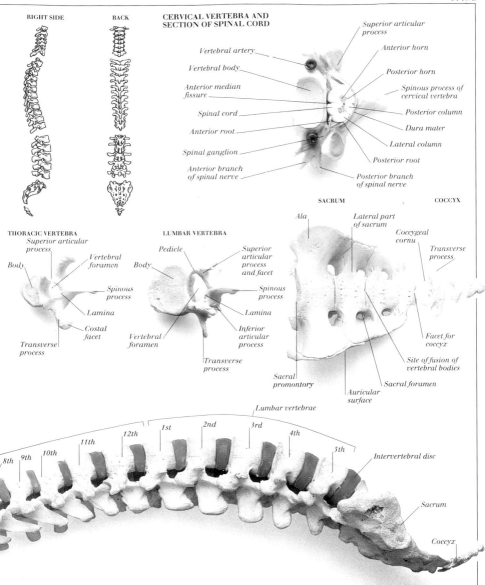

RIGHT SIDE

BACK

CERVICAL VERTEBRA AND SECTION OF SPINAL CORD

Superior articular process

Vertebral artery

Anterior horn

Vertebral body

Posterior horn

Anterior median fissure

Spinous process of cervical vertebra

Spinal cord

Posterior column

Anterior root

Dura mater

Spinal ganglion

Lateral column

Anterior branch of spinal nerve

Posterior root

Posterior branch of spinal nerve

SACRUM

COCCYX

Ala

Lateral part of sacrum

Coccygeal cornu

THORACIC VERTEBRA

Superior articular process

Vertebral foramen

Transverse process

Body

Spinous process

Lamina

Costal facet

Transverse process

LUMBAR VERTEBRA

Pedicle

Body

Superior articular process and facet

Spinous process

Lamina

Inferior articular process

Vertebral foramen

Transverse process

Sacral promontory

Facet for coccyx

Site of fusion of vertebral bodies

Sacral foramen

Auricular surface

Lumbar vertebrae

1st *2nd* *3rd* *4th* *5th*

8th *9th* *10th* *11th* *12th*

Intervertebral disc

Sacrum

Coccyx

Bones and joints

BONES FORM the body's hard, strong skeletal framework. Each bone has a hard, compact exterior surrounding a spongy, lighter interior. The long bones of the arms and legs, such as the femur (thigh bone), have a central cavity containing bone marrow. Bones are composed chiefly of calcium, phosphorus, and a fibrous substance known as collagen. Bones meet at joints, which are of several different types. For example, the hip is a ball-and-socket joint that allows the femur a wide range of movement, whereas finger joints are simple hinge joints that allow only bending and straightening. Joints are held in place by bands of tissue called ligaments. Movement of joints is facilitated by the smooth hyaline cartilage that covers the bone ends and by the synovial membrane that lines and lubricates the joint.

LIGAMENTS SURROUNDING HIP JOINT

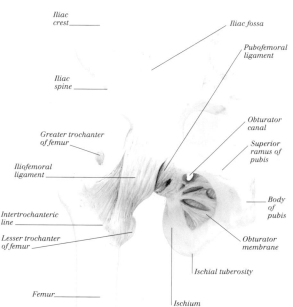

Iliac crest

Iliac fossa

Pubofemoral ligament

Iliac spine

Greater trochanter of femur

Iliofemoral ligament

Obturator canal

Superior ramus of pubis

Body of pubis

Intertrochanteric line

Lesser trochanter of femur

Obturator membrane

Femur

Ischial tuberosity

Ischium

SECTION THROUGH LEFT FEMUR

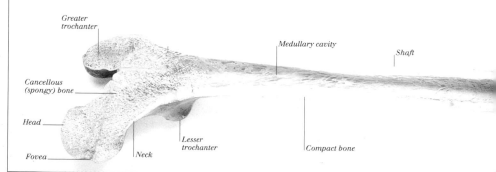

Greater trochanter

Medullary cavity

Shaft

Cancellous (spongy) bone

Head

Fovea

Neck

Lesser trochanter

Compact bone

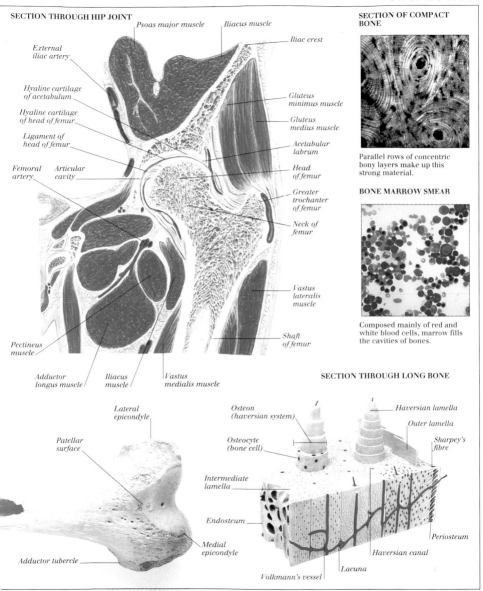

SECTION THROUGH HIP JOINT

Psoas major muscle

Iliacus muscle

Iliac crest

External iliac artery

Hyaline cartilage of acetabulum

Hyaline cartilage of head of femur

Ligament of head of femur

Femoral artery

Articular cavity

Gluteus minimus muscle

Gluteus medius muscle

Acetabular labrum

Head of femur

Greater trochanter of femur

Neck of femur

Vastus lateralis muscle

Shaft of femur

Pectineus muscle

Adductor longus muscle

Iliacus muscle

Vastus medialis muscle

SECTION OF COMPACT BONE

Parallel rows of concentric bony layers make up this strong material.

BONE MARROW SMEAR

Composed mainly of red and white blood cells, marrow fills the cavities of bones.

SECTION THROUGH LONG BONE

Lateral epicondyle

Patellar surface

Osteon (haversian system)

Osteocyte (bone cell)

Intermediate lamella

Endosteum

Adductor tubercle

Medial epicondyle

Volkmann's vessel

Lacuna

Haversian canal

Periosteum

Sharpey's fibre

Outer lamella

Haversian lamella

225

Muscles 1

THERE ARE THREE MAIN TYPES OF MUSCLE: skeletal muscle (also called voluntary muscle because it can be consciously controlled); smooth muscle (also called involuntary muscle because it is not under voluntary control); and the specialized muscle tissue of the heart. Humans have more than 600 skeletal muscles, which differ in size and shape according to the jobs they do. Skeletal muscles are attached either directly or indirectly (via tendons) to bones, and work in opposing pairs (one muscle in the pair contracts while the other relaxes) to produce body movements as diverse as walking, threading a needle, and an array of facial expressions. Smooth muscles occur in the walls of internal body organs and perform actions such as forcing food through the intestines, contracting the uterus (womb) in childbirth, and pumping blood through the blood vessels.

SUPERFICIAL SKELETAL MUSCLES

FRONT VIEW

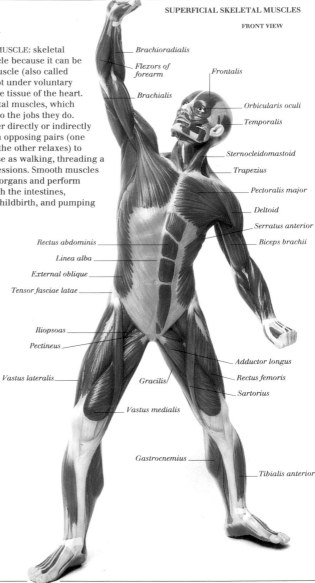

- Brachioradialis
- Flexors of forearm
- Brachialis
- Frontalis
- Orbicularis oculi
- Temporalis
- Sternocleidomastoid
- Trapezius
- Pectoralis major
- Deltoid
- Serratus anterior
- Biceps brachii
- Rectus abdominis
- Linea alba
- External oblique
- Tensor fasciae latae
- Iliopsoas
- Pectineus
- Adductor longus
- Rectus femoris
- Sartorius
- Vastus lateralis
- Gracilis
- Vastus medialis
- Gastrocnemius
- Tibialis anterior

SOME OTHER MUSCLES IN THE BODY

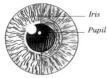

- Iris
- Pupil

IRIS
The muscle fibres contract and dilate (expand) to alter pupil size.

TONGUE
Interlacing layers of muscle allow great mobility.

ILEUM
Opposing muscle layers transport semi-digested food.

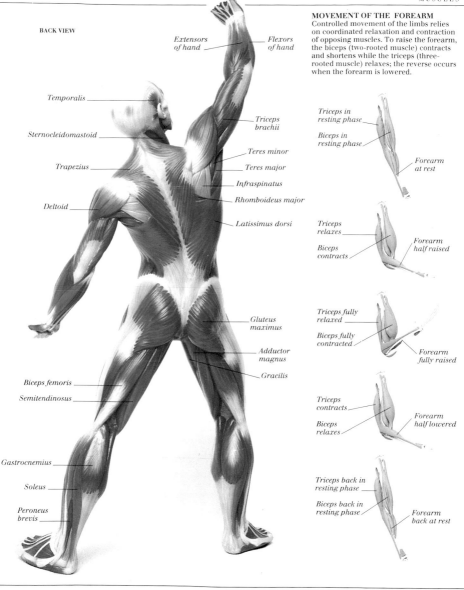

BACK VIEW

Extensors
of hand

Flexors
of hand

Temporalis

Sternocleidomastoid

Trapezius

Deltoid

Triceps
brachii

Teres minor

Teres major

Infraspinatus

Rhomboideus major

Latissimus dorsi

Gluteus
maximus

Adductor
magnus

Gracilis

Biceps femoris

Semitendinosus

Gastrocnemius

Soleus

Peroneus
brevis

MOVEMENT OF THE FOREARM
Controlled movement of the limbs relies
on coordinated relaxation and contraction
of opposing muscles. To raise the forearm,
the biceps (two-rooted muscle) contracts
and shortens while the triceps (three-
rooted muscle) relaxes; the reverse occurs
when the forearm is lowered.

Triceps in
resting phase

Biceps in
resting phase

Forearm
at rest

Triceps
relaxes

Biceps
contracts

Forearm
half raised

Triceps fully
relaxed

Biceps fully
contracted

Forearm
fully raised

Triceps
contracts

Biceps
relaxes

Forearm
half lowered

Triceps back in
resting phase

Biceps back in
resting phase

Forearm
back at rest

Muscles 2

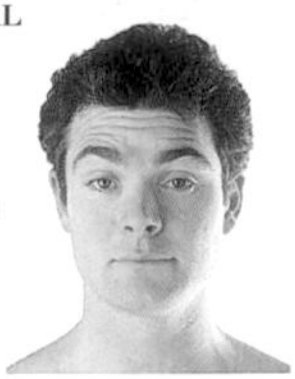

SKELETAL MUSCLE FIBRE

Myofibril
Motor end plate
Synaptic knob
Schwann cell
Motor neuron
Node of Ranvier
Sarcomere
Nucleus
Sarcoplasmic reticulum
Sarcolemma
Endomysium

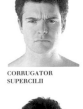

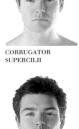

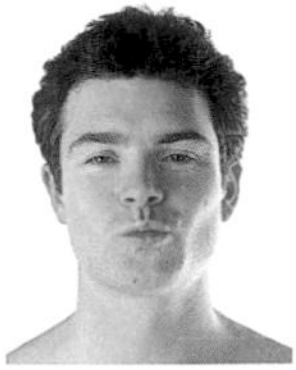

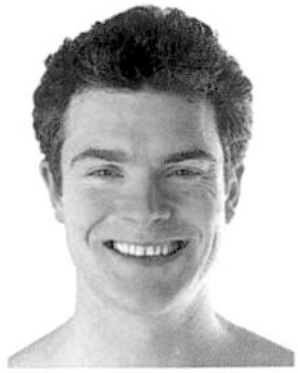

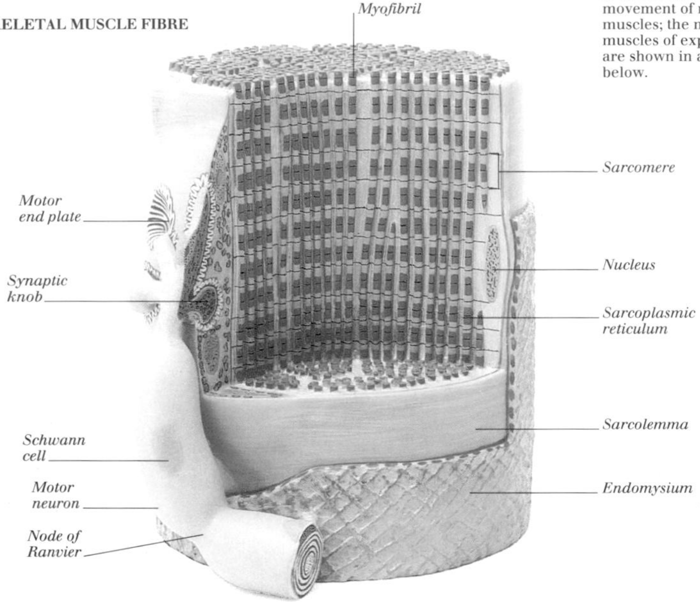

TYPES OF MUSCLE

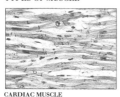

CARDIAC MUSCLE

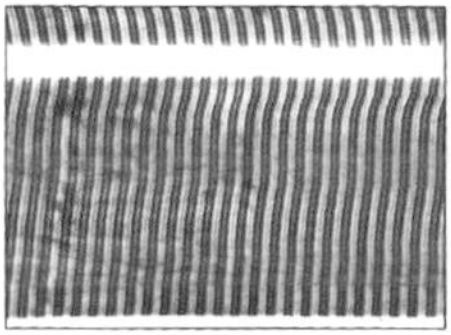

SKELETAL MUSCLE

SMOOTH MUSCLE

CONTRACTION OF SKELETAL MUSCLE

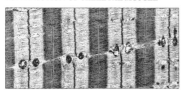

RELAXED STATE

CONTRACTED STATE

MUSCLES OF FACIAL EXPRESSION

A single expression is the result of movement of many muscles; the main muscles of expression are shown in action below.

FRONTALIS

CORRUGATOR SUPERCILII

ORBICULARIS ORIS

ZYGOMATICUS MAJOR

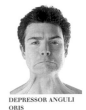

DEPRESSOR ANGULI ORIS

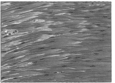

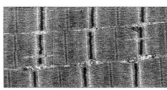

**MUSCLES OF
HEAD AND NECK**

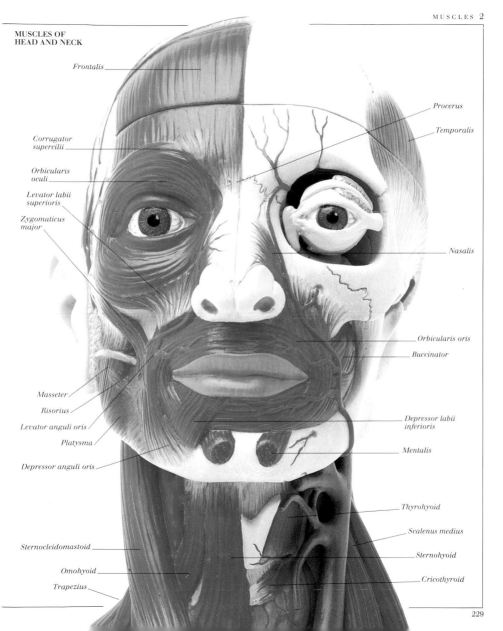

Frontalis

Procerus

Temporalis

Corrugator
supercilii

Orbicularis
oculi

Levator labii
superioris

Zygomaticus
major

Nasalis

Orbicularis oris

Buccinator

Masseter

Risorius

Levator anguli oris

Platysma

Depressor labii
inferioris

Mentalis

Depressor anguli oris

Thyrohyoid

Scalenus medius

Sternocleidomastoid

Sternohyoid

Omohyoid

Cricothyroid

Trapezius

Hands

THE HUMAN HAND is an extremely versatile tool, capable of delicate manipulation as well as powerful gripping actions. The arrangement of its 27 small bones, moved by 37 skeletal muscles that are connected to the bones by tendons, allows a wide range of movements. Our ability to bring the tips of our thumbs and fingers together, combined with the extraordinary sensitivity of our fingertips due to their rich supply of nerve endings, makes our hands uniquely dextrous.

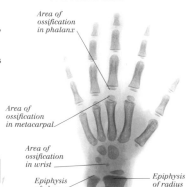

Area of ossification in phalanx

Area of ossification in metacarpal

Area of ossification in wrist

Epiphysis of ulna

Epiphysis of radius

Areas of cartilage in the wrist and at the ends of the finger bones are the sites of growth and have still to ossify.

BONES OF HAND

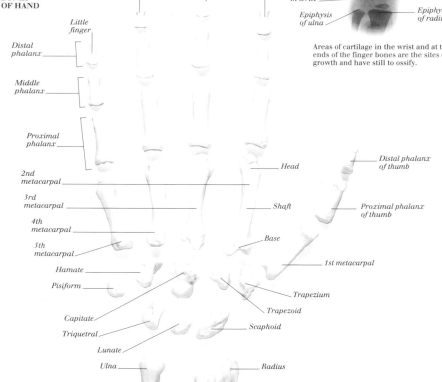

Ring finger

Middle finger

Index finger

Little finger

Distal phalanx

Middle phalanx

Proximal phalanx

2nd metacarpal

3rd metacarpal

4th metacarpal

5th metacarpal

Hamate

Pisiform

Capitate

Triquetral

Lunate

Ulna

Head

Shaft

Base

Trapezium

Trapezoid

Scaphoid

Radius

Distal phalanx of thumb

Proximal phalanx of thumb

1st metacarpal

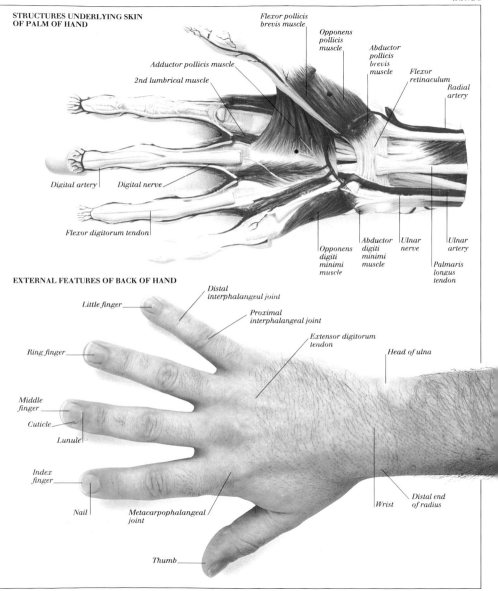

STRUCTURES UNDERLYING SKIN OF PALM OF HAND

Flexor pollicis brevis muscle

Opponens pollicis muscle

Abductor pollicis brevis muscle

Flexor retinaculum

Radial artery

Adductor pollicis muscle

2nd lumbrical muscle

Digital artery

Digital nerve

Flexor digitorum tendon

Opponens digiti minimi muscle

Abductor digiti minimi muscle

Ulnar nerve

Ulnar artery

Palmaris longus tendon

EXTERNAL FEATURES OF BACK OF HAND

Distal interphalangeal joint

Little finger

Proximal interphalangeal joint

Extensor digitorum tendon

Head of ulna

Ring finger

Middle finger

Cuticle

Lunule

Index finger

Nail

Metacarpophalangeal joint

Wrist

Distal end of radius

Thumb

Feet

THE FEET AND TOES are essential elements in body movement. They bear and propel the weight of the body during walking and running, and also help to maintain balance during changes of body position. Each foot has 26 bones, more than 100 ligaments, and 33 muscles, some of which are attached to the lower leg. The heel pad and the arch of the foot act as shock absorbers, providing a cushion against the jolts that occur with every step.

LIGAMENTS OF FOOT

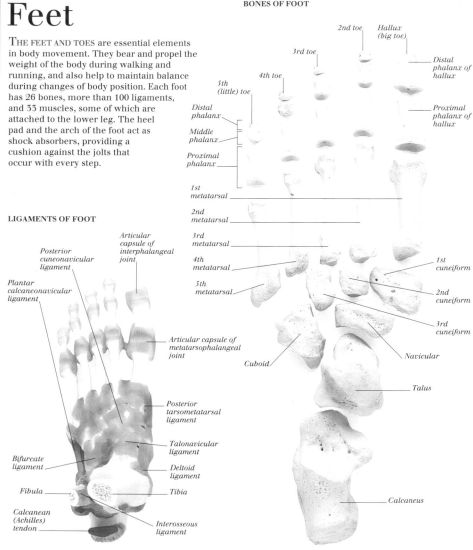

2nd toe

Hallux (big toe)

3rd toe

4th toe

5th (little) toe

Distal phalanx of hallux

Distal phalanx

Middle phalanx

Proximal phalanx

Proximal phalanx of hallux

1st metatarsal

2nd metatarsal

3rd metatarsal

4th metatarsal

5th metatarsal

1st cuneiform

2nd cuneiform

3rd cuneiform

Articular capsule of interphalangeal joint

Posterior cuneonavicular ligament

Plantar calcaneonavicular ligament

Articular capsule of metatarsophalangeal joint

Cuboid

Navicular

Talus

Posterior tarsometatarsal ligament

Talonavicular ligament

Bifurcate ligament

Deltoid ligament

Fibula

Tibia

Calcaneus

Calcanean (Achilles) tendon

Interosseous ligament

STRUCTURES UNDERLYING SKIN OF FOOT

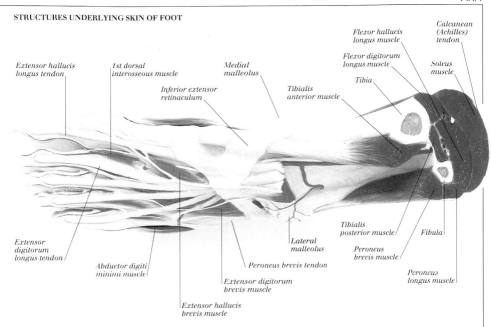

Extensor hallucis longus tendon

1st dorsal interosseous muscle

Medial malleolus

Inferior extensor retinaculum

Flexor hallucis longus muscle

Flexor digitorum longus muscle

Tibialis anterior muscle

Tibia

Calcanean (Achilles) tendon

Soleus muscle

Extensor digitorum longus tendon

Abductor digiti minimi muscle

Lateral malleolus

Extensor digitorum brevis muscle

Extensor hallucis brevis muscle

Peroneus brevis tendon

Tibialis posterior muscle

Peroneus brevis muscle

Fibula

Peroneus longus muscle

EXTERNAL FEATURES OF FOOT

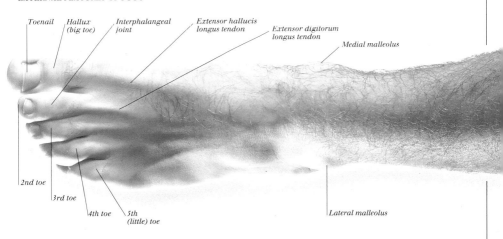

Toenail

Hallux (big toe)

Interphalangeal joint

Extensor hallucis longus tendon

Extensor digitorum longus tendon

Medial malleolus

2nd toe

3rd toe

4th toe

5th (little) toe

Lateral malleolus

Skin and hair

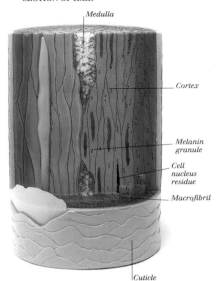

Skin is the body's largest organ, a waterproof barrier that protects the internal organs against infection, injury, and harmful sun rays. The skin is also an important sensory organ and helps to control body temperature. The outer layer of the skin, known as the epidermis, is coated with keratin, a tough, horny protein that is also the chief constituent of hair and nails. Dead cells are shed from the skin's surface and are replaced by new cells from the base of the epidermis, the region that also produces the skin pigment, melanin. The dermis contains most of the skin's living structures, and includes nerve endings, blood vessels, elastic fibres, sweat glands that cool the skin, and sebaceous glands that produce oil to keep the skin supple. Beneath the dermis lies the subcutaneous tissue (hypodermis), which is rich in fat and blood vessels. Hair shafts grow from hair follicles situated in the dermis and subcutaneous tissue. Hair grows on every part of the skin apart from the palms of the hands and soles of the feet.

Medulla

Cortex

Melanin granule

Cell nucleus residue

Macrofibril

Cuticle

SECTIONS OF DIFFERENT TYPES OF SKIN

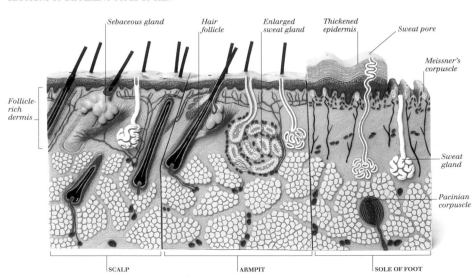

Sebaceous gland · Hair follicle · Enlarged sweat gland · Thickened epidermis · Sweat pore · Meissner's corpuscle · Follicle-rich dermis · Sweat gland · Pacinian corpuscle

SCALP · ARMPIT · SOLE OF FOOT

SECTION OF SKIN

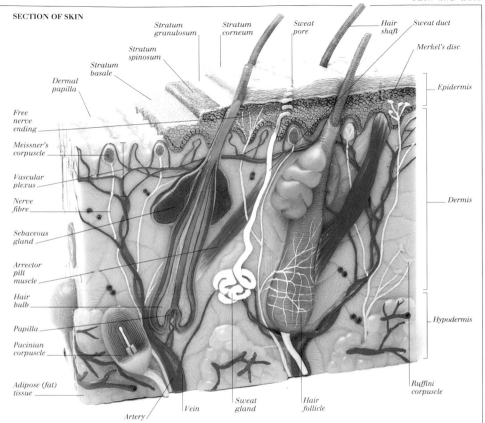

Stratum granulosum

Stratum corneum

Sweat pore

Hair shaft

Sweat duct

Stratum spinosum

Merkel's disc

Stratum basale

Dermal papilla

Epidermis

Free nerve ending

Meissner's corpuscle

Vascular plexus

Nerve fibre

Dermis

Sebaceous gland

Arrector pili muscle

Hair bulb

Papilla

Pacinian corpuscle

Hypodermis

Adipose (fat) tissue

Ruffini corpuscle

Artery

Vein

Sweat gland

Hair follicle

PHOTOMICROGRAPHS OF SKIN AND HAIR

SECTION OF SKIN
The flaky cells at the skin's surface are shed continuously.

SWEAT PORE
This allows loss of fluid as part of temperature control.

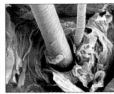

SKIN HAIR
Two hairs pushing through the outer layer of skin.

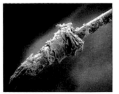

HEAD HAIR
The root and part of the shaft of a hair from the scalp.

Brain

THE BRAIN IS THE MAJOR ORGAN of the central nervous system and the control centre for all the body's voluntary and involuntary activities. It is also responsible for the complexities of thought, memory, emotion, and language. In adults, this complex organ is a mere 1.4 kg (3 lb) in weight, containing over 10 thousand million nerve cells. Three distinct regions can easily be seen – the brainstem, the cerebellum, and the large cerebrum. The brainstem controls vital body functions, such as breathing and digestion. The cerebellum's main functions are the maintenance of posture and the coordination of body movements. The cerebrum, which consists of the right and left cerebral hemispheres joined by the corpus callosum, is the site of most conscious and intelligent activities.

MRI SCAN OF TRANSVERSE SECTION THROUGH BRAIN

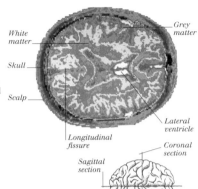

White matter
Skull
Scalp
Grey matter
Lateral ventricle
Longitudinal fissure
Coronal section
Sagittal section

SAGITTAL SECTION THROUGH BRAIN

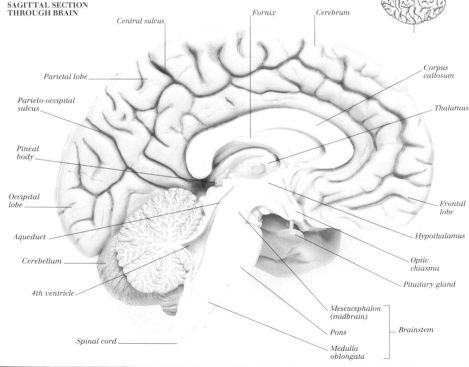

Central sulcus
Fornix
Cerebrum
Parietal lobe
Parieto-occipital sulcus
Pineal body
Occipital lobe
Aqueduct
Cerebellum
4th ventricle
Spinal cord
Corpus callosum
Thalamus
Frontal lobe
Hypothalamus
Optic chiasma
Pituitary gland
Mesencephalon (midbrain)
Pons
Medulla oblongata
Brainstem

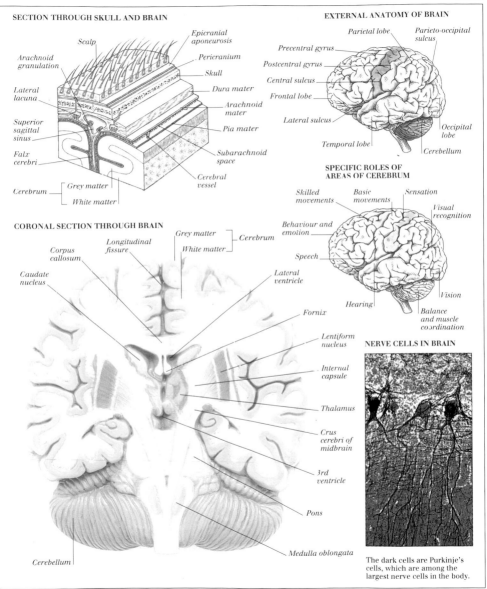

SECTION THROUGH SKULL AND BRAIN

- *Scalp*
- *Epicranial aponeurosis*
- *Arachnoid granulation*
- *Pericranium*
- *Skull*
- *Lateral lacuna*
- *Dura mater*
- *Arachnoid mater*
- *Superior sagittal sinus*
- *Pia mater*
- *Falx cerebri*
- *Subarachnoid space*
- *Cerebrum* { *Grey matter* / *White matter* }
- *Cerebral vessel*

EXTERNAL ANATOMY OF BRAIN

- *Parietal lobe*
- *Parieto-occipital sulcus*
- *Precentral gyrus*
- *Postcentral gyrus*
- *Central sulcus*
- *Frontal lobe*
- *Lateral sulcus*
- *Occipital lobe*
- *Temporal lobe*
- *Cerebellum*

SPECIFIC ROLES OF AREAS OF CEREBRUM

- *Skilled movements*
- *Basic movements*
- *Sensation*
- *Visual recognition*
- *Behaviour and emotion*
- *Speech*
- *Vision*
- *Hearing*
- *Balance and muscle coordination*

CORONAL SECTION THROUGH BRAIN

- *Corpus callosum*
- *Longitudinal fissure*
- *Grey matter* / *White matter* } *Cerebrum*
- *Caudate nucleus*
- *Lateral ventricle*
- *Fornix*
- *Lentiform nucleus*
- *Internal capsule*
- *Thalamus*
- *Crus cerebri of midbrain*
- *3rd ventricle*
- *Pons*
- *Medulla oblongata*
- *Cerebellum*

NERVE CELLS IN BRAIN

The dark cells are Purkinje's cells, which are among the largest nerve cells in the body.

237

Nervous system

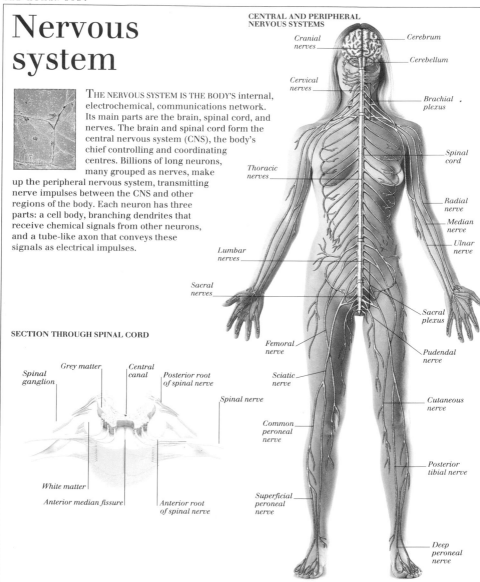

THE NERVOUS SYSTEM IS THE BODY'S internal, electrochemical, communications network. Its main parts are the brain, spinal cord, and nerves. The brain and spinal cord form the central nervous system (CNS), the body's chief controlling and coordinating centres. Billions of long neurons, many grouped as nerves, make up the peripheral nervous system, transmitting nerve impulses between the CNS and other regions of the body. Each neuron has three parts: a cell body, branching dendrites that receive chemical signals from other neurons, and a tube-like axon that conveys these signals as electrical impulses.

CENTRAL AND PERIPHERAL NERVOUS SYSTEMS

Cranial nerves

Cerebrum

Cerebellum

Cervical nerves

Brachial plexus

Spinal cord

Thoracic nerves

Radial nerve

Median nerve

Ulnar nerve

Lumbar nerves

Sacral nerves

Sacral plexus

Femoral nerve

Pudendal nerve

Sciatic nerve

Spinal nerve

Cutaneous nerve

Common peroneal nerve

Posterior tibial nerve

Superficial peroneal nerve

Deep peroneal nerve

SECTION THROUGH SPINAL CORD

Spinal ganglion

Grey matter

Central canal

Posterior root of spinal nerve

White matter

Anterior median fissure

Anterior root of spinal nerve

STRUCTURE OF A MOTOR NEURON

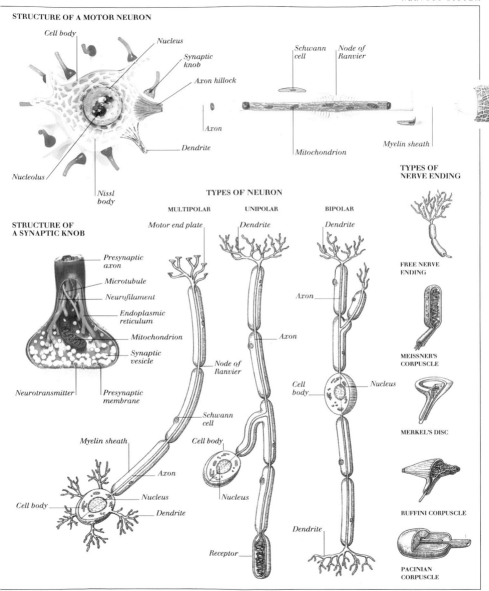

Cell body
Nucleus
Synaptic knob
Axon hillock
Schwann cell
Node of Ranvier
Axon
Dendrite
Mitochondrion
Myelin sheath
Nucleolus
Nissl body

TYPES OF NERVE ENDING

FREE NERVE ENDING

MEISSNER'S CORPUSCLE

MERKEL'S DISC

RUFFINI CORPUSCLE

PACINIAN CORPUSCLE

TYPES OF NEURON

MULTIPOLAR
UNIPOLAR
BIPOLAR

Motor end plate
Dendrite
Dendrite
Axon
Axon
Axon
Node of Ranvier
Cell body
Nucleus
Schwann cell
Cell body
Nucleus
Dendrite
Nucleus
Receptor

STRUCTURE OF A SYNAPTIC KNOB

Presynaptic axon
Microtubule
Neurofilament
Endoplasmic reticulum
Mitochondrion
Synaptic vesicle
Neurotransmitter
Presynaptic membrane
Myelin sheath
Axon
Cell body
Nucleus
Dendrite

Eye

THE EYE IS THE ORGAN OF SIGHT. The two eyeballs, protected within bony sockets called orbits and on the outside by the eyelids, eyebrows, and tear film, are directly connected to the brain by the optic nerves. Each eye is moved by six muscles, which are attached around the eyeball. Light rays entering the eye through the pupil are focused by the cornea and lens to form an image on the retina. The retina contains millions of light-sensitive cells, called rods and cones, which convert the image into a pattern of nerve impulses. These impulses are transmitted along the optic nerve to the brain. Information from the two optic nerves is processed in the brain to produce a single coordinated image.

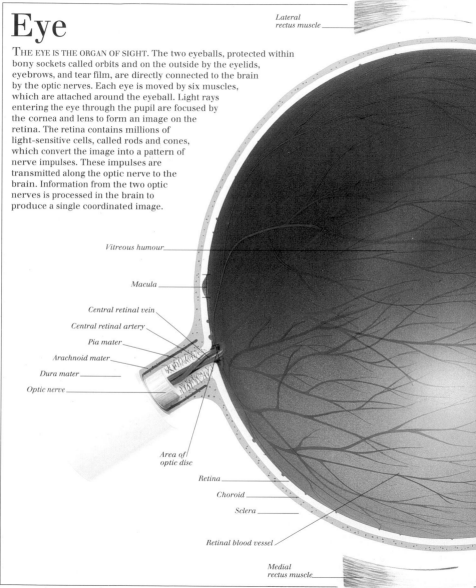

Lateral rectus muscle

Vitreous humour

Macula

Central retinal vein

Central retinal artery

Pia mater

Arachnoid mater

Dura mater

Optic nerve

Area of optic disc

Retina

Choroid

Sclera

Retinal blood vessel

Medial rectus muscle

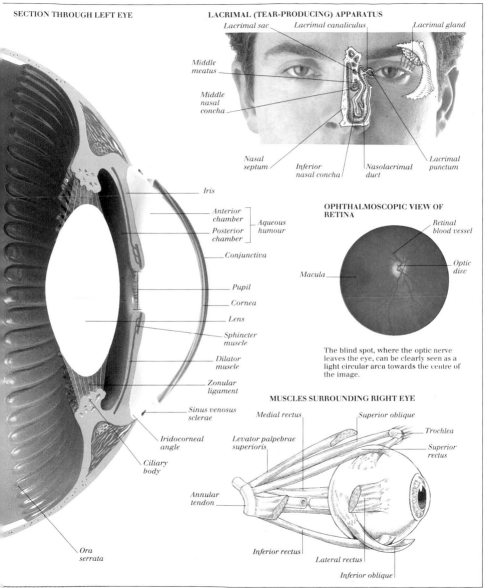

SECTION THROUGH LEFT EYE

Iris

Anterior chamber
Posterior chamber } Aqueous humour

Conjunctiva

Pupil

Cornea

Lens

Sphincter muscle

Dilator muscle

Zonular ligament

Sinus venosus sclerae

Iridocorneal angle

Ciliary body

Ora serrata

LACRIMAL (TEAR-PRODUCING) APPARATUS

Lacrimal sac

Lacrimal canaliculus

Lacrimal gland

Middle meatus

Middle nasal concha

Nasal septum

Inferior nasal concha

Nasolacrimal duct

Lacrimal punctum

OPHTHALMOSCOPIC VIEW OF RETINA

Retinal blood vessel

Optic disc

Macula

The blind spot, where the optic nerve leaves the eye, can be clearly seen as a light circular area towards the centre of the image.

MUSCLES SURROUNDING RIGHT EYE

Medial rectus

Superior oblique

Levator palpebrae superioris

Trochlea

Superior rectus

Annular tendon

Inferior rectus

Lateral rectus

Inferior oblique

241

Ear

THE EAR IS THE ORGAN OF HEARING AND BALANCE. The outer ear consists of a flap called the auricle or pinna and the auditory canal. The main functional parts – the middle and inner ears – are enclosed within the skull. The middle ear consists of three tiny bones, known as auditory ossicles, and the eustachian tube, which links the ear to the back of the nose. The inner ear consists of the spiral-shaped cochlea, and also the semicircular canals and the vestibule, which are the organs of balance. Sound waves entering the ear travel through the auditory canal to the tympanic membrane (eardrum), where they are converted to vibrations that are transmitted via the ossicles to the cochlea. Here, the vibrations are converted by millions of microscopic hairs into electrical nerve signals to be interpreted by the brain.

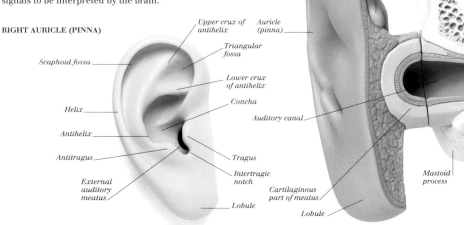

RIGHT AURICLE (PINNA)

Temporal bone

Cartilage of auricle

Upper crux of antihelix

Auricle (pinna)

Triangular fossa

Scaphoid fossa

Lower crux of antihelix

Concha

Helix

Auditory canal

Antihelix

Antitragus

Tragus

Intertragic notch

Mastoid process

External auditory meatus

Cartilaginous part of meatus

Lobule

Lobule

OSSICLES OF MIDDLE EAR

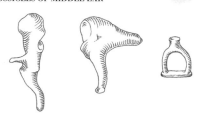

MALLEUS (HAMMER)   INCUS (ANVIL)   STAPES (STIRRUP)

These three tiny bones connect to form a bridge between the tympanic membrane and the oval window. With a system of membranes they convey sound vibrations to the inner ear.

INTERNAL STRUCTURE OF AMPULLA

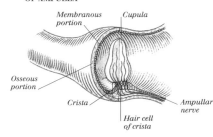

Membranous portion

Cupula

Osseous portion

Crista

Hair cell of crista

Ampullar nerve

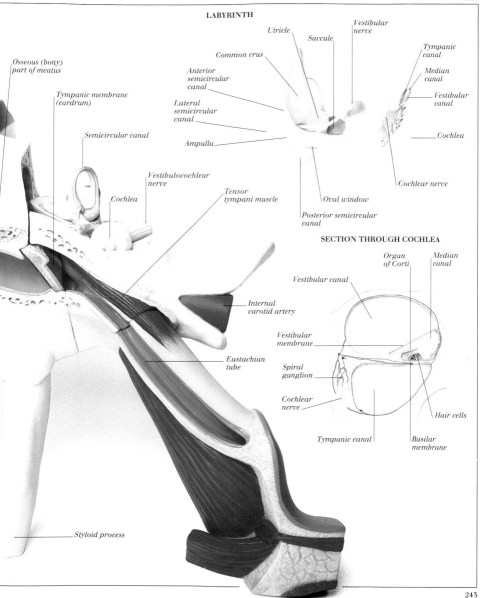

LABYRINTH

Osseous (bony) part of meatus

Tympanic membrane (eardrum)

Semicircular canal

Cochlea

Vestibulocochlear nerve

Common crus

Anterior semicircular canal

Lateral semicircular canal

Ampulla

Utricle

Saccule

Vestibular nerve

Tympanic canal

Median canal

Vestibular canal

Cochlea

Cochlear nerve

Tensor tympani muscle

Oval window

Posterior semicircular canal

Internal carotid artery

Eustachian tube

Styloid process

SECTION THROUGH COCHLEA

Organ of Corti

Median canal

Vestibular canal

Vestibular membrane

Spiral ganglion

Cochlear nerve

Tympanic canal

Basilar membrane

Hair cells

Nose, mouth, and throat

WITH EVERY BREATH, air passes through the nasal cavity down the pharynx (throat), larynx ("voice box"), and trachea (windpipe) to the lungs. The nasal cavity warms and moistens air, and the tiny layers in its lining protect the airway against damage by foreign bodies. During swallowing, the tongue moves up and back, the larynx rises, the epiglottis closes off the entrance to the trachea, and the soft palate separates the nasal cavity from the pharynx. Saliva, secreted from three pairs of salivary glands, lubricates food to make swallowing easier; it also begins the chemical breakdown of food, and helps to produce taste. The senses of taste and smell are closely linked. Both depend on the detection of dissolved molecules by sensory receptors in the olfactory nerve endings of the nose and in the taste buds of the tongue.

STRUCTURE OF TONGUE

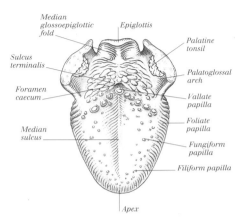

Median glossoepiglottic fold
Epiglottis
Palatine tonsil
Sulcus terminalis
Palatoglossal arch
Foramen caecum
Vallate papilla
Median sulcus
Foliate papilla
Fungiform papilla
Filiform papilla
Apex

STRUCTURES SURROUNDING PHARYNX

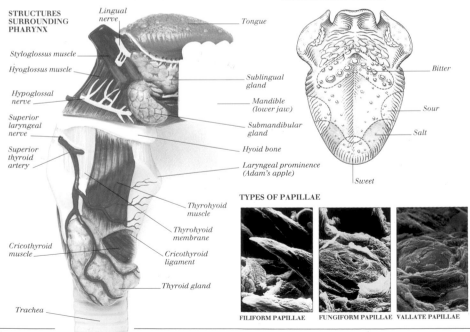

Lingual nerve
Tongue
Styloglossus muscle
Hyoglossus muscle
Sublingual gland
Hypoglossal nerve
Mandible (lower jaw)
Superior laryngeal nerve
Submandibular gland
Superior thyroid artery
Hyoid bone
Laryngeal prominence (Adam's apple)
Thyrohyoid muscle
Thyrohyoid membrane
Cricothyroid muscle
Cricothyroid ligament
Thyroid gland
Trachea

TASTE AREAS ON TONGUE

Bitter
Sour
Salt
Sweet

TYPES OF PAPILLAE

FILIFORM PAPILLAE   FUNGIFORM PAPILLAE   VALLATE PAPILLAE

SECTION THROUGH NOSE, MOUTH, AND THROAT

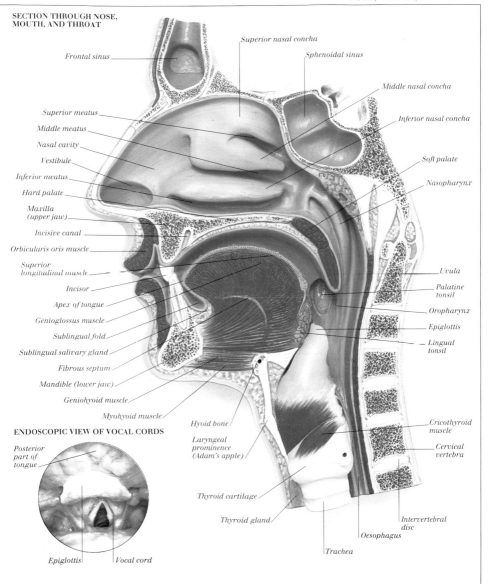

Frontal sinus

Superior nasal concha

Sphenoidal sinus

Middle nasal concha

Inferior nasal concha

Superior meatus

Middle meatus

Nasal cavity

Vestibule

Inferior meatus

Hard palate

Maxilla (upper jaw)

Incisive canal

Orbicularis oris muscle

Superior longitudinal muscle

Incisor

Apex of tongue

Genioglossus muscle

Sublingual fold

Sublingual salivary gland

Fibrous septum

Mandible (lower jaw)

Geniohyoid muscle

Myohyoid muscle

Soft palate

Nasopharynx

Uvula

Palatine tonsil

Oropharynx

Epiglottis

Lingual tonsil

Cricothyroid muscle

Cervical vertebra

Intervertebral disc

Oesophagus

Trachea

Thyroid gland

Thyroid cartilage

Laryngeal prominence (Adam's apple)

Hyoid bone

ENDOSCOPIC VIEW OF VOCAL CORDS

Posterior part of tongue

Epiglottis

Vocal cord

Teeth

THE 20 PRIMARY TEETH (also called deciduous or milk teeth) usually begin to erupt when a baby is about six months old. They start to be replaced by the permanent teeth when the child is about six years old. By the age of 20, most adults have a full set of 32 teeth although the third molars (commonly called wisdom teeth) may never erupt. While teeth help people to speak clearly and give shape to the face, their main function is the chewing of food. Incisors and canines shear and tear the food into pieces; premolars and molars crush and grind it further. Although tooth enamel is the hardest substance in the body, it tends to be eroded and destroyed by acid produced in the mouth during the breakdown of food.

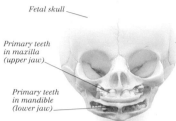

Fetal skull

Primary teeth in maxilla (upper jaw)

Primary teeth in mandible (lower jaw)

FETAL JAWS
By the sixth week of embryonic development areas of thickening occur in each jaw; these areas give rise to tooth buds. By the time the fetus is six months old, enamel has formed on the tooth buds.

DEVELOPMENT OF JAW AND TEETH

Maxilla (upper jaw)

Mandible (lower jaw)

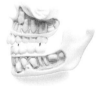
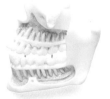

A NEWBORN BABY'S JAWS
The primary teeth can be seen developing in the jaw bones; they begin to erupt around the age of six months.

A FIVE-YEAR-OLD CHILD'S TEETH
There is a full set of 20 erupted primary teeth; the permanent teeth can be seen developing in the upper and lower jaws.

A NINE-YEAR-OLD CHILD'S TEETH
Most of the teeth are primary teeth but the permanent incisors and first molars have now emerged.

AN ADULT'S TEETH
By the age of 20, the full set of 32 permanent teeth (including the wisdom teeth) should be in position.

THE PERMANENT TEETH

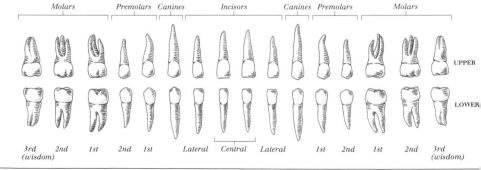

Molars   *Premolars*   *Canines*   *Incisors*   *Canines*   *Premolars*   *Molars*

UPPER

LOWER

3rd (wisdom)   *2nd*   *1st*   *2nd*   *1st*   *Lateral*   *Central*   *Lateral*   *1st*   *2nd*   *1st*   *2nd*   *3rd (wisdom)*

STRUCTURE OF A TOOTH

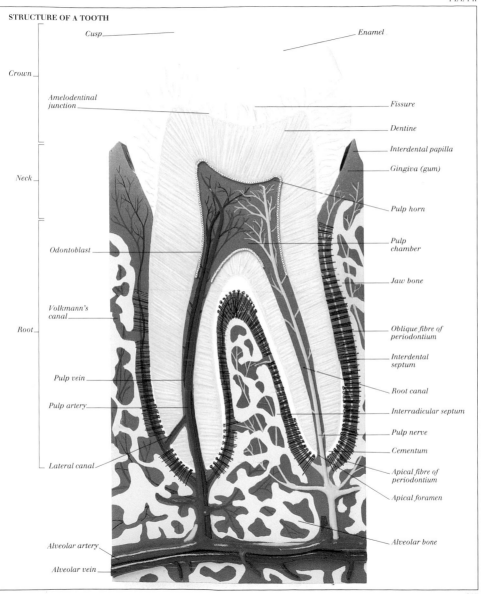

Cusp

Enamel

Crown

Ameloedentinal junction

Fissure

Dentine

Interdental papilla

Neck

Gingiva (gum)

Pulp horn

Odontoblast

Pulp chamber

Jaw bone

Volkmann's canal

Oblique fibre of periodontium

Root

Interdental septum

Pulp vein

Root canal

Pulp artery

Interradicular septum

Pulp nerve

Cementum

Lateral canal

Apical fibre of periodontium

Apical foramen

Alveolar artery

Alveolar bone

Alveolar vein

Digestive system

THE DIGESTIVE SYSTEM BREAKS DOWN FOOD into particles so tiny that blood can take nourishment to all parts of the body. The system's main part is a 9 m (30 ft) tube from mouth to rectum; muscles in this alimentary canal force food along. Chewed food first travels through the oesophagus to the stomach, which churns and liquidizes food before it passes through the duodenum, jejunum, and ileum – the three parts of the long, convoluted small intestine. Here, digestive juices from the gallbladder and pancreas break down food particles; many filter out into the blood through tiny fingerlike villi that line the small intestine's inner wall. Undigested food in the colon forms faeces that leave the body through the anus.

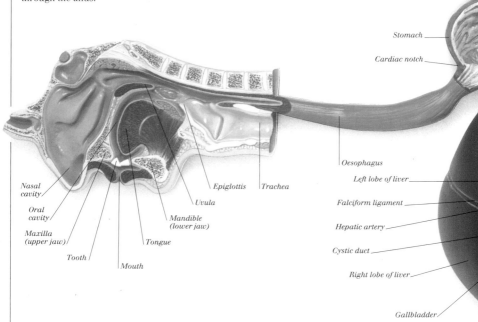

Stomach

Cardiac notch

Oesophagus

Left lobe of liver

Falciform ligament

Hepatic artery

Cystic duct

Right lobe of liver

Gallbladder

Nasal cavity

Oral cavity

Maxilla (upper jaw)

Tooth

Mouth

Tongue

Mandible (lower jaw)

Uvula

Epiglottis

Trachea

ENDOSCOPIC VIEWS INSIDE ALIMENTARY CANAL

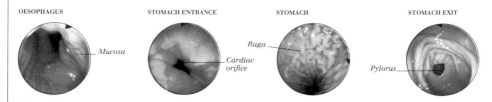

OESOPHAGUS

Mucosa

STOMACH ENTRANCE

Cardiac orifice

STOMACH

Ruga

STOMACH EXIT

Pylorus

ALIMENTARY CANAL

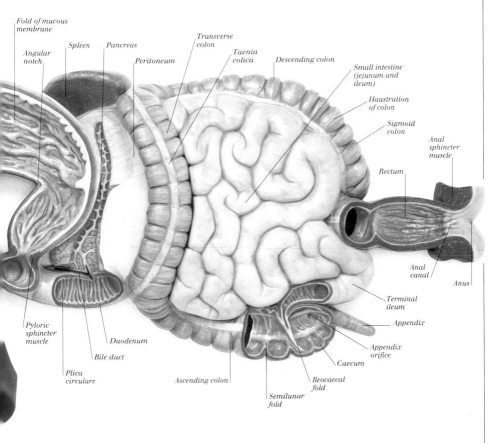

Fold of mucous membrane

Angular notch

Spleen

Pancreas

Peritoneum

Transverse colon

Taenia colica

Descending colon

Small intestine (jejunum and ileum)

Haustration of colon

Sigmoid colon

Anal sphincter muscle

Rectum

Anal canal

Anus

Terminal ileum

Appendix

Appendix orifice

Caecum

Ileocaecal fold

Semilunar fold

Ascending colon

Duodenum

Bile duct

Plica circulare

Pyloric sphincter muscle

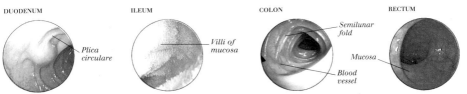

DUODENUM

Plica circulare

ILEUM

Villi of mucosa

COLON

Semilunar fold

Blood vessel

RECTUM

Mucosa

Heart

THE HEART IS A HOLLOW MUSCLE in the middle of the chest that pumps blood around the body, supplying cells with oxygen and nutrients. A muscular wall, called the septum, divides the heart lengthways into left and right sides. A valve divides each side into two chambers: an upper atrium and a lower ventricle. When the heart muscle contracts, it squeezes blood through the atria and then through the ventricles. Oxygenated blood from the lungs flows from the pulmonary veins into the left atrium, through the left ventricle, and then out via the aorta to all parts of the body. Deoxygenated blood returning from the body flows from the vena cava into the right atrium, through the right ventricle, and then out via the pulmonary artery to the lungs for reoxygenation. At rest the heart beats between 60 and 80 times a minute; during exercise or at times of stress or excitement the rate may increase to 200 beats a minute.

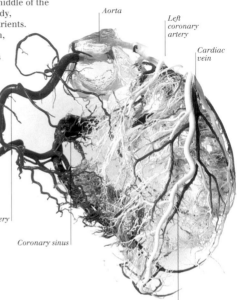

Aorta

Left coronary artery

Cardiac vein

Right coronary artery

Coronary sinus

Main branch of left coronary artery

SECTION THROUGH HEART WALL

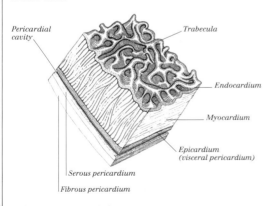

Pericardial cavity

Trabecula

Endocardium

Myocardium

Epicardium (visceral pericardium)

Serous pericardium

Fibrous pericardium

HEARTBEAT SEQUENCE

ATRIAL DIASTOLE

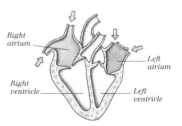

Right atrium

Left atrium

Right ventricle

Left ventricle

Deoxygenated blood enters the right atrium while the left atrium receives oxygenated blood.

STRUCTURE OF HEART

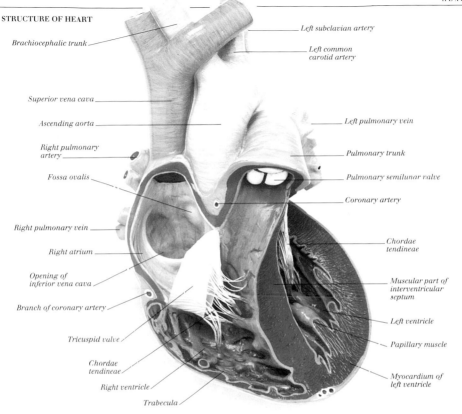

Brachiocephalic trunk

Left subclavian artery

Left common carotid artery

Superior vena cava

Ascending aorta

Left pulmonary vein

Right pulmonary artery

Pulmonary trunk

Fossa ovalis

Pulmonary semilunar valve

Coronary artery

Right pulmonary vein

Chordae tendineae

Right atrium

Opening of inferior vena cava

Muscular part of interventricular septum

Branch of coronary artery

Left ventricle

Papillary muscle

Tricuspid valve

Chordae tendineae

Myocardium of left ventricle

Right ventricle

Trabecula

ATRIAL SYSTOLE (VENTRICULAR DIASTOLE)

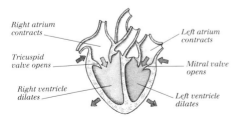

Right atrium contracts

Left atrium contracts

Tricuspid valve opens

Mitral valve opens

Right ventricle dilates

Left ventricle dilates

Left and right atria contract, forcing blood into the relaxed ventricles.

VENTRICULAR SYSTOLE

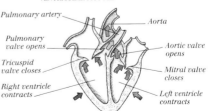

Pulmonary artery

Aorta

Pulmonary valve opens

Aortic valve opens

Tricuspid valve closes

Mitral valve closes

Right ventricle contracts

Left ventricle contracts

Ventricles contract and force blood to the lungs for oxygenation and via the aorta to the rest of the body.

Circulatory system

THE CIRCULATORY SYSTEM consists of the heart and blood vessels, which together maintain a continuous flow of blood around the body. The heart pumps oxygen-rich blood from the lungs to all parts of the body through a network of tubes called arteries, and smaller branches called arterioles. Blood returns to the heart via small vessels called venules, which lead in turn into larger tubes called veins. Arterioles and venules are linked by a network of tiny vessels called capillaries, where the exchange of oxygen and carbon dioxide between blood and body cells takes place. Blood has four main components: red blood cells, white blood cells, platelets, and liquid plasma.

ARTERIAL SYSTEM OF BRAIN

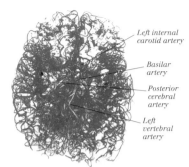

Left internal carotid artery

Basilar artery

Posterior cerebral artery

Left vertebral artery

CIRCULATORY SYSTEM OF HEART AND LUNGS

Superior vena cava

Aorta

Right ventricle

Left ventricle

CIRCULATORY SYSTEM OF LIVER

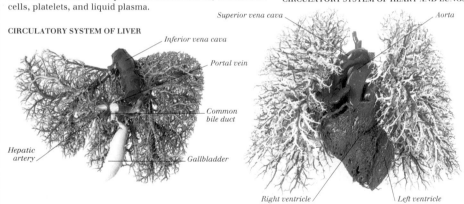

Inferior vena cava

Portal vein

Common bile duct

Hepatic artery

Gallbladder

SECTION OF MAIN ARTERY

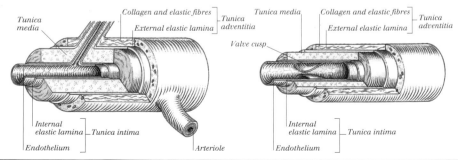

Tunica media

Collagen and elastic fibres

External elastic lamina

Tunica adventitia

Internal elastic lamina

Tunica intima

Endothelium

Arteriole

SECTION OF MAIN VEIN

Tunica media

Collagen and elastic fibres

External elastic lamina

Tunica adventitia

Valve cusp

Internal elastic lamina

Tunica intima

Endothelium

PRINCIPAL ARTERIES AND VEINS OF CIRCULATORY SYSTEM

Internal jugular vein

Common carotid artery

Brachiocephalic vein

Subclavian vein

Subclavian artery

Axillary vein

Arch of aorta

Cephalic vein

Axillary artery

Pulmonary artery

Superior vena cava

Coronary artery

Pulmonary vein

Brachial artery

Basilic vein

Gastric artery

Hepatic artery

Hepatic portal vein

Splenic artery

Median cubital vein

Superior mesenteric artery

Inferior vena cava

Radial artery

Anterior median vein

Ulnar artery

Gastroepiploic vein

Palmar vein

Palmar arch

Digital vein

Digital artery

Inferior mesenteric vein

Common iliac artery

Superior mesenteric vein

External iliac artery

Common iliac vein

Internal iliac artery

Femoral artery

External iliac vein

Popliteal artery

Internal iliac vein

Peroneal artery

Femoral vein

Great saphenous vein

Anterior tibial artery

Short saphenous vein

Posterior tibial artery

Lateral plantar artery

Dorsal metatarsal artery

Dorsal venous arch

Digital vein

TYPES OF BLOOD CELLS

RED BLOOD CELLS
These cells are biconcave in shape to maximize their oxygen-carrying capacity.

WHITE BLOOD CELLS
Lymphocytes are the smallest white blood cells; they form antibodies against disease.

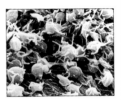

PLATELETS
Tiny cells that are activated whenever blood clotting or repair to vessels is necessary.

BLOOD CLOTTING

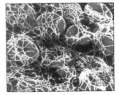

Filaments of fibrin enmesh red blood cells as part of the process of blood clotting.

Respiratory system

THE RESPIRATORY SYSTEM supplies the oxygen needed by body cells and carries off their carbon dioxide waste. Inhaled air passes via the trachea (windpipe) through two narrower tubes, the bronchi, to the lungs. Each lung comprises many fine, branching tubes called bronchioles that end in tiny clustered chambers called alveoli. Gases cross the thin alveolar walls to and from a network of tiny blood vessels. Intercostal (rib) muscles and the muscular diaphragm below the lungs operate the lungs like bellows, drawing air in and forcing it out at regular intervals.

BRONCHIOLE AND ALVEOLI

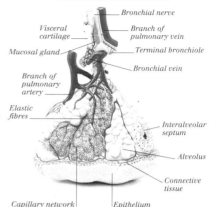

Bronchial nerve
Visceral cartilage
Branch of pulmonary vein
Mucosal gland
Terminal bronchiole
Branch of pulmonary artery
Bronchial vein
Elastic fibres
Interalveolar septum
Alveolus
Connective tissue
Capillary network
Epithelium

SEGMENTS OF BRONCHIAL TREE

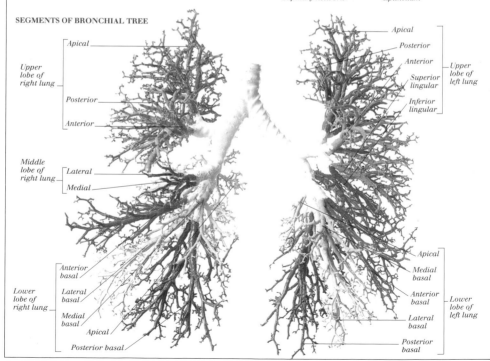

Apical
Upper lobe of right lung
Posterior
Anterior

Middle lobe of right lung
Lateral
Medial

Lower lobe of right lung
Anterior basal
Lateral basal
Medial basal
Apical
Posterior basal

Apical
Posterior
Anterior
Superior lingular
Inferior lingular
Upper lobe of left lung

Apical
Medial basal
Anterior basal
Lateral basal
Posterior basal
Lower lobe of left lung

STRUCTURES OF THORACIC CAVITY

GASEOUS EXCHANGE IN ALVEOLUS

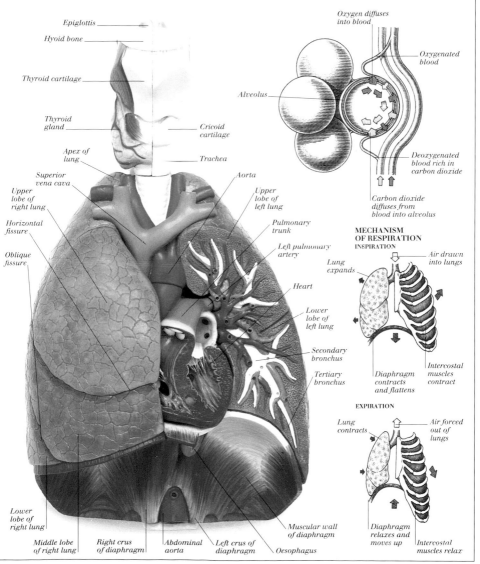

Epiglottis

Hyoid bone

Thyroid cartilage

Thyroid gland

Cricoid cartilage

Apex of lung

Trachea

Superior vena cava

Aorta

Upper lobe of right lung

Upper lobe of left lung

Horizontal fissure

Pulmonary trunk

Oblique fissure

Left pulmonary artery

Heart

Lower lobe of left lung

Secondary bronchus

Tertiary bronchus

Lower lobe of right lung

Middle lobe of right lung

Right crus of diaphragm

Abdominal aorta

Left crus of diaphragm

Oesophagus

Muscular wall of diaphragm

Oxygen diffuses into blood

Oxygenated blood

Alveolus

Deoxygenated blood rich in carbon dioxide

Carbon dioxide diffuses from blood into alveolus

MECHANISM OF RESPIRATION

INSPIRATION

Lung expands

Air drawn into lungs

Diaphragm contracts and flattens

Intercostal muscles contract

EXPIRATION

Lung contracts

Air forced out of lungs

Diaphragm relaxes and moves up

Intercostal muscles relax

Urinary system

THE URINARY SYSTEM FILTERS WASTE PRODUCTS from the blood and removes them from the body via a system of tubes. Blood is filtered in the two kidneys, which are fist-sized, bean-shaped organs. The renal arteries carry blood to the kidneys; the renal veins remove blood after filtering. Each kidney contains about one million tiny units called nephrons. Each nephron is made up of a tubule and a filtering unit called a glomerulus, which consists of a collection of tiny blood vessels surrounded by the hollow Bowman's capsule. The filtering process produces a watery fluid that leaves the kidney as urine. The urine is carried via two tubes called ureters to the bladder, where it is stored until its release from the body through another tube called the urethra.

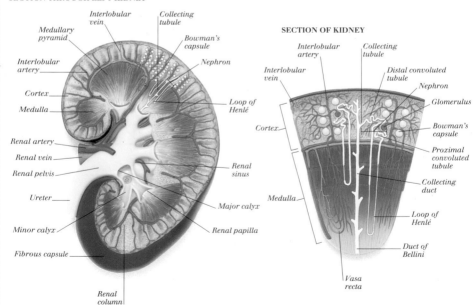

ARTERIAL SYSTEM OF KIDNEYS

Aorta

Coeliac trunk

Superior mesenteric artery

Right renal artery

Left renal artery

Right ureter

Left ureter

SECTION THROUGH LEFT KIDNEY

Interlobular vein

Medullary pyramid

Collecting tubule

Bowman's capsule

Interlobular artery

Nephron

Cortex

Medulla

Loop of Henlé

Renal artery

Renal vein

Renal pelvis

Renal sinus

Ureter

Major calyx

Minor calyx

Renal papilla

Fibrous capsule

Renal column

SECTION OF KIDNEY

Interlobular artery

Collecting tubule

Interlobular vein

Distal convoluted tubule

Nephron

Cortex

Glomerulus

Bowman's capsule

Proximal convoluted tubule

Collecting duct

Medulla

Loop of Henlé

Duct of Bellini

Vasa recta

MALE URINARY TRACT

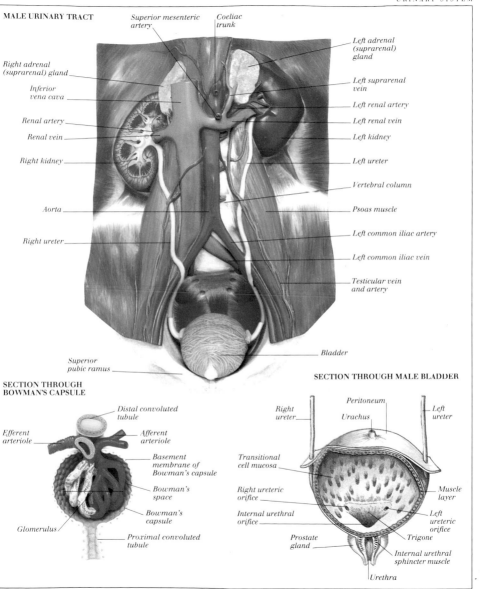

Superior mesenteric artery

Coeliac trunk

Left adrenal (suprarenal) gland

Right adrenal (suprarenal) gland

Inferior vena cava

Left suprarenal vein

Renal artery

Left renal artery

Renal vein

Left renal vein

Right kidney

Left kidney

Left ureter

Vertebral column

Aorta

Psoas muscle

Left common iliac artery

Right ureter

Left common iliac vein

Testicular vein and artery

Bladder

Superior pubic ramus

SECTION THROUGH BOWMAN'S CAPSULE

Distal convoluted tubule

Efferent arteriole

Afferent arteriole

Basement membrane of Bowman's capsule

Bowman's space

Bowman's capsule

Glomerulus

Proximal convoluted tubule

SECTION THROUGH MALE BLADDER

Right ureter

Peritoneum

Urachus

Left ureter

Transitional cell mucosa

Right ureteric orifice

Muscle layer

Internal urethral orifice

Left ureteric orifice

Prostate gland

Trigone

Internal urethral sphincter muscle

Urethra

Reproductive system

SEX ORGANS LOCATED IN THE PELVIS create new human lives. Each month a ripe egg is released from one of the female's ovaries into a fallopian tube leading to the uterus (womb), a muscular pear-sized organ. A male produces minute tadpole-like sperm in two oval glands called testes. When the male is ready to release sperm into the female's vagina, many millions pass into his urethra and leave his body through the fleshy penis. The sperm travel up through the vagina into the uterus and fallopian tubes, and one sperm may enter and fertilize an egg. The fertilized egg becomes embedded in the uterus wall and starts to grow into a new human being.

SECTION THROUGH OVARY

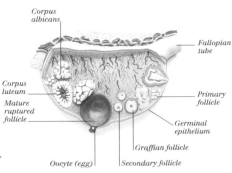

Corpus albicans

Fallopian tube

Corpus luteum

Mature ruptured follicle

Primary follicle

Germinal epithelium

Graffian follicle

Secondary follicle

Oocyte (egg)

SECTION THROUGH FEMALE PELVIC REGION

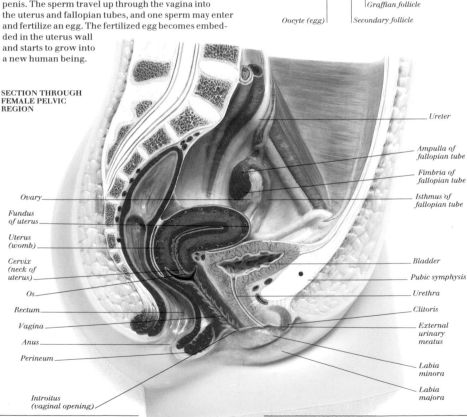

Ureter

Ampulla of fallopian tube

Fimbria of fallopian tube

Isthmus of fallopian tube

Ovary

Fundus of uterus

Uterus (womb)

Cervix (neck of uterus)

Os

Rectum

Vagina

Anus

Perineum

Introitus (vaginal opening)

Bladder

Pubic symphysis

Urethra

Clitoris

External urinary meatus

Labia minora

Labia majora

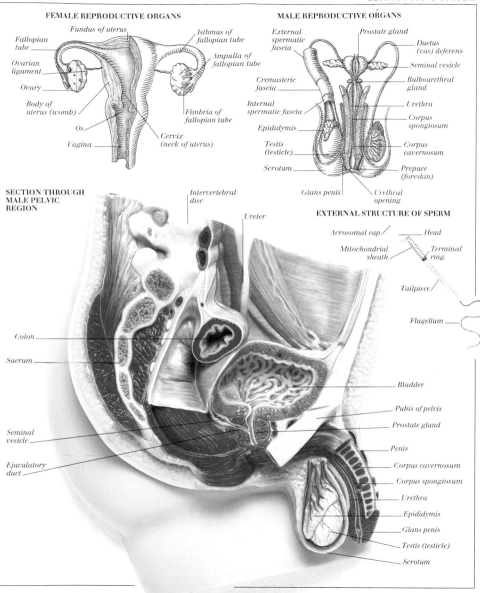

FEMALE REPRODUCTIVE ORGANS

Fundus of uterus

Fallopian tube

Isthmus of fallopian tube

Ovarian ligament

Ampulla of fallopian tube

Ovary

Body of uterus (womb)

Os

Fimbria of fallopian tube

Vagina

Cervix (neck of uterus)

MALE REPRODUCTIVE ORGANS

External spermatic fascia

Prostate gland

Ductus (vas) deferens

Seminal vesicle

Cremasteric fascia

Bulbourethral gland

Internal spermatic fascia

Urethra

Epididymis

Corpus spongiosum

Testis (testicle)

Corpus cavernosum

Scrotum

Prepuce (foreskin)

Glans penis

Urethral opening

SECTION THROUGH MALE PELVIC REGION

Intervertebral disc

Ureter

EXTERNAL STRUCTURE OF SPERM

Acrosomal cap

Head

Mitochondrial sheath

Terminal ring

Tailpiece

Flagellum

Colon

Sacrum

Bladder

Pubis of pelvis

Prostate gland

Seminal vesicle

Penis

Corpus cavernosum

Corpus spongiosum

Ejaculatory duct

Urethra

Epididymis

Glans penis

Testis (testicle)

Scrotum

Development of a baby

A FERTILIZED EGG IS NOURISHED AND PROTECTED as it develops into an embryo and then a fetus during the 40 weeks of pregnancy. The placenta, a mass of blood vessels implanted in the uterus lining, delivers nourishment and oxygen, and removes waste through the umbilical cord. Meanwhile, the fetus lies snugly in its amniotic sac, a bag of fluid that protects it against any sudden jolts. In the last weeks of the pregnancy, the rapidly growing fetus turns head-down: a baby ready to be born.

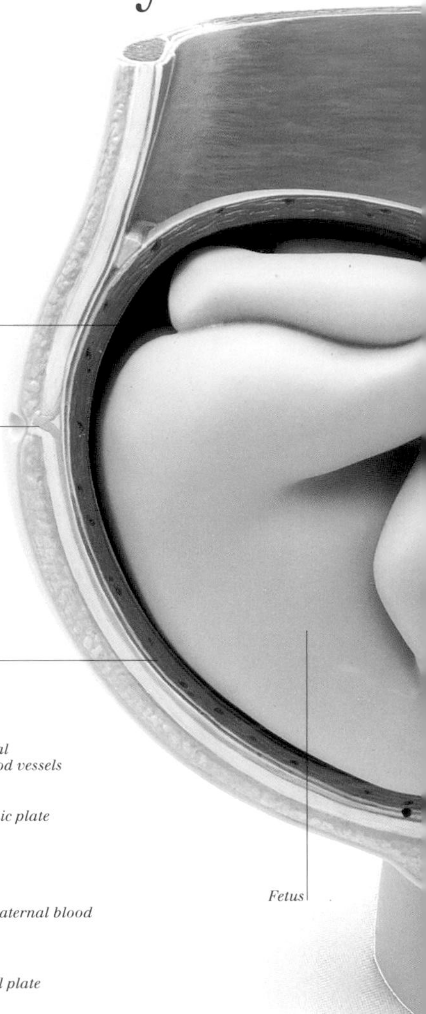

EMBRYO AT FIVE WEEKS

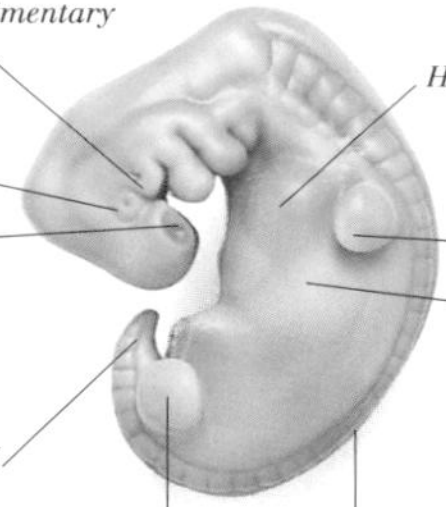

Rudimentary ear

Rudimentary eye

Rudimentary mouth

Heart bulge

Arm bud

Rudimentary liver

Tail bud

Leg bud

Rudimentary vertebra

Amniotic fluid

Umbilicus (navel)

Uterine wall

Fetus

SECTION THROUGH PLACENTA

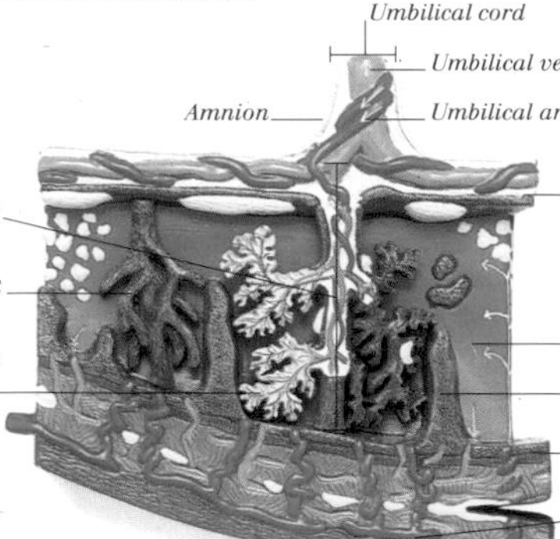

Umbilical cord

Umbilical vein

Amnion

Umbilical artery

Fetal blood vessels

Chorionic plate

Chorion

Trophoblast

Chorionic villus

Pool of maternal blood

Septum

Decidual plate

Maternal blood vessel

Myometrium

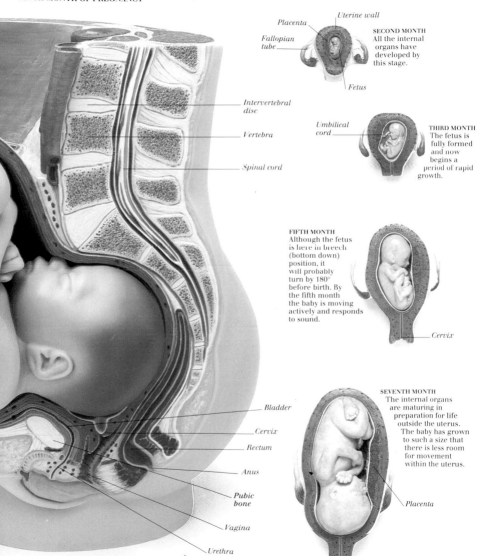

**SECTION THROUGH PELVIS IN
NINTH MONTH OF PREGNANCY**

THE DEVELOPING FETUS

Placenta

Uterine wall

Fallopian tube

SECOND MONTH
All the internal organs have developed by this stage.

Fetus

Intervertebral disc

Vertebra

Spinal cord

Umbilical cord

THIRD MONTH
The fetus is fully formed and now begins a period of rapid growth.

FIFTH MONTH
Although the fetus is here in breech (bottom down) position, it will probably turn by 180° before birth. By the fifth month the baby is moving actively and responds to sound.

Cervix

Bladder

Cervix

Rectum

Anus

SEVENTH MONTH
The internal organs are maturing in preparation for life outside the uterus. The baby has grown to such a size that there is less room for movement within the uterus.

Pubic bone

Placenta

Vagina

Urethra

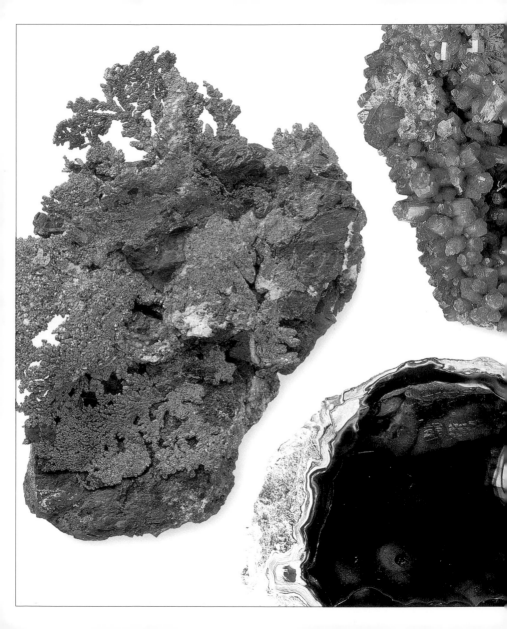

GEOLOGY, GEOGRAPHY, AND METEOROLGY

EARTH'S PHYSICAL FEATURES   264
THE ROCK CYCLE   266
MINERALS   268
MINERAL FEATURES   270
VOLCANOES   272
IGNEOUS AND METAMORPHIC ROCKS   274
SEDIMENTARY ROCKS   276
FOSSILS   278
MINERAL RESOURCES   280
WEATHERING AND EROSION   282
CAVES   284
GLACIERS   286
RIVERS   288
RIVER FEATURES   290
LAKES AND GROUNDWATER   292
COASTLINES   294
OCEANS AND SEAS   296
THE OCEAN FLOOR   298
THE ATMOSPHERE   300
WEATHER   302

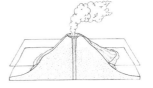

Earth's physical features

MOST OF THE EARTH'S SURFACE (about 70 per cent) is covered with water. The largest single body of water, the Pacific Ocean, alone covers about 30 per cent of the surface. Most of the land is distributed as seven continents; these are (from largest to smallest) Asia, Africa, North America, South America, Antarctica, Europe, and Australasia. The physical features of the land are remarkably varied. Among the most notable are mountain ranges, rivers, and deserts. The largest mountain ranges – the Himalayas in Asia and the Andes in South America – extend for thousands of kilometres. The Himalayas include the world's highest mountain, Mount Everest (8,848 metres). The longest rivers are the River Nile in Africa (6,695 kilometres) and the Amazon River in South America (6,437 kilometres). Deserts cover about 20 per cent of the total land area. The largest is the Sahara, which covers nearly a third of Africa. The Earth's surface features can be represented in various ways. Only a globe can correctly represent areas, shapes, sizes, and directions, because there is always distortion when a spherical surface – the Earth's, for example – is projected on to the flat surface of a map. Each map projection is therefore a compromise: it shows some features accurately but distorts others. Even satellite mapping does not produce completely accurate maps, although they can show physical features with great clarity.

EXAMPLES OF MAP PROJECTIONS

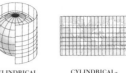

CYLINDRICAL PROJECTION

CYLINDRICAL-PROJECTION MAP

SATELLITE MAPPING OF THE EARTH

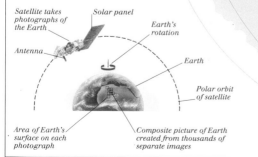

Satellite takes photographs of the Earth

Solar panel

Earth's rotation

Antenna

Earth

Polar orbit of satellite

Area of Earth's surface on each photograph

Composite picture of Earth created from thousands of separate images

180° 160° 120° 80°

Great Slave Lake
Great Bear Lake
Lake Superior
Mackenzie-Peace River
Greenland

Bering Sea

Hudson Bay
Baffin Island

NORTH AMERICA

Rocky Mountains

Sonoran Desert

Lake Huron
Lake Ontario
Lake Erie
Lake Michigan

Sierra Madre

Chihuahuan Desert

Gulf of Mexico

Appalachian Mountains

ATLANTIC OCEAN

Mississippi-Missouri River

Caribbean Sea

Guiana Highlands

Ama River

Braz High

PACIFIC OCEAN

Andes

SOUTH AMERICA

Atacama Desert

Gran Chaco

Ma Gro

Parana River

Pampas

Patagonia

80°

180° 160° 120° 80°

WEST OF GREENW MERIDIAN

CONICAL
PROJECTION

CONICAL-
PROJECTION MAP

AZIMUTHAL
PROJECTION

AZIMUTHAL-
PROJECTION MAP

MODIFIED
AZIMUTHAL-PROJECTION MAP

SATELLITE MAP OF THE EARTH

160°   180°
120°
80°
40°
0°
0°

*ARCTIC
OCEAN*

*Ural
Mountains*

*Kara
Kum*

*River
Ob Irtysh*

*River
Lena*

ARCTIC CIRCLE
(66° 52'N)

Aral Sea

Caucasus

Carpathians

Alps

*River
Amur*

Pyrenees

E U R O P E

Black Sea

A S I A

Lake Baikal

*Atlas
Mountains*

*Mediterranean
Sea*

*Sea of
Japan*

Sahara

Honshu

TROPIC OF
CANCER
(23° 30'N)

*Red
Sea*

Gobi Desert

*Yellow River
(Huang He)*

PACIFIC
OCEAN

Pamirs

A F R I C A

*Caspian
Sea*

*Thar
Desert*

Himalayas

*South
China
Sea*

*Yangtze
River (Chang
Jiang)*

*Arabian
Desert*

River Nile

*Takla Makan
Desert*

*River
Mekong*

Borneo

New Guinea

EQUATOR
(0°)

Lake Victoria

Sumatra

*River Congo
(Zaire)*

*Lake
Tanganyika*

Madagascar

INDIAN
OCEAN

*Australian
Desert*

AUSTRALASIA

*Namib
Desert*

TROPIC OF
CAPRICORN
(23° 30'S)

Lake Nyasa

*Kalahari
Desert*

Drakensberg

New Zealand

ANTARCTIC CIRCLE
(66° 52'S)

ANTARCTICA

0°
0°
40°
80°
120°
160°
180°

GREENWICH
MERIDIAN

EAST OF GREENWICH
MERIDIAN

265

The rock cycle

THE ROCK CYCLE IS A CONTINUOUS PROCESS through which old rocks are transformed into new ones. Rocks can be divided into three main groups: igneous, sedimentary, and metamorphic. Igneous rocks are formed when magma (molten rock) from the Earth's interior cools and solidifies (see pp. 274-275). Sedimentary rocks are formed when sediment (rock particles, for example) becomes compressed and cemented together in a process known as lithification (see pp. 276-277). Metamorphic rocks are formed when igneous, sedimentary, or other metamorphic rocks are changed by heat or pressure (see pp. 274-275). Rocks are added to the Earth's surface by crustal movements and volcanic activity. Once exposed on the surface, the rocks are broken down into rock particles by weathering (see pp. 282-283). The particles are then transported

HEXAGONAL BASALT
COLUMNS, ICELAND

by glaciers, rivers, and wind, and deposited as sediment in lakes, deltas, deserts, and on the ocean floor. Some of this sediment undergoes lithification and forms sedimentary rock. This rock may be thrust back to the surface by crustal movements or forced deeper into the Earth's interior, where heat and pressure transform it into metamorphic rock. The metamorphic rock in turn may be pushed up to the surface or may be melted to form magma. Eventually, the magma cools and solidifies – below or on the surface – forming igneous rock. When the sedimentary, igneous, and metamorphic rocks are exposed once more on the Earth's surface, the cycle begins again.

STAGES IN THE ROCK CYCLE

Magma extruded as lava, which solidifies to form igneous rock

Lava flow

Vent

Main conduit

Secondary conduit

Lava

Ash

THE ROCK CYCLE

Igneous rock

Cooling and solidification (crystallization)

Weathering, transport, and deposition

Sediment

Heat and pressure (metamorphism)

Weathering, transport, and deposition

Weathering, transport, and deposition

Compression and cementation (lithification)

Magma

Melting

Heat and pressure (metamorphism)

Metamorphic rock

Sedimentary rock

Rock surrounding magma changed by heat to form metamorphic rock

Intense heat of rising magma melts some of the surrounding rock

Sedimentary rock crushed and folded to form metamorphic rock

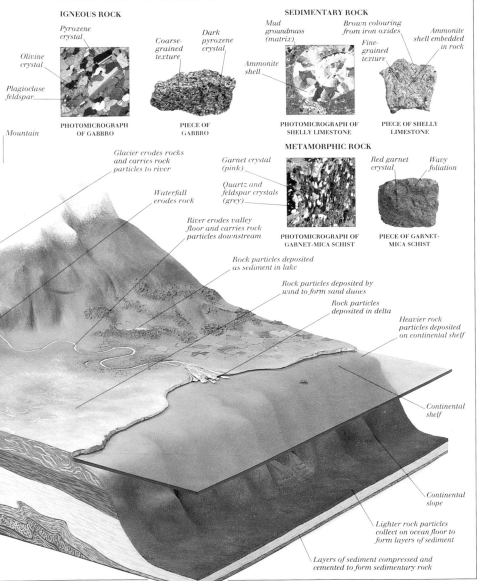

IGNEOUS ROCK

Pyroxene crystal

Olivine crystal

Plagioclase feldspar

PHOTOMICROGRAPH OF GABBRO

Coarse-grained texture

Dark pyroxene crystal

PIECE OF GABBRO

SEDIMENTARY ROCK

Mud groundmass (matrix)

Ammonite shell

PHOTOMICROGRAPH OF SHELLY LIMESTONE

Brown colouring from iron oxides

Fine-grained texture

Ammonite shell embedded in rock

PIECE OF SHELLY LIMESTONE

METAMORPHIC ROCK

Garnet crystal (pink)

Quartz and feldspar crystals (grey)

PHOTOMICROGRAPH OF GARNET-MICA SCHIST

Red garnet crystal

Wavy foliation

PIECE OF GARNET-MICA SCHIST

Mountain

Glacier erodes rocks and carries rock particles to river

Waterfall erodes rock

River erodes valley floor and carries rock particles downstream

Rock particles deposited as sediment in lake

Rock particles deposited by wind to form sand dunes

Rock particles deposited in delta

Heavier rock particles deposited on continental shelf

Continental shelf

Continental slope

Lighter rock particles collect on ocean floor to form layers of sediment

Layers of sediment compressed and cemented to form sedimentary rock

Minerals

A MINERAL IS A NATURALLY OCCURRING SUBSTANCE that has a characteristic chemical composition and specific physical properties, such as habit and streak (see pp. 270-271). A rock, by comparison, is an aggregate of minerals and need not have a specific chemical composition. Minerals are made up of elements (substances that cannot be broken down chemically into simpler substances), each of which can be represented by a chemical symbol. Minerals can be divided into two main groups: native elements and compounds. Native elements are made up of a pure element. Examples include gold (chemical symbol Au), silver (Ag), copper (Cu), and carbon (C); carbon occurs as a native element in two forms, diamond and graphite. Compounds are combinations of two or more elements. For example, sulphides are compounds of sulphur (S) and one or more other elements, such as lead (Pb) in the mineral galena, or antimony (Sb) in the mineral stibnite.

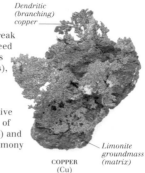

Dendritic (branching) copper

Limonite groundmass (matrix)

COPPER
(Cu)

SULPHIDES

Cubic galena crystal

GALENA
(PbS)

Dendritic (branching) gold

Kimberlite groundmass (matrix)

Quartz vein

GOLD
(Au)

White diamond

DIAMOND
(C)

Hexagonal graphite crystal

GRAPHITE
(C)

OXIDES/HYDROXIDES

Milky quartz groundmass (matrix)

Smoky quartz crystal

SMOKY QUARTZ
(SiO$_2$)

Rounded bauxite grains in groundmass (matrix)

Mass of specular haematite crystals

SPECULAR HAEMATITE
(Fe$_2$O$_3$)

BAUXITE
(FeO(OH) and Al$_2$O$_3$.2H$_2$O)

Prismatic stibnite crystal

Quartz groundmass (matrix)

STIBNITE
(Sb$_2$S$_3$)

Perfect octahedral pyrites crystal

Quartz crystal

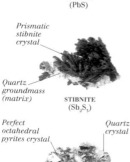

PYRITES
(FeS$_2$)

Parallel bands of onyx

ONYX
(SiO$_2$)

Kidney ore haematite

Specular crystals of haematite

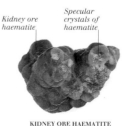

KIDNEY ORE HAEMATITE
(Fe$_2$O$_3$)

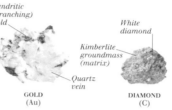

PHOSPHATES

Limonite groundmass (matrix)

Rock groundmass (matrix)

Radiating wavellite crystals

WAVELLITE
(Al₃(PO₄)₂(OH,F)₃.5H₂O)

Prismatic pyromorphite crystals

PYROMORPHITE
(Pb₅(PO₄)₃Cl)

CARBONATES

Striated cerussite crystal

Dog tooth calcite crystal

CERUSSITE
(PbCO₃)

CALCITE
(CaCO₃)

SULPHATES

Rock groundmass (matrix)

Radiating crystal mass of daisy gypsum

Radiating cyanotrichite crystals

CYANOTRICHITE
Cu₄Al₂(SO₄)(OH)₁₂.2H₂O)

DAISY GYPSUM
(CaSO₄.2H₂O)

MOLYBDATE

Tabular wulfenite crystal

Dark rock groundmass (matrix)

WULFENITE
(PbMoO₄)

SILICATES

Feldspar groundmass (matrix)

Transparent bicolored tourmaline crystal

Dodecahedral sodalite crystal

SODALITE
(Na₈Al₆Si₆O₂₄Cl₂)

TOURMALINE
(Na(Mg,Fe,Li,Mn,Al)₃Al₆(BO₃)₃Si₆.O₁₈(OH,F)₄)

Striated surface of olivine crystal

OLIVINE
(Fe₂SiO₄ - Mg₂SiO₄)

Striated prismatic epidote crystal

EPIDOTE
(Ca₂(Al,Fe)₃(SiO₄)₃(OH))

Tabular muscovite crystal

Orthoclase crystal

MUSCOVITE
(KAl₂(Si₃Al)O₁₀(OH,F)₂)

ORTHOCLASE
(KAlSi₃O₈)

HALIDES

Cubic fluorite crystal

Cubic rock salt crystal

GREEN FLUORITE
(CaF₂)

ORANGE HALITE (ROCK SALT)
(NaCl)

Mineral features

MINERALS CAN BE IDENTIFIED BY STUDYING features such as fracture, cleavage, crystal system, habit, hardness, colour, and streak. Minerals can break in different ways. If a mineral breaks in an irregular way, leaving rough surfaces, it possesses fracture. If a mineral breaks along well-defined planes of weakness, it possesses cleavage. Specific minerals have distinctive patterns of cleavage; for example, mica cleaves along one plane. Most minerals form crystals, which can be categorized into crystal systems according to their symmetry and number of faces. Within each system, several different but related forms of crystal are possible; for example, a cubic crystal can have six, eight, or twelve sides. A mineral's habit is the typical form taken by an aggregate of its crystals. Examples of habit include botryoidal (like a bunch of grapes) and massive (no definite form). The relative hardness of a mineral may be assessed by testing its resistance to scratching. This property is usually measured using Mohs scale, which increases in hardness from 1 (talc) to 10 (diamond). The colour of a mineral is not a dependable guide to its identity as some minerals have a range of colours. Streak (the colour the powdered mineral makes when rubbed across an unglazed tile) is a more reliable indicator.

CLEAVAGE

Cleavage in one direction

CLEAVAGE ALONG ONE PLANE

Cleavage in three directions, forming a block cube

CLEAVAGE ALONG THREE PLANES

Horizontal cleavage

Vertical cleavage

CLEAVAGE ALONG TWO PLANES

Cleavage in four directions, forming a double-pyramid crystal

CLEAVAGE ALONG FOUR PLANES

CRYSTAL SYSTEMS

Cubic iron pyrites crystal

Tetragonal idocrase crystal

Representation of tetragonal system

TETRAGONAL SYSTEM

Representation of cubic system

CUBIC SYSTEM

Hexagonal beryl crystal

Representation of hexagonal/trigonal system

HEXAGONAL/TRIGONAL SYSTEM

Orthorhombic barytes crystal

Representation of orthorhombic system

ORTHORHOMBIC SYSTEM

Monoclinic selenite crystal

Representation of monoclinic system

Triclinic axinite crystal

Representation of triclinic system

MONOCLINIC SYSTEM

TRICLINIC SYSTEM

FRACTURE

Fire opal with conchoidal (shell-like) fracture

Nickel-iron with hackly (jagged) fracture

CONCHOIDAL FRACTURE

HACKLY FRACTURE

Orpiment with uneven fracture

Garnierite with splintery fracture

UNEVEN FRACTURE

SPLINTERY FRACTURE

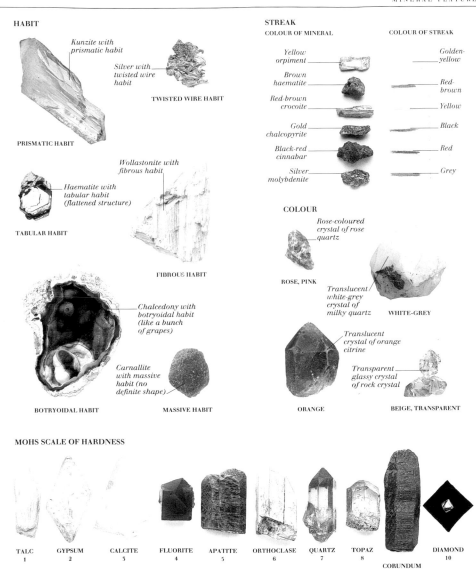

HABIT

Kunzite with prismatic habit

Silver with twisted wire habit

TWISTED WIRE HABIT

PRISMATIC HABIT

Wollastonite with fibrous habit

Haematite with tabular habit (flattened structure)

TABULAR HABIT

FIBROUS HABIT

Chalcedony with botryoidal habit (like a bunch of grapes)

Carnallite with massive habit (no definite shape)

BOTRYOIDAL HABIT

MASSIVE HABIT

STREAK

COLOUR OF MINERAL

Yellow orpiment

Brown haematite

Red-brown crocoite

Gold chalcopyrite

Black-red cinnabar

Silver molybdenite

COLOUR OF STREAK

Golden-yellow

Red-brown

Yellow

Black

Red

Grey

COLOUR

Rose-coloured crystal of rose quartz

ROSE, PINK

Translucent white-grey crystal of milky quartz

WHITE-GREY

Translucent crystal of orange citrine

Transparent glassy crystal of rock crystal

ORANGE

BEIGE, TRANSPARENT

MOHS SCALE OF HARDNESS

TALC	GYPSUM	CALCITE	FLUORITE	APATITE	ORTHOCLASE	QUARTZ	TOPAZ	CORUNDUM	DIAMOND
1	2	3	4	5	6	7	8	9	10

Volcanoes

Folded, rope-like surface

VOLCANOES ARE VENTS OR FISSURES in the Earth's crust through which magma (molten rock that originates from deep beneath the crust) is forced on to the surface as lava. They occur most commonly along the boundaries of crustal plates; most volcanoes lie in a belt called the "Ring of Fire", which runs along the edge of the Pacific Ocean. Volcanoes can be classified according to the violence and frequency of their eruptions. Non-explosive volcanic eruptions generally occur where crustal plates pull apart. These eruptions produce runny basaltic lava that spreads quickly over a wide area to form relatively flat cones. The most violent eruptions take place where plates collide. Such eruptions produce thick rhyolitic lava and may also blast out clouds of dust and pyroclasts (lava fragments). The lava does not flow far before cooling and therefore builds up steep-sided, conical volcanoes. Some volcanoes produce lava and ash eruptions, which build up composite volcanic cones. Volcanoes that erupt frequently are described as active; those that erupt rarely are termed dormant; and those that have stopped erupting altogether are termed extinct. As well as the volcanoes themselves, other features associated with volcanic regions include geysers, hot mineral springs, solfataras, fumaroles, and bubbling mud pools.

HORU GEYSER, NEW ZEALAND

PAHOEHOE (ROPY LAVA)

VOLCANO TYPES

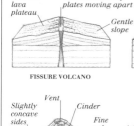

Basaltic lava plateau

Fissure created by plates moving apart

Gentle slope

FISSURE VOLCANO

Gentle slope built up by numerous basaltic lava flows

Vent

BASIC SHIELD VOLCANO

Steep, convex sides caused by thick lava cooling quickly

Vent

DOME VOLCANO

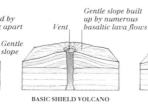

Slightly concave sides

Vent

Cinder

Fine ash

ASH-CINDER VOLCANO

Lava

Vent

Ash

Steep conical shape

Secondary conduit

COMPOSITE VOLCANO

Caldera (volcanic crater)

New cone

Old cone

Ash

CALDERA VOLCANO

Layers of sedimentary rocks

Metamorphic rocks (rocks altered by heat and pressure)

HOW VOLCANIC PLUGS BECOME EXPOSED

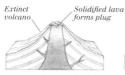

Extinct volcano

Solidified lava forms plug

PLUG FORMATION

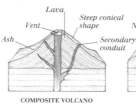

Plug exposed

Volcanic cone slowly eroded away

INITIAL EROSION AROUND PLUG

Resistant lava plug remains

Volcanic cone completely eroded away

COMPLETE DENUDATION OF PLUG

LAPILLI (LAVA FRAGMENTS)

Small piece of solidified lava

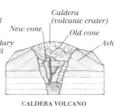

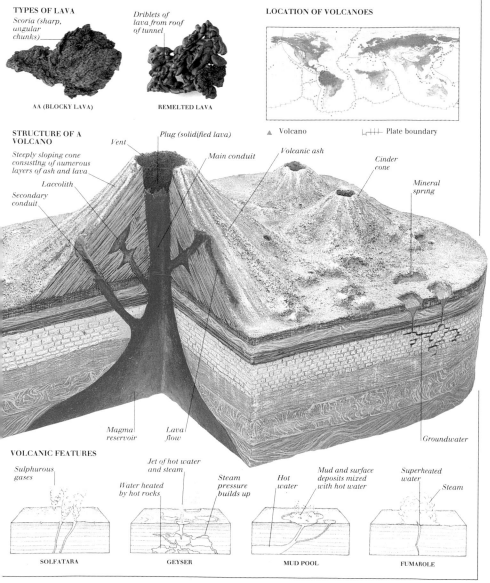

TYPES OF LAVA

Scoria (sharp, angular chunks)

AA (BLOCKY LAVA)

Driblets of lava from roof of tunnel

REMELTED LAVA

LOCATION OF VOLCANOES

▲ Volcano   Plate boundary

STRUCTURE OF A VOLCANO

Steeply sloping cone consisting of numerous layers of ash and lava

Laccolith

Secondary conduit

Vent

Plug (solidified lava)

Main conduit

Volcanic ash

Cinder cone

Mineral spring

Magma reservoir

Lava flow

Groundwater

VOLCANIC FEATURES

Sulphurous gases

Jet of hot water and steam

Water heated by hot rocks

Steam pressure builds up

Hot water

Mud and surface deposits mixed with hot water

Superheated water

Steam

SOLFATARA

GEYSER

MUD POOL

FUMAROLE

273

Igneous and metamorphic rocks

IGNEOUS ROCKS ARE FORMED WHEN MAGMA (molten rock that originates from deep beneath the Earth's crust) cools and solidifies. There are two main types of igneous rock: intrusive and extrusive. Intrusive rocks are formed deep underground where magma is forced into cracks or between rock layers to form structures such as sills, dykes, and batholiths. The magma cools slowly to form coarse-grained rocks such as gabbro and pegmatite. Extrusive rocks are formed above the Earth's surface from lava (magma that has been ejected in a volcanic eruption). The molten lava cools quickly, producing fine-grained rocks such as rhyolite and basalt. Metamorphic rocks are those that have been altered by intense heat (contact metamorphism) or extreme pressure (regional metamorphism). Contact metamorphism occurs when rocks are changed by heat from, for example, an igneous intrusion or lava flow. Regional metamorphism occurs when rock is crushed in the middle of a folding mountain range. Metamorphic rocks can be formed from igneous rocks, sedimentary rocks, or even from other metamorphic rocks.

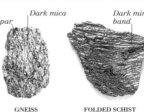

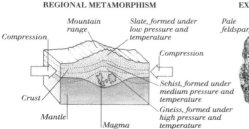

Cinder cone

Large eroded lava flow

Cedar-tree laccolith

Butte

Plug

Cone sheet

Ring dyke

Batholith

Dyke

Sill

Dyke swarm

Lopolith

IGNEOUS ROCK STRUCTURES

CONTACT METAMORPHISM

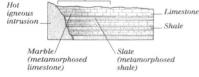

Metamorphic aureole (region where contact metamorphism occurs)

Hot igneous intrusion

Limestone

Shale

Marble (metamorphosed limestone)

Slate (metamorphosed shale)

REGIONAL METAMORPHISM

Mountain range

Slate, formed under low pressure and temperature

Compression

Compression

Crust

Mantle

Magma

Schist, formed under medium pressure and temperature

Gneiss, formed under high pressure and temperature

EXAMPLES OF METAMORPHIC ROCKS

Pale feldspar

Dark mica

Dark mineral band

Pale calcite

GNEISS

FOLDED SCHIST

SKARN

EXAMPLES OF EXTRUSIVE IGNEOUS ROCKS

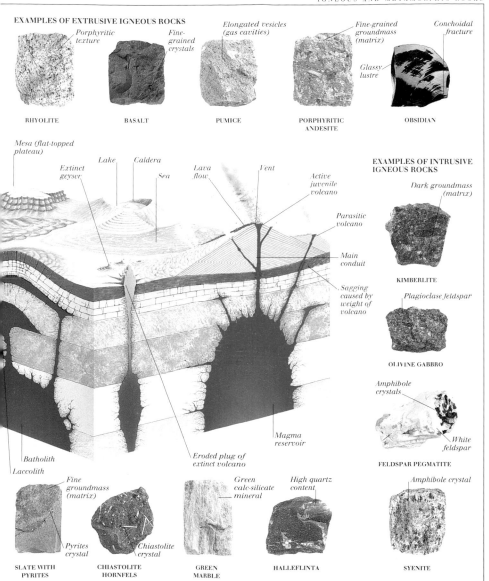

Porphyritic texture

Fine-grained crystals

Elongated vesicles (gas cavities)

Fine-grained groundmass (matrix)

Conchoidal fracture

Glassy lustre

RHYOLITE

BASALT

PUMICE

PORPHYRITIC ANDESITE

OBSIDIAN

Mesa (flat-topped plateau)

Extinct geyser

Lake

Caldera

Sea

Lava flow

Vent

Active juvenile volcano

Parasitic volcano

Main conduit

Sagging caused by weight of volcano

Batholith

Laccolith

Eroded plug of extinct volcano

Magma reservoir

EXAMPLES OF INTRUSIVE IGNEOUS ROCKS

Dark groundmass (matrix)

KIMBERLITE

Plagioclase feldspar

OLIVINE GABBRO

Amphibole crystals

White feldspar

FELDSPAR PEGMATITE

Amphibole crystal

SYENITE

Fine groundmass (matrix)

Pyrites crystal

Chiastolite crystal

Green calc-silicate mineral

High quartz content

SLATE WITH PYRITES

CHIASTOLITE HORNFELS

GREEN MARBLE

HALLEFLINTA

Sedimentary rocks

SEDIMENTARY ROCKS ARE FORMED BY THE ACCUMULATION and consolidation of sediments (see pp. 266-267). There are three main types of sedimentary rock. Clastic sedimentary rocks, such as breccia or sandstone, are formed from other rocks that have been broken down into fragments by weathering (see pp. 282-283), which have then been transported and deposited elsewhere. Organic sedimentary rocks – for example, coal (see pp. 280-281) – are derived from plant and animal remains. Chemical sedimentary rocks are formed by chemical processes. For example, rock salt is formed when salt dissolved in water is deposited as the water evaporates. Sedimentary rocks are laid down in layers, called beds or strata. Each new layer is laid down horizontally over older ones. There are usually some gaps in the sequence, called unconformities. These represent periods in which no new sediments were being laid down, or when earlier sedimentary layers were raised above sea level and eroded away.

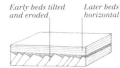

Early beds tilted and eroded / Later beds horizontal

ANGULAR UNCONFORMITY

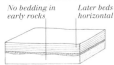

No bedding in early rocks / Later beds horizontal

NONCONFORMITY

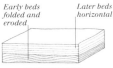

Early beds folded and eroded / Later beds horizontal

DISCONFORMITY

THE GRAND CANYON, USA

SEDIMENTARY LAYERS OF THE GRAND CANYON REGION

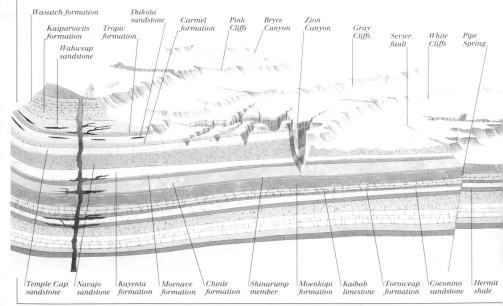

Wasatch formation *Dakota sandstone* *Carmel formation* *Pink Cliffs* *Bryce Canyon* *Zion Canyon* *Gray Cliffs* *Sevier fault* *White Cliffs* *Pipe Spring*

Kaiparowits formation *Tropic formation*

Wahweap sandstone

Temple Cap sandstone *Navajo sandstone* *Kayenta formation* *Moenave formation* *Chinle formation* *Shinarump member* *Moenkopi formation* *Kaibab limestone* *Toroweap formation* *Coconino sandstone* *Hermit shale*

EXAMPLES OF SEDIMENTARY ROCKS

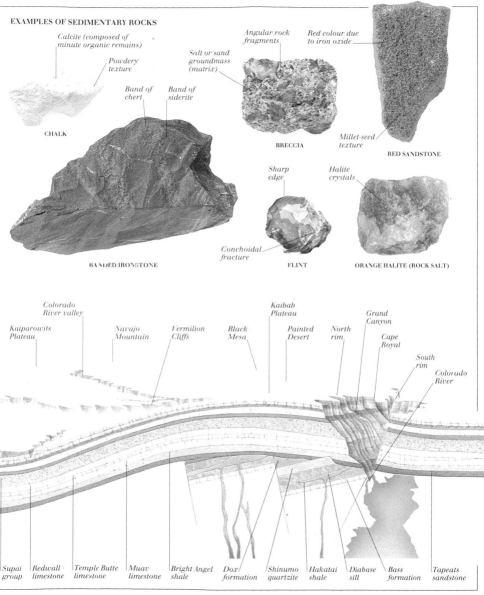

Calcite (composed of minute organic remains)

Powdery texture

CHALK

Band of chert

Band of siderite

BANDED IRONSTONE

Angular rock fragments

Salt or sand groundmass (matrix)

BRECCIA

Red colour due to iron oxide

Millet-seed texture

RED SANDSTONE

Sharp edge

Conchoidal fracture

FLINT

Halite crystals

ORANGE HALITE (ROCK SALT)

Colorado River valley

Kaibab Plateau

Grand Canyon

Kaiparowits Plateau

Navajo Mountain

Vermilion Cliffs

Black Mesa

Painted Desert

North rim

Cape Royal

South rim

Colorado River

Supai group

Redwall limestone

Temple Butte limestone

Muav limestone

Bright Angel shale

Dox formation

Shinumo quartzite

Hakatai shale

Diabase sill

Bass formation

Tapeats sandstone

Fossils

FOSSILS ARE THE REMAINS of plants and animals that have been preserved in rock. A fossil may be the preserved remains of an organism itself, an impression of it in rock, or preserved traces (known as trace fossils) left by an organism while it was alive, such as organic carbon outlines, fossilized footprints, or droppings. Most dead organisms soon rot away or are eaten by scavengers. For fossilization to occur, rapid burial by sediment is necessary. The organism decays, but the harder parts – bones, teeth, and shells, for example – may be preserved and hardened by minerals from the surrounding sediment. Fossilization may also occur even when the hard parts of an organism are dissolved away to leave an impression called a mould. The mould is filled by minerals, thereby creating a cast of the organism. The study of fossils (palaeontology) can not only show how living things have evolved, but can also help to reveal the Earth's geological history – for example, by aiding in the dating of rock strata.

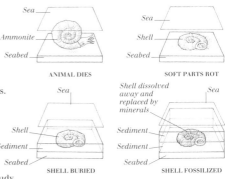

PROCESS OF FOSSILIZATION

ANIMAL DIES

SOFT PARTS ROT

SHELL BURIED

SHELL FOSSILIZED

EXAMPLES OF FOSSILS

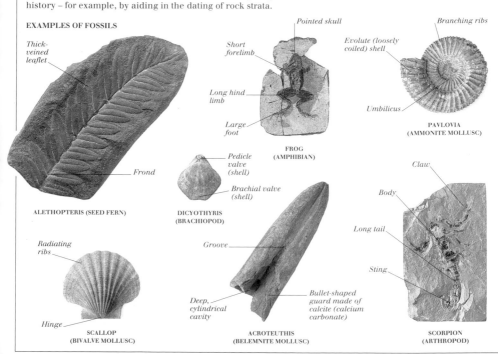

ALETHOPTERIS (SEED FERN)

DICYOTHYRIS (BRACHIOPOD)

FROG (AMPHIBIAN)

PAVLOVIA (AMMONITE MOLLUSC)

SCALLOP (BIVALVE MOLLUSC)

ACROTEUTHIS (BELEMNITE MOLLUSC)

SCORPION (ARTHROPOD)

THE FOSSIL RECORD

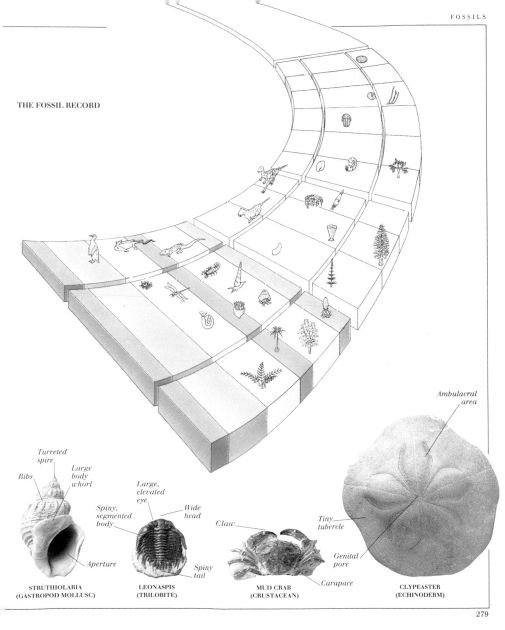

Ambulacral area

Turreted spire

Ribs

Large body whorl

Large, elevated eye

Spiny, segmented body

Wide head

Claw

Tiny tubercle

Genital pore

Aperture

Spiny tail

Carapace

STRUTHIOLARIA (GASTROPOD MOLLUSC)

LEONASPIS (TRILOBITE)

MUD CRAB (CRUSTACEAN)

CLYPEASTER (ECHINODERM)

Mineral resources

MINERAL RESOURCES CAN BE DEFINED AS naturally occurring substances that can be extracted from the Earth and are useful as fuels and raw materials. Coal, oil, and gas – collectively called fossil fuels – are commonly included in this group, but are not strictly minerals, because they are of organic origin. Coal formation begins when vegetation is buried and partly decomposed to form peat. Overlying sediments compress the peat and transform it into lignite (soft brown coal). As the overlying sediments accumulate, increasing pressure and temperature eventually transform the lignite into bituminous and hard anthracite coals. Oil and gas are usually formed from organic matter that was deposited in marine sediments. Under the effects of heat and pressure, the compressed organic matter undergoes complex chemical changes to form oil and gas. The oil and gas percolate upwards through water-saturated, permeable rocks and they may rise to the Earth's surface or accumulate below an impermeable layer of rock that has been folded or faulted to form a trap – an anticline (upfold) trap, for example. Minerals are inorganic substances that may consist of a single chemical element, such as gold, silver, or copper, or combinations of elements (see pp. 268-269). Some minerals are concentrated in mineralization zones in rock associated with crustal movements or volcanic activity. Others may be found in sediments as placer deposits – accumulations of high-density minerals that have been weathered out of rocks, transported, and deposited (on river-beds, for example).

OIL RIG, NORTH SEA

Stalk *Leaf*

PLANT MATTER

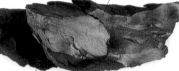

Decayed plant matter

About 60% carbon   PEAT   *About 70% carbon*

Crumbly texture   LIGNITE (BROWN COAL)   *Powdery texture*

About 80% carbon

Shiny surface   BITUMINOUS COAL   *About 95% carbon*

ANTHRACITE COAL

HOW COAL IS FORMED

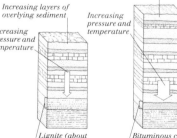

Vegetation

Increasing pressure and temperature

Increasing layers of overlying sediment

Increasing pressure and temperature

Increasing layers of overlying sediment

Increasing pressure and temperature

Peat (about 60% carbon)

PEAT

Lignite (about 70% carbon)

LIGNITE (BROWN COAL)

Bituminous coal (about 80% carbon)

BITUMINOUS COAL

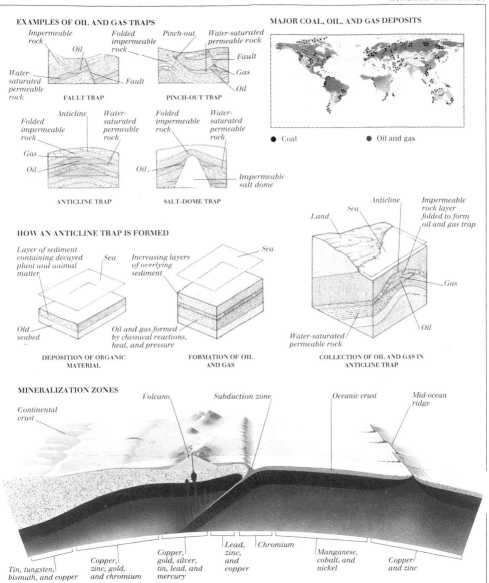

EXAMPLES OF OIL AND GAS TRAPS

Impermeable rock

Oil

Folded impermeable rock

Water-saturated permeable rock

Water-saturated permeable rock

Fault

FAULT TRAP

Pinch-out

Water-saturated permeable rock

Fault

Gas

Oil

PINCH-OUT TRAP

Anticline

Folded impermeable rock

Water-saturated permeable rock

Gas

Oil

ANTICLINE TRAP

Folded impermeable rock

Water-saturated permeable rock

Oil

Impermeable salt dome

SALT-DOME TRAP

MAJOR COAL, OIL, AND GAS DEPOSITS

● Coal   ● Oil and gas

HOW AN ANTICLINE TRAP IS FORMED

Layer of sediment containing decayed plant and animal matter

Sea

Old seabed

DEPOSITION OF ORGANIC MATERIAL

Increasing layers of overlying sediment

Sea

Oil and gas formed by chemical reactions, heat, and pressure

FORMATION OF OIL AND GAS

Land

Sea

Anticline

Impermeable rock layer folded to form oil and gas trap

Gas

Oil

Water-saturated permeable rock

COLLECTION OF OIL AND GAS IN ANTICLINE TRAP

MINERALIZATION ZONES

Continental crust

Volcano

Subduction zone

Oceanic crust

Mid-ocean ridge

Tin, tungsten, bismuth, and copper

Copper, zinc, gold, and chromium

Copper, gold, silver, tin, lead, and mercury

Lead, zinc, and copper

Chromium

Manganese, cobalt, and nickel

Copper and zinc

Weathering and erosion

WEATHERING IS THE BREAKING DOWN of rocks on the Earth's surface. There are two main types: physical (or mechanical) and chemical. Physical weathering may be caused by temperature changes, such as freezing and thawing, or by abrasion from material carried by winds, rivers, or glaciers. Rocks may also be broken down by the actions of animals and plants, such as the burrowing of animals and the growth of roots. Chemical weathering causes rocks to decompose by changing their chemical composition – for example, rainwater may dissolve certain minerals in a rock. Erosion is the wearing away and removal of land surfaces by water, wind, or ice. It is greatest in areas of little or no surface vegetation, such as deserts, where sand dunes may form.

FORMATION OF A HAMADA (ROCK PAVEMENT)

Wind blows away small particles

Larger particles aggregate

Hamada forms

FIRST STAGE

SECOND STAGE

FINAL STAGE

FEATURES OF WEATHERING AND EROSION

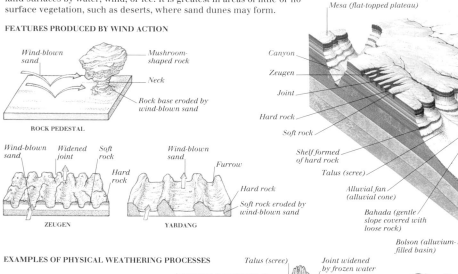

Mesa (flat-topped plateau)

Canyon

Zeugen

Joint

Hard rock

Soft rock

Shelf formed of hard rock

Talus (scree)

Alluvial fan (alluvial cone)

Bahada (gentle slope covered with loose rock)

Bolson (alluvium-filled basin)

FEATURES PRODUCED BY WIND ACTION

Wind-blown sand

Mushroom-shaped rock

Neck

Rock base eroded by wind-blown sand

ROCK PEDESTAL

Wind-blown sand

Widened joint

Soft rock

Hard rock

ZEUGEN

Wind-blown sand

Furrow

Hard rock

Soft rock eroded by wind-blown sand

YARDANG

EXAMPLES OF PHYSICAL WEATHERING PROCESSES

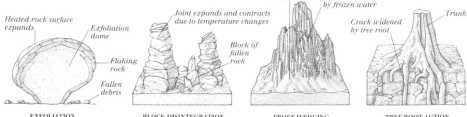

Heated rock surface expands

Exfoliation dome

Flaking rock

Fallen debris

EXFOLIATION (ONION-SKIN WEATHERING)

Joint expands and contracts due to temperature changes

Block of fallen rock

BLOCK DISINTEGRATION

Talus (scree)

FROST WEDGING

Joint widened by frozen water

Trunk

Crack widened by tree root

TREE ROOT ACTION

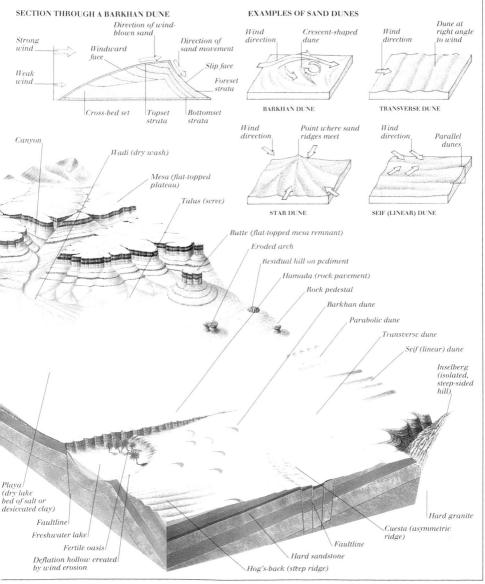

SECTION THROUGH A BARKHAN DUNE

Strong wind

Weak wind

Direction of wind-blown sand

Windward face

Direction of sand movement

Slip face

Foreset strata

Cross-bed set

Topset strata

Bottomset strata

EXAMPLES OF SAND DUNES

Wind direction

Crescent-shaped dune

Wind direction

Dune at right angle to wind

BARKHAN DUNE

TRANSVERSE DUNE

Wind direction

Point where sand ridges meet

Wind direction

Parallel dunes

STAR DUNE

SEIF (LINEAR) DUNE

Canyon

Wadi (dry wash)

Mesa (flat-topped plateau)

Talus (scree)

Butte (flat-topped mesa remnant)

Eroded arch

Residual hill on pediment

Hamada (rock pavement)

Rock pedestal

Barkhan dune

Parabolic dune

Transverse dune

Seif (linear) dune

Inselberg (isolated, steep-sided hill)

Playa (dry lake bed of salt or desiccated clay)

Faultline

Freshwater lake

Fertile oasis

Deflation hollow created by wind erosion

Hog's-back (steep ridge)

Hard sandstone

Faultline

Cuesta (asymmetric ridge)

Hard granite

283

Caves

CAVES COMMONLY FORM in areas of
limestone, although on coastlines they
also occur in other rocks. Limestone is
made of calcite (calcium carbonate),
which dissolves in the carbonic acid
naturally present in rainwater, and in
humic acids from the decay of
vegetation. The acidic water
trickles down through cracks and
joints in the limestone and between rock layers,
breaking up the surface terrain into clints (blocks of
rock), separated by grikes (deep cracks), and punctuated
by sink-holes (also called swallow-holes or potholes) into
which surface streams may disappear. Underground,
the acidic water dissolves the rock around crevices,
opening up a network of passages and caves, which can become large
caverns if the roofs collapse. Various features are formed when the dissolved
calcite is redeposited; for example, it may be redeposited along an underground
stream to form a gour (series of calcite ridges), or in caves and passages to form
stalactites and stalagmites. Stalactites develop where calcite is left behind as
water drips from the roof; where the drops land, stalagmites build up.

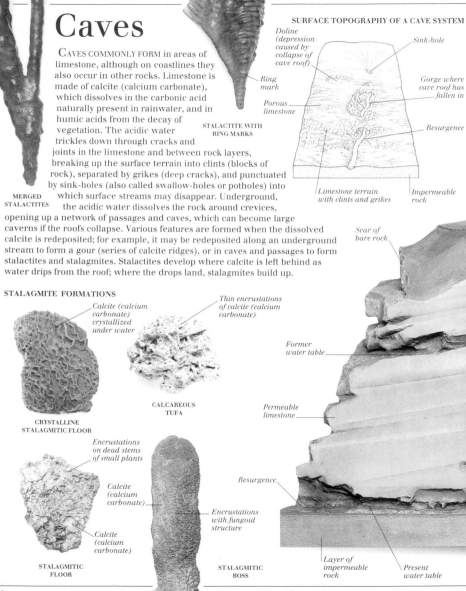

**STALACTITE WITH
RING MARKS**

Ring
mark

Porous
limestone

**MERGED
STALACTITES**

SURFACE TOPOGRAPHY OF A CAVE SYSTEM

Doline
(depression
caused by
collapse of
cave roof)

Sink-hole

Gorge where
cave roof has
fallen in

Resurgence

Limestone terrain
with clints and grikes

Impermeable
rock

Scar of
bare rock

Former
water table

Permeable
limestone

Resurgence

Layer of
impermeable
rock

Present
water table

STALAGMITE FORMATIONS

Calcite (calcium
carbonate)
crystallized
under water

Thin encrustations
of calcite (calcium
carbonate)

**CRYSTALLINE
STALAGMITIC FLOOR**

**CALCAREOUS
TUFA**

Encrustations
on dead stems
of small plants

Calcite
(calcium
carbonate)

Encrustations
with fungoid
structure

Calcite
(calcium
carbonate)

**STALAGMITIC
FLOOR**

**STALAGMITIC
BOSS**

DEVELOPMENT OF A CAVE SYSTEM

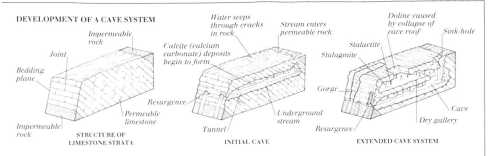

Impermeable rock

Joint

Bedding plane

Impermeable rock

Permeable limestone

STRUCTURE OF LIMESTONE STRATA

Water seeps through cracks in rock

Calcite (calcium carbonate) deposits begin to form

Stream enters permeable rock

Resurgence

Tunnel

Underground stream

INITIAL CAVE

Doline caused by collapse of cave roof

Sink-hole

Stalactite

Stalagmite

Gorge

Resurgence

Cave

Dry gallery

EXTENDED CAVE SYSTEM

INTERCONNECTED CAVE SYSTEM

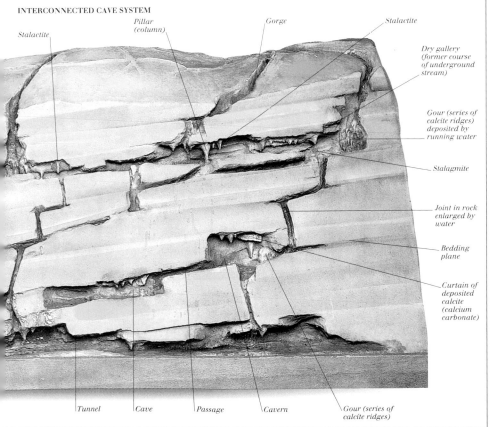

Stalactite

Pillar (column)

Gorge

Stalactite

Dry gallery (former course of underground stream)

Gour (series of calcite ridges) deposited by running water

Stalagmite

Joint in rock enlarged by water

Bedding plane

Curtain of deposited calcite (calcium carbonate)

Tunnel

Cave

Passage

Cavern

Gour (series of calcite ridges)

Glaciers

GLACIER BAY, ALASKA

A VALLEY GLACIER IS A LARGE MASS OF ICE that forms on land and moves slowly downhill under its own weight. It is formed from snow that collects in cirques (mountain hollows also known as corries) and compresses into ice as more and more snow accumulates. The cirque is deepened by frost wedging and abrasion (see pp. 282-283), and arêtes (sharp ridges) develop between adjacent cirques. Eventually, so much ice builds up that the glacier begins to move downhill. As the glacier moves it collects moraine (debris), which may range in size from particles of dust to large boulders. The rocks at the base of the glacier erode the glacial valley, giving it a U-shaped cross-section. Under the glacier, *roches moutonnées* (eroded outcrops of hard rock) and drumlins (rounded mounds of rock and clay) are left behind on the valley floor. The glacier ends at a terminus (the snout), where the ice melts as fast as it arrives. If the temperature increases, the ice melts faster than it arrives, and the glacier retreats. The retreating glacier leaves behind its moraine and also erratics (isolated single boulders). Glacial streams from the melting glacier deposit eskers and kames (ridges and mounds of sand and gravel), but carry away the finer sediment to form a stratified outwash plain. Lumps of ice carried on to this plain melt, creating holes called kettles.

VALLEY GLACIER

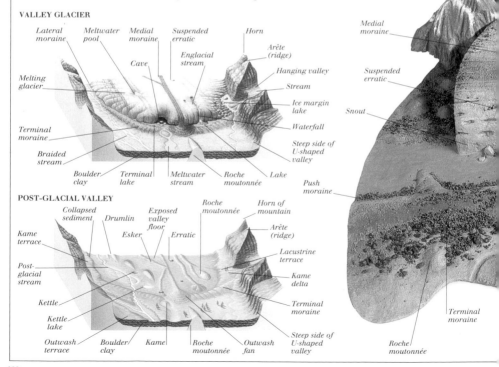

Lateral moraine · Meltwater pool · Medial moraine · Suspended erratic · Horn · Medial moraine · Arête (ridge) · Cave · Englacial stream · Hanging valley · Suspended erratic · Melting glacier · Stream · Ice margin lake · Snout · Terminal moraine · Waterfall · Braided stream · Steep side of U-shaped valley · Boulder clay · Terminal lake · Meltwater stream · Roche moutonnée · Lake · Push moraine

POST-GLACIAL VALLEY

Collapsed sediment · Drumlin · Exposed valley floor · Roche moutonnée · Horn of mountain · Kame terrace · Esker · Erratic · Arête (ridge) · Post-glacial stream · Lacustrine terrace · Kame delta · Kettle · Terminal moraine · Kettle lake · Terminal moraine · Outwash terrace · Boulder clay · Kame · Roche moutonnée · Outwash fan · Steep side of U-shaped valley · Roche moutonnée

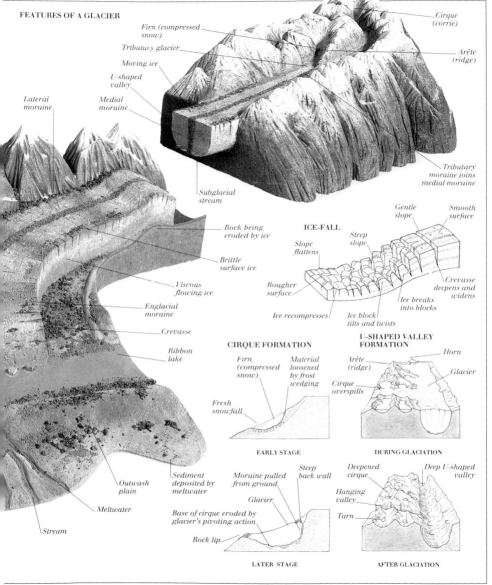

FEATURES OF A GLACIER

Firn (compressed snow)

Tributary glacier

Moving ice

U-shaped valley

Medial moraine

Lateral moraine

Cirque (corrie)

Arête (ridge)

Tributary moraine joins medial moraine

Subglacial stream

Rock being eroded by ice

Brittle surface ice

Viscous flowing ice

Englacial moraine

Crevasse

Ribbon lake

Outwash plain

Meltwater

Stream

Sediment deposited by meltwater

ICE-FALL

Slope flattens

Rougher surface

Ice recompresses

Ice block tilts and twists

Ice breaks into blocks

Steep slope

Gentle slope

Smooth surface

Crevasse deepens and widens

CIRQUE FORMATION

Firn (compressed snow)

Material loosened by frost wedging

Fresh snowfall

EARLY STAGE

Moraine pulled from ground

Steep back wall

Glacier

Base of cirque eroded by glacier's pivoting action

Rock lip

LATER STAGE

U-SHAPED VALLEY FORMATION

Arête (ridge)

Cirque overspills

Horn

Glacier

DURING GLACIATION

Deepened cirque

Deep U-shaped valley

Hanging valley

Tarn

AFTER GLACIATION

Rivers

RIVERS FORM PART of the water cycle – the continuous circulation of water between the land, sea, and atmosphere. The source of a river may be a mountain spring or lake, or a melting glacier. The course that the river subsequently takes depends on the slope of the terrain and on the rock types and formations over which it flows. In its early, upland stages, a river tumbles steeply over rocks and boulders and cuts a steep-sided V-shaped valley. Farther downstream, it flows smoothly over sediments and forms winding meanders, eroding sideways to create broad valleys and plains. On reaching the coast, the river may deposit sediment to form an estuary or delta (see pp. 290-291).

RIVER CAPTURE

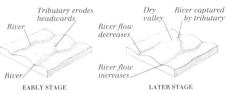

Tributary erodes headwards
River
River
River flow decreases
EARLY STAGE

Dry valley
River captured by tributary
River flow increases
LATER STAGE

THE WATER CYCLE

Precipitation falls on high ground
Water carried downstream by river
Wind
Water vapour released into atmosphere by trees and other plants
Wind
Water vapour forms clouds

SATELLITE IMAGE OF GANGES RIVER DELTA, BANGLADESH

River Ganges

Ganges delta

Water evaporates from sea

Water stored in sea

River flows into sea

Water seeps underground and flows to sea

Water evaporates from lake

Water seeps underground and flows to sea

Infertile swampland
Distributary
Large volume of sediment

RIVER DRAINAGE PATTERNS

RADIAL   **CENTRIPETAL**   **PARALLEL**   **DENDRITIC**

DERANGED   **TRELLISED**   **ANNULAR**   **RECTANGULAR**

Seabed

Sea

Sediment layers

STAGES IN A RIVER'S DEVELOPMENT

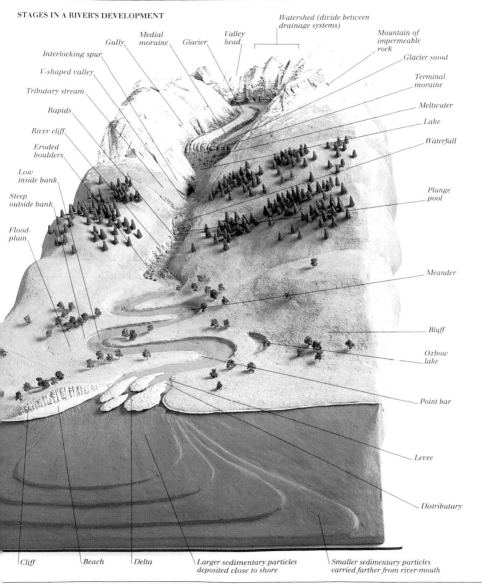

Watershed (divide between drainage systems)

Medial moraine

Gully

Valley head

Glacier

Mountain of impermeable rock

Glacier snout

Interlocking spur

Terminal moraine

V-shaped valley

Meltwater

Tributary stream

Lake

Rapids

Waterfall

River cliff

Eroded boulders

Plunge pool

Low inside bank

Steep outside bank

Flood-plain

Meander

Bluff

Oxbow lake

Point bar

Levee

Distributary

Cliff

Beach

Delta

Larger sedimentary particles deposited close to shore

Smaller sedimentary particles carried farther from river-mouth

River features

RIVERS ARE ONE OF THE MAJOR FORCES that shape the landscape. Near its source, a river is steep (see pp. 288-289). It erodes downwards, carving out V-shaped valleys and deep gorges. Waterfalls and rapids are formed where the river flows from hard rock to softer, more easily eroded rock. Farther downstream, meanders may form and there is greater sideways erosion, resulting in a broad river valley. The river sometimes erodes through the neck of a meander to form an oxbow lake. Sediment deposited on the valley floor by meandering rivers and during floods helps to create a flood-plain. Floods may also deposit sediment on the banks of the river to form levees. As a river spills into the sea or a lake, it deposits large amounts of sediment, and may form a delta. A delta is an area of sand-bars, swamps, and lagoons through which the river flows in several channels called distributaries – the Mississippi delta, for example. Often, a rise in sea level may have flooded the river-mouth to form a broad estuary, a tidal section where seawater mixes with fresh water.

HOW WATERFALLS AND RAPIDS ARE FORMED

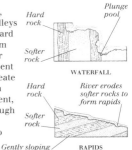

Hard rock
Softer rock
Plunge pool

WATERFALL

Hard rock
Softer rock
River erodes softer rocks to form rapids
Gently sloping rock strata

RAPIDS

A RIVER VALLEY DRAINAGE SYSTEM

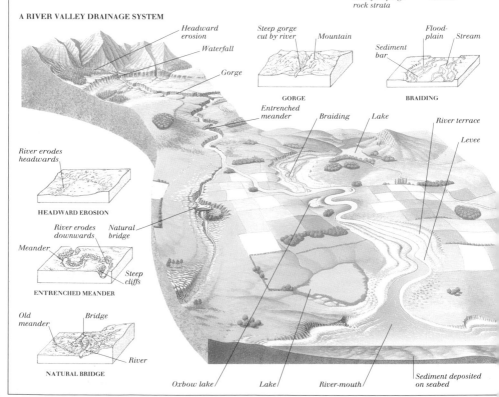

Headward erosion
Waterfall
Gorge

Steep gorge cut by river
Mountain

Flood-plain
Stream
Sediment bar

GORGE

BRAIDING

Entrenched meander
Braiding
Lake
River terrace
Levee

River erodes headwards

HEADWARD EROSION

River erodes downwards
Natural bridge

Meander
Steep cliffs

ENTRENCHED MEANDER

Old meander
Bridge
River

NATURAL BRIDGE

Oxbow lake
Lake
River-mouth
Sediment deposited on seabed

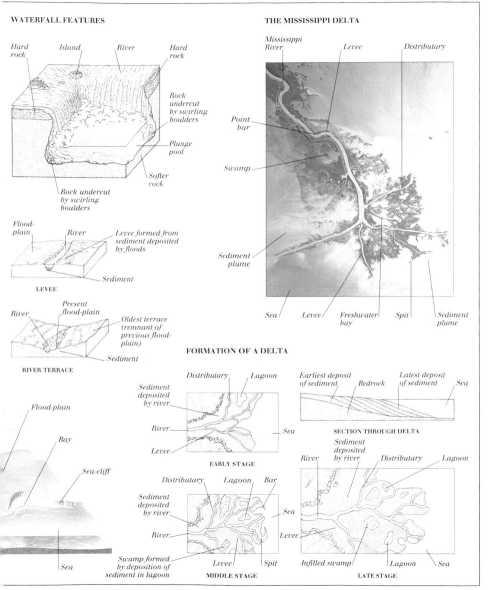

WATERFALL FEATURES

Hard rock

Island

River

Hard rock

Rock undercut by swirling boulders

Plunge pool

Softer rock

Rock undercut by swirling boulders

Flood-plain

River

Levee formed from sediment deposited by floods

Sediment

LEVEE

River

Present flood-plain

Oldest terrace (remnant of previous flood-plain)

Sediment

RIVER TERRACE

Flood-plain

Bay

Sea-cliff

Sea

THE MISSISSIPPI DELTA

Mississippi River

Levee

Distributary

Point bar

Swamp

Sediment plume

Sea

Levee

Freshwater bay

Spit

Sediment plume

FORMATION OF A DELTA

Distributary

Lagoon

Sediment deposited by river

River

Levee

Sea

EARLY STAGE

Earliest deposit of sediment

Bedrock

Latest deposit of sediment

Sea

SECTION THROUGH DELTA

Distributary

Lagoon

Bar

Sediment deposited by river

River

Sea

Swamp formed by deposition of sediment in lagoon

Levee

Spit

MIDDLE STAGE

Sediment deposited by river

River

Distributary

Lagoon

Levee

Infilled swamp

Lagoon

Sea

LATE STAGE

Lakes and groundwater

NATURAL LAKES OCCUR WHERE a large quantity of water collects in a hollow in impermeable rock, or is prevented from draining away by a barrier, such as moraine (glacial deposits) or solidified lava. Lakes are often relatively short-lived landscape features, as they tend to become silted up by sediment from the streams and rivers that feed them. Some of the more long-lasting

lakes are found in deep rift valleys formed by vertical movements of the Earth's crust (see pp. 58-59) – for example, Lake Baikal in Russia, the world's largest freshwater lake, and the Dead Sea in the Middle East, one of the world's saltiest lakes. Where water is able to drain away, it sinks into the ground until it reaches a layer of impermeable rock, then accumulates in the permeable rock above it; this water-saturated permeable rock is called an aquifer. The saturated zone varies in depth according to seasonal and climatic changes. In wet conditions, the water

LAKE BAIKAL, RUSSIA

stored underground builds up, while in dry periods it becomes depleted. Where the upper edge of the saturated zone – the water table – meets the ground surface, water emerges as springs. In an artesian basin, where the aquifer is below an aquiclude (layer of impermeable rock), the water table throughout the basin is determined by its height at the rim. In the centre of such a basin, the water table is above ground level. The water in the basin is thus trapped below the water table and can rise under its own pressure along faultlines or well shafts.

EXAMPLES OF SPRINGS

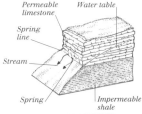

LIMESTONE SPRING

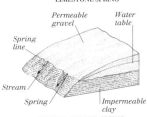

COASTAL (VALLEY) SPRING

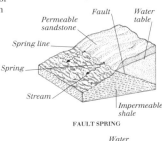

FAULT SPRING

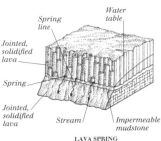

LAVA SPRING

STRUCTURE OF AN ARTESIAN BASIN

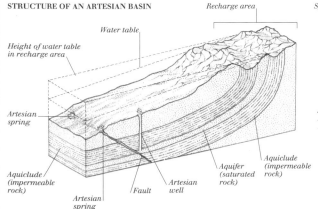

FEATURES OF A GROUNDWATER SYSTEM

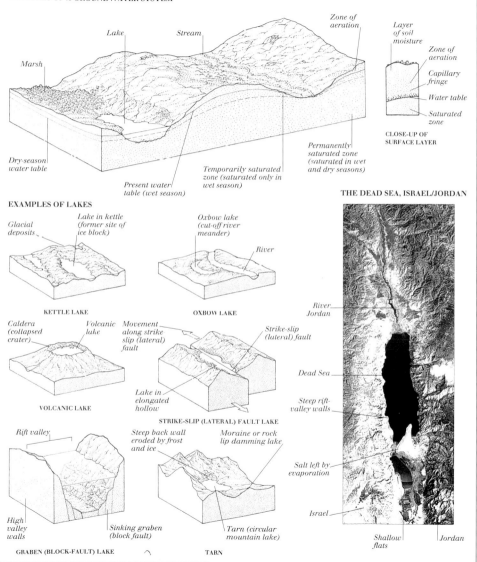

Lake

Stream

Zone of aeration

Marsh

Layer of soil moisture

Zone of aeration

Capillary fringe

Water table

Saturated zone

CLOSE-UP OF SURFACE LAYER

Dry-season water table

Present water table (wet season)

Temporarily saturated zone (saturated only in wet season)

Permanently saturated zone (saturated in wet and dry seasons)

EXAMPLES OF LAKES

Glacial deposits

Lake in kettle (former site of ice block)

KETTLE LAKE

Oxbow lake (cut-off river meander)

River

OXBOW LAKE

Caldera (collapsed crater)

Volcanic lake

VOLCANIC LAKE

Movement along strike-slip (lateral) fault

Strike-slip (lateral) fault

Lake in elongated hollow

STRIKE-SLIP (LATERAL) FAULT LAKE

Rift valley

High valley walls

Sinking graben (block fault)

GRABEN (BLOCK-FAULT) LAKE

Steep back wall eroded by frost and ice

Moraine or rock lip damming lake

Tarn (circular mountain lake)

TARN

THE DEAD SEA, ISRAEL/JORDAN

River Jordan

Dead Sea

Steep rift-valley walls

Salt left by evaporation

Israel

Shallow flats

Jordan

293

Coastlines

COASTLINES ARE AMONG THE MOST RAPIDLY changing landscape features. Some are eroded by waves, wind, and rain, causing cliffs to be undercut and caves to be hollowed out of solid rock. Others are built up by waves transporting sand and small rocks in a process known as longshore drift, and by rivers depositing sediment in deltas. Additional influences include the activities of living organisms such as coral, crustal movements, and sea-level variations due to climatic changes. Rising land or a drop in sea level creates an emergent coastline, with cliffs and beaches stranded above the new shoreline. Sinking land or a rise in sea level produces a drowned coastline, typified by fjords (submerged glacial valleys) or submerged river valleys.

FEATURES OF A SEA-CLIFF

Cliff-top

Cliff-face

High tide level

Low tide level

Offshore deposits

Wave-cut platform

Undercut area of cliff

Mature river

FEATURES OF WAVES

Wave height

Crest

Wavelength

Trough

Shorter wavelength near beach

Circular orbit of water and suspended particles

Orbit deformed into ellipse as water gets shallower

Headland

Bedding plane

LONGSHORE DRIFT

Movement of material along beach

Build-up of material against groyne

Pebble

Backwash

Beach

Groyne

Sea-cliff

Remnants of former headland

Swash zone

Swash

Waves approaching shore at an oblique angle

Estuary

DEPOSITIONAL FEATURES OF COASTLINES

Bay-head beach

Wave direction

Headland

Wave direction

Tombolo

Island

Wave direction

Cuspate foreland

Wave direction

Barrier beach

Lagoon

BAY-HEAD BEACH

TOMBOLO

CUSPATE FORELAND

BARRIER BEACH

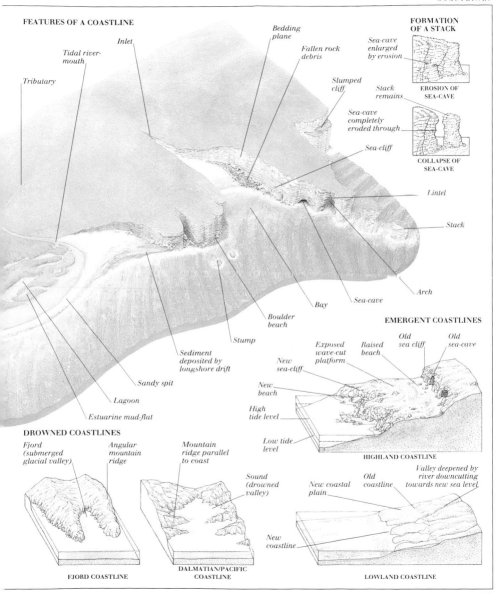

FEATURES OF A COASTLINE

Tributary

Tidal river-mouth

Inlet

Bedding plane

Fallen rock debris

Slumped cliff

Sea-cave enlarged by erosion

Sea-cave completely eroded through

Sea-cliff

Lintel

Stack

Arch

Sea-cave

Bay

Boulder beach

Stump

Sediment deposited by longshore drift

Sandy spit

Lagoon

Estuarine mud-flat

FORMATION OF A STACK

EROSION OF SEA-CAVE

Stack remains

COLLAPSE OF SEA-CAVE

EMERGENT COASTLINES

Exposed wave-cut platform

Raised beach

Old sea cliff

Old sea-cave

New sea-cliff

New beach

High tide level

Low tide level

HIGHLAND COASTLINE

DROWNED COASTLINES

Fjord (submerged glacial valley)

Angular mountain ridge

Mountain ridge parallel to coast

Sound (drowned valley)

New coastal plain

Old coastline

Valley deepened by river downcutting towards new sea level

New coastline

FJORD COASTLINE

DALMATIAN/PACIFIC COASTLINE

LOWLAND COASTLINE

Oceans and seas

OCEANS AND SEAS COVER ABOUT 70 PER CENT of the Earth's surface and account for about 97 per cent of its total water. These oceans and seas play a crucial role in regulating temperature variations and determining climate. Their waters absorb heat from the Sun, especially in tropical regions, and the surface currents distribute it around the Earth, warming overlying air masses and neighbouring land in winter and cooling them in summer. The oceans are never still. Differences in temperature and salinity drive deep current systems, while surface currents are generated by winds blowing over the oceans. All currents are deflected – to the right in the Northern Hemisphere, to the left in the Southern Hemisphere – as a result of the Earth's rotation. This deflective factor is known as the Coriolis force. A current that begins on the surface is immediately deflected. This current in turn generates a current in the layer of water beneath, which is also deflected. As the movement is transmitted downwards, the deflections form an Ekman spiral. The waters of the oceans and seas are also moved by the constant ebb and flow of tides. These are caused by the gravitational pull of the Moon and Sun. The highest tides (Spring tides) occur at full and new Moon; the lowest tides (neap tides) occur at first and last quarter.

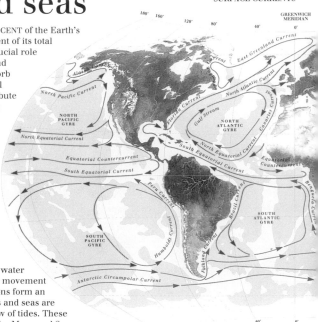

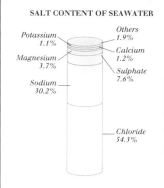

SALT CONTENT OF SEAWATER

Potassium 1.1%

Magnesium 3.7%

Sodium 30.2%

Others 1.9%

Calcium 1.2%

Sulphate 7.6%

Chloride 54.3%

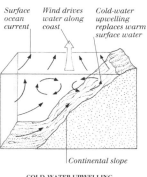

Surface ocean current

Wind drives water along coast

Cold-water upwelling replaces warm surface water

Continental slope

COLD-WATER UPWELLING (SOUTHERN HEMISPHERE)

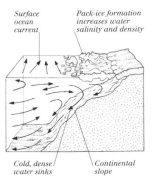

Surface ocean current

Pack-ice formation increases water salinity and density

Cold, dense water sinks

Continental slope

POLAR BOTTOM WATER

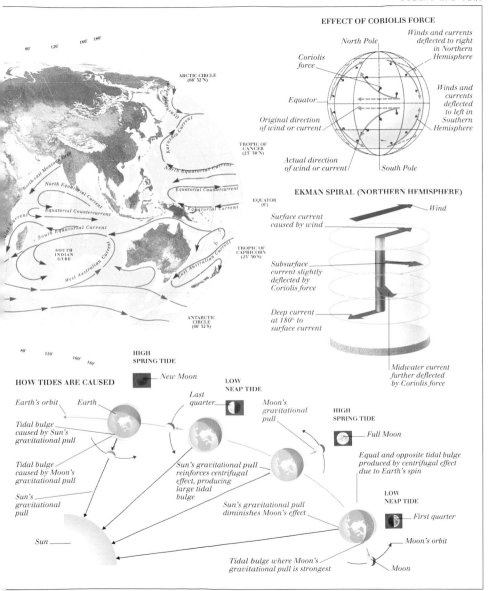

EFFECT OF CORIOLIS FORCE

North Pole

Coriolis force

Winds and currents deflected to right in Northern Hemisphere

Equator

Winds and currents deflected to left in Southern Hemisphere

Original direction of wind or current

Actual direction of wind or current

South Pole

EKMAN SPIRAL (NORTHERN HEMISPHERE)

EQUATOR (0°)

Wind

Surface current caused by wind

Subsurface current slightly deflected by Coriolis force

Deep current at 180° to surface current

Midwater current further deflected by Coriolis force

ARCTIC CIRCLE (66° 52'N)

TROPIC OF CANCER (23° 30'N)

Kuroshio Current

Northeast Monsoon Drift

North Equatorial Current

North Equatorial Current

Equatorial Countercurrent

Equatorial Countercurrent

South Equatorial Current

South Equatorial Current

SOUTH INDIAN GYRE

West Australian Current

West Australian Current

TROPIC OF CAPRICORN (23° 30'S)

ANTARCTIC CIRCLE (66° 52'S)

80° 120° 160° 180°

HIGH SPRING TIDE

New Moon

HOW TIDES ARE CAUSED

LOW NEAP TIDE

Last quarter

Earth's orbit

Earth

Moon's gravitational pull

HIGH SPRING TIDE

Full Moon

Tidal bulge caused by Sun's gravitational pull

Tidal bulge caused by Moon's gravitational pull

Sun's gravitational pull reinforces centrifugal effect, producing large tidal bulge

Equal and opposite tidal bulge produced by centrifugal effect due to Earth's spin

Sun's gravitational pull

Sun's gravitational pull diminishes Moon's effect

LOW NEAP TIDE

First quarter

Moon's orbit

Sun

Tidal bulge where Moon's gravitational pull is strongest

Moon

The ocean floor

THE OCEAN FLOOR COMPRISES TWO SECTIONS: the continental shelf and slope, and the deep-ocean floor. The continental shelf and slope are part of the continental crust, but may extend far into the ocean. Sloping quite gently to a depth of about 140 metres, the continental shelf is covered in sandy deposits shaped by waves and tidal currents. At the edge of the continental shelf, the seabed slopes down to the abyssal plain, which lies at an average depth of about 3,800 metres. On this deep-ocean floor is a layer of sediment made up of clays, fine oozes formed from the remains of tiny sea creatures, and occasional mineral-rich deposits. Echo-sounding and remote sensing from satellites has revealed that the abyssal plain is divided by a system of mountain ranges, far bigger than any on land – the mid-ocean ridge. Here, magma (molten rock) wells up from the Earth's interior and solidifies, widening the ocean floor (see pp. 58-59). As the ocean floor spreads, volcanoes that have formed over hot spots in the crust move away from their magma source; they become extinct and are increasingly submerged and eroded. Volcanoes eroded below sea level remain as seamounts (underwater mountains). In warm waters, a volcano that projects above the ocean surface often acquires a fringing coral reef, which may develop into an atoll as the volcano becomes submerged.

CONTINENTAL-SHELF FLOOR

Bedrock exposed by tidal scour

Shoreline

Parallel strips of coarse material left by strong tidal currents

Sand deposited in wavy pattern by weaker currents

Irregular patches of fine sand deposited by weakest currents

FEATURES OF THE OCEAN FLOOR

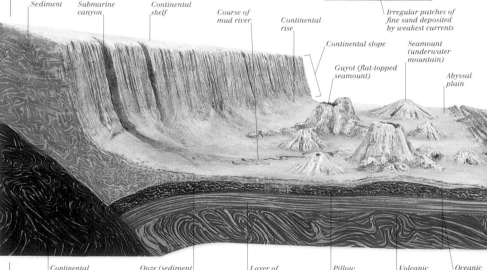

Sediment

Submarine canyon

Continental shelf

Course of mud river

Continental rise

Continental slope

Guyot (flat-topped seamount)

Seamount (underwater mountain)

Abyssal plain

Continental crust

Ooze (sediment consisting of remains of tiny sea creatures)

Layer of volcanic rock

Pillow lava

Volcanic crystalline rock

Oceanic crust

KEY

- ☐ Calcareous ooze
- ☐ Pelagic clay
- ☐ Glacial sediments
- ☐ Siliceous ooze
- ☐ Terrigenous sediments
- ☐ Continental margin sediments
- ▨ Metalliferous muds
- ☐ Major nodule fields

DEEP-OCEAN FLOOR SEDIMENTS

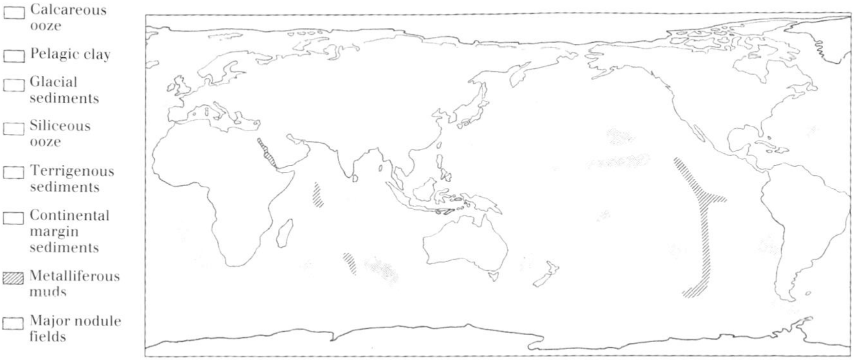

ECHO-SOUND PROFILE OF OCEAN FLOOR

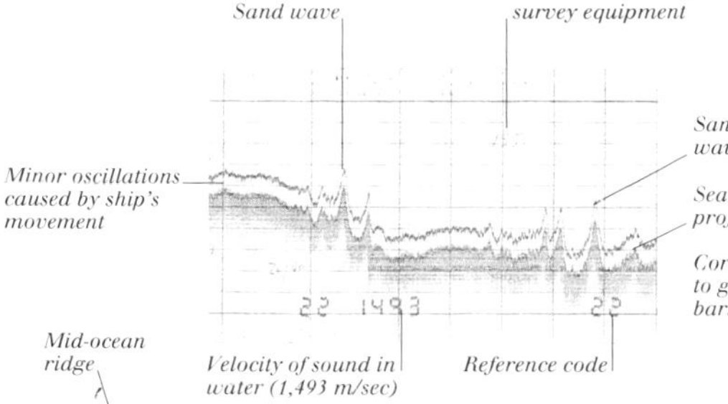

Sand wave

Event mark indicates synchronization of survey equipment

Sand wave

Seabed profile

Minor oscillations caused by ship's movement

22 1493 23

Velocity of sound in water (1,493 m/sec)

Reference code

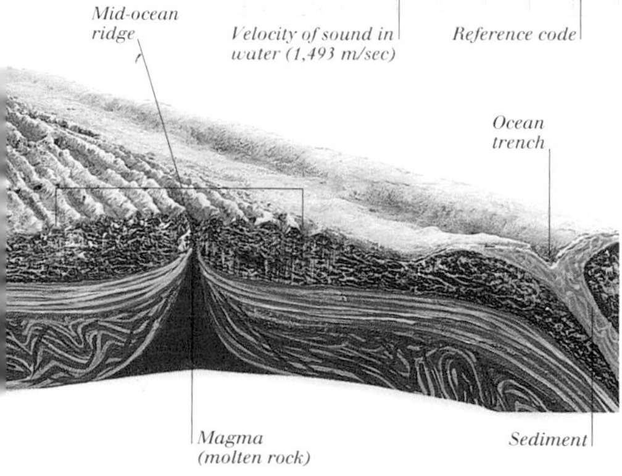

Mid-ocean ridge

Ocean trench

Magma (molten rock)

Sediment

DEVELOPMENT OF AN ATOLL

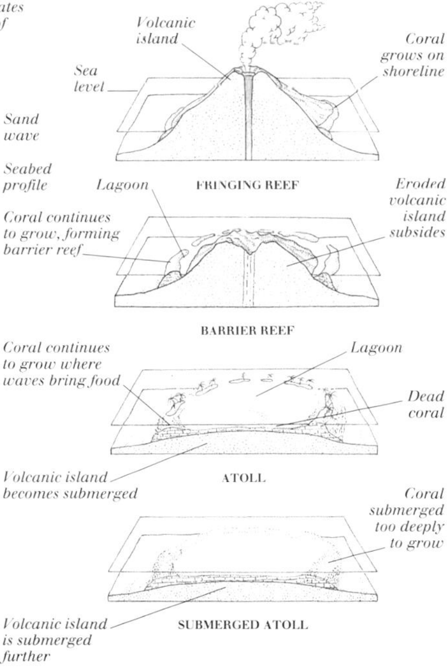

Volcanic island

Sea level

Coral grows on shoreline

FRINGING REEF

Lagoon

Coral continues to grow, forming barrier reef

Eroded volcanic island subsides

BARRIER REEF

Coral continues to grow where waves bring food

Lagoon

Dead coral

Volcanic island becomes submerged

ATOLL

Coral submerged too deeply to grow

Volcanic island is submerged further

SUBMERGED ATOLL

299

The atmosphere

JET STREAM

THE EARTH IS SURROUNDED BY ITS ATMOSPHERE, a blanket of gases that enables life to exist on the planet. This layer has no definite outer edge, gradually becoming thinner until it merges into space, but over 80 per cent of atmospheric gases are held by gravity within about 20 kilometres of the Earth's surface. The atmosphere blocks out much harmful ultraviolet solar radiation, and insulates the Earth against extremes of temperature by limiting both incoming solar radiation and the escape of re-radiated heat into space. This natural balance may be distorted by the greenhouse effect, as gases such as carbon dioxide have built up in the atmosphere, trapping more heat. Close to the Earth's surface, differences in air temperature and pressure cause air to circulate between the equator and poles. This circulation, together with the Coriolis force, gives rise to the prevailing surface winds and the high-level jet streams.

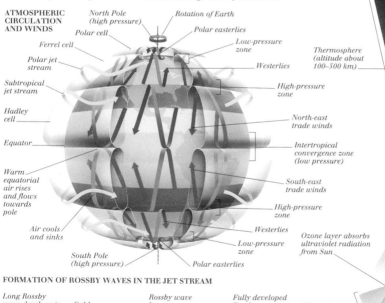

ATMOSPHERIC CIRCULATION AND WINDS

Exosphere (altitude above about 500 km)

Corona

North Pole (high pressure)

Rotation of Earth

Polar cell

Polar easterlies

Ferrel cell

Low-pressure zone

Polar jet stream

Thermosphere (altitude about 100–500 km)

Westerlies

Subtropical jet stream

High-pressure zone

Hadley cell

North-east trade winds

Equator

Intertropical convergence zone (low pressure)

Warm equatorial air rises and flows towards pole

South-east trade winds

High-pressure zone

Air cools and sinks

Westerlies

Low-pressure zone

Ozone layer absorbs ultraviolet radiation from Sun

South Pole (high pressure)

Polar easterlies

FORMATION OF ROSSBY WAVES IN THE JET STREAM

Long Rossby wave develops in polar jet stream

Cold air

Rossby wave becomes more pronounced

Fully developed Rossby wave

Mesosphere (altitude about 50–100 km)

Warm air

Stratosphere (altitude about 10–50 km)

INITIAL UNDULATION

DEEPENING WAVE

DEVELOPED WAVE

Troposphere (altitude up to about 10 km)

STRUCTURE OF THE ATMOSPHERE

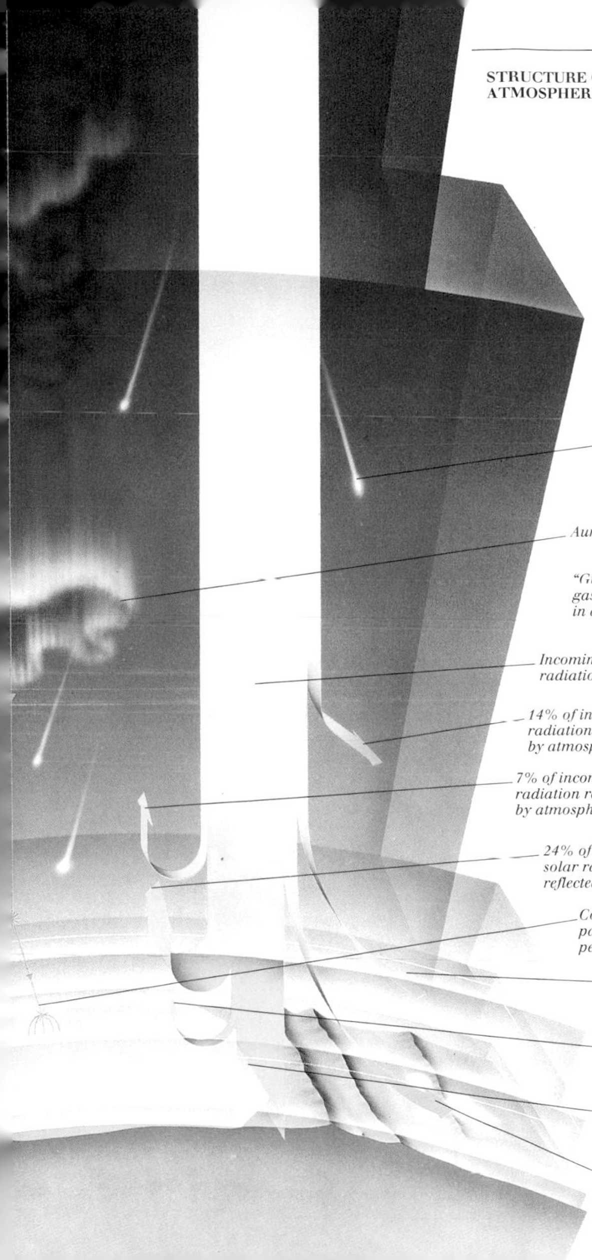

GLOBAL WARMING

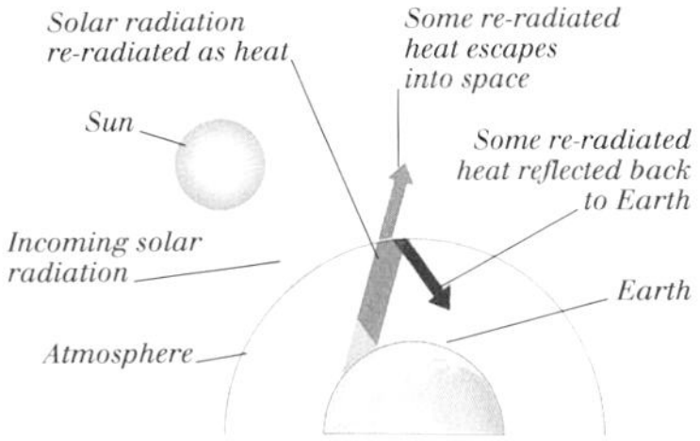

Solar radiation
re-radiated as heat

Some re-radiated
heat escapes
into space

Sun

Some re-radiated
heat reflected back
to Earth

Incoming solar
radiation

Earth

Atmosphere

**NATURALLY MODERATED
GREENHOUSE EFFECT**

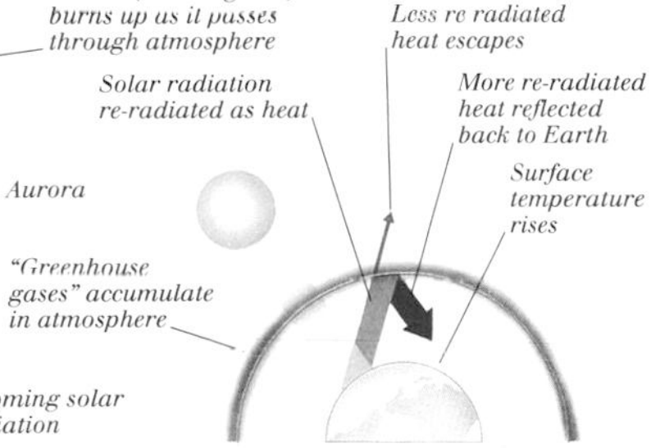

Meteor (shooting star)
burns up as it passes
through atmosphere

Less re-radiated
heat escapes

Solar radiation
re-radiated as heat

More re-radiated
heat reflected
back to Earth

Aurora

Surface
temperature
rises

"Greenhouse
gases" accumulate
in atmosphere

Incoming solar
radiation

**UNBALANCED GREENHOUSE
EFFECT**

14% of incoming solar
radiation absorbed
by atmosphere

7% of incoming solar
radiation reflected
by atmosphere

COMPOSITION OF THE LOWER ATMOSPHERE

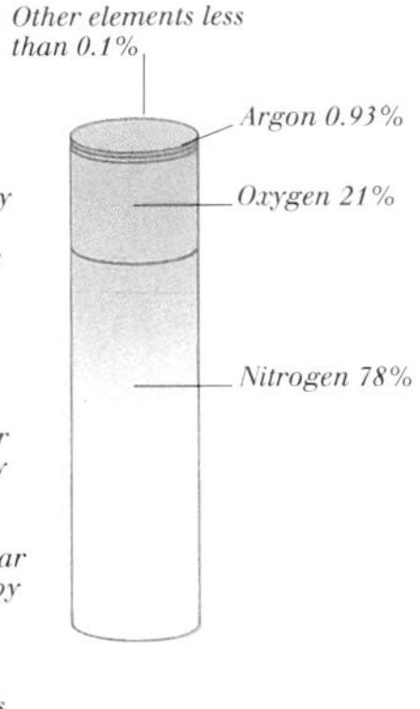

24% of incoming
solar radiation
reflected by clouds

Other elements less
than 0.1%

Argon 0.93%

Cosmic rays (high-energy
particles from space)
penetrate to stratosphere

Oxygen 21%

Some absorbed
heat re-radiated
by atmosphere

4% of incoming solar
radiation reflected by
oceans and land

Nitrogen 78%

51% of incoming
solar radiation absorbed
by Earth's surface

Some absorbed heat
re-radiated by clouds

Weather

WEATHER IS DEFINED AS THE ATMOSPHERIC CONDITIONS at a particular time and place; climate is the average weather conditions for a given region over time. Weather is assessed in terms of temperature, wind, cloud cover, and precipitation, such as rain or snow. Fine weather is associated with high-pressure areas, where air is sinking. Cloudy, wet, changeable weather is common in low-pressure zones with rising, unstable air. Such conditions occur at temperate latitudes, where warm air meets cool air along the polar fronts. Here, spiralling low-pressure cells known as depressions (mid-latitude cyclones) often form. A depression usually contains a sector of warmer air, beginning at a warm front and ending at a cold front. If the two fronts merge, forming an occluded front, the warm air is pushed upwards. An extreme form of low-pressure cell is a hurricane (also called a typhoon or tropical cyclone), which brings torrential rain and exceptionally strong winds.

TYPES OF OCCLUDED FRONT

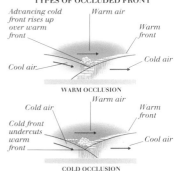

Advancing cold front rises up over warm front *Warm air* *Warm front* *Cool air* *Cold air*

WARM OCCLUSION

Cold air *Warm air* *Warm front* *Cold front undercuts warm front* *Cool air*

COLD OCCLUSION

FORMS OF PRECIPITATION

Water droplets less than 0.5 mm in diameter fall as drizzle *Water droplets coalesce to form raindrops 0.5–5.0 mm in diameter* *Rising air*

RAIN FROM CLOUDS NOT REACHING FREEZING LEVEL

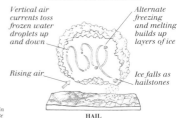

Coalesced water droplets fall as rain *Ice crystal* *Snowflakes grown from ice crystals fall as snow* *Snowflakes melt to fall as rain* *Rising air*

RAIN AND SNOW FROM CLOUDS REACHING FREEZING LEVEL

TYPES OF CLOUD

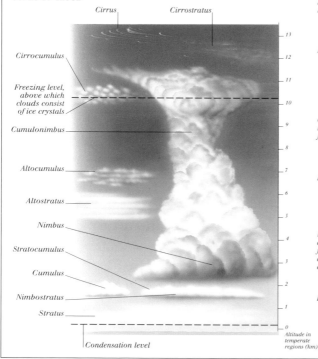

Cirrus *Cirrostratus* *Cirrocumulus* *Freezing level, above which clouds consist of ice crystals* *Cumulonimbus* *Altocumulus* *Altostratus* *Nimbus* *Stratocumulus* *Cumulus* *Nimbostratus* *Stratus* *Condensation level*

13 *12* *11* *10* *9* *8* *7* *6* *5* *4* *3* *2* *1* *0*

Altitude in temperate regions (km)

Vertical air currents toss frozen water droplets up and down *Alternate freezing and melting builds up layers of ice* *Rising air* *Ice falls as hailstones*

HAIL

STRUCTURE OF A HURRICANE

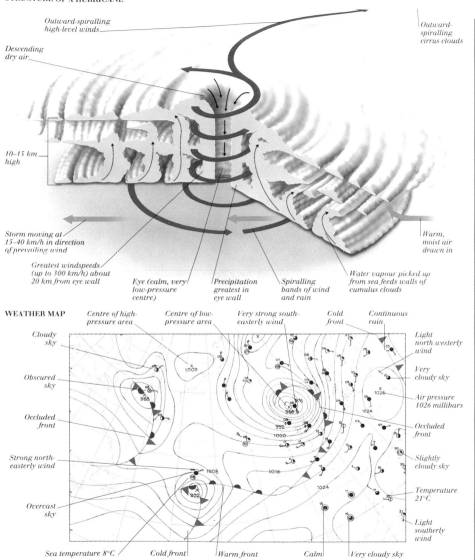

Outward-spiralling high-level winds

Outward-spiralling cirrus clouds

Descending dry air

10–15 km high

Storm moving at 15–40 km/h in direction of prevailing wind

Warm, moist air drawn in

Greatest windspeeds (up to 300 km/h) about 20 km from eye wall

Eye (calm, very low-pressure centre)

Precipitation greatest in eye wall

Spiralling bands of wind and rain

Water vapour picked up from sea feeds walls of cumulus clouds

WEATHER MAP

Centre of high-pressure area

Centre of low-pressure area

Very strong south-easterly wind

Cold front

Continuous rain

Cloudy sky

Light north westerly wind

Obscured sky

Very cloudy sky

Air pressure 1026 millibars

Occluded front

Occluded front

Strong north-easterly wind

Slightly cloudy sky

Temperature 21°C

Overcast sky

Light southerly wind

Sea temperature 8°C

Cold front

Warm front

Calm

Very cloudy sky

Physics and Chemistry

The Variety of Matter 306
Atoms and Molecules 308
The Periodic Table 310
Chemical Reactions 312
Energy 314
Electricity and Magnetism 316
Light 318
Force and Motion 320

The variety of matter

PLANT AND INSECT (LIVING MATTER)

MATTER IS ANYTHING THAT HAS A MASS. It includes everything from natural substances, such as minerals or living organisms, to synthetic materials. Matter can exist in three distinct states – solid, liquid, and gas. A solid is rigid and retains its shape. A liquid is fluid, has a definite volume, and will take the shape of its container. A gas (also fluid) fills a space, so its volume will be the same as the volume of its container. Most substances can exist as a solid, a liquid, or a gas: the state is determined by temperature. At very high temperatures, matter becomes plasma, often considered to be a fourth state of matter. All matter is composed of microscopic particles, such as atoms and molecules (see pp. 308-309). The arrangement and interactions of these particles give a substance its physical and chemical properties, by which matter can be identified. There is a huge variety of matter because particles can arrange themselves in countless ways, in one substance or by mixing with others. Natural glass, for example, seems to be a solid but is, in fact, a supercool liquid: the atoms are not locked into a pattern and can flow. Pure substances known as elements (see p. 310) combine to form compounds or mixtures. Mixtures called colloids are made up of larger particles of matter suspended in a solid, liquid, or gas, while a solution is one substance dissolved in another.

TYPES OF COLLOID

HAIR GEL (SOLID IN LIQUID)

SHAVING FOAM (AIR IN LIQUID)

MIST (LIQUID IN GAS)

EXAMPLES OF MATTER

The element silicon in pure crystalline form

Polythene is made by combining natural materials in new ways

Low pressure gases

Central electrode

Streaks of plasma (mixture of electrons and charged atoms)

Voltage tears electrons from atoms of low pressure gases inside

POLYTHENE (SYNTHETIC POLYMER)

PURE SILICON (SEMICONDUCTOR)

BALL CONTAINING HIGH-TEMPERATURE GAS (PLASMA)

Obsidian is molten volcanic rock that cools quickly, so atoms cannot form a regular pattern

Solid crystals dissolve in liquid water

Water

Potassium permanganate crystals

Azurite is found naturally with deposits of copper ore

OBSIDIAN (NATURAL GLASS)

AZURITE (CRYSTALLINE MINERAL)

POTASSIUM PERMANGANATE AND WATER (SOLUTION)

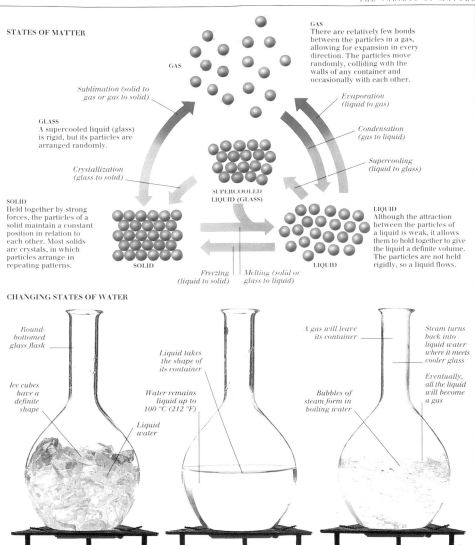

STATES OF MATTER

GAS
There are relatively few bonds between the particles in a gas, allowing for expansion in every direction. The particles move randomly, colliding with the walls of any container and occasionally with each other.

GAS

Sublimation (solid to gas or gas to solid)

Evaporation (liquid to gas)

GLASS
A supercooled liquid (glass) is rigid, but its particles are arranged randomly.

Condensation (gas to liquid)

Crystallization (glass to solid)

Supercooling (liquid to glass)

SUPERCOOLED LIQUID (GLASS)

SOLID
Held together by strong forces, the particles of a solid maintain a constant position in relation to each other. Most solids are crystals, in which particles arrange in repeating patterns.

LIQUID
Although the attraction between the particles of a liquid is weak, it allows them to hold together to give the liquid a definite volume. The particles are not held rigidly, so a liquid flows.

SOLID

LIQUID

Freezing (liquid to solid) *Melting (solid or glass to liquid)*

CHANGING STATES OF WATER

Round-bottomed glass flask

Liquid takes the shape of its container

A gas will leave its container

Steam turns back into liquid water where it meets cooler glass

Ice cubes have a definite shape

Water remains liquid up to 100 °C (212 °F)

Bubbles of steam form in boiling water

Eventually, all the liquid will become a gas

Liquid water

SOLID STATE: ICE
The solid state of water, ice, forms when liquid water is cooled sufficiently. Ice cubes are rigid, with a definite shape and volume.

LIQUID STATE: WATER
When the temperature of a substance rises above its freezing point, it melts to become a liquid. Ice changes to water.

GASEOUS STATE: STEAM
Above its boiling point, a substance will become a gas. When heated sufficiently, liquid water turns to steam, a colourless gas.

Atoms and molecules

FALSE-COLOUR IMAGE OF ACTUAL GOLD ATOMS

ATOMS ARE THE smallest individual parts of an element (see pp. 310-311). They are tiny, with diameters in the order of one ten-thousand-millionth of a metre (10^{-10} m). Two or more atoms join together (bond) to form a molecule of a substance known as a compound. For example, when atoms of the elements hydrogen and fluorine join together, they form a molecule of the compound hydrogen fluoride. So molecules are the smallest individual parts of a compound. Atoms themselves are not indivisible – they possess an internal structure. At their centre is a dense nucleus, consisting of protons, which have a positive electric charge (see p. 316), and neutrons, which are uncharged. Around the nucleus are the negatively charged electrons. It is the electrons that give a substance most of its physical and chemical properties. They do not follow definite paths around the nucleus. Instead, electrons are said to be found within certain regions, called orbitals. These are arranged around the nucleus in "shells", each containing electrons of a particular energy. For example, the first shell (1) can hold up to two electrons, in a so-called s-orbital (1s). The second shell (2) can hold up to eight electrons, in s-orbitals (2s) and p-orbitals (2p). If an atom loses an electron, it becomes a positive ion (cation). If an electron is gained, an atom becomes a negative ion (anion). Ions of opposite charges will attract and join together, in a type of bonding known as ionic bonding. In covalent bonding, the atoms bond by sharing their electrons in what become molecular orbitals.

ATOMIC ORBITALS

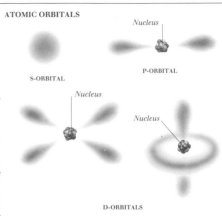

Nucleus

S-ORBITAL

P-ORBITAL

Nucleus

Nucleus

Nucleus

D-ORBITALS

MOLECULAR ORBITALS

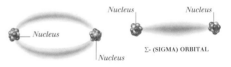

Nucleus

Nucleus

Nucleus

Σ- (SIGMA) ORBITAL

Nucleus

π- (PI) ORBITAL

Nucleus

SP³-HYBRID ORBITAL

EXAMPLE OF IONIC BONDING

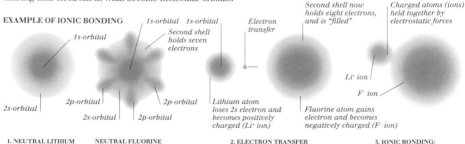

1s-orbital

2s-orbital

2p-orbital   2p-orbital

2s-orbital   2p-orbital

1. NEUTRAL LITHIUM ATOM (Li)

1s-orbital   1s-orbital

Second shell holds seven electrons

NEUTRAL FLUORINE ATOM (F)

Electron transfer

Lithium atom loses 2s electron and becomes positively charged (Li⁺ ion)

2. ELECTRON TRANSFER

Second shell now holds eight electrons, and is "filled"

Li⁺ ion

F⁻ ion

Fluorine atom gains electron and becomes negatively charged (F⁻ ion)

Charged atoms (ions) held together by electrostatic forces

3. IONIC BONDING: LITHIUM FLUORIDE MOLECULE (LiF)

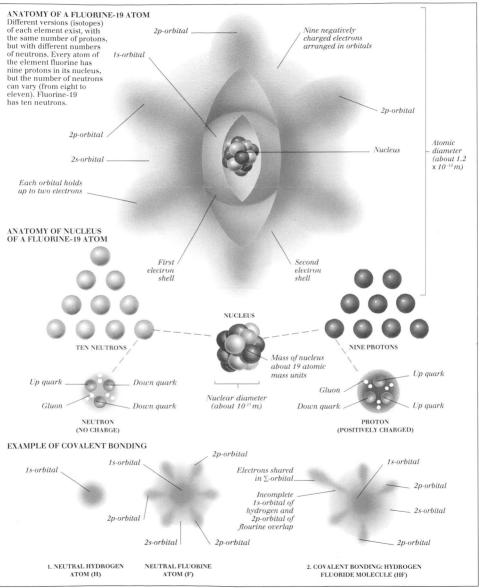

ANATOMY OF A FLUORINE-19 ATOM
Different versions (isotopes) of each element exist, with the same number of protons, but with different numbers of neutrons. Every atom of the element fluorine has nine protons in its nucleus, but the number of neutrons can vary (from eight to eleven). Fluorine-19 has ten neutrons.

2p-orbital

1s-orbital

Nine negatively charged electrons arranged in orbitals

2p-orbital

2p-orbital

2s-orbital

Nucleus

Atomic diameter (about 1.2 x 10⁻¹⁰ m)

Each orbital holds up to two electrons

ANATOMY OF NUCLEUS OF A FLUORINE-19 ATOM

First electron shell

Second electron shell

NUCLEUS

TEN NEUTRONS

NINE PROTONS

Mass of nucleus about 19 atomic mass units

Up quark

Down quark

Nuclear diameter (about 10⁻¹⁵ m)

Gluon

Down quark

Up quark

Gluon

Down quark

Up quark

NEUTRON (NO CHARGE)

PROTON (POSITIVELY CHARGED)

EXAMPLE OF COVALENT BONDING

1s-orbital

1s-orbital

2p-orbital

1s-orbital

2p-orbital

Electrons shared in Σ-orbital

2p-orbital

2s-orbital

Incomplete 1s-orbital of hydrogen and 2p-orbital of flourine overlap

2s-orbital

2p-orbital

2p-orbital

1. NEUTRAL HYDROGEN ATOM (H)

NEUTRAL FLUORINE ATOM (F)

2. COVALENT BONDING: HYDROGEN FLUORIDE MOLECULE (HF)

The periodic table

AN ELEMENT is a substance that consists of atoms of one type only. The 92 elements that occur naturally, and the 17 elements created artificially, are often arranged into a chart called the periodic table. Each element is defined by its atomic number – the number of protons in the nucleus of each of its atoms (it is also the number of electrons present). Atomic number increases along each row (period) and down each column (group). The shape of the table is determined by the way in which electrons arrange themselves around the nucleus: the positioning of elements in order of increasing atomic number brings together atoms with a similar pattern of orbiting electrons (orbitals). These appear in blocks. Electrons occupy shells of a certain energy (see pp. 308-309). Periods are ordered according to the filling of successive shells with electrons, while groups reflect the number of electrons in the outer shell (valency electrons). These outer electrons are important – they decide the chemical properties of the atom. Elements that appear in the same group have similar properties because they have the same number of electrons in their outer shell. Elements in Group 0 have "filled shells", where the outer shell holds its maximum number of electrons, and are stable. Atoms of Group I elements have just one electron in their outer shell. This makes them unstable – and ready to react with other substances.

METALS AND NON-METALS
Elements at the left-hand side of each period are metals. Metals easily lose electrons and form positive ions. Non-metals, on the right of a period, tend to become negative ions. Semi-metals, which have properties of both metals and non-metals, are between the two.

RELATIVE ATOMIC MASS
Atomic mass (formerly atomic weight) is the mass of each atom of an element. It is equal to the number of protons plus the number of neutrons (electrons have negligible mass). The figures given are the averages for all the different versions (isotopes) of each element, measured relative to the mass of carbon-12.

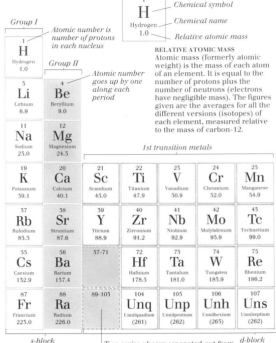

Atomic number

1
H
Hydrogen
1.0

Chemical symbol
Chemical name
Relative atomic mass

Atomic number is number of protons in each nucleus

Atomic number goes up by one along each period

1st transition metals

Two series always separated out from the table to give it a coherent shape

s-block ... *d-block*

Group I

1						
H Hydrogen 1.0						
3 **Li** Lithium 6.9	4 **Be** Beryllium 9.0					
11 **Na** Sodium 23.0	12 **Mg** Magnesium 24.5					
19 **K** Potassium 39.1	20 **Ca** Calcium 40.1	21 **Sc** Scandium 45.0	22 **Ti** Titanium 47.9	23 **V** Vanadium 50.9	24 **Cr** Chromium 52.0	25 **Mn** Manganese 54.9
37 **Rb** Rubidium 85.5	38 **Sr** Strontium 87.6	39 **Y** Yttrium 88.9	40 **Zr** Zirconium 91.2	41 **Nb** Niobium 92.9	42 **Mo** Molybdenum 95.9	43 **Tc** Technetium 99.0
55 **Cs** Caesium 132.9	56 **Ba** Barium 137.4	57-71	72 **Hf** Hafnium 178.5	73 **Ta** Tantalum 181.0	74 **W** Tungsten 183.9	75 **Re** Rhenium 186.2
87 **Fr** Francium 225.0	88 **Ra** Radium 226.0	89-103	104 **Unq** Unnilquadium (261)	105 **Unp** Unnilpentium (262)	106 **Unh** Unnilhexium (263)	107 **Uns** Unnilseptium (262)

Group II (heading above column 2)

SODIUM:
GROUP 1 METAL
Soft, silvery, and highly reactive metal

MAGNESIUM:
GROUP 2 METAL
Silvery, reactive metal

CHROMIUM:
1ST TRANSITION METAL
Hard, silvery metal

TYPES OF ELEMENT KEY:

- [ ] Alkali metals
- [ ] Alkaline earth metals
- [ ] Transition metals
- [ ] Lanthanides (rare earths)
- [ ] Actinides
- [ ] Poor metals
- [ ] Semi-metals
- [ ] Non-metals
- [ ] Noble gases

Radioactive metal

PLUTONIUM:
ACTINIDE SERIES METAL

57 **La** Lanthanum 158.9	58 **Ce** Cerium 140.1	59 **Pr** Praseodymium 140.9	60 **Nd** Neodymium 144.2
89 **Ac** Actinium 227.0	90 **Th** Thorium 252.0	91 **Pa** Protactinium 251.0	92 **U** Uranium 238.0

ALLOTROPES OF CARBON
Some elements exist in more than one form – these are known as allotropes. Carbon powder, graphite, and diamond are allotropes of carbon. They all consist of carbon atoms, but have very different physical properties.

DIAMOND

Bright yellow crystal

IODINE: GROUP 7 SOLID NON-METAL

Purple-black solid turns to gas easily

SULPHUR: GROUP 6 SOLID NON-METAL

Group 0

GRAPHITE   CARBON POWDER

| *Boron and carbon groups* | | *Nitrogen and oxygen groups* | | *Halogens* | |
| Group III | Group IV | Group V | Group VI | Group VII | |

| | | | | | 2
He
Helium
4.0 | *Period* |

| 5
B
Boron
10.8 | 6
C
Carbon
12.0 | 7
N
Nitrogen
14.0 | 8
O
Oxygen
16.0 | 9
F
Fluorine
19.0 | 10
Ne
Neon
20.2 | *Short period* |

2nd transition metals   *3rd transition metals*

| 13
Al
Aluminium
27.0 | 14
Si
Silicon
28.1 | 15
P
Phosphorus
31.0 | 16
S
Sulphur
32.1 | 17
Cl
Chlorine
55.5 | 18
Ar
Argon
40.0 | |

| 26
Fe
Iron
55.9 | 27
Co
Cobalt
58.9 | 28
Ni
Nickel
58.7 | 29
Cu
Copper
63.5 | 50
Zn
Zinc
65.4 | 51
Ga
Gallium
69.7 | 52
Ge
Germanium
72.6 | 55
As
Arsenic
74.9 | 54
Se
Selenium
79.0 | 55
Br
Bromine
79.9 | 36
Kr
Krypton
85.8 | *Long period* |

| 44
Ru
Ruthenium
101.0 | 45
Rh
Rhodium
102.9 | 46
Pd
Palladium
106.4 | 47
Ag
Silver
107.9 | 48
Cd
Cadmium
112.4 | 49
In
Indium
114.8 | 50
Sn
Tin
118.7 | 51
Sb
Antimony
121.8 | 52
Te
Tellurium
127.6 | 53
I
Iodine
126.9 | 54
Xe
Xenon
131.5 |

| 76
Os
Osmium
190.2 | 77
Ir
Iridium
192.2 | 78
Pt
Platinum
195.1 | 79
Au
Gold
197.0 | 80
Hg
Mercury
200.6 | 81
Tl
Thallium
204.4 | 82
Pb
Lead
207.2 | 83
Bi
Bismuth
209.0 | 84
Po
Polonium
210.0 | 85
At
Astatine
210.0 | 86
Rn
Radon
222.0 |

| 108
Uno
Unniloctium
(265) | 109
Une
Unnilennium
(266) |

d-block   *p-block*

Atomic mass is estimated, as element exists fleetingly

Shiny semi-metal

NOBLE GASES
Group 0 contains elements that have a filled (complete) outer shell of electrons, which means the atoms do not need to lose or gain electrons by bonding with other atoms. This makes them stable and they do not easily form ions or react with other elements. Noble gases are also called rare or inert gases.

Unreactive, colourless gas glows red in discharge tube

Yellow, unreactive precious metal

Soft, shiny, reactive metal

NEON: GROUP 0 COLOURLESS GAS

GOLD:
3RD TRANSITION METAL   TIN:
GROUP 4 POOR METAL   ANTIMONY:
GROUP 5 SEMI-METAL

| 61
Pm
Promethium
147.0 | 62
Sm
Samarium
150.4 | 63
Eu
Europium
152.0 | 64
Gd
Gadolinium
157.5 | 65
Tb
Terbium
158.9 | 66
Dy
Dysprosium
162.5 | 67
Ho
Holmium
164.9 | 68
Er
Erbium
167.5 | 69
Tm
Thulium
168.9 | 70
Yb
Ytterbium
175.0 | 71
Lu
Lutetium
175.0 |

| 93
Np
Neptunium
237.0 | 94
Pu
Plutonium
242.0 | 95
Am
Americium
243.0 | 96
Cm
Curium
247.0 | 97
Bk
Berkelium
247.0 | 98
Cf
Californium
251.0 | 99
Es
Einsteinium
254.0 | 100
Fm
Fermium
253.0 | 101
Md
Mendelevium
256.0 | 102
No
Nobelium
254.0 | 103
Lr
Lawrencium
257.0 |

f-block

Chemical reactions

A CHEMICAL REACTION TAKES PLACE whenever bonds between atoms are broken or made. In each case, atoms or groups of atoms rearrange, making new substances (products) from the original ones (reactants). Reactions happen naturally, or can be made to happen; they may take years, or only an instant. Some of the main types are shown here. A reaction usually involves a change in energy (see pp. 314-315). In a burning reaction, for example, the making of new bonds between atoms releases energy as heat and light. This type of reaction, in which heat is given off, is an exothermic reaction. Many reactions, like burning, are irreversible, but some can take place in either direction, and are said to be reversible. Reactions can be used to form solids from solutions: in a double decomposition reaction, two compounds in solution break down and re-form into two new substances, often creating a precipitate (insoluble solid); in displacement, an element (eg. copper) displaces another element (eg. silver) from a solution. The rate (speed) of a reaction is determined by many different factors, such as temperature, and the size and shape of the reactants. To describe and keep track of reactions, internationally recognized chemical symbols and equations are used. Reactions are also used in the laboratory to identify matter. An experiment with candle wax, for example, demonstrates that it contains carbon and hydrogen.

SALT FORMATION (ACID ON METAL)

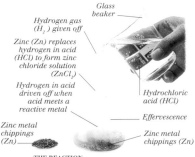

Glass beaker

Hydrogen gas (H_2) given off

Zinc (Zn) replaces hydrogen in acid (HCl) to form zinc chloride ($ZnCl_2$)

Hydrogen in acid driven off when acid meets a reactive metal

Hydrochloric acid (HCl)

Effervescence

Zinc metal chippings (Zn)

Zinc metal chippings (Zn)

THE REACTION
Hydrochloric acid added to zinc produces zinc chloride and hydrogen.
$Zn + 2HCl \rightarrow ZnCl_2 + H_2$

DISPLACEMENT

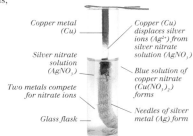

Copper metal (Cu)

Silver nitrate solution ($AgNO_3$)

Two metals compete for nitrate ions

Glass flask

Copper (Cu) displaces silver ions (Ag^+) from silver nitrate solution ($AgNO_3$)

Blue solution of copper nitrate ($Cu(NO_3)_2$) forms

Needles of silver metal (Ag) form

THE REACTION
Copper metal added to silver nitrate solution produces copper nitrate and silver metal.
$Cu + 2AgNO_3 \rightarrow Cu(NO_3)_2 + 2Ag$

BURNING MATTER

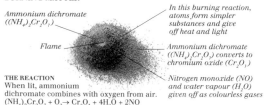

Ammonium dichromate ($(NH_4)_2Cr_2O_7$)

Flame

In this burning reaction, atoms form simpler substances and give off heat and light

Ammonium dichromate ($(NH_4)_2Cr_2O_7$) converts to chromium oxide (Cr_2O_3)

Nitrogen monoxide (NO) and water vapour (H_2O) given off as colourless gases

THE REACTION
When lit, ammonium dichromate combines with oxygen from air.
$(NH_4)_2Cr_2O_7 + O_2 \rightarrow Cr_2O_3 + 4H_2O + 2NO$

A REVERSIBLE REACTION

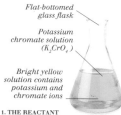

Flat-bottomed glass flask

Potassium chromate solution (K_2CrO_4)

Bright yellow solution contains potassium and chromate ions

1. THE REACTANT
Potassium chromate dissolves in water to form potassium ions and chromate ions.
$K_2CrO_4 \rightarrow 2K^+ + CrO_4^{2-}$

Pipette

Hydrochloric acid (HCl) added in drops

Acid causes reaction to take place

Chromate ions converted to orange dichromate ions

Potassium dichromate (KCr_2O_7) forms

2. THE REACTION
Addition of hydrochloric acid changes chromate ions into dichromate ions.
$2CrO_4^{2-} \rightarrow Cr_2O_7^{2-}$

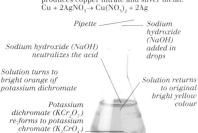

Pipette

Sodium hydroxide (NaOH) added in drops

Sodium hydroxide (NaOH) neutralizes the acid

Solution turns to bright orange of potassium dichromate

Potassium dichromate (KCr_2O_7) re-forms to potassium chromate (K_2CrO_4)

Solution returns to original bright yellow colour

3. REVERSING
Addition of sodium hydroxide changes dichromate ions back into chromate ions.
$Cr_2O_7^{2-} \rightarrow 2CrO_4^{2-}$

FERMENTATION

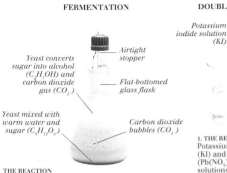

Yeast converts sugar into alcohol (C₂H₅OH) and carbon dioxide gas (CO₂) — *Airtight stopper*

Flat-bottomed glass flask

Yeast mixed with warm water and sugar (C₆H₁₂O₆)

Carbon dioxide bubbles (CO₂)

THE REACTION
Yeast converts sugar and warm water into alcohol and carbon dioxide.
$$C_6H_{12}O_6 \rightarrow 2C_2H_5OH + 2CO_2$$

DOUBLE DECOMPOSITION

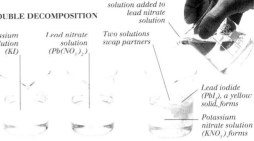

Potassium iodide solution (KI) *Lead nitrate solution (Pb(NO₃)₂)* *Two solutions swap partners*

Potassium iodide solution added to lead nitrate solution

Lead iodide (PbI₂), a yellow solid, forms

Potassium nitrate solution (KNO₃) forms

1. THE REACTANTS
Potassium iodide in water (KI) and lead nitrate in water (Pb(NO₃)₂) each form colourless solutions.

2. THE REACTION
When the solutions are mixed, lead iodide, a precipitate, and potassium nitrate solution are formed.
$$2KI + Pb(NO_3)_2 \rightarrow PbI_2 + 2KNO_3$$

TESTING CANDLE WAX, AN ORGANIC COMPOUND

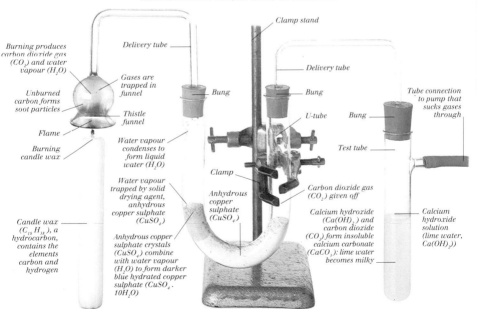

Burning produces carbon dioxide gas (CO₂) and water vapour (H₂O)

Delivery tube

Clamp stand

Delivery tube

Unburned carbon forms soot particles

Gases are trapped in funnel

Bung

Bung

U-tube

Bung

Tube connection to pump that sucks gases through

Flame

Thistle funnel

Burning candle wax

Water vapour condenses to form liquid water (H₂O)

Test tube

Clamp

Carbon dioxide gas (CO₂) given off

Candle wax (C₁₈H₃₈), a hydrocarbon, contains the elements carbon and hydrogen

Water vapour trapped by solid drying agent, anhydrous copper sulphate (CuSO₄)

Anhydrous copper sulphate (CuSO₄)

Anhydrous copper sulphate crystals (CuSO₄) combine with water vapour (H₂O) to form darker blue hydrated copper sulphate (CuSO₄ . 10H₂O)

Calcium hydroxide (Ca(OH)₂) and carbon dioxide (CO₂) form insoluble calcium carbonate (CaCO₃): lime water becomes milky

Calcium hydroxide solution (lime water, Ca(OH)₂)

1. THE BURNING REACTION
Burning wax produces carbon dioxide gas and water vapour.
$$2C_{18}H_{38} + 55O_2 \rightarrow 36CO_2 + 38H_2O$$

2. TESTING FOR WATER VAPOUR
A solid drying agent traps water vapour, proving the presence of hydrogen in the candle wax.
$$CuSO_4 + 10H_2O \rightarrow CuSO_4 . 10H_2O$$

3. TESTING FOR CARBON DIOXIDE
Calcium hydroxide in solution reacts with carbon dioxide, forming a carbonate and turning milky.
$$Ca(OH)_2 + CO_2 \rightarrow CaCO_3 + H_2O$$

Energy

ANYTHING THAT HAPPENS – from a pin-drop to an explosion
– requires energy. Energy is the capacity for "doing work"
(making something happen). Various forms of energy exist,
including light, heat, sound, electrical, chemical, nuclear,
kinetic, and potential energies. The Law of Conservation
of Energy states that the total amount of energy in the
Universe is fixed – energy cannot be created or destroyed.
It means that energy can only change from one form to
another (energy transfer). For example, potential energy
is energy that is "stored", and can be used in the future.
An object gains potential energy when it is lifted; as the
object is released, potential energy changes into the energy
of motion (kinetic energy). During transference, some of
the energy converts into heat. A combined heat and power
station can put some of the otherwise "waste" heat to useful
effect in local schools and housing. Most of the Earth's
energy is provided by the Sun, in the form of electromagnetic
radiation (see pp. 316-317). Some of this energy transfers to
plant and animal life, and ultimately to fossil fuels, where
it is stored in chemical form. Our bodies obtain energy from
the food we eat, while energy needed for other tasks, such
as heating and transport, can be obtained by burning fossil
fuels – or by harnessing natural forces like wind or moving
water – to generate electricity. Another source is nuclear
power, where energy is released by reactions in the nucleus
of an atom. All energy is measured by the international
unit, the joule (J). As a guide, one joule is about equal to
the amount of energy needed to lift an apple one metre.

SANKEY DIAGRAM SHOWING ENERGY FLOW IN A COAL-FIRED COMBINED HEAT AND POWER STATION

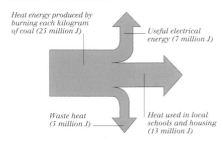

Heat energy produced by burning each kilogram of coal (25 million J)
Useful electrical energy (7 million J)
Waste heat (5 million J)
Heat used in local schools and housing (13 million J)

CROSS-SECTION OF HYDROELECTRIC POWER STATION WITH FRANCIS TURBINE

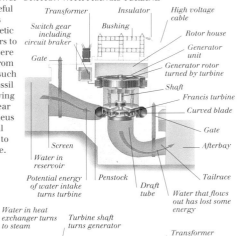

CROSS-SECTION OF NUCLEAR POWER STATION WITH PRESSURIZED WATER REACTOR

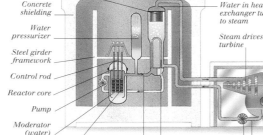

ENERGY SYSTEMS

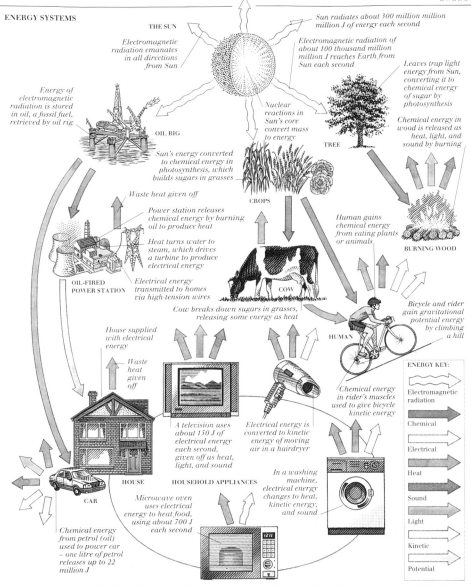

THE SUN

Sun radiates about 300 million million million J of energy each second

Electromagnetic radiation emanates in all directions from Sun

Electromagnetic radiation of about 100 thousand million million J reaches Earth from Sun each second

Leaves trap light energy from Sun, converting it to chemical energy of sugar by photosynthesis

Energy of electromagnetic radiation is stored in oil, a fossil fuel, retrieved by oil rig

OIL RIG

Nuclear reactions in Sun's core convert mass to energy

TREE

Chemical energy in wood is released as heat, light, and sound by burning

Sun's energy converted to chemical energy in photosynthesis, which builds sugars in grasses

CROPS

Waste heat given off

Power station releases chemical energy by burning oil to produce heat

Heat turns water to steam, which drives a turbine to produce electrical energy

Human gains chemical energy from eating plants or animals

BURNING WOOD

OIL-FIRED POWER STATION

Electrical energy transmitted to homes via high-tension wires

COW

Cow breaks down sugars in grasses, releasing some energy as heat

House supplied with electrical energy

HUMAN

Bicycle and rider gain gravitational potential energy by climbing a hill

Waste heat given off

Chemical energy in rider's muscles used to give bicycle kinetic energy

ENERGY KEY:

A television uses about 150 J of electrical energy each second, given off as heat, light, and sound

Electrical energy is converted to kinetic energy of moving air in a hairdryer

Electromagnetic radiation

Chemical

Electrical

HOUSE

HOUSEHOLD APPLIANCES

In a washing machine, electrical energy changes to heat, kinetic energy, and sound

Heat

CAR

Microwave oven uses electrical energy to heat food, using about 700 J each second

Sound

Light

Chemical energy from petrol (oil) used to power car – one litre of petrol releases up to 22 million J

Kinetic

Potential

315

Electricity and magnetism

ELECTRICAL EFFECTS result from an imbalance of electric charge.
There are two types of electric charge, named positive (carried by
protons) and negative (carried by electrons). If charges are opposite
(unlike), they attract one another, while like charges repel. Forces
of attraction and repulsion (electrostatic forces) exist between
any two charged particles. Matter is normally uncharged, but if

electrons are gained, an object will gain an
overall negative charge; if they are removed,
it becomes positive. Objects with an overall
negative or positive charge are said to have
an imbalance of charge, and exert the same
forces as individual negative and positive
charges. On this larger scale, the forces will
always act to regain the balance of charge.
This causes static electricity. Lightning, for
example, is produced by clouds discharging a
huge excess of negative electrons. If charges

LIGHTNING

are "free" – in a wire or material that allows
electrons to pass through it – the forces cause a flow of charge
called an electric current. Some substances exhibit the strange
phenomenon of magnetism – which also produces attractive and
repulsive forces. Magnetic substances consist of small regions
called domains. Normally unmagnetized, they can be magnetized
by being placed in a magnetic field. Magnetism and electricity
are inextricably linked, a fact put to use in motors and generators.

VAN DE GRAAFF (ELECTROSTATIC) GENERATOR

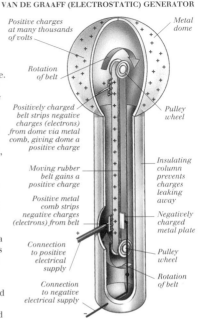

Positive charges at many thousands of volts

Metal dome

Rotation of belt

Positively charged belt strips negative charges (electrons) from dome via metal comb, giving dome a positive charge

Pulley wheel

Moving rubber belt gains a positive charge

Insulating column prevents charges leaking away

Positive metal comb strips negative charges (electrons) from belt

Negatively charged metal plate

Connection to positive electrical supply

Pulley wheel

Connection to negative electrical supply

Rotation of belt

CURRENT ELECTRICITY

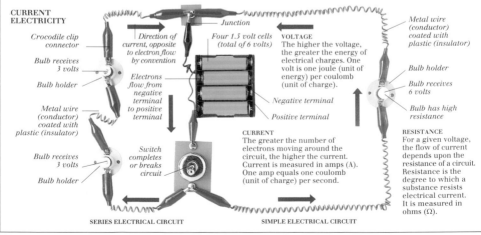

Crocodile clip connector

Direction of current, opposite to electron flow by convention

Junction

Four 1.5 volt cells (total of 6 volts)

Metal wire (conductor) coated with plastic (insulator)

Bulb receives 3 volts

Electrons flow from negative terminal to positive terminal

VOLTAGE
The higher the voltage, the greater the energy of electrical charges. One volt is one joule (unit of energy) per coulomb (unit of charge).

Bulb receives 6 volts

Bulb holder

Bulb holder

Negative terminal

Bulb receives 6 volts

Metal wire (conductor) coated with plastic (insulator)

Positive terminal

Bulb has high resistance

Bulb receives 3 volts

Switch completes or breaks circuit

CURRENT
The greater the number of electrons moving around the circuit, the higher the current. Current is measured in amps (A). One amp equals one coulomb (unit of charge) per second.

RESISTANCE
For a given voltage, the flow of current depends upon the resistance of a circuit. Resistance is the degree to which a substance resists electrical current. It is measured in ohms (Ω).

Bulb holder

SERIES ELECTRICAL CIRCUIT

SIMPLE ELECTRICAL CIRCUIT

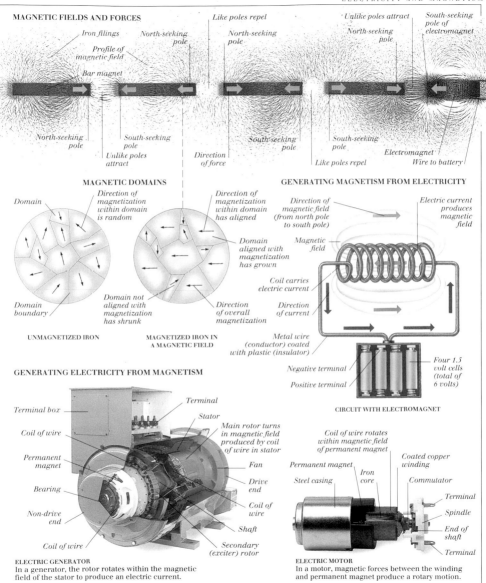

MAGNETIC FIELDS AND FORCES

Iron filings
Profile of magnetic field
Bar magnet
North-seeking pole
North-seeking pole
Like poles repel
North-seeking pole
Unlike poles attract
North-seeking pole
South-seeking pole of electromagnet

North-seeking pole
South-seeking pole
Unlike poles attract
Direction of force
South-seeking pole
South-seeking pole
Like poles repel
Electromagnet
Wire to battery

MAGNETIC DOMAINS

Domain
Direction of magnetization within domain is random
Domain boundary

Direction of magnetization within domain has aligned
Domain aligned with magnetization has grown
Domain not aligned with magnetization has shrunk
Direction of overall magnetization

UNMAGNETIZED IRON

MAGNETIZED IRON IN A MAGNETIC FIELD

GENERATING MAGNETISM FROM ELECTRICITY

Direction of magnetic field (from north pole to south pole)
Electric current produces magnetic field
Magnetic field
Coil carries electric current
Direction of current
Metal wire (conductor) coated with plastic (insulator)
Negative terminal
Positive terminal
Four 1.5 volt cells (total of 6 volts)

CIRCUIT WITH ELECTROMAGNET

GENERATING ELECTRICITY FROM MAGNETISM

Terminal box
Coil of wire
Permanent magnet
Bearing
Non-drive end
Coil of wire
Terminal
Stator
Main rotor turns in magnetic field produced by coil of wire in stator
Fan
Drive end
Coil of wire
Shaft
Secondary (exciter) rotor

ELECTRIC GENERATOR
In a generator, the rotor rotates within the magnetic field of the stator to produce an electric current.

Coil of wire rotates within magnetic field of permanent magnet
Permanent magnet
Steel casing
Iron core
Coated copper winding
Commutator
Terminal
Spindle
End of shaft
Terminal

ELECTRIC MOTOR
In a motor, magnetic forces between the winding and permanent magnet produce a rotary motion.

Light

INFRA-RED IMAGE
OF A HOUSE

LIGHT IS A FORM OF ENERGY. It is a
type of electromagnetic radiation, like X-
rays or radio waves. All electromagnetic
radiation is produced by electric charges
(see pp. 316-317): it is caused by the effects
of oscillating electric and magnetic fields as they travel
through space. Electromagnetic radiation is considered to
have both wave and particle properties. It can be thought
of as a wave of electricity and magnetism. In that case,
the difference between the various forms of
radiation is their wavelength. Radiation can
also be said to consist of particles, or packets
of energy, called photons. The difference
between light and X-rays, for instance, is
the amount of energy that each photon
carries. The complete range of radiation is
referred to as the electromagnetic spectrum,
extending from low energy, long wavelength
radio waves to high energy, short wavelength
gamma rays. Light is the only part of the
electromagnetic spectrum that is visible.
White light from the Sun is made up of all
the visible wavelengths of radiation, which
can be seen when it is separated by using a
prism. Light, like all forms of electromagnetic
radiation, can be reflected (bounced back)
and refracted (bent). Different parts of the
electromagnetic spectrum are produced in
different ways. Sometimes visible light –
and infra-red radiation – is generated by the
vibrating particles of warm or hot objects.
The emission of light in this way is called
incandescence. Light can also be produced
by fluorescence, a phenomenon in which
electrons gain and lose energy within atoms.

MAXWELLIAN DIAGRAM OF ELECTROMAGNETIC RADIATION AS WAVES

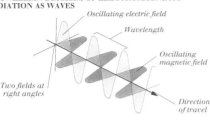

Oscillating electric field
Wavelength
Oscillating magnetic field
Two fields at right angles
Direction of travel

ELECTROMAGNETIC RADIATION AS PARTICLES

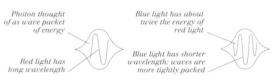

Photon thought of as wave packet of energy
Blue light has about twice the energy of red light
Red light has long wavelength
Blue light has shorter wavelength: waves are more tightly packed
PHOTON OF RED LIGHT
PHOTON OF BLUE LIGHT

SPLITTING WHITE LIGHT INTO THE SPECTRUM

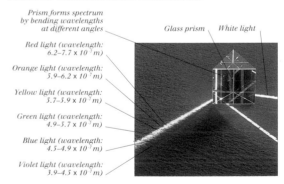

Prism forms spectrum by bending wavelengths at different angles
Glass prism
White light
Red light (wavelength: $6.2–7.7 \times 10^{-7}$ m)
Orange light (wavelength: $5.9–6.2 \times 10^{-7}$ m)
Yellow light (wavelength: $5.7–5.9 \times 10^{-7}$ m)
Green light (wavelength: $4.9–5.7 \times 10^{-7}$ m)
Blue light (wavelength: $4.5–4.9 \times 10^{-7}$ m)
Violet light (wavelength: $3.9–4.5 \times 10^{-7}$ m)

THE ELECTROMAGNETIC SPECTRUM

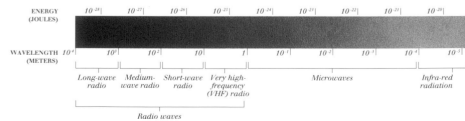

ENERGY (JOULES): 10^{-28} | 10^{-27} | 10^{-26} | 10^{-25} | 10^{-24} | 10^{-23} | 10^{-22} | 10^{-21} | 10^{-20}

WAVELENGTH (METERS): 10^{4} | 10^{1} | 10^{2} | 10 | 1 | 10^{-1} | 10^{-2} | 10^{-3} | 10^{-4} | 10^{-5}

Long-wave radio | Medium-wave radio | Short-wave radio | Very high-frequency (VHF) radio | Microwaves | Infra-red radiation

Radio waves

ARTIFICIAL LIGHT SOURCES

FLUORESCENT TUBE

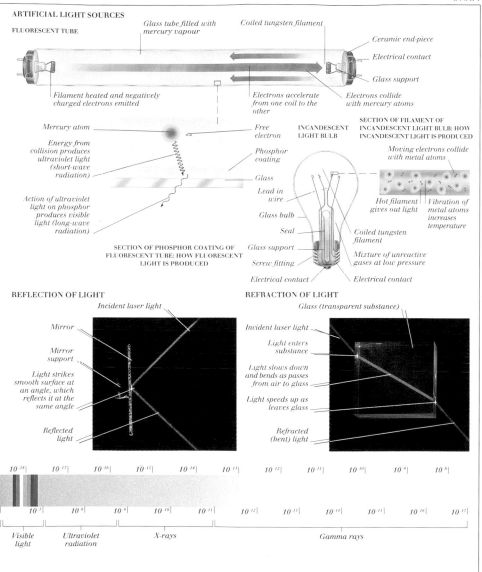

Glass tube filled with mercury vapour

Coiled tungsten filament

Ceramic end-piece

Electrical contact

Glass support

Filament heated and negatively charged electrons emitted

Electrons accelerate from one coil to the other

Electrons collide with mercury atoms

Mercury atom

Free electron

Energy from collision produces ultraviolet light (short-wave radiation)

Action of ultraviolet light on phosphor produces visible light (long-wave radiation)

SECTION OF PHOSPHOR COATING OF FLUORESCENT TUBE: HOW FLUORESCENT LIGHT IS PRODUCED

INCANDESCENT LIGHT BULB

Phosphor coating

Glass

Lead in wire

Glass bulb

Seal

Glass support

Screw fitting

Electrical contact

Coiled tungsten filament

Mixture of unreactive gases at low pressure

Electrical contact

SECTION OF FILAMENT OF INCANDESCENT LIGHT BULB: HOW INCANDESCENT LIGHT IS PRODUCED

Moving electrons collide with metal atoms

Hot filament gives out light

Vibration of metal atoms increases temperature

REFLECTION OF LIGHT

Incident laser light

Mirror

Mirror support

Light strikes smooth surface at an angle, which reflects it at the same angle

Reflected light

REFRACTION OF LIGHT

Glass (transparent substance)

Incident laser light

Light enters substance

Light slows down and bends as passes from air to glass

Light speeds up as leaves glass

Refracted (bent) light

10^{-18} | 10^{-17} | 10^{-16} | 10^{-15} | 10^{-14} | 10^{-13} | 10^{-12} | 10^{-11} | 10^{-10} | 10^{-9} | 10^{-8} |

10^{-7} | 10^{-8} | 10^{-9} | 10^{-10} | 10^{-11} | 10^{-12} | 10^{-13} | 10^{-14} | 10^{-15} | 10^{-16} | 10^{-17} |

Visible light | Ultraviolet radiation | X-rays | Gamma rays

Force and motion

FORCES ARE PUSHES OR PULLS that change the motion of objects. To make a stationary object move, or a moving object stop, a force is needed. A force is also required to change the speed or direction of an object. This change in speed or direction is known as acceleration. Acceleration depends on the size (magnitude) of the force, and on the mass of the object. The effects of forces were first summarized by Isaac Newton in his three laws of motion. The international unit of force, named after him, is the newton (N), which is approximately equal to the weight of one apple. Gravity – the force of attraction between any two masses – can be measured using a newton meter (spring balance). Forces are put to useful effect in machines. A simple machine, such as a wheel and axle, is a device that changes the size or direction of an applied force. It allows an applied force (the effort) to produce another force (the load). A lever uses a bar that turns on a fulcrum to exert force. In all simple machines, there is a relationship between force and distance. A small force (in a compound pulley, for instance) moves through a large distance to lift a heavy object a small distance. This is called the Law of Simple Machines.

SIMPLE MACHINES

Single-pulley system (simple pulley)

Two-pulley system (simple pulley)

Four-pulley system (compound pulley)

Pulley wheel

Simple pulley only changes direction of a force

Effort is the same size as the load (10 N) and is pulled the same distance

One rope attached to load

Load of 10 N

Pulley wheel

Effort is half the load (5 N), but the rope must be pulled twice the distance

Two ropes share the force and distance

Pulley wheel

Load of 10 N

Two pulley wheels

Effort is one quarter of the load (2.5 N), but the rope must be pulled four times the distance

Four ropes share the force and distance

Two pulley wheels

Load of 10 N

SIMPLE AND COMPOUND PULLEYS

NEWTON METERS (SPRING BALANCES)

Weight is measured using a spring

When weight pulls downwards, pointer moves along scale and measures force

Weight is 10 N

Weight is 20 N

Mass of 1 kg

Mass of 2 kg

WEIGHT AND MASS
The "mass" of an object is a measure of the quantity of matter that it possesses. Mass is usually measured in grams (g) or kilograms (kg). The "weight" of an object is the force exerted on the object's mass by gravity. Since weight is a force, its unit is the newton (N).

Wheel and axle multiplies the effort

Force is transmitted to the wheels by the chain

Pedal

Effort, provided by cyclist's muscles, is smaller than the load, but moves through a greater distance

Crank

A larger force, the load, is produced at the axle

WHEEL AND AXLE

A screw, acting like a wedge wrapped around a shaft, multiplies the effort

Effort, a turning force supplied through a screwdriver

Pitch (the angle of the screw thread)

The smaller the angle of pitch, the less force is required, but more turns are needed to move it through a greater distance

A larger force, the load, pulls the screw into wood

SCREW

Effort pushes axe into wood

A larger force, the load, moves through a smaller distance to push wood apart

Axe blade has wedge shape

Wedge multiplies effort

WEDGE

NEWTON'S THREE LAWS OF MOTION

NEWTON'S FIRST LAW
When no force acts on a body, it will continue in a state of rest or uniform motion.

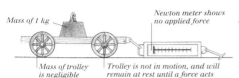

Constant speed

Mass of 1 kg — *Newton meter shows no applied force*

Mass of trolley is negligible — *Trolley is not in motion, and will remain at rest until a force acts*

Mass of 1 kg — *Newton meter shows no applied force*

Trolley is in motion, and will continue at a constant speed in a straight line until a force acts

NO FORCE, NO ACCELERATION: STATE OF REST **NO FORCE, NO ACCELERATION: UNIFORM MOTION**

NEWTON'S SECOND LAW
When a force acts on a body, the motion of the body will change. The size of the change will depend upon the mass of the object and the magnitude of the applied force.

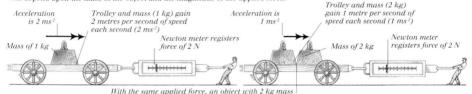

Acceleration is 2 ms⁻² *Trolley and mass (1 kg) gain 2 metres per second of speed each second (2 ms⁻²)* *Newton meter registers force of 2 N*

Mass of 1 kg

Trolley and mass (2 kg) gain 1 metre per second of speed each second (1 ms⁻²) *Acceleration is 1 ms⁻²* *Newton meter registers force of 2 N* *Mass of 2 kg*

With the same applied force, an object with 2 kg mass accelerates at half the rate of object with 1 kg mass

FORCE AND ACCELERATION: SMALL MASS, LARGE ACCELERATION **FORCE AND ACCELERATION: LARGE MASS, SMALL ACCELERATION**

NEWTON'S THIRD LAW
If one object exerts a force on another, an equal and opposite force, called the reaction force, is applied by the second object on the first.

Newton meters pull on each other with equal and opposite forces

Acceleration: the trolley and mass accelerate at 2 ms⁻² *Newton meter registers force of 2 N to the left* *Newton meter registers force of 2 N to the right*

Mass of 1 kg

Person experiences a reaction force

ACTION AND REACTION

THREE CLASSES OF LEVER

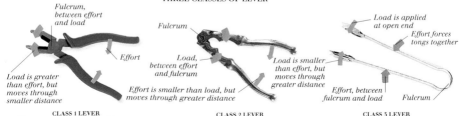

Fulcrum, between effort and load

Effort

Load is greater than effort, but moves through smaller distance

CLASS 1 LEVER
Pliers consist of two class 1 levers.

Fulcrum

Load, between effort and fulcrum

Effort is smaller than load, but moves through greater distance

CLASS 2 LEVER
Nutcrackers consist of two class 2 levers.

Load is applied at open end *Effort forces tongs together*

Load is smaller than effort, but moves through greater distance

Effort, between fulcrum and load *Fulcrum*

CLASS 3 LEVER
Tongs consist of two class 3 levers.

RAIL AND ROAD

STEAM LOCOMOTIVES · · · · · · · · · · · · · · 324
DIESEL TRAINS · · · · · · · · · · · · · · · · · 326
ELECTRIC AND HIGH-SPEED TRAINS · · · · · 328
TRAIN EQUIPMENT · · · · · · · · · · · · · · · 330
TRAMS AND BUSES · · · · · · · · · · · · · · · 332
THE FIRST CARS · · · · · · · · · · · · · · · · 334
ELEGANCE AND UTILITY · · · · · · · · · · · · 336
MASS-PRODUCTION · · · · · · · · · · · · · · · 338
THE "PEOPLE'S CAR" · · · · · · · · · · · · · · 340
EARLY ENGINES · · · · · · · · · · · · · · · · · 342
MODERN ENGINES · · · · · · · · · · · · · · · · 344
ALTERNATIVE ENGINES · · · · · · · · · · · · · 346
BODYWORK · 348
MECHANICAL COMPONENTS · · · · · · · · · · · 350
CAR TRIM · 352
HYBRID CAR · · · · · · · · · · · · · · · · · · · 354
RACING CARS · · · · · · · · · · · · · · · · · · · 356
BICYCLE ANATOMY · · · · · · · · · · · · · · · 358
BICYCLES · 360
THE MOTORCYCLE · · · · · · · · · · · · · · · · 362
THE MOTORCYCLE CHASSIS · · · · · · · · · · 364
MOTORCYCLE ENGINES · · · · · · · · · · · · · 366
COMPETITION MOTORCYCLES · · · · · · · · · 368

Steam locomotives

WAGONS THAT ARE PULLED along tracks have been used to transport material since the 16th century, but these trains were drawn by men or horses until the invention of the steam locomotive. Steam locomotives enabled the basic railway system to realize its true potential. In 1804, Richard Trevithick built the world's first working steam locomotive in South Wales. It was not entirely successful, but it encouraged others to develop new designs. By 1829, the British engineer Robert Stephenson had built the "Rocket", considered to be the forerunner of the modern locomotive. The "Rocket" was a self-sufficient unit, carrying coal to heat the boiler and a water supply for generating steam. Steam passed from the boiler to force the pistons back and forth, and this movement turned the driving wheels, propelling the train forwards. Used steam was then expelled in characteristic "chuffs". Later steam locomotives, like "Ellerman Lines" and the "Mallard", worked in a similar way, but on a much larger scale. The simple design and reliability of steam locomotives ensured that they changed very little in 120 years of use, before being replaced from the 1950s by more efficient diesel and electric power (see pp. 326-329).

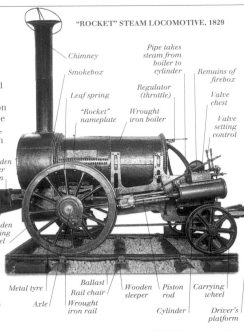

"ROCKET" STEAM LOCOMOTIVE, 1829

Chimney
Smokebox
Pipe takes steam from boiler to cylinder
Remains of firebox
Leaf spring
Regulator (throttle)
Valve chest
"Rocket" nameplate
Wrought iron boiler
Valve setting control
Wooden buffer beam
Wooden driving wheel
Metal tyre
Ballast
Rail chair
Wooden sleeper
Piston rod
Carrying wheel
Axle
Wrought iron rail
Cylinder
Driver's platform
Stay

"ELLERMAN LINES", 1949 (CUTAWAY VIEW)

Vacuum reservoir
Panel brace
Water tank
Coal space
Tender hand brake
Cab
Firebox
Brick arch
Water filler
Panel sheeting
Hand rail
Buffer
Brake vacuum pipe
Wheel guard
Axle
Axle box
Tender wheel
Brake rigging
Water float to indicate water level
Water float lever
Step
Axle box cover
Footplate
Coupling
Coil spring
Trailing wheel
Grate
Fire drawn into fire tubes

TENDER

CAB INTERIOR OF "MALLARD" EXPRESS STEAM LOCOMOTIVE, 1938

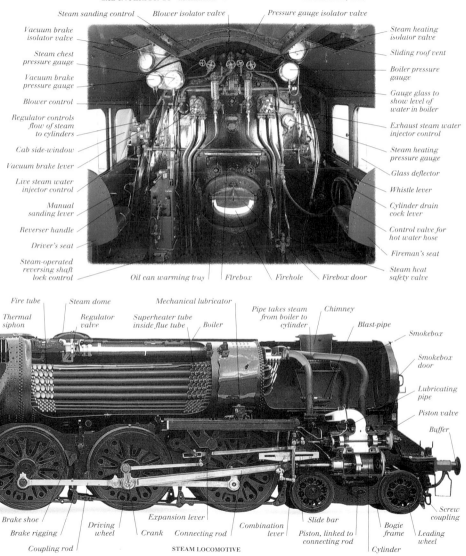

Steam sanding control

Blower isolator valve

Pressure gauge isolator valve

Steam heating isolator valve

Vacuum brake isolator valve

Steam chest pressure gauge

Sliding roof vent

Boiler pressure gauge

Vacuum brake pressure gauge

Blower control

Gauge glass to show level of water in boiler

Regulator controls flow of steam to cylinders

Exhaust steam water injector control

Cab side-window

Steam heating pressure gauge

Vacuum brake lever

Glass deflector

Live steam water injector control

Whistle lever

Manual sanding lever

Cylinder drain cock lever

Reverser handle

Control valve for hot water hose

Driver's seat

Fireman's seat

Steam-operated reversing shaft lock control

Oil can warming tray

Firebox

Firehole

Firebox door

Steam heat safety valve

Fire tube

Steam dome

Mechanical lubricator

Pipe takes steam from boiler to cylinder

Chimney

Thermal siphon

Regulator valve

Superheater tube inside flue tube

Boiler

Blast-pipe

Smokebox

Smokebox door

Lubricating pipe

Piston valve

Buffer

Screw coupling

Brake shoe

Expansion lever

Slide bar

Bogie frame

Leading wheel

Brake rigging

Driving wheel

Crank

Connecting rod

Combination lever

Piston, linked to connecting rod

Coupling rod

STEAM LOCOMOTIVE

Cylinder

Diesel trains

RUDOLF DIESEL FIRST DEMONSTRATED the diesel engine in Germany in 1898, but it was not until the 1940s that diesel locomotives were successfully established on both passenger and freight services, in the US. Early diesel locomotives like the "Union Pacific" were more expensive to build than steam locomotives, but were more efficient and cheaper to operate, especially where oil was plentiful. One feature of diesel engines is that the power output cannot be coupled directly to the wheels. To convert the mechanical energy produced by diesel engines, a transmission system is needed. Almost all diesel locomotives have electric transmissions, and are known as "diesel-electric" locomotives. The diesel engine works by drawing air into the cylinders and compressing it to increase its temperature; a small quantity of diesel fuel is then injected into it. The resulting combustion drives the generator (more recently an alternator) to produce electricity, which is fed to electric motors connected to the wheels. Diesel-electric locomotives are essentially electric locomotives that carry their own power plants, and are used worldwide today. The "Deltic" diesel-electric locomotive, similar to the one shown here, replaced classic express steam locomotives, and ran at speeds up to 160 kph (100 mph).

FRONT VIEW OF "UNION PACIFIC" DIESEL-ELECTRIC LOCOMOTIVE, 1950s

Exhaust vent | Windscreen wiper | Horn | Cab front window | Head-light | Name of operating railroad | Cab door | Illuminated locomotive unit number | Railroad crest

Cab step | Step | Motor-driven bogie axle | Air-brake coupling hose | Centre buck-eye coupler

PROTOTYPE "DELTIC" DIESEL-ELECTRIC LOCOMOTIVE, 1956

Engine room vent | Inspection hatch | Engine exhaust port | Radiator fan | Engine room window | Engine room vent

DELTIC

Fuel tank | Water for heating boiler | Inspection socket | Folding step | Drain for radiator coolant | Radiator coolant | Sand box | Telescopic damper | Drain for control reservoir

DIESEL ENGINE OF BRITISH RAIL CLASS 20
DIESEL-ELECTRIC LOCOMOTIVE

EXAMPLES OF FREIGHT CARS

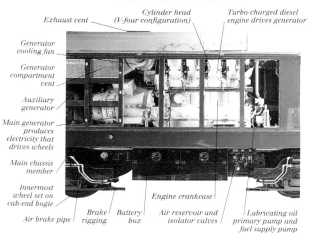

Exhaust vent

Cylinder head
(V-four configuration)

Turbo-charged diesel
engine drives generator

Generator
cooling fan

Generator
compartment
vent

Auxiliary
generator

Main generator
produces
electricity that
drives wheels

Main chassis
member

Innermost
wheel set on
cab-end bogie

Air brake pipe

Brake
rigging

Battery
box

Engine crankcase

Air reservoir and
isolator valves

Lubricating oil
primary pump and
fuel supply pump

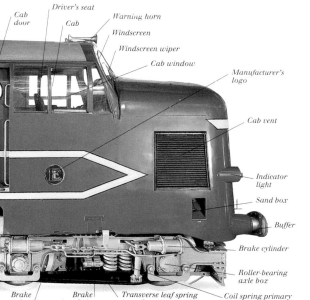

Cab
door

Driver's seat

Cab

Warning horn

Windscreen

Windscreen wiper

Cab window

Manufacturer's
logo

Cab vent

Indicator
light

Sand box

Buffer

Brake cylinder

Roller-bearing
axle box

Brake
shoe

Brake
actuating chain

Transverse leaf spring
secondary suspension

Coil spring primary
suspension

BOX CAR

HOPPER CAR

REFRIGERATOR CAR

LIVESTOCK CAR

FLAT CAR WITH BULKHEADS

AUTOMOBILE CAR

Electric and high-speed trains

THE FIRST ELECTRIC LOCOMOTIVE ran in 1879 in Berlin, Germany. In Europe, electric trains developed as a more efficient alternative to the steam locomotive and diesel-electric power. Like diesels, electric trains employ electric motors to drive the wheels but, unlike diesels, the electricity is generated externally at a power station. Electric current is picked up either from a catenary (overhead cable) via a pantograph, or from a third rail. Since it does not carry its own power-generating equipment, an electric locomotive has a better power-to-weight ratio and greater acceleration than its diesel-electric equivalent. This makes electric trains suitable for urban routes with many stops. They are also faster, quieter, and less polluting. The latest electric French TGV (Train à Grande Vitesse) reaches 300 kph (186 mph); other trains, like the London to Paris and Brussels "Eurostar", can run at several voltages and operate between different countries. Simpler electric trains perform special duties – the "People Mover" at Gatwick Airport in Britain runs between terminals.

HOW ALTERNATING CURRENT (AC) ELECTRIC TRAINS WORK

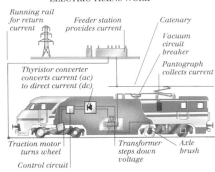

Running rail for return current

Feeder station provides current

Catenary

Vacuum circuit breaker

Thyristor converter converts current (ac) to direct current (dc)

Pantograph collects current

Traction motor turns wheel

Control circuit

Transformer steps down voltage

Axle brush

FRONT VIEW OF ITALIAN STATE RAILWAYS CLASS 402 ELECTRIC LOCOMOTIVE

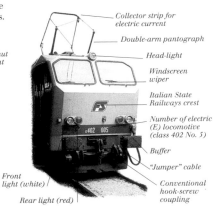

Collector strip for electric current

Double-arm pantograph

Head-light

Windscreen wiper

Italian State Railways crest

Number of electric (E) locomotive (class 402 No. 5)

Buffer

"Jumper" cable

Conventional hook-screw coupling

FRONT VIEW OF PARIS METRO

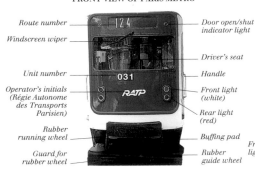

Route number

Windscreen wiper

Unit number

Operator's initials (Régie Autonome des Transports Parisien)

Rubber running wheel

Guard for rubber wheel

Door open/shut indicator light

Driver's seat

Handle

Front light (white)

Rear light (red)

Buffing pad

Rubber guide wheel

SIDE VIEW OF GATWICK EXPRESS "PEOPLE MOVER"

Pneumatic rubber wheel

Concrete track

Front light (white)

Rear light (red)

Automatic door

No driver (train controlled by central computer)

"EUROSTAR" MULTI-VOLTAGE ELECTRIC TRAIN

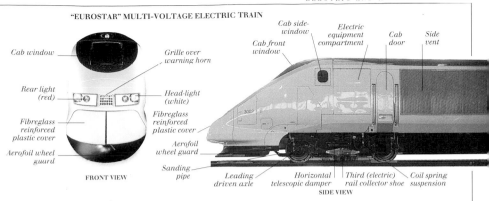

Cab window

Grille over warning horn

Rear light (red)

Head-light (white)

Fibreglass reinforced plastic cover

Fibreglass reinforced plastic cover

Aerofoil wheel guard

Aerofoil wheel guard

Sanding pipe

FRONT VIEW

Cab side-window

Electric equipment compartment

Cab door

Side vent

Cab front window

3002

Leading driven axle

Horizontal telescopic damper

Third (electric) rail collector shoe

Coil spring suspension

SIDE VIEW

TGV ELECTRIC HIGH-SPEED TRAIN

Luggage rack

Reading light

Double-glazed and tinted side-window

Sliding curtain

Seat

Main overhead lighting

Automatic electric carriage end door

Antimacassar

Headrest

Armrest

Centre gangway

INTERIOR OF TGV

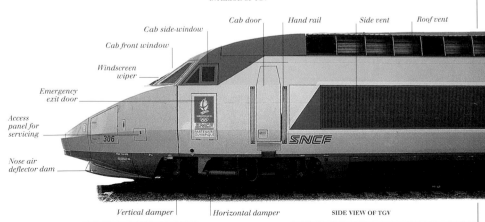

Cab door

Hand rail

Side vent

Roof vent

Cab side-window

Cab front window

Windscreen wiper

Emergency exit door

Access panel for servicing

306

SNCF

Nose air deflector dam

Vertical damper

Horizontal damper

SIDE VIEW OF TGV

Train equipment

MECHANICAL SEMAPHORE SIGNAL

MODERN RAILWAY TRACK consists of two parallel steel rails clipped on to a support called a sleeper. Sleepers are usually made of reinforced concrete, although wood and steel are still used. The distance between the inside edges of the rails is the track gauge. It evolved in Britain, which uses a gauge of 1,435 mm (4 ft 8 1/2 in), known as the standard gauge. As engineering grew more sophisticated, narrower gauges were adopted because they cost less to build. The loading gauge, which is equally important, determines the size of the largest loaded vehicle that may pass through tunnels and under bridges with adequate clearance. Safe train operation relies on following a signalling system. At first, signalling was based on a simple time interval between trains, but it now depends on maintaining a safe distance between successive trains travelling in the same direction. Most modern signals are colour lights, but older mechanical semaphore signals are still used. On the latest high-speed lines, train drivers receive control instructions by electronic means. Signalling depends on reliable control of the train by effective braking. For fast, modern trains, which have considerable momentum, it is essential that each vehicle in the train can be braked by the driver or by a train control system, such as Automatic Train Protection (ATP). Braking is achieved by the brake shoe acting on the wheel rim (rim brakes), by disc brakes, or, increasingly, by electrical braking.

Red, square-ended arm in raised position means "all clear"

Red glass

Green glass

Actuating lever system

Motor operating "home" stop signal

Green glass

Yellow glass

Yellow, "distant" warning arm in horizontal position means "caution"

Tubular steel post

Ladder

Electrical relay box

FOUR-ASPECT COLOUR LIGHT SIGNAL

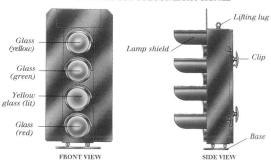

Glass (yellow)

Glass (green)

Yellow glass (lit)

Glass (red)

FRONT VIEW

Lifting lug

Lamp shield

Clip

Base

SIDE VIEW

HOW A MODERN MAIN-LINE SIGNALLING SYSTEM WORKS

Red "stop" light instructs next train not to enter this section of track

Green "all clear" light instructs train B to proceed into this section of track

Green "all clear" light instructs train B to proceed into this section of track

Green "all clear" light instructs train B to proceed into this section of track

Pantograph

Catenary

Train B

Track

EXAMPLES OF INTERNATIONAL TRACK GAUGES

EXAMPLES OF INTERNATIONAL LOADING GAUGES

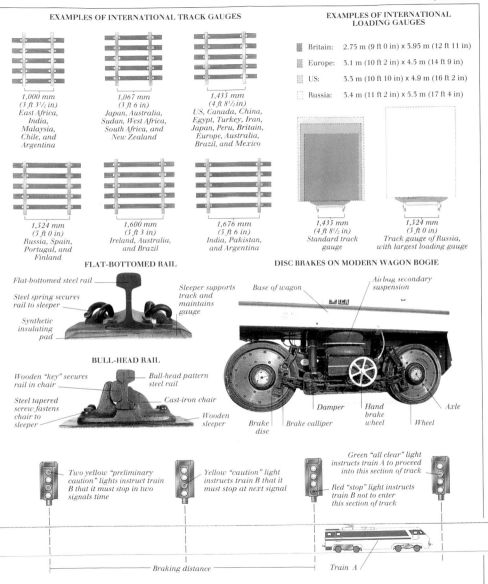

1,000 mm
(3 ft 3¹/₂ in)
East Africa,
India,
Malaysia,
Chile, and
Argentina

1,067 mm
(3 ft 6 in)
Japan, Australia,
Sudan, West Africa,
South Africa, and
New Zealand

1,435 mm
(4 ft 8¹/₂ in)
US, Canada, China,
Egypt, Turkey, Iran,
Japan, Peru, Britain,
Europe, Australia,
Brazil, and Mexico

Britain: 2.75 m (9 ft 0 in) x 3.95 m (12 ft 11 in)

Europe: 3.1 m (10 ft 2 in) x 4.5 m (14 ft 9 in)

US: 3.3 m (10 ft 10 in) x 4.9 m (16 ft 2 in)

Russia: 3.4 m (11 ft 2 in) x 5.3 m (17 ft 4 in)

1,524 mm
(5 ft 0 in)
Russia, Spain,
Portugal, and
Finland

1,600 mm
(5 ft 3 in)
Ireland, Australia,
and Brazil

1,676 mm
(5 ft 6 in)
India, Pakistan,
and Argentina

1,435 mm
(4 ft 8¹/₂ in)
Standard track
gauge

1,524 mm
(5 ft 0 in)
Track gauge of Russia,
with largest loading gauge

FLAT-BOTTOMED RAIL

DISC BRAKES ON MODERN WAGON BOGIE

Flat-bottomed steel rail

Steel spring secures
rail to sleeper

Synthetic
insulating
pad

Sleeper supports
track and
maintains
gauge

Base of wagon

Air bag secondary
suspension

BULL-HEAD RAIL

Wooden "key" secures
rail in chair

Steel tapered
screw fastens
chair to
sleeper

Bull-head pattern
steel rail

Cast-iron chair

Wooden
sleeper

Brake
disc

Brake calliper

Damper

Hand
brake
wheel

Axle

Wheel

Two yellow "preliminary
caution" lights instruct train
B that it must stop in two
signals time

Yellow "caution" light
instructs train B that it
must stop at next signal

Green "all clear" light
instructs train A to proceed
into this section of track

Red "stop" light instructs
train B not to enter
this section of track

Braking distance

Train A

Trams and buses

METROLINK TRAM, MANCHESTER, BRITAIN

AS CITY POPULATIONS exploded in the 1800s, there was an urgent need for mass transportation. Trams were an early solution. The first trams, like buses, were horse-drawn, but in 1881, electric street tramways appeared in Berlin, Germany. Electric trams soon became widespread throughout Europe and North America. Trams run on rails along a fixed route, using electric motors that receive power from overhead cables. As road networks developed, motorized buses offered a flexible alternative to trams. By the 1930s, they had replaced tram systems in many cities. City buses typically have doors at both front and rear to make loading and unloading easier. Double-decker designs are popular, occupying the same amount of street space as single-decker buses but able to transport twice the number of people. Buses are also commonly used for inter-city travel and touring. Tour buses have reclining seats, large windows, luggage space, and toilets. Recently, as city traffic has become increasingly congested, many city planners have designed new tram routes to run alongside bus routes as part of an integrated transport system.

EARLY TRAM, c.1900

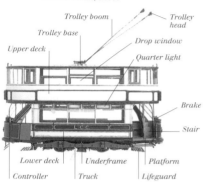

Trolley boom · Trolley head · Trolley base · Drop window · Upper deck · Quarter light · Brake · Stair · Lower deck · Underframe · Platform · Controller · Truck · Lifeguard

MCW METROBUS, LONDON, BRITAIN

Square roof dome · Upper deck air intake · Window vent · Mirror for driver to see upstairs · Upper deck windscreen · Route number · Route information · Operator's logo · Destination screen · Destination screen · Nearside mirror · Offside mirror · Asymmetric windscreen · Nearside mirror · Windscreen wiper · Licence holder · Sidelight · Turning indicator · Head-light · Grille · Front bumper · Fog light · Number plate · Manufacturer's badge · Entrance door · Emergency door control · Turning indicator

LONDON NORTHERN
41
ARCHWAY STN.
PAY DRIVER
mcw
KYV 739X
LONDON NORTHERN

FRONT VIEW

SINGLE-DECKER BUS, NEW YORK, US

Wheelchair access

Sliding window

Sloped roof dome

Marker light

Repeater indicator

Tinted glass

Entrance door

Side mirror

Route number

Head-light

Bumper

Turning indicator

Air intake

Tyre

Axle

Exit door

Access panel

Sidelight

Entrance door

Number plate

Bumper

SIDE VIEW

FRONT VIEW

DOUBLE-DECKER TOUR BUS, PARIS, FRANCE

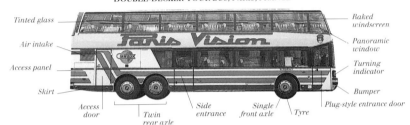

Tinted glass

Raked windscreen

Air intake

Panoramic window

Access panel

Turning indicator

Skirt

Bumper

Access door

Twin rear axle

Side entrance

Single front axle

Tyre

Plug-style entrance door

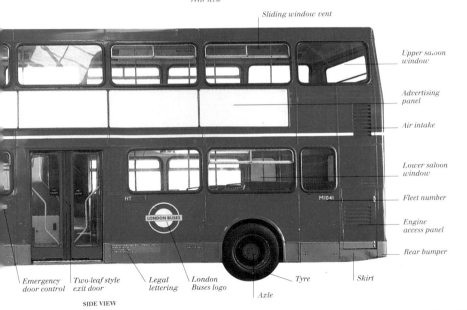

Sliding window vent

Upper saloon window

Advertising panel

Air intake

Lower saloon window

Fleet number

Engine access panel

Rear bumper

Emergency door control

Two-leaf style exit door

Legal lettering

London Buses logo

Tyre

Skirt

Axle

SIDE VIEW

The first cars

THE EARLIEST ROAD VEHICLE powered by an engine, the Cugnot steam traction engine, was built in 1770. More practical steam carriages, such as the Bordino, were available in the early 19th century, but they were heavy and cumbersome. Restrictive laws and the introduction of railways, faster and able to carry more passengers, saw the decline of "cars" powered by steam. It was not until 1860 that the first practical power unit for road vehicles was developed, with the invention of the internal combustion engine by the Belgian Etienne Lenoir. By around 1890, Karl Benz and Gottlieb Daimler in Germany, and Albert de Dion and Armand Peugeot in France were building cars for sale to the public. These early cars, despite being primitive, expensive, and produced in limited numbers, heralded the age of the motor car.

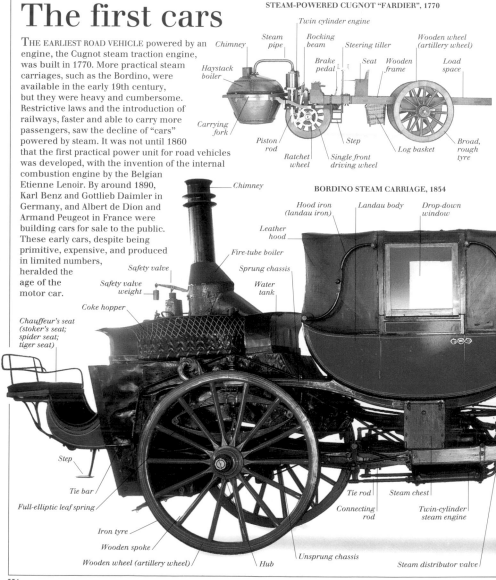

STEAM-POWERED CUGNOT "FARDIER", 1770

Twin cylinder engine

Chimney
Steam pipe
Rocking beam
Steering tiller
Wooden wheel (artillery wheel)

Haystack boiler
Brake pedal
Seat
Wooden frame
Load space

Carrying fork

Piston rod
Ratchet wheel
Single front driving wheel
Step
Log basket
Broad, rough tyre

BORDINO STEAM CARRIAGE, 1854

Chimney

Hood iron (landau iron)
Landau body
Drop-down window

Leather hood

Fire-tube boiler

Sprung chassis

Safety valve

Safety valve weight

Water tank

Coke hopper

Chauffeur's seat (stoker's seat; spider seat; tiger seat)

Step

Tie bar

Full-elliptic leaf spring

Iron tyre

Wooden spoke

Wooden wheel (artillery wheel)

Hub

Tie rod

Connecting rod

Unsprung chassis

Steam chest

Twin-cylinder steam engine

Steam distributor valve

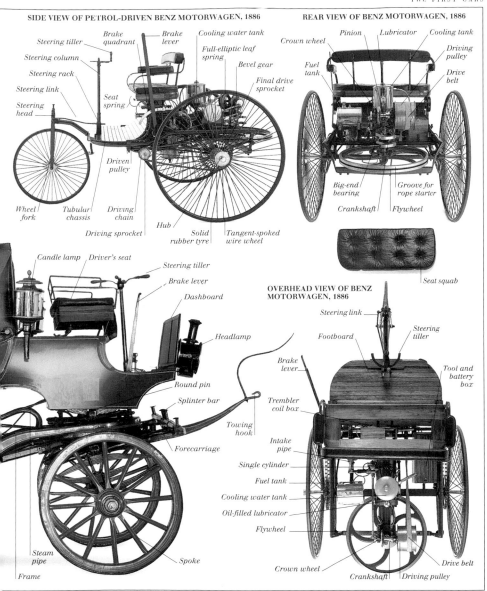

SIDE VIEW OF PETROL-DRIVEN BENZ MOTORWAGEN, 1886

Steering tiller
Brake quadrant
Brake lever
Cooling water tank
Steering column
Full-elliptic leaf spring
Bevel gear
Steering rack
Steering link
Final drive sprocket
Steering head
Seat spring
Driven pulley
Wheel fork
Tubular chassis
Driving chain
Hub
Driving sprocket
Solid rubber tyre
Tangent-spoked wire wheel

REAR VIEW OF BENZ MOTORWAGEN, 1886

Pinion
Lubricator
Cooling tank
Crown wheel
Driving pulley
Fuel tank
Drive belt
Big-end bearing
Groove for rope starter
Crankshaft
Flywheel
Seat squab

OVERHEAD VIEW OF BENZ MOTORWAGEN, 1886

Candle lamp
Driver's seat
Steering tiller
Steering link
Brake lever
Footboard
Steering tiller
Dashboard
Headlamp
Brake lever
Tool and battery box
Round pin
Trembler coil box
Splinter bar
Towing hook
Intake pipe
Forecarriage
Single cylinder
Fuel tank
Cooling water tank
Oil-filled lubricator
Flywheel
Steam pipe
Spoke
Crown wheel
Crankshaft
Driving pulley
Drive belt
Frame

Elegance and utility

1904 OLDSMOBILE SINGLE-CYLINDER ENGINE

DURING THE FIRST DECADE OF THE 20TH CENTURY, the motorist who could afford it had a choice of some of the finest cars ever made. These handbuilt cars were powerful and luxurious, using the finest woods, leathers, and cloths, and bodywork made to the customer's individual requirements; some had six-cylinder engines as big as 15 litres. The price of such cars was several times that of an average house, and their yearly running costs were also very high. As a result, basic, utilitarian cars became popular. Costing perhaps one-tenth of the price of a luxury car, these cars had very little trim and often had only single-cylinder engines.

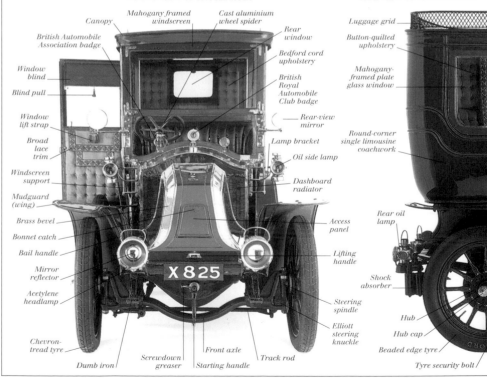

Oil bottle dripfeed
Crankcase
Exhaust pipe
Starting handle bracket
Cylinder head
Cylinder
Starter cog
Carburettor
Engine timing gear
Crankshaft
Flywheel
Gear band

FRONT VIEW OF 1906 RENAULT

Canopy
Mahogany framed windscreen
Cast aluminium wheel spider
Rear window
British Automobile Association badge
Bedford cord upholstery
Window blind
British Royal Automobile Club badge
Blind pull
Window lift strap
Rear-view mirror
Broad lace trim
Lamp bracket
Oil side lamp
Windscreen support
Dashboard radiator
Mudguard (wing)
Brass bevel
Access panel
Bonnet catch
Bail handle
Lifting handle
Mirror reflector
Acetylene headlamp
Chevron-tread tyre
Steering spindle
Elliott steering knuckle
Dumb iron
Screwdown greaser
Front axle
Starting handle
Track rod

X 825

SIDE VIEW OF 1906 RENAULT

Luggage grid
Button-quilted upholstery
Mahogany-framed plate glass window
Round-corner single limousine coachwork
Rear oil lamp
Shock absorber
Hub
Hub cap
Beaded edge tyre
Tyre security bolt

1904 OLDSMOBILE TRIM AND BODYWORK

1904 OLDSMOBILE CHASSIS

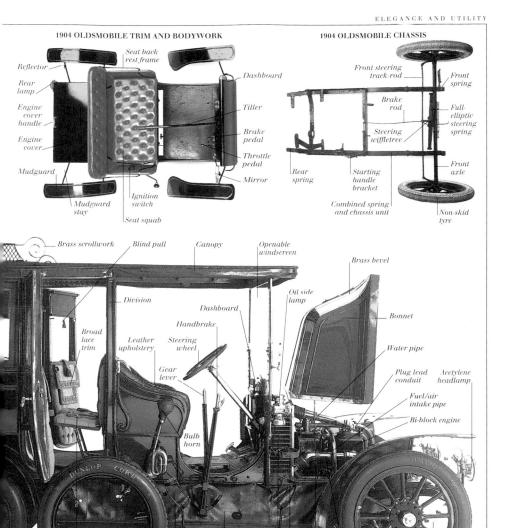

Reflector
Rear lamp
Engine cover handle
Engine cover
Mudguard
Mudguard stay
Seat back rest frame
Ignition switch
Seat squab
Dashboard
Tiller
Brake pedal
Throttle pedal
Mirror

Front steering track-rod
Brake rod
Steering wiffletree
Rear spring
Starting handle bracket
Combined spring and chassis unit
Front spring
Full-elliptic steering spring
Front axle
Non-skid tyre

Brass scrollwork
Blind pull
Canopy
Openable windscreen
Brass bevel
Division
Oil side lamp
Bonnet
Broad lace trim
Leather upholstery
Dashboard
Handbrake
Steering wheel
Water pipe
Gear lever
Plug lead conduit
Acetylene headlamp
Fuel/air intake pipe
Bi-block engine
Bulb horn
Spare tyre
Jump seat (opera seat; strapontin)
Rim clamp
Tyre carrier
Running board
Leather valance
Tyre strap
Dashboard radiator
Bonnet stay
Exhaust manifold
Starting handle
Wooden artillery wheel

Mass-production

THE FIRST CARS WERE HAND-ASSEMBLED from individually built parts, a time-consuming procedure that required skilled mechanics and made cars very expensive. This problem was solved, in America, by a Detroit car manufacturer named Henry Ford; he introduced mass-production by using standardized parts, and later combined these with a moving production line. The work was brought to the workers, each of whom performed one simple task in the construction process as the chassis moved along the line. The first mass-produced car, the Ford Model T, was launched in 1908 and was available in a limited range of body styles and colours. However, when the production line was introduced in 1914, the colour range was cut back; the Model T became available, as Henry Ford said, in "any colour you like, so long as it's black". Ford cut the production time for a car from several days to about 12 hours, and eventually to minutes, making cars much cheaper than before. As a result, by 1920 half the cars in the world were Model T Fords.

Throttle lever
Openable windscreen
Steering wheel
Ignition lever
Windscreen stay
Dashboard
Side lamp
Spring shock absorber
Bulb horn
Mudguard (wing)
Headlamp
Radiator
Front transverse leaf spring
Number plate
Starting handle
Steering knuckle
Front axle
Steering spindle connecting-rod

STAGES OF FORD MODEL T PRODUCTION

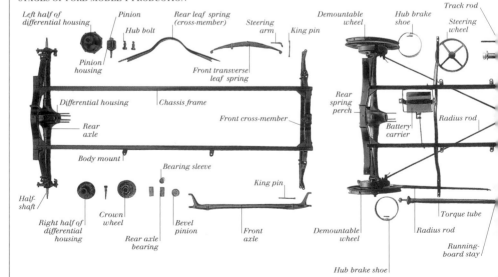

Left half of differential housing
Pinion
Rear leaf spring (cross-member)
Steering arm
King pin
Demountable wheel
Hub brake shoe
Track rod
Steering wheel
Hub bolt
Pinion housing
Front transverse leaf spring
Differential housing
Chassis frame
Rear spring perch
Battery carrier
Radius rod
Rear axle
Front cross-member
Body mount
Bearing sleeve
King pin
Half-shaft
Crown wheel
Bevel pinion
Front axle
Demountable wheel
Radius rod
Torque tube
Right half of differential housing
Rear axle bearing
Running-board stay
Hub brake shoe

SIDE VIEW OF 1913 FORD MODEL T

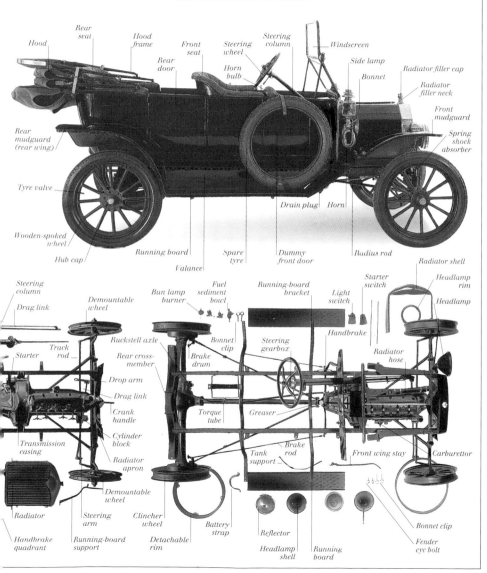

Hood

Rear seat

Hood frame

Front seat

Rear door

Steering wheel

Steering column

Windscreen

Side lamp

Bonnet

Radiator filler cap

Radiator filler neck

Horn bulb

Front mudguard

Spring shock absorber

Rear mudguard (rear wing)

Tyre valve

Drain plug

Horn

Wooden-spoked wheel

Hub cap

Running board

Spare tyre

Dummy front door

Radius rod

Valance

Radiator shell

Steering column

Drag link

Demountable wheel

Bun lamp burner

Fuel sediment bowl

Running-board bracket

Light switch

Starter switch

Headlamp rim

Headlamp

Starter

Track rod

Ruckstell axle

Rear cross-member

Bonnet clip

Brake drum

Steering gearbox

Handbrake

Radiator hose

Drop arm

Drag link

Crank handle

Cylinder block

Torque tube

Greaser

Transmission casing

Radiator apron

Tank support

Brake rod

Front wing stay

Carburettor

Demountable wheel

Radiator

Steering arm

Clincher wheel

Battery strap

Reflector

Bonnet clip

Fender eye bolt

Handbrake quadrant

Running-board support

Detachable rim

Headlamp shell

Running board

The "people's car"

THE MOST POPULAR CAR in the history of car manufacture is the Volkswagen Beetle, originally called the KdF Wagen. The car was developed in Germany in the 1930s by Dr. Ferdinand Porsche. At that time, Germany had only half the number of cars of Britain or France, and Adolf Hitler took a personal interest in the development of the Volkswagen ("people's car"). The intention was to provide a new industry, new jobs, and a car so cheap that anyone in work could afford it. Dr. Porsche designed a car that was cheap to build and run; its rear-mounted, air-cooled engine cut down the number of parts needed and also reduced weight. However, few civilians managed to obtain the Beetle before the outbreak of the Second World War in 1939. After the war, the Beetle proved so popular that eventually more than 20 million were sold.

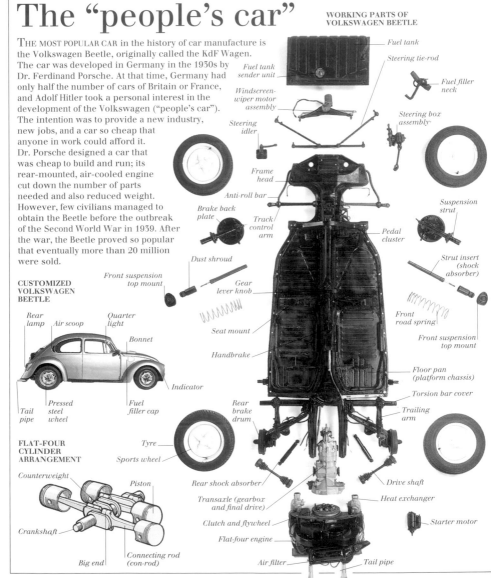

CUSTOMIZED VOLKSWAGEN BEETLE

Rear lamp
Air scoop
Quarter light
Bonnet
Indicator
Tail pipe
Pressed steel wheel
Fuel filler cap

FLAT-FOUR CYLINDER ARRANGEMENT

Counterweight
Piston
Crankshaft
Big end
Connecting rod (con-rod)

Fuel tank sender unit
Windscreen-wiper motor assembly
Steering idler
Frame head
Anti-roll bar
Brake back plate
Track control arm
Dust shroud
Front suspension top mount
Gear lever knob
Seat mount
Handbrake
Rear brake drum
Tyre
Sports wheel
Rear shock absorber
Transaxle (gearbox and final drive)
Clutch and flywheel
Flat-four engine
Air filter

Fuel tank
Steering tie-rod
Fuel filler neck
Steering box assembly
Suspension strut
Pedal cluster
Strut insert (shock absorber)
Front road spring
Front suspension top mount
Floor pan (platform chassis)
Torsion bar cover
Trailing arm
Drive shaft
Heat exchanger
Starter motor
Tail pipe

BODY SHELL OF VOLKSWAGEN BEETLE

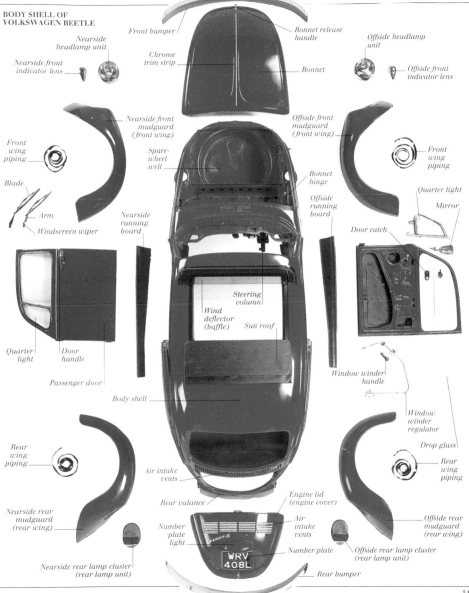

Front bumper

Bonnet release handle

Nearside headlamp unit

Chrome trim strip

Offside headlamp unit

Nearside front indicator lens

Bonnet

Offside front indicator lens

Nearside front mudguard (front wing)

Offside front mudguard (front wing)

Front wing piping

Spare-wheel well

Bonnet hinge

Front wing piping

Blade

Offside running board

Quarter light

Mirror

Arm

Nearside running board

Door catch

Windscreen wiper

Steering column

Wind deflector (baffle)

Sun roof

Quarter light

Door handle

Passenger door

Body shell

Window winder handle

Window winder regulator

Drop glass

Rear wing piping

Air intake vents

Rear wing piping

Nearside rear mudguard (rear wing)

Rear valance

Engine lid (engine cover)

Air intake vents

Offside rear mudguard (rear wing)

Number plate light

Number plate

Offside rear lamp cluster (rear lamp unit)

WRV 408L

Nearside rear lamp cluster (rear lamp unit)

Rear bumper

Early engines

STEAM AND ELECTRICITY were used to power cars until early this century, but neither power source was ideal. Electric cars had to stop frequently to recharge their heavy batteries, and steam cars gave smooth power delivery but were too complicated for the average motorist to use. A rival power source, the internal combustion engine, was invented in 1860 by Etienne Lenoir (see pp. 334-335). This engine converted the force of a controlled explosion into rotary motion, to turn the wheels of a vehicle. Early variations on this basic model included sleeve valves, separately cast cylinders, and the two-stroke combustion cycle. Today, many internal combustion engines, including the Wankel rotary and diesels (see pp. 346-347), use the four-stroke cycle, first demonstrated by Nikolaus Otto in 1876. The Otto cycle, often described as "suck, squeeze, bang, blow", has proved the best method of ensuring that the engine turns over smoothly and that exhaust emissions are controllable.

BERSEY ELECTRIC CAB, 1896

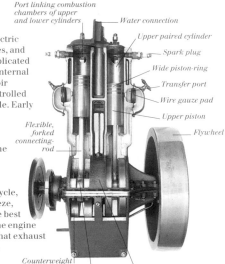

Port linking combustion chambers of upper and lower cylinders

Water connection

Upper paired cylinder

Spark plug

Wide piston-ring

Transfer port

Wire gauze pad

Upper piston

Flywheel

Flexible, forked connecting-rod

Counterweight

Big end

Crankcase

Mounting for tray of 40 batteries

Housing for electric motors

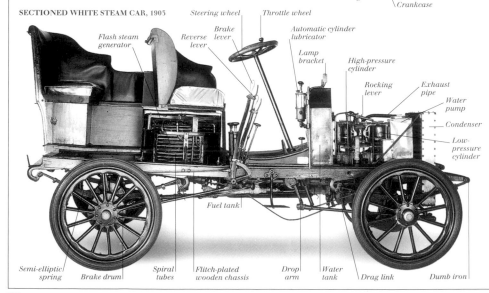

SECTIONED WHITE STEAM CAR, 1903

Steering wheel

Throttle wheel

Brake lever

Reverse lever

Flash steam generator

Automatic cylinder lubricator

Lamp bracket

High-pressure cylinder

Rocking lever

Exhaust pipe

Water pump

Condenser

Low-pressure cylinder

Fuel tank

Semi-elliptic spring

Brake drum

Spiral tubes

Flitch-plated wooden chassis

Drop arm

Water tank

Drag link

Dumb iron

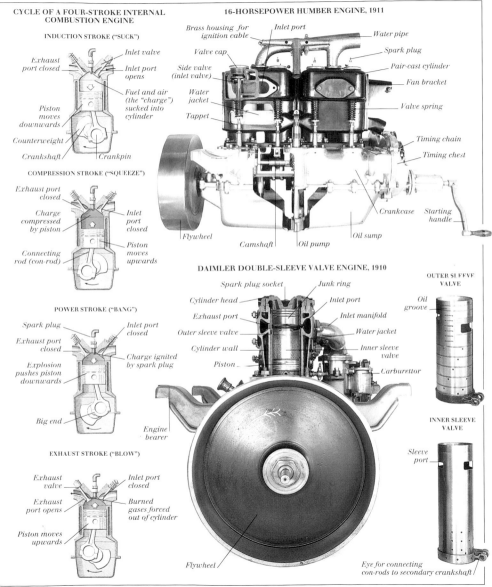

CYCLE OF A FOUR-STROKE INTERNAL COMBUSTION ENGINE

INDUCTION STROKE ("SUCK")

Exhaust port closed
Inlet valve
Inlet port opens
Fuel and air (the "charge") sucked into cylinder
Piston moves downwards
Counterweight
Crankshaft
Crankpin

COMPRESSION STROKE ("SQUEEZE")

Exhaust port closed
Charge compressed by piston
Inlet port closed
Piston moves upwards
Connecting rod (con-rod)

POWER STROKE ("BANG")

Spark plug
Inlet port closed
Exhaust port closed
Explosion pushes piston downwards
Charge ignited by spark plug
Big end

EXHAUST STROKE ("BLOW")

Exhaust valve
Inlet port closed
Exhaust port opens
Burned gases forced out of cylinder
Piston moves upwards

16-HORSEPOWER HUMBER ENGINE, 1911

Brass housing for ignition cable
Inlet port
Water pipe
Valve cap
Spark plug
Side valve (inlet valve)
Pair-cast cylinder
Water jacket
Fan bracket
Tappet
Valve spring
Timing chain
Timing chest
Crankcase
Starting handle
Flywheel
Camshaft
Oil pump
Oil sump

DAIMLER DOUBLE-SLEEVE VALVE ENGINE, 1910

Spark plug socket
Junk ring
Cylinder head
Inlet port
Exhaust port
Inlet manifold
Outer sleeve valve
Water jacket
Cylinder wall
Inner sleeve valve
Piston
Carburettor
Engine bearer
Flywheel

OUTER SLEEVE VALVE

Oil groove

INNER SLEEVE VALVE

Sleeve port

Eye for connecting con-rods to secondary crankshaft

Modern engines

TODAY'S PETROL ENGINE WORKS on the same basic principles as the first car engines of a century ago, although it has been greatly refined. Modern engines, often made from special metal alloys, are much lighter than earlier engines. Computerized ignition systems, fuel injectors, and multi-valve cylinder heads achieve a more efficient combustion of the fuel/air mixture (the charge) so that less fuel is wasted. As a result of this greater efficiency, the power and performance of a modern engine are increased, and the level of pollution in the exhaust gases is reduced. Exhaust pollution levels today are also lowered by the increasing use of special filters called catalytic converters, which absorb many exhaust pollutants. The need to produce ever more efficient engines means that it can take up to seven years to develop a new engine for a family car, at a cost of many millions of pounds.

FRONT VIEW OF A FORD COSWORTH V6 12-VALVE

Idle control valve
Plenum chamber
Valve rocker
Power steering pump reservoir
Oil dipstick
Steering pump pulley
High-tension ignition lead (spark plug lead)
Cogged drive belt
Fan
Alternator
Crankshaft pulley
Viscous coupling
Oil sump

FRONT VIEW OF A FORD COSWORTH V6 24-VALVE

Idle control valve
Plenum chamber
Exhaust gas recirculation valve
Camshaft timing gear
Camshaft chain
Steering pump drive pulley
Air conditioning pump
Belt tensioner
Alternator cooling fan
Drive belt
Oil sump
Crankshaft pulley

SECTIONED VIEW OF A JAGUAR STRAIGHT 6

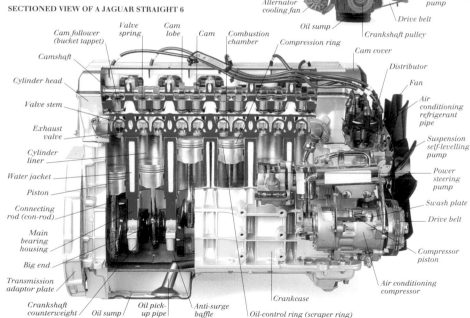

Valve spring
Cam lobe
Cam
Combustion chamber
Compression ring
Cam cover
Cam follower (bucket tappet)
Camshaft
Distributor
Cylinder head
Fan
Valve stem
Air conditioning refrigerant pipe
Exhaust valve
Suspension self-levelling pump
Cylinder liner
Power steering pump
Water jacket
Piston
Swash plate
Connecting rod (con-rod)
Drive belt
Main bearing housing
Compressor piston
Big end
Transmission adaptor plate
Air conditioning compressor
Crankshaft counterweight
Oil sump
Oil pick-up pipe
Anti-surge baffle
Crankcase
Oil-control ring (scraper ring)

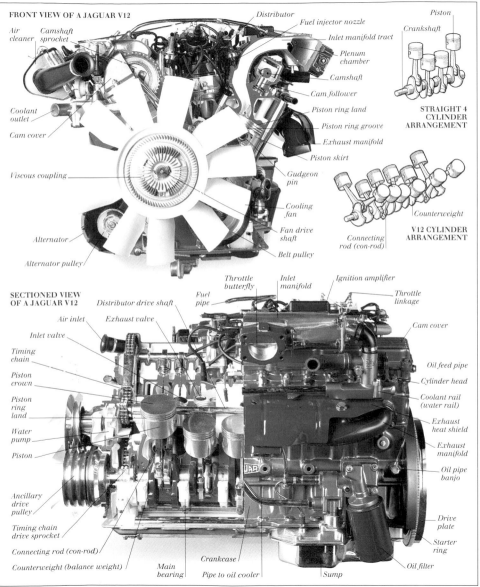

FRONT VIEW OF A JAGUAR V12

Distributor

Fuel injector nozzle

Piston

Crankshaft

Air cleaner

Camshaft sprocket

Inlet manifold tract

Plenum chamber

Camshaft

Cam follower

Piston ring land

Piston ring groove

Exhaust manifold

Piston skirt

Gudgeon pin

Cooling fan

Fan drive shaft

Belt pulley

Coolant outlet

Cam cover

Viscous coupling

Alternator

Alternator pulley

STRAIGHT 4 CYLINDER ARRANGEMENT

Counterweight

V12 CYLINDER ARRANGEMENT

Connecting rod (con-rod)

SECTIONED VIEW OF A JAGUAR V12

Throttle butterfly

Inlet manifold

Ignition amplifier

Throttle linkage

Fuel pipe

Distributor drive shaft

Air inlet

Inlet valve

Exhaust valve

Cam cover

Oil feed pipe

Cylinder head

Coolant rail (water rail)

Exhaust heat shield

Exhaust manifold

Oil pipe banjo

Timing chain

Piston crown

Piston ring land

Water pump

Piston

Ancillary drive pulley

Timing chain drive sprocket

Connecting rod (con-rod)

Counterweight (balance weight)

Main bearing

Pipe to oil cooler

Crankcase

Sump

Oil filter

Drive plate

Starter ring

Alternative engines

THE MOST COMMON TYPE OF ALTERNATIVE ENGINE is the diesel engine, which, instead of igniting the compressed fuel/air mixture with a spark, uses compression alone, heating the mixture to the point where it explodes. A diesel engine's fuel consumption is low in comparison with similarly sized piston engines, despite its heavier, reinforced moving parts and cylinder block. Another type of engine is the rotary-combustion, first successfully developed by Felix Wankel in the 1950s. Its two trilobate (three-sided) rotors revolve in housings shaped in a fat figure-of-eight. The four sequences of the four-stroke cycle, which occur consecutively in a piston engine, occur simultaneously in a rotary engine, producing power in a continuous stream.

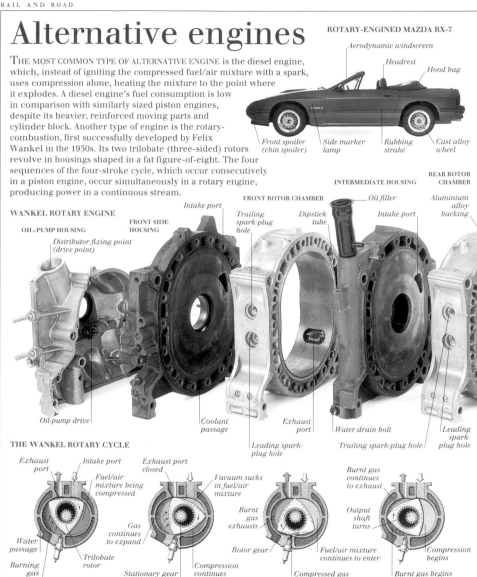

ROTARY-ENGINED MAZDA RX-7
Aerodynamic windscreen
Headrest
Hood bag
Front spoiler (chin spoiler)
Side marker lamp
Rubbing strake
Cast alloy wheel

WANKEL ROTARY ENGINE
OIL-PUMP HOUSING
FRONT SIDE HOUSING
Distributor fixing point (drive point)
Intake port
Trailing spark-plug hole
FRONT ROTOR CHAMBER
Dipstick tube
INTERMEDIATE HOUSING
Oil filler
Intake port
REAR ROTOR CHAMBER
Aluminium alloy backing
Oil-pump drive
Coolant passage
Exhaust port
Leading spark-plug hole
Water drain bolt
Trailing spark-plug hole
Leading spark-plug hole

THE WANKEL ROTARY CYCLE
Exhaust port
Intake port
Fuel/air mixture being compressed
Water passage
Burning gas expands
Trilobate rotor
Gas continues to expand
Stationary gear (fixed gear)
Exhaust port closed
Vacuum sucks in fuel/air mixture
Compression continues
Burnt gas exhausts
Rotor gear
Compressed gas ignites
Burnt gas continues to exhaust
Output shaft turns
Fuel/air mixture continues to enter
Compression begins
Burnt gas begins to expand

FORD TURBOCHARGED DIESEL ENGINE

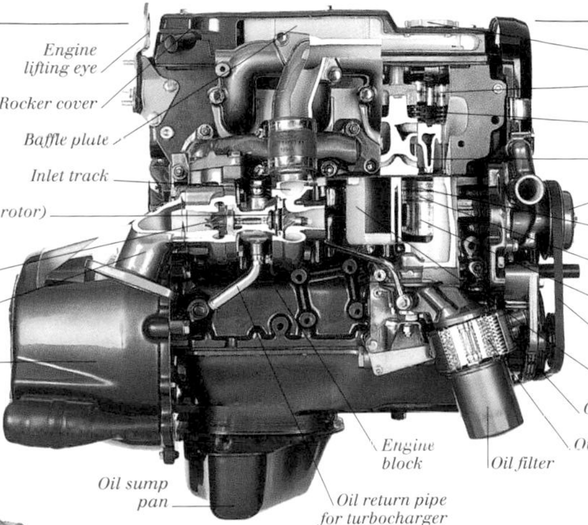

Engine lifting eye

Rocker cover

Baffle plate

Inlet track

Turbo impeller (inlet rotor)

Turbo propeller (exhaust rotor)

Exhaust

Bell housing

Oil filler cap

Cam follower

Valve return spring

Water jacket

Water pump pulley

Compression ring

Oil-control ring

Piston

Ancillary drive belt

Water jacket

Oil cooler

Oil cooler matrix

Oil filter

Engine block

Oil sump pan

Oil return pipe for turbocharger

REAR SIDE HOUSING

Chrome plating

Exhaust port

ROTOR AND SEALS

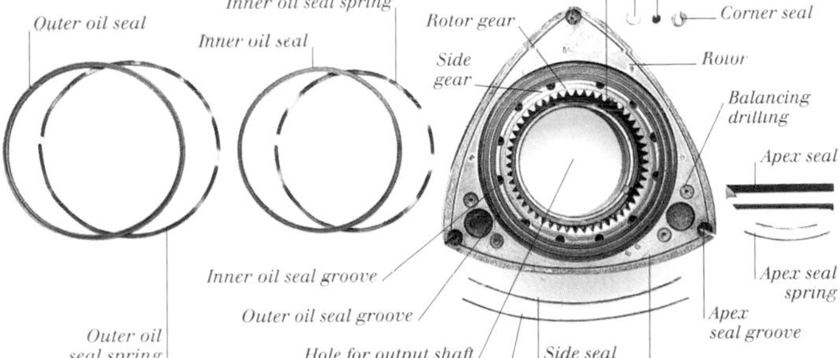

Outer oil seal

Inner oil seal spring

Inner oil seal

Rotor bearing

Rotor gear

Side gear

Corner seal spring

Corner seal insert

Corner seal

Rotor

Balancing drilling

Apex seal

Inner oil seal groove

Outer oil seal groove

Outer oil seal spring

Hole for output shaft

Side seal spring

Side seal

Side seal groove

Apex seal spring

Apex seal groove

OUTPUT SHAFT

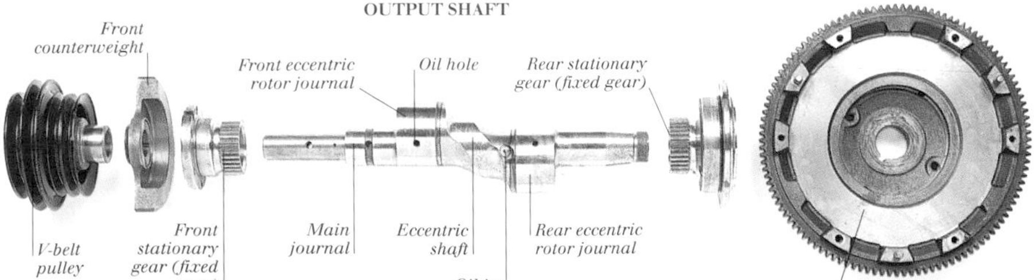

Front counterweight

Front eccentric rotor journal

Oil hole

Rear stationary gear (fixed gear)

V-belt pulley

Front stationary gear (fixed gear)

Main journal

Eccentric shaft

Rear eccentric rotor journal

Oil jet

Flywheel with balance weight

347

Bodywork

RENAULT LOGO

THE BODY OF A MODERN mass-produced car is built on the monocoque (single-shell) principle, in which the roof, side panels, and floor are welded into a single integral unit. This bodyshell protects and supports the car's internal parts. Steel and glass are used to construct the bodyshell, creating a unit that is both light and strong. Its lightness helps to conserve energy, while its strength protects the occupants. Modern bodywork is designed with the aid of computers, which are used to predict factors such as aerodynamic efficiency and impact-resistance. High-technology is also employed on the production line, where robots are used to assemble, weld, and paint the body.

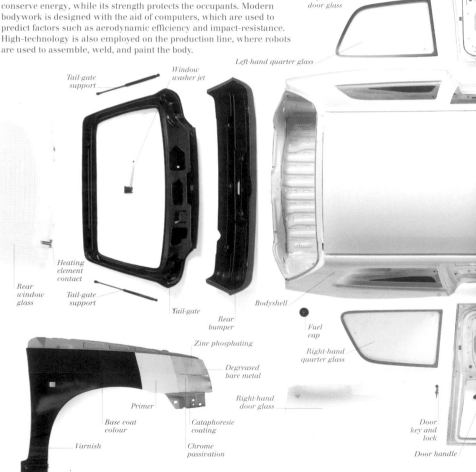

Door handle

Door lock

Left-hand door glass

Left-hand quarter glass

Tail-gate support

Window washer jet

Heating element contact

Rear window glass

Tail-gate support

Tail-gate

Rear bumper

Bodyshell

Fuel cap

Zinc phosphating

Right-hand quarter glass

Degreased bare metal

Primer

Right-hand door glass

Base coat colour

Cataphoresic coating

Door key and lock

Varnish

Chrome passivation

Door handle

Left-hand door

Left-hand mirror assembly

Door hinge

Electric window motor

Rear hatch

Aerial

Side marker lamp

SIDE VIEW OF A RENAULT CLIO

Spoiler bumper

Bonnet-release cable

Bonnet

Bonnet catch

Bonnet hinge

Windscreen glass

Front bumper

Window winder cable

Window winder handle

Door hinge

Right-hand door

Right-hand mirror assembly

Bonnet

Headrest

Headlamp

Spoiler bumper

Fog-lamp

FRONT VIEW OF A RENAULT CLIO

Mechanical components

A TYPICAL MODERN CAR has several thousand individual mechanical components. These are assembled to form the car's various mechanical systems: engine and exhaust, transmission, steering, suspension, and brakes. To ensure that each system functions properly, components are manufactured to extremely fine tolerances – to within a five-hundredth of a millimetre (about one ten-thousandth of an inch) in some cases.

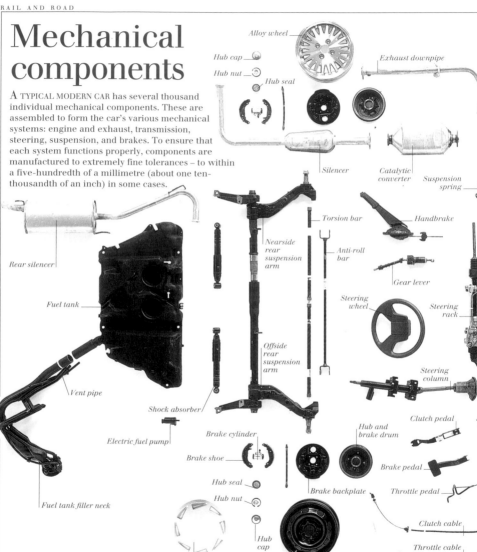

Alloy wheel

Hub cap

Hub nut

Hub seal

Exhaust downpipe

Silencer

Catalytic converter

Suspension spring

Rear silencer

Torsion bar

Handbrake

Nearside rear suspension arm

Anti-roll bar

Gear lever

Fuel tank

Steering wheel

Steering rack

Offside rear suspension arm

Steering column

Vent pipe

Shock absorber

Electric fuel pump

Brake cylinder

Brake shoe

Hub and brake drum

Clutch pedal

Brake pedal

Fuel tank filler neck

Hub seal

Hub nut

Hub cap

Brake backplate

Throttle pedal

Clutch cable

Throttle cable

Wheel trim

Steel wheel

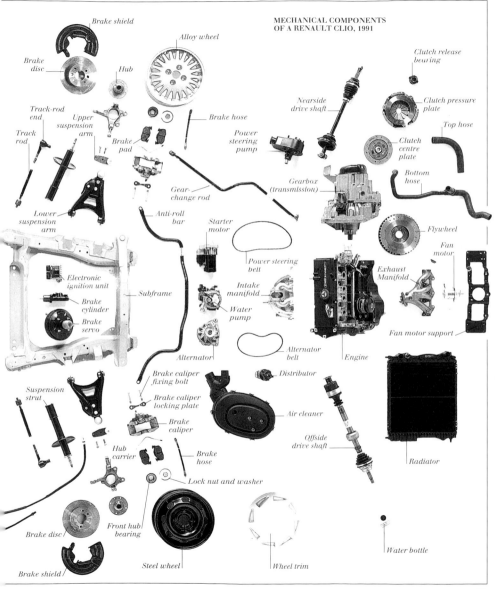

**MECHANICAL COMPONENTS
OF A RENAULT CLIO, 1991**

Brake shield

Alloy wheel

Clutch release
bearing

Brake
disc

Hub

Nearside
drive shaft

Clutch pressure
plate

Track-rod
end

Upper
suspension
arm

Brake hose

Clutch
centre
plate

Top hose

Track
rod

Brake
pad

Power
steering
pump

Bottom
hose

Gear-
change rod

Gearbox
(transmission)

Flywheel

Lower
suspension
arm

Anti-roll
bar

Starter
motor

Fan
motor

Electronic
ignition unit

Power steering
belt

Exhaust
Manifold

Subframe

Intake
manifold

Brake
cylinder

Water
pump

Brake
servo

Alternator

Alternator
belt

Engine

Fan motor support

Brake caliper
fixing bolt

Distributor

Suspension
strut

Brake caliper
locking plate

Brake
caliper

Air cleaner

Hub
carrier

Brake
hose

Offside
drive shaft

Radiator

Lock nut and washer

Brake disc

Front hub
bearing

Brake shield

Steel wheel

Wheel trim

Water bottle

551

Car trim

A MODERN CAR HAS TWO TYPES OF TRIM, according to the materials used: hard (chrome and plastics) and soft (upholstery materials). Safety and comfort are priorities in the trim's design: seats help the occupants to maintain a comfortable posture, rubber seals keep out dirt and moisture, and headlamps light the way. Older cars had interior or leather panelling cut and fitted by craftsmen; modern cars use precisely moulded plastics and seat fabrics cut by robot-controlled lasers to reduce costs and production time. Doors are now trimmed off the production line so that complex wiring can be built in.

TRIM OF A RENAULT CLIO, 1991

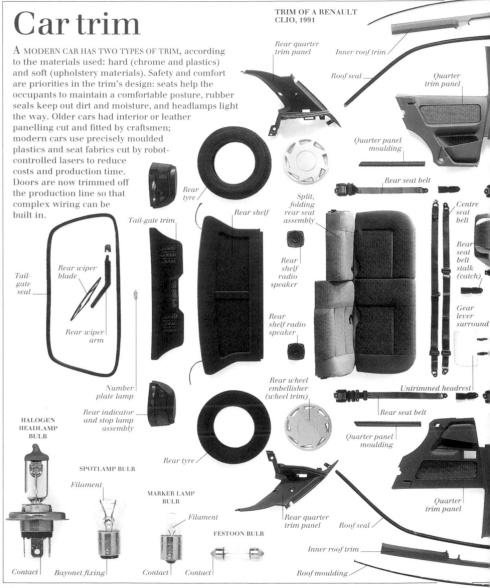

Rear quarter trim panel

Inner roof trim

Roof seal

Quarter trim panel

Quarter panel moulding

Rear seat belt

Rear tyre

Rear shelf

Split, folding rear seat assembly

Centre seat belt

Rear seat belt stalk (catch)

Tail-gate trim

Rear shelf radio speaker

Gear lever surround

Tail-gate seal

Rear wiper blade

Rear wiper arm

Rear shelf radio speaker

Number plate lamp

Rear wheel embellisher (wheel trim)

Untrimmed headrest

Rear seat belt

Rear indicator and stop lamp assembly

HALOGEN HEADLAMP BULB

Quarter panel moulding

SPOTLAMP BULB

Filament

Rear tyre

Quarter trim panel

MARKER LAMP BULB

Filament

Rear quarter trim panel

Roof seal

FESTOON BULB

Inner roof trim

Contact

Bayonet fixing

Contact

Contact

Roof moulding

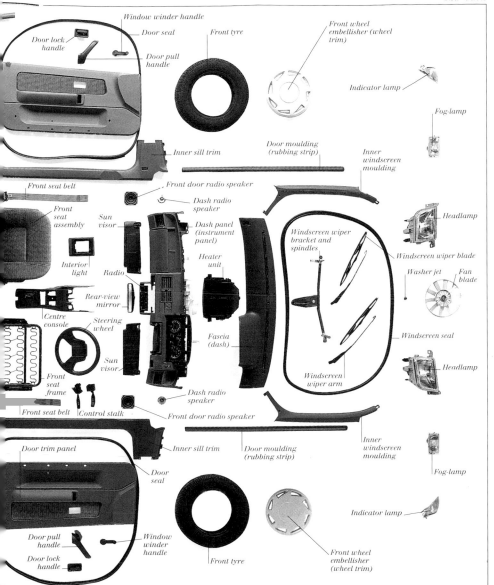

Window winder handle

Door seal

Front tyre

Front wheel embellisher (wheel trim)

Door lock handle

Door pull handle

Indicator lamp

Fog-lamp

Inner sill trim

Door moulding (rubbing strip)

Inner windscreen moulding

Front seat belt

Front door radio speaker

Dash radio speaker

Headlamp

Front seat assembly

Sun visor

Dash panel (instrument panel)

Windscreen wiper bracket and spindles

Windscreen wiper blade

Heater unit

Washer jet

Fan blade

Interior light

Radio

Centre console

Rear-view mirror

Steering wheel

Windscreen seal

Front seat frame

Sun visor

Fascia (dash)

Headlamp

Front seat belt

Control stalk

Dash radio speaker

Front door radio speaker

Windscreen wiper arm

Inner windscreen moulding

Door trim panel

Inner sill trim

Door moulding (rubbing strip)

Fog-lamp

Door seal

Door pull handle

Window winder handle

Indicator lamp

Door lock handle

Front tyre

Front wheel embellisher (wheel trim)

Hybrid car

THERE HAVE BEEN SEVERAL proposed alternatives to conventional petrol- or diesel-powered cars, including cars that use solar or battery power. The object is to lower harmful emissions and conserve natural resources. One of the alternatives already in production is the hybrid car. A hybrid vehicle uses two or more fuels. Examples include diesel-electric trains and mopeds. The latter combine the power of a petrol engine with pedal power. In a hybrid car, petrol consumption is reduced by the provision of additional power by an electric motor during acceleration. The motor is driven by power from on-board batteries that are recharged by an engine-driven generator when the car is decelerating or cruising. Some hybrid cars transfer energy from the wheels to a flywheel during braking. The flywheel drives the generator, which recharges the batteries.

HONDA INSIGHT

Aerial

Aerodynamic roof

Windscreen

Wing mirror

Plastic front wings

Front air dam

Plastic bumper

Aerodynamic underside components

Cooling intake

Aluminium bonnet

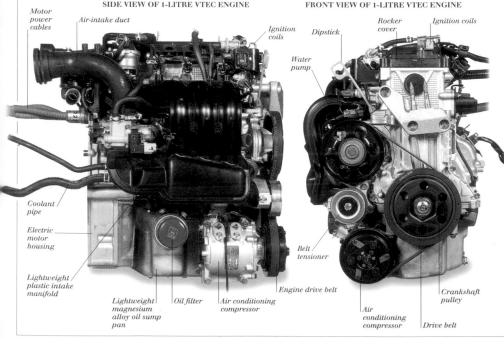

SIDE VIEW OF 1-LITRE VTEC ENGINE

Motor power cables

Air-intake duct

Ignition coils

Coolant pipe

Electric motor housing

Lightweight plastic intake manifold

Lightweight magnesium alloy oil sump pan

Oil filter

Air conditioning compressor

FRONT VIEW OF 1-LITRE VTEC ENGINE

Dipstick

Rocker cover

Ignition coils

Water pump

Belt tensioner

Engine drive belt

Air conditioning compressor

Crankshaft pulley

Drive belt

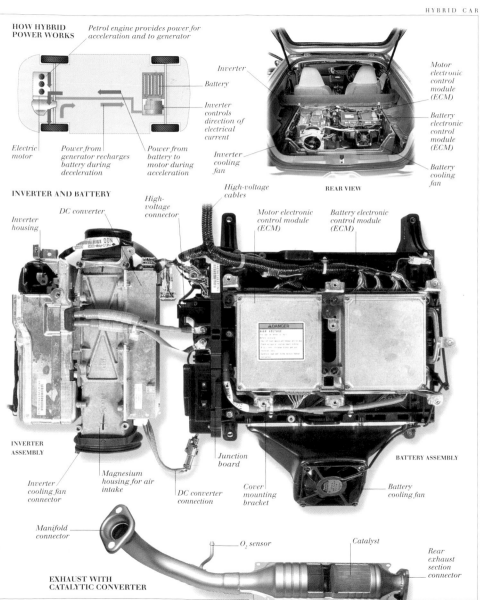

HOW HYBRID POWER WORKS

Petrol engine provides power for acceleration and to generator

Electric motor

Power from generator recharges battery during deceleration

Power from battery to motor during acceleration

Inverter

Battery

Inverter controls direction of electrical current

Inverter cooling fan

High-voltage cables

REAR VIEW

Motor electronic control module (ECM)

Battery electronic control module (ECM)

Battery cooling fan

INVERTER AND BATTERY

DC converter

Inverter housing

High-voltage connector

Motor electronic control module (ECM)

Battery electronic control module (ECM)

ADANGER
HIGH VOLTAGE

INVERTER ASSEMBLY

Inverter cooling fan connector

Magnesium housing for air intake

DC converter connection

Junction board

Cover mounting bracket

BATTERY ASSEMBLY

Battery cooling fan

Manifold connector

O₂ sensor

Catalyst

Rear exhaust section connector

EXHAUST WITH CATALYTIC CONVERTER

Racing cars

SINCE MOTORING BEGAN, racing cars have been a major focus of innovation in car design. Features that are now commonplace, such as disc brakes, turbochargers, and even safety belts, were used first on competition cars. Research into racing cars has contributed to a new understanding of engine performance, aerodynamics, and tyre adhesion, and has led to the development of ultra-light materials such as carbon-fibre for car bodies. A modern McLaren Formula One car has a low, streamlined body and an open cockpit but, unlike its forerunner, it also has front and rear wings that push the wheels firmly on to the track, huge tyres for extra grip, and electronic sensors that continually relay information to the pits about the car's performance.

72° V10 ENGINE

Fuel injection trumpet guard

Cam cover

Gearbox fixing stud

Water and oil pump assembly

Mercedes-Benz

Harmonically-tuned exhaust system

Cylinder head

Stressed cylinder block

BACK VIEW OF MCLAREN MERCEDES MP4-13

Upper flap

Grooved racing tyre

Warning light

Half-shaft

West

BRIDGESTONE

Rear wing end-plate

One-piece side pod and engine cover

Side pod air outlet

Diffuser

Exhaust pipe

Differential

Engine air intake

On-board TV mini-camera

Head rest

SIDE VIEW OF MCLAREN MERCEDES MP4-13

Engine cover

Winglet

Rear wing end-plate

LOCTITE

CAMOZZI

WARSTEIN

BRIDGESTONE

Alloy wheel

Wheel nut

POTENZA

ENKEI

Mobil 1

Mercedes-Benz

Hakkinen

BOSS
HUGO BOSS

E

West

We

Side pod

OVERHEAD VIEW OF MCLAREN MERCEDES MP4-13

Front wing end-plate

Front wing

Nose cover

Lower wishbone

Front brake duct

Grooved racing tyre

Rear-view mirror

Driver's radio aerial

Upper wishbone

Turning vane

One-piece side pod and engine cover

Radius arm

Rear wing endplate

Slot

Upper flap

Rear wing upper mainplane

Safety harness

Driver protection

Grooved racing tyre

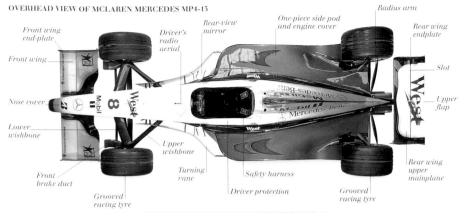

FRONT VIEW OF MCLAREN MERCEDES MP4-13

Rear wing upper mainplane

Engine air intake

Rear-view mirror

Driver's radio aerial

Radiator air intake

Front brake duct

Upper wishbone

Grooved racing tyre

Lower wishbone

End-plate

Rear-view mirror

Forward rollover structure

Steering link

Wing supports

Front wing

Driver's radio aerial

Alloy wheel

High nose

Turning vane

Wheel nut

Front wing end-plate

Mobil

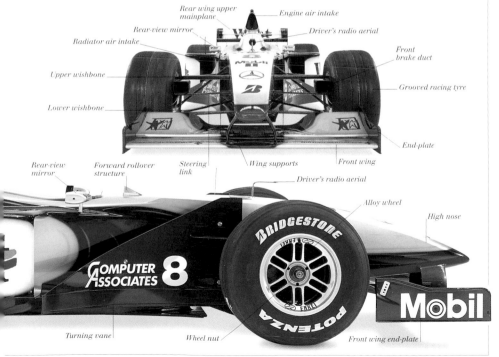

Bicycle anatomy

THE BICYCLE IS A TWO-WHEELED, light-weight machine, which is propelled by human power. It is efficient, cheap, easily manufactured, and one of the world's most popular forms of transport. The first pedal-driven bicycle was built in Scotland in 1839. Since then the basic design – of a frame, wheels, brakes, handlebars, and saddle – has been gradually improved, with the addition of a chain, gear system, and pneumatic tyres (tyres inflated with air). The recent invention of the mountain bike (all-terrain bike) has been an important development. With its strong, rugged frame, wide tyres, and 21 gears, a mountain bike enables riders to reach rough and hilly areas that were previously inaccessible to cyclists.

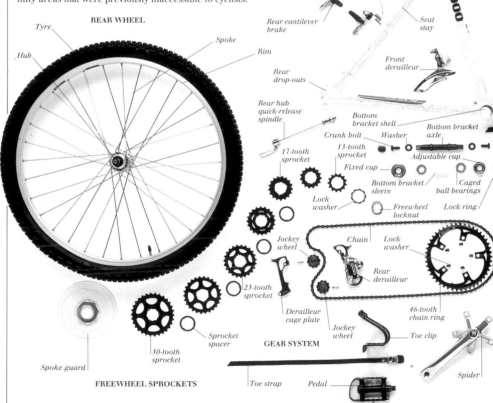

Saddle

Seat post

Seat post quick-release bolt

Cable guide

Straddle wire

Seat tube

Seat stay

REAR WHEEL

Tyre

Spoke

Hub

Rim

Rear cantilever brake

Rear drop-outs

Front derailleur

Rear hub quick-release spindle

Bottom bracket shell

Crank bolt

Washer

Bottom bracket axle

13-tooth sprocket

Adjustable cup

17-tooth sprocket

Fixed cup

Bottom bracket sleeve

Caged ball bearings

Lock washer

Freewheel locknut

Lock ring

Jockey wheel

Chain

Lock washer

Rear derailleur

23-tooth sprocket

Derailleur cage plate

Jockey wheel

46-tooth chain ring

Toe clip

Sprocket spacer

GEAR SYSTEM

30-tooth sprocket

Spoke guard

Spider

FREEWHEEL SPROCKETS

Toe strap

Pedal

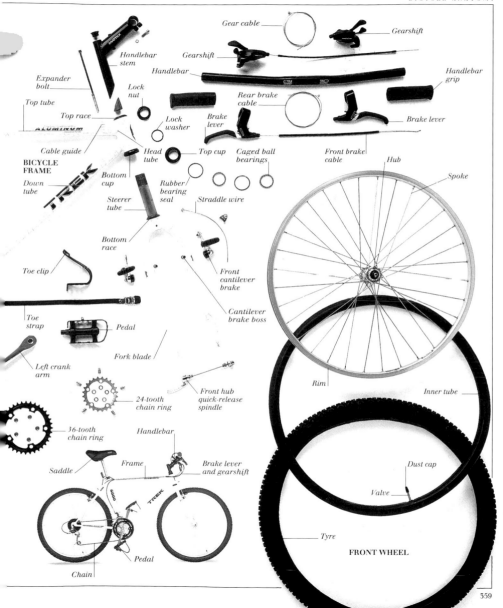

Gear cable

Gearshift

Handlebar
stem

Gearshift

Handlebar

Handlebar
grip

Expander
bolt

Lock
nut

Rear brake
cable

Top tube

Brake
lever

Brake lever

Top race

ALUMINUM

Lock
washer

Cable guide

Head
tube

Top cup

Caged ball
bearings

Front brake
cable

Hub

BICYCLE
FRAME

Spoke

Down
tube

Bottom
cup

Rubber
bearing
seal

Straddle wire

Steerer
tube

Bottom
race

Toe clip

Front
cantilever
brake

Cantilever
brake boss

Toe
strap

Pedal

Fork blade

Rim

Inner tube

Left crank
arm

24-tooth
chain ring

Front hub
quick-release
spindle

36-tooth
chain ring

Handlebar

Saddle

Frame

Brake lever
and gearshift

Dust cap

Valve

Tyre

Pedal

FRONT WHEEL

Chain

Bicycles

ALTHOUGH ALL BICYCLES are made up of the same
basic components, they can vary greatly in design. A
racing bike, such as the Eddy Merckx model, with its
light frame and steep head- and seat-angles, is built for
speed. Its design forces the rider to adopt the "aerotuck",
a crouched, aerodynamic position. While a touring bike
resembles the racing bike in many respects, it is designed
for comfort and stability on long-distance journeys.
Touring bikes are characterized by more relaxed frame
angles, heavy chain stays that support the rear panniers,
and a long wheelbase (the distance between the wheel
axles) for reliable handling. All-round bicycles, known
as "hybrids", combine the light weight and speed of sports
bikes with the rugged durability of mountain bikes (see
pp. 358-359). Bicycles that are not designed for conventional
road use include time-trial bikes, which have a short
head tube, sloping top tube, "aero" handlebars, and
aerodynamic tubing. Most Human Powered Vehicles
(HPVs) are recumbents – the rider has a recumbent
position – which maximize power output and minimize
drag (resistance). Essential to the safety of all
riders are helmets, and both front and rear
lights; locks protect against theft.

FRONT AND REAR LIGHTS

HELMET

Hard outer shell

Red rear light

Air vent

White front light

Polystyrene padding

Quick-release strap

EDDY MERCKX RACING BICYCLE

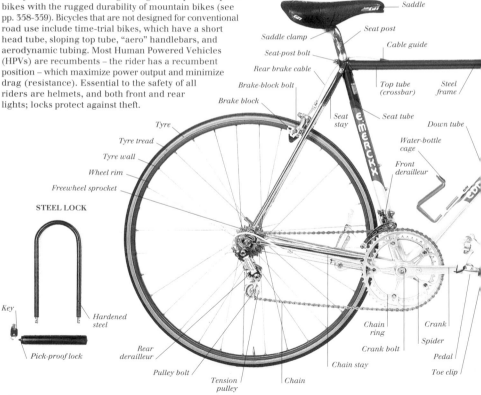

Saddle

Saddle clamp

Seat post

Cable guide

Seat-post bolt

Rear brake cable

Brake-block bolt

Brake block

Top tube (crossbar)

Steel frame

Seat stay

Seat tube

Down tube

Tyre

Tyre tread

Tyre wall

Wheel rim

Freewheel sprocket

Water-bottle cage

Front derailleur

STEEL LOCK

Key

Hardened steel

Pick-proof lock

Rear derailleur

Pulley bolt

Tension pulley

Chain

Chain ring

Crank

Spider

Crank bolt

Pedal

Chain stay

Toe clip

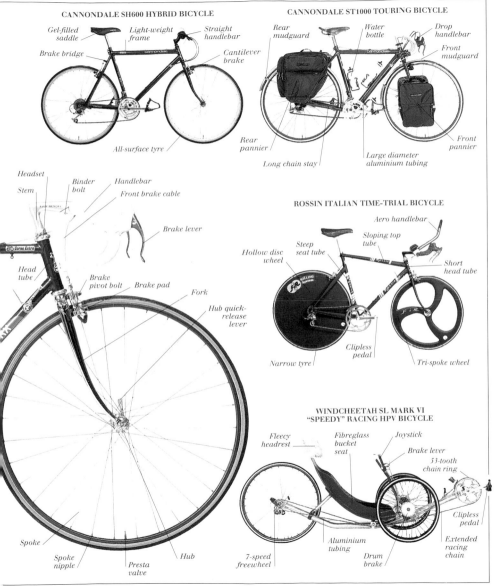

CANNONDALE SH600 HYBRID BICYCLE

Gel-filled saddle

Light-weight frame

Straight handlebar

Brake bridge

Cantilever brake

All-surface tyre

CANNONDALE ST1000 TOURING BICYCLE

Rear mudguard

Water bottle

Drop handlebar

Front mudguard

Rear pannier

Front pannier

Long chain stay

Large diameter aluminium tubing

Headset

Binder bolt

Handlebar

Stem

Front brake cable

Brake lever

Head tube

Brake pivot bolt

Brake pad

Fork

Hub quick-release lever

Spoke

Spoke nipple

Presta valve

Hub

ROSSIN ITALIAN TIME-TRIAL BICYCLE

Aero handlebar

Sloping top tube

Steep seat tube

Hollow disc wheel

Short head tube

Clipless pedal

Narrow tyre

Tri-spoke wheel

WINDCHEETAH SL MARK VI "SPEEDY" RACING HPV BICYCLE

Fleecy headrest

Fibreglass bucket seat

Joystick

Brake lever

53-tooth chain ring

Clipless pedal

7-speed freewheel

Aluminium tubing

Drum brake

Extended racing chain

The motorcycle

THE MOTORCYCLE HAS EVOLVED from a motorized cycle – a basic bicycle with an engine – into a sophisticated, high-performance machine. In 1901, the Werner brothers established the most viable location for the engine by positioning it low in the centre of the chassis (see pp. 364-365): the new Werner became the basis for the modern motorcycle. Motorcycles are used for many purposes – for commuting, delivering messages, touring, and racing – and different machines have been developed according to the demands of different types of riders. The Vespa scooter, for instance, which is small-wheeled, economical, and easy-to-ride, was designed to meet the needs of the commuter. Sidecars provided transport for the family until the arrival of cheap cars caused their popularity to decline. Enthusiast riders generally favour larger capacity machines that are capable of greater performance and offer more comfort. Four-cylinder machines have been common since the Honda CB750 appeared in 1969. Despite advances in motorcycle technology, many riders are attracted to the traditional looks of motorcycles like the twin-cylinder Harley-Davidson. The Harley-Davidson Glides exploit the style of the classic American V-twin engine, where the cylinders are placed in a V-formation.

1901 WERNER MOTORCYCLE

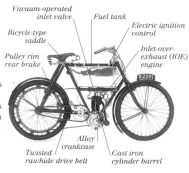

Vacuum-operated inlet valve · Fuel tank · Electric ignition control · Bicycle-type saddle · Inlet-over-exhaust (IOE) engine · Pulley rim rear brake · A2201 · Alloy crankcase · Twisted rawhide drive belt · Cast iron cylinder barrel

1988 HARLEY-DAVIDSON FLHS ELECTRA GLIDE

1965 BMW R/60 WITH 1952 STEIB CHAIR

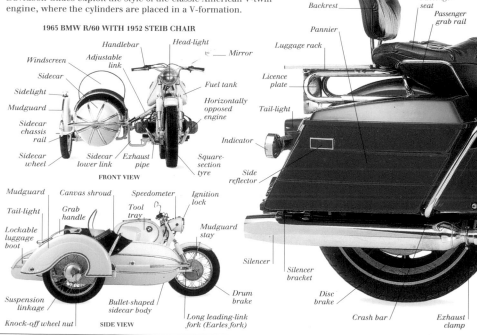

Backrest · Passenger seat · Passenger grab rail · Pannier · Luggage rack · Licence plate · Tail-light · Indicator · Side reflector · Silencer · Silencer bracket · Disc brake · Crash bar · Exhaust clamp

Handlebar · Head-light · Mirror · Windscreen · Adjustable link · Sidecar · Fuel tank · Sidelight · Horizontally opposed engine · Mudguard · Sidecar chassis rail · Sidecar wheel · Sidecar lower link · Exhaust pipe · Square-section tyre · FRONT VIEW

Mudguard · Canvas shroud · Speedometer · Ignition lock · Tail-light · Grab handle · Tool tray · Lockable luggage boot · Mudguard stay · Suspension linkage · Bullet-shaped sidecar body · Drum brake · Knock-off wheel nut · SIDE VIEW · Long leading-link fork (Earles fork)

1969 HONDA CB750

1963 VESPA GRAND SPORT 160 MARK 1

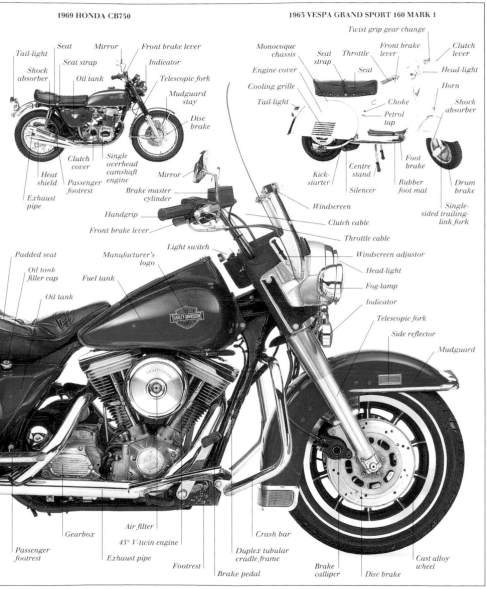

Tail-light
Seat
Mirror
Front brake lever
Shock absorber
Seat strap
Indicator
Oil tank
Telescopic fork
Mudguard stay
Disc brake
Clutch cover
Single overhead camshaft engine
Mirror
Heat shield
Passenger footrest
Brake master cylinder
Exhaust pipe
Handgrip
Front brake lever
Light switch

Twist grip gear change
Monocoque chassis
Seat strap
Throttle
Front brake lever
Clutch lever
Engine cover
Seat
Head-light
Cooling grille
Horn
Tail-light
Choke
Shock absorber
Petrol tap
Kick-starter
Centre stand
Foot brake
Silencer
Rubber foot mat
Drum brake
Windscreen
Single-sided trailing-link fork
Clutch cable
Throttle cable
Windscreen adjustor
Head-light
Fog-lamp
Indicator
Telescopic fork
Side reflector
Mudguard

Padded seat
Oil tank filler cap
Oil tank
Manufacturer's logo
Fuel tank

Passenger footrest
Gearbox
Air filter
45° V-twin engine
Exhaust pipe
Footrest
Brake pedal
Crash bar
Duplex tubular cradle frame
Brake calliper
Disc brake
Cast alloy wheel

The motorcycle chassis

THE MOTORCYCLE CHASSIS is the main "body" of the motorcycle, to which the engine is attached. Consisting of the frame, wheels, suspension, and brakes, the chassis performs various functions. The frame, which is built from steel or alloy, keeps the wheels in line to maintain the handling of the motorcycle, and serves as a structure for mounting other components. The engine and gearbox unit is bolted into place, while items such as the seat, the mudguards, and the fairing are more easily removable. Suspension cushions the rider from irregularities in the road surface. In most suspension systems, coil springs controlled by an oil damper separate the main mass of the motorcycle from the wheels. At the front, the spring and damper are usually incorporated in a telescopic fork; the rear employs a pivoted swingarm. The suspension also helps to retain maximum contact between the tyres and the road, necessary to effective braking and steering. Drum brakes were common until the 1970s, but modern motorcycles use disc brakes, which are more powerful.

1985 HONDA VF750 WITH BODYWORK

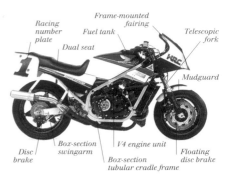

Racing number plate
Frame-mounted fairing
Fuel tank
Telescopic fork
Dual seat
Mudguard
Disc brake
Box-section swingarm
V4 engine unit
Floating disc brake
Box-section tubular cradle frame

1985 HONDA VF750 WITH BODYWORK REMOVED

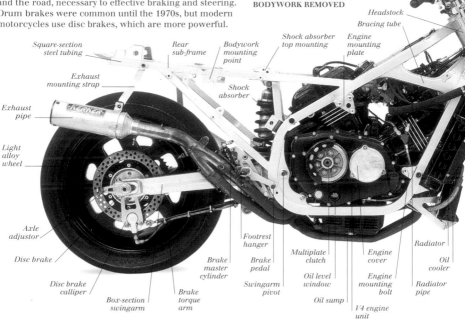

Square-section steel tubing
Rear sub-frame
Bodywork mounting point
Shock absorber top mounting
Engine mounting plate
Brake master cylinder
Headstock
Bracing tube
Exhaust mounting strap
Shock absorber
Exhaust pipe
Light alloy wheel
Axle adjustor
Disc brake
Disc brake calliper
Box-section swingarm
Brake master cylinder
Brake torque arm
Footrest hanger
Brake pedal
Swingarm pivot
Multiplate clutch
Oil level window
Oil sump
Engine cover
Engine mounting bolt
V4 engine unit
Radiator
Oil cooler
Radiator pipe

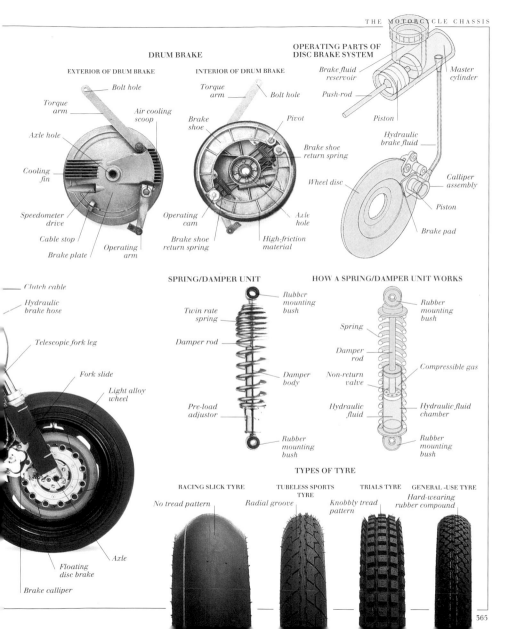

DRUM BRAKE

OPERATING PARTS OF DISC BRAKE SYSTEM

EXTERIOR OF DRUM BRAKE

Bolt hole
Torque arm
Air cooling scoop
Axle hole
Cooling fin
Speedometer drive
Cable stop
Brake plate
Operating arm

INTERIOR OF DRUM BRAKE

Torque arm
Bolt hole
Brake shoe
Pivot
Brake shoe return spring
Wheel disc
Operating cam
Axle hole
Brake shoe return spring
High-friction material

Brake fluid reservoir
Master cylinder
Push-rod
Piston
Hydraulic brake fluid
Calliper assembly
Piston
Brake pad

Clutch cable
Hydraulic brake hose
Telescopic fork leg
Fork slide
Light alloy wheel
Floating disc brake
Axle
Brake calliper

SPRING/DAMPER UNIT

Rubber mounting bush
Twin rate spring
Damper rod
Damper body
Pre-load adjustor
Rubber mounting bush

HOW A SPRING/DAMPER UNIT WORKS

Rubber mounting bush
Spring
Damper rod
Non-return valve
Compressible gas
Hydraulic fluid
Hydraulic fluid chamber
Rubber mounting bush

TYPES OF TYRE

RACING SLICK TYRE
No tread pattern

TUBELESS SPORTS TYRE
Radial groove

TRIALS TYRE
Knobbly tread pattern

GENERAL-USE TYRE
Hard-wearing rubber compound

365

Motorcycle engines

MOTORCYCLE ENGINES must be light-weight and compact, and have a good power output. They have between one and six cylinders, can be cooled by air or water, and the capacity of the combustion chamber varies from 49cc (cubic centimetres) to 1500cc. Two types of internal combustion engine are common: the four-stroke, which is used in cars (see pp. 342-343), and the two-stroke. A basic two-stroke engine has only three moving parts – the crankshaft, the connecting rod, and the piston – but the power output is high. The engine fires every two strokes (rather than every four), giving a "power stroke" every revolution (see p. 343). Power is conveyed from the engine to the rear wheel by the transmission system. This usually consists of a clutch, a gearbox, and a final drive system. Clutches are multiplate devices, which run in oil. Gearboxes have five or six speeds and are operated by foot pedal. Shaft and belt drive systems are used in some cases, but chain drive to the rear wheel is most common.

EXTERIOR OF STANDARD TWO-STROKE ENGINE

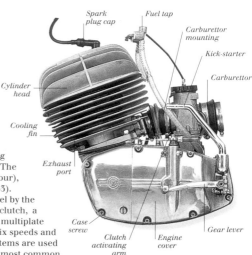

Spark plug cap
Fuel tap
Carburettor mounting
Kick-starter
Carburettor
Cylinder head
Cooling fin
Exhaust port
Case screw
Clutch activating arm
Engine cover
Gear lever

TRANSMISSION SYSTEM

GEARBOX

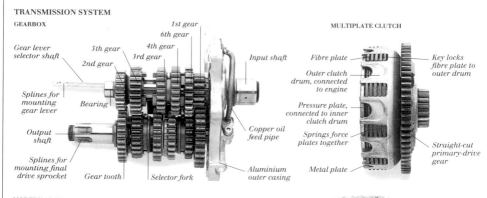

Gear lever selector shaft
5th gear
2nd gear
4th gear
3rd gear
1st gear
6th gear
Input shaft
Splines for mounting gear lever
Bearing
Output shaft
Splines for mounting final drive sprocket
Gear tooth
Selector fork
Copper oil feed pipe
Aluminium outer casing

MULTIPLATE CLUTCH

Fibre plate
Outer clutch drum, connected to engine
Pressure plate, connected to inner clutch drum
Springs force plates together
Metal plate
Key locks fibre plate to outer drum
Straight-cut primary-drive gear

MODERN "O RING" DRIVE CHAIN

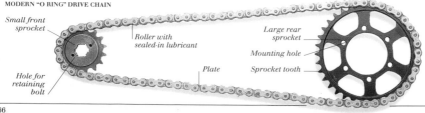

Small front sprocket
Roller with sealed-in lubricant
Large rear sprocket
Mounting hole
Plate
Sprocket tooth
Hole for retaining bolt

VELOCETTE OVERHEAD VALVE (OHV) ENGINE

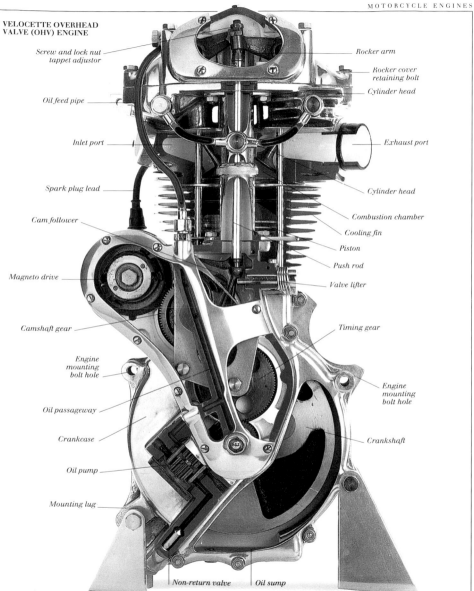

Screw and lock nut tappet adjustor

Oil feed pipe

Inlet port

Spark plug lead

Cam follower

Magneto drive

Camshaft gear

Engine mounting bolt hole

Oil passageway

Crankcase

Oil pump

Mounting lug

Rocker arm

Rocker cover retaining bolt

Cylinder head

Exhaust port

Cylinder head

Combustion chamber

Cooling fin

Piston

Push rod

Valve lifter

Timing gear

Engine mounting bolt hole

Crankshaft

Non-return valve

Oil sump

Competition motorcycles

THERE ARE MANY TYPES of motorcycle sport and in each, a specialist machine has evolved to perform to specific requirements. Races take place on roads or tracks or "off-road", in fields, dirt tracks, and even the desert. "Grand Prix" world championships in road-racing are contested by three classes: 125cc, 250cc two-strokes; the top class of 500cc two-strokes; and 900cc four-stroke machines. The latest racing sidecars have more in common with racing cars than motorcycles. The rider and passenger operate within an all-enclosing, aerodynamic fairing. The Suzuki RGV500 shown here, like other Grand Prix machines, carries advertising, which helps to cover the cost of developing motorcycle technology. In Speedway, which originated in the US in 1902, motorcycles operate without brakes or a gearbox. Off-road competition motorcycles have less emphasis on high power output. In Motocross, for example, which is held on rough terrain, they must have high ground clearance, flexible long-travel suspension, and tyres with a chunky tread pattern.

1992 HUSQVARNA MOTOCROSS TC610

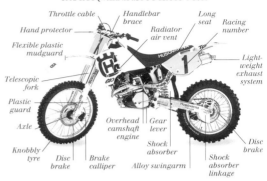

Throttle cable
Handlebar brace
Long seat
Racing number
Hand protector
Radiator air vent
Flexible plastic mudguard
Light-weight exhaust system
Telescopic fork
Plastic guard
Axle
Overhead camshaft engine
Gear lever
Disc brake
Knobbly tyre
Disc brake
Brake calliper
Shock absorber
Alloy swingarm
Shock absorber linkage

1992 SUZUKI RGV500
SIDE VIEW

Exhaust pipe
Racing number
Air vent
One-piece seat and tail unit
Shock absorber
Minimal seat padding
Arched alloy swingarm

Exhaust pipe
Vent
Handlebar
Footrest
Rear brake pedal
Drive chain
Wide, slick tyre
REAR VIEW

Exhaust pipe
Silencer
Shock absorber mounting
Three-spoke alloy wheel
Exhaust pipe
Axle adjustor
Disc brake
Rear brake calliper
Slick racing tyre
Drive chain
Footrest
Brake pedal
Disc brake master cylinder
Light-weight alloy frame

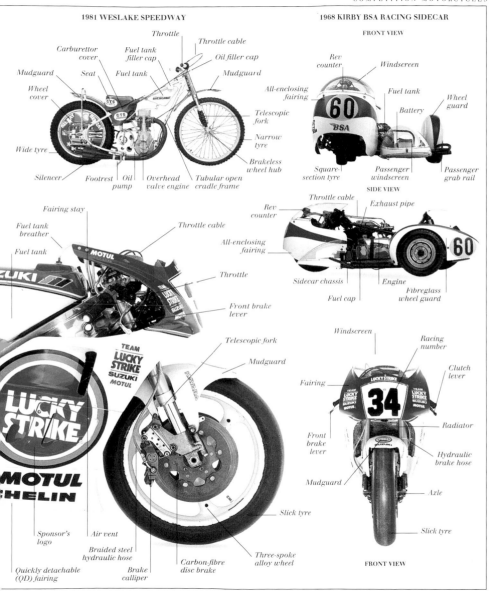

1981 WESLAKE SPEEDWAY

Throttle
Throttle cable
Carburettor cover
Fuel tank filler cap
Oil filler cap
Mudguard
Seat
Fuel tank
Mudguard
Wheel cover
Telescopic fork
Narrow tyre
Wide tyre
Brakeless wheel hub
Silencer
Footrest
Oil pump
Overhead valve engine
Tubular open cradle frame

Fairing stay
Throttle cable
Fuel tank breather
Fuel tank
Throttle
Front brake lever
Telescopic fork
Mudguard
LUCKY STRIKE
SUZUKI
MOTUL
MICHELIN
Sponsor's logo
Air vent
Braided steel hydraulic hose
Slick tyre
Quickly detachable (QD) fairing
Brake calliper
Carbon-fibre disc brake
Three-spoke alloy wheel

1968 KIRBY BSA RACING SIDECAR

FRONT VIEW

Rev counter
Windscreen
Fuel tank
Wheel guard
All-enclosing fairing
Battery
60
BSA
Square-section tyre
Passenger windscreen
Passenger grab rail

SIDE VIEW

Throttle cable
Exhaust pipe
Rev counter
All-enclosing fairing
60
Sidecar chassis
Engine
Fibreglass wheel guard
Fuel cap

Windscreen
Racing number
Clutch lever
Fairing
34
Radiator
Front brake lever
Hydraulic brake hose
Mudguard
Axle
Slick tyre

FRONT VIEW

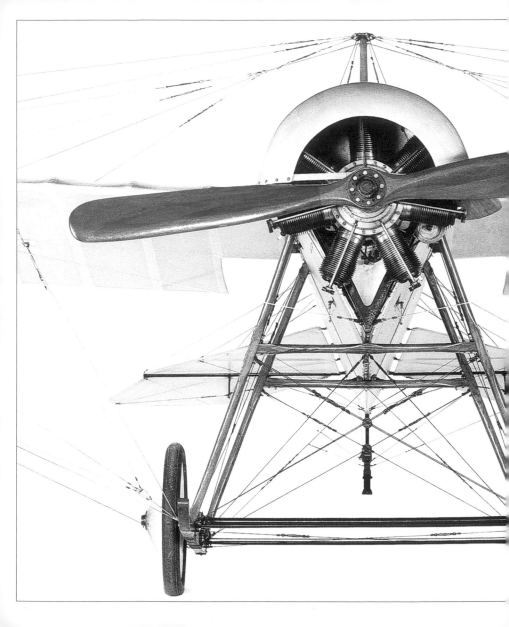

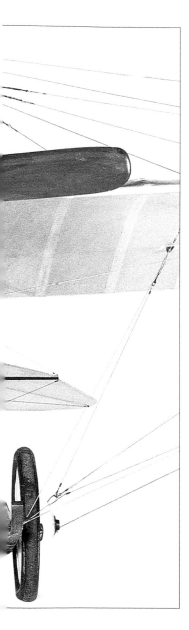

SEA AND AIR

SHIPS OF GREECE AND ROME 372
VIKING SHIPS 374
MEDIEVAL WARSHIPS AND TRADERS 376
THE EXPANSION OF SAIL 378
A SHIP OF THE LINE 380
RIGGING 382
SAILS 384
MOORING AND ANCHORING 386
ROPES AND KNOTS 388
PADDLEWHEELS AND PROPELLERS 390
ANATOMY OF AN IRON SHIP 392
THE BATTLESHIP 394
FRIGATES AND SUBMARINES 396
PIONEERS OF FLIGHT 398
EARLY MONOPLANES 400
BIPLANES AND TRIPLANES 402
WORLD WAR I AIRCRAFT 404
EARLY PASSENGER AIRCRAFT 406
WORLD WAR II AIRCRAFT 408
MODERN PISTON AERO-ENGINES 410
MODERN JETLINERS 1 412
MODERN JETLINERS 2 414
SUPERSONIC JETLINERS 416
JET ENGINES 418
MODERN MILITARY AIRCRAFT 420
HELICOPTERS 422
LIGHT AIRCRAFT 424
GLIDERS, HANG-GLIDERS, AND MICROLIGHTS 426

Ships of Greece and Rome

ROMAN ANCHOR

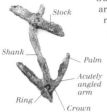

Stock

Shank

Palm

Acutely angled arm

Ring

Crown

IN THE EXPANSIVE EMPIRES OF GREECE AND ROME, powerful fleets were needed for battle, trade, and communication. Greek galleys were powered by a sail and many oars. A new armament, the embolos (ram), was fitted on to the galley bow. As ramming duels required fast and manoeuvrable boats, extra rows of oarsmen were added, culminating in the trireme. During the fifth and fourth centuries B.C., the trireme dominated the Mediterranean. It was powered by 170 oarsmen, rowing with one oar each. The oarsmen were ranged on three levels, as the model opposite shows. The trireme also carried archers and soldiers for boarding. Galleys were pulled out of the water when not in use, and were kept in dockyard ship-sheds. The merchant ships of the Greeks and Romans were mighty vessels too. The full-bodied Roman corbita, for example, could hold up to 400 tons and carried a cargo of spices, gems, silk, and animals. The construction of these boats was based on a stout hull with planking secured by mortice and tenon. Some of these ships embarked on long voyages, sailing even as far as India. To make them easier to steer, corbitas set a fore sail called an "artemon". It flew from a forward-leaning mast that was a forerunner of the long bowsprits carried by the great clipper ships of the 19th century.

ATTIC VASE SHOWING A GALLEY

Roband (rope band)

Ceruchi (lift)

ROMAN CORBITA

Double halyard

Heraldic device

Bullseye

Fore mast

Ring

Antenna (yard)

Buntline

Ruden (brail line)

Brace

Artemon (fore sail)

Fore stay

Oculus (eye)

Anchor

Tabling

Sheet

Bolt rope

Prow

Windlass

Scala (ladder)

Bronze mast truck

Keraia (yard)

Catena (riding bitt)

Kalos (brailing rope)

Ancorale (anchor rope; anchor rode)

Kubernetes (helmsman)

Mast

Sternpost

Hatch board

Embolos (ram; beak)

Pedalia (twin rudder)

Deck beam

Ophthalmos (eye)

Oar port sleeve

Zosteres (rubbing strake)

Kope (oar)

Cargo hold

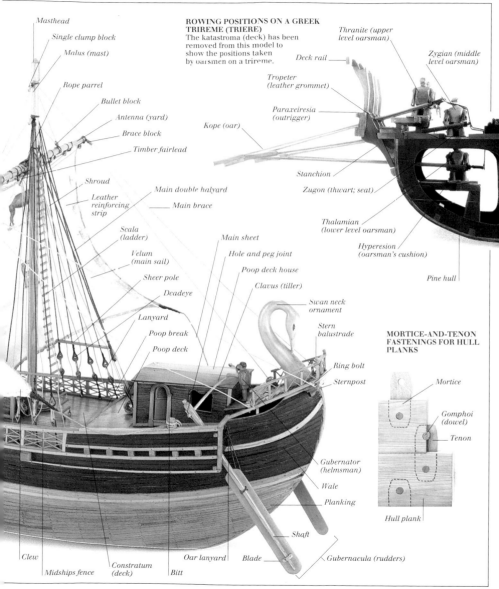

Masthead

Single clump block

Malus (mast)

Rope parrel

Bullet block

Antenna (yard)

Brace block

Timber fairlead

Shroud

Leather reinforcing strip

Main double halyard

Main brace

Scala (ladder)

Velum (main sail)

Main sheet

Hole and peg joint

Poop deck house

Sheer pole

Deadeye

Clavus (tiller)

Lanyard

Swan neck ornament

Poop break

Stern balustrade

Poop deck

Ring bolt

Sternpost

Clew

Midships fence

Constratum (deck)

Bitt

Oar lanyard

Blade

Gubernator (helmsman)

Wale

Planking

Shaft

Gubernacula (rudders)

ROWING POSITIONS ON A GREEK TRIREME (TRIERE)
The katastroma (deck) has been removed from this model to show the positions taken by oarsmen on a trireme.

Thranite (upper level oarsman)

Zygian (middle level oarsman)

Deck rail

Tropeter (leather grommet)

Paraxeiresia (outrigger)

Kope (oar)

Stanchion

Zugon (thwart; seat)

Thalamian (lower level oarsman)

Hyperesion (oarsman's cushion)

Pine hull

MORTICE-AND-TENON FASTENINGS FOR HULL PLANKS

Mortice

Gomphoi (dowel)

Tenon

Hull plank

Viking ships

IN THE DARK AGES and early medieval times, the longships of Scandinavia were one of the most feared sights for people of northern Europe. The Vikings launched raids from Scandinavia every summer in longships equipped with a single steering oar on the right, or "steerboard", side (hence "starboard"). A longship had one row of oars on each side and a single sail. The hull had clinker (overlapping) planks. Prowheads adorned fighting ships during campaigns of war. The sailing longship was also used for local coastal travel. The karv below was probably built as transport for an important family, while the smaller faering (top right) was a rowing boat only. The fleet of William of Normandy that invaded England in 1066 owed much to the Viking boatbuilding tradition, and has been depicted in the Bayeux Tapestry (above). Seals used by port towns and royal courts through the ages provide an excellent record of contemporary ship design. The seal opposite shows how ships changed from the Viking period to the end of the Middle Ages. The introduction of the fighting platform – the castle – and the addition of extra masts and sails changed the character of the medieval ship. Note also that the steering oar has been replaced by a centred rudder.

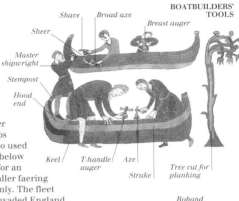

BOATBUILDERS' TOOLS

Shave
Broad axe
Breast auger
Sheer
Master shipwright
Stempost
Hood end
Keel
T-handle auger
Axe
Strake
Tree cut for planking

Roband

Leather diagonal reinforcement

Square sail of homespun yarn

Leech (leach)

VIKING KARV (COASTER)

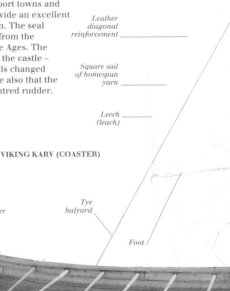

Zoomorphic head
Eye
Tooth

Braiding
Serpentine neck
Lozenge-shaped recess
Rectangular cross-band

Snake-tail ornament

Sternpost

Boss (rudder pivot)

DRAGON PROWHEAD

Steering oar (side rudder)

Tiller

Tye halyard

Foot

Oar

Starboard (steerboard) side

Keel

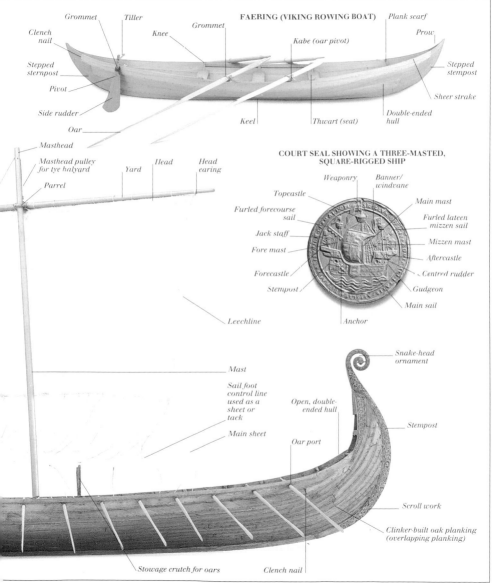

FAERING (VIKING ROWING BOAT)

Grommet
Tiller
Clench nail
Knee
Grommet
Plank scarf
Prow
Kabe (oar pivot)
Stepped sternpost
Stepped stempost
Pivot
Side rudder
Sheer strake
Oar
Keel
Thwart (seat)
Double-ended hull

Masthead
Masthead pulley for tye halyard
Yard
Head
Head earing
Parrel

COURT SEAL SHOWING A THREE-MASTED, SQUARE-RIGGED SHIP

Weaponry
Banner/windvane
Topcastle
Main mast
Furled forecourse sail
Furled lateen mizzen sail
Jack staff
Fore mast
Mizzen mast
Aftercastle
Forecastle
Centred rudder
Stempost
Gudgeon
Main sail
Leechline
Anchor

Snake-head ornament
Mast
Sail foot control line used as a sheet or tack
Open, double-ended hull
Stempost
Main sheet
Oar port
Scroll work
Clinker-built oak planking (overlapping planking)
Stowage crutch for oars
Clench nail

Medieval warships and traders

FROM THE 16TH CENTURY, SHIPS WERE BUILT WITH A NEW FORM OF HULL, constructed from carvel (edge-to-edge) planking. Warships of the time, like King Henry VIII of England's Mary Rose, boasted awesome fire power. This ship carried both long-range cannon in bronze, and short-range, anti-personnel guns in iron. Elsewhere, ships took on a multiformity of shapes. Dhows transported slaves from East Africa to Arabia, their fore-and-aft rigged lateen sails allowing them to sail close to the wind around the lands of the Indian Ocean. The Chinese sailed to East Africa and Arabia in junks, trading goods that were carried in watertight compartments. New astronomical tools helped medieval sailors to find their way. Cross-staves and astrolabes were used to measure the altitude of the sun or stars. One of a choice of four cross-pieces was slid up or down the staff of the cross-stave – which was graduated in degrees of altitude – until its top aligned with the celestial body and its base with the horizon. The sighting rule of the astrolabe was simply lined up with a known body, and its altitude read from marks on the metal disc. With sundials, the sailor could use the shadow of the sun to show the time of day.

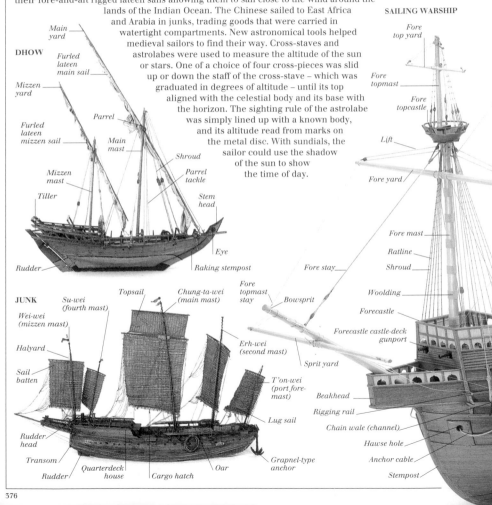

DHOW

Main yard

Furled lateen main sail

Mizzen yard

Furled lateen mizzen sail

Parrel

Main mast

Shroud

Parrel tackle

Mizzen mast

Tiller

Stem head

Rudder

Eye

Raking stempost

SAILING WARSHIP

Fore top yard

Fore topmast

Fore topcastle

Lift

Fore yard

Fore mast

Ratline

Shroud

Fore stay

Fore topmast stay

Bowsprit

Woolding

Forecastle

Forecastle castle-deck gunport

Sprit yard

Beakhead

Rigging rail

Chain wale (channel)

Hawse hole

Anchor cable

Stempost

JUNK

Su-wei (fourth mast)

Wei-wei (mizzen mast)

Halyard

Sail batten

Rudder head

Transom

Quarterdeck house

Rudder

Topsail

Chung-ta-wei (main mast)

Erh-wei (second mast)

T'on-wei (port fore-mast)

Lug sail

Cargo hatch

Oar

Grapnel-type anchor

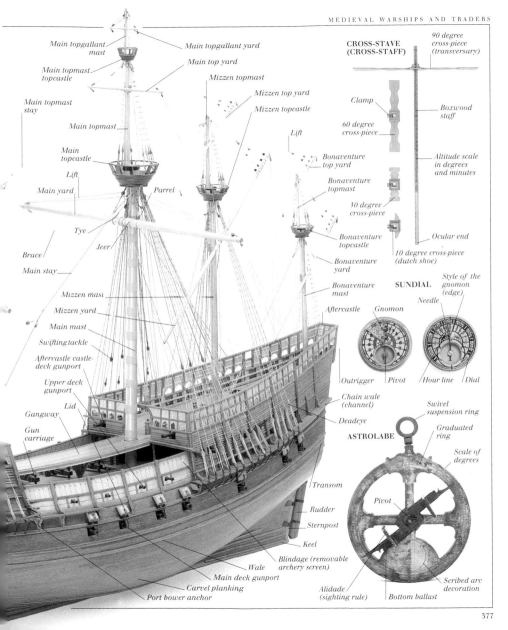

Main topgallant mast

Main topgallant yard

Main topmast topcastle

Main top yard

Mizzen topmast

Main topmast stay

Mizzen top yard

Mizzen topcastle

Main topmast

Lift

Main topcastle

Bonaventure top yard

Lift

Bonaventure topmast

Main yard

Parrel

Bonaventure topcastle

Tye

Bonaventure yard

Jeer

Brace

Bonaventure mast

Main stay

Mizzen mast

Aftercastle

Mizzen yard

Main mast

Swifting tackle

Aftercastle castle-deck gunport

Upper deck gunport

Lid

Outrigger

Gangway

Chain wale (channel)

Gun carriage

Deadeye

Transom

Rudder

Sternpost

Keel

Wale

Blindage (removable archery screen)

Main deck gunport

Carvel planking

Port bower anchor

CROSS-STAVE (CROSS-STAFF)

90 degree cross-piece (transversary)

Clamp

Boxwood staff

60 degree cross-piece

30 degree cross-piece

Altitude scale in degrees and minutes

Ocular end

10 degree cross-piece (dutch shoe)

SUNDIAL

Style of the gnomon (edge)

Gnomon

Needle

Pivot

Hour line

Dial

ASTROLABE

Swivel suspension ring

Graduated ring

Scale of degrees

Pivot

Alidade (sighting rule)

Bottom ballast

Scribed arc decoration

The expansion of sail

BY THE 18TH CENTURY, SAILING SHIPS had become fast and effective floating fortresses. The navies of the north European powers competed with each other by building heavily-armed fighting ships called "men-of-war". The distinctive round stern of the ship below, with its open gallery, balcony, and elaborate wood carving is typical of the period. Hulls around this time were semicircular in cross section, although many boat designers were soon to return to the V-shaped hulls used by the Vikings. Ships of the period carried more sail than ever before. A labyrinth of rigging supported the masts and yards from which the profusion of square sails were set. Ships grew higher, as extra masts were fitted above the lower mast, and the bowsprit became longer to allow the ship to carry staysails, spritsails, and jibsails. Ships went into battle in single file, so that broadsides from the multiple decks of guns would have maximum effect. Ships were classified by rates, the rating of a vessel depending on how many guns it had. A first rate ship had more than 100 guns. The guns fired solid round shot, usually made of iron.

Gilded truck

Main topgallant mast

Main topgallant shroud

WOODEN SAILING SHIP

Bolster

Trestle trees

Main topmast

Main topmast backstay

Mizzen topmast

Main topmast shroud

Mizzen topmast stay

Cap

Lift

Mizzen topmast shroud

Mizzen top

Main top

Main top rail

Mast-head

Mizzen yard

Hounds

Futtock shroud

BOW

Mizzen backstay

Vang

Fiddle block

Mizzen shroud

Mizzen stay

Brace

Mizzen mast

Lift

Taffrail

Mizzen shroud

Main shroud

Foot rope

Poop rail

Studding sail boom

Main top rail

Main mast

Studding sail yard (stuns'l yard)

Jacob's ladder

Rope preventer

Rudder chain

Rudder

Wash cant

Sternpost

Knee of the head

Hawse hole

Pintle strap

Gudgeon strap

Ship's wheel

Binnacle box

Keel

Channel

Chain

Step

Boat slide

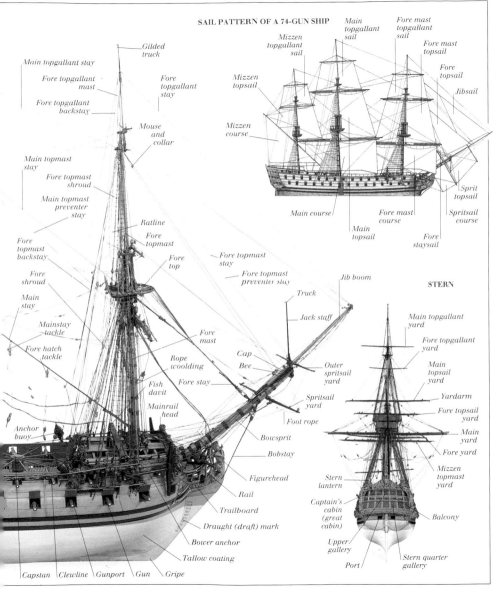

SAIL PATTERN OF A 74-GUN SHIP

Main topgallant sail

Fore mast topgallant sail

Mizzen topgallant sail

Fore mast topsail

Fore topsail

Mizzen topsail

Jibsail

Mizzen course

Main course

Fore mast course

Sprit topsail

Main topsail

Main topgallant stay

Fore topgallant stay

Gilded truck

Fore topgallant mast

Fore topgallant stay

Fore staysail

Spritsail course

Fore topgallant backstay

Mouse and collar

Main topmast stay

Fore topmast shroud

Main topmast preventer stay

Ratline

Fore topmast

Fore mast

Fore topmast stay

Jib boom

STERN

Fore topmast backstay

Fore top

Fore topmast preventer stay

Truck

Main topgallant yard

Fore shroud

Main stay

Jack staff

Fore topgallant yard

Mainstay tackle

Fore hatch tackle

Cap

Bee

Fore mast

Rope woolding

Fore stay

Outer spritsail yard

Main topsail yard

Yardarm

Fore topsail yard

Main yard

Fore yard

Spritsail yard

Foot rope

Fish davit

Mainrail head

Anchor buoy

Bowsprit

Bobstay

Figurehead

Rail

Trailboard

Draught (draft) mark

Bower anchor

Tallow coating

Stern lantern

Captain's cabin (great cabin)

Upper gallery

Port

Mizzen topmast yard

Balcony

Stern quarter gallery

Capstan | Clewline | Gunport | Gun | Gripe

379

A ship of the line

THE 74-GUN WOODEN SHIP WAS A MAINSTAY of British and French battlefleets in the late 18th and early 19th centuries. This "ship of the line" was heavy enough to fight with the most potent of rivals, yet nimble too. The length of such a ship was determined by the number of guns required for each deck, allowing enough room for crews to man them. The gun deck was about 52 m (170 ft) long. The decks had to be very strong to carry the weight of the guns. The deck planks have been removed on the vessel pictured below, to show just how close together the beams had to be to make the hull strong enough. Only timber with a perfect grain was used. The upper deck was open at the waist, but afore and abaft were officers' cabins. The forecastle and quarterdeck carried light guns and acted as platforms for working rigging and for reconnaissance. The ship's longboats (launches) were carried on booms between the gangways.

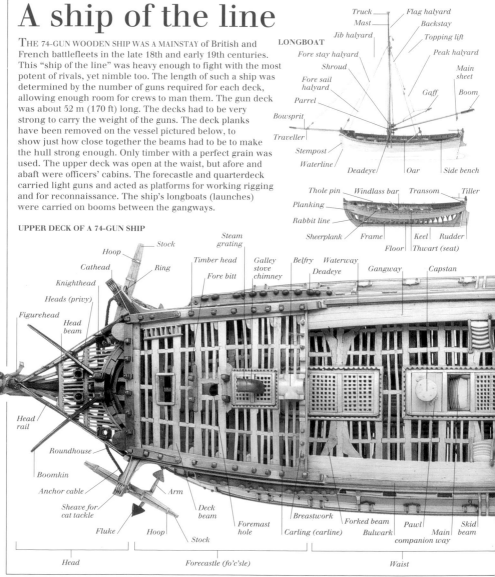

LONGBOAT

UPPER DECK OF A 74-GUN SHIP

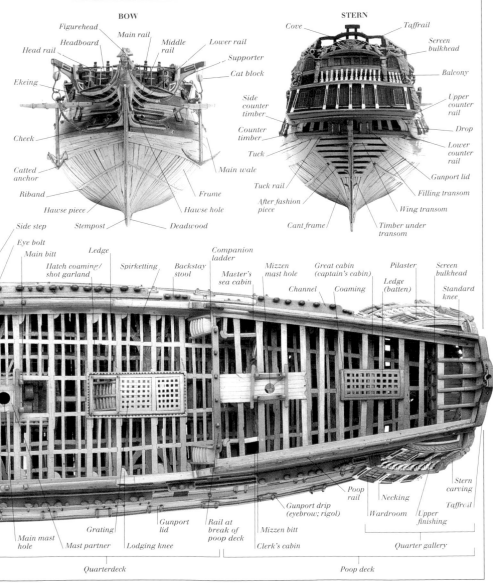

BOW

Figurehead
Main rail
Middle rail
Lower rail
Headboard
Head rail
Supporter
Ekeing
Cat block
Cheek
Catted anchor
Riband
Frame
Hawse piece
Hawse hole
Side step
Stempost
Deadwood
Eye bolt
Main bitt
Main wale

STERN

Cove
Taffrail
Screen bulkhead
Balcony
Upper counter rail
Side counter timber
Drop
Counter timber
Lower counter rail
Tuck
Gunport lid
Tuck rail
Filling transom
After fashion piece
Wing transom
Cant frame
Timber under transom

Ledge
Companion ladder
Hatch coaming/ shot garland
Spirketting
Backstay stool
Master's sea cabin
Mizzen mast hole
Great cabin (captain's cabin)
Pilaster
Screen bulkhead
Channel
Coaming
Ledge (batten)
Standard knee
Poop rail
Stern carving
Necking
Taffrail
Gunport drip (eyebrow; rigol)
Wardroom
Upper finishing
Main mast hole
Mast partner
Grating
Gunport lid
Lodging knee
Rail at break of poop deck
Mizzen bitt
Clerk's cabin
Quarter gallery

Quarterdeck
Poop deck

Rigging

BOWSPRIT AND JIB BOOM

MOST SAILING SHIPS HAVE TWO TYPES OF RIGGING. Standing rigging – kept taut by rigging screws or old-fashioned lanyards and deadeyes – refers to the ropes, wires, and chains that support the masts and yards (horizontal spars). Running rigging, which includes types of block and tackle, halyards, and sheets, is used to hoist, lower, or trim sails.

Outer jib stay
Inner jib stay
Inner jib tack
Bowsprit cap
Fore topmast
staysail tack
Bowsprit
Foot
rope
Boom guy block
Spear
Martingale
backrope
Martingale
(dolphin striker)
Lizard
Chain bobstay

Fore stay
Jib boom
Fore stay
Whisker boom
Jib boom

Upper deadeye
Lower deadeye
Butterfly plate
Chain plate

**OTHER RIGGING
FITTINGS**

Handle

Eye
plate
lug

Parallel
shaft

BELAYING PIN

MAST BAND

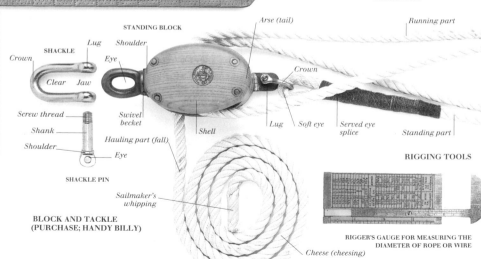

Arse (tail)
Running part
STANDING BLOCK
SHACKLE
Lug
Shoulder
Shoulder
Crown
Eye
Crown
Clear   Jaw
Swivel
becket
Lug   Soft eye
Served eye
splice
Standing part
Screw thread
Shank
Shell
Shoulder
Eye
Hauling part (fall)

SHACKLE PIN

Sailmaker's
whipping

**BLOCK AND TACKLE
(PURCHASE; HANDY BILLY)**

Cheese (cheesing)

RIGGING TOOLS

RIGGER'S GAUGE FOR MEASURING THE
DIAMETER OF ROPE OR WIRE

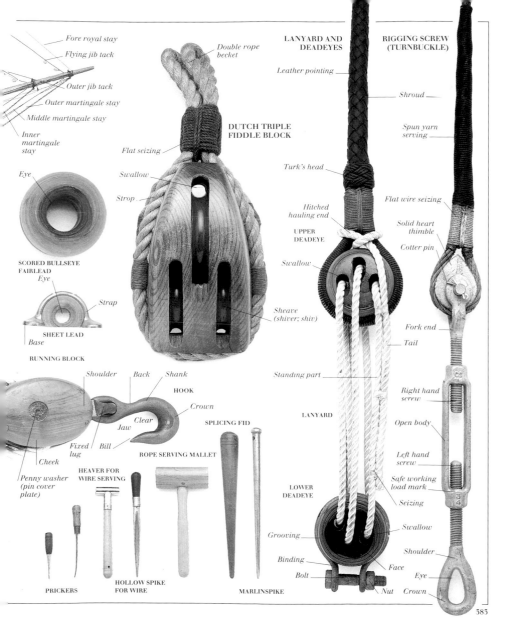

Fore royal stay

Flying jib tack

Outer jib tack

Outer martingale stay

Middle martingale stay

Inner martingale stay

LANYARD AND DEADEYES

RIGGING SCREW (TURNBUCKLE)

Double rope becket

Leather pointing

Shroud

Spun yarn serving

DUTCH TRIPLE FIDDLE BLOCK

Flat seizing

Swallow

Strop

Eye

SCORED BULLSEYE FAIRLEAD

Eye

Strap

SHEET LEAD

Base

RUNNING BLOCK

Turk's head

Hitched hauling end

UPPER DEADEYE

Swallow

Sheave (shiver; shiv)

Flat wire seizing

Solid heart thimble

Cotter pin

Fork end

Tail

Standing part

LANYARD

Right hand screw

Open body

Left hand screw

Safe working load mark

Seizing

Shoulder   Back   Shank

HOOK

Crown

Clear

Jaw

Bill

Fixed lug

Cheek

Penny washer (pin cover plate)

HEAVER FOR WIRE SERVING

SPLICING FID

ROPE SERVING MALLET

LOWER DEADEYE

Grooving

Binding

Bolt

Swallow

Face

Shoulder

Eye

Crown

Nut

PRICKERS

HOLLOW SPIKE FOR WIRE

MARLINSPIKE

Sails

THERE ARE TWO MAIN TYPES OF SAIL, often used in combination. Square sails are driving sails. They are usually attached by parrels to yards, square to the mast to catch the following wind. On fore-and-aft sails, such as lateen and lug sails, the luff (leading edge) usually abuts a mast or a stay. The head of the sail may abut a gaff, and the foot a boom. Around the world, a great range of rigs (sail patterns), such as the ketch, lugger, and schooner, have evolved to suit local needs. Sails are made from strips of cloth, cut to give the sail a belly and strong enough to resist the most violent of winds. Cotton and flax are the traditional sail materials, but synthetic fabrics are now commonly used.

SECTION OF A SAIL

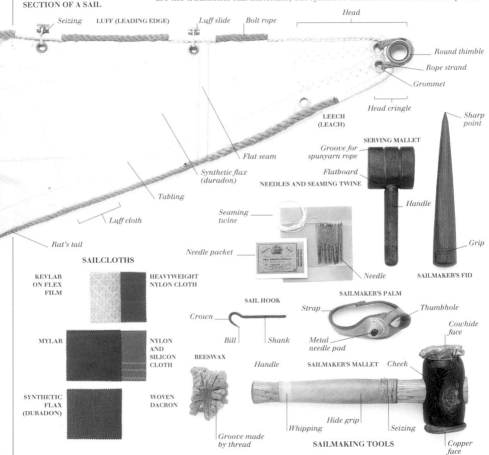

Seizing LUFF (LEADING EDGE) Luff slide Bolt rope Head

Round thimble

Rope strand

Grommet

Head cringle

Sharp point

LEECH (LEACH)

SERVING MALLET

Groove for spunyarn rope

Flat seam

Flatboard

Synthetic flax (duradon)

NEEDLES AND SEAMING TWINE

Handle

Tabling

Seaming twine

Luff cloth

Needle packet

Rat's tail

Grip

Needle

SAILMAKER'S FID

SAILCLOTHS

KEVLAR ON FLEX FILM

HEAVYWEIGHT NYLON CLOTH

SAIL HOOK

SAILMAKER'S PALM

Crown

Strap

Thumbhole

MYLAR

NYLON AND SILICON CLOTH

Bill   Shank

Metal needle pad

Cowhide face

BEESWAX

SYNTHETIC FLAX (DURADON)

WOVEN DACRON

Handle

SAILMAKER'S MALLET

Cheek

Groove made by thread

Whipping

Hide grip

Seizing

SAILMAKING TOOLS

Copper face

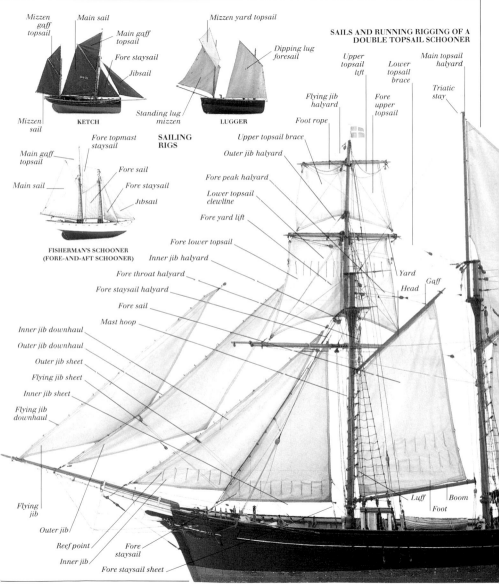

Mizzen gaff topsail

Main sail

Main gaff topsail

Fore staysail

Jibsail

Mizzen sail

KETCH

Mizzen yard topsail

Dipping lug foresail

Standing lug mizzen

LUGGER

**SAILS AND RUNNING RIGGING OF A
DOUBLE TOPSAIL SCHOONER**

Main gaff topsail

Fore topmast staysail

**SAILING
RIGS**

Main sail

Fore sail

Fore staysail

Jibsail

**FISHERMAN'S SCHOONER
(FORE-AND-AFT SCHOONER)**

Upper topsail lift

Flying jib halyard

Foot rope

Upper topsail brace

Outer jib halyard

Fore peak halyard

Lower topsail clewline

Fore yard lift

Fore lower topsail

Inner jib halyard

Fore throat halyard

Fore staysail halyard

Fore sail

Mast hoop

Inner jib downhaul

Outer jib downhaul

Outer jib sheet

Flying jib sheet

Inner jib sheet

Flying jib downhaul

Flying jib

Outer jib

Reef point

Inner jib

Fore staysail

Fore staysail sheet

Lower topsail brace

Fore upper topsail

Main topsail halyard

Triatic stay

Yard

Head

Gaff

Luff

Foot

Boom

385

Mooring and anchoring

FOR LARGE VESSELS IN OPEN WATER, ANCHORAGE IS ESSENTIAL. By holding a ship securely to the seabed, an anchor prevents the vessel from being at the mercy of wave, tide, and current. The earliest anchors were nothing more than stones. In later years, many anchors had a standard design, much like the Admiralty pattern anchor shown on this page. The Danforth anchor is somewhat different. It has particularly deep flukes to give it great holding power. On large sailing ships, anchors were worked by teams of sailors. They turned the drum of a capstan by pushing on bars slotted into the revolving cylinder. This, in turn, lifted or lowered the anchor chain. In calm harbours and estuaries, ships can moor (make fast) without using anchors. Berthing ropes can be attached to bollards both inboard and on the quayside. Berthing ropes are joined to each other by bends, like those opposite.

STONE ANCHOR
(KILLICK)

Rope
hole

TYPES
OF ANCHOR

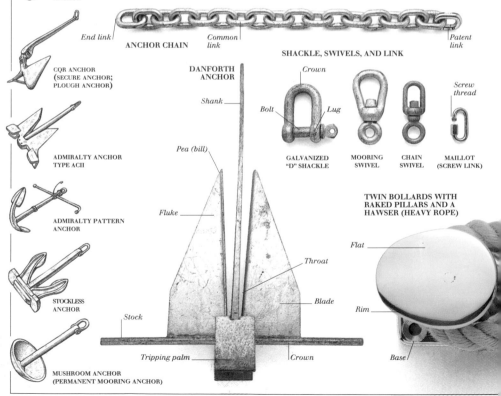

CLOSE-
STOWING
ANCHOR

CQR ANCHOR
(SECURE ANCHOR;
PLOUGH ANCHOR)

ADMIRALTY ANCHOR
TYPE ACII

ADMIRALTY PATTERN
ANCHOR

STOCKLESS
ANCHOR

MUSHROOM ANCHOR
(PERMANENT MOORING ANCHOR)

End link
ANCHOR CHAIN
Common
link
Patent
link

SHACKLE, SWIVELS, AND LINK

DANFORTH
ANCHOR

Shank

Pea (bill)

Fluke

Stock

Tripping palm

Crown

Throat

Blade

Crown

Crown
Bolt
Lug

GALVANIZED
"D" SHACKLE

MOORING
SWIVEL

CHAIN
SWIVEL

Screw
thread

MAILLOT
(SCREW LINK)

TWIN BOLLARDS WITH
RAKED PILLARS AND A
HAWSER (HEAVY ROPE)

Flat

Rim

Base

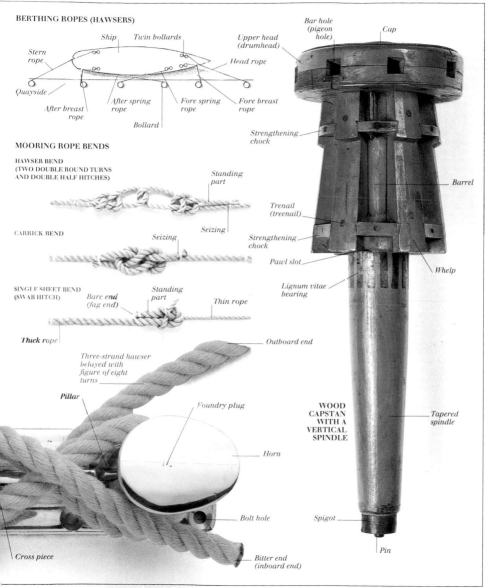

BERTHING ROPES (HAWSERS)

Ship

Twin bollards

Stern rope

Upper head (drumhead)

Head rope

Quayside

After breast rope

After spring rope

Fore spring rope

Fore breast rope

Bollard

Bar hole (pigeon hole)

Cap

Strengthening chock

Barrel

Trenail (treenail)

Strengthening chock

Pawl slot

Whelp

Lignum vitae bearing

MOORING ROPE BENDS

HAWSER BEND (TWO DOUBLE ROUND TURNS AND DOUBLE HALF HITCHES)

Standing part

Seizing

CARRICK BEND

Seizing

Seizing

SINGLE SHEET BEND (SWAB HITCH)

Bare end (fag end)

Standing part

Thin rope

Thick rope

Three-strand hawser belayed with figure of eight turns

Outboard end

Pillar

Foundry plug

Horn

Bolt hole

WOOD CAPSTAN WITH A VERTICAL SPINDLE

Tapered spindle

Spigot

Cross piece

Bitter end (inboard end)

Pin

Ropes and knots

ALL KINDS OF ROPES ARE USED AT SEA, from thin twines and yarns to thick hawsers. Synthetic fibres have been developed specifically for use at sea. Nylon ropes stretch, and so are ideal for anchoring; polypropylene has little stretch, so is ideal for halyards and sheets. Different types of knots are used for different purposes. Knots that join two ropes are called bends; hitches join a rope to another object; and bowlines produce an eye (loop) in the end of a rope. Ropes can be joined by splicing (unravelling the ends and weaving them together) or seizing (lashing the ropes together side by side).

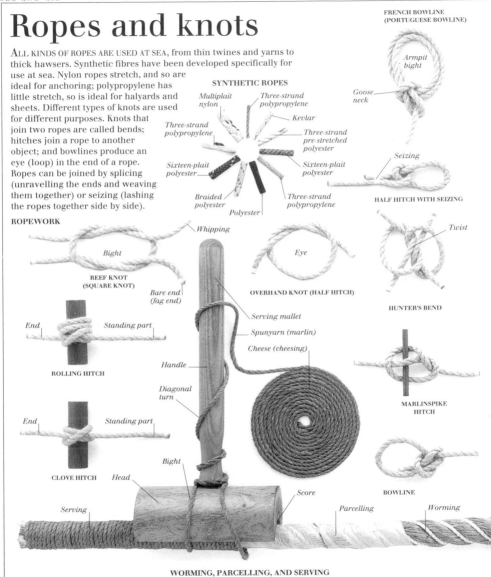

SYNTHETIC ROPES

Multiplait nylon

Three-strand polypropylene

Three-strand polypropylene

Kevlar

Three-strand pre-stretched polyester

Sixteen-plait polyester

Sixteen-plait polyester

Braided polyester

Three-strand polypropylene

Polyester

FRENCH BOWLINE (PORTUGUESE BOWLINE)

Armpit bight

Goose neck

Seizing

HALF HITCH WITH SEIZING

ROPEWORK

Whipping

Bight

REEF KNOT (SQUARE KNOT)

Bare end (fag end)

Eye

OVERHAND KNOT (HALF HITCH)

Twist

HUNTER'S BEND

End

Standing part

Serving mallet

Spunyarn (marlin)

Cheese (cheesing)

ROLLING HITCH

Handle

Diagonal turn

MARLINSPIKE HITCH

End

Standing part

CLOVE HITCH

Head

Bight

Score

BOWLINE

Serving

Parcelling

Worming

WORMING, PARCELLING, AND SERVING

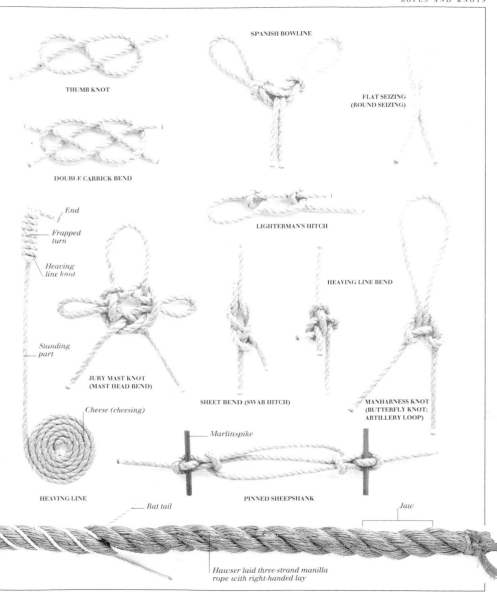

SPANISH BOWLINE

THUMB KNOT

FLAT SEIZING
(ROUND SEIZING)

DOUBLE CARRICK BEND

End

Frapped turn

Heaving line knot

LIGHTERMAN'S HITCH

HEAVING LINE BEND

Standing part

JURY MAST KNOT
(MAST HEAD BEND)

SHEET BEND (SWAB HITCH)

MANHARNESS KNOT
(BUTTERFLY KNOT;
ARTILLERY LOOP)

Cheese (cheesing)

Marlinspike

HEAVING LINE

PINNED SHEEPSHANK

Jaw

Rat tail

Hawser laid three-strand manilla rope with right-handed lay

Paddle wheels and propellers

THE INVENTION OF THE STEAM ENGINE IN THE 18TH CENTURY made mechanically driven ships fitted with paddle wheels or propellers a viable alternative to sails. Paddle wheels have fixed or feathered floats, and the model shown below features both types. Feathered floats give more propulsive power than fixed floats because they are almost upright at all times in the water. Paddle wheels were superseded by the propeller on ocean-going vessels in the mid-19th century. Propellers are more efficient, work better in rough water, and are less vulnerable in collisions. The first propellers were two-bladed but later three- and four-bladed versions are more powerful; the shape and pitch of blades have also been refined over the years. At the beginning of the 18th century, tillers were superseded on many larger ships by the ship's wheel as a means of steering.

SHIP'S WHEEL

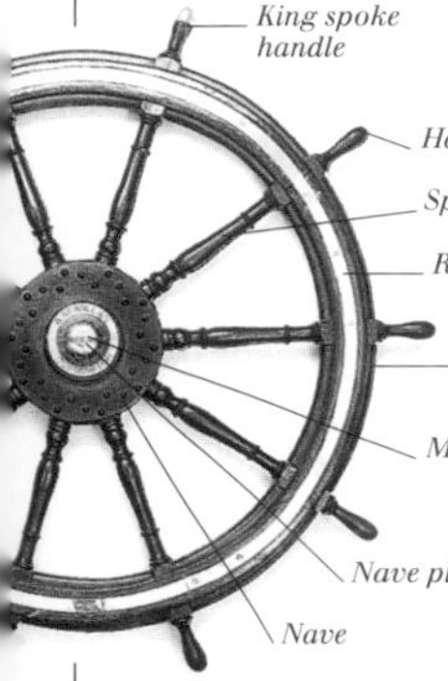

King spoke handle

Handle

Spoke

Rim plate

Felloe (rim section)

Maker's name

Nave plate

Nave

PADDLE WHEEL WITH FIXED FLOATS

Wrist pin

Limb

Fixed float

Hub

Deck beam

OSCILLATING STEAM ENGINE

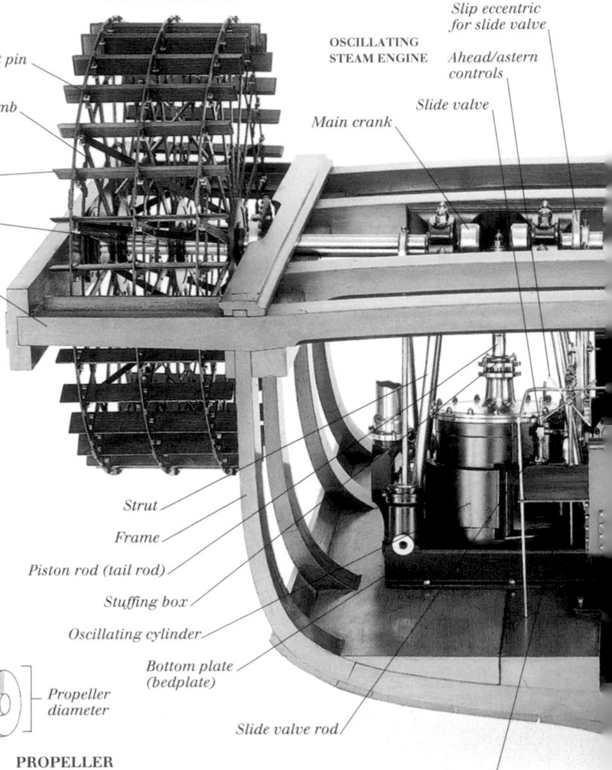

Slip eccentric for slide valve

Ahead/astern controls

Slide valve

Main crank

THREE-BLADED PROPELLER

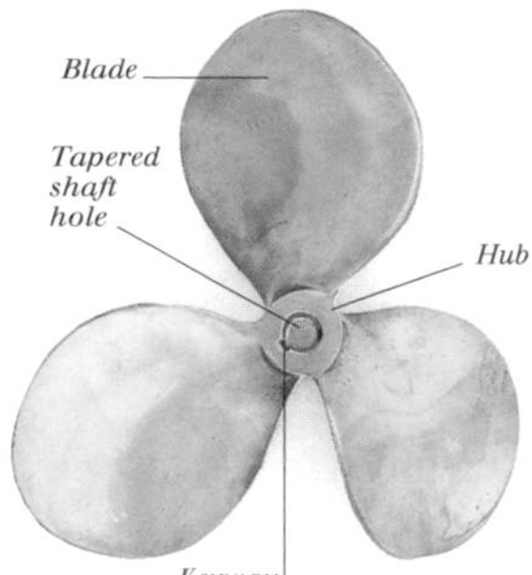

Blade

Tapered shaft hole

Hub

Keyway

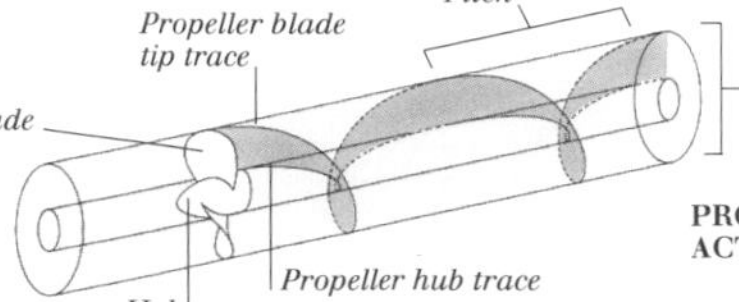

Strut

Frame

Piston rod (tail rod)

Stuffing box

Oscillating cylinder

Bottom plate (bedplate)

Slide valve rod

Control platform

Propeller blade tip trace

Pitch

Blade

Propeller diameter

Hub

Propeller hub trace

PROPELLER ACTION

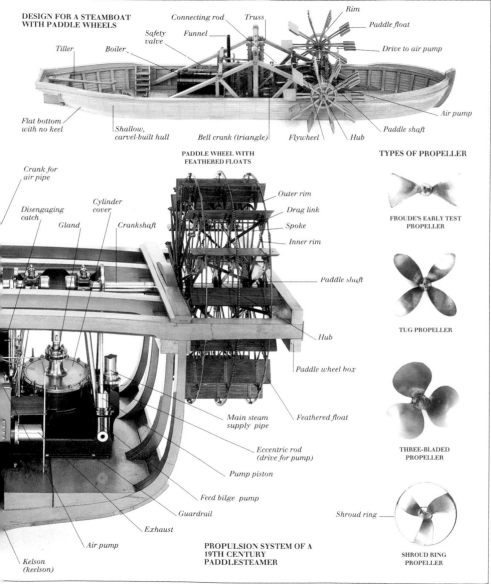

**DESIGN FOR A STEAMBOAT
WITH PADDLE WHEELS**

Rim

Connecting rod Truss

Paddle float

Safety
valve Funnel

Drive to air pump

Tiller Boiler

Air pump

Flat bottom
with no keel

Shallow,
carvel-built hull

Bell crank (triangle) Flywheel Hub

Paddle shaft

**PADDLE WHEEL WITH
FEATHERED FLOATS**

TYPES OF PROPELLER

Crank for
air pipe

Outer rim

Disengaging
catch

Drag link

Cylinder
cover

Spoke

Gland Crankshaft

Inner rim

**FROUDE'S EARLY TEST
PROPELLER**

Paddle shaft

Hub

TUG PROPELLER

Paddle wheel box

Main steam
supply pipe

Feathered float

Eccentric rod
(drive for pump)

Pump piston

**THREE-BLADED
PROPELLER**

Feed bilge pump

Guardrail

Exhaust

Shroud ring

Air pump

Kelson
(keelson)

**PROPULSION SYSTEM OF A
19TH CENTURY
PADDLESTEAMER**

**SHROUD RING
PROPELLER**

Anatomy of an iron ship

IRON PARTS WERE USED IN THE HULLS OF WOODEN SHIPS AS EARLY AS 1675, often in the same form as the wooden parts that they replaced. Eventually, as on the tea clipper Cutty Sark (below), iron rigging was found to be stronger than the traditional rope. The first "ironclads" were warships whose wooden hulls were protected by iron armour plates. Later ironclads actually had iron hulls. The model opposite is based on the British warship HMS Warrior, launched in 1860, the first battleship built entirely of iron. The plan of the iron paddlesteamer (bottom), built somewhat later, shows that this vessel was a sailing ship; but it also boasted a steam propulsion plant amidships that turned two side paddlewheels. Early iron hulls were made from plates that were painstakingly rivetted together (as below), but by the 20th century vessels began to be welded together, whole sections at a time. The Second World War "liberty ship" was one of the first of these "production-line vessels".

TEA CLIPPER

Steel yard | Iron wire stay | Steel lower mast | Steel bowsprit

Wooden planking with copper sheathing | Forged iron anchor

RIVETTED PLATES

Pan head rivet

Plate

Button head rivet (snap head) | Seam

LIBERTY SHIP

Gun section

Accommodation section | Cargo derrick | Weld line

Stern section | Midships section | Cargo hold | Bow section

PLAN OF AN IRON PADDLESTEAMER

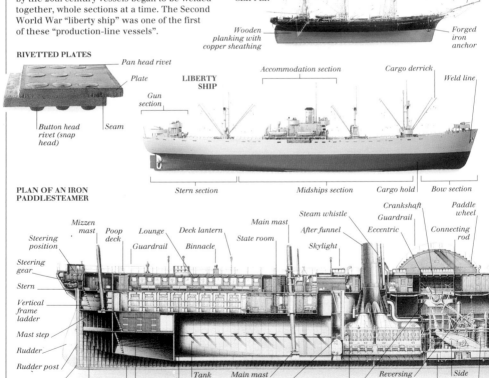

Crankshaft | Paddle wheel
Steam whistle | Guardrail
Main mast | Eccentric | Connecting rod
Mizzen mast | Poop deck | Lounge | Deck lantern | After funnel
Steering position | Guardrail | Binnacle | State room | Skylight
Steering gear
Stern
Vertical frame ladder
Mast step
Rudder
Rudder post
Heel of rudder post | Bar keel | Afterpeak | Tank | Main mast step | Box boiler | Reversing wheel | Side lever
Stern framing | Cabin | Donkey boiler | Foundation | Bottom plate | Cylinder

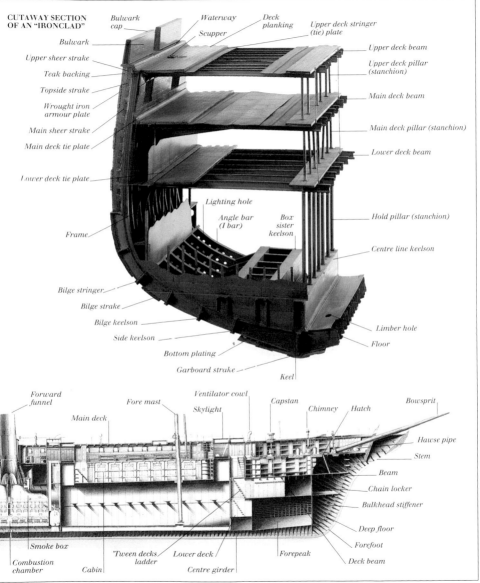

CUTAWAY SECTION OF AN "IRONCLAD"

Bulwark cap

Waterway

Deck planking

Upper deck stringer (tie) plate

Bulwark

Scupper

Upper sheer strake

Teak backing

Topside strake

Wrought iron armour plate

Main sheer strake

Main deck tie plate

Lower deck tie plate

Frame

Lighting hole

Angle bar (I bar)

Box sister keelson

Bilge stringer

Bilge strake

Bilge keelson

Side keelson

Bottom plating

Garboard strake

Keel

Upper deck beam

Upper deck pillar (stanchion)

Main deck beam

Main deck pillar (stanchion)

Lower deck beam

Hold pillar (stanchion)

Centre line keelson

Limber hole

Floor

Forward funnel

Fore mast

Ventilator cowl

Skylight

Capstan

Chimney

Hatch

Bowsprit

Main deck

Hawse pipe

Stem

Beam

Chain locker

Bulkhead stiffener

Deep floor

Forefoot

Deck beam

Smoke box

Combustion chamber

Cabin

'Tween decks ladder

Lower deck

Centre girder

Forepeak

393

The battleship

IN THE EARLY YEARS OF THE 20TH CENTURY, sea warfare – attacking enemy vessels or defending a ship – was revolutionized by the introduction of Dreadnought-type battleships like the Brazilian vessel below. These new ships combined the latest advances in steam propulsion, gunnery, and armour plating. The gun turret was designed to fire shells over huge distances. It was protected by armour 30 cm (12 in) thick. The measurements given for the guns of this ship refer to the bore diameter. Where "weight" is quoted, this is the weight of the shell that the gun fires. Torpedoes – as portrayed on the upper cigarette card (right) – were self-propelled underwater missiles, often steered by gyro-control. Depth charges were designed in the First World War for use against submerged U-boats. They are canisters filled with explosives that are detonated by depth-sensitive pistols. The lower cigarette card shows depth charges being fired by a "thrower", fired from a torpedo tube, and rolled from the stern. Ship's shields were fitted to warships from the late 19th century onwards. The shield shown opposite depicts a traditional ship's cannon.

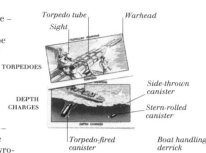

TORPEDOES

DEPTH CHARGES

Torpedo tube

Sight

Warhead

Side-thrown canister

Stern-rolled canister

Torpedo-fired canister

Boat handling derrick

BRAZILIAN BATTLESHIP

Rangefinder
Light screen
Compass
Compass and rangefinder platform
Ship's wheel
Navigating bridge
Conning tower
Captain's shelter/ chart house
Arms of Brazil
Weather shutter for gun
Jack staff
30 cm (12 in) gun
Skylight

Forward funnel
Lifeboat
"F" turret

Gunnery spotting top
Purchase wire
Searchlight
Searchlight platform
Leading block
Tripod mast
Boat winch

Stem (false ram bow)
Porthole
Belt armour
Forward accommodation ladder
Sighting hood
"A" turret
Turret barbette
Open gun mounting
12 cm (4.7 in) gun
Steam launch
Guest boat boom

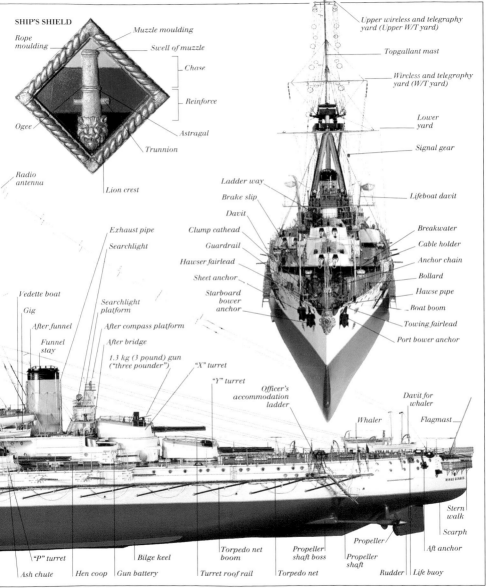

SHIP'S SHIELD

Rope moulding

Muzzle moulding

Swell of muzzle

Chase

Reinforce

Ogee

Astragal

Trunnion

Lion crest

Radio antenna

Upper wireless and telegraphy yard (Upper W/T yard)

Topgallant mast

Wireless and telegraphy yard (W/T yard)

Lower yard

Signal gear

Ladder way

Brake slip

Davit

Clump cathead

Guardrail

Hawser fairlead

Sheet anchor

Starboard bower anchor

Lifeboat davit

Breakwater

Cable holder

Anchor chain

Bollard

Hawse pipe

Boat boom

Towing fairlead

Port bower anchor

Exhaust pipe

Searchlight

Vedette boat

Gig

After funnel

Funnel stay

Searchlight platform

After compass platform

After bridge

1.3 kg (3 pound) gun ("three pounder")

"X" turret

"Y" turret

Officer's accommodation ladder

Whaler

Davit for whaler

Flagmast

Stern walk

Scarph

"P" turret

Ash chute

Hen coop

Bilge keel

Gun battery

Torpedo net boom

Turret roof rail

Propeller shaft boss

Torpedo net

Propeller shaft

Propeller

Rudder

Aft anchor

Life buoy

Frigates and submarines

FROM THE MID-19TH CENTURY, ARMOURED SHIPS provided a new challenge to enemy craft. In response, huge revolving gun turrets were developed. These could fire in any direction, could be loaded from the breech very rapidly, and, instead of cannonballs, they discharged exploding shells. Modern fighting ships, like the frigate, combine heavy ship-borne armament with light helicopter weaponry. Submarines function below the surface of the sea. Their speed and ability to fire missiles from under water are their major assets. The nuclear submarine can stay under water for several years without refuelling.

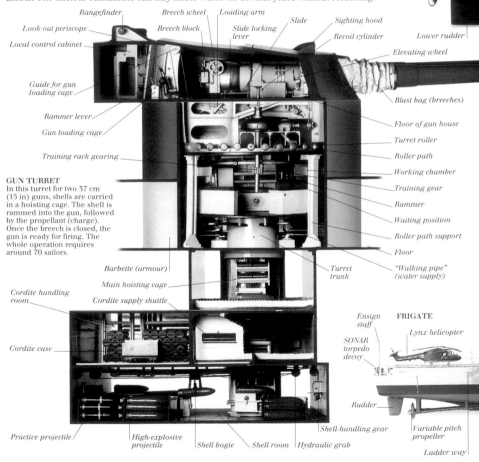

Stabilizer fin
Aft hydroplane
Propeller

Rangefinder
Look out periscope
Local control cabinet
Breech wheel
Breech block
Loading arm
Slide locking lever
Slide
Sighting hood
Recoil cylinder
Lower rudder
Elevating wheel

Guide for gun loading cage
Rammer lever
Gun loading cage
Training rack gearing

Blast bag (breeches)
Floor of gun house
Turret roller
Roller path
Working chamber
Training gear
Rammer
Waiting position
Roller path support
Floor

GUN TURRET
In this turret for two 37 cm (15 in) guns, shells are carried in a hoisting cage. The shell is rammed into the gun, followed by the propellant (charge). Once the breech is closed, the gun is ready for firing. The whole operation requires around 70 sailors.

Barbette (armour)
Main hoisting cage
Cordite handling room
Cordite supply shuttle
Cordite case

Turret trunk
"Walking pipe" (water supply)

Ensign staff
SONAR torpedo decoy

FRIGATE
Lynx helicopter

Rudder

Practice projectile
High-explosive projectile
Shell bogie
Shell room
Hydraulic grab
Shell-handling gear
Variable pitch propeller
Ladder way

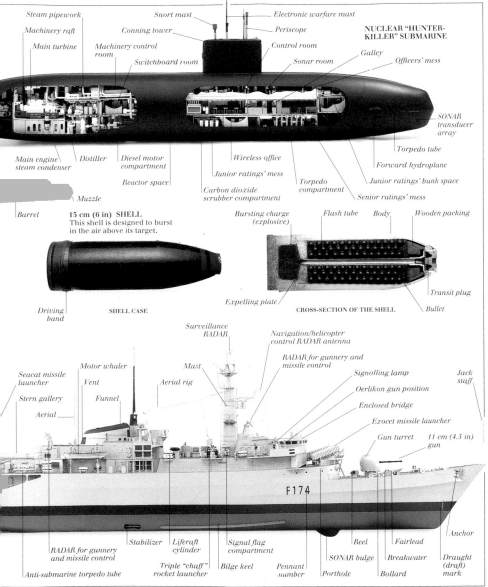

Steam pipework

Machinery raft

Main turbine

Machinery control room

Switchboard room

Snort mast

Conning tower

Periscope

Electronic warfare mast

NUCLEAR "HUNTER-KILLER" SUBMARINE

Control room

Sonar room

Galley

Officers' mess

SONAR transducer array

Torpedo tube

Forward hydroplane

Junior ratings' bunk space

Senior ratings' mess

Wireless office

Junior ratings' mess

Torpedo compartment

Main engine steam condenser

Distiller

Diesel motor compartment

Reactor space

Carbon dioxide scrubber compartment

Muzzle

Barrel

15 cm (6 in) SHELL
This shell is designed to burst in the air above its target.

Bursting charge (explosive)

Flash tube

Body

Wooden packing

Transit plug

Bullet

Driving band

SHELL CASE

Expelling plate

CROSS-SECTION OF THE SHELL

Surveillance RADAR

Navigation/helicopter control RADAR antenna

RADAR for gunnery and missile control

Seacat missile launcher

Stern gallery

Aerial

Motor whaler

Vent

Funnel

Mast

Aerial rig

Signalling lamp

Oerlikon gun position

Enclosed bridge

Exocet missile launcher

Gun turret

11 cm (4.5 in) gun

Jack staff

F174

RADAR for gunnery and missile control

Anti-submarine torpedo tube

Stabilizer

Liferaft cylinder

Triple "chaff" rocket launcher

Bilge keel

Signal flag compartment

Pennant number

Porthole

Reel

SONAR bulge

Breakwater

Bollard

Fairlead

Anchor

Draught (draft) mark

Pioneers of flight

FLIGHT HAS FASCINATED MANKIND for centuries, and countless unsuccessful flying machines have been designed. The first successful flight was made by the French Montgolfier brothers in 1783, when they flew a balloon over Paris. The next major advance was the development of gliders, notably by the Englishman Sir George Cayley, who in 1845 designed the first glider to make a sustained flight, and by the German Otto Lilienthal, who became known as the world's first pilot because he managed to achieve controlled flights. However, powered flight did not become a practical possibility until the invention of lightweight, petrol-driven internal combustion engines at the end of the 19th century. Then, in 1903, the American brothers Orville and Wilbur Wright made the first powered flight in their Wright Flyer biplane, which used a four-cylinder, petrol-driven engine. Aircraft design advanced rapidly, and in 1909 the Frenchman Louis Blériot made his pioneering flight across the English Channel (see pp. 400-401). The American Glenn Curtiss also achieved several "firsts" in his Model-D Pusher and its variants, most notably winning the world's first competition for airspeed at Reims in 1909.

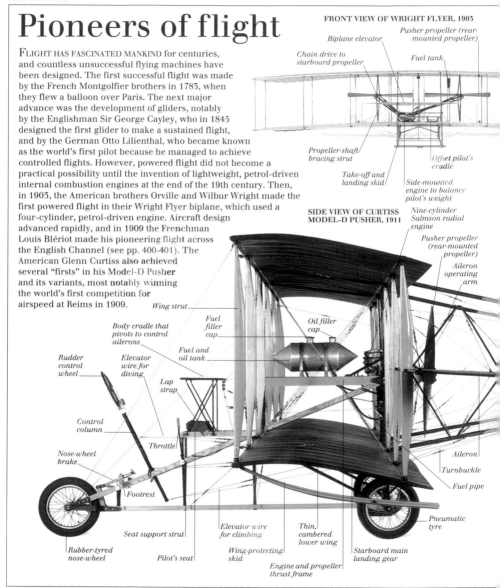

FRONT VIEW OF WRIGHT FLYER, 1903

Pusher propeller (rear-mounted propeller)

Biplane elevator

Chain drive to starboard propeller

Fuel tank

Propeller-shaft bracing strut

Offset pilot's cradle

Take-off and landing skid

Side-mounted engine to balance pilot's weight

SIDE VIEW OF CURTISS MODEL-D PUSHER, 1911

Nine-cylinder Salmson radial engine

Pusher propeller (rear-mounted propeller)

Aileron operating arm

Wing strut

Fuel filler cap

Oil filler cap

Body cradle that pivots to control ailerons

Fuel and oil tank

Rudder control wheel

Elevator wire for diving

Lap strap

Control column

Throttle

Nose-wheel brake

Aileron

Turnbuckle

Fuel pipe

Pneumatic tyre

Footrest

Seat support strut

Elevator wire for climbing

Thin, cambered lower wing

Rubber-tyred nose-wheel

Pilot's seat

Wing-protecting skid

Engine and propeller thrust frame

Starboard main landing gear

SIDE VIEW OF WRIGHT FLYER, 1903

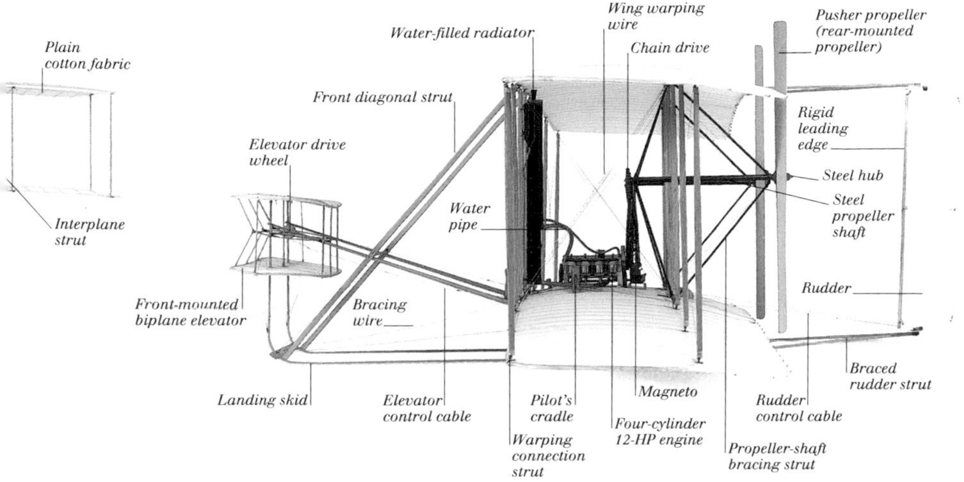

Plain
cotton fabric

Water-filled radiator

Wing warping
wire

Pusher propeller
(rear-mounted
propeller)

Front diagonal strut

Chain drive

Elevator drive
wheel

Rigid
leading
edge

Interplane
strut

Water
pipe

Steel hub

Steel
propeller
shaft

Front-mounted
biplane elevator

Bracing
wire

Rudder

Landing skid

Elevator
control cable

Pilot's
cradle

Magneto

Rudder
control cable

Braced
rudder strut

Warping
connection
strut

Four-cylinder
12-HP engine

Propeller-shaft
bracing strut

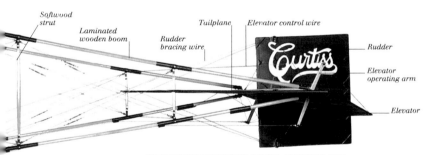

Softwood
strut

Laminated
wooden boom

Tailplane

Elevator control wire

Rudder
bracing wire

Rudder

Elevator
operating arm

Elevator

FRONT VIEW OF CURTISS MODEL-D PUSHER, 1911

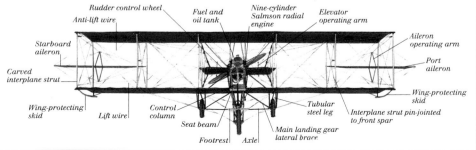

Rudder control wheel

Fuel and
oil tank

Nine-cylinder
Salmson radial
engine

Elevator
operating arm

Anti-lift wire

Aileron
operating arm

Starboard
aileron

Port
aileron

Carved
interplane strut

Wing-protecting
skid

Wing-protecting
skid

Lift wire

Control
column

Tubular
steel leg

Interplane strut pin-jointed
to front spar

Seat beam

Footrest

Axle

Main landing gear
lateral brace

Early monoplanes

RUMPLER MONOPLANE, 1908

MONOPLANES HAVE ONE WING on each side of the fuselage. The principal disadvantage of this arrangement in early, wooden-framed aircraft was that single wings were weak and required strong wires to brace them to king-posts above and below the fuselage. However, single wings also had advantages: they experienced less drag than multiple wings, allowing greater speed; they also made aircraft more manoeuvrable because single wings were easier to warp (twist) than double wings, and warping the wings was how pilots controlled the roll of early aircraft. By 1912, the French pilot Louis Blériot had used a monoplane to make the first flight across the English Channel, and the Briton Robert Blackburn and the Frenchman Armand Deperdussin had proved the greater speed of monoplanes. However, a spate of crashes caused by broken wings discouraged monoplane production, except in Germany, where all-metal monoplanes were developed in 1917. The wings of all-metal monoplanes did not need strengthening by struts or bracing wires, but despite this, such planes were not widely adopted until the 1930s.

FRONT VIEW OF BLACKBURN MONOPLANE, 1912

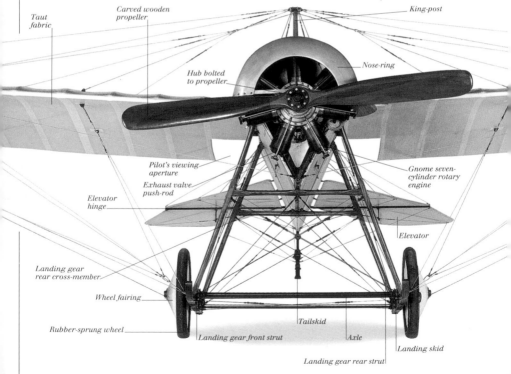

Taut fabric

Carved wooden propeller

King-post

Hub bolted to propeller

Nose-ring

Pilot's viewing aperture

Gnome seven-cylinder rotary engine

Exhaust valve push-rod

Elevator hinge

Elevator

Landing gear rear cross-member

Wheel fairing

Rubber-sprung wheel

Tailskid

Landing gear front strut

Axle

Landing skid

Landing gear rear strut

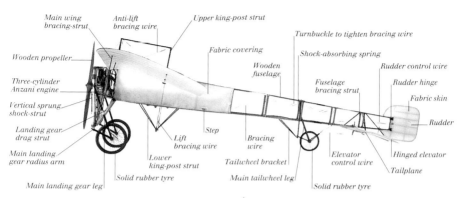

Main wing bracing-strut

Anti-lift bracing wire

Upper king-post strut

Fabric covering

Turnbuckle to tighten bracing wire

Wooden propeller

Shock-absorbing spring

Wooden fuselage

Rudder control wire

Three-cylinder Anzani engine

Fuselage bracing strut

Rudder hinge

Vertical sprung shock-strut

Fabric skin

Landing gear drag strut

Rudder

Main landing gear radius arm

Step

Lift bracing wire

Bracing wire

Elevator control wire

Hinged elevator

Lower king-post strut

Tailwheel bracket

Tailplane

Main landing gear leg

Solid rubber tyre

Main tailwheel leg

Solid rubber tyre

SIDE VIEW OF BLÉRIOT XI, 1909

Anti-lift bracing wire

Leading edge

Rib

Bracing wire anchor bolt

Concave undersurface

Turnbuckle to tighten bracing wire

Lift bracing wire

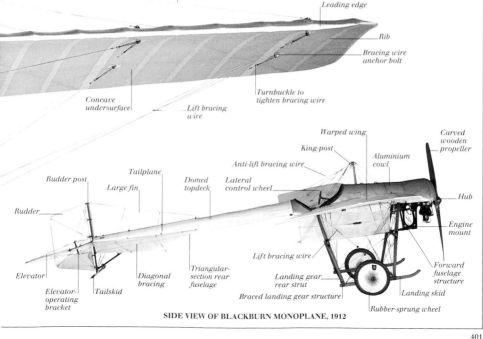

Warped wing

Carved wooden propeller

King-post

Aluminium cowl

Anti-lift bracing wire

Tailplane

Domed topdeck

Lateral control wheel

Rudder post

Large fin

Hub

Rudder

Engine mount

Lift bracing wire

Elevator

Triangular-section rear fuselage

Diagonal bracing

Landing gear rear strut

Forward fuselage structure

Elevator-operating bracket

Tailskid

Braced landing gear structure

Landing skid

Rubber-sprung wheel

SIDE VIEW OF BLACKBURN MONOPLANE, 1912

401

Biplanes and triplanes

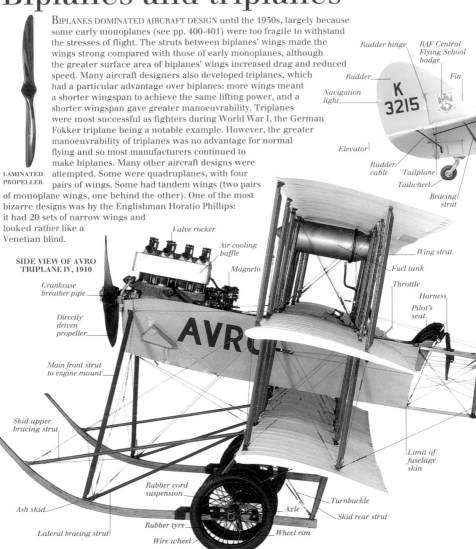

BIPLANES DOMINATED AIRCRAFT DESIGN until the 1930s, largely because some early monoplanes (see pp. 400-401) were too fragile to withstand the stresses of flight. The struts between biplanes' wings made the wings strong compared with those of early monoplanes, although the greater surface area of biplanes' wings increased drag and reduced speed. Many aircraft designers also developed triplanes, which had a particular advantage over biplanes: more wings meant a shorter wingspan to achieve the same lifting power, and a shorter wingspan gave greater manoeuvrability. Triplanes were most successful as fighters during World War I, the German Fokker triplane being a notable example. However, the greater manoeuvrability of triplanes was no advantage for normal flying and so most manufacturers continued to make biplanes. Many other aircraft designs were attempted. Some were quadruplanes, with four pairs of wings. Some had tandem wings (two pairs of monoplane wings, one behind the other). One of the most bizarre designs was by the Englishman Horatio Phillips: it had 20 sets of narrow wings and looked rather like a Venetian blind.

LAMINATED PROPELLER

Rudder hinge

RAF Central Flying School badge

Rudder

Navigation light

K 3215

Fin

Elevator

Rudder cable

Tailplane

Tailwheel

Bracing strut

SIDE VIEW OF AVRO TRIPLANE IV, 1910

Valve rocker

Air cooling baffle

Magneto

Wing strut

Fuel tank

Throttle

Harness

Pilot's seat

Crankcase breather pipe

Directly driven propeller

Main front strut to engine mount

AVRO

Skid upper bracing strut

Limit of fuselage skin

Ash skid

Rubber cord suspension

Axle

Turnbuckle

Skid rear strut

Lateral bracing strut

Rubber tyre

Wire wheel

Wheel rim

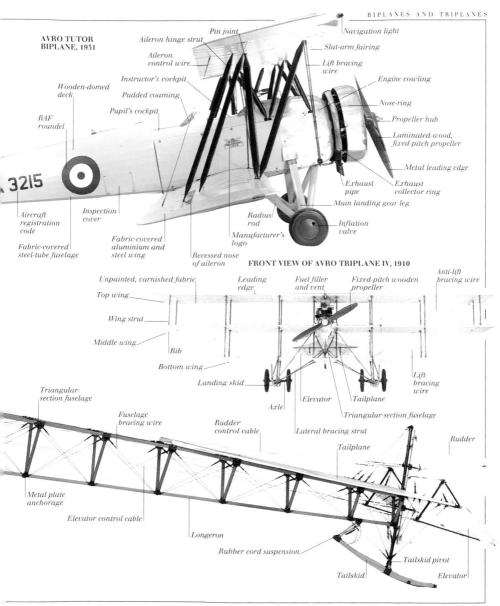

AVRO TUTOR BIPLANE, 1931

Pin joint

Aileron hinge strut

Navigation light

Aileron control wire

Slat-arm fairing

Instructor's cockpit

Lift bracing wire

Wooden-domed deck

Engine cowling

Padded coaming

Nose-ring

Pupil's cockpit

Propeller hub

RAF roundel

Laminated-wood, fixed-pitch propeller

Metal leading edge

3215

Exhaust pipe

Exhaust collector ring

Aircraft registration code

Inspection cover

Main landing gear leg

Radius rod

Inflation valve

Fabric-covered steel-tube fuselage

Fabric-covered aluminium and steel wing

Manufacturer's logo

Recessed nose of aileron

FRONT VIEW OF AVRO TRIPLANE IV, 1910

Unpainted, varnished fabric

Leading edge

Fuel filler and vent

Fixed-pitch wooden propeller

Anti-lift bracing wire

Top wing

Wing strut

Middle wing

Rib

Bottom wing

Landing skid

Lift bracing wire

Axle

Elevator

Tailplane

Triangular-section fuselage

Fuselage bracing wire

Rudder control cable

Lateral bracing strut

Triangular-section fuselage

Tailplane

Rudder

Metal plate anchorage

Elevator control cable

Longeron

Rubber cord suspension

Tailskid pivot

Tailskid

Elevator

World War I aircraft

WHEN WORLD WAR I STARTED in 1914, the main purpose of military aircraft was reconnaissance. The British-built BE 2, of which the BE 2B was a variant, was well-suited to this duty; it was very stable in flight, allowing the occupants to study the terrain, take photographs, and make notes. The BE 2 was also one of the first aircraft to drop bombs. One of the biggest problems for aircraft designers during the war was mounting machine-guns. On aircraft that had front-mounted propellers, the field of fire was restricted by the propeller and other parts of the aircraft. The problem was solved in 1915 by the Dutchman Anthony Fokker, who designed an interrupter gear that prevented a machine-gun from firing when a propeller blade passed in front of the barrel. The German LVG CVI had a forward-firing gun to the right of the engine, as well as a rear-cockpit gun, and a bombing capability. It was one of the most versatile aircraft of the war.

FLYING
HELMET

Interplane-strut attachment
Intermediate leading-edge rib
Airspeed-indicator tube
Leading edge

Wingtip

Airspeed-indicator tube
Airspeed pitot tube
Main rib
Interplane strut
Interplane-strut attachment
Root
Trailing edge

Upper side of lower wing
Attachment lug

Cabane strut fairing
Engine air intake (ram scoop)
Observer's windscreen

BE 2B, 1914

Top-wing centre section

Wooden propeller
Air-cooled V8 engine
Crankcase
Buffed metal cowling
Silencing heat exchanger
Exhaust pipe
Landing gear front strut
Ash skid

Cabane strut
Lift bracing wire
Pilot's windscreen
Plywood skin
Control column
Padded coaming

Elevator rocking arm
Step
Step
Lateral control wire
Reconnaissance camera bracket

Pneumatic rubber tyre
Wheel cover
V-strut
Bomb rack
Lower-wing attachment
112 lb (51 kg) bomb

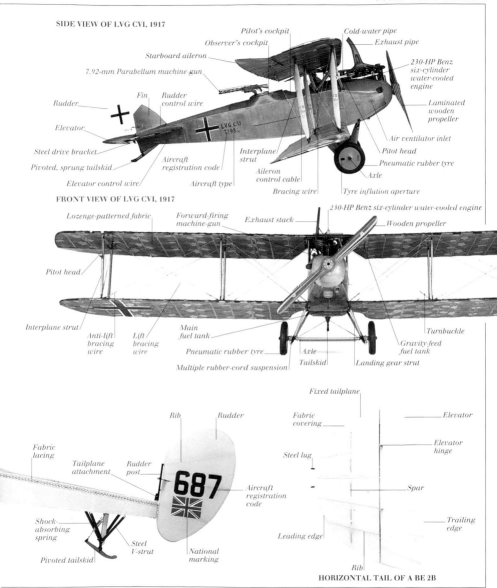

SIDE VIEW OF LVG CVI, 1917

Pilot's cockpit

Observer's cockpit

Cold-water pipe

Exhaust pipe

Starboard aileron

7.92-mm Parabellum machine-gun

230-HP Benz six-cylinder water-cooled engine

Fin

Rudder control wire

Rudder

Laminated wooden propeller

Elevator

Air ventilator inlet

Steel drive bracket

Interplane strut

Pitot head

Pivoted, sprung tailskid

Aircraft registration code

Pneumatic rubber tyre

Aileron control cable

Elevator control wire

Axle

Aircraft type

Elevator control wire

Bracing wire

Tyre inflation aperture

FRONT VIEW OF LVG CVI, 1917

Lozenge-patterned fabric

Forward-firing machine-gun

Exhaust stack

230-HP Benz six-cylinder water-cooled engine

Wooden propeller

Pitot head

Interplane strut

Anti-lift bracing wire

Lift bracing wire

Main fuel tank

Turnbuckle

Gravity-feed fuel tank

Pneumatic rubber tyre

Axle

Landing gear strut

Multiple rubber-cord suspension

Tailskid

Fabric lacing

Rib

Rudder

Fixed tailplane

Fabric covering

Elevator

Elevator hinge

Tailplane attachment

Rudder post

Steel lug

Aircraft registration code

Spar

Shock-absorbing spring

Steel V-strut

Trailing edge

Leading edge

Pivoted tailskid

National marking

Rib

HORIZONTAL TAIL OF A BE 2B

Early passenger aircraft

FRONT VIEW OF LOCKHEED ELECTRA, 1934

UNTIL THE 1930s, most passenger aircraft were biplanes, with two pairs of wings and a wooden or metal framework covered with fabric or, sometimes, plywood. Such aircraft were restricted to low speeds and low altitudes because of the drag on their wings. Many had an open cockpit, situated behind or in front of an enclosed – but unpressurized – cabin that carried a maximum of ten people. The passengers usually sat in wicker chairs that were not bolted to the floor, and the journey could be bumpy when flying through turbulence. Warm clothing, and ear plugs to reduce the effects of prolonged noise, were often required. During the 1930s, powerful, streamlined, all-metal monoplanes, such as the Lockheed Electra shown here, became widespread. By 1939, the advent of pressurized cabins allowed fast flights at high altitudes, where there is less turbulence.

Flying boats were still necessary on many routes until 1945 because of inadequate runways and the frequency of emergency sea-landings. World War II, however, resulted in enough good runways being built for land-planes to become standard on all major airline routes.

Green starboard navigation light

Flush-riveted metal-skinned wing

Leading edge

Fuel-jettison valve

Static discharge wick

Split flap in landing position

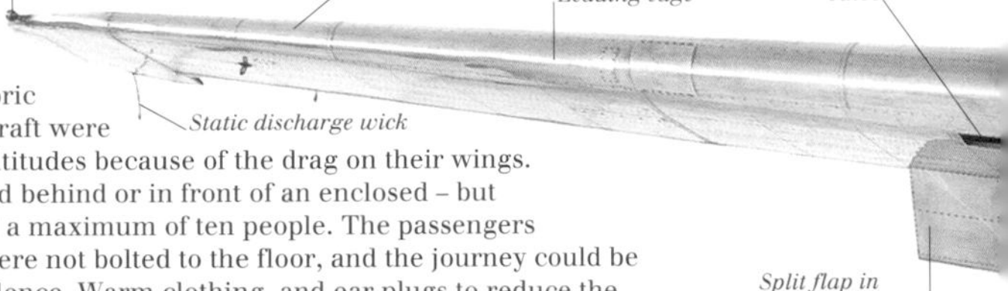

PASSENGER CABIN TRIM PANELS

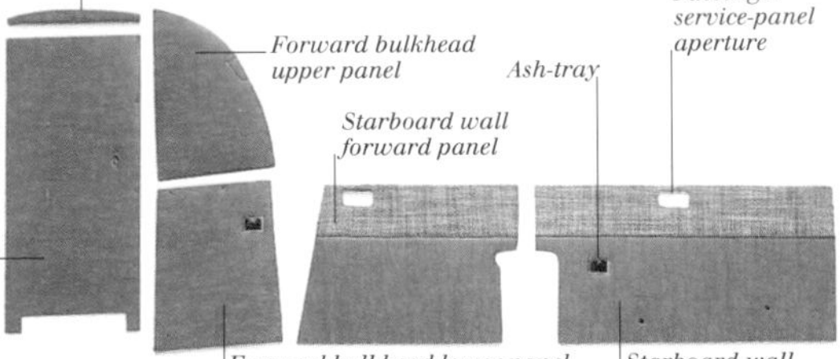

Roof trim panel

Forward bulkhead upper panel

Ash-tray

Passenger service-panel aperture

Starboard wall forward panel

Cockpit door panel

Forward bulkhead lower panel

Starboard wall mid-forward panel

SIDE VIEW OF LOCKHEED ELECTRA, 1934

Cockpit windscreen

Sliding window

Emergency escape hatch

Oil tank

Steel firewall

Passenger window

Air intake

Ventilator exit

Nose

Propeller pitch-change cylinder

Blade counterweight

Spinner mounting disc

Variable-pitch propeller

Exhaust collector ring

Landing gear door

Electrically driven split flap

Passenger door

Pratt & Whitney nine-cylinder radial engine

Red port navigation light

Exhaust pipe

Static discharge wick

Aileron

Main landing gear

Brake pipe

Aluminium wheel

Mudguard

Metal-skinned wing

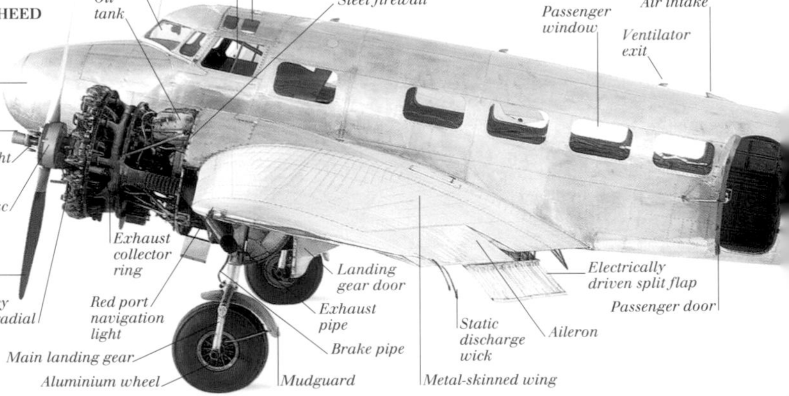

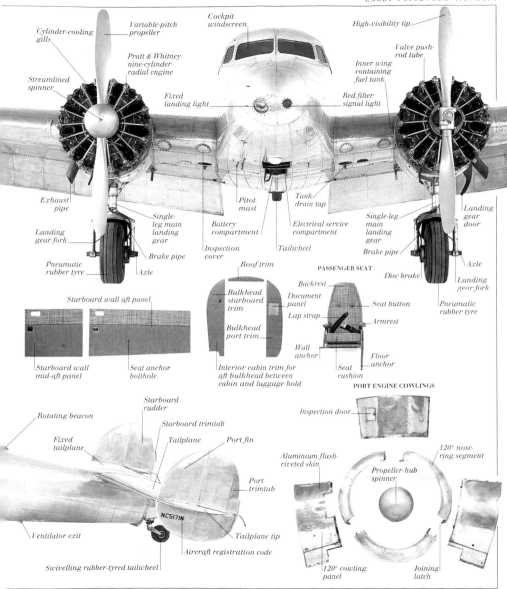

Variable-pitch propeller

Cylinder-cooling gills

Cockpit windscreen

High-visibility tip

Pratt & Whitney nine-cylinder radial engine

Valve push-rod tube

Streamlined spinner

Inner wing containing fuel tank

Fixed landing light

Red filter signal light

Exhaust pipe

Single-leg main landing gear

Pitot mast

Tank drain tap

Single-leg main landing gear

Landing gear door

Landing gear fork

Battery compartment

Electrical service compartment

Brake pipe

Axle

Pneumatic rubber tyre

Brake pipe

Axle

Landing gear fork

Inspection cover

Tailwheel

Disc brake

Pneumatic rubber tyre

Roof trim

PASSENGER SEAT

Starboard wall aft panel

Bulkhead starboard trim

Backrest

Document panel

Seat button

Lap strap

Armrest

Bulkhead port trim

Wall anchor

Floor anchor

Starboard wall mid-aft panel

Seat anchor bolthole

Interior cabin trim for aft bulkhead between cabin and luggage hold

Seat cushion

PORT ENGINE COWLINGS

Rotating beacon

Starboard rudder

Inspection door

Starboard trimtab

Fixed tailplane

Tailplane

Port fin

Aluminium flush-riveted skin

120° nose-ring segment

Propeller-hub spinner

Port trimtab

Ventilator exit

NC5171N

Tailplane tip

Swivelling rubber-tyred tailwheel

Aircraft registration code

120° cowling panel

Joining latch

World War II aircraft

WHEN WORLD WAR II began in 1939, air forces had already replaced most of their fabric-skinned biplanes with all-metal, stressed-skin monoplanes. Aircraft played a far greater role in military operations during World War II than ever before. The wide range of aircraft duties, and the introduction of radar tracking and guidance systems, put pressure on designers to improve aircraft performance. The main areas of improvement were speed, range, and engine power. Bombers became larger and more powerful – converting from two to four engines – in order to carry a heavier bomb load; the US B-17 Flying Fortress could carry up to 6.2 tonnes (6.1 tons) of bombs over a distance of about 3,200 km (2,000 miles). Some aircraft increased their range by using drop tanks (fuel tanks that were jettisoned when empty to reduce drag). Fighters needed speed and manoeuvrability: the Hawker Tempest shown here had a maximum speed of 700 kph (435 mph), and was one of the few Allied aircraft capable of catching the German jet-powered V1 "flying bomb". By 1944, Britain had introduced its first turbojet-powered aircraft, the Gloster Meteor fighter, and Germany had introduced the fastest fighter in the world, the turbojet-powered Me 262, which had a maximum speed of 868 kph (540 mph).

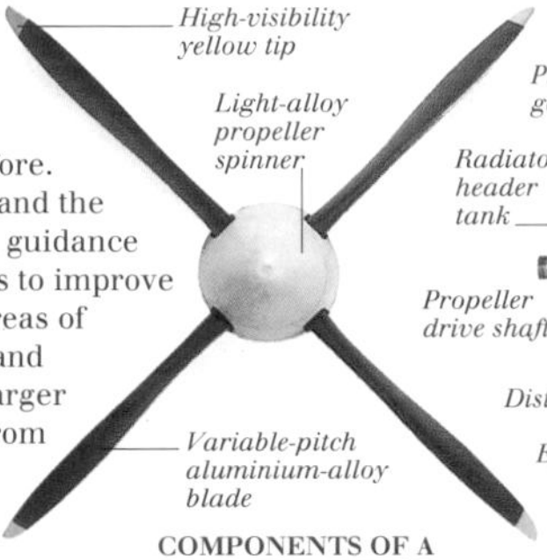

PROPELLER

High-visibility yellow tip

Light-alloy propeller spinner

Variable-pitch aluminium-alloy blade

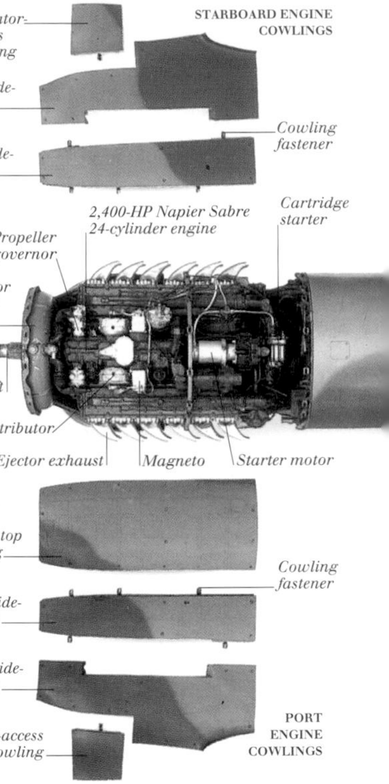

COMPONENTS OF A HAWKER TEMPEST MARK V, c.1943

Radiator-access cowling

Lower side-cowling

Upper side-cowling

STARBOARD ENGINE COWLINGS

Cowling fastener

2,400-HP Napier Sabre 24-cylinder engine

Cartridge starter

Propeller governor

Radiator header tank

Propeller drive shaft

Distributor

Ejector exhaust

Magneto

Starter motor

Engine top cowling

Upper side-cowling

Lower side-cowling

Radiator-access cowling

Cowling fastener

PORT ENGINE COWLINGS

SECTIONED B-17G FLYING FORTRESS BOMBER, c.1943

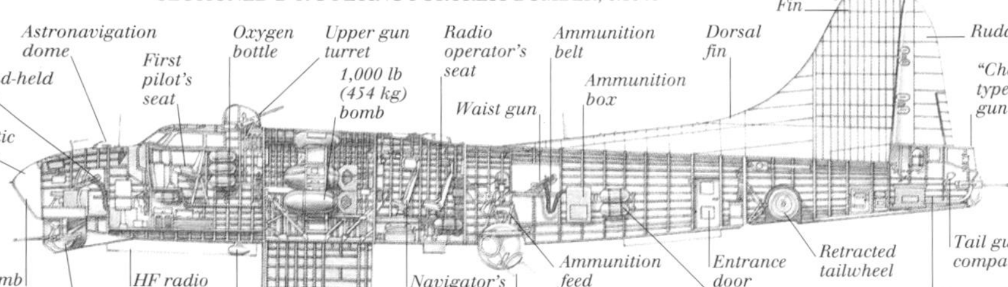

VHF aerial

Fin

Rudder

Astronavigation dome

First pilot's seat

Oxygen bottle

Upper gun turret

Radio operator's seat

Ammunition belt

Dorsal fin

"Cheyenne-type" tail-gun turret

Hand-held gun

1,000 lb (454 kg) bomb

Waist gun

Ammunition box

Plastic nose

Bomb aimer's viewing panel

Chin gun turret

HF radio aerial

Bomb door

Direction-finding-aerial fairing

Navigator's seat

Sperry ball gun turret

Ammunition feed

Entrance door

Oxygen bottle

Retracted tailwheel

Tail gunner's compartment

Ammunition feed

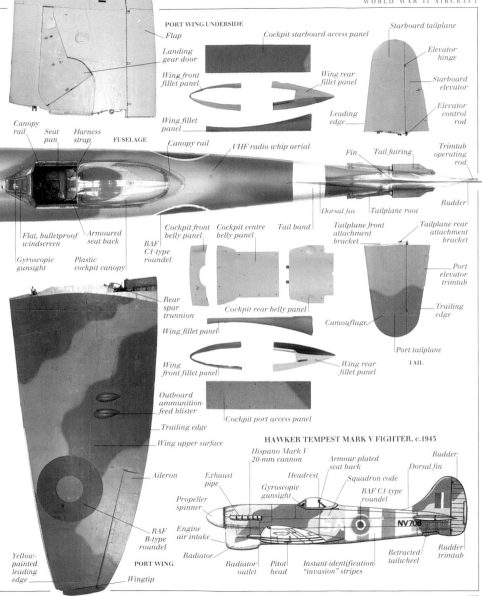

PORT WING UNDERSIDE
Flap
Landing gear door
Wing front fillet panel
Wing fillet panel
Cockpit starboard access panel
Wing rear fillet panel
Leading edge

Starboard tailplane
Elevator hinge
Starboard elevator
Elevator control rod

Canopy rail
Seat pan
Harness strap
FUSELAGE
Canopy rail
VHF radio whip aerial
Fin
Tail fairing
Trimtab operating rod
Dorsal fin
Tailplane root
Rudder

Flat, bulletproof windscreen
Armoured seat back
Gyroscopic gunsight
Plastic cockpit canopy
Cockpit front belly panel
RAF C1-type roundel
Cockpit centre belly panel
Tail band
Tailplane front attachment bracket
Tailplane rear attachment bracket
Port elevator trimtab

Rear spar trunnion
Cockpit rear belly panel
Wing fillet panel
Wing front fillet panel
Wing rear fillet panel
Camouflage
Trailing edge
Port tailplane
TAIL

Outboard ammunition-feed blister
Cockpit port access panel
Trailing edge
Wing upper surface

HAWKER TEMPEST MARK V FIGHTER, c.1943

Aileron
Hispano Mark V 20-mm cannon
Armour-plated seat back
Headrest
Squadron code
Rudder
Dorsal fin
RAF C1-type roundel
Exhaust pipe
Gyroscopic gunsight
Propeller spinner
Engine air intake
RAF B-type roundel
NV703
Radiator
Radiator outlet
Pitot head
Instant-identification "invasion" stripes
Retracted tailwheel
Rudder trimtab
Yellow-painted leading edge
Wingtip
PORT WING

Modern piston aero-engines

MID WEST TWO-STROKE, THREE-CYLINDER ENGINE

PISTON ENGINES today are used mainly to power the vast numbers of light aircraft and microlights, as well as crop-sprayers and crop-dusters, small helicopters, and fire-bombers (which dump water on large fires). Virtually all heavier aircraft are now powered by jet engines. Modern piston aero-engines work on the same basic principles as the engine used by the Wright brothers in the first powered flight in 1903. However, today's engines are more sophisticated than earlier engines. For example, modern aero-engines may use a two-stroke or a four-stroke combustion cycle; they may have from one to nine air- or water-cooled cylinders, which may be arranged horizontally, in-line, in V formation, or radially; and they may drive the aircraft's propeller either directly or through a reduction gearbox. One of the more unconventional types of modern aero-engine is the rotary engine shown here, which has a trilobate (three-sided) rotor spinning in a chamber shaped like a fat figure-of-eight.

MID WEST 75-HP TWO-STROKE, THREE-CYLINDER ENGINE

Spark plug

Coolant outlet

Cylinder head

Piston

Cylinder barrel

Exhaust manifold

Exhaust port

Cylinder liner

Upper crankcase

Reduction gearbox

Driven gear

Propeller drive flange

Gearbox drive splines

Connecting rod (con-rod)

Small end

Pump drive belt

Coolant pump

Generator rotor

Torsional vibration damper

Sprag clutch

Big end

Counterweight

Crankshaft

Stator

Ignition trigger housing

Gearbox mounting plate

Lower crankcase

Engine mounting plate

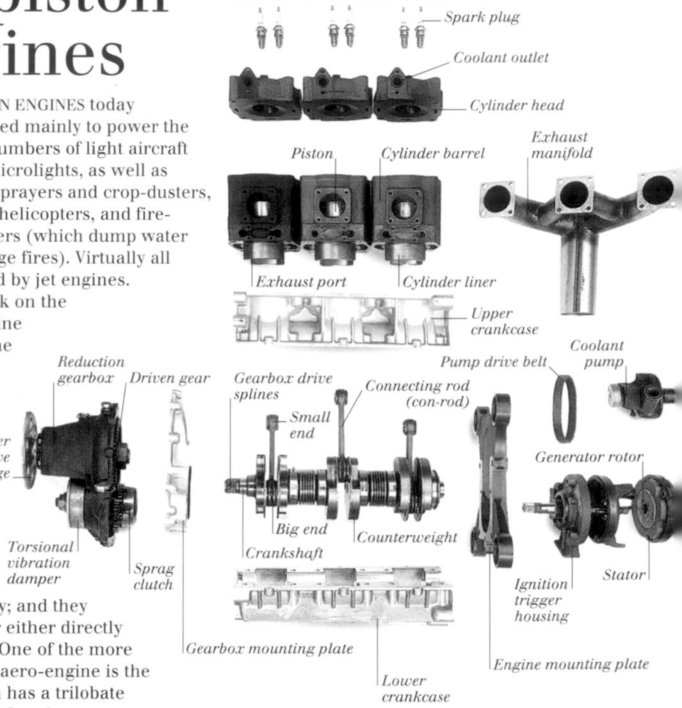

ROTOR AND HOUSINGS OF A MID WEST SINGLE-ROTOR ENGINE

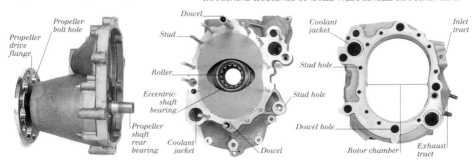

Propeller drive flange

Propeller bolt hole

Dowel

Stud

Coolant jacket

Inlet tract

Roller

Stud hole

Eccentric-shaft bearing

Stud hole

Propeller shaft rear bearing

Coolant jacket

Dowel

Dowel hole

Rotor chamber

Exhaust tract

GEARBOX CASE

FRONT HOUSING (FRONT END-PLATE)

TROCHOID HOUSING

MID WEST 90-HP TWIN-ROTOR ENGINE

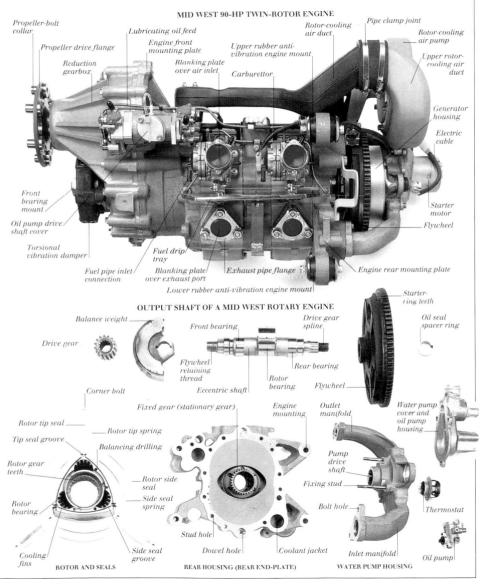

Propeller-bolt collar

Propeller drive flange

Reduction gearbox

Lubricating oil feed

Engine front mounting plate

Blanking plate over air inlet

Upper rubber anti-vibration engine mount

Carburettor

Rotor-cooling air duct

Pipe clamp joint

Rotor-cooling air pump

Upper rotor-cooling air duct

Generator housing

Electric cable

Starter motor

Flywheel

Engine rear mounting plate

Front bearing mount

Oil pump drive shaft cover

Torsional vibration damper

Fuel pipe inlet connection

Fuel drip tray

Blanking plate over exhaust port

Exhaust pipe flange

Lower rubber anti-vibration engine mount

OUTPUT SHAFT OF A MID WEST ROTARY ENGINE

Balance weight

Drive gear

Front bearing

Drive gear spline

Starter-ring teeth

Oil seal spacer ring

Flywheel retaining thread

Rear bearing

Rotor bearing

Eccentric shaft

Flywheel

Corner bolt

Fixed gear (stationary gear)

Engine mounting

Outlet manifold

Water pump cover and oil pump housing

Rotor tip seal

Rotor tip spring

Tip seal groove

Balancing drilling

Rotor gear teeth

Rotor side seal

Side seal spring

Pump drive shaft

Fixing stud

Rotor bearing

Bolt hole

Thermostat

Cooling fins

Side seal groove

Stud hole

Dowel hole

Coolant jacket

Inlet manifold

Oil pump

ROTOR AND SEALS

REAR HOUSING (REAR END-PLATE)

WATER PUMP HOUSING

Modern jetliners 1

BAE-146 JETLINER

MODERN JETLINERS HAVE ENABLED ordinary people to travel to places where once only the wealthy could afford to go. Compared with the first jetliners (which were introduced in the 1940s), modern ones are much quieter, burn fuel more efficiently, and produce less air pollution. These advances are largely due to the replacement of turbojet engines with turbofan engines (see pp. 418-419). The greater power of turbofan engines at low speeds enables modern jetliners to carry more fuel and passengers than turbojet aircraft; a modern Boeing 747-400 (popularly known as a "jumbo jet") can fly 400 people for 13,700 km (8,500 miles) without needing to refuel. Jetliners fly at high altitudes, typically cruising at 8,000-11,000 m (26,000-36,000 ft), where they can use fuel efficiently and usually avoid bad weather. The pilot always controls the aircraft during take-off and landing, but at other times the aircraft is usually controlled by an autopilot. Autopilots are complex on-board mechanisms that detect deviations from an aircraft's route and make appropriate adjustments to the flight controls. Flight decks are also equipped with radars that warn pilots of approaching hazards, such as mountain ranges, bad weather, and other aircraft.

Shoulder cowling

Engine pylon

Hinged cowling panel

Nose cowling

Fan duct nozzle

Fire extinguisher discharge indicator

Core-engine jet pipe

Oil-filler door

Push-in door for hand-held fire extinguisher

TURBOFAN ENGINE COWLING

Drain mast

STRUCTURAL COMPONENTS OF A BAE-146 JETLINER

Oil-filler door for integrated-drive generator

FUSELAGE NOSE-SECTION

FUSELAGE MID-SECTION

Electrically heated, birdproof windshield

Side window

Anchor for open door

Rain gutter

Hinge

Peephole

Finger recess

Static air-pressure plate

Forward main door aperture

Passenger window aperture

VHF omni-range and instrument-landing-system antennas

Light-alloy door frame

Main external operating handle

Multiple-pinned lock

Floor level

Radome

Toilet service connector

FORWARD MAIN DOOR

Anchor for open door

Air temperature probe

Stall warning vane

Pitot head for dynamic air pressure

Overwing
fuel-filler cap

Systems
connector

Overwing fuel-
filler cap

Fuel contents
indicator

STARBOARD
WING
ASSEMBLY

Centre-line (spine)
of aircraft

Single-piece skin
over inboard wing

Rubber sealing strip

Rubber sealing strip

Trailing edge

Trailing edge
of fixed wing

Spoiler anchorage

Hydraulic actuator
attachment

Pivot point

Flap-track fairing

Screw
joint

Aft section

MOVABLE FLAP TRACK AND FAIRING

Upper carriage
attached to flap

Hinge

**INBOARD LIFT
SPOILERS**

Stainless-steel
flap seal

Track roller

Anchor
bearing

Track

Tab-hinge line

FOWLER FLAP

Leading edge

Root

Gearbox
mount

Bellcrank
lever

Gearbox unit

Carriage
drive nut

Flap drive
screw

Lower carriage

Main spar
bridge

Leading
edge

Wing-root mount
containing central
fuel tank

Inboard
tab

Skin lap-
joint

Root rib

Attachment structure for
wing-to-fuselage fairing

Cabin air-pressure
discharge valve

Floor
level

Fairing of
landing gear bay

Fairing of landing
gear pivot

Yellow anti-
corrosion paint

Modern jetliners 2

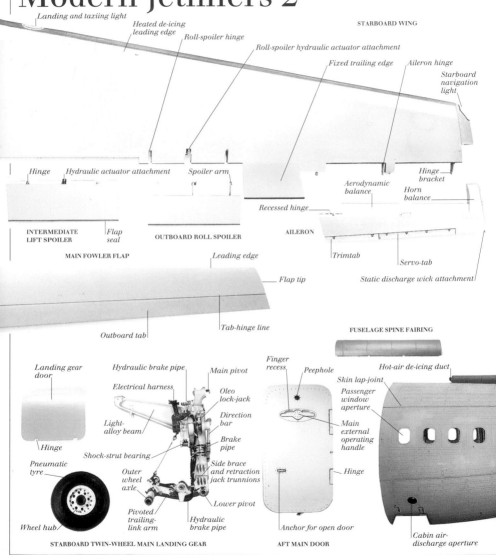

Landing and taxiing light

Heated de-icing leading edge

Roll-spoiler hinge

STARBOARD WING

Roll-spoiler hydraulic actuator attachment

Fixed trailing edge

Aileron hinge

Starboard navigation light

Hinge

Hydraulic actuator attachment

Spoiler arm

Hinge bracket

Aerodynamic balance

Horn balance

Recessed hinge

INTERMEDIATE LIFT SPOILER

Flap seal

OUTBOARD ROLL SPOILER

AILERON

MAIN FOWLER FLAP

Leading edge

Trimtab

Servo-tab

Flap tip

Static discharge wick attachment

Outboard tab

Tab-hinge line

FUSELAGE SPINE FAIRING

Landing gear door

Hydraulic brake pipe

Main pivot

Finger recess

Peephole

Hot-air de-icing duct

Electrical harness

Oleo lock-jack

Skin lap-joint

Passenger window aperture

Light-alloy beam

Direction bar

Main external operating handle

Hinge

Brake pipe

Pneumatic tyre

Shock-strut bearing

Outer wheel axle

Side brace and retraction jack trunnions

Hinge

Lower pivot

Wheel hub

Pivoted trailing-link arm

Hydraulic brake pipe

Anchor for open door

Cabin air-discharge aperture

STARBOARD TWIN-WHEEL MAIN LANDING GEAR

AFT MAIN DOOR

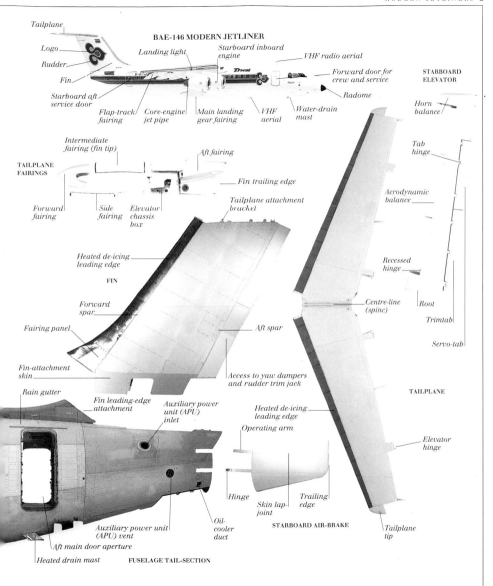

BAE-146 MODERN JETLINER

Tailplane

Logo

Rudder

Fin

Starboard aft
service door

Flap-track
fairing

Core-engine
jet pipe

Landing light

Main landing
gear fairing

Starboard inboard
engine

VHF
aerial

Water-drain
mast

VHF radio aerial

Forward door for
crew and service

Radome

STARBOARD
ELEVATOR

Horn
balance

Tab
hinge

Aerodynamic
balance

Recessed
hinge

Centre-line
(spine)

Root

Trimtab

Servo-tab

TAILPLANE
FAIRINGS

Intermediate
fairing (fin tip)

Forward
fairing

Side
fairing

Elevator
chassis
box

Aft fairing

Fin trailing edge

Tailplane attachment
bracket

FIN

Heated de-icing
leading edge

Forward
spar

Fairing panel

Aft spar

Fin-attachment
skin

Access to yaw dampers
and rudder trim jack

TAILPLANE

Rain gutter

Fin leading-edge
attachment

Auxiliary power
unit (APU)
inlet

Heated de-icing
leading edge

Operating arm

Elevator
hinge

Auxiliary power unit
(APU) vent

Oil-
cooler
duct

Hinge

Skin lap-
joint

Trailing
edge

Aft main door aperture

Heated drain mast

FUSELAGE TAIL-SECTION

STARBOARD AIR-BRAKE

Tailplane
tip

Supersonic jetliners

COMPUTER-
DESIGNED SST

SUPERSONIC AIRCRAFT FLY FASTER than the speed of sound
(Mach 1). There are many supersonic military aircraft, but only
two supersonic passenger-carrying aircraft (also called SSTs, or
supersonic transports) have been produced: the Russian Tu-144,
and Concorde, produced jointly by Britain and France.
The Tu-144 was withdrawn in 1978, after only
seven months in service. Concorde has
remained in service since 1976, with a break for modifications
from July 2000 until October 2001. Its features include a droop
nose, which is lowered during take-off and landing to aid
visibility from the cockpit, and the pumping of fuel between forward and aft trim
tanks to help stabilize the aircraft. Concorde has a narrow fuselage and short-
span wings to reduce drag during supersonic flight. Its noisy turbojet engines
with afterburners enable it to carry 100 passengers at a cruising speed of Mach 2
at 15,000-18,000 m (50,000-60,000 ft). Once an aircraft is flying faster than Mach 1,
it produces a continuous air-pressure wave, which is heard as a "sonic boom".

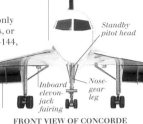

Strake

Fin

Standby
pitot head

Starboard
outboard
engine air-intake

Inboard
elevon-
jack
fairing

Nose-
gear
leg

FRONT VIEW OF CONCORDE

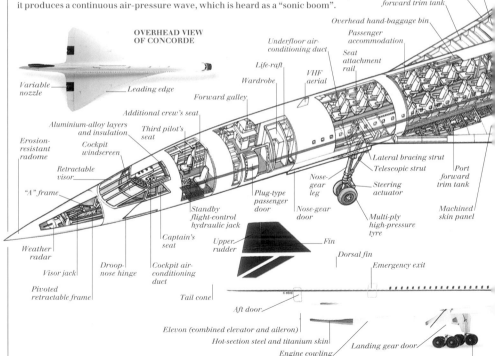

OVERHEAD VIEW
OF CONCORDE

Variable
nozzle

Leading edge

Aluminium-alloy layers
and insulation

Erosion-
resistant
radome

Cockpit
windscreen

Retractable
visor

"A" frame

Additional crew's seat

Third pilot's
seat

Weather
radar

Visor jack

Pivoted
retractable frame

Droop-
nose hinge

Captain's
seat

Cockpit air-
conditioning
duct

Upper
rudder

Tail cone

Aft door

Standby
flight-control
hydraulic jack

Plug-type
passenger
door

Nose-
gear
leg

Nose-gear
door

Fin

Underfloor air-
conditioning duct

Life-raft

Wardrobe

Forward galley

VHF
aerial

Passenger
accommodation

Seat
attachment
rail

Overhead hand-baggage bin

Toilets

Electrothermal
de-icing panel

Starboard
forward trim tank

Lateral bracing strut

Telescopic strut

Steering
actuator

Multi-ply
high-pressure
tyre

Port
forward
trim tank

Machined
skin panel

Dorsal fin

Emergency exit

Elevon (combined elevator and aileron)

Hot-section steel and titanium skin

Engine cowling

Landing gear door

Bogie main landing gear

416

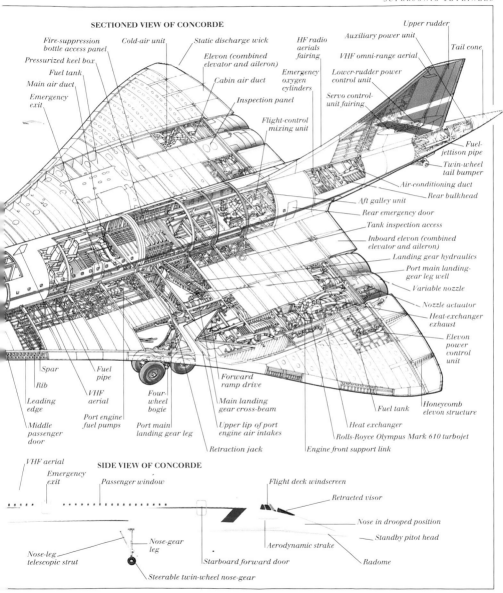

SECTIONED VIEW OF CONCORDE

Fire-suppression bottle access panel
Cold-air unit
Static discharge wick
HF radio aerials fairing
Auxiliary power unit
Upper rudder
Tail cone

Pressurized keel box
Elevon (combined elevator and aileron)
VHF omni-range aerial

Fuel tank
Cabin air duct
Emergency oxygen cylinders
Lower-rudder power control unit

Main air duct
Inspection panel
Servo control-unit fairing

Emergency exit

Flight-control mixing unit

Fuel-jettison pipe

Twin-wheel tail bumper

Air-conditioning duct

Rear bulkhead

Aft galley unit
Rear emergency door

Tank inspection access

Inboard elevon (combined elevator and aileron)

Landing gear hydraulics

Port main landing-gear leg well

Variable nozzle

Nozzle actuator

Heat-exchanger exhaust

Elevon power control unit

Spar
Fuel pipe
Forward ramp drive

Rib

Leading edge
VHF aerial
Four-wheel bogie
Main landing gear cross-beam

Middle passenger door
Port engine fuel pumps
Port main landing gear leg
Upper lip of port engine air intakes
Heat exchanger
Honeycomb elevon structure
Fuel tank

Retraction jack
Rolls-Royce Olympus Mark 610 turbojet
Engine front support link

SIDE VIEW OF CONCORDE

VHF aerial
Emergency exit
Passenger window
Flight deck windscreen

Retracted visor

Nose in drooped position

Standby pitot head

Nose-gear leg

Nose-leg telescopic strut
Starboard forward door
Aerodynamic strake
Radome

Steerable twin-wheel nose-gear

417

Jet engines

JET ENGINES ARE USED BY MOST MILITARY and heavy aircraft, and by many helicopters. The simplest type of jet engine, or gas turbine, is the turbojet. It works by continuously burning a mixture of fuel and air in a combustion chamber to produce a jet of hot exhaust gas that is expelled through a nozzle to produce thrust. The hot gas also spins turbine blades, which, in turn, spin the blades of an air compressor; the compressor forces air into the combustion chamber. Many of the fastest aircraft use turbojets, with additional booster units called afterburners, but their use is restricted by their high noise emission. Most jetliners use turbofan jet engines, which are quieter. An enormous fan, driven by a low-pressure turbine, feeds some air into the compressor but feeds most of it through bypass ducts to join the exhaust jetstream in the tail cone. The bypass stream produces most of the thrust. Many smaller, propeller-driven aircraft use turboprop jet engines, in which the engine powers a propeller.

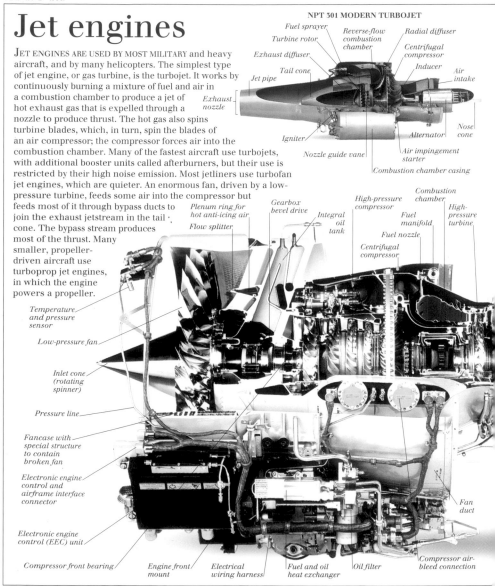

Fuel sprayer
Turbine rotor
Reverse-flow combustion chamber
Radial diffuser
Centrifugal compressor
Exhaust diffuser
Inducer
Air intake
Tail cone
Jet pipe
Exhaust nozzle
Nose cone
Igniter
Alternator
Nozzle guide vane
Air impingement starter
Combustion chamber casing

Combustion chamber
High-pressure compressor
High-pressure turbine
Gearbox bevel drive
Fuel manifold
Plenum ring for hot anti-icing air
Integral oil tank
Fuel nozzle
Flow splitter
Centrifugal compressor

Temperature and pressure sensor

Low-pressure fan

Inlet cone (rotating spinner)

Pressure line

Fancase with special structure to contain broken fan

Electronic engine control and airframe interface connector

Electronic engine control (EEC) unit

Compressor front bearing
Engine front mount
Electrical wiring harness
Fuel and oil heat exchanger
Oil filter
Compressor air-bleed connection
Fan duct

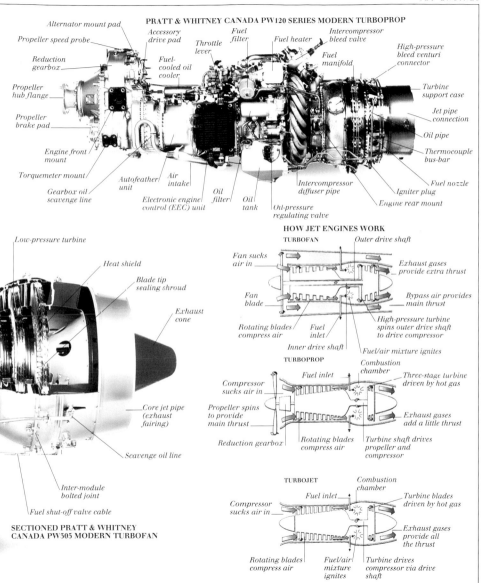

PRATT & WHITNEY CANADA PW120 SERIES MODERN TURBOPROP

Alternator mount pad
Propeller speed probe
Accessory drive pad
Throttle lever
Fuel filter
Fuel heater
Intercompressor bleed valve
High-pressure bleed venturi connector
Reduction gearbox
Fuel-cooled oil cooler
Fuel manifold
Propeller hub flange
Turbine support case
Jet pipe connection
Oil pipe
Propeller brake pad
Thermocouple bus-bar
Engine front mount
Fuel nozzle
Torquemeter mount
Autofeather unit
Air intake
Intercompressor diffuser pipe
Igniter plug
Gearbox oil scavenge line
Electronic engine control (EEC) unit
Oil filter
Oil tank
Oil-pressure regulating valve
Engine rear mount

Low-pressure turbine
Heat shield
Blade tip sealing shroud
Exhaust cone
Core jet pipe (exhaust fairing)
Scavenge oil line
Inter-module bolted joint
Fuel shut-off valve cable

SECTIONED PRATT & WHITNEY CANADA PW305 MODERN TURBOFAN

HOW JET ENGINES WORK

TURBOFAN
Fan sucks air in
Outer drive shaft
Exhaust gases provide extra thrust
Fan blade
Bypass air provides main thrust
Rotating blades compress air
Fuel inlet
High-pressure turbine spins outer drive shaft to drive compressor
Inner drive shaft
Fuel/air mixture ignites

TURBOPROP
Compressor sucks air in
Fuel inlet
Combustion chamber
Three-stage turbine driven by hot gas
Propeller spins to provide main thrust
Exhaust gases add a little thrust
Reduction gearbox
Rotating blades compress air
Turbine shaft drives propeller and compressor

TURBOJET
Compressor sucks air in
Fuel inlet
Combustion chamber
Turbine blades driven by hot gas
Exhaust gases provide all the thrust
Rotating blades compress air
Fuel/air mixture ignites
Turbine drives compressor via drive shaft

Modern military aircraft

MODERN MILITARY AIRCRAFT ARE AMONG THE MOST SOPHISTICATED and expensive products of the 21st century. Fighters need computer-operated controls for manoeuvrability, powerful engines, and effective air-to-air weapons. Most modern fighters also have guided missiles, radar, and passive, infra-red sensors. These developments enable today's fighters to engage in combat with adversaries that are outside visual range. Bombers carry a large weapon load and enough fuel for long-range flights. A few military aircraft, such as the Tornado and the F-14 Tomcat, have variable-sweep ("swing") wings. During take-off and landing their wings are fully extended, but for high-speed flight and low-level attacks the wings are pivoted fully back. A recent development is the "stealth" bomber, which is designed to absorb or deflect enemy radar in order to remain undetected. Earlier bombers, such as the Tornado, use terrain-following radars to fly so close to the ground that they avoid enemy radar detection.

FRONT VIEW OF A PANAVIA TORNADO

Instrument landing system aerial

Birdproof windscreen

Air data probe

Wing-root glove fairing

Port variable-incidence air intake

Starboard inboard stores pylon

Taileron

Starboard main landing gear door

Main landing gear leg

Laser ranger and marked-target seeker

Starboard nose-gear door

Steerable twin-wheel nose-gear

Radome containing ground-mapping, attack, and terrain-following radars

Taxiing light

Wing extended for take-off and landing

Wing pivoted back for high-speed flight

SWING-WING F-14 TOMCAT FIGHTER

SIDE VIEW OF A PANAVIA TORNADO GR1A (RECONNAISSANCE VERSION), 1986

Pilot's cockpit

Navigator's instrument console

Navigator's cockpit

Single canopy over both cockpits

Engine air intake

Navigation light

Flat, birdproof windscreen

High-velocity air duct to disperse rain

Upper "request identification" aerial

Air data probe

RESCUE

Radome containing ground-mapping, attack, and terrain-following radars

UHF aerial

Angle-of-attack probe

Tacan (tactical air navigation) aerial

Emergency canopy release handle

Nose-gear door

Steerable nose-gear leg

Pitot head

Twin nose-wheel

Hinged auxiliary air intake

Cold air intake (ram scoop)

Heat exchanger exhaust duct

Window covering infra-red reconnaissance camera

NORTHROP B-2 ("STEALTH" BOMBER), 1989

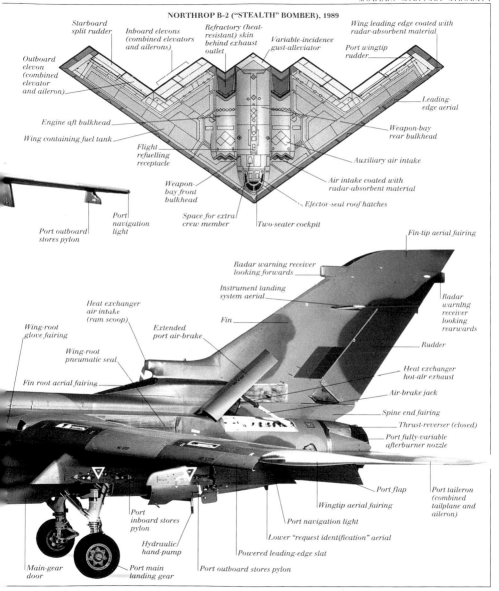

Starboard split rudder

Inboard elevons (combined elevators and ailerons)

Refractory (heat-resistant) skin behind exhaust outlet

Variable-incidence gust-alleviator

Wing leading edge coated with radar-absorbent material

Port wingtip rudder

Outboard elevon (combined elevator and aileron)

Leading-edge aerial

Engine aft bulkhead

Wing containing fuel tank

Flight refuelling receptacle

Weapon-bay rear bulkhead

Auxiliary air intake

Weapon-bay front bulkhead

Space for extra crew member

Air intake coated with radar-absorbent material

Ejector-seat roof hatches

Port navigation light

Two-seater cockpit

Port outboard stores pylon

Fin-tip aerial fairing

Radar warning receiver looking forwards

Instrument landing system aerial

Heat exchanger air intake (ram scoop)

Extended port air-brake

Fin

Radar warning receiver looking rearwards

Wing-root glove fairing

Wing-root pneumatic seal

Rudder

Heat exchanger hot-air exhaust

Fin root aerial fairing

Air-brake jack

Spine end fairing

Thrust-reverser (closed)

Port fully-variable afterburner nozzle

Port flap

Port taileron (combined tailplane and aileron)

Port inboard stores pylon

Wingtip aerial fairing

Hydraulic hand-pump

Port navigation light

Lower "request identification" aerial

Powered leading-edge slat

Main-gear door

Port main landing gear

Port outboard stores pylon

Helicopters

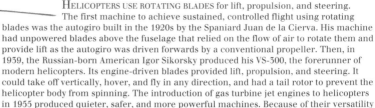

HELICOPTERS USE ROTATING BLADES for lift, propulsion, and steering. The first machine to achieve sustained, controlled flight using rotating blades was the autogiro built in the 1920s by the Spaniard Juan de la Cierva. His machine had unpowered blades above the fuselage that relied on the flow of air to rotate them and provide lift as the autogiro was driven forwards by a conventional propeller. Then, in 1939, the Russian-born American Igor Sikorsky produced his VS-300, the forerunner of modern helicopters. Its engine-driven blades provided lift, propulsion, and steering. It could take off vertically, hover, and fly in any direction, and had a tail rotor to prevent the helicopter body from spinning. The introduction of gas turbine jet engines to helicopters in 1955 produced quieter, safer, and more powerful machines. Because of their versatility in flight, helicopters are today used for many purposes, including crop-spraying, traffic surveillance, and transporting crews to deep-sea oil rigs, as well as acting as gunships, air ambulances, and air taxis.

BELL 47G-3B1

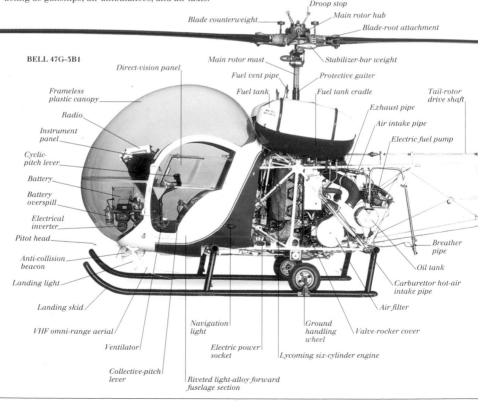

BELL 47G-3B1

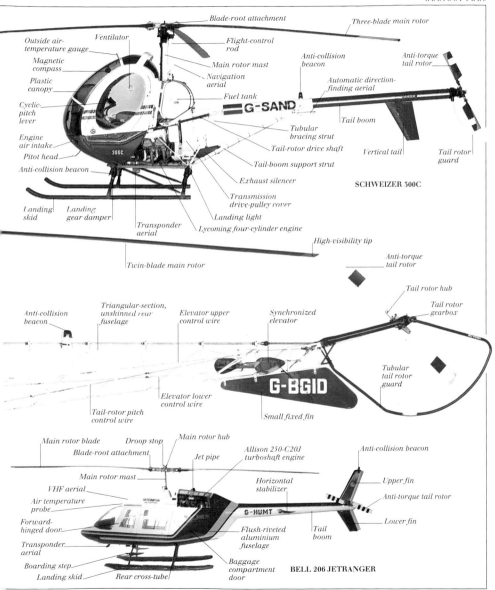

Blade-root attachment

Three-blade main rotor

Outside air-temperature gauge

Ventilator

Flight-control rod

Anti-collision beacon

Anti-torque tail rotor

Magnetic compass

Main rotor mast

Automatic direction-finding aerial

Plastic canopy

Navigation aerial

Cyclic-pitch lever

Fuel tank

G-SAND

Tail boom

Tail rotor guard

Engine air intake

Tubular bracing strut

Tail-rotor drive shaft

Vertical tail

Pitot head

Tail-boom support strut

Anti-collision beacon

Exhaust silencer

SCHWEIZER 300C

Landing skid

Landing gear damper

Transmission drive-pulley cover

Transponder aerial

Landing light

Lycoming four-cylinder engine

High-visibility tip

Twin-blade main rotor

Anti-torque tail rotor

Tail rotor hub

Anti-collision beacon

Triangular-section, unskinned rear fuselage

Elevator upper control wire

Synchronized elevator

Tail rotor gearbox

G-BGID

Tubular tail rotor guard

Elevator lower control wire

Tail-rotor pitch control wire

Small fixed fin

Main rotor blade

Droop stop

Main rotor hub

Blade-root attachment

Jet pipe

Allison 250-C20J turboshaft engine

Anti-collision beacon

Main rotor mast

Horizontal stabilizer

Upper fin

VHF aerial

Anti-torque tail rotor

Air temperature probe

G-HUMT

Lower fin

Forward-hinged door

Tail boom

Transponder aerial

Flush-riveted aluminium fuselage

Boarding step

Baggage compartment door

BELL 206 JETRANGER

Landing skid

Rear cross-tube

423

Light aircraft

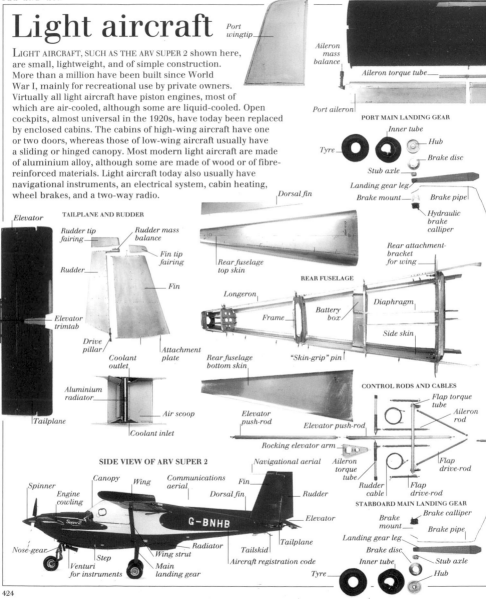

LIGHT AIRCRAFT, SUCH AS THE ARV SUPER 2 shown here, are small, lightweight, and of simple construction. More than a million have been built since World War I, mainly for recreational use by private owners. Virtually all light aircraft have piston engines, most of which are air-cooled, although some are liquid-cooled. Open cockpits, almost universal in the 1920s, have today been replaced by enclosed cabins. The cabins of high-wing aircraft have one or two doors, whereas those of low-wing aircraft usually have a sliding or hinged canopy. Most modern light aircraft are made of aluminium alloy, although some are made of wood or of fibre-reinforced materials. Light aircraft today also usually have navigational instruments, an electrical system, cabin heating, wheel brakes, and a two-way radio.

Port wingtip

Aileron mass balance

Aileron torque tube

Port aileron

PORT MAIN LANDING GEAR

Inner tube

Hub

Tyre

Brake disc

Stub axle

Landing gear leg

Brake mount

Brake pipe

Hydraulic brake calliper

Rear attachment-bracket for wing

Dorsal fin

TAILPLANE AND RUDDER

Elevator

Rudder tip fairing

Rudder mass balance

Fin tip fairing

Rudder

Rear fuselage top skin

Fin

Elevator trimtab

Drive pillar

Coolant outlet

Attachment plate

Rear fuselage bottom skin

REAR FUSELAGE

Longeron

Frame

Battery box

Diaphragm

Side skin

"Skin-grip" pin

CONTROL RODS AND CABLES

Flap torque tube

Aileron rod

Aluminium radiator

Air scoop

Coolant inlet

Elevator push-rod

Elevator push-rod

Rocking elevator arm

Aileron torque tube

Flap drive-rod

Rudder cable

Flap drive-rod

Tailplane

SIDE VIEW OF ARV SUPER 2

Navigational aerial

Spinner

Canopy

Wing

Communications aerial

Fin

Dorsal fin

Rudder

Engine cowling

Elevator

STARBOARD MAIN LANDING GEAR

Brake mount

Brake calliper

Brake pipe

G-BNHB

Landing gear leg

Brake disc

Nose-gear

Step

Radiator

Tailplane

Inner tube

Stub axle

Venturi for instruments

Wing strut

Main landing gear

Tailskid

Aircraft registration code

Tyre

Hub

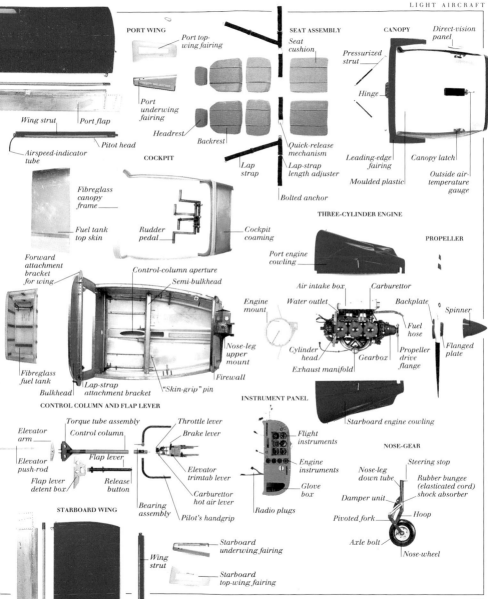

PORT WING

Port top-wing fairing

Port underwing fairing

Headrest

Wing strut

Port flap

Airspeed-indicator tube

Pitot head

SEAT ASSEMBLY

Seat cushion

Backrest

Quick-release mechanism

Lap strap

Lap-strap length adjuster

Bolted anchor

CANOPY

Direct-vision panel

Pressurized strut

Hinge

Leading-edge fairing

Moulded plastic

Canopy latch

Outside air-temperature gauge

COCKPIT

Fibreglass canopy frame

Fuel tank top skin

Rudder pedal

Cockpit coaming

THREE-CYLINDER ENGINE

Port engine cowling

Air intake box

Water outlet

Carburettor

Engine mount

Cylinder head

Exhaust manifold

Gearbox

Backplate

Fuel hose

Propeller drive flange

PROPELLER

Spinner

Flanged plate

Forward attachment bracket for wing

Control-column aperture

Semi-bulkhead

Nose-leg upper mount

Fibreglass fuel tank

Bulkhead

Lap-strap attachment bracket

"Skin-grip" pin

Firewall

Starboard engine cowling

CONTROL COLUMN AND FLAP LEVER

Torque tube assembly

Control column

Elevator arm

Elevator push-rod

Flap lever

Flap lever detent box

Release button

Throttle lever

Brake lever

Elevator trimtab lever

Carburettor hot air lever

Bearing assembly

Pilot's handgrip

INSTRUMENT PANEL

Flight instruments

Engine instruments

Glove box

Radio plugs

NOSE-GEAR

Steering stop

Nose-leg down tube

Damper unit

Pivoted fork

Axle bolt

Rubber bungee (elasticated cord) shock absorber

Hoop

Nose-wheel

STARBOARD WING

Wing strut

Starboard underwing fairing

Starboard top-wing fairing

Gliders, hang-gliders, and microlights

NOSE SHELL

Instrument panel

Grommet for front pylon strut

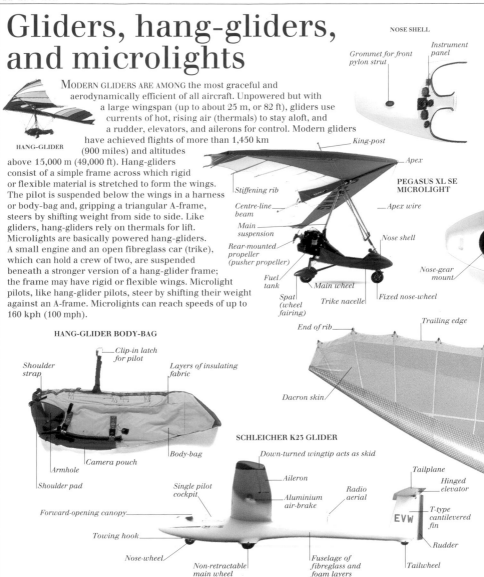

HANG-GLIDER

MODERN GLIDERS ARE AMONG the most graceful and aerodynamically efficient of all aircraft. Unpowered but with a large wingspan (up to about 25 m, or 82 ft), gliders use currents of hot, rising air (thermals) to stay aloft, and a rudder, elevators, and ailerons for control. Modern gliders have achieved flights of more than 1,450 km (900 miles) and altitudes above 15,000 m (49,000 ft). Hang-gliders consist of a simple frame across which rigid or flexible material is stretched to form the wings. The pilot is suspended below the wings in a harness or body-bag and, gripping a triangular A-frame, steers by shifting weight from side to side. Like gliders, hang-gliders rely on thermals for lift. Microlights are basically powered hang-gliders. A small engine and an open fibreglass car (trike), which can hold a crew of two, are suspended beneath a stronger version of a hang-glider frame; the frame may have rigid or flexible wings. Microlight pilots, like hang-glider pilots, steer by shifting their weight against an A-frame. Microlights can reach speeds of up to 160 kph (100 mph).

King-post

Apex

PEGASUS XL SE MICROLIGHT

Apex wire

Stiffening rib

Centre-line beam

Main suspension

Rear-mounted propeller (pusher propeller)

Nose shell

Fuel tank

Main wheel

Spat (wheel fairing)

Trike nacelle

Nose-gear mount

Fixed nose-wheel

Trailing edge

End of rib

Dacron skin

HANG-GLIDER BODY-BAG

Clip-in latch for pilot

Shoulder strap

Layers of insulating fabric

Armhole

Camera pouch

Body-bag

Shoulder pad

SCHLEICHER K23 GLIDER

Down-turned wingtip acts as skid

Single pilot cockpit

Aileron

Tailplane

Hinged elevator

Radio aerial

Aluminium air-brake

EVW

T-type cantilevered fin

Forward-opening canopy

Towing hook

Rudder

Nose-wheel

Non-retractable main wheel

Fuselage of fibreglass and foam layers

Tailwheel

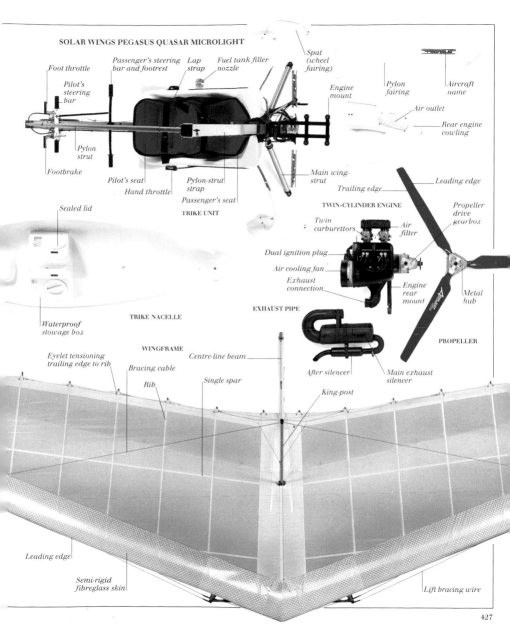

SOLAR WINGS PEGASUS QUASAR MICROLIGHT

Foot throttle

Pilot's steering bar

Passenger's steering bar and footrest

Lap strap

Fuel tank filler nozzle

Spat (wheel fairing)

Engine mount

Pylon fairing

Aircraft name

Air outlet

Rear engine cowling

Pylon strut

Footbrake

Pilot's seat

Hand throttle

Passenger's seat

Pylon-strut strap

TRIKE UNIT

Main wing-strut

Trailing edge

Leading edge

Propeller drive gearbox

Sealed lid

TWIN-CYLINDER ENGINE

Twin carburettors

Air filter

Dual ignition plug

Air cooling fan

Exhaust connection

Engine rear mount

Metal hub

Waterproof stowage box

TRIKE NACELLE

EXHAUST PIPE

After silencer

Main exhaust silencer

PROPELLER

WINGFRAME

Eyelet tensioning trailing edge to rib

Bracing cable

Rib

Centre-line beam

Single spar

King-post

Leading edge

Semi-rigid fibreglass skin

Lift bracing wire

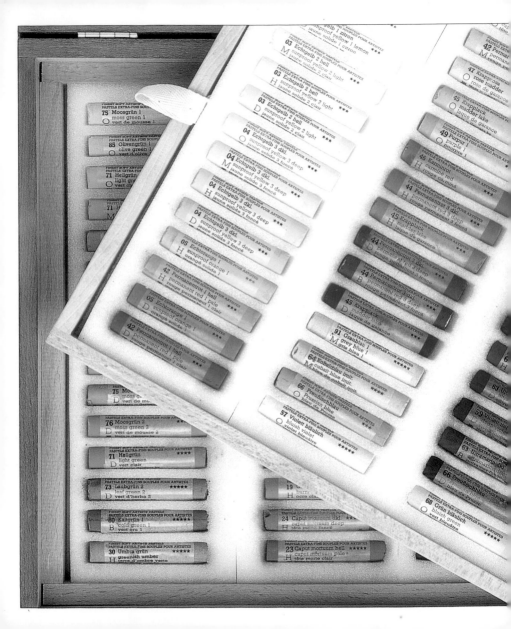

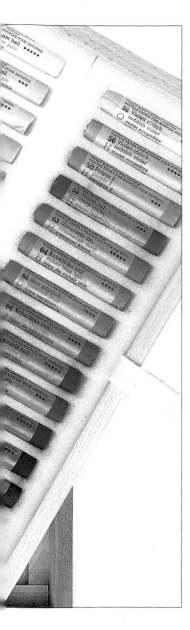

THE VISUAL ARTS

DRAWING 430

TEMPERA 432

FRESCO 434

OILS 436

WATERCOLOUR 438

PASTELS 440

ACRYLICS 442

CALLIGRAPHY 444

PRINTMAKING 1 446

PRINTMAKING 2 448

MOSAIC 450

SCULPTURE 1 452

SCULPTURE 2 454

Drawing

DRAWINGS CAN BE FINISHED WORKS OF ART, or preparatory studies for paintings and other visual arts. They can be made using a wide variety of drawing instruments such as pencils, graphite sticks, chalks, charcoal, pens and inks, and silver wires. The most common drawing instrument is the graphite pencil. A graphite pencil consists of a thin rod of graphite mixed with clay, encased in wood. Charcoal is one of the oldest drawing instruments. It is produced by firing twigs of willow, vine, or other woods at high temperatures in airtight containers. Erasers can be used to rub out marks made by drawing materials such as graphite pencils or charcoal, or to achieve a particular effect – such as smudging. Fixative is often applied – using a mouth diffuser or aerosol spray fixative – to prevent smudging once a drawing is finished. Silver lines can be produced by drawing silver wire across specially prepared paper – a technique known as silverpoint. The lines are permanent and cannot be erased. In time the silver lines oxidize and turn brown.

FIXATIVE AND MOUTH DIFFUSER

Hinge

Liquid fixative consisting of dissolved resin

Fixative is sucked into tube and sprayed on to drawing

CHALK, CRAYON, AND CHARCOAL

Calcite (calcium carbonate) mixed with pigment

BLUE CHALK

Iron oxide mixed with chalk

SANGUINE CRAYON

Carbonized wood

WILLOW CHARCOAL

ERASERS

Hard texture

PLASTIC ERASER

Soft texture

PUTTY ERASER

DRAWING INSTRUMENTS

Medium-soft, light line

Very soft, dark line

2B GRAPHITE PENCIL

8B GRAPHITE PENCIL

SILVER WIRE IN A METAL HOLDER

DRAWING BOARD

DRAWING MATERIALS

Graphite stick

Coloured pencil

Bulldog clip

Dip pen

Drawing board

Paper

Drawing clip

Pencil sharpener

Sketch book

Ink bottle

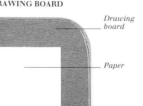

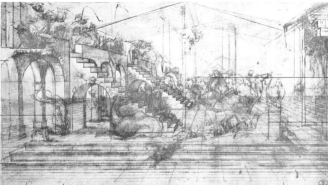

Silver lines
oxidize to a
light brown
colour

Figures drawn
in ink on top
of lines

Line drawn
in silverpoint
using a rule

Vanishing
point located
on head of
man riding
rearing horse

Lines of
squared
pavement slabs
recede toward
a single
vanishing
point

Complex perspective
drawing done as a
preparatory study
for a painting

EXAMPLE OF A SILVERPOINT DRAWING
The Adoration of the Magi, Leonardo da Vinci, 1481
Pen and ink over silverpoint on paper
16.5 x 29.2 cm (6½ x 11½ in)

Paper prepared
with size (glue)
and pigment

One of a series
of drawings
recording
London during
1944–1945

Charcoal lines
softened by
rubbing and
smudging

Charcoal
gives strong,
expressive lines

Handmade, tinted
paper

Broad charcoal
mark

Lines rapidly
drawn on site

EXAMPLE OF A CHARCOAL DRAWING
St. Paul's and the River, David Bomberg, 1945
Charcoal on paper
50.8 x 65.8 cm (20 x 25⅛ in)

Tempera

ILLUMINATED MANUSCRIPT

THE TERM TEMPERA is applied to any paint in which pigment is tempered (mixed) with a water-based binding medium – usually egg yolk. Egg tempera is applied to a smooth surface such as vellum (for illuminated manuscripts) or more commonly to hardwood panels prepared with gesso – a mixture of chalk and size (glue). Hog hair brushes are used to apply the gesso. A layer of gesso grosso (coarse gesso) is followed by successive layers of gesso sotile (fine gesso) that are sanded between coats to provide a smooth, yet absorbent ground. The paint is applied with fine sable brushes in thin layers, using light brushstrokes. Tempera dries quickly to form a tough skin with a satin sheen. The luminous white surface of the gesso combined with the overlaid paint produces the brilliant crispness and rich colours particular to this medium. Egg tempera paintings are frequently gilded with gold. Leaves of finely beaten gold are applied to a bole (reddish-brown clay) base and polished by burnishing.

MATERIALS FOR GILDING

Parchment for protecting gold leaf from draughts

Brush

Bowl containing diluted bole

Gold leaf

Gilder's knife

Gilder's tip for picking up gold leaf

Gilder's cushion

Surface prepared with gesso

Gold leaf smoothed and polished with a burnisher

Gold leaf applied in overlapping layers

Bole brushed on to gesso

Burnisher

Agate tip

MATERIALS FOR TEMPERA PANEL PAINTING

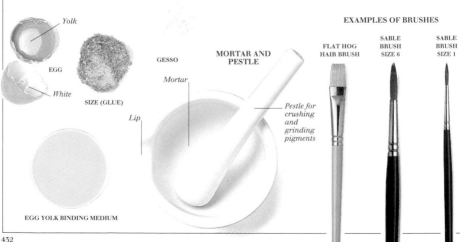

Yolk

EGG

White

GESSO

SIZE (GLUE)

Lip

MORTAR AND PESTLE

Mortar

Pestle for crushing and grinding pigments

EGG YOLK BINDING MEDIUM

EXAMPLES OF BRUSHES

FLAT HOG HAIR BRUSH

SABLE BRUSH SIZE 6

SABLE BRUSH SIZE 1

EXAMPLE OF A TEMPERA PAINTING
Presentation in the Temple, Ambrogio Lorenzetti, 1342
Tempera on wood, 257 x 168 cm (8 ft 5⅛ in x 5 ft 6⅛ in)

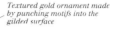

*Altarpiece
commissioned for
Siena Cathedral, Italy*

*Textured gold ornament made
by punching motifs into the
gilded surface*

*The red tinge of
the bole is just
visible beneath
the gold*

*Edge of a sheet
of gold leaf*

VERDACCIO

*Crisp edge
characteristic of
tempera painting*

*Vine black used
to create the
dim cathedral
interior*

*Highlights on
the beard made
by applying thin
layers of white
over dried paint*

VERMILION AND
LEAD WHITE

*Red drapery
painted in
vermilion*

*Raised right hand
and pointing finger
is the gesture of
prophecy*

VERMILION

*Receding floor
tiles create the
impression of
depth*

*Patch of discoloured
varnish, left from
last cleaning*

RED EARTH
(IRON OXIDE)

EXAMPLES OF PIGMENTS

*Warm flesh
tones achieved
by layering
vermilion and
white over an
undercoat of
verdaccio*

*Patterned gold
halo glitters in
candlelight*

MALACHITE   ULTRAMARINE
LAPIS LAZULI

*Ultramarine
lapis lazuli, as
costly as gold,
was reserved for
significant
figures such as
the Virgin Mary*

*Craquelure
(pattern of
cracks in
the paint)*

VINE BLACK   LEAD TIN YELLOW

DETAIL FROM "PRESENTATION
IN THE TEMPLE"

Fresco

FRESCO IS A METHOD OF WALL PAINTING. In buon fresco (true fresco), pigments are mixed with water and applied to an intonaco (layer of fresh, damp lime-plaster). The intonaco absorbs and binds the pigments as it dries making the picture a permanent part of the wall surface. The intonaco is applied in sections called giornate (daily sections). The size of each giornata depends on the artist's estimate of how much can be painted before the plaster sets. The junctions between giornate are sometimes visible on a finished fresco. The range of colours used in buon fresco are limited to lime-resistant pigments such as earth colours (below). Slaked lime (burnt lime mixed with water), bianco di San Giovanni (slaked lime that has been partly exposed to air), and chalk can be used to produce fresco whites. In fresco secco (dry fresco), pigments are mixed with a binding medium and applied to dry plaster. The pigments are not completely absorbed into the plaster and may flake off over time.

CROSS-SECTION SHOWING FRESCO LAYERS

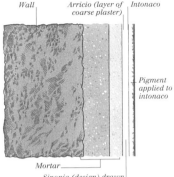

Wall

Arricio (layer of coarse plaster)

Intonaco

Pigment applied to intonaco

Mortar

Sinopia (design) drawn on surface of arricio

EXAMPLES OF EARTH COLOUR PIGMENTS

EXAMPLES OF FRESCO BRUSHES

INGREDIENTS FOR FRESCO WHITES

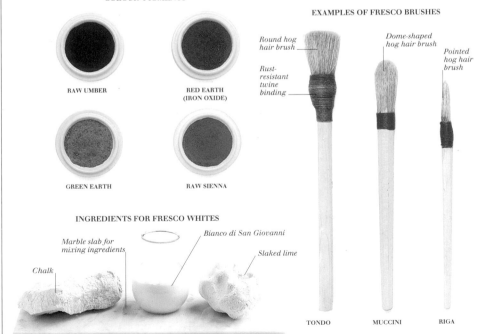

RAW UMBER

RED EARTH (IRON OXIDE)

GREEN EARTH

RAW SIENNA

Round hog hair brush

Rust-resistant twine binding

Dome-shaped hog hair brush

Pointed hog hair brush

Marble slab for mixing ingredients

Bianco di San Giovanni

Slaked lime

Chalk

TONDO

MUCCINI

RIGA

EXAMPLE OF A FRESCO
The Expulsion of the Merchants from the Temple, Giotto, c.1306
Fresco, 200 x 185 cm (78 x 72 in)

One of a series
of frescoes in the
Arena Chapel,
Padua, Italy

Temple acts as
a backdrop for
the action

Patches of azurite
blue have turned
green due to
reaction with
carbon dioxide

Bianco di San
Giovanni often
used for fresco
whites

Gold leaf applied
to apostle's halo

Hairline junction
between giornate
is visible

Green earth
pigment applied
to robe

Child painted
on top of
apostle's robe

Red earth
pigment applied
in buon fresco
has retained
rich hue

Azurite blue applied in fresco secco has
flaked off to reveal the plaster beneath

Dry, matt surface characteristic
of buon fresco

Paint applied
in buon fresco
to child's face

A fresco was
generally
worked in
zones from
the top down

Artist has to finish giornata
before plaster dries

Junction between giornate

Area with little
detail can be
painted quickly,
allowing a
larger giornata
to be completed

White dove
represents
the Holy Ghost

Paint applied
in fresco secco
to child's body
has flaked off

Sinopia (design)
sketched in
red earth

Highly detailed
area takes a
longer time to
paint, restricting
the size of the
giornata

**DETAIL FROM "THE
EXPULSION"**

GIORNATE (DAILY SECTIONS) IN "THE EXPULSION"

Oils

OIL PAINTS ARE MADE BY MIXING and grinding
pigment with a drying vegetable oil such as
linseed oil. The paint can be applied to many
different surfaces and textures – the most
common being canvas. Before painting, the
canvas is stretched on a wooden frame and
its surface is prepared with layers of size (glue)
and primer. The two main types of brushes used

KIDNEY-SHAPED PALETTE

in oil painting are stiff hog hair bristle brushes –
generally used for covering large areas; and soft hair
brushes made from sable or synthetic material – generally
used for fine detail. Other tools, including painting knives, can also
be used to achieve different effects. Oil paint can be applied thickly
(a technique known as impasto), or can be thinned down using
a solvent – such as turpentine or white spirit. Varnishes are
sometimes applied to finished paintings to protect their
surface and to give them a matt or gloss finish.

DAMMAR RESIN VARNISH

Crystals are dissolved and applied to painting to protect its surface

COMMERCIAL OIL PAINTS

CADMIUM RED

Lightfast opaque colour

ULTRAMARINE

Transparent colour

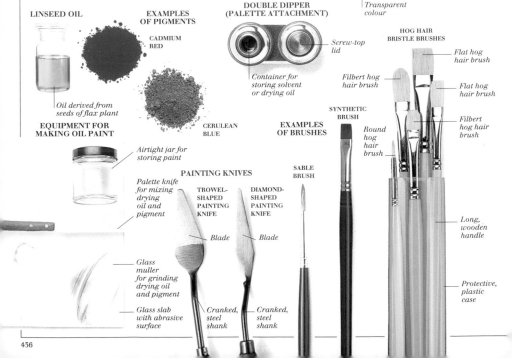

LINSEED OIL

Oil derived from seeds of flax plant

EQUIPMENT FOR MAKING OIL PAINT

EXAMPLES OF PIGMENTS

CADMIUM RED

CERULEAN BLUE

DOUBLE DIPPER (PALETTE ATTACHMENT)

Screw-top lid

Container for storing solvent or drying oil

HOG HAIR BRISTLE BRUSHES

Flat hog hair brush

Filbert hog hair brush

Flat hog hair brush

SYNTHETIC BRUSH

Filbert hog hair brush

EXAMPLES OF BRUSHES

Round hog hair brush

Airtight jar for storing paint

PAINTING KNIVES

Palette knife for mixing drying oil and pigment

TROWEL-SHAPED PAINTING KNIFE

DIAMOND-SHAPED PAINTING KNIFE

SABLE BRUSH

Blade

Blade

Long, wooden handle

Glass muller for grinding drying oil and pigment

Glass slab with abrasive surface

Cranked, steel shank

Cranked, steel shank

Protective, plastic case

EXAMPLE OF AN OIL PAINTING
Fritillarias, Vincent van Gogh, 1886
Oil on canvas, 73.5 x 60.5 cm (29 x 24 in)

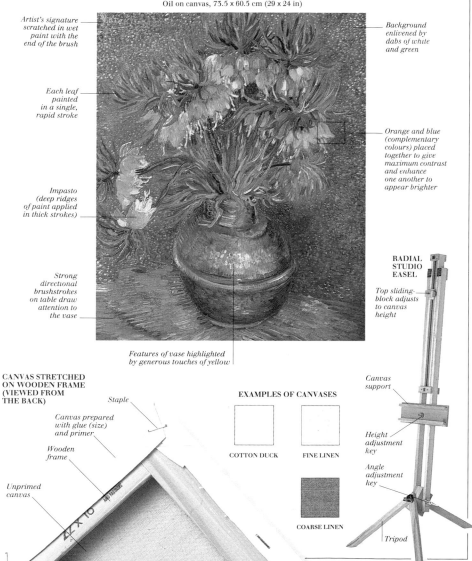

Artist's signature scratched in wet paint with the end of the brush

Each leaf painted in a single, rapid stroke

Impasto (deep ridges of paint applied in thick strokes)

Strong directional brushstrokes on table draw attention to the vase

Background enlivened by dabs of white and green

Orange and blue (complementary colours) placed together to give maximum contrast and enhance one another to appear brighter

Features of vase highlighted by generous touches of yellow

RADIAL STUDIO EASEL

Top sliding-block adjusts to canvas height

Canvas support

Height adjustment key

Angle adjustment key

Tripod

CANVAS STRETCHED ON WOODEN FRAME (VIEWED FROM THE BACK)

Staple

Canvas prepared with glue (size) and primer

Wooden frame

Unprimed canvas

EXAMPLES OF CANVASES

COTTON DUCK

FINE LINEN

COARSE LINEN

Watercolour

WATERCOLOUR PAINT IS MADE OF GROUND PIGMENT mixed with a water-soluble binding medium, usually gum arabic. It is usually applied to paper using soft hair brushes such as sable, goat hair, squirrel, and synthetic brushes. Watercolours are often diluted and applied as overlaying washes (thin, transparent layers) to build up depth of colour. Washes can be laid in a variety of ways to create a range of different effects. For example, a wet-in-wet wash can be achieved by laying a wash on top of another wet wash. The two washes blend together to give a fused effect. Sponges are used to modify washes by soaking up paint so that areas of pigment are lightened or removed from the paper. Watercolours can also be applied undiluted – a technique known as dry brush – to create a broken-colour effect. Watercolours are generally transparent and allow light to reflect from the surface of the paper through the layers of paint to give a luminous effect. They can be thickened and made opaque by adding body colour (Chinese white).

Natural sap from acacia tree

NATURAL SPONGE

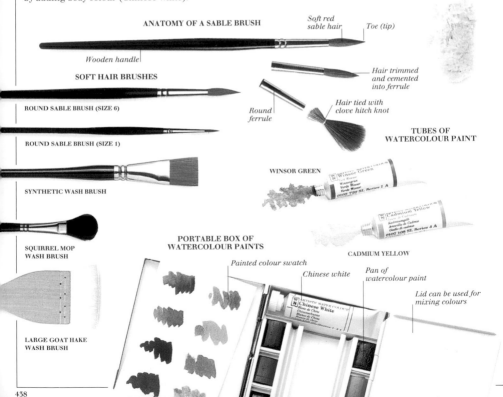

ANATOMY OF A SABLE BRUSH

Soft red sable hair

Toe (tip)

Wooden handle

SOFT HAIR BRUSHES

Hair trimmed and cemented into ferrule

ROUND SABLE BRUSH (SIZE 6)

Round ferrule

Hair tied with clove hitch knot

ROUND SABLE BRUSH (SIZE 1)

TUBES OF WATERCOLOUR PAINT

SYNTHETIC WASH BRUSH

WINSOR GREEN

SQUIRREL MOP WASH BRUSH

PORTABLE BOX OF WATERCOLOUR PAINTS

CADMIUM YELLOW

Painted colour swatch

Chinese white

Pan of watercolour paint

Lid can be used for mixing colours

LARGE GOAT HAKE WASH BRUSH

EXAMPLE OF A WATERCOLOUR
Burning of the Houses of Parliament, Turner, 1854
Watercolour on paper, 29.2 x 44.5 cm (11½ x 17½ in)

Transparent washes laid on top of each other to create tonal depth

Transparent washes allow light to reflect off the surface of the paper to give a luminous effect

Highlight scratched out with a scalpel

Paper shows through thin wash to give flames added highlight

Crowd painted with thin strokes laid over a pale wash

Undiluted paint applied, then partly washed out, to create the impression of water

EXAMPLES OF WASHES

WASH OVER DRY BRUSH
Wash laid over paint applied with dry brush gives two-tone effect

GRADED WASH
Strong wash applied to tilted paper gives graded effect

DRY BRUSH
Undiluted paint dragged across surface of paper gives broken effect

WET-IN-WET
Two diluted washes left to run together to give fused effect

EXAMPLES OF WATERCOLOUR PAPERS

SMOOTH-TEXTURED PAPER

MEDIUM-TEXTURED PAPER

ROUGH-TEXTURED PAPER

COLOUR WHEEL OF WATERCOLOUR PAINTS

Yellow (primary colour)

Secondary colours made by mixing yellow and blue

Secondary colours made by mixing red and yellow

Blue (primary colour)

Red (primary colour)

Secondary colours made by mixing blue and red

Pastels

PASTELS ARE STICKS OF PIGMENT made by mixing ground pigment with chalk and a binding medium, such as gum arabic. They vary in hardness depending on the proportion of the binding medium to the chalk. Soft pastel – the most common form of pastel – contains just enough binding medium to hold the pigment in stick form. Pastels can be applied directly to any support (surface) with sufficient tooth (texture). When a pastel is drawn over a textured surface, the pigment crumbles and lodges in the fibres of the support. Pastel marks have a particular soft, matt quality and are suitable for techniques such as blending, scumbling, and feathering. Blending is a technique of rubbing and fusing two or more colours on the support using fingers or various tools such as tortillons (paper stumps), soft hair brushes, putty erasers, and soft bread. Scumbling is a technique of building up layers of pastel colours. The side or blunted tip of a soft pastel is lightly drawn over an underpainted area so that patches of the colour beneath show through. Feathering is a technique of applying parallel strokes of colour with the point of a pastel, usually over an existing layer of pastel colour. A thin spray of fixative can be applied – using a mouth diffuser (see pp. 430-431) or aerosol spray fixative – to a finished pastel painting, or in between layers of colour, to prevent smudging.

EQUIPMENT FOR MAKING PASTELS

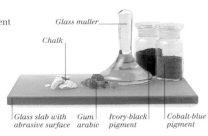

Glass muller

Chalk

Glass slab with abrasive surface | *Gum arabic* | *Ivory-black pigment* | *Cobalt-blue pigment*

EXAMPLES OF SOFT PASTELS

COBALT-BLUE HALF PASTEL

VERMILION HALF PASTEL

OLIVE-GREEN FULL PASTEL

MAUVE FULL PASTEL

EQUIPMENT USED WITH PASTELS

BOXED PASTEL SET

Boxed set containing a mixture of portrait and landscape colours

Foam compartments protect the pastels

Soft pastel

Wooden tray

PUTTY ERASER

AEROSOL SPRAY FIXATIVE

SOFT HAIR BRUSH

Soft bread suitable for erasing and blending

BREAD

TORTILLONS (PAPER STUMPS)

Soft point used for blending

Tight roll of paper

EXAMPLE OF A PASTEL PAINTING
Woman Drying her Neck, Edgar Degas, c.1898
Pastel on cardboard, 62.5 x 65.5 cm (24½ x 25½ in)

Pastels applied directly to support

Rich colour of fabric created by overlaying yellows and oranges

Broken colours, characteristic of scumbling technique

Colours are blended together using fingers or tools such as tortillons

Built up layers of pastel

Toned colour of paper visible beneath thinly applied pastels

Pure bright colours laid side by side produce strong contrasts

DETAIL FROM "WOMAN DRYING HER NECK"

Feathering technique used to produce skin tones

EXAMPLES OF TEXTURED PAPERS AND PASTEL BOARDS

WATERCOLOUR PAPER (ROUGH TEXTURE)

GLASS PAPER

WATERCOLOUR PAPER (MEDIUM TEXTURE)

EXAMPLES OF COLOURED AND TINTED PAPERS

INGRES PAPER

FLOCKED PASTEL BOARD

CANSON PAPER

Acrylics

ACRYLIC PAINT IS MADE BY MIXING PIGMENT with a synthetic resin. It can be thinned with water but dries to become water insoluble. Acrylics are applied to many surfaces, such as paper and acrylic-primed board and canvas. A variety of brushes, painting knives, rollers, air-brushes, plastic scrapers, and other tools are used in acrylic painting. The versatility of acrylics makes them suitable for a wide range of techniques. They can be used opaquely or – by adding water – in a transparent, watercolour style. Acrylic mediums can be added to the paint to adjust its consistency for special effects such as glazing and impasto (ridges of paint applied in thick strokes) or to make it more matt or glossy. Acrylics are quick-drying, which allows layers of paint to be applied on top of each other almost immediately.

EXAMPLES OF BRUSHES

Sable brush

Hog hair sash brush

Synthetic hog hair brush

Synthetic sable brush

Hog hair brush

Goat hair brush

Synthetic wash brush

Ox hair brush

EXAMPLES OF PAINTS USED IN ACRYLICS

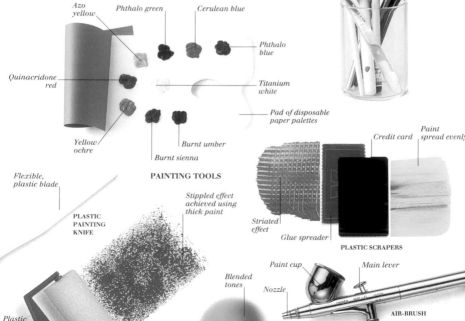

Azo yellow

Phthalo green

Cerulean blue

Phthalo blue

Quinacridone red

Titanium white

Yellow ochre

Burnt umber

Burnt sienna

Pad of disposable paper palettes

Credit card

Paint spread evenly

Flexible, plastic blade

PAINTING TOOLS

Stippled effect achieved using thick paint

Striated effect

Glue spreader

PLASTIC PAINTING KNIFE

PLASTIC SCRAPERS

Paint cup

Main lever

Blended tones

Nozzle

Plastic handle

SPONGE ROLLER

Uniform tone

AIR-BRUSH

Air hose

EXAMPLE OF AN ACRYLIC PAINTING
A Bigger Splash, David Hockney, 1967
Acrylic on canvas, 242.5 x 243.8 cm (95½ x 96 in)

Paint applied evenly using a roller

Cotton duck canvas support (surface)

Flatness of rollered areas enhanced by adding gel medium to the paint

Masking tape stuck on to canvas to define main shapes, and paint applied within these areas using a roller

Thin strip of pool edge left unpainted

Splash painted using thicker paint and small brush

Imprecise edge on end of spring board where paint has seeped under masking tape

EXAMPLES OF ACRYLIC PAINTS AND TECHNIQUES

Opaque effect

Extruded (squeezed) effect

Paint applied using painting knife

PURPLE ACRYLIC PAINT

Transparent, watercolour effect

YELLOW ACRYLIC PAINT

Translucent, impasto glaze

ORANGE ACRYLIC PAINT

Thick impasto with coarse texture

BLUE ACRYLIC PAINT DILUTED WITH WATER

GREEN ACRYLIC PAINT MIXED WITH GEL MEDIUM

RED ACRYLIC PAINT MIXED WITH TEXTURE PASTE

Calligraphy

CALLIGRAPHY IS BEAUTIFULLY FORMED LETTERING. The term applies to written text and illumination (the decoration of manuscripts using gold leaf and colour). The essential materials needed to practise calligraphy are a writing tool, ink, and a writing surface. Quills are among the oldest writing tools. They are usually made from goose or turkey feathers, and are noted for their flexibility and ability to produce fine lines. A quill point, however, is not very durable and constant recutting and trimming is required. The most commonly used writing instrument in western calligraphy is a detachable, metal nib held in a penholder. The metal nib is very durable, and there are a wide range of different types. Particular types of nibs – such as copperplate, speedball, and roundhand nibs – are used for specific styles of lettering. Some nibs have integral ink reservoirs and others have reservoirs that are detachable. Brushes are also used for writing, and for filling in outlined letters and painting decoration. Other writing tools used in calligraphy are fountain pens, felt-tip pens, rotring pens, and reed pens. Calligraphy inks may come in liquid form, or as a solid ink stick. Ink sticks are ground down in distilled water to form a liquid ink. The most common writing surfaces for calligraphy are good quality, smooth -surfaced papers. To achieve the best writing position, the calligrapher places the paper on a drawing board set at an angle.

EQUIPMENT USED IN BRUSH LETTERING

Brush rest

Wolf hair brush

Goat hair brush

BRUSHES AND BRUSH REST

Liquid ink made by grinding down ink stick in distilled water

Solid carbon ink stick

Ink stone

INK STICK AND STONE

Feather

PENS, NIBS, AND BRUSHES USED IN CALLIGRAPHY

PENHOLDER

FELT-TIP PEN

AUTOMATICPEN

REED PEN

SQUARE SABLE BRUSH

POINTED SABLE BRUSH

COPPERPLATE NIB

SPEEDBALL NIB

ROUNDHAND NIB AND DETACHABLE INK RESERVOIR

Feather stripped for better handling

Barrel

Hand-cut point

GOOSE-FEATHER QUILL

GOAT HAIR BRUSH

WOLF HAIR BRUSH

FOUNTAIN PEN AND INK

Bottle of permanent black ink

Barrel

Clip

Nib

Outer cap

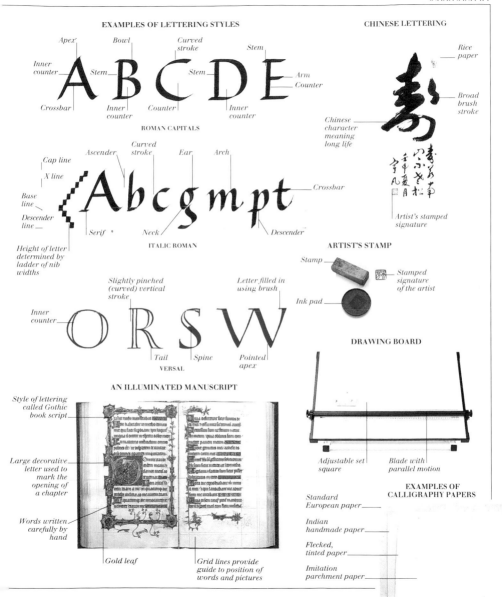

EXAMPLES OF LETTERING STYLES

CHINESE LETTERING

Apex

Bowl

Curved stroke

Stem

Inner counter

Stem

Stem

Arm

Counter

Crossbar

Inner counter

Counter

Inner counter

ROMAN CAPITALS

Rice paper

Broad brush stroke

Chinese character meaning long life

Artist's stamped signature

Cap line

X line

Ascender

Curved stroke

Ear

Arch

Base line

Crossbar

Descender line

Serif

Neck

Descender

Height of letter determined by ladder of nib widths

ITALIC ROMAN

ARTIST'S STAMP

Stamp

Stamped signature of the artist

Ink pad

Slightly pinched (curved) vertical stroke

Letter filled in using brush

Inner counter

DRAWING BOARD

Tail

Spine

Pointed apex

VERSAL

AN ILLUMINATED MANUSCRIPT

Style of lettering called Gothic book script

Large decorative letter used to mark the opening of a chapter

Words written carefully by hand

Gold leaf

Grid lines provide guide to position of words and pictures

Adjustable set square

Blade with parallel motion

EXAMPLES OF CALLIGRAPHY PAPERS

Standard European paper

Indian handmade paper

Flecked, tinted paper

Imitation parchment paper

Printmaking 1

PRINTS ARE MADE BY FOUR BASIC printing processes – intaglio, lithographic, relief, and screen. In intaglio printing, lines are engraved or etched into the surface of a metal plate. Lines are engraved by hand using sharp metal tools. They are etched by corroding the metal plate with acid, using acid-resistant ground to protect the areas not to be etched. The plate is then inked and wiped, leaving the grooves filled with ink and the surface clean. Dampened paper is laid over the plate, and both paper and plate are passed through the rollers of an etching press. The pressure of the rollers forces the paper into the grooves, so that it takes up the ink, leaving an impression on the paper. Lithographic printing is based on the antipathy between grease and water. An image is drawn on a surface – usually a stone or metal plate – with a greasy medium, such as tusche (lihographic ink). The greasy drawing is fixed on to the plate by applying an acidic solution, such as gum arabic. The surface is then dampened and rolled with ink. The ink adheres only to the greasy areas and is repelled by the water. Paper is laid on the plate and pressure is applied by means of a press. In relief printing, the non-printing areas of a wood or linoleum block are cut away using gouges, knives, and other tools. The printing areas are left raised in relief and are rolled with ink. Paper is laid on the inked block and pressure is applied by means of a press or by burnishing (rubbing) the back of the paper. The most common forms of relief printing are woodcut, wood engraving, and linocut.
In screen printing, the printing surface is a mesh stretched across a wooden frame. A stencil is applied to the mesh to seal the non-printing areas and ink is scraped through the mesh to produce an image.

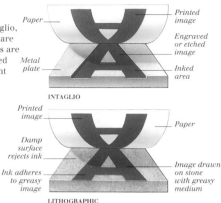

INTAGLIO

Paper — *Printed image* — *Metal plate* — *Engraved or etched image* — *Inked area*

LITHOGRAPHIC

Printed image — *Damp surface rejects ink* — *Ink adheres to greasy image* — *Paper* — *Image drawn on stone with greasy medium*

RELIEF

Paper — *Raised figure* — *Wood block* — *Printed image* — *Inked surface*

SCREEN

Ink forced through mesh — *Paper* — *Wooden frame* — *Stencil* — *Printed image*

LEATHER
INK DABBER

EQUIPMENT USED IN
INTAGLIO PRINTING

ROCKER   SCRIBER   ROULETTE   SCRAPER   BURNISHER   CLAMP

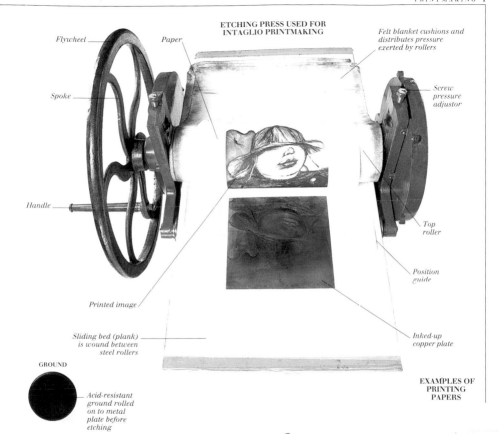

ETCHING PRESS USED FOR
INTAGLIO PRINTMAKING

Flywheel

Paper

*Felt blanket cushions and
distributes pressure
exerted by rollers*

Spoke

*Screw
pressure
adjustor*

Handle

*Top
roller*

*Position
guide*

Printed image

*Sliding bed (plank)
is wound between
steel rollers*

*Inked-up
copper plate*

GROUND

*Acid-resistant
ground rolled
on to metal
plate before
etching*

EXAMPLES OF
PRINTING
PAPERS

GROUND ROLLER

*Gelatine
roller*

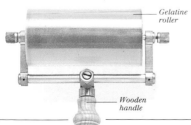

*Wooden
handle*

EXAMPLE OF AN INTAGLIO PRINT
Annie with a Sun Hat, Jock McFadyen, 1993
Etched copper plate, 41 x 40 cm (16 x 15¾ in)

Printmaking 2

EXAMPLE OF A LITHOGRAPHIC STONE AND PRINT
Crown Gateway 2, Mandy Bonnell, 1987
Lithograph, 50 x 40 cm (19½ x 15¾ in)

IMAGE DRAWN ON STONE    LITHOGRAPIC PRINT

EXAMPLE OF A SCREEN PRINT
Sea Change, Patrick Hughes, 1992
Screen print, 77 x 94.5 cm (30 x 37 in)

SCREEN AND SQUEEGEE

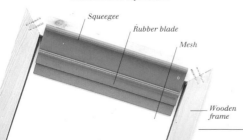

Squeegee

Rubber blade

Mesh

Wooden frame

EQUIPMENT USED IN LITHOGRAPHIC PRINTING

CRAYON AND HOLDER

LITHOGRAPHIC PENCIL

TUSCHE (LITHOGRAPHIC INK) PEN

ERASING STICK

EXPANDABLE SPONGE

TUSCHE (LITHOGRAPHIC INK) STICK

RUBBING INK

INK ROLLER

MILD ACIDIC SOLUTION

GUM ARABIC SOLUTION

WATER-BASED SCREEN PRINTING INKS

BLUE ACRYLIC INK

RED ACRYLIC INK

BROWN TEXTILE INK

EQUIPMENT USED IN RELIEF PRINTING

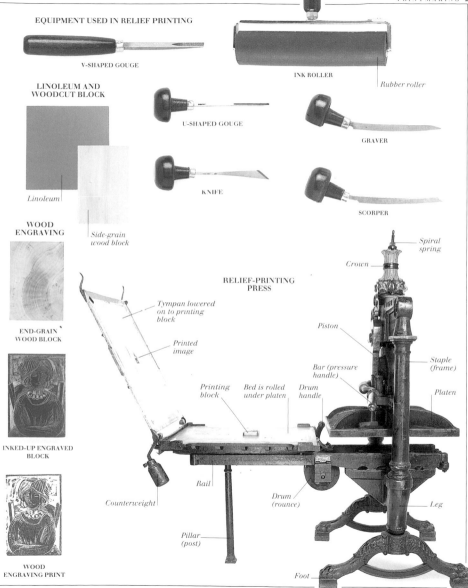

V-SHAPED GOUGE

INK ROLLER

Rubber roller

LINOLEUM AND WOODCUT BLOCK

U-SHAPED GOUGE

GRAVER

KNIFE

SCORPER

Linoleum

WOOD ENGRAVING

Side-grain wood block

END-GRAIN WOOD BLOCK

INKED-UP ENGRAVED BLOCK

WOOD ENGRAVING PRINT

RELIEF-PRINTING PRESS

Spiral spring

Crown

Piston

Staple (frame)

Tympan lowered on to printing block

Printed image

Bar (pressure handle)

Drum handle

Platen

Printing block

Bed is rolled under platen

Rail

Drum (rounce)

Leg

Counterweight

Pillar (post)

Foot

Mosaic

MOSAIC IS THE ART OF MAKING patterns and pictures from tesserae (small, coloured pieces of glass, marble, and other materials). Different materials are cut into tesserae using different tools. Smalti (glass enamel) and marble are cut into pieces using a hammer and a hardy (a pointed blade) embedded in a log. Vitreous glass is cut into pieces using a pair of nippers. Mosaics can be made using a direct or indirect method. In the direct method, the tesserae are laid directly into a bed of cement–based adhesive. In the indirect method, the design is drawn in reverse on paper or cloth. The tesserae are then stuck face-down on the paper or cloth using water-soluble glue. Adhesive is spread with a trowel on to a solid surface – such as a wall – and the back of the mosaic is laid into the adhesive. Finally, the paper or cloth is soaked off to reveal the mosaic. Gaps between tesserae can be filled with grout. Grout is forced into gaps by dragging a grouting squeegee across the face of the mosaic. Mosaics are usually used to decorate walls and floors, but they can also be applied to smaller objects.

EQUIPMENT FOR BREAKING MARBLE

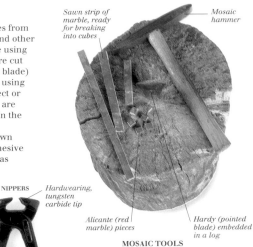

Sawn strip of marble, ready for breaking into cubes

Mosaic hammer

NIPPERS — *Hardwearing, tungsten carbide tip*

Alicante (red marble) pieces

Hardy (pointed blade) embedded in a log

MOSAIC TOOLS

CEMENT-BASED ADHESIVE

GROUT

EXAMPLE OF A MOSAIC (DIRECT METHOD)
Seascape, Tessa Hunkin, 1993
Smalti mosaic on board
80 cm (31½ in) diameter

SMALTI (GLASS ENAMEL)

RED SMALTI

Handle with rubber grip

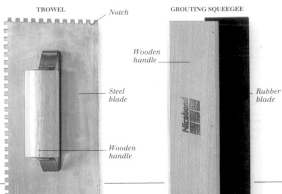

YELLOW SMALTI

TROWEL

Notch

GROUTING SQUEEGEE

Wooden handle

BLUE SMALTI

Steel blade

Rubber blade

Wooden handle

Gold-leaf smalti

STAGES IN THE CREATION OF A MOSAIC (INDIRECT METHOD)

MOSAIC POT

Geometric design

Grout

COLOUR SKETCH
A colour sketch is drawn
in oil pastel to give a clear
impression of how the finished
mosaic will look.

REVERSE IMAGE
Tesserae are glued face-down
on reverse image on paper.
Mosaic is then attached to solid
surface and paper is removed.

MOSAIC MOSQUE DESIGN

Floral design

Geometric border

*Andamenti
(line along
which tesserae
are laid)*

*Gold tessera
with ripple
finish*

*Gold tessera
placed upside-
down*

VITREOUS GLASS

**GREEN VITREOUS
GLASS WITH GOLD LEAF**

*Plain
finish*

**RED VITREOUS
GLASS**

*Grout fills
the gaps
between the
tesserae*

*Ripple
finish*

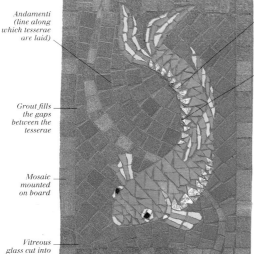

SHEETS OF VITREOUS GLASS

**BLUE VITREOUS
GLASS**

*Mosaic
mounted
on board*

*Vitreous
glass cut into
triangular
shape with
nippers*

FINISHED MOSAIC
Goldfish, Tessa Hunkin, 1993
Vitreous glass mosaic on board
35.5 x 25.5 cm (14 x 10 in)

*Border of square
vitreous glass*

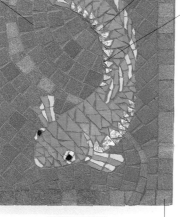

Sculpture 1

THE TWO TRADITIONAL METHODS OF MAKING SCULPTURE are carving and modelling.
A carved sculpture is made by cutting away the surplus from a block of hard material
such as stone, marble, or wood. The tools used for carving vary according to the
material being carved. Heavy steel points, claws, and chisels that are struck with a
lump hammer are generally used for stone and marble. Sharp gouges and chisels
that are struck with a wooden mallet are used for wood. Sculptures formed from hard
materials are generally finished by filing with rasps, rifflers, and other abrasive
implements. Modelling is a process by which shapes are built up, using malleable
materials such as clay, plaster, and wax. The material is cut with wire-ended tools
and modelled with the fingers or a variety of hardwood and metal implements. For
large or intricate modelled sculptures an armature (frame), made from metal or
wood, is used to provide internal support. Sculptures formed in soft materials may
harden naturally or can be made more durable by firing in a kiln. Modelled
sculptures are often first designed in wax or another material to be cast later in a
metal (see pp. 454-455) such as bronze. The development of many new materials in
the 20th century has enabled sculptors to experiment with new techniques such as
construction (joining preformed pieces of material such as machine components,
mirrors, and furniture) and kinetic (mobile) sculpture.

*1.1 kg
(2½ lb)
iron head*

*Ash
handle*

LUMP HAMMER

CALLIPERS

EXAMPLES OF WOODCARVING TOOLS

Curved leg

*Gap measures
distance between
two points on a
sculpture*

CABINET RASP

STRAIGHT GOUGE

SALMON BEND GOUGE

Wing nut

**WIDE
MARBLE
CLAW**

**NARROW
MARBLE
CLAW**

POINT

CHISEL

*Stone for
sharpening
woodcarving
tools*

FLAT CHISEL

**EXAMPLES OF RIFFLERS
(FOR STONE, MARBLE, AND WOOD)**

BULLNOSE CHISEL

*Cedar
box*

30 CM (12 IN) RIFFLER

*Surface for
sharpening
stonecarving
tools*

**ARKANSAS
HONE-STONE**

**CARVING
MALLET**

15 CM (6 IN) RIFFLER

DIAMOND WHETSTONE

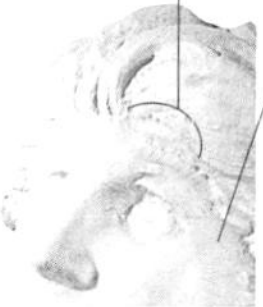

Tiny holes along
the hairline made
with a point

Soft skin texture tooled
with a fine-toothed
marble claw

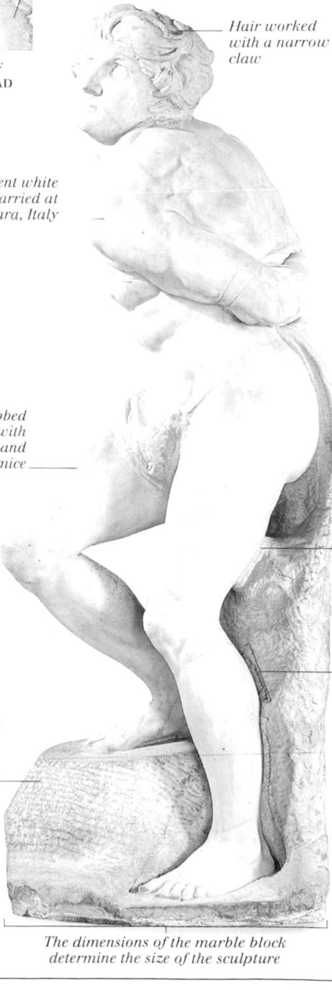

EXAMPLE OF A CARVED WOOD SCULPTURE
Mary Magdalene, Donatello, 1454-1455
Poplar wood, height 188 cm (6 ft 2 in)

EXAMPLE OF A CARVED MARBLE SCULPTURE
The Rebel Slave, Michelangelo, 1513-1516
Marble, height 213 cm (7ft)

Hair worked
with a narrow
claw

DETAIL OF
SLAVE'S HEAD

Delicately
modelled
hand carved
with a chisel

Translucent white
marble, quarried at
Carrara, Italy

Hair
highlighted
with gold
leaf

Figure cut
from single
length of
poplar

Deep
ridges of
hair cut
with a
gouge

Surface rubbed
smooth with
rifflers and
pumice

Strut gives added
support to long
slender limb

Wood prepared
with gesso
(chalk and glue)
and painted

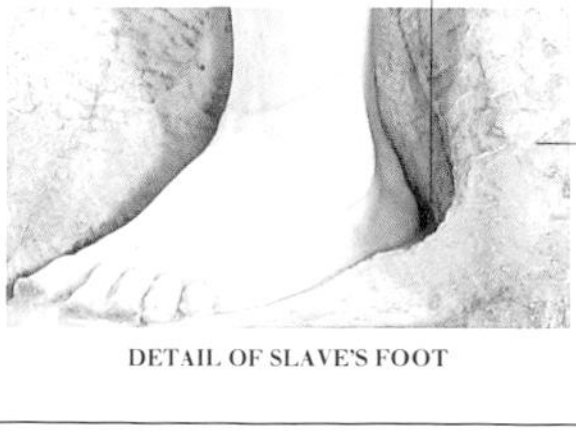

Series of tiny
punch holes,
made with a
fine point,
outline the
form

Base scored with
jagged parallel
cuts made with
point and lump
hammer

Foot carved in
deep relief

Rough surface
made by driving
a point into the
marble at an
oblique angle

The dimensions of the marble block
determine the size of the sculpture

DETAIL OF SLAVE'S FOOT

Sculpture 2

EXAMPLES OF MODELLING TOOLS

WIRE-ENDED CUTTING TOOL

CURVED MOULDING TOOL

SPATULA-ENDED WAX MODELLING TOOL

ROUNDED WAX MODELLING TOOL

EXAMPLES OF BRONZE FINISHING TOOLS

HOOKED RIFFLER   POINTED RIFFLER

SPIRIT LAMP (FOR HEATING WAX MODELLING TOOLS)

Wick _____

Brass holder

Glass bowl _____

Methylated spirit

STAGES IN THE LOST-WAX METHOD OF CASTING
Based on Mars, Giambologna, c.1546

Wax-covered wire armature

ORIGINAL MODEL
An original, solid wax model is made and preserved so that numerous replicas can be cast.

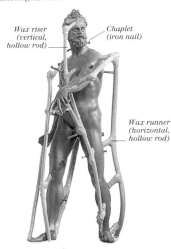

Wax riser (vertical, hollow rod)

Chaplet (iron nail)

Wax runner (horizontal, hollow rod)

HOLLOW WAX FIGURE IS CAST
A new, hollow wax model is cast from the original model. It is filled with a plaster core that is held in place with nails. Wax runners and risers are attached.

Fire-resistant clay _____

FIGURE IS BAKED IN CASTING MOULD
The model is encased in clay and baked. The wax melts away (through the channels made by the wax rods) and is replaced by molten bronze.

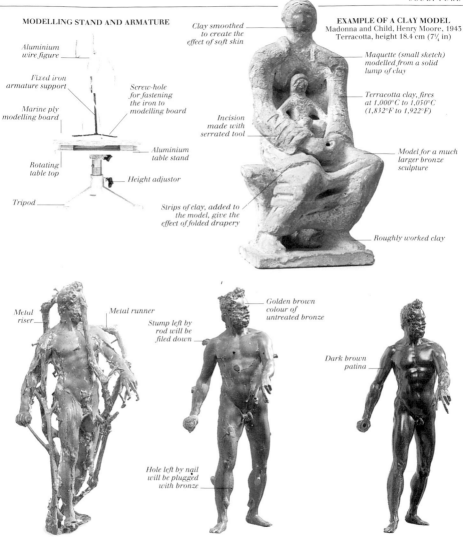

MODELLING STAND AND ARMATURE

Aluminium wire figure

Fixed iron armature support

Marine ply modelling board

Screw-hole for fastening the iron to modelling board

Rotating table top

Aluminium table stand

Height adjustor

Tripod

EXAMPLE OF A CLAY MODEL
Madonna and Child, Henry Moore, 1943
Terracotta, height 18.4 cm (7¼ in)

Clay smoothed to create the effect of soft skin

Maquette (small sketch) modelled from a solid lump of clay

Terracotta clay, fires at 1,000°C to 1,050°C (1,832°F to 1,922°F)

Incision made with serrated tool

Model for a much larger bronze sculpture

Strips of clay, added to the model, give the effect of folded drapery

Roughly worked clay

Metal riser

Metal runner

Golden brown colour of untreated bronze

Stump left by rod will be filed down

Dark brown patina

Hole left by nail will be plugged with bronze

STATUE IS STRIPPED OF CLAY
When the bronze has cooled, the clay mould is broken open to reveal the bronze statue with solid metal runners and risers.

STATUE IS FINISHED
The nails are pulled out and a large hole is made to remove the plaster core. When the metal rods have been sawn off, the sculpture is filed to refine the surface.

STATUE IS CLEANED
Finally the work is cleaned and polished. An artificial patina (colouring) is achieved by treating the surface with chemicals.

ARCHITECTURE

ANCIENT EGYPT	458
ANCIENT GREECE	460
ANCIENT ROME 1	462
ANCIENT ROME 2	464
MEDIEVAL CASTLES AND HOUSES	466
MEDIEVAL CHURCHES	468
GOTHIC 1	470
GOTHIC 2	472
RENAISSANCE 1	474
RENAISSANCE 2	476
BAROQUE AND NEOCLASSICAL 1	478
BAROQUE AND NEOCLASSICAL 2	480
BAROQUE AND NEOCLASSICAL 3	482
ARCHES AND VAULTS	484
DOMES	486
ISLAMIC BUILDINGS	488
SOUTH AND EAST ASIA	490
THE 19TH CENTURY	492
THE EARLY 20TH CENTURY	494
MODERN BUILDINGS 1	496
MODERN BUILDINGS 2	498

Ancient Egypt

THE CIVILIZATION OF THE ANCIENT EGYPTIANS (which lasted from about 3100 BC until it was finally absorbed into the Roman empire in 30 BC) is famous for its temples and tombs. Egyptian temples were often huge and geometric, like the Temple of Amon-Re (below and right). They were usually decorated with hieroglyphs (sacred characters used for picture-writing) and painted reliefs depicting gods, Pharaohs (kings), and queens. Tombs were particularly important to the Egyptians, who believed that the dead were resurrected in the after-life. The tombs were often decorated – as, for example, the surround of the false door opposite – in order to give comfort to the dead. The best-known ancient Egyptian tombs are the pyramids, which were designed to symbolize the rays of the sun. Many of the architectural forms used by the ancient Egyptians were later adopted by other civilizations; for example, columns and capitals were later used by the ancient Greeks (see pp. 460-461) and ancient Romans (see pp. 462-465).

FRONT VIEW OF HYPOSTYLE HALL, TEMPLE OF AMON-RE

Cornice decorated with cavetto moulding
Campaniform (open papyrus) capital
Architrave
Papyrus-bud capital
Socle
Side aisle
Central nave
Side aisle

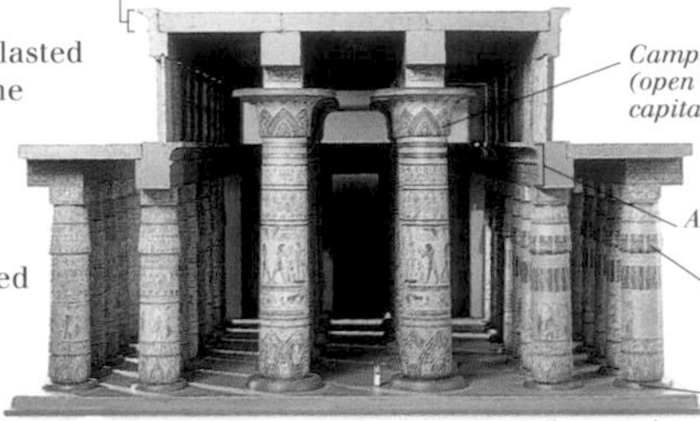

SIDE VIEW OF HYPOSTYLE HALL, TEMPLE OF AMON-RE, KARNAK, EGYPT, c.1290 BC

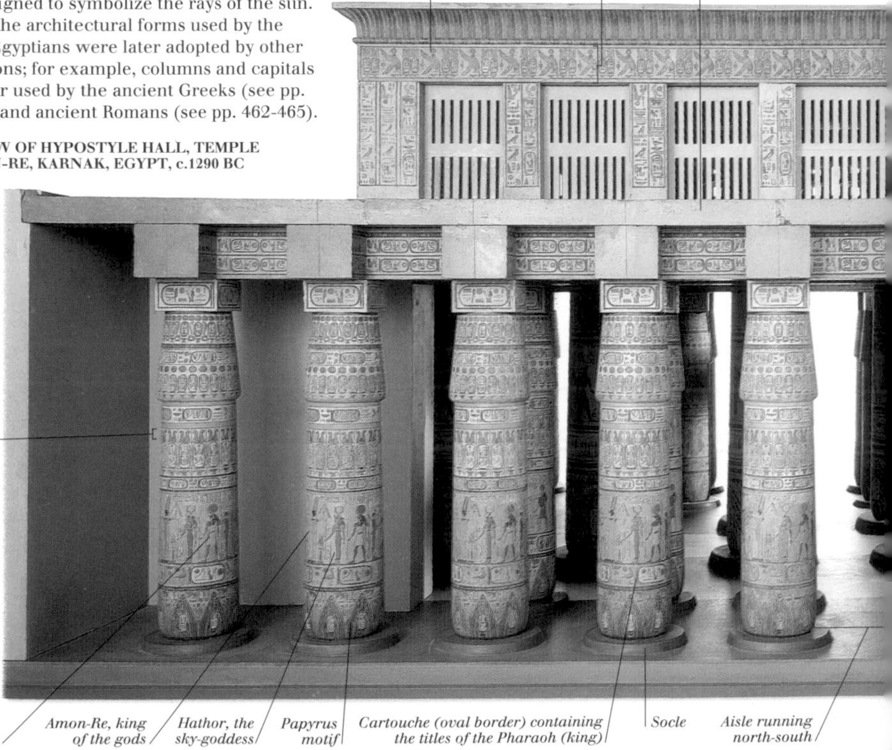

Horus, the sun-god
Architrave
Stone slab forming flat roof of side aisle
Kepresh crown with disc
Chons, the moon-god
Amon-Re, king of the gods
Hathor, the sky-goddess
Papyrus motif
Cartouche (oval border) containing the titles of the Pharaoh (king)
Socle
Aisle running north-south

LIMESTONE FALSE DOOR WITH HIEROGLYPHS, TOMB OF KING TJETJI, GIZA, EGYPT, c.2400 BC

Hieroglyph representing a house

Lintel

Disc representing sun or light

Eroded image of Tjetji

Limestone stela (slab)

Hoe-shaped hieroglyph representing "mr" sound

Head of false door

Image of Tjetji's wife

Image of Tjetji's daughter

PLANT CAPITAL OF THE PTOLEMAIC-ROMAN PERIOD, EGYPT, 332-30 BC

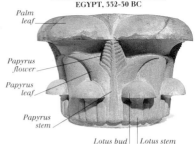

Palm leaf

Papyrus flower

Papyrus leaf

Papyrus stem

Lotus bud

Lotus stem

Cornice decorated with cavetto moulding

Bead moulding

Trellis window

Rectangular pier decorated with hieroglyphs

Elevated roof of central nave

Clerestory

Disc representing sun or light

Architrave

Square abacus

Papyrus-bud capital

Papyriform column

Shaft

Scene depicting a Pharaoh (king) paying homage to the god Amon-Re

Central nave

ANCIENT EGYPTIAN BUILDING DECORATION

DECORATED WINDOW, MEDINET HABU, EGYPT, C.1198 BC

ROPE AND PATERAE DECORATION

CAPITAL WITH THE HEAD OF THE SKY-GODDESS HATHOR, TEMPLE OF ISIS, PHILAE, EGYPT, 283-47 BC

LOTUS AND PAPYRUS FRIEZE DECORATION

Ancient Greece

THE CLASSICAL TEMPLES OF ANCIENT GREECE were built
according to the belief that certain forms and proportions
were pleasing to the gods. There were three main ancient
Greek architectural orders (styles), which can be
distinguished by the decoration and proportions of their
columns, capitals (column tops), and entablatures
(structures resting on the capitals). The oldest is the
Doric order, which dates from the seventh century BC
and was used mainly on the Greek mainland and in the
western colonies, such as Sicily and southern Italy. The
Temple of Neptune, shown here, is a classic example of
this order. It is hypaethral (roofless) and peripteral
(surrounded by a single row of columns). About a
century later, the more decorative Ionic order developed
on the Aegean Islands. Features of this order include
volutes (spiral scrolls) on capitals and acroteria
(pediment ornaments). The Corinthian order was invented
in Athens in the fifth century BC and is typically identified
by an acanthus leaf on the capitals. This order was later
widely used in ancient Roman architecture.

CAPITALS OF THE THREE ORDERS OF ANCIENT GREEK ARCHITECTURE

Abacus

Echinus

Annulet

Trachelion (neck)

DORIC CAPITAL, THE PROPYLAEUM (GATEWAY), THE ACROPOLIS, ATHENS, GREECE, 449 BC

Coussinet (cushion)

Abacus

Lesbian leaf pattern

Cyma reversa profile

Volute

Echinus with egg and dart decoration

Eye

Palmette

IONIC CAPITAL, THE PROPYLAEUM (GATEWAY), TEMPLE OF ATHENA POLIAS, PRIENE, GREECE, c.334 BC

Mask

Abacus

Volute

Cauliculus

Acanthus leaf

Bell-shaped core

CORINTHIAN CAPITAL FROM A STOA (PORTICO), PROBABLY FROM ASIA MINOR

TEMPLE OF NEPTUNE, PAESTUM, ITALY, c.460 BC

Raking cornice

Trachelion (neck)

Taenia

Triglyph

Metope

Glyph (channel)

Pediment

Doric
entablature

Pteron
(external
colonnade)

Euthynteria

Drum

Stylobate

Column of the Doric order

PLAN OF THE TEMPLE OF NEPTUNE, PAESTUM

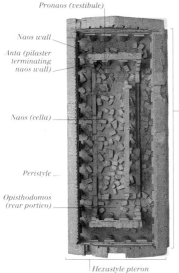

Pronaos (vestibule)

Naos wall

Anta (pilaster terminating naos wall)

Naos (cella)

Peristyle

Opisthodomos (rear portico)

Pteron (external colonnade)

Hexastyle pteron (colonnade of six columns)

ANCIENT GREEK BUILDING DECORATION

Volute

FACADE, TREASURY OF ATREUS, MYCENAE, GREECE, 1350-1250 BC

Meander

FRETWORK, PARTHENON, ATHENS, GREECE, 447-456 BC

ACROTERION, TEMPLE OF APHAIA, AEGINA, GREECE, 490 BC

Griffon (gryphon)

Raking cornice

ANTEFIXA, TEMPLE OF APHAIA, AEGINA, GREECE, 490 BC

Palmette

Volute

Regula (short fillet beneath taenia)   Eaves

Cornice

Frieze

Architrave

Capital

Shaft

Crepidoma (stepped base)

Entasis (slight curve of a column)   Intercolumniation   Fluting

Ancient Rome 1

ANCIENT ROMAN BUILDING DECORATION

IN THE EARLY PERIOD OF THE ROMAN EMPIRE extensive use
was made of ancient Greek architectural ideas, particularly
those of the Corinthian order (see pp. 460-461). As a result,
many early Roman buildings – such as the Temple of Vesta
(opposite) – closely resemble ancient Greek buildings. A
distinctive Roman style began to evolve in the first century
AD. This style developed the interiors of buildings (the Greeks
had concentrated on the exterior) by using arches, vaults, and
domes inside the buildings, and by ornamenting internal walls.
Many of these features can be seen in the Pantheon. Exterior
columns were often used for decorative, rather than structural,
purposes, as in the Colosseum and the Porta Nigra (see
pp. 464-465). Smaller buildings had timber frames with
wattle-and-daub walls, as in the mill (see pp. 464-465).
Roman architecture remained influential for many centuries,
with some of its principles being used in the 11th century in
Romanesque buildings (see pp. 468-469) and also in the 15th
and 16th centuries in Renaissance buildings (see pp. 474-477).

FESTOON, TEMPLE OF VESTA,
TIVOLI, ITALY, C.80 BC

RICHLY DECORATED
ROMAN OVUM

INTERIOR OF THE PANTHEON,
ROME, ITALY, 118-c.128

*Inner dome,
following the
curve of a
depressed arch*

*Outer
saucer
dome*

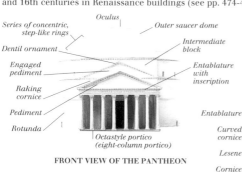

*Series of concentric,
step-like rings*

Oculus

Outer saucer dome

Dentil ornament

*Intermediate
block*

*Engaged
pediment*

*Entablature
with
inscription*

*Raking
cornice*

Pediment

Entablature

Rotunda

*Octastyle portico
(eight-column portico)*

*Curved
cornice*

FRONT VIEW OF THE PANTHEON

Lesene

Cornice

SIDE VIEW OF THE PANTHEON

*Triangular
pediment*

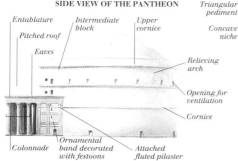

Entablature

*Intermediate
block*

*Upper
cornice*

Pitched roof

*Concave
niche*

Eaves

*Relieving
arch*

*Opening for
ventilation*

Cornice

Colonnade

*Ornamental
band decorated
with festoons*

*Attached
fluted pilaster*

Marble veneer   *Segmental pediment*   *Pedestal*

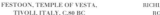

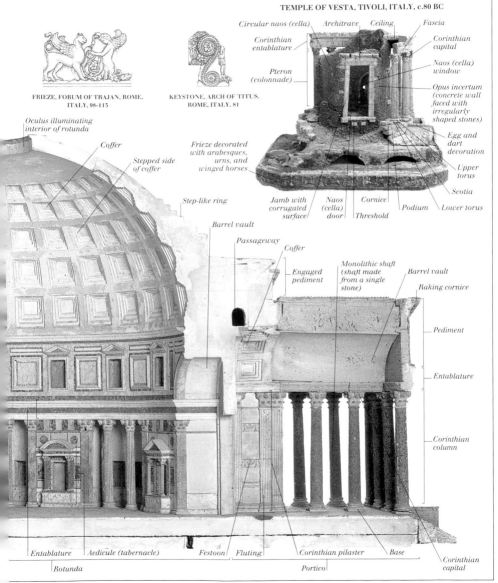

FRIEZE, FORUM OF TRAJAN, ROME, ITALY, 98-113

KEYSTONE, ARCH OF TITUS, ROME, ITALY, 81

TEMPLE OF VESTA, TIVOLI, ITALY, c.80 BC

Circular naos (cella)

Corinthian entablature

Pteron (colonnade)

Architrave

Ceiling

Fascia

Corinthian capital

Naos (cella) window

Opus incertum (concrete wall faced with irregularly shaped stones)

Egg and dart decoration

Upper torus

Scotia

Lower torus

Jamb with corrugated surface

Naos (cella) door

Cornice

Threshold

Podium

Frieze decorated with arabesques, urns, and winged horses

Oculus illuminating interior of rotunda

Coffer

Stepped side of coffer

Step-like ring

Barrel vault

Passageway

Coffer

Engaged pediment

Monolithic shaft (shaft made from a single stone)

Barrel vault

Raking cornice

Pediment

Entablature

Corinthian column

Entablature

Aedicule (tabernacle)

Festoon

Fluting

Corinthian pilaster

Base

Corinthian capital

Rotunda

Portico

Ancient Rome 2

SIDE VIEW OF A ROMAN MILL

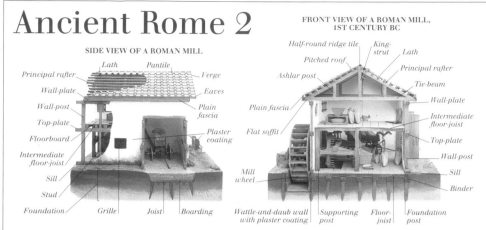

Lath
Pantile
Principal rafter
Verge
Wall-plate
Eaves
Wall-post
Plain
fascia
Top-plate
Plaster
coating
Floorboard
Intermediate
floor-joist
Sill
Stud
Foundation
Grille
Joist
Boarding

Half-round ridge tile
King-strut
Lath
Pitched roof
Ashlar post
Principal rafter
Tie-beam
Plain fascia
Wall-plate
Intermediate
floor-joist
Flat soffit
Top-plate
Wall-post
Mill
wheel
Sill
Binder
Wattle-and-daub wall
with plaster coating
Supporting
post
Floor-
joist
Foundation
post

THE COLOSSEUM (FLAVIAN AMPHITHEATRE), ROME, ITALY, 70-82

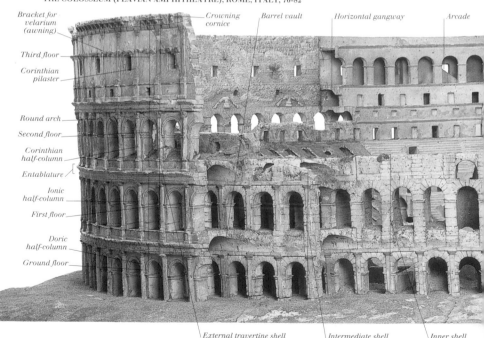

Bracket for
velarium
(awning)
Crowning
cornice
Barrel vault
Horizontal gangway
Arcade
Third floor
Corinthian
pilaster
Round arch
Second floor
Corinthian
half-column
Entablature
Ionic
half-column
First floor
Doric
half-column
Ground floor
External travertine shell
Intermediate shell
Inner shell

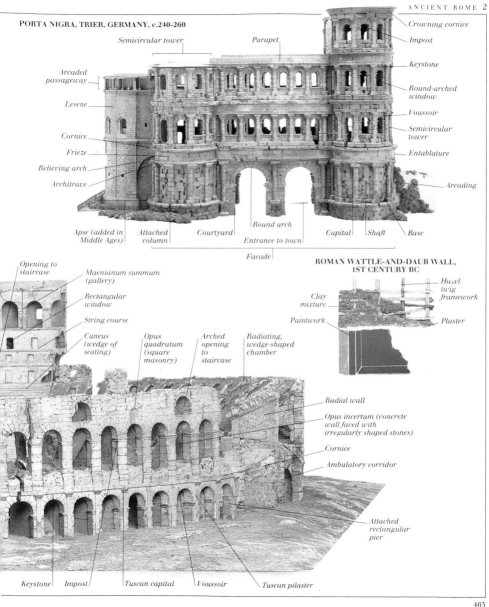

PORTA NIGRA, TRIER, GERMANY, c.240-260

Crowning cornice

Impost

Semicircular tower

Parapet

Keystone

Arcaded passageway

Round-arched window

Lesene

Voussoir

Semicircular tower

Cornice

Entablature

Frieze

Relieving arch

Architrave

Arcading

Apse (added in Middle Ages)

Attached column

Courtyard

Capital

Shaft

Base

Round arch

Entrance to town

Facade

Opening to staircase

Maenianum summum (gallery)

ROMAN WATTLE-AND-DAUB WALL, 1ST CENTURY BC

Hazel twig framework

Rectangular window

Clay mixture

String course

Paintwork

Plaster

Cuneus (wedge of seating)

Opus quadratum (square masonry)

Arched opening to staircase

Radiating, wedge-shaped chamber

Radial wall

Opus incertum (concrete wall faced with irregularly shaped stones)

Cornice

Ambulatory corridor

Attached rectangular pier

Keystone

Impost

Tuscan capital

Voussoir

Tuscan pilaster

Medieval castles and houses

WARFARE WAS COMMON IN EUROPE in the Middle Ages, and many monarchs and nobles built castles as a form of defence. Typical medieval castles have outer walls surrounding a moat. Inside the moat is a bailey (courtyard), protected by a chemise (jacket-wall). The innermost and strongest part of a medieval castle is the keep. There are two main types of keep: towers called donjons, such as the Tour de César and Coucy-le-Château, and rectangular keeps ("hall-keeps"), such as the Tower of London. Castles were often guarded by salients (projecting fortifications), like those of the Bastille. Medieval houses typically had timber cruck (tent-like) frames, wattle-and-daub walls, and pitched roofs, like those on medieval London Bridge (opposite).

DONJON, TOUR DE CESAR, PROVINS, FRANCE, 12TH CENTURY

Oculus
Loophole
Battlements (crenellations)
Conical spire
Hemispherical cupola
Flying buttress
Gallery
Hexahedral hall
Squinch
Semicircular turret
Vaulted room
Fireplace
Main entrance
Bailey
Staircase to chemise (jacket-wall)
Embrasure
Chemise (jacket-wall)
Plain impost
Depressed cupola
Vaulted staircase
Motte

SALIENT, CAERNARVON CASTLE, BRITAIN, 1285-1325

Loophole

CRUCK-FRAMED HOUSE, BRITAIN, c.1200

Timber cruck frame

TOWER OF LONDON, BRITAIN, FROM 1070

Blind, rounded relieving arch
Merlon
Battlements (crenellations)
Tetrahedral spire
Crenel
Loophole
Rectangular turret
Wooden staircase leading to entrance above ground level
Quoin
Timber-framed house
Cornice
Buttress
Round-arched window with twin openings
Cruck frame
Paling

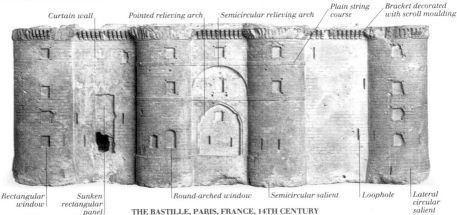

THE BASTILLE, PARIS, FRANCE, 14TH CENTURY

Curtain wall
Pointed relieving arch
Semicircular relieving arch
Plain string course
Bracket decorated with scroll moulding
Rectangular window
Sunken rectangular panel
Round-arched window
Semicircular salient
Loophole
Lateral circular salient

MEDIEVAL LONDON BRIDGE, BRITAIN, 1176 (WITH 14TH-CENTURY BATTLEMENTED BUILDING, NONESUCH HOUSE, AND TWO-TOWERED GATE)

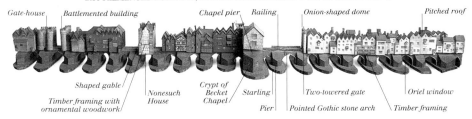

Gate-house | Battlemented building | Chapel pier | Railing | Onion-shaped dome | Pitched roof

Shaped gable | Nonesuch House | Crypt of Becket Chapel | Starling | Two-towered gate | Oriel window

Timber framing with ornamental woodwork | Pier | Pointed Gothic stone arch | Timber framing

DONJON, COUCY-LE-CHATEAU, AISNE, FRANCE, 1225-1245

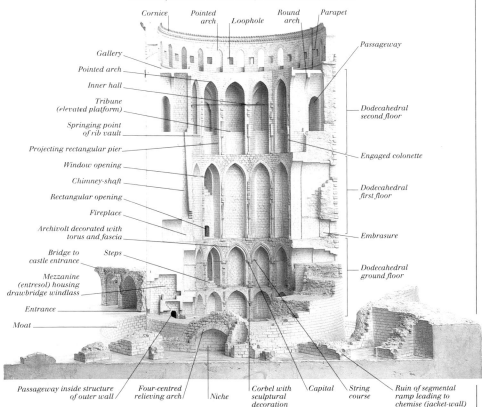

Cornice | Pointed arch | Loophole | Round arch | Parapet

Passageway

Gallery | Pointed arch | Inner hall

Tribune (elevated platform) | Springing point of rib vault | Projecting rectangular pier | Window opening | Chimney-shaft | Rectangular opening | Fireplace | Archivolt decorated with torus and fascia | Bridge to castle entrance | Steps | Mezzanine (entresol) housing drawbridge windlass | Entrance | Moat

Dodecahedral second floor | Engaged colonette | Dodecahedral first floor | Embrasure | Dodecahedral ground floor

Passageway inside structure of outer wall | Four-centred relieving arch | Niche | Corbel with sculptural decoration | Capital | String course | Ruin of segmental ramp leading to chemise (jacket-wall)

467

Medieval churches

ABBEY OF ST. FOI, CONQUES, FRANCE, c.1050-c.1150

DURING THE MIDDLE AGES, large numbers of churches were built in Europe. European churches of this period typically have high vaults supported by massive piers and columns. In the 10th century, the Romanesque style developed. Romanesque architects adopted many Roman or early Christian architectural ideas, such as cross-shaped ground-plans – like that of Angoulême Cathedral (opposite) – and the basilican system of a nave with a central vessel and side aisles. In the mid-12th century, flying buttresses and pointed vaults appeared. These features later became widely used in Gothic architecture (see pp. 470-471). Bagneux Church (opposite) has both styles: a Romanesque tower, and a Gothic nave and choir.

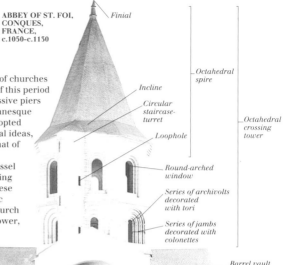

Finial

Octahedral spire

Incline

Circular staircase-turret

Loophole

Octahedral crossing tower

Round-arched window

Series of archivolts decorated with tori

Series of jambs decorated with colonettes

CHURCH-ROOF BOSS, BRITAIN

ROMANESQUE CAPITALS

"THE FLIGHT INTO EGYPT" CAPITAL, CATHEDRAL OF ST. LAZARE, AUTUN, FRANCE, 1120-1130

"CHRIST IN MAJESTY" CAPITAL, BASILICA OF ST. MADELEINE, VEZELAY, FRANCE, 1120-1140

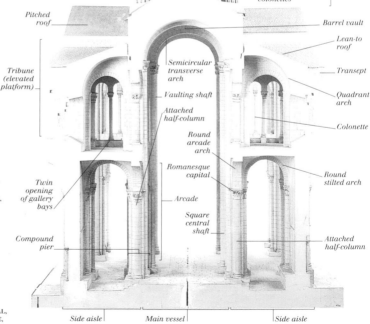

Pitched roof

Tribune (elevated platform)

Semicircular transverse arch

Vaulting shaft

Attached half-column

Round arcade arch

Romanesque capital

Twin opening of gallery bays

Arcade

Square central shaft

Compound pier

Barrel vault

Lean-to roof

Transept

Quadrant arch

Colonette

Round stilted arch

Attached half-column

Side aisle

Main vessel

Side aisle

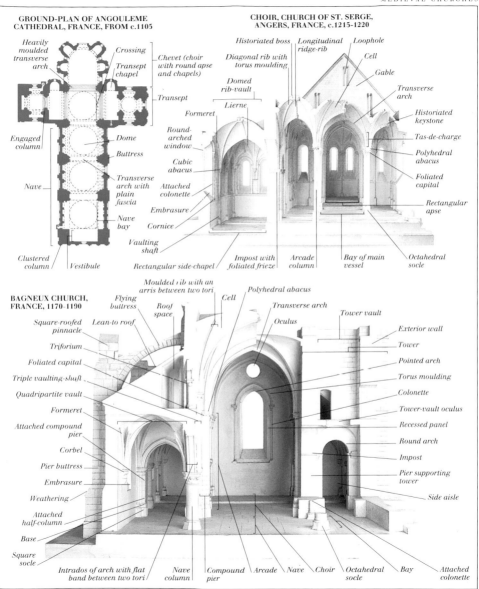

GROUND-PLAN OF ANGOULEME CATHEDRAL, FRANCE, FROM c.1105

- Heavily moulded transverse arch
- Crossing
- Chevet (choir with round apse and chapels)
- Transept chapel
- Transept
- Engaged column
- Dome
- Buttress
- Nave
- Transverse arch with plain fascia
- Attached colonette
- Embrasure
- Cornice
- Nave bay
- Clustered column
- Vestibule
- Vaulting shaft
- Rectangular side-chapel

CHOIR, CHURCH OF ST. SERGE, ANGERS, FRANCE, c.1215-1220

- Historiated boss
- Longitudinal ridge-rib
- Loophole
- Diagonal rib with torus moulding
- Cell
- Gable
- Domed rib-vault
- Transverse arch
- Lierne
- Formeret
- Round-arched window
- Historiated keystone
- Tas-de-charge
- Cubic abacus
- Polyhedral abacus
- Foliated capital
- Rectangular apse
- Impost with foliated frieze
- Arcade column
- Bay of main vessel
- Octahedral socle

BAGNEUX CHURCH, FRANCE, 1170-1190

- Moulded rib with an arris between two tori
- Flying buttress
- Cell
- Polyhedral abacus
- Transverse arch
- Tower vault
- Roof space
- Oculus
- Exterior wall
- Square-roofed pinnacle
- Lean-to roof
- Tower
- Triforium
- Pointed arch
- Foliated capital
- Torus moulding
- Triple vaulting-shaft
- Colonette
- Quadripartite vault
- Tower-vault oculus
- Formeret
- Recessed panel
- Attached compound pier
- Round arch
- Corbel
- Impost
- Pier buttress
- Pier supporting tower
- Embrasure
- Weathering
- Side aisle
- Attached half-column
- Base
- Square socle
- Intrados of arch with flat band between two tori
- Nave column
- Compound pier
- Arcade
- Nave
- Choir
- Octahedral socle
- Bay
- Attached colonette

469

Gothic 1

GOTHIC STAINED GLASS WITH FOLIATED SCROLL MOTIF, ON WOODEN FORM

GOTHIC BUILDINGS are characterized by rib vaults, pointed or lancet arches, flying buttresses, decorative tracery and gables, and stained-glass windows. Typical Gothic buildings include the Cathedrals of Salisbury and old St. Paul's in England, and Notre Dame de Paris in France (see pp. 472-473). The Gothic style developed out of Romanesque architecture in France (see pp. 468-469) in the mid-12th century, and then spread throughout Europe. The decorative elements of Gothic architecture became highly developed in buildings of the English Decorated style (late 13th-14th century) and the French Flamboyant style (15th-16th century). These styles are exemplified by the tower of Salisbury Cathedral and the staircase in the Church of St. Maclou (see pp. 472-473), respectively. In both of these styles, embellishments such as ballflowers and curvilinear (flowing) tracery were used liberally. The English Perpendicular style (late 14th-15th century), which followed the Decorated style, emphasized the vertical and horizontal elements of a building. A notable feature of this style is the hammer-beam roof.

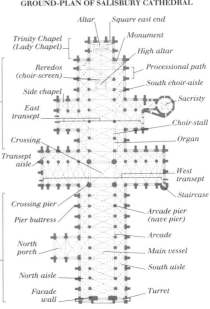

Altar
Square east end
Trinity Chapel (Lady Chapel)
Monument
High altar
Reredos (choir-screen)
Processional path
Side chapel
South choir-aisle
East transept
Sacristy
Choir
Choir-stall
Crossing
Organ
Transept aisle
West transept
Crossing pier
Staircase
Pier buttress
Arcade pier (nave pier)
North porch
Arcade
Nave
Main vessel
North aisle
South aisle
Facade wall
Turret

GOTHIC TORUS WITH BALLFLOWERS

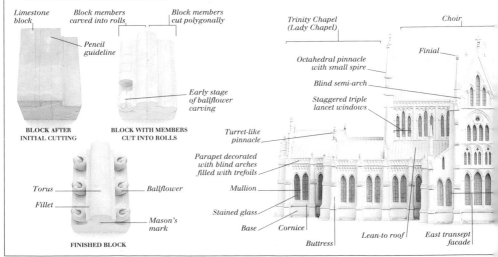

Limestone block
Block members carved into rolls
Block members cut polygonally
Pencil guideline
Early stage of ballflower carving

BLOCK AFTER INITIAL CUTTING
BLOCK WITH MEMBERS CUT INTO ROLLS

Torus
Ballflower
Fillet
Mason's mark

FINISHED BLOCK

Trinity Chapel (Lady Chapel)
Choir
Finial
Octahedral pinnacle with small spire
Blind semi-arch
Staggered triple lancet windows
Turret-like pinnacle
Parapet decorated with blind arches filled with trefoils
Mullion
Stained glass
Base
Cornice
Lean-to roof
East transept facade
Buttress

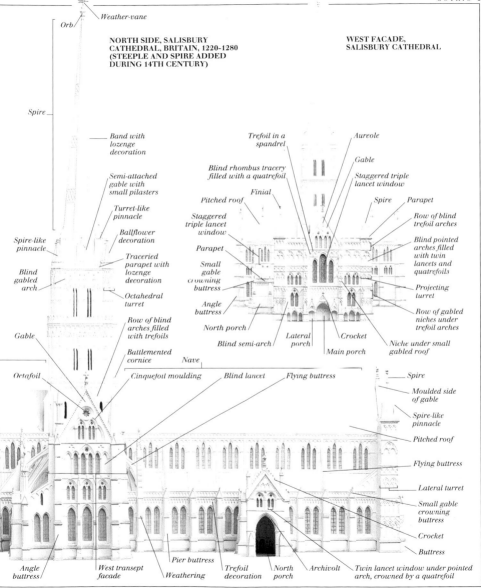

Weather-vane

Orb

**NORTH SIDE, SALISBURY
CATHEDRAL, BRITAIN, 1220–1280
(STEEPLE AND SPIRE ADDED
DURING 14TH CENTURY)**

**WEST FACADE,
SALISBURY CATHEDRAL**

Spire

Band with
lozenge
decoration

Semi-attached
gable with
small pilasters

Turret-like
pinnacle

Ballflower
decoration

Spire-like
pinnacle

Traceried
parapet with
lozenge
decoration

Blind
gabled
arch

Octahedral
turret

Row of blind
arches filled
with trefoils

Gable

Battlemented
cornice

Trefoil in a
spandrel

Aureole

Gable

Blind rhombus tracery
filled with a quatrefoil

Staggered triple
lancet window

Pitched roof

Finial

Staggered
triple lancet
window

Spire

Parapet

Parapet

Row of blind
trefoil arches

Small
gable
crowning
buttress

Blind pointed
arches filled
with twin
lancets and
quatrefoils

Angle
buttress

Projecting
turret

North porch

Row of gabled
niches under
trefoil arches

Blind semi-arch

Lateral
porch

Crocket

Main porch

Niche under small
gabled roof

Nave

Octofoil

Cinquefoil moulding

Blind lancet

Flying buttress

Spire

Moulded side
of gable

Spire-like
pinnacle

Pitched roof

Flying buttress

Lateral turret

Small gable
crowning
buttress

Crocket

Buttress

Angle
buttress

West transept
facade

Pier buttress

Weathering

Trefoil
decoration

North
porch

Archivolt

Twin lancet window under pointed
arch, crowned by a quatrefoil

Gothic 2

**CURVILINEAR (FLOWING) TRACERY FROM A
BALUSTRADE, 14TH OR 15TH CENTURY**

Cyma reversa
(reversed ogee curve)

Cavetto
moulding

Plain fascia

Moulded
cornice

Cavetto
moulding with
elongated
lower part

Ogee
curve

Mouchette
(curved
dagger)

Cusp

Drop
shape

Cavetto moulding

**SPIRAL STAIRCASE TO ORGAN, CHURCH OF
ST. MACLOU, ROUEN, FRANCE, c.1519**

Trefoil

Flamboyant
tracery

Mouchette
(curved dagger)

Cherub

Foliated
scrollwork

Crocket

Pointed arch

Figure

Octahedral
spire

Winding
cornice

Rectangular
buttress

Niche

Attached gable

Gabled
canopy

Attached
gable

Parapet

Statue

Square
pillar

Base

Dagger

Basket arch

Round
arch

Turret-like
pinnacle

Socle

Base decorated
with ovolo
mouldings

Cross
motif

Angle
buttress

Lancet window
with twin lancets
and crowned
with a quatrefoil

**TOWER AND PART OF THE NAVE
AND CHOIR, OLD ST. PAUL'S
CATHEDRAL, LONDON,
BRITAIN, 1087-1666**

Tower

Niche

Pointed arch
filled with
geometrical tracery

Turret-like
pinnacle

Gable

Parapet decorated
with quatrefoils

Flying
buttress

Couronnement

Pointed arch filled
with tracery and
three lancet windows

Mullion

Pitched roof

Clerestory
wall

Lancet window

Blind lancet arch

Lean-to
roof

Window filled
with early English
Perpendicular-
style tracery

Buttress

Outer wall
of side aisle

Octahedral
chapter-house

Oculus

Cloister

Weathering

Early English-style window

Oculus filled
with multifoil

Nave

Transept facade

Choir

472

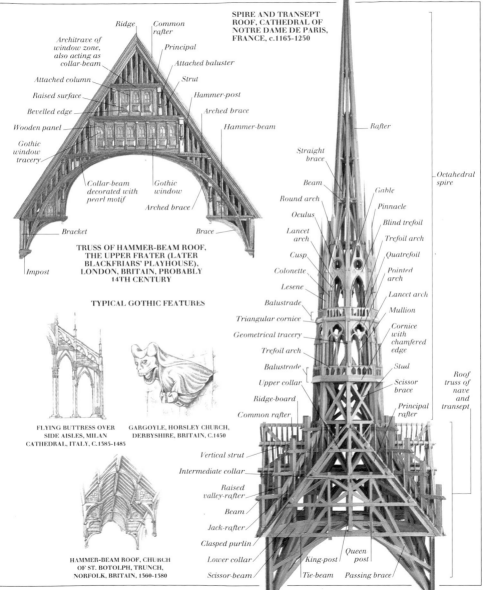

SPIRE AND TRANSEPT ROOF, CATHEDRAL OF NOTRE DAME DE PARIS, FRANCE, c.1163-1250

Ridge

Common rafter

Architrave of window zone, also acting as collar-beam

Principal

Attached baluster

Attached column

Strut

Raised surface

Hammer-post

Bevelled edge

Arched brace

Wooden panel

Hammer-beam

Gothic window tracery

Collar-beam decorated with pearl motif

Gothic window

Arched brace

Bracket

Brace

Impost

Rafter

Straight brace

Beam

Gable

Round arch

Oculus

Pinnacle

Lancet arch

Blind trefoil

Cusp

Trefoil arch

Colonette

Quatrefoil

Lesene

Pointed arch

Balustrade

Lancet arch

Triangular cornice

Mullion

Geometrical tracery

Cornice with chamfered edge

Trefoil arch

Balustrade

Stud

Upper collar

Scissor brace

Ridge-board

Principal rafter

Common rafter

Vertical strut

Intermediate collar

Raised valley-rafter

Beam

Jack-rafter

Clasped purlin

Lower collar

Scissor-beam

King-post

Queen post

Tie-beam

Passing brace

Octahedral spire

Roof truss of nave and transept

TRUSS OF HAMMER-BEAM ROOF, THE UPPER FRATER (LATER BLACKFRIARS' PLAYHOUSE), LONDON, BRITAIN, PROBABLY 14TH CENTURY

TYPICAL GOTHIC FEATURES

FLYING BUTTRESS OVER SIDE AISLES, MILAN CATHEDRAL, ITALY, C.1385-1485

GARGOYLE, HORSLEY CHURCH, DERBYSHIRE, BRITAIN, C.1450

HAMMER-BEAM ROOF, CHURCH OF ST. BOTOLPH, TRUNCH, NORFOLK, BRITAIN, 1380-1380

Renaissance 1

THE RENAISSANCE was a European movement – lasting roughly from the 14th century to the mid-17th century – in which the arts and sciences underwent great changes. In architecture, these changes were marked by a return to the classical forms and proportions of ancient Roman buildings. The Renaissance originated in Italy, and the buildings most characteristic of its style can be found there, such as the Palazzo Strozzi shown here. Mannerism is a branch of the Renaissance style that distorts the classical forms; an example is the Laurentian Library staircase. As the Renaissance style spread to other European countries, many of its features were incorporated into the local architecture; for example, the Château de Montal in France (see pp. 476-477) incorporates aedicules (tabernacles).

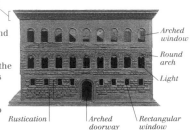

Crowning cornice

Arched window

Round arch

Light

Rustication

Arched doorway

Rectangular window

SIDE VIEW OF PALAZZO STROZZI, FLORENCE, ITALY, 1489 (BY G. DA SANGALLO, B. DA MAIANO, AND CRONACA)

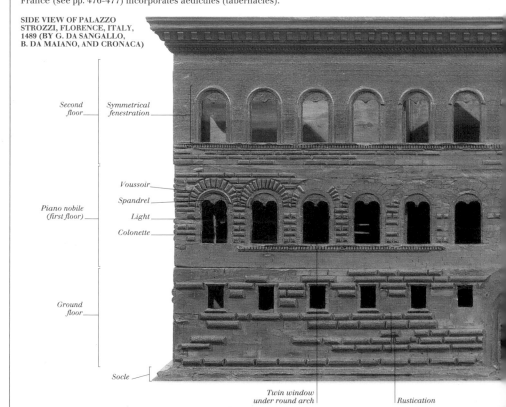

Second floor

Symmetrical fenestration

Voussoir

Spandrel

Piano nobile (first floor)

Light

Colonette

Ground floor

Socle

Twin window under round arch

Rustication

DETAILS FROM ITALIAN RENAISSANCE BUILDINGS

PANEL FROM DRUM OF DOME,
FLORENCE CATHEDRAL, 1420-1436

COFFERING IN DOME,
PAZZI CHAPEL,
FLORENCE, 1429-1461

STAIRCASE,
LAURENTIAN LIBRARY,
FLORENCE, 1559

PORTICO, VILLA ROTUNDA,
VICENZA, 1567-1569

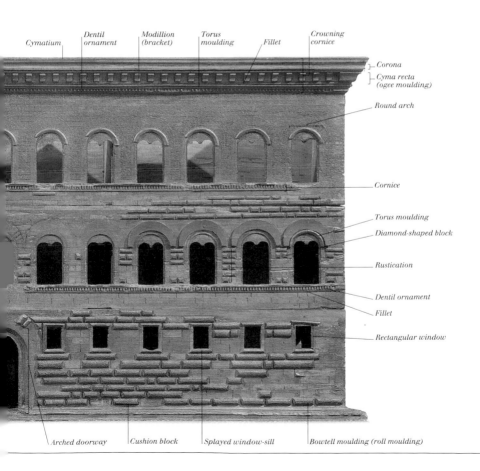

Cymatium

Dentil ornament

Modillion (bracket)

Torus moulding

Fillet

Crowning cornice

Corona

Cyma recta (ogee moulding)

Round arch

Cornice

Torus moulding

Diamond-shaped block

Rustication

Dentil ornament

Fillet

Rectangular window

Arched doorway

Cushion block

Splayed window-sill

Bowtell moulding (roll moulding)

Renaissance 2

DETAILS FROM EUROPEAN RENAISSANCE BUILDINGS

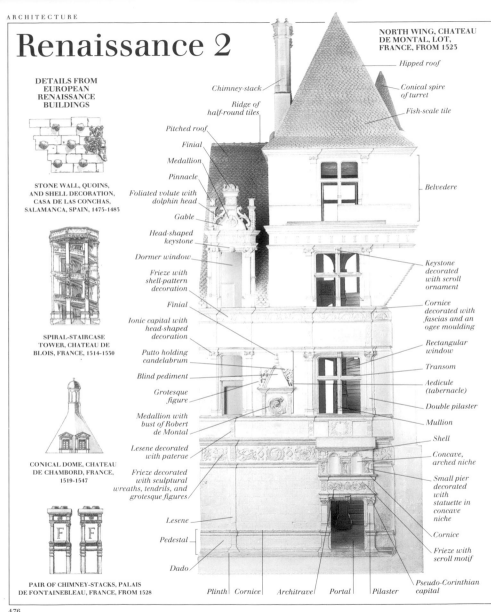

STONE WALL, QUOINS, AND SHELL DECORATION, CASA DE LAS CONCHAS, SALAMANCA, SPAIN, 1475-1483

SPIRAL-STAIRCASE TOWER, CHATEAU DE BLOIS, FRANCE, 1514-1550

CONICAL DOME, CHATEAU DE CHAMBORD, FRANCE, 1519-1547

PAIR OF CHIMNEY-STACKS, PALAIS DE FONTAINEBLEAU, FRANCE, FROM 1528

Hipped roof

Chimney-stack

Conical spire of turret

Ridge of half-round tiles

Fish-scale tile

Pitched roof

Finial

Medallion

Pinnacle

Belvedere

Foliated volute with dolphin head

Gable

Head-shaped keystone

Dormer window

Keystone decorated with scroll ornament

Frieze with shell-pattern decoration

Finial

Cornice decorated with fascias and an ogee moulding

Ionic capital with head-shaped decoration

Rectangular window

Putto holding candelabrum

Transom

Blind pediment

Aedicule (tabernacle)

Grotesque figure

Double pilaster

Medallion with bust of Robert de Montal

Mullion

Lesene decorated with paterae

Shell

Frieze decorated with sculptural wreaths, tendrils, and grotesque figures

Concave, arched niche

Small pier decorated with statuette in concave niche

Lesene

Cornice

Pedestal

Frieze with scroll motif

Dado

Pseudo-Corinthian capital

Plinth Cornice Architrave Portal Pilaster

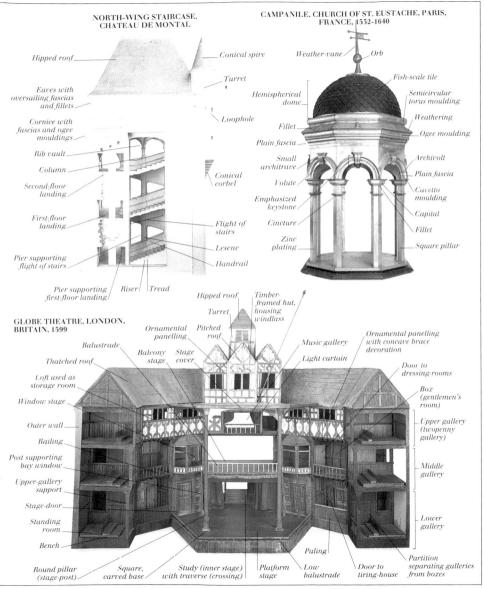

NORTH-WING STAIRCASE, CHATEAU DE MONTAL

Hipped roof

Conical spire

Turret

Eaves with oversailing fascias and fillets

Loophole

Cornice with fascias and ogee mouldings

Rib vault

Column

Conical corbel

Second-floor landing

First-floor landing

Flight of stairs

Lesene

Handrail

Pier supporting flight of stairs

Pier supporting first-floor landing

Riser

Tread

CAMPANILE, CHURCH OF ST. EUSTACHE, PARIS, FRANCE, 1532-1640

Weather-vane

Orb

Fish-scale tile

Hemispherical dome

Semicircular torus moulding

Fillet

Weathering

Plain fascia

Ogee moulding

Small architrave

Archivolt

Volute

Plain fascia

Emphasized keystone

Cavetto moulding

Cincture

Capital

Zinc plating

Fillet

Square pillar

GLOBE THEATRE, LONDON, BRITAIN, 1599

Hipped roof

Timber-framed hut, housing windlass

Turret

Ornamental panelling

Pitched roof

Music gallery

Ornamental panelling with concave brace decoration

Balustrade

Balcony stage

Stage cover

Light curtain

Door to dressing-rooms

Thatched roof

Box (gentlemen's room)

Loft used as storage room

Window stage

Upper gallery (twopenny gallery)

Outer wall

Railing

Middle gallery

Post supporting bay window

Upper-gallery support

Stage-door

Standing room

Lower gallery

Bench

Round pillar (stage-post)

Square, carved base

Study (inner stage) with traverse (crossing)

Platform stage

Low balustrade

Door to tiring-house

Partition separating galleries from boxes

Paling

Baroque and neoclassical 1

THE BAROQUE STYLE EVOLVED IN THE EARLY 17TH CENTURY in Rome. It is characterized by curved outlines and ostentatious decoration, as can be seen in the Italian church details (right). The baroque style was particularly widely favoured in Italy, Spain, and Germany. It was also adopted in Britain and France, but with adaptations. The British architects Sir Christopher Wren and Nicholas Hawksmoor, for example, used baroque features – such as the concave walls of St. Paul's Cathedral and the curved buttresses of the Church of St. George in the East (see pp. 480-481) – but they did so with restraint. Similarly, the curved buttresses and volutes of the Parisian Church of St. Paul-St. Louis are relatively plain. In the second half of the 17th century, a distinct classical style (known as neoclassicism) developed in northern Europe as a reaction to the excesses of baroque. Typical of this new style were churches such as the Madeleine (a proposed facade is shown below), as well as secular buildings such as the Cirque Napoleon (opposite) and the buildings of the British architect Sir John Soane (see pp. 482-483). In early 18th-century France, an extremely lavish form of baroque developed, known as rococo. The balcony from Nantes (see pp. 482-483) with its twisted ironwork and head-shaped corbels is typical of this style.

SCROLLED BUTTRESS,
CHURCH OF ST. MARIA DELLA
SALUTE, VENICE, 1631-1682

STATUE OF THE ECSTASY OF
ST. THERESA, CHURCH OF ST. MARIA
DELLA VITTORIA, ROME, 1645-1652

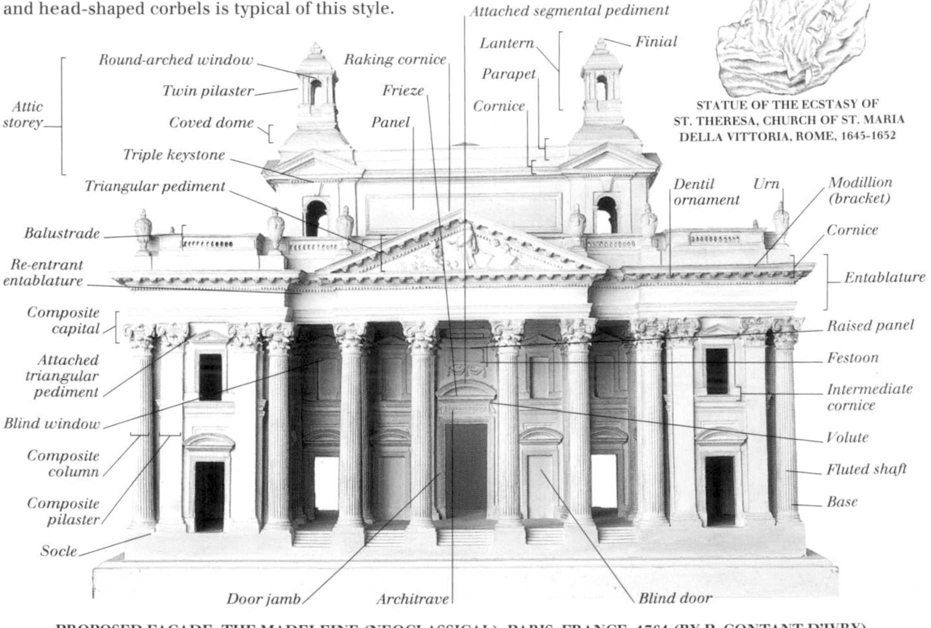

Attached segmental pediment

Round-arched window
Twin pilaster
Attic storey
Coved dome
Triple keystone
Triangular pediment
Balustrade
Re-entrant entablature
Composite capital
Attached triangular pediment
Blind window
Composite column
Composite pilaster
Socle

Raking cornice
Frieze
Panel

Lantern
Parapet
Cornice

Finial

Dentil ornament
Urn
Modillion (bracket)
Cornice
Entablature
Raised panel
Festoon
Intermediate cornice
Volute
Fluted shaft
Base

Door jamb
Architrave
Blind door

PROPOSED FACADE, THE MADELEINE (NEOCLASSICAL), PARIS, FRANCE, 1764 (BY P. CONTANT D'IVRY)

CIRQUE NAPOLEON (NEOCLASSICAL), PARIS, FRANCE, 1852 (BY J.I. HITTORFF)

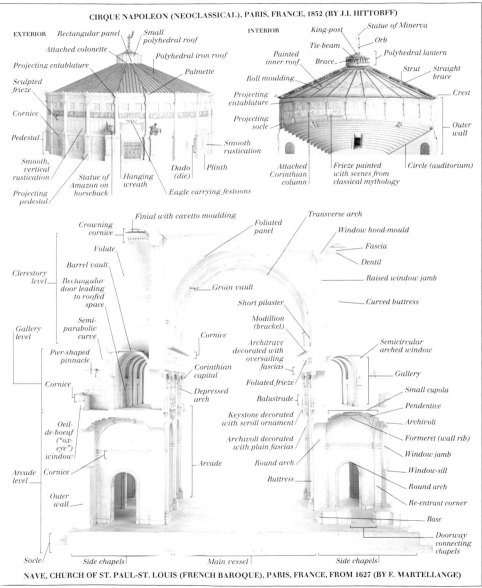

EXTERIOR

Rectangular panel

Small polyhedral roof

Attached colonette

Polyhedral iron roof

Projecting entablature

Palmette

Sculpted frieze

Cornice

Pedestal

Smooth, vertical rustication

Statue of Amazon on horseback

Hanging wreath

Dado (die)

Plinth

Smooth rustication

Projecting pedestal

Eagle carrying festoons

INTERIOR

King-post

Statue of Minerva

Tie-beam

Orb

Painted inner roof

Brace

Polyhedral lantern

Roll moulding

Strut

Straight brace

Projecting entablature

Crest

Projecting socle

Outer wall

Attached Corinthian column

Frieze painted with scenes from classical mythology

Circle (auditorium)

Finial with cavetto moulding

Crowning cornice

Foliated panel

Transverse arch

Volute

Window hood-mould

Clerestory level

Barrel vault

Fascia

Rectangular door leading to roofed space

Groin vault

Dentil

Raised window jamb

Semi-parabolic curve

Curved buttress

Gallery level

Short pilaster

Modillion (bracket)

Pier-shaped pinnacle

Cornice

Architrave decorated with oversailing fascias

Semicircular arched window

Cornice

Corinthian capital

Foliated frieze

Gallery

Depressed arch

Balustrade

Small cupola

Oeil-de-boeuf ("ox-eye") window

Keystone decorated with scroll ornament

Pendentive

Archivolt

Archivolt decorated with plain fascias

Formeret (wall rib)

Arcade

Window jamb

Arcade level

Cornice

Round arch

Window-sill

Outer wall

Buttress

Round arch

Re-entrant corner

Base

Doorway connecting chapels

Socle

Side chapels

Main vessel

Side chapels

NAVE, CHURCH OF ST. PAUL-ST. LOUIS (FRENCH BAROQUE), PARIS, FRANCE, FROM 1627 (BY F. MARTELLANGE)

Baroque and neoclassical 2

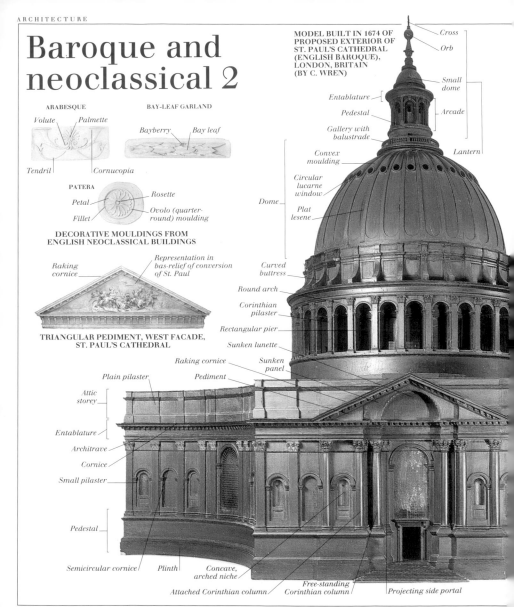

ARABESQUE

Volute *Palmette*
Tendril *Cornucopia*

BAY-LEAF GARLAND

Bayberry *Bay leaf*

PATERA

Petal *Rosette*
Fillet *Ovolo (quarter-round) moulding*

DECORATIVE MOULDINGS FROM ENGLISH NEOCLASSICAL BUILDINGS

Raking cornice *Representation in bas-relief of conversion of St. Paul*

TRIANGULAR PEDIMENT, WEST FACADE, ST. PAUL'S CATHEDRAL

Plain pilaster
Attic storey
Entablature
Architrave
Cornice
Small pilaster
Pedestal
Semicircular cornice *Plinth* *Concave, arched niche*
Attached Corinthian column

MODEL BUILT IN 1674 OF PROPOSED EXTERIOR OF ST. PAUL'S CATHEDRAL (ENGLISH BAROQUE), LONDON, BRITAIN (BY C. WREN)

Cross
Orb
Small dome
Entablature
Pedestal
Arcade
Gallery with balustrade
Lantern
Convex moulding
Circular lucarne window
Dome
Plat lesene
Curved buttress
Round arch
Corinthian pilaster
Rectangular pier
Sunken lunette
Raking cornice
Sunken panel
Pediment
Free-standing Corinthian column
Projecting side portal

CHURCH OF ST. GEORGE IN THE EAST (ENGLISH BAROQUE), LONDON, BRITAIN, 1714-1734 (BY N. HAWKSMOOR)

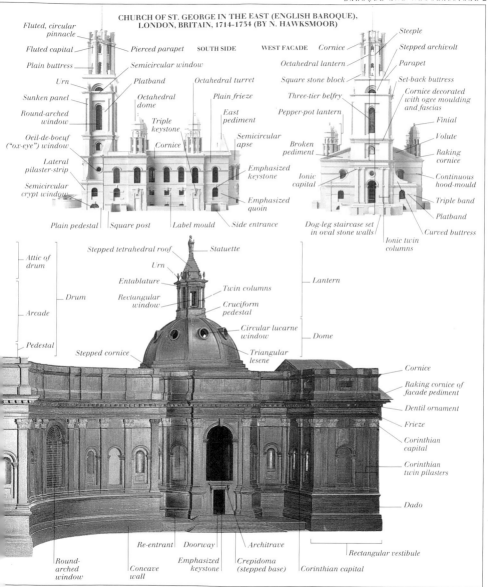

SOUTH SIDE

Fluted, circular pinnacle
Fluted capital
Plain buttress
Urn
Sunken panel
Round-arched window
Oeil-de-boeuf ("ox-eye") window
Lateral pilaster-strip
Semicircular crypt window
Pierced parapet
Semicircular window
Platband
Octahedral dome
Triple keystone
Cornice
Octahedral turret
Plain frieze
East pediment
Semicircular apse
Emphasized keystone
Emphasized quoin
Plain pedestal
Square post
Label mould
Side entrance

WEST FACADE

Steeple
Cornice
Stepped archivolt
Octahedral lantern
Parapet
Square stone block
Set-back buttress
Three-tier belfry
Cornice decorated with ogee moulding and fascias
Pepper-pot lantern
Finial
Volute
Broken pediment
Raking cornice
Ionic capital
Continuous hood-mould
Triple band
Emphasized keystone
Platband
Dog-leg staircase set in oval stone walls
Curved buttress
Ionic twin columns

Attic of drum
Drum
Arcade
Pedestal
Stepped tetrahedral roof
Urn
Entablature
Rectangular window
Statuette
Twin columns
Cruciform pedestal
Circular lucarne window
Triangular lesene
Lantern
Dome
Stepped cornice
Cornice
Raking cornice of facade pediment
Dentil ornament
Frieze
Corinthian capital
Corinthian twin pilasters
Dado
Re-entrant
Doorway
Architrave
Round-arched window
Concave wall
Emphasized keystone
Crepidoma (stepped base)
Corinthian capital
Rectangular vestibule

Baroque and neoclassical 3

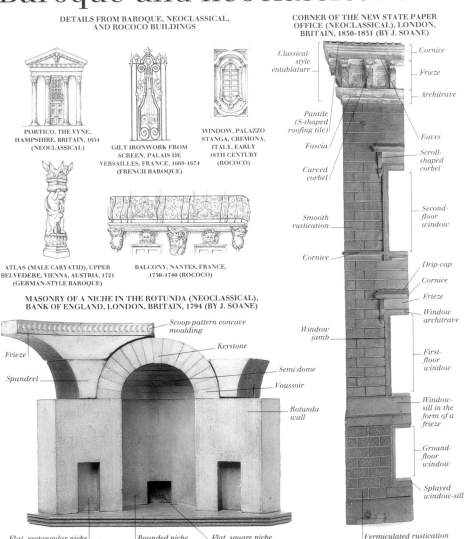

DETAILS FROM BAROQUE, NEOCLASSICAL, AND ROCOCO BUILDINGS

PORTICO, THE VYNE, HAMPSHIRE, BRITAIN, 1654 (NEOCLASSICAL)

GILT IRONWORK FROM SCREEN, PALAIS DE VERSAILLES, FRANCE, 1669-1674 (FRENCH BAROQUE)

WINDOW, PALAZZO STANGA, CREMONA, ITALY, EARLY 18TH CENTURY (ROCOCO)

ATLAS (MALE CARYATID), UPPER BELVEDERE, VIENNA, AUSTRIA, 1721 (GERMAN-STYLE BAROQUE)

BALCONY, NANTES, FRANCE, 1730-1740 (ROCOCO)

MASONRY OF A NICHE IN THE ROTUNDA (NEOCLASSICAL), BANK OF ENGLAND, LONDON, BRITAIN, 1794 (BY J. SOANE)

Scoop-pattern concave moulding

Keystone

Frieze

Spandrel

Semi-dome

Voussoir

Rotunda wall

Flat, rectangular niche

Rounded niche

Flat, square niche

CORNER OF THE NEW STATE PAPER OFFICE (NEOCLASSICAL), LONDON, BRITAIN, 1830-1831 (BY J. SOANE)

Classical-style entablature

Cornice

Frieze

Architrave

Pantile (S-shaped roofing tile)

Fascia

Curved corbel

Eaves

Scroll-shaped corbel

Smooth rustication

Second-floor window

Cornice

Drip-cap

Cornice

Frieze

Window architrave

Window jamb

First-floor window

Window-sill in the form of a frieze

Ground-floor window

Splayed window-sill

Vermiculated rustication

TYRINGHAM HOUSE (NEOCLASSICAL), BUCKINGHAMSHIRE, BRITAIN, 1793-1797 (BY J. SOANE)

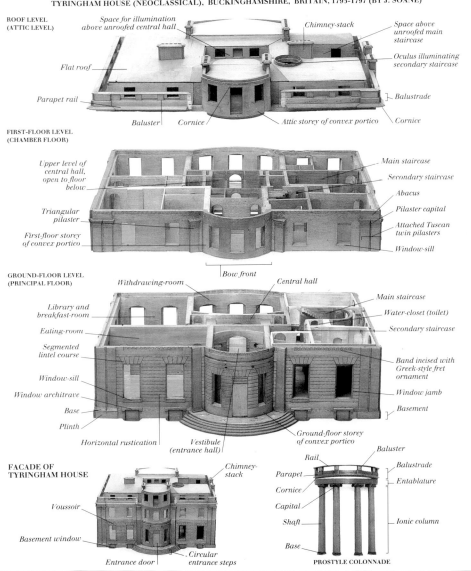

ROOF LEVEL (ATTIC LEVEL)

Space for illumination above unroofed central hall
Chimney-stack
Space above unroofed main staircase
Oculus illuminating secondary staircase
Flat roof
Parapet rail
Balustrade
Baluster
Cornice
Attic storey of convex portico
Cornice

FIRST-FLOOR LEVEL (CHAMBER FLOOR)

Upper level of central hall, open to floor below
Main staircase
Secondary staircase
Abacus
Triangular pilaster
Pilaster capital
First-floor storey of convex portico
Attached Tuscan twin pilasters
Window-sill
Bow front

GROUND-FLOOR LEVEL (PRINCIPAL FLOOR)

Withdrawing-room
Central hall
Library and breakfast-room
Main staircase
Eating-room
Water-closet (toilet)
Secondary staircase
Segmented lintel course
Window-sill
Band incised with Greek-style fret ornament
Window architrave
Window jamb
Base
Basement
Plinth
Horizontal rustication
Vestibule (entrance hall)
Ground-floor storey of convex portico

FACADE OF TYRINGHAM HOUSE

Voussoir
Chimney-stack
Basement window
Circular entrance steps
Entrance door

Rail
Baluster
Parapet
Balustrade
Cornice
Entablature
Capital
Shaft
Ionic column
Base
PROSTYLE COLONNADE

483

Arches and vaults

PARTS OF AN ARCH

ARCHES ARE CURVED STRUCTURES used to bridge spans and to support the weight of upper parts of buildings, such as domes, as in St. Paul's Cathedral (below) and the antique temple (opposite). The voussoirs (wedge-shaped blocks) that form an arch (right) support each other and convert the downward force of the weight of the building into an outward force. This outward force is in turn transferred to buttresses, piers, or abutments. A vault is an arched roof or ceiling. There are four main types of vault (opposite). A barrel vault is a single vault, semicircular in cross-section; a groin vault consists of two barrel vaults intersecting at right-angles; a rib vault is a groin vault reinforced by ribs; and a fan vault is a rib vault in which the ribs radiate from the springing point (where the arch begins) like a fan.

Voussoir Keystone Crown Abutment

Abutment
Intrados (soffit)
Impost
Abutment
Springing point
Span

Keystone
Extrados
Haunch
Intrados (soffit)
Abutment

FRONT   **SIDE**

ARCHES AND BASE OF DOME, ST. PAUL'S CATHEDRAL, LONDON, BRITAIN, 1675-1710 (BY C. WREN)

Inner dome   *Colonnade*
Pilaster   *Passageway*
Base   *Cornice*
Pendentive   *Opening to passageway*   *Pedestal of outer dome*
"Whispering Gallery"

Upper arch (concealing difference in heights between main arch and minor arches)
Round arch
Triangular buttress
Moulded bracket

Extrados
Intrados (soffit)
Springing point
Impost
Barrel vault
Semi-dome
Upper barrel-vaulted passage opening on to side aisle
Abutment

Passage leading to side aisle
Strut built into masonry to strengthen pier (added in the 20th century)

Minor arch leading to side aisle   *Main arch leading to nave*   *Pier*   *Minor arch*

TYPES OF ARCH

HORSESHOE ARCH (MOORISH ARCH), GREAT MOSQUE, CORDOBA, SPAIN, 785

BASKET ARCH (SEMI-ELLIPTICAL ARCH), PALATINE CHAPEL, AIX-LA-CHAPELLE, FRANCE, 790-798

TUDOR ARCH, TOWER OF LONDON, BRITAIN, C.1086-1097

LANCET ARCH, WESTMINSTER ABBEY, LONDON, BRITAIN, 1503-1519

TREFOIL ARCH, BEVERLEY MINSTER, YORKSHIRE, BRITAIN, C.1300

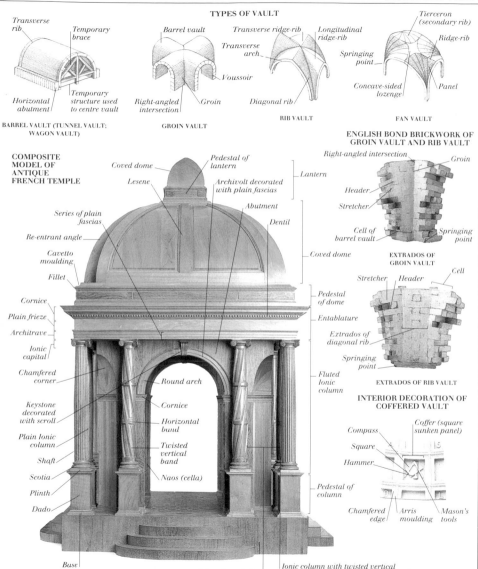

TYPES OF VAULT

Transverse rib
Temporary brace
Horizontal abutment
Temporary structure used to centre vault

BARREL VAULT (TUNNEL VAULT; WAGON VAULT)

Barrel vault
Transverse arch
Voussoir
Right-angled intersection
Groin

GROIN VAULT

Transverse ridge-rib
Longitudinal ridge-rib
Diagonal rib

RIB VAULT

Tierceron (secondary rib)
Ridge-rib
Springing point
Concave-sided lozenge
Panel

FAN VAULT

ENGLISH BOND BRICKWORK OF GROIN VAULT AND RIB VAULT

Right-angled intersection
Groin
Header
Stretcher
Cell of barrel vault
Springing point

EXTRADOS OF GROIN VAULT

Stretcher
Header
Cell
Extrados of diagonal rib
Springing point

EXTRADOS OF RIB VAULT

INTERIOR DECORATION OF COFFERED VAULT

Compass
Square
Hammer
Coffer (square sunken panel)
Chamfered edge
Arris moulding
Mason's tools

COMPOSITE MODEL OF ANTIQUE FRENCH TEMPLE

Coved dome
Lesene
Series of plain fascias
Re-entrant angle
Cavetto moulding
Fillet
Cornice
Plain frieze
Architrave
Ionic capital
Chamfered corner
Keystone decorated with scroll
Plain Ionic column
Shaft
Scotia
Plinth
Dado

Pedestal of lantern
Archivolt decorated with plain fascias
Abutment
Dentil
Lantern
Coved dome
Pedestal of dome
Entablature
Fluted Ionic column
Pedestal of column

Round arch
Cornice
Horizontal band
Twisted vertical band
Naos (cella)

Base
Intercolumniation
Ionic column with twisted vertical bands (wreaths) and horizontal bands

Domes

A DOME IS A CONVEX ROOF. Domes are categorized according to the shapes of both the base and the section through the centre of the dome. The base may be circular, square, or polygonal (many-sided), depending on the plan of the drum (the walls on which the dome rests). The section of a dome may be the same shape as any arch (see pp. 484-485). Various types of dome are illustrated here: a hemispherical dome, which has a circular base and a semicircular section; a saucer dome, which has a circular base and a segmental (less than a semicircle) section; a polyhedral dome, which is a dome on a polygonal base whose sides meet at the top of the dome; and an onion dome, which has a circular or polygonal base and an ogee-shaped section. Many domes have a lantern (a turret with windows) to provide light inside.

LANTERN AND UPPER DOME TIMBERING, ST. PAUL'S CATHEDRAL

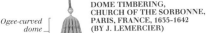

DOME TIMBERING, CHURCH OF THE SORBONNE, PARIS, FRANCE, 1635-1642 (BY J. LEMERCIER)

Ogee-curved dome

Straight brace

Window zone

Deeply projecting pier buttress

Cornice

Depressed hood-mould

Pedestal

Circular lucarne window

Floorboard

Ashlar piece

Floor-joist

Hood-mould

Pin

Waisted-oval lucarne window

Short strut

Mortise-and-tenon joint

Ogee-curved window-frame

Principal rafter

Straight brace

Vertical post

Tie-beam

Circular baseplate

Common rafter

Shaft connecting lantern and church interior

ROOF WITH LANTERN AND ONION DOME

Weathercock

Ellipsoid orb

Keeled lesene

Onion dome

Fish-scale tile

Oversailing fascia

Octahedral base

Sloping roof

Tetrahedral capital

Round arch

Attached pillar

Return

Vertical band

Window

Torus

Oversailing fascia

Fillet

Lantern

Octahedral base of lantern

Tetrahedral roof

REPRESENTATION OF DOME METALLING, CHURCH OF THE SORBONNE

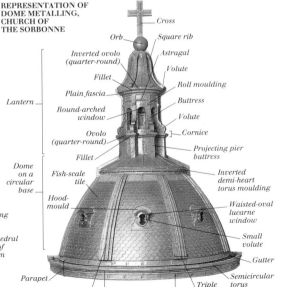

Cross

Orb

Square rib

Inverted ovolo (quarter-round)

Astragal

Fillet

Volute

Plain fascia

Roll moulding

Round-arched window

Buttress

Lantern

Volute

Ovolo (quarter-round)

Cornice

Fillet

Projecting pier buttress

Dome on a circular base

Fish-scale tile

Inverted demi-heart torus moulding

Hood-mould

Waisted-oval lucarne window

Small volute

Gutter

Parapet

Semicircular torus moulding

Small roll

Fillet

Plain fascia

Triple lesene

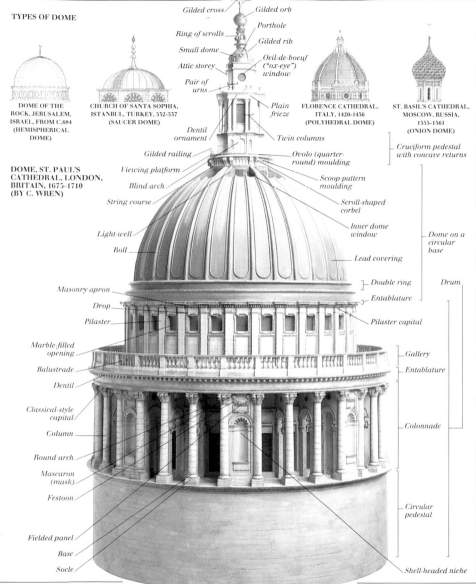

DOMES

TYPES OF DOME

DOME OF THE
ROCK, JERUSALEM,
ISRAEL, FROM C.684
(HEMISPHERICAL
DOME)

CHURCH OF SANTA SOPHIA,
ISTANBUL, TURKEY, 532-537
(SAUCER DOME)

FLORENCE CATHEDRAL,
ITALY, 1420-1436
(POLYHEDRAL DOME)

ST. BASIL'S CATHEDRAL,
MOSCOW, RUSSIA,
1555-1561
(ONION DOME)

DOME, ST. PAUL'S
CATHEDRAL, LONDON,
BRITAIN, 1675-1710
(BY C. WREN)

Gilded cross

Gilded orb

Porthole

Ring of scrolls

Gilded rib

Small dome

Attic storey

Oeil-de-boeuf
("ox-eye")
window

Pair of
urns

Plain
frieze

Dentil
ornament

Twin columns

Gilded railing

Ovolo (quarter-
round) moulding

Viewing platform

Scoop-pattern
moulding

Blind arch

String course

Scroll-shaped
corbel

Light-well

Inner dome
window

Roll

Lead covering

Double ring

Masonry apron

Entablature

Drop

Pilaster

Pilaster capital

Marble-filled
opening

Gallery

Balustrade

Entablature

Dentil

Classical-style
capital

Colonnade

Column

Round arch

Mascaron
(mask)

Festoon

Circular
pedestal

Fielded panel

Base

Socle

Shell-headed niche

Cruciform pedestal
with concave returns

Dome on a
circular
base

Drum

487

Islamic buildings

OPUS SECTILE
MOSAIC DESIGN

THE ISLAMIC RELIGION was founded by the prophet Mohammed, who was born in Mecca (in present-day Saudi Arabia) about 570 AD. In the following three centuries, Islam spread from Arabia to North Africa and Spain, as well as to India and much of the rest of Asia. The worldwide influence of Islam remains strong today. Common characteristics of Islamic buildings include ogee arches and roofs, onion domes, and walls decorated with carved stone, paintings, inlays, or mosaics. The most important type of Islamic building is the mosque – the place of worship – which generally has a minaret (tower) from which the muezzin (official crier) calls Muslims to prayer. Most mosques have a mihrab (decorative niche) that indicates the direction of Mecca. As figurative art is not allowed in Islam, buildings are ornamented with geometric and arabesque motifs, and inscriptions (frequently Koranic verses).

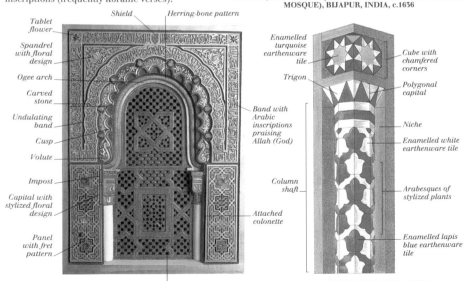

Bud-like onion dome
Depressed arch surrounding mihrab
Painted roof pavilion
Turkish-crescent finial
Lotus-flower pendentive
Arabic inscription
Crest
Painted minaret with censer (incense burner)
Spandrel
Series of recessed arches
Semi-dome
Arched niche within a niche
Mural resembling tomb
Polyhedral niche
Recessed colonettes

MIHRAB, JAMI MASJID (PRINCIPAL OR CONGREGATIONAL MOSQUE), BIJAPUR, INDIA, c.1636

Tablet flower
Shield
Herring-bone pattern
Spandrel with floral design
Ogee arch
Carved stone
Undulating band
Cusp
Volute
Impost
Capital with stylized floral design
Panel with fret pattern
Band with Arabic inscriptions praising Allah (God)
Column shaft
Attached colonette
Jali (latticed screen) with geometrical patterns

ARCH, THE ALHAMBRA, GRANADA, SPAIN, 1333-1354

Enamelled turquoise earthenware tile
Trigon
Cube with chamfered corners
Polygonal capital
Niche
Enamelled white earthenware tile
Arabesques of stylized plants
Enamelled lapis blue earthenware tile

MIHRAB WITH COLUMN, EL-AINYI MOSQUE, CAIRO, EGYPT, 15TH CENTURY

EXAMPLES OF ISLAMIC MOSAICS, EGYPT AND SYRIA

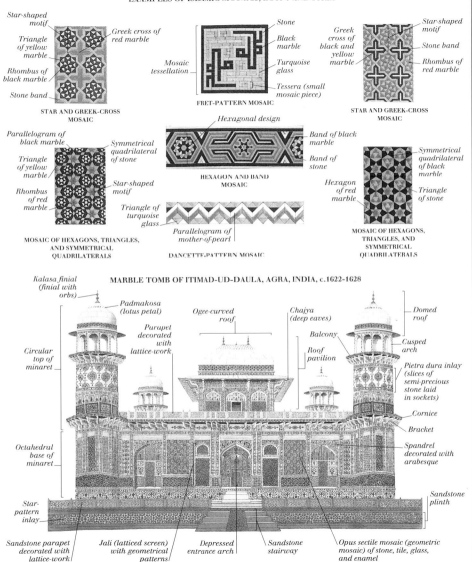

Star-shaped motif

Triangle of yellow marble

Rhombus of black marble

Stone band

Greek cross of red marble

STAR AND GREEK-CROSS MOSAIC

Stone

Black marble

Turquoise glass

Mosaic tessellation

Tessera (small mosaic piece)

FRET-PATTERN MOSAIC

Greek cross of black and yellow marble

Star-shaped motif

Stone band

Rhombus of red marble

STAR AND GREEK-CROSS MOSAIC

Parallelogram of black marble

Triangle of yellow marble

Rhombus of red marble

Symmetrical quadrilateral of stone

Star-shaped motif

MOSAIC OF HEXAGONS, TRIANGLES, AND SYMMETRICAL QUADRILATERALS

Hexagonal design

Band of black marble

Band of stone

HEXAGON AND BAND MOSAIC

Triangle of turquoise glass

Parallelogram of mother-of-pearl

DANCETTE-PATTERN MOSAIC

Symmetrical quadrilateral of black marble

Hexagon of red marble

Triangle of stone

MOSAIC OF HEXAGONS, TRIANGLES, AND SYMMETRICAL QUADRILATERALS

MARBLE TOMB OF ITIMAD-UD-DAULA, AGRA, INDIA, c.1622-1628

Kalasa finial (finial with orbs)

Padmakosa (lotus petal)

Parapet decorated with lattice-work

Ogee-curved roof

Chajya (deep eaves)

Balcony

Roof pavilion

Domed roof

Cusped arch

Circular top of minaret

Pietra dura inlay (slices of semi-precious stone laid in sockets)

Cornice

Bracket

Octahedral base of minaret

Spandrel decorated with arabesque

Star-pattern inlay

Sandstone plinth

Sandstone parapet decorated with lattice-work

Jali (latticed screen) with geometrical patterns

Depressed entrance arch

Sandstone stairway

Opus sectile mosaic (geometric mosaic) of stone, tile, glass, and enamel

South and east Asia

THE TRADITIONAL ARCHITECTURE of south and east Asia has been profoundly influenced by the spread from India of Buddhism and Hinduism. This influence is shown both by the abundance and by the architectural styles of temples and shrines in the region. Many early Hindu temples consist of rooms carved from solid rock-faces. However, free-standing structures began to be built in southern India from about the eighth century AD. Many were built in the Dravidian style, like the Temple of Virupaksha (opposite) with its characteristic antarala (terraced tower), perforated windows, and numerous arches, pilasters, and carvings. The earliest Buddhist religious monuments were Indian stupas, which consisted of a single hemispherical dome surmounted by a chattravali (shaft) and surrounded by railings with ornate gates. Later Indian stupas and those built elsewhere were sometimes modified; for example, in Sri Lanka, the dome became bell-shaped, and was called a dagoba. Buddhist pagodas, such as the Burmese example (right), are multistoreyed temples, each storey having a projecting roof. The form of these buildings probably derived from the yasti (pointed spire) of the stupa. Another feature of many traditional Asian buildings is their imaginative roof-forms, such as gambrel (mansard) roofs, and roofs with angle-rafters (below).

DETAILS FROM EAST ASIAN BUILDINGS

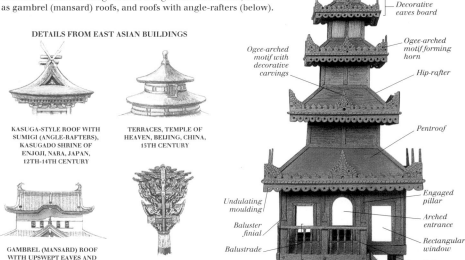

Gilded band

Gilded iron hti (crown)

Dubika (mast)

Arrow motif

Torus moulding with spiral carving

Decorative eaves board

Ogee-arched motif with decorative carvings

Ogee-arched motif forming horn

Hip-rafter

Pentroof

Undulating moulding

Baluster finial

Balustrade

Pillar

Engaged pillar

Arched entrance

Rectangular window

Baluster

Straight brace

KASUGA-STYLE ROOF WITH SUMIGI (ANGLE-RAFTERS), KASUGADO SHRINE OF ENJOJI, NARA, JAPAN, 12TH-14TH CENTURY

TERRACES, TEMPLE OF HEAVEN, BEIJING, CHINA, 15TH CENTURY

GAMBREL (MANSARD) ROOF WITH UPSWEPT EAVES AND UNDULATING GABLES, HIMEJI CASTLE, HIMEJI, JAPAN, 1608-1609

CORNER CAPITAL WITH ROOF BEAMS, POPCHU-SA TEMPLE, POPCHU-SA, SOUTH KOREA, 17TH CENTURY

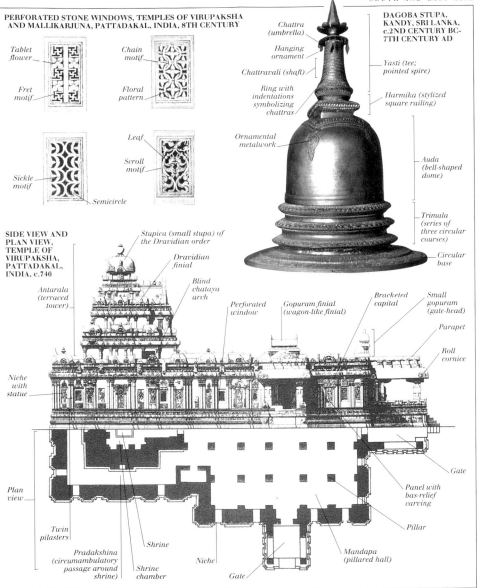

PERFORATED STONE WINDOWS, TEMPLES OF VIRUPAKSHA AND MALLIKARJUNA, PATTADAKAL, INDIA, 8TH CENTURY

Tablet flower

Chain motif

Fret motif

Floral pattern

Leaf

Scroll motif

Sickle motif

Semicircle

DAGOBA STUPA, KANDY, SRI LANKA, c.2ND CENTURY BC– 7TH CENTURY AD

Chattra (umbrella)

Hanging ornament

Chattravali (shaft)

Ring with indentations symbolizing chattras

Ornamental metalwork

Yasti (tee; pointed spire)

Harmika (stylized square railing)

Auda (bell-shaped dome)

Trimala (series of three circular courses)

Circular base

SIDE VIEW AND PLAN VIEW, TEMPLE OF VIRUPAKSHA, PATTADAKAL, INDIA, c.740

Stupica (small stupa) of the Dravidian order

Dravidian finial

Blind chataya arch

Antarala (terraced tower)

Perforated window

Gopuram finial (wagon-like finial)

Bracketed capital

Small gopuram (gate-head)

Parapet

Roll cornice

Niche with statue

Gate

Panel with bas-relief carving

Plan view

Pillar

Twin pilasters

Shrine

Pradakshina (circumambulatory passage around shrine)

Shrine chamber

Niche

Gate

Mandapa (pillared hall)

491

The 19th century

BUILDINGS OF THE 19TH CENTURY are characterized by the use of new materials and by a great diversity of architectural styles. From the end of the 18th century, iron and steel became widely used as alternatives to wood for the framework of buildings, as in the flax-spinning mill shown here. Built in Britain in 1796, this mill exemplifies an architectural style that became common throughout the industrialized world for more than a century. The Industrial Revolution also brought mass-production of building parts – a development that enabled the British architect Sir Joseph Paxton to erect London's Crystal Palace (a building made entirely of iron and glass) in only nine months, ready for the Great Exhibition of 1851. The 19th century saw a widespread revival of older architectural styles. For example, in the USA and Germany, Neo-Greek architecture was fashionable; in Britain and France, Neo-Baroque, Neo–Byzantine, and Neo-Gothic styles (as seen in the Palace of Westminster and Tower Bridge) were dominant.

FLAX-SPINNING MILL, SHREWSBURY, BRITAIN, 1796 (BY C. BAGE)

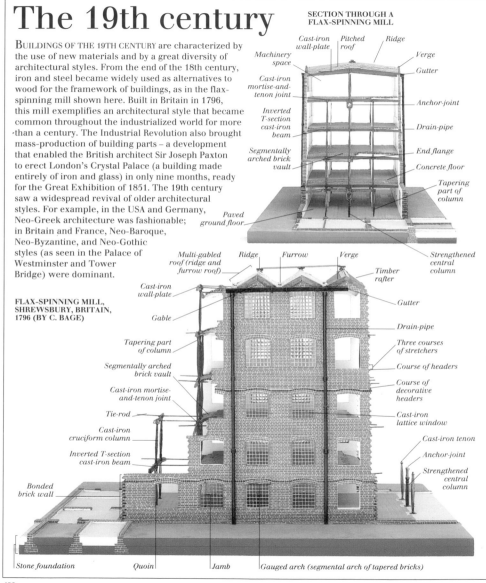

Cast-iron wall-plate
Pitched roof
Ridge
Verge
Gutter
Machinery space
Cast-iron mortise-and-tenon joint
Anchor-joint
Inverted T-section cast-iron beam
Drain-pipe
Segmentally arched brick vault
End flange
Concrete floor
Tapering part of column
Paved ground floor
Strengthened central column

Multi-gabled roof (ridge and furrow roof)
Ridge
Furrow
Verge
Timber rafter
Cast-iron wall-plate
Gutter
Gable
Drain-pipe
Tapering part of column
Three courses of stretchers
Segmentally arched brick vault
Course of headers
Cast-iron mortise-and-tenon joint
Course of decorative headers
Tie-rod
Cast-iron lattice window
Cast-iron cruciform column
Cast-iron tenon
Inverted T-section cast-iron beam
Anchor-joint
Strengthened central column
Bonded brick wall
Stone foundation
Quoin
Jamb
Gauged arch (segmental arch of tapered bricks)

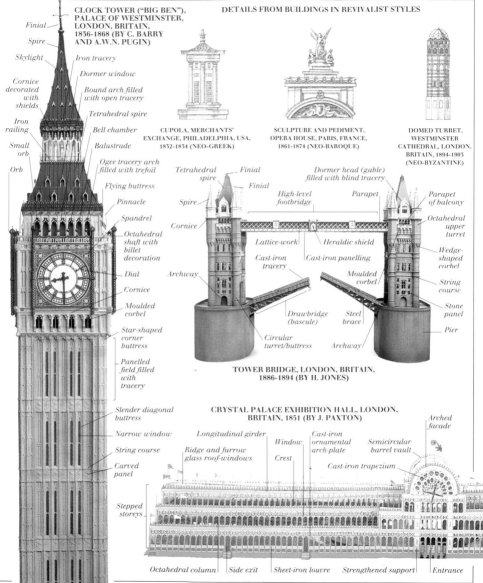

CLOCK TOWER ("BIG BEN"), PALACE OF WESTMINSTER, LONDON, BRITAIN, 1836-1868 (BY C. BARRY AND A.W.N. PUGIN)

Finial
Spire
Skylight
Cornice decorated with shields
Iron railing
Small orb
Orb

Iron tracery
Dormer window
Round arch filled with open tracery
Tetrahedral spire
Bell chamber
Balustrade
Ogee tracery arch filled with trefoil
Flying buttress
Pinnacle
Spandrel
Octahedral shaft with billet decoration
Dial
Cornice
Moulded corbel
Star-shaped corner buttress
Panelled field filled with tracery

Slender diagonal buttress
Narrow window
String course
Carved panel

Stepped storeys

DETAILS FROM BUILDINGS IN REVIVALIST STYLES

CUPOLA, MERCHANTS' EXCHANGE, PHILADELPHIA, USA, 1832-1834 (NEO-GREEK)

SCULPTURE AND PEDIMENT, OPERA HOUSE, PARIS, FRANCE, 1861-1874 (NEO-BAROQUE)

DOMED TURRET, WESTMINSTER CATHEDRAL, LONDON, BRITAIN, 1894-1903 (NEO-BYZANTINE)

Tetrahedral spire
Finial
Finial
High-level footbridge
Parapet
Parapet of balcony
Cornice
Spire
Lattice-work
Heraldic shield
Octahedral upper turret
Cast-iron tracery
Cast-iron panelling
Wedge-shaped corbel
Archway
Moulded corbel
String course
Drawbridge (bascule)
Steel brace
Stone panel
Circular turret/buttress
Archway
Pier

TOWER BRIDGE, LONDON, BRITAIN, 1886-1894 (BY H. JONES)

CRYSTAL PALACE EXHIBITION HALL, LONDON, BRITAIN, 1851 (BY J. PAXTON)

Longitudinal girder
Window
Cast-iron ornamental arch-plate
Semicircular barrel vault
Arched facade
Ridge and furrow glass roof-windows
Crest
Cast-iron trapezium

Octahedral column
Side exit
Sheet-iron louvre
Strengthened support
Entrance

The early 20th century

EMPIRE STATE
BUILDING, NEW
YORK, USA, 1929-1931
(BY R. H. SHREVE,
T. LAMB, AND
A. L. HARMON)

ARCHITECTURE OF THE EARLY 20TH CENTURY is notable for radical new types of steel-and-glass buildings – particularly skyscrapers – and the widespread use of steel-reinforced concrete. The steel-framed skyscraper was pioneered in Chicago in the 1880s, but did not become widespread until the first decades of the 20th century. As construction techniques were refined, skyscrapers became higher and higher; for example, the Empire State Building (right) of 1929-1931 has 102 storeys. Many buildings of this period were constructed from lightweight concrete slabs, which could be supported by cantilever beams or by pilotis (stilts), as in the Villa Savoye (below). The early 20th century also produced a great variety of architectural styles, some of which are illustrated opposite. Despite their diversity, the styles of this period generally had one thing in common: they were completely new, with few links to past architectural styles. This originality is in marked contrast to 19th-century architecture (see pp. 492-493), much of which was revivalist.

Radio mast

Circular lantern

Art deco splayed seashell form

Stepped plinth

Chamfered corner

Colonnaded storey

Ornamentation

Set-back

Ziggurat-style step-back

Steel mullion

Flush window

Vertical pier

Regular fenestration

Window-sill

Solid-panel infill

Curved wall

Fan-like art deco decoration

Decorated stone lintel

Stone structure-line

VILLA SAVOYE, POISSY, FRANCE, 1929-1931 (BY LE CORBUSIER)

TOP VIEW

Fixed table

Parapet

Slab floor

Ramp

Handrail

Flat roof

Flat roof

Screen

Window-sill

Curved wall

Directional skylight

Terrace

Raised planting bed

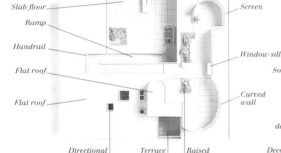

SIDE VIEW

Terrace

Cement-rendered wall of lightweight slabs

Solarium

Sliding pane of glass

Mullion

Piano nobile (first floor)

Reinforced-concrete pilotis (stilt)

Rooms for staff

Ribbon window of long living-room

Curved glazing

Covered driveway

Limestone and granite cladding

Flat roof

Parapet

Stepped cornice

Plinth

Ground-floor entrance

Base

Square bay

MIDWAY GARDENS, CHICAGO, USA, 1914 (BY F. L. WRIGHT)

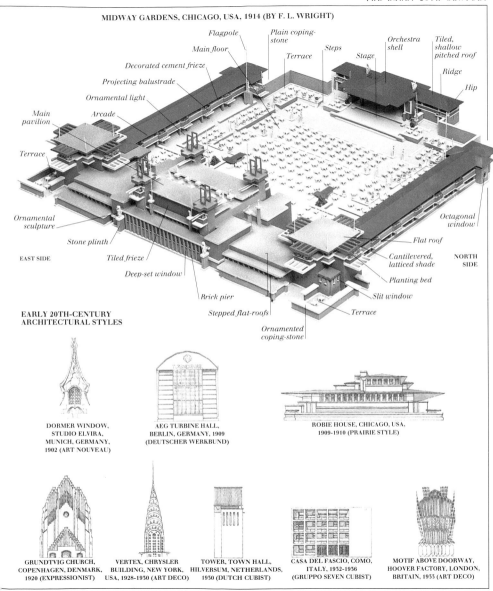

- Flagpole
- Plain coping-stone
- Main floor
- Terrace
- Steps
- Stage
- Orchestra shell
- Tiled, shallow pitched roof
- Decorated cement frieze
- Ridge
- Projecting balustrade
- Hip
- Ornamental light
- Main pavilion
- Arcade
- Terrace
- Ornamental sculpture
- Octagonal window
- Stone plinth
- Flat roof
- EAST SIDE
- Tiled frieze
- Cantilevered, latticed shade
- NORTH SIDE
- Deep-set window
- Planting bed
- Brick pier
- Slit window
- Stepped flat-roofs
- Terrace
- Ornamented coping-stone

EARLY 20TH-CENTURY ARCHITECTURAL STYLES

DORMER WINDOW, STUDIO ELVIRA, MUNICH, GERMANY, 1902 (ART NOUVEAU)

AEG TURBINE HALL, BERLIN, GERMANY, 1909 (DEUTSCHER WERKBUND)

ROBIE HOUSE, CHICAGO, USA, 1909-1910 (PRAIRIE STYLE)

GRUNDTVIG CHURCH, COPENHAGEN, DENMARK, 1920 (EXPRESSIONIST)

VERTEX, CHRYSLER BUILDING, NEW YORK, USA, 1928-1930 (ART DECO)

TOWER, TOWN HALL, HILVERSUM, NETHERLANDS, 1930 (DUTCH CUBIST)

CASA DEL FASCIO, COMO, ITALY, 1932-1936 (GRUPPO SEVEN CUBIST)

MOTIF ABOVE DOORWAY, HOOVER FACTORY, LONDON, BRITAIN, 1933 (ART DECO)

Modern buildings 1

ARCHITECTURE SINCE ABOUT THE 1950s is generally known as modern architecture. One of its main influences has been functionalism – a belief that a building's function should be apparent in its design. Both the Centre Georges Pompidou (below and opposite) and the Hong Kong and Shanghai Bank (see pp. 498-499) are functionalist buildings: on each, elements of engineering and the building's services are clearly visible on the outside. In the 1980s, some architects rejected functionalism in favour of post-modernism, in which historical styles – particularly neoclassicism – were revived, using modern building materials and techniques. In many modern buildings, walls are made of glass or concrete hung from a frame, as in the Kawana House (right); this type of wall construction is known as curtain walling. Other modern construction techniques include the intricate interlocking of concrete vaults – as in the Sydney Opera House (see pp. 498-499) – and the use of high-tension beams to create complex roof shapes, such as the paraboloid roof of the Church of St. Pierre de Libreville (see pp. 498-499).

Solar panel

Concrete frame

Pile foundation

Raft　*Composite cladding-panel*

SIDE VIEW

Rocker-beam

Curtain walling

Lattice-beam

Floor-beam connection　*Floor*

FRONT VIEW

SERVICES FACADE, CENTRE GEORGES POMPIDOU, PARIS, FRANCE, 1977 (BY R. PIANO AND R. ROGERS)

Metal-faced, fire-resistant panel　*Air-conditioning duct*　*Cooling tower*

Water-pipe

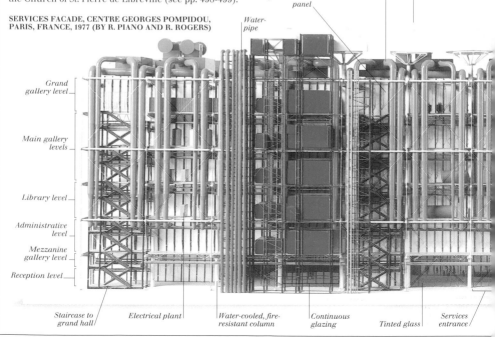

Grand gallery level

Main gallery levels

Library level

Administrative level

Mezzanine gallery level

Reception level

Staircase to grand hall　*Electrical plant*　*Water-cooled, fire-resistant column*　*Continuous glazing*　*Tinted glass*　*Services entrance*

PRINCIPAL FACADE, CENTRE GEORGES POMPIDOU

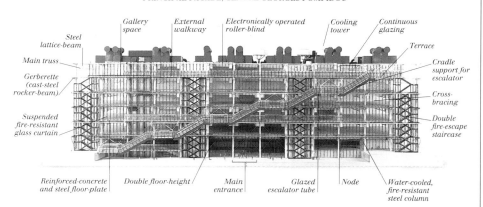

Gallery space

External walkway

Electronically operated roller-blind

Cooling tower

Continuous glazing

Terrace

Steel lattice-beam

Main truss

Cradle support for escalator

Gerberette (cast-steel rocker-beam)

Cross-bracing

Suspended fire-resistant glass curtain

Double fire-escape staircase

Reinforced-concrete and steel floor-plate

Double floor-height

Main entrance

Glazed escalator tube

Node

Water-cooled, fire-resistant steel column

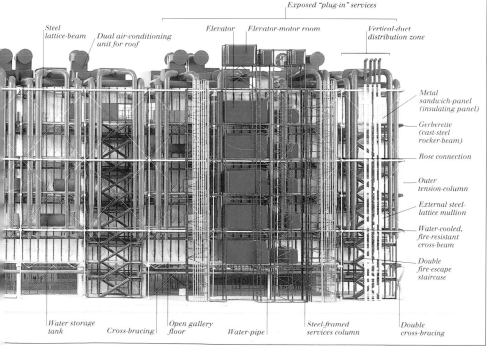

Exposed "plug-in" services

Steel lattice-beam

Dual air-conditioning unit for roof

Elevator

Elevator-motor room

Vertical-duct distribution zone

Metal sandwich-panel (insulating panel)

Gerberette (cast-steel rocker-beam)

Rose connection

Outer tension-column

External steel-lattice mullion

Water-cooled, fire-resistant cross-beam

Double fire-escape staircase

Water storage tank

Cross-bracing

Open gallery floor

Water-pipe

Steel-framed services column

Double cross-bracing

Modern buildings 2

HONG KONG AND SHANGHAI BANK, HONG KONG, 1981-1985 (BY N. FOSTER)

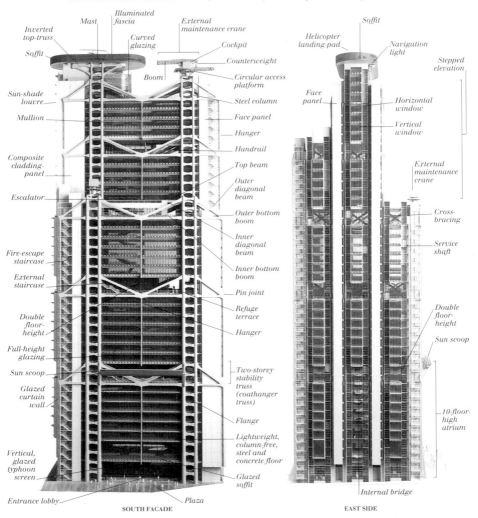

Inverted top-truss
Mast
Illuminated fascia
Curved glazing
External maintenance crane
Cockpit
Soffit
Helicopter landing-pad
Navigation light
Soffit
Stepped elevation
Counterweight
Boom
Circular access platform
Sun-shade louvre
Steel column
Face panel
Mullion
Face panel
Hanger
Horizontal window
Vertical window
Composite cladding-panel
Handrail
Top beam
Escalator
Outer diagonal beam
External maintenance crane
Outer bottom boom
Cross-bracing
Inner diagonal beam
Service shaft
Fire-escape staircase
Inner bottom boom
External staircase
Pin joint
Double floor-height
Refuge terrace
Double floor-height
Full-height glazing
Hanger
Sun scoop
Sun scoop
Two-storey stability truss (coathanger truss)
Glazed curtain wall
Flange
10-floor-high atrium
Vertical, glazed typhoon screen
Lightweight, column-free, steel and concrete floor
Glazed soffit
Entrance lobby
Plaza
Internal bridge

SOUTH FACADE

EAST SIDE

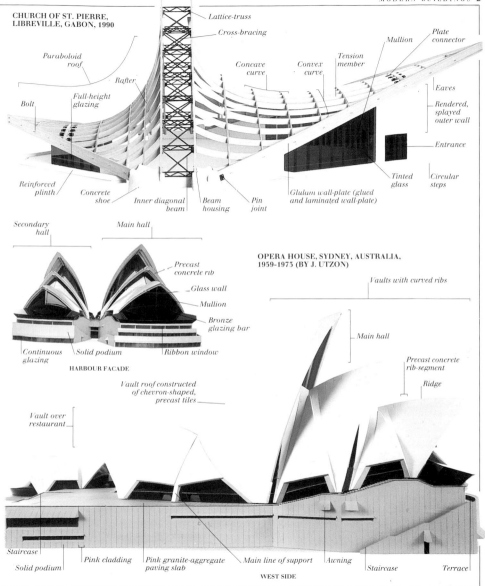

CHURCH OF ST. PIERRE, LIBREVILLE, GABON, 1990

Lattice-truss

Cross-bracing

Plate connector

Mullion

Paraboloid roof

Rafter

Concave curve

Convex curve

Tension member

Eaves

Bolt

Full-height glazing

Rendered, splayed outer wall

Entrance

Reinforced plinth

Concrete shoe

Inner diagonal beam

Beam housing

Pin joint

Glulam wall-plate (glued and laminated wall-plate)

Tinted glass

Circular steps

Secondary hall

Main hall

Precast concrete rib

Glass wall

Mullion

Bronze glazing bar

OPERA HOUSE, SYDNEY, AUSTRALIA, 1959-1973 (BY J. UTZON)

Vaults with curved ribs

Main hall

Precast concrete rib-segment

Ridge

Continuous glazing

Solid podium

Ribbon window

HARBOUR FACADE

Vault roof constructed of chevron-shaped, precast tiles

Vault over restaurant

Staircase

Solid podium

Pink cladding

Pink granite-aggregate paving slab

Main line of support

Awning

Staircase

Terrace

WEST SIDE

499

MUSIC

MUSICAL NOTATION 502
ORCHESTRAS 504
BRASS INSTRUMENTS 506
WOODWIND INSTRUMENTS 508
STRINGED INSTRUMENTS 510
GUITARS 512
KEYBOARD INSTRUMENTS 514
PERCUSSION INSTRUMENTS 516
DRUMS 518
ELECTRONIC INSTRUMENTS 520

Musical notation

MUSICAL NOTATION IS ANY METHOD by which sounds are written down so that they can be read and performed by others. The present-day conventional system of notation uses a five-line stave (staff) – divided by vertical lines into sections known as bars – on which notes, rests, clefs, key signatures, time signatures, accidentals, and other symbols are written. A note indicates the duration of a sound and, according to its position on the stave, its pitch. Notes can be arranged on the stave in order of pitch to form a scale. A silence in the music is indicated by a rest. The clef, which is placed at the begininng of a stave, fixes the pitch. The key signature, which is placed after the clef, indicates the key. The time signature, placed after the key signature, shows the number of beats in a bar. Accidentals are used to indicate the raising or lowering of the pitch of a note.

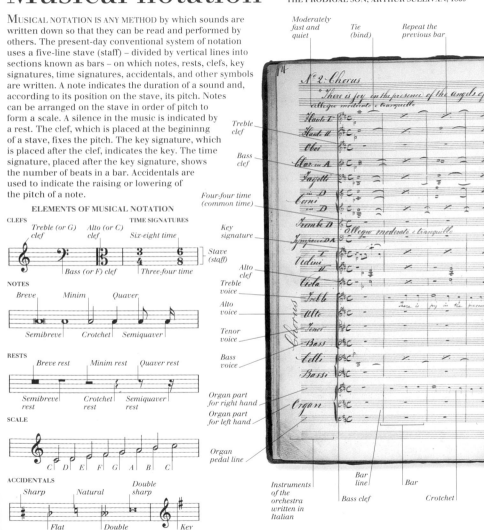

ELEMENTS OF MUSICAL NOTATION

CLEFS

Treble (or G) clef
Alto (or C) clef
Bass (or F) clef

TIME SIGNATURES

Six-eight time
$\frac{3}{4}$
Three-four time
$\frac{6}{8}$

NOTES

Breve
Minim
Quaver
Semibreve
Crotchet
Semiquaver

RESTS

Breve rest
Minim rest
Quaver rest
Semibreve rest
Crotchet rest
Semiquaver rest

SCALE

C D E F G A B C

ACCIDENTALS

Sharp
Natural
Double sharp
Flat
Double flat
Key signature

Labels around the manuscript:
Moderately fast and quiet
Tie (bind)
Repeat the previous bar
Treble clef
Bass clef
Four-four time (common time)
Key signature
Stave (staff)
Alto clef
Treble voice
Alto voice
Tenor voice
Bass voice
Organ part for right hand
Organ part for left hand
Organ pedal line
Instruments of the orchestra written in Italian
Bar line
Bar
Bass clef
Crotchet

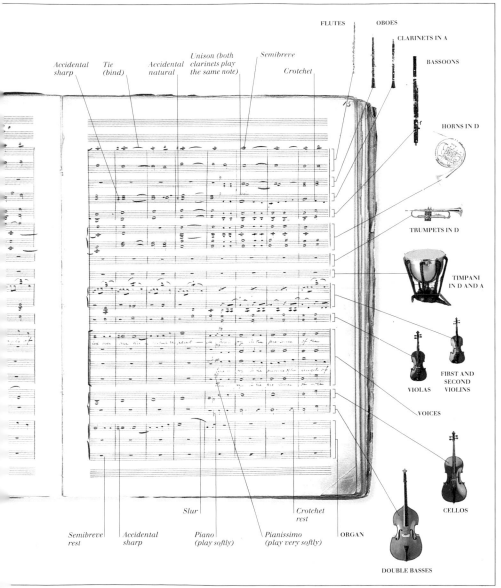

FLUTES

OBOES

CLARINETS IN A

BASSOONS

HORNS IN D

TRUMPETS IN D

TIMPANI IN D AND A

FIRST AND SECOND VIOLINS

VIOLAS

VOICES

CELLOS

ORGAN

DOUBLE BASSES

Accidental sharp

Tie (bind)

Accidental natural

Unison (both clarinets play the same note)

Semibreve

Crotchet

Semibreve rest

Accidental sharp

Piano (play softly)

Slur

Pianissimo (play very softly)

Crotchet rest

Orchestras

AN ORCHESTRA IS A GROUP of musicians that plays music written for a specific combination of instruments. The number and type of instruments included in the orchestra depends on the style of music being played. The modern orchestra (also known as a symphony orchestra) is made up of four sections of instruments – stringed, woodwind, brass, and percussion. The stringed section consists of violins, violas, cellos (violoncellos), double basses, and sometimes a harp (see pp. 510-511). The main instruments of the woodwind section are flutes, oboes, clarinets, and bassoons – the piccolo, cor anglais, bass clarinet, saxophone, and double bassoon (contrabassoon) can also be included if the music requires them (see pp. 508-509). The brass section usually consists of horns, trumpets, trombones, and the tuba (see pp. 506-507). The main instruments of the percussion section are the timpani (see pp. 518-519). The side drum, bass drum, cymbals, tambourine, triangle, tubular bells, xylophone, vibraphone, tam-tam (gong), castanets, and maracas can also be included in the percussion section (see pp. 516-517). The musicians are usually arranged in a semi-circle – strings spread along the front, woodwind and brass in the centre, and percussion at the back. A conductor stands in front of the musicians and controls the tempo (speed) of the music and the overall balance of the sound, ensuring that no instruments are too loud or too soft in relation to the others.

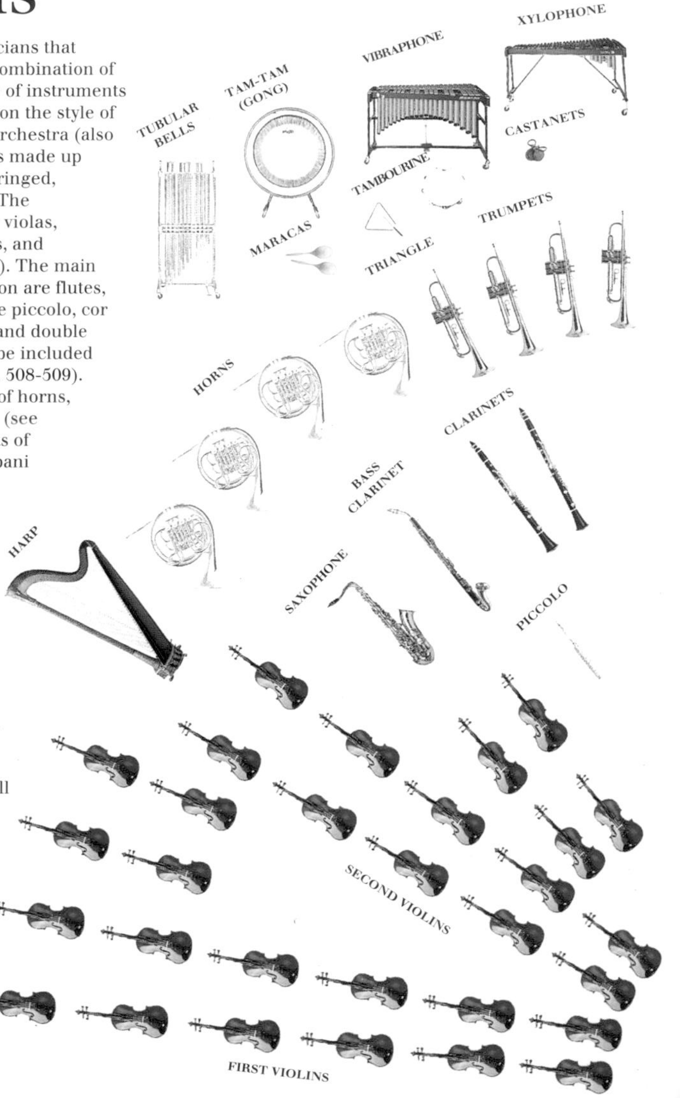

TUBULAR BELLS

TAM-TAM (GONG)

VIBRAPHONE

XYLOPHONE

CASTANETS

TAMBOURINE

MARACAS

TRIANGLE

TRUMPETS

HORNS

CLARINETS

BASS CLARINET

HARP

SAXOPHONE

PICCOLO

SECOND VIOLINS

FIRST VIOLINS

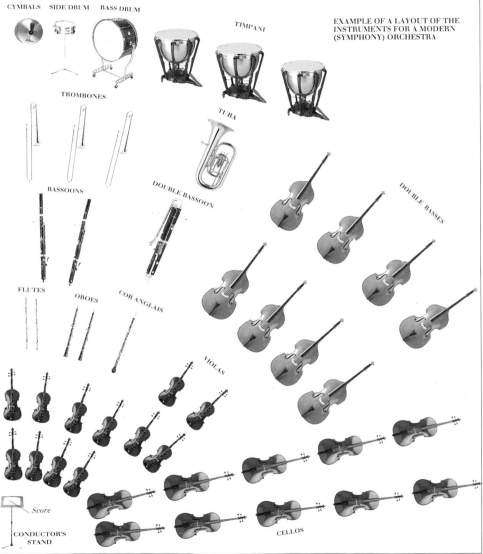

CYMBALS SIDE DRUM BASS DRUM

TIMPANI

**EXAMPLE OF A LAYOUT OF THE
INSTRUMENTS FOR A MODERN
(SYMPHONY) ORCHESTRA**

TROMBONES

TUBA

BASSOONS

DOUBLE BASSOON

DOUBLE BASSES

FLUTES

OBOES

COR ANGLAIS

VIOLAS

Score

CONDUCTOR'S
STAND

CELLOS

505

Brass instruments

BUGLE

BRASS INSTRUMENTS ARE WIND INSTRUMENTS that are made of metal, usually brass. Although they appear in many different shapes and sizes, all brass instruments have a mouthpiece, a length of hollow tube, and a flared bell. The mouthpiece of a brass instrument may be cup-shaped, as in the cornet, or cone-shaped, as in the horn. The tube may be wide or narrow, mainly conical, as in the horn and tuba, or mainly cylindrical, as in the trumpet and trombone. The sound of a brass instrument is made by the player's lips vibrating against the mouthpiece, so that the air vibrates in the tube. By changing lip tension, the player can vary the vibrations and produce notes of different pitches. The range of notes produced by a brass instrument can be extended by means of a valve system. Most brass instruments, such as the trumpet, have piston valves that divert the air in the instrument along an extra piece of tubing (known as a valve slide) when pressed down. The total length of the tube is increased and the pitch of the note produced is lowered. Instead of valves, the trombone has a movable slide that can be pushed away from or drawn toward the player. The sound of a brass instrument can also be changed by inserting a mute into the bell of the instrument.

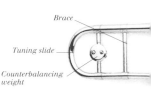

Brace

Tuning slide

Counterbalancing weight

SIMPLIFIED DIAGRAM SHOWING HOW A PISTON VALVE SYSTEM WORKS

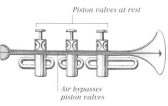

Piston valves at rest

Air bypasses piston valves

PISTON VALVES AT REST

First piston valve pressed down

Second and third piston valves at rest

Air diverted through first valve slide

PISTON VALVE PRESSED DOWN

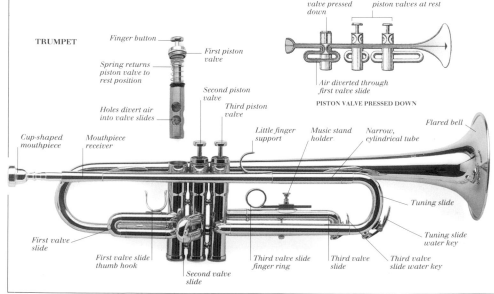

TRUMPET

Finger button

First piston valve

Spring returns piston valve to rest position

Second piston valve

Third piston valve

Holes divert air into valve slides

Little finger support

Music stand holder

Narrow, cylindrical tube

Flared bell

Cup-shaped mouthpiece

Mouthpiece receiver

Tuning slide

First valve slide

First valve slide thumb hook

Second valve slide

Third valve slide finger ring

Third valve slide

Tuning slide water key

Third valve slide water key

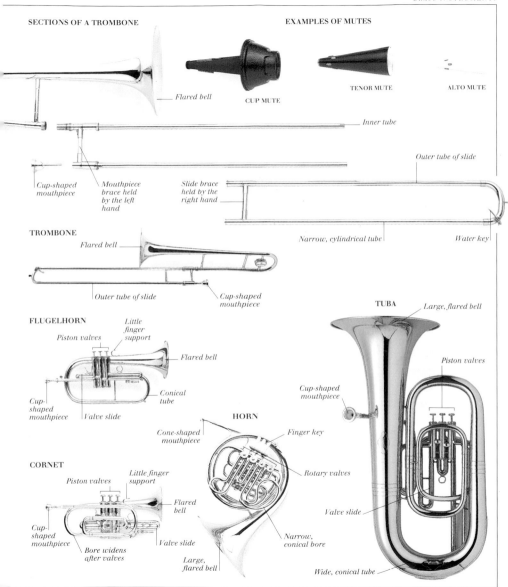

SECTIONS OF A TROMBONE

EXAMPLES OF MUTES

CUP MUTE

TENOR MUTE

ALTO MUTE

Flared bell

Inner tube

Outer tube of slide

Cup-shaped mouthpiece

Mouthpiece brace held by the left hand

Slide brace held by the right hand

Narrow, cylindrical tube

Water key

TROMBONE

Flared bell

Outer tube of slide

Cup-shaped mouthpiece

FLUGELHORN

Piston valves

Little finger support

Flared bell

Cup-shaped mouthpiece

Valve slide

Conical tube

TUBA

Large, flared bell

Piston valves

Cup-shaped mouthpiece

Valve slide

HORN

Cone-shaped mouthpiece

Finger key

Rotary valves

CORNET

Piston valves

Little finger support

Flared bell

Cup-shaped mouthpiece

Bore widens after valves

Valve slide

Narrow, conical bore

Large, flared bell

Wide, conical tube

Woodwind instruments

WOODWIND INSTRUMENTS ARE wind instruments that are generally made of wood, although some are made of metal or plastic. The sound of a woodwind instrument is produced by the vibration of air in a hollow tube. The air is made to vibrate by blowing across a blow hole – as in the flute and piccolo – or by blowing through a single reed – as in the clarinet and saxophone – or a double reed – as in the bassoon, cor anglais, and oboe. The pitch of a woodwind instrument can be changed by opening or closing holes cut into the tube of the instrument.

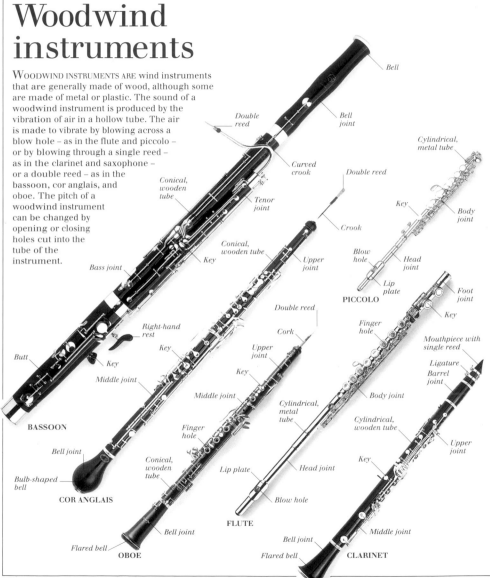

Bell

Double reed

Bell joint

Curved crook

Conical, wooden tube

Tenor joint

Cylindrical, metal tube

Double reed

Key

Body joint

Blow hole

Head joint

Crook

Conical, wooden tube

Upper joint

Lip plate

PICCOLO

Bass joint

Key

Double reed

Finger hole

Foot joint

Key

Right-hand rest

Cork

Key

Upper joint

Mouthpiece with single reed

Butt

Key

Key

Middle joint

Upper joint

Ligature

Barrel joint

Body joint

BASSOON

Finger hole

Middle joint

Cylindrical, metal tube

Cylindrical, wooden tube

Bell joint

Conical, wooden tube

Lip plate

Head joint

Key

Upper joint

Bulb-shaped bell

COR ANGLAIS

Finger hole

Blow hole

FLUTE

Bell joint

Middle joint

Flared bell

OBOE

Bell joint

Flared bell

CLARINET

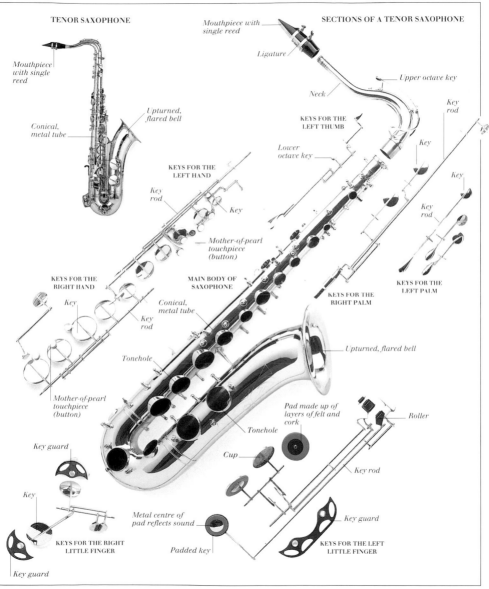

TENOR SAXOPHONE

Mouthpiece with single reed

Conical, metal tube

Upturned, flared bell

Mouthpiece with single reed

Ligature

Neck

SECTIONS OF A TENOR SAXOPHONE

Upper octave key

Key rod

KEYS FOR THE LEFT THUMB

Lower octave key

Key

Key

Key rod

KEYS FOR THE LEFT HAND

Key rod

Key

Mother-of-pearl touchpiece (button)

KEYS FOR THE RIGHT HAND

Key

Key rod

MAIN BODY OF SAXOPHONE

Conical, metal tube

Tonehole

Mother-of-pearl touchpiece (button)

KEYS FOR THE RIGHT PALM

KEYS FOR THE LEFT PALM

Upturned, flared bell

Tonehole

Pad made up of layers of felt and cork

Roller

Cup

Key guard

Key

Metal centre of pad reflects sound

KEYS FOR THE RIGHT LITTLE FINGER

Padded key

Key rod

Key guard

KEYS FOR THE LEFT LITTLE FINGER

Key guard

Stringed instruments

STRINGED INSTRUMENTS PRODUCE SOUND by the vibration of stretched strings. This may be done by drawing a bow across the strings, as in the violin; or by plucking the strings, as in the harp and guitar (see pp. 512-513). The four modern members of the bowed string family are the violin, viola, cello (violoncello), and double bass. Each consists of a hollow, wooden body, a long neck, and four strings. The bow is a wooden stick with horsehair stretched across its length. The vibrations made by drawing the bow across the strings are transmitted to the hollow body, and this itself vibrates, amplifying and enriching the sound produced. The harp consists of a set of strings of different lengths stretched across a wooden frame. The strings are plucked by the player's thumbs and fingers – except the little finger of each hand – which produces vibrations that are amplified by the harp's soundboard. The pitch of the note produced by any stringed instrument depends on the length, weight, and tension of the string. A shorter, lighter, or tighter string gives a higher note.

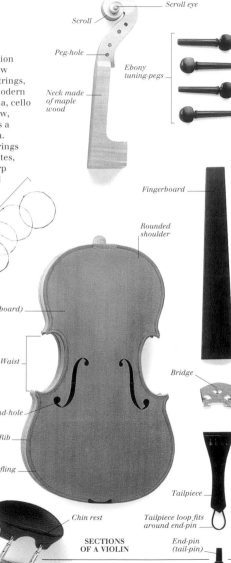

Scroll eye

Scroll

Peg-hole

Neck made of maple wood

Ebony tuning-pegs

Strings

Fingerboard

Rounded shoulder

Belly (soundboard)

Waist

Sound-hole

Rib

Purfling

Bridge

Tailpiece

Chin rest

Tailpiece loop fits around end-pin

End-pin (tail-pin)

SECTIONS OF A VIOLIN

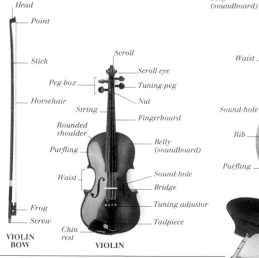

Head

Point

Stick

Scroll

Scroll eye

Peg-box

Tuning-peg

Horsehair

Nut

String

Fingerboard

Rounded shoulder

Belly (soundboard)

Purfling

Waist

Sound-hole

Bridge

Tuning adjustor

Frog

Tailpiece

Screw

Chin rest

VIOLIN BOW

VIOLIN

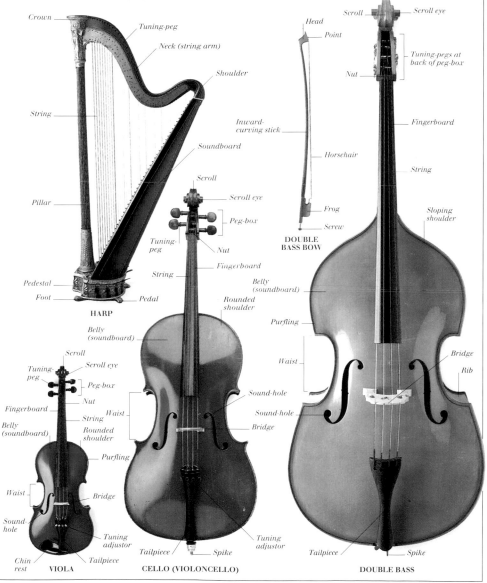

Crown

Tuning-peg

Neck (string arm)

Shoulder

String

Soundboard

Pillar

Pedestal

Foot

Pedal

HARP

Scroll

Scroll eye

Peg-box

Tuning-peg

Nut

Fingerboard

String

Belly (soundboard)

Rounded shoulder

Head

Point

Scroll

Scroll eye

Tuning-pegs at back of peg-box

Nut

Inward-curving stick

Horsehair

Frog

Screw

Fingerboard

String

Sloping shoulder

DOUBLE BASS BOW

Belly (soundboard)

Purfling

Waist

Bridge

Rib

Sound-hole

Sound-hole

Bridge

Belly (soundboard)

Scroll

Tuning-peg

Scroll eye

Peg-box

Nut

Fingerboard

String

Waist

Rounded shoulder

Purfling

Waist

Bridge

Sound-hole

Chin rest

Tuning adjustor

Tailpiece

Tailpiece

Spike

Tuning adjustor

Tailpiece

Spike

VIOLA

CELLO (VIOLONCELLO)

DOUBLE BASS

Guitars

THE GUITAR IS A PLUCKED stringed instrument
(see pp. 510-511). There are two types of guitar –
acoustic and electric. Acoustic guitars have hollow
bodies and six or twelve strings. Plucking the strings
produces vibrations that are amplified by their hollow
bodies. Electric guitars usually have solid bodies and
six strings. Pick-ups placed under the strings convert
their vibrations into electronic signals that are magnified
by an amplifier, and sent to a loudspeaker where they are
converted into sounds (see pp. 520-521). Electric bass
guitars are very similar in structure to electric guitars,
and produce sound in the same way, but have four
strings and play bass notes.

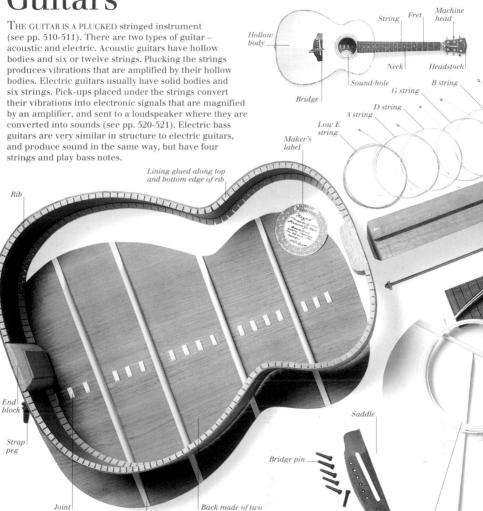

Hollow body

String Fret Machine head

Neck Headstock

Sound-hole B string

G string

Bridge D string

A string

Low E string

Maker's label

Lining glued along top and bottom edge of rib

Rib

End block

Strap peg

Joint

Transverse (crosswise) strut strengthens back

Back made of two pieces of cherry wood joined together

Saddle

Bridge pin

Bridge Binding

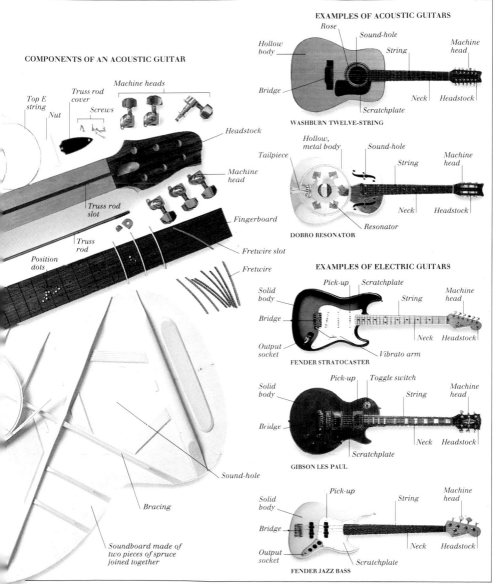

COMPONENTS OF AN ACOUSTIC GUITAR

Top E string
Nut
Truss rod cover
Screws
Machine heads
Headstock
Machine head
Truss rod slot
Truss rod
Position dots
Fingerboard
Fretwire slot
Fretwire
Sound-hole
Bracing
Soundboard made of two pieces of spruce joined together

EXAMPLES OF ACOUSTIC GUITARS

Rose
Hollow body
Sound-hole
String
Machine head
Bridge
Neck
Headstock
Scratchplate

WASHBURN TWELVE-STRING

Hollow, metal body
Tailpiece
Sound-hole
String
Machine head
Neck
Headstock
Resonator

DOBRO RESONATOR

EXAMPLES OF ELECTRIC GUITARS

Pick-up
Scratchplate
Solid body
String
Machine head
Bridge
Neck
Headstock
Output socket
Vibrato arm

FENDER STRATOCASTER

Pick-up
Toggle switch
Solid body
String
Machine head
Bridge
Neck
Headstock
Scratchplate

GIBSON LES PAUL

Pick-up
Solid body
String
Machine head
Bridge
Neck
Headstock
Output socket
Scratchplate

FENDER JAZZ BASS

513

Keyboard instruments

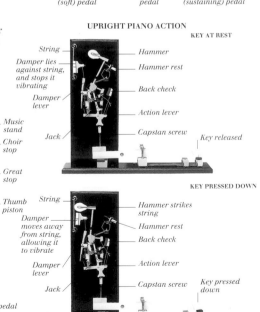

ORGAN PIPE

KEYBOARD INSTRUMENTS are instruments that are sounded by means of a keyboard. The organ and piano are two of the principal members of the keyboard family. The organ consists of pipes which are operated by one or more manuals (keyboards) and a pedal board. The pipes are lined up in rows (known as ranks or registers) on top of a wind chest. The sound of the organ is made when air is admitted into a pipe by pressing a key or pedal. The piano consists of wire strings stretched over a metal frame, and a keyboard and pedals that operate hammers and dampers. The piano frame is either vertical – as in the upright piano – or horizontal – as in the grand piano. When a key is at rest, a damper lies against the string to stop it vibrating. When a key is pressed down, the damper moves away from the string as the hammer strikes it, causing the string to vibrate and sound a note.

UPRIGHT PIANO

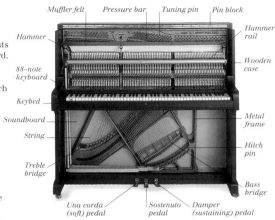

Muffler felt
Pressure bar
Tuning pin
Pin block
Hammer rail
Hammer
88–note keyboard
Wooden case
Keybed
Soundboard
Metal frame
String
Hitch pin
Treble bridge
Bass bridge
Una corda (soft) pedal
Sostenuto pedal
Damper (sustaining) pedal

UPRIGHT PIANO ACTION

KEY AT REST

String
Damper lies against string, and stops it vibrating
Hammer
Hammer rest
Back check
Damper lever
Action lever
Jack
Capstan screw
Key released

KEY PRESSED DOWN

String
Hammer strikes string
Damper moves away from string, allowing it to vibrate
Hammer rest
Back check
Action lever
Damper lever
Jack
Capstan screw
Key pressed down

ORGAN CONSOLE

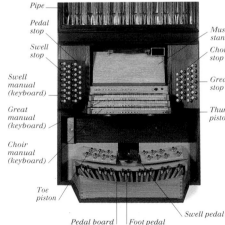

Pipe
Pedal stop
Swell stop
Music stand
Choir stop
Swell manual (keyboard)
Great stop
Great manual (keyboard)
Thumb piston
Choir manual (keyboard)
Toe piston
Pedal board
Foot pedal
Swell pedal

CONCERT GRAND PIANO (VIEWED FROM ABOVE)

CONCERT GRAND PIANO
(FRONT VIEW)

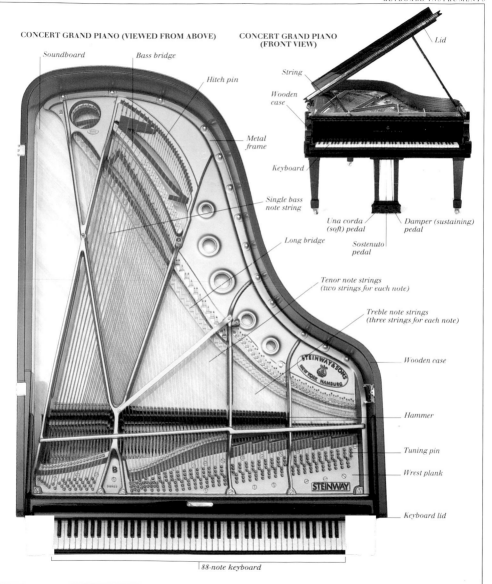

Soundboard

Bass bridge

Hitch pin

Metal
frame

Single bass
note string

Long bridge

Lid

String

Wooden
case

Keyboard

Una corda
(soft) pedal

Sostenuto
pedal

Damper (sustaining)
pedal

Tenor note strings
(two strings for each note)

Treble note strings
(three strings for each note)

Wooden case

Hammer

Tuning pin

Wrest plank

Keyboard lid

STEINWAY & SONS
NEW YORK · HAMBURG

STEINWAY

88-note keyboard

Percussion instruments

TEMPLE BLOCKS

PERCUSSION INSTRUMENTS are a large group of instruments that produce sound by being struck, shaken, scraped, or clashed together. Most percussion instruments – such as the tam-tam (gong), cymbals, and maracas – do not have a definite pitch and are used for rhythm and impact, and the distinctive timbre (colour) of their sound. Other percussion instruments – such as the xylophone, vibraphone, and tubular bells – are tuned to a definite pitch and can play melody, harmony, and rhythms. The xylophone and vibraphone each have two rows of bars that are arranged in a similar way to the black and white keys of a piano. Metal tubes are suspended below the bars to amplify the sound. The vibraphone has electrically operated fans that rotate in the tubes and produce a vibrato (wavering pitch) effect.

Tube struck with mallet

Hollow, metal tube

Damper bar

Metal frame

Mechanism linking pedal and damper bar

Row of tubes graduated in length and pitch

Damper pedal

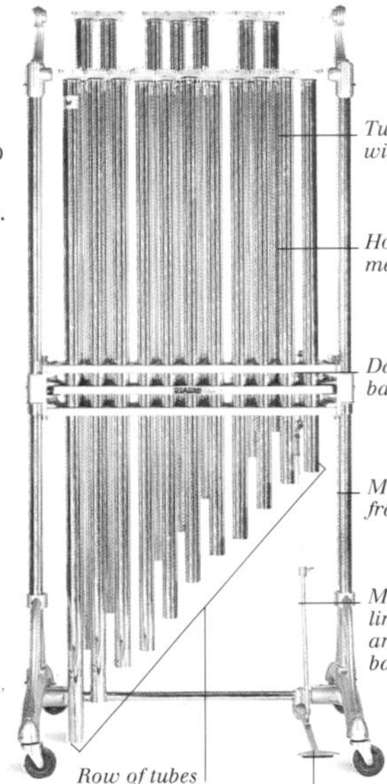

EXAMPLES OF BEATERS

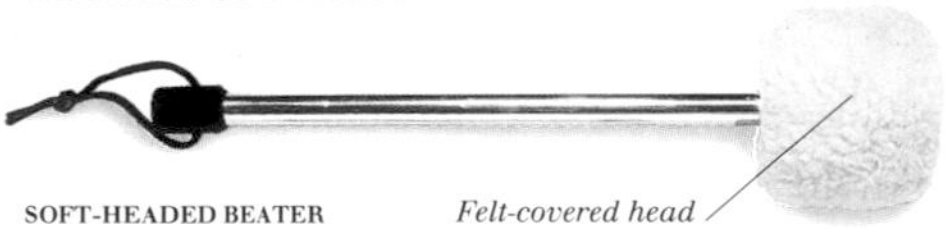

SOFT-HEADED BEATER   Felt-covered head

Rosewood head

HARD-HEADED BEATER

Leather-covered head

MALLET

TAM-TAM (GONG)

Tam-tam struck in centre with soft-headed beater

Cord

Metal frame

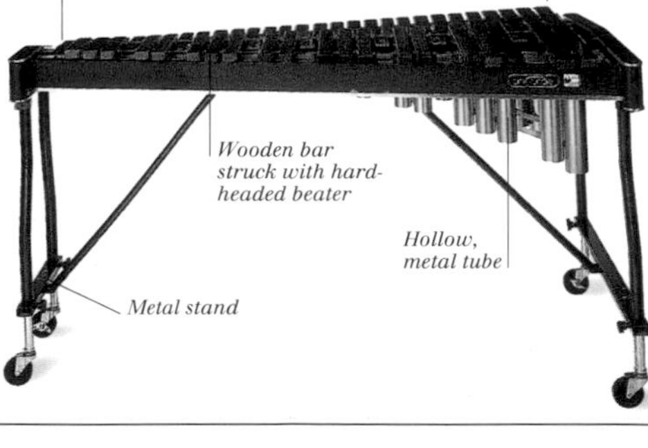

Row of bars graduated in length and pitch

XYLOPHONE

Wooden bar struck with hard-headed beater

Hollow, metal tube

Metal stand

PAISTE

Rim

Large, metal disc

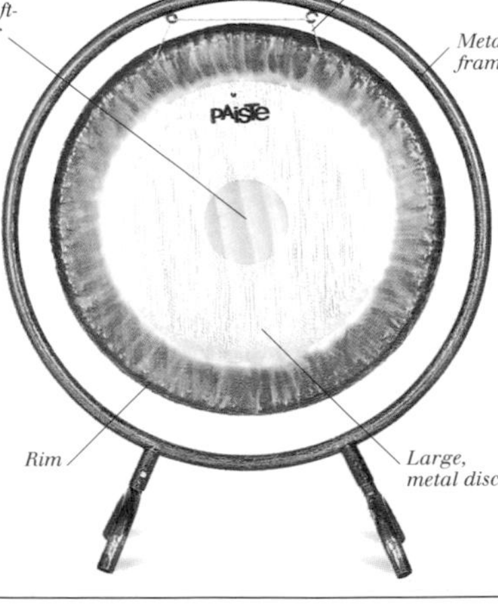

CYMBALS

Leather strap fits around player's hand

Pad protects hands from vibrations

Zildjian

Thin, convex disc of copper and tin alloy

SECTIONS OF A MARACA

Wooden handle

Lead shot

Hollow, wooden head

CLAVES

Hardwood sticks clashed together to give a sharp crack

TRIANGLE

Steel rod bent into triangular shape

Steel beater

CASTANETS

Cord

Hollowed wood

VIBRAPHONE

Row of bars graduated in length and pitch

Metal bar struck with soft-headed beater

musser

Metal frame

Damper pedal

Metal tube containing electrically operated fan that produces vibrato (wavering pitch) effect

Electric cable

Drums

A DRUM IS A percussion instrument that consists of a drumhead, made of skin or plastic, stretched over one or both ends of a hollow vessel (the body-shell). Drums are played in most parts of the world and are made in a number of different shapes and sizes. They can be divided into three groups according to the shape of the body-shell: frame drums (e.g., tambourines), bowl-shaped drums (e.g., timpani), and tubular drums (e.g., congas). Drums are usually sounded by striking the drumhead with the hands or with beaters, such as a hard-headed stick. The drumhead vibrates, and its vibrations are amplified by the hollow body-shell. The snare drum has wires – known as snares – stretched across the lower drumhead; the snares vibrate against the lower drumhead when the drum is played. Most drums, such as congas, do not have a definite pitch and can play only rhythms (see pp. 516-517). Other drums, such as timpani, have a definite pitch and can play melody, harmony, and rhythms. They can be tuned by adjusting the tension of the drumhead. Different types of drum can be combined together with other percussion instruments to form a drum kit. The basic components of the drum kit are bass drum, tom-toms, floor tom (tenor drum), snare drum, and cymbals.

TAMBOURINE

DRUM KIT

Crash cymbal

Tension key

Tension rod

Tom-tom

Lug

Hi-hat cymbal

Snare drum

Tripod stand

SNARE DRUM (VIEWED FROM BELOW)

Snare mounting

Adjustable damper

Lug

Transparent lower drumhead

Upper drumhead

Snare

Stick

Snare release lever

Chain

Tension screw

Felt-covered beater

Pedal

Pedal

EXAMPLES OF BEATERS

Acorn

HARD-HEADED STICK

Taper

SOFT-HEADED STICK

Felt-covered head

WIRE BRUSH

Wire bristles

CONGAS

Metal hoop

Drumhead

Tension rod

Wooden body-shell

Tripod stand

Leg

Ride cymbal

Tension key

Tom-tom

Height adjustment key

Tension rod

Lug

Floor tom (tenor drum)

Tension rod

Lug

Wooden body-shell

Height adjustment key

Leg

Bass drum

Rubber foot

TIMPANUM (KETTLE DRUM)

Drumhead

Tension rod

Metal hoop

Tuning gauge

Copper body-shell

Strut

Tension rod

Crown

Tuning pedal

Castor

Electronic instruments

ELECTRONIC DRUMS

ELECTRONIC INSTRUMENTS generate electronic signals
that are magnified by an amplifier, and sent to a loudspeaker
where they are converted into sounds. Synthesizers, and other
electronic instruments, simulate the characteristic sounds of
conventional instruments, and also create entirely new sounds.
Most electronic instruments are keyboard instruments, but electronic
wind and percussion instruments are also popular. A digital sampler
records and stores sounds from musical instruments or other sources.
When the sound is played back, the pitch of the original sound can be
altered. A keyboard can be connected to the sampler so that a tune can
be played using the sampled sounds. With a MIDI (Musical Instrument
Digital Interface) system, a computer can be linked with other electronic
instruments, such as keyboards and electronic drums, to make sounds
together or in sequence. It is also possible, using music software, to
compose and play music on a home computer.

Drum pad

Height adjustment key

Tripod

HOME KEYBOARD

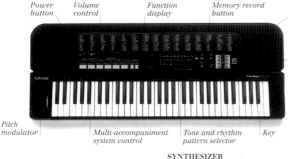

Power button   *Volume control*   *Function display*   *Memory record button*   *Tone editor control*

Demonstration tune button

Pitch modulator   *Multi-accompaniment system control*   *Tone and rhythm pattern selector*   *Key*

SYNTHESIZER

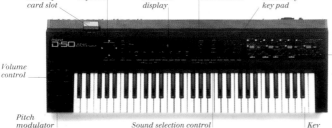

Memory card slot   *Joystick*   *Function display*   *Edit control*   *Data entry key pad*

Sound structure guide

Volume control

Pitch modulator   *Sound selection control*   *Key*

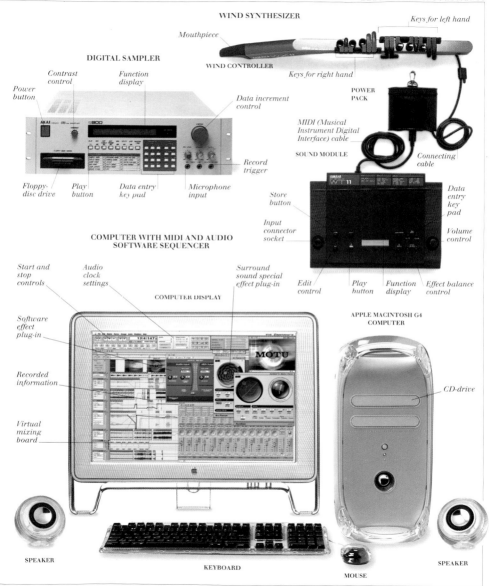

WIND SYNTHESIZER

Keys for left hand

Mouthpiece

WIND CONTROLLER

Keys for right hand

DIGITAL SAMPLER

POWER
PACK

Contrast
control

Function
display

Power
button

Data increment
control

MIDI (Musical
Instrument Digital
Interface) cable

Connecting
cable

SOUND MODULE

Record
trigger

Data
entry
key
pad

Floppy-
disc drive

Play
button

Data entry
key pad

Microphone
input

Store
button

Volume
control

Input
connector
socket

**COMPUTER WITH MIDI AND AUDIO
SOFTWARE SEQUENCER**

Start and
stop
controls

Audio
clock
settings

Surround
sound special
effect plug-in

Edit
control

Play
button

Function
display

Effect balance
control

COMPUTER DISPLAY

APPLE MACINTOSH G4
COMPUTER

Software
effect
plug-in

Recorded
information

CD-drive

Virtual
mixing
board

SPEAKER

KEYBOARD

SPEAKER

MOUSE

521

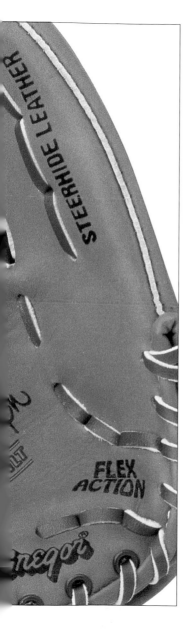

SPORTS

SOCCER 524

AMERICAN FOOTBALL 526

AUSTRALIAN RULES AND GAELIC FOOTBALL ... 528

RUGBY 530

BASKETBALL 532

VOLLEYBALL, NETBALL, AND HANDBALL ... 534

BASEBALL 536

CRICKET 538

HOCKEY, LACROSSE, AND HURLING 540

ATHLETICS 542

RACKET SPORTS 544

GOLF 546

ARCHERY AND SHOOTING 548

ICE HOCKEY 550

ALPINE SKIING 552

EQUESTRIAN SPORTS 554

JUDO AND FENCING 556

SWIMMING AND DIVING 558

CANOEING, ROWING, AND SAILING 560

ANGLING 562

Soccer

GAMES INVOLVING KICKING A BALL have a long history and were recorded in China as early as 300 BC; in medieval Europe, street football was banned as a menace to the public; only in 1863 were the rules established, specifically banning carrying the ball for all players except the goalkeeper, and separating rugby from soccer. Soccer, officially termed association football, is a team sport in which players attempt to score goals by passing and dribbling the ball down the field past opposing defenders, and kicking or heading the ball into the goal net, outwitting the defending goalkeeper. Each team consists of ten outfield players (defenders, midfielders, and strikers) and a goalkeeper. Players from the opposing team may challenge the player in possession of the ball, but an illegal or foul tackle results in a penalty if a foul occurs inside the penalty area or a free kick if outside the penalty area. The round ball used in soccer is more easily controlled than the oval balls used in American, Canadian, and Australian rules football and in rugby. The result is a more "open" or flowing game which is played and watched by millions of people worldwide.

ASSISTANT REFEREE'S FLAG

Lightweight, brightly coloured fabric

Handle with rubber grip

REFEREE'S EQUIPMENT

Red card

Yellow card

Referee's whistle

Stop-watch

PITCH MARKINGS

SOCCER PITCH

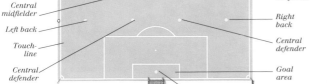

46–91 m
(150–300 ft)

Goal-line

Corner flag

Corner arc

Penalty area

Penalty mark

Referee

Halfway-line flag

Striker

Striker

Left midfielder

Central midfielder

Left back

Touch-line

Central defender

Goal

Goalkeeper

Penalty arc

Assistant referee

Centre circle

Centre spot

Halfway line

Striker

Right midfielder

Right back

Central defender

Goal area

Halfway line

1.5 m
(5 ft)

HALFWAY-LINE FLAG

Corner arc

CORNER FLAG

7.3 m
(24 ft)

Goal-line

GOAL

GOALKEEPER

Goalkeeper's shirt

Shorts

Glove

Shin guard

Sock

Soccer boot

SOCCER STRIP

Open-neck collar

Lightweight, man-made fabric team shirt

Team logo

Manufacturer's logo

Ribbed welt

Sponsor's logo

Manufacturer's name

Edge cut to fit perfectly

MAKING A SOCCER BALL

Hole punched in panel for stitching

Ball size number

lotto

Motta

Mitre

F.I.F.A. APPROVED

MULTIPLEX

Mitre

MULTIPLEX®

Waxed thread

22–23 cm (8¹⁄₂–9 in)

Needle

Bladder valve

Bladder made from latex rubber

Long cotton sock

Club crest

Team shorts

Synthetic bootlace

Laminated panel

Panels sewn together with ball inside out

Interchangeable nylon stud

SOCCER BOOT

American football

In AMERICAN AND CANADIAN FOOTBALL, the object of the game is to get the ball across the opponent's goal line, either by passing or carrying it across (a touch-down), or by kicking it between their goalposts (a field goal). An American football team has 11 players on the field at a time, although up to 40 players can appear for each side in a single game. The agile "offence" tries to score points, and the heavy hitting "defence" holds back the opposition. When in possession of the ball, a team has four chances ("downs"), to move at least ten yards (nine metres) up the field to make a "first down". The opposition gains possession if they fail, or by tackling and intercepting the ball. Canadian football is played on a larger field, with 12 men on each side. A team has only three chances to achieve a first down. Otherwise, the game is very similar to American football. Helmets, face masks, and layers of body padding are worn by the players for protection.

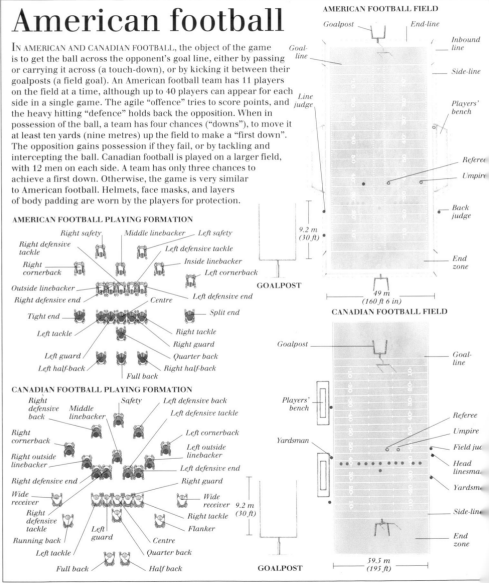

AMERICAN FOOTBALL FIELD

Goalpost — End-line — Goal-line — Inbound line — Side-line — Line judge — Players' bench — Referee — Umpire — Back judge — End zone

9.2 m (30 ft)

GOALPOST

49 m (160 ft 6 in)

AMERICAN FOOTBALL PLAYING FORMATION

Right safety — Middle linebacker — Left safety — Right defensive tackle — Left defensive tackle — Right cornerback — Inside linebacker — Left cornerback — Outside linebacker — Right defensive end — Centre — Left defensive end — Tight end — Split end — Left tackle — Right tackle — Right guard — Left guard — Quarter back — Left half-back — Right half-back — Full back

CANADIAN FOOTBALL PLAYING FORMATION

Right defensive back — Middle linebacker — Safety — Left defensive back — Left defensive tackle — Right cornerback — Left cornerback — Left outside linebacker — Right outside linebacker — Left defensive end — Right defensive end — Right guard — Wide receiver — Wide receiver — Right defensive tackle — Right tackle — Flanker — Left guard — Centre — Running back — Quarter back — Left tackle — Half back — Full back

9.2 m (30 ft)

GOALPOST

CANADIAN FOOTBALL FIELD

Goalpost — Goal-line — Players' bench — Referee — Umpire — Yardsman — Field judge — Head linesman — Yardsman — Side-line — End zone

59.5 m (195 ft)

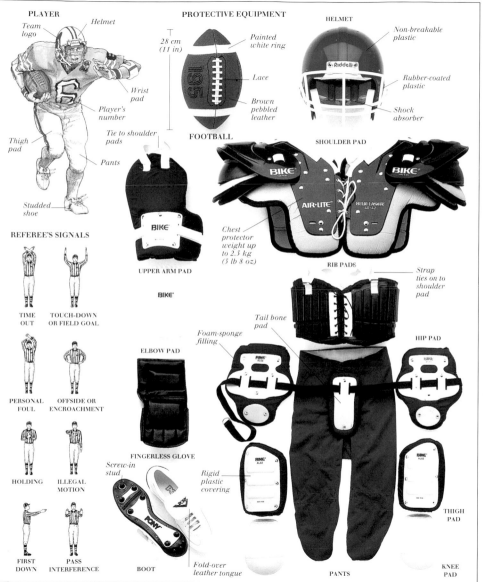

PLAYER

Team logo

Helmet

Wrist pad

Player's number

Thigh pad

Pants

Tie to shoulder pads

Studded shoe

REFEREE'S SIGNALS

TIME OUT

TOUCH-DOWN OR FIELD GOAL

PERSONAL FOUL

OFFSIDE OR ENCROACHMENT

HOLDING

ILLEGAL MOTION

FIRST DOWN

PASS INTERFERENCE

PROTECTIVE EQUIPMENT

28 cm (11 in)

Painted white ring

Lace

Brown pebbled leather

FOOTBALL

UPPER ARM PAD

BIKE

ELBOW PAD

FINGERLESS GLOVE

Screw-in stud

Fold-over leather tongue

BOOT

HELMET

Non-breakable plastic

Rubber-coated plastic

Shock absorber

SHOULDER PAD

BIKE

BIKE

AIR·LITE

BLUE·LASER 40-42

Chest protector weight up to 2.5 kg (5 lb 8 oz)

RIB PADE

Strap ties on to shoulder pad

Tail bone pad

Foam-sponge filling

HIP PAD

Rigid plastic covering

THIGH PAD

PANTS

KNEE PAD

527

Australian rules and Gaelic football

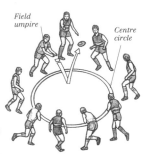

Field umpire

Centre circle

VARIETIES OF FOOTBALL have developed all over the world and Australian rules football is considered to be one of the roughest versions, allowing full body tackles although participants wear no protective padding. The game is played on a large, oval pitch by two sides, each of 18 players. Players can kick or punch the ball, which is shaped like a rugby ball, but cannot throw it. Running with the ball is permitted, as long as the ball touches the ground at least once every ten metres. The full backs defend two sets of posts. Teams try to score "goals" (six points) between the inner posts or "behinds" (one point) inside the outer posts. Each game has four quarters of 25 minutes, and the team with the most points at the end of the allotted time is the winner. In Gaelic football, an Irish version of soccer (see pp. 524–525), a size 5 soccer ball is used. Each team can have 15 players on the field at a time. Players are allowed to catch, fist, and kick the ball, or dribble it using their hands or feet, but cannot throw it. Teams are awarded three points for getting the ball into the net, and one point for getting it through the posts above the crossbar. Gaelic football is rarely played outside of Ireland.

SCORING

GOAL (6 POINTS)

AUSTRALIAN RULES FOOTBALL FIELD

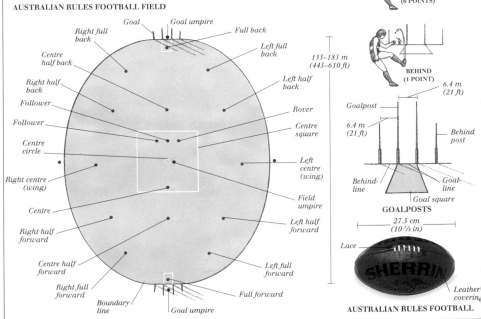

Goal
Goal umpire
Right full back
Full back
Left full back
Centre half back
Right half back
Left half back
Follower
Rover
Follower
Centre square
Centre circle
Left centre (wing)
Right centre (wing)
Left centre (wing)
Field umpire
Centre
Left half forward
Right half forward
Centre half forward
Left full forward
Right full forward
Full forward
Boundary line
Goal umpire

135–185 m (445–610 ft)

BEHIND (1 POINT)

6.4 m (21 ft)

Goalpost

6.4 m (21 ft)

Behind post

Behind- line

Goal line

Goal square

GOALPOSTS

27.5 cm (10 ⁷⁄₈ in)

Lace

Leather covering

AUSTRALIAN RULES FOOTBALL

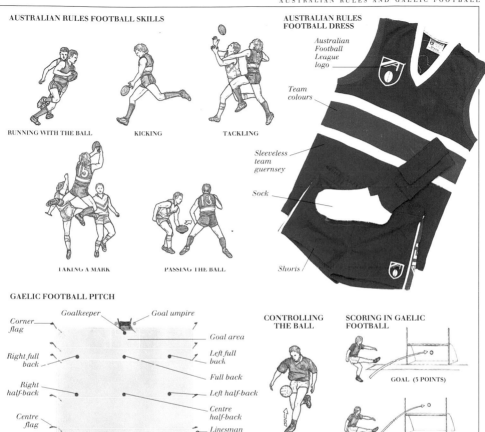

AUSTRALIAN RULES FOOTBALL SKILLS

RUNNING WITH THE BALL

KICKING

TACKLING

TAKING A MARK

PASSING THE BALL

AUSTRALIAN RULES FOOTBALL DRESS

Australian Football League logo

Team colours

Sleeveless team guernsey

Sock

Shorts

GAELIC FOOTBALL PITCH

Corner flag

Goalkeeper

Goal umpire

Goal area

Right full back

Left full back

Full back

Right half-back

Left half-back

Centre half-back

Centre flag

Linesman

Linesman

Right midfielder

Left midfielder

Midfield line

Referee

Left half-forward

Right half-forward

Centre half-forward

Right full-forward

Left full-forward

Full forward

80–90 m
260–295 ft)

CONTROLLING THE BALL

SCORING IN GAELIC FOOTBALL

GOAL (3 POINTS)

POINT (1 POINT)

22–23 cm
(8½–9 in)

6.4 m
(21ft)

Goalpost

Crossbar

Parallelogram

GOAL

o'neills
all-ireland

GAELIC FOOTBALL

529

Rugby

RUGBY IS PLAYED WITH AN OVAL BALL, which may be carried, thrown, or kicked. There are two codes of rugby, both played at amateur and professional levels. Rugby Union is played by two teams of 15 players. They can score points in two ways: by placing the ball by hand over the opponents' goal-line (a try, scoring four points) or by kicking it over the crossbar of the opponent's goal (a conversion of a try, scoring two points; a penalty kick, scoring three points; or a drop-kick, scoring three points). Rugby League developed from the Union game but is played by 13 players. In League games, a try scores four points; a conversion scores two points; a drop goal scores one point, and a penalty kick scores two points. Scrummages occur in both codes when play stops following an infringement.

RUGBY UNION SCRUMMAGE

Loose-head prop
Hooker
Scrum-half
Flanker
Flanker
Lock forward
Lock forward
Tight-head prop
Number 8

RUGBY UNION GOALPOST

Upright
Crossbar
Protective padding
5.5 m (18 ft)
3 m (9 ft 10 in)

RUGBY LEAGUE SCRUMMAGE

Blind-side prop
Hooker
Open-side prop
Scrum-half
Second-row forward
Second-row forward
Loose forward

RUGBY LEAGUE GOALPOST

Upright
Crossbar
Protective padding
5.5 m (18 ft)

RUGBY UNION PITCH

Goal
Dead-ball line
Touch in-goal line
Goal-line
5 m line
Scrum-half
10 m line
Loose-head prop
Flanker
Lock forward
Centre
Left wing
Centre
Full back
Touch-line
Referee
Hooker
Tight-head prop
Touch judge
Flanker
Lock forward
Right wing
Number 8
Fly-half
In-goal area
68 m (225 ft) maximum

RUGBY LEAGUE PITCH

Goal
Dead-ball line
Touch in-goal
Goal-line
10 m line
Referee
Touch judge
Blind-side prop
Second-row forward
Loose forward
Left wing
Full back
Touch in-goal line
Touch-line
Hooker
Open-side prop
Touch judge
Second-row forward
Scrum-half
Stand-off half
Centre
Centre
Right wing
68m (225 ft) maximum

RUGBY

RUGBY SCORING AND SKILLS

GOAL

TRY

PASS

PLACE KICK

FLYING TACKLE

Goal-line

RUGBY UNION PLAYER

Shirt in team colour

Knee-high sock

Team shorts

Studded boot

RUGBY UNION BALL

Laminated leather panel covered with textured plastic

Four-panel construction

28–30 cm (11–12 in)

RUGBY LEAGUE BALL

Eight-panel construction

Laminated leather panel covered with textured plastic

28 cm (11 in)

RUGBY LEAGUE SHIRT

Button-up collar

Team crest

Short sleeve

RUGBY UNION SHIRT

GILBERT

CITY

Team crest

RUGBY BOOT

Ankle support

Circular stud

Team colour

RUGBY SHIRTS

551

Basketball

BASKETBALL IS A BALL GAME for two teams of five players, originally devised
in 1890 by James Naismath for the Y.M.C.A. in Springfield, Massachusetts, U.S.A.
The object of the game is to take possession of the ball and score points by throwing
the ball into the opposing team's basket. A player moves the ball up and down the
court by bouncing it along the ground or "dribbling"; the ball may be passed
between players by throwing, bouncing, or rolling. Players may not run with or kick
the ball, although pivoting on one foot is allowed. The game begins with the referee
throwing the ball into the air and a player from each team jumping up to try and
"tip" the ball to a team-mate. The length of the game and the number of periods
played varies at different levels. There are amateur, professional, and international
rules. No game ends in a draw. An extra period of five minutes is played, plus as
many extra periods as are necessary to break the tie. In addition to the five players
on court, each team has up to seven substitutes, but players may only leave the
court with the permission of the referee. Basketball is a non-contact sport and fouls
on other players are penalized by a throw-in awarded against the offending team; a
free throw at the basket is awarded when a player is fouled in the act of shooting.
Basketball is a fast-moving game, requiring both physical and mental coordination.
Skilful tactical play matters more than simple physical strength and the agility of
the players makes the game an excellent spectator sport.

CHEST PASS

DRIBBLE

OVERHEAD PASS

LAY-UP SHOT

INTERNATIONAL BASKETBALL COURT

Back-board

End-line

Restraining
circle

Player's
bench

Referee

Time-keeper

Clock
operator

Scorer

Referee

Right
forward

Three-
point line

Basket

Semi-circle

Right
guard

Left guard

Centre

Centre-line

Left forward

Centre circle

Free-throw
line

Side-line

15 m (49 ft)

BASKET AND BACK-BOARD

Back-board

Metal
rim

Cord
net

1.8 m
(6 ft)

BASKET AND BACK-BOARD
STRUCTURE

3.05 m
(10 ft)

JUMP SHOT

LONG PASS

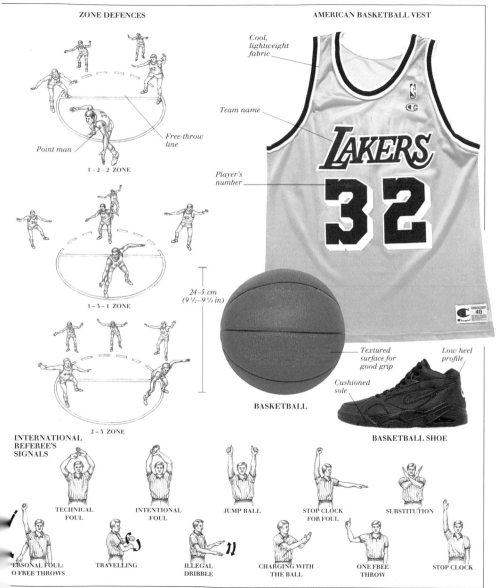

ZONE DEFENCES

Point man

Free-throw line

1 – 2 – 2 ZONE

1 – 3 – 1 ZONE

24–5 cm
(9¹/₂–9¹/₄ in)

2 – 3 ZONE

AMERICAN BASKETBALL VEST

Cool, lightweight fabric

Team name

Player's number

LAKERS

32

48

Textured surface for good grip

Cushioned sole

Low heel profile

BASKETBALL

BASKETBALL SHOE

INTERNATIONAL REFEREE'S SIGNALS

TECHNICAL FOUL

INTENTIONAL FOUL

JUMP BALL

STOP CLOCK FOR FOUL

SUBSTITUTION

PERSONAL FOUL: O FREE THROWS

TRAVELLING

ILLEGAL DRIBBLE

CHARGING WITH THE BALL

ONE FREE THROW

STOP CLOCK

Volleyball, netball, and handball

VOLLEYBALL, NETBALL, AND HANDBALL are fast-moving team sports played with balls on courts with a hard surface. In volleyball, the object of the game is to hit the ball over a net strung across the centre of the court so that it touches the ground on the opponent's side. The team of six players can take three hits to direct the ball over the net, although the same player cannot hit the ball twice in a row. Players can hit the ball with their arms, hands or any other part of their upper body. Teams score points only while serving. The first team to score 15 points, with a two-point margin over their opponent, wins the game. Netball is one of the few sports played exclusively by women. Similar to basketball (see pp.532–533), it is played on a slightly larger court with seven players instead of five. A team moves the ball towards the goal by throwing, passing, and catching it with the aim of throwing the ball through the opponents' goal net. Players are confined by their playing position to specific areas of the court. Team handball is one of the world's fastest games. Each side has seven players. A team moves the ball by dribbling, passing, or bouncing it as they run. Players may stop, catch, throw, bounce, or strike the ball with any part of the body above the knees. Each team tries to score goals by directing the ball past the opposition's goalkeeper into the net, which is similar to a soccer net.

OVERHAND SERVE **SPIKE (SMASH)**

UNDERHAND SERVE **FOREARM PASS (DIG)**

VOLLEYBALL KIT

Team colours

VOLLEYBALL COURT

End-line

Linesman

Clear space

Linesman

Side-line

Players' bench

Referee

Scorer

Net

Left forward

Back zone

Left back

Linesman

Attack zone

Attack line

Umpire

Centre forward

Right forward

Centre back

Linesman

Service area

Server

9 m (29 ft 6 in)

Ribbed cuff

Cotton-knit jersey

Elasticated waist

Leather covering

21 cm (8¼ in)

VOLLEYBALL

Shorts

Elasticated knit fabric

Injected moulded padding

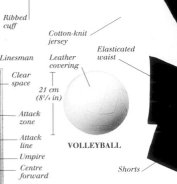

Tape *Net* *Antenna*

Men's: 2.4 m (8 ft) Women's: 2.2 m (7 ft 4 in)

Post

VOLLEYBALL NET

KNEE PADS

NETBALL COURT

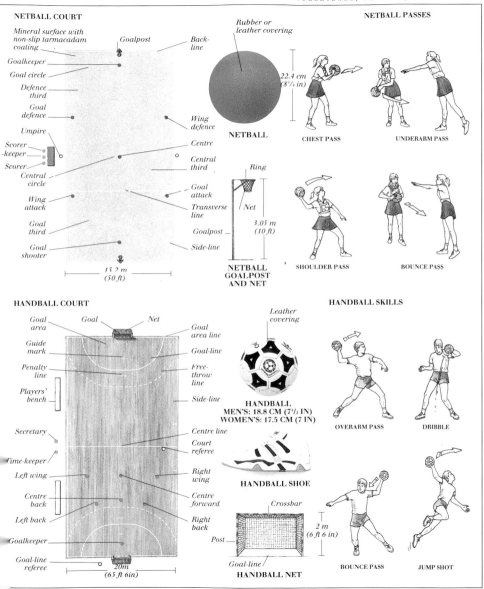

Mineral surface with non-slip tarmacadam coating

Goalpost

Back-line

Goalkeeper

Goal circle

Defence third

Goal defence

Umpire

Scorer-keeper

Scorer

Central circle

Wing attack

Goal third

Goal shooter

Wing defence

Centre

Central third

Goal attack

Transverse line

Goalpost

Side-line

15.2 m (50 ft)

NETBALL PASSES

Rubber or leather covering

22.4 cm (8¼ in)

NETBALL

CHEST PASS

UNDERARM PASS

Ring

Net

3.05 m (10 ft)

Goalpost

NETBALL GOALPOST AND NET

SHOULDER PASS

BOUNCE PASS

HANDBALL COURT

Goal area

Goal

Net

Guide mark

Penalty line

Players' bench

Secretary

Time-keeper

Left wing

Centre back

Left back

Goalkeeper

Goal-line referee

Goal area line

Goal-line

Free-throw line

Side-line

Centre line

Court referee

Right wing

Centre forward

Right back

20m (65 ft 6in)

HANDBALL SKILLS

Leather covering

HANDBALL
MEN'S: 18.8 CM (7½ IN)
WOMEN'S: 17.5 CM (7 IN)

OVERARM PASS

DRIBBLE

HANDBALL SHOE

Crossbar

2 m (6 ft 6 in)

Post

Goal-line

HANDBALL NET

BOUNCE PASS

JUMP SHOT

535

Baseball

BASEBALL IS A BALL GAME for two teams of nine players.
The batter hits the ball thrown by the opposing team's pitcher,
into the area between the foul lines. He then runs round all four
fixed bases in order to score a run, touching or "tagging" each base
in turn. The pitcher must throw the ball at a height between the
batter's armpits and knees, a height which is called the "strike
zone". A ball pitched in this area that crosses over the "home plate"
is called a "strike" and the batter has three strikes in which to try
and hit the ball (otherwise he is "struck out"). The fielding team
tries to get the batting team out by catching the ball before it
bounces, tagging a player of the batting team with the ball who
is running between bases, or by tagging a base before the player
has reached it. Members of the batting team may stop safely at a
base as long as it is not occupied by another member of their team.
When the batter runs to first base, his team-mate at first base must
run on to second – this is called "force play". A game consists of
nine innings and each team will bat once during an inning. When
three members of the batting team are out, the teams swap roles.
The team with the greatest number of runs wins the game.

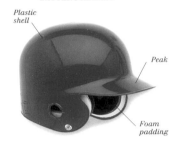

BATTER'S HELMET

Plastic
shell

Peak

Foam
padding

Wire coated
in strong
nylon

Plastic-coated
foam padding

CATCHER'S MASK

BASEBALL PITCH

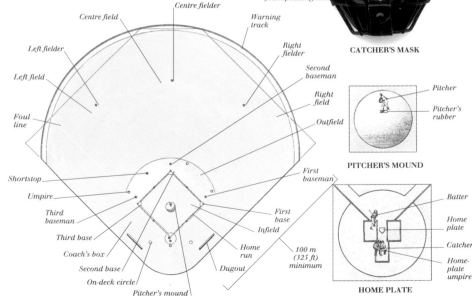

Centre fielder

Centre field

Left fielder

Warning
track

Right
fielder

Left field

Second
baseman

Foul
line

Right
field

Outfield

Shortstop

First
baseman

Umpire

First
base

Third
baseman

Infield

Third base

Home
run

Coach's box

100 m
(325 ft)
minimum

Second base

Dugout

On-deck circle

Pitcher's mound

Pitcher

Pitcher's
rubber

PITCHER'S MOUND

Batter

Home
plate

Catcher

Home-
plate
umpire

HOME PLATE

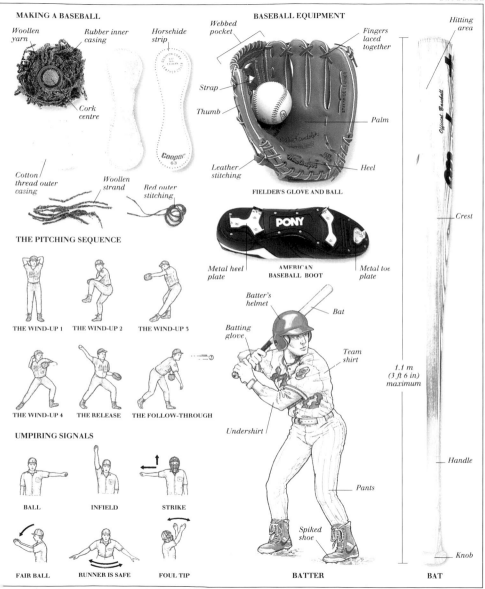

MAKING A BASEBALL

Woollen yarn

Rubber inner casing

Horsehide strip

Cork centre

Cotton thread outer casing

Woollen strand

Red outer stitching

BASEBALL EQUIPMENT

Webbed pocket

Fingers laced together

Strap

Thumb

Palm

Leather stitching

Heel

FIELDER'S GLOVE AND BALL

PONY

Metal heel plate

AMERICAN BASEBALL BOOT

Metal toe plate

THE PITCHING SEQUENCE

THE WIND-UP 1

THE WIND-UP 2

THE WIND-UP 3

THE WIND-UP 4

THE RELEASE

THE FOLLOW-THROUGH

UMPIRING SIGNALS

BALL

INFIELD

STRIKE

FAIR BALL

RUNNER IS SAFE

FOUL TIP

Batter's helmet

Bat

Batting glove

Team shirt

Undershirt

Pants

Spiked shoe

BATTER

Hitting area

Official Baseball

Crest

1.1 m (3 ft 6 in) maximum

Handle

Knob

BAT

537

Cricket

CRICKET IS A BALL GAME PLAYED by two teams of eleven players on a pitch with two sets of three stumps (wickets). The bowler bowls the ball down the pitch to the batsman of the opposing team, who must defend the wicket in front of which he stands. The object of the game is to score as many runs as possible. Runs can be scored individually by running the length of the playing strip, or by hitting a ball which lands outside the boundary ("six"), or which lands inside the boundary but bounces or rolls outside ("four"); the opposing team will bowl and field, attempting to dismiss the batsmen. A batsman can be dismissed in one of several ways: by the bowler hitting the wicket with the ball ("bowled"); by a fielder catching the ball hit by the batsman before it touches the ground ("caught"); by the wicket-keeper or another fielder breaking the wicket while the batsman is attempting a run and is therefore out of his ground ("stumped" or "run out"); by the batsman breaking the wicket with his own bat or body ("hit wicket"); by a part of the batsman's body being hit by a ball that would otherwise have hit the wicket ("leg before wicket" ["lbw"]). A match consists of one or two innings and each innings ends when the tenth batsman of the batting team is out, when a certain number of overs (a series of six balls bowled) have been played, or when the captain of the batting team "declares" ending the innings voluntarily.

FORWARD DEFENSIVE STROKE

BACKWARD DEFENSIVE STROKE

ON-DRIVE

OFF-DRIVE

PULL

HOOK

SQUARE CUT

LEG GLANCE

POSSIBLE FIELD POSITIONS FOR AN AWAY SWING BOWLER TO A RIGHT-HANDED BATSMAN (IN RED) AND OTHER FIELD POSITIONS

Long on

Long off

Umpire

Bowler

Boundary line

Non-striking batsman

Deep mid-wicket

Extra cover

Mid-on

Silly mid-on

Mid-off

Forward short leg

Silly mid-off

Square leg

Cover

Deep square leg

Point

Square-leg umpire

Gulley

Batsman

Third man

Long leg

Bowler

Leg slip

Second slip

Wicket-keeper

Return crease

First slip

Fine leg

Sight screen

CRICKET PITCH

Wicket-keeper

Wicket

Bowling crease

Batsman

20 m (66 ft)

Umpire

Non-striking batsman

CRICKET BALL AND WICKET

Leather skin

Seam

BALL

Bail

WICKET

Stump

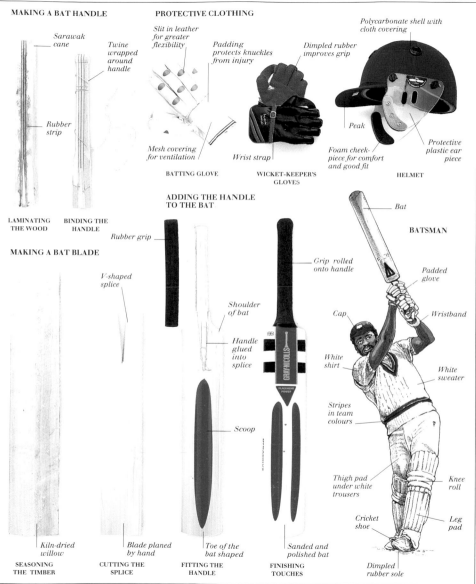

MAKING A BAT HANDLE

Sarawak cane

Twine wrapped around handle

Rubber strip

LAMINATING THE WOOD

BINDING THE HANDLE

MAKING A BAT BLADE

V-shaped splice

Kiln-dried willow

SEASONING THE TIMBER

Blade planed by hand

CUTTING THE SPLICE

PROTECTIVE CLOTHING

Slit in leather for greater flexibility

Padding protects knuckles from injury

Mesh covering for ventilation

BATTING GLOVE

Dimpled rubber improves grip

Wrist strap

WICKET-KEEPER'S GLOVES

Polycarbonate shell with cloth covering

Peak

Foam cheek-piece for comfort and good fit

Protective plastic ear piece

HELMET

ADDING THE HANDLE TO THE BAT

Rubber grip

Shoulder of bat

Handle glued into splice

Scoop

Toe of the bat shaped

FITTING THE HANDLE

Grip rolled onto handle

GRAY·NICOLLS

Sanded and polished bat

FINISHING TOUCHES

Bat

BATSMAN

Padded glove

Wristband

Cap

White shirt

White sweater

Stripes in team colours

Thigh pad under white trousers

Knee roll

Cricket shoe

Leg pad

Dimpled rubber sole

Hockey, lacrosse, and hurling

ALL OVER THE WORLD, TEAM GAMES have evolved which require that a ball be struck or carried, and tossed at the end of a stick. Early forms of these games include hurling, shinty, bandy, and pelota. Hockey is played by men and women: two teams of eleven players try to gain and keep possession of the ball and score goals by using the hockey stick to propel the ball into their opponents' goal net. Skills such as passing, pushing, or hitting the ball by slapping or lifting it in a flicking movement, and shooting at goal are crucial. Hockey is played indoors and outdoors on grass or synthetic pitches. Lacrosse is played internationally as a 12-a-side game for women and as 10-a-side game for men. The women's pitch has no absolute boundaries but the men's pitch has clearly defined side-lines and end-lines. The ball is kept in play by being carried, thrown or batted with the crosse, and rolled or kicked in any direction. In men's and women's lacrosse, play can continue behind the marked goal areas. Similar skills are required in hurling – a Gaelic field game played on the same pitch as Gaelic football (see pp. 528–529), using the same goalposts and net. In hurling, the ball may be struck with or carried on the hurley and, when off the ground, may be struck with the hand or kicked. Goals (three points) are scored when the ball passes between the posts and under the crossbar; one point is scored when it passes between the posts and over the crossbar.

GOALKEEPER'S EQUIPMENT

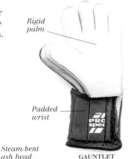

Air vent

Hard shell

Face mask

HELMET

Strap

Rigid palm

Padded wrist

GAUNTLET

HOCKEY STICK AND BALL

STICK

Handle

Tape

Slazenger FLEXI

Steam-bent ash head

Blade

91 cm (3 ft)

Stitched seam

7–7.5 cm (2¹/₄–3 in)

BALL

HOCKEY FIELD

Centre forward

Inside right

Right wing

Right half

Right back

Side-line

Corner flag

Shooting circle

Goal

Penalty spot

Five yard mark

Goal-line

Inside left

Left wing

Umpire

Centre half

Left half

Left back

Goalkeeper

55 m (180 ft)

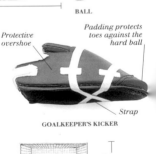

Padding protects toes against the hard ball

Protective overshoe

Strap

GOALKEEPER'S KICKER

2.1 m (7 ft)

HOCKEY GOAL

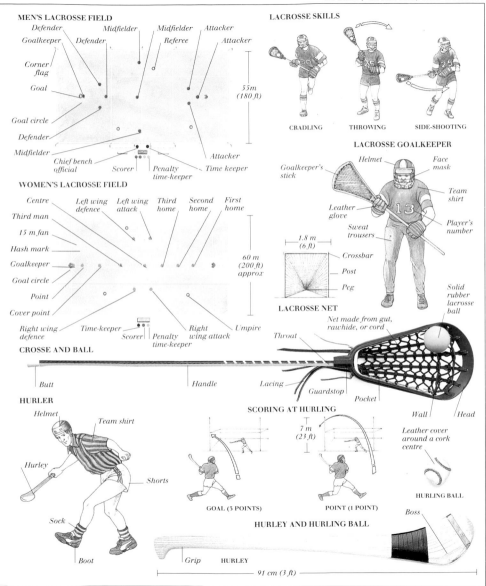

MEN'S LACROSSE FIELD

Defender
Goalkeeper
Defender
Midfielder
Midfielder
Referee
Attacker
Attacker

Corner flag

Goal

55m (180 ft)

Goal circle

Defender

Midfielder

Chief bench official
Scorer
Penalty time-keeper
Attacker
Time keeper

WOMEN'S LACROSSE FIELD

Centre
Left wing defence
Left wing attack
Third home
Second home
First home

Third man

15 m fan

Hash mark

Goalkeeper

Goal circle

Point

Cover point

60 m (200 ft) approx

Right wing defence
Time-keeper
Scorer
Penalty time-keeper
Right wing attack
Umpire

CROSSE AND BALL

Butt
Handle
Lacing
Guardstop
Pocket

HURLER

Helmet
Team shirt

Hurley

Shorts

Sock

Boot

LACROSSE SKILLS

CRADLING
THROWING
SIDE-SHOOTING

LACROSSE GOALKEEPER

Goalkeeper's stick
Helmet
Face mask

Team shirt

Leather glove

Sweat trousers

Player's number

1.8 m (6 ft)
Crossbar
Post
Peg

LACROSSE NET

Net made from gut, rawhide, or cord
Throat

Solid rubber lacrosse ball

Wall
Head

Leather cover around a cork centre

HURLING BALL

SCORING AT HURLING

7 m (23 ft)

GOAL (3 POINTS)
POINT (1 POINT)

Boss

HURLEY AND HURLING BALL

Grip
HURLEY
91 cm (3 ft)

Athletics

THE SPORTS that make up athletics are divided into two main groups: track events – which include sprinting, middle, and long distance running, relay running, hurdling, and walking – and field events which require jumping and throwing skills. Contests designed to test the speed, strength, agility, and stamina of athletes were held by the ancient Greeks over 4,000 years ago. However, the abolition of the Olympic Games in 393 AD meant that athletics were neglected until the revival of large-scale competitions in the mid-nineteenth century. Modern stadia offer areas reserved for the long jump, triple jump, and pole vault usually situated outside the running track. The javelin, shot, hammer, and discus are thrown within the track area. Most athletes specialize in one or two events but, in the heptathlon, women compete in seven events, held over two days: 200 m and 800 m races, 100 m hurdles, javelin, shot put, high jump, and long jump. In the decathlon, men compete in ten events over two days: 100 m, 400 m, and 1,500 m races, 110 m hurdles, javelin, discus, shot put, pole vault, high jump, and long jump.

FIELD EVENT EQUIPMENT

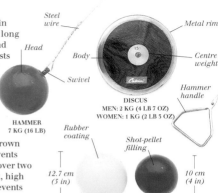

Steel wire

Metal rim

Head

Body

Centre weight

Swivel

DISCUS
MEN: 2 KG (4 LB 7 OZ)
WOMEN: 1 KG (2 LB 3 OZ)

Hammer handle

HAMMER
7 KG (16 LB)

Rubber coating

Shot-pellet filling

12.7 cm (5 in)

10 cm (4 in)

MEN'S SHOT
7 KG (16 LB)

WOMEN'S SHOT
4 KG (8 LB 12 OZ)

JAVELIN   Cord grip   Shaft   Tip

Men: 2.6 m (8 ft 6 in)
Women: 2.3 m (7 ft 6 in)

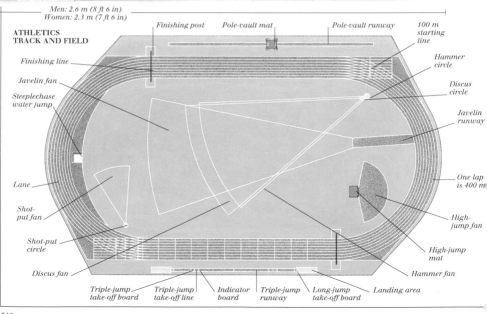

ATHLETICS TRACK AND FIELD

Finishing post

Pole-vault mat

Pole-vault runway

100 m starting line

Finishing line

Hammer circle

Javelin fan

Discus circle

Steeplechase water jump

Javelin runway

Lane

One lap is 400 m

Shot-put fan

High-jump fan

Shot-put circle

High-jump mat

Discus fan

Hammer fan

Triple-jump take-off board

Triple-jump take-off line

Indicator board

Triple-jump runway

Long-jump take-off board

Landing area

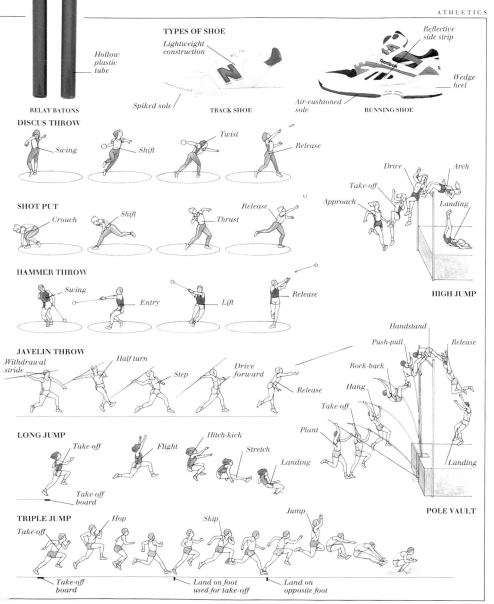

TYPES OF SHOE

Hollow
plastic
tube

Lightweight
construction

Reflective
side strip

Wedge
heel

RELAY BATONS

Spiked sole

Air-cushioned
sole

TRACK SHOE

RUNNING SHOE

DISCUS THROW

Swing

Shift

Twist

Release

SHOT PUT

Crouch

Shift

Thrust

Release

HAMMER THROW

Swing

Entry

Lift

Release

Drive

Arch

Take-off

Approach

Landing

HIGH JUMP

JAVELIN THROW

Withdrawal
stride

Half turn

Step

Drive
forward

Release

Handstand

Push-pull

Release

Rock-back

Hang

Take-off

Plant

Landing

LONG JUMP

Take-off

Flight

Hitch-kick

Stretch

Landing

Take-off
board

POLE VAULT

TRIPLE JUMP

Hop

Skip

Jump

Take-off

Take-off
board

Land on foot
used for take-off

Land on
opposite foot

Racket sports

PROTECTIVE
EYEWEAR

THE OBJECT OF ALL RACKET SPORTS is to make shots the opponent cannot return. Games are played by two players (singles) or four players (doubles). Racket shape and size is tailored to each sport, but all rackets are constructed of wood, plastic, aluminium, or high-performance materials such as fibreglass and carbon graphite. Racket strings are usually synthetic, although natural gut is still used. Tennis is played on a court divided by a low net. Opposing players serve alternate games. At least six games must be won to gain a set, and two or sometimes three sets are needed to win a match. Tennis courts may be concrete, grass, clay, or synthetic, each surface requiring a different style of play. Badminton is an indoor sport that is played with light, flexible rackets and a feather shuttlecock on a court with a high net. Players can score points only on their serve. The first to reach 15 points (11 points for women's singles) wins the game. Two games are needed to win a match. Squash and racketball are both played in enclosed courts. One player hits the ball against the front wall, and the other tries to return it before it bounces on the floor more than once. Squash rackets have smaller, rounder heads and stiffer frames than badminton rackets. In America, the game is played on a narrower court than an international court using a much harder ball. Squash games are played to nine points (international) or 15 points (American). In racketball, players use a ball that is larger and bouncier than a squash ball. The racket is thick and sturdy, with a large head, short handle, and a thong that loops around the wrist. Points can be won only when serving, and the first player to reach 21 points wins.

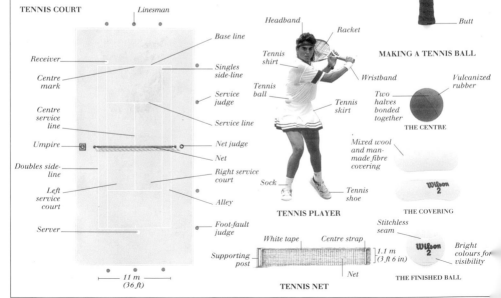

TENNIS RACKET
Synthetic string
Frame
Head
Logo
Throat
Grip
Butt

TENNIS COURT
Linesman
Base line
Receiver
Singles side-line
Centre mark
Service judge
Centre service line
Service line
Umpire
Net judge
Net
Doubles side-line
Right service court
Left service court
Alley
Server
Foot-fault judge
11 m
(36 ft)

Headband
Racket
Tennis shirt
Wristband
Tennis ball
Tennis skirt
Two halves bonded together
Sock
Tennis shoe
TENNIS PLAYER

MAKING A TENNIS BALL
Vulcanized rubber
THE CENTRE
Mixed wool and man-made fibre covering
Wilson 2
THE COVERING
Stitchless seam
Wilson 2
Bright colours for visibility
THE FINISHED BALL

White tape
Centre strap
Supporting post
Net
1.1 m (3 ft 6 in)
TENNIS NET

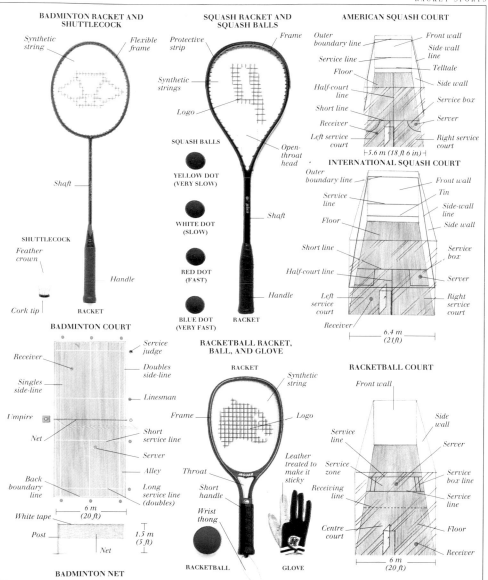

BADMINTON RACKET AND SHUTTLECOCK

Synthetic string

Flexible frame

Shaft

SHUTTLECOCK

Feather crown

Cork tip

RACKET

Handle

SQUASH RACKET AND SQUASH BALLS

Protective strip

Frame

Synthetic strings

Logo

Open-throat head

Shaft

Handle

RACKET

SQUASH BALLS

YELLOW DOT (VERY SLOW)

WHITE DOT (SLOW)

RED DOT (FAST)

BLUE DOT (VERY FAST)

AMERICAN SQUASH COURT

Outer boundary line

Front wall

Service line

Side wall line

Floor

Telltale

Half-court line

Side wall

Short line

Service box

Receiver

Server

Left service court

Right service court

├ 5.6 m (18 ft 6 in) ┤

INTERNATIONAL SQUASH COURT

Outer boundary line

Front wall

Service line

Tin

Floor

Side-wall line

Side wall

Short line

Service box

Half-court line

Server

Left service court

Right service court

Receiver

6.4 m (21 ft)

BADMINTON COURT

Service judge

Doubles side-line

Receiver

Linesman

Singles side-line

Umpire

Short service line

Net

Server

Alley

Back boundary line

Long service line (doubles)

6 m (20 ft)

White tape

1.5 m (5 ft)

Post

Net

BADMINTON NET

RACKETBALL RACKET, BALL, AND GLOVE

RACKET

Synthetic string

Frame

Logo

Leather treated to make it sticky

Throat

Short handle

Wrist thong

RACKETBALL

GLOVE

JAGUAR

RACKETBALL COURT

Front wall

Side wall

Service line

Server

Service zone

Service box line

Receiving line

Service line

Centre court

Floor

Receiver

6 m (20 ft)

Golf

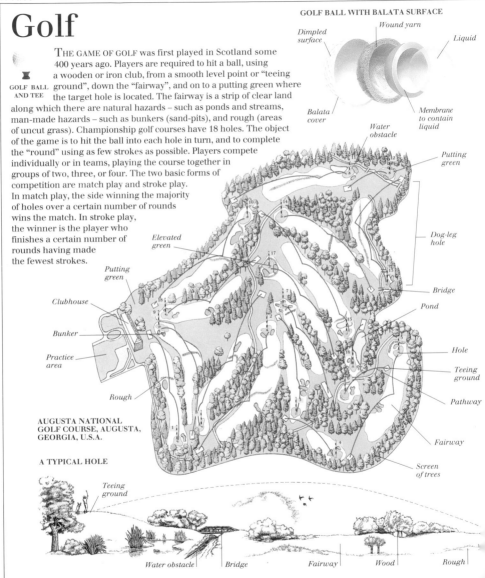

GOLF BALL AND TEE

THE GAME OF GOLF was first played in Scotland some 400 years ago. Players are required to hit a ball, using a wooden or iron club, from a smooth level point or "teeing ground", down the "fairway", and on to a putting green where the target hole is located. The fairway is a strip of clear land along which there are natural hazards – such as ponds and streams, man-made hazards – such as bunkers (sand-pits), and rough (areas of uncut grass). Championship golf courses have 18 holes. The object of the game is to hit the ball into each hole in turn, and to complete the "round" using as few strokes as possible. Players compete individually or in teams, playing the course together in groups of two, three, or four. The two basic forms of competition are match play and stroke play. In match play, the side winning the majority of holes over a certain number of rounds wins the match. In stroke play, the winner is the player who finishes a certain number of rounds having made the fewest strokes.

GOLF BALL WITH BALATA SURFACE

Dimpled surface

Wound yarn

Liquid

Balata cover

Membrane to contain liquid

Water obstacle

Putting green

Elevated green

Dog-leg hole

Putting green

Bridge

Clubhouse

Pond

Bunker

Hole

Practice area

Teeing ground

Rough

Pathway

AUGUSTA NATIONAL GOLF COURSE, AUGUSTA, GEORGIA, U.S.A.

Fairway

A TYPICAL HOLE

Screen of trees

Teeing ground

Water obstacle | Bridge | Fairway | Wood | Rough

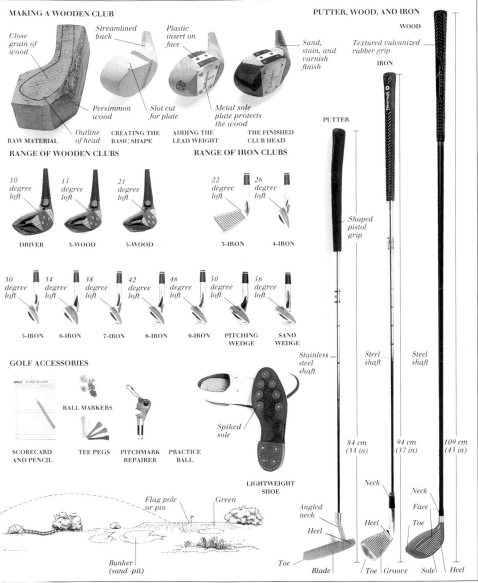

MAKING A WOODEN CLUB

Close grain of wood

Streamlined back

Plastic insert on face

Sand, stain, and varnish finish

Persimmon wood

Slot cut for plate

Metal sole plate protects the wood

Outline of head

RAW MATERIAL

CREATING THE BASIC SHAPE

ADDING THE LEAD WEIGHT

THE FINISHED CLUB HEAD

RANGE OF WOODEN CLUBS

10 degree loft

15 degree loft

21 degree loft

DRIVER

3-WOOD

5-WOOD

30 degree loft

34 degree loft

38 degree loft

42 degree loft

46 degree loft

50 degree loft

56 degree loft

5-IRON

6-IRON

7-IRON

8-IRON

9-IRON

PITCHING WEDGE

SAND WEDGE

RANGE OF IRON CLUBS

22 degree loft

26 degree loft

3-IRON

4-IRON

GOLF ACCESSORIES

GOLF SCORE RECORD

BALL MARKERS

SCORECARD AND PENCIL

TEE PEGS

PITCHMARK REPAIRER

PRACTICE BALL

Spiked sole

LIGHTWEIGHT SHOE

Flag pole or pin

Green

Bunker (sand-pit)

PUTTER, WOOD, AND IRON

WOOD

Textured vulcanized rubber grip

IRON

PUTTER

Shaped pistol grip

Stainless steel shaft

Steel shaft

Steel shaft

84 cm (33 in)

94 cm (37 in)

109 cm (43 in)

Neck

Neck

Angled neck

Face

Heel

Toe

Heel

Heel

Toe

Toe

Groove

Sole

Heel

Blade

Archery and shooting

Target shooting and archery evolved as practice for hunting and battle skills. Modern bows, although designed according to the principles of early hunting bows, use laminates, fibreglass, dacron, and carbon, and are equipped with sights and stabilizers. Competitors in target archery shoot over distances of 30 m (100 ft), 50 m (165 ft), 70 m (230 ft), and 90 m (300 ft) for men, and 30 m (100 ft), 50 m (165 ft), 60 m (200 ft), and 70 m (230 ft) for women. The closer the shot is to the centre of the target, the higher the score. The individual scores are added up, and the archer with the highest total wins the competition. Crossbows are used in match competitions over 10 m (33 ft), and 30 m (100 ft). Rifle shooting is divided into three categories: smallbore, bigbore, and air rifle. Contests take place over a variety of distances and further subdivisions are based on the type of shooting position used: prone, kneeling, or standing. The Olympic biathlon combines cross-country skiing and rifle shooting over a course of approximately 20 km (12$\frac{1}{2}$ miles). Additional magazines of ammunition are carried in the butt of the rifles. Bigbore rifles fitted with a telescopic sight can be used for hunting and running game target shooting. Pistol shooting events, using rapid-fire pistols, target pistols, and air pistols, take place over 10 m (33 ft), 25 m (82 ft), and 50 m (165 ft) distances. In rapid-fire pistol shooting, a total of 60 shots are fired from a distance of 25 m (83 ft).

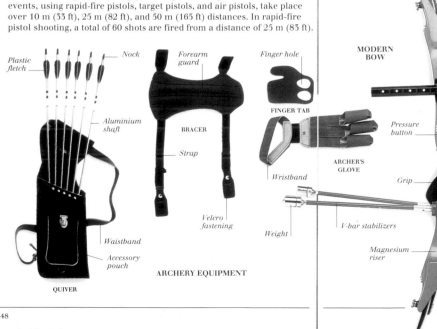

CROSSBOW AND BOLT

Laminated fibreglass bow

Bolt

Bolt rest

45 mm (1¼ in)

Stirrup held between feet when drawing bow

CROSSBOW TARGET

Sight

Hardwood laminate limb

Dacron string

MODERN BOW

Sight

Pressure button

Grip

V-bar stabilizers

Magnesium riser

Plastic fletch

Nock

Forearm guard

Finger hole

Aluminium shaft

BRACER

Strap

FINGER TAB

Wristband

ARCHER'S GLOVE

Velcro fastening

Weight

Waistband

Accessory pouch

ARCHERY EQUIPMENT

QUIVER

SMALLBORE BIATHLON RIFLE

Rifle sight without magnifying lens

Fore sight

Barrel

Trigger

Trigger guard

5.6 mm (0.22 in) calibre bullet

Magazine

Extra magazine stored in rifle butt

155 mm (6 in)

SMALLBORE FREE RIFLE TARGET FOR 50 M (165 FT) RANGE

BIGBORE HUNTING RIFLE

Bolt handle

Bolt

Telescopic sight

Open sight

Open sight

7.62 mm (0.3 in) calibre bullet

1 m (39 in)

BIGBORE RIFLE TARGET FOR 300 M (1000 FT) RANGE

Sling fixing point

AIR PISTOL

Cocking lever and barrel

Wooden grip shaped to fit the hand

Piston

155 mm (6 in)

TARGET PISTOL

197 mm (7¼ in)

AIR-PISTOL TARGET FOR 10 M (33 FT) RANGE

Back sight

Fore sight

Hammer

Firing pin

Sight pin

PISTOL TARGET FOR 18 M (60 FT) RANGE

Trigger

Air-pistol pellet

Sight ring attachment

Magazine

9 mm (0.35 in) calibre bullet

Nock

Metal tip

FIELD ARROW

Feathering

Straw butt

White inner 2 points

Wooden shaft

Blue outer 5 points

Aluminium longrod stabilizer

Yellow inner 10 points (bull's-eye)

ARCHERY TARGET

Ice hockey

ICE HOCKEY IS PLAYED by two teams of six players on an ice rink, with a goal net at each end. The object of this fast, and often dangerous, game is to hit a frozen rubber puck into the opposing team's net with a ice hockey stick. The game begins when the referee drops the puck between the sticks of two players from opposing teams, who "face off". The rink is divided into three areas: defending, neutral, and attacking zones. Players may move with the puck and pass the puck to one another along the ice, but may not pass it more than two zones across the rink markings. A goal is scored when the puck entirely crosses the goal-line between the posts and under the crossbar of the goal. A team may field up to 20 players although only six players are allowed on the ice at one time; substitutions occur frequently. Each game consists of three periods of 20 minutes, divided by breaks of 15 minutes.

GOALKEEPER

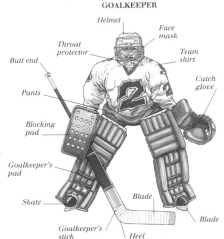

Helmet
Face mask
Throat protector
Team shirt
Butt end
Catch glove
Pants
Blocking pad
Goalkeeper's pad
Skate
Blade
Blade
Goalkeeper's stick
Heel

ICE HOCKEY RINK

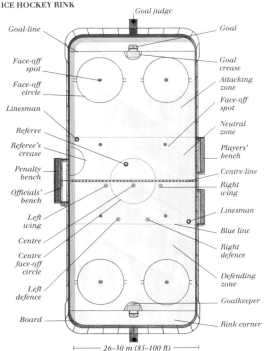

Goal judge
Goal-line
Goal
Face-off spot
Goal crease
Face-off circle
Attacking zone
Linesman
Face-off spot
Referee
Neutral zone
Referee's crease
Players' bench
Penalty bench
Centre-line
Officials' bench
Right wing
Left wing
Linesman
Centre
Blue line
Centre face-off circle
Right defence
Left defence
Defending zone
Board
Goalkeeper
Rink corner

— 26–30 m (85–100 ft) —

THE FACE-OFF

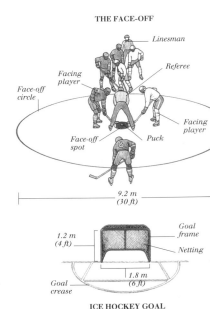

Linesman
Referee
Facing player
Face-off circle
Facing player
Face-off spot
Puck

9.2 m
(30 ft)

Goal frame
1.2 m
(4 ft)
Netting
1.8 m
(6 ft)
Goal crease

ICE HOCKEY GOAL

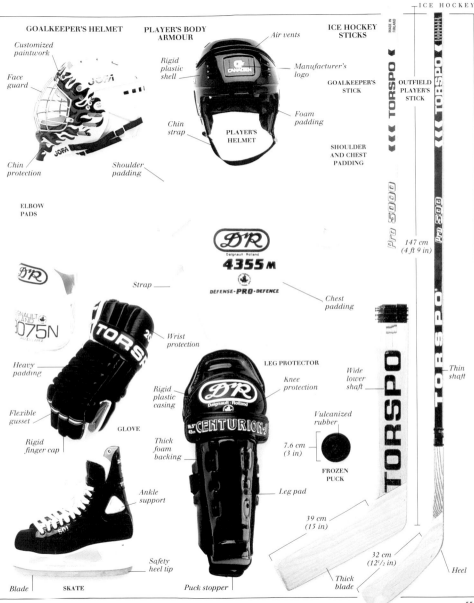

GOALKEEPER'S HELMET

Customized paintwork

Face guard

Chin protection

PLAYER'S BODY ARMOUR

Rigid plastic shell

Chin strap

Shoulder padding

Air vents

Manufacturer's logo

Foam padding

PLAYER'S HELMET

ICE HOCKEY STICKS

MADE IN FINLAND

GOALKEEPER'S STICK

OUTFIELD PLAYER'S STICK

SHOULDER AND CHEST PADDING

147 cm (4 ft 9 in)

ELBOW PADS

Pro 5000

Pro 500

Strap

4355 M

Dalgnault · Rolland

DÉFENSE · PRO · DEFENCE

Chest padding

3075N

Heavy padding

Flexible gusset

Rigid finger cap

GLOVE

Wrist protection

Rigid plastic casing

CENTURION

Thick foam backing

LEG PROTECTOR

Knee protection

Wide lower shaft

Vulcanized rubber

7.6 cm (3 in)

FROZEN PUCK

Leg pad

Thin shaft

Ankle support

Safety heel tip

Blade   SKATE

Puck stopper

39 cm (15 in)

32 cm (12½ in)

Thick blade

Heel

Alpine skiing

COMPETITIVE ALPINE SKIING is divided into four disciplines: downhill, slalom, giant slalom, and super-giant slalom (Super-G). Each one tests different skills. In downhill skiing, competitors race down a slope marked out by control flags, known as "gates", and are timed on a single run only. Competitors wear crash helmets, one-piece Lycra suits, and long skis with flattened tips to minimize air resistance. Slalom and giant slalom skiers negotiate a twisting course requiring balance, agility, and quick reactions. Courses are defined by pairs of gates. Racers must pass through each pair of gates to complete the course successfully. Competitors are timed on two runs over different courses, and the skier who completes the courses in the shortest time wins. The equipment and protective guards used by slalom skiiers are shown opposite. In Super-G races, competitors ski a single run that combines the technical challenge of slalom with the speed of downhill. The course requires skiers to complete medium-to-long radius turns at high speed, and contain up to two jumps. Clothing is the same as for downhill, but slightly shorter skis are used.

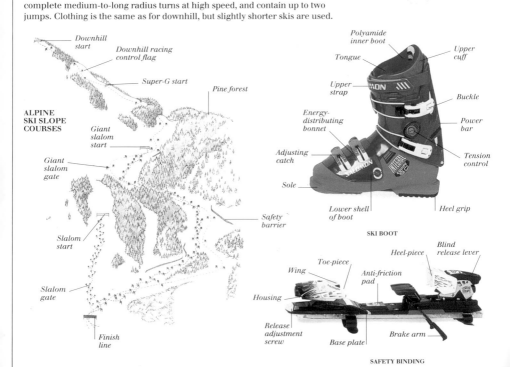

Ski goggles

Helmet

One-piece lycra ski suit

Wrist strap

Ski pole

Basket

Ski boot

Safety binding

Tail

Ski glove

ALPINE SKI SLOPE COURSES

Downhill start

Downhill racing control flag

Super-G start

Pine forest

Giant slalom start

Giant slalom gate

Slalom start

Slalom gate

Safety barrier

Finish line

Polyamide inner boot

Tongue

Upper cuff

Upper strap

Buckle

Energy-distributing bonnet

Power bar

Adjusting catch

Tension control

Sole

Lower shell of boot

Heel grip

SKI BOOT

Blind release lever

Heel-piece

Toe-piece

Wing

Anti-friction pad

Housing

Release adjustment screw

Base plate

Brake arm

SAFETY BINDING

SLALOM CLOTHING AND EQUIPMENT

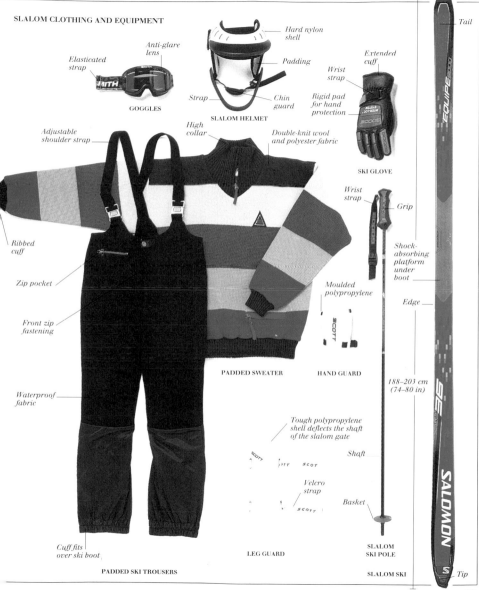

Anti-glare lens

Elasticated strap

GOGGLES

Hard nylon shell

Padding

Strap

Chin guard

SLALOM HELMET

Extended cuff

Wrist strap

Rigid pad for hand protection

SKI GLOVE

Tail

Adjustable shoulder strap

High collar

Double-knit wool and polyester fabric

Wrist strap

Grip

Ribbed cuff

Zip pocket

Front zip fastening

Shock-absorbing platform under boot

Edge

Moulded polypropylene

PADDED SWEATER

HAND GUARD

Waterproof fabric

188–203 cm (74–80 in)

Tough polypropylene shell deflects the shaft of the slalom gate

Shaft

Velcro strap

Basket

Cuff fits over ski boot

LEG GUARD

SLALOM SKI POLE

PADDED SKI TROUSERS

SLALOM SKI

Tip

Equestrian sports

EQUESTRIAN SPORTS HAVE TAKEN place throughout the world for centuries: events involving mounted horses were recorded in the Olympic Games of 642 BC. Showjumping, however, is a much more recent innovation, and the first competitions were held at the beginning of the 1900s. In this sport, horse and rider must negotiate a course of variable, unfixed obstacles, making as few mistakes as possible. Showjumping fences consist of wooden stands, known as standards or wings, that support planks or poles. Parts of the fence are designed to collapse on impact, preventing injury to the horse and rider. Judges penalise competitors for errors, such as knocking down obstacles, refusing jumps, or deviating from the course. Depending on the type of competition, the rider with the fewest faults, most points, or fastest time wins. There are two basic forms of horse racing – flat races and races with jumps, such as steeplechase or hurdle-races. Thoroughbred horses are used in this sport, as they have great strength and stamina and can achieve speeds of up to 65 kph (40 mph). Jockeys wear "silks" – caps and jackets designed in distinctive colours and patterns which help identify the horses. In harness racing, the horse is driven from a light, two-wheeled carriage called a sulky, and different races are held for each of these types of gait. In pacing races, the horses wear hobbles to prevent them from breaking into a trot or gallop. Breeds such as the Standardbred and the French Trotter have been developed especially for this sport.

SHOWJUMPING SADDLE

High cantle
Deep seat
Pommel
Forward-cut flap
Knee roll

SHOWJUMPING FENCES

Standard
Foot
Plank

UPRIGHT PLANKS

Standard
Foot
Pole

UPRIGHT POLES

Back pole
Standard
Foot
Pole

TRIPLE BAR (STAIRCASE)

Standard
Foot
Pole

HOG'S-BACK

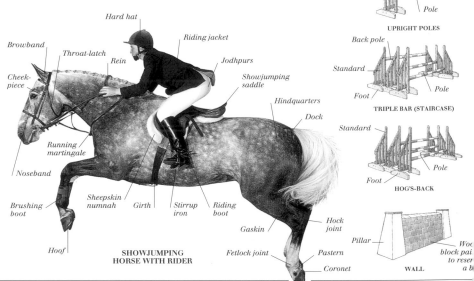

Hard hat
Riding jacket
Browband
Throat-latch
Rein
Jodhpurs
Cheek-piece
Showjumping saddle
Hindquarters
Dock
Running martingale
Noseband
Brushing boot
Sheepskin numnah
Girth
Stirrup iron
Riding boot
Hock joint
Gaskin
Hoof
SHOWJUMPING HORSE WITH RIDER
Fetlock joint
Pastern
Coronet
Pillar
Woo block pai to reser a b
WALL

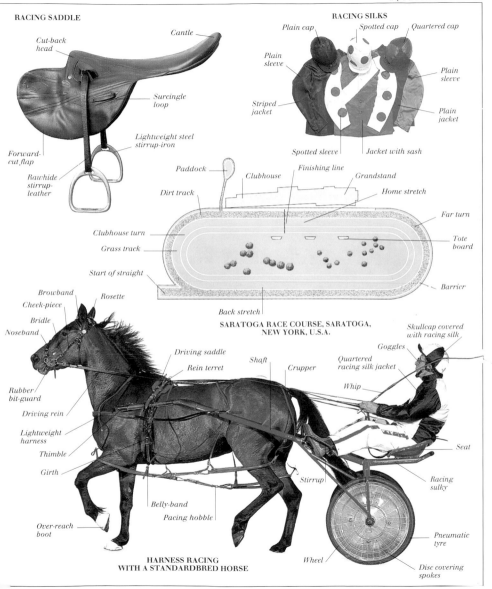

RACING SADDLE

Cut-back head

Cantle

Surcingle loop

Lightweight steel stirrup-iron

Forward-cut flap

Rawhide stirrup-leather

RACING SILKS

Plain cap

Spotted cap

Quartered cap

Plain sleeve

Plain sleeve

Striped jacket

Plain jacket

Spotted sleeve

Jacket with sash

Paddock

Clubhouse

Finishing line

Grandstand

Dirt track

Home stretch

Clubhouse turn

Far turn

Grass track

Tote board

Start of straight

Barrier

Back stretch

SARATOGA RACE COURSE, SARATOGA, NEW YORK, U.S.A.

Browband

Rosette

Driving saddle

Shaft

Crupper

Skullcap covered with racing silk

Cheek-piece

Rein terret

Goggles

Bridle

Quartered racing silk jacket

Noseband

Driving saddle

Whip

Rubber bit-guard

Driving rein

Lightweight harness

Seat

Thimble

Girth

Stirrup

Racing sulky

Belly-band

Pacing hobble

Over-reach boot

Pneumatic tyre

Wheel

Disc covering spokes

HARNESS RACING WITH A STANDARDBRED HORSE

555

Judo and fencing

COMBAT SPORTS ARE BASED ON THE SKILLS used in fighting. In these sports, the competitors may be unarmed – as in judo and boxing – or armed – as in fencing and kendo. Judo is a system of unarmed combat developed in the East. Translated from the Japanese the name means "the gentle way". Students learn how to turn an opponent's force to their own advantage. The usual costume is loose white trousers and a jacket, fastened with a cloth belt. The colour of belt indicates the student's level of expertise, from white-belted novices to the expert "black belts". Competitions take place on a mat or "shiaijo", 9 or 10 m (30 or 33 ft) square in size, bounded by "danger" and "safety" areas to prevent injury. Competitors try to throw, pin, or master their opponent by applying pressure to the arm joints or neck. Judo bouts are strictly monitored, and competitors receive points for superior technique, not for injuring their opponent. Fencing is a combat sport using swords, which takes place on a narrow "piste" 14 m (46 ft) long. Competitors try to touch specific target areas on their opponent with their sword or "foil" while avoiding being touched themselves. The winner is the one who scores the greatest number of hits. Fencers wear clothing made from strong white material, which affords maximum protection while allowing freedom of movement, steel mesh masks with padded bibs to protect the fencer's neck, and a long white glove on their sword hand. Fencing foils do not have sharpened blades, and their tips end in a blunt button to prevent injuries. Three types of swords are used – foils, épées, and sabres. Official foil and épée competitions always use an electric scoring system. The sword tips are connected to lights by a long wire that passes underneath each fencer's jacket. A bulb flashes when a hit is made.

SIDE FOUR QUARTER
HOLD

SINGLE WING

BODY DROP

ONE ARM SHOULDER
THROW

SHOULDER WHEEL

SWEEPING LOW
THROW

STOMACH THROW

KNEE WHEEL

JUDO KIT

JUDO MAT

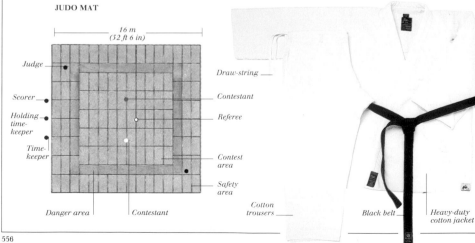

16 m
(52 ft 6 in)

Judge

Scorer

Holding
time-
keeper

Time-
keeper

Danger area

Contestant

Draw-string

Contestant

Referee

Contest
area

Safety
area

Cotton
trousers

Black belt

Heavy-duty
cotton jacket

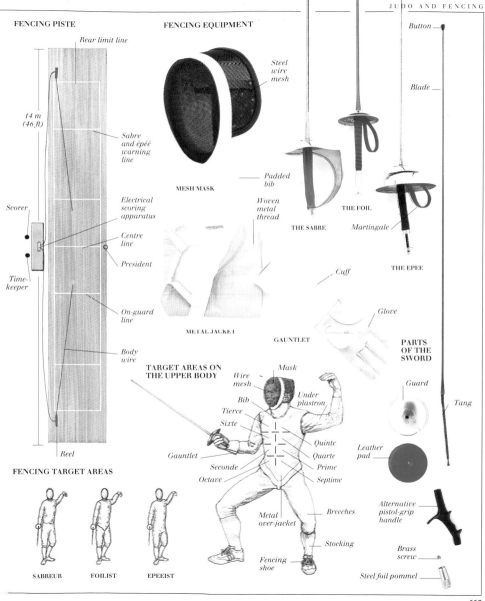

FENCING PISTE

Rear limit line

14 m
(46 ft)

Sabre
and épéé
warning
line

Scorer

Electrical
scoring
apparatus

Centre
line

President

Time-
keeper

On-guard
line

Body
wire

Reel

FENCING TARGET AREAS

SABREUR   FOILIST   EPEEIST

FENCING EQUIPMENT

Steel
wire
mesh

MESH MASK

Padded
bib

Woven
metal
thread

METAL JACKET

Cuff

GAUNTLET

Glove

Button

Blade

THE FOIL

THE SABRE

Martingale

THE EPEE

**PARTS
OF THE
SWORD**

Guard

Tang

Leather
pad

Alternative
pistol-grip
handle

Brass
screw

Steel foil pommel

**TARGET AREAS ON
THE UPPER BODY**

Wire
mesh

Mask

Under
plastron

Bib

Tierce

Sixte

Quinte

Quarte

Prime

Septime

Gauntlet

Seconde

Octave

Metal
over-jacket

Breeches

Stocking

Fencing
shoe

Swimming and diving

SWIMMING GOGGLES

SWIMMING WAS INCLUDED in the first modern Olympic Games in 1896 and diving events were added in 1904. Swimming is both an individual and a team sport and races take place over a predetermined distance in one of the four major categories of stroke – freestyle (usually front crawl), butterfly, breaststroke, and backstroke. Competition pools are clearly marked for racing and anti-turbulence lane lines are used to separate the swimmers and help keep the water calm. The first team or individual to finish the race is the winner. Competitive diving is divided into men's and women's springboard and platform (highboard) events. There are six official groups of dives: forward dives, backward dives, armstand dives, twist dives, reverse dives, and inward dives. Competitors perform a set number of dives and after each one a panel of judges awards marks according to the quality of execution and the degree of difficulty.

STYLES OF DIVES

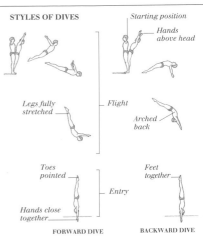

Starting position

Hands above head

Legs fully stretched

Flight

Arched back

Toes pointed

Entry

Hands close together

FORWARD DIVE

Feet together

BACKWARD DIVE

SWIMMING POOL

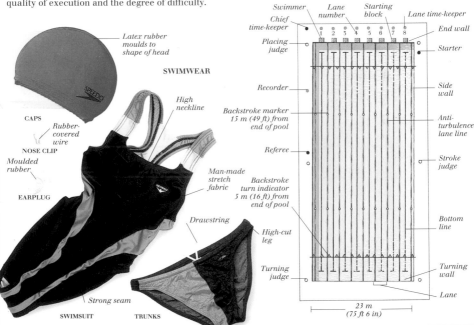

Latex rubber moulds to shape of head

SWIMWEAR

CAPS

High neckline

Rubber-covered wire

NOSE CLIP

Moulded rubber

Man-made stretch fabric

EARPLUG

Drawstring

High-cut leg

Strong seam

SWIMSUIT

TRUNKS

Swimmer

Lane number

Starting block

Lane time-keeper

Chief time-keeper

End wall

Placing judge

Starter

Recorder

Side wall

Backstroke marker 15 m (49 ft) from end of pool

Anti-turbulence lane line

Referee

Stroke judge

Backstroke turn indicator 5 m (16 ft) from end of pool

Bottom line

Turning judge

Turning wall

Lane

23 m (75 ft 6 in)

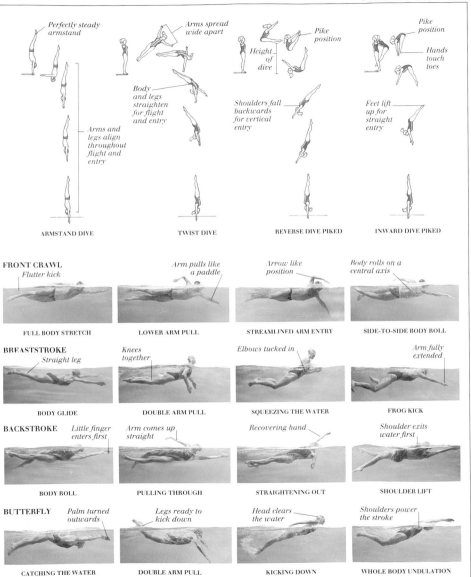

Perfectly steady armstand

Arms spread wide apart

Pike position

Pike position

Body and legs straighten for flight and entry

Height of dive

Hands touch toes

Arms and legs align throughout flight and entry

Shoulders fall backwards for vertical entry

Feet lift up for straight entry

ARMSTAND DIVE

TWIST DIVE

REVERSE DIVE PIKED

INWARD DIVE PIKED

FRONT CRAWL
Flutter kick

Arm pulls like a paddle

Arrow like position

Body rolls on a central axis

FULL BODY STRETCH

LOWER ARM PULL

STREAMLINED ARM ENTRY

SIDE-TO-SIDE BODY ROLL

BREASTSTROKE
Straight leg

Knees together

Elbows tucked in

Arm fully extended

BODY GLIDE

DOUBLE ARM PULL

SQUEEZING THE WATER

FROG KICK

BACKSTROKE
Little finger enters first

Arm comes up straight

Recovering hand

Shoulder exits water first

BODY ROLL

PULLING THROUGH

STRAIGHTENING OUT

SHOULDER LIFT

BUTTERFLY
Palm turned outwards

Legs ready to kick down

Head clears the water

Shoulders power the stroke

CATCHING THE WATER

DOUBLE ARM PULL

KICKING DOWN

WHOLE BODY UNDULATION

Canoeing, rowing, and sailing

WATERBORNE SPORTS are as varied as the crafts used. There are two disciplines in rowing; sweep rowing, in which each rower has one oar and sculling, in which rowers use two oars. There are a number of different Olympic and competitive rowing events for both men and women. The number of rowers and weight classes vary. Some rowing events use a coxswain; a steersman who does not row but directs the crew. Kayaks and canoes are used in straight sprint and slalom races. Slalom races take place over a course consisting of 20 to 25 gates, including at least six upstream gates. In yacht racing, competitors must complete prescribed courses, organized by the race committees, in the shortest possible time, using sail power only. Olympic events include classes for keel boats, dinghies, and catamarans.

SAILING GEAR

Buoyancy aid

Sleeveless long johns

Long-sleeved jacket

Neoprene material

Belt

GLOVE

Bootlace

Ribbed top

Non-slip sole

BOOT

ONE-PERSON KAYAK AND PADDLE

Blade

Rim

Shaft

Cockpit

Back strap

Stern

High density polythene

Toggle

Right rail

Nose cone

Bow

Left rail

Seat

Cockpit rim

**SINGLE SCULL AND OARS
(WITH CLOTH DECKING REMOVED)**

Adjusting screw

Gate clamp

Gate

Spoon   Blade   Colours

Neck

Shaft

Stroke-side oar

Rigger

Grip

Bow-side oar

Button

Loom

Stretcher

Sycamore beam

Water shoot

Keel

Sternpost

Spruce beam

Diagonal frame

Aluminium beam

Bung

Aft shoulder

Shoe

Kelson (keelson)

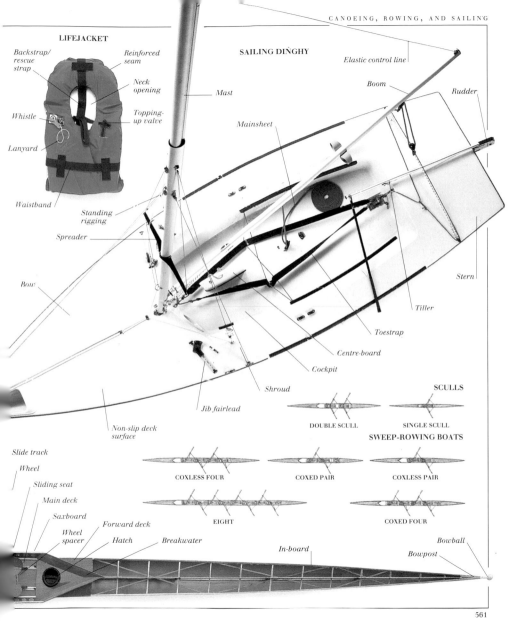

LIFEJACKET

Backstrap/rescue strap

Reinforced seam

Neck opening

Whistle

Topping-up valve

Lanyard

Waistband

Standing rigging

Spreader

Bow

SAILING DINGHY

Elastic control line

Boom

Rudder

Mast

Mainsheet

Stern

Tiller

Toestrap

Centre-board

Cockpit

Shroud

Jib fairlead

Non-slip deck surface

Slide track

Wheel

Sliding seat

Main deck

Saxboard

Wheel spacer

Forward deck

Hatch

Breakwater

In-board

Bowball

Bowpost

SCULLS

DOUBLE SCULL

SINGLE SCULL

SWEEP-ROWING BOATS

COXLESS FOUR

COXED PAIR

COXLESS PAIR

EIGHT

COXED FOUR

Angling

ANGLING MEANS FISHING WITH A ROD, reel, line, and lure. There are several different types of angling: freshwater coarse angling, for members of the carp family and pike; freshwater game angling, for salmon and trout; and sea angling, for sea fish such as flatfish, bass, and mackerel. Anglers use a variety of methods of catching fish. These include bait fishing, in which bait (food to allure the fish) is placed on a hook and cast into the water; fly fishing, in which a natural or artificial fly is used to lure the fish; and spinning, in which a lure that looks like a small fish revolves as it is pulled through the water. The angler uses the rod, reel, and line to cast the lure over the water. The reel controls the line as it spills off the spool and as it is wound back. Weights may be fixed to the line so that it will sink. Swivels are attached to prevent the line from twisting. When a fish bites, the hook must become embedded in its mouth and remain there while the catch is reeled in.

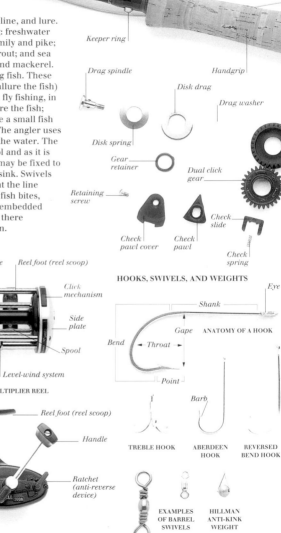

BUTT SECTION

Keeper ring

Drag spindle

Handgrip

Disk drag

Drag washer

Disk spring

Gear retainer

Dual click gear

Retaining screw

Check slide

Check pawl cover

Check pawl

Check spring

REELS

Spool-release button

Reel foot (reel scoop)

Plate-nut

Click mechanism

Mechanical brake

Side plate

Centrifugal brake

Spool

Handle

Star drag

Level-wind system

MULTIPLIER REEL

Reel foot (reel scoop)

Unskirted spool

Handle

Line

Ratchet (anti-reverse device)

Tension nut (drag adjustment)

Handgrip

Reel

Bail arm

FIXED-SPOOL REEL

HOOKS, SWIVELS, AND WEIGHTS

Eye

Shank

Gape   ANATOMY OF A HOOK

Bend

Throat

Point

Barb

TREBLE HOOK

ABERDEEN HOOK

REVERSED BEND HOOK

EXAMPLES OF BARREL SWIVELS

HILLMAN ANTI-KINK WEIGHT

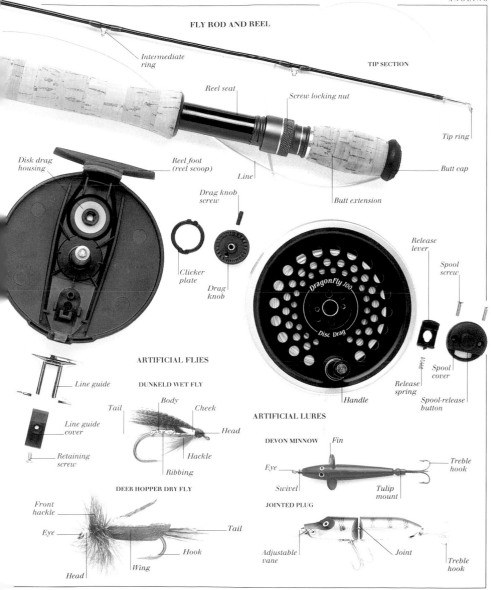

FLY ROD AND REEL

Intermediate ring

TIP SECTION

Reel seat

Screw locking nut

Tip ring

Disk drag housing

Reel foot (reel scoop)

Line

Butt cap

Drag knob screw

Butt extension

Release lever

Spool screw

DragonFly 100

Disc Drag

Clicker plate

Drag knob

Handle

Release spring

Spool cover

Spool-release button

Line guide

ARTIFICIAL FLIES

DUNKELD WET FLY

Tail

Body

Cheek

Head

Line guide cover

Hackle

Ribbing

Retaining screw

ARTIFICIAL LURES

DEVON MINNOW

Fin

Eye

Treble hook

Swivel

Tulip mount

DEER HOPPER DRY FLY

Front hackle

Eye

Tail

Hook

JOINTED PLUG

Wing

Head

Adjustable vane

Joint

Treble hook

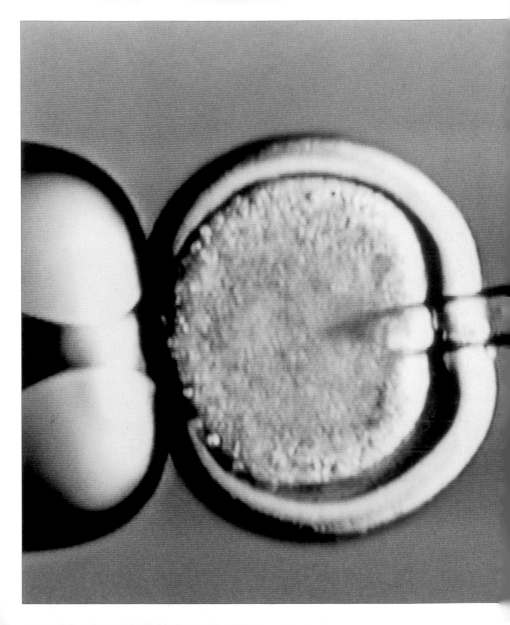

THE MODERN WORLD

PERSONAL COMPUTER · 566
HAND-HELD COMPUTER · · · · · · · · · · · · · · · · · 568
FLATBED SCANNER · 570
FAX MACHINE · 572
INKJET PRINTER · 574
THE INTERNET · 576
ELECTRONIC GAMES · · · · · · · · · · · · · · · · · · · 578
DIGITAL CAMERA · 580
DIGITAL VIDEO CAMERA · · · · · · · · · · · · · · · · 582
HOME CINEMA · 584
PERSONAL MUSIC · 586
MOBILE PHONE · 588
GLOBAL POSITIONING SYSTEM · · · · · · · · · · · 590
VACUUM CLEANER · 592
IRON AND WASHER-DRYER · · · · · · · · · · · · · · 594
MICROWAVE COMBINATION OVEN · · · · · · · · 596
TOASTER · 598
DRILL · 600
HOUSE OF THE FUTURE · · · · · · · · · · · · · · · · 602
RENEWABLE ENERGY · · · · · · · · · · · · · · · · · · 604
CLONING TECHNOLOGY · · · · · · · · · · · · · · · · 606
ROBOTS · 608
HIGH-PERFORMANCE MICROSCOPES · · · · · · · 610
SPACE TELESCOPE · 612
PROBING THE UNIVERSE · · · · · · · · · · · · · · · · 614

Personal computer

PERSONAL COMPUTERS (PCs) fall into two main types: IBM-compatible PCs, known simply as PCs, and Apple Macintosh PCs, known as "Macs". They differ in the way files and programs, and the user's access to them, are organized, and programs must be tailored for each type. However, in most other respects PCs and Macs have much in common. Both contain microchips, or integrated circuits, that store and process data. The "brain" of any PC is a chip known as the central processing unit (CPU), which performs mathematical operations in order to run program instructions and receive, store, and output data. The most powerful CPUs today perform over a billion calculations a second. Data can be input via CDs and other storage media, as well as via modems. Highly portable laptop PCs are also in widespread use. Most PCs are able to communicate with many other devices, from video cameras (see pp. 582–83) to personal data assistants (see pp. 568–69).

APPLE POWER MAC G4 1GHz DUAL PROCESSOR

Liquid crystal display (LCD)

System unit

Keyboard

Mouse

REAR VIEW OF SYSTEM UNIT

Lockable cover latch

Headphone socket

Modem port

Speaker socket

Ethernet network

Firewire ports

Universal serial bus (USB) ports

Access covers for PCI expansion slots

FRONT VIEW OF SYSTEM UNIT

Carrying handle

CD/DVD drive

Cooling vent

Zip expansion bay

Power socket

Cooling vent

Security lock port

Power button

Reset button

Speaker

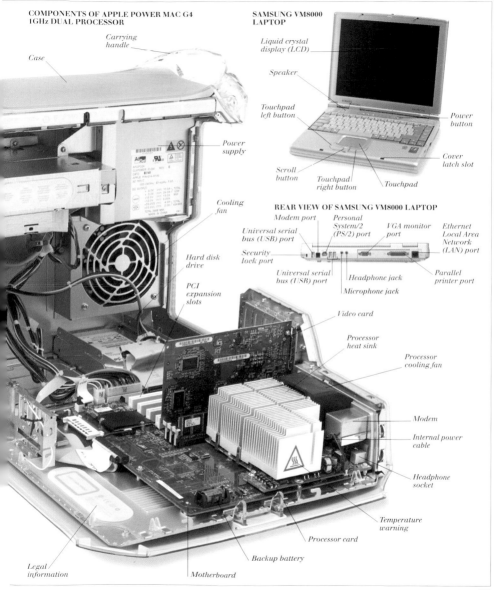

COMPONENTS OF APPLE POWER MAC G4 1GHz DUAL PROCESSOR

Carrying handle

Case

Power supply

Cooling fan

Hard disk drive

PCI expansion slots

Video card

Processor heat sink

Processor cooling fan

Modem

Internal power cable

Headphone socket

Temperature warning

Processor card

Backup battery

Legal information

Motherboard

SAMSUNG VM8000 LAPTOP

Liquid crystal display (LCD)

Speaker

Touchpad left button

Power button

Cover latch slot

Scroll button

Touchpad right button

Touchpad

REAR VIEW OF SAMSUNG VM8000 LAPTOP

Modem port

Personal System/2 (PS/2) port

VGA monitor port

Ethernet Local Area Network (LAN) port

Universal serial bus (USB) port

Security lock port

Universal serial bus (USB) port

Headphone jack

Microphone jack

Parallel printer port

Hand-held computer

PERSONAL DIGITAL ASSISTANTS (PDAs), or hand-held computers, are one of the many small electronic devices that began to be developed during the last years of the 20th century. There are two main types of PDA: those with integral keyboards and those without. PDAs with keyboards are larger and heavier than their keyboardless counterparts, which can be easily held in one hand. The latter employ a combination of touch-screen technology and handwriting-recognition programs to receive instructions and data. In order to write data into the PDA screen with a stylus, users must usually learn to use a special alphabet that the computer understands. PDAs are not intended to replace personal computers (PCs) – there is a high risk of losing data if the batteries are not recharged or replaced before they go flat. The contents of a PDA's memory needs to be regularly backed up on to a PC. Besides their basic programs, such as address book, calendar, and note pad, PDAs are increasingly absorbing the functions of other small electronic devices, such as MP3 players (see pp. 586–587), Global Positioning System (GPS) receivers (see pp. 590–591), and mobile phones (see pp. 588–589). Some can also access e-mail and the Internet.

Backlit liquid crystal display (LCD)

Applications launcher icon

Menu icon

Writing area

Power button/ backlight control/light-emitting diode (LED) indicator

Calculator icon

Zoom in/out icon

PALM M500 PDA

Alarm vibrator motor

FRONT CASE

Front bezel

Power button/ backlight control/ light-emitting diode (LED) indicator

BOTTOM VIEW OF PALM M500 PDA

Date book button

Scroll down buttton

"To Do" list button

Front case

Rear case

Address book button

HotSync™ connector

Note pad button

APPLICATION BUTTON ASSEMBLY

Date book button

Scroll up button

Note pad button

Writing tip

Address book button

STYLUS

Scroll down buttton

"To Do" list button

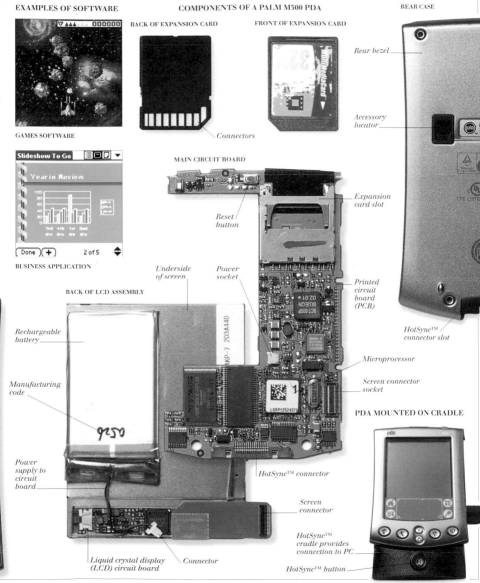

EXAMPLES OF SOFTWARE

COMPONENTS OF A PALM M500 PDA

REAR CASE

GAMES SOFTWARE

BACK OF EXPANSION CARD

FRONT OF EXPANSION CARD

Rear bezel

Accessory locator

Connectors

BUSINESS APPLICATION

MAIN CIRCUIT BOARD

Expansion card slot

Reset button

Underside of screen

Power socket

Printed circuit board (PCB)

HotSync™ connector slot

BACK OF LCD ASSEMBLY

Rechargeable battery

Manufacturing code

9250

Power supply to circuit board

Microprocessor

Screen connector socket

PDA MOUNTED ON CRADLE

HotSync™ connector

Screen connector

HotSync™ cradle provides connection to PC

Liquid crystal display (LCD) circuit board

Connector

HotSync™ button

Flatbed scanner

SCANNERS CONVERT physical images into electronic form, allowing them to be sent over the Internet, displayed on a website, stored on a computer, and manipulated using specialized software. Scanners work by detecting and analysing light reflected from an opaque image, such as a photographic print. Some can also scan photographic transparencies by analysing light that has passed through the image. Flatbed scanners contain a unit, called the scan head, that contains a lamp, mirrors, a lens, and an array of CCDs (Charge-Coupled Devices). The carriage passes beneath the image; the lamp shines light on to or through the original; the mirrors reflect the light on to the lens, which focuses it on to the CCD array. Each CCD detects the brightness of light from a particular pixel (picture element) along a horizontal strip and converts this data into an electric signal. For colour images, the light is usually passed through red, green, and blue filters and then directed to the CCD array so that it can be broken down into its component colours. This information is then converted to digital form. The quality of the image depends on its resolution, measured in dpi (Dots Per Inch).

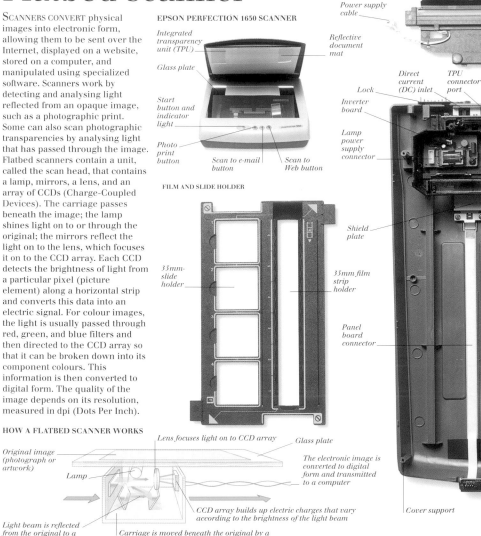

EPSON PERFECTION 1650 SCANNER

Integrated transparency unit (TPU)

Glass plate

Start button and indicator light

Photo print button

Scan to e-mail button

Scan to Web button

Power supply cable

Reflective document mat

Direct current (DC) inlet

TPU connector port

Lock

Inverter board

Lamp power supply connector

FILM AND SLIDE HOLDER

35mm-slide holder

35mm film strip holder

Shield plate

Panel board connector

HOW A FLATBED SCANNER WORKS

Original image (photograph or artwork)

Lamp

Lens focuses light on to CCD array

Glass plate

The electronic image is converted to digital form and transmitted to a computer

CCD array builds up electric charges that vary according to the brightness of the light beam

Light beam is reflected from the original to a series of mirrors

Carriage is moved beneath the original by a stepper motor in a rapid series of tiny steps

Cover support

UNDERSIDE OF SCAN HEAD COVER

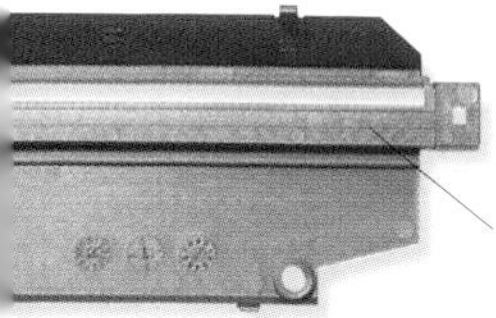

COMPONENTS OF AN
EPSON PERFECTION
1650 SCANNER

Underside of lamp housing

TPU connector

Hinge

LID ASSEMBLY

Glass plate

Lens assembly

Universal serial bus (USB) port

Ferrite core

Integrated transparency unit (TPU)

Scan head

Reflective document mat

Mirror

FCC cable

Carriage shaft

FCC cable slot

Finger recess

UNDERSIDE OF COVER

Underside of control panel

THE EFFECT OF SCANNING AT
DIFFERENT RESOLUTIONS

Pixel

OVERHEAD VIEW

Idler pulley

Control panel circuit board

15 DPI
Lowest resolution at which you may scan.

72 DPI
Used for websites and screen images.

300 DPI
Used for printing books and magazines.

Fax machine

FAX (FACSIMILE) MACHINES TRANSMIT and receive images of documents over the telephone network. Like a scanner (see pp. 570–571, a fax machine scans the original document in a series of horizontal strips, each composed of many pixels (picture elements). A page fed into the machine passes over a lamp whose light is reflected off the page on to an array of about 1,800 tiny CCDs (Charge-Coupled Devices). Each CCD detects the brightness of light reflected from a pixel in the current horizontal strip of the page and produces a corresponding electric signal. The signals are processed and transmitted to another fax machine, which reproduces the pixellated image as a series of black dots interspersed with unprinted, white areas.

COMPONENTS OF BROTHER T-78 FAX MACHINE

UNDERSIDE OF CONTROL PANEL CASING

Document pressure bar assembly

BROTHER T-78 FAX MACHINE

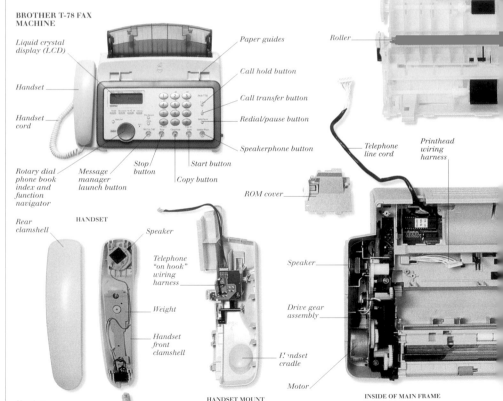

Liquid crystal display (LCD)

Handset

Handset cord

Rotary dial phone book index and function navigator

Message manager launch button

Stop button

Start button

Copy button

Paper guides

Call hold button

Call transfer button

Redial/pause button

Speakerphone button

Roller

Telephone line cord

Printhead wiring harness

ROM cover

HANDSET

Rear clamshell

Speaker

Telephone "on hook" wiring harness

Weight

Handset front clamshell

Speaker

Drive gear assembly

Handset cradle

Motor

HANDSET MOUNT

INSIDE OF MAIN FRAME

Handset cord

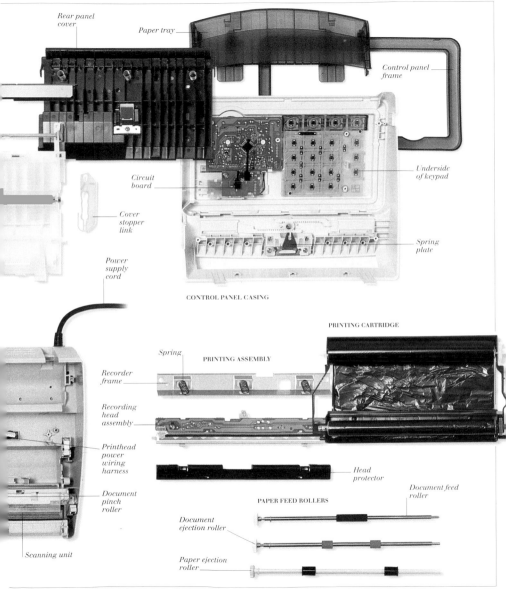

Rear panel cover

Paper tray

Control panel frame

Underside of keypad

Circuit board

Cover stopper link

Spring plate

Power supply cord

CONTROL PANEL CASING

PRINTING CARTRIDGE

Spring

PRINTING ASSEMBLY

Recorder frame

Recording head assembly

Printhead power wiring harness

Document pinch roller

Head protector

Document feed roller

PAPER FEED ROLLERS

Document ejection roller

Paper ejection roller

Scanning unit

573

Inkjet printer

INKJET PRINTERS EXPEL ink droplets from hundreds of tiny jets, or nozzles, on to a medium, such as paper, to print an image. Each droplet corresponds to a single pixel (picture element). Black-and-white printers use only black ink, while colour printers overprint combinations of the printing colours (cyan, yellow, magenta, and black) to create a full colour range. The printhead containing the nozzles moves sideways across the paper, creating a line of pixels, before the paper moves slightly forward so the next line can be printed. Two basic methods are used to eject ink: thermal, in which ink is heated to form an expanding bubble that expels a droplet from the nozzle, and piezoelectric, in which an electric current expands a crystal causing it to push out the ink droplet. The printer shown here can print digital photographs directly from a memory card.

EPSON STYLUS PHOTO 895 COLOUR INKJET PRINTER

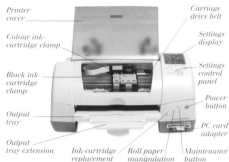

OVERHEAD VIEW WITH OUTER CASING REMOVED

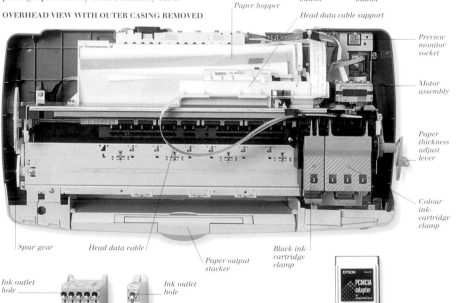

INK CARTRIDGES

PC CARD ADAPTER

PAPER FEED COMPONENTS

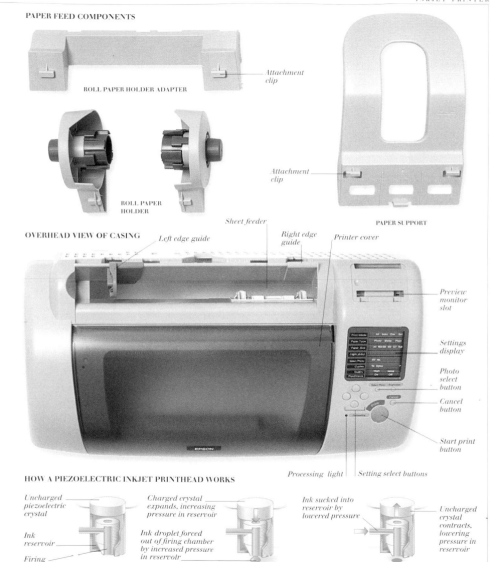

Attachment clip

ROLL PAPER HOLDER ADAPTER

ROLL PAPER HOLDER

Attachment clip

PAPER SUPPORT

OVERHEAD VIEW OF CASING

Sheet feeder

Left edge guide

Right edge guide

Printer cover

Preview monitor slot

Settings display

Photo select button

Cancel button

Start print button

Processing light *Setting select buttons*

HOW A PIEZOELECTRIC INKJET PRINTHEAD WORKS

Uncharged piezoelectric crystal

Charged crystal expands, increasing pressure in reservoir

Ink sucked into reservoir by lowered pressure

Uncharged crystal contracts, lowering pressure in reservoir

Ink reservoir

Ink droplet forced out of firing chamber by increased pressure in reservoir

Firing chamber

INKJET NOZZLE

DROPLET EJECTED

CHAMBER REFILLED

The Internet

THE INTERNET CONSISTS OF TENS of thousands of computer networks linked together to form one huge, global network, allowing any computer on one network to communicate with any computer on another. The two main services used on the Internet are e-mail and the World Wide Web. E-mail allows text messages to be sent – along with attached computer files, images, or video clips, for example – to other computers on the Internet. The Web consists of billions of pages made up of digital files that are stored on computers across the world and can be viewed using a Web browser. The Web also provides interactive access to various services, such as banking and shopping.

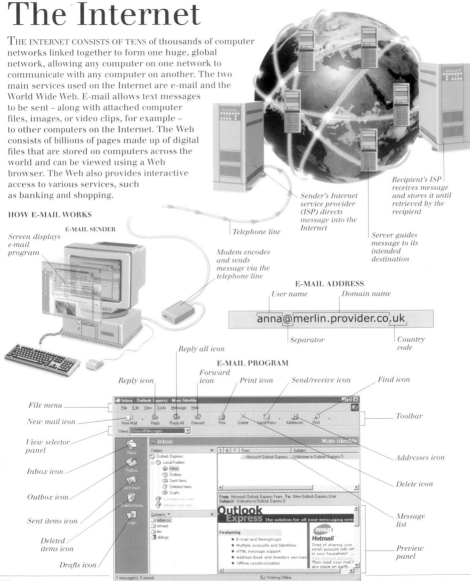

Recipient's ISP receives message and stores it until retrieved by the recipient

Sender's Internet service provider (ISP) directs message into the Internet

Server guides message to its intended destination

Telephone line

HOW E-MAIL WORKS

E-MAIL SENDER

Screen displays e-mail program

Modem encodes and sends message via the telephone line

E-MAIL ADDRESS

User name   *Domain name*

anna@merlin.provider.co.uk

Separator   *Country code*

E-MAIL PROGRAM

Reply all icon

Forward icon

Reply icon   *Print icon*   *Send/receive icon*   *Find icon*

File menu

New mail icon

View selector panel

Inbox icon

Outbox icon

Sent items icon

Deleted items icon

Drafts icon

Toolbar

Addresses icon

Delete icon

Message list

Preview panel

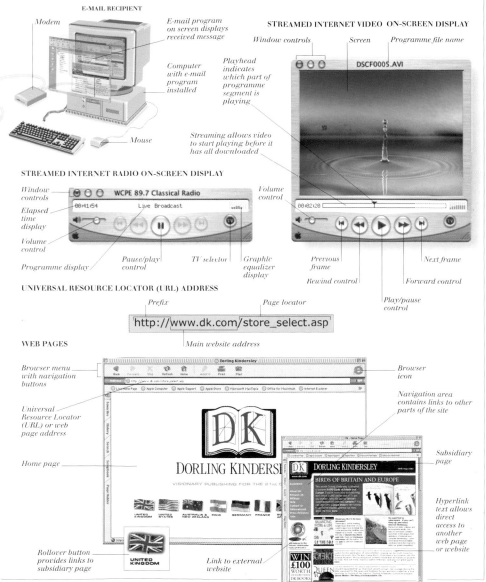

E-MAIL RECIPIENT

Modem

E-mail program on screen displays received message

Computer with e-mail program installed

Mouse

Playhead indicates which part of programme segment is playing

Streaming allows video to start playing before it has all downloaded

STREAMED INTERNET VIDEO ON-SCREEN DISPLAY

Window controls

Screen

Programme file name

DSCF000S.AVI

00:02:20

Previous frame

Next frame

Rewind control

Forward control

Play/pause control

STREAMED INTERNET RADIO ON-SCREEN DISPLAY

Window controls

Elapsed time display

Volume control

WCPE 89.7 Classical Radio

00:41:54

Live Broadcast

Volume control

Programme display

Pause/play control

TV selector

Graphic equalizer display

UNIVERSAL RESOURCE LOCATOR (URL) ADDRESS

Prefix

Page locator

http://www.dk.com/store_select.asp

Main website address

WEB PAGES

Browser menu with navigation buttons

Universal Resource Locator (URL) or web page address

Home page

Dorling Kindersley

Back Forward Stop Refresh Home AutoFill Print Mail

http://www.dk.com/store_select.asp

Live Home Page   Apple Computer   Apple Support   Apple Store   Microsoft MacTopia   Office for Macintosh   Internet Explorer

DK

DORLING KINDERSLEY

VISIONARY PUBLISHING FOR THE 21st C

UNITED KINGDOM   UNITED STATES   AUSTRALIA & NEW ZEALAND   INDIA   GERMANY   FRANCE

UNITED KINGDOM

Browser icon

Navigation area contains links to other parts of the site

Subsidiary page

Hyperlink text allows direct access to another web page or website

DK   DORLING KINDERSLEY

BIRDS OF BRITAIN AND EUROPE

WIN £100 WORTH of DK BOOKS

Rollover button provides links to subsidiary page

Link to external website

Electronic games

VIDEO GAMES HAVE BEEN around since the early 1970s. They are played on PCs, arcade machines, home consoles, and portable handheld players. All these types of players have certain components in common. They need devices such as joysticks and control pads with buttons for controlling movement and action on screen. The game itself is stored in the form of digital information on CD, DVD or microchip – which may be integral or stored in a removable cartridge – or on an internal hard disk. A central processing unit (CPU) (see pp. 566–567) is needed to process commands from the player, while specialized graphics chips are used to process the complex mapping and texturing functions that make modern games appear so realistic.

GAME BOY ADVANCE

Left shoulder button

Directional button pad

Screen

Outside of lower clamshell

Right shoulder button

'A' button

'B' button

Battery terminal

Start button

Select button

Speaker panel

LOWER CLAMSHELL

Ribbon cable connector

Left shoulder button

Button contact

On/off switch

UPPER CLAMSHELL AND DISPLAY

GAME BOY ADVANCE GAMES

High-resolution colour graphics

Fantasy quest story line

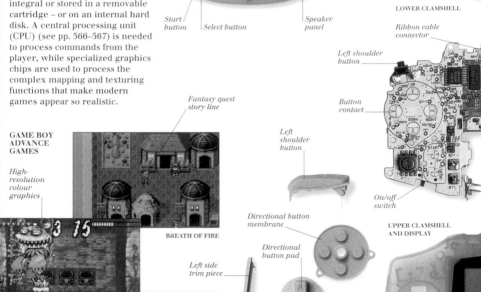

Left shoulder button

BREATH OF FIRE

Directional button membrane

Directional button pad

Left side trim piece

WARIO LAND 4

Score panel

DOOM

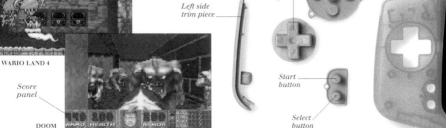

Start button

Select button

Game cartridge

PLAYSTATION 2

Memory card slot

Console

Dual shock controller

Controller port

CD

Disc loading tray

Wrist-strap attachment

Battery tray

MOTHERBOARD

Right shoulder button

Memory microchip

MICROSOFT XBOX

CONSOLE

Disc tray

Power button

Analogue thumbstick

Universal serial bus (USB) ports

8-way D-pad

32-bit central processing unit (CPU)

Mylar cone speaker

Right shoulder button

Analogue action buttons

CONTROLLER

Colour liquid crystal display (LCD) screen

Volume control dial

NINTENDO CUBE

Name plate

Power indicator light

"B" button

"A" button

CD eject button

Cooling vent

Power button

A and B button membrane

Handle

Right side trim piece

TV connector

ADVANCE

Digital camera

FOR MORE THAN 200 YEARS, CAMERAS recorded pictures as chemical changes in silver-containing substances, on a strip of flexible, celluloid film. The digital camera records pictures in electronic form. At its heart is a specialized integrated circuit known as a charge-coupled device (CCD). This has millions of micro-units known as pixels. It works in the opposite way to a miniature computer or TV screen. Instead of electric signals making pixels shine, when light hits a pixel it generates a tiny electrical signal, according to the light's colour and brightness. The signals from the CCD's millions of pixels are analogue: they vary continuously in a wave-like fashion. They are converted by a microchip to digital codes of numbers, represented as on-off electronic pulses. The digital signals are processed and fed both to the in-camera memory chip, which holds a temporary version, and the memory stick, which can be removed to download its contents into a computer or television. The rest of the camera is similar to the traditional design.

FRONT VIEW OF SONY CYBER-SHOT DSC-P1 DIGITAL CAMERA

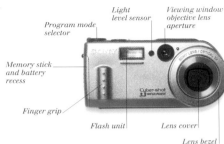

Light level sensor

Viewing window objective lens aperture

Program mode selector

Memory stick and battery recess

Finger grip

Flash unit

Lens cover

Lens bezel

LENS ZOOM AND FOCUS

CCD ribbon connector

CCD window

Lens mounting bracket

CCD board

CCD microchip

Drive gear access hole

Zoom motor

098B

Drive pin

Locating pin

Lens inner barrel (zoom/focus)

Achromatic multi-lens

Viewing window objective lens aperture

Flash unit aperture

SONY

Cyber-shot
3.3 MEGA PIXELS

Finger grip

FRONT PANEL

HOW A DIGITAL CAMERA WORKS

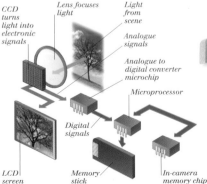

CCD turns light into electronic signals

Lens focuses light

Light from scene

Analogue signals

Analogue to digital converter microchip

Microprocessor

Digital signals

LCD screen

Memory stick

In-camera memory chip

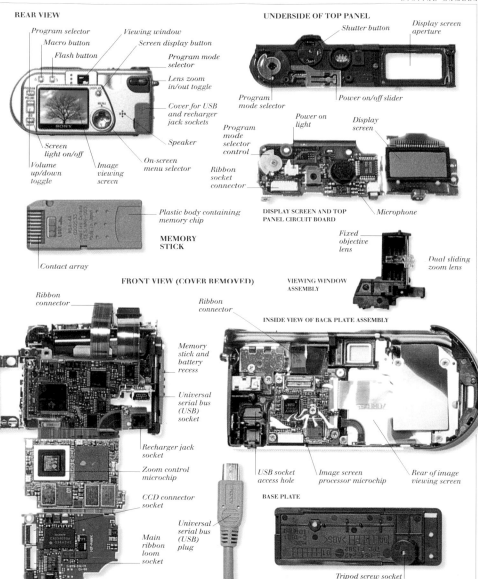

REAR VIEW

Program selector
Macro button
Flash button
Viewing window
Screen display button
Program mode selector
Lens zoom in/out toggle
Cover for USB and recharger jack sockets
Speaker
On-screen menu selector
Image viewing screen
Screen light on/off
Volume up/down toggle

UNDERSIDE OF TOP PANEL

Shutter button
Display screen aperture
Program mode selector
Power on/off slider

Program mode selector control
Power on light
Display screen
Ribbon socket connector
Microphone

DISPLAY SCREEN AND TOP PANEL CIRCUIT BOARD

Plastic body containing memory chip
Contact array

MEMORY STICK

Fixed objective lens
Dual sliding zoom lens

VIEWING WINDOW ASSEMBLY

FRONT VIEW (COVER REMOVED)

Ribbon connector
Ribbon connector
Memory stick and battery recess
Universal serial bus (USB) socket
Recharger jack socket
Zoom control microchip
CCD connector socket
Main ribbon loom socket
Universal serial bus (USB) plug

INSIDE VIEW OF BACK PLATE ASSEMBLY

USB socket access hole
Image screen processor microchip
Rear of image viewing screen

BASE PLATE

Tripod screw socket

581

Digital video camera

A VIDEO CAMERA, OR CAMCORDER, records a scene as a sequence of 25 still images per second, along with sound. It comprises a camera to capture light from the scene, a viewfinder through which the scene may be viewed, a screen on which the recorded scene may be viewed, charge-coupled devices (CCDs) to convert the visual data into an electric signal, and a means of storing the signal. Digital video cameras convert the signal into digital form – a series of separate measurements of the initial analogue (continuously varying) signal. They record the digital signal on tape, hard disk, or DVD. Digital recordings can be copied accurately, whereas analogue recordings tend to "fade" with each copy.

SONY DIGITAL HANDYCAM

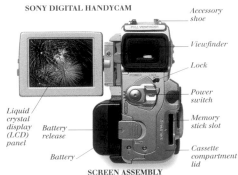

Accessory shoe

Viewfinder

Lock

Power switch

Memory stick slot

Cassette compartment lid

Liquid crystal display (LCD) panel

Battery release

Battery

SCREEN ASSEMBLY

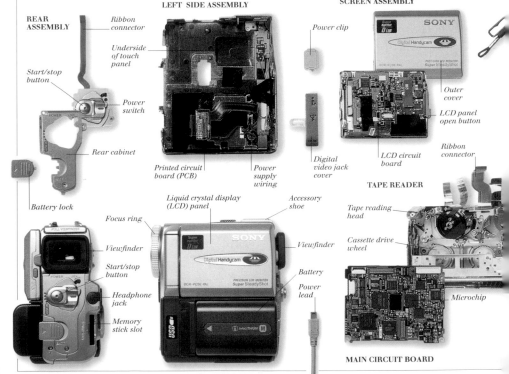

LEFT SIDE ASSEMBLY

REAR ASSEMBLY

Ribbon connector

Underside of touch panel

Start/stop button

Power switch

Rear cabinet

Printed circuit board (PCB)

Power supply wiring

Power clip

Digital video jack cover

Outer cover

LCD panel open button

Ribbon connector

LCD circuit board

TAPE READER

Tape reading head

Cassette drive wheel

Battery lock

Focus ring

Liquid crystal display (LCD) panel

Accessory shoe

Viewfinder

Start/stop button

Headphone jack

Memory stick slot

Viewfinder

Battery

Power lead

Microchip

MAIN CIRCUIT BOARD

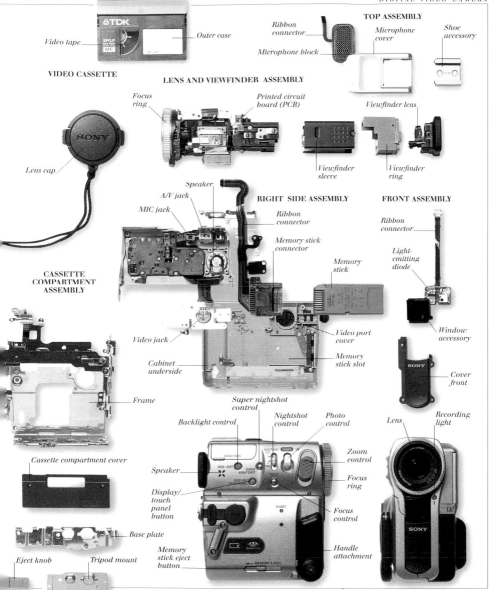

VIDEO CASSETTE

Video tape

Outer case

TOP ASSEMBLY

Ribbon connector

Microphone cover

Microphone block

Shoe accessory

LENS AND VIEWFINDER ASSEMBLY

Focus ring

Printed circuit board (PCB)

Viewfinder lens

Viewfinder sleeve

Viewfinder ring

Lens cap

SONY

CASSETTE COMPARTMENT ASSEMBLY

Speaker

A/V jack

MIC jack

RIGHT SIDE ASSEMBLY

Ribbon connector

Memory stick connector

Memory stick

FRONT ASSEMBLY

Ribbon connector

Light-emitting diode

Window accessory

Video jack

Video port cover

Cabinet underside

Memory stick slot

Frame

Cover front

Cassette compartment cover

Super nightshot control

Backlight control

Nightshot control

Photo control

Lens

Recording light

Speaker

Zoom control

Focus ring

Display/touch panel button

Focus control

Base plate

Eject knob

Tripod mount

Memory stick eject button

Handle attachment

SONY

Home cinema

HOME CINEMA REPLICATES a real "movie theatre" with visuals from a plasma wide-screen, and acoustics from strategically sited loudspeakers that give the viewer/listener the sense of being surrounded by sound. The source for sound and vision is a DVD (Digital Versatile Disc). Its player uses standard CD (Compact Disc) digital technology, but with a higher density of laser-read microscopic pits – more than 20 billion such pits in multi-level spiral tracks that, stretched out, would extend for about 40 kilometres. It is hard for the human ear to discern the direction of low-pitched sounds, so these emanate from a central bass speaker, often built into or below the screen unit. The direction of high-pitched sounds, like people screaming and tyres squealing, is easier to detect. Mid- and high-frequency speakers are positioned around the viewer, so these sounds fit the location of the action. Plasma screens use fluorescent tube ("strip-light") technology. Tiny three-cell pixels, each about one millimetre across, contain red, green and blue phosphor chemicals and a gas mix. Where electric pulses coincide for a split second in the criss-cross matrix of wire electrodes, the gas energizes and emits ultraviolet light, which in turn makes the phosphor glow.

SPEAKER UNITS

Large, heavy cabinet emphasizes deep-pitched sounds

Small cabinet for discrete mounting on stand or shelf

Bass ports emit vibrating air of low-frequency sound waves

Acoustically transparent covering allows all sounds to pass through

TWEETER (MID AND HIGH NOTES)　　　WOOFER (DEEP NOTES)

HOW SURROUND SOUND WORKS

DVD player under screen

Woofer (bass unit)

Front left sound channel

Rear left sound channel

Plasma screen

Front right sound channel

Region of most realistic sound reception

Rear right sound channel

WIDE-SCREEN PLASMA DISPLAY

Mid-grey bezel

HOW A PLASMA SCREEN WORKS

Rear dielectric sandwich

Phosphor lining cell

Front dielectric sandwich

Red cell

Green cell

Blue cell (glowing)

Inert gas in cell

Main screen

Rear panel

Rear energized electrode

Rear un-energized electrode

Cell barrier

Pixel boundary

Front energized electrode

Front un-energized electrode

Damped anti-shock swivel base

16:9 (width:height) screen proportions fit human field of vision

Anti-glare screen surface

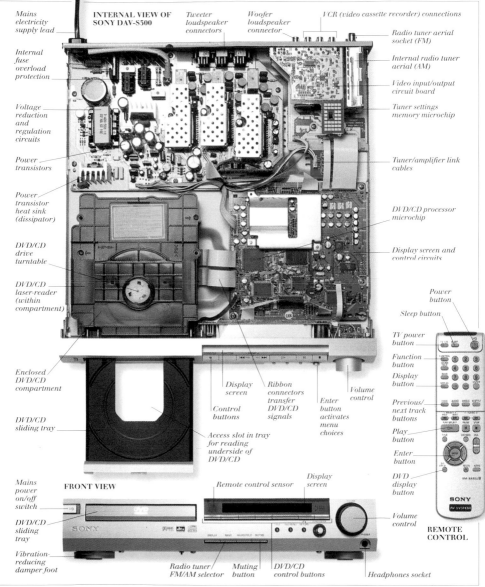

Mains electricity supply lead

INTERNAL VIEW OF SONY DAV-S500

Tweeter loudspeaker connectors

Woofer loudspeaker connector

VCR (video cassette recorder) connections

Radio tuner aerial socket (FM)

Internal fuse overload protection

Internal radio tuner aerial (AM)

Video input/output circuit board

Voltage reduction and regulation circuits

Tuner settings memory microchip

Power transistors

Tuner/amplifier link cables

Power transistor heat sink (dissipator)

DVD/CD processor microchip

DVD/CD drive turntable

Display screen and control circuits

DVD/CD laser-reader (within compartment)

Power button

Sleep button

TV power button

Enclosed DVD/CD compartment

Function button

Display button

DVD/CD sliding tray

Display screen

Ribbon connectors transfer DVD/CD signals

Volume control

Previous/ next track buttons

Control buttons

Enter button activates menu choices

Play button

Access slot in tray for reading underside of DVD/CD

Enter button

Mains power on/off switch

FRONT VIEW

Remote control sensor

Display screen

DVD display button

DVD/CD sliding tray

Volume control

Vibration-reducing damper foot

Radio tuner FM/AM selector

Muting button

DVD/CD control buttons

Headphones socket

SONY

AV SYSTEM

REMOTE CONTROL

Personal music

THE FIRST SOURCE OF SOUND and music small and light enough to carry, and functioning without external electricity, was the transistor radio of the 1950s. In the 1970s, the magnetic audio cassette tape allowed recorded music to be played via portable tape players such as Sony's *Walkman*. Also, new metal alloys permitted the tiny but high-power magnets needed for lightweight earphones. In the mid 1980s optical CDs (compact discs) brought recorded sound into the digital era. Sony's MD or minidisc introduced re-recordable CDs combining magnetic and optical technology. From the mid 1990s music could be stored in all-electronic digital form in a memory "chip", usually in the file format called MP3. These files can be sent to and from computers and via the Internet.

SONY PORTABLE MINIDISC PLAYER MZ-EP11

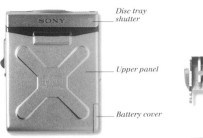

- Disc tray shutter
- Upper panel
- Battery cover

MINIDISC

- Access window sliding cover
- Read/write access window

SONY HEADPHONES

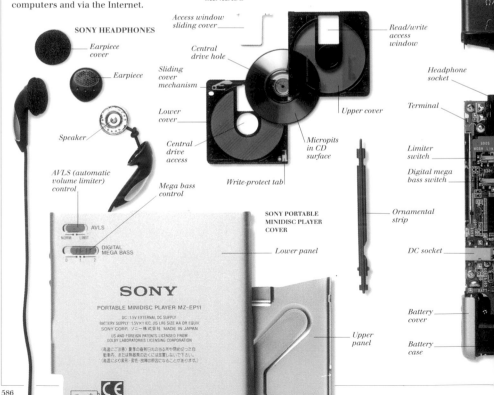

- Earpiece cover
- Earpiece
- Central drive hole
- Sliding cover mechanism
- Lower cover
- Speaker
- Central drive access
- Upper cover
- Micropits in CD surface
- AVLS (automatic volume limiter) control
- Mega bass control
- Write-protect tab
- Headphone socket
- Terminal
- Limiter switch
- Digital mega bass switch
- Ornamental strip
- DC socket

SONY PORTABLE MINIDISC PLAYER COVER

- Lower panel
- Upper panel
- Battery cover
- Battery case

AVLS
NORM LIMIT
DIGITAL MEGA BASS

SONY

PORTABLE MINIDISC PLAYER MZ-EP11

DC: 1.5V EXTERNAL DC SUPPLY
BATTERY SUPPLY: 1.5V×1 IEC, JIS LR6 SIZE AA DR EQUIV.
SONY CORP. ソニー株式会社 MADE IN JAPAN

US AND FOREIGN PATENTS LICENSED FROM
DOLBY LABORATORIES LICENSING CORPORATION

（高温にご注意）夏季の閉め切った自動車内、または熱器具の近くには放置しないで下さい。
（高温による変形・故障の原因になることがあります。）

CE

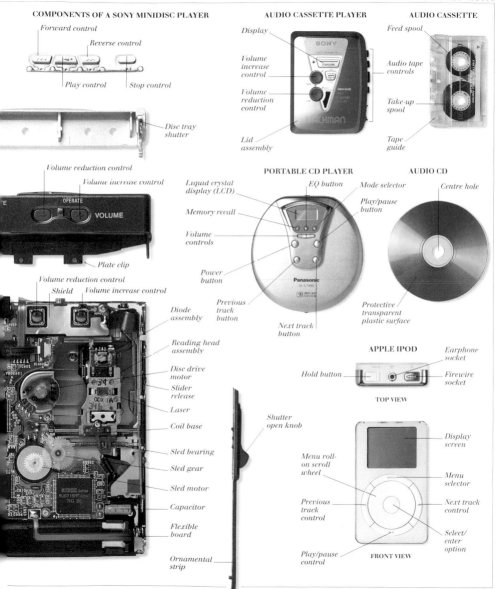

COMPONENTS OF A SONY MINIDISC PLAYER

Forward control

Reverse control

Play control

Stop control

Disc tray shutter

Volume reduction control

Volume increase control

OPERATE VOLUME

Plate clip

Volume reduction control

Shield   Volume increase control

Diode assembly

Reading head assembly

Disc drive motor

Slider release

Laser

Coil base

Sled bearing

Sled gear

Sled motor

Capacitor

Flexible board

Ornamental strip

AUDIO CASSETTE PLAYER

Display

Volume increase control

Volume reduction control

Lid assembly

SONY

WALKMAN

AUDIO CASSETTE

Feed spool

Audio tape controls

Take-up spool

Tape guide

PORTABLE CD PLAYER

Liquid crystal display (LCD)

EQ button

Mode selector

Play/pause button

Memory recall

Volume controls

Power button

Previous track button

Next track button

Panasonic

AUDIO CD

Centre hole

Protective transparent plastic surface

APPLE IPOD

Earphone socket

Hold button

Firewire socket

TOP VIEW

Shutter open knob

Display screen

Menu roll-on scroll wheel

Menu selector

Previous track control

Next track control

Play/pause control

Select/ enter option

FRONT VIEW

587

Mobile phone

IN THE EARLY 1990S, THE MOBILE PHONE (or cellphone) was
still a rare luxury, but by the end of the decade it outsold
almost every other electrical gadget – as a professional tool,
domestic convenience, and even a fashion accessory. A typical
mobile phone has also shrunk in size, due to improvements in
rechargeable batteries, which now store more electricity for
longer in a smaller package, and to smaller, more efficient
electronics that use less electricity. A "mobile" is basically a
low-power radio receiver-transmitter, plus a tiny microphone
to convert sounds into electrical signals, and a small speaker
that does the reverse. A liquid crystal display (LCD) shows
numbers, letters, and symbols. Newer models have a larger
screen for more complex images in colour, and some incorporate
other functions such as Internet access, radio, and an audio
player. When the mobile phone is activated, it sends out a radio
pulse that is answered by nearby mast transmitter-receivers.
The phone locks onto the clearest signal and uses this while
within range (the range of each transmitter is known as a
cell). The phone continuously monitors signal strength and
switches to an alternative transmitter when necessary.

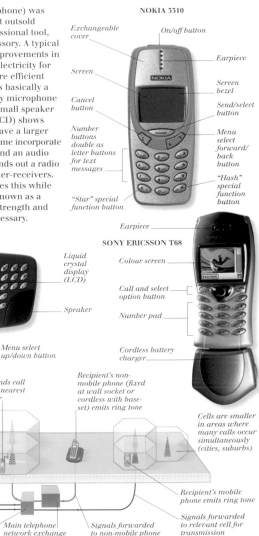

NOKIA 3510

Exchangeable cover

On/off button

Earpiece

Screen

Screen bezel

Cancel button

Send/select button

Number buttons double as letter buttons for text messages

Menu select forward/ back button

"Hash" special function button

"Star" special function button

NOKIA 5510

Upper number pad

Letter keys

Special function buttons

Liquid crystal display (LCD)

Speaker

Screen surround

Power button

Call-send button

Menu select up/down button

Earpiece

SONY ERICSSON T68

Colour screen

Call and select option button

Number pad

Cordless battery charger

HOW A MOBILE PHONE WORKS

Phone locks onto signals from local mast within home cell

Caller sends call signal to nearest cell tower

Recipient's non-mobile phone (fixed at wall socket or cordless with base-set) emits ring tone

Cells are smaller in areas where many calls occur simultaneously (cities, suburbs)

Phone out of signal range – no reception

Activated phone auto-switches to signals from next cell as it moves across cell boundary

Landlines (or tower-to-tower links) carry phone signals to local exchange

Local mobile phone network exchange

Main telephone network exchange

Signals forwarded to non-mobile phone

Recipient's mobile phone emits ring tone

Signals forwarded to relevant cell for transmission

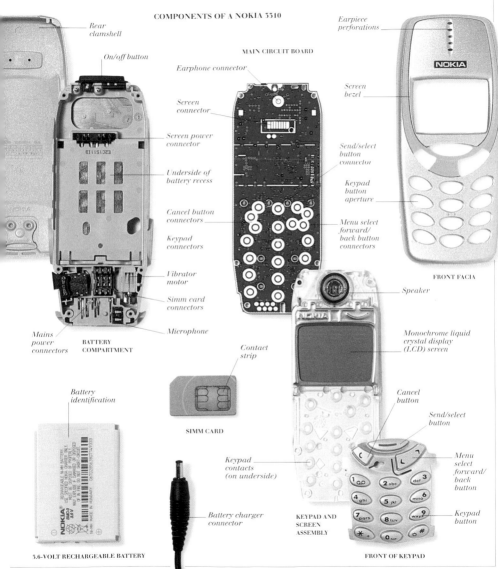

COMPONENTS OF A NOKIA 3310

Rear clamshell

On/off button

Earpiece perforations

MAIN CIRCUIT BOARD

Earphone connector

Screen connector

Screen power connector

Underside of battery recess

Cancel button connectors

Keypad connectors

Vibrator motor

Simm card connectors

Mains power connectors

BATTERY COMPARTMENT

Microphone

Screen bezel

Send/select button connector

Keypad button aperture

Menu select forward/ back button connectors

FRONT FACIA

Speaker

Monochrome liquid crystal display (LCD) screen

Cancel button

Send/select button

Menu select forward/ back button

Keypad button

KEYPAD AND SCREEN ASSEMBLY

FRONT OF KEYPAD

Contact strip

SIMM CARD

Keypad contacts (on underside)

Battery identification

Battery charger connector

3.6-VOLT RECHARGEABLE BATTERY

589

Global positioning system

THE GLOBAL POSITIONING SYSTEM (GPS) is a network of 24 navigation satellites orbiting the Earth that people can use to pinpoint their position. The satellites orbit at a height of 20,000 kilometres (12,500 miles). A GPS receiver picks up signals from any of these satellites that are above the horizon. It uses information in each signal to work out how far away it is from the satellite. It can calculate its position on the Earth's surface when it has information from at least three satellites. A basic GPS receiver shows the latitude and longitude of its position on its screen. A more advanced receiver shows the position on a digital map. Some receivers display extra information, such as the distance that has been travelled and the average speed of the vehicle in which the receiver is installed.

Cigarette lighter adapter and speaker cable

Antenna

GARMIN STREET PILOT III GPS

Page key

On/off and screen control button

Enter key

Quit key

Rocker pad

Menu key

Speak key

Liquid crystal display (LCD) screen

HOW GPS WORKS

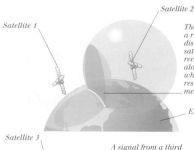

Satellite 1

Satellite 2

Zoom keys

Find key

Route key

The receiver takes a reading of its distance from two satellites. The receiver is located along the plane where the two resultant spheres meet

Earth

Satellite 3

A signal from a third satellite defines two positions on that plane. The position on the earth's surface is read as the correct location

IN-CAR MOUNTING BRACKET ASSEMBLY

QUICK-RELEASE BASE

MOUNTING BRACKET

Locking lever

Release catch

Ratcheted base

Speaker plug

Power plug

COMPONENTS OF A GARMIN STREET PILOT III GPS

GARMIN GPS V

Adjustable antenna

Power backlight key

Rocker keypad

Liquid crystal display (LCD) screen

Data plug

Antenna

Memory battery

Data plug socket

Main printed circuit board (PCB)

Rear case

USB PROGRAMMER ASSEMBLY

Shielded receiver

Data cartridge

Universal serial bus (USB) programmer

Front case

Liquid crystal display (LCD) assembly

Underside of control pad

SPARE FUSES

Vacuum cleaner

IN A CONVENTIONAL VACUUM CLEANER, an electric motor spins a fan that sucks in air carrying dust and debris. The air is forced through tiny pores in a dust bag, trapping most particles. In the 1990s, James Dyson's dual cyclone "bag-less" design did away with the dust bag – and the reduced airflow caused by clogging of its pores. An electrically-driven fan creates a partial vacuum within the machine. Air is forced at more than 100 kilometres per hour past a rotating brush that loosens dirt. The airflow passes along the wand and hose to the outer part of a cylinder-shaped bin. As the air whirls around at 300 kilometres per hour (like a mini-hurricane or cyclone), centrifugal force flings larger particles outwards, to fall to the bin's base. The air then passes through perforations into the cone-shaped, narrower inner bin, where a second cyclone spins even faster, almost 1,000 kilometres per hour, flinging off yet smaller particles. The now almost-clean air exits via two microporous filters.

Wand handle and brushbar controls

Upper wand

Lower wand

Motorized brushbar floor tool

DYSON DC05 MOTORHEAD

CYCLONE ASSEMBLY

Air intake from hose

Air exit to bin/cyclone cover

Hose electricity connector

Inner cyclone cone

Hose slider

WASHABLE PRE-MOTOR FILTER

Microporous filter

Bin upper seal seating

Perforated shroud

Bin handle clip

Hose slider seating

Central retaining screw

DUST COLLECTION BIN

Inner bin fin

Bin upper seal

Hose electricity supply

Post-motor micropore filter

Filter rim casing

Bin base

Bin lower seal

Inner bin dust collection area

Bin handle

Polycarbonate plastic bin body

Bin cover retaining clip

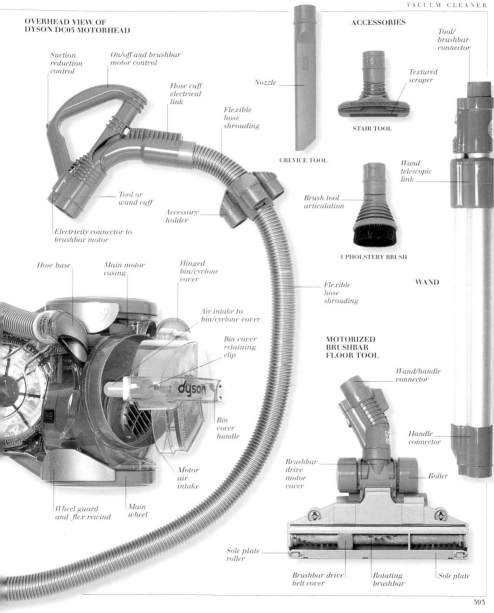

**OVERHEAD VIEW OF
DYSON DC05 MOTORHEAD**

*Suction
reduction
control*

*On/off and brushbar
motor control*

*Hose cuff
electrical
link*

*Flexible
hose
shrouding*

*Tool or
wand cuff*

*Accessory
holder*

*Electricity connector to
brushbar motor*

Hose base

*Main motor
casing*

*Hinged
bin/cyclone
cover*

*Air intake to
bin/cyclone cover*

*Bin cover
retaining
clip*

*Bin
cover
handle*

*Motor
air
intake*

*Wheel guard
and flex rewind*

*Main
wheel*

ACCESSORIES

Nozzle

*Tool/
brushbar
connector*

*Textured
scraper*

STAIR TOOL

CREVICE TOOL

*Wand
telescopic
link*

*Brush tool
articulation*

UPHOLSTERY BRUSH

*Flexible
hose
shrouding*

WAND

**MOTORIZED
BRUSHBAR
FLOOR TOOL**

*Wand/handle
connector*

*Handle
connector*

*Brushbar
drive
motor
cover*

Roller

*Sole plate
roller*

*Brushbar drive
belt cover*

*Rotating
brushbar*

Sole plate

Iron and washer-dryer

IN THE DAYS BEFORE WASHING MACHINES, laundry was done by hand – washed in a barrel, squeezed in a roller-mangle, hung on a line, and smoothed with an iron heated on the hob or stove. In the 1880s electrically heated irons were one of the first home electrical appliances. Today's iron still applies heat, sometimes moistened with steam, to dampen and flatten garment fibres. Machines with electric heaters and motors took the strain out of washing from the 1910s. Up to the 1960s, three machines were needed to wash, spin, and dry. Now clothes are swirled in a rotating ribbed tub of hot water, then spun fast to throw off most of the water, before slowly tumbling in electrically heated air to dry – all in one appliance.

FRONT VIEW OF A MIELE WASHER-DRYER

Detergent tray

Control panels

Door

Filter access flap

COMPONENTS OF A STEAM IRON

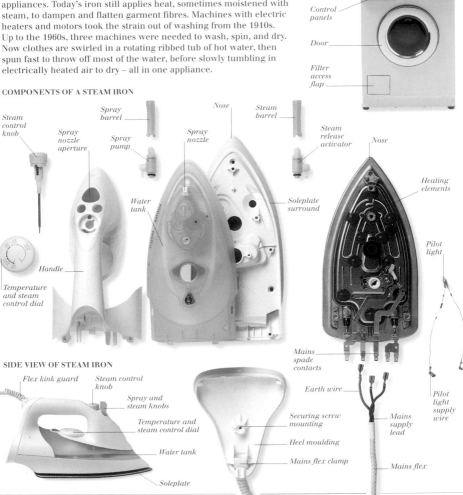

Steam control knob

Spray nozzle aperture

Spray barrel

Spray pump

Spray nozzle

Nose

Steam barrel

Steam release activator

Nose

Heating elements

Water tank

Soleplate surround

Pilot light

Handle

Temperature and steam control dial

Mains spade contacts

SIDE VIEW OF STEAM IRON

Flex kink guard

Steam control knob

Spray and steam knobs

Temperature and steam control dial

Water tank

Soleplate

Earth wire

Securing screw mounting

Heel moulding

Mains flex clamp

Mains supply lead

Pilot light supply wire

Mains flex

COMPONENTS OF A MIELE WASHER-DRYER

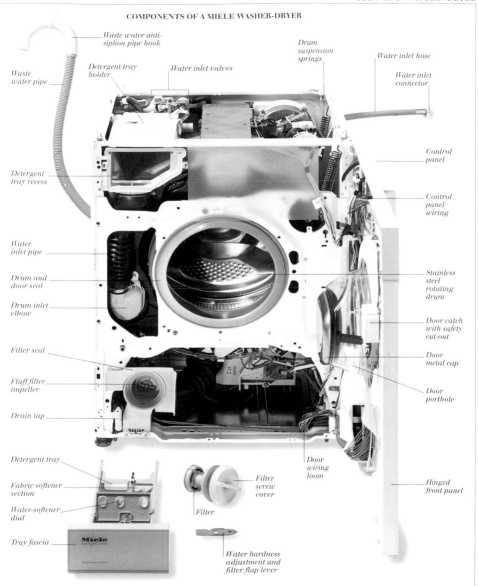

Waste water anti-siphon pipe hook

Detergent tray holder

Water inlet valves

Drum suspension springs

Water inlet hose

Water inlet connector

Waste water pipe

Detergent tray recess

Control panel

Control panel wiring

Water inlet pipe

Drum and door seal

Drum inlet elbow

Stainless steel rotating drum

Door catch with safety cut-out

Door metal cap

Filter seal

Fluff filter impeller

Drain tap

Door porthole

Detergent tray

Door wiring loom

Hinged front panel

Fabric softener section

Filter screw cover

Water-softener dial

Filter

Tray fascia

Miele

Water hardness adjustment and filter flap lever

Microwave combination oven

CONVENTIONAL OVENS use electrically warmed elements or a flame to heat food. In a microwave oven heat energy is created by electromagnetic waves produced by a magnetron and led by waveguides into the oven compartment. These microwaves cannot pass through the compartment's metal casing, being reflected within and spread evenly by a fan. But they do pass through most types of plastic, ceramics, and glass. Therefore platters or containers made from these materials are suitable for use in microwave ovens. A combination oven also has conventional heating elements, to grill and "brown" in the traditional fashion, either alone or in conjunction with microwaves.

MICROWAVE COMBINATION OVEN

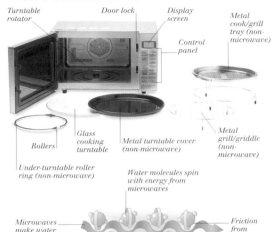

Turntable rotator

Door lock

Display screen

Control panel

Metal cook/grill tray (non-microwave)

Glass cooking turntable

Metal turntable cover (non-microwave)

Rollers

Under-turntable roller ring (non-microwave)

Metal grill/griddle (non-microwave)

HOW MICROWAVES HEAT FOOD

Hydrogen atom

Oxygen atom

Each water molecule in food has two hydrogen atoms and one oxygen atom

Microwaves make water molecules vibrate

Water molecules spin with energy from microwaves

Friction from spinning molecules creates heat

SIDE VIEW OF MICROWAVE COMBINATION OVEN

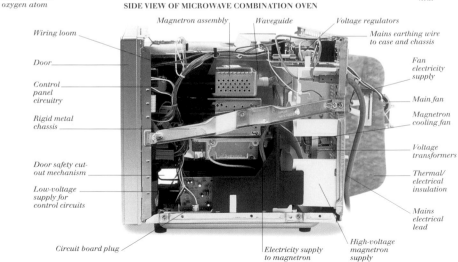

Magnetron assembly

Waveguide

Voltage regulators

Wiring loom

Mains earthing wire to case and chassis

Door

Fan electricity supply

Control panel circuitry

Main fan

Rigid metal chassis

Magnetron cooling fan

Voltage transformers

Door safety cut-out mechanism

Thermal/electrical insulation

Low-voltage supply for control circuits

Mains electrical lead

Circuit board plug

High-voltage magnetron supply

Electricity supply to magnetron

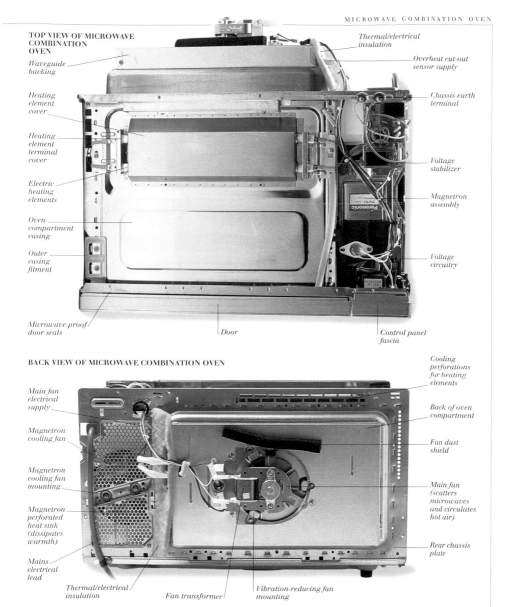

TOP VIEW OF MICROWAVE COMBINATION OVEN

Thermal/electrical insulation

Overheat cut-out sensor supply

Waveguide backing

Chassis earth terminal

Heating element cover

Heating element terminal cover

Voltage stabilizer

Electric heating elements

Magnetron assembly

Oven compartment casing

Outer casing fitment

Voltage circuitry

Microwave-proof door seals

Door

Control panel fascia

BACK VIEW OF MICROWAVE COMBINATION OVEN

Cooling perforations for heating elements

Main fan electrical supply

Back of oven compartment

Magnetron cooling fan

Fan dust shield

Magnetron cooling fan mounting

Main fan (scatters microwaves and circulates hot air)

Magnetron perforated heat sink (dissipates warmth)

Rear chassis plate

Mains electrical lead

Thermal/electrical insulation

Fan transformer

Vibration-reducing fan mounting

Toaster

MOST ELECTRIC TOASTERS not only grill slices of bread, they also pop them up when ready. While the slices rest on a spring-loaded rack, electric heating elements toast the bread. At the same time, a bimetallic strip heats and expands. One of the two metals in this strip expands more quickly than the other, causing the strip to curve. As it bends, it completes an electrical circuit and activates an electromagnet. The magnet attracts a catch, releasing the spring that holds the rack down in the toaster. The elements switch off, and the toasted slices pop up.

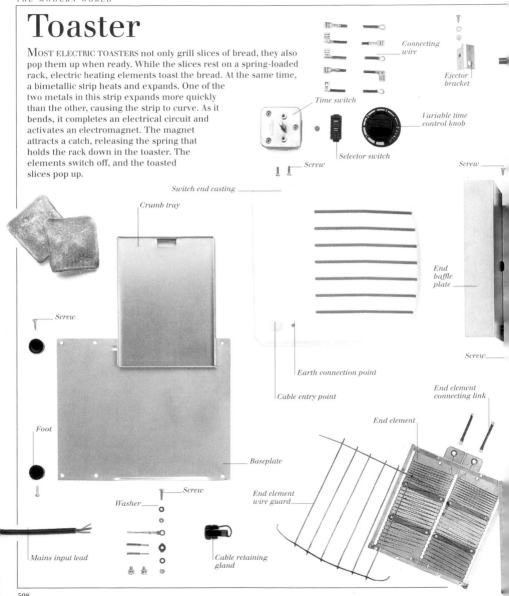

Connecting wire

Ejector bracket

Time switch

Variable time control knob

Selector switch

Screw

Screw

Switch end casting

Crumb tray

End baffle plate

Screw

Screw

Earth connection point

End element connecting link

Cable entry point

End element

Foot

Baseplate

Screw

End element wire guard

Washer

Mains input lead

Cable retaining gland

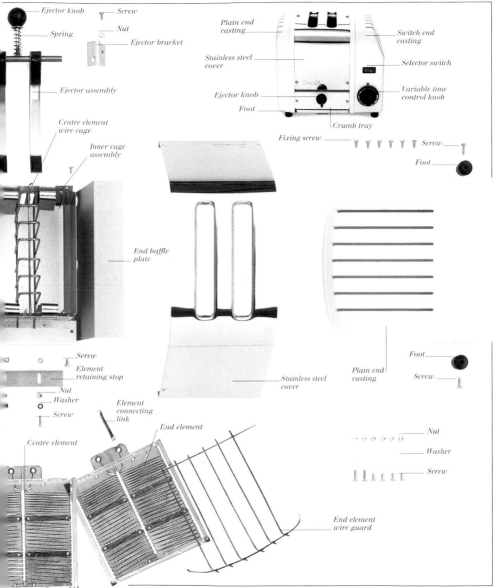

Ejector knob

Screw

Spring

Nut

Ejector bracket

Ejector assembly

Centre element wire cage

Inner cage assembly

Plain end casting

Switch end casting

Stainless steel cover

Selector switch

Ejector knob

Variable time control knob

Foot

Crumb tray

Fixing screw

Screw

Foot

End baffle plate

Screw

Element retaining stop

Nut

Washer

Screw

Foot

Plain end casting

Screw

Element connecting link

Stainless steel cover

End element

Centre element

Nut

Washer

Screw

End element wire guard

Drills

THE ELECTRICALLY POWERED MOTOR OF A POWER DRILL, cooled by a fan, turns a shaft at high speed. The shaft connects, in turn, to a system of gears that rotates a chuck even faster. Clamped by the chuck, a sharp bit cuts out the hole, and at the same time the bit's screw-shaped grooves channel the waste out of the hole. For drilling hard materials, many power drills have a hammer mechanism: when this is operated a ratchet in the gearcase causes the chuck and bit to pound in and out as they drill. A hand drill, although slower and less forceful than a power drill, is easier to control. For cutting wide holes, carpenters often prefer a brace-and-bit. This acts like a lever: the bowed handle of the brace moves a larger distance than the bit, turning the bit with extra force.

MOTOR ASSEMBLY

Armature spindle

Commutator

Armature

Fan

Motor case

Motor case

Field coils

Spring

Screw

Washer

Brush

Lead wire

Hammer mechanism actuator

Brush holder

Top insert blank

Screw hole

Electromagnetic induction capacitor

Triac device

Hammer actuator position

Chuck key holder

Gearcase position

Motor position

Screw

INTERNAL VIEW OF CLAMSHELL

Lock button

Trigger position

On/off trigger

TRIGGER MECHANISM

Washer

Cable

Spring

599

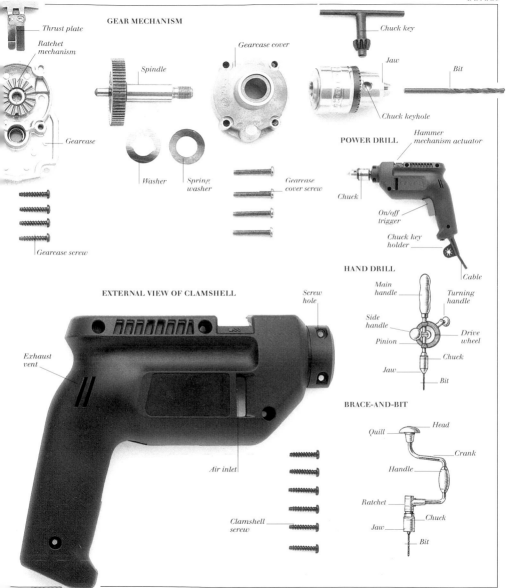

GEAR MECHANISM

Thrust plate

Ratchet mechanism

Spindle

Gearcase cover

Chuck key

Jaw

Bit

Gearcase

Chuck keyhole

Washer

Spring washer

Gearcase cover screw

Gearcase screw

POWER DRILL

Hammer mechanism actuator

Chuck

On/off trigger

Chuck key holder

Cable

EXTERNAL VIEW OF CLAMSHELL

Screw hole

Exhaust vent

Air inlet

Clamshell screw

HAND DRILL

Main handle

Turning handle

Side handle

Drive wheel

Pinion

Chuck

Jaw

Bit

BRACE-AND-BIT

Quill

Head

Crank

Handle

Ratchet

Chuck

Jaw

Bit

House of the future

HOUSES IN THE FUTURE are likely to be more environmentally friendly and energy-efficient than older dwellings, by making better use of materials and intelligent control systems. The Integer house was designed by Cole Thompson Associates, Bree Day Partnership, and Paul Hodgkins Associates, and built in conjunction with the Building Research Establishment in the UK. One of its key features is a large conservatory that warms one side of the house. Extensive use is made of recycled, natural, and renewable materials and energy. The walls are made from timber and insulated with fibre from recycled newspaper; waste water from the bathrooms is saved and used to flush the toilets; and a wind turbine and solar panels contribute some of the electricity requirements. Many elements were prefabricated off site for ease of construction. The Integer house uses only half the energy and a third less water than a traditionally built house.

WALL CONSTRUCTION

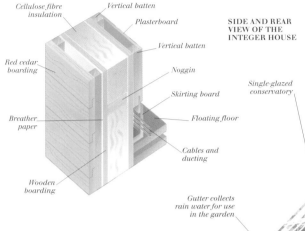

Cellulose fibre insulation

Vertical batten

Plasterboard

Vertical batten

Red cedar boarding

Noggin

Skirting board

Floating floor

Breather paper

Cables and ducting

Wooden boarding

SIDE AND REAR VIEW OF THE INTEGER HOUSE

Single-glazed conservatory

Gutter collects rain water for use in the garden

Composter for recycling kitchen waste

FRONT VIEW OF THE INTEGER HOUSE

Turfed roof helps to regulate temperature

Passive stack vents from bathroom and toilet

Automatic louvres cool conservatory

Small windows reduce heat loss

Red cedar walls that do not require painting or staining

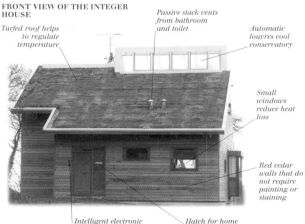

Intelligent electronic door-lock

Hatch for home deliveries

ROOF CONSTRUCTION

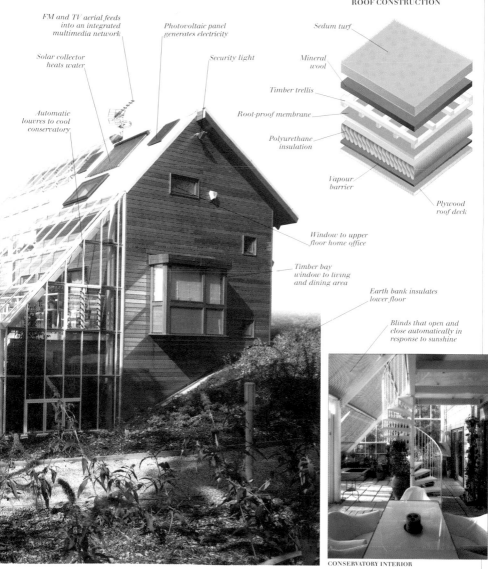

*FM and TV aerial feeds
into an integrated
multimedia network*

*Solar collector
heats water*

*Automatic
louvres to cool
conservatory*

*Photovoltaic panel
generates electricity*

Security light

Sedum turf

*Mineral
wool*

Timber trellis

Root-proof membrane

*Polyurethane
insulation*

*Vapour
barrier*

*Plywood
roof deck*

*Window to upper
floor home office*

*Timber bay
window to living
and dining area*

*Earth bank insulates
lower floor*

*Blinds that open and
close automatically in
response to sunshine*

CONSERVATORY INTERIOR

Renewable energy

RENEWABLE ENERGY COMES from sources that do not become depleted as we use the energy. When a fossil fuel such as coal is burned, it is gone forever, but a renewable source remains available no matter how much is used. The tides, waves, flowing water, sunlight, and the wind are all renewable sources of energy. Wind and water energy are captured by a device called a turbine. The turbine spins and drives an electricity generator. Energy from sunlight, or solar energy, is changed into electricity in two main ways. One uses mirrors to concentrate solar energy and magnify its heating effect which is used to change water into steam to drive turbines. Photovoltaic cells change sunlight directly into electricity. A cell is made from two layers of silicon. One gives out electrons (negative particles) and the other receives them. Sunlight knocks electrons out of atoms where the two layers meet, separating them from the positive particles. The electrons are attracted to one layer of the cell, the positive particles to the other layer. Electrons are naturally attracted to the positive particles, but to come together again, the electrons must flow out of the cell, through an external electric circuit, or load, and back to the other side of the cell, creating a charge. The cell supplies electric current for as long as light keeps falling on it.

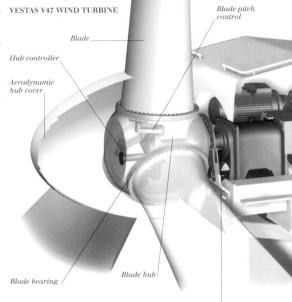

VESTAS V47 WIND TURBINE

Blade pitch control

Blade

Hub controller

Aerodynamic hub cover

Blade bearing

Blade hub

Rotor lock

TIDAL POWER

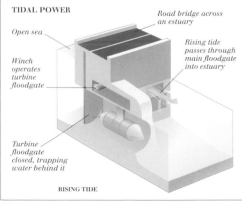

Road bridge across an estuary

Open sea

Winch operates turbine floodgate

Rising tide passes through main floodgate into estuary

Turbine floodgate closed, trapping water behind it

RISING TIDE

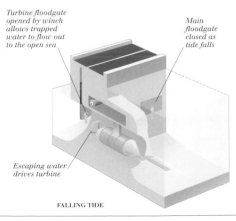

Turbine floodgate opened by winch allows trapped water to flow out to the open sea

Main floodgate closed as tide falls

Escaping water drives turbine

FALLING TIDE

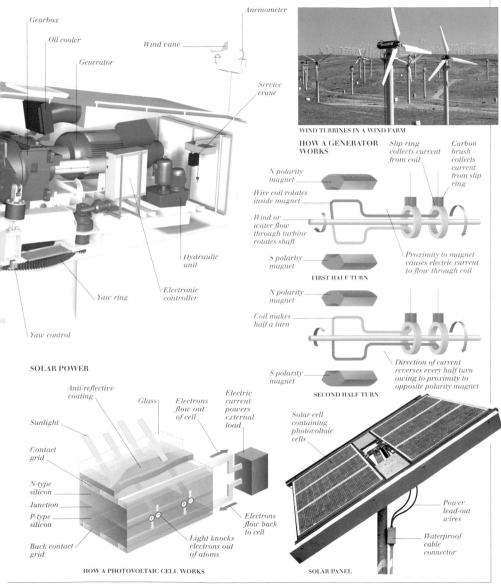

Gearbox

Oil cooler

Generator

Anemometer

Wind vane

Service crane

Hydraulic unit

Electronic controller

Yaw ring

Yaw control

WIND TURBINES IN A WIND FARM

HOW A GENERATOR WORKS

Slip ring collects current from coil

Carbon brush collects current from slip ring

N polarity magnet

Wire coil rotates inside magnet

Wind or water flow through turbine rotates shaft

S polarity magnet

Proximity to magnet causes electric current to flow through coil

FIRST HALF TURN

N polarity magnet

Coil makes half a turn

S polarity magnet

Direction of current reverses every half turn owing to proximity to opposite polarity magnet

SECOND HALF TURN

SOLAR POWER

Anti-reflective coating

Glass

Electrons flow out of cell

Electric current powers external load

Sunlight

Contact grid

N-type silicon

Junction

P-type silicon

Back contact grid

Light knocks electrons out of atoms

Electrons flow back to cell

Solar cell containing photovoltaic cells

Power lead-out wires

Waterproof cable connector

HOW A PHOTOVOLTAIC CELL WORKS

SOLAR PANEL

Cloning technology

IN A LIVING CELL THE GENETIC MATERIAL DNA (deoxyribonucleic acid) contains thousands of units called genes that carry instructions for development, growth, and repair of the living creature. During normal reproduction, half the mother's genetic material contained in an egg cell joins with half the genetic material from the father carried in a sperm cell, to form a unique new genome (set of genes) for a new life. During the early stages of embryo development, the fertilized egg divides into stem cells, which have the potential to become specialized into the hundreds of cell types in a body. Through therapeutic cloning, stem cells can be produced in a laboratory. It is hoped that in the future this technology can be used to grow new tissue that can be transplanted back into the donor to treat illness, without fear of rejection – when the body recognizes a transplanted part as "foreign" because it has different genes, and tries to destroy it. In another form of cloning, performed experimentally using animals, genetic material from a donor animal has been inserted into an egg from another animal that has been emptied of its own genetic material, to produce an animal genetically identical to the donor.

NORMAL REPRODUCTION

Spare cells from egg development

Nucleus with mother's genetic material

Egg cell membrane

Egg cell

Nucleus with mother's genetic material

Polar body (spare genetic material) forms as part of final egg cell division

THERAPEUTIC CLONING

Egg cell with polar body

Zona pellucida (outer casing of egg cell)

Fragments of DNA stain as dark "bar code" bands

"Plug" of zona removed

Suction through micro-pipette holds egg steady

Gentle suction through micro-needle

GEL IMAGE SHOWING DNA PROFILE

Micro-needle inserted through egg cell membrane

Zona plug discarded

Polar body removed

Egg genetic material in nucleus removed

Discarded parts no longer needed

Egg cell provides conditions for multiplication

Zona (casing)

Egg cell

Egg cell nucleus containing genetic material

GENETIC MATERIAL REMOVED FROM EGG

"Enucleated" egg cell (lacks nucleus with genetic material)

Stem cells (unspecialized or undifferentiated cells) collected from donor

Donor genetic material introduced into egg cell

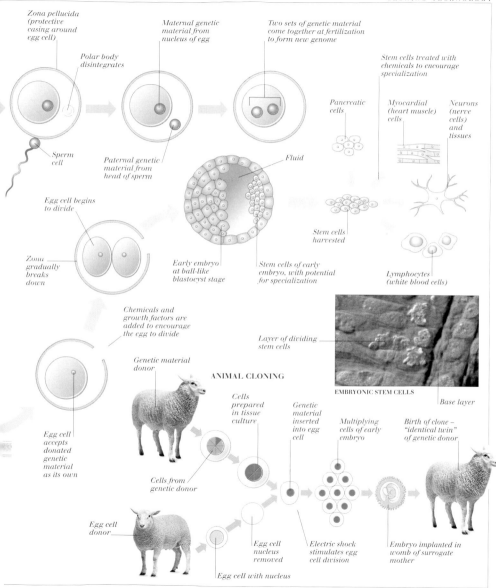

Zona pellucida (protective casing around egg cell)

Polar body disintegrates

Maternal genetic material from nucleus of egg

Two sets of genetic material come together at fertilization to form new genome

Stem cells treated with chemicals to encourage specialization

Pancreatic cells

Myocardial (heart muscle) cells

Neurons (nerve cells) and tissues

Sperm cell

Paternal genetic material from head of sperm

Fluid

Egg cell begins to divide

Stem cells harvested

Zona gradually breaks down

Early embryo at ball-like blastocyst stage

Stem cells of early embryo, with potential for specialization

Lymphocytes (white blood cells)

Chemicals and growth factors are added to encourage the egg to divide

Layer of dividing stem cells

Genetic material donor

ANIMAL CLONING

EMBRYONIC STEM CELLS

Cells prepared in tissue culture

Genetic material inserted into egg cell

Multiplying cells of early embryo

Birth of clone – "identical twin" of genetic donor

Base layer

Egg cell accepts donated genetic material as its own

Cells from genetic donor

Egg cell donor

Egg cell nucleus removed

Electric shock stimulates egg cell division

Embryo implanted in womb of surrogate mother

Egg cell with nucleus

Robots

ROBOTS ARE MACHINES THAT CAN carry out a variety of tasks on their own, with little or no human control. Most robots are mechanical arms used to build things in factories. The end of the robot's arm can be fitted with different tools for gripping, drilling, cutting, welding, and painting. Robot toys have become popular, too. They incorporate sensors that respond to sounds and sometimes touch. Some of them can even understand spoken words. The Aibo robot dog can understand 75 voice commands. Scientists are also trying to create more advanced human-like robots that can see, hear, learn, and make their own decisions. Cog, a robot that has been progressively developed at the Massachusetts Institute of Technology since the 1990s, is one of these "humanoid" robots.

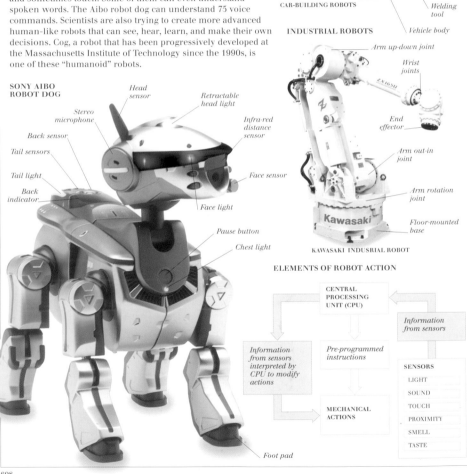

CAR-BUILDING ROBOTS

Welding tool

Vehicle body

INDUSTRIAL ROBOTS

Arm up-down joint

Wrist joints

End effector

Arm out-in joint

Arm rotation joint

Floor-mounted base

Kawasaki

KAWASAKI INDUSRIAL ROBOT

SONY AIBO ROBOT DOG

Head sensor

Retractable head light

Stereo microphone

Infra-red distance sensor

Back sensor

Face sensor

Tail sensors

Tail light

Back indicator

Face light

Pause button

Chest light

Foot pad

ELEMENTS OF ROBOT ACTION

CENTRAL PROCESSING UNIT (CPU)

Information from sensors

Information from sensors interpreted by CPU to modify actions

Pre-programmed instructions

SENSORS

LIGHT

SOUND

TOUCH

MECHANICAL ACTIONS

PROXIMITY

SMELL

TASTE

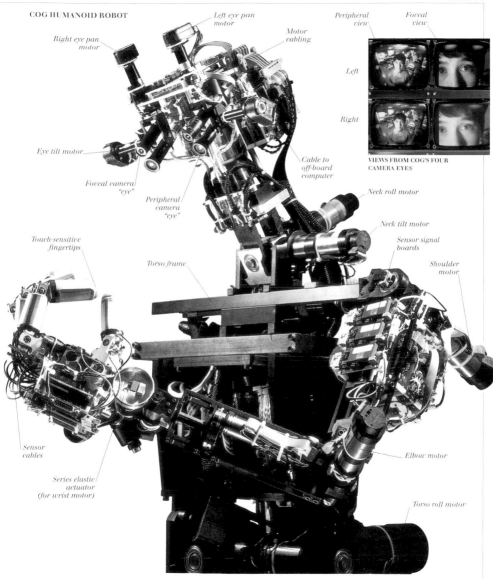

COG HUMANOID ROBOT

Left eye pan motor

Motor cabling

Right eye pan motor

Peripheral view

Foveal view

Left

Right

VIEWS FROM COG'S FOUR CAMERA EYES

Eye tilt motor

Cable to off-board computer

Foveal camera "eye"

Neck roll motor

Peripheral camera "eye"

Neck tilt motor

Sensor signal boards

Touch-sensitive fingertips

Shoulder motor

Torso frame

Sensor cables

Series elastic actuator (for wrist motor)

Elbow motor

Torso roll motor

High-performance microscopes

OPTICAL MICROSCOPES FORM A MAGNIFIED image by using
lenses to bend light. Some special-purpose optical microscopes
used in industry and research are designed for observing
particular materials, such as living cells. They produce
magnifications of up to about 1,000. Electron microscopes
produce magnifications of as much as 1.5 million. Their images
are formed by means of electrons focused by magnetic lenses.
There are two main types: scanning electron microscopes
(SEMs) scan electrons back and forth across the surface of a
specimen; transmission electron microscopes (TEMs) transmit
electrons through a thin slice of the specimen.

**FEI TECNAI G² TRANSMISSION ELECTRON
MICROSCOPE**

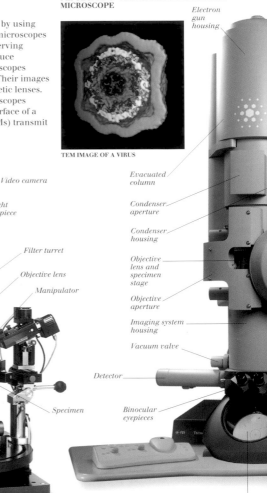

TEM IMAGE OF A VIRUS

OPTICAL MICROSCOPE IMAGE
OF DYING NERVE CELLS

Video camera

Right
eyepiece

Filter turret

Objective lens

Manipulator

Left eyepiece

Manipulator

Specimen
stage

Specimen

Electron
gun
housing

Evacuated
column

Condenser
aperture

Condenser
housing

Objective
lens and
specimen
stage

Objective
aperture

Imaging system
housing

Vacuum valve

Detector

Binocular
eyepieces

Viewing screen

OLYMPUS BX51WI OPTICAL MICROSCOPE

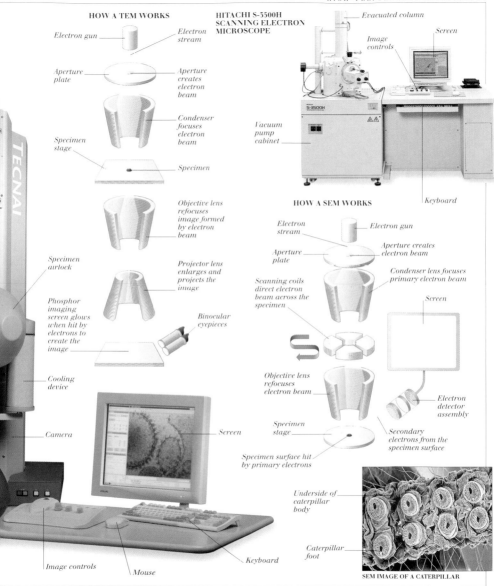

HOW A TEM WORKS

Electron gun

Electron stream

Aperture plate

Aperture creates electron beam

Condenser focuses electron beam

Specimen stage

Specimen

Objective lens refocuses image formed by electron beam

Projector lens enlarges and projects the image

Specimen airlock

Phosphor imaging screen glows when hit by electrons to create the image

Binocular eyepieces

Cooling device

Camera

Screen

Image controls

Mouse

Keyboard

HITACHI S-3500H SCANNING ELECTRON MICROSCOPE

Evacuated column

Image controls

Screen

Vacuum pump cabinet

Keyboard

HOW A SEM WORKS

Electron stream

Electron gun

Aperture plate

Aperture creates electron beam

Scanning coils direct electron beam across the specimen

Condenser lens focuses primary electron beam

Screen

Objective lens refocuses electron beam

Specimen stage

Electron detector assembly

Secondary electrons from the specimen surface

Specimen surface hit by primary electrons

Underside of caterpillar body

Caterpillar foot

SEM IMAGE OF A CATERPILLAR

Space telescope

SPACE TELESCOPES ORBIT THE EARTH hundreds of kilometres above the ground, their instruments collecting light from stars and galaxies. Telescopes in space have a clearer view than those on Earth, because they are unaffected by the Earth's atmosphere, which absorbs or distorts much of this radiation. There are a variety of types of space telescopes designed to observe different types of light. The Hubble Space Telescope observes infra-red, ultraviolet, and visible light. It can detect objects that are 100 times fainter than those any telescopes on Earth can see. When this 11,000-kilogram (242-ton), 13-metre (50-foot) long telescope was launched by the Space Shuttle in 1990, it was found that its primary mirror was faulty and its images were blurred. Astronauts fitted extra optics to correct the problem in 1993.

IMAGES TAKEN FROM HUBBLE   *Pillar of gas*

CONE NEBULA

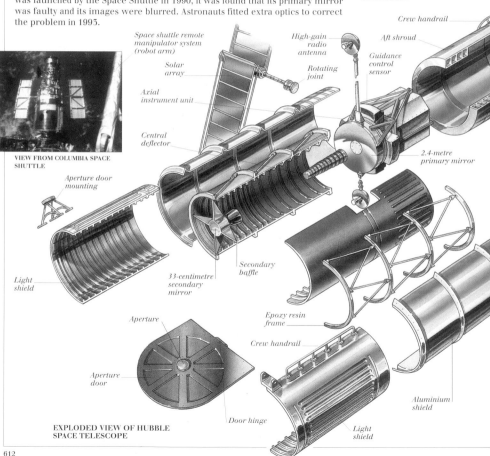

VIEW FROM COLUMBIA SPACE SHUTTLE

Space shuttle remote manipulator system (robot arm)

Solar array

Axial instrument unit

Central deflector

High-gain radio antenna

Rotating joint

Aft shroud

Guidance control sensor

2.4-metre primary mirror

Aperture door mounting

Light shield

33-centimetre secondary mirror

Secondary baffle

Aperture

Epoxy resin frame

Crew handrail

Aperture door

Door hinge

Light shield

Crew handrail

Aluminium shield

EXPLODED VIEW OF HUBBLE SPACE TELESCOPE

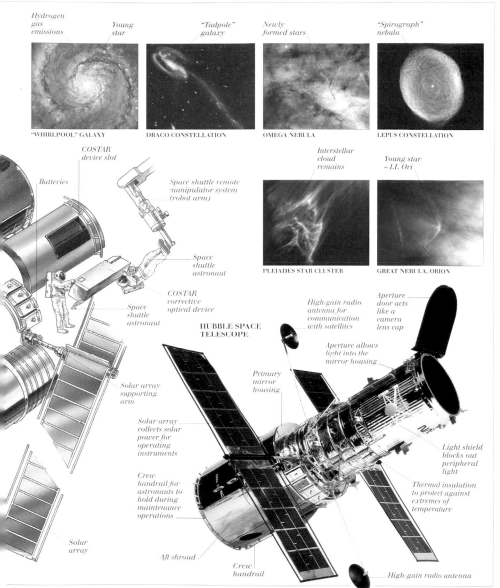

Hydrogen gas emissions

Young star

"Tadpole" galaxy

Newly formed stars

"Spirograph" nebula

"WHIRLPOOL" GALAXY

DRACO CONSTELLATION

OMEGA NEBULA

LEPUS CONSTELLATION

Interstellar cloud remains

Young star – LL Ori

COSTAR device slot

Batteries

Space shuttle remote manipulator system (robot arm)

Space shuttle astronaut

COSTAR corrective optical device

Space shuttle astronaut

PLEIADES STAR CLUSTER

GREAT NEBULA, ORION

Aperture door acts like a camera lens cap

High-gain radio antenna for communication with satellites

HUBBLE SPACE TELESCOPE

Aperture allows light into the mirror housing

Primary mirror housing

Solar array supporting arm

Solar array collects solar power for operating instruments

Crew handrail for astronauts to hold during maintenance operations

Light shield blocks out peripheral light

Thermal insulation to protect against extremes of temperature

Solar array

Aft shroud

Crew handrail

High-gain radio antenna

613

Probing the Universe

SPACE PROBES HAVE VISITED every planet in the Solar
System except Pluto. They take close-up photographs
and gather information that cannot be collected from
Earth-based equipment. Some probes fly past or go
into orbit around planets or moons. Others are
designed to land. Two Voyager space probes flew
past most of the outer planets in the 1970s and 1980s.
Two Viking spacecraft landed on Mars in 1976.
The Magellan spacecraft orbited Venus from 1989
and mapped its surface. The Pathfinder spacecraft
landed on Mars in 1997 and released a rover vehicle
to explore the surface. The Cassini space probe with
a mini-probe called Huygens is due to arrive at
Saturn in 2004. Huygens will be dropped onto
Titan, one of Saturn's moons.

*High-gain
antenna*

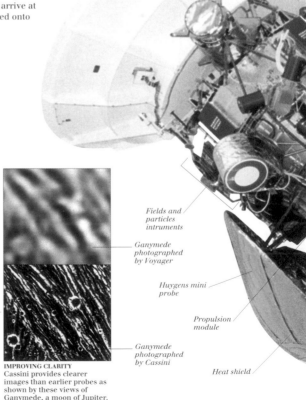

Fields and
particles
intruments

Ganymede
photographed
by Voyager

Huygens mini
probe

Propulsion
module

Heat shield

THE LAUNCH OF THE CASSINI SPACE PROBE
ON OCTOBER 10TH, 1997

JUPITER AND ITS MOON IO PHOTOGRAPHED
BY CASSINI

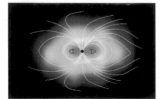

A MAP OF JUPITER'S VAST MAGNETIC FIELD
PRODUCED BY CASSINI'S INSTRUMENTS

Ganymede
photographed
by Cassini

IMPROVING CLARITY
Cassini provides clearer
images than earlier probes as
shown by these views of
Ganymede, a moon of Jupiter.

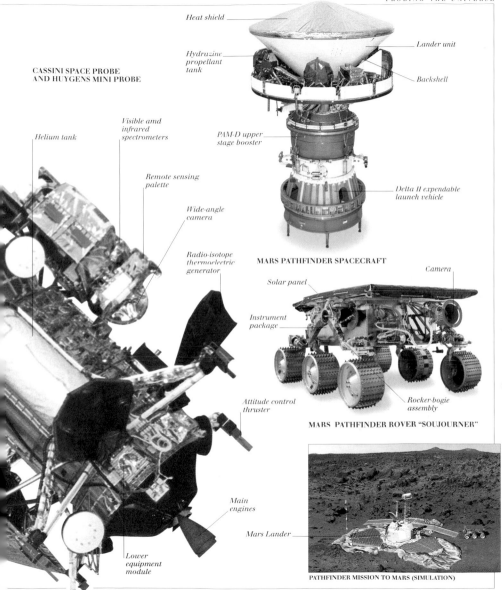

Heat shield

Lander unit

Hydrazine
propellant
tank

Backshell

CASSINI SPACE PROBE
AND HUYGENS MINI PROBE

Helium tank

Visible amd
infrared
spectrometers

PAM-D upper
stage booster

Remote sensing
palette

Wide-angle
camera

Delta II expendable
launch vehicle

Radio-isotope
thermoelectric
generator

MARS PATHFINDER SPACECRAFT

Camera

Solar panel

Instrument
package

Attitude control
thruster

Rocker-bogie
assembly

MARS PATHFINDER ROVER "SOUJOURNER"

Main
engines

Mars Lander

Lower
equipment
module

PATHFINDER MISSION TO MARS (SIMULATION)

615

Political map of the world

This map depicts the political boundaries of the world's nations. There are currently 193 independent countries in the world – a marked increase from the 82 that existed in 1950. With the trend towards greater fragmentation, this figure is likely to increase. There are also some 60 overseas dependencies still in existence, with various forms of local administration, but all belonging to a sovereign state. The largest country in the world is the Russian Federation, which covers 17,075,400 sq. km (6,592,800 sq. mi.), while the smallest is the Vatican City, covering 0.44 sq. km (0.17 sq. mi.). Under the Antarctic Treaty of 1959, no countries are permitted territorial claims in Antarctica.

ABBREVIATIONS	
AFGH.	Afghanistan
ALB.	Albania
AUT.	Austria
AZ. OR AZERB.	Azerbaijan
B. & H.	Bosnia & Herzegovina
BELG.	Belgium
BELO.	Belorussia
BOTS.	Botswana
BULG.	Bulgaria
CAMB.	Cambodia
C.A.R.	Central African Republic
CRO.	Croatia
CZ. REP.	Czech Republic
DOM. REP.	Dominican Republic
EST.	Estonia
HUNG.	Hungary
KYRG.	Kyrgyzstan
LAT.	Latvia
LIECH.	Liechtenstein
LITH.	Lithuania
LUX.	Luxemburg
MACED.	Macedonia
MOLD.	Moldavia
NETH.	Netherlands
NETH. ANT.	Netherlands Antilles
PORT.	Portugal
ROM.	Romania
RUSS. FED.	Russian Federation
SERB. & MON.	Serbia & Montenegro
SLVK.	Slovakia
SLVN.	Slovenia
S.M.	San Marino
SWITZ.	Switzerland
TAJ.	Tajikistan
THAI.	Thailand
TURKMEN.	Turkmenistan
U.A.E.	United Arab Emirates
UZBEK.	Uzbekistan
VAT. CITY	Vatican City
ZIMB.	Zimbabwe

KEY

CONTINENTS

Europe

Africa

Asia

Australasia & Oceania

North & Central America

South America

Antarctica

LABEL STYLES

Eg. MEXICO — Independent state

Eg. FAEROE ISLANDS
(to Denmark) — Self-governing territory
(parent state)

Eg. ANDAMAN ISLANDS
(part of India) — Non self-governing territory
(parent state)

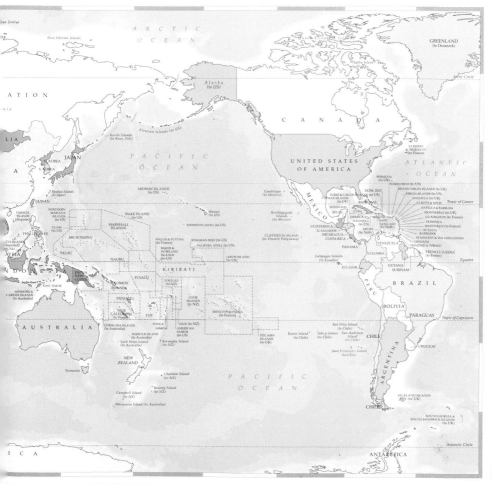

Time zones

The world is divided into 24 time zones, measured in relation to 12 noon Greenwich Mean Time (GMT), on the Greenwich Meridian (0°). Time advances by one hour for every 15° longitude east of Greenwich (and goes back one hour for every 15° west), but the system is adjusted in line with administrative boundaries. Numbers on the map indicate the number of hours that must be added to, or subtracted from GMT to calculate the time in each zone. Thus, eastern USA (–5) is 5 hours behind GMT.

TYPES OF CALENDAR

GREGORIAN

The 365-day Gregorian calendar was introduced by Pope Gregory XIII in 1582 and is now in use throughout most of the Western world. Every four years (leap year) an extra day is added. Below are the names of the months (and number of days).

January (31)	July (31)
February (28, 29 in	August (31)
leap years)	September (30)
March (31)	October (31)
April (30)	November (30)
May (31)	December (31)
June (30)	

JEWISH

The Jewish calendar is a lunar calendar adapted to the solar year. It normally has 12 months but in leap years,which occur seven times in every cycle of 19 years, there are 13 months. The years are reckoned from the Creation (which is placed at 3761 BC); the months are Nisan, Iyyar, Sivan, Thammuz, Ab, Elul, Tishri, Hesvan, Kislev, Tebet, Sebat, and Adar, with an intercalary month (First Adar) being added in leap years.

MUSLIM

The Muslim calendar is based on a year of 12 months, each month beginning roughly at the time of the New Moon. The months are Muharram, Safar, Rabi'I, Rabi'II, Jumada I, Jumada II, Rajab, Sha'ban, Ramadan, Shawwal, Dhu l-Qa'dah, and Dhu l-Hijja.

CHINESE

The Chinese calendar is a lunar calendar, with a year consisting of 12 months. Intercalary months are added to keep the calendar in step with the solar year of 365 days. Months are referred to by a number within a year, but also by animal names that, from ancient times, have been attached to years and hours of the day.

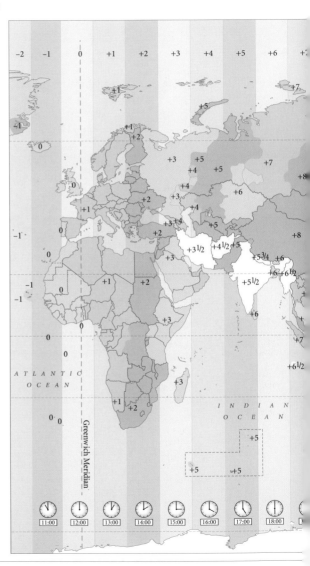

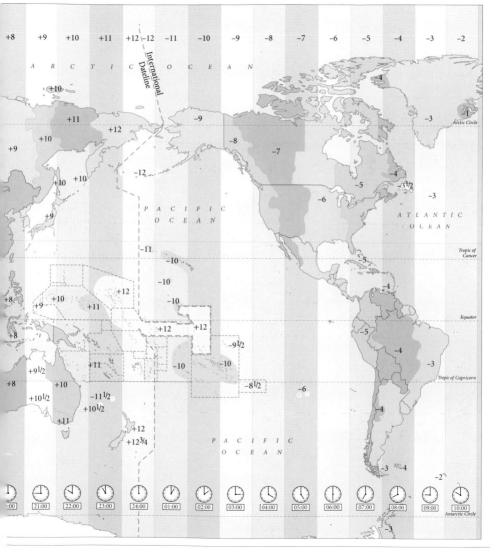

Useful data

UNITS OF MEASUREMENT

METRIC UNIT	EQUIVALENT
Length	
1 centimetre (cm)	10 millimetres (mm)
1 metre (m)	100 centimetres
1 kilometre (km)	1,000 metres
Mass	
1 kilogram (kg)	1,000 grams (g)
1 tonne (t)	1,000 kilograms
Area	
1 square centimetre (cm^2)	100 square millimetres (mm^2)
1 square metre (m^2)	10,000 square centimetres
1 hectare	10,000 square metres
1 square kilometre (km^2)	1,000,000 square metres
Volume	
1 cubic centimetre (cc)	1 millilitre (ml)
1 litre (l)	1,000 millilitres
1 cubic metre (m^3)	1,000 litres
Capacity (liquid and dry measures)	
1 centilitre (cl)	10 millilitres (ml)
1 decilitre (dl)	10 centilitres
1 litre (l)	10 decilitres
1 decalitre (dal)	10 litres
1 hectolitre (hl)	10 decalitres
1 kilolitre (kl)	10 hectolitres

IMPERIAL UNIT	EQUIVALENT
Length	
1 foot (ft)	12 inches (in)
1 yard (yd)	3 feet
1 rod (rd)	5.5 yards
1 mile (mi)	1,760 yards
Mass	
1 dram (dr)	27.344 grains (gr)
1 ounce (oz)	16 drams
1 pound (lb)	16 ounces
1 hundredweight (cwt) (long)	112 pounds
1 hundredweight (cwt) (short)	100 pounds
1 ton (long)	2,240 pounds
1 ton (short)	2,000 pounds
Area	
1 square foot (ft^2)	144 square inches (in^2)
9 square feet	1 square yard (yd^2)
1 acre	4,840 square yards
1 square mile	640 acres
Volume	
1 cubic foot	1,728 cubic inches
1 cubic yard	27 cubic feet
Capacity (liquid and dry measures)	
1 fluidram (fl dr)	60 minims (min)
1 fluid ounce (fl oz)	8 fluidrams
1 gill (gi)	5 fluid ounces
1 pint (pt)	4 gills
1 quart (qt)	2 pints
1 gallon (gal)	4 quarts
1 peck (pk)	2 gallons
1 bushel (bu)	4 pecks

NUMBER SYSTEMS

ROMAN	ARABIC
I	1
II	2
III	3
IV	4
V	5
VI	6
VII	7
VIII	8
IX	9
X	10
XI	11
XII	12
XIII	13
XIV	14
XV	15
XX	20
XXI	21
XXX	30
XL	40
L	50
LX	60
LXX	70
LXXX	80
XC	90
C	100
CI	101
CC	200
CCC	300
CD	400
D	500
DC	600
DCC	700
DCCC	800
CM	900
M	1,000
MM	2,000

METRIC - IMPERIAL CONVERSIONS

TO CONVERT	INTO	MULTIPLY BY
Length		
Centimetres	inches	0.3937
Metres	feet	3.2810
Kilometres	miles	0.6214
Metres	yards	1.0940
Mass		
Grams	ounces	0.0352
Kilograms	pounds	2.2050
Tonnes	long tons	0.9843
Tonnes	short tons	1.1025
Area		
Square centimetres	square inches	0.1550
Square metres	square feet	10.7600
Hectares	acres	2.4710
Square kilometres	square miles	0.3861
Square metres	square yards	1.1960
Volume		
Cubic centimetres	cubic inches	0.0610
Cubic metres	cubic feet	35.3100
Capacity		
Litres	pints	1.7600
Litres	gallons	0.2200

IMPERIAL - METRIC CONVERSIONS

TO CONVERT	INTO	MULTIPLY BY
Length		
Inches	centimetres	2.5400
Feet	metres	0.3048
Miles	kilometres	1.6090
Yards	metres	0.9144
Mass		
Ounces	grams	28.3500
Pounds	kilograms	0.4536
Long tons	tonnes	1.0160
Short tons	tonnes	0.9070
Area		
Square inches	square centimetres	6.4520
Square feet	square metres	0.0929
Acres	hectares	0.4047
Square miles	square kilometres	2.5900
Square yards	square metres	0.8361
Volume		
Cubic inches	cubic centimetres	16.3900
Cubic feet	cubic metres	0.0283
Capacity		
Pints	litres	0.5683
Gallons	litres	4.5460

RULES OF ALGEBRA

EXPRESSION	COMMENTS	EXPRESSION BECOMES
$a + a$	Simple addition	$2a$
$a + b = c + d$	Subtract b from either side	$a = c + d - b$
$ab = cd$	Divide both sides by b	$a = cd \div b$
$(a + b)(c + d)$	Multiplication of bracketed terms	$ac + ad + bc + bd$
$a^2 + ab$	Use parentheses	$a(a + b)$
$(a + b)^2$	Expand brackets	$a^2 + 2ab + b^2$
$a^2 - b^2$	Difference of two squares	$(a + b)(a - b)$
$1/a + 1/b$	Find common denominator	$(a + b)/ab$
$a/b \div c/d$	Dividing by a fraction is the same as multiplying by its reciprocal	$a/b \times d/c$

POWERS OF TEN USED WITH SCIENTIFIC UNITS

FACTOR	NAME	PREFIX	SYMBOL
10^{18}	quintillion	exa-	E
10^{15}	quadrillion	peta-	P
10^{12}	trillion	tera-	T
10^9	billion	giga-	G
10^6	million	mega-	M
10^5	thousand	kilo-	k
10^2	hundred	hecto-	h
10^1	ten	deca-	da
10^{-1}	one tenth	deci-	d
10^{-2}	one hundredth	centi-	c
10^{-3}	one thousandth	milli-	m
10^{-6}	one millionth	micro-	μ
10^{-9}	one billionth	nano-	n
10^{-12}	one trillionth	pico-	p
10^{-15}	one quadrillionth	femto-	f
10^{-18}	one quintillionth	atto-	a

Note: The American system of numeration for denominations above one million is used in this book. In this system, each of the denominations above one billion (1,000 millions) is 1,000 times the preceding one.

BIOLOGY SYMBOLS

SYMBOL	MEANING
○	female individual (used in inheritance charts)
□	male individual (used in inheritance charts)
♀	female
♂	male
×	crossed with; hybrid
+	wild type
F_1	offspring of the first generation
F_2	offspring of the second generation

TEMPERATURE SCALES

To convert from Celsius (C) to Fahrenheit (F): $F = (C \times 9 \div 5) + 32$
To convert from Fahrenheit to Celsius: $C = (F - 32) \times 5 \div 9$
To convert from Celsius to Kelvin (K): $K = C + 273$
To convert from Kelvin to Celsius: $C = K - 273$

Celsius	20	-10	0	10	20	30	40	50	60	70	80	90	100
Fahrenheit	-4	14	32	50	68	86	104	122	140	158	176	194	212
Kelvin	253	263	273	283	293	303	313	323	333	343	353	363	373

MATHEMATICAL SYMBOLS

SYMBOL	EXPLANATION
+	addition
−	subtraction
×	multiplication
÷	division
=	equals
≠	does not equal
>	greater than
<	less than
≥	greater than or equal to
≤	less than or equal to
∞	infinity
%	per cent
π	pi (3.1416)
°	degree
≈	is approximately equal to
∠	angle
∥	parallel to
Σ	summation
u,u	vectors
f(x)	function
!	factorial
√	square root
$\mathcal{E}$	universal set
A ∩ B	intersection
A ∪ B	unison
A ⊂ B	subset
∅	null set

PHYSICS SYMBOLS

SYMBOL	MEANING
α	alpha particle
β	beta ray
γ	gamma ray; photon
ε	electromotive force
η	efficiency; viscosity
λ	wavelength
μ	micro-; permeability
ν	frequency; neutrino
ρ	density; resistivity
σ	conductivity
c	velocity of light
e	electronic charge

CHEMISTRY SYMBOLS

SYMBOL	MEANING
+	plus; together with
−	single bond
•	single bond; single unpaired electron; two separate parts or compounds regarded as loosely joined
=	double bond
≡	triple bond
R	group
X	halogen atom
Z	atomic number

SCIENTIFIC NOTATION

NUMBER	NUMBER BETWEEN 1 AND 10	POWER OF TEN	SCIENTIFIC NOTATION
10	1	10^1	1×10^1
150	1.5	$10^2 (= 100)$	1.5×10^2
274,000,000	2.74	$10^8 (= 100,000,000)$	2.74×10^8
0.0023	2.3	$10^{-3} (= 0.001)$	2.3×10^{-3}

TRIGONOMETRY

Angle A (degrees)	sin A	cos A	tan A
0	0	1	0
30	1/2	$\sqrt{3}/2$	$1/\sqrt{3}$
45	$1/\sqrt{2}$	$1/\sqrt{2}$	1
60	$\sqrt{3}/2$	1/2	$\sqrt{3}$
90	1	0	∞

Shapes: Plane

Two-dimensional shapes are termed plane (or flat) shapes. Plane shapes constructed with straight sides, as illustrated here, are called polygons. They are categorized according to the number of sides they have – for example, three-sided polygons are known as triangles. A polygon that has sides of equal length and internal angles of equal size, such as a square, is said to be regular.

SCALENE TRIANGLE
A triangle (three-sided polygon) with no equal sides or angles.

ISOSCELES TRIANGLE
A triangle with only two sides and two angles equal.

RIGHT-ANGLED TRIANGLE
A triangle with one angle as a right angle (90°).

EQUILATERAL TRIANGLE
A regular triangle. All angles are 60°.

SQUARE
A regular quadrilateral. All angles are 90°.

RHOMBUS
A quadrilateral with all sides equal and two pairs of equal angles.

RECTANGLE
A quadrilateral with four right angles and opposite sides of equal length.

PARALLELOGRAM
A quadrilateral with two pairs of parallel sides.

TRAPEZIUM
A quadrilateral with one pair of parallel sides.

PENTAGON
A five-sided polygon. A regular pentagon is shown above.

HEXAGON
A six-sided polygon. A regular hexagon is shown above.

OCTAGON
An eight-sided polygon. A regular octagon is shown above.

AREAS AND PERIMETERS

The formulae for calculating the areas and perimeters of simple plane shapes were devised by Classical Greek mathematicians.

CIRCLE
r = radius
d = diameter = 2 × r

Circumference = 2 × π × r
Area = π × r²
(π = 3.1416)

TRIANGLE
Height = h
Sides = a, b, c

Perimeter = a + b + c
Area = ½ × b × h

RECTANGLE
Sides = a, b

Perimeter = 2 × (a + b)
Area = a × b

Shapes: Solid

Three-dimensional shapes are known as solid shapes, and include spheres, cubes, and pyramids. A solid shape with a polygon at each face is called a polyhedron.

TETRAHEDRON
A four-sided polyhedron. A regular tetrahedron is shown.

CUBE
A regular hexahedron. All sides are equal and all angles are 90°.

OCTAHEDRON
A polyhedron with eight sides.

PRISM
A polyhedron of constant cross-sections in planes perpendicular to its longitudinal axis.

PYRAMID
A polygonal base and triangular sides that meet at a point.

TORUS
A doughnut-like, ring shape.

SPHERE
A round shape, as in a ball or an orange.

HEMISPHERE
Formed when a sphere is cut exactly in half.

SPHEROID
An egg-shaped solid object whose cross-section is a circle or an ellipse.

CONE
An elliptical or circular base with sides tapering to a single point.

RIGHT CYLINDER
A tube-shaped, solid figure. A right cylinder has parallel faces.

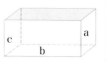

HELIX
A twisted curve. The distance moved in one revolution is its pitch.

SURFACE AREAS AND VOLUMES

Volume refers to the amount of space that a solid object occupies. Its surface area is the sum of the area of each of its faces.

CYLINDER
Surface area =
$2 \times \pi \times r \times h + 2\pi r^2$
Volume = $\pi \times r^2 \times h$

Height = h
Radius = r

CONE
Surface area =
$\pi \times r \times l + \pi r^2$
Volume = $\frac{1}{3} \times \pi \times r^2 \times l$

Height = h
Radius = r
Side = l

RECTANGULAR BLOCK
Surface area =
$2 (a \times b + b \times c + a \times c)$
Volume = $a \times b \times c$

Sides = a, b, c

Index

A

Aa lava 273
A and B button membrane 579
Abacus
  Ancient Egyptian temple 459
  Ancient Greek building 460
  Medieval church 469
  Neoclassical building 483
Abalone 176
Abaxial epidermis 159
Abaxial surface
  Butterwort leaf 161
  Fern pinnule 121
  Mulberry leaf 130
  Water hyacinth leaf 158
  Water lily leaf 159
  Welwitschia leaf 123
Abbey of St. Foi 468
Abdomen
  Crab 172
  Crayfish 172
  Human 211
  Insect 168-169
  Rattlesnake 185
  Scorpion 170
  Shrimp 172
  Spider 171
Abdominal aorta 215, 255
Abdominal artery 173
Abdominal cavity 215
Abdominal segment
  Butterfly 169
  Crayfish 172
  Eurypterid fossil 79
  Extinct shrimp 79
Abductor digiti minimus muscle 231, 233
Abductor pollicis brevis muscle 231
Aberdeen hook 562
Abies Concolor 66
Abomasum 198
Aboral surface
  Sea urchin 175
  Starfish 174
Abortive ovule 151
Abortive seed 146
Abrasion
  Glacier 286
  Weathering and erosion 282
Absolute magnitude
  Hertzsprung-Russell diagram 23
  Stars 22
Absorption lines 22-23
Absorptive hyphae 114
Abutment 484-485
Abyssal plain 298
Acacia tree sap 438
Acadagnostus 64
Acamar 19
Acanthostachys strobilacea 112-113
Acanthotegus 88
Acanthus leaf 460
Accelerated electron 319
Acceleration 320-321
  Electric train 328
  Motorcycle 364
Access door 333
Accessory drive pad 419
Accessory locator 569
Accessory pouch 569
Accessory shoe 582, 585
Access slot 565
Access window sliding cover 586

Access panel 329, 333
Accidentals 502-503
Accretion disc 27-29
AC electric train 328
Acer pseudoplatanus 131, 151
Acer sp. 127
Acetabularia sp. 116
Acetabular labrum 225
Acetabulum
  Eryops 81
  Ornithischian 82
  Saurischian 82
Acetylene headlamp 336-337
Acheres 150
Achernar 20
Achilles tendon 232-233
Achromatic multi-lens 580
Acid
  Intaglio printing 446
  Reversible reaction 312
  Salt formation 312
Acidalia Planitia 43
Acidic solution 446, 448
Acid-resistant ground 446-447
Acid-secreting stomach cell 217
Acipenser sturio 180
Acorn 131
Acoustic guitar 512-513
Acropolis 460
Acrosomal cap 259
Acroterion 460-461
Acroteuthis 278
Acrux
  Centaurus and Crux 21
  Southern stars 21
Acrylic ink 448
Acrylic paint techniques 443
Acrylic-primed board 442
Acrylics 442-443
Actinia equina 166
Actinides 310
Actinium 310
Actinothoe sphyrodeta 166
Action 321
Action lever 514
Active galaxy 12
Active volcano 272
  Igneous and metamorphic rocks 275
  Mountain building 62
Actuating lever system 330
Acuminate leaf apex 136-137
Acute leaf apex 137
Adam's apple 212, 244-245
Adam's ring
  Neptune's rings 50
  Structure of Neptune 51
Adaptation 112
  Dryland plants 156-157
  Wetland plants 158-159
Adaxial epidermis 159
Adaxial surface
  Butterwort leaf 161
  Mulberry leaf 130
  Tree mallow leaf 131
  Water hyacinth leaf 158
  Water lily leaf 159
  Welwitschia leaf 123
Addresses icon 576
Adjustable antenna 591
Adductor longus muscle 225, 226
Adductor magnus muscle 227
Adductor muscle 173

Adductor pollicis muscle 231
Adductor tubercle 225
Adenine 216
Adhara 18, 21
Adipose tissue 215, 235
Address book button 568
Addresses icon 576
Adjustable antenna 591
Adjustable damper 518
Adjustable link 562
Adjustable vane 563
Adjusting screw 560
Admiralty anchor Type ACII 386
Admiralty pattern anchor 386
Adrenal gland 215, 257
Adventitious buds 154
Adventitious roots
  Aechmea miniata 162
  Canadian pond weed 158
  Couch grass 113
  Fern 121
  Horsetail 120
  Ivy 131
  Monocotyledon 126
  Potato 128
  Rock stonecrop 128
  Tree fern 112
  Vegetative reproduction 154-155
  Water fern 158
  Water hyacinth 158
  Water lily 159
Advertising 568
Advertising panel 333
Aechmea miniata 162
Aedicule
  Ancient Roman building 465
  Renaissance building 474, 476
AEG Turbine Hall 495
Aegyptopithecus 75
Aeration zone 293
Aerial
  Frigate 397
  Honda Insight 354
  Renault Clio 349
Aerial mammals 104
Aerial rig 397
Aerial root 162
Aerial shoot 155
Aerial stem 119, 155
Aerobic respiration 256
Aerodynamic balance 414-415
Aerodynamic hub cover 604
Aerodynamic roof 334
Aerodynamic tubing 360
Aerodynamic underside components 354
Aerodynamic windscreen 346
Aerofoil guard 329
Aerofoil 442
"Aero" handlebars 360-561
Aerosol spray fixative 430, 440
"Aerotuck" position 360
Aesculus hippocastanum 130
Aesculus parviflora 137
Afferent arteriole 257
A-frame
  Concorde 416
  Gliders, hang-gliders, and microlights 426
Africa
  Cretaceous period 72-73
  Earth's physical features 264-265
  Great Rift Valley 60
  Jurassic period 70
  Late Carboniferous period 66
  Middle Ordovician

period 64
  Quaternary period 76-77
  Tertiary period 74-75
  Triassic period 68
African elephant 200-201
African plate 59
Aft anchor 395
Aft door 416
Afterbay 314
After breast rope 387
Aft bridge 395
Afterburner
  Jet engine 418
  Supersonic jetliner 416
Afterburner nozzle 421
Aftercastle
  Sailing warship 377
  Square-rigged ship 375
Aftercastle castle-deck gunport 377
After compass platform 395
After fashion piece 381
After funnel
  Battleship 395
  Iron paddlesteamer 392
Afterpeak 392
After silencer 427
After spring rope 387
Aft fairing 415
Aft galley unit 417
Aft hydroplane 396
Aft main door 414-415
Aft shoulder 560
Aft shroud 612, 613
Aft spar 415
Agate burnisher tip 432
Aggregate fruits 148-149
  Bramble 130
  Development 146-147
Aghulas current 297
Agnatha 178
Agropyron repens 113
Ahead/astern controls 390
Aileron
  ARV light aircraft 424
  BAe-146 components 414
  Curtiss biplane 398-399
  Hawker Tempest components 409
  Lockheed Electra airliner 406
  LVG CVI fighter 405
  Schleicher glider 426
Aileron control wire 403
Aileron hinge strut 403
Aileron mass balance 424
Aileron operating arm 398
Aino Planitia 36-37
Air
  Atmosphere 300
  Oceans and seas 296
  Weather 302-303
Air ambulance 422
Airbag suspension 351
Air bladder 117
Air-brake
  BAe-146 components 415
  Schleicher glider 426
  Tornado 421
Air-brake coupling hose 326
Air-brake jack 421
Air brushes 442
Air chamber 118
Air cleaner
  Jaguar V12 engine 345
  Renault Clio 351
Air compression 326
Air-conditioning 496-497
Air conditioning compressor 344, 354
Air-conditioning duct 417
Air conditioning pump 344
Air conditioning refrigerant pipe 344

Air-cooled engine
  Motorcycle engine 366
  V8 engine 404
Air cooling baffle 402
Air cooling fan 427
Air cooling scoop 365
Air-cushioned sole 543
Air data probe 420
Air exit 592
Air filter
  Bell-47 helicopter 422
  Harley Davidson FLHS Electra Glide 363
  Pegasus Quasar microlight 427
  Volkswagen Beetle 340
Air hose 442
Air impingement starter 418
Air inlet
  Jaguar V12 engine 345
  Power drill 601
Air intake
  Concorde 416
  Double-decker tour bus 333
  Formula One racing car 356, 357
  Lockheed Electra airliner 406
  MCW Metrobus 332-333
  Modern military aircraft 420-421
  Single-decker bus 333
  Turbojet engine 418
  Turboprop engine 419
  Vacuum cleaner 592, 593
Air intake box 425
Air-intake duct 354
Air intake vent 541
Air mass 296
Air outlet 356, 427
Air passage
  Lambeosaurus 99
  Parasaurolophus 99
Air pistol 548-549
Air plants 162
Air pressure 303
Air pump
  Oscillating steam engine 391
  Steamboat 391
Air reservoir valve 327
Air resistance 552
Air rifle shooting 548
Air sac
  Chicken's egg 192
  Scots pine 122
Air scoop
  ARV Super 2 424
  Volkswagen Beetle 340
Air spaces
  Clubmoss stem 120
  Mare's tail stem 135
  Moss 119
  Root 132
  Stem 135
  Wetland plants 158-159
Airspeed-indicator tube
  ARV light aircraft 425
  BE 2B wings 404
Airspeed pitot tube 404
Air taxi 422
Air temperature 300
Air temperature probe
  BAe-146 components 412
  Bell Jetranger helicopter 423
Air vent
  Bicycle helmet 560
  Hockey helmet 540
  Suzuki RGV 500 568-569
Air ventilator inlet 405
Aisle
  Ancient Egyptian temple 458
  Cathedral dome 484

Gothic church 470, 472-473
  Medieval church 468-469
Akna Montes 37
Ala 213, 223
Alar groove 213
Alba Fossae 43
Alba Patera 43
Albategnius 40
Albertosaurus 84
Albireo 20
Albumen 192
Albumen gland 177
Alcohol fermentation 313
Alcor 19
Alcyone 20
Aldebaran 18, 21
Alderamin 19
Alethopteris 67, 278
Algae 56, 112, 116-117
Algae M6, 112, 116-117
  Desmid 112
  Earth's evolution 56
  Fossil record 279
  Lichen symbiote 114
Algal cell 114
Algal layer 114
Algebra 621
Algedi 20
Algenib 19, 20
Algieba 18
Algol 19, 20
Alhambra 488
Alhena 18, 21
Alicante 450
Alidade 377
Alimentary canal 248-249
Alioth 18
  The Plough 19
Alkaid 18
  The Plough 19
Alkali metals 310
Allantoic fluid 192
Allantois 192-193
"All clear" position 330
All-enclosing fairing 369
Alley 544-545
Alligator 186
Allison 250-C20J turboshaft engine 423
Allium sp. 143
Allosaurus 71, 85
Allotropes 311
Alloy disc 517
Alloy frame 368
Alloy wheel
  Formula One racing car 356, 357
  Honda VF750 364-365
  Renault Clio 350-351
  Suzuki RGV500 568-369
All-round bicycle 560
All-terrain bicycle 358
Alluvial cone 282
Alluvial fan 282
Alluvium-filled basin 282
Almach 19, 20
  Pegasus and Andromeda 19
Al Nair 19, 20
Alnilam 18
  Orion 18
Alnitak
  Horsehead Nebula 19
  Orion 18
Alouatta seniculus 203
Alpha Centauri 21
Alpha Hydri 20
Alpha Mensae 20
Alphard 18, 21
Alpha Regia 36-37
Alpha ring 48
Alphecca 18, 21
Alpheratz 19, 20
  Pegasus and Andromeda 19
Alphonsus 40
Alpine skiing 552-553
Alps 60, 265

624

Alrami 21
Alsatian dog 195
Alstroemeria aurea 129
Altair 19, 20
Altar 92
Alternating current 328
Alternative engines 346-347
Alternator
  Diesel train 326
  Ford V6 12-valve engine 344
  Jaguar V12 engine 345
  NPT 301 turbojet 418
  Renault Clio 351
Alternator belt 351
Altitude scale 377
Alto clef 502
Altocumulus cloud 302
Alto voice 502
Altostratus cloud 302
Alto voice 502
Aludra 21
Alula 191
Aluminium 311
  Earth's composition 39
  Earth's crust 58
Aluminium alloy backing 346
Aluminium arrow shaft 548
Aluminium beam 560
Aluminium bonnet 354
Aluminium cowl 401
Aluminium flush-riveted skin 407
Aluminium gearbox casing 366
Aluminium racket 544
Aluminium shield 612
Aluminium wheel 406
Aluminium wire figure 455
Alveolar artery and vein 247
Alveolar bone 247
Alveoli 254-255
Amaryllis 155
Amateur rules 552
Amazon Basin 39
Amazonis Planitia 43
Amazon River 264
Ambiens muscle
  Albertosaurus 84
  Iguanodon 97
Ambulacral groove 79, 175
Ambulatory corridor 465
Ameloentinal junction 247
American alligator 186
American beaver 197
American black bear 195
American football 524, 526-527
American squash court 545
American squash game 544
Americium 311
Ammonia
  Jupiter's atmosphere 45
  Saturn's atmosphere 47
  Structure of Neptune 51
  Structure of Uranus 49
Ammonite 278-279
Ammonite shell 267
Ammonium dichromate 312
Ammonium hydrosulphide
  Jupiter's atmosphere 45
  Saturn's atmosphere 47
Ammophila arenaria 113
Ammunition 548-549
Ammunition box 408
Amnion 192-193, 260
Amniotic egg 80
Amniotic fluid 192, 260

Amniotic sac 260
Amoebocyte 166
Amphibia 182
Amphibian 80-81, 182-183
  Earth's evolution 56
  Fossil 278-279
  Primitive 68-69, 78
Amphioxe 275
Amphitheatre 464-465
Amplification
  Drums 518
  Electronic instruments 520
  Guitar 512
  Stringed instruments 510
  Vibraphone 516
  Xylophone 516
Amplifier 520
Amps 316
Ampulla
  Ear 242-243
  Fallopian tube 258-259
  Sea urchin 175
  Starfish 174
Ampullar nerve 242
Anal canal 249
Anal clasper 169
Anal fin
  Bony fish 180-181
  Lamprey 178
Anal fin ray 180
Anal flap 200
Analogue action buttons 579
Analogue thumb stick 579
Anal sphincter muscle 249
Anchisaurus 88-89
Anchor
  74-gun ship 380
  BAe-146 components 412, 414
  Battleship 394-395
  Frigate 397
  Junk 376
  Roman corbita 372
  Square-rigged ship 375
  Tea clipper 392
  Types 386
  Wooden sailing ship 379
Anchor bearing 413
Anchor buoy 379
Anchor cable
  74-gun ship 380
  Sailing warship 576
Anchor chain 386, 395
Anchoring 386-387
Anchor-joint 492
Anchor rode 372
Anchor rope 372-373
Ancient Egyptian building 458-459
Ancient Greek building 460-461, 462
Ancient Greeks 542
Ancient Roman building 462-465, 474
Ancillary drive belt 347
Ancillary drive pulley 345
Ancorale 372
Andamenti 451
Andes
  Cretaceous period 73
  Earth's external features 39
  Jurassic period 71
  Quaternary period 77
  Satellite map 264
  Tertiary period 75
  Triassic period 69
Andreoecium 140-141, 143
Andromeda 19, 20
Andromeda Galaxy 14, 19
Anemometer 605
Anemonia viridis 166
Anemophilous pollination 144

Angiogram 214
Angiospermophyta 112, 126
Angiosperms 279
Angle 572
Angle bar 393
Angle buttress 471, 472
Angle-of-attack probe 420
Anglerfish 180
Angling 562-563
Angoulême Cathedral 468-469
Angular mountain ridge 295
Angular notch 249
Angular process 194
Angular unconformity 276
Anhydrous copper sulphate 313
Animal cloning 607
Animal life
  Electromagnetic radiation 314
  Primitive 78
Animal remains
  Fossils 278
  Sedimentary rocks 276
Animal stances 82
Animals 56, 67, 78
Anions 308
Ankle
  Anchisaurus 89
  Corythosaurus 98
  Edmontonia 95
  Herrerasaurus 86
  Human 211
  Iguanodon 96
  Pachycephalosaurus 100
  Psittacosaurus 103
  Stegoceras 101
  Stegosaurus 92
  Triceratops 102
  Tyrannosaurus 84
Ankle joint
  Brachiosaurus 90
  Diplodocus 90
  Euoplocephalus 94
  Human 219
  Parasaurolophus 98
  Plateosaurus 88
  Stegoceras 101
  Struthiomimus 87
  Triceratops 102
  Tyrannosaurus 84
Ankylosaurs 83, 92, 94-95
Anne's Spot 47
Annual growth ring 125
Annuals 128
Annular river drainage 288
Annular tendon 241
Annulet 460
Annulus
  Fern 121
  Mushroom 115
Annulus of trunk 201
Ant 168
Anta 461
Antarala 490-491
Antarctica
  Cretaceous period 72-73
  Earth's physical features 264-265
  Jurassic period 70
  Late Carboniferous period 66
  Quaternary period 76-77
  Tertiary period 74-75
  Triassic period 68
Antarctic Circle
  Satellite map 265
  Surface currents 297
Antarctic circumpolar current 296
Antares 18, 21
Antefixa 461

Antelope 198
Antenna
  Battleship 395
  Crab 172
  Crayfish 173
  Frigate 397
  Global positioning system 590, 591
  Insects 168-169
  Malacostraca 172
  Roman corbita 372-373
  Shrimp 172
  Volleyball net 534
Antennule 173
Anterior antebrachial muscle 86
Anterior aorta 170
Anterior arch 222
Anterior brachial muscle
  Brachiosaurus 91
  Gallimimus 86
Anterior branch of spinal nerve 223
Anterior chamber 241
Anterior chamber of cloaca 185
Anterior crural muscle
  Brachiosaurus 91
  Gallimimus 86
Anterior dorsal fin
  Bony fish 181
  Dogfish 179
  Lamprey 178
Anterior fontanelle 220
Anterior horn 223
Anterior median fissure 223, 238
Anterior median vein 253
Anterior nasal spine 220-221
Anterior petal 141
Anterior root 238
Anterior semicircular canal 243
Anterior sepal 141
Anterior tentacle 177
Anterior tibial artery 253
Anterior tibial muscle
  Albertosaurus 84
  Iguanodon 97
Anterior tubercle 222
Anterior wing of shell 176
Antheridium 117
  Fern 121
  Moss 119
Antherozoids 116-117
  Fern 121
  Moss 119
Anthers 140-145, 145
  Dicotyledons 126-127
  Fertilization 146-147
  Pollination process 144-145
Anthozoa 166
Anthracite coal 280
Anthriscus sp. 135
Anthropoids 202
Antharium andreanum 143
Antibodies 253
Anticlinal fold 60
Anticline 60-61, 62
Anticline trap 280-281
Anticlinorium 61
Anti-collision beacon 422-423
Anti-corrosion paint 413
Anticyclonic-storm system
  Cloud features of Neptune 50
  Jupiter 44-45
  Structure of Saturn 47
Anti-friction pad 552
Anti-glare lens 553
Anti-glare screen surface 584
Antihelix 242
Anti-lift bracing wire
  Avro triplane 403

Blackburn monoplane 401
Blériot XI monoplane 401
LVG CVI fighter 405
Anti-lift wire 599
Antimacassar 329
Antimony 311
Antipodal cell 147
Anti-reflective coating 605
Anti-reverse drive 562
Anti-roll bar
  Renault Clio 351
  Volkswagen Beetle 340
Anti-submarine torpedo tube 397
Anti-surge baffle 344
Anti-torque tail rotor 423
Antitragus 242
Anti-vibration engine mount 411
Antler hammer 109
Antler harpoon 109
Antlia 18, 21
Antoniadi 41
Antorbital fenestra
  Baryonyx 83
  Camarasaurus 91
  Diplodocus 90
  Plateosaurus 88
Anura 182
Anus
  Barnacle 173
  Bony fish 181
  Butterfly 169
  Cow 198
  Crayfish 173
  Dolphin 205
  Domestic cat 195
  Elephant 200
  Human 249, 258, 261
  Octopus 176
  Rabbit 196
  Sea urchin 175
  Snail 177
  Spider 170
  Starfish 174
  Tortoise 187
Anvil 242
Aorta
  Anterior 170
  Bony fish 181
  Dogfish 179
  Dolphin 205
  Dorsal 179, 181, 182
  Human 215, 250 251, 252, 255, 256-257
  Posterior 170
  Spider 170
  Ventral 179
Apatite 271
Ape 108, 202-203
Aperture 610, 612, 613
Aperture door 612, 613
Aperture door mounting 612
Aperture plate 611
Apex
  Beetle wing 168
  Butterfly wing 169
  Calligraphy characters 445
  Clubmoss shoot 120
  Fern frond 121
  Fern pinnule 121
  Horsetail shoot 120
  Leaf 136-137, 154-155
  Lung 255
  Moss 119
  Pegasus XL SE microlight 426
  Pine shoot 125
  Snail shell 177
  Tongue 244-245
Apex wire 426
Aphelion 30-31
Aphrodite Terra 36-37
Apical bud
  Bulb 155

Pine shoot 125
Apical foramen 247
Apical meristem 134
Apical notch
  Seaweed 116
  Thalloid liverwort 118
Apollo 41
Aponixis 146
Apophysis 119
Apothecium 114
Appalachian mountains
  Late Cretaceous period 67
  Mountain building 62
  Quaternary period 77
  Satellite map 264
  Tertiary period 75
  Triassic period 69
Apparent magnitude 22
Appendix
  Chimpanzee 202
  Human 249
  Rabbit 196
Appendix orifice 249
Apple 148-149
Apple Ipod 587
Apple Macintosh G4 computer 521
Apple Macintosh PCs 566
Apple Power Mac G4 1GHz dual processor 567
Application button assembly 568
Applications launcher icon 568
Approach 543
Apse 465, 469, 481
Aquarius 19, 20
Aquatic mammals 104
Aqueduct 256
Aqueous humour 241
Aquiclude 292
Aquifer 292
Aquiferous system 166
Aquila 19, 20
Ara 20
Ara araurana 190
Arabesque
  Islamic building 488-489
  Neoclassical moulding 480
Arabia
  Cretaceous period 72
  Jurassic period 70
Arabian Desert 265
Arabic number system 591
Arachnids 170-171
Arachnoid granulation 237
Arachnoid mater 237, 240
Aral Sea 265
Araneae 170
Araucaria araucana 68
Arcade
  Ancient Roman building 464-465
  Baroque church 479-481
  Gothic building 470-471
  Medieval church 468-469
  Twentieth-century building 495
Arcadia Planitia 43
Arch 484-485
  Ancient Roman building 462, 464-465
  Asian building 490-491
  Baroque church 479, 480
  Calligraphy characters 445
  Cathedral dome 487
  Features of a coastline 295
  French temple 484-485
  Gothic church 470-473

High jump 543
Islamic building 488-489
Medieval building 466-469
Nineteenth-century building 492-493
Renaissance building 474-475
Archaeopteryx 57, 84, 85
Arched brace 473
Arched doorway 474, 475
Arched facade 493
Archegoniophore 118
Archegonium
  Fern 121
  Liverwort 118
  Moss 119
  Scots pine 122
Archery 548-549
Archery screen 377
Archimedes 40
Architrave
  Ancient Egyptian temple 458-459
  Ancient Greek temple 461
  Ancient Roman building 465, 465
  Baroque church 479-481
  French temple 485
  Gothic building 473
  Neoclassical building 478, 482-483
  Renaissance building 476-477
Archivolt
  Baroque church 479, 481
  French temple 485
  Gothic church 471
  Medieval building 467-468
  Renaissance building 477
Arch of aorta 253
Arch of Titus 463
Arch-plate 493
Archway 493
  Medieval church 469
  Moulding 485
Arctic Circle
  Satellite map 265
  Surface currents 297
Arctic Ocean 265
Arcturus 18, 21
  Hertzsprung-Russell diagram 23
Area measurements 590
Areas 622, 623
Areola 160
Areole 156
Arête 286-287
Argentina 331
Argon
  Atmospheric composition 301
  Mars' atmosphere 43
  Mercury's atmosphere 35
  Periodic table 311
  Venus' atmosphere 37
Argyre Planitia 43
Ariel 48
Aries 19, 20
Aril
  Lychee fruit 148
  Yew seed 123
A ring 46-47
Aristarchus 40
Aristillus 40
Aristoteles 40
Arkab Prior 21
Arkansas hone-stone 452
Arm
  74-gun ship 380
  Calligraphy characters 445

Gorilla 203
Human 210
Lion 194
Roman anchor 372
Starfish 174
Volkswagen Beetle 341
Armature
  Power drill motor 600
  Sculpture 452, 454-455
Armature spindle 600
Arm bud 260
Armed sports 556-557
Armour
  Battleship 394
  Gun turret 396
  Ironclad 393
Armoured dinosaurs 92
Armoured seat back 409
Arm out-in joint 608
Armpit 211, 234
Armpit bight 388
Armrest 329, 407
Arm rotation joint 608
Arms of Brazil 394
Armstand dive 558-559
Arm up-down joint 608
Arrector pili muscle 235
Arricrio 434
Arrow head 109
Arse 382
Arsenic 311
Arsia Mons 43
Arsinoitherium 57, 75, 104-105
Art deco style 495
  Twentieth-century building 494, 495
Artemon 372
Arterial system
  Brain 252
  Kidney 256
Arteriole 252
Artery
  Abdominal 173
  Alveolar 247
  Anterior tibial 253
  Axillary 253
  Basilar 252
  Brachial 253
  Central retinal 240
  Common carotid 215, 251, 253
  Common iliac 215, 253, 257
  Coronary 250-251, 253
  Digital 231, 253
  Dorsal metatarsal 253
  Epibranchial 179
  External iliac 215, 225, 253
  Femoral 225, 253
  Gastric 253
  Hepatic 248, 252-253
  Interlobular 256
  Internal carotid 243, 252
  Internal iliac 215, 253
  Lateral plantar 253
  Orbital 179
  Peroneal 253
  Popliteal 253
  Posterior cerebral 252
  Posterior tibial 253
  Pulmonary 182, 251, 253, 254-255
  Pulp 247
  Radial 231, 253
  Renal 256-257
  Splenic 253
  Sternal 173
  Subclavian 215, 251, 253
  Superior mesenteric 253, 256
  Superior thyroid 244
  Testicular 257
  Ulnar 231, 253
  Umbilical 260
  Vertebral 223, 252

Artesian water 292
Arthropoda 168, 170, 172, 278
Articular capsule 232
Articular cavity
  Hip joint 225
  Metatarsophalangeal joint 232
Artificial elements 310
Artificial fly 562-563
Artificial light 319
Artificial lure 563
Artillery loop 389
Artillery wheel 334
Artist's easel 437
Artist's signature 437, 445
Artist's stamp 445
Art nouveau style 495
Arundinaria nitida 131
Arytenoid cartilage 245
Arzachel 40
Ascender 445
Ascending aorta 251
Ascending colon 249
Ascraeus Mons 43
Asexual reproduction 154
Ash
  Mountain building 62
  Rock cycle 266
  Volcano 272-273
Ash chute 395
Ash-cinder volcano 272
Ash eruptions 272
Ash head 540
Ashlar 464, 486
Asia
  Cretaceous period 72-73
  Earth's physical features 264-265
  Himalaya formation 62-63
  Hominids 108
  Jurassic period 70
  Middle Ordovician period 64
  Quaternary period 76-77
  Tertiary period 74-75
  Triassic period 68
Asian buildings 490-491
Asian elephant 200-201
Asparagus setaceous 64
Ass 198
Association football 524-525
Astatine 311
Asterias rubens 175
Asterina gibbosa 175
Asteroids 52-53
  Solar System 30
Asteroxylon 78-79
Asthenosphere 58-59
Astragal
  Church of the Sorbonne 486
  Ship's shield 395
Astragalus 183
Astrolabe 376, 377
Astronavigation dome 408
Asymmetric ridge 283
Atacama Desert 264
Atalanta Planitia 36
Athletics 542-543
Atlantic Ocean 264-265
  Quaternary period 77
  Tertiary period 75
Atlas
  Baroque building 482
  Horse 199
  Human 222
  Moon 40
Atlas mountains
  Earth's external features 39
  Quaternary period 77
  Satellite map 265

Atmosphere
  Earth 38-39, 64, 300-301
  Jupiter 45
  Mars 43
  Mercury 34-35
  Neptune 51
  Pluto 51
  Saturn 47
  Uranus 49
  Venus 37
  Water cycle 288
Atoll 298-299
Atoll development 299
Atomic mass 309, 310
Atomic number 310
Atomic weight 310
Atoms 306, 308-309, 596
  Chemical properties 310
  Chemical reactions 312
  Periodic table 310
Atrial diastole 250
Atrial systole 251
Atrium
  Hong Kong and Shanghai Bank 498
  Human 215, 250-251
  Sponge 166
Attached column
  Ancient Roman building 465
  Baroque church 480
  Gothic building 473
  Medieval building 468-469
  Neoclassical building 479
Attachment-bracket 424
Attachment clip 575
Attachment lug 404
Attachment plate 424
Attack line 534
Attack radar 420
Attic
  Baroque church 480-481
  Cathedral dome 487
  Neoclassical building 478, 483
Attic vase 372
Attitude control thruster 615
Attraction 316-317
"A" turret 394
Auda 491
Audio cassette 587
Audio cassette player 587
Audio clock settings 521
Audio software sequencer 521
Audio tape controls 587
Auditorium 479
Auditory canal 242
Auditory meatus
  Chimpanzee 202
  Seat 204
Auger 374
Augusta National Golf course 546
Aureole 471
Auricle 242
Auricular surface 223
Auriga 18, 21
Aurora 38, 301
Australasia 264-265
Australia
  Cretaceous period 72-73
  Jurassic period 70
  Late Carboniferous period 66
  Middle Ordovician period 64
  Quaternary period 76-77
  Railway track gauge 331
  Satellite map 265
  Tertiary period 74-75

Triassic period 68
Australian Desert 265
Australian rules football 524, 528-529
Australopithecus 77, 108
  Lower jaw 107
  Tertiary period 74
Autofeather unit 419
Autogiro 422
Automatic cylinder lubricator 342
Automatic direction-finding aerial 423
Automatic door 328-329
Automatic louvres 602, 605
Automatic pen 444
Automatic Train Protection (ATP) 330
Automobile freight car 327
Autopilot 412
Autumn wood xylem 134
Auxiliary air intake 420-421
Auxiliary generator 327
Auxiliary power unit 417
Auxiliary power unit inlet 415
Aves 188
Avimimus 87
AVLS (automatic volume limiter control) 586
Avogadro 41
Avro triplane IV 402-403
Avro Tutor biplane 402-403
Away swing bowler 538
Awning 499
Axe 109, 374
Axial gland 175
Axial instrument unit 612
Axial tilt
  Earth 38
  Jupiter 44
  Mars 42
  Mercury 34
  Moon 40
  Neptune 50
  Pluto 51
  Saturn 46
  Uranus 48
  Venus 36
Axilla 211
Axillary artery 253
Axillary bud 134
  Dicotyledon stem 127
  Durmast oak 131
  Leaf scars 154
Axillary vein 253
Axinite 270
Axis
  Azolla sp. 158
  Horse 199
  Human 222
  Seed 152-153
  Pine cone 122
Axis of rotation
  Jupiter 44
  Mars 42
  Mercury 34
  Moon 40
  Neptune 50
  Pluto 51
  Pulsar 28
  Saturn 46
  Uranus 48
  Venus 36
Axle
  Avro triplane 402-403
  Blackburn monoplane 400
  Bus 333
  Curtiss biplane 399
  Honda VF750 365
  Lockheed Electra airliner 407
  LVG CVI fighter 405
  Steam locomotive 324

Axle bolt 425
Axon 239
Aythya fuligula 188
Azimuthal map projection 265
Azo yellow 442
Azurite 306

B

B-17G Flying Fortress bomber 408
Baboon 202
Bach 35
Back
  Block and tackle 383
  Elephant 200
  Horse 198
  Human 210
  Lion 195
Back-board 552
Back bone 222
Back check 514
Back contact grid 605
Background radiation 10
Back judge 526
Backlight control 583
Back line 535
Backlit liquid crystal display (LCD) 568
Back pocket 528
Backrest
  ARV light aircraft 425
  Lockheed Electra passenger seat 407
Backs
  Handball 535
  Hockey 540
  Soccer 524
  Volleyball 534
Back sight 549
Backstay 378, 379, 380
Backstay stool 381
Back strap 560, 561
Backstroke 558-559
Backup battery 567
Backward defensive stroke 538
Backward dive 558
Backwash 294
Back zones 534
Bacteria 56
Bactrian camel 199
Baculum 144
Badger 194
Badminton 544-545
BAe-146 jetliner components 412-415
Baffin Island 264
Baffle 341
Baffle plate 347
Bage, C. 492
Baggage compartment door 423
Bagneux Church 468-469
Bahada 282
Bail 558
Bail arm 562
Bailey 466
Bail handle 336
Bailly 40
Baird's beaked whale 205
Bait fishing 562
Balaenoptera musculus 205
Balance 232
Balance and muscle coordination 237
Balance weight
  Jaguar V12 engine 345
  Mid West rotary engine 411
Balancing drilling
  Mid West rotary engine 411
  Wankel rotary engine 347
Balanophyllia regia 167
Balata surface 546

Balcony 493
  Islamic tomb 489
  Nineteenth-century building 493
  Renaissance theatre 477
  Rococo style 478, 482
  Sailing ship 378, 379, 381
Baleen whale 204
Ball
  American football 526
  Australian rules football 528
  Baseball 537
  Basketball 533
  Cricket 538
  Gaelic football 528-529
  Golf 546
  Handball 535
  Hockey 540
  Hurling 541
  Lacrosse 541
  Netball 535
  Racketball 545
  Rugby 524, 530-531
  Soccer 524
  Squash 545
  Tennis 544
  Volleyball 534
Ballast 324
Ball bearings 358-359
Ballflowers 470-471
Ball marker 547
Ball size number 525
Baltica 65
Baltimore oriole 193
Baluster
  Asian building 490
  Gothic building 473
  Neoclassical building 485
Balustrade
  Asian building 490
  Baroque church 479-480
  Cathedral dome 487
  Gothic church 472-473
  Neoclassical building 478, 483
  Nineteenth-century building 493
  Renaissance theatre 477
  Twentieth-century building 495
Balzac 35
Bamboo 131
Banana 146
Banded ironstone 277
Banded milk snake 184
Bandy 540
Bank of England 482
Banner 375
Bar
  Musical notation 502
  Relief-printing press 449
Barb
  Angling 562
  Cnidocyte 167
Barberry 130-131
Barbette
  Battleship 394
  Gun turret 396
Bar code 606
Bare end
  Reef knot 388
  Single sheet bend 387
Barium 310
Bark
  Bishop pine stem 125
  Epiphyte 162
  Lichen 114
  Perennials 130-131
  Stem 134
  Woody plants 130-131
Bar keel 392
Barkhan dune 283

Bar line 502
Barnacle 172-173
Barnard's Star 23
Baroque style 478-483
Barosaurus 82
Barrel
  Gun turret 397
  Wood capstan 387
Barrel joint 508
Barrel vault 484-485
  Ancient Roman building 463-464
  Baroque church 479
  Medieval church 468
  Nineteenth-century building 493
Barrier beach 294
Barrier reef 299
Barry, C. 493
Bars 516-517
Bar swivel 562
Baryonyx 83, 84-85
Baryte 270
Basal disc 167
Basal scale 114
Basalt 274-275
Basaltic lava 272
Bascule 493
Base
  Ancient Greek temple 461
  Ancient Roman building 463, 465
  Asian building 490
  Baroque church 479, 481
  Dome 484, 486, 487
  French temple 485
  Gothic church 470, 472
  Medieval church 469
  Neoclassical building 478, 483
  Renaissance theatre 477
  Sheet lead 383
  Twentieth-century building 494
  Twin bollards 386
Baseball 536-537
Base line
  Calligraphy lettering 445
  Tennis 544
Basement 483
Basement membrane of Bowman's capsule 257
Base of phalanx 230
Base plate 552, 581
Bases 556
Basic movements 237
Basic shield volcano 272
Basidium 115
Basilar artery 252
Basilar membrane 243
Basilican system 468
Basilica of St. Madeleine 468
Basilic vein 253
Basket
  Basketball 532
  Ski pole 552-553
Basket arch 472, 484
Basketball 532-533
Basket star 174
Basking shark 179
Bas-relief carving 491
Bass angling 562
Bass bridge
  Concert grand piano 515
  Upright piano 514
Bass clarinet 504
Bass clef 502
Bass drum 504-505, 518-519
Bass formation 277
Bass joint 508
Bass notes 512
Bassoon 503, 504-505, 508

Bass ports 584
Bass voice 502
Bastille 466
Bat
  Baseball 537
  Cricket 539
Bat (animal) 105
Batholiths 274-275
Batsman 538-539
Batten
  74-gun ship 381
  Junk 376
  Wall construction 602
Batter 536-537
Battery
  Bell-47 helicopter 422
  Bersey electric cab 342
  Digital video camera 582
  Hubble Space Telescope 613
  Inverter 355
  Kirby BSA racing sidecar 369
Battery assembly 555
Battery box 327, 424
Battery carrier 338
Battery case 580
Battery charger connector 589
Battery clip 581
Battery compartment 407
Battery cooling fan 555
Battery electronic control module (ECM) 555
Battery identification 589
Battery lid 586
Battery overspill 422
Battery release 582
Battery strap 339
Battery terminal 578
Battery tray 579
Batting gloves
  Baseball 537
  Cricket 539
Battlemented cornice 471
Battlements 466-467
Battleship 394-395
Bauxite 268
Bay
  Building 468, 469, 494
  Coastline features 295
  River features 291
Bay-head beach 294
Bay-leaf garland 480
Bayonet fixing 352
Bay window 477
"B" button 578-579
BE 2B bomber 404-405
Beach
  Coastline 294-295
  River development 289
Beacon 407, 422-423
Beaded edge tyre 336
Beadlet anemone 166
Bead moulding 459
Beak
  Ankylosaurus 94
  Attic vase 372
  Bird 188-190
  Ceratopsian 100
  Chelonian 186
  Dolphin 204
  Euoplocephalus 94
  Hatching chick 192-193
  Iguanodon 97
  Moss 119
  Octopus 176
  Ornithopod 96
  Panoplosaurus 94
  Protoceratops 102
  Psittacosaurus 103
  Stegosaurus 92
Beaked whale 204
Beaker 312
Beam
  BAe-146 jetliner 414
  Gothic church 473

High-tension 496
Iron paddlesteamer 393
Modern building 497-499
Nineteenth-century building 492
Single skull 560
Bean
  Black 153
  Broad 152
Bear 104, 106, 194-195
Bearing
  Electric generator 317
  Jaguar V12 engine 345
  Motorcycle gearbox 366
  Rotary engine output shaft 411
Bearing assembly 425
Bearing housing 344
Bearing mount 411
Bearing seal 359
Bearing sleeve 338
"Beast feet" 84
Beaded gold 452
Beaters 516, 518-519
Beats 502
Bcckct 383
Becket Chapel 467
Bed
  Relief printing press 449
  Sedimentary rocks 277
Bedding plane
  Cave system 285
  Coastline 294-295
Bedford cord upholstery 336
Bedplate 390
Bedrock 298
  Delta formation 291
Bee 168, 379
Bee hummingbird 193
Bee pollination 144-145
Beeswax 384
Beethoven 35
Beetle 168
Begonia 129, 155
Begonia x tuberhybrida 129, 155
Behaviour 108, 237
Belaying pin 382
Belemnites 71, 278-279
Belfry
  74-gun ship 380
  Church of St. George in the East 481
Bell 508
Bell 206 Jetranger 423
Bell 47G-3B1 422-423
Bellatrix 18
Bell chamber 493
Bell crank 391
Bell housing 347
Bell joint 508
Bello 35
Bell Regio
  Radar map of Venus 36
  Structure of Venus 37
Belly
  Bird 188
  Caiman 186
  Dolphin 204
  Elephant 201
  Horse 198
  Lion 195
  Lizard 184
  Sail 384
  Viola 511
  Violin 510
Belly-band 555
Belt
  Jupiter 44-45
  Structure of Saturn 47
Belt armour 394
Belt colour 556
Belt drive 366
Belt pulley 345
Belt tensioner 344, 364

Belvedere 476
Bench officials
  Ice hockey 550
  Lacrosse 541
Bending 318
Bends 587
Benguela current 297
  Satellite map 264
Benz, Karl 354
Benz Motorwagen 355
Benz six-cylinder engine 405
Berardius bairdi 205
Berberis sp. 130-131
Berkelium 311
Berries 148-149
Bersey electric cab 342
Berthing ropes 387
Beryl 270
Beryllium 310
Beta Hydri 20
Beta Mensae 20
Beta Pictoris 21
Beta ring 48
Betelgeuse 18, 21
  Hertzsprung-Russell diagram 23
  Orion 18
  Universe 10-11
Betula grossa 74
Betula lenta 76
Betulites 74
Bevel 444
Bevel gear 335
Bevel pinion 338
Beverley Minster 484
Bezel 584
Bhagirathi Parbat 62
Bianco di San Giovanni 454-455
Biathlon rifle 549
Bib 557
Bi-block engine 337
Biceps brachii muscle 226
Biceps femoris muscle 227
Bicycle 360-361
Bicycle anatomy 358-359
Bicycle riding 315
Biennials 128
Biflagellate cell 116
Bifurcate ligament 232
"Big Ben" 493
Bighorn rifle shooting 548-549
Big end
  Flat-four cylinder arrangement 340
  Four-stroke cycle 343
  Jaguar straight six engine 344
  Mid West engine 410
  Trojan engine 342
Big-end bearing 335
Bight 388
Big toe 232-233
Bile duct 189, 249
Bilge keel 395, 397
Bilge keelson 393
Bill
  Danforth anchor 386
  Running block 383
  Sail hook 384
Bilobed leaves 123
Bin base 592
Bin cover handle 593
Bin cover retaining clip 592, 593
Binder 464
Binder bolt 361
Binding 385
  Acoustic guitar 512
  Iron paddlesteamer 392
Binding medium 440
Bin handle 592
Bin handle clip 592
Bin lower seal 592
Binnacle box 378
Binocular eyepieces 610, 611

Bin upper seal 592
Bin upper seal seating 592
Biology symbols 591, 621
Bipedal dinosaur 84, 96, 100
Bipinnate leaf 137
Biplane elevator 398-399
Biplanes 402-403, 408
Bipolar neuron 239
Birch 74, 76
Bird 84, 188-191
  Beak 190
  Earth's evolution 57
  Feathers 191
  Feet 190
  Fossil record 279
  Wing 191
"Bird feet" 96
Bird-hipped dinosaur 82, 92, 96
Bird of prey 188
Bird pollination 144
Bishop pine 124-125
Bismuth 281, 311
Bit 601
Biternate leaves 137
Bit-guard 555
Bitt
  74-gun ship 380-381
  Roman corbita 373
Bitter end, Hawser 387
Bituminous coal 280
Bivalves 79, 176, 278-279
Blackbacked gull 193
Black bean 153
Black belt 556
Blackberry 130, 146-147
Blackburn monoplane 400-401
Blackburn, Robert 400
Black dwarf 24 25
Blackheaded gull 189
Black ink cartridge 574
Black ink-cartridge clamp 574
Black holes 28-29
  Galaxies 12
  Massive stars 26-27
Black Mesa 277
Black rhinoceros 199
Black Sea 265
Blackstonia perfoliata 144
Black walnut 137
Black widow spider 171
Bladder
  Bony fish 181
  Chimpanzee 202
  Dolphin 205
  Domestic cat 195
  Elephant 200
  Human 215, 257, 258-259, 261
  Lizard 185
  Rabbit 196
  Soccer ball 525
  Swim 178, 180-181
  Tortoise 187
  Urinary 181
Bladder wrack 117
Blade
  Butterwort 161
  Calligraphy drawing board 445
  Danforth anchor 386
  Dicotyledon leaf 127
  Fencing foil 557
  Golf clubs 547
  Hockey stick 540
  Kayak paddle 560
  Leaf surfaces 136, 138
  Monocotyledon leaf 127
  Propeller 390
  Roman rudder 373
  Sculling oar 560
  Seaweed 116-117
  Vegetative reproduction 154
  Venus fly trap 160
  Volkswagen Beetle 341

Wetland plants 158-159
Wind turbine 604
Blade bearing 604
Blade counterweight 406, 422
Blade hub 604
Blade pitch control 604
Blade-root attachment 422-423
Blade tip sealing shroud 419
Blanking plate 411
Blast bag 396
Blastocyst 607
Blast-pipe 325
Blending 440
Blériot XI monoplane 401
Blériot, Louis
    Early monoplane 400
    Pioneers of flight 398
Blindage 377
Blind arch
    Asian building 491
    Cathedral dome 487
    Gothic church 470
Blind door 478
Blind pull 336-337
Blind release bar 552
Blinds 603
Blind-side prop 530
Blind spot 241
Blind tracery 493
Blind trefoil 473
Blind window 478
Block and tackle 582-583
Block carving 470
Block cube 270
Block disintegration 282
Block-fault lake 293
Block-fault mountain 62
Blocking pad 550
Blocks 510
Blood cells 253
Blower control 525
Blower isolator valve 325
Blow hole 508
Blowhole 205
Blubber 204
Blue-and-yellow macaw 190
Blue cell 584
Blue-green alga 56, 78
Blue light 318
Blue line 550
Blue supergiant star
    Hertzsprung-Russell diagram 23
    Stellar black hole 29
Bluff 289
Blunt button 556-557
BMW R/60 motorcycle 362
Board
    Ice hockey rink 550
    Modelling 455
    Pastels 441
Boarding 464
Board mounting 450-451
Boat boom 395
Boatbuilder's tools 374
Boat handling derrick 395
Boat slide 378
Boat winch 394
Bobstay 379
Body
    Anchisaurus 89
    Discus 542
    Dunkeld wet fly 563
    Motorcycle 364-365
    Sauropodomorpha 88
    Stringed instruments 510
Body-bag 426
Body cells 216-217
Body cradle 598
Body drop 556
Body joint
    Flute 508

Piccolo 508
Body mount 558
Body organs 214-215
Body padding 526
Body sections
    Insect 168
    Scorpion 170
    Spider 170-171
Body-shell 518-519
Bodyshell
    Renault Clio 348-349
    Volkswagen Beetle 341
Body tackles 528
Body temperature regulation
    Dinosaurs 92
    Mammals 104
Body wire 557
Bodywork 348-349
    Racing cars 356
    Volkswagen Beetle 341
Bodywork mounting point 364
Boeing 747-400 412
Bogie axle 326
Bogie frame 325
Bogie main landing gear 416
Boiler
    Box boiler 392
    Donkey boiler 392
    Steamboat with paddle wheels 391
    Steam locomotives 324-325
Boiler pressure gauge 325
Boiler water level 325
Bole base 432-433
Bollard
    Battleship 395
    Frigate 397
    Mooring and anchoring 386-387
Bolson 282
Bolster 378
Bolt
    Church of St. Pierre 499
    Lower deadeye 383
    Shackle 386
Bolted anchor 425
Bolt hole
    Drum brake 365
    Mid West rotary engine 411
    Twin bollards 387
Bolt rest 548
Bolt rope 372, 384
Bolts 548-549
Bomb 404, 408
Bomb aimer's viewing panel 408
Bomb door 408
Bomber
    Modern military aircraft 420
    World War I aircraft 404-405
    World War II aircraft 408-409
Bomb rack 404
Bonaventure mast 377
Bonaventure topcastle 377
Bonaventure topmast 377
Bonaventure yard 377
Bonaventure yard 377
Bonded brick wall 492
Bonding
    Chemical reactions 312
    Covalent 309
    English bond 485
    Gases 307
    Ionic 308
    Liquids 307
Bone cell 217, 225
Bone marrow smear 225
Bones
    Fossil 278

Human 224-225, 230, 252
Bone structure 108
Bone surface 80
Bonnet
    1906 Renault 337
    Ford Model T 339
    Renault Clio 349
    Volkswagen Beetle 340-341
Bonnet catch 336, 349
Bonnet clip 339
Bonnet-release cable 349
Bonnet-release handle 341
Bonnet stay 337
Bony crest
    Baryonyx 83
    Corythosaurus 98
    Lambeosaurus 99
    Parasaurolophus 99
Bony dorsal shield 78
Bony fish 180-181
Bony frill 100
Bony nodule
    Pachycephalosaurus 100
    Prenocephale 100
Bony ridge 100
Bony shelf 100, 101
Bony spike 100
Bony strut 83
Bony studs 92
Bony tendons 96
Boom
    Battleship 394-395
    Curtiss Model-D pusher 399
    Double topsail schooner 385
    Guest boat boom 394
    Hong Kong and Shanghai Bank 498
    Longboat 380
    Rigging 382
    Sailing dinghy 561
Boom guy block 382
Boomkin 380
Boötes 18, 21
Boots
    American football 527
    Baseball 537
    Hurling 541
    Riding 554
    Rugby 551
    Sailing 560
    Ski 552
    Soccer 525
Bordino Steam Carriage 334-335
Borealis Planitia 35
Borneo 265
Boron 311
Boss
    Church roof 468-469
    Hurley 541
    Viking karv 374
Bothriolepis 65
Botryoidal habit 270-271
Bottom ballast 377
Bottom bracket 358
Bottom hose 351
Bottom plate 590, 592-593
Bottom race 359
Bottomset strata 283
Boudin 60-61
Boulder beach 295
Boulder clay 286
Bounce pass 535
Boundary
    Cricket 538
    Mantle-crust 39
    Outer core-mantle 39
Boundary line
    Australian rules football 528
    Badminton 545
    Cricket 538
    Squash 545

Bow
    74-gun ship 381
    Kayak 560
    Sailing dinghy 561
    Stringed instruments 510
    Wooden sailing ship 378
Bowball 561
Bow drill 109
Bower anchor
    Battleship 395
    Sailing warship 377
    Wooden sailing ship 379
Bow front 483
Bowl 445
Bowler 538
Bowline 388, 389
Bowling crease 538
Bowman's capsule 256
Bowman's space 257
Bow ornament 375
Bowpost 561
Bows 548
Bow section 392
Bow-side oar 560
Bowsprit
    Iron paddlesteamer 393
    Longboat 380
    Rigging 382
    Sailing warship 376
    Tea clipper 392
    Wooden sailing ship 378-379
Bowsprit cap 382
Bowtell moulding 475
Box 477
Box boiler 392
Box fold 61
Box freight car 327
Boxing 556
Box-leaved milkwort 144
Box-section tubular cradle frame 364
Box sister keelson 393
Boxwood staff 377
Brace
    Asian building 490
    Barrel vault 485
    Double topsail schooner 385
    "Ellerman Lines" steam locomotive 324
    Gothic building 473
    Neoclassical building 479
    Nineteenth-century building 493
    Roman corbita 372
    Sailing warship 377
    Trombone 506
    Wooden sailing ship 378
Brace-and-bit 600-601
Brace block 373
Bracer 548
Brachial artery 253
Brachialis muscle 226
Brachial plexus 238
Brachial valve 278
Brachiocephalic trunk 251
Brachiocephalic vein 253
Brachiopods 278-279
Brachioradialis muscle 226
Brachiosaurus 88, 90-91
Brachylophosaurus 98
Bracing 513
Bracing strut 401-402, 423
Bracing tube 364
Bracing wire
    Blériot XI monoplane 401
    LVG CVI fighter 405
    Wright Flyer 399
Bracken 121

Bracket
    Baroque church 479
    Cathedral dome 484
    Gothic building 473
    Islamic tomb 489
    Medieval building 466
    Neoclassical building 478
    Renaissance building 475
Bracket shell 58
Bracteoles
    Dehiscent fruit 151
    Ice-plant 129
    Live-for-ever 129
Bracts 141-143
    Bromeliad 113
    Dicotyledon flower 127
    Durmast oak 131
    Florists' chrysanthemum 129
    Guzmania lingulata 163
    Ice-plant 129
    Indehiscent fruit 150
    Live-for-ever 129
    Peruvian lily 129
    Rose 131
    Slender thistle 129
    Wind-pollinated plant 144
Bract scales 122
Braided polyester 388
Braided stream 286
Braiding
    Dragon prowhead 374
    River features 290
Brailing rope 372
Brail line 372
Brain
    Bird 189
    Bony fish 181
    Butterfly 169
    Chimpanzee 202
    Crayfish 173
    Dogfish 179
    Dolphin 205
    Domestic cat 195
    Elephant 200
    Hominid 108
    Human 236-237
    Lizard 185
    Octopus 176
    Rabbit 196
    Spider 170
Braincase 108
Brain cavity 100
Brainstem 236
Brake 352, 350
    Brake actuating chain 327
    Brake arm 552
    Brake back plate 340, 350
    Brake block 360
    Brake bridge 361
Brake cable 365
Brake calliper
    ARV light aircraft 424
    Disc brake 365
    Harley-Davidson FLHS Electra Glide 363
    Honda VF750 364-365
    Husqvarna Motocross TC610 368
    Renault Clio 351
    Suzuki RGV500 368-369
    Wagon bogie 331
Brake cylinder 327, 350-351
Brake disc
    ARV light aircraft 424
    Renault Clio 351
    Wagon bogie 331
Brake drum 359-340, 342
Brake duct 357
Brake fluid 365
Brake hose 351
Brakeless wheel hub 369
Brake lever
    ARV light aircraft 425

Benz Motorwagen 335
Bicycle 359
Eddy Merckx racing bicycle 361
Harley-Davidson FLHS Electra Glide 363
Kirby BSA 369
Suzuki RGV500 369
White Steam Car 342
"Windcheetah" racing HPV bicycle 361
Brake master cylinder
    Harley-Davidson FLHS Electra Glide 363
    Honda VF750 364
    Suzuki RGV500 368
Brake mount 424
Brake pad
    Disc brake 365
    Eddy Merckx racing bicycle 361
    Renault Clio 351
    Wagon bogie 331
Brake pedal
    Harley-Davidson FLHS Electra Glide 363
    Honda VF750 364
    Oldsmobile bodywork 337
    Renault Clio 350
    Steam-powered Cugnot 334
    Suzuki RGV500 368
Brake pipe
    ARV light aircraft 424
    BAe-146 components 414
    Lockheed Electra airliner 406-407
    Renault Clio 350
Brake plate 365
Brake quadrant 335
Brake rigging
    British Rail Class 20 diesel engine 327
    "Ellerman Lines" steam locomotive 324-325
Brake rod 337, 339
Brake servo 351
Brake shield 351
Brake shoe 330
    "Deltic" diesel-electric locomotive 327
    Drum brake 365
    "Ellerman Lines" steam locomotive 325
    Renault Clio 350
Brake slip 395
Brake torque arm 364
Brake vacuum pump 324
Braking
    Motorcycle 364
    Train 330
Braking control system 330
Braking distance 331
Bramante 35
Bramble 130, 146-147
Branched leaf venation 127
Branches
    Bishop pine 124
    Clubmoss 120
    Crab cactus 129
    Dicotyledons 127
    Horsetail 120
    Perennials 130-131
    Seaweed 117
    Sporophore 114
    Woody plants 130-131
Branchial heart 176
Branching bracteole 151
Branchiostegal ray 181
Branchlet 114
Branch tracery 471
Brassavola nodosa 162
Brass bevel 336-337
Brass housing for ignition cable 343

Brassica sp. 132
Brass instruments 504–505, 506–507
Brazil 331
Brazilian battleship 394–395
Brazilian current 296
Brazilian Highlands 264
Bread 598
Breakfast-room 483
Breakwater
  Battleship 395
  Frigate 397
  Single scull 561
Breast
  Bird 188
  Horse 199
  Human 211
Breast auger 374
Breast bone 218
Breast stroke 558–559
Breastwork 380
Breather paper 602
Breather pipe 422
Breccia 276–277
Breech 396
Breech block 396
Breccia 557
Breech wheel 396
Breve rest 502
Brick arch 324
Brick pier 495
Brick vault 492
Brick wall 492
Bridge
  Acoustic guitar 512–513
  Battleship 394–395
  Cello 511
  Double bass 511
  Electric guitar 513
  Frigato 397
  Golf course 546
  London Bridge 466–467
  Medieval castle 467
  Modern building 498
  Viola 511
  Violin 510
Bridge pin 512
Bridges 330
Bridle 555
Bright Angel shale 277
B ring 46–47
Britain 331
Brittle stars 174–175
Broad axe 374
Broad bean 133, 152
Broad disc 79
Broad lace trim 336–337
Broadside 378
Broken pediment 481
Bromeliads 112–113
  Epiphytic 162–163
Bromine 311
Bronchi 254
Bronchial nerve 254
Bronchial tree 254
Bronchial vein 254
Bronchiole and alveoli 254
Bronchus
  Frog 182
  Human 215, 255
Bronze casting 452
Bronze finishing tools 454
Bronze mast truck 372
Bronze statue 455
Broomrape 163
Brother T-78 fax machine 572, 573
Browband 554–555
Brow horn 102
Brow horn core 103
Brown alga 116
Brown scales 121
Brown seaweed 116–117
Brow ridge
  Australopithecus 108
  Gorilla 203
  Homo sapiens 108

Browser icon 577
Browser menu 577
Brush 452, 444, 600
Brushbar 592, 593
Brushbar drive belt cover 593
Brushbar motor control 593
Brush holder 600
Brushing boot 554
Brush lettering equipment 444
Brush rest 444
Brush tool articulation 595
Bryce Canyon 276
Bryophyta 118
Bryophytes 112, 118–119
Bryozoans 279
Bryum sp. 112
Buccal cavity
  Bird 189
  Chimpanzee 202
  Dolphin 205
  Domestic cat 195
  Elephant 200
  Pachycephalosaurus 100
  Rabbit 196
  Tortoise 187
Buccal mass 176
Buccinator muscle 229
Bucket seat 361
Bucket tappet 344
Bud
  Adventitious 154
  Aechmea miniata 162
  Apical meristem 134
  Begonia 129
  Bishop pine 124
  Broomrape 163
  Clematis flower 131
  Dicotyledons 127
  Durmast oak 131
  Horse chestnut 130
  Larkspur 141
  Lily 140
  Lime 143
  London plane 134
  Moss 119
  Oxalis sp. 121
  Pine needle 125
  Rhizome 155
  Root tuber 154–155
  Rose 131
  Rowan twig 131
  Stolon 154
  Water lily 159
Buddhist style 490
Budh Planitia 35
Bud scale
  Bishop pine 124
  Dicotyledon stem 127
  London plane 134
  Pine shoot apex 125
Buffer
  "Deltic" diesel-electric locomotive 327
  "Ellerman Lines" steam locomotive 324–325
  Italian State Railways Class 402 328
  "Rocket" steam locomotive 324
Buffing pad 328
Bugle 506
Bulb
  Renault Clio 352
  Vegetative reproduction 154–155
Bulb horn
  1906 Renault 337
  Ford Model T 338
Bulbil 154–155
Bulbourethral gland 259
Bulkhead
  ARV Super 2 425

Flat freight car 327
Bulkhead stiffener 393
Bulkhead trim 407
Bulldog clip 430
Bullet 397, 549
Bullet block 373
Bullet-shaped guard 278
Bull-head rail 331
Bullnose chisel 452
Bull's-eye 549
Bulwark
  74-gun ship 380
  Ironclad 393
Bumblebee 168
Bumper
  Bus 332–333
  Honda Insight 354
  Renault Clio 353
  Volkswagen Beetle 341
Bung 313, 560
Bunkers 546–547
Bunk space 397
Bun lamp burner 339
Buntline 372
Buon fresco 434–435
Buoy 379
Buoyant wetland plants 158
Burmese pagoda 490
Burning reaction 312, 313, 315
Burnisher 432, 446
Bursting charge 397
Buses 332–333
Bush 605
Bushes 150–151
Bushing 314
Butt
  Bassoon 508
  Lacrosse crosse 541
  Tennis racket 544
Butt cap 563
Butte
  Igneous rock structures 274
  Weathering and erosion 283
Buttercup 127, 132–133
Butterfly 168
Butterfly knot 389
Butterfly plate 382
Butterfly swimming stroke 558–559
Butterwort 160–161
Butt extension 563
Buttock
  Horse 198
  Human 210
Button contact 578
Button head rivet 392
Button-quilted upholstery 336
Buttress 484
  Baroque church 478–481
  Dome 486
  Gothic church 470–473
  Medieval building 466, 468–469
  Nineteenth-century building 493
Butt section 562

C

3C275 (quasar) 11
Caardius tenuiflorus 129
Cab 324, 327
Cabane strut 404
Cabbage 152
Cab-end bogie 327
Cabin
  74-gun ship 380–381
  Iron paddlesteamer 392–393
  Wooden sailing ship 379
Cabin air-discharge aperture 414

Cabin air duct 417
Cabin air-pressure discharge valve 413
Cabinet rasp 452
Cabinet underside 583
Cabin trim 406–407
Cable 600–601
Cable guide 358–359, 360
Cable holder 395
Cable retaining gland 598
Cables and ducting 602
Cable stop 365
Cacti
  Desert survivors 112
  Dryland adaptation 156
  Herbaceous flowering plants 129
Cadmium 311
Cadmium red 436
Cadmium yellow 438
Caecum
  Bird 189
  Brachiosaurus 90
  Chimpanzee 202
  Cow 198
  Digestive 176, 173
  Gut 170
  Human 249
  Octopus 176
  Pyloric 181–174
  Rabbit 196
  Rectal 174
Caelum 18
Caernarvon Castle 466
Caesium 310
Caiman 186–187
Calamus 191
Calcanean tendon 232–233
Calcaneum 183, 199
Calcareous ooze 299
Calcareous plates 172
Calcareous tufa 284
Calcite (cah ium carbonate)
  Blue chalk 430
  Carbonates 269
  Cave 284–285
  Fossils 278
  Mohs scale 271
  Sedimentary rocks 277
  Testing candle wax 313
Calcite curtain 285
Calcite ossicle 174
Calcite ridge 284–285
Calcium 310
  Earth's composition 39
  Earth's crust 58
  Seawater salt content 296
Calcium line 23
Calculator icon 568
Caldera
  Igneous rock structures 275
  Lake formation 293
  Volcano 272
Caledonian mountains
  Late Carboniferous period 67
  Triassic period 69
Calendars 618
Calf 210
Californian purple sea urchin 175
Californium 311
Call and select option button 588
Call hold button 572
Calliactis parasitica 166
Calligraphy 444–445
Calliper assembly 365
Callipers 452
Callisto 42
Call-send button 588
Call transfer button 572
Caloris Basin 34–35
Caloris Montes 35

Calypte helenae 193
Calyptra 119
Calyx 140
  Allium sp. 143
  Centaury 144
  Human 256
  Simple succulent berry 149
Cam 344
Camarasaurus 91
Cambium 126
Cambrian period
  Fossil record 279
  Geological timescale 56
Camcorder 582
Cam cover
  Jaguar straight six engine 344
  Jaguar V12 engine 345
  72° VTO engine 356
Camellia 137
Camels 198–199
Camera 611, 615
  Digital 580–581
  Digital video 582–583
Camera pouch 426
Cam follower
  Ford diesel engine 347
  Jaguar straight six engine 344
  Jaguar V12 engine 345
  Velocette OHV engine 367
Cam lobe 344
Camouflage 409
Camouflage coloration 192
Campaniform capital 458
Campanile 477
Camptosaurus 70, 97
Camshaft 343–345
Camshaft gear 367
Camshaft sprocket 345
Camshaft timing gear 344
Canada 331
Canadian football 524, 526–527
Canadian pond weed 158–159
Canal
  Sea urchin 175
  Starfish 174
Canals 42
Canaries current 296
Cancel button 575, 588
Cancellous bone 224
Cancer 18, 21
Candelabrum 476
Candle lamp 335
Candle wax 312–313
Canes Venatici 18, 21
Canine tooth
  Bear 106, 194
  Chimpanzee 202
  Human 246
  Hyaenodon 107
  Lion 194
  Opossum 106
  Smilodon 107
  Toxodon 106
Canis familiaris 195
Canis Major 18, 21
Canis Minor 18, 21
Canister 394
Cannon 376, 594
Cannon bone 198–199
Cannondale bicycle 361
Canoeing 560–561
Canopus 15
Canopy
  1906 Renault 336–337
  ARV light aircraft 424–425
  Bell-47 helicopter 422
  Daimler engine 354
  Ford Model T 339
  Hawker Tempest

components 409
Oldsmobile engine 336
Schleicher glider 426
Schweizer helicopter 423
Canopy latch 425
Canopy rail 409
Canson paper 441
Cant frame 381
Cantilever beam 494
Cantilever brake 358, 361
Cantilever brake boss 359
Cantilevered brake 495
Cantle
  Racing saddle 555
  Showjumping saddle 554
Canvas
  Acrylic paint 442
  Oil paint 436
  Preparation 437
Canvas shroud 362
Canvas support 437
Canyon
  Sedimentary rocks 276–277
  Weathering and erosion 282–283
Cap
  Alga 116
  Fungus 114–115
  Radicle tip 155
  Wood capstan 387
  Wooden sailing ship 378–379
Capacitor 587
Capacity measurements 590
Cape gooseberry 149
Capella 18, 21
Cape Royal 277
Capillary fringe 293
Capillary network 254
Capital
  Ancient Egyptian building 458–459
  Ancient Greek building 458, 460–461
  Ancient Roman building 458, 465, 465
  Asian building 490, 491
  Baroque church 479, 481
  Cathedral dome 487
  Domed roof 486
  French temple 485
  Islamic mosque 488
  Medieval building 467–469
  Neoclassical building 478, 483
  Ptolemaic–Roman period 459
  Renaissance building 476–477
  Romanesque style 468
Capitate bone 230
Capitulum 129, 142
Cap line 445
Capricornus 19, 20
Capstan 387
  74-gun ship 380
  Iron paddlesteamer 393
  Wooden sailing ship 379
Capstan screw 514
Capsule
  Dry fruit 150–151
  Moss 112, 119
Captain's cabin 379, 381
Captain's seat 416
Captain's shelter 394
Capybara 196–197
Carapace 173, 187
Carbon
  Atomic mass 510
  Bows 548
  Candle wax 312–313
  Coal formation 280

Minerals 268
Periodic table 311
Small stars 24–25
Structure of red
supergiant 26
Carbonates 269
Carbon atom 138
Carbon bush 605
Carbon dioxide
Earth's atmosphere 300
Gas 312–313
Mars' atmosphere 43
Photosynthesis 138
Respiratory system 255
Scrubber compartment
397
Structure of comet 53
Venus' atmosphere 37
Carbon graphite racket
544
Carbonic acid 284
Carboniferous period 56–
57, 66-67
Reptiles 80
Carbon ink stick 444
Carbonized wood 430
Carbon monoxide
Mars' atmosphere 43
Venus' atmosphere 37
Carbon powder 311
Carbon-rich earth layers
66
Car-building robots 608
Carburettor
ARV light aircraft 425
Mid West twin-rotor
engine 411
Pegasus Quasar
microlight 427
Two-stroke engine 366
Carburettor cover 369
Carburettor hot-air intake
pipe 422
Carburettor hot air lever
425
Cardiac notch 248
Cardiac region of stomach
179
Cardiac stomach 174
Cardiac vein 250
Carduus tenuiflorus 129
Cargo-carrying boat
Dhow 376
Junk 376
Liberty ship 392
Roman corbita 372–373
Tea clipper 392
Cargo derrick 592
Cargo hatch 376
Cargo hold 372, 392
Car, hybrid 354
Caribbean plate 59
Caribbean Sea 264
Carina 21
Carinal canal 120
Carina plate 173
Carling 380
Carmel formation 276
Carnallite 271
Carnassial teeth 194
Carnivores 104, 194–195
Jurassic period 70
Theropod 84
Triassic period 68
Carnivorous plants 160–
161
Pitcher plant 113
Carotid canal 220
Carp 180
Carpals
Bird 189
Bird's wing 191
Domestic cat 195
Elephant 201
Frog 183
Hare 197
Horse 199
Kangaroo 206
Lizard 184

Platypus 206
Rhesus monkey 202
Seal 204
Carp angling 562
Carpathian mountains 77,
265
Carpels 140–141
Dehiscent fruit 151
Fertilization 146–147
Fruit development 148–
149
Insect-pollinated plant
144
Lemon fruit 148
Ovary 140
Stigma 140
Style 140
Carpel wall 148, 151
Carpophore 151
Carpus
Crab 172
Crayfish 173
Human 218
Carrara white marble 453
Carriage 413, 570
Carriage drivebelt 574
Carriage shaft 571
Carrick bend 587, 589
Carrion crow 193
Carrot 128, 132
Carrying fork 334
Carrying handle 366, 567
Carrying wheel 324
Cartilage
Auricle 242
Bony fish 180
Meatus 242
Wrist 230
Cartilaginous fish 178–
179, 180
Cartouche 458
Cartridge starter 408
Caruncle 213
Carved sculpture 452, 453
Carved stone 488
Carvel-built hull 376, 391
Carvel planking 376, 377
Carving
Asian building 490-491
Gothic building 470
Sculpture 452
Carving mallet 452
Caryopses 113, 150
Casa de las Conchas 476
Casa del Fascio 495
Case 567
Caspian Sea 265
Cassette compartment
assembly 83
Cassette compartment
cover 583
Cassette compartment lid
582
Cassini Division 46, 47
Cassini space probe 614–
615
Cassiopeia 19
Cassowaries 188
Cast alloy wheel 346
Cast aluminium wheel
spider 336
Castanea sativa 136, 150
Castanets 504, 517
Casting 452, 454
Cast-iron 492–493
Cast-iron chair 331
Cast iron cylinder barrel
363
Caste-deck gunport 376–
377
Castles, 574, 466-467
Castor 18, 21
Castor canadensis 197
Cat 104, 194-195
Catalyst 355
Catalytic converter 344,
350, 356
Catamaran 560
Cataphoresic coating 348

Cataphyll 152
Cat block 581
Catcher's mask 556
Catch glove 550
Catena 572
Catenary 328, 330
Caterpillar 168, 169, 611
Eggs 192
Catharina 40
Cathead
74-gun ship 580
Battleship 395
Cathedral of St. Lazare
468
Cations 308
Catkin 144
Catted anchor 581
Cattle 104, 198
Caucasus 265
Caudal fin 178, 179, 180–
181
Caudal musculature 90, 95
Caudal plate 92-93
Caudal spike 92-93
Caudal vertebrae
Ankylosaurus 95
Archaeopteryx 85
Crocodile 186
Diplodocus 90
Domestic cat 195
Elephant 201
Eryops 81
Euoplocephalus 95
Gallimimus 86
Hare 197
Horse 199
Iguanodon 96
Kangaroo 206
Kentrosaurus 93
Lizard 184–185
Parasaurolophus 98
Plateosaurus 89
Platypus 206
Rhesus monkey 202
Seal 204
Stegoceras 101
Stegosaurus 93
Struthiomimus 87
Triceratops 102
Tuojiangosaurus 93
Tyrannosaurus 84-85
Westlothiana 81
Caudate nucleus 237
Caudex 113
Caudo-femoral muscle 97
Cauliculus 460
Caulophryne jordani 180
Cave bear skull 77
Caves 284-285
Coastline 294-295
Glacier 286
Cavetto moulding
Ancient Egyptian
building 458-459
Baroque church 479
French temple 485
Gothic building 472
Renaissance building
477
Cavies 196
Cayley, Sir George 398
CCD board 580
CCD connector socket 581
CCD microchip 580
CCD ribbon connector
580
CCD (Charge-Coupled
Devices) 570, 572
CCD window 589
C clef 502
CD 579
CD-drive 521
CD/DVD drive 566
CDs 586, 587
Cedar-tree laccolith 274
Ceilings 463, 484
Celestial equator
Stars of northern skies
18-19

Stars of southern skies
20-21
Celestial poles 18
Celestial sphere 18
Cell
Alga 116-117
Body 217
Building 469, 485
Chusan palm leaf 130
Clubmoss stem 120
Collar 166
Dicotyledon 126-127
Epidermal 166
Epiphytic orchid 162
Fern rachis 121
Horsetail stem 120
Leaf 126, 139
Marram grass 113
Monocotyledon 126-127
Moss 119
Mushroom 115
Photosynthesis 138-139
Pine 124-125
Pore 166
Root 132-133
Sinus 112
Spirogyra sp. 117
Stem 134-135
Wetland plants 158-159
Cella 461, 463, 485
Cell body 239
Cell membrane 217
Cell nuclear membrane
216
Cell nucleus 217
Cell nucleus residue 254
Cello 503-505, 510
Cells 607
Cellulose fibre insulation
602
Cell wall
Alga 112, 116
Leaf 139
Palisade mesophyll 139
Root 132
Spirogyra sp. 117
Stem surface 156
Celsius temperature scale
590
Cement-based adhesive
450
Cement gland 173
Cement-reinforced wall
494
Cenozoic era 57, 74, 76
Fossil record 279
Censer 488
Centaurium erythraea 144
Centaurus 18, 21
Centaurus A (radio
galaxy) 21
Centaurus and Crux 21
Central Asia 64
Central bulge 12, 14
Central canal 258
Central computer control
528
Central deflector 612
Central drive access 586
Central drive hole 586
Central electrode 306
Central nervous system
258
Central peak
Degas and Brönte 34
Venus' craters 36
Central processing unit
566, 579
Central retinal artery 240
Central retinal vein 240
Central shield 187
Central sulcus 236-237
Centre
American football 526
Australian football 528
Basketball 532
Canadian football 526
Lacrosse 541

Netball 535
Rugby 550
Centre-board 561
Centre buck-eye coupler
326
Centre circle
Australian rules football
528
Basketball 532
Ice hockey 550
Netball 535
Soccer 524
Centre console 353
Centre court 545
Centred rudder 375
Centre element 599
Centre field 556
Centre flag 529
Centre forward 540
Centre gangway 329
Centre Georges Pompidou
496-497
Centre girder 393
Centre half 540
Centre half-back 528, 529
Centre half-forward 528,
529
Centre hole 587
Centre line 413, 415
Fencing piste 557
Ice hockey 550
Soccer 524
Centre-line beam 426-427
Centre line keelson 393
Centrifugal brake 562
Centrifugal compressor
418
Centrifugal effect 297
Centriole 217
Centripetal river drainage
288
Centrum 187
Cephalaspis 65
Cephalic groove 173
Cephalic vein
Human 253
Octopus 176
Cephalopods 176, 279
Cephalothorax
Crayfish 173
Malacostraca 172
Scorpion 170
Shrimp 172
Spider 170-171
Cepheus 19
Ceramic end-piece 319
Ceratopsia 83, 103
Ceratosaurus 85
Ceraunius Tholus 43
Cercidiphyllum sp. 72
Cerebellum 212, 236-237,
238
Cerebral areas 237
Cerebral ganglion 169,
177
Cerebral vessel 257
Cerebrum 212, 236-237,
238
Cereoid cactus 129
Cerium 310
Ceropegia woodii 157
Ceruchi 372
Cerussite 269
Cervical musculature
Euoplocephalus 94
Gallimimus 86
Cervical nerves 238
Cervical plate 92-93
Cervical rib 84, 96, 100-
101, 103
Cervical vertebrae
Archaeopteryx 85
Arsinoitherium 104
Bird 189
Brachiosaurus 91
Crocodile 100
Domestic cat 195
Elephant 201
Eryops 80

Hare 197
Horse 199
Human 212, 222, 245
Iguanodon 96
Kangaroo 206
Kentrosaurus 93
Lizard 184
Parasaurolophus 99
Plateosaurus 88
Platypus 206
Rhesus monkey 202
Seal 204
Stegoceras 101
Stegosaurus 93
Struthiomimus 87
Toxodon 106
Tuojiangosaurus 93
Tyrannosaurus 84
Cervix 258-259
Cervus elephas 199
Cetaceans 204-205
Cetiosaurus 91
Cetorhinus maximus 179
Cetus 19, 20
Chaffinch 193
Chain
Bicycle 358-359, 360-
361
Drum kit 518
Motorcycle 366
Wheel and axle 320
Wooden sailing ship
378
Chain bobstay 382
Chain drive
Motorcycle clutch 362
Werner motorcycle 366
Wright Flyer 398-399
Chain locker 393
Chain motif 491
Chain plate 382
Chain swivel 386
Chain wale 376-377
Chajya 489
Chalcedony 271
Chalk 430
Tempera 432
Gesso 434
Pastel making 440
Fresco 434
Sedimentary rocks 277
Chamber
Building 465, 491
Gun turret 396
Chambers
Seaweed 116
Stomach 198
Substomatal 139
Chamfered corner 485,
488, 494
Championship golf
courses 546
Change 521
Chang Jiang 265
Channel
74-gun ship 581
Sailing warship 376-377
Temple of Neptune 460
Wooden sailing ship
378
Channelled wrack 116
Chapel
Baroque church 479
Gothic church 470
Medieval church 469
Chapel pier 467
Chaplet 454
Chapter-house 472
Charcoal drawing 430-431
Charentais melon 149
Charge
Four-stroke cycle 343
Modern engines 344
Charged atom 306, 308
Charged particle 316
Charging with ball 533
Charon 50
Chart house 394
Chase 395

Chassis
  First cars 354-355
  Ford Model T 338
  Kirby BSA sidecar 369
  Microwave
    combination oven 596
  Monocoque 363
  Motorcycle 362, 364-
    365
  Oldsmobile chassis
    337
  Panhard-system
  Volkswagen Beetle 340
  White Steam Car 342
Chassis earth terminal
  597
Chassis electrical plug
  357
Chassis frame 338
Chassis number 327
Chataya arch 491
Châteaux 474, 476-477
Chattra 491
Chattravali 490-491
Chauffeur's seat 354
Checkerbloom 136
Check pawl 562
Check
  74-gun ship 381
  Dunkeld wet fly 563
  Horse 199
  Human 212
  Running block 383
  Sailmaker's mallet 384
  Stegosaurus 92
Cheek horn 103
Cheek-piece
  Harness racer 555
  Showjumper 554
Cheek pouch 98, 196
Cheek teeth
  Ankylosaurs 92
  Carnivores 194
  Ornithopods 96
  Tetralophodon 104
  Theropods 84
Cheese 382, 588-589
Cheiracanthus 65
Cheirolepis 65
Chekhov 35
Chela 170, 172, 173
Chelicera 79
Chelicerae 170-171
Chelicerates 279
Cheliped
  Crab 172
  Crayfish 173
Chelonia 186
Chemical bond 307
Chemical change 280-281
Chemical energy 314-315
Chemical equations 312
Chemical properties
  Electrons 308, 310
  Substances 306
Chemical reactions 312-
  313
Chemical sedimentary
  rocks 276
Chemical symbols 312,
  591
  Periodic table 310-311
Chemical weathering 282
Chemise 466-467
Chemistry symbols 621
Cherry 148
Cherry wood 512
Chert 277
Cherub 472
Chervil 135
Chest
  Gorilla 203
  Human 211, 214
  Lion 194
Chestnut 198
Chest padding 551
Chest pass 532, 533
Chest protector 527
Chevet 469

Chevron 81, 85, 87, 89, 93,
  95-96, 98, 101-102
Chevron fold 61
Chevron-tread tyre 356
Chi1 Orionis 18
Chi2 Orionis 18
Chiastolite hornfels 275
Chihuahuan Desert 264
Chile 331
Chimney
  Bordino Steam Carriage
    354
  "Ellerman Lines" steam
    locomotive 525
  Iron paddlesteamer 393
  "Rocket" steam
    locomotive 324
Chimney-shaft 467
Chimney-stack 476, 483
Chimpanzee 202-203
Chin
  Bird 188
  Human 211, 212
China
  Ball games 524
  Late Carboniferous
    period 66-67
  Middle Ordovician
    period 64-65
  Ornithopod 96
  Railway track gauge
    331
  Thyreophorans 92
Chinese calendar 618
Chinese characters 445
Chinese junk 376
Chinese white 438
Chin groove 199
Chin gun turret 408
Chinle formation 276
Chin rest 510-511
Chin spoiler 346
Chipmunk 196
Chirostenotes 87
Chisel 452-453
  Chlamydosaurus sp. 116
Chlorenchyma 120
Chloride 296
Chlorine 311
Chlorophyll 138
  Chloroplast 139
  Photosynthesis pigment
    116, 138, 162
Chlorophyta 116
Chloroplast 138-139
  Alga 112
  Chlamydomonas sp.
    116
  Envelope 139
  Epiphytic orchid 162
  Internal view 139
  Spirogyra sp. 117
Choanocyte 166
Choir 468-469, 470, 472
Choir manual 514
Choir screen 470
Choir-stall 470
Choir stop 514
Chondrichthyes 178
Chondrostean fish 69
Chong Ch'ol 35
Chordae tendineae 251
Chorioallantoic
  membrane 192
Chorion 260
Choroid 241
Christian architecture 468
Christmas rose 139
Chromate ion 312
Chrome passivation 348
Chrome plating 347
Chrome trim strip 341
Chromium
  Mineralization zones
    281
  Oxide 312
  Periodic table 310
Chromosphere 32-33

Chrysalis 168
Chrysanthemum
  morifolium 129
Chryse Planitia 43
Chrysler Building 495
Chrysocyon brachyurus
  195
Chuck 601
Chuck key 601
Chung-ta-wei 376
Church
  Santa Sophia 487
  Sorbonne 486
  St. Botolph 473
  St. Eustache 477
  St. George in the East
    478, 481
  St. Maclou 470, 472
  St. Maria della Salute
    478
  St. Maria della Vittoria
    478
  St. Paul-St. Louis 478-
    479
  St. Pierre de Libreville
    496, 499
  St. Serge 469
Church-roof boss 468
Chusan palm 127, 130
Ciconia ciconia 188
Cigarette lighter adapter
  and speaker cable 590
Ciliary body 241
Cincture 477
Cinder 272
Cinder cone
  Igneous rock structures
    274
  Volcanic structure 275
Cinema, home 584-585
Cinnabar 271
Cinquefoil moulding 471
Circle 478, 622
Circle area measurement
  590
Circuit 316
Circuit board 573, 581,
  582, 585, 589
Circuit board plug 596
Circuit breaker 314
Circular mountain lake
  293
Circulatory system 252-
  253
Circumference 622
Cirque 286-287
Cirque formation 287
Cirque Napoleon 478-479
Cirri 172
Cirrocumulus cloud 302
Cirrostratus cloud 302
Cirrus 173
Cirrus cloud
  Neptune 50
  Structure of Mars 43
  Weather 302-303
Citrus limon 148
City bus 332
Civet 194
Cladding 494, 496, 498-
  499
Cladode 129
  Cladonia floerkeana 114
  Cladonia portentosa 114
Clam 176
Clamp
  Cross-stave 377
  Intaglio printing 313
  U-tube 446
Clamshell 572, 578, 589
Clarinet 503-504, 508
Classical-style
  architecture 474, 478,
    482
Clastic sedimentary rocks
  276
Claves 517
Clavicle
  Bird 189

Bony fish 181
  Eryops 80
  Human 211, 218
  Kangaroo 206
  Rhesus monkey 202
Clavius 40
Clavus 573
Claw
  Albertosaurus 84
  Anchisaurus 89
  Archaeopteryx 85
  Beetle 168
  Bird 188
  Bumblebee 168
  Caiman 187
  Chick 193
  Crab 172
  Crayfish 173
  Dinosaur 83
  Herrerasaurus 86
  Kangaroo 207
  Lizard 184
  Marble sculpture 452
  Pachycephalosaurus
    100
  Psittacosaurus 103
  Scorpion 170
  Spider 171
  Stegoceras 101
  Terrapin 187
  Tyrannosaurus 84
Clawed feet 190, 206
Clay 298
Clay daub 465
Clay modelling 452, 455
Clay mounds 286
Clear space 354
Cleavage 270
Clef 502
  Cleithrolepis granulatus
    69
Cleithrum 80
Clematis 130-131, 137
Clench nail 375
Cleomedes 40
Cleopatra Patera 37
Clerestory 459, 472, 479
Clew 373
Clewline 379, 385
Cliffs
  Coastlines 294-295
  River's stages 289
  Sedimentary rocks 276-
    277
Climate
  Carboniferous period
    66
  Geological time 56
  Oceans and seas 296
  Weather 302
Climate change
  Coastline 294
  Geological time 56
Clincher wheel 339
Clinker-built hull 375
Clinker-built oak planking
    375
Clints 284-285
Clitoris 258
Cloaca
  Bird 189
  Brachiosaurus 90
  Dogfish 179
  Euoplocephalus 95
  Frog 182
    87
  Lizard 185
  Spider 170
  Tortoise 187
Cloacal opening 185
Clock operator 532
Clock tower 493
Cloister 472
Cloning technology 606-
  607
Close-stowing anchor 386
Cloud deck 50-51
Cloud features
  Neptune 50

Saturn 46
Venus 36
Clouds
  Earth's atmosphere 301
  Jupiter 44-45
  Mars 42-43
  Neptune 50-51
  Saturn 46-47
  Uranus 48-49
  Venus 36-37
  Water cycle 288
  Weather 302-303
Cloud shadow 50
Clouds of dust and gas
  Life of massive star 24
  Milky Way 14-15
  Nebulae and star
    clusters 16-17
  Origin and expansion of
    Universe 11
  Small stars 24
Cloud-top temperature
  Structure of Jupiter 45
  Structure of Neptune 51
  Structure of Saturn 47
  Structure of Uranus 49
Clove hitch 388
Clover leaf roof 198
Clubmosses 64, 66, 120-
  121
Clump cathead 395
Clustered column 469
Clutch 364, 366
Clutch and flywheel 340
Clutch cable 350, 363, 365
Clutch centre plate 351
Clutch cover 363
Clutch lever 363, 369
Clutch pedal 350
Clutch pressure plate 351
Clutch release bearing
  351
Clutch spring 351
CNS 238
Coal
  Earth's evolution 57
  Mineral resources 280-
    281
  Power stations 314
  Sedimentary rocks 276
  Steam locomotive 324
Coal-forming forests 57
Coal measures 61
Coaming 381
Coastal spring 292
Coaster 574-575
Coastlines 294-295
  Cave 284
Coastline 294
Coastline change
  Geological time 56
Cobalt
  Mineralization zones
    281
  Periodic table 311
Cobra lily 160-161
  Coccosteus 65
Coccygeal cornu 223
Coccygeal vertebrae 222
Coccyx 218, 222
Cochlea 242-243
Cocking lever 549
Cockpit
  Avro biplane 403
  Kayak 560
  LVG CVI fighter 405
  Modern military
    aircraft 420-421
  Sailing dinghy 561
  Schleicher glider 426
Cockpit canopy 409
Cockpit coaming 425
Cocoa 148
Coconino sandstone 276
  Cocos nucifera 135
Cocos plate 59
Cod 180
  Codiaeum variegatum 143
Coelenterata 166
Coeliac trunk 256-257
  Coelodonta 76-77, 104

Coelophysis 68
  Coelurus 87
Coenobium 116
Coffer 463, 485
Coffered vault 485
Coffering 485
Cogged drive belt 344
Cog humanoid robot 609
Coil base 587
Coil spring
  "Ellerman Lines" steam
    locomotive 524
  Motorcycle 364
Coil suspension spring
  "Deltic" diesel-electric
    locomotive 327
  "Eurostar" multi-
    voltage electric train
    329
  Wagon bogie 331
Coke hopper 334
Cold air intake 420
Cold-air unit 417
Cold front 302-303
Cold occlusion 302
Cold occluded front 302
Cold-water upwelling 296
Calcapotra 168
  Coleus sp. 134
Collagen and elastic fibres
  252
Collapsed crater 293
Collar
  Cathedral of Notre
    Dame de Paris 473
  Sea anemone 167
  Snail 177
Collar-beam 473
Collar bone 211, 218
Collar cell 166
Collar of horsetail 120
Collecting duct 256
Collecting tubule 256
Collective lever 422
Collenchyma 126, 134-135
Collefing plates 272
Colloids 306
Colon
  Butterfly 169
  Cow 198
  Human 215, 249, 259
  Rabbit 196
Colonette
  Gothic church 473
  Islamic building 488
  Medieval building 467-
    469
  Neoclassical building
    479
  Renaissance building
    474
Colonnade
  Ancient Greek building
    460-461
  Ancient Roman
    building 462-463
  Cathedral dome 484,
    487
  Neoclassical building
    483
Colonnaded storey 494
Colorado River
  Earth's evolution 57
  Grand Canyon 277
  Valley 277
Coloseum 462, 464-465
Colour 270
Colour changes 312-313
Colour ink cartridge 574
Colour ink-cartridge
  clamp 574
Colour light signals 330
Colour liquid crystal
  display (LCD) screen
  579
Colour screen 588
Colour wheel 439
Colpus 144
Columba 18, 21

Columella 119, 145
Column
Ancient Egyptian
building 458-459
Ancient Greek building
458, 460
Ancient Roman
building 458, 462-463,
465
Baroque church 480-
481
Cathedral dome 487
Cave system 285
French temple 485
Gothic church 473
Islamic mosque 488
Medieval church 468-
469
Modern building 496-
498
Monocotyledonous
flower 126
Neoclassical building
478-479, 483
Nineteenth-century
building 492-493
Renaissance building
477
Coma 52-53
Coma Berenices 18, 21
Combat sports 556-557
Combination lever 325
Combustion 326
Combustion chamber
Capacity 366-367
Iron paddlesteamer
393
Jaguar straight six
engine 344
Jet engines 418-419
Combustion cycle 410
Comets 30, 52-53
Common bile duct 252
Common blackheaded
gull 189
Common brittle star 175
Common carotid artery
215, 251, 253
Common centaury 144
Common crus 243
Common digital extensor
muscle 84, 97
Common elder 143
Common English ivy 131
Common horse chestnut
130
Common horsetail 120
Common Iguana 82
Common iliac artery 215,
253, 257
Common iliac vein 215,
253, 257
Common ivy 137
Common lime 143
Common link 386
Common mulberry 130
Common peroneal nerve
238
Common rafter 473, 486
Common starfish 175
Common tern 193
Common time 502
Communication 108
Communications aerial
424
Commutator 600
Commuters 363
Compact bone 224-225
Compact disc 584, 586,
587
Companion cells 132-134
Companion ladder 381
Companion way 380
Compass
Battleship 394
Vault decoration 485
Compass and rangefinder
platform 394
Competent bed rock 61

Competition motorcycles
368-369
Competitions
Archery 548
Diving 558
Judo 556
Rowing 560
Skiing 552-553
Complete mesentery 167
Composite capital 478
Composite column 478
Composite pilaster 478
Composite volcano 272
Composter 602
Compound eye
Beetle 168
Bumblebee 168
Butterfly 169
Crab 172
Crayfish 173
Damselfly 168
Malacostraca 172
Shrimp 172
Compound inflorescence
131, 142
Compound leaf 130-131,
136
Compound pier 468-469
Compound pulleys 320
Compounds 268, 306, 308
Compound succulent fruit
148-149
Compound umbel 143
Compressible gas 365
Compression
Faults and folds 60
Glacier 286
Igneous and
metamorphic rocks 274
Mineral resources 280
Mountain building 62
Rock cycle 266
Compression ring
Ford diesel engine 347
Jaguar straight six
engine 344
Compression stroke 343
Compressor 418
Compressor piston 344
Compsognathus 70
Computer
and E-mail program
577
Electronic instruments
520
Hand-held 568-569
Modern bodywork 348
Computer display 521
Computerized ignition
system 344
Concave brace 477
Concave moulding 482
Concave wall 478, 481
Conceptacles 116-117
Concert grand piano 515
Concha
Ear 242
Nasal 221, 241
Conchoidal fracture
Extrusive igneous rocks
275
Fracture 270
Sedimentary rocks 277
Concorde 416-417
Concrete 492, 494, 496-
499
Concrete shielding 314
Concrete shoe 499
Concrete track 328
Concrete wall 463, 465,
496
Condensation 307
Nuclear power station
314
Testing candle wax 313
Condensation level 302
Condenser 342
Condenser aperture 610
Condenser housing 611

Condenser lens 611
Conducting tissue 119
Conductor
Electrical circuit 316
Generating magnetism
317
Orchestra 504
Conductor's stand 505
Condylactis sp. 166
Condyle
Carnivore 194
Human 220
Cone 623
Cones
Bishop pine 124
Gymnosperms 122
Igneous and
metamorphic rocks 274
Pine 122
Scots pine 122
Smooth cypress 123
Volcanoes 272-273
Welwitschia 123
Yew 123
Cone sheet 274
Cone stalk surface area
measurement 590
Cone volume
measurement 590
Congas 519
Congo Basin 39
Conical bore 507
Conical dome 476
Conical map projection
265
Conical spire 466, 476
Conical volcano 272
Conifer
Cretaceous period 72
Earth's evolution 57
Fossil record 279
Gymnosperm 122-125
Jurassic period 70
Triassic period 68
Coniferophyta 122
Conjugation 117
Conjunctiva 241
Connecting rod
Bordino Steam Carriage
334
Flat-four cylinder
arrangement 340
Four-stroke cycle 343
Iron paddlesteamer 392
Jaguar straight six
engine 344
Jaguar V12 engine 345
Mid West two-stroke
engine 410
Steamboat with paddle
wheels 391
Connecting wire 598
Connective tissue cells
Connectors 569
Conning tower 394, 397
Conocephalum conicum
118
Con-rod 340, 343-345
Conservation of Energy
Law 314
Conservatory 602, 603
Console 579
Constellations 18-21, 613
Constrictor snakes 184
Construction sculpture
452
Contact 352
Contact array 581
Contact grid 605
Contact metamorphism
274
Contact strip 589
Contant d'Ivry 478
Contest area 556
Contests
Head-butting 100
Shooting 548

Continental crust 58-59
Mineralization zones
281
Mountain building 62-
63
Ocean floor 298
Continental drift 58
Continental margin
sediments 299
Continental rise 298
Continental Sea 73, 75
Continental shelf
Ocean floor 298
Prehistoric Earth 69, 71
Rock cycle 267
Continental slope
Ocean floor 298
Offshore currents 296
Rock cycle stages 267
Continents
Formation of the Earth
38, 56
Earth's physical
features 264-265
Geological time 56
Contrabassoon 504-505
Contractile vacuole 116
Contrast control 521
Control cabinet 396
Control circuit 328
Control buttons 585
Control column
ARV light aircraft 425
BE 2B bomber 404
Curtiss biplane 398-399
Control-column aperture
425
Control flag 552
Controller 332, 579
Control line 561
Control panel 571, 595,
596
Control panel boards 597
Control panel casing 573
Control panel fascia 597
Control panel microchips
596
Control panel frame 573
Control panels 594
Control panel wiring 595
Control reservoir drain
326
Control rod 314, 424
Control room 397
Control stalk 553
Convection cell 33
Convection current 38
Convective zone 24, 33
Converging plates 63
Conversion 550
Convex portico 483
Cook/grill tray 596
Cooking 108
Cooksonia 56
Cooksonia hemisphaerica
64
Coolant 314
Coolant inlet 424
Coolant jacket 410-411
Coolant outlet
ARV light aircraft 424
Jaguar V12 engine 345
Mid West two-stroke
engine 410
Coolant passage 346
Coolant pipe 554
Coolant pump 410
Coolant rail 345
Cooling device 611
Cooling fan 345, 567
Cooling fin
Drum brake 365
Mid West rotary engine
411
Two-stroke engine 366
Velocette OHV engine
367
Cooling intake 554

Cooling perforations 597
Cooling tank 335
Cooling tower
Centre Georges
Pompidou 496-497
Nuclear power station
314
Cooling vent 566
Cooling water tank 335
Co-orbital moons 46
Coping-stone 495
Copper
Mineral resources 280-
281
Minerals 268
Periodic table 311-312
Copper body-shell 519
Copper face 384
Copper nitrate solution
312
Copper ore 306
Copper plate nib 444
Copper sheathing 392
Copper sulphate 313
Copulatory bursa
Butterfly 169
Snail 177
Copy button 572
Coracoid
Bird 189
Diplodocus 90
Euoplocephalus 94
Gallimimus 86
Triceratops 102
Turtle 187
Tyrannosaurus 84
Coral 78, 166-167
Atoll development 299
Fossil record 279
Corallina officinalis 117
Coral reef
Earth's evolution 56
Ocean floor 298
Cor Anglais 504-505, 508
Corbel
Cathedral dome 487
Medieval building 467,
469
Neoclassical building
482
Nineteenth-century
building 493
Renaissance building
477
Rococo style 478
Corbita 372-373
Cor Caroli 18, 21
Cordaites 67
Cordate leaf bases 136-
137
Cordite case 396
Cordite handling room 396
Cordite supply shuttle 396
Cordless battery charger
588
Core
Earth 38-39
Helix Nebula 17
Massive stars 26-27
Moon 40
Neutron stars and black
holes 28-29
Small stars 24-25
Structure of comet 53
Structure of Earth 63
Structure of Jupiter 45
Structure of Mars 43
Structure of Mercury 35
Structure of Neptune 51
Structure of Pluto 51
Structure of Saturn 47
Structure of Uranus 49
Structure of Venus 37
Core-engine jet pipe 412,
415
Core jet pipe 419
Core temperature
Structure of Earth 39

Structure of Jupiter 45
Structure of main
sequence star 24
Structure of red giant
25
Structure of red
supergiant 26
Structure of Saturn 47
Structure of Sun 33
Structure of Uranus 49
Corinthian capital 460,
463, 479, 481
Corinthian column 463-
464, 479-480
Corinthian entablature
463
Corinthian order 460, 462
Corinthian pilaster 463-
464, 480-481
Coriolis force 296-297,
300
Cork
Oboe 508
Stems 154-155
Woody dicotyledons 127
Corms 154-155
Corn 112
Cornea 241
Corner arc 524
Corner seal 347
Cornet 506
Cornice
Ancient Egyptian
temple 458-459
Ancient Greek building
460-461
Ancient Roman
building 462-465
Asian building 491
Baroque church 479-
481
Dome 484, 486
French temple 485
Gothic church 470-473
Islamic tomb 489
Medieval building 466-
467, 469
Neoclassical building
478-479, 482-483
Nineteenth-century
building 493
Renaissance building
477
Twentieth-century
building 494
Cornucopia 480
Corolla 140, 142-143
Corona
Earth's atmosphere 300
Palazzo Strozzi 475
Sun's atmosphere 32-33
Corona Australis 19
Corona Borealis 18, 21
Coronal section through
brain 236-237
Coronal suture 220
Coronary artery 250-251,
253
Coronary sinus 250
Corona temperature 33
Coronet 198, 554
Coronoid process 96, 106,
194, 220
Corpus albicans 258
Corpus callosum 236-237
Corpus cavernosum 259
Corpus luteum 258
Corpus spongiosum 259
Corridor 465
Corries 286-287
Corrugator supercilii
muscle 228-229
Cortex
Apical meristem 154
Canadian pond weed
158-159
Clubmoss stem 120
Dicotyledon 127
Epiphytic orchid 162

Hair 234
Horsetail stem 120
Kidney 256
Lichen 114
Monocotyledon 127
Moss 119
Pine 125
Radicle 152
Rhizome 155
Root 152-153
Stems 154-155
Water hyacinth 158
Water lily 159
Corundum 271
Corvus 18, 21
Corvus corone 193
Corynactis viridis 166
Corythosaurus 96, 98
Cosmic background radiation 10
Cosmic ray 301
COSTAR corrective optical device 613
COSTAR device slot 613
Costal cartilage 218
Costal facet 225
Costal margin 168, 169
Costal shield 187
Cotter pin 383
Cotton duck canvas 437, 443
Cotyledon 126, 152-153
Development 152
Dicotyledon 126
Dry fruit seed 150-151
Embryo development 147
Epigeal germination 153
Hypogeal germination 152
Monocotyledon 126
Pine 122
Root development 152
Seed 152-153
Succulent fruit seed 148-149
Couch grass 113
Couc-le-Château 466-467
Coulomb 316
Counter
Calligraphy lettering 445
Counterbalancing weight 506
Counter rail 381
Counter timber 381
Counterweight
Flat-four cylinder arrangement 340
Four-stroke cycle 343
Hong Kong and Shanghai Bank 498
Jaguar V12 engine 345
Output shaft 347
Relief printing press 449
Rotary engine output shaft 410
Trojan engine 342
V12 cylinder arrangement 345
Country code 576
Coupling
Conventional hook-screw 328
"Ellerman Lines" steam locomotive 324
Coupling rod 325
Couronnement 472
Course
Asian building 491
Medieval building 466-467
Neoclassical building 483
Nineteenth-century building 492-493
Court referee 535

Court
Basketball 532
Handball 535
Netball 535
Volleyball 534
Court seal 375
Courtship display 188
Courtyard 465, 466
Coussinet 460
Covalent bonding 308-309
Cove 581
Cover for USB and recharger jack sockets 581
Cover front 583
Cover latch 566
Cover latch port 567
Cover point 541
Cover stopper link 573
Cover support 570
Coverts 188, 191
Cow 198
Cowhide face 384
Cowling fastener 408
Cowling panel 407, 412
Coxa
Beetle 168
Crayfish 173
Scorpion 170
Coxswain 560
CPU 566, 579
CQR anchor 386
Crab 172
Crab apple 126
Crab cactus 129
Crab Nebula 28
Cracks 284-285
Cradle frame
Honda VF 750 364
Weslake Speedway motorcycle 369
Cradling 541
Crane 498
Cranial nerves 238
Cranium
Ankylosaurus 94
Archaeopteryx 85
Australopithecus 108
Bat 105
Camarasaurus 91
Diplodocus 90
Elephant 201
Eryops 80
Euoplocephalus 94
Homo sapiens 108
Hyaenodon 107
Iguanodon 96
Kentrosaurus 93
Lambeosaurus 99
Moeritherium 105
Opossum 106
Pachycephalosaurus 100
Panoplosaurus 94
Parasaurolophus 99
Plateosaurus 88
Prenocephale 100
Protoceratops 102
Stegoceras 100
Stegosaurus 93
Struthiomimus 87
Styracosaurus 102
Toxodon 106
Triceratops 103
Tuojiangosaurus 93
Tyrannosaurus 84
Crank 320
Brace-and-bit 601
Eddy Merckx racing bicycle 360
"Ellerman Lines" steam locomotive 325
Crank bolt 358, 360
Crankcase
BE 2B bomber 404
British Rail Class 20 diesel engine 327

Humber engine 343
Jaguar straight six engine 344
Jaguar V12 engine 345
Mid West two-stroke engine 410
Oldsmobile engine 336
Trojan engine 342
Velocette OHV engine 367
Werner motorcycle 362
Crankcase breather pipe 402
Crank handle 339
Crankpin 345
Crankshaft
Benz Motorwagen 335
Flat-four cylinder arrangement 340
Four-stroke cycle 343
Iron paddlesteamer 392
Mid West two-stroke engine 410
Oldsmobile engine 336
Oscillating steam engine 391
Straight four cylinder arrangement 345
Two-stroke engine 366
Velocette OHV engine 367
Crankshaft counterweight 344
Crankshaft pulley 344, 345
Crash bar 362-363
Crash cymbal 518
Crash helmet 552
Crater
Mercury's North Pole 35
Northern stars 18
Oceanus Procellarum 40
Southern stars 21
Surface features of Mars 42
Crayfish 172-173
Crayon 448
Creeping stems 154
Clubmoss 120
Strawberry 128
Cremasteric fascia 259
Cremocarp 150-151
Crenellation 466
Crepidoma 461, 481
Crescent-shaped dune 283
Crest
Building 479, 488, 493
Fold formation 60
Horse 199
Lizard 184
Ship's shield 395
Crested porcupine 197
Cretaceous period 72-73
Fossil record 279
Geological time 56-57
Crevasse 287
Crevice 284
Crevice tool 593
Crew handrail 612, 613
Crew's seat 416
Cricket (animal) 168
Cricket (game) 538-539
Cricoid cartilage 255
Cricothyroid ligament 244
Cricothyroid muscle 229, 244-245
C ring 46-47
Cringle 384
Crista 242
Crocket 471-472
Crocodile clip connector 516
Crocodiles 68, 73, 186-187
Crocodylus niloticus 186
Crocoite 271
Cronaca 474
Crook 508

Crop 189
Bird 189
Butterfly 169
Octopus 176
Snail 177
Crop-duster 410
Crops 315
Crop-sprayer 410, 422
Cross
Baroque church 480
Dome 486-487
Motif 472
Crossandra nilotica 145
Crossbar
Calligraphy characters 445
Eddy Merckx racing bicycle 360
Gaelic football 529
Handball 535
Hurling 540
Rugby 530
Cross-bed set 283
Crossbow 548
Cross-bracing 497-499
Cross-country skiing 548
Crosse 540-541
Crossing 469-470, 477
Crossing tower 468
Cross-member 338-339
Cross-piece 376-377, 387
Cross-staff 377
Cross-stave 376-377
Cross tube 423
Cross wall of hypha 115
Crosswise strut 512
Crotchet rest 502-503
Croton 136
Crouch 543
Crow 193
Crown
Bird 188
Building 484, 490
Danforth anchor 386
Harp 511
Head 212
Relief-printing press 449
Roman anchor 372
Sail hook 384
Shackle 386
Teeth 247
Timpanum 519
Crowning cornice
Ancient Roman building 464, 465
Baroque church 479
Renaissance building 474-475
Crown wheel
Benz Motorwagen 335
Ford Model T 338
Cruciform column 492
Cruciform pedestal 481, 487
Crück frame 466
Crumb tray 598-599
Crupper 555
Crusafontia 56
Crus cerebri of midbrain 237
Crus of diaphragm 255
Crust
Moon 41
Ocean floor 298
Pulsar 28
Regional metamorphism 274
Structure of comet 53
Structure of Earth 58-59
Structure of Mars 43
Structure of Mercury 35
Structure of Venus 37
Crustaceans 172-173
Arthropoda 170

Cretaceous period 72-73
Fossil 279
Crustal movement
Coastline 294
Faults and folds 60
Mineralization zones 280
Mountain building 62
Rock cycle 266
Volcano 272
Crustal plate boundary 59
Crustal plates 58-59, 60
Crustose lichen 114
Crutch
Viking karv 375
Crux-Centaurus Arm 14
Crypt 467
Crypt-window 481
Crystalline external crust 28
Crystalline stalagmitic floor 284
Crystallization 307
Crystal Palace Exhibition Hall 492-493
Crystals
Faults 60
Intrusive igneous rocks 275
Mineral features 270-271
Minerals 268-269
Solids 307
Crystal systems 270
Ctenidium 176
CT scan 214
Cube 623
Cubic crystal 270
Cubic system 270
Cubital fossa 211
Cuboid bone 232
Cucumis melo 149
Cud 198
Cuesta 283
Culm 151
Cumulonimbus cloud 302
Cumulus cloud 302
Cuneate leaf base 136-137
Cuneus 625
Cup 509
Cup mute 507
Cupola 466, 479, 493
Cupressus glabra 123
Cup-shaped mouthpiece 506-507
Cup surrounding stomata 157
Cupula 242
Cupule 150
Curium 311
Current 296-297
Current electricity 316
Curtain 477, 497
Curtain wall 466, 496, 498
Curtiss, Glenn 398
Curtiss Model-D Pusher 398-599
Curved buttress 478-481
Curved cornice 462
Curvilinear tracery 470, 472
Cuscuta europaea 163
Cusp
Asian building 488
Gothic building 472-473
Structure of a tooth 247
Cuspate fold 61
Cuspate foreland 294
Cusped arch 488
Cuspidate leaf apex 137
Cutaneous nerve 238
Cuticle
Bishop pine needle 124
Dryland plants 156

Golden barrel cactus 156
Hair 234
Haworthia truncata 157
Leaf 139
Lithops bromfieldii 157
Marram grass 113
Monocotyledon leaf 126
Nail 231
Rose stem 135
Rush stem 135
Wetland plants 158
Cuttlefish 176
Cutty Sark 392
Cyanotrichite 269
Cycadophyta 122
Cycads 68, 122-123, 279
Cycas revoluta 68, 123
Cycas sp. 68
Cyclic-pitch lever 422-423
Cyclone assembly 592
Cyclonic storm
Structure of Earth 39
Structure of Mars 43
Structure of Neptune 50
Cyclostomata 178
Cygnus 19, 20
Cylinder
Diesel train 326
Early engines 342-343
"Ellerman Lines" steam locomotive 325
Iron paddlesteamer 392
Modern piston aero-engines 410
Motorcycle 362, 366
Oldsmobile engine 336
"Rocket" steam locomotive 324
Cylinder barrel
Mid West two-stroke engine 410
Werner motorcycle 362
Cylinder block 339
Cylinder-cooling gills 407
Cylinder drain cock lever 325
Cylinder head
72° V10 engine 356
ARV light aircraft 425
British Rail Class 20 diesel engine 327
Daimler engine 345
Jaguar straight six engine 344
Jaguar V12 engine 345
Mid West two-stroke engine 410
Oldsmobile engine 336
Two-stroke engine 366
Velocette OHV engine 567
Cylinder liner
Jaguar Straight six engine 344
Mid West two-stroke engine 410
cylinder shape 623
Cylinder surface area measurement 592
Cylinder volume measurement 590
Cylindrical fault 61
Cylindrical map projection 264
Cyma recta 475
Cyma reversa 460, 472
Cymatium 475
Cymbals 504-505, 516-517
Drum kit 518
Cyme 129, 143
Cypress 123
Cypselus 150
Cyrillus 40
Cystic duct 248
Cytoplasm
Chlamydomonas sp. 116
Diatom 116

Human 217
Palisade mesophyll 139
Root cell 132
Thalassiosira sp. 116
Cytosine 216

D

Dacron 548
Dacron sailcloth 584
Dacron skin 426
Dactylus 172 173
Dado
  Baroque church 481
  French temple 485
  Neoclassical building 479
  Renaissance building 476
Dagger 472
Dagoba stupa 490-491
Daimler double-sleeve valve engine 343
Daimler, Gottlieb 334
Daisy gypsum 269
Dakota sandstone 276
D'Alembert 41
Dalmatian coastline 295
Da Maiano, B. 474
Damped anti-shock swivel base 584
Damper
  Piano 514
  TGV electric high-speed train 329
  Wagon bogie 331
Damper bar 516
Damper body 565
Damper pedal
  Concert grand piano 515
  Tubular bells 516
  Upright piano 514
  Vibraphone 517
Damper unit 425
Damp lime-plaster 434
Damselfly 168
Dancette-pattern mosaic 489
Dandelion 150
Danforth anchor 386
Danger area 554
Danilova 36
Dark mica 274
Dark nebulae 16
Darlingtonia californica 160-161
Dart sac 177
Darwin 43
Da Sangallo, G. 474
Dash 353
Dashboard
  1906 Renault 337
  Bordino Steam Carriage 335
  Ford Model T 338
Dashboard radiator 336-337
Dash panel 353
Dash radio speaker 353
Data cartridge 591
Data entry key pad
  Digital sampler 521
  Synthesizer 520
  Wind synthesizer 521
Data increment control 521
Data plug 591
Data plug socket 591
Date book button 568
Daucus carota 128, 132
Daughter bulbs 154
Daughter plants 154
Davit 395
D-block 310-311
DC converter 355
DC converter connection 355

DC current 328
DC socket 586
Dead-ball line 550
Deadeye
  74-gun ship 380
  Longboat 380
  Rigging 382-383
  Roman corbita 373
  Sailing warship 377
Deadnettle 135
Dead organisms 278
Dead plant encrustations 284
Dead Sea 292-293
Deadwood 381
Debris
  Glacier 286-287
  Mountain building 62
  Ray crater 34
Decathlon 542
Decidual plate 260
Deciduous plants 130-131
Deciduous teeth 246
Deciduous trees 72
Deck
  Greek trireme 373
  Roman corbita 373
Deck beam
  74-gun ship 380
  Ironclad 393
  Paddle steamer 390, 393
  Roman corbita 372
Deck house 373, 376
Deck lantern 392
Deck planking 393
Deck rail 373
Decorative letter 445
Deep cracks 284-285
Deep current systems 296-297
Deepened valley 295
Deep floor 393
Deep mid wicket 538
Deep-ocean floor 298
Deep-ocean floor sediments 299
Deep peroneal nerve 238
Deep relief carving 453
Deep square leg 538
Deer 104, 198-199
Deer hopper dry fly 563
Defence 526, 535
Defenders
  Ice hockey 550
  Lacrosse 541
  Soccer 524
Defending zones 550
Defensive back 526
Defensive end 526
Defensive tackle 526
Deflation hollow 283
Degreased bare metal 348
Dehiscence 150-151
  Fern spore 121
  Pollen sac 144
Dehiscent fruits 150-151
Dehydration 152
De-icing leading edge 414, 415
Deimos 42
Deinonychus 73
Deinotherium 77
Dekla Tessera 37
de la Cierva, Juan 422
Deleted items icon 576
Delete icon 576
Delphinium 150
Delphinium orientalis 141
Delphinium sp. 151
Delphinus 19, 20
Delta
  Coastline 294
  River features 290
  River 288-289
  Rock cycle 266-267
Delta Andromedae 19
Delta Crucis 21
Delta formation 291

Delta Hydri 20
Delta II expendable launch vehicle 615
Delta ring 48
Deltavjatia vjatkensis 81
"Deltic" diesel-electric locomotive 326-327
Deltoid leaf 137
Deltoid ligament 252
Deltoid muscle 226-227
Demountable wheel 338-339
Dendrite 239
Dendritic copper 268
Dendritic gold 268
Dendritic river drainage 288
Deneb 19, 20
  Hertzsprung-Russell diagram 23
Deneb Algedi 19, 20
Deneb Kaitos 19, 20
Denebola 18, 21
Dens 222
Density
  Formation of black hole 29
  Massive stars 26-27
  Small stars 24-25
  Stellar black hole 29
Dentary 181
Dentary bone 96, 102, 107
Dentate leaf margin
  Hogweed 129
  Ice-plant 129
  Live-for-ever 129
  Mulberry 130
  Rock stonecrop 128
Dentil
  Ancient Roman building 462
  Baroque church 479, 481
  Cathedral dome 487
  French temple 485
  Neoclassical building 478
  Renaissance building 475
Dentine 247
Deoxyribonucleic acid strand 139
Deperdussin, Armand 400
Depressed arch
  Ancient Roman building 462
  Islamic building 488-489
Depressions 302
Depressor anguli oris muscle 228-229
Depressor labii inferioris muscle 229
Depth charge 394
Derailleur cage plate 358
Deranged river drainage 288
Dermal armour 95
Dermal papilla 235
Dermis 234-235
Derrick 392, 395
Descender 445
Descending colon 249
Desert 39, 57
  Carboniferous to Permian period 66
  Earth's physical features 264-265
  Rock cycle 266
  Weathering and erosion 282-283
Desertification 57, 76
Desiccated clay 283
Design
  Fresco 434-435
  Modelled sculpture 452
  Mosaic 449

Destination screen 352
Detachable bud 154
Detachable ink reservoir 444
Detachable rim 359
Detector 610
Detergent tray 594, 595
Detergent tray holder 595
Detergent tray recess 595
Deuterium nucleus 22
Devonian fish 65
Devonian period 64-65, 80
  Fossil record 279
  Geological time 56
  Primitive life 78
Devon minnow 563
Dewlap 184
Dextral strike-slip fault 61
Dhow 376
Diabase sill 277
Diagonal bracing 401
Diagonal reinforcement 374
Diagonal strut 599
Diagonal turn 588
Dial
  Clocktower 493
  Sundial 377
Diameter 622
  Atoms 508
  Earth 30
  Fluorine-19 atom 309
  Fluorine-19 nucleus 309
  Jupiter 26, 44
  Jupiter's moons 44
  Life of massive star 26-27
  Life of small star 21-26
  Mars 30
  Mars' moons 42
  Mercury 30
  Moon 40
  Neptune 51
  Neptune's moons 50
  Planets 30-31
  Pluto 51
  Saturn 27, 46
  Saturn's moons 46
  Stars 22
  Uranus 27, 48
  Uranus' moons 48
  Venus 30
Diamond 311
  Mineral features 270-271
  Native elements 268
Diamond-shaped painting knife 436
Diamond whetstone 452
Diaphragm
  ARV Super 2 424
  Chimpanzee 202
  Domestic cat 195
  Elephant 200
  Human 215, 254-255
  Rabbit 196
Diastema 106
Diatom 116
Diceros bicornis 199
Dichasial cyme 143
Dickinsonia antarctica 70, 112-113
Dicloelosia bilobata 65
Dicotyledon 126-127, 141-143
Dicyothyris 278
Didelphis 106
Didelphis virginiana 207
Dielectric sandwich 584
Diesel fuel injection 326
Diesel motor compartment 397
Diesel, Rudolph 326
Diesel train 324, 326-327

Differential 556
Differential housing 338
Diffuser 356
Digestive caecum 173, 176
Digestive enzymes 160
Digestive gland
  Snail 177
  Spider 170
Digestive glands/zones
  Butterwort 161
  Monkey cup 161
  Venus fly trap 160
Digestive system
  Cow 198
  Human 248-249
Digit 105
Digital artery 231, 253
Digital camera 580-581
Digital extensor muscle 94
Digital flexor muscle 84
Digital nerve 231
Digital sampler 520-521
Digital vein 253
Digital video camera 582-583
Digital video jack cover 582
Digitate leaf 137
Digits
  Bird 189
  Bird's wing 191
  Frog 182
  Kangaroo 207
  Rabbit 196-197
  Rat 196
  Salamander 182
  Seal 204
Dilator muscle 241
Dilsea carnosa 117
Dimetrodon loomisi 67
Dinghy 560
Dinosaur cladogram 83
Dinosaur 56-57, 80, 82-83
  Fossil record 279
Diode assembly 587
Dionaea muscipula 160
Dione 46
Dip 60
Diplodocus 70, 88, 90-91
Dip pen 430
Dipping bed rock 60-61
Dipping log fore-sail 385
Diprotodon 76
Dip-slip fault 61
Dipstick 554
Dipstick tube 346, 356
Dipterus valenciennesi 81
Direct current 328
Direct current (DC) inlet 571
Directional button membrane 578
Directional button pad 578
Direction bar 414
Direction-finding-aerial fairing 408
Direct method mosaic creation 450
Direct-vision panel
  ARV light aircraft 425
  Bell-47 helicopter 422
Dirt track motorcycle racing 368
Disc
  Basal 167
  Crab 166-167
  Liverwort 118
  Pedal 167
  Sea anemone 166-167
  Starfish 174
  Starfish fossil 79
Disc brake
  Harley-Davidson FLHS Electra Glide 362-363
  Honda CB750 565
  Honda VF750 564

Husqvarna Motocross TC610 368
Lockheed Electra airliner 407
Motorcycle 364-365
Suzuki RGV500 368-369
Disc brake calliper 364, 368-369
Disc cover 579
Disc drive motor 587
Disc florets 129, 142, 145
Disc loading tray 579
Discoformity 276
Discovery Rupes 35
Disc tray 579
Disc tray shutter 586, 587
Discus 542-543
Disk drag 562-563
Displacement reactions 312
Display 578, 587
Display button 585
Display screen 581, 585, 587, 596
Display screen and control circuits 585
Display/touch panel button 583
Distal convoluted tubule 256-257
Distal end of radius 231
Distal interphalangeal joint 231
Distal phalanx 219, 230, 252
Distal tarsal 183
Distance lines
  Gaelic football 529
  Rugby 530
Distance running 542
Distance signalling 330
Distilled water 444
Distiller 397
Distributary
  River features 290-291
  Rivers 288-289
Distributor
  Hawker Tempest Mark V 408
  Jaguar straight six engine 344
  Jaguar V12 engine 345
  Renault Clio 351
Distributor drive shaft 345
Distributor fixing point 346
Diving 558-559
DNA 139, 216, 606
Dobro resonator 513
Dock 554
Document ejection roller 575
Document feed roller 573
Document panel 407
Document pinch roller 573
Document pressure bar assembly 572
Document table 571
Dodder 163
Dog 104, 194-195
Dogfish 178-179, 192
Dog-leg hole 546
Dog-leg staircase 481
Doline 284-285
Dolomedes fimbriatus 171
Dolphins 204-205
Dolphin striker 382
Domain name 576
Dome 484, 486-487
  Ancient Roman building 462
  Asian building 490-491
  Baroque church 480-481
  French temple 485
  Islamic building 488
  Medieval building 467, 469

Neoclassical building 478
Renaissance building 475-477
Domed receptacle 142
Domed roof 489
Domed topdeck 401
Domed turret 495
Dome metalling 486
Dome of the Rock 487
Dome timbering 486
Dome volcano 62, 272
Donjon 466-467
Donkey boiler 392
Donor genetic material 606, 607
Door
  Ancient Egyptian tomb 458-459
  Ancient Roman building 463
  Baroque church 479
  Bell 206 jetliner 423
  Double-decker touring bus 333
  Gatwick Express "People Mover" 528
  MCW Metrobus 332-333
  Microwave combination oven 596
  Neoclassical building 478
  Renaissance theatre 477
  Renault Clio 349
  Single-decker bus 333
  TGV electric high-speed train 329
  Washer-dryer 594
Door catch 541
Door catch with safety cut-out 595
Door frame 412
Door glass 348
Door handle 341, 348
Door hinge 612
Door jamb 478
Door key and lock 348
Door lock 596, 602
Door metal cap 595
Door moulding 353
Door porthole 595
Door safety cut-out mechanism 596
Door trim panel 353
Doorway 474-475, 479, 481, 495
Door wiring loom 595
Doppler 41
Dorado 21
Doric capital 460
Doric column 460, 464
Doric half-column 464
Doric order 460
Dormancy
  Horse chestnut bud 130
  Seed 152
Dormant volcano 272
Dormer head 493
Dormer window 476, 493, 495
Dorsal abdominal artery 173
Dorsal aorta
  Bony fish 181
  Dogfish 179
  Frog 182
Dorsal blood vessel 169
Dorsal fin
  ARV light aircraft 424
  Bony fish 181
  Concorde 416
  Dogfish 179
  Dolphin 205
  Lamprey 178
  World War II aircraft 408-409
Dorsal fin ray 181
Dorsal interosseous muscle 231

Dorsal lobe 158
Dorsal mantle cavity 176
Dorsal margin of shell 176
Dorsal metatarsal artery 253
Dorsal plate 78, 92-93
Dorsal scale 184, 186
Dorsal scute 95
Dorsal spine base 78
Dorsal venous arch 253
Dorsal vertebrae
  Archaeopteryx 85
  Brachiosaurus 90
  Diplodocus 90
  Eryops 80
  Euoplocephalus 94
  Gallimimus 86
  Iguanodon 96
  Kentrosaurus 93
  Parasaurolophus 99
  Pareiasaur 81
  Plateosaurus 88
  Stegoceras 101
  Stegosaurus 93
  Struthiomimus 87
  Tuojiangosaurus 93
  Tyrannosaurus 84
Dorsum 213
Double-arm pantograph 328
Double bass 503-505, 510, 511
Double bassoon 504-505
Double-decker bus 332-333
Double decomposition reaction 312-313
Double-dipper palette attachment 436
Double-ended hull 375
Double flat 502
Double halyard 373
Double helix 216
Double planet system
  Earth 38
  Pluto 50
Double-pyramid crystal 270
Double reed 508
Double rope becket 383
Doubles 544
Double samaras
  Dry fruit 150-151
  Sycamore 131
Double scull 561
Double sharp 502
Double topsail schooner 385
Dowel
  Mid West single rotor engine 410
  Mortice-and-tenon fastening 373
Dowel hole 410-411
Downfolds 60
Downhaul 385
Downhill skiing 552
"Downs" 526
Downthrow 60
Down tube 360
Dox formation 277
Dpad, 8-way 579
Dpi (Dots Per Inch) 570
Draco 19, 20
Draft mark
  Frigate 397
  Wooden sailing ship 379
Drafts icon 576
Draft tube 314
Drag
  Biplanes and triplanes 402
  Cycling 360
  Early monoplane 400
  Early passenger aircraft 406
Drag knob 563

Drag link
  19th century paddlesteamer 391
  Ford Model T 339
  White Steam Car 342
Dragon prowhead 374
Drag spindle 562
Drag washer 562
Drainage systems divide 289
Drain mast 412, 415
Drain-pipe 492
Drain plug 339
Drakensberg 265
Draught mark 379, 397
Dravidian finial 491
Dravidian style 490
Drawbridge 493
Drawbridge windlass 467
Drawing 430-431
Drawing board 430, 444-445
Drawing instruments 430
Drawing materials 430
Dreadnought-type battleship 394
Dressing-room 477
Dribbling
  Basketball 532
  Gaelic football 528
  Handball 534-535
  Soccer 524
Drill 600-601
D ring 46-47
Drip-cap 482
Drive 543
Drive belt 354, 355, 344, 362
Drive bracket 405
Drive chain 366, 368
Drive end 317
Drive gear 411
Drive gear access hole 580
Drive gear assembly 572
Driven gear 410
Driven pulley 355
Drive pillar 429
Drive pin 580
Drive plate 345
Drive point 346
Driver 547
Driver protection 557
Driverless train 328
Driver's platform 324
Driver's radio aerial 557
Driver's seat
  Bordino Steam Carriage 335
  "Deltic" diesel-electric locomotive 327
  "Mallard" express steam locomotive 325
  Paris Metro 328
Drive shaft
  Jet engine 419
  Renault Clio 351
  Volkswagen Beetle 340
Drive sprocket mounting spline 366
Drive-wheel 601
Driving band 397
Driving chain 335
Driving pulley 335
Driving rein 555
Driving saddle 555
Driving sprocket 335
Driving wheel 324-325
Drizzle 302
Dromiceiomimus 86
Droop nose 416
Droop stop 422-423
Drop 385
Drop arm
  Ford Model T 339
  White Steam Car 342
Drop-down window 334

Drop handlebar 361
Drop-kick 530
Drop tank 408
Drop window 332
Drowned coastline 294-295
Drowned valley 295
Drum 486
  Ancient Greek building 460
  Baroque church 481
  Cathedral dome 487
  Relief printing press 449
  Washer-dryer 595
Drum and door seal 595
Drum brake
  BMW R/60 362
  Motorcycle 364-365
  Vespa Grand Sport 160 Mark 1 363
  "Windcheetah" racing HPV bicycle 361
Drumhead 387
Drum inlet elbow 595
Drumlins 286
Drum pad 520
Drums 518-519, 520
Drum suspension springs 595
Drupelets 146-149
Drupes 131, 148-149
Dry air 303
Dry brush 438-439
Dry capacity measurements 590
Dry fresco 434-435
Dry fruits 150-151
  Couch grass 113
  Durmast oak 131
  Sycamore 131
Dry gallery 284-285
Drying agent 313
Dry lake bed 283
Dryland plants 156-157
Dryopteris filix-mas 120-121
Dryosaurus 70
Dry pericarps 150
Dry season 293
Dry wash 283
Dual click gear 562
Dual ignition plug 427
Dual seat 364
Dual shock controller 579
Dual sliding zoom lens 581
Dubhe 18
  The Plough 19
Dubika 490
Duck 188
Duct 496, 497
Duct of Bellini 256
Ductus deferens 259
Dugout 536
Dumb iron 336, 342
Dummy front door 339
Dunkeld wet fly 563
Duodenum
  Bird 189
  Cow 198
  Elephant 200
  Frog 182
  Human 215, 248-249
  Rabbit 196
  Tortoise 187
Duplex tubular cradle frame 363
Duradon 384
Dura mater 223, 237, 240
Durmast oak 131
Dust
  Asteroids, comets, and meteoroids 52-53
  Mars 42-43
  Moon 41

Nebulae and star clusters 16-17
NGC 2997 (spiral galaxy) 12
Overhead view of our galaxy 14
Solar system 30
Venus' atmosphere 37
Dust cap 359
Dust cloud
  Geological time 56
  Large Magellanic Cloud 12
  Mars 42-43
  Milky Way 14-15
  Nebulae and star clusters 16-17
  Origin and expansion of Universe 11
  Volcano 272
Dust collection bin 592
Dust lane
  Centaurus A 13
  Horsehead Nebula 16
  NGC 2997 (spiral galaxy) 12
  Optical image of Rings and dust lanes 48
  Trifid Nebula 16
Dust particles 53
Dust shroud 340
Dust storm 43
Dust tail 52-53
Dutch cubist style 495
Dutch shoe 377
Dutch triple fiddle block 383
DVD/CD control buttons 585
DVD/CD drive turntable 585
DVD/CD laser-reader 585
DVD/CD on-screen menu display button 585
DVD/CD processor microchip 585
DVD/CD sliding tray 585
DVD/CD stop button 585
DVD display button 585
DVD player 584-585
Dwarf crocodile 82
Dwarf shoot 124-125
Dyke 274
Dyke swarm 274
Dynastes hercules 12
Dyson DC05 vacuum cleaner 592-593
Dysprosium 311

E

Ear
  Calligraphy characters 445
  Elephant 200
  Gorilla 203
  Hare 196
  Horse 198
  Human 210, 212, 242-243
  Kangaroo 207
  Rabbit 196
  Rat 196
Eardrum
  Chick 193
  Frog 182
  Human 243
  Lizard 184
Earles fork 362
Early desertification 57
Early engines 342-343
Early English
  Perpendicular-style tracery 472
Early English-style window 472
Early monoplanes 400-401

Early passenger aircraft 406-407
Early tram 332
Early voyagers 374-375
Earphone connector 589
Earphone socket 587
Earpiece 586, 588
Earpiece cover 586
Earplug 558
Earth 38-39
  Cretaceous period 73
  Energy emission from Sun 22
  Jurassic period 71
  Objects in Universe 11
  Phases of the Moon 41
  Primitive life 78-79
  Quaternary period 77
  Solar eclipse 32
  Solar System 30
  Tertiary period 75
  Tides 297
  Triassic period 69
Earth-ball fungus 115
Earth bank 603
Earth connection 598
Earth formation 56-57
Earth pigments 434
Earthmoving anatomy 63
Earthquake region 59
Earthquakes
  Crustal movement 58
  Faults and folds 60
  Mountain building 62-63
Earth's atmosphere 38-39, 78, 300-301
Earth's composition 39
Earth's core 38-39, 63
Earth's crust 38-39, 58-59
  Igneous and metamorphic rocks 274
  Lake formation 292
  Volcano 272
Earth's crustal plates 62, 64
Earth's energy 314
Earth's evolution 56-57
Earth's external features 59
Earth's formation 38, 56, 64
Earth's interior
  Ocean floor 298
  Rock cycle 266
  Structure 39
Earth's layers 58
Earth's magnetic field 38
Earth's mantle 38-39, 58-59
Earth's orbit 297
Earth's physical features 264-265
Earth's rotation 38
  Atmospheric circulation and winds 300
  Oceans and seas 296
  Satellite mapping 264
Earth's satellite 38
Earth's surface
  Atmosphere 300-301
  Earth's physical features 264
  Formation of the Earth 38-39
  Geological time 56
  Mineral resources 280
  Mountain building 62
  Oceans and seas 296
  Precambrian to Devonian period 64
  Rock cycle 266
Earth's tilt 38
Earth wire 594
Earwig 168
East Africa 331
East Asian buildings 490-491
East Australian current 297

East Greenland current 296
Eaves
  Ancient Greek building 461
  Ancient Roman building 462, 464
  Islamic tomb 489
  Modern building 499
  Neoclassical building 482
  Renaissance building 477
Eaves board 490
Eccentric 392
Eccentric rod 591
Eccentric rotor journal 347
Eccentric shaft 347, 411
Eccentric-shaft bearing 410
Echidna nebulosa 180
Echidnas 206
Echinocactus grusonii 156
Echinoderms 174, 279
Echinus 460
Echinus esculentus 175
Echo-sounding 298
Ecliptic
  Inclination of planetary orbits 31
  Stars of northern skies 18-19
  Stars of southern skies 20-21
ECM 355
Ecphora 75
Ectoderm 167
Eddy Merckx racing bicycle 360-361
Edible sea urchin 175
Edmontonia 95
Eel 180
Efferent arteriole 256-257
Effervescence 312
Effort 320-321
Egg cells 606-607
Eggs 192-193
  Amphibian 78, 80
  Baltimore oriole 193
  Bee hummingbird 193
  Bird 188
  Butterfly 168
  Capsule 192
  Carrion crow 193
  Case 192
  Chaffinch 193
  Chicken 192
  Common tern 193
  Dinosaur 82
  Dogfish 192
  Frog 182-183, 192
  Giant stick insect 192
  Greater backblacked gull 193
  Hatching 192-193
  Human 258, 260
  Indian stick insect 192
  Leaf insect 192
  Maiasaura 98
  Membrane 193
  Ostrich 193
  Quail 192-193
  Reptile 66, 184
  Titanosaurid 91
  Willow grouse 193
Egg tempera 432
Egg-tooth 192-193
Egg white 192
Egg yolk binding medium 432
Egypt 331
Egyptian building 458-459
Eichhornia crassipes 158
Eighteenth-century building 492
  Baroque 481
  Neoclassical 478, 482-483

Eighth-century building 490-491
Einsteinium 311
Eisila Regio 36-37
Ejaculatory duct 259
Ejecta
  Degas and Brönte 34
  Features of supernova 27
  Ray crater 34
  Venusian craters 32
Eject knob 585
Ejector assembly 599
Ejector exhaust 408
Ejector-seat roof hatches 421
Ekeing 381
Ekman spiral 296-297
El-Ainyi Mosque 488
Elapsed time display 577
Elasmobranchs 178
Elastic fibre 252, 254
Elastic rocks 60
Elbow
  Anchisaurus 89
  Corythosaurus 98
  Edmontonia 95
  Gorilla 203
  Horse 199
  Human 210
  Iguanodon 97
  Lion 194
  Psittacosaurus 103
  Stegoceras 101
  Stegosaurus 92
  Triceratops 102
Elbow guard 553
Elbow joint
  Brachiosaurus 91
  Diplodocus 90
  Eryops 80
  Euoplocephalus 94
  Human 218
  Parasaurolophus 99
  Plateosaurus 88
  Stegoceras 101
  Triceratops 102
  Tyrannosaurus 84
Elbow motor 609
Elbow pad 527, 551
Elder 130-131, 140 143
Electrical braking 330
Electrical cells 316-317
Electrical charge
  imbalance 316
Electrical circuit 316
  Toaster 598
Electrical contact 319
Electrical effects 316
Electrical energy 314-315
Electrical harness 414
Electrical inverter 422
Electrical plant 496
Electrical relay 596
Electrical relay box 330
Electrical service
  compartment 407
Electrical supply 316
Electrical wiring harness 418
Electric bass guitars 512
Electric cable 517
Electric car 342
Electric charge 308
Electric coil 317
Electric current 516-517, 328, 603
Electric equipment
  compartment 329
Electric fuel pump 422
Electric generator 317
Electric guitar 512-513
Electric heating elements 597
Electric ignition control 362
Electricity 316-317
Electricity connector to
  brushbar motor 593

Electricity generation
  Diesel train 326
  Electric train 326
  Magnetism 517
Electricity supply 590
Electric locomotive 324, 328-329
Electric motor
  Diesel train 326
  Electric train 328
  Tram 332
Electric motor/generator 357
Electric motor housing 354
Electric power line 328, 402
Electric power socket 422
Electric scoring system 556-557
Electric street tramway 332
Electric toaster 598
Electric train 528-329
Electric tram 332
Electric transmission 326
Electric window motor 349
Electrode 306
Electromagnet 317, 598
Electromagnetic
  induction capacitor 600
Electromagnetic radiation 314-315, 318
Electromagnetic
  spectrum 318-319
Electron 308, 316
  Atomic number 310
  Fluorine-19 309
Electron beam 611
Electron detector
  assembly 611
Electron gun 611
Electron gun housing 610
Electronic controller 605
Electronic control signals 330
Electronic control-unit
  connector 356
Electronic drums 520
Electronic engine control
  (EEC) unit 418-419
Electronic games 578-579
Electronic ignition unit 351
Electronic impulses 584
Electronic instruments 520-521
Electronic signals 512
Electronic warfare mast 397
Electrons 603
Electron shell 308-309, 310
Electron steam 611
Electron transfer 308
Electrostatic forces 308, 316
Electrostatic generator 316
Electrothermal de-icing
  panel 416
Element retaining stop 599
Elements 306, 308
  Atomic mass 310
  Minerals 268
  Periodic table 310-311
Elephant 90, 104, 200-201
Elephas maximus 200
Elevated green 546
Elevating wheel 396
Elevation 498
Elevator
  ARV light aircraft 424
  BAe-146 components 415
  Bell-47 helicopter 423

Biplanes and triplanes 402-403
  Curtiss biplane 399
  Early monoplanes 400-401
  Hawker Tempest
    components 409
  Schleicher glider 426
  World War I aircraft 405
  Wright Flyer 399
Elevator arm 425
Elevator chassis box 415
Elevator control cable 399, 403
Elevator control rod 409
Elevator control wire
  Bell-47 helicopter 47
  Blériot XI monoplane 401
  Curtiss biplane 399
  LVG CVI fighter 405
Elevator drive wheel 399
Elevator hinge
  BAe-146 components 415
  BE 2B tail 405
  Blackburn monoplane 400
  Hawker Tempest
    components 409
Elevator operating arm 399
Elevator-operating
  bracket 401
Elevator push-rod 424-425
Elevator rocking arm 404
Elevator trimtab 424, 409
Elevator wire 398
Eleventh-century building 466, 468
Elevon 416-417, 421
Elevon-jack fairing 415
Elevon power control unit 417
"Ellerman Lines" steam
  locomotive 324-325
Elliott steering knuckle 336
Ellipsoid orb 486
Elliptical galaxy 11-12
Elliptical orbit 30
Elliptic leaf 137
Elm 144, 150
El Nath 18, 21
Elodea canadensis 158-159
Elodea sp. 159
Elongating root 133, 153
Elrathia 64
Eltanin 19
Elytron 168
E-mail 576, 577
E-mail address 576
E-mail program 576, 577
E-mail sender 576
Emarginate apex 156
Embellisher 553
Embolos 372
Embrasure 466-467, 469
Embryo 607
  Cotyledon 152-153
  Dry fruit seed 150-151
  Fertilization 146-147
  Germination 152-153
  Human 260
  Reptile 80
  Seed leaf 152
  Succulent fruit seed 148-149
Embryonic root 150, 152-153
Embryonic shoot 147
  Epigeal germination 153
  Hypogeal germination 152
  Pea seed 150
  Pine 122
  Seed axis 152-153

Embryo sac 146-147
Emergency canopy
  release handle 420
Emergency door control 332-333
Emergency escape hatch 406
Emergency exit 416-417
Emergency oxygen
  cylinder 417
Emergent coastlines 294-295
Emission nebula 11-12, 14, 16-17
Empire State Building 494
Enamel
  Islamic buildings 488, 489
  Teeth 247
Enceladus 46
Encke 40
Encke Division 46-47
Enclosed bridge 397
Enclosed DVD/CD
  compartment 585
Encroachment 527
End 388-389
End baffle plate 598-599
End block 512
End effector 608
End element 598-599
End-grain wood block 449
End-line
  American football 526
  Basketball 532
  Men's Lacrosse 540
  Volleyball 534
End link 586
Endocardium 250
Endocarp 146-147, 148-149
Endoderm 167
Endodermis
  Bishop pine needle 124
  Canadian pond weed 158-159
  Dicotyledon 127
  Epiphytic orchid 162
  Fern rachis 121
  Horsetail stem 120
  Mare's tail stem 135
  Monocotyledon 127
  Pine root 125
  Root 132-133
  Water hyacinth root 158
Endomysium 228
Endoperidium 115
Endoplasmic reticulum 239
Endopod 172
Endopterygotes 168
Endoscopic view
  Alimentary canal 248
  Vocal cords 245
Endoskeleton 174
Endosperm 147
Endosteum 225
Endothecium 144
Endothelium 252
End-pin 510
End-plate
  Formula One racing car 356-357
  Modern piston aero-
    engine 410-411
End-plate aerodynamic
  skirt 357
End zone 526
En échelon fractures 60-61
Energized electrode 584
Energy 314-315
  Chemical reactions 312
  Electron shells 310
  Light 318
  Renewable 604-605
Energy conversion 138
Energy emission from
  Sun 22
Engaged column 469

Engaged pediment 462-463
Engine 342-347, 410-411, 418-419
  1906 Renault 357
  1-litre VTEC 354
  72° V10 356
  ARV light aircraft 425
  BAe-146 jetliner 415
  BMW R/60 362
  Bordino Steam Carriage 334
  Diesel 326
  Early monoplane 400-401
  Hawker Tempest
    components 408
  Helicopter 422-423
  Honda CB750 363
  Honda VF750 364
  Kirby BSA 369
  Lockheed Electra
    airliner 406-407
  Motorcycles 362, 364, 366-367
  Oldsmobile engine 336
  Pegasus Quasar
    microlight 427
  Pioneers of flight 398-399
  Renault Clio 350-351
  Velocette overhead
    valve (OHV) 367
  Volkswagen Beetle 340
Engine aft bulkhead 421
Engine air intake
  BE 2B bomber 404
  Concorde 416
  Formula One racing car 356, 357
  Hawker Tempest
    fighter 409
  Schweizer helicopter 423
  Tornado 420
Engine and propeller
  thrust frame 398
Engine bearer 343
Engine block 347
Engine cover
  Formula One racing car 356, 357
  Honda VF750 374
  Oldsmobile bodywork 337
  Two-stroke engine 366
  Vespa Grand Sport 160
    Mark 1 363
  Volkswagen Beetle 341
Engine cowling
  ARV light aircraft 424-425
  Avro biplane 405
  Concorde 416
  Hawker Tempest
    components 408
  Lockheed Electra
    airliner 407
  Pegasus Quasar
    microlight 427
Engine crankcase 327
Engine drive belt 354
Engineering 496
Engine front mount 418-419
Engine front support link 417
Engine fuel pump 417
Engine instruments 425
Engine lid 341
Engine lifting eye 347
Engine mounting
  ARV light aircraft 425
  Blackburn monoplane 401
  Honda VF750 364
  Modern piston aero-
    engine 411

Pegasus Quasar
microlight 427
Velocette OHV engine
567
Engine pylon 412
Engine rear mount
Pegasus Quasar
microlight 427
Turboprop engine 419
Engine room 526
Engine timing gear 336
Englacial moraine 287
Englacial stream 286
England 92
English baroque style
480-481
English bond brickwork
485
English Decorated style
470
English ivy 131
English Perpendicular
style 470, 472
Engraving 446
Enif 19, 20
Pegasus and
Andromeda 19
Ensign staff 396
Entablature
Ancient Greek building
460
Ancient Roman
building 462-465
Baroque church 480-
481
Cathedral dome 487
French temple 485
Neoclassical building
478-479, 482-483
Entasis 461
Enter button 585
Enter key 590
Enteromorpha linza 117
Entomophilous
pollination 144
Entrance
Islamic tomb 489
Medieval building 466-
467
Modern building 496-
499
Neoclassical building
483
Nineteenth-century
building 493
Twentieth century
building 494
Entrenched meander 290
Entresol 467
Enucleated egg cell 606
Enzyme 160
Eocene epoch
Fossil record 279
Geological timescale 57
Eon
Fossil record 279
Geological time 56-57
Épée 556-557
Epibranchial artery 179
Epicardium 250
Epicentre 63
Epicotyl 152-153
Epicranial aponeurosis
237
Epidermal cell 166
Epidermis
Apical meristem 134
Canadian pond weed
stem 159
Clubmoss stem 120
Dicotyledon 126-127
Epiphytic orchid 162
Fern rachis 121
Flower 142
Horsetail stem 120
Human 234-235
Leaf 139
Marram grass 113
Monocotyledon 126-127

Moss 119
Multi-layered 162
Pine needle 124
Pine stem 125
Prickle 135
Radicle 152
Rhizome 155
Root 132-133
Stem 134-135
Water hyacinth 158
Water lily 159
Epididymis 259
Epidote 269
Epigeal germination 152-
153
Epiglottis
Elephant 200
Human 212, 244-245,
248, 255
Epiphysis 230
Epiphytes 112, 162-163
Epithelial cell 217
Epithelium 254
Epioccipital bone 102
Epoch
Fossil record 279
Geological time 56-57
Epoxy resin frame 612
Epsilon Centauri 21
Epsilon Crucis 21
Epsilon Hydri 20
Epsilon ring 48-49
Epson Perfection 1650
scanner 570, 571
Epson Stylus Photo 895
colour inkjet printer
574
EQ button 587
Equal-shock intensity
lines 63
Equator
Atmosphere 300
Quaternary period 76
Saturn 47
Satellite map 265
Surface currents 297
Equatorial air 300
Equatorial current 296-
297
Equatorial furrow 144
Equatorial Zone 45
Equestrian sports 554-555
Equisetites sp. 66
Equilateral triangle 622
Equisetum arvense 70, 120
Equuleus 19, 20
Era
Fossil record 279
Geological time 56-57
Eraser 430
Erasing stick 448
Erbium 311
Erect limb stance 82
Erfi-wei 376
Eridanus 19, 20
E ring 46
Erosion 282-283
Coastline 294-295
Lake formation 293
Ocean floor 298
River features 290-291
Rock cycle 267
Sedimentary rocks 276
Eryops 80-81
Escalator 497-498
Esker 286
Estonioceras perforatum
65
Estuarine mud-flat 295
Estuary 288, 290-294
Eta Centauri 21
Eta Mensae 20
Eta Orionis 18
Eta ring 48
Eta Sagittarii 21
Etching 446
Ethernet Local Area
Network (LAN) port 567
Ethernet network 566

Euathlus emilia 170
Euoplocephalus 94-95
Eurasia 76
Eurasian plate 59
Europa 44
Europe
Cretaceous period 72-73
Earth's physical
features 264-265
Electric train 328
Electric train 332
Jurassic period 70
Loading gauge 331
Middle Ordovician
period 64
Quaternary period 76
Railway track gauge
331
Tertiary period 74-75
Triassic period 68
European field elm 144
European hard-screw
coupling 402
Europium 311
"Eurostar" multi-voltage
electric train 328-329
Europierid fossil 79
Eustachian tube 243
Eustreptospondylus 85
Euthynteria 460
Evacuated column 610,
611
Evaporation 307
Event horizon 28-29
Evergreens 130-131
Everlasting pea 129
Evolute shell 278
Evolution
Earth 56-57
Living things 278
Exchangeable cover 588
Excretory pore 177
Excurrent pore 166
Exfoliation 282
Exhaust
Catalytic converter 355
Ford diesel engine 347
Modern mechanics 350-
351
Paddlesteamer 391
Exhaust clamp 362
Exhaust collector ring
403, 406
Exhaust cone 419
Exhaust connection 427
Exhaust diffuser 418
Exhaust downpipe 350
Exhaust fairing 419
Exhaust gas recirculation
valve 344
Exhaust heat shield 345
Exhaust manifold
1906 Renault 337
ARV light aircraft 425
Jaguar V12 engine 345
Mid West two-stroke
engine 410
Renault Clio 351
Exhaust nozzle 418
Exhaust pipe
Avro biplane 403
Bell-47 helicopter 422
BMW R/60 362
Brazilian battleship 395
Harley-Davidson FLHS
Electra Glide 363
Formula One racing car
356
Hawker Tempest
fighter 409
Honda CB750 363
Honda VF750 364
Kirby BSA 369
Kawasaki Electra
airliner 406-407
Oldsmobile engine 336
Pegasus Quasar
microlight 427
Suzuki RGV500 368

White Steam Car 342
World War I aircraft
404-405
Exhaust pipe flange 411
Exhaust port
"Deltic" diesel-electric
locomotive 326
Four-stroke cycle 343
Mid West 75-HP engine
410
Two-stroke engine 367
Velocette OHV engine
367
Wankel engine 347
Wankel rotary cycle 346
Exhaust silencer 423, 427
Exhaust stack 405
Exhaust steam water
injector control 325
Exhaust stroke 343
Exhaust system 368
Exhaust tract 410
Exhaust valve 343-345
Exhaust valve push-rod
400
Exhaust vent
British Rail Class 20
diesel engine 327
Drill 601
"Union Pacific"
locomotive 326
Exine 144-145
Exit door 333
Exocarp 146-149
Exoccipital bone 183
Exocet missile launcher
397
Exodermis 162
Exoperidium 115
Exopod 172
Exoskeleton
Insect 168
Malacostraca 172
Spider 171
Exosphere 300
Exothermic reactions 312
Expander bolt 359
Expandable sponge 448
Expansile jaw 85
Expansion card 569
Expansion card slot 569
Expansion lever 325
Expansion of sail 378-379
Expelling plate 397
Expiration 255
Exploding shell 396, 397
Expressionist style 495
Extended cave system 285
Extended port air-brake
421
Extensor digitorum brevis
muscle 233
Extensor digitorum
longus tendon 233
Extensor digitorum
tendon 231
Extensor hallucis brevis
muscle 233
Extensor hallucis longus
tendon 233
Extensors of hand 227
External anatomy
Body 210-211
Brain 237
Ear 242-243
Foot 233
Hand 231
Sperm 259
External auditory meatus
Homo erectus 108
Homo sapiens 108, 220,
242
External crust 28
External elastic lamina
252
External iliac artery 215,
225, 253
External iliac vein 215,
253

External nostril 184
External oblique muscle
226
External occipital crest
220
External pubo-ischio-
femoral muscle 97
External skeleton
Insect 168
Malacostraca 172
Spider 171
External spermatic fascia
259
External urinary meatus
258
Extinct geyser 275
Extinction
Dinosaur 56, 74, 82, 104
Life 66
Pleistocene mammals
76
Extinct volcano 62, 272
Igneous rock structures
275
Mountain building 62
Ocean floor 298
Extradors 484-485
Extra period 532
Extrusive rocks 274, 275
Eye
Allosaurus 85
Amphibian 182
Anchisaurus 89
Angling hook 562
Beetle 168
Bird 188
Bony fish 181
Brachiosaurus 91
Bumblebee 168
Butterfly 169
Caiman 186
Carnivore 194
Chick 192-193
Corythosaurus 98
Crab 172
Crayfish 173
Crocodilian 186
Deer hopper dry fly 563
Devon minnow 563
Dhow 376
Dogfish 178
Dolphin 204
Elephant 201
Figurehead 374
Forward-facing 194
Frog 182
Gallimimus 86
Gorilla 203
Greek and Roman ships
372
Herrerasaurus 86
Horse 198
Human 211, 212, 240-
241
Iguanodon 97
Kangaroo 207
Knot 388
Lamprey 178
Lion 194
Lizard 184
Median 170
Octopus 177
Pachycephalosaurus
100
Psittacosaurus 103
Rabbit 196
Rat 196
Rattlesnake 185
Rigging 382-383
Salamander 182
Scallop 176
Scorpion 170
Seal 204
Shrimp 172
Simple 170-171
Snail 177
Snake 185
Spider 170
Stegoceras 101

Stegosaurus 92
Terrapin 187
Triceratops 102
Trilobite fossil 78
Tyrannosaurus 84
Westlothiana 87
Eyeball 241
Eye bolt 381
Eyebrow
74-gun ship 381
Human 212
Eyelash 212
Eyelid
Caiman 186
Human 213
Snake 184
Terrapin 187
Eye pam motor 609
Eyepieces 610, 611
Eye plate lug 382
Eyespot 116
Eye tilt motor 609

F

F-14 Tomcat fighter 420
Fabric 384
Fabric covering
Aluminium and steel
wing 403
BE 2B tail 405
Blériot XI monoplane
401
Steel-tube fuselage 403
Fabric lacing 405
Fabric skin 401
Fabric softener section
595
Fabry 41
Façade
Ancient Greek building
461
Ancient Roman
building 465
Baroque church 480-
481
Gothic church 470-472
Modern building 496-
499
Neoclassical building
478, 483
Nineteenth-century
building 493
Renaissance building
474
Façade pediment 481
Façade wall 470
Face
Deadeye 383
Human 211
Sailmaker's mallet 384
Face mask
American football 526
Fencing 557
Hockey goalkeeper 540
Ice hockey goalkeeper
550
Lacrosse goalkeeper
541
Slalom skiing 553
Facet 222-223
Facia 589
"Facing off" 550
Faering 374-375
Fag end 387, 388
Fahrenheit temperature
scale 590
Fairing 364, 369
Fairing of landing gear
413
Fairing panel 415
Fairlead
Battleship 395
Frigate 397
Rigging 383
Roman corbita 373
Fairway 546
Falciform ligament 248

Falco tinnunculus 189
Falkland current 296
Fall 382
Fallopian tube 258-259,
  261
False acacia 156
False anthers 141
False door 458-459
False fruit 148-149
False ram bow 594
"False ribs" 218
False septum 151
Falx cerebri 237
Fan
  Jaguar straight six
    engine 344
  Jet engines 418-419
  Microwave
    combination oven 596-
    597
  Power drill 600
Fan blade
  Renault Clio 353
  Turbofan 419
Fancase 418
Fan drive shaft 345
Fan duct nozzle 412
Fan dust shield 597
Fan fold 61
Fang 170
Fan transformer 597
Fan motor 351
Fan vault 484-485
Farming axe 109
Fascia
  Ancient Roman
    building 463-464
  Baroque church 479,
    481
  Dome 486
  French temple 485
  Gothic building 472
  Medieval building 467,
    469
  Modern building 498
  Neoclassical building
    482
  Renaissance building
    476-477
  Renault Clio 353
Fat
  Cells 217
  Tissue 215, 235
Faultline
  Lake formation 292
  Mountain building 62-
    63
  Weathering and erosion
    283
Fault plane 60
Faults 60-61, 292
  Mineral resources 280
  Mountain building 62
  Oil and gas traps 281
  Showjumping
    competitions 554
Fault spring 292
Fault structure 60
Fault trap 281
Fax machine 572-573
F-block 311
FCC cable 571
C clef 502
Feather 188, 191
Feathered float 391
Feathering 440-441
Feather shuttlecock 544-
  545
Feather star 174
Feed bilge pump 591
Feeder station 328
Feed spool 587
Feet
  Human 232-233
  Theropods 84
Fei Tecnai G2
  transmission electron
  microscope 610
Feldspar 267, 269, 275

Felloe 390
Felt blanket 447
Felt-covered beater 516,
  518-519
Felt-tip pen 444
Female
  Body 210, 211
  Pelvis 218, 258
  Reproductive organs
    259
Female apex 119
Female cones
  Bishop pine 124
  Gymnosperm 122
  Pine 122, 124
  Smooth cypress 123
  Yew 123
Female flower organs
  140-143
Female flower remains
  148
Female flowers 143, 144,
  148
Female gametes
  Fertilization 146-147
  Gymnosperm 122
  Scots pine 122
  Seaweed 116-117
  Yew 123
Female receptacles 117
Female reproductive
  organs
  Fern 121
  Fruit 148
  Moss 119
  Plants 144
Femoral artery 225, 253
Femoral musculature 86
Femoral nerve 238
Femoral vein 253
Femoro-tibial muscle 84
Femur
  Albertosaurus 84
  Archaeopteryx 85
  Beetle 168
  Bird 189
  Brachiosaurus 90
  Butterfly 169
  Crocodile 186
  Dinosaur 82
  Domestic cat 195
  Elephant 201
  Euoplocephalus 94
  Frog 183
  Gallimimus 86
  Hare 197
  Horse 199
  Human 218-219, 224-
    225
  Iguanodon 96-97
  Kangaroo 206
  Lizard 184
  Parasaurolophus 98
  Pareiasaur 81
  Plateosaurus 88
  Platypus 206
  Rhesus monkey 202
  Scorpion 170
  Seal 204
  Spider 171
  Stegoceras 101
  Struthiomimus 87
  Toxodon 107
  Triceratops 102
  Tuojiangosaurus 93
  Turtle 187
  Tyrannosaurus 84
Fencing 556-557
Fender eye bolt 539
Fender jazz bass guitar
  513
Fender stratocaster guitar
  513
Fenestration 474, 494
Fermentation 313
Fermium 311

Fern 120-121
  Fossil 66, 279
  Life-cycle 121
  Prehistoric Earth 68, 70,
    72
  Tree fern 112-113
Ferrel cell 300
Ferrite core 571
Fertile horsetail stem 120
Fertile oasis 283
Fertilization 146-147
  Fern 121
  Gymnosperm 122
  Scots pine 122
  Seaweed 117
Festoon
  Ancient Roman
    building 462-463
  Cathedral dome 487
  Neoclassical building
    478-479
Fetal skull 220
Fetlock 199, 554
Fetus 260-261
Fibre 134-135
Fibreglass 548
  Bow 548
  Bucket seat 361
  Canopy frame 425
  Fuel tank 425
  Racket 544
  Reinforced plastic cover
    329
  Wheel guard 369
Fibre insulation 602
Fibre plate 566
Fibrils 52
Fibrin 253
Fibrous capsule 256
Fibrous habit 271
Fibrous pericardium 250
Fibrous septum 245
Fibula
  Albertosaurus 84
  Brachiosaurus 90
  Crocodile 186
  Diplodocus 90
  Domestic cat 195
  Elephant 201
  Eryops 81
  Hare 197
  Horse 199
  Human 219, 232-233
  Iguanodon 96-97
  Kangaroo 206
  Lizard 184
  Parasaurolophus 99
  Plateosaurus 88
  Platypus 206
  Rhesus monkey 202
  Seal 204
  Stegoceras 101
  Struthiomimus 87
  Toxodon 107
  Triceratops 102
  Turtle 187
  Tyrannosaurus 84
Ficulare 183
Ficus carica 148
Ficus sp. 137
Fid 383, 384
Fiddle block 378, 383
Field arrow 549
Field coil 600
Fielder's glove 537
Field events 542
Field goal 526-527
Fielding 538
Fielding team 556
Field judge 526
Field positions 538
Fields and particles
  instruments 614
Field umpire 528
Fifteenth century
  Mihrab 488

Renaissance building
  474-475
  Style 462, 470
  Terrace 490
  Tracery 472
Fig 137, 148
Fighters 404-405, 408-409,
  420
Fighting 556
Fighting platform 374
Figurehead
  74-gun ship 380-381
  Wooden sailing ship
    379
Figure of eight turns 387
Filament
  Alga 116
  Dicotyledon flower 126-
    127
  Fern 121
  Fertilization 146-147
  Flowers 140-141, 143
  Fungal 114-115
  Jellyfish 167
  Light bulb 319
  Nebulae and star
    clusters 16-17
  Sun 32-33
  Moss 119
  Pollination 144
Filbert hog hair brush 436
File menu 576
Filicinophyta 120
Filiform papilla 244
Filing 455
Filled shell 310-311
Fillet
  Ancient Greek temple
    461
  Dome 486
  French temple 485
  Gothic building 470
  Neoclassical moulding
    480
  Renaissance building
    475, 477
Filling transom 381
Film and transparency
  holder 570
Filter 576
Filter access flap 594
Filter rim casing 592
Filter 576
Filter screen 595
Filter turret 610
Fimbria 258-259
Fin
  Anal 178, 181
  ARV light aircraft 424
  Avro biplane 402
  BAe-146 components
    415
  Blackburn monoplane
    401
  Caudal 178-181
  Concorde 416
  Devon minnow 563
  Dorsal 178-179, 181,
    205
  Helicopter 423
  Lockheed Electra
    airliner 407
  Lungfish 81
  LVG CVI fighter 405
  Pectoral 178, 180-181
  Pelvic 179-181
  Schleicher glider 426
  Tornado 421
  Ventral 179
  World War II aircraft
    408-409
Fish
  Bony 180-181
  Breathing 180
  Cartilaginous 178
  Fossil 279
  Holostean 73
  Jawless 178-179
Fish davit 379
Fisherman's schooner 385
Fishing tackle 109

Fine-toothed marble claw
  453
Finger
  Anchisaurus 89
  Gorilla 203
  Human 211
  Iguanodon 97
  Pachycephalosaurus 100
  Psittacosaurus 103
  Stegoceras 101
  Theropod 84
Fingerboard 510-511, 513
Finger-claw 85, 85
Finger grip 580
Finger hole 508
Finger key 507
Fingerless glove 527
Fingernail 231
Finger recess 571
Finger tab 548
Finial
  Asian building 490-491
  Baroque church 479,
    481
  Gothic church 470-471
  Islamic building 488-
    489
  Medieval building 468
  Neoclassical building
    478
  Nineteenth-century
    building 493
  Renaissance building
    476
Finishing line 542, 554-
    555
Fin leading-edge
  attachment 415
Finned tail 80
Fin-root aerial fairing 421
Fin tip 415
Fin tip fairing 421, 424
Fin trailing edge 415
Fir 66
Fire 108
Fireball 10
Firebox 324-325
Fire-escape 497-498
Fire extinguisher 528
Fire-extinguisher
  discharge indicator 412
Fire-hole 325
Fire-making tools 109
Fireman's seat 325
Fire opal 270
Fireplace 466-467
Fire-resistant clay 454
Fire-resistant curtain 497
Fire-resistant panel 496
Fire-tube boiler 334
Fire tubes 324-325
Firing 452
Firewire ports 560
Firewire socket 587
Firing 452
Firewire ports 560
Firewire socket 587
Firing chamber 575
Firing pin 549
Firm 287
First century 462-464
"first down" 526- 527
First pilot's seat 408
First quarter 41
First rate ship 378
First slip 538
First transition metals 310
First violin 503, 504-505
First wheel set 329
Fish
  Bony 180-181
  Breathing 180
  Cartilaginous 178
  Fossil 279
  Holostean 73
  Jawless 178-179

Fish-scale tile 476-477,
  486
Fishtail nectaries 160
Fissure 247
Fissures 157
Fissure volcano 272
Five-line stave 502
Five yard mark 540
Fixative 430, 440
Fixed float 390
Fixed gear 346-347, 411
Fixed lug 585
Fixed objective lens 581
Fixed-spool reel 562
Fixing screw 599
Fjord 294-295
Flagella 166
Flagellum
  Beetle 168
  Chlamydomonas sp.
    116
  Moss 119
  Seaweed gametes 117
  Snail 177
  Sperm 259
Flag halyard 380
Flagmast 395
Flag pin 547
Flagpole 495
Flaking rock 282
Flamboyant tracery 472
Flame 312-313
Flamingo 188, 190
Flamsteed 40
Flange 492, 498
Flanged plate 425
Flank
  Bird 188
  Cow 198
Flanker
  Canadian football 526
  Rugby 530
Flank spike 95
Flap
  ARV light aircraft 425
  Formula One racing car
    356, 357
  Hawker Tempest
    components 409
  Lockheed Electra
    airliner 406
  Tornado 421
Flap drive screw 413
Flap lever 425
Flap seal 413, 414
Flap tip 414
Flap torque tube 424
Flap track 413
Flap-track fairing 413, 415
Flared bell
  Brass instruments 506-
    507
  Woodwind instruments
    508-509
Flash steam generator 342
Flash tube 397
Flash unit 580
Flask 512-513
Flat
  Musical notation 502
  Twin bollards 386
Flatbed scanner 570-571
Flatboard 384
Flat bottom 591
Flat-bottomed rail 331
Flat chisel 452
Flat cone 272
Flatfish angling 562
Flat-four engine 340
Flat freight car 327
Flat horse-races 554
Flat laminae 158
Flat roof
  Ancient Egyptian
    building 458
  Neoclassical building
    483
  Twentieth-century
    building 494-495

Flat seam 584
Flat seizing 385, 389
Flat soffit 464
Flattened pericarp 151
Flattened petiole 160
Flattened stem 129
Flat-topped plateau 275, 282
Flat-topped seamount 298
Flat wire seizing 383
Flavian amphitheatre 464
Flax-spinning mill 492
Fleet number 553
Flesh-eaters 194
Flesh-eating dinosaur 70
Flesh tones 433
Fleshy aril 148
Fleshy axis 143
Fleshy fruit 146-147
Fleshy hair 140
Fleshy infolded receptacle 148
Fleshy scale leaf 155
Fletch 548
Flexible hose shrouding 593
Flex kink guard 594
Flexor digitorum longus muscle 255
Flexor digitorum tendon 231
Flexor hallucis longus muscle 233
Flexor pollicis brevis muscle 231
Flexor retinaculum muscle 231
Flexors of forearm 226
Flexors of hand 227
Flexor tubercle 85
Flex rewind 593
Flight 543
Flight-control hydraulic jack 416
Flight-control mixing unit 417
Flight-control rod 423
Flight controls 412
Flight feathers 188, 191
Flight instruments 425
Flight refuelling receptacle 421
Flint 277
Flint tools 108-109
Flipper
  Dolphin 204
  Seal 204
Flitch-plated wooden chassis 342
Float 390-391
Floating disc brake 364-365
Floating floor 602
"Floating" rib 218
Flocked pastel board 441
Floodgate 604
Flood-plain 289-291
Floods 290
Floor
  Gun turret 596
  Ironclad 393
  Longboat 380
  Modern building 496-498
  Nineteenth-century building 492
  Twentieth-century building 494-495
Floor anchor 407
Floorboard 464, 486
Floor-joist 464
Floor-mounted base 608
Floor pan 340
Floor tom 518-519
Florence Cathedral 475, 487
Florets 142
  Florists' chrysanthemum 129

Ultraviolet light 145
Florida current 296
Florists' chrysanthemum 129
Flower bud
  Aechmea miniata 162
  Broomrape 163
  Bulb 155
  Clematis 131
  Florists' chrysanthemum 129
  Hibiscus 127
  Ice-plant 129
  Live-for-ever 129
  Oxalis sp. 157
  Peruvian lily 129
  Rose 131
  Water lily 159
  Wind pollination 144
Flowering plant 57, 70, 72
Flowering shoot 155
Flowers 140-143
  Brassavola nodosa 162
  Bromeliad 113
  Broomrape 163
  Buds 140-141, 143
  Clematis 131
  Colour 140, 144-145
  Dicotyledons 126-127, 141-143
  Dodder 163
  Epiphytes 162-163
  Everlasting pea 129
  Florists' chrysanthemum 129
  Guzmania lingulata 163
  Ice-plant 129
  Involucre 129
  Monocotyledons 126, 140-141, 143
  Peruvian lily 129
  Pollination 144-145
  Rose 131
  Russian vine 131
  Scented 144
  Stem arrangements 143
  Ultraviolet light 145
  Vegetative reproduction 154
  Water lily 159
  Yew 125
Flower scars 154
Flower spike 143, 155
Flower stalk
  Brassavola nodosa 162
  Bulbil 154
  Clematis 131
  Dry fruit 150-151
  Fertilization 146-147
  Florists' chrysanthemum 129
  Fruit development 146-147
  Monocotyledons 140-141, 143
  Oxalis sp. 157
  Rose 131
  Rowan 131
  Russian vine 131
  Succulent fruit 148-149
  Sycamore 151
  Water lily 159
Flow splitter 418
Fluff filter impeller 595
Fluid 306
Fluke
  74-gun ship 380
  Danforth anchor 386
Fluorescent light 318-319
Fluorine 308-309, 311
Fluorite 271
  Halides 269
Flush-riveted aluminium fuselage 423
Flush-riveted metal-skinned wing 406
Flush window 494
Flute 503, 504-505, 508

Fluted pilaster 462
Fluted pinnacle 481
Fluted shaft 478
Flute tube 525
Fluting 461, 463
Flutter kick 559
Fly 168
Fly fishing 562
Fly-half 550
Flying boat 406
Flying buttress
  Gothic building 470-473
  Medieval building 466, 468-469
  Nineteenth-century building 493
Flying Fortress bomber 408
Flying helmet 404
Flying jib 385
Flying reptile 70
Flying tackle 551
Fly rod 562-563
Flywheel
  Benz Motorwagen 335
  Early engines 342-343
  Etching press 447
  Mid West rotary engine 411
  Oldsmobile engine 336
  Renault Clio 351
  Steamboat 391
Flywheel retaining thread 411
Flywheel with balance weight 347
FM and TV aerial 603
Focker, Anthony 404
Fo'c'sle 380
Focus 63
Focus control 583
Focus ring 583
Fog 42-43
Fog-lamp 349, 353
Fog light 332, 363
Foil 556-557
Foilist 557
Foil pommel 557
Folded rock 60, 266
  Impermeable rock 281
  Mineral resources 280
  Strata 60-61
Folded schist 274
Folding mountain range 274
Folding step 326
Fold mountains 62
Fold of mucous membrane 249
Folds 60-61
Foliage leaf
  Bishop pine 124
  Bud 124
  Bulb 155
  Germination 152-153
  Monocotyledon 126
  Parasitic plant 162
  Pine 124-125
  Rhizome 155
  Seedling 152-153
  Stem bulbil 155
  Yew 123
Foliated capital 469
Foliated frieze 469, 479
Foliated panel 479
Foliated scrollwork 472
Foliate papilla 244
Foliose lichen 114
Foliose thallus 114
Follicle
  Dehiscent dry fruit 150-151
  Hair 235
  Ovary 258
Fomalhaut 19, 20
Fontanelle 220
Food storage
  Bulb 155

Corm 155
Embryo 147
Rhizome 155
Root tuber 155
Scale leaf 155
Seed 152
Succulent 156-157
Swollen stem 113, 155
Foot
  Anchisaurus 89
  Bird 190
  Caiman 186-187
  Corythosaurus 98
  Cow 198
  Diplodocus 90
  Duck 188
  Elephant 90
  Gorilla 203
  Harp 511
  Herrerasaurus 86
  Horse 198
  Human 210
  Iguanodon 96
  Kangaroo 207
  Pachycephalosaurus 100
  Relief-printing press 449
  Sails 374, 385
  Slug 176
  Snail 177
  Stegoceras 101
  Stegosaurus 92
  Toaster 598-599
  Tyrannosaurus 84
  Tube 174
  Webbed 188
  Westlothiana 81
Football 524-525
Footboard 335
Foot brake 363
Footbridge 493
Foot-fault judge 544
Foot mat 363
Foot pad 608
Foot pedal 366, 514
Footplate 324
Footrest
  Curtiss biplane 398-399
  Suzuki RGV500 368
  Weslake Speedway motorcycle 369
Footrest hanger 364
Foot rope 378-379, 382, 385
Foot throttle 427
Foramen caecum 244
Foramen magnum 220
Foraminifers 279
Force 320-321
  "Force play" 536
Ford Cosworth V6 12-valve engine 344
Ford Cosworth V6 24-valve engine 344
Ford, Henry 338
Ford Model T 338-339
Ford turbocharged diesel engine 347
Fore-and-aft rigged lateen sails 376
Fore-and-aft sails 384
Fore-and-aft schooner 385
Forearm
  Gorilla 203
  Horse 199
  Human 210
  Movement 227
Forearm guard 548
Forearm pass 534
Fore bitt 380
Fore breast rope 387
Forecarriage 335
Forecastle
  74-gun ship 380
  Sailing warship 376
  Square-rigged ship 375
Forecastle castle-deck gunport 376

Forefoot
  Caiman 186
  Diplodocus 90
  Edmontonia 95
  Elephant 90
  Iron paddlesteamer 393
  Stegosaurus 92
Fore hatch tackle 379
Forehead
  Bird 188
  Dolphin 204
  Elephant 200-201
  Horse 199
  Human 211, 212
Foreleg
  Caiman 186
  Elephant 201
  Lizard 184
  Terrapin 187
Forelimb
  Anchisaurus 89
  Bird 188
  Corythosaurus 98
  Edmontonia 95
  Frog 182
  Hare 196
  Herrerasaurus 86
  Iguanodon 97
  Kangaroo 207
  Pachycephalosaurus 100
  Psittacosaurus 103
  Rabbit 196
  Rat 196
  Salamander 182
  Stegoceras 101
  Stegosaurus 92
  Thyreophorans 92
  Triceratops 102
  Tyrannosaurus 84
Forelock 199
Fore lower topsail 385
Foremast
  Iron paddlesteamer 392
  Roman corbita 372
  Sailing warship 376
  Square-rigged ship 375
  Wooden sailing ship 379
Fore mast course 379
Foremast hole 380
Fore mast topgallant sail 379
Fore mast topsail 379
Forepeak 393
Fore royal stay 383
Fore sail 372, 385
Fore sail halyard 380
Foreset strata 283
Fore shroud 379
Foresight
  Rifle 549
  Target pistol 549
Foreskin 259
Fore spring rope 387
Fore stay
  Rigging 382
  Roman corbita 372
  Sailing warship 376
  Wooden sailing ship 379
Fore staysail 379, 385
Fore staysail halyard 385
Fore staysail stay 376
Fore topmast staysail 385
Fore topmast staysail tack 382
Fore topsail 379
Fore upper topsail 385
Forewing 169
Fore yard 376, 379
Fore yard lift 385
Forged iron anchor 392

Fork
  ARV Super 2 425
  Eddy Merckx racing bicycle 361
  Harley-Davidson FLHS Electra Glide 363
  Honda CB750 363
  Motorcycle 364
  Vespa Grand Sport 160 Mark 1 363
Fork blade 359
Forked beam 580
Forked connecting-rod 342
Fork end 383
Fork slide 365
Formeret 469, 479
Fornax 19, 20
Fornix 236-237
Fortifications 466
Forum of Trajan 463
Forward bulkhead panel 406
Forward control 577, 587
Forward deck 561
Forward defensive stroke 538
Forward dive 558
Forward door 415, 417
Forward-facing eyes 194
Forward fairing 415
Forward-firing machine-gun 405
Forward funnel 393, 395
Forward fuselage structure 401
Forward galley 416
Forward hydroplane 397
Forward main door 412
Forward ramp drive 417
Forward rollover structure 357
Forwards 532, 534-535
Forward short leg 538
Forward spar 415
Fossa ovalis 251
Fossil fuel 280-281, 314-315
Fossilization 278
Fossil record 279
Fossils 278-279
  Acanthostega skull 80
  Ankylosaurus tail cuib 95
  Birch leaf 74, 76
  Blue green algae 78
  Brachiopod 65
  Clubmoss 66
  Eurypterid 79
  Fern 66
  Graptolite 65
  Horsetail 66
  Hyaenodon skull 107
  Jawless fish 79
  Land plant 64
  Lungfish 81
  Nautiloid 65
  Palm bark 74
  Shark teeth 67
  Starfish 79
  Swamp plant 64
  Sweetgum leaf 76
  Titanosaurid egg 91
  Trilobite 78
Fossil skeleton
  Archaeopteryx 85
  Bat 105
  Parasaurolophus 98
  Pareiasaur 81
  Struthiomimus 87
  Westlothiana 81
Foul line 536
Fouls 532
Foul tackle 524
Foul tip 557
Foundation
  Ancient Roman building 464

659

Iron paddlesteamer 392
Modern building 496
Nineteenth-century building 492
Foundry plug 587
Fountain pen 444
Four-aspect colour light signal 330
Four-chambered heart 104
Four-cylinder 12-HP engine 399
Four-cylinder motorcycle 363
Four-footed dinosaur 88, 92, 96, 100
Four-pulley system 520
Four-stroke combustion engine 366
Four-stroke cycle 343
Fourteenth century 474
Arch 488
Gothic building 471-473
Medieval building 466-467
Roof 490
Style 470
Fourth mast 376
Four-wheel bogie 417
Fovea 224
Foveal camera 609
Foveal view 609
Fowler flap 413, 414
Foxes 194
Fracastorius 40
Fracture 270
Fractured rock 34
Fragaria x ananassa 128, 150
Fra Mauro 40
Frame
74-gun ship 381
ARV light aircraft 424
Bicycle 358-359
Cannondale SH600
Digital video 585
Hybrid bicycle 361
Concert grand piano 515
Concorde 416
Harley-Davidson FLHS Electra Glide 363
Honda VF750 364
Ironclad 393
Longboat 380
Medieval house 466
Minidisc player 587
Modelled sculpture 452
Modern building 496
Motorcycle 364
Oscillating steam engine 390
Racing bicycle 360
Racket 544-545
Relief-printing press 449
Single scull 560
Steam-powered Cugnot 335
Steel 494
Upright piano 514
Weslake Speedway motorcycle 369
Frame angle 360
Frame drum 518
Frame head 340
Frame-mounted fairing 364
Fram Rupes 35
Francis turbine 314
Francium 310
Frapped turn 589
Free nerve ending 235, 239
Freestyle swimming stroke 558
Free-throw line 532-533, 535
Freewheel 361

Freewheel lock nut 358
Freewheel sprocket 360
Freezing 307
Freezing level 302
Freight car 527
Freight service 326
French baroque style 479, 482
French bowline 388
French Flamboyant style 470
French TGV train 328-329
French trotter 554
Fresco 434-435
Freshwater bay 291
Freshwater angling 562
Freshwater lake
Lakes and groundwater 292
Weathering and erosion 283
Freshwater turtle 186
Fret 512-513
Fret-pattern mosaic 488-489
Fretwork 461, 491
Frieze
Ancient Egyptian building 459
Ancient Greek building 461
Ancient Roman building 463, 465
Baroque church 479, 481
Cathedral dome 487
French temple 485
Medieval church 469
Neoclassical building 478-479, 482
Renaissance building 476
Twentieth-century building 495
Frigate 396-397
F ring 46-47
Fringed crumble cap 115
Fringilla coelebs 193
Fringing reef 299
Frog 182-183
Double bass bow 511
Eggs 183, 192
Fossil 278
Violin bow 510
Frog kick 559
Frond
Fern 120-121
Seaweed 116-117
Tree fern 112-113
Front air dam 354
Frontal bone
Bony fish 181
Chimpanzee 202
Human 212-213, 220-221
Frontalis muscle 226, 228-229
Frontal lobe 236-237
Frontal notch 213
Frontal process 221
Frontal rib 161
Frontal sinus 212, 245
Front axle
1906 Renault 336-337
Ford Model T 338
Honda VF750 363
Husqvarna Motocross TC610 368
Kirby BSA 369
Front bezel 568, 584
Front brake cable
Bicycle 359
Eddy Merckx racing bicycle 361
Front brake lever 363
Front bumper 332
Front cantilever brake 359
Front case 568
Front crawl 558-559

Front cylinder exhaust pipe 368
Front derailleur 358-360
Front leg 168-169
Front light
Bicycle 360
Paris Metro 328
Italian State Railways Class 402 328
Frontoparietal bone 183
Frontozygomatic suture 220
Front spring 337
Front wheel
Bicycle 359
Front wing 168
Frost wedging 282, 286-287
Frozen rubber puck 550-551
Fruit
Bramble 130
Couch grass 113
Development 146-147
Dry 150-151
Durmast oak 131
Peach 131
Pitcher plant 113
Rowan 131
Succulent 148-149
Sycamore 151
Fruit wall 148-149, 150-151
Fruticose lichen 114
Fruticose thallus 114
Fucoxanthin 116
Fucus spiralis 116
Fucus vesiculosus 116, 117
Fuel and heat exchanger 418
Fuel and oil heat exchanger 418
Fuel and oil tank 398-399
Fuel cap 548, 569
Fuel contents indicator 340
Fuel-cooled oil cooler 419
Fuel drip tray 411
Fuel filler cap
Curtiss biplane 398
Volkswagen Beetle 340
Fuel filler neck 340
Fuel filter 419
Fuel heater 419
Fuel hose 425
Fuel injection 344, 356
Fuel inlet 419
Fuel-jettison pipe 417
Fuel-jettison valve 406
Fuel manifold 418-419
Fuel nozzle 418-419
Fuel pipe
Concorde 417
Curtiss biplane 398
Jaguar V12 345
Fuel reservoir 568
Fuel sediment bowl 339
Fuel shut-off valve cable 419
Fuel sprayer 418
Fuel supply pump 327
Fuel tank
Avro triplane 402
Benz Motorwagen 335
BMW R/60 362
Concorde 417
"Deltic" diesel-electric locomotive 326
Harley-Davidson FLHS Electra Glide 363
Helicopter 422-423
Honda VF750 364
Lockheed Electra airliner 407
LVG CVI fighter 405
Pegasus XL SE microlight 426

Renault Clio 350
Suzuki RGV500 369
Volkswagen Beetle 340
Werner motorcycle 362
Weslake Speedway motorcycle 369
White Steam Car 342
Wright Flyer 398
Fuel tank breather 369
Fuel tank cradle 422
Fuel tank filler cap 369
Fuel tank filler neck 350
Fuel tank filler nozzle 427
Fuel tank sender unit 340
Fuel tank top skin 425
Fuel tap 566
Fuel vent pipe 422
Fulcrum 320-321
Full back
American football 526
Australian rules football 527
Canadian football 526
Gaelic football 529
Rugby 530
Full back line 529
Full-elliptic leaf spring 334-335
Full-elliptic suspension spring 337
Full forward 528-529
Fumaroles 272-273
Funaria hygrometrica 119
Funaria sp. 119
Functionalism 496
Function button 385
Function display 520-521
Fundus 258
Fungal filament 114-115
Fungi 112, 114-115, 133
Fungia fungites 167
Fungiform papilla 244
Fungoid-structure encrustations 284
Funicle 150
Funnel
Battleship 395
Frigate 397
Iron paddlesteamer 392-393
Lizard 185
Octopus 176-177
Steamboat with paddle wheels 391
Funnel guide 126
Funnel stay 395
Furcula 189
Furled forecourse sail 375
Furled lateen main sail 376
Furled lateen mizzen sail 375, 376
Furnerius 40
Furrow 282
Furud 21
Fused carpels 140, 144, 151
Fused petals 142, 145
Fused receptacles 149
Fuselage 401, 409, 424
Fuselage bottom skin 424
Fuselage bracing wire 403, 426
Fuselage mid-section 412
Fuselage nose-section 412
Fuselage skin 402
Fuselage spine fairing 414
Fuselage tail-section 415
Fuselage top skin 424
Fuses 591
Fusion crust 52
Futtock shroud 378

G

Gabbro 267, 274
Gable
Gothic building 470-473

Medieval building 467, 469
Nineteenth-century building 492-493
Renaissance building 476
Gabled arch 471
Gacrux 21
Gadolinium 311
Gaelic football 528-529
Gaff 380, 385
Gagarin 41
Gait 554
Galactic centre 14, 18, 20
Galactic nucleus 12-13
Galactic plane 14-15
Galaxy 10-15, 613
Galena 268
Galeocerdo cuvier 179
Galilean moons 44
Galium aparine 150
Gallbladder
Domestic cat 195
Human 248, 252
Rabbit 196
Tortoise 187
Galle ring 50-51
Gallery
74-gun ship 381
Ancient Roman building 465
Baroque church 479-480
Cathedral dome 487
Frigate 397
Medieval building 466-468
Modern building 496-497
Renaissance theatre 477
Wooden sailing ship 378-379
Galley 372-397
Gallimimus 82, 84, 86-87
Gallium 311
Galois 41
Galvanized "D" shackle 386
Gambrel roof 490
Game Boy Advance 578, 579
Game Boy Advance games 578
Game cartridge 579
Game target shooting 548
Gamete 154
Brown seaweed 116-117
Bryophyte 118-119
Fern 120-121
Fertilization 146-147
Gymnosperm 122
Moss 112
Pine 122
Vegetative reproduction 154
Yew 123
Gametophyte
Bryophyte 118-119
Fern 120-121
Liverwort 118
Moss 112, 119
Gamma 18, 21
Gamma Centauri 21
Gamma Hydri 20
Gamma Mensae 20
Gamma radiation 10
Gamma ray 22, 318-319
Gamma ring 48
Ganges pauis 63
Ganges River delta 288
Ganglion 173, 177
Gangway
74-gun ship 380
Colosseum 464
Sailing warship 377
Ganymede 44, 614

Gape
Angling hook 562
Dolphin 204
Garboard strake 393
Gargoyle 473
Garmin GPS V 591
Garmin Street Pilot III GPS 590, 591
Garnet 267
Garnet-mica schist 267
Garnierite 270
Garudimimus 86
Gas 306-307
Asteroids, comets, and meteoroids 52-53
Chemical reactions 313
Massive stars 26-27
Mineral resources 280-281
NGC 2997 (spiral galaxy) 12
Small stars 24-25
Stellar black hole 29
Gas blanket 306
Gas cloud
Earth's formation 56
Milky Way 14
Nebulae and star clusters 16-17
Origin and expansion of Universe 10-11
Gas current 29
Gas deposit 57, 281
Gaseous exchange in alveolus 255
Gaseous water 49
Gas exchange 154
Leaf 138-139
Photosynthesis process 138
Root 132
Sunken stoma 156-157
Wetland plants 158
Gas formation 280-281
Gas giants
Jupiter 44-45
Neptune 50-51
Saturn 46-47
Solar System 30-31
Uranus 48-49
Gaskin 198, 554
Gas loop 52-53
Gas molecule 53
Gassendi 40
Gas shell 16-17, 25
Gas tail 52-53
Gastralia 85, 87
Gas traps 281
Gastric artery 253
Gastrocnemius muscle
Albertosaurus 84
Euoplocephalus 95
Human 226-227
Iguanodon 97
Gastroepiploic vein 253
Gastropod mollusc 75
Gastropods 176, 279
Gastrovascular cavity 167
Gas turbine 418
Gate
Building 467, 490-491
Canoeing 560
Downhill skiing 552
Hydroelectric power station 314
Gate clamp 560
Gate-house 467
Gateway 467
Gatwick Express "People Mover" 328
Gavialis gangeticus 186
G clef 502
Gear 587
Gear band 336

Gearbox
ARV light aircraft 425
Ford Model T 339
Harley-Davidson FLHS
Electra Glide 363
Motorcycle 364, 366
Renault Clio 351
Volkswagen Beetle 340
Wind turbine 605
Gearbox bevel drive 418
Gearbox case 410
Gearbox drive spline 410
Gearbox fixing stud 356
Gearbox mount 413
Gearbox oil scavenge line
419
Gearbox unit 413
Gear cable 359
Gearcase 601
Gearcase position 600
Gear change 363
Gear-change rod 351
Gear lever
1906 Renault 337
Husqvarna Motocross
TC610 368
Renault Clio 350
Two-stroke engine 366
Gear lever knob 340
Gear lever surround 352
Gear ratios 361
Gear rotator 562
Gear shift 359
Gear system 358, 366
Gears
Drills 600
Motorcycle 366
Gelatine roller 447
Gemini 18
Gomma 118
Generative nucleus 147
Generator 317
British Rail class 20
diesel engine 327
Diesel train 326
Electric train 326
Nuclear power station
314
Van de Graaff 316
Wind turbine 605
Generator cooling fan 327
Generator housing 411
Generator rotor
Hydroelectric power
station 314
Mid West engine 410
Generator unit 314
Genetic material 606, 607
Genioglossus muscle 245
Geniohyoid muscle 245
Genome 607
Genital plate 175
Gentlemen's room 477
Geographic pole 38
Geological time 56–57, 279
Geranium pratense 144
Gerberette 497
Gerbil 196
Germanium 311
German-style baroque
482
Germany 326
Germinal epithelium 258
Germination 152–153
Cabbage seed 132
Epigeal 152–153
Fern spore 121
Hypogeal 152–153
Mushroom spore 115
Pine 122
Pollen grain 146–147
Gesso 432, 453
Geyser 272–273, 275
Gharial 186
Ghost anemone 166
Giant redwood 112
Giant saloon 552
Giant stars 22–23, 26
Gibbon 202

Gibson Les Paul guitar
513
Gig 595
Gilded band 490
Gilded cross 487
Gilded orb 487
Gilded rib 487
Gilded truck 378–379
Gilding materials 431,
432
Gill
Bivalves 176
Bony fish 180–181
Dogfish 178–179
Fungi 114–115
Lamprey 178
Newt 182
Salamander 182
Tadpole 183
Gill filament 180
Gill opening 178
Gill raker 180
Gill slit 178–180
Gilt ironwork 482, 490
Ginger 155
Gingiva 247
Ginkgo 68, 70, 72, 122–
123, 279
Ginkgo biloba 68, 123
Ginkgophyta 122
Ginkgo pluripartita 72
Giornate 434–435
Giraffa camelopardalis
199
Giraffe 198–199
Girder 493
Girdle 116
Girdle scar 123
Girth
Harness racer 555
Showjumper 554
Gizzard
Bird 189
Brachiosaurus 91
Euoplocephalus 94
Gallimimus 86
Glabella
Human skull 213, 221
Trilobite fossil 78
Glacial deposits 286–287,
292–293
Glacial periods 56–57, 76
Glacial sediments 299
Glacial streams 286
Glacier Bay 286
Glacier features 286–287
Glaciers 286–287
Prehistoric Earth 66, 76
River's stages 289
Rock cycle 266–267
Weathering and erosion
282
Glacier snout 286, 289
Gladiolus 154–155
Glans penis 259
Gland
19th century
paddlesteamer 391
Axial 175
Butterwort 161
Cement 173
Green 173
Monkey cup 161
Mucous 177
Pedal 177
Poison 170, 176
Rectal 179
Salivary 177
Silk 170
Venus fly trap 160
Glans penis 259
Glass 507
Buildings 492, 494
Photovoltaic cell 605
Tesserae 450
Glass bulb 319
Glass cooking turntable
596
Glass curtain 497
Glass deflector 325

Glass enamel 450
Glass flask 312
Glass mosaic 489
Glass muller 436, 440
Glass pane 494
Glass paper 441
Glass plate 570, 571
Glass prism 518
Glass slab 436, 440
Glass tube 319
Glass wall 496, 499
Glazing
Acrylic paints 442
Modern building 496–
499
Twentieth-century
building 494
Glazing bar 499
Gleba 114–115
Glechoma hederacea 154
Gleditsia triacanthos 137
Glenoid cavity 180
Gliders 426–427
Global positioning system
(GPS) 590–591
Global warming 301
Globe 264
Globe Theatre 477
Globular cluster 12, 16, 21
Globule 24, 26
Glomerulus 256–257
Gloriosa superba 145
Glory lily 145
Gloss finish
Acrylics 442
Oil painting 436
Glossopteris 67
Gloster Meteor fighter 408
Glove box 425
Gloves
American football 527
Baseball fielder 557
Cricket batsman 559
Cricket wicket keeper
559
Fencing 556–557
Ice hockey 551
Lacrosse goalkeeper
541
Racketball 545
Sailing 560
Skiing 552–553
Soccer goalkeeper 525
Glucose 138
Glulam wall-plate 499
Gluon 309
Gluteal fold 210
Gluteus maximus muscle
227
Gluteus medius muscle
225
Gluteus minimus muscle
225
Glyph 460
Gnathostomata 178, 180
Gneiss 274
Gnetophytes 122
Gnome seven-cylinder
rotary engine 400
Gnomon 377
Goal
Australian rules football
528
Gaelic football 529
Hockey 540
Hurling 541
Ice hockey 550
Lacrosse 541
Rugby 550–551
Soccer 524
Goal area
Gaelic football 529
Handball 535
Soccer 524
Goal attack 535
Goal circle 535, 541
Goal crease 541, 550
Goal defence 535
Goal judge 550

Goalkeeper
Australian rules football
528
Football rules 524
Gaelic football 529
Handball 534–535
Hockey 540
Ice hockey 550
Lacrosse 541
Netball 535
Soccer 525
Goalkeeper's equipment
540
Goalkeeper's gloves 525
Goalkeeper's helmet 550–
551
Goalkeeper's kicker 540
Goalkeeper's pad 540
Goalkeeper's shirt 525,
550
Goalkeeper's stick 550
Goal line
American football 526
Australian rules football
528
Handball 535
Hockey 540
Ice hockey 550
Rugby 550
Soccer 524
Goal line referee 535
Goal net 524, 534, 550
Goalposts
American football 526
Australian rules football
528
Gaelic football 529
Netball 535
Rugby 550
Goal shooter 535
Goal square 528
Goal third 535
Goal umpire 528–529
Goat 198
Goat hair brush 438, 442
Goat hake wash brush 438
Gobi Desert 265
Goggles
Harness racing 555
Ice hockey 550
Swimming 558
Gold 31, 268, 280–281, 438
Gold chalcopyrite 271
Golden barrel cactus 156
Gold leaf 432
Fresco 435
Illumination 444–445
Smalti 450
Vitreous glass 451
Wood sculpture 454
highlighting 455
Golf 546–547
Golgi complex 217
Gomphoi 373
Gonad
Jellyfish 167
Octopus 176
Sea anemone 167
Sea urchin 175
Starfish 174
Gondwanaland
Cretaceous period 72
Jurassic period 70–71
Late Carboniferous
period 66–67
Middle Ordovician
period 64–65
Gong 504, 516
Goniastrea aspera 167
Gonopore
Barnacle 173
Sea urchin 175
Snail 177
Starfish 174
Goose-feather quill 444
Goosegrass 150
Goose neck 388

Gopher 196
Gopuram finial 491
Gorge
Cave 284–285
River features 290
Gorilla 202–203
Gothic architecture 468,
470–473
Gothic book script
lettering 445
Gothic stone arch 467
Gothic torus 486
Gouge
Relief printing 446, 449
Woodcarving 454–455
Gour 284–285
Goya 35
GPS 590–591
Grab handle 362
Graben 61
Graben lake 293
Gracilis muscle 226–227
Graded wash 439
Graffian follicle 258
Graffias 21
Gran Chaco 264
Grand Canyon 57, 226–227
Grand piano 514–515
"Grand Prix" world
championships 366
Grandstand 555
Granite-aggregate slab
499
Granite cladding 494
Granular stalk 114
Granum 139
Grape hyacinth 155
Graphic equalizer display
577
Graphite 268, 311
Graphite pencil 430
Graphite stick 430
Grapnel-type anchor 376
Grasping tail 202
Grass 113
Grate 524
Graver 449
Gravitation (gravity)
Atmosphere 300
Force and motion 320
Neutron stars and black
holes 28
Oceans and seas 296–
297
Universe 10
Gravitational pull 296–297
Gravity-feed fuel tank 405
Gray Cliffs 276
Grease 446
Greaser 339
Great Bear Lake 264
Great cabin 379, 381
Great Dark Spot 50–51
Greater blackbacked gull
193
Greater flamingo 190
Greater omentum 214
Greater palatine foramen
220
Greater trochanter of
femur 224–225
Greater wing coverts 188
Greater wing of sphenoid
bone 220–221
Great Lakes 264
Great manual 514
Great Mosque 484
Great Red Spot 44–45
Great Rift Valley 60
Great saphenous vein 253
Great stop 514
Greek ship 372–373
Greek-style fret ornament
483
Green (golf) 547
Green alga 112, 116–117
Green calc-silicate
mineral 275

Green cell 584
Green chlorophyll
pigment 116, 158
Green earth 434–435
Green fluorite 269
Greenhouse effect 36,
300–301
"Greenhouse gas" 301
Greenland
Cretaceous period 73
Late Carboniferous
period 66
Middle Ordovician
period 64
Satellite map 264
Green light 318, 330–331
Green seaweed 117
Green snakelock
anemone 166
Green starboard
navigation light 406
Greenwich Meridian
Satellite map 264–265
Currents 296
Gregorian calendar 681
Grey matter 236–237, 238
Grey squirrel 197
Grey whale 204
Grid lines 445
Griffon 461
Grikes 284
Grille
"Eurostar" warning
horn 329
Roman Mill 464
Grill/griddle 596
Grimaldi 40
Grip
Sailmaker's fid 384
Sailmaker's mallet 384
Gripe 379
Groin
Arches and vaults 485
Human body 211
Groin pad 527
Groin vault 479, 484–485
Grommet 373, 375, 384,
426
Groove
Rope starter 335
Serving mallet 384
Grooved racing tyre 356,
357
Groove for FCC cable 571
Grooving 383
Grotesque figure 476
Ground handling wheel
422
Ground ivy 154
Ground-mapping radar
420
Groundmass 268–269
Ground roller 447
Groundwater 292–293
Volcanic structure 273
Grout 450–451
Growing point 155
Growing tip 79
Growth line
Fossilised jawless fish
78
Snail 177
Groyne 294
Grundtvig Church 495
Gruppo Seven Cubist 495
Grus 19, 20
Gryphon 461
Gryposaurus 96, 99
Guanine 216
Guard
American football 526
Basketball 552
Fencing foil 557
Guard cell 138–139
Guardrail 391–392, 395
Guardstop 541
Gubernator 373
Gudgeon 375

Gudgeon pin 345
Gudgeon strap 378
Guest boat boom 394
Guiana Highlands 264
Guidance control sensor 612
Guide hair 126
Guide mark 555
Guide wheel 528
Guinevere Planitia 36, 37
Guitars 510, 512-513
Gula Mons 37
Gulf of Mexico 264
Gulf Stream 296
Gull 189, 193
Gulley 558
Gully 289
Gum 247
Gum arabic 438
  Lithographic printing 446, 448
  Pastel making 440
Gun
  1.5 kg gun 595
  3 pound gun 595
  4.5 in gun 597
  4.7 in gun 594
  11 cm gun 597
  12 cm gun 594
  12 in gun 594
  30 cm gun 594
  Battleship 594
  Frigate 597
  Measurements 594
  Sailing warship 376
  Wooden sailing ship 378, 379
Gun battery 595
Gun carriage 377
Gun deck 380
Gun loading cage 396
Gunnery control radar dish 397
Gunnery spotting top 594
Gunport 381
  Sailing warship 376-377
  Wooden sailing ship 379
Gun position 597
Gun section 392
Gunship 422
Gun turret 596-597
  Battleship 594
  Frigate 597
  World War II aircraft 408
Gut caecum 170
Gutenberg discontinuity 59
Gutter 486, 492, 602
Guyot 298
Guzmania lingulata 162-163
Gymnosperm 122-125
Gynoecium 140
Gypsum 271
Gyroscopic gunsight 409

H

Habit 270-271
Habitat 112
  Dryland plants 156-157
  Wetland plants 158-159
Hackle 563
Hackly fracture 270
Hadar 21
Hadley cell 300
Hadrosaur 96, 98-99
  Hadrosaurus 96, 99
Haemal spine 180
Haematite 268
Hafnium 310
Hagfish 178
Hail 302
Hair 254-235
  Cobra lily 160

Golden barrel cactus 156
Inflorescence 140, 142
Insulating 104, 107
Mammal 104
Marram grass 113
Monocotyledon 126
Pitcher plant 113
Root 132
Venus fly trap 160
Water fern leaf 158
Hair bulb 255
Hair cell 242 245
Hairdryer 315
Hair follicle 254-255
Hair gel 306
Hair-like sepal 142
Hair shaft 255
Hakatai shale 277
Half-back 526, 529
Half-back flank 528
Half-column 464, 468-469
Half-court line 545
Half-forward 529
Half-forward flank 528
Half-fruit 151
Half hitch 388
Half-shaft
  Ford Model T 338
  Formula One racing car 356
  Half turn 543
Halite crystal 277
Hall
  Asian building 491
  Hypostyle 458
  Medieval building 466-467
  Modern building 496, 499
  Neoclassical building 483
Halleflinta 275
Halley's Comet 52
"Hall-keeps" 466
Hallux
  Anchisaurus 89
  Archaeopteryx 85
  Herrerasaurus 86
  Human 232
  Tyrannosaurus 84
Halo 14
Halogen headlamp bulb 352
Halogens 311
Halo ring 44
Halyard
  Double topsail schooner 385
  Junk 376
  Longboat 380
  Rigging 582
  Roman corbita 372, 375
  Viking karv 374
Hamada 282-283
Hamal 19, 20
Hamate bone 230
Hammer 242, 285
  Antler 109
  Athletics 542
  Concert grand piano 515
  Mosaic 450
  Target pistol 549
  Upright piano 514
Hammer actuator 600-601
Hammer-beam roof 470, 473
Hammerhead shark 179
Hammer throw 543
Hand
  Anchisaurus 89
  Human 210
  Iguanodon 97
  Pachycephalosaurus 100
  Primate 203
  Stegoceras 101

Tyrannosaurus 84
Handball 534-535
Handbrake 337, 339-340, 350
Handbrake control shaft 338
Handbrake quadrant 339
Hand brake wheel 331
Hand drill 600-601
Hand-held computer 568
Hand-held gun 408
Handle
  Belaying pin 382
  Brace-and-bit 601
  Nintendo Cube 579
  Steam iron 594
Handlebars
  Bicycle 358-359
  BMW R/60 562
  Cannondale SH600 hybrid bicycle 361
  Cannondale ST 1000 touring bicycle 361
  Eddy Merckx racing bicycle 361
  Suzuki RGV500 368
Handle connector 593
Handle attachment 583
Handling
  Motorcycle 360
  Touring bicycle 564
Hand protector 368
Hand rail
  "Ellerman Lines" steam locomotive 324
  Modern building 498
  Renaissance building 477
  Sailmaker's mallet 384
  Serving mallet 384, 388
  Ship's wheel 390
Handset 572
Handset cord 572
Handset cradle 572
Handset mount 572
Handstand 543
Hand throttle 427
Handy Billy 382-385
"Handy man" 108
Hanger 498
Hang-gliders 426-427
Hanging valley 286-287
Hapteron 116-117
Hard disk drive 567
Hard endocarp 146-147, 149
Hard granite 283
Hard hat 554
Hard-headed beater 516, 518-519
Hard metals 310
Hardness 270-271
Hard palate 212, 245
Hard rock 60
  Faults and folds 60
  Glacier 286
  River features 290-291
  Weathering and erosion 282
Hard trim 552
Hardwood implements 452
Hardwood laminate limb 548
Hardwood panels 432
Hardwood sticks 517
Hardy 450
Hare 196-197
Harley-Davidson FLHS
  Electra Glide 362-363
Harmika 491
Harmon, A.L. 494
Harmonically-tuned exhaust system 356

Harmony
  Drums 518
  Percussion instruments 516
Harness
  Avro triplane IV 402
  Equestrian sports 555
Harness racing 554
Harness strap 409
Harp 504, 510-511
Harpoon point 109
Harpsichord score 521
Hash mark 541
Hash special function button 588
Hastate leaf 128
Hatch
  Cargo 376
  For home deliveries 602
  Iron paddlesteamer 393
  Single scull 561
Hatch board 372
Hatch coaming 381
Hatching egg 192-193
Hatchling 98
Hathor Mons 37
Haunch 484
Haustoria 163
Haustration of colon 249
Haversian system 225
Hawker Tempest 408-409
Hawksmoor, N. 478, 481
Haworthia truncata 157
Hawse hole
  74-gun ship 381
  Sailing warship 376
  Wooden sailing ship 378
Hawse piece 381
Hawse pipe 393, 395
Hawser 586-587
Hawser fairlead 395
Hawthorne 35
Haystack boiler 334
Haze 37, 47
Head
  74-gun ship 380
  Allosaurus 85
  Beetle 168
  Brace-and-bit 601
  Bumblebee 168
  Butterfly 169
  Caterpillar 169
  Ceratopsian 100
  Deer hopper dry fly 563
  Double bass bow 511
  Double topsail schooner 385
  Dunkeld wet fly 563
  Femur 224-225
  Frog 182
  Hammer 542
  Human 211, 212-213
  Insect 168
  Lacrosse crosse 541
  Lamprey 178
  Pachycephalosaurus 100
  Phalanx 230
  Prosauropod 88
  Racing bicycle 360
  Racing saddle 554
  Rattlesnake 185
  Sail 375, 384
  Sauropodomorph 88
  Serving mallet 388
  Snail 177
  Sperm 259
  Stegoceras 101
  Stegosaurus 92
  Tennis racket 544
  Thyreophoran 92
  Ulna 231
  Violin bow 510
Headband 544
Head beam 380
Headboard 381
Head-butting contest 100
Head crest 96

Head cringle 384
Head data cable 574
Head data cable support 574
Head earing 375
Headers
  Brickwork 485
  Nineteenth-century building 492
Head horn 94
Head joint 508
Headlamp
  Bordino Steam Carriage 335
  Bulbs 552
  Ford Model T 338-339
  Renault Clio 349, 353
  Volkswagen Beetle 341
Headland 294
Head-light
  BMW R/60 562
  "Eurostar" multi-voltage electric train 329
  Harley-Davidson FLHS Electra Glide 363
  Italian State Railways Class 402 328
  MCW Metrobus 332
  Single-decker bus 333
  "Union Pacific" locomotive 326
  Vespa Grand Sport 160 Mark 1 363
Head linesman 526
Headphone jack 567, 582
Headphones 586
Headphone socket 566, 567, 585, 586
Head protector 573
Head rail 380-381
Headrest
  ARV light aircraft 425
  Formula One racing car 356
  Hawker Tempest fighter 409
  Mazda RX-7 346
  Renault Clio 349, 352
  TGV electric high-speed train 329
  "Windcheetah" racing HPV bicycle 361
Head rope 387
Headset 561
Headstock
  Acoustic guitar 512-513
  Electric guitar 513
  Honda VF750 564
Head tube 359-361
Headward erosion 290
Headwaters 288
Hearing 237, 242
Heart
  Bird 189
  Bony fish 181
  Branchial 176
  Butterfly 169
  Chimpanzee 202
  Crayfish 173
  Dogfish 179
  Dolphin 205
  Domestic cat 195
  Elephant 200
  Euoplocephalus 94
  Frog 182
  Gallimimus 86
  Human 214-215, 250-251
  Lizard 185
  Mammal 104
  Octopus 176
  Rabbit 196
  Snail 177
  Spider 170
  Systemic 176
  Tortoise 187
Heartbeat sequence 250-251

Heart bulge 260
Heartwood 125
Heat 314-315
  Chemical reactions 312
  Global warming 300-301
  Igneous and metamorphic rocks 274
Heat absorption 92
Heated filament 519
Heater element contacts 348
Heater unit 353
Heat exchanger
  Concorde 417
  Nuclear power station 314
  Volkswagen Beetle 340
Heat exchanger air intake 421
Heat exchanger exhaust duct 420
Heat exchanger hot-air exhaust 421
Heating element cover 597
Heating elements 594
Heating element terminal cover 597
Heat radiation 92
Heat shield
  Jet engine 419
  Motorcycle 363
  Space probes 614, 615
Heat trapping 300
Heaver for wire serving 383
Heaving line 389
Heavy chemical elements 27
Hedera colchica 137
Hedera helix 131, 137
Heel
  Horse 198
  Human 210
  Rudder post 392
Heel moulding 594
Heine 35
Heka 18
Helen Planitia 36
Helianthus annulus 142
Heliconia peruviana 143
Helioprion bessonowi 67
Helicopter landing-pad 498
Helicopters 396, 410, 422-423
Helium
  Jupiter 44-45
  Massive stars 26
  Mercury's atmosphere 35
  Neptune's atmosphere 51
  Pluto's atmosphere 51
  Periodic table 311
  Saturn 46-47
  Small stars 24-25
  Sun 32
  Uranus' atmosphere 49
Helium-3 nucleus 22
Helium-4 nucleus 22
Helium line 23
Helix 242, 623
Helix Nebula 17
Helleborus niger 139
Hellenic plate 59
Helmet
  American football 526-527
  Baseball batter 536
  Bicycle 360
  Cricket 559
  Hockey goal keeper 540
  Hurling 541
  Ice hockey 550-551
  Lacrosse goalkeeper 541
  Skiing 542

642

Helmsman 372-373
Hemicyclaspis 56
Hemisphere 623
Hemispherical dome 477,
  486-487, 490-491
Hen coop 395
Hepaticae 118
Hepatic artery 248, 252-
  253
Hepatic portal vein 253
Heptathlon 542
Heracleum sp. 151
Heracleum sphondylium
  129
Heraldic device 372
Herbaceous plants 126,
  128-129
  Structure 112-113
  Woody 150-151
Herbaceous stems 154
Herbivores
  Carnivora 194
  Jurassic period 70
  Marginocephalian 100
  Ornithopods 96
  Prosauropods 88-89
  Sauropodomorphian 88
  Triassic period 68
Hercules 19, 20, 40
Herds 88
Hermaphrodite duct 177
Hermit shale 276
Herodotus 40
Herrerasaurids 68, 86
Herring-bone pattern 488
Hertzsprung 41
Hertzsprung-Russell
  diagram 22-23
Hesperidium 148
Hestia Rupes 37
Heterocentrotus
  mammillus 175
Heterodontosaurus 83
Heteropoda venatoria 171
Hexagon 622
Hexagonal system 270
HF radio aerial 408
HF radio aerials fairing
  417
Hibiscus 126-127
Hide 105
Hide grip 384
Hieroglyphs 458-459
High altar 470
High-altitude cloud 45, 50
Highboard diving 558
High-density minerals 280
High-energy particle 301
High-energy radiation 22
High-explosive projectile
  596
High-gain antenna 614
High-gain radio antenna
  612, 615
High-jump 542
Highland coastline 295
High-level jet streams 300
High nose 357
High-performance
  microscopes 610-
  611 High-pressure areas
  302-303
High-pressure bleed
  venturi connector 419
High-pressure
  compressor 418
High-pressure cylinder
  342
High-pressure turbine 418
High-pressure zone 300
High-resolution colour
  graphics 578
High-speed trains 328-329
High Spring tide 296-297
High temperature gas 306
High-tension beam 496
High-tension ignition lead
  344
High tension wire 315

High tide 296-297
High-velocity air duct 420
High voltage cable 314,
  355
High-voltage connector
  355
High-voltage magnetron
  supply 611
Hi-hat cymbal 518
Hilbert 41
Hillman anti-kink weight
  562
Hilum
  Dehiscent fruit seed
    151
  Epigeal germination
    153
  Hypogeal germination
    152
  Succulent fruit seed
    148-149
Himalayas
  Earth's physical
    features 264-265
  Geological time 56-57
  Formation 60, 62-62
  Mountain building 62-
    63
  Quaternary period 77
  Tertiary period 74
Himeji Castle 490
Hind foot
  Caiman 187
  Stegosaurus 92
Hindgut 173
Hind leg
  Amphibian 182
  Beetle 168
  Bumblebee 168
  Butterfly 169
  Caiman 187
  Elephant 200
  Frog 182
  Iguanodon 97
  Lizard 185
  Rabbit 196
  Terrapin 187
Hind limb
  Anchisaurus 89
  Corythosaurus 98
  Edmontonia 95
  Frog 182
  Iguanodon 96
  Kangaroo 207
  Pachycephalosaurus
    100
  Prosauropod 88
  Psittacosaurus 103
  Rabbit 197
  Rat 196
  Salamander 182
  Stegoceras 101
  Stegosaurus 92
  Theropods 84
  Thyreophoran 92
  Triceratops 102
  Tyrannosaurus 84
Hindlimb bone 105
Hind wing 168-169
  ARV light aircraft 425
  BAe-146 components
    412-415
Hinge 571
Hinge bracket 414
Hinge cell 153, 160
Hinged bin/cyclone cover
  593
Hingeless bivalve shell 79
Hingeline 60
Hip
  Anchisaurus 89
  Human 211
  Kangaroo 207
  Lion 195
  Midway Gardens 495
  Stegosaurus 92
Hip girdle 80
Hip joint 218, 224-225

Brachiosaurus 90
Diplodocus 90
Gallimimus 86
Parasaurolophus 98
Plateosaurus 88
Stegoceras 101
Struthiomimus 87
Hip pad 527
Hippeastrum sp. 155
Hipped roof 476-477
Hippocampus kuda 180
Hippophae rhamnoides
  156
Hippopotamus 198
Hippopotamus amphibius
  77
Hippuris vulgaris 135
Hip-rafter 490
Hispano Mark V 20-mm
  cannon 409
Historiated boss 469
Historiated keystone 469
Hitachi S-3500H scanning
  electron microscope
  611
Hitched hauling end 383
Hitch-kick 543
Hitch pin
  Concert grand piano
    515
  Upright piano 514
Hittorff, J.I. 479
Hobbles 554
Hock 195, 198
Hockey 540-541
Hock joint 554
Hog hair brush 432, 434
Hog's-back 283
Hog's-back jump 554
Hogweed 129, 150-151
Hohenbuehelia petaloides
  115
Hoisting cage 396
Holden 587 button 587
Holden 45
Holdfast 116-117
Holding 527
Holding timekeeper 556
Hold pillar 393
Hole and peg joint 373
Hollow disc wheel 361
Hollow pith cavity 120
Holmium 311
Holocene epoch
  Fossil record 279
  Geological timescale 57
Holostean fish 73
Homarus sp. 75
Home cinema 584-585
Home computer system
  520-521
Homeosaurus pulchellus
  71
Home page 577
Home plate 536
Home run 556
"Home" signal 330
Hominid 74-75, 108-109,
  202
Homocephale 101
Homo erectus 108
Homo habilis 108
Homo sapiens 57, 76, 108-
  109
Honda CB750 362-363
Honda Insight 354
Honda VF750 364-365
Hone-stone 452
Honesty 150-151
Honeycomb coral 167
Honey guides 140-141,
  145
Honey locust 137
Hong Kong and Shanghai
  Bank 496, 498
Honshu 265
Hood
  Battleship 394
  Ford Model T 339

Gun turret 396
Jellyfish 167
  Pitcher plant 160
Hood bag 346
Hood end 574
Hood frame 339
Hood iron 334
Hood-mould 479, 481, 486
Hoof 198, 554
Hoofbone 105, 198
Hoof-like nail 36-37
Hook
  Angling 562
  Cricket 558
  Deer hopper dry fly 563
  Devon minnow 563
  Rigging 383
  Sail 384
Hooked beak 190
Hooked pericarps 150
Hooked riffler 454
Hooker 530
Hoop 380, 425
Hoover Factory 495
Hop 543
Hopper freight car 327
Horizon 376
Horizontal bed rock 61
Horizontal cleavage 270
Horizontal damper 329
Horizontal fissure 255
Horizontally opposed
  engine 362
Horizontal movement 60
Horizontal stabilizer 423
Horn
  Ford Model T 339
  Glacier 286-287
  Mooring 387
  Musical instrument
    503, 504
  "Union Pacific"
    locomotive 326
  Vespa Grand Sport 160
    Mark 1 363
Horn balance 414, 415
Horn bulb 339
"Horned faces" 100
Horny beak 96
Horse 104-105, 198-199
Horse chestnut 130, 137
Horse-drawn vehicle 332
Horsehair bow 510-511
Horsehead Nebula 16
Horse riding 554-555
Hox's shoe arch 181
Horsetail 120-121
Horsley Church 473
Horst 61
Horu Geyser 272
Hose base 593
Hose cuff electrical link
  593
Hose electricity supply
  connector 592
Hose slider 592
Hose slider seating 592
Host plants 162-163
Hot-air de-icing duct 414
Hot mineral springs 272
Hot spot
  Black holes 29
  Earth's crust 58
  Ocean floor 298
HotSync™ button 569
HotSync™ connector 568,
  569
HotSync™ connector slot
  569
Hot Sync™ Cradle 569
Hot water jet 273
Hound 378
Hour line 377
Household appliances 315
House of the future 602-
  603
Housing
  Alpine skiing 552
  Electric motor 342

House spider 171
Howe 36
Howea forsteriana 126
Howler monkey 202
Hti 490
Huang He 265
Huayangosaurus 93
Hub
  1906 Renault 336
  ARV light aircraft 424
  Benz Motorwagen 335
  Bicycle wheels 358-359
  Blackburn monoplane
    400-401
  Bordino Steam Carriage
    334
  Eddy Merckx racing
    bicycle 361
  Paddle wheel 390-591
  Pegasus Quasar
    microlight 427
  Propellers 390
  Renault Clio 351
  Wright Flyer 399
Hub and brake drum 350
Hub bearing 351
Hubble Space Telescope
  612-613
Hub bolt 338
Hub brake shoe 338
Hub cap
  1906 Renault 336
  Ford Model T 339
  Renault Clio 350
Hub carrier 351
Hub controller 604
Hub nut 350
Hub quick release lever
  361
Hub seal 350
Hudson Bay 264
Hull
  Carvel-built 376, 591
  Clinker-built 375
  Cross-section 378
  Double-ended 375
  Greek and Roman ships
    372-373
  Iron and wood 392
Hull plank 373
Human body 210-211
Human classification 108
Human Powered Vehicles
  (HPV) 358, 360
Humans 57, 76, 108, 202,
  315
Humber engine 343
Humboldt current 296
Humerus
  Archaeopteryx 85
  Arsinoitherium 104
  Bird 189, 191
  Brachiosaurus 91
  Crocodile 186
  Diplodocus 90
  Domestic cat 195
  Elephant 201
  Eryops 80
  Euoplocephalus 94
  Frog 183
  Gallimimus 86
  Hare 197
  Horse 199
  Human 218
  Iguanodon 96
  Kangaroo 206
  Kentrosaurus 93
  Pareiasaur 81
  Plateosaurus 88
  Stegoceras 100
  Struthiomimus 87
  Toxodon 106
  Triceratops 102
  Tyrannosaurus 84
Humic acid 284
Hunter-killer submarine
  396-397
Hunter's bend 388
Hunting 108, 548

Huntsman spider 171
Hurdle races 554
Hurdling 542
Hurling 540-541
Hurricane 302-303
Husk 150
Husqvarna Motocross
  TC610 368
Huygens space probe 614
Hyaenodon 74, 107
Hyaline cartilage 225
Hybrid bicycle 360-361
Hybrid car 354
Hybrid power 355
Hydra 18, 21
Hydrated copper sulphate
  313
Hydraulic actuator
  attachment 413, 414
Hydraulic brake calliper
  424
Hydraulic brake hose 369
Hydraulic brake pipe 414
Hydraulic fluid
  Disc brake 365
  Spring/damper unit 365
Hydraulic grab 396
Hydraulic hand-pump 421
Hydraulic hose 369
Hydraulic unit 605
Hydrazine propellant tank
  615
Hydrocarbon 313
Hydrochloric acid 312
Hydrochoerus
  hydrochaeris 197
Hydroelectric power
  station 314
Hydrogen 308, 310
  Candle wax 312-313
  Covalent bonding 309
  Jupiter's atmosphere 45
  Massive stars 26
  Mercury's atmosphere
    35
  Nebulae and star
    clusters 16-17
  Neptune's atmosphere
    51
  Nuclear fusion in Sun
    22
  Salt formation 312
  Saturn's atmosphere 47
  Small stars 24-25
  Sun 32
  Uranus' atmosphere 49
Hydrogen alpha line 23
Hydrogen atom 138, 596
Hydrogen beta line 23
Hydrogen fluoride 308
Hydrogen gamma line 23
Hydrogen gas 312
Hydrogen nucleus 22
Hydrogen requirement
  138
Hydrogen sulphide 51
Hydroplane 396-397
Hydroxide 268
Hydrus 20
Hyena 194
Hymenoptera 168
Hyoglossus muscle 244
Hyoid bone 244-245, 255
Hypacrosaurus 99
Hypanal temple 460-
  461
Hypereision 373
Hyperlink 577
Hyphae
  Fungus 114-115
  Mycorrhizal association
    133
Hypocotyl 152-153
Hypodermis
  Gynosperm 125
  Human 235
Hypogeal germination
  152-153
Hypoglossal nerve 244

Hypogymnia physodes 114
Hypostyle hall 458-459
Hypothalamus 256
Hypsilophodon 72, 82
Hypural 180
Hystrix africaeaustralis 197

I

I bar 393
IBM-compatible PCs 566
Ice 66, 307
Glacier 286-287
Weathering and erosion 282
Ice age 56
Ice-age mammals 76
Ice block
Ice-fall 287
Lake formation 293
Ice-cap 287
Ice crystal 302
Ice cube 307
Ice erosion 287
Ice-fall 287
Ice hockey 550-551
Ice margin lake 286
Ice-plant 128-129
Ice sheet 76
Ichthyosaur 70-71
Ichthyostega 56, 80
Icons 576
Icterus galbula 193
Idle control valve 344
Idocrase 270
Igneous intrusion 274
Igneous rock 266-267, 274-275
Igniter 418
Igniter plug 419
Ignition amplifier 345
Ignition coils 354
Ignition control 562
Ignition lever 338
Ignition lock 362
Ignition switch 337
Ignition trigger housing 410
Iguana iguana 82
Iguanodon 73, 96-97
Ileocaecal fold 249
Ileum
Bird 189
Frog 182
Human 226, 249
Rabbit 196
Iliac crest 224-225
Iliac fossa 224
Iliac spine 224
Iliacus muscle 225
Ilio-femoral muscle 84, 97
Ilio-fibular muscle 84, 97
Ilio-ischial joint 82
Iliopsoas muscle 226
Ilio-pubic joint 82
Ilio-tibial muscle
Albertosaurus 84
Euoplocephalus 94
Iguanodon 97
Ilium
Archaeopteryx 85
Bird 189
Diplodocus 90
Eryops 81
Euoplocephalus 94
Frog 183
Gallimimus 86
Human 218
Iguanodon 96-97
Kentrosaurus 93
Ornithischian 82
Parasaurolophus 98
Plateosaurus 88
Saurischian 82
Stegoceras 100-101
Stegosaurus 93
Struthiomimus 87

Toxodon 107
Tuojiangosaurus 93
Tyrannosaurus 84
Illuminated manuscript 432
Illumination 444-445
Image controls 611
Image screen processor microchip 581
Image viewing screen 581
Imaging system housing 610
Imaging the body 214
Imago 168
Immature pitcher 161
Immature spur 141
Impasto 436-437, 442
Impeller 347
Imperial-Metric conversions 591, 620
Imperial unit measurements 590
Impermeable clay 292
Impermeable mudstone 292
Impermeable rock
Cave 284-285
Lake 292
Mineral resources 280-281
River's stages 289
Impermeable salt dome 281
Impermeable shale 292
Impost
Ancient Roman building 465
Cathedral dome 484
Gothic building 473
Islamic building 488
Medieval building 466, 469
In-board 561
Inboard elevon 417, 421
Inboard elevon-jack fairing 418
Inboard end 587
Inboard engine 415
Inboard lift spoilers 413
Inboard trimtab 413
Inbound line 526
Inbox icon 576
Incandescent light 318-319
In-car mounting bracket assembly 590
Incident laser light 319
Incisive canal 245
Incisor teeth
Bear 194
Chimpanzee 202
Elephant 201
Human 245, 246
Lion 194
Rabbit 196
Rodent 196
Toxodon 106
Incline 468
Incompetent bed rock 61
Incomplete mesentery 167
Incurrent pore 166
Incus 242
Indehiscent fruit 150
Index finger 230-231
India
Cretaceous period 72-73
Jurassic period 70
Himalaya formation 62-63
Late Carboniferous period 66
Middle Ordovician period 64
Mountain building 62-63
Quaternary period 76-77
Railway track gauge 331

Tertiary period 74-75
Thyreophorans 92
Triassic period 68
Indian ocean 73, 75, 77, 265
Indian stick insect 192
Indicator
"Deltic" diesel-electric locomotive 327
Bus 333
Harley-Davidson FLHS Electra Glide 363
Honda CB750 363
MCW Metrobus 332
Volkswagen Beetle 340
Indicator assembly 352
Indicator board 542
Indicator lamp 353
Indicator lens 341
Indirect method mosaic creation 450-451
Indium 311
Indo-Australian plate 59
Inducer 418
Induction stroke 343
Indus 20
Indusium 121
Industrial Revolution 492
Industrial robots 608
Inert gas 311, 584
Inferior articular process 223
Inferior concha 212, 241
Inferior extensor retinaculum 233
Inferior meatus 245
Inferior mesenteric vein 253
Inferior nasal concha 221, 241, 245
Inferior oblique muscle 241
Inferior orbital fissure 221
Inferior rectus muscle 241
Inferior vena cava 215, 252-253, 257
Infertile swamp 288
Infield 536-537
Infilled swamp 291
Inflated petiole 158
Inflation valve 403
Inflorescences 140
Aechmea miniata 162
Bromeliad 113
Catkin 144
Compound 142-143
Couch grass 113
Dodder 163
Stem arrangements 143
Inflorescence stalk 140-143
Aechmea miniata 162
Brassavola nodosa 162
Everlasting pea 129
Indehiscent fruit 150
Peach 131
Peruvian lily 129
Rowan 131
Russian vine 131
Succulent fruit 148
Vegetative reproduction 154-155
Wind-pollinated plant 144
Inflorescence types
Capitulum 129, 142
Compound umbel 143
Dichasial cyme 143
Raceme 129
Single flower 143
Spadix 143
Spherical umbel 143
Spike 143, 155, 162
Infraorbital foramen 221
Infraorbital margin 213, 221
Infra-red radiation 318-319

Energy emission from Sun 22
Infra-red map of our galaxy 15
Infra-red sensor 608
Infraspinatus muscle 227
Infratemporal fenestra
Baryonyx 83
Camarasaurus 91
Diplodocus 90
Heterodontosaurus 83
Lambeosaurus 99
Panoplosaurus 94
Parasaurolophus 99
Plateosaurus 88
Protoceratops 102
Triceratops 103
Infratemporal foramen 106-107
Ingres paper 441
Initial cave 285
Ink 430, 444
Ink-cartridge replacement button 574
Ink cartridges 574
Ink dabber 446
Inkjet nozzle 575
Inkjet printer 574-575
Ink outlet hole 574
Ink pad 445
Ink reservoir 444, 446
Ink roller 448, 449
Ink sac 176
Ink stick 444
Ink stone 444
Inlay 488-489
Inlet 295
Inlet cone 418
Inlet manifold
Daimler engine 343
Jaguar V12 engine 345
Mid West single-rotor engine 411
Inlet manifold tract 345
Inlet-over-exhaust (IOE) engine 362
Inlet port 345, 367
Inlet rotor 347
Inlet tract 410
Inlet valve 343, 345, 362
Inner bin fin 592
Inner bud scales 134
Inner cage assembly 599
Inner clutch drum 366
Inner core 38-39, 41
Inner counter 445
Inner cyclone cone 592
Inner dome 484
Inner floret 129, 142
Inner jib downhaul 385
Inner jib halyard 385
Inner jib stay 382
Inner jib tack 382
Inner layer of cortex
Dicotyledon 127
Epiphytic orchid 162
Monocotyledon 127
Wetland plants 158-159
Inner mantle 44-47
Inner martingale stay 383
Inner membrane 139
Inner planetary orbits 31
Inner posts 528
Inner tepal 126, 140, 143
Inner tube 359, 424, 507
Inner vane 191
Innings 536, 538
Inorganic substances 280
Inscription 488
Insectivorous plants 113, 160-161
Insects 168-169, 279
Cretaceous 72-75
Plant food 160-161
Pollinators 144-145
Inselberg 283
Insoluble solids 312
Inspection cover
Avro biplane 403

Lockheed Electra airliner 407
Inspection door 407
Inspection panel 417
Inspiration 255
Instep 211
Instructor's cockpit 403
Instrument console 420
Instrument landing system aerial 420-421
Instrument package 615
Instrument panel
ARV light aircraft 425
Bell-47 helicopter 422
Renault Clio 353
Schweizer helicopter 426
Insulating column 316
Insulating hair 104, 107
Insulation 300
Insulator
Electric circuit 316
Generating magnetism 317
Hydroelectric power station 314
Intaglio printing 446-447, 448
Intake manifold 351, 354
Intake pipe 335
Intake port 346
Integral ink reservoir 444
Integrated transparency unit (TPU) 570, 571
Integrated transport system 332
Integument
Ovule 147
Scots pine 122
Intelligent electronic door-lock 602
Intentional foul 533
Interalveolar septum 254
Intercellular leaf space 139
Interception 526
Inter-City travel 332
Intercolumniation 461, 485
Intercompressor bleed valve 419
Intercompressor diffuser pipe 419
Intercostal muscle 91, 255
Interdental papilla 247
Interdental septum 247
Interglacial period 76
Integer house 602, 603
Interior light 353
Interlobular artery 256
Interlobular vein 256
Interlocking spur 289
Intermediate housing 346
Intermediate lamella 225
Intermediate ring 563
Internal capsule 237
Internal carotid artery 245, 252
Internal combustion engine
First cars 334
Motorcycle engine 366
Pioneers of flight 398
Internal crust 28
Internal elastic lamina 252
Internal fuse overload protection 585
Internal iliac artery 253, 255
Internal iliac vein 253
Internal jugular vein 253
Internal power cable 567
Internal skeleton 174
Internal spermatic fascia 259
Internal urethral orifice 257
Internal urethral sphincter muscle 257

International referees signals 533
International rules 532
International squash 544-545
International track gauge 331
Internet 576-577
Internet service provider (ISP) 576
Internode
Canadian pond weed 158-159
Horsetail 120
Ice-plant 129
Live-for-ever 129
London plane 134
Rhizome 155
Rock stonecrop 128
Rose stem 130
Stem 134
Stolon 154
Interopercular bone 181
Interosseous ligament 232
Interphalangeal joint
Baryonyx 85
Human 231, 233
Interplane strut 399, 404-405
Interradicular septum 247
Interrupter gear 404
Interstellar cloud remains 613
Intertragic notch 242
Intertrochanteric line 225
Intertropical convergence zone 300
Interventricular septum 251
Intervertebral disc 212, 218, 223, 245, 261
Intestinal muscle 226
Intestine
Bony fish 181
Butterfly 169
Chimpanzee 202
Cow 198
Crayfish 173
Dogfish 179
Dolphin 205
Elephant 200
Frog 182
Gallimimus 86
Human 214
Large 195, 202
Lizard 185
Sea urchin 175
Small 182, 185, 187, 195, 198, 200, 202
Spider 170
Tortoise 187
Intrados 469, 484
Intoitus 258
Intrusive rocks 26, 275
Invasion stripes 409
Invertebrates
Earth's evolution 56
Fossil record 279
Insects 168-169
Marine 65
Inverted ovolo 486
Inverter 355
Inverter board 570
Inverter cooling fan 355
Inverter cooling fan connector 555
Inverter housing 355
Inward dive 558, 559
Io 44
Iodine 311
Ion 308
Ionic bonding 308
Ionic capital 460
Baroque church 481
French temple 485
Renaissance building 476
Ionic column
Baroque church 481

French temple 485
Neoclassical building
  485
Ionic half-column 464
Ionic order 460
Iota Centauri 21
Iota Pegasi 19
Iota Sagittarii 21
Ipomoea batatas 154
Iran 331
Ireland 331
Iridium 311
Iridocorneal angle 241
Iris
  Human 213, 226, 241
  Linear leaf 137
  Octopus 177
Iris lazica 137
Iron 311
  Earth's composition 39
  Earth's crust 58
  Golf club 547
  Magnetic domains 317
  Meteorite 52
  Nineteenth-century
    buildings 492
  Structure of Mercury 35
  Structure of Venus 37
Iron armature support
  455
Ironclad 392-393
Iron club 546-547
Iron filings 317
Iron hull 392-393
Iron oxide
  Earth pigments 434
  Flesh-coloured
    pigments 433
  Sanguine crayon 430
  Sedimentary rocks 267,
    277
Iron oxide dust 42
Iron paddlesteamer 392-
  393
Iron pyrite 79, 270
Iron railing 495
Iron roof 479
Iron ship 392-393
Iron, steam 594
Iron tracery 493
Iron tyre 334
Ironwork 478, 482
Irregular galaxy 10-12, 15
Irreversible reactions 312
Ischial tuberosity 224
Ischium
  Archaeopteryx 85
  Bird 189
  Crayfish 173
  Diplodocus 90
  Eryops 81
  Euoplocephalus 94
  Frog 183
  Human 218, 224
  Iguanodon 96
  Ornithischian 82
  Parasaurolophus 98
  Plateosaurus 88
  Saurischian 82
  Stegoceras 100-101
  Stegosaurus 93
  Struthiomimus 87
  Triceratops 102
  Tyrannosaurus 84
Ishtar Terra 36-37
Islamic buildings 488-489,
  492
Islamic mosaic 489
Islands 291, 294
Isocline 61
Isolated single boulders
  286
Isolated steep-sided hill
  283
Isolator valve 325, 327
Isosceles triangle 622
Isoseismal lines 63
Isotopes 310
ISP 576
Israel 293

Isthmus
  Reproductive system
    258-259
  Water hyacinth 158
Italian State Railways
  Class 402 328
Italic Roman lettering 445
Itonaco 434
Ivy 130-131, 137

J

Jack 514
Jacket-wall 466
Jack-rafter 473
Jack staff
  Battleship 394
  Frigate 397
  Square-rigged ship 375
  Wooden sailing ship 379
Jacob's ladder 378
Jagged fracture 270
Jaguar straight six engine
  344
Jaguar V12 engine 345
Jali 488-489
Jamb
  Ancient Roman temple
    463
  Baroque church 479
  Medieval church 468
  Neoclassical building
    478, 482-483
  Nineteenth-century
    building 492
Jami Masjid 488
Javelin 542-543
Jaw
  Brace-and-bit 601
  Hand drill 601
  Human 212, 220-221
  Power drill 601
  Rope 389
Jawbone
  Allosaurus 85
  Australopithecus 107-
    108
  Ceratopsian 100
  Dolphin 204
  Horse 105
  Human 220, 247
  Ornithopod 96
  Shark 178
  Snake 184
  Theropods 94
Jawless fish 78, 178-179,
  180
Jeer 377
Jejunum 249
Jelly 192
Jellyfish 78, 166-167
  Earth's evolution 56
  Fossil record 279
Jet engine 412, 418-419
Jetliners 412-415
Jet pipe 418-419, 423
Jet pipe connection 419
Jetstream 300, 418
Jewel anemone 166
Jewel Box 11
Jewish calendar 618
Jib boom 379, 382
Jib fairhead 561
Jib halyard 380
Jibsail 378, 379, 385
Jib sheet 385
Jib stay 382
Jib tack 382, 383
Jockey 554-555
Jockey wheel 358
Jodhpurs 554
Joint
  Cave 284-285
  Coastline 295
  Faults and folds 61
  Jointed plug 19
  Weathering and erosion
    282

Jointed leg 79, 168
Jointed pincer 79
Jointed solidified lava 292
Jointed stem 131
Joints 224-225, 608
Joist 464, 486
Jones, H. 495
Jordan 293
Joule 314, 316
Journal 347
Joystick 361, 520
Judo 556-557
Jugal bar 201
Jugal bone 96, 102-103
Jugal plate 94
Juglans nigra 137
Jugular vein 215
Juice sac 148
"Jumbo jet" 412
Jumps 552, 554
Jump seat 337
Jump shot 532, 533
Junction
  Electrical circuit 316
  Giornata 434-435
  Photovoltaic cell 605
Junction board 555
Juncus sp. 135
Junior ratings' mess 397
Junk 376
Junk ring 343
Jupiter 30-31, 44-45, 614
Jurassic period 70-71
  Fossil record 279
  Geological time 57
Jury mast knot 389
Justicia aurea 144
Juvenile volcano 275

K

Kabe 375
Kaibab limestone 276
Kaibab Plateau 277
Kaiparowits formation 276
Kaiparowits Plateau 277
Kalahari Desert 265
*Kalanchoe
  daigremontiana* 154
Kalasa finial 489
Kalos 372
Kame delta 286
Kame terrace 286
Kangaroo 206-207
Kappa Pegasi 19
Kara Kum 265
Karv 374
Kasugado Shrine of Enjoji
  490
kasuga-style roof 490
Katastroma 373
Kaus Australis 19, 20
Kaus Borealis 21
Kaus Meridionalis 21
Kawana House 496
Kawasaki industrial robot
  608
Kayak 560
Kayenta formation 276
Kazakstania 65
Kedrostis africana 113
Keel
  Battleship 395
  Bird 189
  Frigate 397
  Ironclad 393
  Iron paddlesteamer 392
  Longboat 380
  Sailing warship 377
  Viking ship 374-375
  Wooden sailing ship
    378
Keel boat 560
Keeled leaves 136
Keeler 41
Keelson (Kelson) 560
  19th century paddle

steamer 391
Ironclad 393
Keep 466
Keeper ring 562
Kelvin temperature scale
  590
Kendo 556
Kentrosaurus 92-93
Kepler 40
Keraia 372
Keratin 234
Kestrel 189
Ketch 384, 385
Kettle 286
Kettle drum 519
Kettle lake 293
  Post-glacial valley 286
Kevlar 384, 388
Key
  Concert grand piano
    515
  Home keyboard 520
  Motorcycle clutch 366
  Musical notation 502
  Steel lock 360
  Synthesizer 520
  Upright piano 514
  Woodwind instruments
    508-509
Keyboard 521, 566, 611
Keyboard instruments
  514-515, 520
Key guard 509
Key pad button 589
Key pad button aperture
  589
Key pad connectors 589
Key pad contacts 589
Key rod 509
Key signature 502
Keystone 484
  Ancient Roman
    building 463, 465
  Baroque church 479,
    481
  French temple 485
  Medieval church 469
  Neoclassical building
    478, 482
  Renaissance building
    476-477
Keyway 590
Kick-shaft 363
Kick-starter 363, 366
Kidney
  Bird 189
  Bony fish 181
  Brachiosaurus 90
  Dogfish 179
  Dolphin 205
  Domestic cat 195
  Elephant 200
  Frog 182
  Gallimimus 86
  Human 215, 256-257
  Lizard 185
  Octopus 176
  Rabbit 196
  Snail 177
  Tortoise 187
Kidney ore haematite 268
Kidney-shaped palette 436
Killer whale 205
Killick 386
Kiln 452
Kimberlite 268, 275
Kinetic energy 314-315
Kinetic sculpture 452
King pin 338
King-post 473, 479
  Early monoplane 400-
    401
Pegasus Quasar
  microlight 427
Pegasus XL SE
  microlight 426
King-post strut 401
King spoke handle 390
King strut 464

King vulture 190
Kirby BSA racing sidecar
  369
Kittiwake 190
Kiwis 188
Knee
  Anchisaurus 89
  Corythosaurus 98
  Faering 373
  Gorilla 203
  Horse 199
  Human 211
  Iguanodon 96
  Kangaroo 207
  Lion 195
  Pachycephalosaurus
    100
  Psittacosaurus 103
  Rabbit 197
  Stegoceras 101
  Stegosaurus 92
  Tyrannosaurus 84
  Wooden ships 381
Knee joint
  Brachiosaurus 90
  Diplodocus 90
  Euoplocephalus 94
  Human 219
  Parasaurolophus 98
  Plateosaurus 88
  Stegoceras 101
  Struthiomimus 87
  Toxodon 107
  Triceratops 102
  Tyrannosaurus 84
Knee of the head 378
Knee roll 539, 554
Knife
  Palette 436
  Relief printing 446, 449
Knighthead 380
Knots 388-389
Knuckle 210
Koala 207
Koch ab 18
Kope 372-373
Korolev 41
Krypton 311
Kuan Han-ch'ing 35
Kubernetes 372
Kunzite 271
Kuroshio current 297

L

Labellum 126, 145
Label mould 481
Lamium sp. 155
Labia 258
Labial palp 168
Labrum 168
Laburnum x watereri 137
Laccolith 273-275
Lacerta 19, 20
Lacertilia 184
Lacrimal apparatus 241
Lacrimal bone
  Bony fish 181
  Human 221
  Protoceratops 102
Lacrimal canaliculus 241
Lacrimal gland 241
Lacrimal punctum 241
Lacrimal sac 241
Lacrosse 540-541
Lacuna
  Bones and joints 225
  Clubmoss 120
  Mare's tail 135
  Wetland plants 158-159
Lacustrine terrace 286
Lada Terra 36, 37
Ladder
  74-gun ship 381
  Battleship 394
  Frigate 396
  Iron paddlesteamer
    392, 393

Roman corbita 372-373
Train equipment 330
Wooden sailing ship
  378
Ladder-way 395-396
Lady Chapel, Salisbury
  Cathedral 470
Lagenorhpha 196
Lagoon
  Atoll development 299
  Coastline 294-295
  River features 290-291
Lagoon Nebula 21
Lagopus lagopus 193
Lagostomus maximus 197
Lake Baikal 265
Lake Erie 264
Lake Huron 264
Lake Michigan 264
Lake Nyasa 265
Lake Ontario 264
Lakes 292-293
  Glacier 286-287
  Groundwater system
    293
  Igneous rock structures
    275
  River features 290
  River's stages 260
  Rock cycle 266-267
  Weathering and erosion
    283
Lake Superior 264
Lake Tanganyika 265
Lake Victoria 265
Lakshmi Planum 37
Lambeosaurus 96, 98-99
Lamb, T. 494
Lamella 159
Lamina 136
  Butterwort 161
  Couch grass 113
  Dicotyledon leaf 127
  Human 222-223
  Leaf 138
  Monocotyledon leaf 127
  Seaweed 116-117
  Succulent 113
  Vegetative reproduction
    154
  Water hyacinth leaf 158
  Water lily leaf 159
Laminaria digitata 116-
  117
Laminates 548
Lamium sp. 155
Lamp 570, 571
Lamp bracket 336, 342
Lamp cluster 341
Lampland 43
Lamprey 178
Lampropeltis ruthveni 184
*Lampropeltis triangulum
  annulata* 184
Lamp shield 330
Lanceolate leaf 120, 131,
  136
Lancet 471
Lancet arch 473, 484
Lancet window 470-472
Land 39
  Amphibians 80
  Animals 64
  Atmosphere 301
  Plants 56, 64
  Rivers 288
  Vertebrates 82
Lander unit 615
Landau body 334
Landau iron 334
Landing 477
Landing and taxiing light
  414
Landing gear 406-407,
  424-425
Landing-gear damper 425

Landing gear door
BAe-146 components
414
Concorde 416
Hawker Tempest
components 409
Lockheed Electra
airliner 406-407
Landing gear drag strut
401
Landing gear fork 407
Landing gear front strut
400, 404
Landing gear hydraulics
417
Landing gear leg 424
Landing gear rear cross-
member 400
Landing gear rear strut
400-401
Landing gear strut 405
Landing light
BAe-146 jetliner
components 414-415
Bell-47 helicopter 422
Lockheed Electra
airliner 407
Schweizer helicopter
423
Landing skid
Avro triplane 403
Blackburn monoplane
400-401
Helicopter 422-423
Wright Flyer 399
Land movement 59
Land plants 56, 78
Landscape features 290-
291, 294
Land surface removal 282
Land turtle 186
Lane
Athletic track 542
Swimming pool 558
Lane time-keeper 558
Langrenus 40
Language 108
Langur 202
Lantern 486
Baroque church 480-
481
French temple 485
Neoclassical building
478-479
Twentieth-century
building 494
Wooden sailing ship
379
Lanthanides 310
Lanthanum 310
Lanyard
Lifejacket 561
Oar 373
Rigging 382-383
Roman corbita 373
Lap 542
Lapilli 272
Lap strap
ARV light aircraft 425
Curtiss biplane 398
Lockheed Electra
passenger seat 407
Pegasus Quasar
microlight 427
Laptop computer 566, 567
Large intestine
Brachiosaurus 90
Chimpanzee 202
Domestic cat 195
Euoplocephalus 94
Human 214
Large Magellanic Cloud
Hydras and Mensa 20
Our galaxy and nearby
galaxies 15
Stars of southern skies
20-21
Large mammals 57
Larkspur 141, 151

Larus marinus 193
Larus ridibundus 193
Larva 168
Laryngeal prominence
212, 244-245
Larynx
Amphibian 182
Human 214-215, 244
Laser 587
Lateen sail 375, 376, 384
Lateral angle 213
Lateral bracing strut 402-
403, 416
Lateral branch
Adventitious roots 158-
159
Horsetail 120
Vegetative reproduction
154
Lateral bud 134
Begonia 129
Dicotyledon 127
Durmast oak 131
Leaf scars 154
London plane tree 134
Rhizome 155
Rowan twig 131
Stem bulbil 155
Stolon 154
Lateral canal
Human 247
Starfish 174
Lateral caudal
musculature 87
Lateral column 223
Lateral control wheel 401
Lateral control wire 404
Lateral dorsal aorta 179
Lateral epicondyle 225
Lateral fault 61
Lateral fault lake 293
Lateral lacuna 257
Lateral line 181
Lateral malleolus 233
Lateral mass 222
Lateral moraine 286-287
Lateral plantar artery 253
Lateral plate 78
Lateral rectus muscle
240-241
Lateral root 133
Broomrape host 163
Carrot 128
Dicotyledon 127
Germination 152-153
Horse chestnut 130
Seedling 152-153
Strawberry 128
Sweet pea 128
Lateral root scar 128
Lateral sepal 141
Lateral shield 187
Lateral shoot 156
Lateral strike-slip fault 61
Lateral sulcus 237
Lateral tepal 126
Lateral vein 136, 159
Lateral ventricle 237
Lath 464
Lathyrus latifolius 129
Lathyrus odoratus 128
Latissimus dorsi muscle
227
Latrodectus mactans 171
Lattice-beam 496-497
Latticed screen 488-489
Latticed shade 495
Lattice-truss 499
Lattice window 494
Lattice-work 495
Laurasia
Cretaceous period 62
Jurassic period 70-71
Late Carboniferous
period 66-67
Laurentia 65
Laurentian Library 474-
475

Lava 62
Igneous and
metamorphic rocks
274-275
Mountain building 62
Rock cycle 266
Volcano 272-273
Lava flow 273
Contact metamorphism
274-275
Mars 42
Rock cycle 266
Lava fragments 272
Lavatera arborea 131
Lava types 273
Lavinia Planitia 36-37
Lawrencium 311
Layering
Fresco 434-435
Pastel colours 440
Lay-up shot 532
LCD circuit board 582
LCD panel open button
582
LCD see Liquid crystal
display (LCD)
Leach 574, 584
Lead
Mineralization zones
281
Minerals 268
Periodic table 311
Lead covering 487
Leading block 594
Leading edge
Avro biplane 403
Avro triplane 403
BAe-146 components
413, 414-415
BE 2B tail 405
BE 2B wings 404
Blackburn monoplane
401
Concorde 416-417
Hawker Tempest
components 409
Lockheed Electra
airliner 406
Northrop B-2 bomber
421
Pegasus Quasar
microlight 427
Wright Flyer 399
Leading-edge aerial 421
Leading-edge fairing 425
Lead-in wire 319
Lead iodide 313
Lead nitrate 313
Lead shot 517
Lead wire 600
Leaf axis 137
Leaf bases 128, 136-137
Aechmea miniata 162
Couch grass 113
Dicotyledon 127
Florists'
chrysanthemum 129
Guzmania lingulata
162-163
Hogweed 129
Monocotyledon 126-127
Sago palm 123
Seedling leaf 152
Water hyacinth 158
Leaf blade
Butterwort 161
Dicotyledon 127
Leaf surface 136, 158
Monocotyledon 127
Vegetative reproduction
154
Venus fly trap 160
Wetland plants 158-159
Leaf insect 192
Leafless branch 120
Leaflets 136-137
Everlasting pea 129
Fern 120-121

Horse chestnut leaf 130
Mahonia 130-131
Monocotyledon 126
Pinna 121, 136-137
Rose 131
Rowan 130
Sago palm 123
Tree fern 112-113
Leaflet stalk 137
Leaf-like structures 141-
143
Dehiscent fruit 151
Dicotyledon flower 127
Guzmania lingulata
163
Ice-plant 129
Live-for-ever 129
Peruvian lily 129
Slender thistle 129
Wind pollination 144
Leaf margin 129
Aechmea miniata 162
Slender thistle 129
Vegetative reproduction
154
Leaf notch 154
Leaf primordium 134
Leaf scar
Begonia 129
Elder 130
Horse chestnut 130
Ice-plant 128-129
London plane 134
Rock stonecrop 128
Leaf shape 136-137
Leaf sheath 129
Leaf spring 338
Leaf spring suspension
327
Leaf stalk 128, 136-137
Chusan palm 130
Clematis 131
Cobra lily 160
Common horse
chestnut 130
Dicotyledon 127
Everlasting pea 129
Florists'
chrysanthemum 129
Kedrostis africana 113
Maidenhair tree 123
Mulberry 130
Oxalis sp. 157
Passion flower 130
Peach 131
Seedling 153
Strawberry 128
String of hearts 157
Tree fern 112
Tree mallow 131
Vegetative reproduction
154-155
Venus fly trap 160
Water lily 159
Wind pollination 144
Leaf succulents
Haworthia truncata 157
Lithops bromfieldii 157
Lithops sp. 156
Leaf trace 127
Leaf venation 129
Leafy liverwort 118
Leafy thallus 114
Lean-to roof 468-470, 472
Leather ball making 525
Leather grommet 373
Leather hood 334
Leather ink dabber 446
Leather pad 557
Leather upholstery 337
Leather valance 337
Leathery exocarps 148
Leaves 136-157
Abaxial surface 123, 130
Adaxial surface 123,
150
Aechmea miniata 162
Apex 136-137

Apical meristem 134
Barberry 150-151
Bishop pine 124
Brassavola nodosa 162
Bromeliad 112-113
Broomrape 163
Butterwort 161
Canadian pond weed
158-159
Carnivorous plants 160-
161
Checkerbloom 156
Chusan palm 130
Classification 156-157
Clematis 130-131
Clubmoss 120
Cobra lily 160
Couch grass 113
Dicotyledon 126-127
Dryland plants 156-157
Durmast oak 131
Epiphyte 162-163
Fern 120-121
Florists'
chrysanthemum 129
Germination 152-153
Guzmania lingulata
162-163
Haworthia truncata 157
Hinge cell 113
Hogweed 129
Horsetail 120
Intercellular space 139
Ivy 131
Kedrostis africana 113
Lithops bromfieldii 157
Liverwort 118
London plane tree 134
Maidenhair tree 123
Margin 136
Marram grass 113
Midrib 136
Monkey cup 161
Monocotyledon 126-127
Moss 112, 119
Mulberry 130
Orange lily 154
Oxalis sp. 157
Parasite host 163
Passion flower 130
Peach 131
Photosynthesis 134,
138-139
Pine 122, 124-125
Pitcher development
161
Pitcher plant 113, 160-
161
Primordia 134
Rock stonecrop 128
Rose 130-131
Rosettes 162-163
Rowan 130
Sago palm 123
Scots pine 122
Seedling 152-153
Slender thistle 129
Smooth cypress 123
Stomata 139
Strawberry 128
Tendrils 161
Toadflax 129
Tree fern 112-113
Tree mallow 131
Vegetative reproduction
154-155
Veins 136, 159
Venus fly trap 160
Water fern 158
Water hyacinth 158
Water lily 159
Welwitschia 122-123
Xerophyte 156-157
Le Corbusier 494
Leda Planitia 36, 37
Ledge 581
Leech 374, 584

Leechline 375
Left edge guide 575
Leg
Amphibian 182
Caiman 186-187
Crab 172
Crayfish 172-173
Crocodilian 186
Elephant 200
Frog 182
Gorilla 203
Human 210
Lizard 184-185
Relief-printing press
449
Salamander 182
Scorpion 170
Shrimp 172
Spider 170-171
Tadpole 183
Terrapin 187
Tripod congas stand
519
"Leg before wicket" 538
Leg bud 260
Leg pad 539, 551
Leg protector 551
Leg slip 538
Legumes 150
Leibnitz 41
Lemercier, J. 486
Lemming 196
Lemon 148
Lemur 202-203
Lemur catta 203
Lenoir, Etienne
Early engines 342
First cars 334
Lens
Digital camera 583
Digital video 583
Flatbed scanner 570
Human body 241
Microscope 610, 611
Lens assembly 583
Lens bezel 580
Lens cap 583
Lens inner barrel
(zoom/focus) 580
Lens mounting bracket
580
Lens zoom and focus 580
Lens zoom in/out toggle
581
Lenticels 130-131, 134
Lentiform nucleus 237
Leo 18, 21
Leo Minor 18, 21
Leonaspsis 279
Leonid meteor shower 52
Leontopithecus rosalia 203
Lepidodendron 66-67
Lepidoptera 168
Lepidotes maximus 73
Leptoceratops 103
Lepus 21
Lesbian leaf pattern 460
Lesene
Ancient Roman
building 462, 465
Baroque church 480-
481
Dome 486
French temple 485
Gothic church 473
Renaissance building
476-477
Lesser trochanter of
femur 225
Lesser wing covert 188
Lesser wing of sphenoid
bone 221
Letronne 40
Letter buttons 588
Lettering 444-445
Letter keys 588
Levator anguli oris
muscle 229

Levator labii superioris muscle 229
Levator palpebrae superioris muscle 241
Levee 289-291
Level-wind system 562
Lever 320-321
Le Verrier ring 50-51
Liang K'ai 55
Libellulium longialatum 73
Liberty ship 392
Libra 18, 21
Library 485, 496
Licence holder 332
Lichens 114-115
Lid
  Moss 119
  Pitchers 161
  Ships for war and trade 377
Lid assembly 571, 587
Lierne 469
Life 56, 78-79, 300
Lifeboat 394
Lifeboat davit 395
Life buoy 395
Life-cycle
  Brown seaweed 117
  Fern 121
  Insect 168
  Moss 119
  Mushroom 115
  Plants 112
  Scots pine 122
Lifeguard 332
Lifejacket 561
Life of massive star 26-27
Life of small star 24-25
Life-raft 416
Liferaft cylinder 397
Lift
  Athletics 543
  Centre Georges Pompidou 497
  Double topsail schooner 385
  Roman corbita 372
  Sailing warship 376-377
  Wooden sailing ship 378
Lift bracing wire
  Biplanes and triplanes 403
  Early monoplane 400-401
  Pegasus Quasar microlight 427
  World War I aircraft 404-405
Lifting handle 336
Lifting lug 330
Lift spoiler 413, 414
Lift wire 399
Ligament
  Bifurcate 232
  Cricothyroid 244
  Deltoid 232
  Falciform 248
  Foot 232
  Hip joint 224
  Iliofemoral 224
  Interosseus 232
  Ovarian 258
  Periodontal 247
  Plantar calcaneonavicular 232
  Posterior cuneonavicular 232
  Posterior tarsometatarsal 232
  Pubofemoral 224
  Talonavicular 232
  Zonular 241
Ligature 508, 509
Light 314-315, 318-319
  Chemical reactions 312

Renaissance building 474
Seed germination 152
Translucent "window" 157
Twentieth-century building 495
Ultraviolet 145
Light aircraft 410, 424-425
Light Emitting Diode 585
Lightfish 589
Light hour 14
Lighting hole 393
Light level sensor 581
Lightning 45, 316
Lights
  Bicycle 360
  MCW Metrobus 332
Light screen 394
Light shield 612, 613
Light switch 339
Lightweight plastic intake manifold 354
Light-well 487
Light year 14
Lignite 280
Lignum vitae bearing 387
Ligulate ray floret 129
Lilienthal, Otto 398
Lilium bulbiferum 154
Lilium sp. 133, 138, 140-141, 155
Lily
  Bulbil 154-155
  Flower 140-141
  Leaf surface 158
Limb
  Mammal 104
  Paddlesteamer 390
  Reptile 80
  Structure of a fold 60
Limber hole 393
Lime 143
Lime-resistant pigment 434
Limestone
  Cave 284
  Contact metamorphism 274
  Faults and folds 60
  Fossilized blue-green alga 78
  Lower Carboniferous 60
Limestone block 470
Limestone cladding 494
Limestone false door 459
Limestone spring 292
Limestone strata 284
Lime water 313
Limiter switch 586
Limonite groundmass 268-269
Limpet 176
Linaria sp. 129
Line 562
Linea alba 226
Linear dune 283
Linear leaf 129, 137
Linebacker 526
Line guide 563
Line judge 526
Line of sight 41
Linesman
  Badminton 545
  Gaelic football 529
  Ice hockey 550
  Soccer 524
  Tennis 544
  Volleyball 534
Lingual nerve 244
Lingual tonsil 245
Link 386
Link to external website 577
Linocut 446
Linoleum block 446, 449
Linseed oil 436

Lintel
  Building 459, 494
  Coastline 295
Lintel course 483
Lion 194-195
Lion crest 395
Lionfish 180
Lip
  Flower 126, 145
  Human 212-213
  Lamprey 178
  Pollination 145
Lip of trunk 200-201
Lip plate 508, 508
Lip tension 506
Liquidambar styraciflua 76
Liquid capacity measurements 590
Liquid crystal display (LCD)
  Apple Power Mac G4 1GHz dual processor 566
  Brother T-78 fax machine 572
  Game Boy Advance 579
  Garmin Street Pilot III GPS 590, 591
  Nokia 5510 588
  Portable CD player 587
  Samsung VM800 laptop 567
  Sony digital handycam 582
Liquid crystal display (LCD) assembly 591
Liquid crystal display (LCD) circuit board 569
Liquid helium 45
Liquid hydrogen 44-47
Liquid ink 444
Liquids 306-307
Litchi chinensis 148
Lithification 266
Lithium 308, 310
Lithium fluoride molecule 308
Lithographic printing 446
Lithographic printing equipment 448
Lithops bromfieldii 157
Lithops sp. 156
Lithosphere 58-59
Little finger 230 -231
Little grebe 190
Little toe 232-233
Live-for-ever 128-129
Liver
  Bird 189
  Bony fish 181
  Chimpanzee 202
  Dogfish 179
  Dolphin 205
  Domestic cat 195
  Euoplocephalus 94
  Frog 182
  Gallimimus 86
  Human 214, 248, 252
  Lizard 185
  Rabbit 196
  Tortoise 187
Liverworts 112, 118-119
Livestock freight car 327
Living organisms 306
Lizard 184-185, 382
"Lizard-feet forms" 88
Lizard-hipped dinosaurs 82, 88-89
Llama 198
Load 320-321
Loading arm 396
Loading gauge 330-331
Load space 334
Lobby 498
Lobe
  Liverwort 118
  Venus fly trap 160
Lobed leaf 129, 131
Lobsters 172

Lobule 242
Local Arm 14
Local control cabinet 396
Locating pin 580
Lock 582
Lockable cover latch 566
Lock button 600
Lock forward 550
Lockheed Electra airliner 406-407
Locking lever 590
Lock nut 551, 559
Locks 360
Lock washer 358-359
Locomotion 104
Locomotives 324-329
Lodging knee 381
Loft 477
Log basket 334
Loin
  Horse 198
  Human 210
London Bridge 466-467
London plane tree 134
Longboat 380
Long bridge 515
Long-distance cycling 360
Long-distance running 542
Longeron 403, 424
Longitudinal channels 120
Longitudinal fissure 236-237
Long jump 542-543
Long leading-link fork 362
Long leg 558
Long off 538
Long on 538
Long pass 532
Long radius turns 552
Longrod stabilizer 549
Longship 374-375
Longshore drift 294-295
Long-travel suspension 368
Long-wave radio 318
Look out periscope 596
Loom 560
Loop 388-389
Looped prominence 32-33
Loophole
  Medieval building 466-469
  Renaissance building 477
Loop of Henlé 256
Loose forward 550
Loose-head prop 550
Lopolith 274
Lora 127, 130
Lorises 202
Lost-wax casting method 454
Lotus flower 488
Lotus petal 489
Loudspeaker 520
Lounge 392
Louvre 493, 498
Love-in-a-mist 150-151
Lowell 43
Lower Carboniferous Limestone 60
Lower crankcase 410
Lower crux of antihelix 242
Lower deadeye 382-383
Lower deck 393
Lower-energy radiation 22
Lower epidermis 139, 159
Lower equipment module 615
Lower eyelid 213
Lower fin 423
Lower haze 37
Lower lobe of lung 215, 254-255

Lower seed axis 152-153
Lower topsail 385
Lower-wing attachment 404
Lower yard 395
Lowland coastline 295
Low Neap tide 297
Low pressure areas 300, 302-303
Low pressure gases 306
Low tides 296-297
Low-voltage supply 596
Loxodonta africana 200
Lozenge 471, 485
Lubricant 366
Lucarne window 480-481, 486
Lufengosaurus 89
Luff 384-385
Lug 382, 586
Lugger 384
Lug sail
  Junk 376
  Sail types 384
Lumbar nerves 238
Lumbar vertebrae
  Crocodile 186
  Domestic cat 195
  Hare 197
  Horse 199
  Human 222-223
  Kangaroo 206
  Platypus 206
  Rhesus monkey 202
  Seal 204
Lumbrical muscle 231
Lump hammer 452-453
Lunae Planum 43
Lunaria annua 151
Lunate bone 230
Lunette 480
Lung
  Amphibian 182
  Bird 189
  Brachiosaurus 91
  Chimpanzee 202
  Dolphin 205
  Domestic cat 195
  Elephant 200
  Euoplocephalus 94
  Frog 182
  Gallimimus 86
  Human 214 215, 252, 254-255
  Lizard 184-185
  Rabbit 196
  Snail 177
  Snake 184
  Spider 170
  Tortoise 187
Lungfish 80, 81
Lunule 231
Lures 562-563
Lutetium 311
LVG CVI fighter 405
Lychee 148
Lycoming four-cylinder engine 423
Lycoming six-cylinder engine 422
Lycopodophyta 64, 120
Lymphocytes 253
Lynx 18, 21
Lynx helicopter 396
Lyra 19, 20
Lysosome 217

M

M22 (globular cluster) 21
Macaques 202
Macaws 190
Mach 41
Machine-gun 404-405
Machine heads 512-513
Mackenzie-Peace River 264
Mackerel angling 562

Maquette 455
Macrobius 40
Macrofibril 234
Macrospicule 33
Macs 566
Macula 240-241
Madagascar 265
Madreporite 174, 175
Madrilus sphinx 205
Maenianum summum 465
Magazine 548-549
Magellanic Cloud 15, 20
Maginus 40
Magma
  Igneous and metamorphic rocks 26
  Mountain building 63
  Ocean floor 298-299
  Rock cycle 266
  Volcanoes 272
Magma reservoir
  Igneous rock structures 275
  Volcanic structure 273
Magnesium 310
  Earth's composition 39
  Earth's crust 58
  Seawater salt content 296
Magnesium alloy oil sump pan 354
Magnesium housing for air intake 355
Magnesium riser 548
Magnet 598, 605
Magnetic axis 28
Magnetic compass 423
Magnetic field 38
Magnetism 316-317
Magneto
  Avro triplane 402
  Hawker Tempest components 408
  Wright Flyer 399
Magneto drive 367
Magneto-optical circuits 587
Magnetosphere 38
Magnetron assembly 596, 597
Magnetron cooling fan 596, 597
Magnetron cooling fan mounting 597
Magnetron perforated heat sink 597
Magnitude 22
Magnolia 57, 72
Mahonia 130-131
Maidenhair tree 122-123
Maillot 586
Main circuit board 569, 582
Main engines 615
Main fan 596, 597
Main fan electrical supply 597
Main frame 572
Main-line signalling system 330-331
Main motor casing 593
Main printed circuit board (PCB) 591
Mainrail head 379
Main ribbon loom socket 581
Main sail
  Dhow 376
  Roman corbita 373
  Sailing rigs 385
  Square-rigged ship 375
Main screen 584
Mains earthing wire 581
Mains electricity supply lead 585
Main sequence star
  Massive stars 26
  Objects in Universe 11
  Small stars 24

Stars 22-23
Mains flex 594
Mains flex clamp 594
Main sheer strake 593
Main sheet
  Longboat 380
  Roman corbita 373
  Sailing dinghy 561
  Viking karv 375
Main shroud 378
Mains lead 597-598
Main spar bridge 413
Mains power connectors 589
Mains power on/off switch 585
Mains spade contacts 594
Main stay 377, 379
Mains supply lead 594
Maintenance button 574
Main topcastle 377
Main topgallant mast 577, 578
Main topgallant sail 579
Main topgallant stay 579
Main top yard 577
Main turbine 397
Main wale 381
Main wheel 426, 593
Main wing bracing-strut 401
Main wing-strut 427
Main yard
  Dhow 376
  Sailing warship 377
  Wooden sailing ship 379
Maize 127
Major calyx 256
Major coverts 188, 191
Malachite 433
Malacostraca 172
Malaysia 331
Male
  Bladder 257
  Body 210, 211
  Pelvis 259
  Reproductive organs 259
  Urinary tract 257
Male apex 119
Male catkin 144
Male cone 122-123, 24
Male fern 120-121
Male flower organs 140-143
Male flowers
  Fertilization 146-147
  Gymnosperms 122
  Painter's palette 143
  Seaweed 116-117
  Succulent fruit 148
  Wind-pollinated plant 144
"Mallard" express steam locomotive 324-325
Mallet
  Marble carving 452
  Ships and sailing 383, 384, 388
  Tubular bells 516
Malleus 242
Malpighian tubule
  Butterfly 169
  Spider 170
Malus 373
Malus sp. 126
Malus sylvestris 149
Mammals 104-107
  Carnivora 194
  Cetacea 204
  Cretaceous period 72
  Earth's evolution 56-57

Fossil record 279
Jurassic period 70
Lagomorpha 196
Large 57
Marsupalia 206
Monotremata 206
Pinnipedia 204
Primates 202
Proboscidea 200
Rodentia 196
Shrew-like 70
Small 56
Tertiary period 74-75
Ungulates 198
Mammoth 107
Mammut 75
Mammuthus 76, 77, 104
Mandapa 491
Mandarinfish 180
Mandible
  Acanthostega 80
  Ankylosaurus 94
  Arsinoitherium 104
  Baryonyx 83
  Bat 105
  Bear 194
  Beetle 168
  Bird 188-189
  Bony fish 181
  Camarasaurus 91
  Chimpanzee 202
  Crayfish 173
  Crocodile 186
  Diplodocus 90
  Elephant 201
  Eryops 80
  Euoplocephalus 94
  Hare 197
  Heterodontosaurus 83
  Horse 199
  Human 220-221, 244-245
  Hyaenodon 107
  Iguanodon 96
  Kangaroo 206
  Lambeosaurus 99
  Lion 194
  Moeritherium 105
  Panoplosaurus 94
  Parasaurolophus 99
  Phiomia 105
  Plateosaurus 88
  Protoceratops 102
  Rattlesnake 185
  Rhesus monkey 202
  Seal 204
  Stegoceras 100-101
  Styracosaurus 102
  Toxodon 106
  Triceratops 103
  Turtle 187
  Tyrannosaurus 84
Mandrills 202-203
Mane 194, 199
Manganese 281, 310
Manharness knot 389
Manifold connector 355
Manilla rope 389
Manipulator 610
Man-of-war 378
Mansard roof 490
Mantle
  Earth 38-39, 58-59, 63
  Mars 43
  Mercury 35
  Moon 41
  Molluscs 176-177
  Neptune 51
  Pluto 51
  Regional metamorphism 274
  Uranus 49
  Venus 37
Manufacturing code 569
Maple 127
Map projections 264-265
Maracas 504, 516-517
Marble 274
Marble block 453

Marble breaking equipment 450
Marble mosaic 489
Marble sculpture 452
Marble tessera 450
Marble veneer 462
Marchantia polymorpha 118
Mare Crisium 40
Mare Fecunditatis 40
Mare Frigoris 40
Mare Humorum 40
Mare Imbrium 40
Mare Ingenii 41
Mare Moscoviense 41
Mare Nectaris 40
Mare Nubium 40
Mare Orientale 41
Mareotis Fossae 43
Mare Serenitatis 40
Mare Smithii 41
Mare's tail 45
Mare Tranquillitatis 40
Mare Vaporum 40
Margaritifer Sinus 43
Margin
  Lamina 116-117, 161
  Leaf 129, 156-157
  Needle 124
  Water lily leaf 159
Marginal shield 187
"Margined heads" 100
Marginocephalians 83, 100-103
Maria 40
Marine invertebrates 65
Marine plants 56
Marine reptiles 57, 70
Marine sediments 280
Marine turtles 186
Mariopteris 66
Markab 19, 20
Markeb 21
Marlin 388
Marlinspike 383, 389
Marmosets 202
Marram grass 113
Mars 30, 42-43
Mars Lander 615
Marsh 293
Marsupials 104, 206-207
Martellange, E. 479
Martingale 382, 557
Martingale stay 383
Mary Rose 376
Mascaron 487
Mask 460, 487, 536
  Ancient Roman building 465
  Cathedral dome 484
  Neoclassical building 482
Masonry apron 487
Mason's mark 470
Mason's tools 485
Mass
  Atoms and molecules 309, 320
  Earth 30
  Jupiter 26, 44
  Mars 30
  Mercury 30
  Neptune 31
  Planets 30-31
  Pluto 31
  Saturn 31
  Uranus 31
  Venus 30
Massive habit 270-271
Massive stars 26-27
Mass measurements 590
Massospondylus 89
Mass-production 338-339, 492
Mass transportation 332

Mast
  Battleship 394
  Frigate 397
  Greek galley 372
  Iron paddlesteamer 392
  Junk 376
  Longboat 380
  Roman corbita 373
  Sailing 561
  Sailing warship 376-377
  Submarine 397
  Tea clipper 382
  Three-masted square-rigged ship 375
  Viking karv 375
  Wooden sailing ship 378-379
Mast band 582
Master cylinder
  Disc brake 365
  Harley-Davidson FLHS Electra Glide 363
  Honda VF750 564
Master shipwright 574
Master's sea cabin 381
Masthead
  Roman corbita 373
  Viking karv 375
  Wooden sailing ship 378
Mast head bend 589
Masthead pulley for tye halyard 375
Mast hoop 585
Mastoid fontanelle 220
Mastoid process 220, 242
Mast partner 581
Mast step 592
Mast truck 372
Matar 19
Match play 546
Maternal blood cord 260
Maternal blood vessel 260
Mathematical symbols 621
Mato Grosso 264
Matter 306-307
  Electrical charge 316
  Identification 312
Mature ruptured follicle 258
Mawsonites spriggi 65
Maxilla
  Ankylosaurus 94
  Baryonyx 83
  Bear 194
  Bony fish 181
  Camarasaurus 91
  Chimpanzee 202
  Diplodocus 90
  Elephant 201
  Eryops 80
  Euoplocephalus 94
  Frog 183
  Horse 199
  Human 212, 220-221, 244-245, 246, 248
  Iguanodon 96
  Lion 194
  Pachycephalosaurus 100
  Prenocephale 100
  Stegoceras 100
  Toxodon 106
Maxillary fenestra 90
Maxilliped 173
Maxwellian diagram 318
Maxwell Montes 36, 57
Mazda RX-7 346
McLaren Mercedes MP4-13 356-357
MCW Metrobus 332-333
ME 262 fighter 408
Meadow cranesbill 144
Meadow rue 137
Meadow sage 145
Meander 461
Meanders 288-289, 290
Measurement units 620
Meatus 242-243

Mechanical semaphore signal 350
Mechanical weathering 282
Mechanics 350-351
Mechanism of respiration 255
Medallion 476
Medial epicondyle 225
Medial malleolus 233
Medial moraine
  Glaciers 286-287
  River's stages 289
Medial rectus muscle 240-241
Median canal 243
Median cubital vein 253
Median eye 170
Median glossoepiglottic fold 244
Median nerve 238
Median sulcus 244
Median wing coverts 188
Medieval castles 466-467
Medieval churches 468-469
Medieval houses 466-467
Medinet Habu, Egypt 459
Mediterranean Sea 74, 265
Mediterranean sea anemone 166
Medium-wave radio 318
Medulla 114, 234, 256
Medulla oblongata 212, 236-237
Medullary cavity 224
Medullary pyramid 256
Medullary ray 125
Medullosa 66
Mega bass control 586
Megaspores 122
Megazostrodon 104
Megrez 19
Meiolania 77
Meissner's corpuscle 234-235, 239
Melanin 234
Melanosaurus 68, 88-89
Melon 149, 205
Melting glacier 286, 289
Meltwater 287, 289
Meltwater pond 286
Membrane
  Chloroplasts 139
  Chorioallantoic 192
  Egg 193
  Shell 192
  Thylakoid 139
Memory card 579
Memory microchip 579
Memory stick 581, 583
Memory stick connector 583
Memory stick cover recess 589
Memory stick eject button 583
Memory stick slot 583
Mendel 41
Mendeleev 41
Mendelevium 311
Meninges 237
Menkalinan 21
Menkar 19, 20
Menkent 21
Mensa 20, 21
Mental foramen 213, 220-221
Mentalis muscle 229
Mental protuberance 221
Mental symphysis 220
Mentolabial sulcus 213
Menu icon 568
Menu key 590
Menu roll-on scroll/wheel 587
Menu select forward/back button 588

Menu select forward/back button connectors 589
Menu selector 587
Menu select up/down button 588
Merak 19
Merchants' Exchange 493
Mercury 30, 34-35
Mercury (metal) 281, 311, 519
Mericarp 151
Meristematic cells 154
Merlon 466
Mermaid's purses 192
Mersenius 40
Merus 172, 173
Merycoidodon 75
Mesa 275, 277, 282
Mesentery 167, 182
Mesocarp 146-147, 148, 148-149
Mesoglea 167
Mesohyal 166
Mesophyll 155
  Bishop pine needle 124
  Dicotyledon leaf 126
  Marram grass 113
  Monocotyledon leaf 126
  Palisade layer 139
  Spongy layer 139
Mesosphere 300
Mesothorax 168
Mesozoic era
  Cretaceous period 72
  Dinosaurs 82
  Fossil record 279
  Geological timescale 57
  Jurassic period 70
  Reptiles 80
  Triassic period 68
Mess 397
Message list 576
Message manager launch button 572
Metacarpals
  Archaeopteryx 85
  Arsinoitherium 104
  Baryonyx 83
  Bird 189, 191
  Brachiosaurus 91
  Cow 198
  Diplodocus 90
  Domestic cat 195
  Elephant 90, 201
  Eryops 80
  Euoplocephalus 94
  Frog 183
  Gallimimus 86
  Hare 197
  Horse 198-199
  Human 218-219, 230
  Kangaroo 206
  Lizard 184
  Parasaurolophus 99
  Plateosaurus 88
  Platypus 206
  Rhesus monkey 202
  Seal 204
  Stegoceras 100
  Toxodon 106
  Triceratops 103
  Tyrannosaurus 84
Metacarpophalangeal joint 85
Metal cook/grill tray 596
Metal grill/griddle 596
Metalliferous muds 299
Metalling 486
Metal modelling implements 452
Metal needle pad 584
Metal nib 444
Metal riser 455
Metal runner 455
Metals 310
Metal tyre 324
Metal wire conductor 316-317
648

Metamorphic aureole 26
Metamorphic rocks 26, 274–275, 266–267
Metamorphosis
Amphibian 182
Frog 183
Insect 168
Metasoma 170
Metatarsals
  Albertosaurus 84
  Archaeopteryx 85
  Brachiosaurus 90
  Crocodile 186
  Domestic cat 195
  Elephant 201
  Eryops 81
  Euoplocephalus 94
  Frog 183
  Hare 197
  Horse 199
  Human 218–219, 232
  Iguanodon 96–97
  Kangaroo 206
  Lizard 184
  Parasaurolophus 98
  Plateosaurus 88
  Platypus 206
  Rhesus monkey 202
  Scorpion 170
  Seal 204
  Spider 171
  Stegoceras 100–101
  Struthiomimus 87
  Toxodon 107
  Triceratops 102
Metathorax 168
Metaxylem 127, 132–133
Meteor 52, 301
Meteorite
  Asteroids, comets, and meteoroids 52
  Earth's atmosphere 38
  Moon 41
  Ray crater 34
Meteorite impact 34, 40
Meteoroids 52–53
  Solar System 30
Methane
  Jupiter 45
  Neptune and Pluto 50–51
  Saturn 47
  Uranus 48–49
Methane cirrus clouds 50–51
Metis Regio 36
Metope 460
Metric-Imperial conversions 620
Metric unit measurements 590
Metrobus 352–353
Metrolink tram 332
Mexican hat plant 154
Mexican mountain king snake 184
Mexican true red-legged tarantula 170
Mexico 331
Mezzanine 467, 496
Miaplacidus 21
Mica 26, 270
Mice 104, 196
Michelangelo 35
Micrasterias sp. 112
Microchip 582
Microfilament 217
Microlights 410, 426–427
Micro-needle 606
Micro-organisms 38, 76
Microphone 581, 589
Microphone block 585
Microphone cover 583
Microphone jack 567
Micro-pipette 606
Micropits 586
Microporous filter 592
Microprocessor 569

Microscopes 610–611
Microsoft XBox 579
Microsporangium 122
Microspores 122
Microsporophyll 122
Microtubule 217, 239
Microwave oven 515
Microwave radiation 10
Microwave combination oven 596–597
Microwaves 318, 596
Midbrain 236
Middle ear ossicles 242
Middle finger 230–231
Middle leg
  Beetle 168
  Bumblebee 168
  Butterfly 169
Middle lobe of lung 215, 254–255
Middle meatus 241, 245
Middle nasal concha 212, 221, 241, 245
Middle phalanx 219, 230, 232
Middle rail 581
Midfielders
  Gaelic football 529
  Lacrosse 541
  Soccer 524
Midgut173
Mid-latitude band 36
Mid-latitude cyclones 302
Mid-ocean ridge 281, 298–299
Mid-off 538
Mid-on 538
Midrib
  Dicotyledon leaf 126–127
  Durmast oak leaf 131
  Fern fronds 121
  Hogweed leaf 129
  Ice-plant leaf 129
  Live-for-ever leaf 129
  Liverwort 118
  Monkey cup 161
  Moss leaf 119
  Spiral wrack 116
  Sweet chestnut leaf 136
  Tree fern 113
  Venus fly trap 160
  Water lily leaf 159
Midships fence 375
Midships section 392
Midwater current 297
Midway Gardens 495
Mid West single-rotor engine 411
Mid West twin-rotor engine 411
Mid West two-stroke engine 410
Miele washer-dryer 594, 595
Mihrab 488
Milan Cathedral 473
Milankovic 43
Milk snake 184
Milk teeth 246
Milky quartz 268, 271
Milky Way 14–15
  Northern stars 18
  Solar System 30
  Stars of southern skies 20
Mill 462, 464, 492
Millstone grit 60–61
Milne 41
Milton 35
Mimas 46
Mimulopsis solmsii 145
Minaret 488–489
Mineral-filled fault 60–61
Mineral-rich deposits 298
Minerals 268–269
  Carnivorous plants 160

Epiphytes 162
Fossils 278
Mineral features 270–271
Mineral resources 280–281
  Photosynthesis 138–139
  Wetland plants 158
  Xylem vessel 134
Mineral spicules 166
Mineral spring 273
Mineral wool 603
Minidisc 586
Minidisc player 586, 587
Minim 502
Minmi 95
Minor calyx 256
Minor coverts 188, 191
Mint 109
Mintaka 18
Miocene epoch
  Fossil record 279
  Geological timescale 57
Mira 19, 20
Mirach 19, 20
Miranda 48
Mizar backstay 378
Mizzen 376
Mizzen course 379
Mizzen mast
  Dhow 376
  Iron paddlesteamer 392
  Junk 376
  Sailing warship 377
  Square-rigged ship 375
  Wooden sailing ship 378
Mizzen sail 375, 385
Mizzen shroud 378
Mizzen stay 378
Mizzen top 378
Mizzen topcastle 377
Mizzen topgallant sail 379
Mizzen topmast 377, 378
Mizzen topsail 378
Mizzen yard 376–377, 378
Moat 466–467
Mobile phone 588–589
Mobile sculpture 452
Modelling 452
Modelling tools 454
Modem 567, 576, 577
Modem port 566, 567
Moderator 314
Modern buildings 496–499
Modern engines 344–345
Modern humans 57
Modern jetliners 412–415
Modern military aircraft 420–421
Modern piston aero-engines 410–411
Mode selector 587
Modified cuticle 157
Modified lateral shoots 156
Modified leaflets 129
Modified leaves
  Barberry 130–131
  Cobra lily 160
  Dryland plants 156–157
  Everlasting pea 129

Golden barrel cactus 156
Pitcher development 161
Spines 156
Strawberry 128
Modified shoots 156
Modified stipules 128–129
Modillion
  Baroque church 479
  Neoclassical building 478
  Renaissance building 475
Moenave formation 276
Moenkopi formation 276
Moeritherium 104
Mohorovic discontinuity 39
Mohs scale 270–271
Molar tooth
  Arsinoitherium 104
  Australopithecus 107
  Bear 106, 194
  Chimpanzee 202
  Elephant 201
  Horse 105
  Human 246
  Hyaenodon 107
  Moeritherium 105
  Opossum 106
  Phiomia 105
  Toxodon 106
Molecular orbitals 308
Molecules 306, 308–309
Molluscs 176–177
  Belemnite 71
  Nautiloid 69
Molten bronze 454
Molten core 39
Molten rock
  Igneous and metamorphic rocks 274
  Matter 306
  Ocean floor 298
  Plate movements 58
  Rock cycle 266
  Volcanoes 272
Molybdate 269
Molybdenum 310
Mongooses 194
Monkey cup 161
Monkeys 202–203
Monoceros 18, 21
Monoclinal fold 60
Monocline 61
Monoclinic system 270
Monocoque chassis 363
Monocoque shell 348
Monocotyledonous petals 140, 143
Monocotyledonous sepals 126, 140, 143
Monocotyledons 126–127, 140–141, 143
Monodon monoceros 205
Monograptus convolutus 65
Monolithic shaft 463
Monoplanes 400–401, 402, 406
Monotremes 206–207
Montes Apenninus 40
Montes Cordillera 41
Montes Jura 40
Montes Rook 41
Monteverdi 35
Montgolfier brothers 398
Monument 470
Moon 40–41
  Objects in Universe 11
  Solar eclipse 32
  Tides 296–297
Moonquake region 41
Moons
  Jupiter 44
  Mars 42
  Neptune 50
  Saturn 46

Solar System 30
Uranus 48
Mooring 386–387
Moorish arch 484
Moraine 286–287, 292–293
Moray eel 180
Morias 57
Mortar 452
Mortice 373
Mortise 486, 492
Morus nigra 130
Mosaic 450–451
  Islamic building 488–489
  Tools 450
Mosque 484, 488
Mosses 112, 114, 118–119
  Epiphytic 162
  Life-cycle 119
  Structure 119
Moth 168
Motherboard 567, 579
Mother's milk 104
Motocross motorcycle 368
Motor 555, 572, 609
Motor air intake 593
Motor assembly 574
Motorcycle chassis 362, 364–365
Motorcycle engines 366–367
Motorcycle racing 368
Motorcycles 362–363
Motorcycle sidecar 362, 369
Motor-driven bogie axle 326
Motor electronic control module (ECM) 355
Motor end plate 228, 239
Motorhead 503, 505
Motorized buses 332
Motor neuron 228, 239
Motor operating signal 330
Motor whaler 397
Motte 466
Mouchette 472
Mould 278
Moulded bracket 484
Moulded corbel 493
Moulding 485
  Ancient Egyptian temple 458–459
  Asian building 490
  Baroque church 480–481
  Dome 486–487
  Gothic church 471–472
  Medieval building 466, 469
  Neoclassical building 479–480, 482
  Renaissance building 475–477
  Ship's shield 395
Moulding tool 454
Moulds 114
Moulting 171
Mounds 286
Mountain bikes 358, 360
Mountain building 56, 58, 62–63
Mountain hollows 286
Mountain lake 288
Mountain ranges
  Earth's physical features 264
  Faults and folds 60
  Geological time 56
  Igneous and metamorphic rocks 274
Mountain building 62
Ocean floor 298
Plate movements 59
Mountain ridge 291
Mountain Star 34
Mountains 62–63, 267

Mountain spring 288
Mounting bracket 590
Mounting bush 365
Mounting splines 366
Mouse 521, 566, 611
Mouse and collar 379
Mouth
  Barnacle 173
  Bony fish 180–181
  Cobra lily 160
  Cow 198
  Crayfish 173
  Dogfish 179
  Dolphin 204
  Elephant 200
  Frog 182
  Gorilla 203
  Horse 199
  Human 211, 212, 244–245, 248
  Jellyfish 167
  Kangaroo 207
  Lamprey 178
  Lizard 184
  Pitcher plant 161
  Rabbit 196
  Rat 196
  Sea anemone 166–167
  Seal 204
  Sea urchin 175
  Snail 177
  Spider 171
  Starfish 174–175
Mouth diffuser 430, 440
Mouthpiece
  Brass instruments 506
  Clarinet 508
  Tenor saxophone 509
  Trumpet 506
  Wind synthesizer 521
Movement
  Gas particles 307
  Objects 320
MP3 586
MRI scan
  Head 214
  Brain 236
Mt. Everest 264
Mu Andromedae 19
Muav limestone 277
Muccini brush 434
Mucosa 248
Mucosal gland 254
Mucous gland 177
Mucronate leaf apex 137
Mucus-secreting duodenal cells 217
Mud 267, 273
Mud crab 279
Mud-flat 295
Mudguard
  1906 Renault 336–337
  BMW R/60 with Steib chair 362
  Cannondale ST 1000 touring bicycle 361
  Ford Model T 338–339
  Harley-Davidson FLHS Electra Glide 363
  Honda VF750 364
  Husqvarna Motocross TC610 368
  Kirby BSA 369
  Lockheed Electra 406
  Motorcycle 364
  Suzuki RGV500 369
  Volkswagen Beetle 341
  Weslake Speedway motorcycle 369
Mudguard stay 337, 362, 363
Mud pools 272–273
Mud river 298
Mulberry 130
Muliphein 21
Mullion
  Gothic church 470, 472–473
  Modern building 497–499

Renaissance building 476
Small-scale rock formation 60-61
Twentieth-century building 494
Multicellular animals 56
Multicellular organisms 78
Multicellular soft-bodied animals 56
Multifoil 472
Multi-gabled roof 492
Multiplait nylon 388
Multiplate clutch 364, 366
Multiple fruits 148-149
Multiplier reel 562
Multi-ply tyre 416
Multipolar neuron 239
Mu Orionis 18
Mu Pegasi 19
Musa 'lacotan' 146
Muscari sp. 155
Musci 118
Muscle 226-229
  Abductor digiti minimus 231, 233
  Adductor longus 225
  Adductor magnus 227
  Adductor pollicis 231
  Adductor pollicis brevis 231
  Anal sphincter 249
  Arrector pili 235
  Cricothyroid 244-245
  Dilator 241
  Dorsal interosseous 233
  Energy system 315
  Extensor digitorum brevis 233
  Extensor hallucis brevis 233
  Flexor digitorum longus 233
  Flexor hallucis longus 233
  Flexor pollicis brevis 231
  Flexor retinaculum 231
  Genioglossus 245
  Geniohyoid 245
  Gluteus medius 225
  Gluteus minimus 225
  Hyoglossus 244
  Iliacus 225
  Inferior oblique 241
  Inferior rectus 241
  Intercostal 255
  Internal urethral sphincter 257
  Lateral rectus 240-241
  Levator palpebrae superioris 241
  Lumbrical 231
  Medial rectus 240-241
  Mylohyoid 245
  Opponens digiti minimi 231
  Opponens pollicis 231
  Orbicularis oris 245
  Papillary 251
  Pectineus 225
  Peroneus brevis 233
  Peroneus longus 233
  Psoas major 225, 257
  Pyloric sphincter 249
  Soleus 233
  Sphincter 241
  Styloglossus 244
  Superior longitudinal 245
  Superior oblique 241
  Superior rectus 241
  Tensor tympani 243
  Thyrohyoid 244
  Tibialis anterior 233
  Tibialis posterior 233
  Urethral sphincter 257
  Vastus lateralis 225

Vastus medialis 225
Muscovite 269
Muscular septum 176
Mushroom anchor 386
Mushroom coral 167
Mushrooms 114, 115
Music 514, 586
Musical Instrument Digital Interface (MIDI) system 520-521
Musical manuscript 502-503
Musical notation 502-503
Musical score 502-503, 505
Music gallery 477
Musicians 504
Music software 520
Muslim calendar 618
Mussels 176
Mutes 506-507
Muttaburrasaurus 97
Muzzle 199, 597
Mycelium 114-115
Mycorrhizal association 133
Myelin sheath 239
Mylar 584
Mylar cone speaker 579
Myocardium 250-251
Myofibril 228
Myohyoid muscle 245
Myometrium 260

N

Nail
  Corythosaurus 98
  Edmontonia 95
  Elephant 90
  Human 231
  Iguanodon 96-97
  Stegosaurus 92
  Triceratops 102
Nair Al Zaurak 19, 20
Naismath, James 532
Namib Desert 265
Naos 461, 463, 485
Nape 188, 210
Napier Sabre 24-cylinder engine 408
Naris
  Anchisaurus 89
  Ankylosaurus 94
  Arsinoitherium 104
  Australopithecus 108
  Baryonyx 83
  Brachiosaurus 91
  Camarasaurus 91
  Corythosaurus 98
  Edmontonia 95
  Eryops 80
  Euoplocephalus 94
  Homo erectus 108
  Homo habilis 108
  Homo sapiens 108
  Hyaenodon 107
  Iguanodon 96
  Lambeosaurus 99
  Moeritherium 105
  Opossum 106
  Panoplosaurus 94
  Parasaurolophus 99
  Plateosaurus 88
  Protoceratops 102
  Smilodon 107
  Stegoceras 100-101
  Styracosaurus 102
  Triceratops 102-103
  Tyrannosaurus 84
Narrow gauge track 331
Narwhal 205
Nasal bone
  Ankylosaurus 94
  Bear 194
  Frog 183

Human 220-221
Lion 194
Panoplosaurus 94
Protoceratops 102
Toxodon 106
Nasal cavity
  Chimpanzee 202
  Domestic cat 195
  Elephant 200
  Human 245, 248
  Rabbit 196
Nasal horn 104
Nasalis 229
Nasal *passage* 200
Nasal plug 205
Nasal septum 213, 221, 241
Nasal tusk 105
Nash 21
Nasion 221
Nasolacrimal duct 241
Nasopharynx 245
Natal cleft 210
Natal cocoon 24, 26
Native elements 268
Natural bridge 290
Natural elements 510
Natural fly 562
Natural forces 314
Natural glass 306
Natural gut strings 544
Natural lakes 292
Natural satellites 40
Natural sponge 438
Nautiloid mollusc 69
  Fossil 65
Navajo Mountain 277
Navajo sandstone 276
Nave
  Ancient Egyptian temple 458-459
  Baroque church 479
  Cathedral dome 484
  Gothic church 470-473
  Medieval church 468-469
  Ship's wheel 390
Navel 211, 260
Nave plate 390
Navicular bone 232
Navigating bridge 594
Navigational aerial 423-424
Navigation area 577
Navigation buttons 577
Navigator's cockpit 420
Navigator's seat 408
Navka 57
Nazea plate 59
Neanderthals 108
Neap tides 296-297
Nebulae 16-17
  Cone 612
  Galaxies 12-13
  Great, Orion 613
  Life of massive star 26
  Milky Way 14-15
  NGC 1566 (Seyfert galaxy) 13
  Omega 613
  Small stars 24
  Structure of nebula 24
Neck
  Acoustic guitar 512-513
  Anchisaurus 89
  Calligraphy character 445
  Corythosaurus 98
  Electric guitar 513
  Golf club 547
  Harp 511
  Horse 199
  Human 211, 224-225, 247, 258-259
  Iguanodon 97
  Pachycephalosaurus 100
  Rat 196
  Sauropodomorpha 88

Sculling oar 560
Stegoceras 101
Stegosaurus 92
Stringed instruments 510
Tenor saxophone 509
Theropod 84
Violin 510
Necking 381
Neck roll motor 609
Neck tilt motor 609
Nectar 142, 160-161
Nectaries 141, 144-145
  160-161
Needles
  Bishop pine 124
  Pine 124-125
  Scots pine 122
  Yew 123
Nefertiti Corona 37
Negative electric charge 316
Negative ions 308, 310
Neo-Baroque style 492-493
Neo-Byzantine style 492-493
Neoclassical style 478-483, 496
Neodymium 310
Neo-Greek style 492-493
Neo-Gothic style 492-493
Neon 35, 311
Nepenthes mirabilis 161
Nephron 256
Neptune 31, 50-51
Neptunides polychromus 12
Neptunium 311
Nerve
  Ampullar 242
  Bronchial 254
  Cervical 238
  Cochlear 243
  Common peroneal 238
  Cranial 238
  Cutaneous 238
  Deep peroneal 238
  Digital 251
  Femoral 238
  Hypoglossal 244
  Lingual 244
  Lumbar 238
  Median 238
  Optic 240
  Posterior tibial 238
  Pudendal 238
  Radial 238
  Sacral 238
  Sciatic 238
  Spinal 223, 238
  Superficial peroneal 238
  Superior laryngeal 244
  Thoracic 238
  Ulnar 231, 238
  Vestibular 243
  Vestibulocochlear 243
Nerve cell 217, 237, 239
Nerve cord 175
Nerve fibre 233
Nerve ring 175
Nervous system 176, 238-239
Nervous tissue 166
Netball 534-535
Neural spine
  Arsinoitherium 104
  Bony fish 180
  Brachiosaurus 90
  Eryops 81
  Euoplocephalus 95
  87
  Iguanodon 96
  Parasaurolophus 98
  Plateosaurus 88
  Stegoceras 100-101
  Stegosaurus 93

Toxodon 106
Triceratops 102
Tuojiangosaurus 93
Tyrannosaurus 85
Neurofilament 239
Neuron 239
Neurotransmitter 239
Neutralization 312
Neutrino 22
Neutron 22, 28
Neutrons 308, 309, 310
Neutron stars 28-29, 26-27
New Guinea 265
New Moon 41
New State Paper Office 482
Newton (N) 320
Newton, Isaac 320
Newton meter 320-321
Newton's Motion laws 320-321
Newts 182
New World monkeys 202-203
New Zealand 265, 272
NGC 1566 (Seyfert galaxy) 13
NGC 2997 (spiral galaxy) 12
NGC 4406 (elliptical galaxy) 11
NGC 4486 (elliptical galaxy) 12
NGC 5236 (spiral galaxy) 11
NGC 5754 (colliding galaxies) 9
NGC 6656 (globular cluster) 21
NGC 6822 (irregular galaxy) 11
Nib types 444
Niche
  Ancient Roman building 462
  Asian temple 491
  Baroque church 480
  Cathedral dome 487
  Gothic church 471-472
  Islamic building 488
  Medieval building 467
  Neoclassical building 482
  Renaissance building 476
Nickel 37, 49, 281, 311
Nickel-iron 270
Nigella damascena 151
Nightshot control 583
Nile crocodile 186
Nimbostratus cloud 302
Nimbus cloud 302
Nineteenth-century buildings 479, 482, 492-493, 494
Nintendo Cube 579
Ninth-century building 490
Niobe Planitia 36, 37
Niobium 310
Nippers 450
Nipple
  Human 211
  Marsupials 206
Nissl body 239
Nitrate ions 512
Nitrates 160
Nitrogen
  Atmospheric composition 301
  Helix Nebula 17
  Mars' atmosphere 43
  Periodic table 311
  Pluto's atmosphere 51
  Venus' atmosphere 37
Nitrogen dioxide gas 312
Nobelium 311
Noble gases 310-311
Nock 548

Noctis Labryrinthus 42, 43
Nocturnal mammals 104
Node
  Bamboo 131
  Brassavola nodosa 162
  Canadian pond weed 158-159
  Couch grass 113
  Dicotyledons 127
  Horsetail 120
  Ice-plant 129
  Live-for-ever 129
  Modern buildings 497
  Rhizome 155
  Rock stonecrop 128
  Rose stem 130
  Stems 154
  Stolon 154
  Strawberry 128
Node of Ranvier 228, 239
Nodule fields 299
Nodules 128
Noggin 602
Nokia 3310 588, 589
Nokia 5510 588
Nonconformity 276
Non-drive end 317
Nonesuch House 467
Non-explosive eruptions 272
Non-flowering plants 68
Non-metals 310
Non-return valve 367
Non-skid tyre 337
North America
  Appalachian Mountains 62
  Cretaceous period 72-73
  Earth's physical features 264
  Jurassic period 70
  Late Carboniferous period 66
  Middle Ordovician period 64
  Quaternary period 76-77
  Tertiary period 74-75
  Triassic period 68
North American Cordillera 71
North American period 56
North American plate 59
North Atlantic current 296
North Atlantic Gyre 296
North Atlantic Ocean 59, 71, 75
North East Africa 64
North-easterly wind 303
North-east monsoon 297
North-east trade winds 300
North Equatorial Belt 45
North Equatorial current 296-297
Northern Hemisphere 296-297
North Galactic Pole 15
North magnetic polar region 28
North Pacific current 296
North Pacific Gyre 296
North polar aurora 45
North polar ice-cap 43
North Pole
  Atmospheric circulation and winds 300
  Coriolis force 297
  Jupiter 44
  Mars 42
  Mercury 34
  The Moon 40
  Neptune 50
  Pluto 51
  Pulsar 28
  Saturn 46
  Uranus 48
  Venus 36

650

North rim 277
North Temperate Zone 45
North Tropical Zone 45
North-westerly wind 303
Nose
　B-17 bomber 408
　Concorde 416-417
　Iron 594
　Horse 198
　Human 211-212, 244-245
　Lion 194
　Lockheed Electra airliner 406
　Rabbit 196
　Rat 196
Noseband 554, 555
Nose clip 558
Nose cone 418, 560
Nose cover 557
Nose cowling 412
Nose-end bogie 327
Nose-gear
　ABV light aircraft 424-425
　Concorde 417
　Tornado 420
Nose horn 102, 103
Nose-ring
　Avro biplane 403
　Blackburn monoplane 400
Nose-wheel
　ABV light aircraft 425
　Curtiss biplane 398
　Pegasus XL SE microlight 426
　Tornado 420
Nostril
　Bird 188
　Chick 193
　Crocodilians 186
　Dolphin 205
　Domestic cat 195
　Elephant 200
　Frog 182
　Gorilla 203
　Horse 198
　Human 213
　Kangaroo 207
　Lion 194
　Lizard 184
　Monkey 202
　Rat 196
　Rattlesnake 185
　Seal 204
Nostril pocket 80
Note pad button 568
Notes 502, 506
Nothosaurian reptile 69
Notre Dame de Paris 470, 475
Nozzle
　Concorde 416-417
　Jet engines 418-419
　Tornado 421
　Vacuum cleaner 593
NPT 301 turbojet 418
N-type silicon 605
Nu Andromedae 19
Nucellus 147
Nuchal plate 187
Nuchal ring 95
Nuchal shield 187
Nuclear energy 314
Nuclear fusion
　Massive stars 26
　Small stars 24
　Stars 22
　Sun 32
Nuclear "hunter-killer" submarine 396-397
Nuclear power station 314
Nuclear reactions 315
Nucleolus 216, 239
Nucleoplasm 216
Nucleus
　Asteroids, comets, and meteoroids 52-53

Atoms and molecules 308, 309
Chlamydomonas sp. 116
Cnidocytes 167
Egg cell 606, 607
Endosperm 147
Fungal cell 115
Galaxies 12-13
Generalized human cell 216
Muscle cell 228
Neuron 239
Overhead view of our galaxy 14
Palisade mesophyll cell 139
Pollen 122
Pollen tube 147
Roots 132
Scots pine pollen 122
Side view of our galaxy 14
Synergid 147
Thalassiosira sp. 116

O

O₂ sensor 355
Oak 74
Oar
　Greek and Roman ships 372-373
　Junk 376
　Longboat 380
　Viking ships 374-375
Oarweed 116-117
Oasis 283
Oberon 48
Objective aperture 610
Objective lens 610, 611
Obiect mass 320
Oblique-slip fault 61
Oboe 504-505, 508
Obovate leaves 137
Observer's cockpit 403
Observer's windscreen 404
Obsidian 275, 306
Obturator canal 224
Obturator membrane 224
Occipital bone 202, 220
Occipital condyle 107, 194, 220
Occipital lobe 236-237
Occluded fronts 302-303
Ocean currents 296-297
Ocean floor 298-299, 266-267
Oceanic crust
　Earth's crust 58-59
　Mineralization zones 281
　Mountain building 62-63
　Ocean floor 298
Oceanic seahorse 180

Ocean ridges 58-59
Oceans 39, 296-297, 301
Ocean trenches
　Ocean floor features 299
　Offshore currents 296
　Plate movements 58
Oceanus Procellarum 40
Ocellus 176
Octafoil 471
Octagon 622
Octahedron 623
Octastyle portico 462
Octave 557
Octopus 176-177
Ocular end 377
Oculus
　Ancient Roman building 462-463
　Gothic church 472-473
　Medieval building 466, 469
　Neoclassical building 483
　Roman corbita 372
Odd-toed ungulates 198-199
Odontoblast 247
Oesophagus
　Barnacle 173
　Bird 189
　Brachiosaurus 91
　Butterfly 169
　Chimpanzee 202
　Cow 198
　Dogfish 179
　Dolphin 205
　Domestic cat 195
　Elephant 200
　Human 212, 215, 245, 248
　Lizard 185
　Rabbit 196
　Snail 177
　Spider 170
　Starfish 174
　Tortoise 187
Off-road motorcycle racing 368
Offshore deposits 294
Ogee 595
Ogee arch 488
Ogee-arched motif 490
Ogee curve 472
Ogee-curved dome 486
Ogee-curved roof 489
Ogee moulding 475-477, 481
Ogee tracery 493
Ohms 316
Oil
　Clutches 366
　Diesel trains 326
　Energy storage 315
　Mineral resources 280-281
Oil bottle dripfeed 336
Oil cooler 347, 364, 605
Oil-cooler duct 415
Oil-cooler matrix 347
Oil damper 364
Oil deposit 281
Oil deposit formation 57
Oil deposits 281
Oil dipstick 344
Oil duct 151
Oil feed 411
Oil feed pipe 345, 366, 367
Oil filter
　1-litre VTEC engine 354
　Ford diesel engine 347
　Jaguar V12 engine 345
　Turbofan engine 418
　Turboprop engine 419

Oil-fired power station 315
Oil formation 280-281
Oil paints 436-437
Oil pipe banjo 345
Oil-pressure regulating valve 419
Oil pump
　Humber engine 343
　Mid West single-rotor engine 411
　Velocette OHV engine 367
　Weslake speedway bike 369
Oil rig 315
Oil side lamp 336-337
Oil sump
　Honda VF750 364
　Humber engine 343
　Modern engines 344-345
　Velocette OHV engine 367
Oil tank
　Bell-47 helicopter components 422
　Harley-Davidson FLHS Electra Glide 363
　Lockheed Electra airliner 406
　Turbofan engine 418
　Turboprop engine 419
Oil traps 281
Oildsmobile 336-337
Old World monkeys 202-203
Olecranon 85
Olenellus 64
Oleo lock-jack 414
Olfactory bulb 181
Oligocene epoch
　Fossil record 70
　Geological timescale 57
Olivine
　Igneous rock 267
　Meteorites 52
　Silicates 269
Olivine gabbro 275
Olympus BX51W1 optical microscope 610
Olympus Mons 42-43
Omasum 198
Omega Centauri 21
Omicron Andromedae 19
Omicron1 Canis Majoris 21
Omicron2 Canis Majoris 21
Omicron Orionis 18
Omicron Sagittarii 21
Omnivores 84
Omohyoid muscle 229
One-toed ungulates 198
Onion dome 467, 486-488
Onion-skin weathering 282
On-screen display 577
Onyx 268
Oocyte 607
Oogonium 117
Oort Cloud 52
Oospheres 116 117
　Fern 121
　Moss 119
Ooze 298
Open cluster 16
Open gun mounting 394
Opera House, Paris 493
Opera House, Sydney 496, 499
Opercula 180
Opercular bone 181
Operculum
　Bony fish 180-181
　Cnidocyte 167
　Giant stick insect eggs 192
　Indian stick insect eggs 192

Leaf insect eggs 192
　Moss 119
Ophidia 184
Ophiothix fragilis 175
Ophiuchus 19, 20
Ophthalmos 372
Opisthodomos 461
Opisthosoma 170-171
Opossums 206, 207
Opponens digiti minimi muscle 231
Opponens pollicis muscle 231
Optical map of our galaxy 14-15
Optical microscope 610
Optic chiasma 236
Optic disc 240-241
Optic nerve 240
Option connector 571
Opus incertum 463, 465
Opus quadratum 465
Opus sectile mosaic 488-489
Oral arm 167
Oral cavity 248
Oral disc 166-167
Oral surface 175
Orange citrine 271
Orange halite 269, 277
Orange light 318
Orangutans 202
Ora serrata 241
Orbit
　Baroque church 480
　Cathedral dome 487
　Gothic church 471
　Neoclassical building 479
　Nineteenth-century building 493
　Renaissance building 477
Orbicularis oculi muscle 226, 229
Orbicularis oris muscle 228-229, 245
Orbicular lamina 158
Orbicular leaves 137
Orbit
　Acanthostega 80
　Ankylosaurus 94
　Archaeopteryx 85
　Arsinoitherium 104
　Australopithecus 108
　Baryonyx 83
　Bear 194
　Bird 189
　Bony fish 181
　Camarasaurus 91
　Chimpanzee 202
　Diplodocus 90
　Elephant 201
　Eryops 80
　Euoplocephalus 94
　Heterodontosaurus 83
　Homo erectus 108
　Homo habilis 108
　Homo sapiens 108
　Horse 199
　Hyaenodon 107
　Iguanodon 96
　Lambeosaurus 99
　Lion 194
　Lizard 184
　Opossum 106
　Outer planetary 31
　Pachycephalosaurus 100
　Panoplosaurus 94
　Parasaurolophus 99
　Plateosaurus 88
　Platypus 206
　Prenocephale 100
　Protoceratops 102
　Rattlesnake 185
　Rhesus monkey 202
　Smilodon 107

Stars of northern skies 18
Stars of southern skies 20
Stegoceras 100-101
Styracosaurus 102
Toxodon 106
Triceratops 103
Tyrannosaurus 84
Orbital artery 179
Orbital cavity 220
Orbital motion 31, 32
Orbital plane
　Earth 38
　Jupiter 44
　Mars 42
　Mercury 34
　Neptune 50
　Pluto 51
　Saturn 46
　The Moon 40
　Uranus 48
　Venus 36
Orbits 30, 508-509, 510
Orbital speed (velocity)
　Mercury 34
　Solar System 30-31
Orb spider 171
Orchestra layout 504-505
Orchestral instruments 504-505
　Musical notation 502-503
Orchestras 504-505
Orchestra shell 495
Orchids 126, 133, 162
Orcinus orca 205
Ordovician period 64-65
　Fossil record 279
　Geological time 56
　Primitive life 78
Organ 514, 502-503
Organic compound 313
Organic material deposition 281
Organic remains 276-277, 280
Organ of Corti 243
Oriel window 467
"O Ring" drive chain 366
Orion 18, 21, 24
Orion Arm 14
Orion Nebula 15, 17, 18
Orion's belt 15-16
Ornament
　Asian building 491
　Baroque church 479, 481
　Cathedral dome 487
　Islamic building 488
　Neoclassical building 483
Ornamental strip 586, 587
Ornithischians 68, 82-83
　Marginocephalians 100
　Ornithopods 96
　Stegosaurs 92-93
　Thyreophorans 92
Ornithomimosaurs 86-87
Ornithopoda 83
Ornithopods 96-97, 98-99
Orobanche sp. 163
Orogenesis 62-63
Oropharynx 245
Orpiment 270-271
Orthoclase 269, 271
Orthorhombic system 270
Os 258-259
Oscillating cylinder 390
Oscillating electric field 318
Oscillating magnetic field 318
Oscillating steam engine 390-391
Osculum 166

Osmium 311
Ossicles 79, 174
Ossicles of middle ear 242
Osteichthyes 180
Osteocyte 225
Osteolaemus tetraspis 82
Osteon 225
Ostiole 117
Ostium
  Crayfish 173
  Sea anemone 167
  Spider 170
  Sponge 166
Ostrich 188, 193
Otters 194
Otto cycle 342
Otto, Nikolaus 342
Ouranosaurus 97
Outboard ammunition-
  feed blister 409
Outboard elevon 421
Outbox icon 576
Outer bud scale 134
Outer casing fitment 597
Outer core 38-39, 41
Outer ear
  Brachiosaurus 91
  Stegoceras 101
  Stegosaurus 92
Outer electrons 310-311
Outer envelope 25-26
Outer fertilized floret 142
Outer jib downhaul 385
Outer jib halyard 385
Outer jib sheet 385
Outer jib stay 382
Outer lamella 225
Outer mantle
  Jupiter 44-45
  Saturn 46-47
Outer tepals
  Glory lily 143
  Lily 140
  Monocotyledons 126
Outfield 536
Outlet manifold 411
Output tray 574
Outrigger 373, 377
Outwash fan 286
Outwash plain 287
Outwash terrace 286
Ovary
  Barnacle 173
  Bony fish 181
  Brachiosaurus 90
  Butterfly 169
  Chimpanzee 202
  Crayfish 173
  Dogfish 179
  Epigeal germination
    153
  Fertilization 146-147
  Flower 140-143
  Gallimimus 86
  Human 258-259
  Hypogeal germination
    152
  Insect pollination 144
  Lizard 185
  Rose 131
  Spider 170
  Succulent fruit 148-149
  Tortoise 188
Ovate leaf
  Ice-plant 129
  Live-for-ever 129
  Strawberry 128
Ovda Regio 36, 57
Oven compartment 597
Overarm pass 535
Overhand knot 588
Overhand serve 534
Overhead camshaft
  engine 368
Overhead pass 532
Overhead valve engine
  (OHV) 367, 369
Over-reach boot 555
Overs 538

Oversailing fascia 477,
  482, 486
Overthrust fold 61
Overturned fold 61
Oviduct
  Barnacle 173
  Brachiosaurus 90
  Butterfly 169
  Crayfish 173
  Dogfish 179
  Lizard 185
  Spider 170
  Tortoise 187
Ovolo 486
Ovolo moulding
  Cathedral dome 487
  Gothic church 472
  Neoclassical building
    480
Ovotestis 177
Ovules 140-143
  Bishop pine 124
  Dehiscent fruit 151
  Fertilization 146
  Pine 122
  Scots pine 122
  Smooth cypress 123
  Yew 123
Ovuliferous scales
  Bishop pine 124
  Pine 122
  Scots pine 122
  Smooth cypress 123
  Yew 123
Ovum
  Ancient Roman
    building 462
  Fertilization 146-147
  Scots pine 122
  Oxalis sp. 157
Oxbow lake 293
River features 290
River's stages 289
"Ox-eye" window
  Baroque church 479,
    481
  Cathedral dome 487
Oxides 268
Oxygen
  Atmospheric
    Atom 596
    Composition 301
  Early micro-organisms
    78
  Earth's composition 39
  Earth's crust 58
  Earth's formation 38, 64
  Helix Nebula 17
  Mars' atmosphere 43
  Mercury's atmosphere
    35
  Periodic table 311
  Photosynthesis 138
  Seed germination 152
  Structure of red
    supergiant 26
  Respiration 255
Oxygenated blood 255
Oxygen bottle 408
Oxygen group 311
Oyashio current 297
Oyster fungus 114
Oysters 176
Ozone 301
Ozone layer 300

P

Pachycephalosaurus 69,
  83, 100
Pachypteris sp. 68
Pachyrhinosaurus 103
Pacific coastline 293
Pacific Ocean 264-265,
  272
Pacific plate 59
Pacing races 554
Pacing sulky 554-555

Pacinian corpuscle 234-
  235
Pack-ice 296
Packing tissue
  Dicotyledon leaf 126
  Fern rachis 121
  Golden barrel cactus
    156
  Haworthia truncata 157
  Horsetail stem 120
  Leaf succulents 157
  Lithops bromfieldii 157
  Monocotyledon leaf 126
  Roots 132-133
  Stem 134-135
  Stem succulents 156
  String of hearts 157
  Water lily leaf 159
Padded coaming
  Avro biplane 403
  BE 2B bomber 404
Paddle
  Eurypterid fossil 79
  Kayak 560
Paddlesteamer
  19th century 390-391
  Iron 392-393
Paddle wheels 390-391,
  392
Padmakosa 489
Page key 590
Page locator 577
Pagoda 490
Pahoehoe 272
Painted Desert 277
Painting knives 436, 442
Painting tools 436
Pair-cast cylinder 343
Paired cylinder 342
Palace of Westminster
  492-493
Palaeocene epoch
  Fossil record 279
  Geological timescale 57
Palaeontology 278
Palaeozoic era
  Fossil record 279
  Geological time 56
Palais de Fontainebleau
  476
Palais de Versailles 482
Palatine Chapel,
  Aix-le-Chapelle 484
Palatine tonsil 212, 244-
  245
Palatoglossal arch 244
Palazzo Stanga 482
Palazzo Strozzi 474-475
Pale calcite 26
Pale feldspar 26
Palette 143, 436
Palette knife 436
Paling 466, 477
Palisade mesophyll 126,
  159
Palladium 311
Palm
  Danforth anchor 386
  Hand 211
  Roman anchor 372
Palm M500 PDA 568-569
Palmar arch 253
Palmaris longus tendon
  231
Palmar vein 253
Palmate leaves 130, 136
Palmate venation 129
Palmette 460-461, 479-480
Palmoxylon 74
Pam-D upper stage
  booster 615
Pamirs 265
Pampas 264
Panavia Tornado GR1A
  420-421
Pancreas
  Bird 189

Bony fish 181
Chimpanzee 202
Dogfish 179
Domestic cat 195
Frog 182
Human 215, 249
Rabbit 196
Tortoise 187
Pandas 194
Panduriform leaves 136
Pane 494
Panel 485
  Asian building 491
  Baroque church 479-
    481
  Cathedral dome 487
  Gothic building 473
  Islamic building 488
  Medieval building 466,
    469
  Modern building 496-
    498
  Neoclassical building
    478-479
  Nineteenth-century
    building 493
  Renaissance building
    475
  Twentieth-century
    building 494
Panel board connector
  570
Pangaea 66, 68-69, 70
Panniers 360, 361, 362
Panoplosaurus 94
Panicle 131
Pantheon 462-463
Pantile 464, 482
Pantograph 328, 330
Pan troglodytes 202
Paper
  Acrylic paint 442
  Calligraphy 444, 445
  Pastels 440
  Printing processes 446,
    447
  Watercolours 438
Paper ejection roller 573
Paper feed components
  575
Paper feed rollers 573
Paper hopper 574
Paper output stacker 574
Paper stumps 440
Paper support 575
Paper tray 573
Papilla
  Flower 140
  Hair 235
  Renal 256
  Tongue 244
Papillary muscle 251
Pappus 142
Papyriform column 459
Parabellum machine-gun
  405
Parabolic dune 283
Paraboloid roof 496, 499
Parachute seed dispersal
  150
Paradise palm 126
Paragaster 166
Parallel dunes 283
Parallelogram 622
Parallel printer port 567
Parallel river drainage
  288
Parallel shaft 382
Parallel venation 126
Parana River 264
Parapet
  Ancient Roman
    building 465
  Asian building 491
  Baroque church 481
  Dome 486
  Gothic church 470-472
  Islamic tomb 489
  Medieval building 467

Neoclassical building
  478, 483
Nineteenth-century
  building 493
Twentieth-century
  building 494
Parapet rail 483
Paraphysis 117, 119
Parasaurolophus 98-99
Parasitic anemone 166
Parasitic cone 272-273
Parasitic plants 162-163
Parasitic volcano 275
Paraxeiresia 373
Parcelling 388
Parchment
  Gilding 432
  Imitation 445
Pareiasaur 81
Parenchyma
  Dicotyledon leaf 126
  Dryland plants 156-157
  Fern rachis 121
  Golden barrel cactus
    156
  Horsetail stem 120
  Monocotyledon leaf 126
  Pine stem 125
  Roots 132
  Stems 134-135
  Water lily leaf 159
Parent plant 154
Parietal bone
  Bony fish 181
  Chimpanzee 202
  Human 220-221
Parietal fenestra 102
Parietal lobe 236-237
Parieto-occipital sulcus
  236-237
Parietosquamosal frill
  102-103
Paripteris 66
Paris Metro 328
Paroccipital process
  Iguanodon 96
  Plateosaurus 88
Parrel
  Dhow 376
  Longboat 380
  Sailing warship 377
  Viking karv 375
Parrel beads 384
Parrel tackle 376
Parthenon 461
Partial solar eclipse 32
Partial veil 115
Particle attraction 307
Particle properties 318
Passiflora caerulea 130
Passing pace 473
Passion flower 130
Passive stack vents 602
Pastels 440-441
Pastern 198-199, 554
Pasteur 41
Patagonia 264
Patella
  Domestic cat 195
  Elephant 201
  Hare 197
  Horse 199
  Human 219
  Platypus 206
  Rhesus monkey 202
  Scorpion 170
  Spider 171
Patellar surface 225
Patera
  Neoclassical building
    480
  Renaissance building
    476
Pause button 608
Paved floor 492
Pavilion 489, 495
Paving slab 499
Pavlova 57
Pavlovia 278

Pavo 20
Pavonis Mons 43
Paw 195
Pawl 380
Pawl slot 587
Paxton, J. 492-493
Pazzi Chapel 475
PCB *see* printed circuit
  board (PCB)
PC card adapter 574
PCI expansion slots 566,
  567
PCs 566
PDAs 568
Pea
  Dry fruit 150
  Danforth anchor 586
Peach 131, 148
Peacock 20
Peak halyard 380
Peat 280
Peccaries 198
Pecopteris 66
Pectineus muscle 225-
  226
Pectoral fin
  Bony fish 180-181
  Lamprey 178
Pectoral fin ray 181
Pectoralis major muscle
  226
Pedal board 514
Pedal cluster 340
Pedal-damper bar
  mechanism 516
Pedal disc 167
Pedal-driven bicycle 358
Pedal gland 177
Pedalia 372
Pedals
  Bass drum 518
  Bicycle 320, 358-359
  Eddy Merckx racing
    bicycle 360
  Harp 511
  Hi-hat cymbal 518
  Piano 514
  Rossin Italian time-trial
    bicycle 361
Pedal stop 514
Pedestal
  Ancient Roman
    building 462
  Baroque church 480-
    481
  Dome 484, 486-487
  French temple 485
  Harp 511
  Neoclassical building
    479
  Renaissance building
    476
Pedice 168
Pedicel
  Brassavola nodosa 162
  Clematis 131
  Dicotyledon flower 127
  Dry fruit 150-151
  Fertilization 146-147
  Florists'
    chrysanthemum 129
  Flowers 140-141, 143
  Fruit development 146-
    147
  Oxalis sp. 157
  Pitcher plant 113
  Rose 131
  Rowan 131
  Russian vine 131
  Succulent fruit 148-149
  Sycamore 131
  Vegetative reproduction
    154
  Water lily 159
Pedicle of vertebra 223
Pedicle valve 278
Pediment
  Ancient Greek building
    460

Ancient Roman
  building 462-465
Baroque church 480-
  481
Neo-Baroque building
  495
Neoclassical building
  478
Renaissance building
  476
Pedipalp 170-171
Peduncle 140, 142-143
  Aechmea miniata 162
  Brassavola nodosa 162
  Everlasting pea 129
  Florists'
    chrysanthemum 129
  Indehiscent fruit 150
  Peach 151
  Peruvian lily 129
  Rowan 151
  Russian vine 131
  Succulent fruit 148-149
  Toadflax 129
  Vegetative reproduction
    154
  Wind-pollinated plant
    144
Peephole 412, 414
Pegasus 19, 20
Pegasus Quasar
  microlight 426-427
Pegasus XL SE microlight
  427
Peg-box 510-511
Pegmatite 26
Peg of vertebra 222
Pelagic clay 299
Pelecypoda 176
Peloneustes philarcus 71
Pelota 540
Peltetia canaliculata 116
Pelvic fin
  Bony fish 180-181
  Dogfish 179
Pelvis
  Bird 189
  Bony fish 181
  Dinosaur 81
  Domestic cat 195
  Elephant 201
  Hare 197
  Horse 199
  Human 256, 258, 259
  Kangaroo 206
  Lizard 184
  Platypus 206
  Rhesus monkey 202
  Seal 204
  Turtle 187
Penalty area 524
Penalty box 524
Penalty kick 550
Penalty spot 529, 540
Pencils 430
Pencil sharpener 450
Pencil slate sea urchin
  175
Pendentive 479, 484, 488
Penguins 188
Penis
  Barnacle 173
  Dolphin 205
  Human 211, 259
  Snail 177
Pennant number 397
Pennsylvanian period 56
Penny washer 383
Pens 430
Penstock 314
Pentagon 622
Pentaradiate symmetry
  174
Pentroof 490
Penumbra 32
Pepo 149
Pepper-pot lantern 481
Perch 180
Percolation 280

Percussion instruments
  516-517
Drums 518-519
Electronic 520
Orchestral
  arrangement 504-505
Perennials 128, 130-151
Pereopod 172-173
Perforated shroud 592
Perianth 140
Pericardial cavity 250
Pericarp 148
  Dry fruit 150-151
  Embryo development
    147
  Fruit development 146-
    147
  Succulent fruit 148-149
  Sycamore 151
Pericranium 237
Pericycle 127, 132
Periderm 125
Peridium 115
Perihelion 30-31
Perimeters 622
Perimeum 258
Periodic table 510-311
Periodontium 247
Periosteum 225
Peripheral camera 609
Peripheral nervous
  system 238
Peripteral temple 460-461
Periscope 396, 397
Perissodactyla 104, 198-
  199
Peristome tooth 119
Peristyle 461
Peritoneum 249, 257
Permeable limestone
  Caves 284-285
  Lake formation 292
Permeable rock 292
Permeable sandstone 292
Permian period 66-67
  Fossil record 279
  Geological time 57
Peroneal artery 253
Peroneus brevis muscle
  227, 233
Peroneus brevis tendon
  253
Peroneus longus muscle
  233
Peroxisome 217
Perseus 19, 20
Perseus Arm 14-15
Persian ivy 137
Personal computer 566-
  567
Personal digital assistants
  (PDAs) 568
Personal music 586-587
Personal System/2 (PS/2)
  port 567
Perspective drawing 431
Peru current 296
Peruvian lily 129
Petal moulding 480
Petals 140-143
  Clematis 131
  Colour 140, 144-145
  Dicotyledons 126-127
  Everlasting pea 129
  Fertilization 146
  Insect pollination 145
  Monocotyledons 126
  Peruvian lily 129
  Rose 131
  Water lily 159
Petavius 40
Petiole 128, 136-137
  Chusan palm 130
  Clematis 131
  Cobra lily 160
  Dicotyledons 127
  Everlasting pea 129
  Florists'

chrysanthemum 129
Horse chestnut 130
Kedrostis africana 113
Maidenhair tree 123
Monocotyledons 126-
  127
Mulberry 130
Oralis sp. 157
Passion flower 130
Peach 131
Rock stonecrop 128
Seedling 153
Strawberry 128
String of hearts 157
Tree fern 112
Tree mallow 151
Vegetative reproduction
  154
Venus fly trap 160
Water hyacinth 158
Water lily 159
Wind-pollinated plant
  144
Petiolule 137
Petrol 315
Peugeot, Armand 354
Phacops 64
Phaeophyta 16
Phaet 21
Phalaenopsis sp. 126
Phalanges
  Cow 198
  Crocodile 186
  Diplodocus 90
  Domestic cat 195
  Elephant 90
  Eryops 80-81
  Frog 183
  Hare 197
  Horse 198-199
  Kangaroo 206
  Lizard 184
  Parasaurolophus 99
  Plateosaurus 88
  Platypus 206
  Rhesus monkey 202
  Seal 204
  Stegoceras 100-101
  Triceratops 102-103
  Turtle 187
  Tyrannosaurus 84
Phalanx
  African elephant 201
  Archaeopteryx 85
  Arsinoitherium 104
  Baryonyx 85, 87
  Horse 105
  Human 219, 230
  Plateosaurus 88
  Stegoceras 100
  Struthiomimus 87
  Toxodon 107
Phallus impudicus 114
Phanerozoic eon 279
Pharyngeal tubercle 220
Pharynx
  Bony fish 180-181
  Dogfish 179
  Human 212, 244
  Sea anemone 167
  Sea urchin 175
Phascolarctos cinereus 207
Phaseolus sp. 153
Phases of the Moon 41
Phekda 19
Phellem
  Pine root 125
  Stem 134-135
  Woody dicotyledon 127
Phi Andromedae 19
Phidias 35
Philippine plate 59
Phillips, Horatio 402
Philtrum 213
Phiomia 104
Phloem 158
  Bishop pine 124-125

Clubmoss stem 120
Dicotyledons 126-127
Dodder host 163
Epiphytic orchid 162
Fern roots 121
Horsetail stem 120
Marram grass 113
Monocotyledons 126-
  127
Parasite host 163
Photosynthesis 138
Pine root/stem 125
Radicle 152
Root 132-133
Sieve tube 134
Stem 134-135
Water hyacinth root 158
Water lily leaf 159
Phloem fibres 134-135
Phloem sieve tube 134
Phobos 42
Phoebe Regio 36
Phoenicopterus ruber 190
Phoenix 19, 20
Phorusrhacus 74
Phosphates 269
Phosphate/sugar band 216
Phosphor imaging screen
  611
Phosphor lining cell 584
Phosphorus 311
Photomicrographs of skin
  and hair 255
Photons 518
Photo print button 570
Photo select button 575
Photosphere 32-33
Photosynthesis 112, 116,
  154, 156, 158-159
Carnivorous plants 160-
  161
Organelle 116, 139
Photosynthetic cells 139
Bishop pine 124
Coconut palm stem 135
Water lily leaf 159
Photosynthetic region 157
Photosynthetic tissue
Cacti 156
Dicotyledon leaf 126
Horsetail stem 120
Marram grass 113
Monocotyledon leaf 126
Rush stem 135
Photovoltaic cell 605
Photovoltaic panel 603
Phyla 116
Phyllode 160
Phylum 16
Physalis peruviana 149
Physeter catodon 205
Physical weathering 282
Physics symbols 621
Pi Canis Majoris 21
Piccolo 504, 508
Pictor 21
Pier 484
Ancient Egyptian
  temple 459
Ancient Roman
  building 465
Baroque church 480
Gothic church 470
Medieval building 467-
  469
Renaissance building
  476-477
Twentieth-century
  building 494-495

Pier buttress 469-471, 486
Pietra dura inlay 489
Piezoelectric inkjet
  printhead 575
Pigments 433, 434, 436
Pigs 104, 198
Pilaster
  74-gun ship 381
  Ancient Greek building
    461
  Ancient Roman
    building 465-465
  Asian temple 490-491
  Baroque church 479-
    481
  Cathedral dome 484,
    487
  Gothic church 471
  Neoclassical building
    478, 483
  Renaissance building
    477
  Twin bollards 387
Pileus 114-115
Pillar
  Asian buildings 490-491
  Domed roof 486
  Gothic church 472
  Ironclad 393
  Renaissance building
    477
Pillow lava 298
Pilotis 494
Pilot light 594
Pilot's cockpit
  LVG CVI fighter 405
  Tornado 420
Pilot's cradle 398-399
Pilot's seat
  Avro biplane 402
  Curtiss biplane 398
Pegasus Quasar
  microlight 427
Pin
  Capstan 387
  Dome timbering 486
Pinaccocyte 166
Pineal body 212, 236
Pine hull 375
Pines 122, 124-125
Pinguicula caudata 161
Pinion
  Benz Motorwagen 335
  Ford Model T 338
  Hand drill 601
Pinna
  Elephant 201
  Everlasting pea 129
  Fern 121
  Gorilla 203
  Human 242-243
  Kangaroo 207
  Leaves 136-137
  Rabbit 196
  Rat 196
  Sago palm 123
  Tree fern 112-113
Pinnacle
  Baroque church 479,
    481
  Gothic church 470, 472-
    473
  Medieval church 469
  Nineteenth-century
    building 493
  Renaissance building
    476
Pinnate leaves 136-137
  Mahonia 130-131
  Rowan 130
  Sago palm 123
Pinned sheepshank 389
Pinnipedia 204
Pinnule 121, 137
Pinocytotic vesicle 217
Pintle strap 378
Pinus muricata 72, 124-
  125
Pinus sp. 122, 124-125

Pinus sylvestris 122
Pi Pegasi 19
Pipette 312
Pips 148-149
Pi Sagittarii 21
Pisanosaurus 68
Pisces 19, 20
Pisces Austrinus 19, 20
Pisiform bone 230
Piste 556, 557
Pistol shooting 548
Piston
  Disc brake 365
  Early engines 342-343
  Ford diesel engine 347
  Mid West two-stroke
    engine 410
  Modern engines 344-
    345
  Relief-printing press
    449
  Steam locomotive 324
  Two-stroke engine 366
  Velocette OHV engine
    367
  Volkswagen Beetle 340
Piston engines 410-411,
  424
Piston rod 324, 334, 390
Piston valves
  Brass instruments 506
  Cornet 507
  "Ellerman Lines" steam
    locomotive 525
  Flugelhorn 507
  Stringed instruments
    510
  Trumpet 506
  Tuba 507
Pisum sativum 150
Pitatus 40
Pitch
  Brass instruments 506
  Drums 518
  Musical notation 502
  Percussion instruments
    516
Propeller action 390
Screw thread angle 320
Woodwind instruments
  508
Pitched roof
  Ancient Roman
    building 462, 464
  Gothic church 471-472
  Medieval building 466-
    468
  Nineteenth-century
    building 492
  Renaissance building
    476-477
  Twentieth-century
    building 495
Pitcher 556
Pitcher plants 113, 160-
  161
Pitches
  Australian rules football
    528
  Baseball 556
  Cricket 538
  Gaelic football 529
  Lacrosse 540
Pitching wedge
  Baseball 557
  Golf 547
Pitfall traps 160
Pith
  Apical meristem 134
  Bishop pine stem 125
  Dicotyledon stem 127
  Epiphytic orchid 162
  Horsetail stem 120
  Monocotyledon root 127
  Pine stem 125
  Stems 134-135
Pith cavity 135

653

Pitot head
ARV light aircraft 425
BAe-146 jetliner
components 412
Bell-47 helicopter 422
Concorde 416-417
Hawker Tempest
fighter 409
LVG CVI fighter 405
Schweizer helicopter
423
Tornado 420
Pitot mast 407
Pituitary gland 212, 236
Pivot
Astrolabe 377
BAe-146 jetliner
components 414
Drum brake 365
Sundial 377
Viking ships 374-375
Pixel 570, 571
Place kick 550
Placenta
Dry fruit 150-151
Fern pinnule 121
Human 260
Succulent fruit 148-149
Placental mammals 74, 104
Placer deposits 280
Plagioclase feldspar 275
Plains viscacha 197
Planck 41
Plane shapes 622
Planetary nebula
Nebulae and star
clusters 17
Small stars 24-25
Planetary orbits 30-31
Planetary rotation 30
Planets
Jupiter 44-45
Mars 42-43
Mercury 34-35
Neptune 50-51
Pluto 50-51
Saturn 46-47
Solar System 30-31
Uranus 48-49
Venus 36-37
Planking
Ironclad 393
Longboat 380
Roman corbita 373
Sailing warship 377
Tea clipper 392
Plantar calcaneonavicular
ligament 252
Plant bodies 116
Plant capital 459
Plant-eating dinosaurs 68, 70
Plant matter 280
Plant remains
Fossils 278-279
Mineral resources 280
Sedimentary rocks 276
Plants 56, 66
Electromagnetic
radiation 314
Flowering 57, 70, 72
Fossil record 279
Non-flowering 68
Plant variety 112-113
Plasma 306
Plasma display 584
Plasma screen 584
Plaster 452, 464-465
Plasterboard 602
Plaster bumper 354
Plastic fletch 548
Plastic front wings 354
Plastic insulator 316, 317
Plastic rackets 544
Plastid 116
Platanus x acerifolia 134
Platband 481

Plate
Etching press 477
Plywood roof deck 603
Motorcycle clutch 366
"O Ring" drive chain
366
Plateau
Neptune's rings 50
Structure of Neptune 51
Plateaus 276-277
Plate clip 587
Plate movements 58-59
Faults and folds 60
Mountain building 62-63
Platen 449
Plateosaurus 69, 88-89
Plate tectonics 58-59
Platform
Cathedral dome 487
Early tram 332
Medieval building 467-468
Modern building 498
Platform diving 558
Platform stage 477
Platinum 311
Plat lesene 480
Plato 40
Platypus 206-207
Platysma 229
Play button 585
Play control 587
Player's bench
American football 526
Basketball 532
Handball 535
Ice hockey 550
Volleyball 534
Playhead 587
Play/pause button 587
Play/pause control 577, 587
Playstation 2 579
Plaza 498
Pleiades 14, 16, 19, 20
Pleistocene epoch
Fossil record 279
Geological timescale 57
Pleistocene period 76
Plenum chamber 344-345
Plenum ring 418
Pleopod 172
Plesiochelys latiscutata 73
Plesiosaurs 70-71
Pleurotus pulmonarius
114
Plica circulare 249
Plicate lamina 127
Pliers 521
Plinth
Baroque church 480
French temple 485
Islamic tomb 489
Modern building 499
Neoclassical building
479, 483
Renaissance building
476
Twentieth-century
building 494-495
Pliocene epoch
Fossil record 279
Geological timescale 57
Plough anchor 386
Plug-ins 521
Plug lead conduit 337
Plugs 272-273
Igneous rock structures
274
Plumage 188
Plume 45
Plumose anemone 166
Plumule 147, 152-153
Plunge 60
Plunge pool 289, 291
Pluto 31, 50-51

Plutonium 310-311
Plywood roof deck 603
Plywood skin 404
Pneumatic tyres 358, 555
Podetium 114
Podium 463, 499
Point
Angling hook 562
Cricket 538
Double bass bow 511
Sailmaker's fid 584
Sculpting tool 452-453
Violin bow 510
Point bar
Mississippi Delta 291
River's stages 289
Pointed arch 466, 467,
469, 472
Pointed hog hair brush
434
Pointed riffler 454
Pointed sable brush 444
Pointing 383
Poison duct 170
Poison gland
Octopus 176
Spider 170
Polacanthus 95
Polar band 36
Polar body 606, 607
Polar bottom water 296
Polar easterlies 300
Polar fronts 302
Polar hood 36
Polaris 14, 18-19
Polar jet stream 300
Polar nuclei 146
Poles 297, 300
Pole star 14, 18
Pole vault 542
Polian vesicle 175
Political map of the world
616-617
Poll 199
Pollen 140, 142, 144-145
Dicotyledon flower 126
Fertilization 146-147
Pollen-forming structures
122
Pollen grains 144-145
Fertilization 146-147
Pine 122
Scots pine 122
Pollen sac wall 144
Pollen tubes
Fertilization 146-147
Scots pine 146-147
Pollination 144-145, 122
Pollux 18, 21
Polonium 311
Polycarbonate plastic bin
592
Polyester 388
Polygala chamaebuxus
144
Polygnotus 35
Polygonum
baldschuanicum 131
Polyhedral dome 486-487
Polypropylene rope 388
Polythene 306
Polytrichum commune 119
Polyurethane insulation
603
Pome 131, 149
Pommel 554
Pond weeds 158
Pons 212, 236-237
Poop break 373
Poop deck
74-gun ship 381
Iron paddlesteamer 392
Roman corbita 373
Poop rail
74-gun ship 381
Wooden sailing ship
378
Poor metals 310-311
Popchu-Sa Temple 490

Popliteal artery 253
Popliteal fossa 210
Porch 470-471
Porcupines 196-197
Pore
Bishop pine needle 124
Blackberry 147
Dryland plants 156-157
Elder stem 130
Epigeal germination
153
False fruit 148
Gas exchange 158, 158
Golden barrel cactus
156
Haworthia truncata 157
Leaf 138-139
Liverwort 118
Monocotyledon leaf 126
Nuclear membrane 217
Perennial bark 130-131
Pollen grain 144-145
Seed 153
Sponge 166
Water absorption 150,
155
Wetland plants 158
Woody plants 130-131
Woody stems 134
Porifera 166
Porocyte 166
Porous limestone 284
Porous stipe 114
Porphyritic andesite 275
Porpoises 204
Porrima 21
Porsche, Ferdinand 340
Port
Trojan two-stroke
engine 342
Wooden sailing ship
379
Portable CD player 587
Portable minidisc player
586
Portal 476, 480
Portal vein 252
Port bower anchor 377,
395
Port foremast 376
Porthole
Battleship 394
Dome 487
Frigate 397
Portico
Ancient Greek building
460-461
Ancient Roman
building 462-463
Neoclassical building
482-485
Renaissance building
475
Portugal 331
Portuguese bowline 388
Position guide 447
Positive electric charge
316
Positive ions 308, 310
Positive metal comb 316
Positive terminal 316, 317
Positron 22
Post 481, 486
Postabdominal spine 169
Postacetabular process 82
Postcentral gyrus 237
Post-crural musculature
90
Posterior antebrachial
musculature 86, 91
Posterior aorta 170
Posterior arch 222
Posterior border of vomer
220
Posterior brachial muscle
86, 91
Posterior branch of spinal
nerve 223

Posterior cerebral artery
252
Posterior chamber 241
Posterior chamber of
cloaca 185
Posterior column 223
Posterior crural muscle 87
Posterior cuneonavicular
ligament 252
Posterior dorsal fin
Bony fish 181
Dogfish 179
Lamprey 178
Posterior horn 223
Posterior nasal aperture
220
Posterior nasal spine 220
Posterior part of tongue
245
Posterior petal 141
Posterior root 223, 238
Posterior semicircular
canal 243
Posterior sepal 141
Posterior tarsometatarsal
ligament 252
Posterior tentacle 177
Posterior tibial artery 253
Posterior tibial nerve 238
Posterior tubercle 222
Posterior vena cava 182
Posterolateral horn 94
Post-glacial stream 286
Post-glacial valley 286
Post-modernism 296, 496
Post-motor micropore
filter 592
Potassium 35, 58, 286, 310
Potassium chromate
solution 312
Potassium dichromate
ions 312
Potassium iodide 312-313
Potassium nitrate 313
Potassium permanganate
306
Potato 128
Potential energy 314, 315
Potholes 284
Pouch 206
Power bar 532
Power drill 600-601
Power button
Hand-held computer
568
Home cinema 585
Inkjet printer 574
Microsoft Xbox 579
Mobile phone 587-588
Personal computer
566-567
Power clip 582
Power indicator light 579
Power lead 582
Power on light 581
Power on/off slider 581
Power output 360, 366
Power plug 591
Power socket 566, 569
Power stations 314, 315
Power steering belt 351
Power steering pump 344,
351
Power stroke 343
Power supply 567, 568
Power supply cord 570,
573
Power supply wiring 582
Power switch 582
Power switch control 582
Power-to-weight ratio
328
Power transistor heat sink
(dissipator) 585
Power transistors 585
Practice projectile 396
Pradakshina 491
Praesepe 8

Prairie style 495
Praseodymium 310
Pratt & Whitney Canada
turbofan engine 418-419
Pratt & Whitney Canada
turboprop engine 419
Pratt & Whitney radial
engine 406-407
Praxiteles 35
Preacetabular process 82
Precambrian period 56,
64-65, 279
Precentral gyrus 237
Precious metals 311
Precipitate 312
Precipitation 288, 302-303
Predatory dinosaurs 84
Predatory theropods 88
Predentary bone
Arsinoitherium 104
Iguanodon 96
Lambeosaurus 99
Moeritherium 105
Protoceratops 102
Triceratops 103
Prefix 577
Prehensile tail 202
Prehistoric foods 109
Pre-load adjustor 365
Premaxilla
Baryonyx 83
Bony fish 181
Chimpanzee 202
Elephant 201
Frog 183
Iguanodon 96
Lambeosaurus 99
Premolars
Australopithecus 107
Bear 106, 194
Chimpanzee 202
Horse 105
Human 246
Lion 194
Prenocephale 100-101
Preopercular bone 181
Preparatory drawing 430-431
Prepubic process
Iguanodon 96
Parasaurolophus 98
Stegosaurus 93
Prepubis
Ornithischian 82
Stegoceras 100-101
Prepuce 259
Preserved remains 278
Press
Etching 447
Lithographic printing
446
Relief-printing 449
Pressed steel wheel 340
Pressure
Formation of black hole
29
Igneous and
metamorphic rocks 274
Mineral resources 280
Stellar black hole 29
Volcanic features 273
Pressure line 418
Pressure plate 366
Pressurized cabin 406
Pressurized keel box 417
Pressurized strut 425
Pressurized water reactor
314
Presta valve 206
Prestatyn axon 259
Presynaptic membrane
259
Preview monitor slot 575
Preview panel 576
Preview monitor socket
574
Previous frame 577

654

Previous/next track
buttons 585
Previous track button 587
Previous track control 587
Prickers 583
Prickle
Blackberry 147
Bramble stem 130
Rose stem 130
Slender thistle 129
Primary bronchus 215
Primary colours 439
Primary-drive gear 366
Primary flight feathers
188, 191
Primary follicle 258
Primary leaf 121
Primary mirror 612
Primary mirror housing
613
Primary mycelium 115
Primary remiges 188, 191
Primary root 132-133
Germination 152-153
Seedling 152-153
Primary teeth 246
Primary thallus 114
Primary xylem 125, 135
Primates 10, 202-203,
279
Primer 348, 436
Primitive crocodilians 68
Primitive life-forms 64
Primitive mammals 206
Principal arteries and
veins 255
Principal rafter
Ancient Roman mill 464
Dome 486
Gothic building 473
Printed circuit board
(PCB)
Digital video camera
582-583
Hand-held computer
569
Printer 574-575
Printer cover 574, 575
Printhead power wiring
harness 573
Printhead wiring harness
572
Print icon 576
Printing assembly 573
Printing block 449
Printing cartridge 573
Printing papers 447
Print making 446-447,
448-449
Prism 318, 623
Prismatic habit 271
Privy 380
Probactosaurus 97
Probes, space 614-615
Proboscidea 104
Proboscis 169, 201
Procambial strand 134
Procerus muscle 229
Processing cooling fan
567
Processing light 575
Processional path 470
Processor card 567
Processor heat sink 567
Procompsognathus 87
Procoptodon 76
Procyon 8, 21
Procyon lotor 195
Production line
Mass-production 338
Modern bodywork 348
Modern trim 352
Programme display 577
Programme file name 577
Program mode selector
580, 581
Program mode selector
control 581
Program selector 581

Projectile 396
Projector lens 611
Prokaryotes 78
Proleg 169
Promethium 311
Prominence 32-33
Pronaos 461
Pro-otic bone 183
Propagative structures
154-155
Propellant 396
Propeller 390-391
ARV light aircraft 425
Battleship 395
Biplanes and triplanes
402-403
Early monoplanes 400-
401
Ford diesel engine 347
Frigate 396
Hawker Tempest
components 408
Lockheed Electra
airliner 406-407
Pegasus Quasar
microlight 427
Pioneers of flight 398-
399
Submarine 396
World War I aircraft
404-405
Propeller-bolt collar 411
Propeller brake pad 419
Propeller drive flange
ARV light aircraft 425
Modern piston aero-
engines 410-411
Propeller drive gearbox
427
Propeller drive shaft 408
Propeller-hub spinner 407
Propeller shaft
Brazilian battleship 395
Wright Flyer 399
Propeller shaft boss 391
Propeller-shaft bracing
strut 398-399
Propeller shaft rear
bearing 410
Propeller speed probe 419
Propeller spinner 408, 409
Propodus 172, 173
Propylaeum 460
Prosauropoda 83
Prosauropods 88
Proscapular process 187
Prosimians 203
Prosimii 202
Prosoma 170, 171
Prostate gland 257, 259
Prostyle colonnade 483
Protactinium 310
Protective clothing
American football 528
Cricket 539
Ice hockey 550-551
Protective eyewear 544
Protective gaiter 422
Protective outer layer 125
Protective root covering
153
Protective scale 154
Protective scale leaf 155
Protein body 112
Protein fibres 166
Protein matrix 166
Protein synthesis site 139
Proterozoic eon 279
Proteus 50
Prothallus 121
Prothorax 168
Protista 112, 116
Protoceratops 102-103
Protogalaxies 10-11
Proton 308, 316
Atomic mass 310
Atomic number 310
Fluorine-19 309
Nuclear fusion 22

Protonema 119
Protostar 24, 26
Protoxylem
Dicotyledon root 127
Monocotyledon root 127
Root 132-133
Proventriculus
Bird 189
Crayfish 173
Prow 372, 375
Prowhead 374
Proxima Centauri 18
Proximal convoluted
tubule 256-257
Proximal interphalangeal
joint 231
Proximal phalanx 250, 232
Proximal phalanx 251
Prunus persica 131
Psathyrella candolleana
115
Pseudocarps 148-149
Pseudo-Corinthian capital
476
Psi Sagittarii 21
Psilotacrosaurus 100, 103
Psoas major muscle 225,
257
Pterapsis 65
Pterichthyodes 65
Pteridium aquilinum 121
Pteris volitans 180
Pteron 460-461, 463
Pterosaurs 70-71
Pterygoid bone 183
Pterygoid hamulus 220
Pterygoid plate 220
Ptolemaeus 40
Ptolemaic-Roman period
459
"P" turret 395
P-type silicon 605
Pubic bone 261
Pubic ramus 257
Pubic symphysis 258
Pubis
Archaeopteryx 85
Bird 189
Diplodocus 90
Eryops 81
Gallimimus 86
Human 218, 224, 259
Iguanodon 96
Ornithischian 82
Plateosaurus 88
Saurischian 82
Stegosaurus 93
Struthiomimus 87
Tyrannosaurus 84
Pubofemoral ligament 224
Pudenda 211
Pudendal nerve 238
Puffballs 114
Pugin, A.W.N. 493
Pulley bolt 360
Pulley rim rear brake 362
Pulley wheel
Simple pulleys 320
Van de Graaff generator
316
Pulmonary artery
Frog 182
Human 251, 253, 254-
255
Pulmonary semilunar
valve 251
Pulmonary trunk 251, 255
Pulmonary vein 251, 253,
254
Pulp artery and vein 247
Pulp chamber 247
Pulp horn 247
Pulp nerve 247
Pulsar 28
Pumice 275
Marble carving 453
Pump
Nuclear power station
314
Testing candle wax 313

Pump drive belt 410
Pump drive shaft 411
Pump piston 391
Pupa 168
Pupil
Caiman 186
Human 213, 226, 241
Pupil's cockpit 403
Puppis 18, 21
Purchase 382-383
Purchase wire 394
Pure substances 306
Purfling 510, 511
Purkinje's cells 257
Purlin 473
Pusher propeller
Pegasus Quasar
microlight 426
Pioneers of flight 398-
399
Push moraine 286
Push-rod 365, 367
Putlet 547
Putting green 546
Putto 476
Putty eraser 430, 440
"P" wave 63
Pygal shield 187
Pygostyle 189
Pylon 514
Pylon fairing 427
Pylon strut 427
Pyloric caecum
Bony fish 181
Starfish 174
Pyloric duct 174
Pyloric region of stomach
179
Pyloric sphincter muscle
249
Pyloric stomach 174
Pyramid 458, 623
Pyrenees 77, 265
Pyrenoid 112, 116
Pyrites 268
Intrusive igneous rocks
275
Pyroclasts 272
Pyromorphite 269
Pyroxene 52, 267
Pyxis 18

Q

Quadrant arch 468
Quadrate bone 181
Quadratojugal bone
Frog 183
Heterodontosaurus 83
Quadrilateral 489
Quadripartite vault 469
Quadrupedal dinosaurs
88, 92, 96, 100
Quadruplanes 402
Quark 309
Quarter back 526
Quarterdeck 380-381
Quarterdeck house 376
Quarter gallery 381
Quarter glass 348
Quarter light 340-341
Quarter panel moulding
352
Quarter trim panel 352
Quartz
Colour 271
Metamorphic rock 267
Oxides/hydroxides 268
Quasar (quasi-stellar
object)
Galaxies 12
Objects in Universe 11
Origin and expansion of
Universe 10-11
Quasar nucleus 13
Quaternary period 57, 76-
77
Fossil record 279

Quatrefoil 471-473
Quaver 502
Quayside 587
Queen-post 473
Quercus palustris 74
Quercus petraea 131
Quick-release base 590
Quick-release mechanism
425
Quick-release strap 360
Quill
Drill 601
Feather 191
Writing tool 444
Quinacridone red 442
Quit key 590
Quiver 548
Quoin
Baroque church 481
Medieval building 466
Nineteenth-century
building 492
Renaissance building
476

R

Rabbit line 580
Rabbits 196-197
Raccoons 194-195
Raceme 129
Rachilla 137
Rachis 136-137
Bipinnate leaf 137
Couch grass 113
Everlasting pea 129
Feather 191
Fern 121
Hogweed 129
Pinnate leaf 136-137
Rowan leaf 130
Tree fern 112
Tripinnate leaf 137
Racing bicycle 360
Racing car 356-357
Racing chain 361
Racing colours 554-555
Racing saddle 554
Racing sidecar 368-369
Racing "silks" 554-555
Racing tyre 365
Formula One racing car
356-357
Suzuki RGV500 368-369
Racketball 544-545
Racket sports 544-545
Radar
Modern jetliners 412
Modern military
aircraft 420-421
World War II aircraft
408
RADAR antenna 397
RADAR for gunnery and
missile control 597
Radial artery 251, 253
Radial canal
Jellyfish 167
Sea urchin 175
Starfish 174
Radial cartilage 180
Radial diffuser 418
Radial engine
Curtiss biplane 398-399
Lockheed Electra
airliner 406-407
Radial groove 565
Radial nerve
Human 238
Sea urchin 175
Radial river drainage 288
Radial spoke 47
Radial studio easel 437
Radial wall 465
Radiation 38
Electromagnetic 314
Energy emission from
Sun 22

Galaxies 12-13
Nebulae and star
clusters 16
Ozone formation 64
Universe 10
Radiative zone
Structure of main
sequence star 24
Structure of Sun 33
Radiator
1906 Renault 336-337
ARV light aircraft 424
Ford Model T 338-339
Hawker Tempest
fighter 409
Honda VF750 364
Kirby BSA 369
Renault Clio 351
Wright Flyer 399
Radiator-access cowling
408
Radiator air vent 368
Radiator apron 339
Radiator coolant 326
Radiator fan 326
Radiator filler neck 339
Radiator header tank 408
Radiator hose 339
Radiator outlet 409
Radiator pipe 364
Radiator shell 339
Radicle
Dry fruit 150
Embryo development
147
Epigeal germination
153
Hypogeal germination
152
Radio
Bell-47 helicopter 422
Renault Clio 353
Streamed Internet 577
Radio aerial 426
Radio antenna 395
Radio galaxies 12-13
Radio image 13
Radio-isotope thermo-
electric generator 615
Radio lobe 13
Radio mast 494
Radio operator's seat 408
Radio plugs 425
Radio speaker 353
Radio tuner aerial socket
(FM) 585
Radio tuner FM/AM
selector 585
Radio-ulna 183
Radio wave beam 28
Radio-wave emission 15
Radio waves
Electromagnetic
spectrum 318
Pulsar 28
Radio image of
Centaurus A 13
Radium 310
Radius
Archaeopteryx 85
Arsinoitherium 104
Baryonyx 85
Bird 188, 191
Circle 622
Crocodile 186
Diplodocus 90
Domestic cat 195
Elephant 90, 201
Eryops 80
Euoplocephalus 94
Hare 197
Horse 199
Human 218, 230-231
Iguanodon 96
Kangaroo 206
Lizard 184
Parasaurolophus 99
Pareiasaur 81
Plateosaurus 88

Platypus 206
Rhesus monkey 202
Seal 204
Stegoceras 100–101
Struthiomimus 87
Toxodon 106
Triceratops 102
Turtle 187
Radius arm 357
Radius rod
  Avro Tutor biplane 403
  Ford Model T 338–339
Radome
  BAe-146 jetliner 415
  Concorde 416–417
  Tornado 420
Radon 311
Radula 176–177
RAF Central Flying School
  badge 402
RAF roundels 403, 409
Raft 496
Rafter
  Ancient Roman mill 464
  Dome 486
  Gothic building 473
  Modern building 499
  Nineteenth-century
    building 492
Raft spider 171
Rail
  Electric tram 332
  Kayak 560
  Neoclassical building
    483
  Relief-printing press
    449
  Train 330–331
  Wooden sailing ship
    379
Rail chair 324
Railing
  Asian building 490–491
  Cathedral dome 487
  Medieval building 467
  Nineteenth-century
    building 493
  Renaissance theatre 477
Railroad crest 326
Railway system 324
Rain 302
Rain erosion 294
Rain gutter 412, 415
Rainwater
  Caves 284
  Weathering and erosion
    282
Raised beach 295
Raja clavata 179
Raked windscreen 333
Raking cornice
  Ancient Greek building
    460–461
  Ancient Roman
    building 462–463
  Baroque church 480–
    481
  Neoclassical building
    478
Raking stempost 376
Ram 572
Ramaria formosa 114
Ramentum 112, 121
Rammer 396
Ramp 467, 494
Ram scoop
  BE 2B bomber 404
  Tornado 420–421
Rangefinder
  Battleship 394
  Gun turret 396
Ranks 514
Ranunculus sp. 127, 132–
  133
Raphe 153
Rapid-fire pistols 548
Rapids
  River features 290
  River's stages 289

Rare earths 310
Rare gases 311
Ras Algethi 20
Ras Alhague 19, 20
Rasp 452
Raspberry 149
Rat 104, 196
Ratchet
  Brace-and-bit 601
  Fixed-spool reel 562
Ratcheted base 590
Ratchet mechanism 601
Ratchet wheel 334
Rating 578
Ratings' mess 397
Ratline 376, 379
Rat's tail 584
Rat tail 589
Rattlesnake 185
Raw sienna 434
Raw umber 434
Ray
  Branchiostegal 181
  Caudal fin 180
  Dorsal fin 181
  Jawless fish 178
  Liverwort 118
  Mercury 34
  Near side of the Moon
    40
  Parenchyma cells 134
  Pectoral fin 181
  Ray crater 34
Ray florets
  Florists'
    chrysanthemum 129
  Sunflower 142, 145
Reactants 312
Reactive metals 310–311
Reactor core 314
Reactor space 397
Read/write access
  window 586
Rear axle 338
Rear axle adjustor 364,
  368
Rear bearing 411
Rear bezel 569
Rear brake 362
Rear brake cable 359, 360
Rear brake calliper 368
Rear brake pedal 368
Rear bulkhead 417
Rear cabinet 582
Rear cantilever brake 358
Rear case 568
Rear chassis plate 597
Rear cylinder exhaust
  pipe 568
Rear derailleur 358, 360
Rear door 339
Rear drop-outs 358
Rear hatch 349
Rear hub quick-release
  spindle 358
Rear indicator 362
Rear lamp
  Oldsmobile trim 337
  Volkswagen Beetle 340
Rear leaf spring 338
Rear light
  Bicycle 360
  Italian State Railways
    Class 402 328
  Paris Metro 328
Rear limit line 557
Rear-mounted propeller
  Pegasus Quasar
    microlight 426
  Pioneers of flight 398–
    399
Rear panel cover 573
Rear oil lamp 336
Rear shelf 352
Rear shock absorber 340
Rear sub-frame 364
Rear tail light 329
Rear-view mirror
  1906 Renault 336

Formula One racing car
  357
Renault Clio 353
Receiver
  American squash 545
  Badminton 545
  International squash
    545
  Racketball 545
  Tennis 544
Receiving line 545
Receptacles
  Algae 116
  Dicotyledon flower 127
  Dry fruit 150–151
  Fertilization 147
  Flower 140–56
  Rose 131
  Seaweed 116–117
  Succulent fruit 148–149
Recessed arch 488
Recessed hinge 414, 415
Rechargeable battery
  Digital camera 581
  Hand-held computer
    569
  Mobile phone 589
Recharge area 292
Recharge jack socket 581
Recoil cylinder 396
Reconnaissance camera
  420
Recorded information 521
Recorder frame 573
Recording head assembly
  573
Recording light 585
Record trigger 521
Rectal caecum 174
Rectal gland 179
Rectangle 622
Rectangular block 623
Rectangular cross-band
  574
Rectangular pier 465, 467,
  480
Rectangular river
  drainage 288
Rectangular window
  Ancient Roman
    building 465
  Asian building 490
  Baroque church 481
  Medieval building 466
  Renaissance building
    474, 476
Rectum
  Bird 189
  Butterfly 169
  Chimpanzee 202
  Cow 198
  Dogfish 179
  Dolphin 205
  Elephant 200
  Frog 182
  Human 215, 248–249,
    258–259, 261
  Lizard 185
  Rabbit 196
  Starfish 174
  Tortoise 187
Rectus abdominis muscle
  226
Rectus femoris muscle
  226
Recumbent fold 61
Red algae 116
Red blood cells 217, 253
Red-brown crocoite 271
Red card 524
Red cedar boarding 602
Red cell 584
Red deer 199
Red dwarf 23
Red earth 433, 434–435
Red filter signal light 407
Red giant
  Small stars 24–25
  Stars 22–23

Red howler monkey 203
Redial/pause button 572
Red light 318
  Main-line signalling
    system 330, 331
Red light photon 318
Red marble 450
Red port navigation light
  406
Red sandstone 277
Red seaweeds 117
Red spot 44–45
Red supergiant
  Massive stars 26–27
  Stars 22–23
Reduction gearbox
  Early piston aero-
    engines 410–411
  Jet engines 419
  Turboprop engine 419
Redwall limestone 277
Red warning light
  Italian State Railways
    Class 402 328
  Paris Metro 328
Redwood trees 70
Reed pen 444
Reef knot 588
Reef point 385
Reel
  Angling equipment 562–
    563
  Fencing piste 557
  Frigate 397
  Reel foot 562–563
  Reel scoop 562–563
  Reel seat 563
Re-entrant angle 485
Re-entrant corner 479
Referee
  American football 526
  Basketball 532
  Gaelic football 529
  Ice hockey 550
  Judo 556
  Lacrosse 541
  Rugby 530
  Soccer 524
  Swimming 558
  Volleyball 534
Referee's crease 550
Referee's equipment 524
Referee's signals
  American football 527
  Basketball 533
Reflection 318
Reflection nebula 16
Reflector
  Ford Model T 339
  Oldsmobile trim 337
Refraction 318–319
Refractory (heat-resistant)
  skin 421
Refrigerator freight car
  327
Régie Autonome des
  Transports Parisien 328
Regional metamorphism
  274
Regional weather 302
Registers 514
Regolith (soil) 41
Regula 461
Regulator
  "Mallard" express
    steam locomotive 325
  "Rocket" steam
    locomotive 324
Regulator valve 325
Regulus 18, 21
Rein 554
Reinforced belt 581
Reinforced concrete 494,
  497
Reinforced plinth 499
Rein terret 555
Relative atomic mass 310
Relay baton 543

Relay running 542
Release 537, 543
Release adjustment screw
  552
Release button 425
Release catch 590
Release lever 563
Release spring 563
Relief 458
Relief printing 446
Relief printing equipment
  449
Relieving arch
  Ancient Roman
    building 462, 465
  Medieval building 466–
    467
Remiges 188, 191
Remote control 585
Remote control sensor
  585
Remote sensing palette
  615
Removable archery
  screen 577
Renaissance buildings
  474–477
Renal artery 256–257
Renal column 256
Renal papilla 256
Renal pelvis 256
Renal sinus 256
Renal vein 256–257
Renault (1906) 336–337
Renault Clio 348–353
Renault logo 348
Renewable energy 604–
  605
Renoir 35
Repeater indicator 333
Repeating pattern 307
Replum 151
Reply all icon 576
Reply icon 576
Reproduction
  Algae 116–117
  Cloning 606–607
  Fertilization 146–147
  Flowering plants 140
  Liverwort 118
  Moss 118–119
  Vegetative 154–155
Reproductive canal 94
Reproductive chamber
  116
Reproductive organs
  259
Reproductive structures
  Flower 140–143
  Pollination 144
Reproductive system 258–
  259
Reptiles 80–81, 184–187
  Carboniferous period
    66
  Dinosaurs 82–83
  Fossil record 279
  Jurassic period 70
  Present-day 82
  Rhynchosaurian 71
  Synapsid skull 67
  Triassic period 68
Reptilia 184, 186
Repulsion 316–317
"Request identification"
  aerial 421
Re-radiated heat 300–301
Reredos 470
Rescue strap 561
Reservoir 314
Reset button 560, 569
Resin canal
  Bishop pine needle 124
  Pine root/stem 125
Resistance 316
Resonator 513
Respiration 255
Respiratory system 254–
  255

Rest
  Musical notation 502
  Newton's first motion
    law 321
Resurgence 284–285
Retaining bolt hole 366
Retaining screw 562, 563
Reticulum
  Digestive system of a
    cow 198
  Southern stars 20
Retina 240–241
Retractable head light 608
Retraction jack 417
Retractor muscle 167
Retreating glacier 286
Retrices 188
Retroarticular process 83
Return 486–487
Rev counter 369
Reversed bend hook 562
Reverse control 587
Reversed dive piked 559
Reverse dip-slip fault 61
Reverse dive 558
Reverse-flow combustion
  chamber 418
Reverse lever 342
Reverser handle 325
Reverse shock wave 27
Reversible reactions 312
Reversing shaft lock
  control 325
Reversing wheel 392
Revivalist style 493–494
Rewind control 577
Rhamphodopsis 65
Rhamphorhynchus sp. 71
Rheas 188
Rhenium 310
Rhesus monkey 202
Rhinoceroses 198–199
Rhizine 114
Rhizoids 118–119
  Alga 116
  Fern 121
  Liverwort 118
  Moss 119
Rhizomes 154–155
  Fern 121
  Herbaceous flowering
    plants 128
  Horsetail 120
  Water hyacinth 158
  Water lily 159
Rhizophore 120
Rho1 Sagittarii 21
Rhodium 311
Rhodophyta 116
Rhomboideus major
  muscle 227
Rhomboid leaves 137
Rhombus 622
Rhopalium 167
Rhynchosaurian reptile 71
Rhynchosaurs 68–69, 71
Rhyolite 274–275
Rhyolitic lava 272
Rhythm
  Drums 518
  Percussion instruments
    516
Rhythm pattern selector
  520
Rib
  Acoustic guitar 512
  Archaeopteryx 85
  Avro triplane 403
  Baroque church 479
  BE 2B tail 405
  BE 2B wings 404
  Bird 189
  Blackburn monoplane
    401
  Bony fish 181
  Brachiosaurus 90
  Concorde 417
  Crocodile 186
  Diplodocus 90

Dome 486-487
Domestic cat 195
Double bass 511
Elephant 201
Eryops 80
Euoplocephalus 94
Galliminus 86
Hare 197
Herbaceous flowering plant 128
Horse 199
Kangaroo 206
Lizard 184
Medieval church 469
Modern building 499
Pareiasaur 81
Pegasus Quasar microlight 426-427
Pegasus XL SE microlight 426
Plateosaurus 88
Platypus 206
Rhesus monkey 202
Seal 204
Snake 185
Stegoceras 101
Struthiomimus 87
Toxodon 107
Triceratops 102
Tyrannosaurus 84
Violin 510
Westlothiana 81

Riband 381
Ribbon cable connector 578
Ribbon connectors 585, 581
Ribbon Lake 287
Ribbon socket connector 581
Ribbon window 499
Rib cage
  Carnivores 195
  Human 218
Ribosome
  Chloroplast 139
  Human cell 217
Rib vault 469, 484-485
  Gothic building 470
  Medieval building 467
  Renaissance building 477
Rice paper 445
Ride cymbal 519
Ridge
  Epigeal germination 153
  False septum 151
  Gothic building 473
  Modern building 499
  Nineteenth-century building 492
  Seed 153
  Twentieth-century building 495
Ridge and furrow roof 492
Ridge-board 473
Ridge-rib 469, 485
Ridges 286-287
Ridge tile 464, 476
Riding bitt 372
Riding jacket 554
Riffler 452, 453, 454
Rifle 548, 549
Rift valley 58
  Lake formation 292-293
Rig 384-385
Riga brush 454
Rigel
  Northern stars 18
  Orion 18
  Southern stars 21
  Star magnitudes 22
Rigger 560
Rigger's gauge 382
Rigging 382-383
  Iron 392
  Sailing dinghy 561
  Wooden sailing ship 378-379

Rigging rail 376
Rigging tools 382-383
Right-angled triangle 622
Right cylinder 623
Right edge guide 575
Right whales 204
Rigid rock 60
Rigol 581
Rim
  Bicycle wheel 358-359
  Kayak paddle 560
  Paddle wheel 591
  Tam-tam 516
  Twin bollards 386
Rim brake 350
Rim clamp 337
Rim of pitcher 161
Rim plate 590
Rim section 590
Rind 149
Ring
  74-gun ship 380
  Mushroom 115
  Roman corbita 572
Ring 1986 U1R 48
Ring 1986 U2R 48
Ring 6 48
Ring bolt 573
Ring canal
  Sea urchin 175
  Starfish 174
Ring dyke 26
Ring finger 230 -231
"Ring of Fire" 272
Ring of trunk 201
Rings
  Jupiter 44-45
  Neptune 50-51
  Saturn 46-47
  Uranus 48-49
Rings 4 and 5 48
Ring scar 150,151
Ring-tailed lemur 203
Rink corner 550
Riojasaurus 80
Ripple finish 451
Riser
  Bronze casting 454, 455
  Staircase 477
Rising air
  Atmospheric circulation and winds 300
  Precipitation 302
Rising land 294
Risorius muscle 229
Rissa tridactyla 190
Ritchey 43
River Amur 265
River banks 289, 290
River-bed 289
River capture 288
River cliff 289, 290
River Congo 265
River course 288
River development 289
River drainage patterns 288
River features 290-291
River flow 290
River Ganges 288
River Jordan 293
River Lena 265
River Mekong 265
River-mouth 290
River Nile 264-265
River Ob-Irtysh 265
Rivers 288-289
  Earth's physical features 264
  River features 290-291
  Rock cycle 266-267
  Weathering and erosion 282
River source
  River features 290
  Rivers 288
River's stages 288-289
River terrace 290-291
River valley 288, 289, 290

Rivetted plates 392
Road spring 340
Roband 372, 374
Robie House 495
Robinia pseudoacacia 136
Robots 608-609
Roche 41
Roches moutonnées 286
Rock compression 60
Rock crystal 271
Rock cycle 266-267
Rock debris 295
Rock deformations 60, 61
Rocker 446
Rocker arm 366
Rocker-beam 496-497
Rocker-bogie assembly 615
Rocker cover 347, 354
Rock erosion 282
Rocker keypad 591
Rocker pad 590
"Rocket" steam locomotive 324
Rocket launcher 397
Rock fracture 60
Rock groundmass 269
Rocking beam 334
Rocking elevator arm 424
Rocking lever 342
Rock layer
  Caves 284
  Faults and folds 60
Rock lip
  Cirque formation 287
  Tarn lake 293
Rock mounds 286
Rock particles 266-267
Rock pavement 282-283
Rock pedestal 282-283
Rock prisms 61
Rocks
  Faults and folds 60-61
  Fossils 278-279
  Igneous and metamorphic rocks 274-275
  Mineral resources 280
  Minerals 268
  Rock cycle 266-267
  Sedimentary rocks 276
  Weathering and erosion 282
Rock salt
  Halides 269
  Sedimentary rocks 276-277
Rock scar 284
Rock stonecrop 128
Rock strata 60, 61
  Fossils 278
Rock stress 60, 61
Rock tension 60, 61
Rocky Mountains 73, 75, 77, 264
Rocky planets
  Mars 42-43
  Mercury 34-35
  Solar System 30-31
  Venus 36-37
Rococo style 478
Rod 562-563
Rodentia 104, 196
Rodents 196-197
Rod-shaped structure 144
Rogers, R. 496
Roll 400
Roller
  Fax machine 572, 573
  Mid West single-rotor engine 410
  Motorized brushbar floor tool 593
  "O Ring" drive chain 366
  Painting tool 442
  Printing equipment 447, 449
  Tenor saxophone 509

Roller-bearing axle box 327
Roller-blind 497
Roller path 396
Rollers 596
Rolling hitch 388
Rollover button 577
Roll paper holder 575
Roll paper holder adapter 575
Roll paper manipulation button 574
Roll spoiler 414
Roll-spoiler hydraulic actuator attachment 414
Rolls-Royce Olympus Mark 610 turbojet 417
Roman anchor 372
Roman architecture 462-465
Roman corbita 572-573
Romanesque style 468, 470
Roman mill 464
Roman number system 591
Roman ships 372-373
ROM cover 572
Roof boss 468
Roof construction 603
Roof dome 552, 553
Roofed space 479
Roofing tile 482
Roofless temple 460
Roof moulding 552
Roofs 484
  Ancient Egyptian temple 458-459
  Ancient Roman building 462
  Asian building 490
  Baroque church 481
  Dome 486
  Gothic building 470-473
  Hammer-beam 470, 473
  Islamic building 488-489
  Medieval building 467, 468
  Modern building 496-499
  Neoclassical building 479, 485
  Nineteenth-century building 492
  Renaissance building 476-477
  Twentieth-century building 494-495
Root
  BAe-146 jetliner components 413, 415
  BE 2B wings 404
  Tooth 247
Root canal 247
Root cap
  Broad bean 133
  Radicle 153
Root growth 282
Root hairs 132
Root nodule 128
Root of tail 198
Root parasite 163
Root-proof membrane 603
Root rib 413
Roots 132-133
  Adventitious 112-113
  Amaryllis 155
  Begonia 155
  Brassavola nodosa 162
  Broomrape host 163
  Carrot 128
  Cell division 133
  Clubmoss 120
  Couch grass 113
  Dehiscent fruit 150
  Dicotyledons 127
  Elongation region 133

Embryo 147
Epigeal germination 153
Epiphytes 162-163
Fern 121
Germination 152-153
Ginger 155
Gladiolus 155
Golden barrel cactus 156
Grape hyacinth 155
Horse chestnut 130
Horsetail 121
Hypogeal germination 152
Ivy 131
Kedrostis africana 113
Lily 155
Monocotyledons 126-127
Mycorrhizal association 133
Oxalis sp. 157
Pine seedling 122
Potato 128
Rock stonecrop 128
Seedling 152-153
String of hearts 157
Sweet pea 128
Sweet potato 155
Vegetative reproduction 154-155
Water hyacinth 158
Water transport 158
Root scar 128
Root succulents 157
Root tip 152-153
  Radicle 152-153
Root tubers 154-155, 157
Rope and paterae decoration 459
Rope band 372
Rope hole 386
Rope moulding 395
Rope parrel 373
Rope preventer 578
Ropes 388-389
Rope serving mallet 383
Rope strand 384
Rope woolding 379
Ropework 388
Rorquals 204
Rosa sp. 130-131, 135
Rose 130-131
Rose quartz 271
Rosette
  Epiphytic plants 162-163
  Neoclassical building 480
Rosette Nebula 11
Rossby waves 300
Rossin Italian time-trial bicycle 361
Rostellum 16
Rostral bone 102, 103
Rostrum
  Crayfish 173
  Dolphin 204
Rotary engine 346-347
  Blackburn monoplane 400
  Modern piston aero-engines 410-411
Rotary valves 507
Rotating beacon 407
Rotating joint 612
Rotational period 36
Rotor
  Mid West rotary engine 411
  Rotor and seals 347
Rotor blade 423
Rotor chamber
  Mid West single-rotor engine 410
  Wankel rotary engine 346
Rotor gear 346-347

Rotor gear teeth 411
Rotor house 314
Rotor hub
  Bell-47 helicopter 422
  Schweizer helicopter 423
Rotor journal 347
Rotor lock 604
Rotor mast 422-423
Rotunda 462-463, 482
Rough 546
Rough endoplasmic reticulum 217
Rough terrain motorcycle racing 368
Rough-textured paper 439, 441
Roulette 446
Rounce 449
Round arch
  Ancient Roman building 464-465
  Baroque church 479-480
  Dome 484, 486-487
  French temple 485
  Gothic church 473
  Medieval building 467-469
  Nineteenth-century building 493
  Renaissance building 474-475
Round-arched window
  Ancient Roman building 465
  Baroque church 481
  Dome 486
  Medieval building 466, 468-469
  Neoclassical building 478
Round ball 524
Round corner single limousine coachwork 336
Roundel
  Avro biplane 403
  Hawker Tempest fighter 409
Roundhead nib 444
Roundhouse 380
Round pin 335
Round shot 378
Round thimble 384
Route information 332
Route key 590
Rover 528
Rowan 130-131
Rowing 560-561
Rowing boat 375
Rowing positions on a Greek trireme 373
Rubber bungee shock absorber 425
Rubber cord suspension 402-403
Rubber guide wheel 328
Rubber mounting bush 365
Rubber puck 550-551
Rubber roller 449
Rubber sealing strip 413
Rubber-sprung wheel 400-401
Rubber tyre 402
Rubber-tyred running wheel 328
Rubber wheel-guard 528
Rubber wheels
  Paris Metro 328
  "People Mover" 528
Rubbing
  Charcoal drawing 431
  Relief printing 446
Rubbing ink 448
Rubbing strake
  Mazda RX-7 346
  Roman corbita 572

657

Rubbing strip 353
Rubens 55
Rubidium 510
Rubus fruticosus 150, 146-147
Rubus idaeus 149
Ruckman 528
Rucknover 528
Ruckstell axle 339
Rudder
  ARV light aircraft 424
  Avro biplane 402
  Avro triplane 405
  BAe-146 jetliner 415
  Battleship 595
  BE 2B bomber 405
  Blackburn monoplane 401
  Blériot XI 401
  Concorde 416-417
  Curtiss biplane 399
  Dhow 376
  Frigate 596
  Greek and Roman ships 372-373
  Iron paddlesteamer 392
  Junk 376
  Lockheed Electra airliner 407
  Longboat 380
  LVG CVI fighter 405
  Northrop B-2 bomber 421
Sailing dinghy 561
Sailing warship 577
Schleicher glider 426
Submarine 396
Tornado 421
Viking boats 374-375
Wooden sailing ship 378
World War II aircraft 408-409
Wright Flyer 399
Rudder cable
  ARV light aircraft 424
  Avro biplane 402
Rudder chain 378
Rudder head 576
Rudder hinge
  Avro biplane 402
  Blériot XI monoplane 401
Rudder mass balance 424
Rudder pedal 425
Rudder post
  BE 2B bomber 405
  Blackburn monoplane 401
  Iron paddlesteamer 392
Rudder power control unit 417
Rudder strut 599
Rudder tip fairing 424
Rudder trimtab 409
Ruden 372
Rudimentary ear 260
Rudimentary eye 260
Rudimentary liver 260
Rudimentary mouth 260
Rudimentary vertebra 260
Ruellia grandiflora 145
Ruffini corpuscle 235, 239
Ruga 248
Rugby 524, 530-531
Rugby League 550-551
Rugby Union 550
Rules of algebra 621
Rumen 198
Ruminants 198
Rumpler monoplane 400
Run 536
Runners
  Bronze casting 454-455
  Rock stonecrop 128
  Strawberry 128
  Vegetative reproduction 154

Running 542
Running back 526
Running block 383
Running board
  Ford Model T 339
  1906 Renault 337
  Volkswagen Beetle 341
Running martingale 554
Running part 582
Running rail 328
Running rigging 582-383, 385
Running shoe 543
Running track 542
Running wheel 328
Runs 538
Rupes 34
Rupes Altai 40
Rush 135
Russian vine 131
Rustication
  Neoclassical building 479, 482-483
  Renaissance building 474-475
Rusts 114
Ruthenium 311

S

62 Sagittarii 21
Sabik 20
Sable brush
  Acrylics 442
  Calligraphy 444
  Oil paints 436
  Tempera 432
  Watercolours 438
Sabres 556-557
Sabreur 557
Sabre warning line 557
Sacajawea 37
Saccule 243
Sacral foramen 223
Sacral nerves 238
Sacral plexus 238
Sacral promontory 223
Sacral vertebra 185
Sacral vertebrae
  Diplodocus 90
  Eryops 81
  Human 223
  Iguanodon 96
  Parasaurolophus 98
  Plateosaurus 88
  Stegoceras 101
Sacristy 470
Sacrum
  Crocodile 186
  Domestic cat 195
  Elephant 201
  Hare 197
  Horse 199
  Human 218, 223, 259
  Kangaroo 206
  Lizard 184
  Rhesus monkey 202
  Seal 204
Saddle
  Acoustic guitar 512
  Bicycle 358-359
  Cannondale SH600 hybrid bicycle 361
  Eddy Merckx racing bicycle 360
  Horse racing 555
  Showjumping 554
  Werner motorcycle 362
Saddle clamp 360
Safety area 556
Safety barrier 552
Safety belt 356
Safety binding 552
Safety harness 557
Safety valve
  Bordino steam carriage 334
  Steamboat 391

Safe working load mark 383
Sagartia elegans 166
Sagitta 20
Sagittal crest 107, 194
Sagittal section through brain 236
Sagittarius 19-21
Sagittarius Arm 14
Sago palm 123
Sahara 39, 264-265
Sail
  Roman corbita 372-373
  Square-rigged ship 375
  Types 584-585
  Viking karv 374
Sail batten 576
Sailcloths 384
Sail foot control line 375
Sail hook 384
Sailing 560-561
Sailing rigs 584-585
Sailing warship 576-377
Sailmaker's whipping 382
Sailmaking tools 384
Sail patterns 379, 384
Saiph 18
Salamanders 182
Salient 466
Salisbury Cathedral 470-471
Saliva 244
Salivary gland
  Butterfly 169
  Snail 177
Salmon 109, 180
Salmon angling 562
Salmon bend gouge 452
Salmson radial engine 398-399
Salt
  Dead Sea 293
  Seawater salt content 296
Saltasaurus 72, 91
Salt-dome trap 281
Salt formation 312
Salt groundmass 277
Salt lakes 292
Samaras
  Dry fruit 150
  Sycamore 131, 150
Samarium 311
Sambucus nigra 130-131, 143
Samotherium 74
Samsung VM8000 laptop 567
San Andreas fault 58, 62-63
Sand-bars 290
Sand box 326, 327
Sand dunes
  Rock cycle 267
  Weathering and erosion 282-283
Sand groundmass 277
Sanding pipe 529
Sand-pits 546
Sandstone
  Marble tomb of Itimad-Ud-Daula 489
  Sedimentary rocks 276
Sand wave 299
Sand wedge 547
Sandy deposits 298
Sandy spit 295
Sanguine crayon 450
Sankey diagram 314
Sappho Patera 37
Sapwood 125
Saratoga Race Course 555
Sarcolemma 24
Sarcomere 24
Sarcophilus harrisii 207
Sarcoplasmic reticulum 24
Sarcorhamphus papa 190
Sarracenia purpurea 113

Sartorius muscle 226
Satellite 264
Satellite map 264-265
Saturated zone 292-293
Saturn 46-47
  Solar System 31
Saucer dome 486-487
  Ancient Roman building 462
Saurischia 82-83, 84, 88
Sauropoda 83
Sauropodomorpha 83, 88
Sauropodomorphs 88-91
Sauropods 70, 88
Savannah 74
Saxboard 561
Saxophone 504, 508-509
Scala 572-573
Scale (musical) 502
Scale leaf scar 124, 155
Scale leaves
  Bishop pine 124
  Bulb 155
  Corm 155
  Epiphytic orchid 162
  Hypogeal germination 152
  Pine 122, 125
  Sago palm 123
  Stem bulbil 155
Scalene triangle 622
Scalenus medius muscle 229
Scale of degrees 377
Scales
  Asteroxylon 79
  Bishop pine 124
  Bony fish 180
  Bract 122
  Brassavola nodosa 162
  Caiman 186
  Cartilaginous fish 178
  Crocodilians 186
  Dicotyledons 127
  False fruit 148
  Fern fronds 121
  Insects 168
  Lepidoptera wings 168
  Lizard 184
  Mushroom 115
  Ovuliferous 122-124
  Pine cone 122
  Pine shoot apex 125
  Rattlesnake 185
  Sago palm 122
  Tree fern 112
  Yew 123
Scallop 176
  Fossil 278
Scalloped hammerhead shark 179
Scalp 234, 236-237
Scaly lichens 114
Scaly skin
  Anchisaurus 89
  Corythosaurus 98
  Dinosaurs 82
  Edmontonia 95
  Ichthyostega 80
  Iguanodon 97
  Pachycephalosaurus 100
  Psittacosaurus 103
  Reptile 80
  Snake 184
  Stegosaurus 92
  Triceratops 102
  Tyrannosaurus 84
  Westlothiana 81
Scandinavia 64, 69
Scandium 310
Scan head 571
Scanner 570-571
Scanning coils 611
Scanning electron microscope (SEM) 610, 611

Scanning unit 573
Scan to e-mail button 570
Scan to web button 570
Scapania undulata 118
Scape 168
Scaphoid bone 230
Scaphoid fossa 242
Scaphonyx fischeri 69
Scapula
  Archaeopteryx 85
  Arsinoitherium 104
  Bird 189
  Bony fish 181
  Brachiosaurus 91
  Crocodile 186
  Diplodocus 90
  Domestic cat 195
  Elephant 201
  Eryops 80
  Euoplocephalus 94
  Gallimimus 86
  Hare 197
  Horse 199
  Human 210, 218
  Iguanodon 96
  Kangaroo 206
  Lizard 184
  Parasaurolophus 99
  Pareiasaur 81
  Plateosaurus 88
  Platypus 206
  Rhesus monkey 202
  Seal 204
  Stegoceras 101
  Struthiomimus 87
  Toxodon 106
  Triceratops 102
  Tuojiangosaurus 93
  Turtle 187
  Tyrannosaurus 84
Scapular muscle 91
Scapular spine 91
Scarlet star 162-163
Scarph 395
Scars
  Horse chestnut 130
  Leaf 128-30, 154
  Rowan twig 131
Scavenge oil line 419
Scelidosauridae 83
Scelidosaurids 71
Scelidosaurus 71
Scent 144
Scheat 19,20
Schedar 19
Schickard 40
Schist 26
Schizocarpic dry fruits 150-151
Schleicher K23 glider 426
Schlumbergera truncata 129
Schooner 384-385
Schrödinger 41
Schubert 35
Schwann cell 228, 239
Schweizer 300c 423
Sciatic nerve 238
Scientific notation 621
Scintigram 214
Scissor brace 473
Sciurus carolinensis 197
Sclera 213, 240
Sclereid 159
Sclerenchyma
  Fern rachis 121
  Horsetail stem 120
  Marram grass 113
  Monocotyledon leaf 126
  Stems 134-135
Sclerenchyma fibres 135
Scleroderma citrinum 115
Sclerotic ring 90, 99
Scooter 50-51
Score 388
Scorecard 552
Score panel 578
Scorer
  Basketball 532
  Fencing contest 557

Judo contest 556
Lacrosse 541
Netball 535
Volleyball 534
Scoria 273
Scoring
  Australian rules football 528
  Badminton 544
  Baseball 536
  Basketball 532
  Cricket 538
  Gaelic football 529
  Hockey 540
  Hurling 540-541
  Netball 534
  Rugby 550-551
  Tennis 544
  Volleyball 534
Scorper 449
Scorpion 170, 278
Scorpiones 170
Scorpius 19, 20
Scotia 463, 485
Scots pine 122
Scraper 46
Scraper ring 344
Scratchplate 513
Scree 282-283
Screen
  Computer 576, 577, 611
  French baroque building 482
  Game Boy Advance 578
  Hydroelectric power station 314
  Islamic building 488-489
  Mobile phone 588
  Screen printing 448
  Streamed Internet video 577
  Twentieth-century building 494
Screen assembly 582
Screen bezel 588, 589
Screen bulkhead 581
Screen connector 569, 589
Screen connector socket 569
Screen display button 581
Screen light on/off 581
Screen panel 581
Screen power connector 589
Screen printing 446, 448
Screen surround 588
Screw 520
  Acoustic guitar 513
  Double bass bow 511
  Power drill 600
  Toaster 598
  Violin bow 510
Screw and lock nut tappet adjustor 367
Screw coupling 325
Screwdown greaser 336
Screw fitting 319
Screw hole 600
Screw joint 413
Screw link 386
Screw locking nut 563
Screw pressure adjustor 447
Scriber 446
Scroll
  Cello 511
  Double bass 511
  Viola 511
  Violin 510
Scroll button 567
Scroll down button 568
Scrolled buttress 478
Scroll motif 470, 491
Scroll moulding 466
Scroll ornament 476, 479, 485
Scroll-shaped corbel 482, 487

Scroll up button 567
Scrollwork 472
Scrotum 211, 259
Scrum-half 530
Scrummages 530
Scull 561
Sculling 560
Scull oar 560
Sculptor 19, 20
Sculptural decoration 467
Sculpture 452-455, 493, 495
Sculptured testa 151
Scumbling 440-441
Scupper 393
Scute 186
Scutellum 168
Scutum 19
Scutum plate 173
Scyphozoa 166
Sea
  Anticline trap 281
  Fossils 278
  Hurricane structure 303
  River features 290-291
Sea anemone 166-167
Sea angling 562
Seabed
  Fossils 278
  Ocean floor 298
  River features 290
  Rivers 288
Seabed profile 299
Sea buckthorn 136
Seacat missile launcher 397
Sea level 66
Sea-level variations 294
Sea lilies 174
Sea lion 204
Seals 204-205
Seam
  Rivetted plates 392
  Sail 384
Seaming twine 384
Seamounts 298
Sea of Japan 265
Searchlight 394-395
Seas 296-297
  Igneous and metamorphic rocks 275
  Rivers 288
  Satellite map 265
Seasons 72
Seat
  1906 Renault 337
  Driver's 325, 328
  Faering 375
  Fireman's 325
  First cars 334-335
  Ford Model T 339
  Greek trireme 373
  Harley-Davidson FLHS Electra Glide 363
  Honda CB750 363
  Honda VF750 364
  Husqvarna Motocross TC610 368
  Kayak 560
  Longboat 380
  Motorcycle 364
  Racing sulky 555
  Renault Clio 352-353
  Showjumping saddle 554
  Suzuki RGV500 368
  TGV electric high-speed train 329
  Vespa Grand Sport 160

Mark 1 363
Weslake Speedway motorcycle 369
Seat angle 360
Seat assembly 425, 553
Seat attachment rail 416
Seat back rest frame 337, 352-353
Seat beam 399
Seat belt catch 352
Seat cushion 407, 425
Sea temperature 303
Seat frame 353
Seating 465
Seat mount 340
Seat pan 409
Seat post 358, 360
Seat post quick-release bolt 358
Seat spring 353
Seat squab 353, 357
Seat stay 358, 360
Seat support strut 398
Seat tube 358, 360, 361
Sea urchins 174-175
Seawater
  River features 290
  Salt content 296
Seaweeds 116-117
Seaworm 78
Sebaceous gland 234-235
Secondary baffle 612
Secondary bronchus 215
Secondary colours 439
Secondary conduit 272-273
  Rock cycle 266
Secondary crater 34
Secondary flight feathers 188, 191
Secondary follicle 258
Secondary mirror 612
Secondary mycelium 115
Secondary phloem 134-135
Secondary remiges 188, 191
Secondary rotor 317
Secondary suspension 327
Secondary thallus 114
Secondary vascular tissue 134
Secondary xylem 125, 134-135
Second-century building 462
Second electron shell 309
Second mast 376
Second-row forward 530
Second slip 538
Second toe 232
Second violins 503, 504-505
Second wheel set 329
Secretory gland 161
Secretory thyroid gland cells 217
Secure anchor 386
Security light 603
Security lock port 566, 567
Sediment
  Coastlines 294-295
  Fossils 278
  Glaciers 286-287
  Lakes 292
  Mineral resources 280
  Mountain building 62-63
  Ocean floor 298-299
  River features 290-291
  Rivers 288
  Rock cycle 266-267
Sedimentary rocks 276-277
  Igneous and metamorphic rocks 274
  Rock cycle 266-267
Sedna Planitia 36-37

Sedum rupestre 128
Sedum spectabile 128-129
Seed
  Apomixis 146
  Apple 149
  Cape gooseberry 149
  Dehydration 152
  Dispersal 148-151
  Dormancy 152
  Dry fruit 150-151
  Embryo development 147
  Fig 148
  Germination 132, 152-153
  Goosegrass 150
  Gymnosperms 122
  Hilum 148-149, 151-153
  Hogweed 151
  Honesty 151
  Larkspur 151
  Lemon 148
  Love-in-a-mist 151
  Melon 149
  Parts 152-153
  Pea 150
  Pine 122
  Raspberry 149
  Root development 132
  Scots pine 122
  Smooth cypress 123
  Strawberry 150
  Succulent fruit 148-149
  Sweet chestnut 150
  Sycamore 131, 151
  Wind dispersal 150
  Wings 150-151
  Yew 123
Seed axis 152-153
Seed coat 132, 152-153
  Dry fruit 150-151
  Embryo development 147
  Epigeal germination 153
  Hypogeal germination 152
  Succulent fruit 148-149
Seed fern 278
Seed leaves 126, 152-153
  Dry fruit 150-151
  Embryo development 147
  Epigeal germination 153
  Hypogeal germination 152
  Pine 122
  Succulent fruit 148-149
Seedlings
  Epigeal germination 153
  Hypogeal germination 152
  Pine 122
Seed-producing organs 148-149
Seed scar 122
Seed stalks 150
Seed wings 151
Segmental arch 492
Segmental pediment 462, 478
Segnosauria 83
Seif dune 283
Seismic activity 58
Seizing 383, 384, 387, 388-389
Selaginella sp. 120Select button 578
Select/enter option 587
Selector fork 366
Selector switch 598-599
Selenite 270
Selenium 311
Self-pollination 144
Semaphore signal 330

Semen 217
Semi-arch 470-471
Semibreve 502-503
Semi-bulkhead 425
Semi-circle 552
Semicircular canals 243
Semicircular tower 465
Semi-conductor 306
Semi-dome 484, 482, 488
Semi-elliptical arch 484
Semi-elliptic leaf spring 342
Semilunar fold 249
Semi-metals 510-511
Seminal receptacle 169
  Spider 170
Seminal vesicle 259
Semiquaver 502
Semi-solid core 37
Semi-solid outer core 41
Semi-sprawling stance 82
  Westlothiana 81
Semitendinosus muscle 227
Send/receive icon 576
Send/select button 588
Send/select button connector 589
Senior ratings' mess 397
Sensor cables 609
Sensors 608
Sensor signal boards 609
Sensory antenna 168
Sensory hinge 160
Sensory tentacle 176
Sent items icon 576
Sepal 140-143
  Clematis 131
  Dicotyledons 126-127
  Dry fruit 150-151
  Everlasting pea 129
  Fertilization 146-147
  Monocotyledons 126
  Peruvian lily 129
  Pitcher plant 113
  Pollination 145
  Rose 131
  Succulent fruit 149
Sepal remains 146-147
Sepal sheath 141
Separated carpels 151
Separator 576
Septime 557
Septum 115
  False 151
  Interventricular 251
  Nasal 213, 241
  Placenta 260
Sequencer 521
Sequoiadendron sp. 70
Series elastic actuator 609
Series electrical circuit 516
Serif 445
Serous pericardium 250
Serpens Caput 18, 21
Serpens Cauda 19, 20
Serpentes 184
Serpentine neck 374
Serrated tooth 84, 85, 88
Serrate leaf margins 129
Serratus anterior muscle 226
Server 534, 544, 545, 576
Server Service 544
Service area 534
Service box line 545
Service court 544, 545
Service crane 605
Service door 415
Service judge 544, 545
Service line 544, 545
Service shaft 498
Service zone 545
Serving 588
Serving mallet 383, 384, 388
Servo control-unit fairing 417

Servo-tab 414, 415
Sesamoid bone 198
Seta 112, 119
Set-back buttress 481
Set square 445
Settings control panel 574
Settings display 574, 575
Setting select buttons 575
Seven Sisters 14
Seventeenth century 474
  Building 479-481, 488
  Capital 490
  Dome 486-487
  Roof 490
  Style 478
  Tomb 489
Seventh century
  Building 491
Sevier fault 276
Sex cells 154
  Fertilization 146-147
  Gametophyte plants 120
  Gymnosperms 122
  Liverwort 118
  Moss 118-119
Sextans 21
Sexual reproduction
  Algae 116, 117
  Bryophytes 119
  Flowering plants 140-147
  Mosses 118-119
  Seaweed 116-117
  Spirogyra sp. 117
Seyfert 41
Seyfert galaxies 12-13
Shackle 382, 386
Shackle pin 383
Shaft
  Ancient Egyptian column 459
  Ancient Greek temple 461
  Ancient Roman building 465, 465
  Arrow 548
  Asian building 490-491
  Badminton racket 545
  Electric generator 317
  Feather 191
  Femur 225
  French temple 485
  Golf club 547
  Harness racer 555
  Hydroelectric power station 314
  Javelin 542
  Kayak paddle 560
  Medieval church 468-469
  Modern building 498
  Neoclassical building 478, 485
  Nineteenth-century building 493
  Phalanx 230
  Power drill 600
  Roman Corbita 373
  Sculling oar 560
  Ski pole 553
  Squash racket 545
Shaft drive 366
Shale
  Contact metamorphism 274
  Grand Canyon 277
Shallow carvel-built hull 391
Shallow flats 293
Shank
  Anatomy of a hook 562
  Danforth anchor 386
  Hook 383
  Roman anchor 372
  Sail hook 384
  Shackle pin 382
Shannon bone 198
Shape
  Chemical reactants 312

Matter 306-307
Periodic table 510
Shapes (plane; solid) 622
Sharks 178-179, 180
Sharp 502
Sharpey's fibre 225
Shaula 19, 20
Shave 374
Shaving foam 306
Shearing 61
Sheave 383
Sheave for cat tackle 380
Sheep 198
Sheepskin numnah 554
Sheer 374
Sheerplank 380
Sheer pole 373
Sheer strake 375, 393
Sheet 372, 375, 382
Sheet anchor 395
Sheet bend 389
Sheet feeder 575
Sheet-iron louvre 493
Sheet lead 383
Shelf formation 282
Shell
  379 cm shell 397
  6 in shell 397
  Building 464, 476
  Chelonians 186
  Crab 172
  Dorsal margin 176
  Egg 192-193
  Exploding 394, 596-597
  Fossil 278
  Massive stars 26
  Mollusc 176-177
  Octopus 176
  Rib 176
  Rudiment 176
  Scallop 176
  Small stars 24-25
  Snail 177
  Standing block 382
  Terrapin 187
  Ventral margin 176
Shell bogie 396
Shell case 397
Shelled invertebrates 56
Shelley 35
Shell-like fracture 270
Shell room 396
Shelly limestone 267
"Shiaijo" 556
Shield 394-395
"Shield bearers" 92
Shielded receiver 591
Shield plate 570
Shield volcano 42
Shin
  Herrerasaurus 86
  Human 211
  Shinarump member 276
Shin guard
  Slalom skiing 553
  Soccer 525
Shinty 540
Shinumo quartzite 277
Ship 387
  74-gun ship 379, 380-381
  Ship's cannon 376, 394
  Ships of Greece and Rome 372-373
Ship of the line 380-381
Ship's shield 394-395
Ship's wheel 378, 390, 394
Shipwright 374
Shiv 383
Shiver 383
Shock absorber
  1906 Renault 336
  American football helmet 527
  ARV light aircraft 425
  Honda CB750 363
  Honda VF750 364
  Renault Clio 350
  Suzuki RGV500 368

Vespa Grand Sport 160
Mark 1 363
Volkswagen Beetle 340
Shock-absorbing platform 553
Shock-absorbing spring 401, 405
Shock-strut 401
Shock waves 27
Path 63
Athletics 543
Basketball 533
Golf 547
Handball 535
Rowing 560
Shoot
Broomrape 163
Embryo 147
Horsetail 120
Hypogeal germination 152
Pine 125
Vegetative reproduction 155
Shoot apex 125
Shooting 548-549
Shooting circle 540
Shooting positions 548
Shoreline
Coastlines 294
Continental-shelf floor 298
Short line 545
Shorts
Australian rules football 529
Hurling 541
Soccer 525
Volleyball 534
Short saphenous vein 253
Shortstop 536
Short-wave radio 318
Shot
Field events equipment 542
Gun 578
Shot garland 381
Shot put 543
Shot-put circle 542
Shot-put fan 542
Shoulder
Anchisaurus 89
Cello 511
Corythosaurus 98
Double bass 511
Gorilla 203
Harp 511
Horse 199
Human 210
Iguanodon 97
Rabbit 196
Rigging 382-383
Stegoceras 101
Stegosaurus 92
Viola 511
Violin 510
Shoulderblade 210, 218
Shoulder button 578, 579
Shoulder cowling 412
Shoulder girdle 80
Shoulder joint
Brachiosaurus 91
Gallimimus 86
Human 218
Parasaurolophus 99
Plateosaurus 88
Triceratops 102
Tyrannosaurus 84
Shoulder motor 609
Shoulder pad 426
Shoulder padding 551
Shoulder pass 535
Shoulder spikes
Edmontonia 95
Euoplocephalus 94
Shoulder wheel throw 556
Showjumping 554
Shreve, R.H. 494
Shrew-like mammals 70

Shrimp 172
Fossil 79
Shrine 490-491
Shroud
Dhow 376
Longboat 380
Rigging 383
Roman corbita 373
Sailing dinghy 561
Sailing warship 376
Shrubs 130-131
Shutter button 581
Shutter for gun 394
Shutter open knob 587
Shuttlecock 544-545
Sickle motif 491
Sidalcea malviflora 136
Side aisle
Cathedral dome 484
Gothic church 472-473
Medieval church 469
Side bench 580
Side brace and retraction jack trunnions 414
Sidecar
BMW R/60 362
Motorcycle racing 368-369
Side chapel 469-470, 479
Side counter timber 381
Side-cowling 408
Side drum 504-505
Side fairing 415
Side forequarter hold 556
Side gear 347
Side housing 346-347
Side lamp 338-339
Sidelight 332, 333, 362
Side-line
American football 526
Badminton 545
Basketball 532
Handball 535
Hockey 540
Men's lacrosse 540
Netball 535
Tennis 541
Volleyball 534
Side marker lamp 346, 549
Side-mounted engine 398
Side plate 562
Side pod 356, 357
Side reflector 362, 363
Siderite band 277
Side rudder 374-375
Side-shooting 541
Side vent 329
Side wall 545, 558
Side-wall line 545
Sideways erosion
River features 290
Rivers 288
Sierra Madre 264
Sierra Nevada 57, 75
Sieve tubes 134
Sieving beak 188
Sif Mons 37
Sight 394
Sight pin 549
Sight screen 538
Sighting hood
Battleship 394
Gun turret 596
Sighting rule 376-377
Sights 548-549
Sigma Canis Majoris 21
Sigmoid colon 249
Signal flag compartment 397
Signal gear 395
Signalling systems 330-331
Sikorsky, Igor 422
Silence 502
Silencer
Harley-Davidson FLHS Electra Glide 362
Renault Clio 350

Suzuki RGV500 368
Vespa Grand Sport 160
Mark 1 363
Weslake Speedway motorcycle 369
Silencing heat exchanger 404
Silicate core 51
Silicate dust 53
Silicate material 39
Silicate rock 39
Silicates 269
Siliceous ooze 299
Silicon 26
Earth's composition 39
Earth's crust 58
Periodic table 311
Variety of matter 306
Siliquas 150-151
Silk gland 170
Sill 26
Ancient Roman mill 464
Renaissance building 475
Twentieth-century building 494
Sill trim 353
Silly mid-off 538
Silly mid-on 538
Silurian period
Fossil record 279
Geological time 56
Silver
Mineral resources 280-281
Minerals 268
Periodic table 311-312
Streak 271
Silver lines 430-431
Silver molybdenite 271
Silver nitrate solution 312
Silverpoint 430, 431
Silver wire 430
Silvery metals 310
Simm card 589
Simm card connectors 589
Simple electrical circuit 316
Simple eye 170-171
Simple leaves 136-137
Entire 130
Hastate 128
Herbaceous flowering plants 128-129
Lanceolate 131
Lobed 131
Simple machines 320
Simple Machines Law 320
Simple pulleys 320
Simple succulent fruits 148-149
Simulated sound 520
Single bass note string 515
Single-celled micro-organisms 78
Single clump block 373
Single cylinder 335
Single-decker bus 332, 333
Single flowers 140-141, 143
Single front driving wheel 334
Single-glazed conservatory 602
Single-leg main landing gear 407
Single overhead cam engine 363
Single-piece skin 413
Single-pulley system 320
Single reed 508, 509
Singles 544
Single scull 560, 561
Single sheet bend 587
Single-sided trailing-link fork 363
Single wing hold 556

Singularity
Formation of black hole 29
Stellar black hole 29
Sinistral strike-slip fault 61
Sink-holes 284-285
Sinking land 294
Sinopia 434, 435
Sinous venosus sclerae 241
Sinuous cell wall 156
Sinus
Frontal 212, 245
Green alga 112
Renal 256
Superior sagittal 212
Sinus Borealis 69
Sinus Iridum 40
Siphon
Octopus 176-177
Sea urchin 175
Siphonoglyph 167
Sirius
Canis Major 21
Northern stars 18
Our galaxy and nearby galaxies 15
Southern stars 21
Spectral absorption lines 23
Star magnitudes 22
Sirius A 23
Sirius B 23
Sixteenth century
Building 476-477
Staircase 472
Style 462, 470
Size (glue) 431, 432, 436
Skarn 26
Skate
Chondrichthyes 178
Ice hockey 550, 551
Skeletal muscle 228
Skeletal muscle fibre 228
Skeleton
Archaeopteryx 85
Arsinoitherium 104-105
Baryonyx hand 85
Bat 105
Bird 189
Bony fish 180-181
Cow's foot 198
Crocodile 186
Diplodocus 90
Domestic cat 195
Elephant 201
Eryops 80-81
Frog 183
Hare 197
Horse 199
Human 218-219
Iguanodon 96
Kangaroo 206
Kentrosaurus 93
Lizard 184
Parasaurolophus 98-99
Pareiasaur 81
Plateosaurus 88-89
Platypus 206
Rhesus monkey 202
Seal 204
Smilodon 107
Stegoceras 101
Styracosaurus 102
Synapsid reptile 67
Tortoise 77
Turtle 187
Skull bones 81
Skullcap 555
Slab
Ancient Egyptian building 458-459
Modern building 499
Twentieth-century building 494
Slaked lime 434
Slalom
Skiing 552
Canoeing 560
Slalom clothing 553

Skilled movements 237
Skin
Amphibian 80, 182
Drumhead 518
Lizard 184
Reptile 80
Snake 184
Succulent fruits 148-149
Waterproof 81
Skin and hair 234-235
"Skin-grip" pin 424-425
Skin lap-joint 413, 414, 415
Skin tones 441
Ski pole 552
Skirting board 602
Skis 552
Skull
Acanthostega 80
Alligator 186
Ankylosaurus 94
Australopithecus 108
Baryonyx 83
Bear 194
Bird 189
Camarasaurus 91
Chimpanzee 202
Crocodilians 186
Diplodocus 90
Domestic cat 195
Elephant 201
Euoplocephalus 94
Fetal 220
Gharial 186
Hadrosaurs 96
Hare 197
Heterodontosaurus 83
Homo erectus 108
Homo habilis 108
Horse 199
Human 108, 212, 218, 220-221, 222, 236-237
Hyaenodon 107
Iguanodon 96
Lambeosaurus 99
Lion 194
Lizard 184
Marginocephalian 100
Moeritherium 105
Octopus 176
Opossum 106
Pachycephalosaurs 100
Pachycephalosaurus 100
Phiomia 105
Plateosaurus 88
Platypus 206
Prenocephale 100
Protoceratops 102
Rattlesnake 185
Rhesus monkey 202
Smilodon 107
Stegoceras 100
Styracosaurus 102
Toxodon 106
Triceratops 102-103
Tuojiangosaurus 93
Turtle 187
Tyrannosaurus 84-85
Westlothiana 81
Sketch book 430
Skid 402, 404
Skid beam 380
Ski goggles 552, 553
Skiing 552, 553

Slalom equipment 553
Slalom gate 552
Slat 421
Slate 274, 275
Sleep button 585
Sleeper 324, 331
Sleeve port 343
Sleeve valve 343
Slender thistle 129
Slick racing tyre 365
Kirby BSA 369
Suzuki RCV500 369
Slide 396
Slide bar 325
Slide brace 507
Slide locking lever 596
Slide release 587
Slide track 561
Slide valve 390
Sliding bed 447
Sliding curtain 329
Sliding seat 561
Sliding window 333
Sling fixing point 549
Slip face 283
Slip faults 61
Slipher 43
Slope structure 60
Sloping roof 486
Slug 176
Slumped cliff 295
Slur 503
Smallbore rifle shooting 548
Smallbore rifle target 549
Small intestine
Brachiosaurus 90
Chimpanzee 202
Cow 198
Domestic cat 195
Elephant 200
Euoplocephalus 94
Frog 182
Human 214, 249
Lizard 185
Tortoise 187
Small Magellanic Cloud
Hydrus and Mensa 20
Our galaxy and nearby galaxies 15
Stars of southern skies 20
Small stars 24-25
Small theropods 87
Small-scale rock deformities 61
Smalti 450
Smalti mosaic 450
Smash 534
Smell 244
Smilodon 107
Smokebox 524, 325
Smoky quartz 268
Smooth cypress 123
Smooth endoplasmic reticulum 216
Smudging 430, 431
Smuts 114
Snail 176-177
Snake-head ornament 375
Snakes 184-185
Snap head 392
Snare 518
Snare drum 518
Snort mast 397
Snout
Anchisaurus 89
Caiman 186
Crocodilians 186
Dogfish 178
Edmontonia 95
Herrerasaurus 86
Iguanodonts 96
Jawless fish fossil 78
Pachycephalosaurus 100
Rat 196
Snow
Glaciers 286-287

Weather 502
Snowflake moray eel 180
Snowflakes 502
Soane, J. 478, 482-483
Sobkou Planitia 35
Soccer 524-525
Soccer kit 525
Socket 575
Socle
  Ancient Egyptian
    temple 458
  Baroque church 479
  Cathedral dome 487
  Gothic church 472
  Medieval church 469
  Neoclassical building
    478-479
  Renaissance building
    474
Sodalite 269
Sodium 35, 58
  Periodic table 310
  Seawater salt content
    296
Sodium hydroxide 312
Sodium lines 23
Soffit 464, 484, 498
Soft eye 382
Soft hair brush 436, 438,
  440
Soft-headed beater 516,
  517, 519
Soft metals 310
Soft palate 212, 245
Soft pastels 440
Soft pedal 514, 515
Soft rock
  River features 290
  Weathering and erosion
    282
Software 569
Software effect plug-in
  591
Solanum tuberosum 128
Solar array 612, 613
Solar array supporting
  arm 613
Solar cell 605
Solar collector 605
Solar day 34
Solar eclipse 32
Solar flare 32-33
Solar panel 496, 605, 615
Solar power 605
Solar radiation 300-301
Solar system 38, 30-31
Solar wind
  Earth's magnetosphere
    38
  Structure of comet 53
  Sun 32
Solarium 494
Solar Wings Pegasus
  Quasar microlight 427
Sole of foot 234
Soleplate 595
Soleplate roller 593
Soleplate surround 594
Soleus muscle 227, 233
Solfataras 272-273
Solid body 512, 513
Solid heart thimble 383
Solidified lava
  Lake formation 292
  Volcanoes 272-273
Solid ink stick 444
Solid rubber tyre 335
Solids 306-307
  Chemical reactions 312
Solid shapes 622
Solutions 306, 312-313
Sombrero 12
Somites 79
SONAR bulge 397
SONAR torpedo decoy 396
SONAR transducer array
  397
Sonic boom 416

Sonoran Desert 264
Sony Aibo robot dog 608
Sony Cyber-Shot DSC-P1
  digital camera 580
Sony DAV-S300 585
Sony Ericsson T68 588
Sony digital handycam
  582
Sony Portable Minidisk
  Player MZ- 586-587
Soot particles 53
Sophocles 35
Soralium 114
Sorbus aucuparia 130-131
Soredia 114
Sori 120-121
Sostenuto pedal 514, 515
Sound 314-315
  Coastline 295
  Electronic instruments
    520
  Musical notation 502
Soundboard
  Acoustic guitar 513
  Concert grand piano
    515
  Harp 511
  Upright piano 514
  Viola 511
  Violin 510
Sound channels 584
Sound-hole
  Acoustic guitar 512-513
  Cello 511
  Double bass 511
  Viola 511
  Violin 510
Sound module 521
South Africa 64
South America 264
  Cretaceous period 72-
    73
  Jurassic period 70
  Late Carboniferous
    period 66
  Middle Ordovician
    period 64
  Quaternary period 76-
    77
  Tertiary period 74-75
  Triassic period 68
South American plate 59
South Asian buildings
  490-491
South Atlantic Gyre 296
  Satellite map 265
South Atlantic Ocean 39,
  73
South-east trade winds
  300
South-easterly wind 303
South Equatorial Belt 45
South equatorial current
  296-297
Southerly wind 303
Southern Hemisphere
  296-297
Southern polar region 64
South Galactic Pole 15
South Indian Gyre 297
South magnetic polar
  region 28
South Pacific Gyre 296
South Pacific Ocean 39
South polar ice-cap
  Structure of Mars 43
  Surface of Mars 42
South Pole
  Atmospheric circulation
    and winds 300
  Coriolis force 297
  Earth 38
  Jupiter 44
  Mars 42
  Mercury 34
  The Moon 40
  Neptune 50
  Pluto 51
  Pulsar 28

Saturn 46
Uranus 48-49
Venus 36
South rim 277
South seeking pole 317
South Temperate Belt 45
South Temperate Zone
  45
South Tropical Zone 45
Space 300-301
Space probes 614-615
Space shuttle astronaut
  613
Space shuttle remote
  manipulator system
  (robot arm) 612, 613
Space telescope 612-613
Spadix 143
Span 484
Spandrel
  Gothic church 471
  Islamic building 488-
    489
  Neoclassical building
    482
  Nineteenth-century
    building 493
  Renaissance building
    474
Spanish bowline 380
Spar
  BAe-146 jetliner
    components 415
  BE 2B tail 405
  Concorde 417
  Pegasus Quasar
    microlight 427
Spare tyre 337, 339
Spare wheel well 341
Spark plug 342-343, 410
Spark plug cap 366
Spark plug hole 346
Spark plug lead 344
Spar trunnion 409
Spat 426-427
Spathe 143
  Horsetails 120
Spawn 182-183, 192
Speaker
  Digital video 583
  Electronic music
    system 521
  Fax machine 572
  Headphones 586
  Nokia mobile phone
    588, 589
  Samsung laptop 567
  Sony digital camera 581
Speaker panel 578
Speakerphone button 572
Speaker plug 591
Speaker socket 566
Speaker units 584
Speak key 590
Spear 382
Spear head 109
Special function buttons
  588
Specimen 610, 611
Specimen airlock 611
Specimen stage 610, 611
Spectral absorption lines
  22-23
Spectral type 22-23
Specular haematite 268
Speech 237
Speed
  Forces 320
  Gearbox 366
Speedball nib 444
Speedometer 362
Speedometer drive 365
Speedway motorcycle
  racing 368
Sperm 258-259
Spermatheca
  Snail 177
  Spider 170

Sperm cell 217, 607
Sperm duct 195
Spermoviduct 177
Sperm whale 204-205
Sperry-ball gun turret
  408
Sphenethmoid bone 183
Sphenoidal fontanelle 220
Sphenoidal sinus 212, 245
Sphenoid bone 220
Sphenopsids 279
Sphenopteris latiloba 72
Sphere 623
Spherical umbel 143
Spheroid 623
Sphincter muscle
  Anal 249
  Iris 241
  Pyloric 249
Sea anemone 167
Urethral 257
Sphyrna lewini 179
Spica 18, 21
Spicule 32, 33
Spicules 166
Spider
  Arachnid 170-171
  Bicycle 358, 360
  Spider seat 334
Spigot 582
Spike
  Aechmea miniata 162
  Dodder 163
  Double bass 511
  Flower 143
  Grape hyacinth 155
  Thyreophorans 92-93
  Volleyball 534
Spiky cupule 150
Spinal column 258
Spinal cord
  Bird 189
  Bony fish 181
  Chimpanzee 202
  Dogfish 179
  Dolphin 205
  Domestic cat 195
  Elephant 200
  Human 212, 217, 223,
    236, 238, 261
  Lizard 185
  Rabbit 196
Spinal ganglion 223, 238,
  243
Spinal nerve 223, 238
Spindle 601
Spine
  Aechmea miniata 162
  Barberry 130-131
  Bromeliad 113
  Calligraphy character
    445
  Cnidocyte 167
  Diatom 116
  Dryland plants 156
  Golden barrel cactus
    156
  Haemal 180
  Herbaceous flowering
    plants 128-129
  Human 218, 222-223
  Mahonia 130-131
  Modern jetliners 413,
    415
  Neural 180
  Sea urchin 174
  Starfish 174
Spine end fairing 421
Spinner
  ARV light aircraft 424-
    425
  Hawker Tempest
    components 408
  Hawker Tempest
    fighter 409
  Lockheed Electra
    airliner 407
  Turbofan engine 418
Spinneret 170-171

Spinner mounting disc
  406
Spinning lure 562
Spinose-dentate margin
  129
Spinous process 222-223
Spiny anteaters 206
Spiny leaflets 130-131
Spiracle
  Acanthostega 80
  Caterpillar 169
  Spider 170
Spiral arm
  Galaxies 12-13
  Milky Way 14
Spiral galaxy
  Galaxies 12-13
  Milky Way 14-15
  Objects in Universe 11
  Origin and expansion of
    Universe 10-11
Spiral ganglion 243
Spiralling clouds 302
Spiralling low-pressure
  cells 302
Spiralling rain 303
Spiralling winds 302-303
Spiral scroll 460
Spiral spring 449
Spiral staircase 472, 476
Spiral tubes 542
Spiral valve 179
Spiral wrack 116
Spire
  Asian building 490-491
  Gothic church 470-471,
    473
  Medieval building 466,
    468
  Nineteenth-century
    building 493
  Renaissance building
    476-477
Spirit lamp 454
Spirketting 381
Spirogyra sp. 117
Spit 291
Splayed window-sill 475,
  482
Spleen
  Bony fish 181
  Chimpanzee 202
  Domestic cat 195
  Elephant 200
  Frog 182
  Human 215, 249
Splenic artery 253
Splenius fibre 585
Splint bone 198
Splinter bar 335
Splintery fracture 270
Split flap 406
Split line 151
Split-open pollen sac 144
Split rudder 421
Spoiler 346, 349
Spoiler anchorage 413
Spoiler arm 414
Spoke
  Bicycle wheel 358-359
  Bordino Steam Carriage
    335
  Eddy Merckx racing
    bicycle 361
  Etching press 447
  Paddle wheel 391
  Ship's wheel 390
Spoked wheel
  Bicycle 358-359
  Pacing sulky 555
Spoke guard 358
Spoke nipple 361
Sponge roller 442
Sponges 166-167
  Fossils 279
Spongocoel 166
Spongy bone 224
Spongy mesophyll 126,
  139

Spongy tissues 156
Spool 562
Spoon 560
Spoon-shaped tooth 91
Sporangia 120-121
Sporangiophore 120
Sporangium 79
Spore-case 79
Spore producing
  structures
  Fern 121
  Fungi 114-115
  Lichen 114
  Moss 112
Spores
  Clubmoss 120
  Fern 120-121
  Fungi 114-115
  Horsetail 120
  Lichen 114
  Liverworts 118
  Mosses 118-119
  Mushroom 115
Sporophores 114-115
Sporophytes
  Clubmoss 120
  Fern 120-121
  Horsetail 120
  Liverworts 118
  Moss 112, 118-119
Sports tyre 365
Sports wheel 340
Sprag clutch 410
Spray and steam knobs
  594
Spray barrel 594
Spray nozzle 594
Spray pump 594
Spreader 561
Spring
  Lakes and
  Groundwater 292
  Motorcycle 366
  Power drill 600
  Toaster 599
Spring and chassis unit
  337
Spring balance 320
Springboard diving 558
Spring/damper unit 365
Springing point 467, 484-
  485
Spring line 292
Spring perch 338
Spring petiole 160
Spring shock absorber
  358-359
Spring tides 296-297
Spring-trap mechanism
  160
Spring washer 601
Spring wood xylem 134
Sprint races 560
Sprinting 542
Spritsail 378
Sprit yard 376
Sprocket 358, 366
Spruce 513
Spruce beam 560
Sprung chassis 334
Spunyarn 388
Spun yarn serving 383
Spur 169
Spur gear 574
Spurious wing 191
Squadron code 409
Squamata 184
Squamosal bone 183
Squamous suture 220
Squamulose lichens 114
Squamulose thallus 114
Square 622
Square cut 538
Square knot 388
Square leg 538
Square-leg umpire 538
Square masonry 465
Square rib 486
Square-rigged ship 375

Square sail 574, 578, 584
Square-section steel
  tubing 364
Square-section tyre 562,
  569
Squash 544, 545
Squeegee 448
Squid 176
Squinch 466
Squirrel 196-197
Squirrel hair brush 458
Squirrel mop wash brush
  458
SST 416-417
St. John's wort 145
St. Basil's Cathedral 487
St. Paul's Cathedral
  Arch 484
  Baroque style 478, 480-
    481
  Dome 480, 486-487
  Old 470, 472
Stabilizer 397, 548
Stabilizer-bar weight 422
Stabilizer fin 396
Stable elements 310, 311
Stack 295
Staff 577, 596
Stage 477, 495
Stage-door 477
Stained glass 470
Stainless steel cover 599
Staircase
  Ancient Roman
    building 465
  Baroque church 481
  Gothic church 470, 472
  Medieval building 466
  Modern building 496-
    497, 499
  Neoclassical building
    483
  Renaissance building
    474-477
Staircase turret 468
Stairs 477
Stair tool 593
Stairway 489
Stalactites 284-285
Stalagmites 284-285
Stalagmitic boss 284
Stalagmitic floor 284
Stalk
  Algae 116-117
  Barnacle 173
  Dicotyledons 127
  Flower 140
  Fungi 114-115
  Liverwort 118
  Monocotyledons 128
  Moss 112, 119
  Pitcher plant 113
  Seaweed 117
  Stem succulent 115
  Water lily 159
Stalked barnacle 173
Stalked secretory glands
  161
Stalk scar 123
Stall warning vane 412
Stamen remains 146-147,
  150
Stamens 140-143
  Anther 140-143
  Dicotyledon flower 126-
    127
  Fertilization 146-147
  Filament 140-143
  Insect-pollination 144
  Monocotyledon flower
    126
  Rose 131
Stamp 445
Stance
  Dinosaurs 82
  Hominids 108
  Westlothiana 81
Stanchion 573, 593
Standard 554

Standardbred horse 554,
  555
Standard European paper
  445
Standard knee 381
Standby pitot head 416-
  417
Standing block 582
Standing lug mizzen 585
Standing part
  Hawser bend 387
  Knots 588, 589
  Rigging 582-585
  Single sheet bend 587
Standing position 548
Standing rigging 582-585
Stand-off half 550
Stapes 242
Staple 449
Starbirth region 16
Starboard side 374
Starch grains 139
  Chlamydomonas sp.
    116
  Orchid root 133
Star clusters 16-17, 613
  Objects in Universe 11
  Our galaxy and nearby
    galaxies 14
Star coral 167
Star drag 562
Star dune 283
Starfish 174-175
  Fossil 79
Star formation in Orion
  24
Starling 467
Star magnitudes 22
Stars 22-23, 613
  Massive stars 26-27
  Milky Way 14-15
  Neutron stars and black
    holes 28-29
  Small stars 24-25
  Star clusters 16, 613
  Sun 32-33
Star-shaped parenchyma
  135
Star-shaped sclereids 159
Stars of northern skies 18-
  19
Stars of southern skies 20-
  21
Start button 572, 578
Start button and indicator
  light 570
Starter 559, 558
Starter cog 336
Starter motor
  Hawker Tempest
    components 408
  Mid West twin-rotor
    engine 411
  Renault Clio 351
  Volkswagen Beetle 540
Starter ring 345
Starting block 558
Starting handle 336-337,
  338, 343
Starting line (100m) 542
Start print button 575
State room 592
Static air-pressure plate
  412
Static discharge wick 406
Static electricity 316
Stationary gear 346-347,
  411
Stator 410
Statue 472, 478
Statue creation 455
Statuette 476, 481
Staurikosaurids 69
  Staurikosaurus 69
Stay 525, 592
Staysail 378, 585
"Stealth" bomber 420-421
Steam 273, 307
  Locomotives 324, 325

Nuclear power station
  314
Oil-fired power station
  315
Steam barrel 594
Steamboat with paddle
  wheels 391
Steam car 334, 342
Steam chest 334
Steam chest pressure
  gauge 325
Steam condenser 397
Steam control knob 594
Steam dome 325
Steam engine 390-391
Steam generator 314
Steam grating 580
Steam iron 594
Steam launch 594
Steam locomotive 324,
  325
Steam pipe 334-335
Steam pipework 597
Steam whistle 392
Steel 492
Steel and concrete floor
  498
Steel and titanium skin
  416
Steel beater 517
Steel brace 493
Steel column 497-498
Steel floor-plate 497
Steel frame 360, 364
Steel girder framework
  314
Steel lattice-beam 497
Steel lock 560
Steel mullion 494
Steel point 452
Steel rails 330
Steel-reinforced concrete
  494
Steel sleeper 330
Steel wheel 340, 350-351
Steeple 471, 481
Steeplechase 554
Steep ridge 283
Steerboard side 374
Steerer tube 359
Steering 350, 564
Steering actuator 416
Steering arm 338-339
Steering box assembly 340
Steering column
  Benz Motorwagen 335
  Ford Model T 339
  Renault Clio 350
  Volkswagen Beetle 341
Steering gear 342
Steering gearbox 339
Steering head 335
Steering idler 340
Steering knuckle 338
Steering link 335
Steering oar 374
Steering pump pulley 344
Steering wheel force 557
Steersman 500
  Stegoceras 100-101
Stegosauria 83
Stegosaurs 71, 92
  Stegosaurus 71, 92

Steib chair 562
Stela 459
Stele
  Dicotyledons 127
  Monocotyledons 127
  Root 132-133
Stellar core 17
Stellar spectral absorption
  lines 22-23
Stellate parenchyma 135
Stem 134-135
  Aechmea miniata 162
  Asteroxylon 79
  Bamboo 131
  Barberry 130-131
  Battleship 394
  Begonia 129
  Bishop pine 124-125
  Brassavola nodosa 162
  Bromeliad 113
  Broomrape 163
  Canadian pond weed
    158-159
  Chusan palm 130
  Clubmoss 120
  Corallina officinalis 117
  Couch grass 113
  Crab cactus 129
  Dicotyledons 126-127
  Dodder 163
  Eddy Merckx racing
    bicycle 361
  Epiphytes 162-163
  Everlasting pea 129
  Florists'
    chrysanthemum 129
  Flower arrangements
    143
  Golden barrel cactus
    156
  Guzmania lingulata
    162-163
  Hogweed 129
  Horsetail 120
  Ice-plant 128-129
  Iron paddlesteamer 393
  Ivy 131
  Kedrostis africana 113
  Live-for-ever 128-129
  Liverwort 118
  Maidenhair tree 123
  Maple 127
  Monocotyledons 126-127
  Moss 119
  Parasitic plants 163
  Passion flower 130
  Peach 131
  Perennials 130-131
  Sago palm 123
  Strawberry 128
  String of hearts 157
  Vegetative reproduction
    154-155
  Water fern 158
  Welwitschia 123
  Woody plants 130-131
  Woody stem 134
  Yew 123
Stem base
  Bulbil 155
  Guzmania lingulata
    162-163
Stem branch 129
Stem bulbils 155
Stem cambium 126
Stem cells 606, 607
Stem head 576
Stempost
  74-gun ship 381
  Dhow 376
  Longboat 380
  Sailing warship 376
  Viking ships 374-375
Stem projections 156
Stem segments 129
Stem succulents 115, 156-
  157

Stem tubers 128, 154
Stencil 446
Step
  74-gun ship 381
  ARV light aircraft 424
  BE 2B bomber 404
  Blériot XI monoplane
    401
  Medieval building 467
  Modern building 499
  Neoclassical building
    483
  Steam-powered Cugnot
    334
  Twentieth-century
    building 495
  Wooden sailing ship
    378
Stephenson, Robert 324
Stepped roof 481
Stepped stempost 375
Stepped stempost 375
Sterile hairs 117, 119
Sterile ray 119
Sterile ray floret 142
Sterile shoot 120
Sterile whorl 116
Stern
  74-gun ship 381
  Iron paddlesteamer 392
  Kayak 560
  Sailing dinghy 561
  Wooden sailing ship
    378-379
  Sterna hirundo 193
Sternal artery 173
Sternal bone 96, 102
Stern balustrade 373
Stern carving 381
Stern framing 392
Stern gallery 597
Stern lantern 579
Sternocleidomastoid
  muscle 226-227, 229
Sternohyoid muscle 229
Sternpost
  Greek galley 372
  Roman corbita 373
  Sailing warship 377
  Single scull 560
  Viking ships 374-375
  Wooden sailing ship
    378
Stern quarter gallery 379
Stern rope 387
Stern section 392
Sternum
  Bird 189
  Domestic cat 195
  Elephant 201
  Hare 197
  Horse 199
  Human 218
  Kangaroo 206
  Seal 204
Stern walk 395
Stibnite 268
Stick insect 192
Stiff brush 436
Stifle 198
Stigma
  Damselfly 168
  Dicotyledon flower 126-
    127
  Fertilization 146-147
  Flower 140-143
  Pollination 144-145
Stigma remains 146-147,
  150-151
Stipule
  Begonia 129
  Everlasting pea 129

Passion flower 130
Rose 131
Seedling leaf 152
St. John's wort 145
Strawberry 128
Stirrup
  Crossbow 548
  Ossicles of middle ear
    242
  Saddle 555
Stoa 460
  Ancient Roman
    building 465, 465
  Islamic building 488
Stock
  74-gun ship 380
  Danforth anchor 386
  Roman anchor 372
Stockless anchor 386
Stöfler 40
Stoker's seat 354
Stolons 154
Stomach
  Barnacle 173
  Bird 189
  Bony fish 181
  Chimpanzee 202
  Cow 198
  Crayfish 173
  Dogfish 179
  Dolphin 205
  Domestic cat 195
  Elephant 200
  Frog 182
  Human 214, 248
  Jellyfish 167
  Lizard 185
  Octopus 176
  Rabbit 196
  Ruminants 198
  Snail 177
  Starfish 174
  Tortoise 187
Stomach throw 556
Stomata
  Dryland plants 156-157
  Golden barrel cactus
    156
  Haworthia truncata 157
  Monocotyledon leaf 126
  Photosynthesis role
    138-139
  Pine needle 124
  Wetland plants 158
Stone
  Succulent fruits 148
  Lithographic printing
    446, 448
  Sculpture 452
Stone canal 174, 175
Stone plate 446, 448
Stony-iron meteorite 52
Stony meteorite 52
Stop button 572
Stop control 597
Stop lamp assembly 352
Stop signal 330
Stopwatch 524
Storage organs
  Bulb 155
  Corm 155
  Rhizome 155
  Scale leaf 155
  Seed 152
  Succulent tissue 156-
    157
  Swollen stem 113, 155
  Tubers 128, 155
  Underground 154-155
Store button 521
Stores pylon 420-421
Stork 188
Storm 303
Straddle wire 358, 359
Straight 555
Straight four cylinder
  arrangement 345
Straight gouge 452
Straight handlebar 361

Strake
Concorde 416-417
Ironclad 393
Roman corbita 372
Viking ships 574-575
Strapontin 557
Strap-shaped leaf 162
Strata 276
Faults and folds 60-61
Sedimentary rocks 276
Stratocumulus cloud 302
Stratosphere
Earth's atmosphere
300-301
Jupiter's atmosphere 45
Mars' atmosphere 43
Saturn's atmosphere 47
Stratum basale 235
Stratum corneum 235
Stratum granulosum 235
Stratum spinosum 235
Stratus cloud 302
Strawberry 128, 150
Straw butt 549
Streak 270-271
Stream
Glaciers 286-287
Groundwater system
293
Spring examples 292
Streamed Internet radio
on-screen display 577
Streamed Internet video
on-screen display 577
Streamlined spinner 407
Strengthening tissue
Fern rachis 121
Horsetail stem 120
Marram grass 113
Monocotyledon leaf 126
Stems 134-135
Water lily leaf 159
Stress 61
Stretcher
Brickwork 485
Nineteenth-century
building 492
Single scull 560
Stretches 555
Striated effect 442
Striation 46
Strike
Baseball 556
Baseball umpire signal
557
Slope structure 60
Striker 524
Strike-slip fault 61
Strike-slip fault lake 293
Strike zone 556
Strindberg 35
String
Acoustic guitar 512-513
Cello 511
Concert grand piano
515
Double bass 511
Electric guitar 513
Harp 511
Upright piano 514
Viola 511
String arm 511
String course
Ancient Roman
building 465
Cathedral dome 487
Medieval building 466-
467
Nineteenth-century
building 493
Stringed instruments 510,
511
Guitar 512, 513
Orchestral
arrangement 504, 505
Strings
Guitar 512-513
Racket 544

Violin 510
Strix aluco 190
Strobili 120
Stroke judge 558
Stroke play 546
Strokes 546
Stroke-side oar 560
Stroma 139
Stroma thylakoid 139
Strongylocentrotus
purpuratus 175
Strontium 310
Strop 383
Strut
Dome 484, 486
Gothic building 473
Marble sculpture
support 453
Neoclassical building
479
Paddlesteamer 390
Timpanum 519
Strut insert 340
Struthio camelus 188
Egg 193
Struthiolaria 279
Struthiomimus 84, 87
Stub axle 424
Stud
Ancient Roman mill 464
Gothic building 473
Mid West single rotor
engine 410
Studding sail boom 378
Studding sail yard 378
Studio Elvira 495
Study 477
Stuffing box 390
Stump
Coastline 295
Wicket 558
Stupa 490-491
Stupica 491
Sturgeon 180
Style 140-143
Fertilization 146-147
Monocotyledon flower
126
Pitcher plant 113
Pollination 144-145
Rowan fruit 131
Style of the gnomon 377
Style remains
Dry fruit 150-151
Fruit development 146-
147
Succulent fruit 148-149
Stylet 107
Stylobate 460
Styloglossus muscle 244
Styloid process 220, 245
Stylus 568
Styracosaurus 102, 103
Subacute leaf apex 136-137
Subarachnoid space 237
Subclavian artery 215,
251, 253
Subclavian vein 253
Subduction 58
Subduction zone 281
Subframe 351
Subgenital pit 167
Subglacial stream 287
Sublimation 307
Sublingual fold 245
Sublingual gland 244-245
Submandibular gland 244
Submarine 396-397
Submarine canyon 298
Submerged atoll 299
Submerged glacial
valleys 294-295
Submerged river valleys
294
Subopercular bone 181
Substitutions 552, 550
Substomatal chamber 139
Substrate 112
Substratum 113

Subsurface current 297
Subtropical jet stream 300
Succulent fruits 148-149,
150
Bramble 130
Development 146-147
Peach 131
Rowan 131
Succulent leaves 128, 157
Succulent plants 156-157
Succulents 112
Leaf 157
Stem 156-157
Stem and root 157
Trailing stem 157
Succulent stem 129
Sucker
Lamprey 178
Octopus 176
Sucking stomach 170
Suction reduction control
593
Sugar
Fermentation 312
Formation 138
Photosynthesis 315
Transport 139
Sulcus terminalis 244
Sulky 554
Sulphates 269, 296
Sulphides 268
Sulphur 39, 268
Sulphur dioxide 37
Sulphuric acid 36-37
Sulphurous gases 273
Sumatra 265
Sumigi 490
Summer petiole 160
Summit caldera 42
Sump 345, 344-345
Sump pan 354
Sun 32, 33, 38
Atmosphere 301
Comet tails 48
Earth's energy 314
Electromagnetic
radiation 314-315
Energy emission from
Sun 22
Light 318
Milky Way 14
Objects in Universe 11
Oceans and seas 296-
297
Ozone formation 64
Solar eclipse 32
Solar System 30-31
Stars 22-23
Sundew 160
Sundial 376, 377
Sunflower 140, 142, 145
Sunken stoma 157
Sunlight and
photosynthesis 138
solar power 605
Sun roof 341
Sun scoop 498
Sunspots 32-33
Sun visor 350, 353
Supai group 277
Superclusters 10
Supercooling 307
Supercool liquid 306-307
Superficial peroneal
nerve 238
Superficial skeletal
muscles 226-227
Superfluid neutrons 28
Super-giant slalom
(Super-G) skiing 552
Supergiant stars
Massive stars 26
Small stars 24-25
Stellar black hole 29
Supergranule 33
Superheater 325
Superior articular facet
222

Superior articular process
222-223
Superior concha 212
Superior laryngeal nerve
244
Superior longitudinal
muscle 245
Superior meatus 245
Superior mesenteric
artery 253, 256
Superior mesenteric trunk
257
Superior mesenteric vein
253
Superior nasal concha 245
Superior oblique muscle
241
Superior orbital fissure
221
Superior ramus of pubis
224, 257
Superior rectus muscle
241
Superior sagittal sinus
212, 237
Superior thyroid artery
244
Superior vena cava 215,
251, 252-253, 255
Supernova
Massive stars 26-27
Nebulae and star
clusters 16
Neutron stars and black
holes 29
Supernova remnant
Nebulae and star
clusters 16-17
X-ray image of Crab
Nebula 28
Supersonic flight 416
Supersonic jetliners 416-
417
Supersonic transport 416-
417
Supporter 581
Supporting tissue
Bishop pine stem 125
Dicotyledon leaf 126
Stems 134-135
Supraoccipital bone 181
Supraoccipital crest 85
Supraoesophageal
ganglion 173
Supraorbital fissure 221
Supraorbital foramen 221
Supraorbital margin 213,
220, 221
Supraorbital notch 213
Supraorbital ridge
Chimpanzee 202
Stegaceras 100
Styracosaurus 102
Suprarenal gland 257
Suprarenal vein 257
Suprascapula 183
Suprasternal notch 211
Surangular bone 102
Surcingle loop 555
Surface areas 623
Surface currents 296-297
Surface deposits 273
Surface layer 293
Surface ocean current 296
Surface streams 284
Surface temperature 39
Stars 22
Structure of main
sequence star 24
Structure of Mars 43
Structure of Mercury 35
Structure of Neptune 51
Structure of red giant
25
Structure of red
supergiant 26
Structure of Venus 37
Sun 33
Surface terrain 284

Surface vegetation 282
Surface winds 300
Surrogate mother 607
Surround sound 584
Surround sound special
effect plug-in 521
Surveillance RADAR 397
Suspended erratic 286
Suspension
"Deltic" diesel-electric
locomotive 327
Microlight 426
Motocross racing 368
Motorcycle 364
Suspension arm 350-351
Suspension linkage 362
Suspension spring 350
Suspension strut 340, 351
Suspension top mount 340
Sustaining pedal 514, 515
Suture 202
Su-wei 376
Suzuki RGV500 368, 369
Swab hitch 387, 389
Swallow 383
Swallow-hole 284
Swamp 290-291
Swan neck ornament 373
Swash plate 344
Swash zone 294
S waves 63
Sweat duct 235
Sweat gland 234-235
Sweat pore 234-235
Sweep rowing boat 561
Sweeping low throw 556
Sweet chestnut 136, 144,
150
Sweetgum 76
Sweet pea 128
Sweet potato 154
Swell manual 514
Swell of muzzle 395
Swell pedal 514
Swell stop 514
Swifting tackle 377
Swim bladder 178, 180-
181
Swimmeret 172
Swimming 558, 559
Swimming pool 558
Swimwear 558
Swingarm 364, 368
"Swing-wings" 420
Switch 316
Switchboard room 597
Switch end casing 598-
599
Switch gear 314
Swivel becket 382
Swivels
Mooring and anchoring
586
Angling 562, 563
Swivel suspension ring
377
Swollen leaf base 154-155
Swollen stem base
Guzmania lingulata
163
Kedrostis africana 113
Oxalis sp. 157
Swollen stem 154-155
Sword 556-557
Sycamore 131, 150-151
Sycamore beam 560
Syconium 148
Syenite 275
Symbiosis
Lichens 114
Mycorrhizal association
133
Symbols
Biology 591
Chemistry 591
Communication 108
Mathematics 591
Music 502, 503

Physics 591
Symphony orchestra 504,
505
Synapsid reptile skull 67
Synaptic knob 228, 259
Synaptic vesicle 239
Syncarpous gynoecium
140
Synchiropus splendidus
180
Synchronized elevator 423
Syncline 60, 61, 62
Synclinorium 61
Synergid nucleus 147
Synsacrum 189
Synthesizer 520
Synthetic brush 436, 438
Synthetic flax 384
Synthetic hog hair brush
442
Synthetic materials 306
Synthetic polymer 306
Synthetic ropes 388
Synthetic sable brush 442
Synthetic strings 544, 545
Synthetic wash brush 458,
442
Syria Planum 42, 43
Systems connector 413
System unit 566

T

Tabernacle 463, 474, 476
Tab hinge 415
Tablet flower 488, 491
Tabling 372, 384
Tabular habit 271
Tacan aerial 420
Tachybaptus ruficollis 190
Tack 375
Tackling
American football 526
Australian rules football
528, 529
Rugby 531
Soccer 524
Tactical air navigation
(Tacan) aerial 420
Tadpoles 182-183, 192
Taenia 460
Taenia colica 249
Taffrail 378, 381
Tail
Amphibian 182
Anchisaurus 89
BE 2B bomber 404
Caiman 187
Calligraphy character
445
Corythosaurus 98
Crocodilians 186
Deer hopper dry fly 563
Dolphin 205
Dunkeld wet fly 563
87
Hare 196
Hawker Tempest
components 409
Herrerasaurus 86
Horse 198
Ichthyostega 80
Iguanodon 96
Iguanodonts 96
Kangaroo 206
Lion 195
Lizard 184-185
Lungfish 81
Monkey 202
Ornithopods 96
Pachycephalosaurus
100
Prehensile 202
Rabbit 196-197
Rat 196
Rattlesnake 185
Rigging 382-383

Salamander 182
Sauropodomorpha 88
Schweizer helicopter 423
Scorpion 170
Ski 552-553
Stegoceras 101
Stegosaurus 95
Tadpole 185
Triceratops 102
Tyrannosaurus 84
Westlothiana 81
Tail area 78
Tail boom 423
Tail bud 260
Tail bumper 417
Tail club 95
Tail cone 416-417, 418
Tail crest 187
Taileron 420-421
Tail fairing 409
Tail feathers 188
Tail fluke 205
Tail-gate 348
Tail gunner's compartment 408
Tail-gun turret 408
Tail-light
  BMW R/60 362
  Harley-Davidson FLHS Electra Glide 362
  Honda CB750 363
  Vespa Grand Sport 160
  Mark 1 363
Tailpiece 510, 511
Tail-pin 510
Tail pipe 340
Tailplane
  ARV light aircraft 424
  BAe-146 jetliner 415
  BE 2B tail 405
  Biplanes and triplanes 402-403
  Blackburn monoplane 401
  Blériot XI monoplane 401
  Curtiss biplane 399
  Hawker Tempest 409
  Lockheed Electra airliner 407
  Schleicher glider 426
Tailplane fairing 415
Tailplane root 409
Tailplane tip 407, 415
Tailrace 314
Tail rod 390
Tail rotor 422-423
Tail-rotor drive shaft 422, 423
Tail rotor gearbox 423
Tail shield 78
Tailskid
  ARV light aircraft 424
  Avro triplane 405
  BE 2B bomber 405
  Blackburn monoplane 400-401
  LVG CVI fighter 405
Tail spike 92
Tail spine 79
Tail unit 368
Tailwheel
  Avro biplane 402
  B-17 bomber 408
  Hawker Tempest fighter 409
  Lockheed Electra airliner 407
  Schleicher glider 426
Tailwheel leg 401
Take-off and landing skid 598
Take-up spool 587
Takla Makan Desert 265
Talc 270-271
Tallow coating 379
Talonavicular ligament 232

Talons 188
Talus 282-283
Talus bone 232
Tamarins 202, 203
Tambourine 504, 518
Tam-tam 504, 516
Tandem wings 402
Tank 592
Tank drain tap 407
Tank inspection access 417
Tank support 339
Tantalum 310
Tantalus Fossae 43
Tapeats sandstone 277
Tape guide 587
Tape reader 582
Tape reading head 582
Tapir 198
Tappet 543
Tappet adjustor 367
Tap root 128
Tarantula Nebula 26-27
  Large Magellanic Cloud 12
Tarantulas 170-171
Target areas 556, 557
Target hole 546
Target pistol 548, 549
Target shooting 548, 549
Tarn 293
  U-shaped valley formation 287
Tarsal bone
  Albertosaurus 84 87
  Iguanodon 97
Tarsals
  Crocodile 186
  Domestic cat 195
  Elephant 201
  Frog 183
  Hare 197
  Horse 199
  Kangaroo 206
  Lizard 184
  Platypus 206
  Rhesus monkey 202
  Seal 204
Tarsiers 202
Tarsomere 13
Tarsometatarsus 189
Tarsus
  Beetle 168
  Bird 188
  Human 219
  Scorpion 170
  Spider 171
Tas-de-charge 469
Tasmanian devil 207
Taste 244
Taste bud 244
Tau Orionis 18
Taurus 19, 20
Taurus mountains 77
Tau Sagittarii 21
Tawny owl 190
Taxiing light 414, 420
Taxus baccata 70, 123
Tea clipper 592
Team crest 531
Team jersey 529
Team name 533
Tear fault 61
Technetium 310
Technosaurus 69
Tee 546
Teeing ground 546
Tee peg 547
Teeth
  Ankylosaurus 92
  Bear 106
  Caiman 186
  Canine 194, 202
  Carnassial 194
  Carnivores 194
  Ceratopsian 100
  Cheek 194
  Chimpanzee 202

Crocodilians 186
Extinct shark 67
Hadrosaur 96
Hominid 108
Horse 105
Human 246-247
Iguanodont 96
Incisor 194, 196, 201, 202
Lamprey 178
Leaf-shaped 88-89
Molar 194, 201, 202
Ornithopod 96
Premolar 194, 202
Rabbit 196
Rodents 196
Theropod 84
Thyreophoran 92
Venus fly-trap 160
Teeth development 246
Tegenaria gigantea 171
Telephone line 576
Telephone line cord 572
Telephone on hook wiring harness 572
Telescope, space 612-613
Telescopic damper 326, 329
Telescopic fork
  Harley-Davidson FLHS Electra Glide 363
  Honda CB750 363
  Husqvarna Motocross TC610 368
  Motorcycle 364
  Suzuki RGV500 368
  Weslake Speedway motorcycle 369
Telescopic sight 548, 549
Telescopic strut 416
Television 315
Telltale 545
Tellurium 311
Tellus Regio 36, 37
Tellus Tessera 37
Telson 172
  Fossil 79
TEM 610, 611
Tempe Fossae 43
Tempera 432, 433
Temperate latitudes 302
Temperature
  Atmosphere 300-301
  Chemical reactions 312-313
  Formation of black hole 29
  Germination 152
  Matter 306-307
  Mineral resources 280
  Oceans and seas 296
  Stellar black hole 29
  Weather 302-305
Temperature and pressure sensor 418
Temperature and steam control dial 594
Temperature changes
  Atmosphere 301
  Oceans and seas 296
  Weathering and erosion 282
Temperature scales 621
Temperature warning 567
Tempered pigment 432
Temple 484-485
  Ancient Egyptian 458
  Ancient Greek 460-461
  Ancient Roman 462-463
  Asian 490
Temple blocks 516
Temple Butte limestone 277
Temple Cap sandstone 276
Temple of Amon-Re 458-459
Temple of Aphaia 461

Temple of Athena Polias 460
Temple of Heaven 490
Temple of Isis 459
Temple of Mallikarjuna 491
Temple of Neptune 460-461
Temple of Vesta 462-463
Temple of Virupaksha 490-491
Tempo 504
Temporal bone
  Chimpanzee 202
  Human 220-221, 242
Temporalis muscle 226-227, 229
Tendon
  Achilles 232-233
  Annular 241
  Calcanean 232-233
  Extensor digitorum longus 233
  Extensor digitorum 231
  Extensor hallucis longus 233
  Flexor digitorum 231, 87
  Palmaris longus 231
  Peroneus brevis 233
Tendril
  Arabesque 480
  Clematis 130
  Dogfish egg 192
  Everlasting pea 129
  Monkey cup 161
  Passion flower 130
Tennis 544
Tennis racket 544
Tenon
  Flax spinning mill 492
  Hull plank fastening 575
Tenor drum 518-519
Tenor joint 508
Tenor mute 507
Tenor note strings 515
Tenor saxophone 509
Tenor voice 502
Tension
  Drums 518
  Faults and folds 60-61
  Mountain building 62
Tension-column 497
Tension control 552
Tension key 518, 519
Tension member 499
Tension pulley 560
Tension rod 518, 519
Tension screw 518
Tensor fasciae latae muscle 226
Tensor tympani muscle 243
Tentacle
  Coelenterates 166
  Jellyfish 167
  Molluscs 176-177
  Scallop 176
  Sea anemone 166-167
  Snail 177
Tenth century
  Building 490
  Style 468
Tepal scar 140
Tepal
  Flower parts 140, 143
  Monocotyledons 126
  Peruvian lily 129
Terbium 311
Teres major muscle 227
Teres minor muscle 227
Tergum plate 173
  Egg 193
Terminal 586
  Bishop pine 124

Horse chestnut 130
London plane 134
Rhizome 155
Root tuber 154-155
Stems 154
Stolon 154
Terminal ileum 249
Terminal lake 286
Terminal moraine
  Glaciers 286
  Rivers 289
Terminal pinna 136
Terminal ring 259
Terminus 286
Terrace
  Asian building 490-491
  Modern building 497-499
  Twentieth-century building 494-495
Terracotta clay 455
Terrain-following radar 420
Terrapin 186-187
Terrestrial animal 74
Terrestrial mammal 104
Terrigenous sediment 299
Tertiary bronchus 215
Tertiary period 57, 74, 75
  Fossil record 279
Tessellation 489
Tessera 450, 489
Test 174-175
Testa 152
  Dry fruit 150-151
  Embryo development 147
  Epigeal germination 155
  Hypogeal germination 152
  Succulent fruit seed 148-149
Testicle 259
Testicular artery 257
Testicular vein 257
Testis
  Barnacle 173
  Dolphin 205
  Domestic cat 195
  Human 259
  Rabbit 196
Test tube 313
Tetanurae 83
Tethus Regio 36
Tethys 46
Tethys Sea
  Cretaceous period 73
  Jurassic period 71
  Tertiary period 74, 75
  Triassic period 69
Tetragonal system 270
Tetrahedron 623
Tetralophodon 75, 104
Text 444
Text messages 588
Textured papers 441
Textured scraper 555
TGV electric high-speed train 529
Thalamian 373
Thalamus 236-237
Thalassiosira sp. 116
Thallium 311
Thalloid liverwort 118
Thallus
  Algae 116-117
  Lichen 114
  Liverwort 118
  Seaweed 116-117
T-handle auger 374
Thar Desert 265
Tharsis Tholus 43
Thatched roof 477
Thaumasia Fossae 43
Themis Regio 36
The Plough 19
Therapeutic cloning 606

Theobroma cacao 148
Therapsids 104
Thermal/electrical insulation 596, 597
Thermal insulation 613
Thermals 426
Thermocouple bus-bar 419
Thermogram 214
Thermosphere
  Earth's atmosphere 300
  Mars' atmosphere 43
  Venus' atmosphere 37
Thermostat 411
Theropoda 83
Theropods 84-87
Thesium alpinum 145
Theta1 Sagittarii 21
Theta Andromedae 19
Theta Pegasi 19
Thetis Regio 36
Thick skull 46
Thigh
  Anchisaurus 89
  Bird 188
  Corythosaurus 98
  Gorilla 203
  Horse 198
  Human 211
  Iguanodon 96
  Kangaroo 207
  Lion 195
  Psittacosaurus 103
  Stegoceras 101
  Stegosaurus 92
  Triceratops 102
  Tyrannosaurus 84
Thigh musculature 90
Thigh pad 527
Thimble
  Harness racing 555
  Rigging 383, 384
Third-century building 465
Third home 541
Third main 538, 541
Third rail 328
Thirteenth century
  Building 467, 469-471
  Style 470
Thirty-five mm file strip holder 570
Thistle funnel 313
Thole pin 380
Thoracic cavity 255
Thoracic leg 169
Thoracic nerve 238
Thoracic pleurae 78
Thoracic segment 79
Thoracic vertebrae
  Crocodile 186
  Domestic cat 195
  Hare 197
  Horse 199
  Human 222
  Kangaroo 206
  Platypus 206
  Rhesus monkey 202
  Seal 204
Thoracolumbar vertebrae
  Elephant 201
  Lizard 184
Thorax
  Cirripedia 172
  Human 211
  Insects 168-169
Thorium 310
Thornback ray 179
Thoroughbred horse 554
Thranite 373
Thread 567
Three-blade main rotor 423
Three-cylinder Anzani engine 401
Three-cylinder engine 425
Three-lobed stigma 143

Three-masted square-
rigged ship 575
Three-point line 552
Three pounder 395
Three-toed ungulates 198
Threshold 463
Throat
Angling hook 562
Bird 188
Danforth anchor 586
Human 212, 244-245
Lacrosse crosse 541
Racketball racket 545
Squash racket 545
Tennis racket 544
Throatlatch 199
Throttle
Avro triplane 402
Curtiss biplane 398
"Rocket" steam
locomotive 324
Suzuki RGV500 363
Vespa Grand Sport 160
Mark 1 363
Weslake Speedway
motorcycle 360
Throttle butterfly 345
Throttle cable 350
Harley-Davidson FLHS
Electra Glide 363
Husqvarna Motocross
TC610 368
Kirby BSA racing
sidecar 369
Suzuki RGV500 369
Weslake Speedway
motorcycle 369
Throttle lever 419, 425
Throttle linkage
Ford Model T 338
Jaguar V12 engine 345
Oldsmobile trim 337
Renault Clio 350
Throttle wheel 342
Throw
Judo 556
Structure of a fault 60
Thrower 394
Throw-in 532
Thrushes 188
Thrust 545
Thrust fault 61
Thrust plate 601
Thrust-reverser 421
Thulium 311
Thumb 211, 230-231
Thumb-claw
Anchisaurus 89
Apatosaurus 83
Baryonyx 85, 89
Massospondylus 83, 89
Plateosaurus 88
Thumbhole 384
Thumb knot 389
Thumb piston 514
Thumb-spike mould 454
Thwart 373, 375, 380
Thylakoid 139
Thymine 216
Thyreophora 83
Thyreophorans 92-93, 94-
95
Thyristor converter 328
Thyrohyoid membrane
244
Thyrohyoid muscle 229,
244
Thyroid cartilage 245,
255
Thyroid gland 214-215,
217, 244-245, 255
Tibetan plateau 63
Tibia
Archaeopteryx 85
Beetle 168
Butterfly 169
Crocodile 186
Diplodocus 90
Domestic cat 195

Elephant 201
Eryops 81
Gallimimus 86
Hare 197
Horse 199
Human 219, 232-233
Iguanodon 96-97
Kangaroo 206
Lizard 184
Parasaurolophus 99
Plateosaurus 88
Platypus 206
Rhesus monkey 202
Scorpion 170
Seal 204
Spider 171
Stegoceras 101
Stegosaurus 93
Struthiomimus 87
Toxodon 107
Triceratops 102
Turtle 187
Tyrannosaurus 84
Tibiale 183
Tibial flexor muscle 97
Tibialis anterior muscle
226, 233
Tibialis posterior muscle
233
Tibiofibula 183
Tibiotarsus 189
Tidal bulge 297
Tidal currents 296-297,
298
Tidal flow 296
Tidal levels 295
Tidal power 604
Tidal river-mouth 295
Tidal scour 298
Tidal waves 58
Tides 294, 297
Tie
Basketball match 532
Bordino Steam Carriage
334
Musical notation 502,
503
Tie-beam
Ancient Roman mill 464
Dome 486
Gothic church 473
Neoclassical building
479
Tie plate 395
Tierceron 485
Tie rod 334, 340
Tiger seat 334
Tiger shark 178-179
Tight end 526
Tight-head prop 530
Tile
Dome 486
Islamic mosque 488
Modern building 499
Neoclassical building
482
Renaissance building
476-477
Tiled roof 495
Tilia sp. 134
Tilia x europaea 143
Tiller
Dhow 376
First cars 334-335
Longboat 380
Oldsmobile trim 337
Roman corbita 373
Sailing dinghy 561
Steamboat with paddle
wheels 391
Viking ships 374-375
Tilt and rotation
Jupiter 44
Mars 42
Mercury 34
The Moon 40
Neptune 50
Pluto 51
Saturn 46

Uranus 48
Venus 36
Timber frame
Ancient Roman
building 462, 464-465
Dome 486
Medieval building 466-
467
Renaissance building
477
Timber head 580
Timber rafter 492
Timber trellis 603
Timbre 516
Time interval signal 330
Timekeeper
Basketball 532
Fencing contest 557
Handball 535
Judo contest 556
Lacrosse 541
Netball 535
Swimming 558
Time signature 502
Time switch 598
Time-trial bicycle 360
Time zones 618-619
Timing chain 343, 345
Timing chest 343
Timing gear 307
Timpani 503, 504, 505,
518
Timpanum 519
Tin 311
Mineralization zones
281
Squash 545
Tinatin Planitia 37
Tinted paper 441
Tip of dodder stem 163
Tip ring 563
Tip section 563
Tissue culture 607
Titania 48
Titanium 310
Titanohyrax 74
Toad 182
Toadflax 129
Toaster 598-599
To Do list button 568
Toe
Albertosaurus 84
Anchisaurus 89
Archaeopteryx 85
Bird 188
Caiman 186-187
Corythosaurus 98
Golf club 547
Gorilla 203
Herrerasaurus 86
Human 211, 232-233
Iguanodon 96-97
Lion 194
Lizard 184
Pachycephalosaurus
100
Psittacosaurus 103
Stegoceras 101
Tyrannosaurus 84
Toe clip 560
Toenail
Elephant 200
Gorilla 203
Human 233
Toe piston 514
Toe strap 358-359
Toggle switch 513
Toilet 416, 483
Tolstoj 35
Tomb 458-459, 489
Tomb of Itimad-ud-daula
489
Tomb of King Tjetji 459
Tombolo 294
Tom-toms 518-519
Tondo brush 434
Tone editor control 520
Tonehole 509
Tone pattern selector 520

Tongs 321
Tongue
Allosaurus 85
Caiman 186
Chimpanzee 202
Corythosaurus 98
Cow 198
Dolphin 205
Domestic cat 195
Elephant 200
Human 212, 226, 244,
248
Iguanodon 97
Lamprey 178
Lion 194
Rabbit 196
Rattlesnake 185
Ski boot 552
T'on-wei 376
Tool and battery box 335
Toolbar 576
Tool/brush-head
connector 593
Tool or wand cuff 593
Tools
Rigging 382-383
Sailmaking 384
Viking boatbuilding 374
Tooth
Acanthostega 80
Anchisaurus 89
Ankylosaurus 94
Arsinoitherium 104
Australopithecus 108
Baryonyx 85
Camarasaurus 91
Diplodocus 90
Dragon prowhead 374
Eryops 80
Euoplocephalus 94
Heterodontosaurus 83
Homo habilis 108
Phiomia 105
Plateosaurus 88
Protoceratops 102
Smilodon 107
Triceratops 103
Tyrannosaurus 84
Toothless beak
Ankylosaurs 92
Corythosaurus 98
Euoplocephalus 94
Gallimimus 86
Theropods 84
Triceratops 102
Topaz 271
Topcastle 375, 377
Topgallant mast
Battleship 395
Sailing warship 377
Wooden sailing ship
378-379
Top hose 351
Topmast 377, 378
Topping lift 380
Topping-up valve 561
Top-plate 464
Top race 359
Topsail
74-gun ship 379
Double topsail
schooner 385
Junk 376
Topset strata 283
Topside strake 393
Top sliding block 437
Tornado GR1A 420-421
Torosaurus 97
Toroweap formation 276
Torpedo 394-397
Torque arm 364, 365
Torquemeter mount 419
Torque tube 358-359

Torque tube assembly
425
Torrential rain 302
Torsional vibration
damper 410-411
Torsion bar 350
Torso frame 609
Torso roll motor 609
Tortillon 440, 441
Tortoise 186
Tortoise skull 77
Torus
Ancient Roman
building 463
Asian building 490
Dome 486
Gothic building 470
Medieval building 467-
469
Renaissance building
475, 477
Shapes: solid 623
Total solar eclipse 32
Tote board 555
Touch-down 526
Touch-in goal line 530
Touch judge 530
Touch line
Rugby 530
Soccer 524
Touchpad 567
Touchpiece 509
Touch-sensitive fingertips
609
Tour buses 332
Tour de César 466
Touring bicycle 360, 361
Tourmaline 269
Tower
Ancient Roman
building 465
Asian building 490-491
Clock 493
Gothic church 472
Islamic building 488
Medieval building 466-
467, 468-469
Modern building 496-
497
Nineteenth-century
building 492-493
Renaissance building
476
Twentieth-century
building 495
Tower Bridge 492-493
Tower vault 469
Towing fairlead 395
Towing hook 335, 426
Town Hall 495
Toxodon 76, 106, 107
TPU connector 571
Trabecula 250-251
Trace fossils 278
Tracery
Gothic building 470-473
Nineteenth-century
building 493
Trachea
Bird 189
Brachiosaurus 91
Chimpanzee 202
Dolphin 205
Domestic cat 195
Elephant 200
Gallimimus 86
Human 212, 215, 244-
245, 248, 255
Lizard 185
Rabbit 196
Spider 170
Tortoise 187
Trachelion 460
Trachycarpus fortunei 127,
130
Track 413
Track control arm 340
Track events 542, 543
Track gauge 330, 331

Track rod
Elegance and utility
336-337
Ford Model T 338-339
Renault Clio 351
Track shoe 543
Traction motor 328
Trade winds 300
Traffic congestion 332
Traffic surveillance 422
Tragus 242
Trailboard 379
Trailing arm 340
Trailing edge
BAe-146 jetliner
components 413, 414,
415
BE 2B tail 405
BE 2B wings 404
Hawker Tempest
components 409
Pegasus Quasar
microlight 426-427
Trailing-link arm 414
Trailing wheel 324
Train equipment 330-331
Training gear 396
Trains
Diesel 326-327
Electric 328-329
High-speed 328-329
Steam 324-325
Trams 332-333
Transaxle 340
Transept
Gothic church 470, 473
Medieval church 468-
469
Transfer port 342
Transformation 168
Transformer 314, 328
Transform fault 59
Transistor 584
Transitional cell mucosa
257
Transition metals 310, 311
Transit plug 597
Translucent crystal 271
Translucent impasto glaze
443
Translucent white marble
453
Translucent "window" 157
Transmission 350-351
Transmission adaptor
plate 344
Transmission electron
microscope (TEM) 610,
611
Transmission system 526,
366
Transom
74-gun ship 381
Junk 376
Longboat 380
North wing, Chateau de
Montal 476
Sailing warship 377
Transparency holder 570
Transparent glassy crystal
271
Transparent lower
drumhead 518
Transparent tissue 160
Transparent wash 439
Transpiration 136
Transponder aerial 423
Transportation lock 571
Transport system 532
Transport tissue
Golden barrel cactus
156
Monocotyledons 126
Photosynthesis 138-139
Transversary 377
Transverse arch 485
Baroque church 479
Medieval church 468-
469

Transverse colon 249
Transverse dune 283
Transverse foramen 222
Transverse leaf spring 338
Transverse line 555
Transverse process
　Human 222-223
　Plateosaurus 89
　Tyrannosaurus 85
Transverse rib 485
Transverse strut 512
Trapezium 17, 622
Trapezium bone 230
Trapezius muscle 226-227, 229
Trapezoid bone 230
Traps
　Butterwort 161
　Cobra lily 160
　Monkey cup 161
　Pitcher plant 113, 160-161
　Sundew 160
　Venus fly trap 160
Traveller 380
Travelling 553
Travertine shell 464
Tray fascia 595
Tread 477
Tread pattern 365
Treasury of Atreus 461
Treble bridge 514
Treble clef 502
Treble hook 562-563
Treble note strings 515
Treble voice 502
Tree 66-67, 130-131
　Energy storage 315
　Epiphytes 162-163
　Gymnosperms 122-125
Tree fern 112-113
Tree mallow 151
Tree root action 282
Treenail 387
Trefoil
　Gothic church 470-473
　Nineteenth-century building 493
Trefoil arch 473, 484
Trellis window 459
Trellised river drainage 288
Trembler coil box 335
Trenail 387
Trestle trees 378
Trevithick, Richard 324
Triac device 600
Trials tyre 365
Triangle
　Shapes: plane 622
　Musical instrument 504, 517
　Steamboat with paddle wheels 391
Triangle mosaic 489
Triangular buttress 484
Triangular fossa 242
Triangular horn 85
Triangular lesene 481
Triangular pediment 462
Triangular-section fuselage
　Avro triplane 403
　Bell-47 helicopter 423
　Blackburn monoplane 401
Triangulum 19, 20
Triangulum Australe 21
Triassic period 68-69
　Fossil record 279
　Geological time 57
Triatic stay 385
Tribune 467-468
Tributary
　Coastlines 295
　Rivers 288
Tributary moraine 287
Tributary stream 289

Triceps brachii muscle 227
Triceratops 100, 102-103
Trichome 156
　Marram grass 113
Triclinic system 270
Tricolpate pollen grain 145
Tricuspid valve 251
Triere 373
Trifid Nebula 16
Trifoliate leaves 128, 130
　Laburnum 137
　Oxalis sp. 157
Triforium 469
Trigger
　Air pistol 549
　Biathlon smallbore rifle 549
　Cnidocyte structure 167
Trigger hair 160
Trigger mechanism 600
Trigger position 600
Triglyph 460
Trigon 488
Trigonal system 270
Trigone 257
Trigonometry 621
Trike nacelle 426-427
Trilete mark 145
Trilobate rotor 546
Tri-lobed tail 81
Trilobites 64, 78
　Earth's evolution 56
　Fossil record 279
Trim 352-353
　1906 Renault 356-357
　Oldsmobile trim 337
　Renault Clio 350-351
　Volkswagen Beetle 341
Trimala 491
Trim piece 579
Trimnall 407, 414, 415
Trim tank 416-417
Trinity Chapel, Salisbury Cathedral 470
Tripinnate leaves 137
Triplanes 402-405
Triple bar jump 554
Triple jump 542
Triple spine 130-151
Tripod mast 394
Tripod mount 583
Tripod screw socket 581
Tripod stand
　Congas 519
　Drum kit 518
　Electronic drums 520
　Modelling stand 455
　Radial studio easel 437
Tripping palm 586
Tripping ring 372
Triquetral bone 230
Trireme 372-373
Tri-spoke wheel 361, 368, 369
Triton 50
Trochanter
　Beetle 168
　Scorpion 170
　Spider 171
Trochoid housing 410
Trojan two-stroke engine 342
Trolley 332
Trombone 504, 505, 506, 507
Tropeter 573
Trophoblast 260
Tropic formation 276
Tropic of Cancer
　Satellite map 265
　Surface currents 297
Tropic of Capricorn
　Satellite map 265
　Surface currents 297

Tropical cyclone 302
Tropical orchids 162
Tropical rainforest 39, 66
Troposphere
　Earth's atmosphere 300
　Jupiter's atmosphere 45
　Mars' atmosphere 43
　Saturn's atmosphere 47
　Venus' atmosphere 37
Trout 180
Trout angling 562
Truck
　Early tram 332
　Greek galley 372
　Longboat 380
　Wooden sailing ship 378-379
Trumpet 504, 506, 503
Truncate leaf base 157
Trunk
　Elephant 200-201
　Mammoth 107
　Phiomia 105
　Tree fern 112
　Woody flowering plant 130-131
Trunnion 395
Truss
　Gothic church 473
　Modern building 497-499
　Steam boat with paddle wheels 391
Truss rod 513
Try 550, 551
T-section beam 492
Tsiolkovsky 41
T-type cantilevered fin 426
Tu-144 416
Tuba 504, 505
Tube feet 174, 175
Tubeless sports tyre 365
Tuber
　Broomrape 143
　Dryland plants 157
　Horsetail 120
　Potato 128
　Vegetative reproduction 155
Tubercle
　Corythosaurus 98
　Golden barrel cactus 156
　Sea urchins 174
　Starfish 174
　Stem projections 156
Tubular bells 504, 516
Tubular chassis 335
Tubular drums 518
Tubular open cradle frame 369
Tubular petioles 160
Tuck 581
Tudor arch 484
Tufted duck 188
Tug propeller 391
Tulip mount 563
Tuner/amplifier link cables 585
Tuner settings memory microchip 585
Tungsten
　Mineralization zones 281
　Periodic table 510
Tungsten carbide tip 450
Tungsten filament 319
Tunica adventitia 252
Tunica intima 252
Tunica media 252
Tunicates 174
Tuning adjustor 510-511
Tuning pedal 519
Tuning peg 510, 511
Tuning pin 514, 515
Tuning slide 506
Tunnel
　Cave 285
　Trains 330

Tunnel vault 485
Tuojiangosaurus 92
Tupelo 137
Turbine
　Energy 314-315
　Floodgate 604
　Jet engines 418-419
　Nuclear "Hunter-Killer" submarine 397
Turbo-charged diesel engine 327
Turbocharger 356
Turbofan engine 418-419
　Landing gear 412
Turbo impeller 347
Turbojet engine 418-419
　Landing gear 412
　Supersonic jetliner 416
Turbo propeller 347
Turboprop engine 418-419
Turdus viscivorus 190
Turfed roof 602, 603
Turgai strait 71
Turkish crescent finial 488
Turk's head 583
Turnbuckle
　Avro triplane 402
　Blackburn monoplane 401
　Curtiss biplane 398
　LVG CVI fighter 405
　Rigging screw 383
Turn indicator 558
Turning force 320
Turning indicator 332, 333
Turning judge 558
Turning vane 357
Turns 555
Turntable 506
Turntable rotator 596
Turpentine 436
Turret 486
　Baroque church 481
　Battleship 394-395
　Gothic church 470-471
　Gun turret 596
　Medieval building 466, 468
　Nineteenth-century building 493
　Renaissance building 476-477
Turtle 72-75, 186-187
Tuscan capital 465
Tuscan pilaster 465, 483
Tusche 446
Tusche pen 448
Tusche stick 448
Tusk
　Elephant 200-201
　Mammoth 107
　Phiomia 105
TV mini-camera 556
TV power button 585
TV selector 577
Tweeter 585
Tweeter loudspeaker connectors 585
Twelfth century
　Building 466-467
　Church 469, 473
　Roof 490
　Style 468, 470
Twentieth-century buildings 494-495
Twin-blade main rotor 423
Twin carbon-fibre disc brake 369
Twin connectors 427
Twin-cylinder engine
　Harley-Davidson 362
　Pegasus Quasar microlight 427
　Steam-powered Cugnot 334
Twin-domed forehead 200
Twine 584
Twin-lobed leaf blade 160

Twin nose-wheel 420
Twin rate spring 365
Twin rear axle 333
Twin rudder 372
Twin-wheel main landing gear 414
Twin-wheel nose-gear 417, 420
Twist 388
Twist dive 558, 559
Twisted wire habit 271
Two-lobed stigma 142
Two-pulley system 320
Two-seater cockpit 421
Two-stroke combustion engine 366
Two-toed ungulates 198
Two-towered gate 467
Tyagaraja 35
Tycho 40
Tye 373
Tye halyard 374
Tympan 449
Tympanic bulla 194
Tympanic canal 243
Tympanic membrane 243
Tympanum
　Frog 182
　Quail chick 193
Typhoon 302
Tyrannosaurus 73, 84-85
Tyre
　1906 Renault 356-357
　ARV light aircraft 424
　Avro triplane 402
　BAe-146 jetliner 414
　Bicycle 358-359
　Blériot XI monoplane 401
　BMW R/60 362
　Cannondale SH600 hybrid bicycle 361
　Curtiss biplane 398
　Double-decker tour bus 333
　Eddy Merckx racing bicycle 360
　First cars 334-335
　General use 365
　Lockheed Electra airliner 407
　MCW Metrobus 333
　Metal 324
　Motocross racing 368
　Motorcycle 365
　Pacing sulky 555
　Pneumatic 358, 555
　Racing car 356-357
　Renault Clio 352-353
　"Rocket" steam locomotive 324
　Rossin Italian time-trial bicycle 361
　Single-decker bus 333
　Slick racing 565
　Suzuki RGV500 368-369
　Trials 565
　Tubeless sports 365
　Volkswagen Beetle 340
　Weslake Speedway motorcycle 369
　World War I aircraft 404-405
Tyre carrier 337
Tyre tread 360, 365, 368
Tyre wall 360
Tyringham House 483

U

UHF aerial 420
UK loading gauges 331
Ulmus minor 144
Ulna
　Archaeopteryx 85
　Arsinoitherium 104
　Baryonyx 85
　Bird 189, 191

Brachiosaurus 91
Crocodile 186
Diplodocus 90
Domestic cat 195
Elephant 90, 201
Eryops 80
Euoplocephalus 94
Gallimimus 86
Hare 197
Horse 199
Human 218, 230
Iguanodon 96
Kangaroo 206
Kentrosaurus 93
Lizard 184
Parasaurolophus 99
Pareiasaur 81
Plateosaurus 88
Platypus 206
Rhesus monkey 202
Seal 204
Stegoceras 100, 101
Stegosaurus 93
Struthiomimus 87
Tuzodon 106
Triceratops 102
Tuojiangosaurus 93
Turtle 187
Tyrannosaurus 84
Ulnar artery 231, 255
Ulnar nerve 231, 238
Ultramarine lapis lazuli 433
Ultraviolet scan 214
Ultraviolet light 145, 319
Ultraviolet radiation 22, 319
Ultraviolet solar radiation 300
Umbels 143
Umbilical artery and vein 260
Umbilical cord 260-261
Umbilicus 211, 260
Umbo 176
Umbra 32
Umbrella 80
Umbriel 48
Umpire
　American football 526
　Badminton 545
　Baseball 536
　Cricket 538
　Hockey 540
　Lacrosse 541
　Netball 535
　Tennis 544
　Volleyball 534
Umpire signals 537
Una corda pedal 514, 515
Unarmed combat 556
Underarm pass 535
Underframe 332
Underground mycelium 115
Underground stem 154
Underground storage organs 154-155
Underground stream 284-285
Underground water
　Lake formation 292
　Rivers 288
Underhand serve 534
Under plastron 557
Under-turntable roller ring 596
Underwater mountains 298
Underwing fairing 425
Unenergized electrode 584
Ungulates 198-199
Unicellular organisms 56
Unified leaf pair 157
Uniform motion 321
"Union Pacific" diesel train 326
Unipolar neuron 239

Unison 503
Unit number 328
Units of measurement 620
Universal resource
locator (URL) address
577
Universal serial bus (USB)
plug 581
Universal serial bus (USB)
ports 566, 567, 570, 579
Universal serial bus (USB)
programmer 591
Universal serial bus (USB)
socket 581
USB socket access hole
581
Universal veil 114–115
Universe 10–11
Unmapped region
Degas and Brönte 34
Structure of Mercury 35
Unnilennium 311
Unnilhexium 310
Unniloctium 311
Unnilpentium 310
Unnilquadium 310
Unnilseptium 310
Unreactive gas mixture
319
Unreactive metals 311
Unstable elements 310
Unukalhai 21
Upcurved edge 191
Upfold 60
Upfold trap 280
Upholstery 336–337
Upholstery brush 593
Uplifted block fault
mountain 62
Upper arm 210
Upper Belvedere 482
Upper Carboniferous Coal
Measures 61
Upper Carboniferous
Millstone Grit 60–61
Upper crankcase 410
Upper crux of antihelix
242
Upper deadeye 382–383
Upper deck 380
Upper epidermis 159
Upper eyelid 213
Upper fin 423
Upper finishing 381
Upper Frater 473
Upper gallery 379
Upper head 387
Upper jaw 212, 220–221,
244–245, 246, 248
Upper joint
Clarinet 508
Cor Anglais 508
Oboe 508
Upper lobe of lung 215,
254–255
Upper number pad 588
Upper octave key 509
Upper rudder 416–417
Upper seed axis 152–153
Upper sheer strake 393
Upper topsail 385
Upper wireless and
telegraphy yard 395
Upright man 108
Upright piano 514
Upright planks jump 554
Upright poles jump 554
Upsilon Sagittarii 21
Upstream gates 560
Upthrow 60
Urachus 257
Ural mountains
Cretaceous period 73
Earth's physical
features 265
Jurassic period 71
Late Carboniferous
period 67
Triassic period 69

Uranium 310
Uranium fuel 314
Uranius Tholus 43
Uranus 48–49
Solar System 31
Ureter
Bird 189
Bony fish 181
Domestic cat 195
Elephant 200
Frog 182
Human 215, 256–259
Lizard 185
Rabbit 196
Snail 177
Ureteric orifice 257
Urethra
Chimpanzee 202
Domestic cat 195
Human 256–257, 259,
261
Rabbit 196
Urethral opening 259
Urethral sphincter muscle
257
Urinary bladder 181
Urinary system 256–257
Urinogenital opening
Bony fish 181
Dolphin 205
URL 577
Urn 478, 481, 487
Urodela 182
Uropod 172
Urostyle 183
Ursa Major 18, 19
Ursa Minor 18, 21
Ursus americanus 194
Ursus spelaeus 77, 106
U-shaped gouge 449
U-shaped valley 286–287
USB programmer
assembly 591
USB see Universal serial
bus (USB)
User name 576
U-shaped valley 286–287
Uterine wall 260–261
Uterus
Chimpanzee 202
Elephant 200
Human 258–259
Utricle 243
U-tube 313
Utzon, J. 499
Uvula 212, 245, 248

V

V1 "flying bomb" 408
V12 cylinder arrangement
345
V4 engine unit
British Rail Class 20
diesel 327
Honda VF750 364
Vacuole
Chlamydomonas sp.
116
Diatom 116
Human cell 216
Palisade mesophyll
159
Vacuum brake lever 325
Vacuum circuit braker
528
Vacuum cleaner 592–593
Vacuum operated inlet
valve 362
Vacuum pump cabinet
611
Vacuum reservoir 324
Vacuum valve 610
Vagina
Chimpanzee 202
Elephant 200
Human 258–259, 261
Snail 177
Spider 170

Valance
1906 Renault 337
Ford Model T 339
Volkswagen Beetle 341
Valency electrons 310
Vallate papillae 244
Vallecular canal 120
Valles Marineris 43
Valley
Coastline 294
Glacier 286–287
Grand Canyon 277
Mountain 62
River features 290
River 288–289
Rock cycle stages 267
Valley floor erosion 267
Valley head 289
Valley rafter 473
Valley spring 292
Válmiki 35
Valve 359
Valve chest 324
Valve cusp 252
Valve lifter 367
Valve return spring 347
Valve rocker 344, 402
Valves
Bivalves 176
Dehiscent fruit 151
Indehiscent fruit 150
Scallop 176
Valve slide 506, 507
Valve spring 343, 344
Valve system 506
Vanadium 310
Van Allen radiation belt 38
Van de Graaff 41
Van de Graaff generator
316
Vane 191
Van Eyck 35
Vang 378
Vanishing point 431
Vapour barrier 603
Variable incidence air
intake 420
Variable incidence gust-
alleviator 421
Variable nozzle 416–417
Variable pitch aluminium-
alloy blade 408
Variable pitch propeller
396
Variable time control
knob 598–599
Variegated lamina 131,
137
Varnish 348, 436
Vasa recta 256
Vascular cambium 154–
155
Vascular plants 279
Vascular plexus 235
Vascular strand 149
Vascular system 162–163
Vascular tissue 130
Aerial shoot 155
Apical meristem 134
Bishop pine 124
Canadian pond weed
159
Clubmoss stem 120
Corm 155
Dicotyledon 127
Dodder 163
Epiphytic orchid 162
Fern rachis 121
Higher plants 118–119
Horsetail stem 120
Marram grass 113
Monocotyledon 126–127
Parasite host 163
Perennials 130–131
Pine needle 124
Pine root/stem 125
Radicle 152
Rhizome 155
Root 152–153

Stem 134–135
Water hyacinth root 158
Water lily leaf 159
Woody plants 130–131
Vas deferens
Domestic cat 195
Human 259
Rabbit 196
Vastitas Borealis 43
Vastus lateralis muscle
225–226
Vastus medialis muscle
225–226
Vault 484–485, 496
Ancient Roman
building 462–464
Baroque church 479
Gothic building 470
Medieval building 467–
469
Modern building 496,
499
Nineteenth-century
building 492–493
Renaissance building
477
Vaulting shaft 468–469
V-belt pulley 347
VCR connections 585
Vedette boat 395
Vega 19, 20
Our galaxy and nearby
galaxies 15
Vegetable oil 436
Vegetative reproduction
154–155
Veil 114–115
Vein
Alveolar 247
Anterior median 253
Axillary 253
Basilic 253
Brachiocephalic 253
Bronchial 254
Cardiac 250
Central retinal 240
Cephalic 176, 253
Common iliac 215, 253,
257
Dicotyledon leaf 126–
127
Digital 253
External iliac 215, 253
Femoral 253
Gastroepiploic 253
Great saphenous 253
Hepatic portal 253
Hogweed leaf 129
Inferior mesenteric 253
Inferior vena cava 215,
252–253, 257
Insect 168, 169
Interlobular 256
Internal iliac 253
Internal jugular 253
Jugular 215
Leaf 136, 138–139
Median cubital 253
Monocotyledon leaf 126
Palmar 253
Portal 252
Pulmonary 251, 253, 254
Pulp 247
Renal 256–257
Short saphenous 253
Subclavian 253
Superior mesenteric
253
Superior vena cava 215,
251, 252–253, 255
Supraorbital 253
Testicular 257
Tree mallow leaf 131
Umbilical 260
Water hyacinth leaf 158
Water lily leaf 159
Vela 18, 21
Velamen 162
Velarium 464

Velar scale 115
Vela Supernova Remnant
17
Vellum 432
Velocette overhead valve
(OHV) engine 367
Velum 373
Vena cava
Frog 182
Inferior 215, 252–253,
257
Superior 215, 251, 252–
253, 255
Vendelinus 40
Veneer 462
Venomous snake 184
Vent
Frigate 397
Igneous rock structures
275
Mountain building 62
Rock cycle 266
Suzuki RGV500 368
Volcano 272–273
Ventilation 462
Ventilator 422, 423
Ventilator exit 406–407
Ventral abdominal artery
173
Ventral antebrachial
muscle 94
Ventral aorta 179
Ventral fin 179
Ventral margin of shell
176
Ventral nerve cord 169,
173
Ventral scale 184, 186
Ventricle
Brain 236–237
Heart 215, 250–251, 252
Ventricular diastole 251
Ventricular systole 251
Venturi 424
Venus 36–37
Solar System 30
Venus fly trap 160
Verdaccio 433
Verge 464, 492
Vermiculated rustication
482
Vermilion 433
Vermilion border of lip
213
Vermilion Cliffs 277
Versal lettering 445
Vertebra 261
Bony fish 180
Frog 183
Lumbar 222–223
Rattlesnake 185
Rudimentary 260
Thoracic 222–223
Turtle 187
Westlothiana 81
Vertebral artery 223, 252
Vertebral body 223
Vertebral column 218,
222, 257
Vertebral foramen 222–
223
Vertebral shield 187
Vertebrates 56, 64, 104
Cervical 212, 222
Lumbar 222–223
Thoracic 222–223
Vertex
Building 495
Human body 212
Vertical air current 302
Vertical batten 602
Vertical cleavage 270
Vertical damper 329
Vertical frame ladder 392
Vertical movement
Faults and folds 60
Lake formation 292
Vertical pupil 186
Vertical ridge 129
Vertical spindle 387

Vertical stroke 445
Very high frequency
(VHF) radio 318
Vesicle 148
Vespa Grand Sport 160
Mark 1 363
Vespa scooter 362, 363
Vessel
Baroque church 479
Gothic church 470
Medieval church 468–
469
Vesta Rupes 37
Vestas A47 wind turbine
604
Vestibular canal 243
Vestibular membrane 243
Vestibular nerve 243
Vestibule
Ancient Greek temple
461
Baroque church 481
Human body 212, 245
Medieval church 469
Neoclassical building
483
Vestibulocochlear nerve
243
Vestibulovaginal region
243
VGA monitor port 567
VHF aerial
B-17 bomber 408–409
BAe-146 jetliner 415
Bell Jetranger
helicopter 423
Concorde 416–417
VHF radio 318
VHF omni-range aerial
Bell-47 helicopter 422
Concorde 417
VHF omni-range and
instrument-landing-
system aerial 412
Vibraphone 504, 516, 517
Vibration-reducing
damper foot 58
Vibration-reducing fan
mounting 597
Vibrations
Brass instruments 506
Stringed instruments
510
Vibrato arm 513
Vibrato effect 516, 517
Vibrator motor 589
Vibrissa
Lion 194
Rabbit 196
Rat 196
Seal 204
Vicia faba 133, 152
Video
Digital 582–583
Streamed Internet 577
Video camera 610
Video card 567
Video cassette 583
Video input/output circuit
board 585
Video jack port 583
Video port cover 583
Video tape 583
Viewfinder 582
Viewfinder lens 583
Viewfinder ring 583
Viewfinder sleeve 583
Viewing screen 610
Viewing window 581
Viewing window objective
lens aperture 580
Viewselector panel 576
Viking ships 374–375
Villa Rotunda 475
Villa Savoye 494
Villi of mucosa 248
Viola 503, 504, 505, 510,
511
Violent eruptions 272
Violet light 318
Violin 503, 504, 505, 510

Violoncello 510-511
Virginia opossum 207
Virgo 18, 21
Virtual mixing board 521
Visceral cartilage 254
Visceral hump 177
Visceral pericardium 250
Viscous coupling 344-345
Visible and infrared
  spectrometers 615
Visible light 318-319
Vision 237
Visor 416-417
Visual recognition 237
Vitreous glass mosaic 451
Vitreous glass tessera 450,
  451
Vitreous humour 240
Vitta 151
Vivaldi 35
Vocal cords 245
Voices 503
Volans 21
Volcanic activity
  Mineralization zones
    280
  Rock cycle 266
Volcanic eruption 26
Volcanic gases 64
Volcanic island 58, 299
Volcanic lake 293
Volcanic lava
  Jupiter 44
  Mars 42
  The Moon 40
  Venus 36
Volcanic mountain 62
Volcanic rock 298, 306
Volcano 58, 63, 272-273
  Jupiter 44
  Locations 273
  Mars 42
  Mineralization zones
    281
  Mountain building 62-
    63
  Ocean floor 298
  Vent 62
  Venus 36
Volkmann's canal 247
Volkmann's vessel 225
Volkswagen Beetle 340-
  341
Volleyball 534-535
Voltage 306, 316
Voltage circuitry 597
Voltage reduction and
  regulation circuits 585
Voltage regulators 596
Voltage stabilizer 597
Voltage transformers 596
Volume 306, 307
Volume control
  Electronic instruments
    520, 521
  Streamed internet radio
    577
  Home cinema 585
  Personal music 587
Volume increase control
  587
Volume reduction control
  587
Volumes 623
Volume up/down toggle
  581
Volute
  Ancient Greek building
    460-461
  Baroque church 479,
    481
  Dome 486
  Islamic building 488
  Neoclassical building
    478, 480
  Renaissance building
    476-477
Volva 114-115
Volvox sp. 116

Vomer 221
Von Kármán 41
Voussoir 484-485
  Ancient Roman
    building 465
  Neoclassical building
    482
  Renaissance building
    474
V-shaped gouge 449
V-shaped valley
  River features 290
  Rivers 288-289
V-strut 404-405
VTEC engine 354
V-twin engine 362, 363
Vulpecula 19
Vulture 190
Vulva 200
Vyāsa 35
Vyne 482

W

Wadi 283
Wagner 35
Wagon 324
Wagon bogie 330
Wagon vault 485
Wahweap sandstone 276
Waist
  74-gun ship 380-381
  Human 210
  Stringed instruments
    510-511
Waistband 548
Waist gun 408
Wale
  74-gun ship 381
  Roman corbita 373
  Sailing warship 376-377
Walkway 497
Wall
  Ancient Greek temple
    461
  Ancient Roman
    building 462, 465
  Baroque building 478-
    479, 481
  Carpel 148, 151
  Cell 112, 117, 132, 139
  Concrete 496
  Fruit 148-151
  Fungal tissue 115
  Glass 496
  Gothic church 470
  Islamic building 488
  Medieval building 466-
    467, 469
  Modern building 498-
    499
  Neoclassical building
    479, 482
  Nineteenth-century mill
    492
  Ovary 140, 150
  Renaissance building
    476-477
  Twentieth-century
    building 494
Wall anchor 407
Wall construction 602
Wall panel 406-407
Wall painting 434
Walrus 204
Walter 40
Wand 592, 593
Wand handle and
  brushbar controls 592
Wand/handle connector
  593
Wand telescopic link 593
Wankel, Felix 346
Wankel rotary engine
  346-347
Wannanosaurus 101
Wardrobe 416
Wardroom 381

Warhead 394
Warm air 300, 302-303
Warm blood
  Mammals 104
  Theropods 84
Warm front 302-303
Warm occlusion 302
Warm periods 56
Warning horn 527, 529
Warning light 328, 556
Warship
  74-gun ship 379, 380-
    381
  Battleship 394-395
  Frigate 396-397
  Ironclad 392-393
  Man-of-war 378-379,
    Sailing warship 376-377
  Submarine 396-397
Wasatch formation 276
Washable pre-motor filter
  592
Wash cant 378
Washer-dryer 594-595
Wash over dry brush 439
Washburn twelve-string
  guitar 513
Washer
  Bicycle 358
  Power drill 600-601
  Toaster 598-599
Washer jet 553
Washes 438, 439
Washing machine 315
Wasp 168
Waste heat 514-515
Waste water anti-siphon
  pipe hook 595
Waste water pipe 595
Water 38, 66
  Absorption 150
  Amphibian 80
  Changing states 307
  "Deltic" diesel-electric
    locomotive 326
  Energy generation 314-
    315
  Epiphyte supply 162
  Fermentation 313
  Lithographic printing
    446
  Mars 42
  Molecule 138
  Oceans and seas 296
  Photosynthesis 138
  Pollination 144
  Reversible reactions
    312
  Seed germination 152-
    153
  Solutions 306
  Storage organs 156-157
  Transport 134, 159
Water and oil pump
  assembly 356
Waterborne sports 560-
  561
Water-closet 483
Watercolour 438-439
Watercolour paint pan 438
Watercolour paper 439,
  441
Watercolour-style acrylic
  painting 442, 443
Water cooled engine 566
Water cycle 288
Water density 296
Water distribution 264
Water droplets 45
Waterfall 291
  Glacier 286
  River 289-290
  Rock cycle 267
Water fern 158
Water float 324
Water hardness
  adjustment and filter
  flap lever 595

Water hyacinth 158
Water ice
  Jupiter's atmosphere
    45
  Mercury's atmosphere
    47
  Structure of comet 53
  Structure of Mars 43
  Structure of Neptune 51
Water-ice fog 42
Water-ice permafrost 43
Water inlet connector 595
Water inlet hose 595
Water inlet pipe 595
Water inlet valves 595
Water jacket
  Daimler engine 343
  Ford diesel engine 347
  Humber engine 343
  Jaguar straight six
    engine 344
Water key 506, 507
Water lily 158-159
Waterline 380
Water obstacle 546
Water outlet 425
Water passage 346
Water pipe
  1906 Renault 357
  Humber engine 343
  Wright Flyer 399
Water pressurizer 314
Waterproof acrylic paint
  442
Waterproof cable
  connector 605
Waterproof covering
  Bishop pine needles
    124
  Golden barrel cactus
    156
  Haworthia truncata 157
  Lithops bromfieldii 157
  Monocotyledon leaf 126
  Rush stem 135
  Wetland plants 158
Waterproof shell 80
Waterproof ski clothing
  553
Waterproof skin 81
Waterproof stowage box
  427
Water pump
  Hybrid car 354
  Jaguar V12 engine 345
  Renault Clio 351
  White Steam Car 342
Water pump pulley 347
Water rail 345
Water reactor 314
Water-retaining cuticle 78
Water salinity 296
Water-saturated
  permeable rock
  Lakes and groundwater
    292
  Mineral resources 280-
    281
Watershed 289
Water shoot 560
Water softener dial 595
Water-soluble glue 450
Water storage tank 497
Water-storing
  parenchyma 156-157
Water supply
  Gun turret 396
  Steam locomotive 324
Water table
  Cave system 284
  Lake formation 292
Water tank
  Bordino Steam Carriage
    334
  "Ellerman Lines" steam
    locomotive 324
  Steam iron 594
  White Steam Car 342
Water vapour

Chemical reactions
  312-313
Hurricane structure 303
Jupiter's atmosphere 45
Mars' atmosphere 43
Saturn's atmosphere 47
Venus' atmosphere 37
Water cycle 288
Water vascular system
  174
Waterway 380, 393
Wattle-and-daub
  Ancient Roman
    building 462, 464-465
  Medieval house 466
Wave 294, 298
  Erosion 294
  Features 294
  Properties 318
Wave-cut platform 295
Waveguide 596, 597
Wavelength 318
Wavellite 269
Wavering pitch 516, 517
Wavy foliation 267
Wavy lamina 159
Wax modelling 452
Wax riser 454
Wax runner 454
Waxy cuticle 156, 157
Waxy fruit skin 149
Waxy laminae 159
Waxy zone 161
Weapon-bay bulkhead 421
Weaponry 375
Weasel 194
Weather 302-303
Weathercock 486
Weathering 282-283
  Gothic church 471-472
  Medieval church 469
  Mineral deposits 280
  Renaissance building
    477
  Rock cycle 266
  Sedimentary rocks 276
Weather radar 416
Weather shutter for gun
  394
Weather-vane 471, 477
Web
  Frog 182
  Internet 576
Webbed feet 188, 190
Web pages 577
Website address 577
Weight
  Arch 484
  All-round bicycle 360
  Bolts 548
  Fax machine handset
    572
  Measurement 320, 590
  Motorcycle engine 366
  Newton meters 320
Weights 562
Wei-wei 376
Welding tool 608
Weld line 592
Welt 122-123
Welwitschia mirabilis 122-
  123
Werner motorcycle 362
Weslake Speedway
  motorcycle 369
West Africa 73
West Australian current
  297
Westerlies 300
Westlothiana 67, 80-81
Westminster Abbey 484
Westminster Cathedral
  493
Wet-in-wet wash 438, 439
Wetland plants 158-159
Wet season 293
Wet wash 438
Wezen 18
  Canis Major 21
Whaler 395

Whales 204-205
Wheat 109, 150
Wheel
  1906 Renault 357
  Alloy 356, 357
  Bicycle 358-359
  Diesel motor output 326
  First cars 334-335
  Force/motion 320
  Ford Model T 338-339
  Harley-Davidson FLHS
  Electra Glide 363
  Mazda RX-7 346
  Motorcycle 364
  Pacing sulky 555
  Paddle 390-391
  Renault Clio 350-351
  Rossin Italian time-trial
    bicycle 361
  Ship 378, 390, 394
  Single scull 561
  Volkswagen Beetle 340
  Weslake Speedway
    motorcycle 369
Wheel axle
  BAe-146 jetliner 414
  Touring bicycle 360
Wheelbase 360
Wheelchair access 333
Wheel fairing
  Blackburn monoplane
    400
  Pegasus Quasar
    microlight 427
  Pegasus XL SE
    microlight 426
Wheel fork 335
Wheel guard 324, 369, 593
Wheel hub 414
Wheel nut 356, 357
Wheel sets 327, 329
Wheel spacer 561
Whelp 387
Whetstone 452
Whip 555
Whipping 384, 388
Whisker
  Lion 194
  Rabbit 196
  Rat 196
  Seal 204
Whisker boom 382
"Whispering Gallery" 484
Whistle
  Iron paddlesteamer 392
  Life jacket 561
  Referee 524
Whistle lever 325
White belt 556
White blood cells 217, 253
White Cliffs 276
White diamond 268
White dwarfs
  Small stars 24-25
  Stars 22-23
White feldspar 275
White-grey crystal 271
White light 318
White matter
  Cerebrum 236-237
  Spinal cord 238
White of eye 213
White oval
  Jupiter 44-45
White Steam Car 342
White spirit 436
White stork 188
White warning light 328
White whale 204
Whorls
  Flower 140
  Green alga cell 116
  Sepals 144, 149
Wicket 538
Wicket-keeper 538
Wide-angle camera 615
Widened joint 282
Wide receiver 526

Wide-screen plasma display 584
Wiener 41
Willow grouse 193
Wind
  Atmosphere 300
  Ekman spiral 297
  Energy generation 514
  Oceans and seas 296-297
  Rock cycle 266-267
  Water cycle 288
  Weather 302
  Weathering and erosion 282-283
  Windspeed 303
Windcheetah SL Mark VI "Speedy" racing HPV bicycle 361
Wind chest 514
Wind controller 521
Wind deflector 341
Wind-dispersed seeds 150-151
Wind erosion 282-283
  Coastline 294
Winding cornice 472
Wind instruments 508, 509
  Brass 506, 507
  Electronic 520
  Woodwind 508, 509
Windlass
  Buildings 467, 477
  Roman corbita 372
Windlass bar 380
Window
  Ancient Egyptian building 459
  Ancient Roman building 463, 465
  Asian building 490-491
  Baroque church 479-481
  Dome 486-487
  Dormer 495
  Double-decker tour bus 333
  "Eurostar" multi-voltage electric train 329
  Gothic building 470-473
  MCW Metrobus 333
  Medieval building 466-469
  Modern building 498, 499
  Neoclassical building 478, 482-483
  Nineteenth-century building 492-493
  Renaissance building 474, 476
  Rococo style 482
  Single-decker bus 333
  TGV electric high-speed train 329
  Twentieth-century building 494-495
Window accessory 585
Window blind 336
Window controls 577
Window-frame 486
Window glass 348
Window jamb 479, 482, 483
Window-sill
  Baroque church 479
  Neoclassical building 482-483
  Twentieth-century building 494
Window stage 477
Wind-pollinated plants 144
Windscreen
  BAe-146 jetliner components 412
  BE 2B bomber 404

BMW R/60 sidecar 362
Concorde 416-417
"Deltic" diesel-electric locomotive 327
Double-decker tour bus 333
Ford Model T 339
Harley-Davidson FLHS Electra Glide 363
Honda Insight 354
Hawker Tempest components 409
Kirby BSA racing sidecar 362
Lockheed Electra airliner 406-407
Tornado 420
Windscreen wiper
  "Deltic" diesel-electric locomotive 327
  "Eurostar" multi-voltage electric train 329
  Italian State Railways Class 402 328
  MCW Metrobus 332
  Paris Metro 328
  TGV electric high-speed train 329
  "Union Pacific" locomotive 326
  Volkswagen Beetle 341
Windsor green 458
Windspeed 303
Wind synthesizer 521
Wind turbine 604, 605
Wind-up 557
Windvane 375, 605
Windward face 283
Wing
  1906 Renault 336
  Alula 191
  ARV light aircraft 424-425
  Australian rules football 528
  Avro biplane 403
  BAe-146 jetliner components 413, 414
  BE 2B bomber 404
  Beetle 168
  Biplanes and triplanes 402
  Bird 188, 191
  Blackburn monoplane 401
  Bones 191
  Bumblebee 168
  Butterfly 169
  Cobra lily 160
  Coverts 188
  Curtiss biplane 398
  Deer hopper dry fly 563
  Developing 192
  Dry fruit 150-151
  Early monoplanes 400
  Feather 188, 191
  Ford Model T 338
  Formula One racing car 357
  Gliders, hang-gliders, and microlights 426
  Handball 535
  Hawker Tempest components 409
  Hockey 540
  Ice hockey 550
  Lockheed Electra airliner 406
  Pine seed 122
  Pitcher plant 113
  Rugby 530
  Scots pine seed 122
  Showjumping fence 554
  Ski boot safety binding 552
  Spurious 191
  Sycamore 151

Wing assembly 413
Wing attack 535, 541
Wing case 168
Wing defence
  Lacrosse 541
  Netball 535
Winged seeds
  Scots pine 122
  Sycamore 151, 151
Winged stem 129
Wing end-plate 357
Wing-feather impression 85
Wing fillet panel 409
Wingframe 427
Winglet 356
Wing mirror 354
Wing piping 541
Wing-protecting skid 398-399
Wing-root glove fairing 420-421
Wing-root mount 413
Wing scar 122
Wing stay 559
Wing strut
  ARV light aircraft 424-425
  Avro triplane 402-403
  Curtiss biplane 398
Wing supports 357
Wingtip
  ARV light aircraft 424
  BE 2B wings 404
  Hawker Tempest components 409
  Schleicher glider 426
Wingtip aerial fairing 421
Wing transom 381
Wing vein 168, 169
Wing warping 400
Wire armature 454, 455
Wire bristle brush 519
Wire coil 605
Wire-ended cutting tool 454
Wire end tools 452
Wire gauze pad 542
Wireless and telegraphy yard 395
Wireless office 397
Wires 518
Wire wheel 402
Wiring loom 596
Wishbone
  Bird 189
  Formula One racing car 357
Withdrawal stride 543
Withdrawing-room 483
Withers 199
Wolf 195
Wolffian duct 179
Wolf hair brush 444
Wollastonite 271
Womb 258-259
Women's lacrosse field 540, 541
Women's shot 542
Wood
  Golf club 547
  Sculpture 454
Wood block 446, 449
Wood capstan 387
Woodcarving 452, 453
Woodcut 446
Wooden arrow 109
Wooden artillery wheel 377
Wooden bar 516
Wooden boarding 602
Wooden body 510
Wooden body-shell 519
Wooden buffer 324
Wooden case 514, 515
Wooden-domed deck 403
Wooden driving wheel 324
Wooden frame
  Harp 511

Printing mesh 446, 448
Sculpture 452
Steam-powered Cugnot "Fardier" 334
Wooden golf clubs 546, 547
Wood engraving 446, 447
Wood engraving print 449
Wooden grip 549
Wooden hearth 109
Wooden "key" 551
Wooden packing 397
Wooden panel 473
Wooden sailing ship 378-379
Wooden sleeper 324, 331
Wooden spoke 334
Wooden-spoked wheel 339
Wooden stands 554
Wooden wheel 334
Woodwind instruments 504, 505, 508, 509
Woodwork 467
Woody flowering plants 126, 130-131
Woody pericarps 150
Woody plants 126
Woody scales
  Bishop pine cone 124
  Smooth cypress 123
Woody stem 134-135
Woofer 584
Woofer loudspeaker connector 585
Woolding 376
Work 314
Working chamber 396
World War I aircraft 404-405
World War II aircraft 408-409
World Wide Web 576
Worming 388
Worms
  Earth's evolution 56
  Fossil record 279
Woven dacron 384
Wrack 116-117
Wren, C. 478
  Baroque church 480
  Cathedral dome 484, 487
Wrest plank
  Concert grand piano 515
  Upright piano 514
Wright brothers
  Modern piston aero engines 410
  Pioneers of flight 398-399
Wright, F. L. 495
Wright Flyer 398-399
Wrist
  Corythosaurus 98
  Elephant 90
  Human 211, 230-231
  Iguanodon 97
  Stegosaurus 92
  Triceratops 102
Wrist joint
  Baryonyx 85
  Brachiosaurus 90
  Diplodocus 90
  Euoplocephalus 94
  Human 218
  Parasaurolophus 99
  Plateosaurus 88
  Robot 608
  Stegoceras 100, 101
  Tyrannosaurus 84
Wrist pin 390
Wrist position 444
Wrist-strap attachment 579
Write-protect tab 586
Writing area 568
Writing tip 568

Writing tools 444
Wrought iron boiler 324
Wrought iron rail 324
Wuerhosaurus 93
Wulfenite 269

X

Xerophytes 156-157
Xιζ Sagittarii 21
Xi Orionis 18
Xi Pegasi 19
X line 445
X-ray 518-519
  Colon 214
  Gallbladder 214
  Hand 230
X-ray emission 28
X-ray image of Crab Nebula 28
"X" turret 395
Xylem
  Bishop pine 124
  Clubmoss stem 120
  Dicotyledons 126-127
  Dodder host 163
  Epiphytic orchid 162
  Fern rachis 121
  Higher plants 118-119
  Horsetail stem 120
  Marram grass 113
  Monocotyledons 126-127
  Pine needle 124
  Pine root/stem 125
  Radicle 152
  Root 132
  Stem 134-135
  Water hyacinth root 158
  Water lily leaf 159
Xylem fibres 134-135

Y

Yacht racing 560
Yangchuanosaurus 85
Yangtze River 265
Yard 382
  Battleship 395
  Double topsail schooner 385
  Greek and Roman ships 372, 373
  Steel 392
  Tea clipper 392
  Viking karv 375
Yardang 282
Yardarm 379
Yardsman 526
Yasti 490, 491
Yaw control 605
Yaw ring 605
Year
  Earth 30
  Jupiter 30
  Mars 30
  Mercury 26, 34
  Neptune 31
  Planets 30-31
  Pluto 31
  Saturn 31
  Uranus 31
  Venus 30
Yeast
  Fermentation 313
  Fungi 114
Yellow card 524
Yellow light 318, 351
Yellow ochre 442
Yellow orpiment 271
Yellow River 265
Yellow warning arm 330
Yellow-wort 144
Yew 123
Y.M.C.A. 552
Yolk 192
Yolk sac 192

Ytterbium 311
Yttrium 310
"Y" turret 395
Yucca 126
Yucca sp. 126

Z

Zagros Mountains 75
Zaire 265
Zea mays 127
Zeami 35
Zebra 198
Zeeman 41
Zeilleria frenzlii 66
Zeta Centauri 21
Zeta Sagittarii 21
Zeugen 282
Ziggurat-style step-back 494
Zinc 281, 312
Zinc phosphating 348
Zinc plating 477
Zingiber officinale 155
Zion Canyon 276
Zip expansion bay 566
Zirconium 310
Zona pellucida 606, 607
Zone
  Jupiter 44-45
  Structure of Saturn 47
Zone defences 533
Zonular ligament 241
Zoom control 583
Zoom control microchip 581
Zoom in/out icon 568
Zoom keys 590
Zoom motor 580
Zoomorphic head 374
Zosteres 372
Zosterophyllum llanoveranum 64
Zubenelgenubi 18, 21
Zubeneschamali 18, 21
Zugon 373
Zygian 373
Zygomatic arch
  Bear 191
  Chimpanzee 202
  Human 213, 220
  Lion 194
  Smilodon 106
  Toxodon 107
Zygomatic bone 220-221
Zygomaticus major muscle 228-229
Zygote
  Bryophyte 118-119
  Fertilization 146-147
  Plant formation 146
  Primitive land plants 120
  Seaweed 116-117

Acknowledgments

Dorling Kindersley would like to thank (in order of sections):

The Universe
(consultant editors – Sue Becklake, Gevorkyan Tatyana Alekseyevna):
John Becklake; the Memorial Museum of Cosmonautics, Moscow; The Cosmos Pavilion, Moscow; The United States Space and Rocket Centre, Alabama; Broadhurst, Clarkson and Fuller Ltd; Susannah Massey

Prehistoric Earth
(consultant editors – William Lindsay, Martyn Bramwell, Dr Ralph E. Molnar, David Lambert):
Dr Monty Reid, Andrew Neuman, and the staff of the Royal Tyrrell Museum of Palaeontology, Drumheller, Alberta; Dr Angela Milner and the staff of the Department of Palaeontology, the Natural History Museum, London; Professor W. Ziegler and the staff, in particular Michael Loderstaedt, of the Naturmuseum Senckenburg, Frankfurt; Dr Alexander Liebau, Axel Hunghrebüller, Reiner Schoch, and the staff of the Institut und Museum für Geologie und Paläontologie der Universität, Tübingen; Rupert Wild of the Institut für Paläontologie, Staatliches Museum für Naturkunde, Stuttgart; Dr Scheiber of the Stadtmuseum, Nördlingen; Professor Dr Dietrich Herm of Staatssammlung für Paläontologie und Historische Geologie, München; Dr Michael Keith-Lucas of the Department of Botany, University of Reading; Richard Walker; American Museum of Natural History, New York

Plants
(consultant editor – Richard Walker):
Diana Miller; Lawrie Springate; Karen Sidwell; Chris Thody; Michelle End; Susan Barnes and Chris Jones of the EMU Unit of the Natural History Museum, London; Jenny Evans of Kew Gardens, London; Kate Biggs of the Royal Horticultural Society Gardens, Wisley, Surrey; Spike Walker of Microworld Services; Neil Fletcher; John Bryant of Bedgebury Pinetum, Kent; Dean Franklin

Animals
(consultant editor – Richard Walker):
David Manning's Animal Ark; Intellectual Animals; Howletts Zoo, Canterbury; John Dunlop; Alexander O'Donnell; Sue Evans of the Royal Veterinary College, London; Dr Geoff Potts and Fred Frettsome of the Marine Biological Association of the United Kingdom, Plymouth; Jeremy Adams of the Booth Museum of Natural History, Brighton; Derek Telling of the Department of Anatomy, University of Bristol; the Natural History Museum, London; Andy Highfield of the Tortoise Trust; Brian Harris of the Aquarium, London Zoo; the Invertebrate Department, London Zoo; Dr Harold McClure of the Yerkes Regional Primate Research Center, Emory University, Atlanta, Georgia; Nielson Lausen of the Harvard Medical School, New England Regional Primates Research Centre, Southborough, Massachusetts; Dr Paul Hopwood of the Department of Veterinary Anatomy, University of Sydney; Dean Franklin

The Human Body
(consultant editors – Dr Frances Williams, Dr Fiona Payne, Richard Cummins FRCS):
Derek Edwards and Dr Martin Collins, British School of Osteopathy; Dr M.C.E. Hutchinson of the Department of Anatomy, United Medical and Dental Schools of Guy's and St Thomas' Hospitals, London. Models – Barry O'Borke (Bodyline Agency) and Pauline Swaine (MOT Model Agency)

Geology, Geography, and Meteorology
(consultant editor – Martyn Bramwell):
Dr John Nudds of the Manchester Museum, Manchester; Dr Alan Wooley and Dr Andrew Clark of the Natural History Museum, London; Graham Bartlett of the National Meteorological Library and Archive, Bracknell; Tony Drake of BP Exploration, Uxbridge; Jane Davies of the Royal Society of Chemistry, Cambridge; Dr Tony Waltham of Nottingham Trent University, Nottingham; staff of the Smithsonian Institute, Washington; staff of the United States Geological Survey, Washington; staff of the National Geographic Society, Washington; staff of Edward Lawrence Associates (Export Ltd), Midhurst; John Farndon; David Lambert

Rail and Road
Rail (consultant editor – John Coiley)
Michael Ashworth of the London Transport Museum

Road (consultant editors – David Burgess-Wise, Hugo Wilson)
The National Motor Museum, Beaulieu; Alf Newell of Renault UK Ltd; David Suter of Cheltenham Cutaway Exhibits Ltd; Francesca Riccini of the Science Museum, London. Signore Amadelli of the Museo dell' Automobile Carlo Biscaretti di Ruffia; Paul Bolton of the Mazda MCL Group; Duncan Bradford of Reg Mills Wire Wheels; John and Leslie Brewster of Autocavan; David Burgess-Wise; Trevor Cass of Garrett Turbo Service; John Corbett of The Patrick Collection; Gary Crumpler of Williams Grand Prix Engineering Ltd; Mollie Easterbrooke and Duncan Gough of Overland Ltd; Arthur Fairley of the Vauxhall Motor Company; Paul Foulkes-Halbard of Filching Manor Motor Museum; Frank Gilbert of I. Wilkinson and Son Ltd; Paolo Gratton of Gratton Museum; Colvin Gunn of Gunn and Son; Judy Hogg of Ecurie Bertelli; Milton Holman of Dream Cars; Ian Matthews of IMAT Electronics; Eric Neal of Jaguar Cars Ltd; Paul Niblett, Keith Davidson, Mark Reumel, and David Woolf of Michelin Tyre plc; Doug Nye; Kevin O'Keefe of O'Keefe Cars; Seat UK; Ian Whitley, Raj Johal and Andy Faiers of the Honda Institute; Roger Smith; Jim Stirling of Ironbridge Gorge Museum, Staffordshire; Jon Taylor; Doug Thompson; Martyn Watkins of Ford Motor Company Ltd; John Cattermole, Customer Services Manager at London Northern Buses; F. W. Evans Cycles Ltd; Trek UK Ltd (Bicycle); Sam Grimmer; Colin Uttley

Physics and Chemistry
(consultant editor – Jack Challoner)

Sea and Air
Sea (consultant editors – Geoff Hales and Harvey B. Loomis):
David Spence, Gillian Hutchinson, David Topliss, Simon Stephens, Robert Baldwin, Jonathan Betts, all of the National Maritime Museum, London; Ian Friel; Simon Turnage of Captain O.M. Watts of London Ltd; Davey and Company Ltd, Great Dunmow; Avon Inflatables Ltd, Llanelli; Musto Ltd, Benfleet; Peter Martin of Spencer Rigging Ltd, Southampton; Peter Rowson of Ratseys Sailmakers, Southampton; Swiftech Ltd, Wallingford; Colin Scattergood of the Barrow Boat Company Ltd, Colchester; Professor J.S. Morrison of the Trireme Trust, Cambridge; The Cutty Sark Maritime Trust; Adrian Daniels of Kelvin Hughes Marine Instruments, London; Arthur Credland of Hull City Council Museums and Art Galleries; The Hull Maritime Society; Gerald Clark; Peter Fitzgerald of the Science Museum, London; Alec Michael of HMB Subwork Ltd, Great Yarmouth, and Ray Ward of the OSEL Group, Great Yarmouth; Richard Bird of UWI, Weybridge; Walker Marine Instruments, Birmingham; The International Sailing Craft Association; The Exeter Maritime Museum; Jane Wilson of the Trinity Lighthouse Company, London; The Imperial War Museum Collections; Thorn Security Ltd; Michael Bach

Air (consultant editor – Bill Gunston):
Aeromega Helicopters, Stapleford; Aero Shopping, London; Avionics Mobile Services Ltd, Watford; Roy Barber and John Chapman of the RAF Museum, Hendon; Mitch Barnes Aviation, London; Mike Beach; British Caledonian Flight Training Ltd; Fred Coates of Helitech (Luton) Ltd; Michael Cuttell and CSE Aviation Ltd, Oxford; Dowty Aerospace Landing Gear, Gloucester; Guy Hartcup of the Airship Association; Anthony Hooley, Chris Walsh, and David Cord of British Aerospace Regional Aircraft Ltd; Ken Huntley of Mid-West Aero Engines Ltd; Imperial War Museum, Duxford; The London Gliding Club, Dunstable; Musée des Ballons, Calvados; Noel Penny Turbines Ltd; Andy Pavey of Aviation Scotland Ltd; Tony Pavey of Thermal Aircraft Developments, London; the Commanding Officer and personnel of RAF St Athan; the Commanding Officer and personnel of RAF Wittering; The Science Museum, London; Ross Sharp of the Science Museum, Wroughton; The Shuttleworth Collection; Skysport Engineering; Mike Smith; Solar Wings Ltd, Marlborough; Julian Temple of Brooklands Museum Trust Ltd; Kelvin Wilson of Flying Start

Architecture
(consultant editor – Alexandra Kennedy):
Stephen Cutler for advice and text; Gavin Morgan of the Museum of London, London; Chris Zeuner of the Weald and Downland Museum, Singleton, Sussex; Alan Hills and James Putnam of the British Museum, London; Dr Simon Penn and Michael Thomas of the Avoncroft Museum of Buildings, Bromsgrove,